T0189200

Lecture Notes in Computer Science

# Lecture Notes in Artificial Intelligence 14172

Founding Editor

Jörg Siekmann

Series Editors

Randy Goebel, *University of Alberta, Edmonton, Canada*
Wolfgang Wahlster, *DFKI, Berlin, Germany*
Zhi-Hua Zhou, *Nanjing University, Nanjing, China*

The series Lecture Notes in Artificial Intelligence (LNAI) was established in 1988 as a topical subseries of LNCS devoted to artificial intelligence.

The series publishes state-of-the-art research results at a high level. As with the LNCS mother series, the mission of the series is to serve the international R & D community by providing an invaluable service, mainly focused on the publication of conference and workshop proceedings and postproceedings.

Danai Koutra · Claudia Plant ·
Manuel Gomez Rodriguez · Elena Baralis ·
Francesco Bonchi
Editors

# Machine Learning and Knowledge Discovery in Databases

## Research Track

European Conference, ECML PKDD 2023
Turin, Italy, September 18–22, 2023
Proceedings, Part IV

 Springer

*Editors*
Danai Koutra (iD)
University of Michigan
Ann Arbor, MI, USA

Claudia Plant (iD)
University of Vienna
Vienna, Austria

Manuel Gomez Rodriguez (iD)
Max Planck Institute for Software Systems
Kaiserslautern, Germany

Elena Baralis (iD)
Politecnico di Torino
Turin, Italy

Francesco Bonchi (iD)
CENTAI
Turin, Italy

ISSN 0302-9743    ISSN 1611-3349 (electronic)
Lecture Notes in Artificial Intelligence
ISBN 978-3-031-43420-4    ISBN 978-3-031-43421-1 (eBook)
https://doi.org/10.1007/978-3-031-43421-1

LNCS Sublibrary: SL7 – Artificial Intelligence

This Springer imprint is published by the registered company Springer Nature Switzerland AG
The registered company address is: Gewerbestrasse 11, 6330 Cham, Switzerland

Paper in this product is recyclable.

# Preface

The 2023 edition of the European Conference on Machine Learning and Principles and Practice of Knowledge Discovery in Databases (ECML PKDD 2023) was held in Turin, Italy, from September 18 to 22, 2023.

The ECML PKDD conference, held annually, acts as a worldwide platform showcasing the latest advancements in machine learning and knowledge discovery in databases, encompassing groundbreaking applications. With a history of successful editions, ECML PKDD has established itself as the leading European machine learning and data mining conference, offering researchers and practitioners an unparalleled opportunity to exchange knowledge and ideas.

The main conference program consisted of presentations of 255 accepted papers and three keynote talks (in order of appearance):

- Max Welling (University of Amsterdam): Neural Wave Representations
- Michael Bronstein (University of Oxford): Physics-Inspired Graph Neural Networks
- Kate Crawford (USC Annenberg): Mapping Generative AI

In addition, there were 30 workshops, 9 combined workshop-tutorials, 5 tutorials, 3 discovery challenges, and 16 demonstrations. Moreover, the PhD Forum provided a friendly environment for junior PhD students to exchange ideas and experiences with peers in an interactive atmosphere and to get constructive feedback from senior researchers. The conference included a Special Day on Artificial Intelligence for Financial Crime Fight to discuss, share, and present recent developments in AI-based financial crime detection.

In recognition of the paramount significance of ethics in machine learning and data mining, we invited the authors to include an ethical statement in their submissions. We encouraged the authors to discuss the ethical implications of their submission, such as those related to the collection and processing of personal data, the inference of personal information, or the potential risks. We are pleased to report that our call for ethical statements was met with an overwhelmingly positive response from the authors.

The ECML PKDD 2023 Organizing Committee supported Diversity and Inclusion by awarding some grants that enable early career researchers to attend the conference, present their research activities, and become part of the ECML PKDD community. A total of 8 grants covering all or part of the registration fee (4 free registrations and 4 with 50% discount) were awarded to individuals who belong to underrepresented communities, based on gender and role/position, to attend the conference and present their research activities. The goal of the grants was to provide financial support to early-career (women) scientists and Master and Ph.D. students from developing countries. The Diversity and Inclusion action also includes the SoBigData Award, fully sponsored by the SoBigData++ Horizon2020 project, which aims to encourage more diverse participation in computer science and machine learning events. The award is intended to cover expenses for transportation and accommodation.

The papers presented during the three main conference days were organized in four different tracks:

- Research Track: research or methodology papers from all areas in machine learning, knowledge discovery, and data mining;
- Applied Data Science Track: papers on novel applications of machine learning, data mining, and knowledge discovery to solve real-world use cases, thereby bridging the gap between practice and current theory;
- Journal Track: papers published in special issues of the journals Machine Learning and Data Mining and Knowledge Discovery;
- Demo Track: short papers introducing new prototypes or fully operational systems that exploit data science techniques and are presented via working demonstrations.

We received 829 submissions for the Research track and 239 for the Applied Data Science Track.

We accepted 196 papers (24%) in the Research Track and 58 (24%) in the Applied Data Science Track. In addition, there were 44 papers from the Journal Track and 16 demo papers (out of 28 submissions).

We want to thank all participants, authors, all chairs, all Program Committee members, area chairs, session chairs, volunteers, co-organizers, and organizers of workshops and tutorials for making ECML PKDD 2023 an outstanding success. Thanks to Springer for their continuous support and Microsoft for allowing us to use their CMT software for conference management and providing support throughout. Special thanks to our sponsors and the ECML PKDD Steering Committee for their support. Finally, we thank the organizing institutions: CENTAI (Italy) and Politecnico di Torino (Italy).

September 2023

Elena Baralis
Francesco Bonchi
Manuel Gomez Rodriguez
Danai Koutra
Claudia Plant
Gianmarco De Francisci Morales
Claudia Perlich

# Organization

## General Chairs

Elena Baralis — Politecnico di Torino, Italy
Francesco Bonchi — CENTAI, Italy and Eurecat, Spain

## Research Track Program Chairs

Manuel Gomez Rodriguez — Max Planck Institute for Software Systems, Germany
Danai Koutra — University of Michigan, USA
Claudia Plant — University of Vienna, Austria

## Applied Data Science Track Program Chairs

Gianmarco De Francisci Morales — CENTAI, Italy
Claudia Perlich — NYU and TwoSigma, USA

## Journal Track Chairs

Tania Cerquitelli — Politecnico di Torino, Italy
Marcello Restelli — Politecnico di Milano, Italy
Charalampos E. Tsourakakis — Boston University, USA and ISI Foundation, Italy
Fabio Vitale — CENTAI, Italy

## Workshop and Tutorial Chairs

Rosa Meo — University of Turin, Italy
Fabrizio Silvestri — Sapienza University of Rome, Italy

## Demo Chairs

Nicolas Kourtellis      Telefonica, Spain
Natali Ruchansky      Netflix, USA

## Local Chairs

Daniele Apiletti      Politecnico di Torino, Italy
Paolo Bajardi       CENTAI, Italy
Eliana Pastor       Politecnico di Torino, Italy

## Discovery Challenge Chairs

Danilo Giordano      Politecnico di Torino, Italy
André Panisson      CENTAI, Italy

## PhD Forum Chairs

Yllka Velaj       University of Vienna, Austria
Matteo Riondato      Amherst College, USA

## Diversity and Inclusion Chair

Tania Cerquitelli      Politecnico di Torino, Italy

## Proceedings Chairs

Eliana Pastor       Politecnico di Torino, Italy
Giulia Preti       CENTAI, Italy

## Sponsorship Chairs

Daniele Apiletti      Politecnico di Torino, Italy
Paolo Bajardi       CENTAI, Italy

## Web Chair

Alessandro Fiori                    Flowygo, Italy

## Social Media and Publicity Chair

Flavio Giobergia                    Politecnico di Torino, Italy

## Online Chairs

Alkis Koudounas                    Politecnico di Torino, Italy
Simone Monaco                      Politecnico di Torino, Italy

## Best Paper Awards Chairs

Peter Flach                        University of Bristol, UK
Katharina Morik                    TU Dortmund, Germany
Arno Siebes                        Utrecht University, The Netherlands

## ECML PKDD Steering Committee

Massih-Reza Amini                  Université Grenoble Alpes, France
Annalisa Appice                    University of Bari, Aldo Moro, Italy
Ira Assent                         Aarhus University, Denmark
Tania Cerquitelli                  Politecnico di Torino, Italy
Albert Bifet                       University of Waikato, New Zealand
Francesco Bonchi                   CENTAI, Italy and Eurecat, Spain
Peggy Cellier                      INSA Rennes, France
Saso Dzeroski                      Jožef Stefan Institute, Slovenia
Tias Guns                          KU Leuven, Belgium
Alípio M. G. Jorge                 University of Porto, Portugal
Kristian Kersting                  TU Darmstadt, Germany
Jefrey Lijffijt                    Ghent University, Belgium
Luís Moreira-Matias                Sennder GmbH, Germany
Katharina Morik                    TU Dortmund, Germany
Siegfried Nijssen                  Université catholique de Louvain, Belgium
Andrea Passerini                   University of Trento, Italy

| | |
|---|---|
| Marco Cotogni | University of Pavia, Italy |
| Gabriele D'Acunto | Sapienza University of Rome, Italy |
| Cassio Fraga Dantas | TETIS, Université Montpellier, INRAE, France |
| Jérôme Darmont | Université Lumière Lyon 2, France |
| George Dasoulas | Harvard University, USA |
| Sébastien Destercke | Université de Technologie de Compiègne, France |
| Shridhar Devamane | Global Academy of Technology, India |
| Claudia Diamantini | Università Politecnica delle Marche, Italy |
| Gianluca Drappo | Politecnico di Milano, Italy |
| Pedro Ferreira | University of Lisbon, Portugal |
| Cèsar Ferri | Universitat Politècnica de València, Spain |
| M. Julia Flores | Universidad de Castilla-La Mancha, Spain |
| Germain Forestier | University of Haute-Alsace, France |
| Elisa Fromont | Université de Rennes 1, France |
| Emanuele Frontoni | University of Macerata, Italy |
| Esther Galbrun | University of Eastern Finland, Finland |
| Joao Gama | University of Porto, Portugal |
| Jose A. Gamez | Universidad de Castilla-La Mancha, Spain |
| David García Soriano | ISI Foundation, Italy |
| Paolo Garza | Politecnico di Torino, Italy |
| Salvatore Greco | Politecnico di Torino, Italy |
| Riccardo Guidotti | University of Pisa, Italy |
| Francesco Gullo | UniCredit, Italy |
| Shahrzad Haddadan | Rutgers Business School, USA |
| Martin Holena | Czech Academy of Sciences, Czech Republic |
| Jaakko Hollmén | Stockholm University, Sweden |
| Dino Ienco | INRAE, France |
| Georgiana Ifrim | University College Dublin, Ireland |
| Felix Iglesias | TU Vienna, Austria |
| Angelo Impedovo | Niuma, Italy |
| Manfred Jaeger | Aalborg University, Denmark |
| Szymon Jaroszewicz | Warsaw University of Technology, Poland |
| Panagiotis Karras | Aarhus University, Denmark |
| George Katsimpras | National Center for Scientific Research Demokritos, Greece |
| Mehdi Kaytoue | Infologic R&D, France |
| Dragi Kocev | Jožef Stefan Institute, Slovenia |
| Yun Sing Koh | University of Auckland, New Zealand |
| Sotiropoulos Konstantinos | Boston University, USA |
| Lars Kotthoff | University of Wyoming, USA |
| Alkis Koudounas | Politecnico di Torino, Italy |
| Tommaso Lanciano | Sapienza University of Rome, Italy |

| Helge Langseth | Norwegian University of Science and Technology, Norway |
| Thien Le | MIT, USA |
| Hsuan-Tien Lin | National Taiwan University, Taiwan |
| Marco Lippi | University of Modena and Reggio Emilia, Italy |
| Corrado Loglisci | University of Bari, Aldo Moro, Italy |
| Manuel López-ibáñez | University of Manchester, UK |
| Nuno Lourenço | CISUC, Portugal |
| Claudio Lucchese | Ca' Foscari University of Venice, Italy |
| Brian Mac Namee | University College Dublin, Ireland |
| Gjorgji Madjarov | Ss. Cyril and Methodius University in Skopje, North Macedonia |
| Luigi Malagò | Transylvanian Institute of Neuroscience, Romania |
| Sagar Malhotra | Fondazione Bruno Kessler, Italy |
| Fragkiskos Malliaros | CentraleSupélec, Université Paris-Saclay, France |
| Giuseppe Manco | ICAR-CNR, Italy |
| Basarab Matei | Sorbonne Université Paris Nord, France |
| Michael Mathioudakis | University of Helsinki, Finland |
| Rosa Meo | University of Turin, Italy |
| Mohamed-Lamine Messai | Université Lumière Lyon 2, France |
| Sara Migliorini | University of Verona, Italy |
| Alex Mircoli | Università Politecnica delle Marche, Italy |
| Atsushi Miyauchi | University of Tokyo, Japan |
| Simone Monaco | Politecnico di Torino, Italy |
| Anna Monreale | University of Pisa, Italy |
| Corrado Monti | CENTAI, Italy |
| Katharina Morik | TU Dortmund, Germany |
| Lia Morra | Politecnico di Torino, Italy |
| Arsenii Mustafin | Boston University, USA |
| Mirco Mutti | Politecnico di Milano/University of Bologna, Italy |
| Amedeo Napoli | University of Lorraine, CNRS, LORIA, France |
| Kleber Oliveira | CENTAI, Italy |
| Gabriella Olmo | Politecnico di Torino, Italy |
| Marios Papachristou | Cornell University, USA |
| Panagiotis Papapetrou | Stockholm University, Sweden |
| Matteo Papini | Universitat Pompeu Fabra, Spain |
| Vincenzo Pasquadibisceglie | University of Bari, Aldo Moro, Italy |
| Eliana Pastor | Politecnico di Torino, Italy |
| Andrea Paudice | University of Milan, Italy |
| Charlotte Pelletier | IRISA - Université Bretagne-Sud, France |
| Ruggero G. Pensa | University of Turin, Italy |
| Simone Piaggesi | University of Bologna/ISI Foundation, Italy |

| | |
|---|---|
| Matteo Pirotta | Meta, France |
| Marc Plantevit | EPITA, France |
| Konstantinos Pliakos | KU Leuven, Belgium |
| Kai Puolamäki | University of Helsinki, Finland |
| Jan Ramon | Inria, France |
| Rita P. Ribeiro | INESC TEC/University of Porto, Portugal |
| Matteo Riondato | Amherst College, USA |
| Antonio Riva | Politecnico di Milano, Italy |
| Shota Saito | University College London, UK |
| Flora Salim | University of New South Wales, Australia |
| Roberto Santana | University of the Basque Country, Spain |
| Lars Schmidt-Thieme | University of Hildesheim, Germany |
| Thomas Seidl | LMU Munich, Germany |
| Kijung Shin | KAIST, South Korea |
| Shinichi Shirakawa | Yokohama National University, Japan |
| Konstantinos Sotiropoulos | Boston University, USA |
| Fabian Spaeh | Boston University, USA |
| Gerasimos Spanakis | Maastricht University, The Netherlands |
| Myra Spiliopoulou | Otto-von-Guericke-University Magdeburg, Germany |
| Jerzy Stefanowski | Poznan University of Technology, Poland |
| Mahito Sugiyama | National Institute of Informatics, Japan |
| Nikolaj Tatti | University of Helsinki, Finland |
| Maximilian Thiessen | TU Vienna, Austria |
| Josephine Thomas | University of Kassel, Germany |
| Kiran Tomlinson | Cornell University, USA |
| Leonardo Trujillo | Tecnológico Nacional de México, Mexico |
| Grigorios Tsoumakas | Aristotle University of Thessaloniki, Greece |
| Genoveva Vargas-Solar | CNRS, LIRIS Lab, France |
| Edoardo Vittori | Politecnico di Milano/Intesa Sanpaolo, Italy |
| Christel Vrain | University of Orléans, France |
| Willem Waegeman | Ghent University, Belgium |
| Yanbang Wang | Cornell University, USA |
| Pascal Welke | University of Bonn, Germany |
| Marcel Wever | LMU Munich, Germany |
| Stefan Wrobel | University of Bonn/Fraunhofer IAIS, Germany |
| Guoxian Yu | Shandong University, China |
| Ilias Zavitsanos | National Center for Scientific Research Demokritos, Greece |
| Ye Zhu | Deakin University, Australia |
| Albrecht Zimmermann | Université de Caen Normandie, France |

## Area Chairs, Research Track

| | |
|---|---|
| Fabrizio Angiulli | University of Calabria, Italy |
| Annalisa Appice | University of Bari, Aldo Moro, Italy |
| Antonio Artés | Universidad Carlos III de Madrid, Spain |
| Martin Atzmueller | Osnabrück University, Germany |
| Christian Böhm | University of Vienna, Austria |
| Michael R. Berthold | KNIME, Switzerland |
| Albert Bifet | Université Paris-Saclay, France |
| Hendrik Blockeel | KU Leuven, Belgium |
| Ulf Brefeld | Leuphana University, Germany |
| Paula Brito | INESC TEC - LIAAD/University of Porto, Portugal |
| Wolfram Burgard | University of Technology Nuremberg, Germany |
| Seshadhri C. | UCSC, USA |
| Michelangelo Ceci | University of Bari, Aldo Moro, Italy |
| Peggy Cellier | IRISA - INSA Rennes, France |
| Duen Horng Chau | Georgia Institute of Technology, USA |
| Nicolas Courty | IRISA - Université Bretagne-Sud, France |
| Bruno Cremilleux | Université de Caen Normandie, France |
| Jesse Davis | KU Leuven, Belgium |
| Abir De | IIT Bombay, India |
| Tom Diethe | AstraZeneca, UK |
| Yuxiao Dong | Tsinghua University, China |
| Kurt Driessens | Maastricht University, The Netherlands |
| Tapio Elomaa | Tampere University, Finland |
| Johannes Fürnkranz | JKU Linz, Austria |
| Sophie Fellenz | RPTU Kaiserslautern-Landau, Germany |
| Elisa Fromont | IRISA/Inria rba - Université de Rennes 1, France |
| Thomas Gärtner | TU Vienna, Austria |
| Patrick Gallinari | Criteo AI Lab - Sorbonne Université, France |
| Joao Gama | INESC TEC - LIAAD, Portugal |
| Rayid Ghani | Carnegie Mellon University, USA |
| Aristides Gionis | KTH Royal Institute of Technology, Sweden |
| Chen Gong | Nanjing University of Science and Technology, China |
| Francesco Gullo | UniCredit, Italy |
| Eyke Hüllermeier | LMU Munich, Germany |
| Junheng Hao | University of California, Los Angeles, USA |
| José Hernández-Orallo | Universitat Politècnica de Valencia, Spain |
| Daniel Hernández-Lobato | Universidad Autonoma de Madrid, Spain |
| Sibylle Hess | TU Eindhoven, The Netherlands |

| | |
|---|---|
| Jaakko Hollmén | Aalto University, Finland |
| Andreas Hotho | University of Würzburg, Germany |
| Georgiana Ifrim | University College Dublin, Ireland |
| Jayaraman J. Thiagarajan | Lawrence Livermore, USA |
| Alipio M. G. Jorge | INESC TEC/University of Porto, Portugal |
| Ross King | Chalmers University of Technology, Sweden |
| Yun Sing Koh | University of Auckland, New Zealand |
| Lars Kotthoff | University of Wyoming, USA |
| Peer Kröger | Christian-Albrechst University of Kiel, Germany |
| Stefan Kramer | JGU Mainz, Germany |
| Jörg Lücke | University of Oldenburg, Germany |
| Niklas Lavesson | Blekinge Institute of Technology, Sweden |
| Bruno Lepri | Fondazione Bruno Kessler, Italy |
| Jefrey Lijffijt | Ghent University, Belgium |
| Marius Lindauer | Leibniz University Hannover, Germany |
| Patrick Loiseau | Inria, France |
| Jose A. Lozano | UPV/EHU, Spain |
| Emmanuel Müller | TU Dortmund, Germany |
| Donato Malerba | University of Bari, Aldo Moro, Italy |
| Fragkiskos Malliaros | CentraleSupelec, France |
| Giuseppe Manco | ICAR-CNR, Italy |
| Pauli Miettinen | University of Eastern Finland, Finland |
| Dunja Mladenic | Jožef Stefan Institute, Slovenia |
| Anna Monreale | University of Pisa, Italy |
| Luis Moreira-Matias | Sennder GmbH, Germany |
| Katharina J. Morik | TU Dortmund, Germany |
| Siegfried Nijssen | Université catholique de Louvain, Belgium |
| Evangelos Papalexakis | UC, Riverside, USA |
| Panagiotis Papapetrou | Stockholm University, Sweden |
| Andrea Passerini | University of Trento, Italy |
| Mykola Pechenizkiy | TU Eindhoven, The Netherlands |
| Jaakko Peltonen | Tampere University, Finland |
| Franz Pernkopf | TU Graz, Austria |
| Bernhard Pfahringer | University of Waikato, New Zealand |
| Fabio Pinelli | IMT Lucca, Italy |
| Goran Radanovic | Max Planck Institute for Software Systems, Germany |
| Jesse Read | École Polytechnique, France |
| Matthias Renz | Christian-Albrechst University of Kiel, Germany |
| Marian-Andrei Rizoiu | University of Technology, Sydney, Australia |
| Celine Robardet | INSA Lyon, France |
| Juho Rousu | Aalto University, Finland |

| Sriparna Saha | IIT Patna, India |
| Ute Schmid | University of Bamberg, Germany |
| Lars Schmidt-Thieme | University of Hildesheim, Germany |
| Michele Sebag | LISN CNRS, France |
| Thomas Seidl | LMU Munich, Germany |
| Junming Shao | University of Electronic Science and Technology of China, China |
| Arno Siebes | Utrecht University, The Netherlands |
| Fabrizio Silvestri | Sapienza University of Rome, Italy |
| Carlos Soares | University of Porto, Portugal |
| Christian Sohler | University of Cologne, Germany |
| Myra Spiliopoulou | Otto-von-Guericke-University Magdeburg, Germany |
| Jie Tang | Tsinghua University, China |
| Nikolaj Tatti | University of Helsinki, Finland |
| Evimaria Terzi | Boston University, USA |
| Marc Tommasi | Lille University, France |
| Heike Trautmann | University of Münster, Germany |
| Herke van Hoof | University of Amsterdam, The Netherlands |
| Celine Vens | KU Leuven, Belgium |
| Christel Vrain | University of Orleans, France |
| Jilles Vreeken | CISPA Helmholtz Center for Information Security, Germany |
| Wei Ye | Tongji University, China |
| Jing Zhang | Renmin University of China, China |
| Min-Ling Zhang | Southeast University, China |

## Area Chairs, Applied Data Science Track

| Annalisa Appice | University of Bari, Aldo Moro, Italy |
| Ira Assent | Aarhus University, Denmark |
| Martin Atzmueller | Osnabrück University, Germany |
| Michael R. Berthold | KNIME, Switzerland |
| Hendrik Blockeel | KU Leuven, Belgium |
| Michelangelo Ceci | University of Bari, Aldo Moro, Italy |
| Peggy Cellier | IRISA - INSA Rennes, France |
| Yi Chang | Jilin University, China |
| Nicolas Courty | IRISA - UBS, France |
| Bruno Cremilleux | Université de Caen Normandie, France |
| Peng Cui | Tsinghua University, China |
| Anirban Dasgupta | IIT Gandhinagar, India |

| | |
|---|---|
| Tom Diethe | AstraZeneca, UK |
| Carlotta Domeniconi | George Mason University, USA |
| Dejing Dou | BCG, USA |
| Kurt Driessens | Maastricht University, The Netherlands |
| Johannes Fürnkranz | JKU Linz, Austria |
| Faisal Farooq | Qatar Computing Research Institute, Qatar |
| Paolo Frasconi | University of Florence, Italy |
| Elisa Fromont | IRISA/Inria rba - Université de Rennes 1, France |
| Glenn Fung | Liberty Mutual, USA |
| Joao Gama | INESC TEC - LIAAD, Portugal |
| Jose A. Gamez | Universidad de Castilla-La Mancha, Spain |
| Rayid Ghani | Carnegie Mellon University, USA |
| Aristides Gionis | KTH Royal Institute of Technology, Sweden |
| Sreenivas Gollapudi | Google, USA |
| Francesco Gullo | UniCredit, Italy |
| Eyke Hüllermeier | LMU Munich, Germany |
| Jingrui He | University of Illinois at Urbana-Champaign, USA |
| Jaakko Hollmén | Aalto University, Finland |
| Andreas Hotho | University of Würzburg, Germany |
| Daxin Jiang | Microsoft, Beijing, China |
| Alipio M. G. Jorge | INESC TEC/University of Porto, Portugal |
| George Karypis | University of Minnesota, USA |
| Eamonn Keogh | UC, Riverside, USA |
| Yun Sing Koh | University of Auckland, New Zealand |
| Parisa Kordjamshidi | Michigan State University, USA |
| Lars Kotthoff | University of Wyoming, USA |
| Nicolas Kourtellis | Telefonica Research, Spain |
| Stefan Kramer | JGU Mainz, Germany |
| Balaji Krishnapuram | Pinterest, USA |
| Niklas Lavesson | Blekinge Institute of Technology, Sweden |
| Chuan Lei | Amazon Web Services, USA |
| Marius Lindauer | Leibniz University Hannover, Germany |
| Patrick Loiseau | Inria, France |
| Giuseppe Manco | ICAR-CNR, Italy |
| Gabor Melli | PredictionWorks, USA |
| Anna Monreale | University of Pisa, Italy |
| Luis Moreira-Matias | Sennder GmbH, Germany |
| Nuria Oliver | ELLIS Alicante, Spain |
| Panagiotis Papapetrou | Stockholm University, Sweden |
| Mykola Pechenizkiy | TU Eindhoven, The Netherlands |
| Jian Pei | Simon Fraser University, Canada |
| Julien Perez | Naver Labs Europe, France |

| | |
|---|---|
| Fabio Pinelli | IMT Lucca, Italy |
| Zhiwei (Tony) Qin | Lyft, USA |
| Visvanathan Ramesh | Goethe University, Germany |
| Zhaochun Ren | Shandong University, China |
| Sriparna Saha | IIT Patna, India |
| Ute Schmid | University of Bamberg, Germany |
| Lars Schmidt-Thieme | University of Hildesheim, Germany |
| Thomas Seidl | LMU Munich, Germany |
| Fabrizio Silvestri | Sapienza University of Rome, Italy |
| Myra Spiliopoulou | Otto-von-Guericke-University Magdeburg, Germany |
| Karthik Subbian | Amazon, USA |
| Liang Sun | Alibaba Group, China |
| Jie Tang | Tsinghua University, China |
| Jiliang Tang | Michigan State University, USA |
| Sandeep Tata | Google, USA |
| Nikolaj Tatti | University of Helsinki, Finland |
| Marc Tommasi | Lille University, France |
| Yongxin Tong | Beihang University, China |
| Vincent S. Tseng | National Yang Ming Chiao Tung University, Taiwan |
| Antti Ukkonen | University of Helsinki, Finland |
| Willem Waegeman | Ghent University, Belgium |
| Fei Wang | Cornell University, USA |
| Jie Wang | University of Science and Technology of China, China |
| Sinong Wang | Meta AI, USA |
| Zheng Wang | Alibaba DAMO Academy, China |
| Lingfei Wu | Pinterest, USA |
| Yinglong Xia | Meta, USA |
| Hui Xiong | Rutgers University, USA |
| Hongxia Yang | Alibaba Group, China |
| Min-Ling Zhang | Southeast University, China |
| Jiayu Zhou | Michigan State University, USA |
| Xingquan Zhu | Florida Atlantic University, USA |
| Fuzhen Zhuang | Institute of Artificial Intelligence, China |
| Albrecht Zimmermann | Université de Caen Normandie, France |

# Program Committee, Research Track

| | |
|---|---|
| Matthias Aßenmacher | LMU Munich, Germany |
| Sara Abdali | Microsoft, USA |
| Evrim Acar | Simula Metropolitan Center for Digital Engineering, Norway |
| Homayun Afrabandpey | Nokia Technologies, Finland |
| Reza Akbarinia | Inria, France |
| Cuneyt G. Akcora | University of Manitoba, Canada |
| Ranya Almohsen | West Virginia University, USA |
| Thiago Andrade | INESC TEC/University of Porto, Portugal |
| Jean-Marc Andreoli | Naverlabs Europe, France |
| Giuseppina Andresini | University of Bari, Aldo Moro, Italy |
| Alessandro Antonucci | IDSIA, Switzerland |
| Xiang Ao | Institute of Computing Technology, CAS, China |
| Héber H. Arcolezi | Inria/École Polytechnique, France |
| Jerónimo Arenas-García | Universidad Carlos III de Madrid, Spain |
| Yusuf Arslan | University of Luxembourg, Luxemburg |
| Ali Ayadi | University of Strasbourg, France |
| Steve Azzolin | University of Trento, Italy |
| Pierre-Luc Bacon | Mila, Canada |
| Bunil K. Balabantaray | NIT Meghalaya, India |
| Mitra Baratchi | LIACS/Leiden University, The Netherlands |
| Christian Bauckhage | Fraunhofer IAIS, Germany |
| Anna Beer | Aarhus University, Denmark |
| Michael Beigl | Karlsruhe Institute of Technology, Germany |
| Khalid Benabdeslem | Université de Lyon, Lyon 1, France |
| Idir Benouaret | Epita Research Laboratory, France |
| Paul Berg | IRISA, France |
| Christoph Bergmeir | Monash University, Australia |
| Gilberto Bernardes | INESC TEC/University of Porto, Portugal |
| Eva Besada-Portas | Universidad Complutense de Madrid, Spain |
| Jalaj Bhandari | Columbia University, USA |
| Asmita Bhat | TU Kaiserslautern, Germany |
| Monowar Bhuyan | Umeå University, Sweden |
| Adrien Bibal | University of Colorado Anschutz Medical Campus, USA |
| Manuele Bicego | University of Verona, Italy |
| Przemyslaw Biecek | Warsaw University of Technology, Poland |
| Alexander Binder | University of Oslo, Norway |
| Livio Bioglio | University of Turin, Italy |
| Patrick Blöbaum | Amazon Web Services, USA |

| | |
|---|---|
| Thomas Bonald | Télécom Paris, France |
| Ludovico Boratto | University of Cagliari, Italy |
| Stefano Bortoli | Huawei Research Center, Germany |
| Tassadit Bouadi | Université de Rennes 1, France |
| Ahcène Boubekki | UiT, Arctic University of Norway, Norway |
| Luc Brogat-Motte | Télécom Paris, France |
| Jannis Brugger | TU Darmstadt, Germany |
| Nhat-Tan Bui | University of Science - VNUHCM, Vietnam |
| Mirko Bunse | TU Dortmund, Germany |
| John Burden | University of Cambridge, UK |
| Wolfram Burgard | University of Technology, Germany |
| Julian Busch | Siemens Technology, Germany |
| Sebastian Buschjäger | TU Dortmund, Germany |
| Oswald C. | NIT Trichy, India |
| Seshadhri C. | UCSC, USA |
| Xin-Qiang Cai | University of Tokyo, Japan |
| Zekun Cai | University of Tokyo, Japan |
| Xiaofeng Cao | University of Technology, Sydney, Australia |
| Giuseppe Casalicchio | LMU Munich, Germany |
| Guilherme Cassales | University of Waikato, New Zealand |
| Oded Cats | TU Delft, The Netherlands |
| Remy Cazabet | Université de Lyon, Lyon 1, France |
| Mattia Cerrato | JGU Mainz, Germany |
| Ricardo Cerri | Federal University of Sao Carlos, Brazil |
| Prithwish Chakraborty | IBM Research, USA |
| Harry Kai-Ho Chan | University of Sheffield, UK |
| Joydeep Chandra | IIT Patna, India |
| Vaggos Chatziafratis | Stanford University, USA |
| Zaineb Chelly Dagdia | UVSQ - Université Paris-Saclay, France |
| Hongyang Chen | Zhejiang Lab, China |
| Huaming Chen | University of Sydney, Australia |
| Hung-Hsuan Chen | National Central University, Taiwan |
| Jin Chen | University of Electronic Science and Technology of China, China |
| Kuan-Hsun Chen | University of Twente, The Netherlands |
| Ling Chen | University of Technology, Australia |
| Lingwei Chen | Wright State University, USA |
| Minyu Chen | Shanghai Jiaotong University, China |
| Xi Chen | Ghent University, Belgium |
| Xiaojun Chen | Institute of Information Engineering, CAS, China |
| Xuefeng Chen | Chongqing University, China |
| Ying Chen | RMIT University, Australia |

| | |
|---|---|
| Yueguo Chen | Renmin University of China, China |
| Yuzhou Chen | Temple University, USA |
| Zheng Chen | Osaka University, Japan |
| Ziheng Chen | Walmart, USA |
| Lu Cheng | University of Illinois, Chicago, USA |
| Xu Cheng | Shanghai Jiao Tong University, China |
| Zhiyong Cheng | Shandong Academy of Sciences, China |
| Yann Chevaleyre | Université Paris Dauphine, France |
| Chun Wai Chiu | Keele University, UK |
| Silvia Chiusano | Politecnico di Torino, Italy |
| Satyendra Singh Chouhan | MNIT Jaipur, India |
| Hua Chu | Xidian University, China |
| Sarel Cohen | Academic College of Tel Aviv-Yaffo, Israel |
| J. Alberto Conejero | Universitat Politècnica de València, Spain |
| Lidia Contreras-Ochando | Universitat Politècnica de València, Spain |
| Giorgio Corani | IDSIA, Switzerland |
| Luca Corbucci | University of Pisa, Italy |
| Roberto Corizzo | American University, USA |
| Baris Coskunuzer | University of Texas at Dallas, USA |
| Fabrizio Costa | Exeter University, UK |
| Gustavo de Assis Costa | Instituto Federal de Goiás, Brazil |
| Evan Crothers | University of Ottawa, Canada |
| Pádraig Cunningham | University College Dublin, Ireland |
| Jacek Cyranka | University of Warsaw, Poland |
| Tianxiang Dai | Huawei European Research Institute, Germany |
| Xuan-Hong Dang | IBM T.J. Watson Research Center, USA |
| Thi-Bich-Hanh Dao | University of Orleans, France |
| Debasis Das | Indian Institute of Technology Jodhpur, India |
| Paul Davidsson | Malmö University, Sweden |
| Marcilio de Souto | LIFO, University of Orleans, France |
| Klest Dedja | KU Leuven, Belgium |
| Elena Demidova | University of Bonn, Germany |
| Caglar Demir | Paderborn University, Germany |
| Difan Deng | Leibniz University Hannover, Germany |
| Laurens Devos | KU Leuven, Belgium |
| Nicola Di Mauro | University of Bari, Aldo Moro, Italy |
| Jingtao Ding | Tsinghua University, China |
| Yao-Xiang Ding | Nanjing University, China |
| Lamine Diop | EPITA, France |
| Gillian Dobbie | University of Auckland, New Zealand |
| Stephan Doerfel | Kiel University of Applied Sciences, Germany |
| Carola Doerr | Sorbonne Université, France |

| | |
|---|---|
| Nanqing Dong | University of Oxford, UK |
| Haizhou Du | Shanghai University of Electric Power, China |
| Qihan Du | Renmin University of China, China |
| Songlin Du | Southeast University, China |
| Xin Du | University of Edinburgh, UK |
| Wouter Duivesteijn | TU Eindhoven, The Netherlands |
| Inês Dutra | University of Porto, Portugal |
| Sourav Dutta | Huawei Research Centre, Ireland |
| Saso Dzeroski | Jožef Stefan Institute, Slovenia |
| Nabil El Malki | IRIT, France |
| Mohab Elkaref | IBM Research Europe, UK |
| Tapio Elomaa | Tampere University, Finland |
| Dominik M. Endres | University of Marburg, Germany |
| Georgios Exarchakis | University of Bath, UK |
| Lukas Faber | ETH Zurich, Switzerland |
| Samuel G. Fadel | Leuphana University, Germany |
| Haoyi Fan | Zhengzhou University, China |
| Zipei Fan | University of Tokyo, Japan |
| Hadi Fanaee-T | Halmstad University, Sweden |
| Elaine Ribeiro Faria | UFU, Brazil |
| Fabio Fassetti | University of Calabria, Italy |
| Anthony Faustine | ITI/LARSyS - Técnico Lisboa, Portugal |
| Sophie Fellenz | RPTU Kaiserslautern-Landau, Germany |
| Wenjie Feng | National University of Singapore, Singapore |
| Zunlei Feng | Zhejiang University, China |
| Daniel Fernández-Sánchez | Universidad Autónoma de Madrid, Spain |
| Luca Ferragina | University of Calabria, Italy |
| Emilio Ferrara | USC ISI, USA |
| Cèsar Ferri | Universitat Politècnica València, Spain |
| Flavio Figueiredo | Universidade Federal de Minas Gerais, Brazil |
| Lucie Flek | University of Marburg, Germany |
| Michele Fontana | University of Pisa, Italy |
| Germain Forestier | University of Haute-Alsace, France |
| Raphaël Fournier-S'niehotta | CNAM, France |
| Benoît Frénay | University of Namur, Belgium |
| Kary Främling | Umeå University, Sweden |
| Holger Froening | University of Heidelberg, Germany |
| Fabio Fumarola | Prometeia, Italy |
| María José Gómez-Silva | Universidad Complutense de Madrid, Spain |
| Vanessa Gómez-Verdejo | Universidad Carlos III de Madrid, Spain |
| Pratik Gajane | TU Eindhoven, The Netherlands |
| Esther Galbrun | University of Eastern Finland, Finland |

| | |
|---|---|
| Claudio Gallicchio | University of Pisa, Italy |
| Chen Gao | Tsinghua University, China |
| Shengxiang Gao | Kunming University of Science and Technology, China |
| Yifeng Gao | University of Texas Rio Grande Valley, USA |
| Luis Garcia | University of Brasilia, Brazil |
| Dominique Gay | Université de La Réunion, France |
| Suyu Ge | University of Illinois at Urbana-Champaign, USA |
| Zhaocheng Ge | Huazhong University of Science and Technology, China |
| Alborz Geramifard | Facebook AI, USA |
| Ahana Ghosh | Max Planck Institute for Software Systems, Germany |
| Shreya Ghosh | Penn State University, USA |
| Flavio Giobergia | Politecnico di Torino, Italy |
| Sarunas Girdzijauskas | KTH Royal Institute of Technology, Sweden |
| Heitor Murilo Gomes | University of Waikato, Sweden |
| Wenwen Gong | Tsinghua University, China |
| Bedartha Goswami | University of Tübingen, Germany |
| Anastasios Gounaris | Aristotle University of Thessaloniki, Greece |
| Michael Granitzer | University of Passau, Germany |
| Derek Greene | University College Dublin, Ireland |
| Moritz Grosse-Wentrup | University of Vienna, Austria |
| Marek Grzes | University of Kent, UK |
| Xinyu Guan | Xian Jiaotong University, China |
| Massimo Guarascio | ICAR-CNR, Italy |
| Riccardo Guidotti | University of Pisa, Italy |
| Lan-Zhe Guo | Nanjing University, China |
| Lingbing Guo | Zhejiang University, China |
| Shanqing Guo | Shandong University, China |
| Karthik S. Gurumoorthy | Walmart, USA |
| Thomas Guyet | Inria, France |
| Huong Ha | RMIT University, Australia |
| Benjamin Halstead | University of Auckland, New Zealand |
| Massinissa Hamidi | LIPN-UMR CNRS 7030, France |
| Donghong Han | Northeastern University, USA |
| Marwan Hassani | TU Eindhoven, The Netherlands |
| Rima Hazra | Indian Institute of Technology, Kharagpur, India |
| Mark Heimann | Lawrence Livermore, USA |
| Cesar Hidalgo | University of Toulouse, France |
| Martin Holena | Institute of Computer Science, Czech Republic |
| Mike Holenderski | TU Eindhoven, The Netherlands |

| | |
|---|---|
| Adrian Horzyk | AGH University of Science and Technology, Poland |
| Shifu Hou | Case Western Reserve University, USA |
| Hongsheng Hu | CSIRO, Australia |
| Yaowei Hu | University of Arkansas, USA |
| Yang Hua | Queen's University Belfast, UK |
| Chao Huang | University of Hong Kong, China |
| Guanjie Huang | Penn State University, USA |
| Hong Huang | Huazhong University of Science and Technology, China |
| Nina C. Hubig | Clemson University, USA |
| Dino Ienco | Irstea Institute, France |
| Angelo Impedovo | Niuma, Italy |
| Roberto Interdonato | CIRAD, France |
| Stratis Ioannidis | Northeastern University, USA |
| Nevo Itzhak | Ben-Gurion University, Israel |
| Raghav Jain | IIT Patna, India |
| Kuk Jin Jang | University of Pennsylvania, USA |
| Szymon Jaroszewicz | Polish Academy of Sciences, Poland |
| Shaoxiong Ji | University of Helsinki, Finland |
| Bin-Bin Jia | Lanzhou University of Technology, China |
| Caiyan Jia | School of Computer and Information Technology, China |
| Xiuyi Jia | Nanjing University of Science and Technology, China |
| Nan Jiang | Purdue University, USA |
| Renhe Jiang | University of Tokyo, Japan |
| Song Jiang | University of California, Los Angeles, USA |
| Pengfei Jiao | Hangzhou Dianzi University, China |
| Di Jin | Amazon, USA |
| Guangyin Jin | National University of Defense Technology, China |
| Jiahui Jin | Southeast University, China |
| Ruoming Jin | Kent State University, USA |
| Yilun Jin | The Hong Kong University of Science and Technology, Hong Kong |
| Hugo Jonker | Open University of the Netherlands, The Netherlands |
| Adan Jose-Garcia | Lille University, France |
| Marius Köppel | JGU Mainz, Germany |
| Vana Kalogeraki | Athens University of Economics and Business, Greece |
| Konstantinos Kalpakis | University of Maryland Baltimore County, USA |

| | |
|---|---|
| Andreas Kaltenbrunner | ISI Foundation, Italy |
| Shivaram Kalyanakrishnan | IIT Bombay, India |
| Toshihiro Kamishima | National Institute of Advanced Industrial Science and Technology, Japan |
| Bo Kang | Ghent University, Belgium |
| Murat Kantarcioglu | UT Dallas |
| Thommen Karimpanal George | Deakin University, Australia |
| Saurav Karmakar | University of Galway, Ireland |
| Panagiotis Karras | Aarhus University, Denmark |
| Dimitrios Katsaros | University of Thessaly, Greece |
| Eamonn Keogh | UC, Riverside, USA |
| Jaleed Khan | University of Galway, Ireland |
| Irwin King | Chinese University of Hong Kong, China |
| Mauritius Klein | LMU Munich, Germany |
| Tomas Kliegr | Prague University of Economics and Business, Czech Republic |
| Dmitry Kobak | University of Tübingen, Germany |
| Dragi Kocev | Jožef Stefan Institute, Slovenia |
| Lars Kotthoff | University of Wyoming, USA |
| Anna Krause | University of Würzburg, Germany |
| Amer Krivosija | TU Dortmund, Germany |
| Daniel Kudenko | L3S Research Center, Germany |
| Meelis Kull | University of Tartu, Estonia |
| Sergey O. Kuznetsov | HSE, Russia |
| Beatriz López | University of Girona, Spain |
| Jörg Lücke | University of Oldenburg, Germany |
| Firas Laakom | Tampere University, Finland |
| Mateusz Lango | Poznan University of Technology, Poland |
| Hady Lauw | Singapore Management University, Singapore |
| Tuan Le | New Mexico State University, USA |
| Erwan Le Merrer | Inria, France |
| Thach Le Nguyen | Insight Centre, Ireland |
| Tai Le Quy | L3S Research Center, Germany |
| Mustapha Lebbah | UVSQ - Université Paris-Saclay, France |
| Dongman Lee | KAIST, South Korea |
| Yeon-Chang Lee | Georgia Institute of Technology, USA |
| Zed Lee | Stockholm University, Sweden |
| Mathieu Lefort | Université de Lyon, France |
| Yunwen Lei | University of Birmingham, UK |
| Vincent Lemaire | Orange Innovation, France |
| Daniel Lemire | TÉLUQ University, Canada |
| Florian Lemmerich | RWTH Aachen University, Germany |

| | |
|---|---|
| Youfang Leng | Renmin University of China, China |
| Carson K. Leung | University of Manitoba, Canada |
| Dan Li | Sun Yat-Sen University, China |
| Gang Li | Deakin University, Australia |
| Jiaming Li | Huazhong University of Science and Technology, China |
| Mark Junjie Li | Shenzhen University, China |
| Nian Li | Tsinghua University, China |
| Shuai Li | University of Cambridge, UK |
| Tong Li | Hong Kong University of Science and Technology, China |
| Xiang Li | East China Normal University, China |
| Yang Li | University of North Carolina at Chapel Hill, USA |
| Yingming Li | Zhejiang University, China |
| Yinsheng Li | Fudan University, China |
| Yong Li | Huawei European Research Center, Germany |
| Zhihui Li | University of New South Wales, Australia |
| Zhixin Li | Guangxi Normal University, China |
| Defu Lian | University of Science and Technology of China, China |
| Yuxuan Liang | National University of Singapore, Singapore |
| Angelica Liguori | University of Calabria, Italy |
| Nick Lim | University of Waikato, Sweden |
| Baijiong Lin | The Hong Kong University of Science and Technology, Hong Kong |
| Piotr Lipinski | University of Wrocław, Poland |
| Marco Lippi | University of Modena and Reggio Emilia, Italy |
| Bowen Liu | Stanford University, USA |
| Chien-Liang Liu | National Chiao Tung University, Taiwan |
| Fenglin Liu | University of Oxford, UK |
| Junze Liu | University of California, Irvine, USA |
| Li Liu | Chongqing University, China |
| Ninghao Liu | University of Georgia, USA |
| Shenghua Liu | Institute of Computing Technology, CAS, China |
| Xiao Fan Liu | City University of Hong Kong, Hong Kong |
| Xu Liu | National University of Singapore, Singapore |
| Yang Liu | Institute of Computing Technology, CAS, China |
| Zihan Liu | Zhejiang University/Westlake University, China |
| Robert Loftin | TU Delft, The Netherlands |
| Corrado Loglisci | University of Bari, Aldo Moro, Italy |
| Mingsheng Long | Tsinghua University, China |
| Antonio Longa | Fondazione Bruno Kessler, Italy |

Grigorios Loukides King's College London, UK
Tsai-Ching Lu HRL Laboratories, USA
Zhiwu Lu Renmin University of China, China
Pedro Henrique Luz de Araujo University of Vienna, Austria
Marcos M. Raimundo University of Campinas, Brazil
Maximilian Münch University of Applied Sciences
 Würzburg-Schweinfurt, Germany
Fenglong Ma Pennsylvania State University, USA
Pingchuan Ma The Hong Kong University of Science and
 Technology, Hong Kong
Yao Ma New Jersey Institute of Technology, USA
Brian Mac Namee University College Dublin, Ireland
Henryk Maciejewski Wrocław University of Science and Technology,
 Poland
Ayush Maheshwari IIT Bombay, India
Ajay A. Mahimkar AT&T, USA
Ayan Majumdar Max Planck Institute for Software Systems,
 Germany
Donato Malerba University of Bari, Aldo Moro, Italy
Aakarsh Malhotra IIIT-Delhi, India
Fragkiskos Malliaros CentraleSupelec, France
Pekka Malo Aalto University, Finland
Hiroshi Mamitsuka Kyoto University, Japan/Aalto University, Finland
Domenico Mandaglio University of Calabria, Italy
Robin Manhaeve KU Leuven, Belgium
Silviu Maniu Université Paris-Saclay, France
Cinmayii G. Manliguez National Sun Yat-Sen University, Taiwan
Naresh Manwani IIIT Hyderabad, India
Giovanni Luca Marchetti KTH Royal Institute of Technology, Sweden
Koji Maruhashi Fujitsu Research, Fujitsu Limited, Japan
Florent Masseglia Inria, France
Sarah Masud IIIT-Delhi, India
Timothée Mathieu Inria, France
Amir Mehrpanah KTH Royal Institute of Technology, Sweden
Wagner Meira Jr. Universidade Federal de Minas Gerais, Brazil
Joao Mendes-Moreira INESC TEC, Portugal
Rui Meng BNU-HKBU United International College, China
Fabio Mercorio University of Milan-Bicocca, Italy
Alberto Maria Metelli Politecnico di Milano, Italy
Carlo Metta CNR-ISTI, Italy
Paolo Mignone University of Bari, Aldo Moro, Italy
Tsunenori Mine Kyushu University, Japan

| | |
|---|---|
| Nuno Moniz | INESC TEC, Portugal |
| Pierre Monnin | Université Côte d'Azur, Inria, CNRS, I3S, France |
| Carlos Monserrat-Aranda | Universitat Politècnica de València, Spain |
| Raha Moraffah | Arizona State University, USA |
| Davide Mottin | Aarhus University, Denmark |
| Hamid Mousavi | University of Oldenburg, Germany |
| Abdullah Mueen | University of New Mexico, USA |
| Shamsuddeen Hassan Muhamamd | University of Porto, Portugal |
| Koyel Mukherjee | Adobe Research, India |
| Yusuke Mukuta | University of Tokyo, Japan |
| Pranava Mummoju | University of Vienna, Austria |
| Taichi Murayama | NAIST, Japan |
| Ankur Nahar | IIT Jodhpur, India |
| Felipe Kenji Nakano | KU Leuven, Belgium |
| Hideki Nakayama | University of Tokyo, Japan |
| Géraldin Nanfack | University of Namur, Belgium |
| Mirco Nanni | CNR-ISTI, Italy |
| Franco Maria Nardini | CNR-ISTI, Italy |
| Usman Naseem | University of Sydney, Australia |
| Reza Nasirigerdeh | TU Munich, Germany |
| Rajashree Nayak | MIT ADT University, India |
| Benjamin Negrevergne | Université Paris Dauphine, France |
| Stefan Neumann | KTH Royal Institute of Technology, Sweden |
| Anna Nguyen | IBM, USA |
| Shiwen Ni | SIAT, CAS, China |
| Siegfried Nijssen | Université catholique de Louvain, Belgium |
| Iasonas Nikolaou | Boston University, USA |
| Simona Nisticò | University of Calabria, Italy |
| Hao Niu | KDDI Research, Japan |
| Mehdi Nourelahi | University of Wyoming, USA |
| Slawomir Nowaczyk | Halmstad University, Sweden |
| Eirini Ntoutsi | Bundeswehr University Munich, Germany |
| Barry O'Sullivan | University College Cork, Ireland |
| Nastaran Okati | Max Planck Institute for Software Systems, Germany |
| Tsuyoshi Okita | Kyushu Institute of Technology, Japan |
| Pablo Olmos | Universidad Carlos III de Madrid, Spain |
| Luis Antonio Ortega Andrés | Autonomous University of Madrid, Spain |
| Abdelkader Ouali | Université de Caen Normandie, France |
| Latifa Oukhellou | IFSTTAR, France |
| Chun Ouyang | Queensland University of Technology, Australia |
| Andrei Paleyes | University of Cambridge, UK |

Menghai Pan  Visa Research, USA
Shirui Pan  Griffith University, Australia
Apostolos N. Papadopoulos  Aristotle University of Thessaloniki, Greece
Chanyoung Park  KAIST, South Korea
Emilio Parrado-Hernandez  Universidad Carlos III de Madrid, Spain
Vincenzo Pasquadibisceglie  University of Bari, Aldo Moro, Italy
Eliana Pastor  Politecnico di Torino, Italy
Anand Paul  Kyungpook National University, South Korea
Shichao Pei  University of Notre Dame, USA
Yulong Pei  TU Eindhoven, The Netherlands
Leonardo Pellegrina  University of Padua, Italy
Ruggero Pensa  University of Turin, Italy
Fabiola Pereira  UFU, Brazil
Lucas Pereira  ITI/LARSyS - Técnico Lisboa, Portugal
Miquel Perello-Nieto  University of Bristol, UK
Lorenzo Perini  KU Leuven, Belgium
Matej Petkovifá  University of Ljubljana, Slovenia
Lukas Pfahler  TU Dortmund, Germany
Ninh Pham  University of Auckland, New Zealand
Guangyuan Piao  Maynooth University, Ireland
Francesco Piccialli  University of Naples Federico II, Italy
Martin Pilát  Charles University, Czech Republic
Gianvito Pio  University of Bari, Aldo Moro, Italy
Giuseppe Pirrò  Sapienza University of Rome, Italy
Francesco S. Pisani  ICAR-CNR, Italy
Srijith P. K.  IIIT Hyderabad, India
Marc Plantevit  EPITA, France
Mirko Polato  University of Turin, Italy
Axel Polleres  Vienna University of Economics and Business, Austria
Giovanni Ponti  ENEA, Italy
Paul Prasse  University of Potsdam, Germany
Mahardhika Pratama  University of South Australia, Australia
Philippe Preux  Inria, France
Ricardo B. Prudencio  Universidade Federal de Pernambuco, Brazil
Chiara Pugliese  CNR-ISTI, Italy
Erasmo Purificato  Otto-von-Guericke-University Magdeburg, Germany
Abdulhakim Qahtan  Utrecht University, The Netherlands
Lianyong Qi  China University of Petroleum, China
Kun Qian  Amazon Web Services, USA
Tieyun Qian  Wuhan University, China

| Chuan Qin | BOSS Zhipin, China |
| Yumou Qiu | Iowa State University, USA |
| Dimitrios Rafailidis | University of Thessaly, Greece |
| Edward Raff | Booz Allen Hamilton, USA |
| Chang Rajani | University of Helsinki, Finland |
| Herilalaina Rakotoarison | Inria, France |
| M. José Ramírez-Quintana | Universitat Politècnica de Valencia, Spain |
| Jan Ramon | Inria, France |
| Rajeev Rastogi | Amazon, India |
| Domenico Redavid | University of Bari, Aldo Moro, Italy |
| Qianqian Ren | Heilongjiang University, China |
| Salvatore Rinzivillo | CNR-ISTI, Italy |
| Matteo Riondato | Amherst College, USA |
| Giuseppe Rizzo | Niuma, Italy |
| Marko Robnik-Sikonja | University of Ljubljana, Slovenia |
| Christophe Rodrigues | Pôle Universitaire Léonard de Vinci, France |
| Federica Rollo | University of Modena and Reggio Emilia, Italy |
| Luca Romeo | University of Macerata, Italy |
| Benjamin Roth | University of Vienna, Austria |
| Céline Rouveirol | LIPN - Université Sorbonne Paris Nord, France |
| Salvatore Ruggieri | University of Pisa, Italy |
| Pietro Sabatino | ICAR-CNR, Italy |
| Luca Sabbioni | Politecnico di Milano, Italy |
| Tulika Saha | University of Manchester, UK |
| Pablo Sanchez Martin | Max Planck Institute for Intelligent Systems, Germany |
| Parinya Sanguansat | Panyapiwat Institute of Management, Thailand |
| Shreya Saxena | Quantiphi, India |
| Yücel Saygin | Sabanci Universitesi, Turkey |
| Patrick Schäfer | Humboldt-Universität zu Berlin, Germany |
| Kevin Schewior | University of Southern Denmark, Denmark |
| Rainer Schlosser | Hasso Plattner Institute, Germany |
| Johannes Schneider | University of Liechtenstein, Liechtenstein |
| Matthias Schubert | LMU Munich, Germany |
| Alexander Schulz | CITEC - Bielefeld University, Germany |
| Andreas Schwung | Fachhoschschule Südwestfalen, Germany |
| Raquel Sebastião | IEETA/DETI-UA, Portugal |
| Pierre Senellart | ENS, PSL University, France |
| Edoardo Serra | Boise State University, USA |
| Mattia Setzu | University of Pisa, Italy |
| Ammar Shaker | NEC Laboratories Europe, Germany |
| Shubhranshu Shekhar | Carnegie Mellon University, USA |

| | |
|---|---|
| Jiaming Shen | Google Research, USA |
| Qiang Sheng | Institute of Computing Technology, CAS, China |
| Bin Shi | Xi'an Jiaotong University, China |
| Jimeng Shi | Florida International University, USA |
| Laixi Shi | Carnegie Mellon University, USA |
| Rongye Shi | Columbia University, USA |
| Harsh Shrivastava | Microsoft Research, USA |
| Jonathan A. Silva | Universidade Federal de Mato Grosso do Sul, Brazil |
| Esther-Lydia Silva-Ramírez | Universidad de Cádiz, Spain |
| Kuldeep Singh | Cerence, Germany |
| Moshe Sipper | Ben-Gurion University of the Negev, Israel |
| Andrzej Skowron | University of Warsaw, Poland |
| Krzysztof Slot | Lodz University of Technology, Poland |
| Marek Smieja | Jagiellonian University, Poland |
| Gavin Smith | University of Nottingham, UK |
| Carlos Soares | University of Porto, Portugal |
| Cláudia Soares | NOVA LINCS, Portugal |
| Andy Song | RMIT University, Australia |
| Dongjin Song | University of Connecticut, USA |
| Hao Song | Seldon, UK |
| Jie Song | Zhejiang University, China |
| Linxin Song | Waseda University, Japan |
| Liyan Song | Southern University of Science and Technology, China |
| Zixing Song | Chinese University of Hong Kong, China |
| Arnaud Soulet | University of Tours, France |
| Sucheta Soundarajan | Syracuse University, USA |
| Francesca Spezzano | Boise State University, USA |
| Myra Spiliopoulou | Otto-von-Guericke-University Magdeburg, Germany |
| Janusz Starzyk | WSIZ, Poland |
| Jerzy Stefanowski | Poznan University of Technology, Poland |
| Julian Stier | University of Passau, Germany |
| Michiel Stock | Ghent University, Belgium |
| Eleni Straitouri | Max Planck Institute for Software Systems, Germany |
| Łukasz Struski | Jagiellonian University, Poland |
| Jinyan Su | University of Electronic Science and Technology of China, China |
| David Q. Sun | Apple, USA |
| Guangzhong Sun | University of Science and Technology of China, China |

| | |
|---|---|
| Mingxuan Sun | Louisiana State University, USA |
| Peijie Sun | Tsinghua University, China |
| Weiwei Sun | Shandong University, China |
| Xin Sun | TU Munich, Germany |
| Maryam Tabar | Pennsylvania State University, USA |
| Anika Tabassum | Virginia Tech, USA |
| Shazia Tabassum | INESC TEC, Portugal |
| Andrea Tagarelli | University of Calabria, Italy |
| Acar Tamersoy | NortonLifeLock Research Group, USA |
| Chang Wei Tan | Monash University, Australia |
| Cheng Tan | Zhejiang University/Westlake University, China |
| Garth Tarr | University of Sydney, Australia |
| Romain Tavenard | LETG-Rennes/IRISA, France |
| Maguelonne Teisseire | INRAE - UMR Tetis, France |
| Evimaria Terzi | Boston University, USA |
| Stefano Teso | University of Trento, Italy |
| Surendrabikram Thapa | Virginia Tech, USA |
| Maximilian Thiessen | TU Vienna, Austria |
| Steffen Thoma | FZI Research Center for Information Technology, Germany |
| Simon Tihon | Euranova, Belgium |
| Kai Ming Ting | Nanjing University, China |
| Abhisek Tiwari | IIT Patna, India |
| Gabriele Tolomei | Sapienza University of Rome, Italy |
| Guangmo Tong | University of Delaware, USA |
| Sunna Torge | TU Dresden, Germany |
| Giovanni Trappolini | Sapienza University of Rome, Italy |
| Volker Tresp | Siemens AG/LMU Munich, Germany |
| Sofia Triantafillou | University of Crete, Greece |
| Sebastian Trimpe | RWTH Aachen University, Germany |
| Sebastian Tschiatschek | University of Vienna, Austria |
| Athena Vakal | Aristotle University of Thessaloniki, Greece |
| Peter van der Putten | Leiden University, The Netherlands |
| Fabio Vandin | University of Padua, Italy |
| Aparna S. Varde | Montclair State University, USA |
| Julien Velcin | Université Lumière Lyon 2, France |
| Bruno Veloso | INESC TEC/University of Porto, Portugal |
| Rosana Veroneze | LBiC, Brazil |
| Gennaro Vessio | University of Bari, Aldo Moro, Italy |
| Tiphaine Viard | Télécom Paris, France |
| Herna L. Viktor | University of Ottawa, Canada |

| | |
|---|---|
| Joao Vinagre | Joint Research Centre - European Commission, Belgium |
| Jordi Vitria | Universitat de Barcelona, Spain |
| Jean-Noël Vittaut | LIP6 - CNRS - Sorbonne Université, France |
| Marco Viviani | University of Milan-Bicocca, Italy |
| Paola Vocca | Tor Vergata University of Rome, Italy |
| Tomasz Walkowiak | Wrocław University of Science and Technology, Poland |
| Ziwen Wan | University of California, Irvine, USA |
| Beilun Wang | Southeast University, China |
| Chuan-Ju Wang | Academia Sinica, Taiwan |
| Deng-Bao Wang | Southeast University, China |
| Di Wang | KAUST, Saudi Arabia |
| Dianhui Wang | La Trobe University, Australia |
| Hongwei Wang | University of Illinois at Urbana-Champaign, USA |
| Huandong Wang | Tsinghua University, China |
| Hui (Wendy) Wang | Stevens Institute of Technology, USA |
| Jiaqi Wang | Penn State University, USA |
| Puyu Wang | City University of Hong Kong, China |
| Qing Wang | Australian National University, Australia |
| Ruijie Wang | University of Illinois at Urbana-Champaign, USA |
| Senzhang Wang | Central South University, China |
| Shuo Wang | University of Birmingham, UK |
| Suhang Wang | Pennsylvania State University, USA |
| Wei Wang | Fudan University, China |
| Wenjie Wang | Shanghai Tech University, China |
| Yanhao Wang | East China Normal University, China |
| Yimu Wang | University of Waterloo, Canada |
| Yue Wang | Microsoft Research, USA |
| Yue Wang | Waymo, USA |
| Zhaonan Wang | University of Tokyo, Japan |
| Zhi Wang | Southwest University, China |
| Zijie J. Wang | Georgia Tech, USA |
| Roger Wattenhofer | ETH Zurich, Switzerland |
| Pascal Weber | University of Vienna, Austria |
| Jörg Wicker | University of Auckland, New Zealand |
| Michael Wilbur | Vanderbilt University, USA |
| Weng-Fai Wong | National University of Singapore, Singapore |
| Bin Wu | Zhengzhou University, China |
| Chenwang Wu | University of Science and Technology of China, China |

| | |
|---|---|
| Di Wu | Chongqing Institute of Green and Intelligent Technology, CAS, China |
| Guoqiang Wu | Shandong University, China |
| Peng Wu | Shanghai Jiao Tong University, China |
| Xiaotong Wu | Nanjing Normal University, China |
| Yongkai Wu | Clemson University, USA |
| Danyang Xiao | Sun Yat-Sen University, China |
| Zhiwen Xiao | Southwest Jiaotong University, China |
| Cheng Xie | Yunnan University, China |
| Hong Xie | Chongqing Institute of Green and Intelligent Technology, CAS, China |
| Yaqi Xie | Carnegie Mellon University, USA |
| Huanlai Xing | Southwest Jiaotong University, China |
| Ning Xu | Southeast University, China |
| Xiaolong Xu | Nanjing University of Information Science and Technology, China |
| Hao Xue | University of New South Wales, Australia |
| Yexiang Xue | Purdue University, USA |
| Sangeeta Yadav | Indian Institute of Science, India |
| Qiao Yan | Shenzhen University, China |
| Yan Yan | Carleton University, Canada |
| Yu Yan | People's Public Security University of China, China |
| Yujun Yan | Dartmouth College, USA |
| Jie Yang | University of Wollongong, Australia |
| Shaofu Yang | Southeast University, China |
| Yang Yang | Nanjing University of Science and Technology, China |
| Liang Yao | Tencent, China |
| Muchao Ye | Pennsylvania State University, USA |
| Michael Yeh | Visa Research, USA |
| Kalidas Yeturu | Indian Institute of Technology Tirupati, India |
| Hang Yin | University of Copenhagen, Denmark |
| Hongwei Yong | Hong Kong Polytechnic University, China |
| Jaemin Yoo | KAIST, South Korea |
| Mengbo You | Iwate University, Japan |
| Hang Yu | Shanghai University, China |
| Weiren Yu | University of Warwick, UK |
| Wenjian Yu | Tsinghua University, China |
| Jidong Yuan | Beijing Jiaotong University, China |
| Aras Yurtman | KU Leuven, Belgium |
| Claudius Zelenka | Christian-Albrechts University of Kiel, Germany |

Akka Zemmari                    University of Bordeaux, France
Bonan Zhang                     Princeton University, USA
Chao Zhang                      Zhejiang University, China
Chuang Zhang                    Nanjing University of Science and Technology,
                                   China
Danqing Zhang                   Amazon, USA
Guoqiang Zhang                  University of Technology, Sydney, Australia
Guoxi Zhang                     Kyoto University, Japan
Hao Zhang                       Fudan University, China
Junbo Zhang                     JD Intelligent Cities Research, China
Le Zhang                        Baidu Research, China
Ming Zhang                      National Key Laboratory of Science and
                                   Technology on Information System Security,
                                   China
Qiannan Zhang                   KAUST, Saudi Arabia
Tianlin Zhang                   University of Manchester, UK
Wenbin Zhang                    Michigan Tech, USA
Xiang Zhang                     National University of Defense Technology,
                                   China
Xiao Zhang                      Shandong University, China
Xiaoming Zhang                  Beihang University, China
Xinyang Zhang                   University of Illinois at Urbana-Champaign, USA
Yaying Zhang                    Tongji University, China
Yin Zhang                       University of Electronic Science and Technology
                                   of China, China
Yongqi Zhang                    4Paradigm, China
Zhiwen Zhang                    University of Tokyo, Japan
Mia Zhao                        Airbnb, USA
Sichen Zhao                     RMIT University, Australia
Xiaoting Zhao                   Etsy, USA
Tongya Zheng                    Zhejiang University, China
Wenhao Zheng                    Shopee, Singapore
Yu Zheng                        Tsinghua University, China
Yujia Zheng                     Carnegie Mellon University, USA
Jiang Zhong                     Chongqing University, China
Wei Zhou                        School of Cyber Security, CAS, China
Zhengyang Zhou                  University of Science and Technology of China,
                                   China
Chuang Zhu                      Beijing University of Posts and
                                   Telecommunications, China
Jing Zhu                        University of Michigan, USA
Jinjing Zhu                     Hong Kong University of Science and
                                   Technology, China

| Junxing Zhu | National University of Defense Technology, China |
| Yanmin Zhu | Shanghai Jiao Tong University, China |
| Ye Zhu | Deakin University, Australia |
| Yichen Zhu | Midea Group, China |
| Zirui Zhuang | Beijing University of Posts and Telecommunications, China |
| Tommaso Zoppi | University of Florence, Italy |
| Meiyun Zuo | Renmin University of China, China |

## Program Committee, Applied Data Science Track

| Jussara Almeida | Universidade Federal de Minas Gerais, Brazil |
| Mozhdeh Ariannezhad | University of Amsterdam, The Netherlands |
| Renato M. Assuncao | ESRI, USA |
| Hajer Ayadi | York University, Canada |
| Ashraf Bah Rabiou | University of Delaware, USA |
| Amey Barapatre | Microsoft, USA |
| Patrice Bellot | Aix-Marseille Université - CNRS LSIS, France |
| Ludovico Boratto | University of Cagliari, Italy |
| Claudio Borile | CENTAI, Italy |
| Yi Cai | South China University of Technology, China |
| Lei Cao | University of Arizona/MIT, USA |
| Shilei Cao | Tencent, China |
| Yang Cao | Hokkaido University, Japan |
| Aniket Chakrabarti | Amazon, USA |
| Chaochao Chen | Zhejiang University, China |
| Chung-Chi Chen | National Taiwan University, Taiwan |
| Meng Chen | Shandong University, China |
| Ruey-Cheng Chen | Canva, Australia |
| Tong Chen | University of Queensland, Australia |
| Yi Chen | NJIT, USA |
| Zhiyu Chen | Amazon, USA |
| Wei Cheng | NEC Laboratories America, USA |
| Lingyang Chu | McMaster University, Canada |
| Xiaokai Chu | Tencent, China |
| Zhendong Chu | University of Virginia, USA |
| Federico Cinus | Sapienza University of Rome/CENTAI, Italy |
| Francisco Claude-Faust | LinkedIn, USA |
| Gabriele D'Acunto | Sapienza University of Rome, Italy |
| Ariyam Das | Google, USA |

| | |
|---|---|
| Jingtao Ding | Tsinghua University, China |
| Kaize Ding | Arizona State University, USA |
| Manqing Dong | eBay, Australia |
| Yushun Dong | University of Virginia, USA |
| Yingtong Dou | University of Illinois, Chicago, USA |
| Yixiang Fang | Chinese University of Hong Kong, China |
| Kaiyu Feng | Beijing Institute of Technology, China |
| Dayne Freitag | SRI International, USA |
| Yanjie Fu | University of Central Florida, USA |
| Matteo Gabburo | University of Trento, Italy |
| Sabrina Gaito | University of Milan, Italy |
| Chen Gao | Tsinghua University, China |
| Liangcai Gao | Peking University, China |
| Yunjun Gao | Zhejiang University, China |
| Lluis Garcia-Pueyo | Meta, USA |
| Mariana-Iuliana Georgescu | University of Bucharest, Romania |
| Aakash Goel | Amazon, USA |
| Marcos Goncalves | Universidade Federal de Minas Gerais, Brazil |
| Francesco Guerra | University of Modena e Reggio Emilia, Italy |
| Huifeng Guo | Huawei Noah's Ark Lab, China |
| Ruocheng Guo | ByteDance, China |
| Zhen Hai | Alibaba DAMO Academy, China |
| Eui-Hong (Sam) Han | The Washington Post, USA |
| Jinyoung Han | Sungkyunkwan University, South Korea |
| Shuchu Han | Stellar Cyber, USA |
| Dongxiao He | Tianjin University, China |
| Junyuan Hong | Michigan State University, USA |
| Yupeng Hou | UC San Diego, USA |
| Binbin Hu | Ant Group, China |
| Jun Hu | National University of Singapore, Singapore |
| Hong Huang | Huazhong University of Science and Technology, China |
| Xin Huang | Hong Kong Baptist University, China |
| Yizheng Huang | York University, Canada |
| Yu Huang | University of Florida, USA |
| Stratis Ioannidis | Northeastern University, USA |
| Radu Tudor Ionescu | University of Bucharest, Romania |
| Murium Iqbal | Etsy, USA |
| Shoaib Jameel | University of Southampton, UK |
| Jian Kang | University of Rochester, USA |
| Pinar Karagoz | METU, Turkey |
| Praveen C. Kolli | Carnegie Mellon University, USA |

| | |
|---|---|
| Deguang Kong | Yahoo Research, USA |
| Adit Krishnan | University of Illinois at Urbana-Champaign, USA |
| Mayank Kulkarni | Amazon, USA |
| Susana Ladra | University of A Coruña, Spain |
| Renaud Lambiotte | University of Oxford, UK |
| Tommaso Lanciano | KTH Royal Institute of Technology, Sweden |
| Md Tahmid Rahman Laskar | Dialpad, Canada |
| Matthieu Latapy | CNRS, France |
| Noah Lee | Meta, USA |
| Wang-Chien Lee | Pennsylvania State University, USA |
| Chang Li | Apple, USA |
| Chaozhuo Li | Microsoft Research Asia, China |
| Daifeng Li | Sun Yat-Sen University, China |
| Lei Li | Hong Kong University of Science and Technology, China |
| Shuai Li | University of Cambridge, UK |
| Xiang Lian | Kent State University, USA |
| Zhaohui Liang | National Library of Medicine, NIH, USA |
| Bang Liu | University of Montreal, Canada |
| Ji Liu | Baidu Research, China |
| Jingjing Liu | MD Anderson Cancer Center, USA |
| Tingwen Liu | Institute of Information Engineering, CAS, China |
| Weiwen Liu | Huawei Noah's Ark Lab, China |
| Andreas Lommatzsch | TU Berlin, Germany |
| Jiyun Luo | Pinterest, USA |
| Ping Luo | CAS, China |
| Xin Luo | Shandong University, China |
| Jing Ma | University of Virginia, USA |
| Xian-Ling Mao | Beijing Institute of Technology, China |
| Mirko Marras | University of Cagliari, Italy |
| Zoltan Miklos | Université de Rennes 1, France |
| Ahmed K. Mohamed | Meta, USA |
| Mukesh Mohania | IIIT Delhi, India |
| Corrado Monti | CENTAI, Italy |
| Sushant More | Amazon, USA |
| Jose G. Moreno | University of Toulouse, France |
| Aayush Mudgal | Pinterest, USA |
| Sepideh Nahali | York University, Canada |
| Wolfgang Nejdl | L3S Research Center, Germany |
| Yifan Nie | University of Montreal, Canada |
| Di Niu | University of Alberta, Canada |
| Symeon Papadopoulos | CERTH/ITI, Greece |

| | |
|---|---|
| Manos Papagelis | York University, Canada |
| Leonardo Pellegrina | University of Padua, Italy |
| Claudia Perlich | TwoSigma, USA |
| Fabio Pinelli | IMT Lucca, Italy |
| Giulia Preti | CENTAI, Italy |
| Buyue Qian | Xi'an Jiaotong University, China |
| Chuan Qin | BOSS Zhipin, China |
| Xiao Qin | Amazon Web Services AI/ML, USA |
| Yanghui Rao | Sun Yat-Sen University, China |
| Yusuf Sale | LMU Munich, Germany |
| Eric Sanjuan | Avignon University, France |
| Maria Luisa Sapino | University of Turin, Italy |
| Emmanouil Schinas | CERTH/ITI, Greece |
| Nasrullah Sheikh | IBM Research, USA |
| Yue Shi | Meta, USA |
| Gianmaria Silvello | University of Padua, Italy |
| Yang Song | Apple, USA |
| Francesca Spezzano | Boise State University, USA |
| Efstathios Stamatatos | University of the Aegean, Greece |
| Kostas Stefanidis | Tampere University, Finland |
| Ting Su | Imperial College London, UK |
| Munira Syed | Procter & Gamble, USA |
| Liang Tang | Google, USA |
| Ruiming Tang | Huawei Noah's Ark Lab, China |
| Junichi Tatemura | Google, USA |
| Mingfei Teng | Amazon, USA |
| Sofia Tolmach | Amazon, Israel |
| Ismail Hakki Toroslu | METU, Turkey |
| Kazutoshi Umemoto | University of Tokyo, Japan |
| Yao Wan | Huazhong University of Science and Technology, China |
| Chang-Dong Wang | Sun Yat-Sen University, China |
| Chong Wang | Amazon, USA |
| Chuan-Ju Wang | Academia Sinica, Taiwan |
| Hongzhi Wang | Harbin Institute of Technology, China |
| Kai Wang | Shanghai Jiao Tong University, China |
| Ning Wang | Beijing Jiaotong University, China |
| Pengyuan Wang | University of Georgia, USA |
| Senzhang Wang | Central South University, China |
| Sheng Wang | Wuhan University, China |
| Shoujin Wang | Macquarie University, Australia |
| Wentao Wang | Michigan State University, USA |

| | |
|---|---|
| Yang Wang | University of Science and Technology of China, China |
| Zhihong Wang | Tsinghua University, China |
| Zihan Wang | Shandong University, China |
| Shi-ting Wen | Ningbo Tech University, China |
| Song Wen | Rutgers University, USA |
| Zeyi Wen | Hong Kong University of Science and Technology, China |
| Fangzhao Wu | Microsoft Research Asia, China |
| Jun Wu | University of Illinois at Urbana-Champaign, USA |
| Wentao Wu | Microsoft Research, USA |
| Yanghua Xiao | Fudan University, China |
| Haoyi Xiong | Baidu, China |
| Dongkuan Xu | North Carolina State University, USA |
| Guandong Xu | University of Technology, Sydney, Australia |
| Shan Xue | Macquarie University, Australia |
| Le Yan | Google, USA |
| De-Nian Yang | Academia Sinica, Taiwan |
| Fan Yang | Rice University, USA |
| Yu Yang | City University of Hong Kong, China |
| Fanghua Ye | University College London, UK |
| Jianhua Yin | Shandong University, China |
| Yifang Yin | A*STAR-I2R, Singapore |
| Changlong Yu | Hong Kong University of Science and Technology, China |
| Dongxiao Yu | Shandong University, China |
| Ye Yuan | Beijing Institute of Technology, China |
| Daochen Zha | Rice University, USA |
| Feng Zhang | Renmin University of China, China |
| Mengxuan Zhang | University of North Texas, USA |
| Xianli Zhang | Xi'an Jiaotong University, China |
| Xuyun Zhang | Macquarie University, Australia |
| Chen Zhao | Baylor University, USA |
| Di Zhao | University of Auckland, New Zealand |
| Yanchang Zhao | CSIRO, Australia |
| Kaiping Zheng | National University of Singapore, Singapore |
| Yong Zheng | Illinois Institute of Technology, USA |
| Jingbo Zhou | Baidu, China |
| Ming Zhou | University of Technology, Sydney, Australia |
| Qinghai Zhou | University of Illinois at Urbana-Champaign, USA |
| Tian Zhou | Alibaba DAMO Academy, China |
| Xinyi Zhou | University of Washington, USA |

| | |
|---|---|
| Yucheng Zhou | University of Macau, China |
| Jiangang Zhu | ByteDance, China |
| Yongchun Zhu | CAS, China |
| Ziwei Zhu | George Mason University, USA |
| Jia Zou | Arizona State University, USA |

## Program Committee, Demo Track

| | |
|---|---|
| Ferran Diego | Telefonica Research, Spain |
| Jan Florjanczyk | Netflix, USA |
| Mikko Heikkila | Telefonica Research, Spain |
| Jesus Omaña Iglesias | Telefonica Research, Spain |
| Nicolas Kourtellis | Telefonica Research, Spain |
| Eduard Marin | Telefonica Research, Spain |
| Souneil Park | Telefonica Research, Spain |
| Aravindh Raman | Telefonica Research, Spain |
| Ashish Rastogi | Netflix, USA |
| Natali Ruchansky | Netflix, USA |
| David Solans | Telefonica Research, Spain |

## Sponsors

## Platinum

**Gold**

**Silver**

**Bronze**

 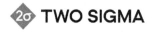

**PhD Forum Sponsor**

**Publishing Partner**

# Invited Talks Abstracts

# Neural Wave Representations

Max Welling

University of Amsterdam, The Netherlands

**Abstract.** Good neural architectures are rooted in good inductive biases (a.k.a. priors). Equivariance under symmetries is a prime example of a successful physics-inspired prior which sometimes dramatically reduces the number of examples needed to learn predictive models. In this work, we tried to extend this thinking to more flexible priors in the hidden variables of a neural network. In particular, we imposed wavelike dynamics in hidden variables under transformations of the inputs, which relaxes the stricter notion of equivariance. We find that under certain conditions, wavelike dynamics naturally arises in these hidden representations. We formalize this idea in a VAE-over-time architecture where the hidden dynamics is described by a Fokker-Planck (a.k.a. drift-diffusion) equation. This in turn leads to a new definition of a disentangled hidden representation of input states that can easily be manipulated to undergo transformations. I also discussed very preliminary work on how the Schrödinger equation can also be used to move information in the hidden representations.

**Biography.** Prof. Dr. Max Welling is a research chair in Machine Learning at the University of Amsterdam and a Distinguished Scientist at MSR. He is a fellow at the Canadian Institute for Advanced Research (CIFAR) and the European Lab for Learning and Intelligent Systems (ELLIS) where he also serves on the founding board. His previous appointments include VP at Qualcomm Technologies, professor at UC Irvine, postdoc at the University of Toronto and UCL under the supervision of Prof. Geoffrey Hinton, and postdoc at Caltech under the supervision of Prof. Pietro Perona. He finished his PhD in theoretical high energy physics under the supervision of Nobel laureate Prof. Gerard 't Hooft. Max Welling served as associate editor-in-chief of IEEE TPAMI from 2011–2015, he has served on the advisory board of the NeurIPS Foundation since 2015 and was program chair and general chair of NeurIPS in 2013 and 2014 respectively. He was also program chair of AISTATS in 2009 and ECCV in 2016 and general chair of MIDL in 2018. Max Welling was a recipient of the ECCV Koenderink Prize in 2010 and the ICML Test of Time Award in 2021. He directs the Amsterdam Machine Learning Lab (AMLAB) and co-directs the Qualcomm-UvA deep learning lab (QUVA) and the Bosch-UvA Deep Learning lab (DELTA).

# Physics-Inspired Graph Neural Networks

Michael Bronstein

University of Oxford, UK

**Abstract.** The message-passing paradigm has been the "battle horse" of deep learning on graphs for several years, making graph neural networks a big success in a wide range of applications, from particle physics to protein design. From a theoretical viewpoint, it established the link to the Weisfeiler-Lehman hierarchy, allowing us to analyse the expressive power of GNNs. We argue that the very "node-and-edge"-centric mindset of current graph deep learning schemes may hinder future progress in the field. As an alternative, we propose physics-inspired "continuous" learning models that open up a new trove of tools from the fields of differential geometry, algebraic topology, and differential equations so far largely unexplored in graph ML.

**Biography.** Michael Bronstein is the DeepMind Professor of AI at the University of Oxford. He was previously a professor at Imperial College London and held visiting appointments at Stanford, MIT, and Harvard, and has also been affiliated with three Institutes for Advanced Study (at TUM as a Rudolf Diesel Fellow (2017–2019), at Harvard as a Radcliffe fellow (2017–2018), and at Princeton as a short-time scholar (2020)). Michael received his PhD from the Technion in 2007. He is the recipient of the Royal Society Wolfson Research Merit Award, Royal Academy of Engineering Silver Medal, five ERC grants, two Google Faculty Research Awards, and two Amazon AWS ML Research Awards. He is a Member of the Academia Europaea, Fellow of the IEEE, IAPR, BCS, and ELLIS, ACM Distinguished Speaker, and World Economic Forum Young Scientist. In addition to his academic career, Michael is a serial entrepreneur and founder of multiple startup companies, including Novafora, Invision (acquired by Intel in 2012), Videocites, and Fabula AI (acquired by Twitter in 2019).

# Mapping Generative AI

Kate Crawford

USC Annenberg, USA

**Abstract.** Training data is foundational to generative AI systems. From Common Crawl's 3.1 billion web pages to LAION-5B's corpus of almost 6 billion image-text pairs, these vast collections – scraped from the internet and treated as "ground truth" – play a critical role in shaping the epistemic boundaries that govern generative AI models. Yet training data is beset with complex social, political, and epistemological challenges. What happens when data is stripped of context, meaning, and provenance? How does training data limit what and how machine learning systems interpret the world? What are the copyright implications of these datasets? And most importantly, what forms of power do these approaches enhance and enable? This keynote is an invitation to reflect on the epistemic foundations of generative AI, and to consider the wide-ranging impacts of the current generative turn.

**Biography.** Professor Kate Crawford is a leading international scholar of the social implications of artificial intelligence. She is a Research Professor at USC Annenberg in Los Angeles, a Senior Principal Researcher at MSR in New York, an Honorary Professor at the University of Sydney, and the inaugural Visiting Chair for AI and Justice at the École Normale Supérieure in Paris. Her latest book, *Atlas of AI* (Yale, 2021) won the Sally Hacker Prize from the Society for the History of Technology, the ASIS&T Best Information Science Book Award, and was named one of the best books in 2021 by *New Scientist* and the *Financial Times*. Over her twenty-year research career, she has also produced groundbreaking creative collaborations and visual investigations. Her project *Anatomy of an AI System* with Vladan Joler is in the permanent collection of the Museum of Modern Art in New York and the V&A in London, and was awarded with the Design of the Year Award in 2019 and included in the Design of the Decades by the Design Museum of London. Her collaboration with the artist Trevor Paglen, *Excavating AI*, won the Ayrton Prize from the British Society for the History of Science. She has advised policymakers in the United Nations, the White House, and the European Parliament, and she currently leads the Knowing Machines Project, an international research collaboration that investigates the foundations of machine learning.

# Contents – Part IV

## Neuro/Symbolic Learning

## Optimization

## Recommender Systems

## Reinforcement Learning

## Representation Learning

# Natural Language Processing

# Unsupervised Deep Cross-Language Entity Alignment

Chuanyu Jiang[1], Yiming Qian[2], Lijun Chen[3], Yang Gu[4], and Xia Xie[1(✉)]

[1] School of Computer Science and Technology, Hainan University, Haikou, China
{cyhhyg,shelicy}@hainanu.edu.cn
[2] Institute of High Performance Computing (IHPC), Agency for Science, Technology
and Research (A*STAR), 1 Fusionopolis Way, #16-16 Connexis, Singapore 138632,
Republic of Singapore
qiany@ihpc.a-star.edu.sg
[3] School of Cyberspace Security, Hainan University, Haikou, China
clara@hainanu.edu.cn
[4] School of Information and Communication Engineering, Hainan University, Haikou,
China
guyangl@hainanu.edu.cn

**Abstract.** Cross-lingual entity alignment is the task of finding the
same semantic entities from different language knowledge graphs. In this
paper, we propose a simple and novel unsupervised method for cross-
language entity alignment. We utilize the deep learning multi-language
encoder combined with a machine translator to encode knowledge graph
text, which reduces the reliance on label data. Unlike traditional methods that only emphasize global or local alignment, our method simultaneously considers both alignment strategies. We first view the alignment
task as a bipartite matching problem and then adopt the re-exchanging
idea to accomplish alignment. Compared with the traditional bipartite
matching algorithm that only gives one optimal solution, our algorithm
generates ranked matching results which enabled many potentials downstream tasks. Additionally, our method can adapt two different types
of optimization (minimal and maximal) in the bipartite matching process, which provides more flexibility. Our evaluation shows, we each
scored 0.966, 0.990, and 0.996 $Hits$@1 rates on the DBP15K dataset in
Chinese, Japanese, and French to English alignment tasks. We outperformed the state-of-the-art method in unsupervised and semi-supervised
categories. Compared with the state-of-the-art supervised method, our
method outperforms 2.6% and 0.4% in Ja-En and Fr-En alignment tasks
while marginally lower by 0.2% in the Zh-En alignment task.

**Keywords:** Knowledge graph · Entity alignment · Unsupervised
learning · Combination optimization · Cross-lingual

---

C. Jiang and Y. Qian—Contribute equally to this work.

D. Koutra et al. (Eds.): ECML PKDD 2023, LNAI 14172, pp. 3–19, 2023.
https://doi.org/10.1007/978-3-031-43421-1_1

# 1   Introduction

Knowledge graph (KG) was first proposed by Google in 2012 [28], and it has been popularized in the fields of question answering, information retrieval, and recommendation system et al. [48]. Each knowledge graph contains structured information in the form of entities, relations, and semantic descriptions. Each entity is represented as a node in the graph, the relationship represents the relationship between connected entities, and the semantic description contains the attribute of each entity [9]. The task of cross-lingual entity alignment is to find entities that are similar to the entities from a knowledge graph in another language. A schematic diagram of cross-lingual entity alignment between knowledge graphs is shown in Fig. 1.

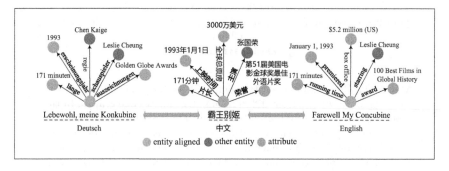

**Fig. 1.** An illustration of between knowledge graphs cross-lingual entity alignment. The orange nodes are entities aligned across three knowledge graphs in three languages. The purple nodes are other entities that connect to the orange node, the green nodes are the attributes associated with the orange node. (Color figure online)

In recent years, deep learning methods are gaining popularity in cross-lingual entity alignment tasks. There are three major methods: supervised learning, semi-supervised learning, and unsupervised learning. The difference between those three methods is the percentage of labeled data available. The supervised methods require all data to be labeled and available in the training. When only a small subset of data is labeled, semi-supervised learning becomes the next optimal choice. It can utilize both labeled and unlabeled data in the training process. In many cases, having even a small amount of annotated data is a luxury where the unsupervised learning method becomes the go-to solution.

For existing unsupervised methods, we find these methods don't sufficiently utilize the extra information or do a relative complexity work to integrate extra information [17,18,20,22,42]. Besides, by [21,22] two methods we find that the global alignment can helps to improve accuracy but ignores the interaction with local information and lacks flexibility in the alignment process. Based on the above findings, we propose an unsupervised method called **U**nsupervised **D**eep **C**ross-Language **E**ntity **A**lignment (UDCEA). Our method conducts the embedding process with combinations of simple machine translation and pre-training language model encoder, which avoids the use of complex technologies like Graph Attention Networks (GAT) [34], graph convolutional network (GCN) [13], et al. In the alignment process, our method makes the global and local information interact. Our alignment strategy not only brings accuracy increases but also improves flexibility in the alignment process. Our method is divided into two modules: feature embedding and alignment.

In the feature embedding module, we are not limited to using the entity name information but further utilize the multi-view information (entity name, structure, and attribute). On the multi-view information, we apply the machine translation (Google translator) engine to translate non-English text into English, which provides a weak alignment between entities across two languages. This practice is quite popular in the unsupervised entity alignment methods [20, 21, 38, 46]. Then we apply a pre-trained multi-language encoder [27] to obtain embedding for multi-view information. From our experiments, we found the encoder model trained in a multi-language fashion scored higher alignment accuracy than the monolingual encoder when the two languages have a distinct difference.

In the alignment module, we are not only adopting the global alignment to conduct alignment and further combining it with the local alignment. The first step is to construct the adjacency matrix for global alignment. The adjacency matrix is built by a simple but efficient method, which is fusing the multi-view information into a unified matrix. Usually, the preliminary adjacency matrix does not have the directional information and so we transposed the adjacency matrix to add the directional information. Next, we utilize the optimization algorithm to handle the adjacency matrix containing directional information, which attains the global information. Finally, we allow the global information interaction with local information (specific operations in 3.3) and get the final ranking alignment results. Our alignment strategy can be deployed to improve existing approaches without heavy modifications. The detailed evaluation is in Sect. 5.3. Our evaluation shows, we improve 1.0% to 5.6% for SEU [21], 15.3% to 16.5% for RREA [24], and 9.9% to 18.3% for HGCN-JE [39] on three language alignment tasks. Furthermore, our method can adapt to different data sizes, which the detailed experiments result is shown in Fig. 5(b).

We evaluated our overall alignment method on the DBP15K dataset [30] which results achieving 0.966, 0.990, and 0.996 accuracy each in Zh-En, Ja-En, and Fr-En datasets. We exceed the state-of-the-art unsupervised and semi-supervised methods in alignment accuracy. Even compared with the state-of-the-art supervised method, our method surpasses them by 2.6% and 0.4% in Ja-En and Fr-En alignment while only marginally lower by 0.2% in the Zh-En alignment. In conclusion, our method contributions are summarized as follows:

- We apply a simple but efficient method to fuse the multi-view information into one unified adjacency matrix.
- We propose a novel method that extracts the ranked matching results from state-of-the-art bipartite matching algorithms.
- We conduct throughout experiments to study the impact of different configurations of machine translation and encoders on the entity alignment task.

- We show our alignment module method is flexible and can be used as an add-on to improve existing entity alignment methods.

## 2    Related Work

The early entity alignment methods [3,7,11] were mainly based on measuring the text similarity between entity pairs augmented by relation information and probability models. These early methods tend to ignore the hide semantic information while suffering scalability issues. As the size of available data increases, so does the degree of knowledge graph complexity. The urge of finding a method to handle large amounts of data leads to wide adaptation of data-driven learning approaches. Based on the amount of annotated available data, we can categorize the learning based approaches into supervised, semi-supervised, and unsupervised three types.

### 2.1    Supervised Entity Alignment

The supervised entity alignment method requires access to fully annotated data for training. The early works deploy translation-based methods such as TransE [1], TransH [35], TransR [16], and TransD [8] to obtain the feature embedding. TransE assumes each entity $h$ on the graph is a linear combination of its adjacent entity $t$ and relation $r$ which can be formulated as $h + r \approx t$. This linear combination approach suffers huge errors when the entities have a 1-to-N or N-to-N relation with other entities. TransH reduced this problem by projecting the entity vector onto a hyperplane which preserved the topology information between vectors. Both TransE and TransH assume the vector of entities and relations in the same space. However, multiple attributes may associate with the same entity so this assumption may not always hold. TransR removed this assumption by projecting the entity and relation vector into different spaces. TransD took a more in-depth division for the projection between entity and relation.

The linear combination between vectors is fast but as dataset size grows, the complexity between entities grows exponentially. To handle this growing complexity, GCN based methods [36,44] start to gain popularity. The drawback of the learning-based entity alignment method is the requirement of an enormous amount of labeled data to properly train a model. One way to reduce this drawback is through semi-supervised learning.

### 2.2    Semi-supervised Entity Alignment

The semi-supervised method solved the label requirement only by utilizing a small number of alignment labels as seed. Then this seed propagates over the knowledge graph to align the rest of the entities. To address the labeled data relative lack problem, semi-supervised alignment methods use the iterative strategy to generate new training data [23,40,45]. With the iterative process starting, more and more pseudo-labeled data will be added to the training sets until reaching the stop criteria. The semi-supervised method relaxed the reliance on the amount of labeled data and this data requirement can be further reduced to zero by unsupervised learning.

### 2.3   Unsupervised Entity Alignment

Unsupervised methods apply external resources to eliminate the need of requiring labeled data in the entity alignment. One popular external resource is machine translation engine [20–22, 38, 46] such as Google translator. Non-English entities are translated into English and then encoded into text embedding. The encoding methods can be statistical (e.g. N-gram [14], and GloVe [25]), or deep learning (e.g. BERT [4], and RoBERTa [19]). Later, [18] suggests these two-step machine translation and encoding process can be replaced by a single pre-trained multilingual model [5]. The external resources can be used to obtain the semantic embedding and further generate the similarity matrix. Finally, the similarity matrix is processed by optimization algorithms such as Hungarian algorithm [21], deferred acceptance algorithm [46], or Sinkhorn algorithm [21,22] to conduct alignment.

## 3   Proposed Method

Our method[1] contains two modules: feature embedding and alignment. The feature embedding module utilizes the machine translator and pre-trained deep multi-language learning encoder to generate feature embedding for each aligned entity. The alignment module first generates the similarity matrix based on feature embedding and then applies the optimization-based method to align two knowledge graphs. The overall flow of our method is shown in Fig. 2.

### 3.1   Base Symbol Definition

Given two knowledge graphs in different languages, named $G_1$ and $G_2$. $E_1 = \{e_{(1,1)}, e_{(1,2)}, ..., e_{(1,m_1)}\}$ and $E_2 = \{e_{(2,1)}, e_{(2,2)}, ..., e_{(2,m_2)}\}$ denote a set of entity in $G_1$ and $G_2$ respectively, which $m_1$ and $m_2$ is the index. Abstractly, we define $E$ to represent entity name information. The goal is to find all entity pairs that share the same semantic information in $E_1$ and $E_2$. An entity of knowledge graph usually has two types of information which are the structure and attribute information. The structure information represents the relation between entities while attribute information usually is to entity description. The attribute information represents the properties that associate with each entity. We further divide the structure and attribute information into target and relation information. For example in Fig. 2, the purple nodes, green nodes, purple arrowheads, and green arrowheads are the structure target (ST), attribute target

---

[1] Our source code is available in https://github.com/chuanyus/UDCEA.

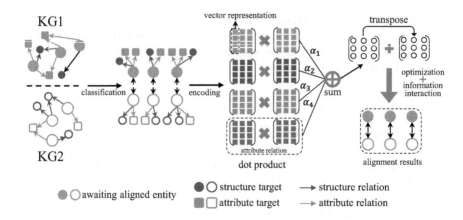

**Fig. 2.** The overall flow of our method. (Color figure online)

(AT), structure relation (SR), and attribute relation (AR) respectively. Here, we denote $ST_1$, $SR_1$, $AT_1$, and $AR_1$ to represent the information from $G_1$. Similarly, we denote $ST_2$, $SR_2$, $AT_2$, and $AR_2$ to represent the information from $G_2$.

## 3.2 Feature Embedding Module

The feature embedding module consists of two steps which are language translation and text encoding. In this process, we choose the $E$, $ST$, $AT$, and $AR$ for embedding and give up the $SR$ feature. Because the $SR$ information generally exists in reality so lacks identity property. In the language translation step, we convert all non-English text into English using Google translator $f_t$. This translation process can be formulated as:

$$(E_i', ST_i', AT_i', AR_i') = f_t\left((E_i, ST_i, AT_i, AR_i)\right), \quad i = 1, 2. \tag{1}$$

where $E_i'$, $ST_i'$, $AT_i'$, and $AR_i'$ is the translated text.

Next, we utilize the multi-language Sentence-BERT [27] encoder $f_e$ to encode these texts. The encoder maps the text to a 768-dimensional dense vector that includes abundant semantic information. This encoding process is formulated as:

$$(V_{(i,E)}, V_{(i,ST)}, V_{(i,AT)}, V_{(i,AR)}) = f_e(E_i', ST_i', AT_i', AR_i'), \quad i = 1, 2. \tag{2}$$

where $V_{(i,E)}$, $V_{(i,ST)}$, $V_{(i,AT)}$, and $V_{(i,AR)}$ is the feature embedding for $E$, $ST$, $AT$ and $AR$ respectively.

### 3.3 Alignment Module

Taking the embedding generated by the feature embedding module, we get the set of vectors $V_{(i,E)}$, $V_{(i,ST)}$, $V_{(i,AT)}$, and $V_{(i,AR)}$ for $E$, $ST$, $AT$, and $AR$ respectively:

$$\begin{cases} V_{(i,E)} = (e_{(i,1)}, e_{(i,2)}, ..., e_{(i,m_i)}), \\ V_{(i,ST)} = (st_{(i,1)}, st_{(i,2)}, ..., st_{(i,m_i)}), \\ V_{(i,AT)} = (at_{(i,1)}, at_{(i,2)}, ..., at_{(i,m_i)}), \\ V_{(i,AR)} = (ar_{(i,1)}, ar_{(i,2)}, ..., ar_{(i,m_i)}), \end{cases} \quad i = 1, 2. \tag{3}$$

Next, the pairwise similarity matrices $S_E$, $S_{ST}$, $S_{AT}$ and $S_{AR}$ for $E$, $ST$, $AT$, and $AR$ are constructed by calculating the dot product between normalized vectors:

$$\begin{cases} S_E = (e_{(1,1)}, e_{(1,2)}, ..., e_{(1,m_1)})^T (e_{(2,1)}, e_{(2,2)}, ..., e_{(2,m_2)}), \\ S_{ST} = (st_{(1,1)}, st_{(1,2)}, ..., st_{(1,m_1)})^T (st_{(2,1)}, st_{(2,2)}, ..., st_{(2,m_2)}), \\ S_{AT} = (at_{(1,1)}, at_{(1,2)}, ..., at_{(1,m_1)})^T (at_{(2,1)}, at_{(2,2)}, ..., at_{(2,m_2)}), \\ S_{AR} = (ar_{(1,1)}, ar_{(1,2)}, ..., ar_{(1,m_1)})^T (ar_{(2,1)}, ar_{(2,2)}, ..., ar_{(2,m_2)}). \end{cases} \tag{4}$$

The weighted summation of the similarity matrices forms a new matrix $S$ which can be used as an adjacency matrix for the later alignment task. We denote the weight parameter $\alpha_E$, $\alpha_{ST}$, $\alpha_{AT}$, and $\alpha_{AR}$ for $S_E$, $S_{ST}$, $S_{AT}$ and $S_{AR}$ respectively. The summation step be expressed as:

$$S = (S_E, S_{ST}, S_{AT}, S_{AR})(\alpha_E, \alpha_{ST}, \alpha_{AT}, \alpha_{AR})^T. \tag{5}$$

where $S$ is the new matrix with dimension of $m_1 \times m_2$. For the case of $S$ is not a square matrix, we add padding to the shorter dimension to convert it into a square matrix. The value in the padding depends on the optimization strategy (minimal or maximal optimization), where positive and negative infinity are used for minimal and maximal optimization respectively. In this way, we can minimize the impact of the padding and get the matrix $\bar{S}$ that dimension is the $n \times n$ ($n$ is the maximum value in $m_1$ and $m_2$). The [46] indicates that directional information can improve alignment accuracy but we notice that the softmax operation is an unnecessary step (specific in 5.2). So the transpose of $\bar{S}$ is directly added to the $\bar{S}$ and forms a new adjacency matrix $A = \bar{S} + \bar{S}^T$ that contains directional information.

Unlike previous methods that only utilize global or local information in alignment, we employ both global and local information to interact. Our method first utilizes an optimization algorithm to get the preliminary alignment results and based this to further align the single entity. Before giving formulas of the final weighting matrix generating, we show an example in Fig. 3.

In Fig. 3, the $(e_{11}, e_{21})$ and $(e_{12}, e_{22})$ are the alignment entity pairs that total similarity degree is $s_1 + s_2$. The $e_{11}$ and $e_{12}$ aligns with $e_{22}$ and $e_{21}$ respectively and receive a new similarity value $s_{12} + s_{21}$. We calculate the value of $(s_{12} + s_{21}) - (s_1 + s_2)$ as the loss of this exchanging operation. The value of loss is greater which means this exchanging more effectivity. We repeat the above exchanging process until exchange all aligned entities in the preliminary alignment results. This step gets a set of losses which includes all the exchanging losses from each step. Then, we sort the loss set and get the $e_{11}$ alignment sequence.

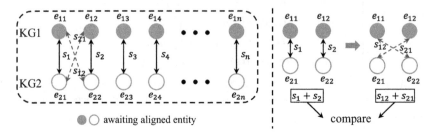

**Fig. 3.** A single entity alignment example. The orange nodes are the awaiting aligned entities that use $e_{11}, e_{12}, ...$ to represent. The $s_1, s_2, ...$ are the similarity degree values between aligned entities. (Color figure online)

Based on the above example, the weighting matrix generates formulas that are the description for all single entity exchanging process calculations. Firstly, the similarity degree of preliminary alignment results needs in the diagonal of matrix $A$. So we use the preliminary alignment results to re-arrange matrix A and get matrix $\bar{A}$. Next, we construct the auxiliary matrix $U$ as:

$$U = \begin{bmatrix} s_1 & s_1 & \dots & s_1 \\ s_2 & s_2 & \dots & s_2 \\ \vdots & \vdots & \dots & \vdots \\ s_n & s_n & \dots & s_n \end{bmatrix} \tag{6}$$

where the $\{s_1, s_2, ..., s_n\}$ is the diagonal elements of $\bar{A}$.

Finally, we attain the weighting matrix $A_{unsorted}$ by the following formula:

$$\begin{aligned} A_{unsorted} &= (\bar{A} + \bar{A}^T) - (U + U^T) \\ &= (\bar{A} - U) + (\bar{A} - U)^T. \end{aligned} \tag{7}$$

Then we sort the elements of each row in $A_{unsorted}$ and obtain a sorted matrix $A_{sorted}$ which indicates the ranked order for the top matching results.

## 4   Experiments

### 4.1   Cross-Lingual Dataset

We pick DBP15K [30] dataset to evaluate our method. This dataset contains knowledge graphs from four languages which are English (En), Chinese (Zh), and Japanese (Ja), and French (Fr). Three language pairs are evaluated which are Zh-En, Ja-En, and Fr-En. Each language pair contains about 15,000 entity pairs.

## 4.2 Comparative

To benchmark the efficiency of our method, we choose 20 state-of-art methods as a comparison. Three categories of methods are evaluated which are supervised, semi-supervised, and unsupervised learning. The supervised learning which utilizes a full training set to conduct alignment, are MuGNN [2], AliNet [31], HGCN-JE [39], RpAlign [6], SSEA [43], RNM [47], FuzzyEA [10], HMAN [41], EPEA [37], and BERT-INT [33]. The semi-Supervised learning method, which only utilized a subset of the training set, are KECG [15], NAEA [45], MRAEA [23], RREA [24]. The unsupervised learning, which doesn't need a training set, are EVA [17], SelfKG [18], UED [20], SEU [21], ICLEA [42], and LightEA [22].

**Table 1.** Comparison of entity alignment results on DBP15K dataset.

| Method | DBP15K$_{Zh-En}$ | | | DBP15K$_{Ja-En}$ | | | DBP15K$_{Fr-En}$ | | |
|---|---|---|---|---|---|---|---|---|---|
| | Hits@1 | Hits@10 | MRR | Hits@1 | Hits@10 | MRR | Hits@1 | Hits@10 | MRR |
| Supervised | | | | | | | | | |
| MuGNN [2] | 0.494 | 0.844 | 0.611 | 0.501 | 0.857 | 0.621 | 0.495 | 0.870 | 0.621 |
| AliNet [31] | 0.539 | 0.826 | 0.628 | 0.549 | 0.831 | 0.645 | 0.552 | 0.852 | 0.657 |
| HGCN-JE [39] | 0.720 | 0.857 | – | 0.766 | 0.897 | - | 0.892 | 0.961 | – |
| RpAlign [6] | 0.748 | 0.889 | 0.794 | 0.730 | 0.890 | 0.782 | 0.752 | 0.900 | 0.801 |
| SSEA [43] | 0.793 | 0.899 | – | 0.830 | 0.930 | – | 0.918 | 0.972 | – |
| RNM [47] | 0.840 | 0.919 | 0.870 | 0.872 | 0.944 | 0.899 | 0.938 | 0.981 | 0.954 |
| FuzzyEA [10] | 0.863 | 0.984 | 0.909 | 0.898 | 0.985 | 0.933 | 0.977 | **0.998** | 0.986 |
| HMAN [41] | 0.871 | 0.987 | – | 0.935 | **0.994** | – | 0.973 | **0.998** | – |
| EPEA [37] | 0.885 | 0.953 | 0.911 | 0.924 | 0.969 | 0.942 | 0.955 | 0.986 | 0.967 |
| BERT-INT [33] | **0.968** | **0.990** | **0.977** | **0.964** | 0.991 | **0.975** | **0.992** | **0.998** | **0.995** |
| Semi-Supervised | | | | | | | | | |
| KECG [15] | 0.478 | 0.835 | 0.598 | 0.490 | 0.844 | 0.610 | 0.486 | 0.851 | 0.610 |
| NAEA [45] | 0.650 | 0.867 | 0.720 | 0.641 | 0.873 | 0.718 | 0.673 | 0.894 | 0.752 |
| MRAEA [23] | 0.757 | 0.930 | 0.827 | 0.758 | 0.934 | 0.826 | 0.780 | 0.948 | 0.849 |
| RREA [24] | **0.801** | **0.948** | **0.857** | **0.802** | **0.952** | **0.858** | **0.827** | **0.966** | **0.881** |
| Unsupervised | | | | | | | | | |
| EVA [17] | 0.761 | 0.907 | 0.814 | 0.762 | 0.913 | 0.817 | 0.793 | 0.942 | 0.847 |
| SelfKG [18] | 0.745 | 0.866 | – | 0.816 | 0.913 | – | 0.959 | 0.992 | – |
| UED [20] | 0.826 | 0.943 | 0.870 | 0.863 | 0.960 | 0.900 | 0.938 | 0.987 | 0.957 |
| SEU [21] | 0.900 | 0.965 | 0.924 | 0.956 | 0.991 | 0.969 | 0.988 | **0.999** | 0.992 |
| ICLEA [42] | 0.921 | 0.981 | – | 0.955 | 0.988 | – | 0.992 | **0.999** | – |
| LightEA-L [22] | 0.952 | 0.984 | 0.964 | 0.981 | **0.997** | 0.987 | 0.995 | 0.998 | 0.996 |
| **UDCEA (ours)** | **0.966** | **0.989** | **0.975** | **0.990** | **0.997** | **0.993** | **0.996** | **0.999** | **0.997** |

*The comparison results are extracted from the corresponding paper.

## 4.3 Evaluation Indicate and Experiment Setting

We use $Hits@n$ and MRR (Mean Reciprocal Rank) to evaluate our approach. $Hits@n$ represents the proportion of truly aligned entity ranking greater or equal to $n$ and MRR is the sum of the reciprocal ranks of all aligned entities divided by the total number of aligned entities. In the embedding generation module, we use Google translator and multi-language encoder [27] as our translator and encoder respectively. In the entity alignment module, the value of $\alpha_E$, $\alpha_{ST}$, $\alpha_{AT}$, and $\alpha_{AR}$ are set to 1.00, 0.75, 0.75, and 0.15 respectively. We choose the Jonker-Volgenant algorithm [12] to conduct a bipartite matching process.

The weight of the four parameters is according to their significance. Naturally, the E most represents the aligned entity, the next is ST and AT, and the final is AR. Based on this idea, we set the weight for the four parameters respectively. In fact, the weight doesn't have a large impact on the alignment result (specific experiments in 5.2). For the optimization algorithm, we choose the Jonker-Volgenant algorithm because it has a relatively fast speed and stability. The time complexity of the Jonker-Volgenant algorithm is $O(n^3)$. If a faster speed is needed, Sinkhorn algorithm [21, 22, 29] is the next best option.

### 4.4 Experimental Results

Our results are shown in Table 1. Experiment results show our method exceeds all baselines in $Hits@1$, $Hits@10$, and MRR and achieves state-of-the-art results. Specifically, compared with unsupervised methods our method outperformed the next highest algorithm by 1.4%, 0.9%, and 0.1% in the $Hits@1$ accuracy. Even for relatively difficult DBP15K$_{Zh-En}$ dataset, we also achieve high accuracy of 0.966. To a certain extent, it shows our method's ability to effectively handle difficult cross-language entity alignment tasks. Moreover, we still obtain an advantage compared with state-of-art semi-supervised and supervised methods. Compared with semi-supervised methods, our method exceeds all methods and keeps an average improvement of above 15% accuracy. Compared with the state-of-the-art supervised method BERT-INT [33], we still surpass it by 2.6% and 0.4% for DBP15K$_{Ja-En}$ and DBP15K$_{Fr-En}$ datasets and only marginally lower by 0.2% in DBP15K$_{Zh-En}$ dataset. These experimental results show the superior performance of our method.

## 5   Ablation Study

In this section, we present a detailed analysis of our method. The total description is as follows:

- Analysis the influence of translator and encoder on results (5.1).
- Analysis the influence of E, ST, AT, and AR on results (5.2).
- Analysis the influence of bi-directional information on results (5.2).
- Analysis the influence of minimal or maximal optimization on results (5.2).
- Evaluation the influence of our alignment method on existing methods (5.3).
- Study the adaptability of our method on data sizes (5.3).

## 5.1   Translator and Encoder Analysis

We analyze the influence of Google translator and multi-language encoder [27] on the entity alignment task. The experiment results are shown in Table 2. For translators, we give up using Google translator and directly utilize the multi-language encoder to encode. The experiment results show that Google translator improves 3.5% and 5.4% accuracy on the Zh-En and Ja-En datasets respectively while decreasing 0.2% accuracy on the Fr-En dataset. It indicates that the translator helps in cross-language entity alignment when the two languages have a distinct difference while the translator has a minimal influence when the two languages are similar. For the encoder, we choose N-Gram [14], GloVe [25], and a monolingual sentence-bert [26] model as the comparison. The experiment results show that the multi-language encoder has an absolute advantage compared with the N-Gram and GloVe encoders, which gives the accuracy a large boost. Compared with the monolingual encoder, the multi-language encoder still improves 3%, 1.1%, and 1.2% accuracy on three datasets. In conclusion, the Google translator and multi-language encoder both have a positive influence on entity alignment mission, which combined can achieve higher accuracy.

**Table 2.** The experiment on translator and encoder. For parameter setting, the n is 2 in the N-Gram model and the dimension is 300 in the GloVe model. The symbol description: MS-B denotes multi-language Sentence-BERT [27], S-B denotes monolingual Sentence-Bert [26].

| Encoder Model | Translation | Zh-En | | Ja-En | | Fr-En | |
|---|---|---|---|---|---|---|---|
| | | *Hits@1* | *Hits@10* | *Hits@1* | *Hits@10* | *Hits@1* | *Hits@10* |
| N-Gram | ✓ | 0.352 | 0.523 | 0.425 | 0.602 | 0.550 | 0.670 |
| GloVe | ✓ | 0.718 | 0.841 | 0.791 | 0.896 | 0.840 | 0.915 |
| S-B | ✓ | 0.936 | 0.978 | 0.979 | 0.994 | 0.984 | 0.994 |
| MS-B | ✓ | **0.966** | **0.989** | **0.990** | **0.997** | 0.996 | 0.999 |
| MS-B | ✗ | 0.931 | 0.987 | 0.936 | 0.978 | **0.998** | **1.000** |

## 5.2   Alignment Module Analysis

We analyze the influence of multi-view information and alignment strategy for accuracy. To further prove the advantage of our alignment strategy, we add the similarity matching alignment method (directly sorted by similarity degree value) as a comparison in all experiments of this part. The experiment results are shown in Fig. 4. In Fig. 4(a), the weight of N, ST, AT, and AR is set to 1.00.

For multi-view information. From Fig. 4(a), we can see that the alignment accuracy gradually increases as the multi-view information is added. The experiment results indicate that the multi-view information is beneficial for improving accuracy. Meanwhile, notice that after adding the ST information that the alignment results have already achieved outstanding results. It indicates our method

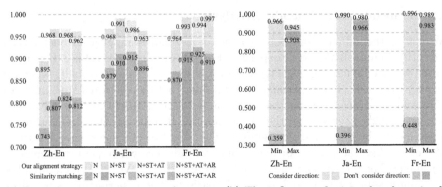

(a) The influence of multi-view information and alignment strategy for accuracy.

(b) The influence of minimal and maximal optimization for accuracy.

**Fig. 4.** The experiment results of alignment module analysis. (Color figure online)

has enough robustness that can adapt to the multi-view information part lack of circumstance. What's more, when we do not consider the weighting of multi-view information (all the weights set to 1.00), we can find that the accuracy may decrease as the multi-view information is added, which indicates that weighting adjustment is necessary. For alignment strategy. In Fig. 4(a), it shows that our alignment strategy achieves higher accuracy than the similarity matching method in all experiments.

The evaluations of the influence of directional information, and minimal, and maximal optimization for alignment results are displayed in Fig. 4(b). The experiment results show that the directional information further improves alignment accuracy. Moreover, adding the directional information makes minimal optimization becomes possible. Here, we found that the apply softmax operation when adding directional information is an unnecessary step and will decrease system accuracy. We adopt the softmax on matrix A and get 0.964, 0.976, and 0.997 alignment results in the Zh-En, Ja-En, and Fr-En datasets respectively. Compared with the results without softmax (0.966, 0.990, and 0.996). The softmax function does not bring benefit in Zh-En and Fr-En datasets and decreases 1.4% accuracy in the Ja-En dataset.

From the experiment results, we can conclude that both minimal and maximal optimization achieves outstanding alignment results. The minimum optimization has a strong reliance on the directional property and increases 61%, 59%, and 55% accuracy in three datasets when adding directional property. In conclusion, our alignment method can adapt maximum or minimum value optimization and further improve alignment process flexibility.

## 5.3  Additional Analysis

We conduct two experiments to show the benefit our alignment strategy brings to the existing alignment methods. Three open source code methods SEU [21],

RREA [24], and HGCN-JE [39] are evaluated. To evaluate the adaptability of our alignment method to data size changes, we use a larger size dataset DBP100K [32]. The DBP100K dataset includes En-De and En-Fr two cross-language pairs, and each language pair includes 100K aligned entity. We sub-sampled 10K, 20K, 30K, 40K, 60K, 80K, and 100K data to see the impact of different dataset sizes on our alignment method. The experiments are displayed in Fig. 5.

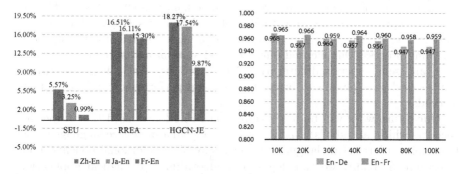

(a) The performance gain of attaching (b) The adapting ability of our method on our algorithm on improving existing entity different data sizes.
alignment methods.

**Fig. 5.** The experiment results of additional analysis. (Color figure online)

The results of Fig. 5(a) indicate that our alignment strategy brings improvement in all existing alignment methods. In those three methods, HGCN-JE received the highest received performance gain of 18.27% accuracy in the Zh-En dataset. The evaluation for the adaptability is shown in Fig. 5(b). As the data size increases, so does the complexity of the data, the maximum performance drop of our method is less than 2.1%.

## 6    Error Mode Analysis

In this section, we are analyzing the entity pairs that our algorithm falsely aligned. Through our analysis and statistics, we list the main four circumstances as follows. 1) Abbreviation: one entity is the other entity abbreviation in aligned entity pairs, such as "société nationale des chemins de fer français ↔ sncf". In fact, it's difficult to recognize even by an expert. 2) Person's name: In different nations, one person may have a different name. Besides, the same name also can correspond to a different person. Such as "李正秀 ↔ lee jung-soo". 3) Drama show/Music record names: one drama show/music record may have a different official name in a different nation or region, which is due to language, culture, marketing et al. Besides that, records may have many informal names such as

"静寂の世界 ↔ a rush of blood to the head". 4) Special characters: some special characters may be due to system error or typo such as " 『z』 の誓い ↔ %22z%22 no chikai".

## 7   Conclusion and Future Research

In this paper, we propose an unsupervised entity alignment method. We first utilize the multi-language encoder combined with Google translator to encode the multi-view information which reduces the reliance on labeled data. Then we adopt the optimization-based method to align the entities. Our method can generate ranked matching results which provides a higher degree of flexibility in the matching process. Our method outperformed state of art methods in unsupervised and semi-supervised categories. Moreover, our novel alignment strategy can be used as a plug-in to bring in additional performance gains to existing methods.

Our future work will be in two directions. Firstly, we used the off-the-shelf encoders which, at today's standard, it is considered a small-size language model. Developing a large-scale language encoder may bring additional benefits to our algorithm. Secondly, we can deploy our algorithm into medical applications where the patient record can be used as a query to conduct a multi-lingual search in the global dataset.

**Acknowledgement.** This work is supported by Hainan Province Science and Technology Special Fund (No. ZDKJ2021042) and A*STAR under its Artificial Intelligence in Medicine Transformation (AIMx) Program (Award H20C6a0032) National Natural Science Foundation of China (No.62362023).

**Ethical Statement.** This work doesn't involve any unethical tasks, all the experiment was done in public datasets.

## References

1. Bordes, A., Usunier, N., Garcia-Durán, A., Weston, J., Yakhnenko, O.: Translating embeddings for modeling multi-relational data. In: Proceedings of the 26th International Conference on Neural Information Processing Systems (NIPS), pp. 2787–2795 (2013)
2. Cao, Y., Liu, Z., Li, C., Liu, Z., Li, J., Chua, T.S.: Multi-channel graph neural network for entity alignment. In: Proceedings of the 57th Annual Meeting of the Association for Computational Linguistics (ACL), pp. 1452–1461 (2019)
3. Cohen, W.W., Richman, J.: Learning to match and cluster large high-dimensional data sets for data integration. In: Proceedings of the Eighth ACM SIGKDD International Conference on Knowledge Discovery and Data Mining, pp. 575–480 (2002)
4. Devlin, J., Chang, M.W., Lee, K., Toutanova, K.: BERT: pre-training of deep bidirectional transformers for language understanding. In: Proceedings of the 2019 Conference of the North American Chapter of the Association for Computational Linguistics (NAACL): Human Language Technologies, Volume 1 (Long and Short Papers), pp. 4171–4186 (2019)

5. Feng, F., Yang, Y., Cer, D., Arivazhagan, N., Wang, W.: Language-agnostic BERT sentence embedding, In: Proceedings of the 60th Annual Meeting of the Association for Computational Linguistics (ACL), pp. 878–891 (2022)
6. Huang, H., et al.: Cross-knowledge-graph entity alignment via relation prediction. Knowl. -Based Syst. **240**(15), 107813 (2022)
7. Jean-Mary, Y.R., Shironoshita, E.P., Kabuka, M.R.: Ontology matching with semantic verification. J. Web Semant. **7**(3), 235–251 (2009)
8. Ji, G., He, S., Xu, L., Liu, K., Zhao, J.: Knowledge graph embedding via dynamic mapping matrix. In: Proceedings of the 53rd Annual Meeting of the Association for Computational Linguistics (ACL) and the 7th International Joint Conference on Natural Language Processing (IJCNLP), pp. 687–696 (2015)
9. Ji, S., Pan, S., Cambria, E., Marttinen, P., Yu, P.S.: A survey on knowledge graphs: representation, acquisition, and applications. IEEE Trans. Neural Netw. Learn. Syst. **33**(2), 494–514 (2021)
10. Jiang, W., Liu, Y., Deng, X.: Fuzzy entity alignment via knowledge embedding with awareness of uncertainty measure. Neurocomputing **468**, 97–110 (2022)
11. Jiménez-Ruiz, E., Grau, B.C.: LogMap: logic-based and scalable ontology matching. In: The International Semantic Web Conference (ISWC), pp. 273–288 (2001)
12. Jonker, R., Volgenant, A.: A shortest augmenting path algorithm for dense and sparse linear assignment problems. Computing **38**, 325–340 (1987)
13. Kipf, T.N., Welling, M.: Semi-supervised classification with graph convolutional networks. In: 5th International Conference on Learning Representations (ICLR) (2017)
14. Kondrak, G.: N-gram similarity and distance. In: International Conference on String Processing and Information Retrieval, pp. 115–126 (2005)
15. Li, C., Cao, Y., Hou, L., Shi, J., Li, J., Chua, T.S.: Semi-supervised entity alignment via joint knowledge embedding model and cross-graph model. In: Proceedings of the 2019 Conference on Empirical Methods in Natural Language Processing and the 9th International Joint Conference on Natural Language Processing (EMNLP-IJCNLP), pp. 2723–2732 (2019)
16. Lin, Y., Liu, Z., Sun, M., Liu, Y., Zhu, X.: Learning entity and relation embeddings for knowledge graph completion. In: Proceedings of the Twenty-Ninth AAAI Conference on Artificial Intelligence, pp. 2181–2187 (2015)
17. Liu, F., Chen, M., Roth, D., Collier, N.: Visual pivoting for (unsupervised) entity alignment. In: Proceedings of the AAAI Conference on Artificial Intelligence, pp. 4257–4266 (2021)
18. Liu, X., et al.: SelfKG: self-supervised entity alignment in knowledge graphs. In: Proceedings of the ACM Web Conference (WWW), pp. 860–870 (2022)
19. Liu, Y., et al.: RoBERTa: a robustly optimized BERT pretraining approach. arXiv:1907.11692 (2019)
20. Luo, S., Yu, S.: An accurate unsupervised method for joint entity alignment and dangling entity detection. In: Findings of the Association for Computational Linguistics: ACL 2022, pp. 2330–2339 (2022)
21. Mao, X., Wang, W., Wu, Y., Lan, M.: From alignment to assignment: frustratingly simple unsupervised entity alignment. In: Proceedings of the 2021 Conference on Empirical Methods in Natural Language Processing (EMNLP), pp. 2843–2853 (2021)
22. Mao, X., Wang, W., Wu, Y., Lan, M.: LightEA: a scalable, robust, and interpretable entity alignment framework via three-view label propagation. In: Proceedings of the 2022 Conference on Empirical Methods in Natural Language Processing (EMNLP), pp. 825–838 (2022)

23. Mao, X., Wang, W., Xu, H., Lan, M., Wu, Y.: MRAEA: an efficient and robust entity alignment approach for cross-lingual knowledge graph. In: Proceedings of the 13th International Conference on Web Search and Data Mining (WSDM), pp. 420–428 (2020)
24. Mao, X., Wang, W., Xu, H., Wu, Y., Lan, M.: Relational reflection entity alignment. In: Proceedings of the 29th ACM International Conference on Information & Knowledge Management (CIKM), pp. 1095–1104 (2020)
25. Pennington, J., Socher, R., Manning, C.D.: GloVe: global vectors for word representation. In: Proceedings of the 2014 Conference on Empirical Methods in Natural Language Processing (EMNLP), pp. 1532–1543 (2014)
26. Reimers, N., Gurevych, I.: Sentence-BERT: sentence embeddings using siamese BERT-networks. In: Proceedings of the 2019 Conference on Empirical Methods in Natural Language Processing and the 9th International Joint Conference on Natural Language Processing (EMNLP-IJCNLP), pp. 3982–3992 (2019)
27. Reimers, N., Gurevych, I.: Making monolingual sentence embeddings multilingual using knowledge distillation. In: Proceedings of the 2020 Conference on Empirical Methods in Natural Language Processing (EMNLP), pp. 4512–4525 (2020)
28. Singhal, A.: Introducing the knowledge graph: Things, not strings (2012). https://www.blog.google/products/search/introducing-knowledge-graph-things-not/, eB/OL
29. Sinkhorn, R.: A relationship between arbitrary positive matrices and doubly stochastic matrices. Ann. Math. Stat. **35**(2), 876–879 (1964)
30. Sun, Z., Hu, W., Li, C.: Cross-lingual entity alignment via joint attribute-preserving embedding. In: The International Semantic Web Conference (ISWC), pp. 628–644 (2017)
31. Sun, Z., et al.: Knowledge graph alignment network with gated multi-hop neighborhood aggregation. In: Proceedings of the AAAI Conference on Artificial Intelligence, pp. 222–229 (2020)
32. Sun, Z., et al.: A benchmarking study of embedding-based entity alignment for knowledge graphs. Proc. VLDB Endowment **13**(11), 2326–2340 (2020)
33. Tang, X., Zhang, J., Chen, B., Yang, Y., Chen, H., Li, C.: BERT-INT: a BERT-based interaction model for knowledge graph alignment. In: Proceedings of the Twenty-Ninth International Joint Conference on Artificial Intelligence (IJCAI), pp. 3174–3180 (2021)
34. Veličković, P., Cucurull, G., Casanova, A., Romero, A., Liò, P., Bengio, Y.: Graph attention networks. In: 6th International Conference on Learning Representations (ICLR) (2018)
35. Wang, Z., Zhang, J., Feng, J., Chen, Z.: Transh: knowledge graph embedding by translating on hyperplanes. In: Proceedings of the Twenty-Eighth AAAI Conference on Artificial Intelligence, pp. 1112–1119 (2014)
36. Wang, Z., Lv, Q., Lan, X., Zhang, Y.: Cross-lingual knowledge graph alignment via graph convolutional networks. In: Proceedings of the 2018 Conference on Empirical Methods in Natural Language Processing (EMNLP), pp. 349–357 (2018)
37. Wang, Z., Yang, J., Ye, X.: Knowledge graph alignment with entity-pair embedding. In: Proceedings of the 2020 Conference on Empirical Methods in Natural Language Processing (EMNLP), pp. 1672–1680. Association for Computational Linguistics (2020)
38. Wu, Y., Liu, X., Feng, Y., Wang, Z., Yan, R., Zhao, D.: Relation-aware entity alignment for heterogeneous knowledge graphs. In: Proceedings of the Twenty-Eighth International Joint Conference on Artificial Intelligence (IJCAI), pp. 5278–5284 (2019)

39. Wu, Y., Liu, X., Feng, Y., Wang, Z., Zhao, D.: Jointly learning entity and relation representations for entity alignment. In: Proceedings of the 2019 Conference on Empirical Methods in Natural Language Processing and the 9th International Joint Conference on Natural Language Processing (EMNLP-IJCNLP), pp. 240–249 (2019)
40. Xin, K., et al.: Ensemble semi-supervised entity alignment via cycle-teaching. In: Proceedings of the AAAI Conference on Artificial Intelligence, pp. 4281–4289 (2022)
41. Yang, H.W., Zou, Y., Shi, P., Lu, W., Lin, J., Sun, X.: Aligning cross-lingual entities with multi-aspect information. In: Proceedings of the 2019 Conference on Empirical Methods in Natural Language Processing and the 9th International Joint Conference on Natural Language Processing (EMNLP-IJCNLP), pp. 4431–4441 (2019)
42. Zeng, K., et al.: Interactive contrastive learning for self-supervised entity alignment. In: Proceedings of the 31st ACM International Conference on Information & Knowledge Management (CIKM), pp. 2465–2475 (2022)
43. Zhu, B., Bao, T., Han, J., Han, R., Liu, L., Peng, T.: Cross-lingual knowledge graph entity alignment by aggregating extensive structures and specific semantics. J. Ambient Intell. Humanized Comput. **14**, 12609–12616 (2022)
44. Zhu, Q., et al.: Collective multi-type entity alignment between knowledge graphs. In: Proceedings of The Web Conference 2020 (WWW), pp. 2241–2252 (2020)
45. Zhu, Q., Zhou, X., Wu, J., Tan, J., Guo, L.: Neighborhood-aware attentional representation for multilingual knowledge graphs. In: Proceedings of the 28th International Joint Conference on Artificial Intelligence (IJCAI), pp. 1943–1949 (2019)
46. Zhu, R., Ma, M., Wang, P.: RAGA: relation-aware graph attention networks for global entity alignment. In: Advances in Knowledge Discovery and Data Mining (PAKDD), pp. 501–513 (2021)
47. Zhu, Y., Liu, H., Wu, Z., Du, Y.: Relation-aware neighborhood matching model for entity alignment. In: Proceedings of the AAAI Conference on Artificial Intelligence, pp. 4749–4756 (2021)
48. Zou, X.: A survey on application of knowledge graph. J. Phys. Conf. Ser. **1487**(1), 012016 (2020)

# Corpus-Based Relation Extraction by Identifying and Refining Relation Patterns

Sizhe Zhou[1], Suyu Ge[2], Jiaming Shen[3], and Jiawei Han[2(✉)]

[1] Shanghai Jiao Tong University, Shanghai, China
`sizhezhou@sjtu.edu.cn`
[2] University of Illinois Urbana-Champaign, Urbana, USA
`{suyuge2,hanj}@illinois.edu`
[3] Google Research, New York, USA
`jmshen@google.com`

**Abstract.** Automated relation extraction without extensive human-annotated data is a crucial yet challenging task in text mining. Existing studies typically use lexical patterns to label a small set of high-precision relation triples and then employ distributional methods to enhance detection recall. This *precision-first* approach works well for common relation types but struggles with unconventional and infrequent ones. In this work, we propose a *recall-first* approach that first leverages high-recall patterns (e.g., a `per:siblings` relation normally requires both the head and tail entities in the `person` type) to provide initial candidate relation triples with weak labels and then clusters these candidate relation triples in a latent spherical space to extract high-quality weak supervisions. Specifically, we present a novel framework, RCLUS, where each relation triple is represented by its head/tail entity type and the shortest dependency path between the entity mentions. RCLUS first applies high-recall patterns to narrow down each relation type's candidate space. Then, it embeds candidate relation triples in a latent space and conducts spherical clustering to further filter out noisy candidates and identify high-quality weakly-labeled triples. Finally, RCLUS leverages the above-obtained triples to prompt-tune a pre-trained language model and utilizes it for improved extraction coverage. We conduct extensive experiments on three public datasets and demonstrate that RCLUS outperforms the weakly-supervised baselines by a large margin and achieves generally better performance than fully-supervised methods in low-resource settings.

**Keywords:** Relation Extraction · Weak Supervision · Latent Space Clustering

## 1 Introduction

Relation extraction, which aims to extract semantic relationships between the head and tail entities as shown in Fig. 1, is crucial to various downstream tasks

---

S. Zhou and S. Ge—Equal contribution.

© The Author(s), under exclusive license to Springer Nature Switzerland AG 2023
D. Koutra et al. (Eds.): ECML PKDD 2023, LNAI 14172, pp. 20–38, 2023.
https://doi.org/10.1007/978-3-031-43421-1_2

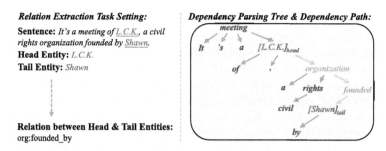

**Fig. 1.** Sentence's relation is explicitly contained in the dependency path. Head entities are indicated in blue while tail entities are indicated in red. The shortest dependency path connecting each pair of head entity and tail entity is indicated in light yellow. (Color figure online)

including hypernymy detection [33], knowledge base construction [25], and question answering [34,38,40]. A common practice of relation extraction is to fine-tune pre-trained language models with massive human annotations as full supervisions. As human annotations are expensive to acquire, potentially outdated or even noisy, such supervised methods are unable to scale. Instead of relying on massive human annotations, weakly-supervised relation extraction has been explored to tackle the data scarcity issue [24,26,47]. To improve the efficiency and minimize the expense of obtaining annotations, weakly-supervised relation extraction leverages only an incomplete set of pre-defined patterns to automatically annotate a portion of the corpus with weak labels as supervision [14,27].

In general, weakly-supervised relation extraction methods can be divided into two types: alignment-based and distributional. Alignment-based approaches obtain weak labels by exactly aligning pre-defined lexical patterns (e.g., certain tokens between entities or entity co-occurrence) with unlabeled examples from the corpus [14,20,24,28]. However, due to such context-agnostic hard matching process, the labels annotated by alignment-based approaches are noisy and suffer from limited recall and semantic drift [8]. Distributional approaches try to tackle such issues by encoding textual patterns with neural models so that the pattern matching can be conducted in a soft matching way [5,26,47]. Typically, distributional approaches utilize the alignment-based weak supervision or scarce human annotations at the initial stage to train neural encoder models [33]. However, such dependence introduces the severe problem of initial noise propagation [44,45]. Besides, the dependence on the initial alignment-based weak supervision along with the noise propagation also causes such distributional approaches to suffer from semantic drift and generalization problems.

To tackle the above mentioned high precision but low recall issue, we propose a novel recall-first framework RCLUS for weakly-supervised relation extraction which takes the sentence, head entity and tail entity as input and return the extracted relations as output (see Fig. 1 for an example). Instead of sticking to the traditional precision-first philosophy for weak supervision, RCLUS starts with initial weak supervisions with high recall and then further refines the weak supervision. Our RCLUS framework features three key designs as follows.

First, instead of relying on annotated data, RCLUS utilizes pre-defined patterns to obtain weak labels. To maximize the recall of weak supervision, RCLUS uses entity types along with relation-indicative words as relation identifiers for weak supervision. The head and tail entity types are usually fixed for a specific relation type. For example, the relation org:founded_by generally specifies the head entity as an organization and the tail entity as a person. Utilizing the entity requirements along with occurrence of relation-indicative words, such as "founder" and "establish", maximizes the recall of the weak supervision.

Second, based on the maximized recall, RCLUS tries to compensate the precision by presenting a novel representation of relation triples and conducting clustering on the representations. As utilizing relation-indicative words for weak supervision ignores the complete semantics for the relation expression, RCLUS adopts the shortest dependency path as the relation-related context within which the relation-indicative words will be searched. For example, the shortest dependency path in Fig. 1 helps neglecting irrelevant information including *It's a meeting of* and *civil rights*. The shortest dependency path is adopted as it retains the most relevant information to the target relation which is hence beneficial to the precision [7,12,35,42]. Furthermore, as the above alignment-based weakly-supervised extraction only focuses on local indicative words in the relation-related contexts, the assigned weak labels still suffer from noise. For example, *William talks with the founder team of the company D.M..* will give $\langle org., company - founder\_team - talks, person \rangle$ which satisfies the entity requirements and contains the indicated word "founder" of relation org:founded_by. However, based on the complete semantics from the sentence expression, it's unclear whether *D.M.* is founded by *William* or not. To prevent such noisy extractions, RCLUS proposes to cluster on a latent space which accommodates the objective to highlight the salient relation-related contexts across the corpus to isolate noisy contexts.

Third, in order to generalize to implicit and other varied expression patterns of relations to further improve the recall of the whole system, RCLUS prompt-tunes a pre-trained language model based on the limited but quality samples selected from the clustering space. To consolidate the pre-defined rules as the foundation for generalization, RCLUS selects quality samples from the clustering for tuning as these samples are noise-reduced and well represent the pre-defined patterns for relations. Meanwhile, RCLUS aggregates sub-prompts to extract relation-related components from the entire sentence and to improve context understanding. Compared with fine-tuning, prompt-tuning has a closer objective to the pre-training objective of language models. Thus, RCLUS can more efficiently distill the knowledge acquired from pre-training for generalizing the relation patterns under low resource setting.

To summarize, our main contributions are as follows: (1) We have proposed a weakly-supervised relation extraction framework based on the novel recall-first philosophy of weak supervision construction and then improve precision to tackle the data scarcity issue, (2) we have designed the relation triple representation extraction and the latent space clustering to mitigate the noisy labeling and noise propagation issues and we have incorporated prompt-tuning to mitigate the generalization issues, and (3) we have conducted extensive experiments on three relation extraction datasets to verify the effectiveness of our framework.

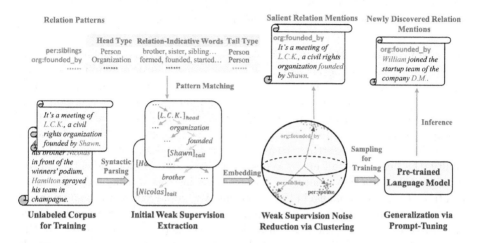

**Fig. 2.** Framework overview. Our model mainly consists of three steps: (1) relation triple representation extraction, (2) latent space clustering, and (3) prompt-tuning with sub-prompts.

## 2   Problem Formulation

Let corpus $S := \{S_1, \ldots, S_N\}$ be a set of sentences with each sentence $S_i$ consists of a word sequence $[w_{i,1}, \ldots, w_{i,n_i}]$. For relation extraction, it is assumed that for each sentence $S_i$, a head entity $W_{h,i}$ and a tail entity $W_{t,i}$ are given, and both of them are represented by a sub-sequence of the sentence. Given $S_i$, $W_{h,i}$ and $W_{t,i}$, the goal of relation extraction is to predict the relation $y_i \in \mathcal{Y}$ between $W_{h,i}$ and $W_{t,i}$ which is the most appropriate based on the sentence, where $\mathcal{Y}$ is a set of pre-defined relations.

## 3   Methodology

In Fig. 2, we outline our framework that extracts relations from corpus in three major steps: (1) *initial weak supervision extraction* which matches the extracted representations of relation triple with pre-defined patterns to obtain weak labels with high recall (Sect. 3.2), (2) *weak supervision noise reduction via clustering* in a latent spherical space which mines salient relation-related contexts to filter the noisy weak labels for improving precision (Sect. 3.3), and (3) *generalization via prompt-tuning* which leverages salient samples from the clustering space to recall implicit and varied relation expressions (Sect. 3.4).

## 3.1   Representation of Relation Triple

We first introduce the concept of representations of relation triples which is fundamental for our initial weak supervision extraction. Then we introduce the method to construct the corresponding embeddings for representations of relation triple which will be used for latent space clustering.

**Representation of Relation Triple.** The relation triple is defined to be in the form of ⟨*head entity, relation, tail entity*⟩. Based on the definition of relation triples, we further define the representation of relation triple which is the example-specific triple containing the essential relation-related information. The formulation of relation triple representations is aimed to automatically annotate examples with most suitable weak labels while maximally reducing the noise under the low resource setting. To assign weak relation labels with maximal suitability, the head and tail entity types along with the relation-indicative words serve as strong relation identifiers. For example, instead of using only the entity mentions *L.C.K.* and *Shawn* in Fig. 1, the entity types `organization` and `person` together with the word *founded* also indicate the relation label `founded_by`. However, directly matching the relation-indicative words (e.g. *founded* above) in the whole sentence will likely get distracted by the noise from parts of sentence which are irrelevant to the target entities' relationship. Previous studies suggest that shortest dependency paths between head and tail entities retain the most relevant information to their relation [7, 12, 35, 42] which makes it perfect to isolate noise from irrelevant contexts. As shown in Fig. 1, the semantics of *founded* in the shortest dependency path between *L.C.K.* and *Shawn* is clearly relevant to entities' semantic relationship. Meanwhile, other parts of the sentence beyond the shortest dependency path such as "a civil right organization" is not relevant to the semantic relationship. Therefore the use of shortest dependency paths further avoids noise from directly matching with relation-indicative words.

Based on the above intuitions, we define a representation of relation triple $K$ as ⟨$h, r, t$⟩ where $h$ indicates the head entity type, $t$ indicates the tail entity type, and $r$ indicates the shortest dependency path starting from head entity mention to tail entity mention. Each valid representation of relation triple $K$ is associated with a relation $y$. For the sentence in Fig. 1, a representation of relation triple would be ⟨*org., organization-founded, person*⟩ associated with relation `org:founded_by`.

**Embedding for Representation of Relation Triple.** Suppose relation triple representation extraction gives $M$ representations of relation triples $\{K_1, \ldots, K_M\}$. For each relation triple representation $K_i = \langle h_i, r_i, t_i \rangle$, we acquire its initial features in the form of relation triple representation embeddings $\left\langle \vec{h}_{h_i}, \vec{h}_{r_i}, \vec{h}_{t_i} \right\rangle$ which includes: head entity embedding $\vec{h}_{h_i}$, dependency path embedding $\vec{h}_{r_i}$ and tail entity embedding $\vec{h}_{t_i}$.

*Head/Tail Entity Embedding:* We derive the embedding for head or tail entity based on their entity type surface names. Namely, head entity embedding

$\vec{h}_{h_i} \in \mathbf{H_h}$ is obtained by retrieving and averaging pre-trained token embeddings[1] of the head entity type surface name $h_i$. The tail entity embedding $\vec{h}_{t_i} \in \mathbf{H_t}$ is constructed likewise. Here $\mathbf{H_h}$ and $\mathbf{H_t}$ denote the semantic spaces for head and tail entities respectively.

*Dependency Path Embedding:* To capture the complete semantics of the dependency information, we construct the contextualized embedding $\vec{h}_{r_i}^{cont}$ as one component of the dependency path embedding $\vec{h}_{r_i}$. To accommodate the word choice variation of the dependency path (e.g., "founded" and "established" alternatively for the same relation `org:founded_by`), we construct masked language modeling embedding $\vec{h}_{r_i}^{mask}$ with BERT [10] to obtain the other component of the dependency path embedding $\vec{h}_{r_i}$.

Assume the dependency path $r_i$ is composed of $m_{r_i}$ words $\{w_{i_K,1}, \ldots, w_{i_K,m_{r_i}}\}$ from original sentence $S_{i_K} \in \mathcal{S}$ which are not necessarily consecutive in $S_{i_K}$ but are necessarily consecutive in the dependency parse tree by definition. To obtain $h_{r_i}^{cont}$, we feed sentence $S_{i_K}$ to pre-trained language model and retrieve the corresponding encoded vecors of $r_i$ as $\{\vec{h}_{w_{i_K},1}, \ldots, \vec{h}_{w_{i_K},m_{r_i}}\}$. $\vec{h}_{r_i}^{cont}$ can be calculated with average pooling.

To obtain $\vec{h}_{r_i}^{mask}$, we replace each word in the dependency path with a mask token [MASK], feed the masked sentence to the pre-trained language model and retrieve the corresponding encoded vectors of $r_i$ as $\{\vec{h}_{mask_{i_K},1}, \ldots, \vec{h}_{mask_{i_K},m_{r_i}}\}$. $\vec{h}_{r_i}^{mask}$ can be similarly calculated with average pooling.

Finally, the dependency path embedding is constructed by the concatenation of two components: $\vec{h}_{r_i} = [\vec{h}_{r_i}^{mask}; \vec{h}_{r_i}^{cont}] \in \mathbf{H_r}$ where $\mathbf{H_r}$ denotes the semantic space for dependency path.

After the above feature acquisition process, for each extracted representation of the relation triple $K_i$, we have obtained the relation triple embedding $\left\langle \vec{h}_{h_i}, \vec{h}_{r_i}, \vec{h}_{t_i} \right\rangle \in \mathbf{H_h} \times \mathbf{H_r} \times \mathbf{H_t}$ for relation triple representation clustering.

## 3.2   Initial Weak Supervision Extraction

Based on weakly-supervised setting and the formulation of relation triple representation, we maintain corresponding entity types and a limited set of relation-indicative words for each relation to construct the pre-defined relation patterns (see the table in Fig. 2 as an example). In contrast to previous weakly-supervised approaches that applies pattern matching in a precision-first manner, we first adopts the philosophy of recall-first and later improve the precision for weak supervision. Given our pursuit of high recall, we assign weak labels once the entity types are matched and the relation-indicative words are captured in the shortest dependency path.

Utilizing the pre-defined relation patterns for constructing initial weak supervision, we first conduct dependency parsing and named entity typing[2] on each

---

[1] For simplicity in feature acquisitions, we adopts BERT-Large [10] as the pre-trained language model for all the encoding.

[2] For convenience, we use the Stanford CoreNLP toolkit [19].

sentence $S_i \in \mathcal{S}$. Based on the parsing results, we find the shortest dependency path between each pair of head entity $W_{h,i}$ and tail entity $W_{t,i}$ so that each sentence $S_i$ will correspond to one candidate representation of relation triple. Second, we align the pre-defined relation patterns and the relation triple representation candidates so that relation triple representations which have the matched entity types and the indicative words will be assigned with a weak label.

## 3.3   Weak Supervision Noise Reduction via Clustering

As the matching-based extraction of the initial weak supervision only focuses on in-sentence indicative words which leads to noisy weak labels and hence low precision, RCLUS introduces latent space clustering which highlights salient relation-related contexts across the corpus for noise filtering. Given the semantic spaces of the head entity, the tail entity and the relation-related context, RCLUS fuses the three semantic spaces onto a joint latent spherical space of much lower dimensionality for clustering. The rationale for such fusing method for clustering are two folds: (1) Angular similarity in spherical space is more effective than Euclidean metrics to capture word semantics [21,23], and (2) clustering while optimizing the projection onto a joint lower dimensional space can force the RCLUS to model the interactions between the head entity, the tail entity and the relation related contexts, discarding irrelevant information in the relation-related contexts. In contrast, a naïve clustering method on the dimension reduced or simply concatenated semantic spaces of the relation triple representations without integrating any clustering promoting objective is weak to guarantee the above suitability.

**Clustering Model.** We use the clustering model to regularize the interactions between the head entity and the tail entity and discard noise in relation-related contexts. We assume that there exists a latent space $\mathbf{Z} \subset \mathbb{S}^{d-1}$[3] with $C$ clusters. Each cluster corresponds to one relation and is represented by a von Mises-Fisher (vMF) distribution [4].

The vMF distribution is controlled by a mean vector $\mu \in \mathbf{Z}$ and a concentration parameter $\kappa \in \mathbb{R}^+ \cup \{0\}$. The vMF probability density function for a unit vector $z$ is given by $p(z|\mu, \kappa) = n_d(\kappa) \cdot \exp(\kappa \cdot \cos(z, \mu))$. Here $n_d(\kappa)$ is the normalization constant defined as

$$n_d(\kappa) = \frac{\kappa^{d/2-1}}{(2\pi)^{d/2} I_{d/2-1}(\kappa)}, \tag{1}$$

where $I_{d/2-1}(\cdot)$ represents the modified Bessel function of the first kind at order $d/2 - 1$.

With the assumption on the relation clusters, we further make assumptions on the generation of relation triple embeddings $\left\langle \vec{h}_{h_i}, \vec{h}_{r_i}, \vec{h}_{t_i} \right\rangle$ as follows: (1) A

---

[3] $\mathbb{S}^{d-1} := \{z \in \mathbb{R}^d | \|z\| = 1\}$. We assume that $d \ll \min(\dim(\mathbf{H_h}), \dim(\mathbf{H_r}), \dim(\mathbf{H_t}))$.

relation type $c$ is uniformly sampled over $C$ relations: $c \sim \text{Uniform}(C)$, (2) a latent embedding $z_i$ is generated from the vMF distribution with mean vector $\mu_c$ and concentration parameter $\kappa$: $z_i \sim \text{vMF}_d(\mu_c, \kappa)$, (3) three functions $g_h(\cdot)$, $g_r(\cdot)$, $g_t(\cdot)$ respectively map the latent embedding $z_i$ to the original relation triple embeddings $\vec{h}_{h_i}$, $\vec{h}_{r_i}$ and $\vec{h}_{t_i}$: $\vec{h}_{h_i} = g_h(z_i), \vec{h}_{r_i} = g_r(z_i), \vec{h}_{t_i} = g_t(z_i)$.

To enhance joint optimization, we follow the autoencoder structure [15] to jointly optimize the decoding mappings $g_h : \mathbf{Z} \to \mathbf{H_h}$, $g_r : \mathbf{Z} \to \mathbf{H_r}$, $g_t : \mathbf{Z} \to \mathbf{H_t}$ and an encoding mapping $f : \mathbf{H_h} \times \mathbf{H_r} \times \mathbf{H_t} \to \mathbf{Z}$.

**Model Training.** To optimize the salient context mining without supervision, we adopt a pre-training and EM optimization process [9] with the reconstruction objective and the clustering-promoting objective.

In the E-step, we update the clustering assignment estimation $q(\mu_c|z_i)$ by computing the posterior distribution as

$$p(\mu_c|z_i) = \frac{p(z_i|\mu_c)p(\mu_c)}{\sum_{c'=1}^{C} p(z_i|\mu_{c'})p(\mu_{c'})} = \frac{\exp(\kappa \cdot z_i^T \cdot \mu_c)}{\sum_{c'=1}^{C} \exp(\kappa \cdot z_i^T \cdot \mu_{c'})} \qquad (2)$$

The target distribution is derived as $q(\mu_c|z_i)$:

$$q(\mu_c|z_i) = \frac{p(\mu_c|z_i)^2/s_c}{\sum_{c'=1}^{C} p(\mu_{c'}|z_i)^2/s_{c'}} \qquad (3)$$

with $s_c := \sum_{j=1}^{K} p(\mu_c|z_j)$. The squaring-then-normalizing formulation is shown to introduce a sharpening effect which shifts the estimation towards the most confident area so that different clusters will have more distinct separation [22,41].

The corresponding clustering-promoting objective is defined as

$$\mathcal{O}_{clus} = \sum_{j=1}^{K} \sum_{c'=1}^{C} q(\mu_{c'}|z_j) \cdot \log p(\mu_{c'}|z_j) \qquad (4)$$

and the reconstruction objective is defined as

$$\mathcal{O}_{recon} = \sum_{j=1}^{K} \sum_{l \in \{h,r,t\}} \cos(\vec{h}_{l_j}, g_l(f(\vec{h}_{h_j}, \vec{h}_{r_j}, \vec{h}_{t_j}))) \qquad (5)$$

The reconstruction objective leads the model to preserve the input space semantics while conducting mappings.

In the M-step, the mapping functions $g_h(\cdot)$, $g_r(\cdot)$, $g_t(\cdot)$, $f(\cdot)$ and cluster distribution parameters are updated by maximizing $\mathcal{O}_{recon} + \lambda\mathcal{O}_{clus}$.

After convergence, there are $C$ well-separated clusters $\{\mu_{c'}\}_{c'=1}^{C}$. Each cluster centroid $\mu_{c'}$ is associated with a cluster of relation triples $\{K_j^{(c')}\}_{j=1}^{M_{c'}}$ where $M_{c'}$ denotes the number of relation triples affiliated with cluster centroid $\mu_{c'}$.

## 3.4    Generalization via Prompt-Tuning

Even with high recall and the improved precision, the weak supervision still suffer from following deficiencies. First of all, the weak supervision extraction by hard matching the pre-defined patterns with the extracted relation triple representations is deficient to handle implicitly expressed relations that need to be inferred from the whole sentence context beyond dependency path. One example for the relation `per:grandparent` is *Alice, the wife of Mike, gave birth to Beck three months before Mike's father, John, visited her.* This example sentence indicates John is the grandparent of Beck by incorporating the `per:mother`, `per:spouse` and `per:father` relations and it is hard to cover such complicated and implicit patterns for applying weak supervision. Second, the pre-defined relation patterns suffer from limited coverage due to the hard matching nature of the weak supervision construction. For example, the set of relation-indicative words for `org:founded_by` is far from completeness.

To tackle the first deficiency, we select samples with salient relation-related contexts from the clustering space for tuning pre-trained language models[4]. These high-quality samples well represent the pre-defined patterns whose noise from initial weak supervision construction is largely reduced after clustering. By tuning the pre-trained language models leveraging these samples, RCLUS is capable to learn the essence of the pre-defined patterns and to generalize to other implicit relation patterns that need to be reasoned from the context.

To tackle the second deficiency, instead of fine-tuning, we tune the language models with prompts. As prompt-tuning has a much closer objective to the pre-training objective, RCLUS is hence much more efficient in distilling the knowledge acquired from pre-training for generalizing the high-quality patterns under low resource setting. Sticking to our philosophy of designing the pre-defined relation patterns, we follow [13] to aggregate three sub-prompts to jointly contribute to the inference of prompt-tuning. As each target relation is generally equivalent to the combination of the head entity type, the tail entity type and the semantic relationship between the head and the tail. The three sub-prompts are hence designed corresponding: (1) the sub-prompt for inferring the head entity type and it consists of a mask and the head entity mention, (2) the sub-prompt for inferring the semantic relationship independent to entity types (e.g., "gave birth to") and it consists of three masks, and (3) the sub-prompt for inferring the tail entity type same as (1). The original sentence and the three sub-prompts will be concatenated in order to tune the pre-trained language model. RCLUS integrates the inference of the three sub-prompts to give the extracted relation. As an example, to give the relation `org:founded_by`, the three sub-prompts will need to predict the head entity as an organization, the tail entity as a person and the semantic relationship between entities as "was founded by".

---

[4] For this work, we use RoBERTa_Large [48] as the backbone model and maintain the consistency between baselines in experiments.

## 4   Experiments

In the following[5] we first show the effectiveness of RCLUS on three relation extraction datasets (Sect. 4.1) and the data sampling for prompt-tuning (Sect. 4.2). Then, we illustrate the clustering results utilizing t-SNE [18] (Sect. 4.3) and study the importance of each component of RCLUS with an ablation study (Sect. 4.4).

### 4.1   Relation Extraction

*Datasets:* We carry out the experiments on three relation extraction datasets: (1) TACRED [46] which is the most widely used large scale dataset for sentence-level relation extraction. There are 41 common relations and 1 NA[6] label for negative samples which are defined to have relations beyond labeled relations.. (2) TACREV [3] which corrects labels of part of dev and test set of TACRED. (3) ReTACRED [36] which refactors the TACRED and modifies some relations for suitability.

Without loss of generality, we sampled 30 relations from original relations of each dataset for the convenience of designing weak supervisions. 27 relations are shared across 3 datasets. For the left 3 relations, the org:country_of_headquarters, the org:stateorprovince_of_headquarters and the org:city_of_headquarters, ReTACRED modifies the *headquarters* to *branch*. The statistics are shown in Table 2.

*Baselines:* We compare RCLUS with: (1) EXACT MATCHING: prediction is given by pre-defined relation patterns. (2) COSINE [44]: weakly-supervised

**Table 1.** $F_1$ scores (%) on full test set with different sizes ($K$ = 4, 8, 16) for each relation label. 3 seeds (212, 32, 96) are used for uniformly random sampling and the median value is taken as the final result for robustness against extreme values. Note that - means for that setting, no size limitation on labeled samples for training is assumed and the evaluation results will be indicated under *Mean* column. Models under such setting is also indicated with *.

| Model | TACRED | | | | TACREV | | | | ReTACRED | | | |
|---|---|---|---|---|---|---|---|---|---|---|---|---|
| K | 4 | 8 | 16 | Mean | 4 | 8 | 16 | Mean | 4 | 8 | 16 | Mean |
| *w/ weak supervision* | | | | | | | | | | | | |
| EXACT MATCHING* | – | – | – | 48.87 | – | – | – | 53.67 | – | – | – | 54.86 |
| COSINE | 23.28 | 26.60 | 37.16 | 29.01 | 21.43 | 30.85 | 41.21 | 31.16 | 28.12 | 35.00 | 44.54 | 35.89 |
| COSINE* | – | – | – | 58.88 | – | – | – | 60.80 | – | – | – | 68.59 |
| RCLUS NOISY | 45.35 | 50.94 | 55.73 | 50.67 | 50.41 | 61.67 | **66.85** | 59.64 | 56.89 | 65.81 | 71.09 | 64.60 |
| RCLUS BALANCED | 45.19 | 55.71 | 59.33 | 53.41 | 55.36 | 58.74 | 64.56 | 59.55 | 53.84 | 65.27 | 71.03 | 63.38 |
| RCLUS | **49.89** | **56.65** | **60.26** | 55.60 | **56.94** | **63.75** | 66.50 | 62.40 | **61.03** | **68.78** | **72.23** | 67.35 |
| *w/ ground truth supervision* | | | | | | | | | | | | |
| FINE-TUNING | 13.62 | 26.09 | 32.07 | 23.93 | 18.75 | 25.21 | 35.12 | 26.36 | 17.36 | 31.77 | 42.63 | 30.59 |
| GDPNET | 13.79 | 28.42 | 43.11 | 28.44 | 15.61 | 24.59 | 42.12 | 27.44 | 19.20 | 35.79 | 52.84 | 35.94 |
| PTR | 39.16 | 49.46 | 54.67 | 47.76 | 47.18 | 51.58 | 59.17 | 52.64 | 51.27 | 62.60 | 71.11 | 61.66 |

---

[5] The code for this work is available at https://github.com/KevinSRR/RClus.
[6] no_relation for TACREV and ReTACRED.

model that utilizes contrastive self-training to extend labeled dataset and de-noise. (3) FINE-TUNING: a RoBERTa_Large [48] backbone plus a classification head whose input is the sequence classification embedding concatenated with the averaged embeddings of head and tail entities. (4) GDPNET [43]: it constructs a multi-view graph on top of BERT. (5) PTR [13]: RCLUS's backbone prompt-tuning model except for some modifications. For training with weak supervision, we assume the negative samples in the train set are known but only $2 \times K \times$ Number of Positive Labels of negative samples can be used.

As RCLUS requires applying pre-defined patterns on positive examples, there will be examples that match with zero or multiple patterns. RCLUS will ignore such examples while RCLUS NOISY will respectively assign negative label and the first matched relation, only not using them for clustering. This is the only difference between RCLUS and RCLUS NOISY. For RCLUS, as prompt-tuning requires data sampled from clusters, it involves sampling of both positive and negative samples whose details are in Sect. 4.2.

For fair comparisons, we study the low-resource setting performance. For weakly-supervised baselines without being denoted with *, we provide small training sets as weakly-labeled data while leaving the remaining data as unlabeled data. For fine-tuning based or prompt-tuning baselines, we provide same sizes of training sets but with ground truth labels. The difference between RCLUS and RCLUS BALANCED is that, after positive data sampling, RCLUS compensate the relations with samples fewer than K using weak supervisions until reaching K while RCLUS BALANCED will cut down exceeded samples at the same time to keep sample size of each positive relations as K.

*Evaluation Metrics:* We follows the micro $F_1$ metric adopted by most of the works that experiment on three datasets. Note that mainstream approaches calculate this metric over positive samples only. We set the training epochs as 20 and the evaluation frequency on dev set as once every 2 epochs. Best checkpoint on dev set is chosen for evaluation.

**Table 2.** Statistics of datasets

| Dataset | #train | #dev | #test |
|---------|--------|------|-------|
| TACRED | 65,044 | 21,226 | 14,637 |
| TACREV | 65,044 | 21,238 | 14,681 |
| ReTACRED | 49,419 | 15,780 | 10,375 |

**Table 3.** Ablation study of RCLUS

| Model | TACREV | | |
|-------|--------|---|---|
| | Precision | Recall | $F_1$ |
| RCLUS | | | |
| w/ Weak | 59.30 | 49.02 | 53.67 |
| w/ Prompt | 48.25 | 75.73 | 58.95 |
| w/ Weak + Prompt | 58.80 | 72.07 | 64.76 |
| w/ Weak + Cluster | 63.62 | 40.61 | 49.57 |
| w/ Weak + Cluster + Prompt | 60.76 | 74.29 | 66.85 |
| w/ Weak + Cluster + Prompt* | 57.85 | 78.47 | 66.61 |

*Experiment Setups:* Baseline implementation details and the pre-defined patterns of RCLUS are uploaded with source codes[7]. Before applying patterns, NER

---

[7] https://github.com/KevinSRR/RClus.

will be leveraged for typing head and tail entity mentions. Sentences with unrecognized mentions will not be considered for training and will be seen as negative sample if in test set.

For the clustering model's decoding function $g_l(\cdot)$ with $l \in \{h, r, t\}$, we implement them as feed-forward neural networks with each layer followed by ReLU activation [1]. We adopt 100, 1000, 2000, 1000, $dim_l$ for the hidden states dimensions of each layer. The $dim_l$ is 1024 for head/tail entity embeddings and 2048 for dependency path embeddings. For encoding mapping $f$, we basically reverse the layout of the three decoding functions and concatenate them to form the latent space vector $z \in \mathbb{R}^{300}$. For the clustering, the concentration parameter $\kappa$ of each vMf distribution is set as 10, the $\lambda$ is chosen as 5. During training, the batchsize is 256 while the learning rate is $5e - 4$. Additionally, we set the tolerance threshold for optimization convergence as 0.001 which means when the ratio of the examples with changed cluster assignment is fewer than this threshold, the training will stop. The pre-training epochs with only objective $\mathcal{O}_{recon}$ is set as 100, and the interval for updating the target assignment distribution $q(\mu_c|z_i)$ is set as 100. The remaining experiment setups are similar to [31].

For prompt-tuning with sub-prompts, we used the verbalizer and the label word set from [13] except that we have modified some prompt templates and search the learning rate from $\{3e - 5, 4e - 5\}$ and we search the max input sequence length from $\{256, 512\}$.

The hyperparameter search space for sampling interval $I$ is $\{2, 3\}$ and the $M_{negative}$ is $\{10000, 20000, 30000\}$. A found good combination is $I$ as 3 and $M_{negative}$ as 30000.

*Main Analysis:* The results are shown in Table 1. Generally, compared with weakly-supervised baselines and supervised baselines with ground truth, our model achieves better performances under low-resource scenarios. The advantage is more significant when compared to weakly-supervised baselines, demonstrating the overall effectiveness.

Compared with PTR which is the backbone of our prompt-tuning method, RCLUS, with weak supervision and clustering, has improved PTR's performance by a large margin. Additionally, RCLUS can be easily adapted for integrating other more powerful prompt-tuning backbones for better performance. This shows the effectiveness of the whole pipeline design as well as the further potential of RCLUS.

Considering different levels of data scarcity, RCLUS's advantage over baselines with ground truth supervision is most significant when ground truth samples are scarce, as the pre-defined patterns and the pattern generalizability of RCLUS will reach a limit while baselines with ground truth supervision can access more patterns from more samples.

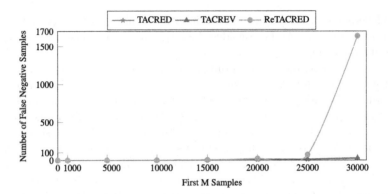

**Fig. 3.** Number of false negative samples among first M samples with smallest max-assignment-probability (consider both negative examples and weakly labeled positive examples).

## 4.2   Positive and Negative Samples

To obtain quality samples for prompt-tuning, RCLUS adopts sampling with intervals. Based on the cluster assignment probability by Eq. 2, sampling with interval $I$ means for each cluster, starting from highest assignment probability in descending order, taking one sample among every $I$ candidate samples. The purpose is to avoid repetitions of similar samples as there are numerous similar or reused samples from the datasets.

As relation triple representation extraction and clustering is targeted at positive samples that fall into the range of defined relations, for model training, RCLUS also needs to obtain quality negative samples. RCLUS follows a min max approach. After the latent space clustering on extracted relation triple representations with positive relations, we apply the trained mapping function $f : \mathbf{H_h} \times \mathbf{H_r} \times \mathbf{H_t} \rightarrow \mathbf{Z}$ to project the unextracted relation triple representations (or negative samples) and sort by their maximal assignment probability among all clusters given by Eq. 2 in ascending order. Then negative relation triples are sampled uniformly from the first $M_{negative}$ sorted relation triple representations.

This method follows the intuition that clusters trained using positive samples well represent the salient features of positive relations. Therefore, negative samples will be projected as outliers. To further enhance the prompt-tuning effectiveness, the range of first $M_{negative}$ samples guarantees minimal distinction between the sampled negative and positive samples. While uniform sampling introduces different levels of difficulty for prompt-tuning to distinguish the sampled positive and negative samples. Figure 3 verifies our intuition as the ratios of false negative samples are 0.070%, 0.093%, and 5.46%, against the overall negative sample ratios as 9.92%, 9.54%, and 15.43% for TACRED, TACREV and ReTACRED respectively.

## 4.3   Cluster Visualization

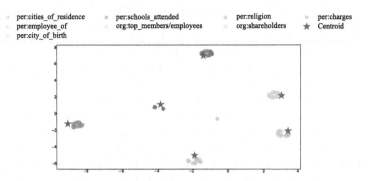

**Fig. 4.** Visualization of the clusters with t-SNE. For clarity, we sample 6 cluster centroids for TACREV dataset and visualize them along with first 40 data points closest to each centroid.

Clustering result visualized with t-SNE [18] is shown in Fig. 4. We can see that clusters generally have well separated boundaries, which means that the clusters well capture the salient features of different relation patterns. In rare cases, relations that have semantically close patterns might have close latent representations. For example, the patterns of `org:employee_of` and `org:shareholders` share the same head and tail entity types and the two relations can generally have similar contexts. So they are in the same cluster as shown by Fig. 4. As our clustering is unsupervised, some clusters may represent more than one relation. However, instead of being leveraged to assign labels, our clustering is only used to filter noisy relation triple representations which are expected to be outliers after clustering. Hence such problem will not influence any relation extraction results. For example, even the above discussed cluster contains samples of `org:employee_of` and `org:shareholders`, we will only sample them with their labels assigned by pattern matching as long as they are not outliers.

## 4.4   Ablation Study

In order to show the importance of each component of RCLUS, an ablation study is conducted with results shown in Table 3. Note that we take 16 for few-shot settings and the seed as 212 if needed. *Weak* refers to weak supervision, *Prompt* refers to prompt-tuning, and *Cluster* refers to latent space clustering. And * denotes RCLUS BALANCED. Generally, each component is indispensable to the whole framework based on the evaluation performance. Specifically, it can be seen that the weak supervision and the clustering are both important for the precision metric as they capture certain patterns and reduce initial weak supervision noise. The weak supervision provides relatively high recall while the clustering provides high precision. Additionally, the prompt-tuning is important for boosting recall as it helps comprehend the whole context, generalize the patterns and infer the implicit relations. This is in accordance with design expectations.

# 5   Related Work

**De-noising for Weakly-Supervised Learning:** Previous methods design probabilistic models to aggregate multiple weak supervisions to achieve denoising yet ignoring the contexts for further improvement [2,27,37]. Other studies either focus on noise transitions without dealing with instance-level de-noising or require too much supervision to be suitable for weakly-supervised relation extraction [29,39]. A recent study proposes a contrastive self-training based denoising method but cannot bypass potential issues of noise propagations from initial weak supervision [44]. Different from them, RCLUS adopts unsupervised relation triple representation clustering which captures salient semantic features of relation expressions to filter noises from weak supervision.

**Prompt-Tuning for Low-Resource Settings:** Enhanced by the birth of GPT-3 [6], prompt-tuning has introduced various studies [11,16,17,30,32]. KNOWPROMPT tries to include prior knowledge on labels into prompts for relation extraction. They focused on extending prompt models' generalizability without making use of weak supervision to boost the performance. In contrast, RCLUS adopts prompt-tuning to achieve generalizability with a strong base on learnt noise-reduced patterns.

# 6   Conclusions

In this work, we propose a novel weakly-supervised relation extraction framework. Specifically, our framework: (1) has designed new relation patterns for a novel *recall-first* philosophy for weak supervision construction, (2) designed a novel representation of relation triple for initial weak supervision construction for high recall and then utilized clustering to mine salient contexts to improve precision, (3) leveraged the samples from clusters for prompt-tuning to enhance generalization and context understanding. Experiments show RCLUS largely outperforms the weakly-supervised baselines and achieves better performance than fully-supervised methods under low-resource settings. We also show the importance of each component of RCLUS and verify design expectations quantitatively and qualitatively.

**Acknowledgements.** Research was supported in part by US DARPA KAIROS Program No. FA8750-19-2-1004 and INCAS Program No. HR001121C0165, National Science Foundation IIS-19-56151, IIS-17-41317, and IIS 17-04532, and the Molecule Maker Lab Institute: An AI Research Institutes program supported by NSF under Award No. 2019897, and the Institute for Geospatial Understanding through an Integrative Discovery Environment (I-GUIDE) by NSF under Award No. 2118329. Any opinions, findings, and conclusions or recommendations expressed herein are those of the authors and do not necessarily represent the views, either expressed or implied, of DARPA or the U.S. Government.

**Ethical Statement.** To the best of our knowledge, there is no specific ethical concern for the methodology of RCLUS. However, since RCLUS is dependent on external entity typing tools, pre-trained language models and also the given corpus, potential errors or bias should be given appropriate awareness and be taken good care of.

# References

1. Agarap, A.F.: Deep learning using rectified linear units (relu). CoRR abs/1803.08375 (2018). http://arxiv.org/abs/1803.08375
2. Aina, L., Gulordava, K., Boleda, G.: Putting words in context: LSTM language models and lexical ambiguity. In: Proceedings of the 57th Annual Meeting of the Association for Computational Linguistics, pp. 3342–3348. Association for Computational Linguistics, Florence, Italy (2019). https://doi.org/10.18653/v1/P19-1324, https://aclanthology.org/P19-1324
3. Alt, C., Gabryszak, A., Hennig, L.: TACRED revisited: a thorough evaluation of the TACRED relation extraction task. In: Proceedings of the 58th Annual Meeting of the Association for Computational Linguistics, pp. 1558–1569. Association for Computational Linguistics, Online (2020). https://doi.org/10.18653/v1/2020.acl-main.142, https://aclanthology.org/2020.acl-main.142
4. Banerjee, A., Dhillon, I.S., Ghosh, J., Sra, S.: Clustering on the unit hypersphere using von Mises-Fisher distributions. J. Mach. Learn. Res. **6**, 1345–1382 (2005)
5. Batista, D.S., Martins, B., Silva, M.J.: Semi-supervised bootstrapping of relationship extractors with distributional semantics. In: Proceedings of the 2015 Conference on Empirical Methods in Natural Language Processing, pp. 499–504. Association for Computational Linguistics, Lisbon, Portugal (2015). https://doi.org/10.18653/v1/D15-1056, https://aclanthology.org/D15-1056
6. Brown, T., et al.: Language models are few-shot learners. In: Larochelle, H., Ranzato, M., Hadsell, R., Balcan, M., Lin, H. (eds.) Advances in Neural Information Processing Systems, vol. 33, pp. 1877–1901. Curran Associates, Inc. (2020). https://proceedings.neurips.cc/paper/2020/file/1457c0d6bfcb4967418bfb8ac142f64a-Paper.pdf
7. Chen, Y.N., Hakkani-Tür, D., Tur, G.: Deriving local relational surface forms from dependency-based entity embeddings for unsupervised spoken language understanding. In: 2014 IEEE Spoken Language Technology Workshop (SLT), pp. 242–247 (2014). https://doi.org/10.1109/SLT.2014.7078581
8. Curran, J., Murphy, T., Scholz, B.: Minimising semantic drift with mutual exclusion bootstrapping. In: Proceedings of the 10th Conference of the Pacific Association for Computational Linguistics, pp. 172–180 (2008)
9. Dempster, A.P., Laird, N.M., Rubin, D.B.: Maximum likelihood from incomplete data via the EM algorithm. J. Royal Stat. Soc. Ser. B (Methodological) **39**(1), 1–38 (1977). http://www.jstor.org/stable/2984875
10. Devlin, J., Chang, M.W., Lee, K., Toutanova, K.: BERT: pre-training of deep bidirectional transformers for language understanding. In: Proceedings of the 2019 Conference of the North American Chapter of the Association for Computational Linguistics: Human Language Technologies, Volume 1 (Long and Short Papers), pp. 4171–4186. Association for Computational Linguistics, Minneapolis, Minnesota (2019). https://doi.org/10.18653/v1/N19-1423, https://aclanthology.org/N19-1423
11. Ding, N., et al.: Prompt-learning for fine-grained entity typing. ArXiv abs/2108.10604 (2021)

12. Küffner, K., Zimmer, R., Fundel, R.: Relex - relation extraction using dependency parse trees. Bioinformatics **23**(3), 365–71 (2007)

13. Han, X., Zhao, W., Ding, N., Liu, Z., Sun, M.: PTR: prompt tuning with rules for text classification. AI Open **3**, 182–192 (2022). https://doi.org/10.1016/j.aiopen.2022.11.003, https://www.sciencedirect.com/science/article/pii/S2666651022000183

14. Hancock, B., Varma, P., Wang, S., Bringmann, M., Liang, P., Ré, C.: Training classifiers with natural language explanations. In: Proceedings of the 56th Annual Meeting of the Association for Computational Linguistics (Volume 1: Long Papers), pp. 1884–1895. Association for Computational Linguistics, Melbourne, Australia (2018). https://doi.org/10.18653/v1/P18-1175, https://aclanthology.org/P18-1175

15. Hinton, G.E., Zemel, R.S.: Autoencoders, minimum description length and Helmholtz free energy. In: Proceedings of the 6th International Conference on Neural Information Processing Systems, pp. 3–10. NIPS'93, Morgan Kaufmann Publishers Inc., San Francisco, CA, USA (1993)

16. Hu, S., Ding, N., Wang, H., Liu, Z., Li, J.Z., Sun, M.: Knowledgeable prompt-tuning: Incorporating knowledge into prompt verbalizer for text classification. In: Annual Meeting of the Association for Computational Linguistics (2021)

17. Lu, Y., Bartolo, M., Moore, A., Riedel, S., Stenetorp, P.: Fantastically ordered prompts and where to find them: Overcoming few-shot prompt order sensitivity. CoRR abs/2104.08786 (2021). https://arxiv.org/abs/2104.08786

18. van der Maaten, L., Hinton, G.: Visualizing data using t-SNE. J. Mach. Learn. Res. **9**(86), 2579–2605 (2008). http://jmlr.org/papers/v9/vandermaaten08a.html

19. Manning, C., Surdeanu, M., Bauer, J., Finkel, J., Bethard, S., McClosky, D.: The Stanford CoreNLP natural language processing toolkit. In: Proceedings of 52nd Annual Meeting of the Association for Computational Linguistics: System Demonstrations, pp. 55–60. Association for Computational Linguistics, Baltimore, Maryland (2014). https://doi.org/10.3115/v1/P14-5010, https://aclanthology.org/P14-5010

20. Mausam, Schmitz, M., Soderland, S., Bart, R., Etzioni, O.: Open language learning for information extraction. In: Proceedings of the 2012 Joint Conference on Empirical Methods in Natural Language Processing and Computational Natural Language Learning, pp. 523–534. Association for Computational Linguistics, Jeju Island, Korea (2012). https://aclanthology.org/D12-1048

21. Meng, Y., et al.: Spherical text embedding. In: Advances in Neural Information Processing Systems (2019)

22. Meng, Y., Shen, J., Zhang, C., Han, J.: Weakly-supervised neural text classification. In: Proceedings of the 27th ACM International Conference on Information and Knowledge Management, pp. 983–992. CIKM '18, Association for Computing Machinery, New York, NY, USA (2018). https://doi.org/10.1145/3269206.3271737, https://doi.org/10.1145/3269206.3271737

23. Meng, Y., Zhang, Y., Huang, J., Zhang, Y., Zhang, C., Han, J.: Hierarchical topic mining via joint spherical tree and text embedding. In: Proceedings of the 26th ACM SIGKDD International Conference on Knowledge Discovery & Data Mining, pp. 1908–1917. KDD '20, Association for Computing Machinery, New York, NY, USA (2020). https://doi.org/10.1145/3394486.3403242, https://doi.org/10.1145/3394486.3403242

24. Nakashole, N., Weikum, G., Suchanek, F.: PATTY: A taxonomy of relational patterns with semantic types. In: Proceedings of the 2012 Joint Conference on Empirical Methods in Natural Language Processing and Computational Natural Language Learning, pp. 1135–1145. Association for Computational Linguistics, Jeju Island, Korea (2012). https://aclanthology.org/D12-1104

25. Nayak, T., Majumder, N., Goyal, P., Poria, S.: Deep neural approaches to relation triplets extraction: a comprehensive survey. Cognitive Comput. **13**, 1215–1232 (2021)

26. Qu, M., Ren, X., Zhang, Y., Han, J.: Weakly-supervised relation extraction by pattern-enhanced embedding learning. In: Proceedings of the 2018 World Wide Web Conference, pp. 1257–1266. WWW '18, International World Wide Web Conferences Steering Committee, Republic and Canton of Geneva, CHE (2018). https://doi.org/10.1145/3178876.3186024, https://doi.org/10.1145/3178876.3186024

27. Ratner, A., Bach, S.H., Ehrenberg, H., Fries, J., Wu, S., Ré, C.: Snorkel: rapid training data creation with weak supervision. Proc. VLDB Endowment **11**(3), 269–282 (2017). https://doi.org/10.14778/3157794.3157797

28. Ratner, A., Sa, C.D., Wu, S., Selsam, D., Ré, C.: Data programming: creating large training sets, quickly. In: Proceedings of the 30th International Conference on Neural Information Processing Systems, pp. 3574–3582. NIPS'16, Curran Associates Inc., Red Hook, NY, USA (2016)

29. Ren, W., Li, Y., Su, H., Kartchner, D., Mitchell, C., Zhang, C.: Denoising multi-source weak supervision for neural text classification. In: Findings of the Association for Computational Linguistics: EMNLP 2020, pp. 3739–3754. Association for Computational Linguistics, Online (2020). https://doi.org/10.18653/v1/2020.findings-emnlp.334, https://aclanthology.org/2020.findings-emnlp.334

30. Schick, T., Schmid, H., Schütze, H.: Automatically identifying words that can serve as labels for few-shot text classification. In: Proceedings of the 28th International Conference on Computational Linguistics, pp. 5569–5578. International Committee on Computational Linguistics, Barcelona, Spain (Online) (2020). https://doi.org/10.18653/v1/2020.coling-main.488, https://aclanthology.org/2020.coling-main.488

31. Shen, J., Zhang, Y., Ji, H., Han, J.: Corpus-based open-domain event type induction. In: Proceedings of the 2021 Conference on Empirical Methods in Natural Language Processing, pp. 5427–5440. Association for Computational Linguistics, Online and Punta Cana, Dominican Republic (2021). https://doi.org/10.18653/v1/2021.emnlp-main.441, https://aclanthology.org/2021.emnlp-main.441

32. Shin, T., Razeghi, Y., IV, R.L.L., Wallace, E., Singh, S.: Eliciting knowledge from language models using automatically generated prompts. ArXiv abs/2010.15980 (2020)

33. Shwartz, V., Goldberg, Y., Dagan, I.: Improving hypernymy detection with an integrated path-based and distributional method. In: Proceedings of the 54th Annual Meeting of the Association for Computational Linguistics (Volume 1: Long Papers), pp. 2389–2398. Association for Computational Linguistics, Berlin, Germany (2016). https://doi.org/10.18653/v1/P16-1226, https://aclanthology.org/P16-1226

34. Simmons, R.F.: Answering English questions by computer: a survey. Commun. ACM **8**(1), 53–70 (1965). https://doi.org/10.1145/363707.363732

35. Socher, R., Karpathy, A., Le, Q.V., Manning, C.D., Ng, A.Y.: Grounded compositional semantics for finding and describing images with sentences. Trans. Assoc. Comput. Linguist. **2**, 207–218 (2014). https://doi.org/10.1162/tacl_a_00177, https://aclanthology.org/Q14-1017

36. Stoica, G., Platanios, E.A., P'oczos, B.: Re-TACRED: addressing shortcomings of the TACRED dataset. In: AAAI Conference on Artificial Intelligence (2021)
37. Varma, P., Ré, C.: Snuba: Automating weak supervision to label training data. Proc. VLDB Endow. **12**(3), 223–236 (2018). https://doi.org/10.14778/3291264.3291268
38. Wang, C., Kalyanpur, A., Fan, J., Boguraev, B.K., Gondek, D.C.: Relation extraction and scoring in deepqa. IBM J. Res. Dev. **56**(3.4), 9:1–9:12 (2012). https://doi.org/10.1147/JRD.2012.2187239
39. Wang, H., Liu, B., Li, C., Yang, Y., Li, T.: Learning with noisy labels for sentence-level sentiment classification. In: Proceedings of the 2019 Conference on Empirical Methods in Natural Language Processing and the 9th International Joint Conference on Natural Language Processing (EMNLP-IJCNLP), pp. 6286–6292. Association for Computational Linguistics, Hong Kong, China (2019). https://doi.org/10.18653/v1/D19-1655, https://aclanthology.org/D19-1655
40. Wang, H., Tian, F., Gao, B., Zhu, C., Bian, J., Liu, T.Y.: Solving verbal questions in IQ test by knowledge-powered word embedding. In: Conference on Empirical Methods in Natural Language Processing (2015)
41. Xie, J., Girshick, R., Farhadi, A.: Unsupervised deep embedding for clustering analysis. In: Proceedings of the 33rd International Conference on International Conference on Machine Learning - Volume 48, pp. 478–487. ICML'16, JMLR.org (2016)
42. Xu, Y., Mou, L., Li, G., Chen, Y., Peng, H., Jin, Z.: Classifying relations via long short term memory networks along shortest dependency paths. In: Proceedings of the 2015 Conference on Empirical Methods in Natural Language Processing, pp. 1785–1794. Association for Computational Linguistics, Lisbon, Portugal (2015). https://doi.org/10.18653/v1/D15-1206, https://aclanthology.org/D15-1206
43. Xue, F., Sun, A., Zhang, H., Chng, E.S.: GDPNet: refining latent multi-view graph for relation extraction. In: AAAI Conference on Artificial Intelligence (2020)
44. Yu, Y., Zuo, S., Jiang, H., Ren, W., Zhao, T., Zhang, C.: Fine-tuning pre-trained language model with weak supervision: a contrastive-regularized self-training approach. ArXiv abs/2010.07835 (2020)
45. Zhang, J., et al.: WRENCH: a comprehensive benchmark for weak supervision. In: Thirty-fifth Conference on Neural Information Processing Systems Datasets and Benchmarks Track (Round 2) (2021). https://openreview.net/forum?id=Q9SKS5k8io
46. Zhang, Y., Zhong, V., Chen, D., Angeli, G., Manning, C.D.: Position-aware attention and supervised data improve slot filling. In: Proceedings of the 2017 Conference on Empirical Methods in Natural Language Processing, pp. 35–45. Association for Computational Linguistics, Copenhagen, Denmark (2017). https://doi.org/10.18653/v1/D17-1004, https://aclanthology.org/D17-1004
47. Zhou, W., et al.: NERO: a neural rule grounding framework for label-efficient relation extraction. In: Proceedings of The Web Conference 2020, pp. 2166–2176. WWW '20, Association for Computing Machinery, New York, NY, USA (2020). https://doi.org/10.1145/3366423.3380282
48. Zhuang, L., Wayne, L., Ya, S., Jun, Z.: A robustly optimized BERT pre-training approach with post-training. In: Proceedings of the 20th Chinese National Conference on Computational Linguistics, pp. 1218–1227. Chinese Information Processing Society of China, Huhhot, China (2021). https://aclanthology.org/2021.ccl-1.108

# Learning to Play Text-Based Adventure Games with Maximum Entropy Reinforcement Learning

Weichen Li[1]([✉]), Rati Devidze[2], and Sophie Fellenz[1] [iD]

[1] University of Kaiserslautern-Landau, Kaiserslautern, Germany
{weichen,fellenz}@cs.uni-kl.de
[2] Max Planck Institute for Software Systems (MPI-SWS), Saarbrücken, Germany
rdevidze@mpi-sws.org

**Abstract.** Text-based adventure games are a popular testbed for language based reinforcement learning (RL). In previous work, deep Q-learning is most often used as the learning agent. Q-learning algorithms are difficult to apply to complex real-world domains, for example due to their instability in training. Therefore, we adapt the Soft-Actor-Critic (SAC) algorithm to the domain of text-based adventure games in this paper. To deal with sparse extrinsic rewards from the environment, we combine the SAC with a potential-based reward shaping technique to provide more informative (dense) reward signals to the RL agent. The SAC method achieves higher scores than the Q-learning methods on many games with only half the number of training steps. Additionally, the reward shaping technique helps the agent to learn the policy faster and improve the score for some games. Overall, our findings show that the SAC algorithm is a well-suited approach for text-based games.

**Keywords:** Language based Reinforcement Learning ·
Soft-Actor-Critic · Reward shaping

## 1 Introduction

Language-based interactions are an integral part of our everyday life. Reinforcement learning (RL) is a promising technique for developing autonomous agents used in real-life applications, such as dialog systems. A game environment can be considered to be a simulated world, where the agent must play their actions by interacting with the environment to achieve some game-specific goal. In games, we can compare the performance of various RL agents using the final game score. Therefore, text-based adventure games are a useful benchmark for developing language-based agents [10].

Figure 1 illustrates the problem setup for this paper. The large and discrete action space is the main difference between text-based adventure games and other RL scenarios. In contrast to other games (e.g., ATARI games), each action is characterized by a sentence or word (e.g., *climb tree*). Also, the action space is

D. Koutra et al. (Eds.): ECML PKDD 2023, LNAI 14172, pp. 39–54, 2023.
https://doi.org/10.1007/978-3-031-43421-1_3

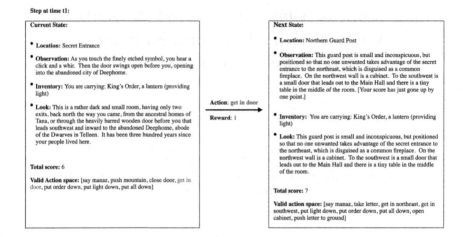

**Fig. 1.** This figure shows one possible state transition for the game *deephome*. At time t1, the RL agent has the current state and valid action space from the Jericho environment. The agent then needs to predict the action (*e.g., get in door*) from the valid action space and move to the next state, where it receives a reward from the game environment, and the total score is updated based on the reward. The state information includes location, observation, inventory, and look.

not fixed. For example, if the agent is in front of the house, the action *open door* is available, whereas if the agent is in the forest, other actions are possible, e.g. *climb tree*, but not *open tree*. Therefore, in addition to the action space, there is the space of valid actions in the current state. This space is much smaller than the space of all actions but can be significantly different in each step. In general, this space of valid actions is unknown to the agent, but a common simplification is to let the agent have the list of valid actions as input and select one from the list. A number of prior works in this domain focused on the described setup [1,2,7,23,25]. Most of those works used deep Q-learning [17] as a learning agent.

In general, Q-learning has several drawbacks. As an off-policy algorithm, it suffers from high variance, and the performance can be unstable [20]. Other online, policy-based learning algorithms are also unsuitable for our scenario since policy-based agents cannot reuse experiences from the training history. Therefore, in this paper, we develop a learning agent based on the soft actor critic (SAC) algorithm [8], which combines the advantages of both value-based and policy-based learning. It can use a replay buffer as in value-based learning, and it is relatively stable in training as a policy-based algorithm. Additionally, the maximum entropy technique encourages exploration. SAC was originally designed for continuous action spaces; however, with slight modifications, it is applicable for discrete action spaces [3]. Nevertheless, it has never been used in the context of text-based adventure games before.

A problem that text-based adventure games have in common with many other RL problems is the sparseness of rewards. Especially at the beginning of training, the agent must perform many actions before receiving feedback. This problem is even more severe in text-based adventure games due to the large and context-dependent action space. To speed up the convergence, it is therefore desirable to have a denser reward function. A popular way to achieve this is through reward shaping. However, finding a good reward function is difficult and requires significant manual effort, background information, or expert knowledge. A well-known reward shaping technique, circumventing the need for external knowledge, is potential-based reward shaping [19] which has strong theoretical guarantees. This enables faster convergence during the training, as we show for several games.

To sum up, our contributions are as follows:

1. We propose to use SAC as an alternative to deep Q-learning for text-based adventure games.
2. We propose a variant of potential-based reward shaping for discrete action spaces that is effective for text-based adventure games.
3. We compare our method on a range of games and show that we can achieve better scores than deep Q-learning with fewer training episodes on many games.
4. Additionally, we show that convergence is faster with reward shaping for some games.

This paper is structured as follows. We will first review existing approaches to text-based adventure games and potential-based reward shaping in Sect. 2. The problem setting and background on soft actor critic RL are introduced in Sect. 3. Section 4 discusses our reward shaping method. We present experimental results in Sect. 5, discuss the current limitations and future work in Sect. 6, and conclude in Sect. 7.

## 2  Related Work

**RL for Text-based adventure games.** Hausknecht *et al.* [10] built the Jericho Interactive Fiction environment, which includes 57 different games that are categorized into possible, difficult, and extreme games. In general, for text-based adventure games, there are *choice-based* agents and *parser-based* agents [10]. Parser-based agents [18] generate actions using verb-object combinations, whereas choice-based agents choose an action from a pre-generated list of actions. Other related work focuses on action generation [1,2,7,23,25]. In this work, we follow the line of choice-based agents, which allows us to concentrate on the RL part of our method.

We compare our experimental results with the deep reinforcement relevance network (DRRN) [12] agent. DRRN is a widely used framework for choice-based and parser-based agents. The basic idea behind DRRN is to encode the actions and states into embedding vectors separately and then use the state and its corresponding action embeddings as inputs into a neural network to approximate the Q-values of all possible actions $Q(s_t, a_t^i)$. The action at each time step is selected by $a_t = argmax_{a_t^i}(Q(s_t, a_t^i))$.

NAIL [11] is an agent that is not choice-based, able to play any unseen text-based game without training or repeated interaction and without receiving a list of valid actions. We compare both DRRN (and variants) and NAIL in our experiments, but only DRRN has the same experimental setup and handicaps as our agent. NAIL serves as a baseline of scores possible without any simplifications of gameplay.

Yao et al. [24] investigate whether the RL agent can make a decision without any semantic understanding. They evaluate three variants based on DRRN: a) only location information is available as observation b) observations and actions are hashed instead of using the pure text c) inverse dynamic loss based vector representations are used. Their results show that the RL agent can achieve high scores in some cases, even without language semantics. In concurrent work, building on this, Gu et al. [6] point out that the RL agent can achieve higher scores by combining semantic and non-semantic representations. Moreover, Tuyls et al. [21] propose a new framework that includes two stages: the exploitation phase and the exploration phase. The exploitation policy uses imitation learning to select the action based on previous trajectories. The goals of the second exploration policy are to explore the actions to find rewards and reach new states. This work manually adds relevant actions into the valid action space.

The **potential-based reward shaping** technique that we use was introduced in the seminal work by Ng et al. [19]. Potential-based reward shaping (PBRS) is one of the most well-studied reward design techniques. The shaped reward function is obtained by modifying the reward using a state-dependent potential function. The technique preserves a strong invariance property: a policy $\pi$ is optimal under shaped reward *iff* it is optimal under extrinsic reward. Furthermore, when using the optimal value function $V^*$ under the original reward function as the potential function, the shaped rewards achieve the maximum possible informativeness.

In a large number of prior studies interested in PBRS, Wiewiora et al. [22] propose the *state-action potential advice* methods, which not only can estimate a good or bad state, but also can advise action. Grzes et al. [5] evaluate the idea of using the online learned abstract value function as a potential function. Moreover, Harutyunyan et al. [9] introduce an arbitrary reward function by learning a secondary Q-function. They consider the difference between sampled next state-action value and the expected next state-action value as dynamic advice. In our work we focus on the classical algorithm by Ng et al. [19] as a robust baseline.

**Rewards in NLP-based RL agents.** One of the challenges of using RL to solve natural language processing (NLP) tasks is the difficulty of designing reward functions. There could be more than one factor that affects the rewards, such as semantic understanding and grammatical correctness. Li et al. [14] define reward considering three factors: "ease of answering", "information flow", and "semantic coherence" for dialogue generation tasks. Reward shaping techniques have also been used in other NLP-based RL tasks; for example, Lin *et al.* [15] use knowledge-based reward shaping for a multi-hop knowledge graph reasoning task. The core difference to our model is that we do not pre-define any function or knowledge as a reward signal, instead shaping the rewards automatically.

## 3   Problem Setting and Background

An environment is defined as a Markov Decision Process (MDP) $M :=$ $(\mathcal{S}, \mathcal{A}, T, \gamma, R)$, where the set of states and actions are denoted by $\mathcal{S}$ and $\mathcal{A}$ respectively. $T : \mathcal{S} \times \mathcal{S} \times \mathcal{A} \to [0, 1]$ captures the state transition dynamics, i.e., $T(s' \mid s, a)$ denotes the probability of landing in state $s'$.

The reward $R$ and terminal signal $d$ come from the game environment, and $\gamma$ is the discount factor. The stochastic policy $\pi : \mathcal{S} \to \Delta(\mathcal{A})$ is a mapping from a state to a probability distribution over actions, i.e., $\sum_a \pi(a|s) = 1$, parameterized by a neural network.

Notice that the valid action space size is variable at each time step. Following Hausknecht *et al.* [10], we differentiate between game state $s$ and observation $o$, where the observation refers only to the text that is output by the game whereas the state corresponds to the locations of players, items, monsters, etc. Our agent only knows the observations and not the complete game state.

### 3.1   SAC for Discrete Action Spaces

Soft-actor-critic [8] combines both advantages of value-based and policy-based learning. The drawback of value-based learning like deep Q-learning is the instability during training where the policy can have high variance [20]. The SAC algorithm includes three elements. The first element are separate predict and critic neural networks, the second is that offline learning can reuse the past collections via replay buffer, which is the same as in deep Q-learning, and the third is that the entropy of the policy is maximized to encourage exploration. The optimal policy aims to find the highest expected rewards and maximize the entropy term $\mathcal{H}(\pi(.|s_t))$:

$$\pi^{\star} = \arg\max_{\pi} \sum_{t=0}^{T} \mathbb{E}_{(s_t, a_t) \sim \rho_\pi} [r(s_t, a_t) + \alpha \mathcal{H}(\pi(.|s_t))]$$

where $s_t$ and $a_t$ denote the state and action at time step $t$ and $\rho$ denotes the state-action marginals of the trajectory distribution induced by a policy $\pi$. The temperature parameter $\alpha$ controls the degree of exploration. The original SAC is evaluated on several continuous control benchmarks. Since we are dealing with discrete text data, we base our method on the framework for discrete action spaces by Christodoulou [3]. The key difference between continuous and discrete action spaces is the computation of the action distribution. For discrete action spaces, it is necessary to compute the probability of each action in the action space. The actor policy is changed from $\pi_\phi(a_t|s_t)$, a distribution over the continuous action space, to $\pi_\phi(s_t)$, a discrete distribution over the discrete action space.

The SAC algorithm has a separate predictor (actor) and critic. In the following, we first describe the two crucial equations for updating the critic and then the actor policy update.

In the critic part, the targets for the Q-functions are computed by

$$y(r, s', d) = r + \gamma(1 - d)\left(\min_{i=1,2}\left(Q_{\hat{\theta}_i}(s')\right) - \alpha \log\left(\pi_\phi(s'_t)\right)\right), \tag{1}$$

where in our scenario, the target Q-values and the policy distribution range over the set of valid actions $A_{valid}(s')$ [10]. We use two Q-functions $Q_{\theta_i}$ and two Q target functions $Q_{\hat{\theta}_i}$, and $i \in \{1,2\}$ is the index of the Q-neural networks. $\gamma \in (0, 1]$ is a discount factor, and $d \in \{0, 1\}$ is 1 if the terminal state has been reached.

The critic learns to minimize the distance between the target soft Q-function and the Q-approximation with stochastic gradients:

$$\nabla J_Q(\theta) = \nabla \mathbb{E}_{a\sim\pi(s), s\sim D} \frac{1}{B} \sum_{i=1,2} (Q_{\theta_i}(s) - y(r, s', d))^2, \tag{2}$$

where $D$ is the replay buffer, and $B$ is the size of mini-batch sampled from $D$. If using double Q-functions, the agent should learn the loss functions of both Q-neural networks with parameters $\theta_1$ and $\theta_2$.

The update of the actor policy is given by:

$$\nabla J_\pi(\phi) = \nabla \mathbb{E}_{s\sim D} \frac{1}{B} \left[\pi_t(s)^T[\alpha \log \pi_\phi(s) - \min_{i=1,2}(Q_{\theta_i}(s))]\right]. \tag{3}$$

where $Q_{\theta_i}(s)$ denotes the actor value by the Q-function (critic policy), and $\log \pi_\phi(s)$ and $\pi_t(s)$ are the expected entropy and probability estimate by the actor policy.

As shown in Algorithm 1 in lines 8 and 9, Eqs. 2 and 3 constitute the basic SAC algorithm without reward shaping, where critic and actor are updated in turn. In the next section, we will explain the reward shaping in lines 2–7 of the algorithm.

## 4　Reward Shaping Method

The original SAC equation is given in Eq. 1. In the following we describe how we are modifying it through reward shaping. The whole algorithm is given by Algorithm 1. We start by reward shaping in line 2. The shaping reward function $F : S \times A \times S \to \mathbb{R}$ [19] is given by

$$F(s, a, s') = \gamma\Phi(s') - \Phi(s), \tag{4}$$

where $s'$ is the target state and $s$ refers to the source state. Two critical criteria of a reward function are *informativeness* and *sparseness* [4]. As mentioned in Sect. 2, when using the optimal value-function $V^*$ under original reward as the potential function, i.e., $\Phi(s) = V^*(s)$, the shaped rewards achieve the maximum possible informativeness.

---

**Algorithm 1.** SAC with potential-based reward shaping

---

**Require:** policy $\pi$; Q-functions $\theta_1, \theta_2, \hat{\theta}_1, \hat{\theta}_2$; replay buffer D; roll-out N
1: **for** step $= 1 \ldots$ max step **do**
    ▷ Update the *critic*:
2:     **if** Reward Shaping is True **then**
3:         $V_{step}(s) \leftarrow \pi(s)^T \left[ (Q_{\hat{\theta}_i}(s) - \alpha \log(\pi(s))) \right]$ (Eq. 7) ▷ Compute soft state val.
4:         $V_{step}(s) \leftarrow (1 - \alpha)V_{step}(s) + \alpha(r + \gamma_r V_{step}(s'))$ (Eq.8) ▷ Update value func.
5:         $F_{step}(s, a, s') \leftarrow \gamma_r V_{step}(s') - V_{step}(s)$ (Eq. 5)      ▷ Compute shaping function
6:         $\hat{R}(s, a) \leftarrow R(s, a) + F_{step}(s, a, s')$ (Eq. 6)         ▷ Compute reshaped reward
7:     **end if**
8:     Update Q-function (Equation 2)
    ▷ Update the *actor*:
9:     Update policy (Equation 3)
10: **end for**

---

Since we do not have access to the optimal value function $V^*$, we use the idea of *dynamic* reward shaping. In particular, Grzes *et al.* [5] generalized the form in Eq. 4 to dynamic potentials, and empirically showed an advantage in helping the agent. The idea is that the RL agent uses the current approximation of the value function as a potential function. More precisely, the shaped function $F$ at learning step can be represented as follows (Algorithm 1, line 5):

$$F(s, a, s') = \gamma_r V(s') - V(s), \tag{5}$$

where $\Phi(s)$ from Eq. 5 is given by $V(s)$. Hence, the new shaped reward $\hat{R}$ : $A \times S \to \mathbb{R}$ is defined as:

$$\hat{R}(s, a) := R(s, a) + F(s, a, s'), \tag{6}$$

where $R(s, a)$ is the original extrinsic reward from the environment (Algorithm 1, line 6).

To shape reward signals, we use the soft state value function instead of the plain value function. This allows us to use reward shaping without a separate neural network for the reward function. Haarnoja *et al.* [8] also mention that it is in principle not necessary to add a separate approximator for the state value although they find it to stabilize results in practice. More precisely, we directly utilize the original form of the soft value function as given in the SAC algorithm for discrete action spaces [3]:

$$V(s) = \pi(s)^T \left[ (Q_{\hat{\theta}_i}(s) - \alpha \log(\pi(s))) \right], \tag{7}$$

where $Q$ denotes the target Q-functions. The soft value has two terms, the expected Q-value at the given state and the entropy regularized probability of all possible actions. The Q-function aims to update the policy to maximize the expected reward. The maximum entropy policy encourages the agent to explore states with more uncertainty under the given constraints [26].

Using Eq. 7, inspired by Grze *et al.* [5], the current value $V(s)$ is updated by simple TD learning:

$$V(s) = (1 - \alpha)V(s) + \alpha(r + \gamma_r V(s')), \tag{8}$$

where, $\alpha$ is the learning rate between 0 and 1, and $\gamma_r$ is the discount rate for TD update. Now, we can rewrite the target Eq. 1 by incorporating Eq. 5:

$$y(r, s', d) = [r + (\gamma_r V(s') - V(s))] + \gamma_r(1 - d)V(s'). \tag{9}$$

This concludes the description of our reward shaping algorithm which relies on the soft value function.

## 5   Experimental Results

### 5.1   Datasets

The experiments are run on the Jericho environment [10][1], which categorizes the games into three groups: possible games, difficult games, and extreme games. In the following experiments, we focused on the possible and difficult games. The learning agent can solve the possible games in a few steps. The difficult games have sparser rewards and require a higher level of long-term decision-making strategies than the possible games.

### 5.2   Experimental Settings

We built a choice-based agent[2]. The agent predicts one of the possible actions from the action space distribution based on the observation of the current time step and the previous action from the last time step. The agent receives the valid action space identified by the world-change detection handicap from the Jericho game environments. Using the same handicaps as the DRRN method, we also use the Load, Save handicap to receive information on inventory and location without changing the game state. As shown in Table 1, we ran the main experiments using the SAC algorithm. In Fig. 3 we compare two additional reward shaping variants:

1. SAC: This is the basic RL agent with the SAC algorithm.

---

[1] https://github.com/microsoft/jericho.
[2] Source code and additional results of our experiments are available at https://github. com/WeichenLi1223/Text-based-adventure-games-using-SAC.

2. SAC+RS: Here we use the reward shaping technique in combination with SAC. This is our SAC with potential-based reward shaping algorithm as given in Algorithm 1.
3. SAC+0.1*RS: This variant is the same as SAC+RS except that it introduces one more parameter $s$ to re-scale the reshape reward, $s * \hat{R}(s, a)$. In the following experiments, we set the value of $s$ as 0.1.

**Neural networks and parameters.** The policy neural network includes three linear layers with two hidden dimensions $D_1 = 512$ and $D_2 = 128$, each hidden layer connects with the ReLU activation function, and the categorical distribution is on top to ensure that the sum of action probabilities is one. The Q-function neural network has also three linear layers with ReLU activation functions. Both policy and Q-function update at each step, and the target Q-functions update the weights from the Q-function every two steps.

**The RL agent parameters** were set as follows: the batch size is 32, and the learning rate of both policy and Q-function neural networks is 0.0003. The discount factor for SAC update is 0.9. When the value of the discount factor is close to 1, the future rewards are more important to the current state. Epsilon-Greedy action selection and a fixed entropy regularization coefficient were used in all of the experiments. For each game, we ran 8 environments in parallel to get the average score of the last 100 episodes, and each model ran three times to compute the average scores. The maximum number of training steps per episode is 100. Since the RL agent interacts with the game environments, the training time depends on the game implementation in the Jericho framework. For example, zork1, and zork3 are comparably fast to train, whereas gold takes an extremely long time compared to the rest of the games. Because of this, we only trained gold for 3,000 steps, yomomma for 10,000 steps, and karn for 20,000 steps. Our comparison methods also use varying step sizes for these games (but they use more training steps than we do). Most of the previous work trained the agent in a maximum of 100,000 steps, whereas the maximum number of training steps for our method is only 50,000 in all experiments. We use the same parameters for all of the games; however, we recommend trying different values for parameters such as learning rate, a discount factor of reward shaping, or the layers of the neural network for individual games to achieve higher scores.

**Input representation.** Following Hausknecht *et al.* [10], the state $s$ includes three elements: (observation, inventory, look) at the current time step. The representation of the elements in the state and the action are tokenized by a SentencePiece [13] model and then use seperate GRUs to learn the embeddings. The embedding size is 128. During training, the agent randomly samples the data from the replay buffer.

### 5.3   Results

We compare our results with the previous choice-based agents using deep Q-learning, and then discuss the effect of reward shaping and its variants.

**Table 1.** The average score of the **last** 100 episodes is shown for three repetitions of each game. The maximum number of training steps is 50,000 for our method. Top (adventureland, detective, pentari) are possible games and rest of the games are diffifult games. RAND, DRRN, and NAIL results are by Hausknecht *et al.* [10], the DRRN in column 6 is the reproduced score by Yao *et al.* [24].

| Game | Hausknecht *et al.* [10] | | | Yao *et al.* [24] | Ours |
|---|---|---|---|---|---|
| | Max | RAND | DRRN | NAIL | DRRN | SAC |
| adventureland | 100 | 0 | 20.6 | 0 | – | **24.8** |
| detective | 360 | 113.7 | 197.8 | 136.9 | **290** | 274.8 |
| pentari | 70 | 0 | 27.2 | 0 | 26.5 | **50.7** |
| balances | 51 | 10 | 10 | 10 | 10 | 10 |
| gold | 100 | 0 | 0 | 3 | – | **6.3** |
| jewel | 90 | 0 | 1.6 | 1.6 | – | **8.8** |
| deephome | 300 | 1 | 1 | 13.3 | **57** | 48.1 |
| karn | 170 | 0 | **2.1** | 1.2 | – | 0.1 |
| ludicorp | 150 | 13.2 | 13.8 | 8.4 | 12.7 | **15.1** |
| zork1 | 350 | 0 | 32.6 | 10.3 | **39.4** | 25.7 |
| zork3 | 7 | 0.2 | 0.5 | 1.8 | 0.4 | **3.0** |
| yomomma | 35 | 0 | 0.4 | 0 | – | **0.99** |

**Comparison to Q-Learning Methods.** Table 1 shows the average game scores of the SAC-based learning agent on twelve different games over three runs. All of the twelve different games over three runs. In comparison with DRRN and Yao *et al.* [24], which are deep Q-learning-based RL agents, seven of the SAC agents can achieve notably higher scores while only using half of the training steps. One game (*balances*) got identical scores. The scores of *detective, deephome, zork1* and *karn* are lower than those using the deep Q-learning agent. The difficult games still include several games where no method has achieved a score higher than a random agent. Same as for the baselines, we compute the average of the last 100 episodes for each run of the game. For each run of one game, eight environments are run in parallel and the average score is computed. The results of the baselines are taken directly from the respective papers.

One key idea behind SAC is maximizing the log probability, which can encourage the agent to explore uncertain states and converge faster. The training progress is shown in Fig. 3 where the game score is plotted over training episodes including standard deviations. We can see that the method converges well except for the games *balance* and *karn* in the additional results, where the agent is not able to learn (see Sect. 6 for a possible explanation). Overall, the results indicate that SAC is well-suited to solve text-based games.

Additionally, we observed that the discount factor is a critical parameter during the experiments. As shown in Fig. 2, using a discount factor 0.9 achieved higher scores than a discount factor of 0.99. When using a discount factor of 0.9

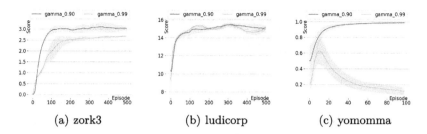

(a) zork3                    (b) ludicorp                    (c) yomomma

**Fig. 2.** This figure shows three examples of training the SAC agent with the discount factor of 0.9 and 0.99, where shaded areas correspond to standard deviations. We can see that the agent with a discount factor of 0.9 outperforms the agent with a discount factor of 0.99.

**Table 2.** This Table shows that reward shaping improves the performance of SAC for many of the games. Compared are SAC with two variants of reward shaping: non-scaled RS and re-scaled reshaped reward 0.1*RS.

| | adventureland | detective | pentari | balances | gold | jewel | deephome | karn | yomomma | ludicorp | zork1 | zork3 |
|---|---|---|---|---|---|---|---|---|---|---|---|---|
| SAC | **24.8** | 274.8 | 50.7 | 10 | 6.3 | 8.8 | 48.1 | 0.1 | **0.99** | **15.1** | 25.7 | 3.0 |
| RS | 23.8 | 276.2 | **51.5** | 10 | **6.7** | **9.9** | **50.1** | 0.0 | 0.98 | 14.4 | **36.0** | 2.8 |
| 0.1*RS | 24.6 | **276.9** | 47.1 | 10 | 6.4 | 9.0 | 49.5 | **0.2** | 0.98 | 14.6 | 25.1 | **3.5** |

the current update is less dependent on expected future rewards. This might be explained by the highly complex and hard to predict game environments.

**Comparison to Reward Shaping.** Table 2 shows the comparison of SAC and two variants of reward shaping. The first three games are possible games, and rest of the games are nine difficult games. According to [10], difficult games tend to have sparser rewards than possible games. Figure 3 presents three examples of the game *detective*, *deephome*, and *zork3*. As Sect. 4 outlines, the potential function is based on the soft state value in our experiments. Eight of the twelve games tested scored higher when using a reshaped reward. For the games *deephome* and *zork3* we can see that shaping the original rewards leads to faster convergence than without reward shaping. Thus, we find the reward shaping technique to be particularly advantageous for difficult games as compared to possible games.

We compare the re-scaled reshaped reward to the non-scaled reshaped reward. The games *ludicorp* and *balances* have a similar performance for both reward types. However, there is a noticeable gap between the re-scaled reward and the original reshaped reward for games like *jewel*, *zork1*, and *zork3*. To quantify the sparseness of rewards received in each game, we checked the number of

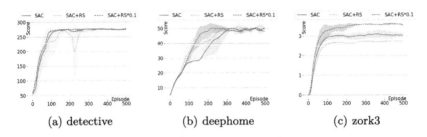

(a) detective          (b) deephome          (c) zork3

**Fig. 3.** This figure illustrates the development of the game scores over training episodes where shaded areas correspond to standard deviations. The figure compares the performance of the SAC agents with and without different reward shaping variants: reshaped reward (SAC+RS) and re-scaled reshaped reward combined SAC (SAC+RS*0.1). This figure shows only three examples; more games are presented in additional results[2].

steps of each agent before it received the first reward and between two consecutive rewards in the game. The average steps per reward [10] of *zork3* and *karn* are 39 and 17, while for *deephome, jewel,* and *zork1* they are 6, 8, and 9. This shows that *zork3* and *karn* have sparser rewards. These results suggest that slightly changed reward values are more beneficial for sparse models.

## 6   Limitations and Future Work

As shown in Table 1, the SAC-based agent improves state of the art on several games, but not all of them. We manually checked the agent-predicted trajectories and the games' walk-throughs. In the following, we discuss examples from the games *balances* and *karn*.

The main limitation we found is that the valid action spaces are often incomplete. An essential part of the game *balances* is understanding and using different spells. However, the valid action space does not include those spells, such as *bozbar tortoise* and *caskly chewed scroll*. As shown in Fig. 4, the agent can only repeat meaningless actions and cannot reach higher scores as the required actions, shown in red, are omitted in the valid action space. One solution to overcome the imperfection of the valid action space handicap is manually adding some relevant actions from game walk-throughs [21]. Additionally, the agent performs poorly when receiving a large valid action space. For example, compared to *ludicorp* or *jewel*, the game *karn* often receives action spaces with many possible actions at a state.

The second limitation is, as Yao *et al.* [24] point out, that the current RL agent needs a more robust semantic understanding. Their experiments found that the agent can even achieve higher scores in three games out of twelve using hash-based nonsemantic representations. We check the actions predicted by the agent during training as shown in Fig. 5 to see whether the agent understands the state description. The agent receives the following description: *"Console Room The console room is the heart of operations of the TARDIS. Dominating the*

---

**Walk-through:**
[search furniture (+5points), learn rezrov, rezrov box, ..., search oats (+ 5 points),..., learn bozbar, bozbar tortoise (+5 points), get chewed scroll,..., examine book, caskly chewed scroll (+5 points),...]

---

**RL trajectories:**
[examine furniture (+5 points), west, north, examine oats(+5 points), south, east, put scroll down, examine scroll, examine spell, examine book, examine book, put all down....]

**Action:** examine spell

**Info:** Which do you mean, the gnusto spell, the frotz spell, the yomin spell or the rezrov spell?

**Valid actions:** [take up, take scroll, put book down, put burin down, put coin down, put box down, put all down, examine book, examine scroll, examine spell]

**Action:** examine book

**Info:** My Spell Book. *gnusto spell:* copy a scroll into your spell book *frotz spell:* cause an object to give off light. *yomin spell:* mind probe. *rezrov spell:* open even locked or enchanted objects. *bozbar spell:* cause an animal to sprout wings.

**Valid actions:**[west, take scroll, put book down, put burin down, put coin down, put box down, put all down, examine book, examine scroll, examine spell]

---

**Fig. 4.** Game balances: The walk-through and RL agent trajectory are shown. The relevant actions, shown in red, are not in the valid action space. (Color figure online)

*room is a six-side console. Located above the console is the scanner. A corridor to the east leads further into the TARDIS. On the west side of the room are the main doors."* And the player's inventory includes a jacket, hat, and scarf. The agent gets stuck in the exact location and repeats the same actions: *put jacket down, take off jacket, take off hat,* and *take card.* The distributions and reshaped rewards change only slightly. The agent tends to require more steps to find practical actions; we assume the agent suffers from making decisions based on semantic understanding. As human players, we can easily decide, like *go east* or *go west.* A further investigation is necessary to ensure the agent learns from language.

In future work, we plan to adapt our method to play with valid actions generated by a large language model (LLM). Action generation is a critical challenge in playing text-based games which requires a high level of language understanding. LLMs are beneficial in generating possible actions [16] since pre-trained LLMs contain rich common sense knowledge. For example, Yao *et al.* [25] fine-tuned the GPT2 model with game walk-throughs. Nevertheless, it is currently unclear whether an LLM could solve the difficult text-based adventure games we consider in this paper. These games are very difficult to solve, even for intelligent humans, and require a high level of common sense reasoning, creativity, problem-solving capabilities, and planning. Thus, we emphasize that these games pose a challenge to even the best available state-of-the-art language models, and their investigation might help to improve the planning capabilities of future systems of this kind.

| State: -Location: console room; -Look: the console room is the heart of operations of the tardis....A corridor to the east leads further into the TARDIS. On the west side of the room are the main doors; -Inventory: you are carrying: a tweed jacket, an incredibly long scarf , ... |
| --- |
| Valid Actions:[west, take card, take key, take yo, take all, take off hat, take off jacket, east, put hat down, put scarf down, put jacket down, put on scarf, pull lever, open drawer] |

| Action: west; Reward: 0 ; Reshaped Reward: -0.0441 | Action: put jacket down; Reward: 0 ; Reshaped Reward: -0.049 |
| --- | --- |
| **Next state: -Location: Rocky clearing;** -Look: you're standing on a relatively flat piece of ground on the side of a mountain. rocky outgrowths stand like walls all around you, ...; -Inventory: you are carrying: a tweed jacket, an incredibly long scarf, the TARDIS key, ...<br><br>**Next state valid actions** :[take off hat, take off scarf, east, take on northwest, take on tardis, close tardis, put hat down, put card down, put scarf down, put yo down, put jacket down, put all down, put on jacket, put hat in tardis, put card in tardis, put scarf in tardis, put yo in tardis, put jacket in tardis,  put all in tardis] | **Next state:** You take off the tweed jacket. Dropped. **-Location: console room;** -Look: the console room is the heart of operations of the tardis ...; -Inventory: you are carrying: an incredibly long scarf, ...<br><br>**Next state valid actions**: [take jacket, take card, take off scarf, take off hat,  east, put scarf down, put yo down, put hat down, put key down, put all down, put on jacket, pull lever, open drawer] |

**Fig. 5.** Game *karn*: Most of the actions in the valid action spaces do not lead the agent to a new location and significantly change reward signals. (In the right column, choosing the action *put jacket down*, labeled in yellow, the agent is still in the same location. In the left column, when the agent moves *west*, labeled in red, the agent goes to a new location.)(Color figure online)

In summary, two directions need to be further explored in the future. First, generating accurate action spaces is crucial to improve agent performance. Second, it is necessary to incorporate semantic information in the agent and ensure it is used to predict the next action.

## 7 Conclusion

The primary motivation of this paper is to effectively adapt the maximum entropy RL to the domain of text-based adventure games and speed up the learning process. The results show that the SAC-based agent achieves significantly higher scores than deep Q-learning for some games while using only half the number of training steps. Additionally, we use a reward-shaping technique to deal with sparse rewards. This allows us to learn intermediate rewards, which speeds up learning at the beginning of training for some games and leads to higher scores than without reward shaping for many games. Our analysis reveals two key limitations involving the valid action space that will be addressed in future work.

**Acknowledgment.** The first author was funded by the German Federal Ministry of Education and Research under grant number 01IS20048. The responsibility for the content of this publication lies with the author. Furthermore, we acknowledge support by the Carl-Zeiss Foundation and the DFG awards BU 4042/2-1 and BU 4042/1-1.

**Ethical Statement.** In this paper, we investigate RL algorithms in text-based adventure games. We ran our experiments on the Jericho Interactive Fiction game environment, which does not contain any tools for collecting and processing personal data and inferring personal information. Therefore, our experiments do not raise concerns about data privacy. Our RL algorithm could in the future lead to systems that are better at advanced planning and decision making. Such agents would pose many hypothetical dangers. However, we believe that our work does not further any malicious goals or use-cases in itself.

# References

1. Ammanabrolu, P., Hausknecht, M.: Graph constrained reinforcement learning for natural language action spaces. In: International Conference on Learning Representations (2020)
2. Ammanabrolu, P., Tien, E., Hausknecht, M., Riedl, M.O.: How to avoid being eaten by a grue: structured exploration strategies for textual worlds. arXiv preprint arXiv:2006.07409 (2020)
3. Christodoulou, P.: Soft actor-critic for discrete action settings. arXiv preprint arXiv:1910.07207 (2019)
4. Devidze, R., Radanovic, G., Kamalaruban, P., Singla, A.: Explicable reward design for reinforcement learning agents. Adv. Neural. Inf. Process. Syst. **34**, 20118–20131 (2021)
5. Grześ, M., Kudenko, D.: Online learning of shaping rewards in reinforcement learning. Neural Netw. **23**(4), 541–550 (2010)
6. Gu, Y., Yao, S., Gan, C., Tenenbaum, J., Yu, M.: Revisiting the roles of text in text games. In: Findings of the Association for Computational Linguistics: EMNLP 2022, pp. 6867–6876. Association for Computational Linguistics, Abu Dhabi, United Arab Emirates (2022)
7. Guo, X., Yu, M., Gao, Y., Gan, C., Campbell, M., Chang, S.: Interactive fiction game playing as multi-paragraph reading comprehension with reinforcement learning. In: Proceedings of the 2020 Conference on Empirical Methods in Natural Language Processing, pp. 7755–7765. Association for Computational Linguistics, Online (2020)
8. Haarnoja, T., Zhou, A., Abbeel, P., Levine, S.: Soft actor-critic: off-policy maximum entropy deep reinforcement learning with a stochastic actor. In: Dy, J.G., Krause, A. (eds.) Proceedings of the 35th International Conference on Machine Learning (ICML 2018), Stockholmsmässan, Stockholm, Sweden, July 10–15, 2018. Proceedings of Machine Learning Research, vol. 80, pp. 1856–1865. PMLR (2018)
9. Harutyunyan, A., Devlin, S., Vrancx, P., Nowé, A.: Expressing arbitrary reward functions as potential-based advice. In: Proceedings of the AAAI Conference on Artificial Intelligence, vol. 29 (2015)
10. Hausknecht, M., Ammanabrolu, P., Côté, M.A., Yuan, X.: Interactive fiction games: a colossal adventure. In: Proceedings of the AAAI Conference on Artificial Intelligence, pp. 7903–7910 (2020)
11. Hausknecht, M., Loynd, R., Yang, G., Swaminathan, A., Williams, J.D.: Nail: a general interactive fiction agent. arXiv preprint arXiv:1902.04259 (2019)
12. He, J., et al.: Deep reinforcement learning with a natural language action space. In: Proceedings of the 54th Annual Meeting of the Association for Computational Linguistics (Volume 1: Long Papers), pp. 1621–1630. Association for Computational Linguistics, Berlin, Germany (2016)

13. Kudo, T., Richardson, J.: SentencePiece: a simple and language independent sub-word tokenizer and detokenizer for neural text processing. In: Proceedings of the 2018 Conference on Empirical Methods in Natural Language Processing: System Demonstrations, pp. 66–71 (2018)
14. Li, J., Monroe, W., Ritter, A., Jurafsky, D., Galley, M., Gao, J.: Deep reinforcement learning for dialogue generation. In: Proceedings of the 2016 Conference on Empirical Methods in Natural Language Processing, pp. 1192–1202. Association for Computational Linguistics, Austin, Texas (2016)
15. Lin, X.V., Socher, R., Xiong, C.: Multi-hop knowledge graph reasoning with reward shaping. In: Proceedings of the 2018 Conference on Empirical Methods in Natural Language Processing, pp. 3243–3253 (2018)
16. Luketina, J., et al.: A survey of reinforcement learning informed by natural language. arXiv preprint arXiv:1906.03926 (2019)
17. Mnih, V., et al.: Playing Atari with deep reinforcement learning. arXiv preprint arXiv:1312.5602 (2013)
18. Narasimhan, K., Kulkarni, T., Barzilay, R.: Language understanding for text-based games using deep reinforcement learning. In: Proceedings of the 2015 Conference on Empirical Methods in Natural Language Processing, pp. 1–11. Association for Computational Linguistics, Lisbon, Portugal (2015)
19. Ng, A.Y., Harada, D., Russell, S.: Policy invariance under reward transformations: theory and application to reward shaping. In: Bratko, I., Dzeroski, S. (eds.) Proceedings of the Sixteenth International Conference on Machine Learning, Bled, Slovenia, June 27–30, 1999, pp. 278–287. Morgan Kaufmann (1999)
20. Sutton, R.S., Barto, A.G.: Reinforcement learning: an introduction. MIT Press (2018)
21. Tuyls, J., Yao, S., Kakade, S.M., Narasimhan, K.: Multi-stage episodic control for strategic exploration in text games. In: The Tenth International Conference on Learning Representations, ICLR 2022. OpenReview.net (2022)
22. Wiewiora, E., Cottrell, G.W., Elkan, C.: Principled methods for advising reinforcement learning agents. In: Proceedings of the 20th International Conference on Machine Learning, pp. 792–799 (2003)
23. Xu, Y., Fang, M., Chen, L., Du, Y., Zhou, J.T., Zhang, C.: Deep reinforcement learning with stacked hierarchical attention for text-based games. Adv. Neural. Inf. Process. Syst. **33**, 16495–16507 (2020)
24. Yao, S., Narasimhan, K., Hausknecht, M.: Reading and acting while blindfolded: the need for semantics in text game agents. In: Proceedings of the 2021 Conference of the North American Chapter of the Association for Computational Linguistics: Human Language Technologies, pp. 3097–3102. Association for Computational Linguistics, Online (2021)
25. Yao, S., Rao, R., Hausknecht, M., Narasimhan, K.: Keep CALM and explore: language models for action generation in text-based games. In: Proceedings of the 2020 Conference on Empirical Methods in Natural Language Processing, pp. 8736–8754. Association for Computational Linguistics, Online (2020)
26. Ziebart, B.D., Bagnell, J.A., Dey, A.K.: Modeling interaction via the principle of maximum causal entropy. In: Fürnkranz, J., Joachims, T. (eds.) Proceedings of the 27th International Conference on Machine Learning, June 21–24, 2010, Haifa, Israel, pp. 1255–1262. Omnipress (2010)

# SALAS: Supervised Aspect Learning Improves Abstractive Multi-document Summarization Through Aspect Information Loss

Haotian Chen[✉], Han Zhang, Houjing Guo, Shuchang Yi, Bingsheng Chen, and Xiangdong Zhou

School of Computer Science, Fudan University, Shanghai, China
{htchen18,hanzhang20,xdzhou}@fudan.edu.cn,
{houjingguo21,scyi21,chenbs21}@m.fudan.edu.cn

**Abstract.** Abstractive multi-document summarization (MDS) aims at summarizing and paraphrasing the salient key information in multiple documents. For dealing with the long-input issue brought by multiple documents, most previous work extracts salient sentence-level information from the input documents and then performs summarizing on the extracted information. However, the aspects of documents are neglected. The limited ability to discover the content on certain aspects hampers the key information seeking and ruins the comprehensiveness of the generated summaries. To solve the issue, we propose a novel **S**upervised **A**spect-**L**earning **A**bstractive **S**ummarization framework (SALAS) and a new aspect information loss (AILoss) to learn aspect information to supervise the generating process heuristically. Specifically, SALAS adopts three probes to capture aspect information as both constraints of the objective function and supplement information to be expressed in the representations. Aspect information is explicitly discovered and exploited to facilitate generating comprehensive summaries by AILoss. We conduct extensive experiments on three public datasets. The experimental results demonstrate that SALAS outperforms previous state-of-the-art (SOTA) baselines, achieving a new SOTA performance on the three MDS datasets. We make our code for SALAS publicly available (https://github.com/Hytn/AspectSum).

**Keywords:** Multi-document summarization · Supervised aspect learning · Aspect information loss

## 1 Introduction

Document summarization (DS) aims to convert a document or multiple thematically related documents into a fluent, condensed, and informative summary [11,18,23]. It is beneficial for a wide range of downstream applications including generating Wikipedia abstracts [15,30], creating news digests [1], and

D. Koutra et al. (Eds.): ECML PKDD 2023, LNAI 14172, pp. 55–70, 2023.
https://doi.org/10.1007/978-3-031-43421-1_4

opinion summarization [2]. The given documents comprise various aspects and can overlap and complement each other [11]. Therefore DS faces more challenges due to capturing and organizing information scattered across the long input (especially entailed by multiple documents) [7,18].

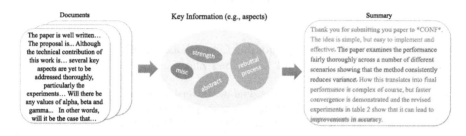

**Fig. 1.** An example for performing multi-document summarization by aspect information.

Traditional methods tackled DS based on feature engineering [7], statistical learning [3], and graph theory [7,20]. Most of them extract salient textual units, structural dependencies among phrases, keywords, or semantic clusters as key information to aid the generation of a final summary [18]. Recently, pre-trained language models (PLMs) significantly facilitate MDS through several paradigms, including adopting extract-then-generate methods [26,28] and applying hierarchical models architecture [15,29]. The former shorten the length of input context by extracting salient texts while the latter improve the capability of models to simultaneously process all information. It is reported that extract-then-generate methods, hierarchical models, most traditional methods, and human performance possess a common background: They believe that a summary can be produced through a top-down method where key information is first detected from the input documents explicitly and then summarized or adopted to guide the summarization [12,19].

However, aspect information is rarely considered or modeled as the key information in these methods. Summaries are often viewed as plain text despite the fact that their summarized documents can be well organized and written down according to the underlying aspects (e.g., writing according to a mind map). As shown in Fig. 1, the detected aspects, as key information, can summarize the input documents and thereby guides the top-down methods to generate a final summary. A pipeline method [30] is proposed to address the issue, which first detects topics described by input documents, and then encodes the detected topics together with the documents to generate a final summary. Despite the improved performance, the method leaves two problems unsolved: (1) the separately-trained pipeline methods can suffer from cascade errors; (2) the aspect information indirectly aids the generator in an implicit way. We argue that aspect information is essential for supervising the generation process of MDS.

In this paper, we propose a novel supervised aspect learning abstractive summarization framework (SALAS) with aspect information loss (AILoss). AILoss enables SALAS to capture aspect information as both constraints of the objective function and sufficient expressive power of representations to guide the generating process. Specifically, we design three linear probes to detect the aspect information expressed by the representations of both input documents and the generated summaries: an encoder probe for documents and two decoder probes for summaries. AILoss considers the detected aspect information from three probes, which not only infuses representations with aspect information but also eliminates the inconsistency between the aspects expressed by documents and summaries. It renders summaries to cover each aspect mentioned in corresponding documents. The aspects and summaries are jointly learned with our proposed AILoss. We evaluate our proposed SALAS on 3 MDS benchmarks. Using the same backbones, SALAS outperforms the strong baseline models and achieves a new state-of-the-art performance on the three benchmarks. Our main contributions are threefold:

- We introduce SALAS, a novel aspect-guided joint learning summarization framework that captures aspect information to guide the generating process.
- We propose aspect information loss (AILoss) to constrain the objective function and give sufficient expressive power to representations, which aids the generating process.
- Experimental results show that SALAS significantly outperforms previous SOTA methods on 3 MDS benchmarks. We further conduct a comprehensive analysis that exhibits the high quality of detected aspects and the effectiveness of modules in SALAS.

## 2    Related Work

### 2.1    Multi-document Summarization

Traditional MDS obtain key information represented by words, sentences, graphs, and semantic clusters to guide the generator [7,20]. With recent significant improvement in SDS brought by large-scale PLMs [13], most researchers tackle MDS based on PLMs in four ways with two underlying purposes: (1) To enhance the long-input processing capability of models, they propose sparse attention [4] and hierarchical model architectures [15,29]. The former is proposed for reducing the memory complexity of transformer-based PLMs while the latter is designed for capturing dependency information among sentences and words. (2) To shorten the length of source input, researchers adopt extract-then-generate methods [26,28] and divide-and-conquer approaches [8]. The former extracts salient texts (key information) from the given documents and then summarizes them, the latter divides the given documents into sections and then individually summarizes them to form a final summary.

The extract-then-generate methods and hierarchical model architectures try to collect and merge the information scattered across the source input in a heuristic way and then summarize the derived key information. Inspired by the paradigm, we focus on exploring and modeling the aspect information, which is objective, definite, concise, and often neglected in previous work, as key information to explicitly supervise the generating process of summaries.

## 2.2   Aspect-Related Text Generation

Little recent work exploits aspect information while generating a generic summary [21]. One line of research focuses on heuristically identifying aspects (e.g., words or phrases) expressed in opinions for opinion summarization and sentiment analysis [25]. Aspect information and its corresponding context will help distinguish the sentiment polarities of reviews about different aspects of a product. A previous work [1] also proposes a summarization system where aspect-level keywords can be automatically extracted without assuming human-annotated data for training the extractor.

More recently, aspect information is manually annotated in some aspect-oriented abstractive summarization datasets in the multi-document setting. It includes WikiAsp for aspect-oriented Wikipedia summarization [9], summaries of popular and aspect-specific customer experience (SPACE) dataset for opinion mining [2], and meta-review dataset (MRED) for structure-controllable meta-review generation [24], which makes human-annotated aspect information sufficient and available for text generators.

Instead of directly applying the heuristically extracted aspect information with noises, we propose modeling the human-annotated accurate aspect information to facilitate abstractive MDS. TWAG [30] explores a pipeline method to model the aspect information for abstractive MDS, which we compare with.

## 3   Methodology

We present the overview of our framework composed of two kinds of aspect probes and a generator with aspect constraints in Fig. 2 and then elaborate on each component in the following sections. In Sect. 3.1, we first formulate the target task and our proposed aspect-guided framework. In Sect. 3.2 and Sect. 3.3, we then introduce two kinds of aspect probes for documents and summaries, respectively. After that, we elaborate on the mechanism of our proposed aspect-guided generator in Sect. 3.4. Finally, we summarize and formulate the training objective in Sect. 3.5.

### 3.1   Task and Framework Formulation

We formulate the task and our proposed solution and then introduce the underlying motivation in this section. In the MDS task, the input document set $\mathcal{D} = \{D_i\}_{i=1}^{n}$ comprises multiple documents and can be expressed by its concatenate context $X$, while the generated output is their summary $y$ of length $T$. Given input documents $X$ and the previously generated tokens $y_{<t}$, the goal

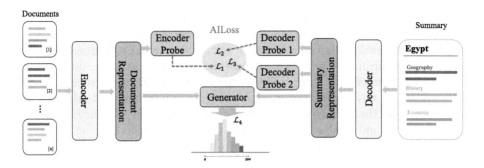

**Fig. 2.** An overview of our framework.

of previous methods in MDS is to train a learning model, which aims to maximize the likelihood of the given optimal summary $y^*$, to generate a sequence of summary tokens $y$ which can be described by,

$$y^* = \arg\max_y P(y \mid \mathcal{D}) = \arg\max_y \prod_{t=1}^{T} P(y_t \mid \mathcal{D}, y_{<t}). \tag{1}$$

However, most documents are well organized and written down according to the underlying aspect information, which guides human-written summaries of multiple documents [30]. That is to say, aspect information is a constraint of the summary-generating process. The constraint is missed in Eq. (1) adopted by previous work, leading to their increased risk of falling into suboptimal results. To solve the issue, we present two kinds of probabilistic models (probes) $P(\mathcal{A} \mid \mathcal{D})$ and $P(\mathcal{A} \mid y)$ to estimate the aspect information $\mathcal{A} = \{a_i\}_{i=1}^{N}$ contained in the representations of input documents and generated words. In each step $t$ of the generating process, the imbalance in the amount of two source aspect information supervises the generator to recover the missing target aspect information. To measure the extent to which aspect information is missed, we introduce aspect information loss (AILoss). Let $d$ be a symmetric "distance" of the amount of aspect information contained by two representations, where $d$ possesses a variety of choices, including $L_2$ distance and symmetric KL-divergence. The AILoss is defined as follows:

**Definition 1 (Aspect Information Loss).** *The aspect information loss between the aspect information represented by source input text $C$ and the target amount of aspect information $P^*$ is*

$$\rho = d\left[P_{\mathcal{A}\mid\mathcal{D}}\left(a_i \mid C\right), P_i^*\right]. \tag{2}$$

*The representation of source input text is $\xi$-informative if $\rho \leq \xi$.*

Note that in some cases, we have restricted access to the exact number of categories of aspects and to the human-annotated aspect information for context, which exacerbates the difficulty of estimating aspect information. Thanks to methods for aspect-level keywords extraction [1] and clustering-based unsupervised representation learning models [10,27], models are able to extract and classify aspect information in a heuristic way. However, noise information will be introduced during the process to confuse the generator. As it remains unclear whether aspect information can facilitate the generation of generic summaries in MDS and which way can effectively exploit the aspect information. In this paper, we demonstrate the effectiveness of both aspect information and our framework in a convincing and clear setting and leave the situation where aspect information is combined with noise to be studied in future work.

### 3.2    Encoder Probe

The encoder probe aims to detect the aspect information contained in representations of the input documents. For input context $X$ and the previously generated words $y_{<t}$, PLMs generate both token and context representations. We obtain the context representations of $X$ and $y_{<t}$ by,

$$\mathbf{h}_{\mathrm{doc}} = \mathrm{PLM}(X), \mathbf{h}_{\mathrm{sum}} = \mathrm{PLM}(y_{<t}), \tag{3}$$

where PLM includes multiple options, such as BERT [6], BART [13], GloVe [22], etc., exhibiting different features explained by representations. To give sufficient expressive power to the context representations, we integrate aspect information into the representations by training them together with an aspect probe,

$$\mathcal{L}_1 = \sum_{a_i \in A} d\Big[P_{\mathcal{A}|\mathcal{D}}\left(a_i \mid X; \phi\right), P_{\mathrm{gold}}(a_i)\Big], \tag{4}$$

where $d$ denotes the distance between the prediction and its corresponding ground truth $P_{\mathrm{gold}}(a_i)$. $A$ represents the set of target aspects that compose the input documents and their corresponding summary. We adopt the commonly used mean square error (MSE) as our loss function to compute the overall distance $\mathcal{L}_1$. Aspect probe $P_{\mathcal{A}|\mathcal{D}}\left(a_i \mid X; \phi\right)$ with trainable parameters $\phi$ maps the input documents to a certain score of each aspect and then derives the corresponding output by the sigmoid function $\sigma$,

$$P_{\mathcal{A}|\mathcal{D}}\left(a_i \mid X; \phi\right) = \sigma\left(\mathbf{W}_i \mathbf{h}_{\mathrm{doc}} + \mathbf{b}_i\right), \tag{5}$$

where $\phi$ consists of $\mathbf{W}$ and $\mathbf{b}$. The output can either be regarded as probability or measurement, which indicates the amount of a certain kind of aspect information existing in the input context.

### 3.3    Decoder Probe

The decoder probe aims to detect the aspect information contained in representations of generated words. We use a similar method to derive aspect information from the previously generated words. Specifically, during the process of generating, the amount of aspect information dynamically changes. If we discard words from the ground truth summary one after another, the corresponding aspect information becomes less and less. Given the target amount of aspect information $P(a_i)$ and the generated words $y_{<t}$ with length $t$, where the ground truth words summarize the current aspect $a_i$ with length $L_i$ and other words describe other aspects with length $L_i^-$, we give out a function $F_i(t)$ to measure the expected amount of increasing information for aspect $a_i$ in the $t$ step ($t$-th newly generated word). We assume that each word equally contributes to the information of each aspect, then $F_i(t)$ can be represented by,

$$F_i(t) = \frac{t - L_i^-}{L_i} P(a_i). \tag{6}$$

Note that the target amount of information $P(a_i)$ can either be ground truth probability (derived by human-annotated aspect labels or introduced from aspects possessed by input documents) which equals 1 or be probability predicted by the aspect probe for input documents. Correspondingly, we propose two decoder probes as follows.

On human-annotated datasets where aspect information is accurate and available, we adopt ground truth aspect information in training where $P(a_i) = 1$. Similar to the motivation and training process of the encoder probe for input documents, we train the first decoder probe $P_{\mathcal{A}|\mathcal{D}}(a_i \mid y_{<t}; \eta)$ and representations of generated words by,

$$\mathcal{L}_2 = \sum_{t=1}^{T} \sum_{a_i \in A} d\left[ P_{\mathcal{A}|\mathcal{D}}(a_i \mid y_{<t}; \eta), \frac{t - L_i^-}{L_i} \right]. \tag{7}$$

During the training process, the probed scores for aspects represent the comprehensiveness of the generated summary and serve as an indicator to discover the missing aspect information in the previously generated words.

We can apply the second decoder probe on any datasets, including those where we have restricted access to aspect labels. It infuses the probed aspect information $P(a_i) = P_{\mathcal{A}|\mathcal{D}}(a_i \mid X; \phi)$ from input documents into representations of the generated words,

$$\mathcal{L}_3 = \sum_{t=1}^{T} \sum_{a_i \in A} d\left[ P_{\mathcal{A}|\mathcal{D}}(a_i \mid y_{<t}; \mu), \frac{t - L_i^-}{L_i} P_{\mathcal{A}|\mathcal{D}}(a_i \mid X; \phi) \right]. \tag{8}$$

Here, we do not propagate gradients of $\mathcal{L}_3$ to the parameters $\phi$ to avoid introducing spurious correlations which can impede the learning process described in Eq. (4).

### 3.4 Aspect-Guided Generator

As we obtain the gap between aspect information in input documents and that in the generated words, we require a generator, which abides by the regularity described in Eq. (6) where the gap is continuously narrowed during the generating process, to recover the missing aspect information when generating the summary. We exhibit two reasons why a generator learns to generate those words that can narrow the gap: (1) The ground truth aspect information in documents is instructive and easily accessible as mentioned in Sect. 3.1. Besides the precious human-annotated aspect information for summaries, it can serve as a supplementary indicator to supervise the generation of summaries. (2) The gap reveals missing aspects. The existence of a gap indicates that salient information of a certain aspect from input documents does not occur in the summary. The learning model minimizes the overall loss to narrow the gap, which constrains the generating process and thus reduces the entropy of the potential words. Therefore, the generation loss for a generated summary is represented by,

$$\mathcal{L}_4 = -\frac{1}{T} \sum_{t=1}^{T} \log P_\Theta \left(y_t \mid y_{<t}, X\right), \tag{9}$$

where $\Theta$ denotes model parameters excluding the parameters of three probes.

### 3.5 Training Objective

The core idea of our proposed learning framework is to train a summarization model under the constraints of aspect information abstracted from the input documents, which not only supervises the generation, but also avoids the isolation between the aspect probes and the generator. Different from the methods that exploit and incorporate aspect information by,

$$y^* = \arg\max_{\mathcal{A}} P(\mathcal{A} \mid \mathcal{D}) \arg\max_{y} P(y \mid \mathcal{D}, \mathcal{A}), \tag{10}$$

which can suffer from the cascade error and impede the interaction between the aspect probe and summarization model. Our proposed training objective is represented by,

$$\arg\max_{\Theta} \prod_{t=1}^{T} P_\Theta \left(y_t \mid X, y_{<t}\right)$$

$$\text{s.t.} \sum_{t=1}^{T} \sum_{a_i \in A} d\left[P_{\mathcal{A}\mid\mathcal{D}}\left(a_i \mid y_{<t}\right), F_i(t)\right] + \sum_{a_i \in A} d\left[P_{\mathcal{A}\mid\mathcal{D}}\left(a_i \mid X\right), P_{\text{gold}}(a_i)\right] \leq \xi, \tag{11}$$

where $i = 0, 1, \ldots, N$. $P(a_i)$ in $F_i(t)$ denotes either ground truth or the probability of $a_i$ probed from $X$ and $\xi$ an upper bound of inconsistency between the target amount of aspect information and that probed from documents and generated words.

To sum up, the overall training objective of our proposed framework is

$$\mathcal{L} = \lambda_1 \mathcal{L}_1 + \lambda_2 \mathcal{L}_2 + \lambda_3 \mathcal{L}_3 + \lambda_4 \mathcal{L}_4, \tag{12}$$

where $\lambda_1, \lambda_2, \lambda_3$, and $\lambda_4$ are hyperparameters to balance and control the influence of different loss components. Parameters $\phi$ are solely optimized with $\mathcal{L}_1$, parameters $\eta$ are solely optimized with $\mathcal{L}_2$ and $\mathcal{L}_3$, and parameters $\Theta$ are optimized with $\mathcal{L}$.

## 4  Experiments

### 4.1  Datasets

We experiment on two datasets as follows.

**MRED** [24] is a highly abstractive dataset focusing on meta-reviews from a peer-reviewing system (ICLR) which contains essential and high-density opinions. It is provided for structure-controllable text generation. The meta-reviews are manually written to summarize the aspects described in different reviews and we use *sent-ctrl* version of MRED.

**WikiAsp** [9] is provided for aspect-based summarization. It contains articles, consisting of section titles and section texts, from various domains of Wikipedia and their corresponding reference documents. The section texts serve as aspect-based summaries of corresponding reference documents. We randomly select 2 out of 20 domain datasets from WikiAsp as evaluation benchmarks. The two datasets are **Historic Place** and **Plant**.

### 4.2  Baselines

We compare SALAS with previous state-of-the-art methods (comprising an extractive model and 4 abstractive models) on the three datasets:

**TextRank** [20] is a common extractive summarization baseline model which uses vertex scores calculated by a graph-based "random-surfer model" to rank sentences.

**TWAG** [30] is a two-step abstractive summarization method that first detects the aspects described by the multiple source documents and then performs summarization based on the detected aspects.

**BertAbs** [16] is an abstractive summarization model with encoder initialized with BERT [5] and transformer decoder randomly initialized.

**Longformer** [4] is a pre-trained language model tackling long input by sparse attention. Following BertAbs [16], We initialize the encoder with Longformer and randomly initialize the transformer decoder.

**BART** [13] is a SOTA abstractive summarization model pre-trained with the objective of denoising autoencoding.

We also compare with other baselines mentioned in the work proposing the corresponding dataset.

### 4.3  Implementation Details

We complete our experiments on a single RTX3090 GPU. We first load the pre-trained models released by Huggingface[1] as the backbones. To keep in line with the basic settings of baselines for fair comparison, we adopt the common hyper-parameters used in the transformer-based baseline models. Specifically, we apply AdamW algorithm [17] to optimize model parameters with a learning rate of 1e-5. We evaluate our generated summaries against the reference manually written

---

[1] https://huggingface.co/models.

ones by calculating the $F_1$-scores of ROUGE$_1$, ROUGE$_2$, and ROUGE$_L$ [14]. Following previous work, we adopt the Rouge evaluation script[2] provided by Huggingface with "use_stemmer" enabled.

## 4.4  Main Results

We compare SALAS with all of the previous SOTA methods on MReD and WikiAsp. We also further implement several common strong baselines for comparison and deeper analysis. Table 1 and Table 2 show the main results of the baseline models and our proposed SALAS. We can observe that SALAS outperforms the existing SOTA baselines on MReD and Wikiasp in BERT, Longformer, and BART backbones, respectively. Specifically, with BERT$_{base}$ and BART$_{large}$ as the PLM, SALAS surpasses BertAbs and BART$_{large}$ by 2.02/0.50/0.48 and 0.58/2.99/0.79 of ROUGE-1/2/L scores respectively, achieving new SOTA performance on MReD. Meanwhile, SALAS yields gains of 2.13/0.69/0.84 and 1.44/0.83/0.84 of ROUGE-1/2/L scores on two randomly selected domains from Wikiasp compared to the previous SOTA methods. The experimental results show the effectiveness of the overall framework of SALAS.

**Table 1.** Performance on MReD. The signal † denotes that the results of models are quoted in the original paper proposing MReD. The rest of the results are based on our implementation.

| Model | R-1 | R-2 | R-L |
|---|---|---|---|
| MMR[†] | 32.37 | 6.28 | 17.58 |
| LexRank[†] | 32.60 | 6.66 | 17.48 |
| TextRank[†] | 33.52 | 7.20 | 17.75 |
| TWAG | 27.82 | 7.22 | 19.99 |
| Longformer | 23.39 | 5.63 | 20.52 |
| BertAbs-BERT$_{base}$ | 23.57 | 6.67 | 18.59 |
| SALAS-BERT$_{base}$ | 25.59 | 7.17 | 19.07 |
| BART$_{large}^{†}$ | 38.59 | 10.61 | 22.93 |
| SALAS-BART$_{large}$ | **39.17** | **13.60** | **23.72** |

We attribute the improvement to the incorporation of aspect information and our proposed joint learning framework for two reasons. First, aspect information significantly improves the performance of models. We observe the performance gaps (the aforementioned gains of ROUGE-1/2/L scores) between models that adopt SALAS framework and models with the same backbones neglecting aspect information. The difference between two kinds of models is that the former incorporates aspect information by constraining the objective function, which indicates that by properly infusing models and constraining the objective function

---

[2] https://github.com/huggingface/transformers/blob/main/examples/pytorch/summarization/.

with aspect information, models are able to achieve more significant improvements. Second, learning aspect information in a joint way largely enhances the effectiveness of models. Compared to TWAG which models aspect information in a two-step way, our proposed SALAS significantly outperforms TWAG by 11.35/6.38/3.73, 10.17/4.12/2.87, and 6.11/2.23/1.51 ROUGE-1/2/L on MReD, Historic Place domain of WikiAsp, and Plant domain of WikiAsp, respectively.

**Table 2.** Performance on Wikiasp. All of the results are based on our implementation.

| Model | Historic Place | | | Plant | | |
|---|---|---|---|---|---|---|
| | R-1 | R-2 | R-L | R-1 | R-2 | R-L |
| TextRank | 10.97 | 2.05 | 7.50 | 14.12 | 1.95 | 8.70 |
| TWAG | 24.36 | 7.07 | 16.98 | 22.51 | 4.68 | 14.99 |
| BERT$_{base}$ | 25.22 | 8.21 | 14.88 | 21.84 | 6.35 | 13.54 |
| Longformer | 33.17 | 10.38 | 18.82 | 25.67 | 6.21 | 15.67 |
| SALAS-Longformer | 34.30 | 10.65 | 19.39 | 25.77 | 6.02 | 15.76 |
| BART$_{large}$ | 32.40 | 10.50 | 19.01 | 27.18 | 6.08 | 15.66 |
| SALAS-BART$_{large}$ | **34.53** | **11.19** | **19.85** | **28.62** | **6.91** | **16.50** |

## 4.5  Results of Ablation Study

We conduct ablation experiments on SALAS to further test the effectiveness of its components. As shown in Table 3, we observe that each component exerts a positive effect on the performance of SALAS on all of the three datasets, demonstrating their effectiveness. Furthermore, the extents of their influence differ from each other. Excluding AILoss leads to the most significant performance drop, which indicates that our modeled aspect information properly guides the generator and constrains the optimization to avoid falling into sub-optimal results.

**Table 3.** Results of ablation study.

| Model | MReD | | | Historic Place | | | Plant | | |
|---|---|---|---|---|---|---|---|---|---|
| | R-1 | R-2 | R-L | R-1 | R-2 | R-L | R-1 | R-2 | R-L |
| SALAS-BART$_{large}$ | **39.17** | **13.60** | **23.72** | **34.53** | **11.19** | **19.85** | **28.62** | **6.75** | **16.39** |
| w/o encoder probe | 39.04 | 12.96 | 23.58 | 33.62 | 11.04 | 19.48 | 28.05 | 6.58 | 16.05 |
| w/o decoder probe | 38.83 | 11.00 | 23.08 | 33.39 | 10.76 | 19.27 | 27.70 | 6.30 | 15.83 |
| w/o AILoss | 38.59 | 10.61 | 22.93 | 32.40 | 10.50 | 19.01 | 27.18 | 6.08 | 15.66 |

When only keeping the encoder probe and removing other constraints, the performance of the model can still be improved. That is to say, the generator requires more aspect information to improve its performance by infusing aspect information into the representations of input documents. Meanwhile, the small improvement indicates that guiding the generator in an implicit way, giving aspect-specific expressive power to the encoded representations without explicit supervision on the decoder, is not effective enough for a generator to capture and decode the corresponding aspect information in representations. The significant performance drop, caused by removing the decoder probe, also reflects the same conclusion.

## 4.6    Analysis and Discussion

The above experimental results confirm the effectiveness of our proposed SALAS, we analyze how SALAS is able to achieve the performance in this section.

**Table 4.** Results of the probed aspects from documents.

| Model | Micro | | | Macro | | |
|---|---|---|---|---|---|---|
| | **Precision** | **Recall** | **F1** | **Precision** | **Recall** | **F1** |
| SALAS | **85.64** | **95.58** | **90.34** | **66.48** | **77.53** | **70.88** |
| TWAG | 83.91 | 69.80 | 76.21 | 63.66 | 54.14 | 57.42 |

**Effectiveness of the Probe.** We evaluate the effectiveness of the aspect probe (encoder probe) that probes aspect information in documents to guide the summarization. As shown in Table 4, compared with TWAG which separates aspect classification from generation. Our joint learned encoder probe not only avoids the cascade error but also achieves better performance on aspect detection. We can observe that our encoder probe outperforms TWAG by 13.46/14.13 macro/micro-F1 score, which demonstrates that SALAS captures the scattered aspect information across documents more accurately than TWAG. Since SALAS recovers missing aspect information and uses it to guide the generator, the increasing quality of aspect information explains how SALAS achieves the current SOTA performance.

**Effectiveness of Guidance from Aspects.** We demonstrate that the performance improvement depends not only on our probed accurate aspect information but also on its effective guidance. As shown in Fig. **??**, strengthening the guidance of aspect information exerts a significant positive effect on the performance of $BART_{large}$. Specifically, the parameters of $BART_{large}$ are optimized with the objective function proposed in Eq. (12), where the value of $\lambda_2$ iterates from 0 to 1 with a step of 0.1. The increasing $\lambda_2$ represents the growing strength of guidance (penalizing the model for missing aspect information). We keep other parameters constant to investigate the relationship between guidance and performance. We observe that (1) the guidance improves the performance of models; (2) the improvement fluctuates when the guidance is weak; (3) After the fluctuation, the stronger guidance leads to a better performance, which has leveled out since exceeding a certain strength.

To sum up, we verify the effectiveness of both our proposed probe and the guidance of aspect information, thus explaining the underlying reason why SALAS achieves the SOTA performance and demonstrating the validity of our idea.

## 5   Conclusion

Multi-document summarization (MDS) is a long-standing task and is challenging due to the requirement of paraphrasing the key information scattered across multiple documents. In this paper, we introduce our supervised aspect learning abstractive summarization (SALAS) model, which captures aspect information to constrain the optimization and aids representation learning. SALAS adopts a multi-task joint learning method to avoid introducing the cascade error and impeding the interaction between aspect detection and generation. The extracted aspect information guides the generating process, improving the comprehensiveness and faithfulness of the generated summaries. The experimental results on three commonly used summarization datasets not only show that SALAS outperforms the strong baseline models but also validate the effectiveness of the probed aspects which are accurate and well guide the generating process.

## References

1. Ahuja, O., Xu, J., Gupta, A., Horecka, K., Durrett, G.: ASPECTNEWS: aspect-oriented summarization of news documents. In: Proceedings of the 60th Annual Meeting of the Association for Computational Linguistics (Volume 1: Long Papers), pp. 6494–6506. Association for Computational Linguistics, Dublin, Ireland (2022). https://doi.org/10.18653/v1/2022.acl-long.449
2. Angelidis, S., Amplayo, R.K., Suhara, Y., Wang, X., Lapata, M.: Extractive opinion summarization in quantized transformer spaces. Trans. Assoc. Comput. Linguist. **9**, 277–293 (2021). https://doi.org/10.1162/tacl-a-00366
3. Arora, R., Ravindran, B.: Latent dirichlet allocation and singular value decomposition based multi-document summarization. In: 2008 Eighth IEEE International Conference on Data Mining, pp. 713–718. IEEE, Pisa, Italy (2008). https://doi.org/10.1109/ICDM.2008.55
4. Beltagy, I., Peters, M.E., Cohan, A.: LongFormer: the long-document transformer. ArXiv (2020). https://doi.org/10.48550/ARXIV.2004.05150
5. Devlin, J., Chang, M.W., Lee, K., Toutanova, K.: BERT: pre-training of deep bidirectional transformers for language understanding. In: Proceedings of the 2019 Conference of the North, pp. 4171–4186. Association for Computational Linguistics, Minneapolis, Minnesota (2019). https://doi.org/10.18653/v1/N19-1423
6. Devlin, J., Chang, M.W., Lee, K., Toutanova, K.N.: BERT: pre-training of deep bidirectional transformers for language understanding. In: Proceedings of the 2019 Conference of the North American Chapter of the Association for Computational Linguistics: Human Language Technologies, Volume 1 (Long and Short Papers), pp. 4171–4186 (2018)

7. Erkan, G., Radev, D.R.: LexRank: graph-based lexical centrality as salience in text summarization. J. Artif. Intell. Res. **22**, 457–479 (2004). https://doi.org/10.1613/jair.1523

8. Grail, Q., Perez, J., Gaussier, E.: Globalizing BERT-based transformer architectures for long document summarization. In: Proceedings of the 16th Conference of the European Chapter of the Association for Computational Linguistics: Main Volume, pp. 1792–1810. Association for Computational Linguistics, Online (2021). https://doi.org/10.18653/v1/2021.eacl-main.154

9. Hayashi, H., Budania, P., Wang, P., Ackerson, C., Neervannan, R., Neubig, G.: WikiAsp: a dataset for multi-domain aspect-based summarization. Trans. Assoc. Comput. Linguist. **9**, 211–225 (2021). https://doi.org/10.1162/tacl-a-00362

10. Hu, X., Wen, L., Xu, Y., Zhang, C., Yu, P.: SelfORE: self-supervised relational feature learning for open relation extraction. In: Proceedings of the 2020 Conference on Empirical Methods in Natural Language Processing (EMNLP), pp. 3673–3682. Association for Computational Linguistics, Online (2020). https://doi.org/10.18653/v1/2020.emnlp-main.299

11. Jin, H., Wang, T., Wan, X.: Multi-granularity interaction network for extractive and abstractive multi-document summarization. In: Proceedings of the 58th Annual Meeting of the Association for Computational Linguistics, pp. 6244–6254. Association for Computational Linguistics, Online (2020). https://doi.org/10.18653/v1/2020.acl-main.556

12. Kiyoumarsi, F.: Evaluation of automatic text summarizations based on human summaries. Proc. Soc. Behav. Sci. **192**, 83–91 (2015). https://doi.org/10.1016/j.sbspro.2015.06.013

13. Lewis, M., et al.: BART: denoising sequence-to-sequence pre-training for natural language generation, translation, and comprehension. In: Proceedings of the 58th Annual Meeting of the Association for Computational Linguistics, pp. 7871–7880 (2020). https://doi.org/10.18653/v1/2020.acl-main.703

14. Lin, C.Y.: ROUGE: a package for automatic evaluation of summaries. In: Text Summarization Branches Out, pp. 74–81. Association for Computational Linguistics, Barcelona, Spain (2004)

15. Liu, Y., Lapata, M.: Hierarchical transformers for multi-document summarization. In: Proceedings of the 57th Annual Meeting of the Association for Computational Linguistics, pp. 5070–5081. Association for Computational Linguistics, Florence, Italy (2019). https://doi.org/10.18653/v1/P19-1500

16. Liu, Y., Lapata, M.: Text summarization with pretrained encoders. In: Proceedings of the 2019 Conference on Empirical Methods in Natural Language Processing and the 9th International Joint Conference on Natural Language Processing (EMNLP-IJCNLP), pp. 3728–3738. Association for Computational Linguistics, Hong Kong, China (2019). https://doi.org/10.18653/v1/D19-1387

17. Loshchilov, I., Hutter, F.: Decoupled weight decay regularization. arXiv preprint arXiv:1711.05101 (2017)

18. Ma, C., Zhang, W.E., Guo, M., Wang, H., Sheng, Q.Z.: Multi-document summarization via deep learning techniques: a survey. ACM Comput. Surv., 3529754 (2022). https://doi.org/10.1145/3529754

19. Mao, Z., et al.: DYLE: dynamic latent extraction for abstractive long-input summarization. In: Proceedings of the 60th Annual Meeting of the Association for Computational Linguistics (Volume 1: Long Papers), pp. 1687–1698. Association for Computational Linguistics, Dublin, Ireland (2022). https://doi.org/10.18653/v1/2022.acl-long.118

20. Mihalcea, R., Tarau, P.: TextRank: bringing order into text. In: Proceedings of the 2004 Conference on Empirical Methods in Natural Language Processing, pp. 404–411 (2004)
21. Over, P., Yen, J.: An introduction to DUC-2004. National Institute of Standards and Technology (2004)
22. Pennington, J., Socher, R., Manning, C.D.: GloVe: global vectors for word representation. In: Proceedings of the 2014 Conference on Empirical Methods in Natural Language Processing (EMNLP), pp. 1532–1543 (2014). https://doi.org/10.3115/v1/D14-1162
23. Radev, D.: A common theory of information fusion from multiple text sources step one: cross-document structure. In: 1st SIGdial Workshop on Discourse and Dialogue, pp. 74–83 (2000). https://doi.org/10.3115/1117736.1117745
24. Shen, C., Cheng, L., Zhou, R., Bing, L., You, Y., Si, L.: MReD: meta-review dataset for structure-controllable text generation. In: Findings of the Association for Computational Linguistics: ACL 2022, pp. 2521–2535. Association for Computational Linguistics, Dublin, Ireland (2022). https://doi.org/10.18653/v1/2022.findings-acl.198
25. Wang, W., Pan, S.J., Dahlmeier, D., Xiao, X.: Recursive neural conditional random fields for aspect-based sentiment analysis. In: Proceedings of the 2016 Conference on Empirical Methods in Natural Language Processing, pp. 616–626 (2016). https://doi.org/10.18653/v1/D16-1059

26. Xu, J., Durrett, G.: Neural extractive text summarization with syntactic compression. In: Proceedings of the 2019 Conference on Empirical Methods in Natural Language Processing and the 9th International Joint Conference on Natural Language Processing (EMNLP-IJCNLP), pp. 3290–3301. Association for Computational Linguistics, Hong Kong, China (2019). https://doi.org/10.18653/v1/D19-1324

27. Yao, L., Haghighi, A., Riedel, S., McCallum, A.: Structured relation discovery using generative models. In: Proceedings of the Conference on Empirical Methods in Natural Language Processing, pp. 1456–1466. EMNLP '11, Association for Computational Linguistics, USA (2011)

28. Zhang, Y., et al.: An exploratory study on long dialogue summarization: what works and what's next. In: Findings of the Association for Computational Linguistics: EMNLP 2021, pp. 4426–4433. Association for Computational Linguistics, Punta Cana, Dominican Republic (2021). https://doi.org/10.18653/v1/2021.findings-emnlp.377

29. Zhu, C., Xu, R., Zeng, M., Huang, X.: A hierarchical network for abstractive meeting summarization with cross-domain pretraining. In: Findings of the Association for Computational Linguistics: EMNLP 2020, pp. 194–203. Association for Computational Linguistics, Online (2020). https://doi.org/10.18653/v1/2020.findings-emnlp.19

30. Zhu, F., Tu, S., Shi, J., Li, J., Hou, L., Cui, T.: TWAG: a topic-guided wikipedia abstract generator. In: Proceedings of the 59th Annual Meeting of the Association for Computational Linguistics and the 11th International Joint Conference on Natural Language Processing (Volume 1: Long Papers), pp. 4623–4635. Association for Computational Linguistics, Online (2021). https://doi.org/10.18653/v1/2021.acl-long.356

# KL Regularized Normalization Framework for Low Resource Tasks

Neeraj Kumar[1(✉)], Ankur Narang[2], and Brejesh Lall[1]

[1] IIT Delhi, New Delhi, India
`neerajkr2k14@gmail.com`,`bsz208607@iitd.ac.in` , `brejesh@ee.iitd.ac.in`
[2] IEEE, New Delhi, India

**Abstract.** Large pretrained models, such as Bert, GPT, and Wav2Vec, have demonstrated great potential for learning representations that are transferable to a wide variety of downstream tasks. It is difficult to obtain a large quantity of supervised data due to the limite d availability of resources and time. In light of this, a significant amount of research has been conducted in the area of adopting large pretrained datasets for diverse downstream tasks via fine tuning, linear probing, or prompt tuning in low resource settings. Normalization techniques are essential for accelerating training and improving the generalization of deep neural networks and have been successfully used in a wide variety of applications. A lot of normalization techniques have been proposed but the success of normalization in low resource downstream NLP and speech tasks is limited. One of the reasons is the inability to capture expressiveness by rescaling parameters of normalization. We propose Kullback-Leibler(KL) Regularized normalization (KL-Norm) which make the normalized data well behaved and helps in better generalization as it reduces over-fitting, generalises well on out of domain distributions and removes irrelevant biases and features with negligible increase in model parameters and memory overheads. Detailed experimental evaluation on multiple low resource NLP and speech tasks, demonstrates the superior performance of KL-Norm as compared to other popular normalization and regularization techniques.

**Keywords:** Normalization · Kullback-Leibler(KL) Regularization · Low resource task · Large pretrained Model

## 1 Introduction

With the coming of large pretrained models in NLP such as Bert [8], GPT [41], Wav2Vec [3], Whisper [37], etc., low resource tasks have become an active area of research and have lots of industry use-cases such as manufacturing, gaming, metaverse, etc. A lot of techniques such as fine tuning, linear probing [24], prompt tuning [55] have been explored to improve the performance of these model in low resource settings. No work has been done in the direction of use of normalization on pretrained models to make it work better for low resource tasks.

D. Koutra et al. (Eds.): ECML PKDD 2023, LNAI 14172, pp. 71–89, 2023.
https://doi.org/10.1007/978-3-031-43421-1_5

The normalization method is one of the fundamental contributions to the deep learning community. It is a method of adaptive reparametrization, motivated by the difficulty of training very deep neural networks [14]. Batch Normalization [20] is the first normalization technique proposed to prevent the training from getting stuck in the saturated regimes of non-linearities and improves the training speed. It gives regularization effects which leads to better generalization of deep neural networks. Beyond Batch Normalization, several normalization techniques have been proposed which work better on various applications such as stylization [19,35,47], recurrent neural networks [2,7], object detection [51] and faster convergence [44], image to image translation [38], neural acoustic modeling [25] and vision related applications [27,31]. Such techniques have gained success in all the fields of artificial intelligence such as NLP, vision, speech and others.

In the traditional batch normalization operation, normalization is done by mean shifting of feature map along with making it the unit variance. To increase the expressivity of network, we use two learnable parameters namely scale $\gamma$ and bias $\beta$ as shown in Equation (5).

$$z = \gamma \odot \frac{x - \mu}{\sqrt{\Sigma}} + \beta \tag{1}$$

Assuming the input data is Gaussian, after passing through the batch normalization, it becomes the unit gaussian and to increase the representative power, we are adding the learnable parameters to shift its mean and increase it variance according to the deep learning tasks.

Now if we expand the Equation (5) and combine the scale and shift with mean and variance, we will get the general equation of normalization (Equation (3)).

$$z = \gamma \odot \frac{x}{\sqrt{\Sigma}} + (\beta - \gamma \odot \frac{\mu}{\sqrt{\Sigma}}) \tag{2}$$

$$z = \alpha \odot x + \zeta \tag{3}$$

Normalization makes the data well behaved by making it unit gaussian such that it helps in faster optimization, larger learning rate and implicit regularization. Equation (3) is the general formulation of normalization where the $\alpha$ and $\zeta$ incorporates the mean and variance which results in the batch normalization as shown in equation (5). There are various ways to make the normalization framework well behaved and effective for deep learning training with different formulation of $\alpha$ and $\zeta$.

We are looking into the normalization framework that works well in low resource setting as it has a lot of industry and research relevance. High resource supervised datasets are time and resource consuming and sometimes impossible to scale in industry set up. With the coming of large pretrained models such as Bert, Wav2Vec, etc. it is possible to achieve good results in low resource setting. Current normalization approaches such as batch normalization, layer normalization have not been effective in low resource set up to make data well behaved, increasing the expressive power of the network and better generalization as shown in experimental section.

In this regard, we propose ***KL-Norm*** *KL Regularized normalization* framework which imposes the prior on the normalization framework through the KL divergence loss [1] to follow gaussian distribution. This has shown promising result in low resource tasks. KL Regularized normalization helps to improve accuracy and training generalization as it reduces overfitting by adding a regularization loss function in the training schedule. It generalizes well on out of domain datasets as compared to other normalization techniques. It filters relevant features and removes the superficial features or biases present in the dataset or pretrained model. An overview of the proposed normalization mechanism is shown in Fig. 2. We specifically make the following contributions:

– We propose a novel KL Regularized normalization framework (KL-Norm) which incorporates rescaling parameter computation by considering regularization loss (Sect. 3). KL-Norm demonstrates better expressiveness due to regularization loss and generalizes well by reducing over-fitting. It incorporates uncertainty which promotes better out of domain data generalization.
– Detailed experimental analysis demonstrates superior accuracy and performance of KL-Norm as compared to other normalization techniques, on low resource downstream NLP tasks including: sentiment classification, characterizing semantic relationships, semantic textual similarity, textual entailment and paraphrase detection as well as downstream speech task such as keyword detection and emotion classification.

## 2    Related Work

We have divided this section into two parts namely low resource NLP and normalization techniques.

***Low Resource NLP and Speech.*** Earlier work in low resource include feature engineering which requires significant efforts while adapting to the new datasets [46]. Other work is transferring knowledge across the domain to increase the data require for training [56]. Adversarial training [15] is one of these approach that uses the knowledge of domain where plentiful data is present and does the out of domain adaptation on low resource data [12]. However, these approaches have not used a pretrained generic language models, but perform pretraining for each task individually. Another set of low resource training involves using language model [6,21]. [18] showed that a classifier that fine-tunes a pretrained BERT model generally has wider optima on the training loss curves in comparison to models trained for the same task from scratch, indicating a more general classifier. In the speech domain, pretrained architectures such as DeepeSpeech [17] and Wav2Vec [3] have been explored for various classification task as intent [52], phoneme [3], speaker and language identification [11]. Another approach of linear probing is used in large pretrained model where the linear layer is added on top of pretrained model with fine tuning the linear layer only. Prompt tuning has gained a lot of attention after the coming of GPT-3 model where the discrete or continuous prompts are used to predict the tasks by the large pretrained model. However, none of them studied the impact of normalization based on KL regularization in low resource setting.

***Normalization Techniques.*** Batch normalization(BN) is the first form for normalization techniques proposed in [20] to normalize the feature maps by computing the batch statistics which helps in training the deep neural networks faster. Normalization works better as the first order optimization algorithms such as SGD works better on isotropic landscape ([36]).

Motivated by this, a lot of normalization techniques have been proposed to deal different scenarios. Layer Normalization(LN) ([2]) and Recurrent batch normalization ([7]) give better performance in recurrent deep learning models. Instance Normalization(IN) [47] and Adaptive Instance Normalization [19] helps in image stylization, Group Normalization [51] improves performance in object detection, Weight Normalization [44] speeds up the convergence by reparametrization of weight vectors in a neural network that decouples the length of those weight vectors from their direction. Batch-Instance Normalization(BIN) [35] controls the styles adaptively to the task and selectively to individual feature maps. SPADE [38] makes this denormalization spatially sensitive. SPADE normalization boils down to "conditional batch normalization which varies on a per-pixel basis". Switchable Normalization [31] are dynamically select BN, LN and IN in proportion and works better in vision tasks. Stochastic Normalization [27] gives regulaization effects and better on vision tasks. [22] provides a meta learning mechanism for instance-level normalization techniques. [25] generates the rescaling parameters by different speakers and environments for adaptive neural acoustic modeling via Layer Normalization. The proposed KL-Norm uses KL Regularized inference based affine parameters to show the expressive power on low resource NLP downstraemed tasks.

# 3    Theoretical Foundation of KL Regularized Normalization

## 3.1    Preliminaries: Batch Normalization

Batch normalization(BN) [20] is first introduced for faster convergence and training stability. By normalizing activations throughout the network, it prevents small changes to the parameters from amplifying into larger and suboptimal changes in activations in gradients; for instance, it prevents the training from getting stuck in the saturated regimes of nonlinearities. It leads to better generalization of network because it has the implicit regularization effect and sometimes the neural netowrk do not requires the explicit regularization techniques such as dropout [45], mixout [30], weight decay [28], etc.

Equation (5) is the batch normalized output(z) with input($x_1 \cdots x_n$) is used to calculate the mean($\mu$) and variance($\sigma^2$). Use of scale($\gamma$) and bias($\beta$) in Equation (5) give flexibility to work with normalized input($\hat{x}$), if there is a need, thus increasing the representation power.

$$\mu = \frac{1}{m} \sum_{i=1}^{m} x_i \quad \sigma^2 = \frac{1}{m} \sum_{i=1}^{m} (x_i - \mu)^2 \qquad (4)$$

$$z = \gamma \odot \frac{x - \mu}{\sqrt{\sigma^2 + \epsilon}} + \beta \qquad (5)$$

At the inference stage, mini-batch estimations $\mu$ and $\sigma^2$ are not available, so BN tracks moving average of the statistics during training (Equation (6)) where $\alpha$ is the coefficient of moving average, $\hat{\mu}$ and $\hat{\sigma}$ moving average versions of $\mu$ and $\sigma$. These moving statistics $\hat{\mu}$ and $\hat{\sigma}$ at iteration t are used to normalize the feature map as given in Equation (7) during inference.

$$\hat{\mu}^{(t)} = \alpha\mu^{(t)} + (1 - \alpha)\hat{\mu}^{(t-1)} \quad \hat{\sigma^2}^{(t)} = \alpha\sigma^{2(t)} + (1 - \alpha)\sigma^{2(\hat{t}-1)} \qquad (6)$$

$$\hat{x} = \frac{x - \hat{\mu}}{\sqrt{\hat{\sigma}^2 + \epsilon}} \qquad (7)$$

In the batch normalization setting the normalized feature map($\hat{x}$) follows the isotropic gaussian distribution [14] with zero mean and unit variance i.e. $\hat{x} \sim \mathcal{N}(0, I)$. The reparamterization of the normalized feature map through rescaling paramters i.e. mean and variance (Equation 12) allows the output to represent the same family of functions of the input as the old parametrization, but the new parametrization has different learning dynamics as shown in Equation (5). This setting is not found useful for low resource setting and not able to capture the expressiveness through normalization and unable to perform well in out of domain generalization.

## 3.2   KL Regularized Batch Normalization

We denote normalized feature map, $z^i$ $i = 1\ldots, K$. To make the data well behaved and capture more representative power through normalization, we impose a prior, $t^i$ which will follow gaussian distribution. Assume the loss with respect to the neural network parameters $\theta$ is denoted by $\mathcal{L}(\theta)$. To impose prior on normalized feature map, we pose the optimization as a constrained problem:

$$\min_{\theta} \quad \mathcal{L}(\theta)$$
$$s.t. \quad \mathrm{E}[d_z(z^i, t^i)] \leq \epsilon_i, \ i = 1, \ldots, K \qquad (8)$$

From above optimization problem, we get a function of $\theta$ and $\lambda$ known as the Lagrangian where $\lambda$'s are langrangian multipliers:

$$\mathcal{L}(\theta, \lambda) = \mathcal{L}(\theta) + \sum_{i=1}^{K} \lambda^i d_z(z^i, t^i) \qquad (9)$$

The primal form of above equation can be written as :

$$\min_{\theta} \ \max_{\lambda} \ \mathcal{L}(\theta, \lambda) \qquad (10)$$

This is a hard problem. Instead of solving this, we solve its dual formulation,

$$\max_{\lambda} \min_{\theta} \mathcal{L}(\theta, \lambda) \tag{11}$$

We apply gradient-based optimization to the following loss ($\mathcal{L}(\theta)$ is the CE loss). In particular, we choose $d_z(z^i, t^i)$ as KL loss between the normalized feature map and the gaussian prior. This will bring the distribution of normalized output closer to gaussian prior and add regularization effect in the network. The $\lambda$ is the hyperparameter which is tuned according to the task. In the proposed normalization setting, the affine parameters i.e. $\gamma$ and $\beta$ can be seen as the rescaling parameters i.e. mean($\mu_v$) and standard deviation($\Sigma_v^{\frac{1}{2}}$) of normalization framework. The rescaling parameters (mean and variance) can be modeled with deep neural network architecture. We have used multi layer perceptron(MLP) to model mean and variance. With this, the KL Regularized normalized output $z$ will defined by the Eq. 13.

$$\mu_v = MLP(x) \quad \Sigma_v^{\frac{1}{2}} = MLP(x) \tag{12}$$

$$z = \Sigma_v^{\frac{1}{2}} \odot \widehat{x} + \mu_v \tag{13}$$

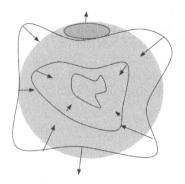 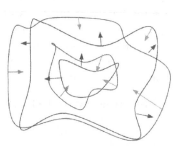

**Fig. 1.** Left:The KL Normalized distribution(black contour) tries to match the fixed prior(blue contour) and seeing a hole. Right : The KL Normalized distribution(pink contour) tries to match the learnable prior(black contour) and is modified to fit the prior. (Color figure online)

We are trying to match the normalized output distribution with prior distribution using the KL loss. In case of fixed gaussian prior, we obtain holes, namely, regions in the latent space where the normalized output assigns low probability while the prior assigns (relatively) high probability as shown in left part of Fig. 1. On the other hand, if we consider a learnable prior, the situation looks different. The optimization allows to change the KL normalized distribution and the prior. As the consequence, both distributions try to match each other as shown in right part of Fig. 1. The problem of holes is then less apparent, especially if the prior is flexible enough. We have imposed the learnable gaussian prior on normalized output through KL divergence loss function which is given by Eq. 14

where $\mu_0$ and $\mu_1$ are $K$−dimensional mean vectors, and $\Sigma_0$ and $\Sigma_1$ are diagonal co-variance matrices.

$$\text{KL}(\mathcal{N}(\mu_0, \Sigma_0) \| \mathcal{N}(\mu_1, \Sigma_1)) = \frac{1}{2}(\text{tr}(\Sigma_1^{-1}\Sigma_0)+$$
$$(\mu_1 - \mu_0)^T \Sigma_1^{-1} (\mu_1 - \mu_0) - K + \log(\frac{\det(\Sigma_1)}{\det(\Sigma_0)})) \tag{14}$$

KL loss has several properties which are useful for better expressivity, generalization in low resource setting. We will discuss each of these properties in the next subsections.

***Regularization Effect of Kullbach-Leibler Loss.*** Thus KL loss acts as a regularizer term means 'keep the representations $z$ sufficiently diverse'. If we don't include the regularizer, the model can learn to cheat and give each datapoint a representation in a different region of euclidean space. With the KL loss, a gaussian prior will be imposed on normalization framework and which results in the data points to follow the gaussian distribution with similar representation close together.

***Out of Domain Generalization.*** The source of uncertainty is provided by the KL divergence between the conditional distribution over latent space given the input and the latent space defined by the learned marginal $p_\phi(z)$; i.e. $\text{KL}[q(z|x)\|p(z)]$. Here, the marginal effectively learns a density model for the data, albeit in the lowerF-dimensional, lower-information latent-space rather than the original input space. Density estimation, whether explicit [9] or implicit [26], has been shown to be useful for out-of-distribution detection.

***Algorithm.*** Figure 2 shows the proposed KL-Norm framework where the two multi-layer perceptron(MLP) layer is used to compute the rescaling parameters(mean($\mu_v$) and statistics($\Sigma_v^{\frac{1}{2}}$)). The normalized feature map($\hat{y}$) is calvulated using mean batch statistics to do affine transformation with rescaling parameters.

We have proposed the algorithm of KL Regularized normalization (Algorithm 1). At the training stage, we compute the mean batch statistics($\mu$ and $\sigma^2$) to get the normalized feature map($\hat{x}$). The rescaling paramters i.e. mean($\mu_v$) and variance($\Sigma_v^{\frac{1}{2}}$) is calculated which goes into linear transformation to get the final output feature map($z$). The moving average statistics is calculated during training to be used at inference. The cross entropy(CE) and Kullbach-Leibler(KL) loss function is used while training with $\beta$ as a hyper-parameter. At the inference, the moving average statistics calculates the normalized feature map. The final output is generated by linear transformation of normalized feature map using rescaling paramters.

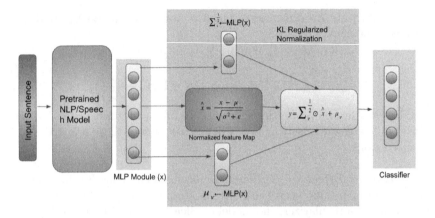

**Fig. 2.** Architecture of proposed KL Regularized normalization framework

## 4    Experiments

### 4.1    Model Architecture

Figure 2 shows the architecture having pretrained Language model, MLP module, KL Regularized normalization and classifier. The pretrained $BERT_{Base}$ (12 layers, 110M parameters) and $BERT_{Large}$ (24 layers, 340M parameters) uncased [8] implementation of [50] are used as our base models which gives 768 dimensional embeddings for sentence representation. The MLP module used to compute the compressed sentence representations is a shallow MLP with 768, $\frac{2304+K}{4}$, $\frac{768+K}{2}$ hidden units with a ReLU non-linearity, where $K$ is [384, 512] gives K dimensional embedding. The MLP module acts as a bottleneck module for incorporating the relevant features in the KL Regularized normalization through the rescaling parameters. The KL Regularized normalization module include two linear layers which are used to calculate the affine/rescaling parameters to go into the normalization. A linear layer classifier is used on top to classify the sentence. Similar to [5], we use a linear annealing schedule for $\beta$ and set it as $\min(1, \text{ epoch} \times \beta_0)$ in each epoch, where $\beta_0$ is the initial value.

For the speech related downstream tasks, we have used encoder of Wav2Vec2.0 pretrained model as base model and added 1d convolution layer with 768 output channel. We have added MLP module having linear layers to compute the affine parameters of KL-Norm. A linear layer classifier is used on top to classify the speech related classes.

---

**Algorithm 1.** KL Regularized Normalization

---

**Input:** mini-batch feature maps of each channel
$\quad$ x $= \{x_i\}_{i=1}^m$;
$\quad$ moving statistics $\hat{\mu}, \hat{\sigma^2}$;
$\quad$ moving statistics update rate $\alpha \in (0,1)$
**Output:** z $=$ KL-NORM(x)
1: **Training:**

$\quad$ – $\mu \leftarrow \frac{1}{m}\sum_{i=1}^m x_i$, $\quad \sigma^2 \leftarrow \frac{1}{m}\sum_{i=1}^m (x_i - \mu)^2$ $\quad$ // mini batch mean and variance
$\quad$ – $\hat{x} \leftarrow \frac{x-\mu}{\sqrt{\sigma^2 + \epsilon}}$ $\quad$ // normalize with mini-batch statistics

$\quad$ – $\mu_v \leftarrow = \mathrm{MLP}(x)$, $\quad \Sigma_v^{\frac{1}{2}} \leftarrow = \mathrm{MLP}(x)$ $\quad$ // rescaling paramters i.e. mean
$\quad$ and variance.
$\quad$ – $z = \Sigma_v^{\frac{1}{2}} \odot \hat{x} + \mu_v$ $\quad\quad\quad\quad\quad\quad$ // KL Regularized normalized output
$\quad$ feature map
$\quad$ – $\hat{\mu} \leftarrow \alpha\mu + (1-\alpha)\hat{\mu}$ $\quad \hat{\sigma^2} \leftarrow \alpha\sigma^2 + (1-\alpha)\hat{\sigma^2}$ $\quad$ // update estimations of
$\quad$ moving statistics

2: **Loss:**

$\quad$ – Loss $=$ CE $+ \beta$ KL

3: **Inference:**

$\quad$ – $\mu_v \leftarrow = \mathrm{MLP}(x)$, $\quad \Sigma_v^{\frac{1}{2}} \leftarrow = \mathrm{MLP}(x)$. $\quad$ // rescaling paramters i.e. mean
$\quad$ and variance.
$\quad$ – $z \leftarrow \Sigma_v^{\frac{1}{2}} \odot \frac{x-\hat{\mu}}{\sqrt{\hat{\sigma^2}+\epsilon}} + \mu_v$ $\quad\quad\quad$ // KL Regularized normalization output
$\quad$ feature map

---

## 4.2 Comparison Methods

We have used the common normalization techniques used in NLP tasks such as batch normalization(BN) [20], layer normalization(LN) [2] and group normalization(GN) [51]. Such techniques do faster convergence and generalize well on NLP datsets. Apart from that, other common regularization techniques have also been used for the comparison namely Dropout [45] and Weight [28] Decay. While experimenting, we replace the KL Regularized normalization with the comparison methods (Fig. 2). We have also performed the experiments with BERT$_\text{Base}$ model given in Fig. 2 without KL Regularized normalization.

## 4.3 Training Details

We have used the pretrained BERT$_\text{Base}$ and BERT$_\text{Large}$ uncased models as the base models to see the effectiveness of the proposed method on down-streamed NLP tasks. We use the default hyper-parameters of BERT, i.e., we use a sequence length of 128, with batch size 8. We use the stable variant of the Adam optimizer [34,54] with the default learning rate of 2e$-$5 through all experiments. We do not use warm-up or weight decay.

**Table 1.** Average results and standard deviation in parentheses over 5 runs on low-resource data in GLUE. $\Delta$ shows the absolute difference between the results of the KL-Norm model with BERT-base.

| Model | MRPC | | STS-B | | RTE |
|---|---|---|---|---|---|
| | Accuracy | F1 | Pearson | Spearman | Accuracy |
| BERT$_{Base}$ | 84.31 (0.2) | 87.01 (0.2) | **84.43 (0.2)** | **83.28 (0.1)** | 64.23 (1.8) |
| +BN [20] | 86.76 (0.5) | 90.49 (0.5) | 82.28 (0.5) | 81.57(0.7) | 66.42 (1.4) |
| +LN [2] | 85.23 (0.3) | 88.12 (0.7) | 84.33 (0.9) | 82.98(1.0) | 65.17 (0.9) |
| +GN [51] | 85.01 (0.2) | 87.98 (0.5) | 82.76 (0.8) | 81.91(1.1) | 65.55 (0.2) |
| +Dropout [45] | 85.55 (0.6) | 88.47 (0.2) | 84.11 (0.8) | 82.65 (0.7) | 65.12 (0.9) |
| +WD [30] | 85.01(0.2) | 86.91(0.2) | 84.02(0.8) | 82.29(0.5) | 65.02(0.8) |
| KL-Norm$_{Base}$ | **87.25 (0.1)** | **91.03 (0.6)** | 82.49 (0.9) | 81.63 (0.8) | **70.42 (0.8)** |
| $\Delta$ | +2.94 | +4.02 | −1.94 | −1.65 | +6.19 |
| BERT$_{Large}$ | 86.76 (0.7) | 90.20 (1.3) | **86.27 (0.3)** | **85.21 (0.1)** | 67.11 (0.8) |
| +BN [20] | 85.53 (0.5) | 85.44 (0.5) | 84.47 (0.3) | 82.73(0.7) | 66.7 7(1.4) |
| +LN [2] | 86.27 (0.5) | 86.41 (0.5) | 86.52 (0.2) | 85.73(0.3) | 67.23 (1.4) |
| +GN [51] | 85.72 (0.3) | 85.87 (0.2) | 85.10 (0.3) | 85.21(0.7) | 66.2 (0.9) |
| +Dropout [45] | 86.51 (0.4) | 89.98 (0.2) | 86.13 (0.8) | 85.02 (0.5) | 67.01 (0.6) |
| +WD [30] | 86.11(0.5) | 89.03(0.4) | 86.18(0.2) | 85.10(0.1) | 68.07(0.9) |
| KL-Norm$_{Large}$ | **87.99 (0.4)** | **91.38 (0.6)** | 86.01 (0.7) | 84.68 (0.9) | **71.01 (0.8)** |
| $\Delta$ | +1.23 | +1.18 | −0.26 | −0.53 | +3.9 |

We have used the Wav2Vec 2.0 [3] pretrained on LibriSpeech 960 h as the base model to see the performance of proposed method on downstream speech related tasks. We have chosen Adam optimizer and set the learning rate of the backbone to 1e−5 for fine tuning and an L2 penalty of 1e−5 was established.

### 4.4   Analysis of Increased Expressive Power

***Glue Benchmarks.*** We have used the three low resource datasets namely MRPC and RTE for the evaluation of the proposed method. Table 1 shows the comparison of the proposed model with the compared models having BERT-base uncased as the base model. It shows that the proposed normalization model outperforms the other method in various evaluation metrics. Our KL-Norm method substantially improves the results and surpasses the prior work in all settings for both BERT$_{Base}$ and BERT$_{Large}$ models. Due to the computational overhead of BERT$_{Large}$, for the rest of this work, we stick to BERT$_{Base}$.

***Low Resource Varying Datasets.*** We have used the four large NLP datasets such as SNLI, MNLI, QNLI, and YELP and subsample the dataset using the random seeds. We then evaluated the performance of NLI datasets under varying sizes of training data (200, 400, 600 800 and 1000 samples). We reported the average and standard deviation across 5 different seeds. Table 2 shows that KL-Norm consistently outperforms all the baselines on low-resource scenarios.

We have also performed the experiments on three large speech related datasets such as Google Speech Command, Crema-D and ESD. We have evaluated the performance under varying size using random seeds. Table 3 have shown the that. KL-Norm performs better as compared to other methods.

**Table 2.** Test accuracies in the low-resource setting on text classification and NLI datasets under varying sizes of training data (200, 400, 600, 800 and 1000 samples). $\Delta$ shows the absolute difference between the results of the KL-Norm model with BERT-base.

| Data | Model | 200 | 400 | 600 | 800 | 1000 |
|---|---|---|---|---|---|---|
| SNLI | BERT$_{Base}$ | 60.07 (0.6) | 66.87 (0.4) | 68.69 (0.9) | 72.47 (0.8) | 72.98 (0.4) |
| | +BN | 58.43 (0.4) | 66.29 (0.5) | 68.76 (0.4) | 71.96 (0.2) | 73.43 (0.5) |
| | +LN | 59.95 (0.3) | 65.26 (0.4) | 68.68 (0.6) | 72.52 (0.1) | 73.01 (0.2) |
| | +GN | 58.60 (0.2) | 66.11 (0.6) | 67.57 (0.5) | 72.01 (0.3) | 73.10 (0.2) |
| | +Dropout | 58.44 (0.4) | 66.76 (0.9) | 68.74 (0.7) | 72.12 (0.5) | 72.58 (0.7) |
| | +WD | 59.23 (0.6) | 66.11 (0.9) | 68.41(0.8) | 72.48 (0.6) | **72.52** (0.3) |
| | +KL-Norm | **62.55** (1.3) | **69.02** (0.6) | **70.47** (0.3) | **73.92** (0.2) | **74.05** (0.7) |
| | $\Delta$ | +2.48 | +2.15 | +1.78 | +1.45 | +1.07 |
| MNLI | BERT$_{Base}$ | 45.53 (1.1) | 51.12 (0.9) | 57.74 (0.8) | 58.83 (0.3) | 60.19 (0.7) |
| | +BN | 46.34 (0.4) | 52.14 (1.3) | 55.7 (0.8) | 56.5 (0.5) | 59.5 (0.7) |
| | +LN | 45.25 (1.3) | 51.42 (1.3) | 57.79 (0.4) | 59.03 (0.6) | 60.32 (0.7) |
| | +GN | 44.17 (1.8) | 50.53 (1.1) | 57.34 (0.6) | 58.60 (0.3) | 59.17 (0.5) |
| | +Dropout | 45.44 (0.8) | 51.32 (1.1) | 57.65 (1.1) | 59.43 (0.4) | 60.08 (0.9) |
| | +WD | 45.72 (0.7) | 51.42 (0.4) | 57.34 (0.7) | 58.88 (0.6) | 60.24 (0.4) |
| | +KL-Norm | **47.65** (0.7) | **53.20** (1.4) | **59.29** (1.2) | **60.17** (0.9) | **61.24** (0.8) |
| | $\Delta$ | +2.12 | +2.08 | +1.55 | +1.34 | +1.05 |
| QNLI | BERT$_{Base}$ | 71.12 (0.6) | 75.30 (0.4) | 75.9 (0.8) | 78.18 (0.2) | 79.51 (0.4) |
| | +BN | 71.70 (0.2) | 74.13 (0.5) | 75.7 (0.3) | 77.12 (0.4) | 77.32 (0.4) |
| | +LN | 71.95 (0.4) | 74.97 (0.8) | 75.8 (0.3) | 78.38 (0.2) | 79.67 (0.4) |
| | +GN | 71.24 (0.4) | 74.16 (0.6) | 75.7 (0.2) | 77.55 (0.1) | 77.45 (0.3) |
| | +Dropout | 71.43 (1.2) | 74.77 (0.4) | 75.23 (0.7) | 78.67 (0.5) | 79.23 (0.3) |
| | +WD | 71.43 (0.3) | 74.61 (0.6) | 75.51 (0.2) | 78.47 (0.9) | 79.33 (0.4) |
| | KL-Norm | **73.20** (0.5) | **76.82** (0.8) | **76.97** (0.3) | **79.12** (0.8) | **80.34** (0.7) |
| | $\Delta$ | +2.08 | +1.52 | +1.07 | +0.94 | +0.83 |
| YELP | BERT$_{Base}$ | **41.58** (0.3) | **44.02** (0.5) | 45.54 (0.5) | 47.62 (0.9) | 47.92 (0.7) |
| | +BN | 38.08 (0.3) | 43.18 (0.7) | 44.56 (0.3) | 45.58 (0.3) | 47.04 (0.8) |
| | +LN | 41.13 (0.4) | 43.37 (0.4) | 46.01 (0.6) | 46.35 (0.5) | 47.94 (0.8) |
| | +GN | 40.34 (0.7) | 43.11 (0.6) | 45.12 (0.2) | 45.79 (0.4) | 47.17 (0.3) |
| | +Dropout | 40.86 (0.3) | 43.37 (0.4) | 45.02 (0.9) | 46.77 (0.7) | 48.02 (0.2) |
| | +WD | 40.77 (0.9) | 43.60 (1.1) | 45.07 (0.6) | 47.12 (1.1) | 47.83 (0.9) |
| | KL-Norm | 41.48 (0.4) | 43.86 (1.1) | **46.10** (0.7) | **48.38** (0.4) | **48.58** (0.4) |
| | $\Delta$ | −0.1 | −0.16 | +0.56 | +0.76 | +0.66 |

## 4.5  Analysis of out of Domain Generalization

We have used various NLP datasets to see the effectiveness of KL Regularized normalization in the out of domain generalization. We have used datasets referred in [32], including SICK [33], ADD1 [39], JOCI [53], MPE [29], MNLI, SNLI, SciTail [23], and three datasets from [49] namely DPR [42], FN+ [40], SPR [43], and Quora Question Pairs (QQP) interpreted as an NLI task as by [13]. We use the same split used in [48] for the experiment. We have trained the model on 6000 samples of SNLI and MNLI datasets and used these dataset as the test set to see the out of domain generalization of the proposed model. The SNLI and MNLI datasets contain three labels of contradiction, neutral, and entailment. However, some of the considered target datasets have only two labels, such as DPR or SciTail. When the target dataset has two labels of *entailed* and *not-entailed*, as in DPR, we consider the predicted contradiction and neutral labels as the not-entailed label. In the case the target dataset has two labels of *entailment* and *neutral*, as in SciTail, we consider the predicted contradiction label as neutral.

**Table 3.** Test accuracies in the low-resource setting on speech classification under varying sizes of training data (300, 600, 900, 1200 and 1500 samples).

| Data | Model | 300 | 600 | 900 | 1200 | 1500 |
|---|---|---|---|---|---|---|
| GoogleC | Wav2vec | 63.21 (0.9) | 83.15 (0.5) | 84.32 (0.7) | 85.58 (0.5) | 86.92 (0.4) |
| | +BN | 64.70 (0.6) | 84.99 (0.7) | 86.81 (0.6) | 87.33 (0.7) | 88.17 (0.9) |
| | +LN | 63.86 (0.4) | 84.11 (0.5) | 85.68 (0.6) | 86.99 (0.2) | 87.73 (0.6) |
| | +GN | 63.14 (0.2) | 84.03 (0.2) | 85.16 (0.4) | 86.45 (0.6) | 87.01(0.1) |
| | +Dropout | 63.11 (0.3) | 83.45 (0.7) | 84.87 (0.4) | 85.63 (0.7) | 86.61 (0.4) |
| | +WD | 63.21 (0.8) | 83.56(0.6) | 84.93(0.5) | 85.77 (0.8) | **86.79** (0.4) |
| | +KL-Norm | **70.16** (0.9) | **87.17** (0.7) | **87.93** (0.8) | **88.44** (0.4) | **89.08** (0.3) |
| | Δ | +6.95 | +4.02 | +3.61 | +2.86 | +2.16 |
| ESD | Wav2Vec | 55.23 (0.7) | 62.02 (0.8) | 72.56 (0.3) | 75.01 (0.4) | 77.12 (0.5) |
| | +BN | 56.82 (0.6) | 62.93 (0.6) | 73.67 (0.4) | 75.43 (0.8) | 77.88 (0.7) |
| | +LN | 56.36 (0.3) | 62.58 (0.7) | 73.11 (0.8) | 75.19 (0.6) | 77.16 (0.4) |
| | +GN | 55.08 (0.3) | 62.11 (0.2) | 72.36 (0.8) | 74.79 (0.6) | 76.52 (0.4) |
| | +Dropout | 54.15 (0.6) | 61.66 (0.8) | 71.56(0.7) | 74.33 (0.2) | 76.21 (0.4) |
| | +WD | 54.34 (0.7) | 61.79 (0.6) | 71.62 (0.4) | 74.72 (0.9) | 76.19 (0.8) |
| | KL-Norm | **59.62** (0.7) | **65.86** (0.8) | **75.67** (0.6) | **77.13** (0.2) | **78.53** (0.7) |
| | Δ | +4.39 | +3.84 | +3.11 | +2.12 | +1.41 |
| Crema | Wav2vec | 52.12 (0.2) | 57.13 (1.2) | 59.74 (0.5) | 63.76 (0.5) | 65.67 (0.6) |
| | +BN | 52.07 (0.2) | 58.03 (0.9) | 59.76 (0.7) | 64.62 (0.8) | 65.26 (0.2) |
| | +LN | 51.38 (0.9) | 57.29 (0.8) | 59.16 (0.7) | 64.01 (0.6) | 64.94 (0.7) |
| | +GN | 51.05 (0.9) | 57.12 (0.4) | 59.21 (0.2) | 63.42 (0.8) | 63.79 (0.6) |
| | +Dropout | 50.61 (0.7) | 56.88 (0.8) | 57.03 (0.8) | 62.67 (0.6) | 63.08 (0.7) |
| | +WD | 50.88 (0.7) | 56.91 (0.7) | 57.28 (0.6) | 62.84 (0.2) | 63.19 (0.4) |
| | +KL-Norm | **55.45** (0.8) | **58.95** (1.3) | **61.21** (0.9) | **64.89** (0.8) | **66.57** (0.6) |
| | Δ | +3.33 | +1.82 | +1.47 | +1.13 | +0.90 |

Table 4 shows that KL-Norm gives an average improvement of 2.62% and 4.5% over accuracy when trained with SNLI and MNLI respectively from BERT$_{Base}$ model. It has shown substantial improvement against all other baseline models. These results support our claim that KL-Norm motivates learning more general features, rather than redundant superficial features, leading to an improved generalization to datasets without these superficial biases.

**Table 4.** Test accuracy of models transferring to new target datasets. All models are trained on SNLI or MNLI and tested on the target datasets.

| Data | SNLI | | | | | | MNLI | | | | | |
|---|---|---|---|---|---|---|---|---|---|---|---|---|
| | BERT$_{Base}$ | +BN | +LN | +GN | +KL-Norm | Δ | BERT$_{Base}$ | +BN | +LN | +GN | +KL-Norm | Δ |
| JOCI | 46.03 | 47.13 | 44.67 | 45.55 | 51.82 | +5.79 | 46.41 | 48.12 | 45.21 | 44.31 | 54.11 | +7.7 |
| ADD1 | 45.61 | 38.75 | 44.7 | 39.81 | 44.14 | −1.47 | 51.22 | 35.65 | 46.42 | 47.21 | 56.67 | +5.45 |
| DPR | 49.22 | 49.12 | 49.18 | 49.11 | 50.31 | +1.09 | 49.95 | 49.31 | 49.4 | 49.3 | 50.11 | +0.16 |
| SPR | 37.07 | 35.43 | 37.48 | 35.55 | 36.12 | +1.7 | 42.37 | 40.45 | 45.12 | 42.11 | 43.17 | +0.80 |
| FN+ | 45.31 | 50.61 | 44.31 | 47.71 | 47.35 | −0.95 | 43.5 | 43.2 | 43.53 | 43.3 | 44.88 | +1.38 |
| SICK | 53.06 | 46.78 | 53.98 | 45.11 | 55.61 | +2.55 | 65.07 | 62.43 | 66.60 | 63.33 | 71.64 | +6.53 |
| MPE | 58.12 | 57.21 | 57.44 | 54.33 | 63.61 | +5.48 | 55.10 | 54.43 | 57.5 | 56.48 | 58.31 | +3.21 |
| SCITAIL | 64.81 | 58.13 | 65.23 | 58.43 | 70.88 | +6.07 | 64.67 | 67.49 | 66.61 | 64.31 | 75.43 | +10.76 |
| QQP | 62.91 | 60.93 | 59.88 | 58.07 | 65.87 | +2.96 | 63.38 | 60.16 | 62.89 | 60.11 | 69.67 | +6.29 |
| SNLI Hard | 64.39 | 63.12 | 65.37 | 63.31 | 67.45 | +3.06 | 54.11 | 53.78 | 54.38 | 53.55 | 56.91 | +2.8 |
| Average | --- | --- | --- | --- | --- | +2.62 | --- | --- | --- | --- | --- | +4.50 |

## 4.6 Impact of KL-Norm on Overfitting

We analyze the effect of KL-Norm on the generalization of model and in reducing overfitting. We analyze the effect of the $\beta$ parameter on training and validation error. We fix the bottleneck size $(K)$ based on the models selected in Sect. 4.4, and we train KL-Norm model on the GLUE benchmark for varying values of $\beta$ and plot the validation and training loss in Fig. 3.

KL-Norm has little effect for the small value of $\beta$ as the validation loss is substantially higher than training loss showing the case of over-fitting. This is because network become too deterministic ($\Sigma \approx 0$) and learns irrelevant features not needed to predict the labels. As we increase the $\beta$, we see the better generalization of the network. As the $\beta$ become too large, again the validation loss increases as it starts blocks relevant features needed to predict the labels.

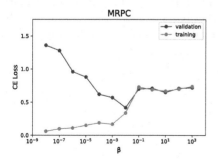
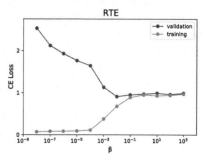

**Fig. 3.** Validation and training losses of VI-Norm for varying $\beta$ and a fixed bottleneck size on GLUE.

## 4.7    Analysis of Removal of Irrelevant Features

We have used [4,10] framework to evaluate whether the debiasing methods are succesful in removing the biases from sentence or not. After debiasing, the trained encoder is frozen and the classifier is retrained to try to extract the biases. If the classifier reaches high accuracy given only bias features, then the encoder's representation has not been successfully debiased. We train a classifier which only sees the representation of the hypothesis sentence and see if it can predict the class of the sentence pair, which is an established criterion to measure known biases in NLI datasets [16]. Thus, we freeze the trained encoders from our model and the BERT baseline and retrain a hypothesis-only classifier on hypotheses from the SNLI and MNLI datasets. For reference, we compare to a hypothesis-only model with a BERT encoder trained end-to-end. Table 5 shows the results which shows that KL-Norm is able to achieve lower accuracy against all baseline models.

**Table 5.** Hypothesis-only accuracy when freezing the encoder from models trained on SNLI/MNLI in Table 2 and retraining a hypothesis-only classifier, and baseline results when the encoder is not frozen (H-only). Lower results show more successful debiasing.

| Model | SNLI | | | MNLI | | |
|---|---|---|---|---|---|---|
| | Train | Dev | Test | Train | Dev | Test |
| H-only | 95.2 | 56.62 | 55.78 | 83.12 | 51.34 | 51.12 |
| BERT$_{Base}$ | 73.2 | 51.87 | 51.17 | 52.7 | 42.68 | 43.55 |
| +BN | 71.1 | 51.91 | 51.11 | 58.5 | 44.68 | 44.03 |
| +LN | 70.9 | 51.98 | 52.26 | 58.5 | 44.68 | 44.03 |
| +GN | 71.9 | 52.75 | 53.08 | 58.7 | 44.91 | 44.72 |
| +KL-Norm | 49.5 | **41.41** | **40.12** | 37.4 | **35.28** | **35.99** |

## 4.8    Analysis of Model Parameters

Table 6 shows the efficiency evaluation of the proposed model in terms of number of model parameters and memory overheads with K = 512. The peak memory overheads increases by 1.92% against all other baseline model. KL-norm has substantially lower memory overheads as compared to weight decay and negligible increment(1.68%) of the model parameters.

**Table 6.** Performance evaluation for all methods. $\Delta\%$ are relative differences with BERT$_{\text{Base}}$.

| Model | Memory | $\Delta\%$ | #Parameters | $\Delta\%$ |
|---|---|---|---|---|
| BERT$_{\text{Base}}$ | 418.74 GB | — | 109.48 M | — |
| +BN | 418.74 GB | 0% | 109.48 M | 0% |
| +LN | 418.74 GB | 0% | 109.48 M | 0% |
| +GN | 418.74 GB | 0% | 109.48 M | 0% |
| +WD | 506.19 GB | 20.88% | 109.48 M | 0% |
| +Dropout | 418.74 GB | 0% | 109.48 M | 0% |
| +KL-Norm | 426.80 GB | 1.92 % | 111.33 M | 1.68% |

## 4.9 Ablation Study

***Analysis of Model without KL Loss.*** Table 7 shows the evaluation on three GLUE datasets without regularization loss($\beta =0$). The architecture just reduces to deterministic dimensionality reduction with an MLP. This evaluation shows the performance increment while adding the regularization loss.

**Table 7.** Average ablation results over 5 runs with std in parentheses on GLUE.

| Model | MRPC | | RTE |
|---|---|---|---|
| | Accuracy | F1 | Accuracy |
| BERT$_{\text{Base}}$ | 84.31 (0.2) | 89.01 (0.2) | 64.23 (1.8) |
| +BN | 86.76 (0.5) | 90.49 (0.5) | 66.42 (1.4) |
| +LN | 85.23 (0.3) | 88.12 (0.7) | 65.17 (0.9) |
| +GN | 85.01 (0.2) | 87.98 (0.5) | 65.55 (0.2) |
| +KL-Norm ($\beta=0$) | 86.27 (0.4) | 90.03 (0.3) | 67.17 (0.8) |
| +KL-Norm | **87.25 (0.1)** | **91.03 (0.6)** | **70.42 (0.8)** |

**Table 8.** Average accuracy over 5 runs with std in parentheses in High resource setting

| Model | MNLI | QNLI | GoogleC |
|---|---|---|---|
| BERT$_{Base}$ | 82.92(0.24) | 90.12(0.12) | – |
| +BN | 82.23 (0.21) | 89.14(0.23) | – |
| +LN | 82.98 (0.18) | 90.34 (0.14) | – |
| +GN | 82.01 (0.13) | 90.01 (0.15) | – |
| +KL-Norm | 82.27 (0.28) | 90.03 (0.09) | – |
| Wav2Vec | – | – | 94.78(0.12) |
| +BN | – | – | 93.12(0.13) |
| +LN | – | – | 94.84(0.17) |
| +GN | – | – | 94.52(0.31) |
| +KL-Norm | – | – | 94.29(0.21) |

***Analysis of Model in High Resource Setting.*** We have done the experiments win high resource setting with two NLP datasets (MNLI and QNLI)and one speech datasets (Google speech Command) to see the behaviour of the proposed model. We found the results are comparable with other normalization techniques as shown in Table 8. The reason is the learnable parameters of traditional normalization techniques is able to make the data well behaved with the proposed KL regularized normalization in higher resource settings.

## 5    Conclusion

In this paper, we have proposed a novel KL Regularized normalization framework, KL-Norm, that calculates the rescaling parameters of normalization along with imposing the gaussian prior through KL loss. It incorporates stochasticity which gives ensemble effect that helps the model to give higher accuracy. Addition of KL loss acts as a regularizer that reduces overfitting and better generalization. It removes the irrelevant features of data. This approach is based on density estimation which performs better on out of domain generalization. Experimental evaluations on low resource downstream NLP tasks using pretrained BERT and speech task using pretrained Wav2Vec2.0 model demonstrate superior performance of the proposed framework against baseline models.

## References

1. Asperti, A., Trentin, M.: Balancing reconstruction error and kullback-leibler divergence in variational autoencoders (2020)
2. Ba, J., Kiros, J., Hinton, G.E.: Layer normalization. arXiv preprint arXiv:1607.06450 (2016)
3. Baevski, A., Zhou, H., Rahman Mohamed, A., Auli, M.: wav2vec 2.0: A framework for self-supervised learning of speech representations. arXiv preprint arXiv:2006.11477 (2020)

4. Belinkov, Y., Poliak, A., Shieber, S., Durme, B.V., Rush, A.M.: On adversarial removal of hypothesis-only bias in natural language inference. In: Proceedings of the Eighth Joint Conference on Lexical and Computational Semantics (SEMEVAL) (2019)
5. Bowman, S., Vilnis, L., Vinyals, O., Dai, A., Jozefowicz, R., Bengio, S.: Generating sentences from a continuous space. In: Proceedings of The 20th SIGNLL Conference on Computational Natural Language Learning (CoNLL) (2016)
6. Chaudhari, P., et al.: Entropy-SGD: biasing gradient descent into wide valleys. In: 5th International Conference on Learning Representations, ICLR 2017, Toulon, France, 24–26 April 2017, Conference Track Proceedings (2017)
7. Cooijmans, T., Ballas, N., Laurent, C., Courville, A.C.: Recurrent batch normalization. arXiv preprint arXiv:1603.09025 (2017)
8. Devlin, J., Chang, M.W., Lee, K., Toutanova, K.: BERT: pre-training of deep bidirectional transformers for language understanding. In: Proceedings of the 2019 Conference of the North American Chapter of the Association for Computational Linguistics (NAACL) (2019)
9. Devries, T., Taylor, G.W.: Learning confidence for out-of-distribution detection in neural networks. arXiv preprint arXiv:1802.04865 (2018)
10. Elazar, Y., Goldberg, Y.: Adversarial removal of demographic attributes from text data. In: Proceedings of the 2018 Conference on Empirical Methods in Natural Language Processing (EMNLP) (2018)
11. Fan, Z., Li, M., Zhou, S., Xu, B.: Exploring wav2vec 2.0 on speaker verification and language identification. arXiv preprint arXiv:2012.06185 (2021)
12. Ganin, Y., et al.: Domain-adversarial training of neural networks. J. Mach. Learn. Res. $17$(1), 2096–2030 (2016). http://dl.acm.org/citation.cfm?id=2946645.2946704
13. Gong, Y., Luo, H., Zhang, J.: Natural language inference over interaction space. In: International Conference on Learning Representations (ICLR) (2017)
14. Goodfellow, I., Bengio, Y., Courville, A.: Deep Learning. MIT Press, Cambridge (2016). http://www.deeplearningbook.org
15. Goodfellow, I., et al.: Generative adversarial nets. In: Advances in Neural Information Processing Systems. vol. 27, pp. 2672–2680 (2014)
16. Gururangan, S., Swayamdipta, S., Levy, O., Schwartz, R., Bowman, S., Smith, N.A.: Annotation artifacts in natural language inference data. In: Proceedings of the 2018 Conference of the North American Chapter of the Association for Computational Linguistics (NAACL) (2018)
17. Hannun, A.Y., et al.: Deep speech: Scaling up end-to-end speech recognition. arXiv preprint arXiv:1412.5567 (2014)
18. Hao, Y., Dong, L., Wei, F., Xu, K.: Visualizing and understanding the effectiveness of BERT. In: Proceedings of the 2019 Conference on Empirical Methods in Natural Language Processing and the 9th International Joint Conference on Natural Language Processing (EMNLP-IJCNLP), pp. 4141–4150. Association for Computational Linguistics, Hong Kong, China (Nov 2019)
19. Huang, X., Belongie, S.J.: Arbitrary style transfer in real-time with adaptive instance normalization. In: 2017 IEEE International Conference on Computer Vision (ICCV), pp. 1510–1519 (2017)
20. Ioffe, S., Szegedy, C.: Batch normalization: Accelerating deep network training by reducing internal covariate shift. arXiv preprint arXiv:1502.03167 (2015)

21. Izmailov, P., Podoprikhin, D., Garipov, T., Vetrov, D., Wilson, A.G.: Averaging weights leads to wider optima and better generalization. In: Silva, R., Globerson, A., Globerson, A. (eds.) 34th Conference on Uncertainty in Artificial Intelligence 2018, UAI 2018, pp. 876–885. 34th Conference on Uncertainty in Artificial Intelligence 2018, UAI 2018, Association For Uncertainty in Artificial Intelligence (AUAI) (2018)

22. Jia, S., Chen, D.J., Chen, H.T.: Instance-level meta normalization. In: 2019 IEEE/CVF Conference on Computer Vision and Pattern Recognition (CVPR), pp. 4860–4868 (2019)

23. Khot, T., Sabharwal, A., Clark, P.: SciTaiL: a textual entailment dataset from science question answering. In: AAAI Conference on Artificial Intelligence (2018)

24. Kim, J.H., Jun, J., Zhang, B.T.: Bilinear attention networks. In: Advances in Neural Information Processing Systems (NeurIPS) (2018)

25. Kim, T., Song, I., Bengio, Y.: Dynamic layer normalization for adaptive neural acoustic modeling in speech recognition. arXiv preprint arXiv:1707.06065 (2017)

26. Kliger, M., Fleishman, S.: Novelty detection with GAN. arXiv preprint arXiv:1802.10560 (2018)

27. Kou, Z., You, K., Long, M., Wang, J.: Stochastic normalization. In: Advances in Neural Information Processing Systems (NeurIPS) (2020)

28. Krogh, A., Hertz, J.A.: A simple weight decay can improve generalization. In: Advances in Neural Information Processing Systems (NeurIPS) (1992)

29. Lai, A., Bisk, Y., Hockenmaier, J.: Natural language inference from multiple premises. In: Proceedings of the Eighth International Joint Conference on Natural Language Processing (IJCNLP) (2017)

30. Lee, C., Cho, K., Kang, W.: Mixout: Effective regularization to finetune large-scale pretrained language models. In: International Conference on Learning Representations (ICLR) (2019)

31. Luo, P., Zhang, R., Ren, J., Peng, Z., Li, J.: Switchable normalization for learning-to-normalize deep representation. IEEE Trans. Pattern Anal. Mach. Intell. **43**, 712–728 (2021)

32. Mahabadi, K.R., Belinkov, Y., Henderson, J.: End-to-end bias mitigation by modelling biases in corpora. In: Proceedings of the 58th Annual Meeting of the Association for Computational Linguistics (ACL) (2020)

33. Marelli, M., Menini, S., Baroni, M., Bentivogli, L., Bernardi, R., Zamparelli, R.: A SICK cure for the evaluation of compositional distributional semantic models. In: Proceedings of the Ninth International Conference on Language Resources and Evaluation (LREC) (2014)

34. Mosbach, M., Andriushchenko, M., Klakow, D.: On the stability of fine-tuning BERT: misconceptions, explanations, and strong baselines. In: International Conference on Learning Representations (ICLR) (2021)

35. Nam, H., Kim, H.E.: Batch-instance normalization for adaptively style-invariant neural networks. In: Advances in Neural Information Processing Systems (NeurIPS) (2018)

36. Nesterov, Y.: Introductory lectures on convex optimization - a basic course. In: Applied Optimization (2004)

37. Niranjan, A., Sharma, M.C., Gutha, S.B.C., Shaik, M.A.B.: End-to-end whisper to natural speech conversion using modified transformer network (2021)

38. Park, T., Liu, M.Y., Wang, T.C., Zhu, J.Y.: Semantic image synthesis with spatially-adaptive normalization. In: Proceedings of the IEEE Conference on Computer Vision and Pattern Recognition (2019)

39. Pavlick, E., Callison-Burch, C.: Most "babies" are "little" and most "problems" are "huge": Compositional entailment in adjective-nouns. In: Proceedings of the 54th Annual Meeting of the Association for Computational Linguistics (ACL) (2016)
40. Pavlick, E., Wolfe, T., Rastogi, P., Callison-Burch, C., Dredze, M., Van Durme, B.: Framenet+: Fast paraphrastic tripling of frameNet. In: Proceedings of the 53rd Annual Meeting of the Association for Computational Linguistics (ACL) (2015)
41. Radford, A., Wu, J., Child, R., Luan, D., Amodei, D., Sutskever, I.: Language models are unsupervised multitask learners (2019)
42. Rahman, A., Ng, V.: Resolving complex cases of definite pronouns: the winograd schema challenge. In: Proceedings of the 2012 Joint Conference on Empirical Methods in Natural Language Processing (EMNPL) (2012)
43. Reisinger, D., Rudinger, R., Ferraro, F., Harman, C., Rawlins, K., Van Durme, B.: Semantic proto-roles. In: Transactions of the Association for Computational Linguistics (TACL) (2015)
44. Salimans, T., Kingma, D.P.: Weight normalization: A simple reparameterization to accelerate training of deep neural networks. In: Advances in Neural Information Processing Systems (NIPS) (2016)
45. Srivastava, N., Hinton, G., Krizhevsky, A., Sutskever, I., Salakhutdinov, R.: Dropout: a simple way to prevent neural networks from overfitting. In: Journal of Machine Learning Research (JMLR) (2014)
46. Tan, S., Zhang, J.: An empirical study of sentiment analysis for Chinese documents. Expert Syst. Appl. **34**(4), 2622–2629 (2008). https://doi.org/10.1016/j.eswa.2007.05.028, http://dx.doi.org/10.1016/j.eswa.2007.05.028
47. Ulyanov, D., Vedaldi, A., Lempitsky, V.: Instance normalization: The missing ingredient for fast stylization. arXiv preprint arXiv:1607.08022 (2016)
48. Wang, Z., Hamza, W., Florian, R.: Bilateral multi-perspective matching for natural language sentences. In: Proceedings of the Twenty-Sixth International Joint Conference on Artificial Intelligence (IJCAI) (2017)
49. White, A.S., Rastogi, P., Duh, K., Van Durme, B.: Inference is everything: recasting semantic resources into a unified evaluation framework. In: Proceedings of the Eighth International Joint Conference on Natural Language Processing (IJCNLP) (2017)
50. Wolf, T., et al.: HuggingFace's transformers: state-of-the-art natural language processing. arXiv:1910.03771 (2019)
51. Wu, Y., He, K.: Group normalization. In: Proceedings of the European Conference on Computer Vision (ECCV) (2018)
52. Yadav, H., Gupta, A., Rallabandi, S.K., Black, A.W., Shah, R.R.: Intent classification using pre-trained embeddings for low resource languages (2021)
53. Zhang, S., Rudinger, R., Duh, K., Van Durme, B.: Ordinal common-sense inference. In: TACL (2017)
54. Zhang, T., Wu, F., Katiyar, A., Weinberger, K.Q., Artzi, Y.: Revisiting few-sample BERT fine-tuning. In: International Conference on Learning Representations (ICLR) (2021)
55. Zhou, K., Yang, J., Loy, C.C., Liu, Z.: Learning to prompt for vision-language models. Int. J. Comput. Vis. **130**, 2337–2348 (2022)
56. Zoph, B., Yuret, D., May, J., Knight, K.: Transfer learning for low-resource neural machine translation. In: Proceedings of the 2016 Conference on Empirical Methods in Natural Language Processing, pp. 1568–1575. Association for Computational Linguistics, Austin, Texas (Nov 2016)

# Improving Autoregressive NLP Tasks via Modular Linearized Attention

Victor Agostinelli[✉] and Lizhong Chen

Oregon State University, Corvallis, OR 97330, USA
{agostinv,chenliz}@oregonstate.edu

**Abstract.** Various natural language processing (NLP) tasks necessitate models that are efficient and small based on their ultimate application at the edge or other resource-constrained environment. While prior research has reduced the size of these models, increasing computational efficiency without considerable performance impacts remains difficult, especially for autoregressive tasks. This paper proposes *modular linearized attention (MLA)*, which combines multiple efficient attention mechanisms, including cosFormer [32], to maximize inference quality while achieving notable speedups. We validate this approach on several autoregressive NLP tasks, including speech-to-text neural machine translation (S2T NMT), speech-to-text simultaneous translation (SimulST), and autoregressive text-to-spectrogram, noting efficiency gains on TTS and competitive performance for NMT and SimulST during training and inference.

**Keywords:** attention linearization · autoregressive inference · text-to-spectrogram · neural machine translation · simultaneous translation

## 1 Introduction

Transformers [37] have provided researchers and industry leaders with new ways to take advantage of sequential data in natural language processing (NLP), computer vision, and a number of other fields [10,12,26]. Constructing efficient transformers that address the bottleneck of classical, quadratic attention mechanisms is a long-standing effort. Associated efficiency gains, however, are often coupled with significant inference quality costs. Prior transformer development has focused on mitigating those costs in several ways, such as carefully limiting available context for each token [29,35,41], making assumptions about the condition of the intermediate $QK^T$ matrix and applying pattern-based attention [3,6,43], or attempting to model the input matrices in a lower dimensional space [39]. Unfortunately, the aforementioned methods often are limited in their scope and can perform poorly when attempting to generalize to new tasks, in many cases due to environmental assumptions.

While truly linearized attention, with no prior environmental assumptions, is possible via several newer methods [7,14], these implementations often struggle to approach the inference quality of quadratic, softmax-based attention. cosFormer [32] is a recently proposed, state-of-the-art attention linearization technique that focuses on providing a tight approximation of softmax functionality

D. Koutra et al. (Eds.): ECML PKDD 2023, LNAI 14172, pp. 90–106, 2023.
https://doi.org/10.1007/978-3-031-43421-1_6

for attention mechanisms. It emphasizes token locality and is proven to maintain long-range dependencies. In spite of its excellent performance on a range of tasks, there are significant limitations associated with cosFormer. These include a lack of validation on decoder cross-attention and suffering from a training to evaluation environment mismatch concerning sequence length availability for most autoregressive tasks. Moreover, that aforementioned token locality emphasis necessarily limits the widespread applicability of cosFormer.

Noting the issues facing current efficient transformers and problems concerning the applicability of individual efficient attention mechanisms, we propose *modular linearized attention (MLA)*, a new design method that combines multiple attention paradigms for different attention blocks in a tight search space. This method avoids the pitfalls of a "one-size-fits-all" approach to efficient transformer construction. To enable *MLA* for cosFormer, we propose an augmentation to its general formulation to allow for its application to decoder cross-attention. Additionally, as cosFormer struggles with most autoregressive tasks with dynamic sequence lengths, we propose several techniques related to predicting the target sequence length. The effectiveness of our approach is demonstrated across multiple tasks, with efficiency gains of up to a 7% increase in decoder throughput during inference for autoregressive text-to-spectrogram (TTS), inference quality gains of 0.6 BLEU for English to German (en-de) speech-to-text neural machine translation (S2T NMT), and even a perplexity reduction of 0.44 during training for English to German speech-to-text simultaneous translation (SimulST).

## 2    Background and Motivation

### 2.1    Fundamentals of Transformers and Attention

The core architecture of Vaswani et al. [37] original transformer has been studied exhaustively, so we will only review its attention-based elements. General transformer attention blocks receive a query $Q$ in $\mathbb{R}^{N_1 \times d_k}$, a key $K$ in $\mathbb{R}^{N_2 \times d_k}$, and a value $V$ in $\mathbb{R}^{N_2 \times d_v}$. Classically, a softmax operator is applied to the product of the query and key to further distance tokens that are less relevant to one another and generate a probability distribution. These attention blocks are usually multi-headed for heads $H$ and the original embedding space is divided between each head before being reformed by concatenating the head outputs. Each attention head projects the input matrices into this new sub-space via weight matrices $W_h^q$ in $\mathbb{R}^{d_k \times d_{kh}}$, $W_h^k$ in $\mathbb{R}^{d_k \times d_{kh}}$, and $W_h^v$ in $\mathbb{R}^{d_v \times d_{vh}}$ for some head $h$ in $H$. A final output projection layer is characterized by $W_O$ in $\mathbb{R}^{Hd_v \times d_{model}}$ and is applied to the concatenation of head outputs. General formulations for multi-head attention calculations of a classical transformer are provided by Eqs. 1 and 2.

$$a_h = softmax(\frac{QW_h^q K^T W_h^k}{\sqrt{d_{kh}}})W_h^v V \tag{1}$$

$$A_{mha} = concat(a_1, a_2, \ldots, a_H)W_O \tag{2}$$

## 2.2  Linear Transformers

The quadratic bottleneck of Vaswani et al. attention mechanism would prove problematic for workloads with long sequences, sometimes precluding the deployment of a transformer-based model. A plethora of efficient transformers exist [6,9,15,18,35,39,41], but Katharopoulos et al. [14] introduce the first attention mechanism of truly $O(n)$ run-time complexity with no prior environmental assumptions by reordering the quadratic attention calculation, as explained by the caption in Fig. 1. This is normally impossible due to the softmax operator removing any associability for the query and key matrices. Katharapoulos et al. elect to replace that softmax operator with a non-linear similarity function that they denote as a function $S$ that is distributable, meaning that $S(Q, K^T) = S_q(Q)S_k(K^T)$. This reordering is demonstrated in a row-wise manner for the output matrix of the attention mechanism via Eqs. 3, 4, and 5 where $A_i$ is equivalent to one output row $i$ in $N_1$ for classical softmax attention and $\tilde{A}_i$ is equivalent to one output row $i$ in $N_1$ for truly linear attention.

Critically, Katharapolous et al. note that their implementation can achieve throughput that is orders of magnitude higher than classical attention for very long sequences. This is accomplished for autoregressive tasks via a data-reuse opportunity present in the $K^T V$ intermediate matrix and the normalization vector of a given autoregressive attention calculation, which is highlighted and explained by Fig. 2.

$$A_i = \sum_j \frac{exp(Q_i K_j^T)}{\sum_j exp(Q_i K_j^T)} V_j \tag{3}$$

$$\tilde{A}_i = \sum_j \frac{S(Q_i K_j^T)}{\sum_j S(Q_i K_j^T)} V_j = \sum_j \frac{S_q(Q_i)S_k(K_j^T)}{\sum_j S_q(Q_i)S_k(K_j^T)} V_j \tag{4}$$

$$\tilde{A}_i = \sum_j \frac{S_q(Q_i)(S_k(K_j^T)V_j)}{S_q(Q_i) \sum_j S_k(K_j^T)} \tag{5}$$

While Katharapolous et al. work is foundational and inspired the development of a number of linearized attention mechanisms (e.g. [7,32]), it can struggle to match the inference quality of other schemes. Their similarity function, defined as $S(M) = ELU(M) + 1$, was settled on seemingly arbitrarily. In response, Choromanski et al. [7] propose Performer, an extremely efficient transformer that makes use of the aforementioned reordering mechanism in addition to several techniques to better emulate softmax-based attention without any prior assumptions. Instead of employing an ELU for their similarity function, Choromanski et al. choose to use positive and orthogonal random feature maps in addition to a customized kernel function to approximate softmax attention. Performer remains a somewhat popular paradigm and has inspired several similar schemes [1,30,42]. Unfortunately, Performer can suffer from some instability depending on the environment due to its stochastic properties [32].

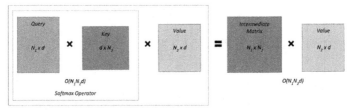

**Classical Softmax Attention**

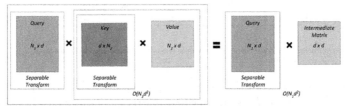

**Reordered Linearized Attention**

**Fig. 1.** Illustration of attention calculation reordering and linearization for one attention head. This mechanism is useful when both $N_1$ and $N_2$ are significantly larger than $d$, which occurs for many applications or for models with many attention heads with smaller samples. When this condition is met, run-time is linearized from $O(N_1 N_2)$ to $O(N_1) + O(N_2)$ for an arbitrary decoding time-step, assuming that neither size is significantly greater than the other.

### 2.3 cosFormer and Re-weighting Mechanisms

Similar to its prominent predecessors, cosFormer, proposed by Qin et al. [32], takes advantage of the reordering opportunities present in linearized attention when the softmax operator is replaced with an approximate similarity function. Additionally, a re-weighting mechanism is proposed that emphasizes locality bias (i.e. a tendency for nearby tokens to attend strongly to one another) observed in the intermediate $QK^T$ matrix of many NLP tasks [8,16] and ensures the positivity of the $QK^T$ matrix. This allows for tight approximation of the softmax operator (i.e. probability distribution concentration, positive $QK^T$ for every score) in linear time and without the random characteristics of Performer. Given that, they employed the decomposable re-weighting function described in Eq. 6 to self-attention blocks, where $N$ is the length of the input sequence and $S_q$ and $S_k$ are ReLU functions. The maximal response of the function in Eq. 6 occurs when the positions in the query and key are equal and tapers off as that positional difference grows, modeling softmax behavior for attention mechanisms exhibiting locality bias.

$$S(Q_i, K_j^T) = S_q(Q_i) S_k(K_j^T) cos(\frac{\pi}{2}(\frac{i-j}{N})) \tag{6}$$

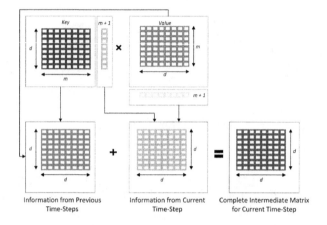

**Fig. 2.** Illustration of one of the data-reuse opportunities present under reordered and linearized attention for the $K^T V$ intermediate matrix for one attention head in decoder self-attention. Past time-steps are represented from decoding time-step 1 to $m$, with the current decoding time-step being represented as $m + 1$.

cosFormer achieves state-of-the-art scores for a number of tasks, including fixed-length autoregressive language modeling on WikiText-103 [2], bi-directional language modeling via insertion into RoBERTa [20] during pre-training, downstream fine-tuning for various text classification tasks on RoBERTa, and competitive results on the Long-Range Arena (LRA) benchmark [36]. The LRA scores are especially superb given the locality-based assumptions baked into cosFormer's re-weighting mechanism that should discourage long-range dependencies.

## 2.4   Motivation for Investigation

While many capable efficient attention mechanisms exist, their widespread applicability is usually limited by prior assumptions (e.g. assuming sparsity or expressivity of low-rank approximations) or by poor inference quality outside of a few tasks. Even for a single application, multiple attention blocks can behave significantly differently such that broadly applying a single efficient attention mechanism may produce poor results. In spite of these difficulties, many complex autoregressive applications such as S2T NMT, SimulST, and TTS, desire efficient attention mechanisms for their associated throughput increases.

Applying a state-of-the-art technique like cosFormer to mitigate inference quality loss for the aforementioned applications is natural. However, some issues exist for cosFormer when it is applied to autoregressive tasks without a fixed length. First and foremost, cosFormer has no method to deal with the mismatch between casual training and the evaluation environment as far as target sequence length availability is concerned. Simply stepping the target sequence length at each decoding time-step (i.e. setting it equal to the current sequence length) is a poor solution for most tasks and leads to unstoppable inference for TTS with absurd distortion and BLEU scores of essentially 0 for en-de NMT and SimulST. Moreover, while locality bias is often present for attention mechanisms, it is not always relevant depending on the application and on the attention mechanism. We will demonstrate later in this paper that applications often do not meet expectations about their emphasis or lack thereof on token locality for various attention blocks. Additionally, cosFormer was never extended to decoder cross-attention, necessarily limiting the scope of its applicability.

Others have attempted to apply cosFormer to new tasks, but have applied this linearization method to autoregressive tasks, in particular, with extremely limited success. Liu et al. [21] worked to apply cosFormer to text-to-text en-de NMT as part of an architecture search enhancement [11]. However, linearizing any of the decoder attention blocks in their study resulted in BLEU scores of 0. Additionally, as they explored the validity of applying cosFormer to new tasks, they varied a number of parameters tied to the models they studied, including number of layers, FFN dimensions, and model embedding dimensions, rendering their evaluation of cosFormer as a methodology somewhat unreliable.

## 3 Proposed Approach

### 3.1 Modular Linearized Attention

In recognizing that cosFormer, and other linearization techniques, are often built with specific properties in mind that are not always present on an application-basis, we propose *modular linearized attention (MLA)*[1]. This method combines efficient attention mechanisms in a modular manner to take advantage of the strengths of different linearization schemes while avoiding applying them to attention blocks that do not exhibit desired characteristics. This paper firmly urges model designers to avoid seeking a "one size fits all" attention linearization solution, as we will later demonstrate that these solutions are typically inferior to a modular combination in terms of inference quality. Equation 7 is a brief formulation of our method for an encoder-decoder transformer-based model $T$.

$$T(eSA(A_t),\ dSA(A_t),\ dCA(A_t)),\ A_t = \{softmax,\ cosFormer,\ ReLU\} \quad (7)$$

As described in Eq. 7, our total search space is denoted as softmax, cosFormer, or simple ReLU attention (identity re-weighting function) for the following attention blocks: $eSA$ for encoder self-attention, $dSA$ for decoder self-attention, and $dCA$ for decoder cross-attention. To determine an appropriate combination of attention blocks for each task, we propose targeted ablation studies on an attention block-basis. It should be noted that a lower level of granularity could be applied for layer-by-layer *MLA* (i.e. applying cosFormer to multiple layers in the decoder while applying simple ReLU to layers with attention blocks that do not emphasize token locality), but we leave this to future work to explore.

---

[1] Materials found at https://github.com/OSU-STARLAB/Modular-Linearized-Attention.

## 3.2    Augmenting CosFormer for Decoder Cross-Attention

In the interest of enabling *MLA* for state-of-the-art linearization techniques that employ sequence length-based re-weighting, in the vein of cosFormer, we propose a generalization of cosFormer for decoder cross-attention. This generalization is defined by Eq. 8, which preserves cosFormer's original design intent behind locality between relative positions by applying them to both sequences being attended to in cross-attention (*M* is set equal to the length of the key and value matrices). Failing to produce this generalization, as in the original cosFormer, would preclude investigation of cosFormer for many possible attention mechanisms, limiting the modular attention search space unnecessarily.

$$S(Q_i, K_j^T) = S_q(Q_i)S_k(K_j^T)cos(\frac{\pi}{2}(\frac{i}{N} - \frac{j}{M})) \tag{8}$$

## 3.3    Closing the Gap: Target Sequence Length Prediction

Any sequence length-based re-weighting mechanism, like the one cosFormer employs, suffers from a mismatch between the training and evaluation environments concerning the availability of the target sequence length in autoregressive tasks. For autoregressive tasks without a fixed sequence length, the target sequence is unbounded and will only cease after an end of sequence prediction. Two obvious paths to close that gap present themselves. One option would be to replicate the stepping behavior of the current sequence length in the re-weighting mechanism at every decoding time-step (i.e. increasing $N$ and/or $M$ in Eq. 8). This adds a number of sequential steps that, in practice, slow down training significantly or introduce massive memory footprints to enable parallelization of those sequential steps. Moreover, this does not reflect the set history of autoregressive applications. For example, during decoder self-attention, the key entry for time-step $m$ is constant for all later time-steps in softmax-based attention, but would differ at later time-steps for this stepping scheme, which is intuitively erroneous. Alternatively, one could attempt to predict the target sequence length in the evaluation environment, and we consider this option to better reflect autoregressive behavior.

This paper proposes a few simple and computationally cheap solutions for target sequence length prediction. The first is a statistical analysis of the training set, producing a simple ratio $\alpha$ to map between the average source length and target length. The second is a lookup table based on a similar statistical analysis on the average length mapping on a token-to-token basis. The third is learned target length prediction via a compact network of a few convolutional layers and ReLU activations. We validate each of these approaches briefly in the following sections on TTS with a model based on TransformerTTS [19] and reduced dimensionality (training and evaluation details are elaborated upon in later sections), with preliminary results for the translation tasks suggesting that observed trends for TTS extend to translation. Ultimately, we conclude that a simple ratio $\alpha$ provides competitive results while remaining computationally negligible, and we choose to employ it for our evaluation in later sections.

Mel-cepstral distortion (MCD) is the quantitative metric of choice for this exploration, as it isolates phonetic differences between the synthesized and reference spectrograms [17,34,38].

**Sequence Length Prediction via Simple Ratio $\alpha$.** A brief analysis of the training set of LJSpeech [13] suggests a ratio $\alpha$ of around 1.25 between the source sequence to the target sequence for average mapping and a ratio $\alpha$ of around 1.5 for close to 90% of training examples containing positive queries and keys in Eq. 8. The primary question facing this method of target length prediction is clear: is mostly guaranteeing a positive query and key matrix (ensured in softmax-based attention) actually as beneficial cosFormer's construction would suggest? As Table 1 demonstrates, this is not necessarily the case. For example, an $\alpha$ of 1.75 would almost always guarantee positive query and key matrices, but the distortion per reference frame in Table 1 is very large and the summed synthesized sequence lengths are nearly 2.5x the summed reference sequence lengths. Given that, we default to average mappings for later evaluations. We note that this method is computationally negligible during evaluation, and fits well into very tight computational budgets.

**Table 1.** MCD values (lower is better) for differing target length to source length ratios for target length predictions. All models were baseline TransformerTTS architectures with their decoder cross-attention mechanism replaced by cosFormer. Reference duration is approximately 273k frames across all 523 test samples in LJSpeech. Distortion is provided as average distortion per reference frame and per dynamic time-aligned frame [5,40], as optimizing for one or the other would lead to clearly erroneous $\alpha$ values, as demonstrated in this table.

| $\alpha$ Length Ratio | Synth. Dur. (frames) | Dist./Ref | Dist./Align |
|---|---|---|---|
| 0.50 | 167k | 7.42 | 7.05 |
| 0.60 | 212k | 7.73 | 6.99 |
| 0.75 | 307k | 8.49 | 6.59 |
| 1.00 | 431k | 9.70 | 5.75 |
| 1.25 | 531k | 10.74 | 5.27 |
| 1.50 | 650k | 12.00 | 4.88 |
| 1.75 | 772k | 13.30 | 4.59 |

**Sequence Length Prediction via Lookup Table.** The lookup table (LUT) is constructed as a set of mappings from input tokens to the average size of their representation in the output sequence via a statistical analysis similar to the one done for a simple ratio $\alpha$. This method tends to excel when the vocabulary size is relatively small and when token mappings are consistent. The former characteristic minimizes the memory footprint of the LUT and ensures a large enough set of samples for each token mapping (unknown tokens used the average token-to-token mapping) while the latter ensures accurate mappings. In the case of the TTS task exemplified in this section, we pre-processed the input text into phonemes [38] and produced reference alignments via the Montreal Forced Aligner (MFA) [27]. Phonemes are well-suited to this methodology as they should have consistent mappings from the source to target sequence that can be taken advantage of and form a tight vocabulary. In practice, as shown in Table 2, this method performed similarly to a simple ratio $\alpha$, and we attribute this unexpected lack of improvement to extreme variance in predicting the length of silences (or "space" phonemes), errors introduced by MFA itself, and that this method does not take advantage of sequence context. A dampening factor that scales the average mappings is briefly explored as a fine-tuning tool to discourage or encourage the provided model to produce an end of sequence prediction.

**Table 2.** MCD values for various LUT dampening factors. All models contained cos-Former attention blocks for decoder cross-attention with softmax self-attention blocks.

| Dampening Factor | Synth. Dur. (frames) | Dist./Ref | Dist./Align |
|---|---|---|---|
| 1.1 | 342k | 8.81 | 6.11 |
| 1.0 | 378k | 9.20 | 5.89 |
| 0.9 | 450k | 9.56 | 5.55 |

**Sequence Length Prediction via Compact Neural Network.** An intuitive solution, training a compact network to predict the target sequence length should acknowledge source sequence context, unlike the other evaluated methodologies, and result in higher quality predictions. The baseline TransformerTTS was augmented with this network (inspired by the very similar network in FastSpeech2 [33], a non-autoregressive TTS solution) at the end of the encoder stack, and for the following experiment the target sequence length predictor was composed of two convolutional layers with a ReLU activation function tied to the end of each of them. Importantly, limiting the size of this network is required for a fair comparison, as if it requires notable computation time and significantly increases the memory footprint of the model, then it is likely unsuitable for applications where linearized attention is desirable in the first place. That limited size necessarily degrades the quality of the target length prediction and, as seen in Table 3, results in inference quality that is just competitive with the previous two methodologies. We leave it to future work to more closely examine the performance to efficiency trade-off for this augmentation.

## 4   Training and Evaluation Details

To demonstrate the effectiveness of *MLA* we formalize the following experiments on Fairseq [28], a language and sequence-modeling toolkit built in PyTorch. TTS experiments employed the Fairseq $S^2$ extension [38], which contains a number of useful tools for pre-processing and evaluation. TTS was thoroughly explored while additional experiments were also conducted for NMT and SimulST tasks.

**Table 3.** MCD values for various cosFormer ablations with learned target length prediction. Ablations made use of softmax for all attention blocks other than the specified linear ones.

| Linearization Scheme | Synth. Dur. (frames) | Dist./Ref | Dist./Align |
|---|---|---|---|
| cosFormer $dSA$ & $dCA$ | 328k | 9.09 | 6.68 |
| cosFormer $dSA$ | 334k | 8.98 | 6.58 |
| cosFormer $dCA$ | 367k | 9.38 | 6.35 |

### 4.1  Model Configurations and Training Hyperparameters

All models trained for the following TTS experiments were based on TransformerTTS [19] with a length predictor augmentation based on the aforementioned schemes. The S2T NMT and SimulST models were based on models within the ESPnet-ST toolkit that focused on end-to-end S2T translation with a modified cross-attention block for a wait-k and fixed pre-decision paradigm [22–24]. All translation models were pre-trained for automatic speech recognition (ASR) and their encoders were used for initialization when training for en-de S2T NMT [4]. All models were trained on four NVIDIA Tesla V100 GPUs. Further details for model parameters and training hyperparameters can be found in the supplementary materials.

**End of Sequence Training for TTS.** End of sequence prediction is engaged with separately for TTS and is a somewhat sensitive part of the training process, with a single positive output resulting in an end of sequence prediction. If the end of sequence linear layer converges to a poor solution, unstoppable inference can occur and significant overgeneration on the order of 3x to 4x the number of reference output frames can be observed. To compensate for this issue, a multiplicative weighting of 5.0 was applied to a separately calculated end of sequence loss that serves as an additional training objective.

**Target Length Prediction Training.** For learned target length prediction, we adopt a very similar approach to FastSpeech2 [33]. Training goals related to target length prediction were added via separately calculated loss values for the predicted target length on a phoneme-by-phoneme basis, generated via the Montreal Forced Aligner [27]. Target sequence length prediction (and cosFormer) was not applied to simultaneous translation tasks, as predicting the target length is not possible without the oracle knowledge on when a speaker would stop.

### 4.2  Evaluation Setup and Metrics

All models were evaluated within Fairseq's framework or with associated extensions. For SimulST, we employed SimulEval [25] as an evaluation framework and evaluated on a wait-k of 3 and a fixed pre-decision ratio of 7 [24]. All TTS evaluations were executed on a single NVIDIA Tesla V100 and all translation evaluations were executed on a Intel Xeon Platinum 8168 CPU.

**Distortion (MCD) and BLEU.** Mel cepstral distortion (MCD) [17] and mel spectral distortion (MSD) have emerged as popular quantitative metrics for speech synthesis [34, 38, 40]. MCD is calculated as demonstrated in Eq. 9 with dimensionality $K$ of 13 and with the Mel-Frequency Cepstrum Coefficients (MFCCs) $c_{i,k}$ and their synthesized counterparts being calculated via classical methods. MSD is calculated similarly, but contains slightly different embedded information. For the sake of brevity, only MCD is included in later sections.

$$MCD_K = \frac{1}{T} \sum_{t=0}^{T} \sqrt{\sum_{k=1}^{K} (c_{i,k} - c'_{i,k})} \tag{9}$$

All translation models were evaluated via BLEU-4 on sacreBLEU [31]. To ensure a fair comparison to other, similar models, all translations were detokenized before scoring.

## 5 Results

### 5.1 TTS Training Results for Targeted Ablations

To determine how well individual attention blocks demonstrate desired characteristics for each of the attention mechanisms in our proposed search space, we refer to the training results in Table 4 for targeted ablations. cosFormer encoder self-attention and decoder cross-attention ablations perform particularly well. However, a simple ReLU similarity function outperforms cosFormer for decoder self-attention. We note that the decoder self-attention ReLU ablation has slightly higher composite loss than full cosFormer, but combining it with cosFormer via *MLA* should eliminate the EOS loss entirely, as any cosFormer decoder attention block perfectly predicts the end of sequences during training.

It was assumed that TTS, as an application, would exhibit a focus on token locality for all attention blocks, but these training results indicate otherwise for decoder self-attention and validate the necessity of an identity re-weighting mechanism as a performance baseline for this design search. It is worth noting that cosFormer ablations generally overestimate their performance when they are embedded within the decoder, as during training (unless otherwise stated) target sequence lengths are known. We underscore the very poor training results of fully linearized models with homogenous attention linearization schemes, demonstrating the potential of *MLA*.

### 5.2 Training and Evaluation Results for Finalized TTS Configurations

Based on the training results in Table 4, we propose a few *MLA* configurations with optimally placed efficient attention mechanisms for this search. The most efficient combination includes cosFormer being applied to encoder self-attention and decoder cross-attention, with decoder self-attention employing a simple

**Table 4.** TTS training results for various linearization schemes and their ablations. All loss values (lower is better) are provided from the best performing checkpoint on the validation split. Composite loss encompasses all training goals, including MAE loss, MSE loss, and EOS loss. EOS loss corresponds to the separately trained end of sequence loss, which is a critical indicator of inference quality. MSE loss is included explicitly as it served as a tie-breaker for checkpoints with otherwise nearly identical training performance.

| Linearization Scheme | Composite Loss | MSE Loss | EOS Loss |
|---|---|---|---|
| Softmax Attention (non-Linear) | 1.021 | 0.364 | 0.026 |
| Full cosFormer | 1.132 | 0.440 | 0.000 |
| cosFormer $eSA$, Softmax $dSA$ & $dCA$ | 1.063 | 0.385 | 0.029 |
| cosFormer $dSA$, Softmax $eSA$ & $dCA$ | 1.158 | 0.455 | 0.000 |
| cosFormer $dCA$, Softmax $eSA$ & $dSA$ | 1.102 | 0.424 | 0.000 |
| Full Simple ReLU | 1.262 | 0.496 | 0.029 |
| Simple ReLU $eSA$, Softmax $dSA$ & $dCA$ | 1.097 | 0.399 | 0.037 |
| Simple ReLU $dSA$, Softmax $eSA$ & $dCA$ | 1.133 | 0.424 | 0.025 |
| Simple ReLU $dCA$, Softmax $eSA$ & $dSA$ | 1.162 | 0.438 | 0.031 |

ReLU baseline. However, linearizing encoder self-attention and decoder self-attention, while clearly benefiting calculated FLOPs in Table 7, does not influence the practical run-time of the model as significantly. As such, a final model configuration with notable throughput increases while also mitigating inference performance degradation would likely only host cosFormer in the decoder cross-attention block. Direct comparisons to the ablations in Table 4 with the final configurations in Table 5 demonstrate the effectiveness of $MLA$ in producing competitive models, especially noting that the fully linearized $MLA$ model produces better composite loss on the validation set (a difference of 0.013 composite loss) when compared to a model with all attention blocks replaced with cosFormer.

All decoder cosFormer attention blocks made use of a simple ratio $\alpha$ of 1.25 during evaluation. Table 6 represents the distortion of these final configurations. While some additional distortion is present in spite of the application of $MLA$, this distortion is mitigated for this search space while still achieving notable throughput increases. As can be observed in Table 7, around a 5.2% decoder throughput increase (decoder run-time tends to dominate encoder run-time for these tasks, SimulST excepted) was produced with mitigated distortion while the largest decoder speedup produced was around 7% with a fully linearized model, demonstrating the capability of $MLA$ to produce significant efficiency gains with relatively small added distortion.

## 5.3 en-de NMT and SimulST Training and Evaluation Results

Both en-de S2T NMT and SimulST were explored less exhaustively than TTS. For all cosFormer blocks, the target length was predicted via a simple ratio $\alpha$ of

**Table 5.** TTS training results for final *MLA* models with best performing checkpoints on the validation set listed. Softmax is provided again for a quick reference point.

| Linearization Scheme | Composite Loss | MSE Loss | EOS Loss |
|---|---|---|---|
| Softmax Attention (non-Linear) | 1.021 | 0.364 | 0.026 |
| cosFormer *eSA* & *dCA*, ReLU *dSA* | 1.119 | 0.433 | 0.000 |
| cosFormer *eSA* & *dCA*, Softmax *dSA* | 1.105 | 0.426 | 0.000 |
| cosFormer *dCA*, Softmax *eSA* & *dSA* | 1.102 | 0.424 | 0.000 |

**Table 6.** MCD values for various final *MLA* configurations, two of which are not fully linearized due to the size of this workload warranting comparisons with non-linear ablations.

| Linearization Scheme | Synth. Dur. (frames) | Dist./Ref | Dist./Align |
|---|---|---|---|
| Softmax Attention (non-Linear) | 285k | 5.52 | 4.69 |
| cosFormer *eSA* & *dCA*, ReLU *dSA* | 273k | 8.10 | 6.57 |
| cosFormer *eSA* & *dCA*, Softmax *dSA* | 293k | 8.35 | 6.43 |
| cosFormer *dCA*, Softmax *eSA* & *dSA* | 297k | 8.20 | 6.30 |

0.6. Concerning NMT, results can be observed in Tables 8 and 9. While homogeneous, fully linearized models suffered from poor accuracy, models featuring modular linearization and including some quadratic elements tended to exhibit mitigated performance degradation, or even competitive prediction quality, compared to fully quadratic models. In particular, we note that a simple ReLU baseline for *dSA* performed competitively with a softmax-based implementation for both S2T NMT and SimulST, exhibiting gains of 0.6 BLEU and 0.44 perplexity respectively (Tables 8 and 10).

We note that cosFormer's superior cross-attention performance during training and evaluation worked in opposition to expectations. While English is a subject-verb-object (SVO) language, German is a subject-object-verb (SOV) language, implying that long-distance dependencies should exist for this tasks's cross-attention block. This validates the necessity of a targeted ablation study to empirically show the capabilities of a given linearization scheme for each attention block.

**Table 7.** Efficiency related results from various *MLA* configurations on the LJSpeech test set. Encoder and decoder throughput (higher is better) was measured via the number of forward calls and the wall-clock time for those calls. FLOPs (lower is better) were calculated and are an estimation of floating point operations for a single sample with a source sequence length of 100 and a target sequence length of 150.

| Linearization Scheme | Enc. Thrpt. (itr/sec) | Dec. Thrpt. (itr/sec) | FLOPs |
|---|---|---|---|
| Softmax Attention (non-Linear) | 1.51 | 72.81 | 1.94G |
| cosFormer *eSA* & *dCA*, ReLU *dSA* | 1.57 | 77.88 | 1.46G |
| cosFormer *eSA* & *dCA*, Softmax *dSA* | 1.58 | 76.53 | 1.60G |
| cosFormer *dCA*, Softmax *eSA* & *dSA* | 1.52 | 76.56 | 1.68G |

**Table 8.** Results from S2T NMT for MuST-C en-de for various linearization schemes with softmax as a baseline. BLEU scores (higher is better) are generated on the tst-COMMON split. Perplexity (lower is better) is generated during training on the validation set. Missing entries were not explored due to resource/time constraints.

| Attention Linearization Scheme | BLEU | ppl(dev) |
|---|---|---|
| Softmax Attention (non-Linear) | 10.47 | 9.36 |
| Full cosFormer | 2.37 | 20.08 |
| Full Simple ReLU | 1.95 | 18.33 |
| cosFormer $dSA$, Softmax Elsew | – | 9.92 |
| Simple ReLU $dSA$, Softmax Elsew | 11.07 | 9.74 |

**Table 9.** Results from S2T NMT for MuST-C en-de for various linearization schemes with slightly different model parameters. These models were trained with an embedding dimension $d_{model}$ of 224 and 4 attention heads.

| Attention Linearization Scheme | BLEU | ppl(dev) |
|---|---|---|
| Full cosFormer | 2.73 | 22.12 |
| cosFormer $eSA$ & $dSA$, Simple ReLU $dCA$ | 1.89 | 23.1 |
| cosFormer $eSA$ & $dSA$, Softmax $dCA$ | 7.71 | 13.35 |

**Table 10.** Results from SimulST for MuST-C en-de for various linearization schemes. Missing entries were not explored due to resource/time constraints.

| Attention Linearization Scheme | BLEU | ppl(dev) |
|---|---|---|
| Softmax Attention (non-Linear) | 9.25 | 10.15 |
| Simple ReLU $eSA$ & $dSA$, Softmax $dCA$ | 7.35 | 12.81 |
| Simple $dSA$, Softmax $eSA$ & $dCA$ | – | 9.71 |

# 6 Conclusion

Attention linearization is a popular method for building efficient transformers for a variety of latency-sensitive tasks. In this paper, we propose *modular linearized attention (MLA)*, which combines multiple efficient attention mechanisms to maximize performance. To enable *MLA* and solve issues in applying cosFormer [32] to autoregressive tasks without a fixed length, we propose several computationally cheap solutions for target sequence length prediction. Moreover, we apply effective attention linearization with sequence length-based re-weighting for the first time to S2T NMT, SimulST, and autoregressive TTS. We achieve up to a 7% decoder throughput increase for TTS with mitigated additional MCD and produce competitive prediction quality for en-de S2T NMT and SimulST, with a up to a 0.6 BLEU score increase and 0.44 perplexity reduction for models featuring *MLA*.

**Acknowledgment.** This research was supported, in part, by the National Science Foundation grants 2223483 and 2223484.

# References

1. Ashtari, P., Sima, D.M., Lathauwer, L.D., Sappey-Marinier, D., Maes, F., Huffel, S.V.: Factorizer: a scalable interpretable approach to context modeling for medical image segmentation. Med. Image Anal. **84**, 102706 (2022)
2. Baevski, A., Auli, M.: Adaptive input representations for neural language modeling (2019)
3. Beltagy, I., Peters, M.E., Cohan, A.: Longformer: The long-document transformer (2020). https://doi.org/10.48550/ARXIV.2004.05150
4. Bentivogli, L., et al.: Cascade versus direct speech translation: Do the differences still make a difference? In: Proceedings of the 59th Annual Meeting of the Association for Computational Linguistics and the 11th International Joint Conference on Natural Language Processing. vol. 1: Long Papers), pp. 2873–2887. Association for Computational Linguistics, Online (Aug 2021). https://doi.org/10.18653/v1/2021.acl-long.224, https://aclanthology.org/2021.acl-long.224
5. Berndt, D.J., Clifford, J.: Using dynamic time warping to find patterns in time series. In: Proceedings of the 3rd International Conference on Knowledge Discovery and Data Mining, pp. 359–370. AAAIWS 1994, AAAI Press (1994)
6. Child, R., Gray, S., Radford, A., Sutskever, I.: Generating long sequences with sparse transformers (2019). https://doi.org/10.48550/ARXIV.1904.10509, https://arxiv.org/abs/1904.10509
7. Choromanski, K., et al.: Rethinking attention with performers (2020). https://doi.org/10.48550/ARXIV.2009.14794, https://arxiv.org/abs/2009.14794
8. Clark, K., Khandelwal, U., Levy, O., Manning, C.D.: What does BERT look at? An analysis of BERT's attention (2019). https://doi.org/10.48550/ARXIV.1906.04341, https://arxiv.org/abs/1906.04341
9. Dai, Z., Yang, Z., Yang, Y., Carbonell, J., Le, Q.V., Salakhutdinov, R.: Transformer-XL: Attentive language models beyond a fixed-length context (2019). https://doi.org/10.48550/ARXIV.1901.02860, https://arxiv.org/abs/1901.02860
10. Dosovitskiy, A., et al.: An image is worth 16x16 words: Transformers for image recognition at scale (2020). https://doi.org/10.48550/ARXIV.2010.11929, https://arxiv.org/abs/2010.11929
11. Hu, C., et al.: RankNAS: Efficient neural architecture search by pairwise ranking (2021)
12. Huang, C.Z.A., et al.: Music transformer (2018). https://doi.org/10.48550/ARXIV.1809.04281, https://arxiv.org/abs/1809.04281
13. Ito, K., Johnson, L.: The LJ speech dataset (2017)
14. Katharopoulos, A., Vyas, A., Pappas, N., Fleuret, F.: Transformers are RNNs: Fast autoregressive transformers with linear attention (2020). https://doi.org/10.48550/ARXIV.2006.16236, https://arxiv.org/abs/2006.16236
15. Kitaev, N., Kaiser, L., Levskaya, A.: Reformer: The efficient transformer (2020). https://doi.org/10.48550/ARXIV.2001.04451, https://arxiv.org/abs/2001.04451
16. Kovaleva, O., Romanov, A., Rogers, A., Rumshisky, A.: Revealing the dark secrets of BERT (2019). https://doi.org/10.48550/ARXIV.1908.08593, https://arxiv.org/abs/1908.08593

17. Kubichek, R.F.: Mel-cepstral distance measure for objective speech quality assessment. In: Proceedings of IEEE Pacific Rim Conference on Communications Computers and Signal Processing. vol. 1, pp. 125–128 (1993)

18. Lee, J., Lee, Y., Kim, J., Kosiorek, A.R., Choi, S., Teh, Y.W.: Set transformer: A framework for attention-based permutation-invariant neural networks (2018). https://doi.org/10.48550/ARXIV.1810.00825, https://arxiv.org/abs/1810.00825

19. Li, N., Liu, S., Liu, Y., Zhao, S., Liu, M., Zhou, M.: Neural speech synthesis with transformer network (2018). https://doi.org/10.48550/ARXIV.1809.08895, https://arxiv.org/abs/1809.08895

20. Liu, Y., et al.: RoBERTa: A robustly optimized BERT pretraining approach (2019)

21. Liu, Z., et al.: Neural architecture search on efficient transformers and beyond (2022)

22. Ma, M., et al.: STACL: simultaneous translation with implicit anticipation and controllable latency using prefix-to-prefix framework. In: Proceedings of the 57th Annual Meeting of the Association for Computational Linguistics, pp. 3025–3036. Association for Computational Linguistics (ACL), Florence, Italy (2019)

23. Ma, X., Pino, J., Cross, J., Puzon, L., Gu, J.: Monotonic multi head attention. In: International Conference on Learning Representations (2020)

24. Ma, X., Pino, J., Cross, J., Puzon, L., Gu, J.: SimulMT to simulST: adapting simultaneous text translation to end-to-end simultaneous speech translation. In: Proceedings of 2020 Asia-Pacific Chapter of the Association for Computational Linguistics and the International Joint Conference on Natural Language Processing (2020)

25. Ma, X., Dousti, M.J., Wang, C., Gu, J., Pino, J.: SimulEval: An evaluation toolkit for simultaneous translation (2020). https://doi.org/10.48550/ARXIV.2007.16193, https://arxiv.org/abs/2007.16193

26. Madani, A., et al.: ProGen: Language modeling for protein generation (2020). https://doi.org/10.48550/ARXIV.2004.03497, https://arxiv.org/abs/2004.03497

27. McAuliffe, M., Socolof, M., Mihuc, S., Wagner, M., Sonderegger, M.: Montreal forced aligner: trainable text-speech alignment using kaldi. In: Interspeech (2017)

28. Ott, M., et al.: fairseq: A fast, extensible toolkit for sequence modeling (2019). https://doi.org/10.48550/ARXIV.1904.01038, https://arxiv.org/abs/1904.01038

29. Parmar, N., et al.: Image transformer (2018). https://doi.org/10.48550/ARXIV. 1802.05751, https://arxiv.org/abs/1802.05751

30. Peng, H., Pappas, N., Yogatama, D., Schwartz, R., Smith, N.A., Kong, L.: Random feature attention (2021). https://doi.org/10.48550/ARXIV.2103.02143, https:// arxiv.org/abs/2103.02143

31. Post, M.: A call for clarity in reporting BLEU scores. In: Proceedings of the Third Conference on Machine Translation: Research Papers, pp. 186–191. Association for Computational Linguistics, Belgium, Brussels (Oct 2018), https://www.aclweb. org/anthology/W18-6319

32. Qin, Z., et al.: cosFormer: Rethinking softmax in attention. In: International Conference on Learning Representations (2022), https://openreview.net/forum? id=Bl8CQrx2Up4

33. Ren, Y., et al.: FastSpeech 2: Fast and high-quality end-to-end text to speech (2020). https://doi.org/10.48550/ARXIV.2006.04558, https://arxiv.org/abs/2006. 04558

34. Skerry-Ryan, R., et al.: Towards end-to-end prosody transfer for expressive speech synthesis with Tacotron (2018). https://doi.org/10.48550/ARXIV.1803. 09047, https://arxiv.org/abs/1803.09047

35. Sukhbaatar, S., Grave, E., Bojanowski, P., Joulin, A.: Adaptive attention span in transformers (2019). https://doi.org/10.48550/ARXIV.1905.07799, https://arxiv.org/abs/1905.07799
36. Tay, Y., et al.: Long range arena : a benchmark for efficient transformers. In: International Conference on Learning Representations (2021). https://openreview.net/forum?id=qVyeW-grC2k
37. Vaswani, A., et al.: Attention is all you need. In: Proceedings of 31st Conference on Neural Information Processing Systems (NIPS 2017) (2017)
38. Wang, C., et al.: fairseq $s^2$: A scalable and integrable speech synthesis toolkit (2021). https://doi.org/10.48550/ARXIV.2109.06912, https://arxiv.org/abs/2109.06912
39. Wang, S., Li, B.Z., Khabsa, M., Fang, H., Ma, H.: Linformer: Self-attention with linear complexity (2020). https://doi.org/10.48550/ARXIV.2006.04768, https://arxiv.org/abs/2006.04768
40. Weiss, R.J., Skerry-Ryan, R., Battenberg, E., Mariooryad, S., Kingma, D.P.: Wavetacotron: Spectrogram-free end-to-end text-to-speech synthesis (2020). https://doi.org/10.48550/ARXIV.2011.03568, https://arxiv.org/abs/2011.03568
41. Wu, Q., Lan, Z., Qian, K., Gu, J., Geramifard, A., Yu, Z.: Memformer: A memory-augmented transformer for sequence modeling (2020). https://doi.org/10.48550/ARXIV.2010.06891, https://arxiv.org/abs/2010.06891
42. Xiong, Y., et al.: Nyströmformer: A nyström-based algorithm for approximating self-attention (2021)
43. Zaheer, M., et al.: Big bird: Transformers for longer sequences (2020). https://doi.org/10.48550/ARXIV.2007.14062, https://arxiv.org/abs/2007.14062

# Enhancing Table Retrieval with Dual Graph Representations

Tianyun Liu[1], Xinghua Zhang[1,2], Zhenyu Zhang[1,2], Yubin Wang[1,2],
Quangang Li[1,2], Shuai Zhang[1,2], and Tingwen Liu[1,2(✉)]

[1] Institute of Information Engineering, Chinese Academy of Sciences, Beijing, China
[2] School of Cyber Security, University of Chinese Academy of Sciences, Beijing,
China
{liutianyun,zhangxinghua,zhangzhenyu1996,wangyubin,
liquangang,zhangshuai0612,liutingwen}@iie.ac.cn

**Abstract.** Table retrieval aims to rank candidate tables for answering
natural language query, in which the most critical problem is how to
learn informative representations for structured tables. Most previous
methods roughly flatten the table and send it into a sequence encoder,
ignoring the structure information of tables and the semantic interaction
between table cells and contexts. In this paper, we propose a dual graph
based method to perceive the semantics and structure of tables, so as
to preferably support the downstream table retrieval task. Inspired by
human cognition, we first decouple a table into the row view and column
view, then build dual graphs from these two views with the consideration
of table contexts. Afterward, intra-graph and inter-graph interactions
are iteratively performed for aggregating and exchanging local row- and
column-oriented features respectively, and an adaptive fusion strategy
is eventually tailor-made for sophisticated table representations. In this
way, the table structure and semantic information are well considered
with dual-graph modeling. Consequently, the input query can match the
target tables based on their full-fledged table representations and achieve
the ultimate ranking results more accurately. Extensive experiments verify the superiority of our dual graphs over strong baselines on two table
retrieval datasets WikiTables and WebQueryTable. Further analyses also
confirm the adaptability for row-/column-oriented tables, and show the
rationality and generalization of dual graphs. The source code is available
at https://github.com/ty33123/DualG.

**Keywords:** table understanding · table retrieval · graph
representation learning

## 1 Introduction

Table retrieval is an important task in information retrieval, which aims to rank
the candidate tables extracted from the web given a natural language query. Due
to valuable semi-structured information in these tabular data, table retrieval has
been used in various research tasks such as knowledge graph construction [12,22],
question answering [3,11], and fact verification [2,15].

© The Author(s), under exclusive license to Springer Nature Switzerland AG 2023
D. Koutra et al. (Eds.): ECML PKDD 2023, LNAI 14172, pp. 107–123, 2023.
https://doi.org/10.1007/978-3-031-43421-1_7

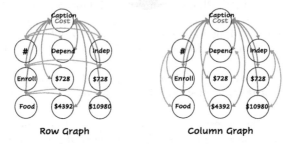

**Fig. 1.** Tabular graph construction for the *table* along with its context (e.g., caption), comprising *Row Graph* and *Column Graph* in our method.

Previous table retrieval methods typically treat a table as plain text by flattening the table with its contexts (e.g., page title, table caption) into a long sequence [4,13,18,19,24], in which the most direct way is arranging these table cells from left to right and from top to bottom. However, unlike natural language processing, flattened tables are still not strictly grammatical and cannot act as native text sequences, and an ideal table understanding model requires the ability of semantic comprehension and structure awareness. Taking the table in Fig. 1 as a concrete example, table cells appearing in the same column or row tend to have similar surface form and some semantic relevance, which are difficult to perceive and capture with these flat-based methods, resulting in sub-optimal performances.

Naturally, tables have a two-dimensional structure, that is, rows and columns organize the table horizontally and vertically. Therefore, there are two orthogonal ways to deliver the association among data cells and need to be accurately understood for downstream tasks like table retrieval. As shown in Fig. 1, data cells "*$4392*" and "*$10980*" share the identical fee type since they appear in the same row "*Food and Housing*", so that establishing the connections between cells and their corresponding row headers is capable of boosting the table representation. Similarly, this phenomenon also exists in columns. Moreover, table context (e.g., page title, table caption) is another information source closely related to the table topic and helps assist table understanding. From the above observations, we believe that the table should be understood from row and column, respectively, with the consideration of table contexts.

To this end, we propose a **Dual-Graph** (DualG) based table representation model for precise table retrieval. Specifically, DualG imitates human cognition and constructs row graph and column graph from horizontal and vertical perspectives, respectively. Meanwhile, table context is also specified as special nodes integrated into these graphs. Next, dual-graph representation learning is devised for the row and column graphs to obtain a full-fledged table representation, where the *intra-graph interaction* mechanism is conducted to aggregate the local row- and column-oriented information in each graph. Beside, we also propose *inter-graph interaction* to enable the exchange of heterogeneous messages between two graphs for the recombination of rows and columns, which avoids the risk of information loss in single row or column graph and facilitates the concise interaction of two views. Finally, an adaptive fusion module is introduced to dynamically fuse the unique information from row and column perspectives for achieving the holistic table representation.

In this way, the informative table representation can be involved into the final retrieval prediction procedure. Specifically, natural language query is matched with both the table representation encoded by dual-graph learning and the semantic-rich table contextual representation, and then the matching features are fed into the ultimate regression network to gain the relevance score between the query and candidate table. As the table is modeled into dual graphs, the row- and column-oriented structures can be delicately captured for enhancing table retrieval. We construct broad experiments on the WikiTables and Web-QueryTable datasets to evaluate our DualG. Experimental results confirm our consistent improvements in comparison with previous state-of-the-art methods. Extensive analyses show that DualG can adaptively fuse the row- and column-aware structures, and a cross-dataset evaluation reveals the better generality.

## 2   Related Work

Flat table-based methods have always been a popular paradigm in the table retrieval field, which flatten the table into a text sequence for representation. Some early approaches are following unsupervised BM25 [14] or feature-based [16,18,26] table retrieval procedure. Researchers have recently explored ways to use BERT [6] for table retrieval. TaBERT [24] jointly learns representations for natural language sentences and structured tables by the content snapshot. BERT4TR [4] combines BERT and table features for joint training. Due to the length limit for BERT, only the most relevant components (rows, columns, cells) are encoded. StruBERT [19] encodes the row or column sequence of a table using horizontal and vertical self-attention. However, these flat table modeling methods cannot fully mine and explore the table structural information, which is essential for table understanding. In other ways, MTR [17] uses a gated multimodal unit (GMU) to learn a joint representation of the query and the different table modalities, and the final table-query relevance is estimated based on the query and unimodal representation.

The development of graph representation learning has brought state-of-the-art research results in many fields. There are also some researchers try to adapt these techniques into table retrieval. MGNETS [5] builds the graph based on the whole corpus, where each unique data cell, context term, and table in the corpus

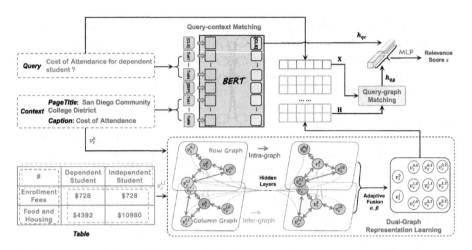

**Fig. 2.** Overview of DualG, we obtain the relevance score ($s$) by query-context matching and query-graph matching, where **H** is achieved by Dual-Graph representation learning and **X** is the initial representation of query. The horizontal purple arrows represent information propagation within the graph (Sect. 3.3), and the vertical green arrows represent an exchange of heterogeneous information between the row graph and column graph (Sect. 3.3).

serve as nodes, and edges represent the membership and co-occurrence relationship. GTR [23] converts the table into a single tabular graph with data cell, virtual row, and column nodes to capture the layout structures. Although the above graph-based algorithms can obtain the intrinsic table structure, they still face the challenges of information fuzziness and entanglement. Because rows and columns may represent different semantic relations in different tables, modeling the global natural layout into a single graph neglects the local row and column properties. In addition, table contexts also have strong indicative effects on table gist and offer vital guidance for table understanding, which prior methods often ignore for modeling the table. Different from the above attempts, we follow the design specification of tables and the expression mechanism of information, propose first to *decouple a table into row view and column view and build dual graph* with its instructive contexts, and then couple two graphs for the holistic table representation.

## 3 Methodology

In this section, we first introduce the studied problem (Sect. 3.1) and then describe our proposed framework DualG for table retrieval.

**Overview.** Figure 2 illustrates the architecture of DualG. In our framework, table retrieval is composed of tabular graph construction (Sect. 3.2), tabular graph representation learning (Sect. 3.3), and relevance prediction (Sect. 3.4). In particular, we consider the table cells and its contexts to build the tabular graphs from row and column views in tabular graph construction. As for tabular graph learning, a systematic dual-graph learning method is proposed to capture the holistic table representation, which contains intra-graph interaction, inter-graph interaction, and adaptive fusion. In prediction module, the relevance score can be obtained by matching the natural language query with the table representation and table contextual features.

## 3.1 Task Definition

In table retrieval task, given a query $q \in Q$, the candidate table set $\mathcal{T} = \{T_1, ..., T_p\}$ is sorted by the relevance to $q$ in descending order, where $T_i$ $(i = 1, .., p)$ is the $i$-th table in the table set. The table $T_i$ consists of $m$ rows and $n$ columns, and several surrounding text (e.g., table caption). The core problem of table retrieval is the calculation of the correlation between $q$ and $T_i$.

## 3.2 Graph Construction

In this subsection, to effectively depict the structured information for the table, we describe how to construct dual graphs: the row graph $\mathcal{G}_r = \{(\mathcal{V}, \mathcal{E}_r)\}$ and the column graph $\mathcal{G}_c = \{(\mathcal{V}, \mathcal{E}_c)\}$. From human perception, $\mathcal{G}_r$ and $\mathcal{G}_c$ should have the same nodes but different edges. So, they are both composed of cell nodes $\mathcal{V}_c$ and context nodes $\mathcal{V}_t$, i.e., $\mathcal{V} = \{\mathcal{V}_c, \mathcal{V}_t\}$. Each data cell in $i$-th row and $j$-th column of table is regarded as a node $v_c^{i,j} \in \mathcal{V}_c$ in the graph. For the merged data cell, we restore the original layout and fill in the same data as the merged cell. As table context (e.g., web page title, table caption) has rich semantic knowledge which is highly relevant to the table topic and helps assist table understanding, we view each context information as a graph node $v_t^k \in \mathcal{V}_t$.

Considering that the first node of a row/column is usually the table header which describes the main content of row/column, It is intuitive to establish the connection between each table cell node and header node in a differentiated way. Herein, when building distinct tabular graphs with row and column structures, we construct two kinds of undirected edges (cell-context edge and cell-cell edge). The specific edges of *row* and *column* graphs are as follows

**Row Graph.** As for the edges $\mathcal{E}_r$ in row graph, we connect each data cell node $v_c^{i,j}$ $(i \in \{0, ..., m\}, j \in \{0, ..., n\})$ in the table with the row header node $v_c^{i,0}$ and the context node $v_t^k$, that is $(v_c^{i,j}, v_c^{i,0}) \in \mathcal{E}_r$ and $(v_c^{i,j}, v_t^k) \in \mathcal{E}_r$, which enables the graph to aggregate information by rows.

**Column Graph.** When connecting $\mathcal{E}_c$, we build the relation between each cell node $v_c^{i,j}$ $(i \in \{0, ..., m\}, j \in \{0, ..., n\})$ and the column header node $v_c^{0,j}$, the context node $v_t^k$, respectively. That is $(v_c^{i,j}, v_c^{0,j}) \in \mathcal{E}_c$ and $(v_c^{i,j}, v_t^k) \in \mathcal{E}_c$. In this graph, the message can be passed by columns.

Figure 1 shows an example of a constructed tabular graph from the table which caption is *Cost of Attendance*. In a tabular graph, the caption as context node connects to all cell nodes, and the first cell of a row/column connects to each cell node of this row/column. To this end, correlation among different rows can be captured by the intermediate context (e.g., table caption) node in our DualG, which is modelled in a column graph. The correlation among different columns can also be captured in row graph by the similar way.

### 3.3   Dual-Graph Representation Learning

As shown in Fig. 2, representation learning for dual graphs (row and column graph) contains three parts: *intra-graph interaction*, *inter-graph interaction* and *adaptive fusion module*, where node information is aggregated within a graph and exchanged between dual graphs. In this way, row- and column-based structures can be finely captured respectively and then fused adaptively for holistic dual-graph representations.

**Intra-Graph Interaction.** Graph convolutional network [9] is a typical graph neural network model that contains a stack of convolutional layers and is employed for different representation learning tasks. To better learn the table representation, we perform it on row and column graphs to learn latent node embeddings, respectively, and learn the representation of each node by aggregating information from its neighbours within a graph. Therefore, intra-graph interactions can be used to understand different cell contents through tabular structures:

$$\mathbf{H}^{(l+1)} = \sigma \left( \tilde{\mathbf{D}}^{-\frac{1}{2}} \tilde{\mathbf{A}} \tilde{\mathbf{D}}^{-\frac{1}{2}} \mathbf{H}^{(l)} \mathbf{W}^{(l)} \right) \tag{1}$$

where $\tilde{\mathbf{A}} = \mathbf{A} + \mathbf{I}$ is the adjacency matrix $\mathbf{A}$ of the graph $\mathcal{G}_r$ ($\mathcal{G}_c$) with added self-connections, $\mathbf{I}$ is the identity matrix, $\tilde{\mathbf{D}}$ is the diagonal node degree matrix with $\tilde{\mathbf{D}}(i,i) = \sum_j \tilde{\mathbf{A}}(i,j)$, $\mathbf{W}^{(l)}$ is the $l$-th layer trainable weight matrix, $\sigma$ is a non-linear activation function, $\mathbf{H}^{(0)}$ is initialized with pretrained word vectors according to each node content. Thus, $l$-th layer hidden representations in $\mathcal{G}_r$ and $\mathcal{G}_c$ can be notated as $\mathbf{H}_r^{(l)}$ and $\mathbf{H}_c^{(l)}$ respectively.

**Inter-Graph Interaction.** To enable heterogeneous information (row- and column-based structures) from different graphs to be gradually fused into an accordant one, we introduce inter-graph interaction to exchange information between dual graphs, which first apply a linear transformation and layer normalization [20] to node representation following $l$-th layer in GCN:

$$\mathbf{H}_r^{(l)} = \text{LayerNorm}(\mathbf{H}_r^{(l)} \mathbf{W}_r^{(l)} + b_r^{(l)}), \tag{2}$$

$$\mathbf{H}_c^{(l)} = \text{LayerNorm}(\mathbf{H}_c^{(l)} \mathbf{W}_c^{(l)} + b_c^{(l)}), \tag{3}$$

$$\mathbf{H}^{(l)} = \text{MLP}([\mathbf{H}_r^{(l)} \| \mathbf{H}_c^{(l)}]), \tag{4}$$

where $\mathbf{W}_r^{(l)}$, $b_r^{(l)}$, $\mathbf{W}_c^{(l)}$ and $b_c^{(l)}$ are trainable parameters. After that, the normalized node representations $\mathbf{H}_r^{(l)}$ and $\mathbf{H}_c^{(l)}$ learned from the row graph $\mathcal{G}_r$ and column graph $\mathcal{G}_c$ are concatenated, which then goes through an MLP layer to combine the heterogeneous information and obtain the final $l$-th layer hidden features $\mathbf{H}^{(l)}$ in dual-graph representation learning, i.e., $\mathbf{H}_r^{(l)} = \mathbf{H}_c^{(l)} = \mathbf{H}^{(l)}$.

**Adaptive Fusion.** A perfect fusion strategy should eliminate redundant data after combining heterogeneous information. So, we introduce a particular fusion module in the last layer of DualG for full-fledged table representation. Concretely, the fusion strategy to adaptive fuse row- and column-based unique features and the dynamic weights are computed as follows:

$$\alpha = \text{sigmoid}(\mathbf{H}_r^{(L)}\mathbf{W}_r^{(L)} + b_r^{(L)}), \tag{5}$$

$$\beta = \text{sigmoid}(\mathbf{H}_c^{(L)}\mathbf{W}_c^{(L)} + b_c^{(L)}). \tag{6}$$

where $\mathbf{H}_r^{(L)}$ and $\mathbf{H}_c^{(L)}$ are row-aware and column-aware node representations after the $L$-th (last) layer of GCN, which do not conduct the inter-graph interaction but direct access to fusion module. Due to the complexity and diversity of tables, we design these vector $\alpha, \beta \in \mathbb{R}^{|\mathcal{V}| \times 1}$ represent the each cell row/column weight, where $\mathbf{H}_r^{(L)}$ and $\mathbf{H}_c^{(L)}$ are calculated with Eq. 1 in row graph $\mathcal{G}_r$ and column graph $\mathcal{G}_c$ respectively at the last layer of GCN. $\alpha$ and $\beta$ represent the adaptive fusion weights of $\mathcal{G}_r$ and $\mathcal{G}_c$ respectively. To enable $\alpha + \beta = 1$, we normalize $\alpha$ and $\beta$ is:

$$\alpha = \alpha/(\alpha + \beta), \tag{7}$$

$$\beta = 1 - \alpha. \tag{8}$$

Then, we can get the final full-fledged table representation $\mathbf{H}^{(L)}$ based on the calculated importance $\alpha$ and $\beta$ for dual graphs:

$$\mathbf{H}^{(L)} = \alpha\mathbf{H}_r^{(L)} + \beta\mathbf{H}_c^{(L)} \tag{9}$$

Inspired by Attention [20], we use the multi-head dual-graph representation method, which allows the model jointly learn relevant information from different representation subspaces. For table representation $\mathbf{H}_h^{(L)}$ in *head h*, we can obtain it with Eq. 1–9. And then we stack the initialized table representation and the multi-head table representations $\mathbf{H}_{mh} = [\mathbf{H}^{(0)}, \mathbf{H}_1^{(L)}, ..., \mathbf{H}_h^{(L)}, .., \mathbf{H}_N^{(L)}]$, and perform mean pooling to get the final table representation $\mathbf{H}$ whose dimension is consistent with $\mathbf{H}_h^{(L)}$.

### 3.4  Prediction

Based on the table representation, we conduct the prediction process in three steps: *query graph matching* to understand the table structure and obtain query-related features, *query context matching* to compute the semantic similarity between the query and table context, and the final matching optimization to combine above results for the final metric.

**Query Graph Matching.** Given the table representation obtained by Section 3.3 and query representation encoded by the pre-trained word vectors which also encode the graph node content, we first apply the linear transformation and layer normalization similar to Eq. 2 to these representations, which maps the table and query representations into the same space for subsequent matching operations. In order to implement query-relevant table features $h_{qg}$. We designed a query-aware attention mechanism:

$$
\begin{aligned}
\mathbf{h}_{qg} &= \text{Attention}(\mathbf{q}, \mathbf{K}, \mathbf{V}) \\
&= \text{softmax}(\mathbf{q}\mathbf{K}^\top / \sqrt{d_k}) \cdot \mathbf{V}
\end{aligned}
\tag{10}
$$

where $\mathbf{q} = \mathbf{X}\mathbf{W}_q$, $\mathbf{K} = \mathbf{H}\mathbf{W}_K$, $\mathbf{V} = \mathbf{H}\mathbf{W}_V$. $\mathbf{X}$ and $\mathbf{H}$ are normalized query, table representations, respectively.

**Query Context Matching.** The table contextual information (e.g., page title and table caption) has valuable semantic knowledge and can provide indicative information for the table data. Therefore, we perform the query context matching to further improve the retrieval. The sentence pairs task in the pre-trained language model (PLM) is a clever interactive semantic similarity computation model. So we concatenate the query with all contexts ($\mathbf{X}_{qc} = [CLS]$ query $[SEP]$ contexts $[SEP]$) and input them into a pre-trained language model (e.g., BERT) to extract semantic similarity features:

$$
\mathbf{h}_{qc} = \text{PLM}(\mathbf{X}_{qc})
\tag{11}
$$

**Training and Inference**

*Training.* After matching the query with tabular graph and table context, respectively. We concatenate the query-related table features $h_{qc}$ and semantic similarity features $h_{qg}$, and feed them into a multi-layer perceptron (MLP) to calculate the relevance score:

$$
s = \text{MLP}([\mathbf{h}_{qc}\|\mathbf{h}_{qg}])
\tag{12}
$$

Following BERT4TR [4], we treat the problem as a regression task and approximate point-wise ranking with a mean square error (MSE) loss as:

$$
\mathcal{L}_{\text{MSE}} = \sum_i (y_i - s_i)^2
\tag{13}
$$

where $y_i$ is the gold relevance score of table $i$ and $s_i$ is the predicted score by Eq. 12.

Otherwise, when the query has only one relevant table, we minimize the cross-entropy loss as training objective, following [23]:

$$
\mathcal{L}_{\text{CE}} = -\sum_i [y_i \log(s_i) + (1-y_i) \log(1-s_i)]
\tag{14}
$$

*Inference.* Given a query $q$, each candidate table $T_i$ is constructed as dual tabular graphs for the table representation which is then passed into query-graph matching process, and then combined with query-context matching for an estimation of relevance score $s_i$.

## 4 Experiments

### 4.1 Datasets

To evaluate the effectiveness of the proposed approach, we conducted extensive experiments on two datasets for table retrieval: WikiTables [26] and WebQueryTable [18]. Query-table pairs of both datasets were collected from different sources.

**WikiTables** is one of the most commonly used datasets for table retrieval task. It contains 60 queries from two source query subsets [1,21], and the tables extracted from Wikipedia[1] (dump date: 2015 October). The dataset has a total of 3120 retrieval pairs (query-table pairs), and each retrieval pair is labelled with 0 (irrelevant), 1 (relevant), and 2 (highly relevant).

**WebQueryTable** uses the search logs of commercial search engines to obtain a list of query-table pair marks the most relevant query-table pair with 1 and the rest of the candidate list with 0, producing 21,113 query-table pairs, each query has only one relevant table. We follow previous work [16,23,26] to separate the dataset as training, validation, and testing with a 7:1:2 split.

### 4.2 Baselines

We compare our method with the following table retrieval baselines and group them into four types:

(1) *Feature-based methods*: **BM25** [14] calculates the score for document and each word in the query. **LTR** [26] uses 18 different discrete features for regression training using a random forest. **T2VW** [25] employ neural language modeling approaches to embed tabular data into vector spaces. **STR** [26] extends LTR by introducing additional 16 features. **Feature + NeuralNet** [18] combines word-level, phrase-level, sentence-level features and neural network architectures to measure the relevance score between query and table. **TabIESim** [16] enhances the retrieval by a combination of intrinsic and extrinsic table similarity based on BM25 and cluster hypothesis [10].

(2) *BERT-based methods*: **BERT4TR** [4] first use the BERT to encode the table, and then the retrieval performance is further improved by combining features [26]. **TaBERT** [24] jointly learns contextual representations for utterance and the structured schema of tables, implicitly capturing the mapping between them based on BERT. **StruBERT** [19] uses horizontal and vertical self-attentions to the encoded column- and row-based table sequences.

---

[1] https://en.wikipedia.org/.

**Table 1.** Main results on WikiTables. **Bold** indicates the best result, <u>underline</u> is the second best, and "-" indicates the result not reported in the original paper. The significant test p-value $< 0.05$ when comparing with GTR.

| Method Type | Method | N@5 | N@10 | N@15 | N@20 | MAP |
|---|---|---|---|---|---|---|
| Feature-based | BM25 [14] | 0.3196 | 0.3377 | 0.3732 | 0.4045 | 0.4260 |
| | LTR [26] | 0.5527 | 0.5456 | 0.5738 | 0.6031 | 0.4112 |
| | T2VW [25] | 0.5974 | 0.6096 | 0.6312 | 0.6505 | 0.4675 |
| | STR [26] | 0.5951 | 0.6293 | 0.6590 | 0.6825 | 0.5141 |
| | TabIESim [16] | 0.6498 | 0.6479 | – | 0.6935 | 0.5124 |
| BERT-based | BERT4TR [4] | 0.6361 | 0.6519 | 0.6558 | 0.6564 | 0.6311 |
| | TaBERT [24] | 0.5926 | 0.6108 | 0.6451 | 0.6668 | 0.6326 |
| | StruBERT [19] | 0.6393 | – | – | – | 0.6378 |
| Multi-modal | MTR [17] | <u>0.6631</u> | <u>0.6813</u> | – | <u>0.7370</u> | 0.6058 |
| Graph-based | MGNETS [5] | 0.6373 | 0.6490 | – | – | 0.6339 |
| | GTR [23] | 0.6554 | 0.6747 | <u>0.6978</u> | 0.7211 | <u>0.6665</u> |
| | DualG (Ours) | **0.6707** | **0.6925** | **0.7259** | **0.7541** | **0.7083** |

**Table 2.** Retrieval performance on WebQueryTable.

| Method | Precision@1 | MAP |
|---|---|---|
| BM25 [14] | 0.4712 | 0.5823 |
| Feature+NN [18] | 0.5415 | 0.6718 |
| BERT4TR [4] | – | 0.7104 |
| GTR [23] | 0.6257 | 0.7369 |
| DualG (Ours) | **0.6363** | **0.7466** |

(3) *Multi-modal methods*: **MTR** [17] views web tables as multimodal objects, which uses gated multimodal units (GMUs) to learn joint-representation.

(4) *Graph-based methods*: **MGNETS** [5] constructs two table-term graphs by mining co-occurrence relation, and conduct GCN on both graph. **GTR** [23] transforms the table into a single tabular graph with data cell, row and column as nodes to capture multi-granular content and the layout structures.

## 4.3   Implementation Details

In our experiments, we use BERT-base [6] to extract semantic similarity features $h_{qc}$. Similar to BERT4TR [4] and GTR [23], the words inside table are initialized by FastText [8] with dimension 300 in query-graph matching. The number of GCN layers $L$ and heads $N$ are set to 2 and 4, respectively. During training, we set the learning rates of BERT and GCN to 1e-5 and 1e-4, respectively. The random seed number is 0. The batch size and the number of maximum epochs

**Table 3.** Ablation studies on WikiTables. N is the abbreviation of NDCG.

|                                    | N@5    | N@10   | N@15   | N@20   | MAP    |
|------------------------------------|--------|--------|--------|--------|--------|
| DualG (Ours)                       | **0.6707** | **0.6925** | **0.7259** | **0.7541** | **0.7083** |
| *w/o* Dual graphs                  | 0.6161 | 0.6610 | 0.6944 | 0.7213 | 0.6849 |
| *w/o* Row graph                    | 0.6403 | 0.6663 | 0.7100 | 0.7406 | 0.6989 |
| *w/o* Column graph                 | 0.6100 | 0.6441 | 0.6951 | 0.7202 | 0.6757 |
| *w/o* Context node                 | 0.6024 | 0.6505 | 0.6925 | 0.7173 | 0.6850 |
| *w/o* Inter-graph interaction      | 0.6117 | 0.6538 | 0.6906 | 0.7225 | 0.6823 |
| *w/o* Adaptive fusion              | 0.6365 | 0.6830 | 0.7121 | 0.7436 | 0.7034 |
| *w* Single graph                   | 0.6163 | 0.6663 | 0.6888 | 0.7178 | 0.6792 |
| *replace* Adaptive fusion          | 0.6349 | 0.6749 | 0.7050 | 0.7373 | 0.6938 |
| *replace* Inter-graph interaction  | 0.6247 | 0.6466 | 0.6799 | 0.7175 | 0.6891 |

are 16 and 5, respectively, on both datasets. Because the WikiTables dataset does not provide a data split, we follow the previous work [4,5,16,17,23,26] and conduct a 5-fold cross-validation on this dataset for evaluation. We use the originally released split for WebqueryTable evaluation. Our framework is implemented with PyTorch and DGL for graph learning.

*Evaluation Metrics.* Due to distinct labeling strategies between two datasets, we use different groups of metrics to evaluate the performance of different methods for WikiTables and WebQueryTable, following previous work [4,23,26]. On WikiTables, we report Normalized Discounted Cumulative Gain (NDCG@n, n={5,10,15,20}) and Mean Average Precision (MAP). Because WebQueryTable only has one positive sample for each query, we report MAP and Precision@1 (P@1). Specifically, MAP and NDCG metrics are calculated using the TREC[2].

### 4.4 Results

From Tables 1 and 2, it can be seen that our proposed DualG method outperforms all other baselines on both datasets. The outstanding results confirm the necessity of capturing the table structural information, and the effectiveness of decoupling the whole table layout into dual graphs (row and column graph), which contributes to the fine-grained row- and column-aware structural features for full-fledged table understanding.

On WikiTables dataset, our method outperforms prior graph-based SOTA GTR [23] by 1.53%, 2.81%, 3.30% on NDCG@{5,15,20} and 4.18% on MAP. The reason is that our approach has the ability to adaptively capture precise row- and column-aware structures based on dual-graph learning instead of the overall layout graph without row/column distinction, and then the thorough

---

[2] https://github.com/usnistgov/trec_eval.

and accurate table representation can be achieved for higher performance. Compared to the multimodal approach, our proposed method outperforms MTR [17] by 1.12% on NDCG@10 and 10.25% on MAP, which shows the limitation of capturing table structure based on multimodal information. It is worth noting that the significant improvement in the MAP metric indicates that DualG has higher precise discrimination on the candidate tables.

In contrast with flat table based methods, our approach outperforms the latest StruBERT [19] by 3.14% on NDCG@5 and 7.05% on MAP. The reason is that flattening tables into sequences loses the structural information. While these approaches adapt a variety of attention mechanisms to achieve an understanding of the table, it fundamentally limits the upper bound of the model. As for the WebqueryTable dataset, our DualG outperforms the existing SOTA by 1.06% on Precision@1 and 0.97% on MAP, which comes to a consistent conclusion.

### 4.5   Analyses

**Ablation Study.** To evaluate the impact of each module in our method, we perform the following ablation studies:

(1) After removing dual-graph representation learning (*w/o* Dual graphs), i.e., the query only matches with table contexts, our DualG reduces by 5.46% on NDCG@5 and 2.34% on MAP. This ablation result shows the significant efficacy of our dual graphs, which is conducive to precise table representation for an accurate matching process. Furthermore, eliminating one of the dual graphs (*w/o* Row/Column graph) leads to a 3.04% and 6.07% decline on NDCG@5, which confirms the necessity of row and column structures.

(2) When removing the context node in our dual graphs (*w/o* Context node), the performance is reduced by 6.83% on NDCG@5 and 2.33% on MAP, which demonstrates that the table context information (e.g., web page title, table caption) can significantly profit the table understanding.

(3) Meanwhile, getting rid of inter-graph interaction when performing dual-graph representation learning results in a 5.90% drop in NDCG@5. The reason is that heterogeneous information is exchanged and propagated between row and column graphs, which contributes to a thorough understanding of table layout.

(4) We replace the adaptive fusion module with an average one (setting alpha and beta to 0.5). As shown in Table 3 (*w/o* Adaptive fusion), the NDCG@5 index declined by 3.43%, which confirms the efficacy of assigning dynamic weights to dual graphs to fuse the unique information.

(5) We merge the edges in row and column graphs into a single graph (*w* Single graph), leading to remarkable declines, which demonstrates the effectiveness of capturing fine-grained row/column information by building dual graphs.

(6) Furthermore, we replace the inter-graph interaction module or the adaptive fusion module with another of these modules and observed that the retrieval performance decreased substantially. The experimental results show that these modules play different roles in DualG as described in the motivation.

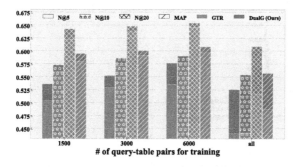

**Fig. 3.** Results of cross-dataset evaluation, training on WebQueryTable and testing on WikiTables. Blue blocks indicate the absolute increase of our method. (Color figure online)

| Year | Award Ceremony | Category | Nominee | Result |
|------|----------------|----------|---------|--------|
| 1954 | Tony Award | Best Performance by a Leading Actor in a Musical | Alfred Drake | Won |
| 1954 | Tony Award | Best Conductor and Musical Director | Louis Adrian | Won |

(a) Relational Table

| | Dependent Student | Independent Student |
|---|---|---|
| Enrollment Fees | $728 | $728 |
| Food and Housing | $4,392 | $10,980 |

(c) Matrix Table

| | |
|---|---|
| Area | 55,673km² |
| State capital | Shimla |
| Language | Hindi |
| District | 12 |
| Population | Census |
| Literacy | 77% |

(b) Entity Table

**Fig. 4.** Example for three types of Table.

**Cross-Dataset Evaluation.** To study the generalization ability, we train our DualG and prior GTR on WebQueryTable, and evaluate on WikiTables. Concretely, we use *1500, 3000, 6000* and *all* query-table pairs from WebQueryTable, which are approximately *half, equal, double* and *quadruple* of WikiTables dataset respectively. As shown in Fig. 3, blue blocks indicate the absolute increase of our method in comparison with GTR [23]. We can observe that our DualG achieves consistent increases on all query-table pairs of different proportions. The DualG shows the prominent superiority on NDCG@5, indicating that our model can rank the related tables ahead even across datasets. In addition, training on the full WebQueryTable tends to produce the worst performance on WikiTables, the reason may be that a large number of training instances exacerbate the data distribution gap between WebQueryTable and WikiTables dataset. Still, our DualG shows the more significant advantages over GTR (e.g., 11.27% increase on NDCG@10) when training on *all* query-table pairs of WebQueryTable. Overall, our superiority comes from the dual graphs based on row view and column view, which contribute to the accurate table understanding and improve the generalization of our DualG.

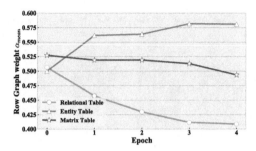

**Fig. 5.** Dynamic changes of row graph weight $\alpha_{mean}$ during training for various tables.

**Case Study.** As shown in Fig. 4, table types can be summarized into *Relational Table*, *Entity Table* and *Matrix Table* [7,23]. To study the adaptability of our DualG for various table types, we give 3 cases from WikiTables dataset corresponding to three table types in Fig. 4, and then record the change trend of fusion weight $\alpha_{mean} = \text{mean}([\text{mean}(\boldsymbol{\alpha}_1), ..., \text{mean}(\boldsymbol{\alpha}_N)])$ for the row graph during training process in Fig. 5. We can observe that: $\alpha_{mean}$ for the relational table tends to decrease with the training epoch, while the entity table shows an uptrend. As the relational table is column information-intensive and DualG properly focuses on a column-aware layout instead of a row-aware one, while the entity table has rich row information and exhibits the opposite trend. The $\alpha_{mean}$ weight for the matrix table converges to about 0.5, which shows DualG can capture both row- and column-aware structures correctly. Overall, our DualG has the powerful potential of adaptability for diversified table layouts.

## 5    Conclusion

This paper proposes a dual-graph based method DualG for enhancing table retrieval, which captures the local row- and column-aware layouts with table contexts (e.g., caption), and then acquires the thorough table representation with tailor-made interaction and fusion mechanism. Experimental results show that the approach is effective and feasible by using it in table retrieval, and the cross-dataset evaluation shows that it has a good generalization ability. Our method further enriches the table retrieval community from graph perspective, and we would like to apply it into related downstream tasks, e.g., table-based question answering and fact verification in the future.

**Acknowledgment.** This work is supported by the National Key Research and Development Program of China (grant No.2021YFB3100600), the Strategic Priority Research Program of Chinese Academy of Sciences (grant No.XDC02040400) and the Youth Innovation Promotion Association of CAS (Grant No. 2021153).

**Ethics Statement.** I understand that using technology can have ethical implications, especially in collection, processing, and privacy of form retrieval data. I acknowledge and recognize the importance of complying with ethical standards and the hazards of potential risks.

In the data collection and processing, my training data comes from two publicly available tabular search datasets. Although we do not collect or store any sensitive information, we should strictly restrict the retrieval text of users and ensure that it does not contain any dangerous information.

In addition, when the model used in police or military related applications, we should pay special attention to its use in these areas, which must conducted in a more responsible manner. To prevent models from providing inaccurate search results for police or military personnel, users are responsible for ensuring that they comply with ethical principles and laws and regulations when using model outputs, and for screening search results.

In summary, I strive to ensure that the model outputs search results in an ethical and responsible manner, and I urge my users to do the same. I will continue to adhere to ethical standards and stay abreast of emerging ethical issues in the fields of machine learning and data mining.

# References

1. Cafarella, M.J., Halevy, A., Khoussainova, N.: Data integration for the relational web. Proc. VLDB Endowment **2**(1), 1090–1101 (2009)
2. Chen, W., et al.: TabFact: a large-scale dataset for table-based fact verification. In: 8th International Conference on Learning Representations, ICLR 2020, Addis Ababa, Ethiopia, 26–30 April 2020. OpenReview.net (2020). https://openreview.net/forum?id=rkeJRhNYDH
3. Chen, W., Zha, H., Chen, Z., Xiong, W., Wang, H., Wang, W.Y.: HybridQA: a dataset of multi-hop question answering over tabular and textual data. In: Findings of the Association for Computational Linguistics: EMNLP 2020. Association for Computational Linguistics, Online (2020). https://doi.org/10.18653/v1/2020.findings-emnlp.91, https://aclanthology.org/2020.findings-emnlp.91
4. Chen, Z., Trabelsi, M., Heflin, J., Xu, Y., Davison, B.D.: Table search using a deep contextualized language model. In: Huang, J., et al. (eds.) Proceedings of the 43rd International ACM SIGIR conference on research and development in Information Retrieval, SIGIR 2020, Virtual Event, China, 25–30 July 2020. ACM (2020). https://doi.org/10.1145/3397271.3401044, https://doi.org/10.1145/3397271.3401044
5. Chen, Z., Trabelsi, M., Heflin, J., Yin, D., Davison, B.D.: MGNETS: multi-graph neural networks for table search. In: Proceedings of the 30th ACM International Conference on Information & Knowledge Management, pp. 2945–2949. Association for Computing Machinery, New York, NY, USA (2021), https://doi.org/10.1145/3459637.3482140
6. Devlin, J., Chang, M.W., Lee, K., Toutanova, K.: BERT: Pre-training of deep bidirectional transformers for language understanding. In: Proceedings of the 2019 Conference of the North American Chapter of the Association for Computational Linguistics: Human Language Technologies. vol. 1 (Long and Short Papers). Association for Computational Linguistics, Minneapolis, Minnesota (2019). https://doi.org/10.18653/v1/N19-1423, https://aclanthology.org/N19-1423

7. Eberius, J., Braunschweig, K., Hentsch, M., Thiele, M., Ahmadov, A., Lehner, W.: Building the dresden web table corpus: a classification approach. In: 2015 IEEE/ACM 2nd International Symposium on Big Data Computing (BDC) (2015). https://doi.org/10.1109/BDC.2015.30

8. Joulin, A., Grave, E., Bojanowski, P., Mikolov, T.: Bag of tricks for efficient text classification. In: Proceedings of the 15th Conference of the European Chapter of the Association for Computational Linguistics. vol. 2, Short Papers. Association for Computational Linguistics, Valencia, Spain (2017). https://aclanthology.org/E17-2068

9. Kipf, T.N., Welling, M.: Semi-supervised classification with graph convolutional networks. In: 5th International Conference on Learning Representations, ICLR 2017, Toulon, France, 24–26 April 2017, Conference Track Proceedings. OpenReview.net (2017). https://openreview.net/forum?id=SJU4ayYgl

10. Kurland, O.: The cluster hypothesis in information retrieval. In: Jones, G.J.F., Sheridan, P., Kelly, D., de Rijke, M., Sakai, T. (eds.) The 36th International ACM SIGIR conference on research and development in Information Retrieval, SIGIR 2013, Dublin, Ireland - July 28 - August 01, 2013. ACM (2013). https://doi.org/10.1145/2484028.2484192, https://doi.org/10.1145/2484028.2484192

11. Li, X., Sun, Y., Cheng, G.: TSQA: Tabular scenario based question answering. Proc. AAAI Conf. Artif. Intell. **35**(15), 13297–13305 (2021). https://ojs.aaai.org/index.php/AAAI/article/view/17570

12. MacDonald, E., Barbosa, D.: Neural relation extraction on wikipedia tables for augmenting knowledge graphs. In: d'Aquin, M., Dietze, S., Hauff, C., Curry, E., Cudré-Mauroux, P. (eds.) CIKM 2020: The 29th ACM International Conference on Information and Knowledge Management, Virtual Event, Ireland, 19–23 October 2020. ACM (2020). https://doi.org/10.1145/3340531.3412164, https://doi.org/10.1145/3340531.3412164

13. Pan, F., Canim, M., Glass, M., Gliozzo, A., Fox, P.: CLTR: an end-to-end, transformer-based system for cell-level table retrieval and table question answering. In: Proceedings of the 59th Annual Meeting of the Association for Computational Linguistics and the 11th International Joint Conference on Natural Language Processing: System Demonstrations. Association for Computational Linguistics, Online (2021). https://doi.org/10.18653/v1/2021.acl-demo.24, https://aclanthology.org/2021.acl-demo.24

14. Robertson, S.E., Walker, S., Jones, S., Hancock-Beaulieu, M.M., Gatford, M., et al.: Okapi at trec-3. Nist Special Publication Sp 109 (1995)

15. Shi, Q., Zhang, Y., Yin, Q., Liu, T.: Logic-level evidence retrieval and graph-based verification network for table-based fact verification. In: Proceedings of the 2021 Conference on Empirical Methods in Natural Language Processing. Association for Computational Linguistics, Online and Punta Cana, Dominican Republic (2021). https://doi.org/10.18653/v1/2021.emnlp-main.16, https://aclanthology.org/2021.emnlp-main.16

16. Shraga, R., Roitman, H., Feigenblat, G., Canim, M.: Ad hoc table retrieval using intrinsic and extrinsic similarities. In: WWW 2020: The Web Conference 2020, Taipei, Taiwan, April 20–24, 2020. ACM/IW3C2 (2020). https://doi.org/10.1145/3366423.3379995, https://doi.org/10.1145/3366423.3379995

17. Shraga, R., Roitman, H., Feigenblat, G., Canim, M.: Web table retrieval using multimodal deep learning. In: Huang, J., (eds.), Proceedings of the 43rd International ACM SIGIR conference on research and development in Information Retrieval, SIGIR 2020, Virtual Event, China, 25–30 July 2020. ACM (2020). https://doi.org/10.1145/3397271.3401120, https://doi.org/10.1145/3397271.3401120

18. Sun, Y., Yan, Z., Tang, D., Duan, N., Qin, B.: Content-based table retrieval for web queries. Neurocomputing **349**, 183–189 (2019). https://doi.org/10.1016/j.neucom.2018.10.033, https://www.sciencedirect.com/science/article/pii/S0925231218312219

19. Trabelsi, M., Chen, Z., Zhang, S., Davison, B.D., Heflin, J.: StruBERT: structure-aware BERT for table search and matching. In: Proceedings of the ACM Web Conference 2022. WWW 2022, Association for Computing Machinery, New York, NY, USA (2022). https://doi.org/10.1145/3485447.3511972, https://doi.org/10.1145/3485447.3511972

20. Vaswani, A., et al.: Attention is all you need. In: Guyon, I., (ed.) Advances in Neural Information Processing Systems 30: Annual Conference on Neural Information Processing Systems 2017, December 4–9, 2017, Long Beach, CA, USA (2017)

21. Venetis, P., et al.: Recovering semantics of tables on the web. Proc. VLDB Endowment **4**(9), 528–538 (2011)

22. Wang, D., Shiralkar, P., Lockard, C., Huang, B., Dong, X.L., Jiang, M.: TCN: table convolutional network for web table interpretation. In: Proceedings of the Web Conference 2021. WWW 2021, Association for Computing Machinery, New York, NY, USA (2021). https://doi.org/10.1145/3442381.3450090, https://doi.org/10.1145/3442381.3450090

23. Wang, F., Sun, K., Chen, M., Pujara, J., Szekely, P.: Retrieving complex tables with multi-granular graph representation learning. In: Proceedings of the 44th International ACM SIGIR Conference on Research and Development in Information Retrieval. Association for Computing Machinery, New York, NY, USA (2021). https://doi.org/10.1145/3404835.3462909

24. Yin, P., Neubig, G., Yih, W.T., Riedel, S.: TaBERT: pretraining for joint understanding of textual and tabular data. In: Proceedings of the 58th Annual Meeting of the Association for Computational Linguistics. Association for Computational Linguistics, Online (2020). https://doi.org/10.18653/v1/2020.acl-main.745, https://aclanthology.org/2020.acl-main.745

25. Zhang, L., Zhang, S., Balog, K.: Table2vec: neural word and entity embeddings for table population and retrieval. In: Piwowarski, B., Chevalier, M., Gaussier, É., Maarek, Y., Nie, J., Scholer, F. (eds.) Proceedings of the 42nd International ACM SIGIR Conference on Research and Development in Information Retrieval, SIGIR 2019, Paris, France, 21–25 July 2019. ACM (2019). https://doi.org/10.1145/3331184.3331333, https://doi.org/10.1145/3331184.3331333

26. Zhang, S., Balog, K.: Ad hoc table retrieval using semantic similarity. In: Champin, P., Gandon, F.L., Lalmas, M., Ipeirotis, P.G. (eds.) Proceedings of the 2018 World Wide Web Conference on World Wide Web, WWW 2018, Lyon, France, 23–27 April 2018. ACM (2018). https://doi.org/10.1145/3178876.3186067, https://doi.org/10.1145/3178876.3186067

# A Few Good Sentences: Content Selection for Abstractive Text Summarization

Vivek Srivastava$^{(\boxtimes)}$, Savita Bhat, and Niranjan Pedanekar

TCS Research, Pune, India
{srivastava.vivek2,savita.bhat,n.pedanekar}@tcs.com

**Abstract.** Abstractive text summarization has been of research interest for decades. Neural approaches, specifically recent transformer-based methods, have demonstrated promising performance in generating summaries with novel words and paraphrases. In spite of generating more fluent summaries, these approaches may yet show poor summary-worthy content selection. In these methods, the extractive content selection is majorly dependent on the reference summary with little to no focus on identifying the summary-worthy segments (SWORTS) in a reference-free setting. In this work, we leverage three metrics, namely, *informativeness*, *relevance*, and *redundancy* in selecting the SWORTS. We propose a novel topic-informed and reference-free method to rank the sentences in the source document based on their importance. We demonstrate the effectiveness of SWORTS selection in different settings such as fine-tuning, few-shot tuning, and zero-shot abstractive text summarization. We observe that self-training and cross-training a pre-trained model with SWORTS selected data shows competitive performance to the pre-trained model. Furthermore, a small amount of SWORTS selected data is sufficient for domain adaptation against fine-tuning on the entire training dataset with no content selection. In contrast to training a model on the source dataset with no content selection, we observe a significant reduction in the time required to train a model with SWORTS that further underlines the importance of content selection for training an abstractive text summarization model.

**Keywords:** Summarization · Fine-tuning · Content Selection

## 1 Introduction

Text summarization aims at generating compact outline text covering salient information from a source document. Recent years have seen an increased focus on the summarization task with advancements in model architectures [9,14], evaluation metrics [36,41], and large-scale datasets [18]. Selecting summary-worthy sentences (hereafter SWORTS) from the source document is a crucial step in ensuring quality outputs. Works such as [8,23] identify this as one of the limitations in generating informative summaries. Variety of approaches such as attention-based sentence selection [8,33], semantic salience-based selection [15], and policy-based reinforcement learning [2], are documented in the literature

Australia leg-spinner Stuart MacGill has announced he will quit international cricket at the end of the ongoing second Test against West Indies. MacGill will retire after 10 years of Test cricket, in which he has taken 207 wickets. The 37-year-old made his Test debut against South Africa 10 years ago and has since gone on to take 207 wickets at an average of 28.28 over 43 Test matches. "Unfortunately now my time is up" MacGill said. "I am incredibly lucky that as well as providing me with amazing opportunities off the field, my job allows me to test myself in one of Australia's most highly scrutinised sporting environments. Bowling with some of crickets all time greats such as Glenn McGrath, Shane Warne, Jason Gillespie and Brett Lee has made my job a lot easier. I want to be sure that exciting young bowlers like Mitchell Johnson enjoy the same privilege," he added. MacGill took the only wicket to fall on a rain-interrupted third day of the Test in Antigua. He had Ramnaresh Sarwan brilliantly caught at slip by Michael Clarke for a well-constructed 65, but otherwise drew blank on a frustrating day for the tourists. The ever dependable Shivnarine Chanderpaul (55 not out) and Dwayne Bravo (29 not out) took the West Indies to the close on 255 for four wickets. They were replying to Australia's 479 for seven declared and with only two days remaining a draw looks the likely outcome in MacGill's farewell appearance. Australia won the first Test in Jamaica by 95 runs.

**Fig. 1.** Example from the CNN-DM dataset. We highlight the sentences identified as non-summary-worthy by our SWORTS selection approach. The underlined phrases cover the facts presented in the first highlighted sentence. The second highlighted sentence captures the sentiment associated with the event (i.e., retirement) and presents very less factual information. (Color figure online)

for selecting suitable candidate sentences. Majority of these approaches, while training, use reference summaries to evaluate and identify candidate sentences. In the case of extractive summarization, identifying SWORTS is typically considered as a sequence labeling task [3] with greedy search approach [19] as the most popular way for labeling sentences. Recent works have demonstrated various issues such as lead bias [10], underfitting [22], and monolingual bias [12] with the greedy labeling approach. Content selection in abstractive summarization is implicit in end-to-end systems.

In this work, we posit that an end-to-end abstractive text summarization system gives little to no control in planning the quality of the output on various aspects such as informativeness and relevance. Also, in a two-stage abstractive summarization system [2,38], the first stage (un)supervised extractive summarization models crudely chop off a large chunk of the summary-worthy sentences which makes the output from these systems unsuitable to be used with an abstractive summarization system. To this extent, we consider a reference-free approach and use topical distribution and inter-sentence relationships to identify summary-worthy sentences from the source document (see Sect. 2). We believe that focused identification of SWORTS ensures better control and planning as well as interpretability of the generated output. In Fig. 1, we present an example document with the identified SWORTS with our approach, highlighting the need for such approaches in abstractive text summarization tasks.

In this work, we explore the effect of content selection in various settings, viz: domain adaptation, self-training, and cross-training. Domain adaptation, where a model trained on a source domain is transformed for a different target domain, has been explored from different dimensions, such as model-centric methods in which feature space, loss functions, or model architectures are altered or augmented [7,25], and data-centric methods involving pseudo labeling and data selection [6,31,32]. Here, we consider a data-centric approach in which we investigate the amount of quality data required to train a system for domain adaptation on unseen domains. In another setup, we self-train an abstractive summarization model pre-trained on a dataset by further fine-tuning the same model using SWORTS selected documents along with the original reference summaries from the same dataset. In a cross-training setting, we consider the source data (for the pre-trained model) and cross-training data to be different but from a similar domain.

These setups help us to investigate the effectiveness of content selection metrics in fine-tuning the existing pre-trained models on novel and unseen datasets. Furthermore, these metrics also help us to reduce the training time owing to the reduced dataset size post content selection. Our contributions are as follows:

1. We define a novel topic-aware formulation for three metrics, namely, *informativeness*, *relevance*, and *redundancy*.
2. We propose a novel topic-informed and reference-free pipeline (COMET) to identify the SWORTS. Also, we present and investigate three variations of COMET for content selection.
3. We extensively experiment to understand the effect of content selection in various settings, such as fine-tuning, few-shot training, and zero-shot inference, exploring domain adaptation and self-training.

## 2    SWORTS Selection

In this section, we present a novel approach to identify SWORTS from the source document for the abstractive text summarization task. Inspired by several existing works [24,27,37], we propose a novel formulation for three metrics (*informativeness*, *relevance*, and *redundancy*) and leverage these metrics for SWORTS selection from the source document in a reference-free setting.

*Notations and Problem Formulation:* Given a source document $D = \{d_1, d_2, ..., d_n\}$ containing $n$ sentences and the document summary $S = \{s_1, s_2, ..., s_m\}$ containing $m$ sentences, we identify a set $D'$ of $k$ sentences s.t. $D' \subseteq D$ and $k \leq n$. The set $D'$ of $k$ sentences is the SWORTS selected data from $D$. Furthermore, the SWORTS selection algorithm considers the source document as the set of $p$ ordered topics i.e., $D = \{t_1, t_2, ..., t_p\}$ where $t_i = \{s_j, s_{j+1}, s_{j+2}, ..., s_{j+l-1}\}$ contains $l$ ordered sentences from the document. Each topic $t_i$ contains a list of sentences in the same order as they appear in the source document (see Sect. 3.4 for a detailed discussion on experimental settings).

## 2.1   Content Selection Metrics

In this section, we define and formulate the three content selection metrics for SWORTS selection. With each formulation, we assign a score to a sentence in the source document $D$. We refer to a sentence $i$ in $D$ as a *document unit* ($d_i$).

**Informativeness:** To a reader, the document unit is informative if it offers a change in the knowledge about the document. Intuitively, informativeness measures the degree to which the document unit provides non-trivial information. A document unit is less informative if it contains the likely semantic units (words or phrases). To measure the informativeness, we consider a document unit to be made up of semantic units (here, $u$-grams, where $u \geq 1$) such that each semantic unit contributes to the overall informativeness of the document unit. Formally, we define the informativeness of a document unit $d_i$ in a topic-segment $t_j$ as:

$$Info(d_i, t_j) = \frac{\sum_{u=1}^{U} w(u, d_i) f_{rep}(u, d_i, t_j)}{n} \qquad (1)$$

such that,

$$w(u, d_i) = \frac{1}{|\text{Unique } u\text{-grams in } d_i|} \qquad (2)$$

where, $f_{rep}(u, d_i, t_j)$ represents the repetitiveness of $u$-grams by measuring the count of $u$-grams in $d_i$ that occurs in the remaining document units in $t_j$. Intuitively, a lower-order $u$-gram is likely to be repeated in the topic segment and will contribute less towards the overall informativeness score of $d_i$ due to the relatively lower $w(u, d_i)$ score whereas the repetition of higher-order $u$-grams in a segment signifies its high importance in conveying the key information. $w(u, d_i)$ controls the degree with which the repetitive behavior of a $u$-gram in a topic-segment denotes its informativeness.

**Relevance:** While approximating a document, we need to keep the key content with minimum loss of information. Leveraging the relevance of each document unit, we condense the source document to deliver the key message. We formally define the relevance of a document unit $d_i$ in a topic-segment $t_j$ as:

$$Rel(d_i, t_j) = \begin{cases} R_{lead}(d_i, t_j), & \text{if } D \text{ starts with } d_i \\ R_{topic}(d_i, t_j), & \text{if } t_j \text{ starts with } d_i \\ R(d_i, t_j), & \text{Otherwise} \end{cases}$$

such that,

$$R_{lead}(d_i, t_j) = \frac{\sum_{v=1}^{p} f_{csim}(\vec{d_i}, \vec{d_1^v})}{p} \qquad (3)$$

$$R_{topic}(\vec{d_i}, \vec{t_j}) = f_{csim}(\vec{d_i}, \vec{d_{-1}^{j-1}}) \qquad (4)$$

$$R(d_i, t_j) = \frac{\sum_{x=1}^{i-1} f_{csim}(\vec{d_i}, \vec{d_x})}{i - 1} \qquad (5)$$

where $f_{csim}(.)$ represents the cosine similarity between the two vectors. In Eq. 3, $\vec{d_1^v}$ represents the vector corresponding to the first document unit of topic segment $v$. Similarly, $\vec{d_{-1}^{j-1}}$ represents the vector corresponding to the last document unit of topic segment $j - 1$. We consider the sentence embedding representation as the document unit vector.

In Eq. 3, we compute the relevance of the leading document unit of a document with respect to the leading document units of the other topic segments of the document. In Eq. 4, the relevance of a leading document unit of a topic is computed with respect to the last document unit of the previous topic segment to capture the continuum of the discussion across topics. In Eq. 5, we consider the relevance of a document unit with respect to the preceding document units in the same topic segment.

**Redundancy:** Redundancy in a document leads to overlap between various semantic units and increased repetitiveness in the document. It further leads to reduced information coverage per semantic units of the document. To measure the redundancy, we consider a document unit to be made up of $Q$ words. Formally, we define the redundancy of a document unit $d_i$ in a topic -segment $t_j$ as:

$$Red(d_i, t_j) = \frac{\sum_{q=1}^{Q} g_{rep}(q, t_j)}{Q * |t_j|} \tag{6}$$

where, $g_{rep}(q, t_j)$ represents the repetitiveness of the word $q$ by measuring the count of document units in $t_j$ where the word $q$ occurs. Intuitively, a document unit comprising of words that occur frequently in the topic segment leads to its high redundancy and that results in the document unit being less summary-worthy.

### 2.2   SWORTS Selection Pipeline

In this section, we present the content selection metrics driven pipeline for SWORTS selection (hereafter, $COMET$) leveraging the three content selection metrics proposed in Sect. 2.1. COMET consists of four major components:

1. **Scoring the document unit:** For a given source document $D$, we compute three topic-informed metric scores for each document unit using the formulation given in Sect. 2.1. We represent this 3-dimensional metric score for $d_i$ as $M^{d_i}$ such that:

$$M^{d_i} = \{Info(d_i), Rel(d_i), Red(d_i)\} \tag{7}$$

2. **Importance ranking of document units:** Next, we propose four different document unit ranking systems leveraging metric combinations from $M^{d_i}$. In each ranking system, we consider the different combinations of the proposed metrics. Formally, the four importance ranking systems for a document unit $d_i$ are defined as follows:

$$Imp_\alpha(d_i) = N_{Info}(Info(d_i)) + N_{Rel}(Rel(d_i)) \tag{8}$$

---

**Algorithm 1.** SWORTS selection for COMET

---

1: **procedure** BLOCKING($d_j$, $Selected_{d_i}$)
2:     $Flag = 0$
3:     **for** i in range($len(Selected_{d_i})$) **do**
4:         **if** $Trigram\_phrase(Selected_{d_i}[i]) \in d_j$ **then**
5:             $Flag = 1$
6:             Break
7:         **if** $Noun\_phrase(Selected_{d_i}[i]) \in d_j$ **then**
8:             $Flag = 1$
9:             Break
10:    **return** $Flag$

1: **procedure** SWORTS_SELECT($D, M$)
2:     $Selected_{d_i} \leftarrow \{\}$
3:     **for** i in range(1, n) **do**
4:         Select the maximum scoring document unit ($d_j$) s.t. $d_j \notin Selected_{d_i}$
5:         **if** $BLOCKING(d_j, Selected_{d_i}) == False$ **then**
6:             $Selected_{d_i}.insert(d_j)$
7:     **return** $Selected_{d_i}$

---

$$Imp_\beta(d_i) = N_{Rel}(Rel(d_i)) - N_{Red}(Red(d_i)) \tag{9}$$

$$Imp_\gamma(d_i) = N_{info}(Info(d_i)) - N_{Red}(Red(d_i)) \tag{10}$$

$$Imp_\delta(d_i) = N_{Info}(Info(d_i)) + N_{Rel}(Rel(d_i)) - N_{Red}(Red(d_i)) \tag{11}$$

where, $N_{Info}(.)$, $N_{Rel}(.)$, and $N_{Red}(.)$ are the functions to scale the metric scores between 0 to 1. We subtract the redundancy score in Eqs. 9, 10, and 11 as the redundancy of the document unit is undesirable while identifying the summary-worthy content.

3. **SWORTS selection:** We use the four document unit ranking systems to identify and select the SWORTS. For a source document $D$, each ranking system independently generates the SWORTS selected data (i.e., $D'_\alpha$, $D'_\beta$, $D'_\gamma$, and $D'_\delta$). We present the SWORTS selection procedure in Algorithm 1. We adopt and modify the trigram blocking [26] strategy to dynamically select the document units from the source documents. Specifically, in addition to the trigram phrases, we consider the noun phrases (comprising more than one token) as the blocking strategy (see details in Algorithm 1). For a document unit $d_j$, if a trigram phrase or a noun phrase from $d_j$ exists in the already selected document units, we drop $d_j$ and do not consider it as SWORTS.

4. **Fluency ranking of SWORTS selected data:** For a source document $D$, we obtain four SWORTS selected documents corresponding to each ranking system. Next, we retrieve the best candidate based on the fluency of each SWORTS selected document. We measure the fluency of a document using the perplexity computed with an auto-regressive language model. Among $D'_\alpha$,

$D'_\beta$, $D'_\gamma$, and $D'_\delta$, we select the document with the least perplexity as the final SWORTS selected document $(D')$ for $D$.

## 2.3  COMET Variants

For each document in a dataset, the COMET pipeline retrieves a varying number of document units. On average, we obtain $K$ document units per document in the dataset. Leveraging the capability of COMET to dynamically prune the source document, we propose three variants of the COMET pipeline for content selection. In the first variant of the COMET pipeline (a.k.a LEAD-K), we select the leading $K$ document units from the source documents. In the next variant (a.k.a ORACLE), we select the top-$K$ document units from the source document based on the ROUGE-1 score between the document units and the reference summary. Lastly, we propose a dynamic version of the second variant (a.k.a DYNAMIC ORACLE or D-ORACLE). Similar to the ORACLE method, we select the document units based on the ROUGE-1 score with the reference summary. But instead of selecting $K$ document units for each document, we dynamically identify the number of document units to select based on the number of document units identified by the COMET pipeline.

## 3  Experimental Setup

In this section, we present the experimental setup to evaluate the effectiveness of the proposed content selection methodology for the abstractive text summarization task. In three different configurations, we experiment with BART [16] and PEGASUS [39] models pre-trained on the CNN-DM [11,20] and XSUM [21] datasets. Both the CNN-DM and the XSUM datasets are popularly used as a benchmark for the abstractive news summarization task. The CNN-DM dataset contains an approximately 3–4 sentence long summary along with the CNN-DailyMail news article whereas the XSUM dataset contains a single sentence summary along with the BBC news article. Next, we discuss the three experimental setups in detail.

### 3.1  Self-training

In the first setup, we experiment with self-training an existing summarization model. We perform the self-training on the SWORTS selected data as the source document along with the original reference summary. Formally, if a summarization model $X$ is trained on the dataset $\hat{D}$, we self-train the model $X$ such that:

$$\hat{X} = \theta_{self}(X, d_i, s_i); \ \forall (d_i, s_i) \in \hat{D} \tag{12}$$

where, $\theta_{self}$ is the self-training of the pre-trained model $X$ on the SWORTS selected document and reference summary pairs from $\hat{D}$. In our experiment, we self-train the pre-trained BART and PEGASUS models on the SWORTS selected datasets.

Furthermore, we evaluate the model's performance on the Factual Inconsistency Benchmark (FIB) [34]. The FIB benchmark contains article-summary pairs from the CNN-DM and XSUM datasets where the reference summaries are manually corrected to remove the factual inconsistency. With the FIB benchmark, we evaluate and compare the performance of self-trained and pre-trained models against the factually corrected reference summaries.

## 3.2    Cross-Training

In the next setup, we experiment with cross-training a pre-trained summarization model on a novel dataset. We cross-train a pre-trained model $Y$ on a randomly sampled set of $r$ document and summary pairs from $\hat{D}$. In this experiment, the model $Y$ is pre-trained on the dataset(s) other than $D$ and $\hat{D}$. Formally,

$$\hat{Y} = \theta_{cross}(Y, r, d_i, s_i); \forall (d_i, s_i) \in \hat{D} \tag{13}$$

where, $\theta_{cross}$ is the cross-training of $Y$ on the SWORTS selected document and reference summary pairs from $\hat{D}$.

In our experiment, we cross-train the BART and PEGASUS models (pre-trained on the XSUM dataset) on the CNN-DM dataset and vice-versa. We experiment with four different sample sizes ($r$) i.e., 0.1%, 1%, 10%, and 100% of the training dataset.

## 3.3    Zero-Shot Adaptation

In the final experiment, we evaluate the zero-shot adaptation capability of the summarization models. In all our experiments, we generate the abstractive summary for a document in the test set with no content selection. Our content selection strategy is restricted to the training and development phases only. Here, we compare the pre-trained BART and PEGASUS models on the XSUM and CNN-DM datasets against the self-trained versions of these models on the same datasets. We experiment with these models on datasets from four different domains:

- **NARRASUM** [40]: It is a narrative summarization dataset to summarize the plot description of movies and TV episodes abstractively. The data is collected from various movie websites and encyclopedias such as Wikipedia and IMDb. We generate the zero-shot summaries for 6121 narrative-summary pairs from the test set and report our findings.
- **PENS** [1]: It is a personalized news headline generation dataset. The dataset is curated from the Microsoft News website and contains English news articles and summaries, other textual content, and user impression logs. We generate the zero-shot summaries for 5000 news articles from the dataset and compare them against the reference summary.
- **Reddit** [13]: This dataset is collected from the Reddit online discussion forum. In contrast to the usual summarization datasets with formal documents as the source, this dataset contains informal discussions from the

TIFU subreddit forum along with TL; DR as the summary. We experiment with 5000 samples from this dataset and report our findings.

- **WikiSum** [5]: The dataset is collected from the article-summary pairs appearing on the WikiHow website. The WikiSum documents are written in simple English, and the summaries (written by the document author) provide non-obvious tips that mimic the advice a knowledgeable, empathetic friend might give[1]. We experiment with 2000 article-summary pairs from the test set of the dataset.

## 3.4  Experimental Settings

We segment a document into a sequence of topics using the sentence similarity-based topic-segmentation algorithm, C99 [4]. We select C99 due to the fast topic segmentation and flexibility to plug and play with different sentence representation models. We use the sentence BERT representations [29] to segment the article into multiple topics. We also use the sentence BERT representations to encode the sentences in the relevance metric computation. To compute the perplexity of the documents for fluency ranking in Sect. 2, we use the pre-trained GPT-2 model [28]. We experiment with BART[2,3] and PEGASUS[4,5] models available on Hugging Face. We train our models on a V100 GPU with a batch size of 8, one epoch, and default arguments from the transformers library[6]. Based on the COMET pipeline, we use the value of $K$ (in LEAD-K and ORACLE) as 74.53% and 81.70% for the CNN-DM and XSUM datasets respectively.

## 4  Results and Analysis

In this section, we present and analyze the results from the three experiments discussed in Sect. 3. We use the following metrics for evaluating different setups:

1. **ROUGE** [30]: We evaluate the model-generated summaries against the reference summary using the ROUGE-1, ROUGE-2, and ROUGE-L F1 metric scores[7].
2. **$\Delta$ROUGE**: We compare the performance of two models based on the percentage change in the ROUGE score. For two systems with ROUGE-1 scores as R and $\hat{R}$, we define $\Delta R1$ as:

$$\Delta R1 = 100 * \frac{R - \hat{R}}{R} \qquad (14)$$

---

[1]  https://www.wikihow.com/.

[2]  https://huggingface.co/facebook/bart-large-cnn.

[3]  https://huggingface.co/facebook/bart-large-xsum.

[4]  https://huggingface.co/google/pegasus-cnn_dailymail.

[5]  https://huggingface.co/google/pegasus-xsum.

[6]  https://github.com/huggingface/transformers/tree/main/examples/pytorch/summarization.

[7]  https://github.com/google-research/google-research/tree/master/rouge.

Similarly, we define the $\Delta R2$ and $\Delta RL$ scores for ROUGE-2 and ROUGE-L metrics, respectively.

3. **Aggregate Performance Change (APC):** While comparing two systems, the $\Delta$ROUGE metric gives three different scores i.e., $\Delta R1$, $\Delta R2$, and $\Delta RL$. We report an aggregate change in the performance between models M1 and $\hat{M}1$ as:

$$APC(M1, \hat{M}1) = \frac{\Delta R1 + \Delta R2 + \Delta RL}{3} \tag{15}$$

where, $\Delta R1$, $\Delta R2$, and $\Delta RL$ scores are computed between the summaries generated by the models M1 and $\hat{M}1$.

4. **$\Delta$Time:** We compare two models based on the time required to train a model on a given dataset. For two systems with training time as T and $\hat{T}$, we define, $\Delta Time$ (or $\Delta T$) as:

$$\Delta Time = 100 * \frac{T - \hat{T}}{T} \tag{16}$$

### 4.1    Self-training

This section presents the self-training results of the BART and PEGASUS models on the SWORTS selected data from the CNN-DM and the XSUM datasets. In Table 1, we report the results of the self-training experiment. We report the ROUGE and APC scores for each model. We compute the APC score for the COMET model (and its variant) against the base model (i.e., pre-trained BART and PEGASUS). We also report the performance of the self-trained models on the FIB benchmark (see Table 2). Some key observations are:

**Focused Training with SWORTS Improves Model Performance.** As shown in Table 1, all COMET variations show comparable performance to the base model, especially in the case of the CNN-DM dataset. CNN-DM dataset has comparatively longer and more high-quality reference summaries than the XSUM dataset [35] which further helps the self-training to generate high-quality summaries (see Appendix for examples of model-generated summaries).

**Table 1.** Self-training results. We highlight the row with the maximum APC among all the COMET variants. We bold the ROUGE metric scores for a better model than the corresponding BASE model. The BASE model represents the pre-trained model on the corresponding dataset.

| Model | CNN-DM | | | | | | | | XSUM | | | | | | | |
| | BART | | | | PEGASUS | | | | BART | | | | PEGASUS | | | |
| | R1 | R2 | RL | APC | R1 | R2 | RL | APC | R1 | R2 | RL | APC | R1 | R2 | RL | APC |
| BASE | 44.16 | 21.28 | 40.9 | - | 44.17 | 21.47 | 41.11 | - | 45.14 | 22.27 | 37.25 | - | 47.21 | 24.56 | 39.25 | - |
| COMET | **44.53** | 21.12 | **41.56** | +0.56 | **44.68** | **21.67** | **41.63** | **+1.11** | 44.20 | 20.87 | 35.58 | -4.28 | 46.72 | 23.92 | 38.67 | -1.70 |
| LEAD-K | 44.09 | 21.11 | **41.16** | -0.10 | 44.01 | 21.07 | 41.03 | -0.80 | **44.86** | **21.54** | 36.29 | -2.15 | **47.26** | 24.32 | 39.09 | -0.42 |
| ORACLE | **44.39** | 21.26 | **41.46** | +0.59 | **44.32** | 21.39 | **41.33** | +0.16 | 44.58 | 21.29 | 35.98 | -3.01 | 46.83 | 24.11 | 38.81 | -1.25 |
| D-ORACLE | **44.46** | **21.34** | **41.52** | +0.82 | 44.14 | 21.25 | 41.10 | -0.37 | 44.51 | 21.23 | 35.95 | -3.18 | 46.91 | 24.15 | 38.86 | -1.09 |

**Table 2.** Zero-shot results on the FIB benchmark with the self-trained models. We highlight the row with the maximum APC among all the COMET variants. We bold the ROUGE metric scores for a better model than the corresponding BASE model.

| Model | CNN-DM | | | | | | | | XSUM | | | | | | | |
| | BART | | | | PEGASUS | | | | BART | | | | PEGASUS | | | |
| | R1 | R2 | RL | APC | R1 | R2 | RL | APC | R1 | R2 | RL | APC | R1 | R2 | RL | APC |
| BASE | 32.15 | 12.93 | 29.12 | - | 32.01 | 13.21 | 27.07 | - | **44.01** | **19.95** | **36.90** | - | **44.99** | **20.93** | **38.08** | - |
| COMET | 33.48 | 13.03 | 30.54 | +3.26 | **35.01** | **14.40** | **31.86** | +12.02 | 42.34 | 18.48 | 35.17 | -5.28 | 44.56 | 20.84 | 37.80 | -0.70 |
| LEAD-K | 34.23 | 14.03 | 30.68 | +6.77 | 33.27 | 13.35 | 30.54 | +5.93 | 42.63 | 18.70 | 35.19 | -4.67 | 43.93 | 20.03 | 37.41 | -2.80 |
| ORACLE | 33.81 | 13.91 | 30.73 | +6.09 | 34.22 | 13.62 | 31.12 | +8.32 | 43.34 | 19.07 | 36.28 | -2.53 | 44.26 | 20.19 | 37.22 | -2.42 |
| D-ORACLE | **35.69** | **15.58** | **32.20** | +14.02 | 34.28 | **14.52** | 31.38 | +10.97 | 43.07 | 18.98 | 36.07 | -3.08 | 44.61 | 20.37 | 37.44 | -1.73 |

**Shorter and More Abstractive Summarization Needs Attention.** For the XSUM dataset, all experiments show comparable but negative APC. We believe this is because of the inherent complexity of the XSUM dataset, which is defined as eXtreme **SUM**marization. In other words, self-training may be of limited use in the case of more abstractive and shorter summary generation which is in line with the observations made with the existing extractive summarization works on this dataset [42]. Further experiments with more training, additional data or external data will be useful in identifying contributing factors for better performance.

**Noisy Data Needs to Be Cleaned!** We consider the FIB Benchmark dataset that contains factually consistent reference summaries. Due to the limited size of the dataset, we present zero-shot inference results for comparison. As shown in Table 2, all COMET variations give better results than the base model in the case of the CNN-DM dataset, whereas the base model performs better in the case of the XSUM dataset similar to observations in Table 1. We hypothesize that this is because the articles, as well as corresponding summaries in the CNN-DM dataset, are comparatively larger and less noisy than the ones in the XSUM dataset.

## 4.2  Cross-training

We present the results for the sampled cross-training experiments with the BART and PEGASUS models in Tables 3, 4, and 5. Some key observations are:

**No Need to Worry About the Training Time!** In Table 3, we present the cross-training results on the original source dataset without any content selection. We report results on four different sample sizes ($r$) of the training dataset. Tables 4 and 5 give a more detailed understanding of the trade-off between the training time and performance. It is observed that only 10% of the dataset may be sufficient to get comparable performance on the ROUGE score with almost 90% saving on the training time. In such a setting, the content selection with COMET further helps to reduce the training time against cross-training on the source dataset with no content selection. In many real-world applications, time and resources spent on training and fine-tuning a model on domain-specific data

**Table 3.** Cross-training results with no content selection. $r$ denotes the sample size of the training dataset used for cross-training.

| Model | $r$ | CNN-DM | | | | | | XSUM | | | | | |
|---|---|---|---|---|---|---|---|---|---|---|---|---|---|
| | | BART | | | PEGASUS | | | BART | | | PEGASUS | | |
| | | R1 | R2 | RL | R1 | R2 | RL | R1 | R2 | RL | R1 | R2 | RL |
| BASE | - | 44.16 | 21.28 | 40.9 | 44.17 | 21.47 | 41.11 | 45.14 | 22.27 | 37.25 | 47.21 | 24.56 | 39.25 |
| ZERO-SHOT | - | 24.99 | 7.42 | 21.55 | 20.84 | 6.93 | 18.13 | 20.73 | 3.51 | 16.64 | 21.15 | 3.89 | 14.24 |
| SOURCE | 0.1% | 38.49 | 16.47 | 35.32 | 30.95 | 12.52 | 27.19 | 29.11 | 9.87 | 21.87 | 24.97 | 6.66 | 17.76 |
| | 1% | 41.51 | 18.86 | 38.53 | 39.4 | 17.64 | 35.96 | 31.26 | 11.66 | 23.53 | 36.7 | 14.8 | 27.72 |
| | 10% | 42.82 | 20.05 | 39.84 | 41 | 18.95 | 37.89 | 32.93 | 13.14 | 25.02 | 39.93 | 17.44 | 30.83 |
| | 100% | 44.08 | 21.14 | 41.12 | 42.71 | 20.19 | 39.62 | 34.74 | 14.93 | 26.51 | 41.58 | 19.16 | 32.89 |

**Table 4.** Cross-training results for the CNN-DM dataset. For a model, we compute the metric scores against the model trained on the 100% training dataset with no content selection (see Model: SOURCE and $r$: 100% in Table 3). We highlight the row with the maximum APC score among all five models. For a given $r$ and the base model, we bold the individual best scores for the metrics.

| $r$ | Model | BART | | | | | PEGASUS | | | | |
|---|---|---|---|---|---|---|---|---|---|---|---|
| | | $\Delta$R1 | $\Delta$R2 | $\Delta$RL | APC | $\Delta$T | $\Delta$R1 | $\Delta$R2 | $\Delta$RL | APC | $\Delta$T |
| 0.1% | SOURCE | -12.68 | -22.09 | -14.10 | -16.29 | -99.91 | -27.53 | -37.98 | -31.37 | -32.39 | -99.92 |
| | COMET | -12.11 | -21.71 | -13.95 | -15.92 | -99.92 | -27.69 | -38.28 | -31.60 | -32.42 | -99.93 |
| | LEAD-K | -13.81 | -22.65 | -15.53 | -17.33 | -99.91 | -28.02 | -38.43 | -31.85 | -32.76 | -99.92 |
| | ORACLE | **-10.93** | **-18.73** | **-12.28** | **-13.98** | -99.91 | **-26.94** | **-36.20** | **-30.38** | -31.17 | -99.92 |
| | D-ORACLE | -11.43 | -19.34 | -12.67 | -14.48 | -99.91 | -27.81 | -36.55 | -31.07 | -31.81 | -99.92 |
| 1% | SOURCE | -5.83 | -10.78 | -6.29 | -7.63 | -99.12 | -7.74 | -12.63 | -9.23 | -9.86 | -99.09 |
| | COMET | -5.17 | -10.12 | -5.73 | -7.01 | **-99.18** | -7.84 | -13.47 | -9.54 | -10.28 | **-99.20** |
| | LEAD-K | -6.57 | -11.44 | -6.97 | -8.32 | **-99.18** | -7.67 | -12.63 | -9.06 | -9.78 | **-99.20** |
| | ORACLE | **-5.19** | **-9.46** | **-5.59** | -6.74 | **-99.18** | -7.25 | -11.98 | -8.55 | -9.26 | -99.16 |
| | D-ORACLE | -5.33 | -9.50 | -5.73 | -6.85 | -99.17 | **-6.88** | **-11.58** | **-8.25** | -8.90 | -99.14 |
| 10% | SOURCE | **-2.85** | **-5.15** | **-3.11** | -3.70 | -90.42 | -4 | -6.14 | -4.36 | -4.83 | -90.51 |
| | COMET | -3.10 | -5.62 | -3.45 | -4.05 | **-91.21** | -3.46 | -5.79 | -3.96 | -4.40 | **-91.59** |
| | LEAD-K | -3.74 | -6.48 | -3.89 | -4.70 | -91 | -3.48 | -5.54 | -3.83 | -4.28 | -91.51 |
| | ORACLE | -3.19 | -5.58 | -3.40 | -4.05 | -90.85 | **-3.39** | **-5.10** | **-3.73** | -4.07 | -90.91 |
| | D-ORACLE | -2.90 | -5.25 | **-3.11** | -3.75 | -90.88 | -3.44 | -5.29 | -3.81 | -4.18 | -90.88 |
| 100% | SOURCE | - | - | - | - | - | - | - | - | - | - |
| | COMET | -0.79 | -1.75 | -0.89 | -1.14 | **-8.74** | 0 | +0.44 | -0.10 | +0.11 | **-8.82** |
| | LEAD-K | -0.58 | -0.80 | -0.51 | -0.63 | -7.19 | -0.35 | -0.24 | -0.47 | -0.12 | -6.11 |
| | ORACLE | 0 | **-0.04** | +0.02 | -0.01 | -3.16 | **+0.09** | **+0.59** | **+0.02** | **+0.23** | -3.02 |
| | D-ORACLE | **+0.02** | -0.14 | **+0.04** | -0.02 | -4.09 | **+0.09** | **+0.59** | **+0.02** | **+0.23** | -3.53 |

are of utmost importance and our findings would be highly beneficial in such scenarios.

**Pre-trained Summarization Models Are Easily Customizable in Similar Domains.** Cross-training involves fine-tuning a model pre-trained on a dataset from the same or similar domain. Results in Tables 4 and 5 show as small

**Table 5.** Cross-training results for the XSUM dataset. For a model, we compute the metric scores against the model trained on the 100% training dataset with no content selection (see Model: SOURCE and $r$: 100% in Table 3). We highlight the row with the maximum APC score among all five models. For a given $r$ and the base model, we bold the individual best scores for the metrics.

| $r$ | Model | BART | | | | | PEGASUS | | | | |
|---|---|---|---|---|---|---|---|---|---|---|---|
| | | $\Delta$R1 | $\Delta$R2 | $\Delta$RL | APC | $\Delta$T | $\Delta$R1 | $\Delta$R2 | $\Delta$RL | APC | $\Delta$T |
| 0.1% | SOURCE | -16.20 | -33.89 | **-17.50** | -22.53 | -99.90 | -39.94 | -65.24 | -46 | -50.39 | -99.92 |
| | COMET | -16.63 | -34.56 | -18.52 | -23.23 | -99.92 | -39.70 | -64.71 | -45.69 | -50.03 | -99.93 |
| | LEAD-K | **-16** | **-32.15** | -18.48 | **-22.21** | -99.92 | -37.68 | -61.84 | -43.72 | -47.74 | -99.93 |
| | ORACLE | -17.21 | -35.09 | -18.59 | -23.63 | -99.92 | -39 | -63.83 | -45.02 | -49.28 | -99.93 |
| | D-ORACLE | -16.75 | -34.62 | -18.18 | -23.18 | -99.92 | **-36.60** | **-60.22** | **-42.41** | -46.41 | -99.93 |
| 1% | SOURCE | **-10.01** | **-21.90** | **-11.24** | **-14.38** | -99.13 | **-11.73** | **-22.75** | **-15.71** | -16.73 | -99.07 |
| | COMET | -10.24 | **-21.90** | -11.58 | -14.57 | **-99.27** | -12.55 | -23.69 | -16.47 | -17.57 | **-99.17** |
| | LEAD-K | -10.67 | -22.77 | -11.69 | -15.04 | -99.24 | -12.09 | -23.17 | -15.93 | -17.06 | -99.14 |
| | ORACLE | -11.08 | -23.30 | -12.22 | -15.53 | -99.22 | -12.69 | -24.06 | -16.60 | -17.78 | -99.09 |
| | D-ORACLE | -10.67 | -22.97 | -11.99 | -15.21 | -99.25 | -12.24 | -23.53 | -16.20 | -17.20 | -99.16 |
| 10% | SOURCE | **-5.21** | -11.98 | **-5.62** | -7.60 | -90.10 | **-3.96** | **-8.97** | **-6.26** | -6.39 | -90.60 |
| | COMET | -5.81 | -12.86 | -6.26 | -8.31 | **-91.90** | -4.56 | -10.02 | -6.99 | -7.19 | **-91.87** |
| | LEAD-K | -5.38 | **-11.92** | -6.11 | -7.80 | -91.21 | -3.99 | -9.34 | -6.47 | -6.6 | -91.39 |
| | ORACLE | -5.87 | -13.52 | -6.63 | -8.67 | -90.61 | -4.59 | -10.17 | -6.68 | -7.14 | -90.92 |
| | D-ORACLE | -6.04 | -13.46 | -6.71 | -8.73 | -90.97 | -4.61 | -10.59 | -7.05 | -7.41 | -91.58 |
| 100% | SOURCE | - | - | - | - | - | - | - | - | | |
| | COMET | -0.94 | -2.07 | -1.01 | -1.34 | **-16.22** | -1.13 | -1.82 | -1.21 | -1.38 | **-12.43** |
| | LEAD-K | **-0.28** | **-0.46** | **-0.75** | -0.49 | -8.43 | **-0.60** | **-0.73** | **-0.51** | -0.61 | -6.64 |
| | ORACLE | -0.89 | -2.27 | -1.20 | -1.45 | -6.55 | -1.34 | -2.19 | -1.55 | -1.69 | -4.63 |
| | D-ORACLE | -1.09 | -2.27 | -1.35 | -1.57 | -8.44 | -1.01 | -1.35 | -1.12 | -1.16 | -6.45 |

as 10% of the dataset is sufficient to get comparable performance on ROUGE score and APC along with additional time saved with content selection. We believe that the models do learn intrinsic properties about the domain and the task which makes it easier to adapt them for different datasets in similar and related domains with limited additional data.

## 4.3   Zero-Shot Adaptation

In order to evaluate the domain generalization capabilities, we consider self-trained COMET variations of BART and PEGASUS models. We present the results in Table 6. We observe that a self-trained model with content selection shows improved zero-shot performance on novel datasets from unseen domains. D-ORACLE consistently performs better than any other COMET variation and the base model. Extrapolating our observation in cross-training and self-training experiments, we believe that a small subset of the training data may be sufficient to get strong results on domain adaptation with additional time saved in training such models with content selection.

## 4.4   Limitations and Opportunities with SWORTS Selection

In the previous section, we highlight several merits of using the content selection over the naive training of the summarization models with an unmodified dataset. We observe the competitive performance of the trained models in several configurations against the base models. We also observe the time saved in training a model with the content selection which deems useful in a real-world setting. Additionally, we also recognize the challenges in the content selection model that guides the COMET variants. One such major limitation is the additional time required for content selection with the COMET pipeline. To mitigate this, we posit that the threshold $K$ which we identify with COMET on the entire training dataset could be identified on a very small subset of the dataset which can be further used with $Lead - K$ and $Oracle$ variants. It would also be interesting to combine the COMET content selection pipeline with other extractive summarization techniques such as MATCHSUM [42] and BERT-Ext [17].

**Table 6.** Zero-shot adaptation results. We compute the APC against the BASE model. We highlight the row with the maximum APC score among all the COMET variants. For a given dataset, we bold the individual best scores for the metrics.

| Model | NARRASUM | | | | PENS | | | | Reddit | | | | WikiSum | | | |
|---|---|---|---|---|---|---|---|---|---|---|---|---|---|---|---|---|
| | R1 | R2 | RL | APC | R1 | R2 | RL | APC | R1 | R2 | RL | APC | R1 | R2 | RL | APC |
| **BART CNN-DM** | | | | | | | | | | | | | | | | |
| BASE | 28.18 | 5.72 | 24.59 | - | 17.96 | 6.65 | 16.21 | - | 17.23 | 3.78 | 14.50 | - | 32.03 | 8.74 | 28.78 | - |
| COMET | 28.40 | 5.80 | 25.14 | +1.47 | **18.08** | **6.75** | **16.43** | +1.17 | 17.68 | 3.80 | 14.91 | +1.98 | **33.97** | 9.46 | **30.52** | +6.78 |
| LEAD-K | **28.85** | 5.81 | **25.34** | +2.33 | 17.28 | 6.39 | 15.67 | -3.67 | 17.86 | 4.00 | 15.06 | 4.44 | 33.52 | 9.30 | 30.13 | +5.24 |
| ORACLE | 28.27 | 5.76 | 24.84 | +0.67 | 17.75 | 6.62 | 16.17 | -0.62 | **18.38** | **4.01** | **15.48** | +6.50 | 33.37 | 9.39 | 30.03 | +5.32 |
| D-ORACLE | 28.80 | **5.87** | 25.30 | +2.56 | 17.87 | 6.69 | 16.21 | +0.03 | 17.92 | 3.87 | 15.12 | +3.55 | 33.55 | **9.50** | 30.26 | +6.19 |
| **PEGASUS CNN-DM** | | | | | | | | | | | | | | | | |
| BASE | 25.16 | 4.97 | 19.97 | - | 19.37 | 7.43 | 16.12 | - | 17.35 | 3.69 | 13.15 | - | 27.68 | 7.36 | 22.73 | - |
| COMET | 25.50 | 5.25 | 22.34 | +6.28 | 20.01 | 7.63 | 18.01 | +5.90 | 18.02 | 3.84 | 14.98 | +7.28 | 28.99 | 7.84 | 25.94 | +8.45 |
| LEAD-K | 26.04 | 5.15 | 22.77 | +7.04 | 19.41 | 7.28 | 17.42 | +2.08 | 17.40 | 3.68 | 14.49 | +3.40 | 29.23 | 7.76 | 26.14 | +8.67 |
| ORACLE | 25.89 | 5.20 | 22.71 | +7.08 | 19.75 | 7.52 | 17.82 | +4.57 | 17.84 | 3.74 | 14.85 | +5.70 | 28.62 | 7.76 | 25.65 | +7.22 |
| D-ORACLE | **26.30** | **5.31** | **23.03** | +8.89 | 19.66 | 7.53 | 17.63 | +4.07 | 17.42 | 3.60 | 14.51 | +2.76 | **29.38** | **8.02** | **26.33** | +10.31 |
| **BART XSUM** | | | | | | | | | | | | | | | | |
| BASE | 16.25 | 2.83 | 13.53 | - | **24.62** | **8.57** | **20.81** | - | 17.87 | 3.65 | 13.91 | - | 15.59 | 4.57 | 13.77 | - |
| COMET | 15.99 | 2.30 | 13.29 | -7.36 | 18.67 | 5.01 | 15.35 | -30.64 | 14.74 | 2.17 | 11.43 | -25.29 | 18.25 | 4.22 | 15.51 | +7.34 |
| LEAD-K | **17.63** | 2.80 | **14.55** | +4.99 | 20.29 | 5.97 | 16.96 | -22.14 | 16.85 | 3.13 | 13.14 | -8.49 | 16.20 | 4.63 | 14.33 | +3.09 |
| ORACLE | 17.50 | **2.88** | 14.45 | +5.41 | 21.98 | 6.83 | 18.23 | -14.47 | **18.21** | **3.69** | 13.99 | +1.19 | 16.48 | 4.80 | 14.50 | +5.34 |
| D-ORACLE | 17.40 | 2.83 | 14.34 | +4.35 | 21.05 | 6.32 | 17.49 | -18.90 | 18.19 | 3.51 | **14.00** | -3.75 | 17.50 | **5.08** | 15.39 | +11.72 |
| **PEGASUS XSUM** | | | | | | | | | | | | | | | | |
| BASE | 14.24 | 2.50 | 11.93 | - | 20.36 | 7.28 | 17.38 | - | 14.36 | 2.43 | 11.71 | - | **16.80** | **4.85** | **14.81** | - |
| COMET | 13.77 | 2.27 | 11.55 | -5.22 | 19.07 | 6.42 | 16.22 | -8.27 | 14.17 | 2.21 | 11.58 | -3.82 | 14.29 | 3.78 | 12.62 | -17.26 |
| LEAD-K | 14.30 | 2.46 | 12.02 | -0.14 | 18.97 | 6.46 | 16.14 | -8.40 | 14.24 | 2.14 | 11.56 | -4.68 | 13.29 | 3.78 | 11.78 | -21.13 |
| ORACLE | 14.94 | 2.62 | 12.49 | +4.80 | 19.03 | 6.48 | 16.18 | -8.14 | 14.57 | 2.40 | 11.96 | +0.78 | 13.38 | 3.78 | 11.89 | -20.71 |
| D-ORACLE | **15.14** | **2.72** | **12.67** | +7.10 | **20.51** | 7.20 | **17.46** | +0.03 | **14.90** | **2.48** | **12.19** | +3.30 | 13.83 | 4.03 | 12.28 | -17.22 |

## 5   Conclusion

In this work, we propose a novel topic-aware and reference-free approach for identifying summary-worthy segments (content selection) from a document. We experiment with multiple variations of content selection for self-training, cross-training, and domain adaptation settings. We leverage three metrics (*informativeness*, *relevance*, and *redundancy*) to identify SWORTS from a document. We find that content selection universally improves the model performance. Specifically, we observe that dynamic content selection (D-ORACLE) performs the best across all variations. From self-training and cross-training experiments, we observe that it is possible to achieve strong and comparable results with lesser data and in lesser training time. Zero-shot domain adaptation observations show that content selection helps in improving model performance beyond the training dataset (and domain). With extensive experimentation, we reiterate the importance of content selection for better summarization. As a part of future work, we will consider evaluating the efficacy of content selection beyond the ROUGE metric with the human-based evaluation in focus. We also plan to study the impact of content selection on summarization with large instruction-tuned language models.

**Ethics Statement.** All the datasets and pre-trained models used in this work are publicly available for research purposes. The authors foresee no ethical concerns or copyright violations with the work presented in this paper.

# References

1. Ao, X., Wang, X., Luo, L., Qiao, Y., He, Q., Xie, X.: Pens: a dataset and generic framework for personalized news headline generation. In: Proceedings of the 59th Annual Meeting of the Association for Computational Linguistics and the 11th International Joint Conference on Natural Language Processing (Volume 1: Long Papers), pp. 82–92 (2021)
2. Chen, Y.C., Bansal, M.: Fast abstractive summarization with reinforce-selected sentence rewriting. In: Proceedings of the 56th Annual Meeting of the Association for Computational Linguistics (Volume 1: Long Papers), pp. 675–686 (2018)
3. Cheng, J., Lapata, M.: Neural summarization by extracting sentences and words. In: Proceedings of the 54th Annual Meeting of the Association for Computational Linguistics (Volume 1: Long Papers), pp. 484–494 (2016)
4. Choi, F.Y.: Advances in domain independent linear text segmentation. In: 1st Meeting of the North American Chapter of the Association for Computational Linguistics (2000)
5. Cohen, N., Kalinsky, O., Ziser, Y., Moschitti, A.: Wikisum: coherent summarization dataset for efficient human-evaluation. In: Proceedings of the 59th Annual Meeting of the Association for Computational Linguistics and the 11th International Joint Conference on Natural Language Processing (Volume 2: Short Papers), pp. 212–219 (2021)
6. Cui, X., Bollegala, D.: Self-adaptation for unsupervised domain adaptation. In: Proceedings-Natural Language Processing in a Deep Learning World (2019)
7. Ganin, Y., et al.: Domain-adversarial training of neural networks. J. Mach. Learn. Res. **17**(1), 2030–2096 (2016)
8. Gehrmann, S., Deng, Y., Rush, A.M.: Bottom-up abstractive summarization. arXiv preprint arXiv:1808.10792 (2018)
9. Gliwa, B., Mochol, I., Biesek, M., Wawer, A.: Samsum corpus: a human-annotated dialogue dataset for abstractive summarization. In: Proceedings of the 2nd Workshop on New Frontiers in Summarization, pp. 70–79 (2019)

10. Grenander, M., Dong, Y., Cheung, J.C.K., Louis, A.: Countering the effects of lead bias in news summarization via multi-stage training and auxiliary losses. In: Proceedings of the 2019 Conference on Empirical Methods in Natural Language Processing and the 9th International Joint Conference on Natural Language Processing (EMNLP-IJCNLP), pp. 6019–6024 (2019)

11. Hermann, K.M., et al.: Teaching machines to read and comprehend. In: Advances in Neural Information Processing Systems, vol. 28 (2015)

12. Jia, R., Zhang, X., Cao, Y., Lin, Z., Wang, S., Wei, F.: Neural label search for zero-shot multi-lingual extractive summarization. In: Proceedings of the 60th Annual Meeting of the Association for Computational Linguistics (Volume 1: Long Papers), pp. 561–570 (2022)

13. Kim, B., Kim, H., Kim, G.: Abstractive summarization of reddit posts with multi-level memory networks. In: Proceedings of the 2019 Conference of the North American Chapter of the Association for Computational Linguistics: Human Language Technologies, Volume 1 (Long and Short Papers), pp. 2519–2531 (2019)

14. Ladhak, F., Durmus, E., Cardie, C., Mckeown, K.: Wikilingua: a new benchmark dataset for cross-lingual abstractive summarization. In: Findings of the Association for Computational Linguistics: EMNLP 2020, pp. 4034–4048 (2020)

15. Lebanoff, L., et al.: Scoring sentence singletons and pairs for abstractive summarization. In: Proceedings of the 57th Annual Meeting of the Association for Computational Linguistics, pp. 2175–2189 (2019)

16. Lewis, M., et al.: Bart: denoising sequence-to-sequence pre-training for natural language generation, translation, and comprehension. In: Proceedings of the 58th Annual Meeting of the Association for Computational Linguistics, pp. 7871–7880 (2020)

17. Liu, Y.: Fine-tune BERT for extractive summarization. arXiv preprint arXiv:1903.10318 (2019)

18. Liu, Y., Liu, P.: SimCLS: a simple framework for contrastive learning of abstractive summarization. In: Proceedings of the 59th Annual Meeting of the Association for Computational Linguistics and the 11th International Joint Conference on Natural Language Processing (Volume 2: Short Papers), pp. 1065–1072 (2021)

19. Nallapati, R., Zhai, F., Zhou, B.: Summarunner: a recurrent neural network based sequence model for extractive summarization of documents. In: Proceedings of the AAAI Conference on Artificial Intelligence, vol. 31 (2017)

20. Nallapati, R., Zhou, B., Gulcehre, C., Xiang, B., et al.: Abstractive text summarization using sequence-to-sequence RNNs and beyond. arXiv preprint arXiv:1602.06023 (2016)

21. Narayan, S., Cohen, S.B., Lapata, M.: Don't give me the details, just the summary! Topic-aware convolutional neural networks for extreme summarization. In: Proceedings of the 2018 Conference on Empirical Methods in Natural Language Processing, pp. 1797–1807 (2018)

22. Narayan, S., Cohen, S.B., Lapata, M.: Ranking sentences for extractive summarization with reinforcement learning. In: Proceedings of the 2018 Conference of the North American Chapter of the Association for Computational Linguistics: Human Language Technologies, Volume 1 (Long Papers), pp. 1747–1759 (2018)

23. Narayan, S., Maynez, J., Adamek, J., Pighin, D., Bratanic, B., McDonald, R.: Stepwise extractive summarization and planning with structured transformers. In: Proceedings of the 2020 Conference on Empirical Methods in Natural Language Processing (EMNLP), pp. 4143–4159 (2020)

24. Padmakumar, V., He, H.: Unsupervised extractive summarization using pointwise mutual information. In: Proceedings of the 16th Conference of the European Chapter of the Association for Computational Linguistics: Main Volume, pp. 2505–2512 (2021)
25. Pan, S.J., Ni, X., Sun, J.T., Yang, Q., Chen, Z.: Cross-domain sentiment classification via spectral feature alignment. In: Proceedings of the 19th International Conference on World Wide Web, pp. 751–760 (2010)
26. Paulus, R., Xiong, C., Socher, R.: A deep reinforced model for abstractive summarization. In: International Conference on Learning Representations (2018)
27. Peyrard, M.: A simple theoretical model of importance for summarization. In: Proceedings of the 57th Annual Meeting of the Association for Computational Linguistics, pp. 1059–1073 (2019)
28. Radford, A., Wu, J., Child, R., Luan, D., Amodei, D., Sutskever, I.: Language models are unsupervised multitask learners (2019)
29. Reimers, N., Gurevych, I.: Sentence-BERT: sentence embeddings using Siamese BERT-networks. In: Proceedings of the 2019 Conference on Empirical Methods in Natural Language Processing and the 9th International Joint Conference on Natural Language Processing (EMNLP-IJCNLP), pp. 3982–3992 (2019)
30. Rouge, L.C.: A package for automatic evaluation of summaries. In: Proceedings of Workshop on Text Summarization of ACL, Spain (2004)
31. Ruder, S., Plank, B.: Learning to select data for transfer learning with Bayesian optimization. In: Proceedings of the 2017 Conference on Empirical Methods in Natural Language Processing, pp. 372–382 (2017)
32. Ruder, S., Plank, B.: Strong baselines for neural semi-supervised learning under domain shift. In: Proceedings of the 56th Annual Meeting of the Association for Computational Linguistics (Volume 1: Long Papers), pp. 1044–1054 (2018)
33. Sotudeh, S., Deilamsalehy, H., Dernoncourt, F., Goharian, N.: Curriculum-guided abstractive summarization. arXiv preprint arXiv:2302.01342 (2023)
34. Tam, D., Mascarenhas, A., Zhang, S., Kwan, S., Bansal, M., Raffel, C.: Evaluating the factual consistency of large language models through summarization. arXiv preprint arXiv:2211.08412 (2022)
35. Tejaswin, P., Naik, D., Liu, P.: How well do you know your summarization datasets? In: Findings of the Association for Computational Linguistics: ACL-IJCNLP 2021, pp. 3436–3449 (2021)
36. Vasilyev, O., Dharnidharka, V., Bohannon, J.: Fill in the blanc: human-free quality estimation of document summaries. In: Proceedings of the First Workshop on Evaluation and Comparison of NLP Systems, pp. 11–20 (2020)
37. Xiao, L., Wang, L., He, H., Jin, Y.: Modeling content importance for summarization with pre-trained language models. In: Proceedings of the 2020 Conference on Empirical Methods in Natural Language Processing (EMNLP), pp. 3606–3611 (2020)
38. Zhang, H., Cai, J., Xu, J., Wang, J.: Pretraining-based natural language generation for text summarization. In: Proceedings of the 23rd Conference on Computational Natural Language Learning (CoNLL), pp. 789–797 (2019)
39. Zhang, J., Zhao, Y., Saleh, M., Liu, P.: Pegasus: pre-training with extracted gap-sentences for abstractive summarization. In: International Conference on Machine Learning, pp. 11328–11339. PMLR (2020)
40. Zhao, C., Brahman, F., Song, K., Yao, W., Yu, D., Chaturvedi, S.: Narrasum: a large-scale dataset for abstractive narrative summarization. arXiv preprint arXiv:2212.01476 (2022)

41. Zhao, W., Peyrard, M., Liu, F., Gao, Y., Meyer, C.M., Eger, S.: Moverscore: text generation evaluating with contextualized embeddings and earth mover distance. In: Proceedings of the 2019 Conference on Empirical Methods in Natural Language Processing (EMNLP) (2019)
42. Zhong, M., Liu, P., Chen, Y., Wang, D., Qiu, X., Huang, X.J.: Extractive summarization as text matching. In: Proceedings of the 58th Annual Meeting of the Association for Computational Linguistics, pp. 6197–6208 (2020)

# Encouraging Sparsity in Neural Topic Modeling with Non-Mean-Field Inference

Jiayao Chen, Rui Wang, Jueying He, and Mark Junjie Li[✉]

College of Computer Science and Software Engineering,
Shenzhen University, Shenzhen, China
{chenjiayao2021,2210273056,hejueying2020}@email.szu.edu.cn
jj.li@szu.edu.cn

**Abstract.** Topic modeling is a popular method for discovering semantic information from textual data, with latent Dirichlet allocation (LDA) being a representative model. Recently, researchers have explored the use of variational autoencoders (VAE) to improve the performance of LDA. However, there remain two major limitations: (1) the Dirichlet prior is inadequate to extract precise semantic information in VAE-LDA models, as it introduces a trade-off between the topic quality and the sparsity of representations; (2) new variants of VAE-LDA models with auxiliary variables generally ignore the correlation between latent variables in the inference process due to the Mean-Field assumption. To address these issues, in this paper, we propose a **Sparsity Reinforced and Non-Mean-Field Topic Model (SpareNTM)** with a bank of auxiliary Bernoulli variables in the generative process of LDA to further model the sparsity of document representations. Thus individual documents are forced to focus on a subset of topics by a corresponding Bernoulli topic selector. Then, instead of applying the mean-field assumption for the posterior approximation, we take full advantage of VAE to realize a non-mean-field approximation, which succeeds in preserving the connection of latent variables. Experiment results on three datasets (20NewsGroup, Wikitext-103, and SearchSnippets) show that our model outperforms recent topic models in terms of both topic quality and sparsity.

**Keywords:** Topic modeling · Latent Dirichlet Allocation · Sparse representation · Variational autoencoders

## 1 Introduction

Topic models are commonly employed to extract semantic information from a collection of documents, and their utility is evident in various natural language processing (NLP) applications such as user interest profiling and event detection. Latent Dirichlet allocation (LDA) [2], a classic topic model, represents each document as a distribution over latent topics and each topic as a distribution over words. Typically, parameter estimations for these latent distributions are trained by variational inference [2] or Gibbs sampling [11]. However, these

ⓒ The Author(s), under exclusive license to Springer Nature Switzerland AG 2023
D. Koutra et al. (Eds.): ECML PKDD 2023, LNAI 14172, pp. 142–158, 2023.
https://doi.org/10.1007/978-3-031-43421-1_9

inference procedures are inflexible in realizing new topic model variants and are computationally expensive for large corpora.

The development of deep learning has led to the exploration of variational autoencoder (VAE) [13] for simplifying the inference process of LDA [19,29]. It should be noted that using Dirichlet is one of the key successes of LDA for encouraging smoothness and sparsity in representations [41]. Dirichlet Variational Autoencoder model (DVAE) [3] has successfully imposed Dirichlet prior constraints on latent terms in VAE networks. However, the use of Dirichlet prior in VAE-LDA models poses a challenge to their topic quality [6] due to the sparsity of the learned document representations. Allocating a smaller Dirichlet prior can generate sparser document-topic distributions, which also force VAE to assign a negligible probability to some existing words in a document, compromising its ability to capture the entire semantic structure [3,29]. As a result, the quality of topics will suffer. Therefore, modeling the sparse structure of texts requires an additional mechanism that goes beyond the Dirichlet prior in VAE-LDA models.

To address this issue, researchers modify the network architecture in VAE-LDA models. Techniques such as batch normalization and dropout layers have been used to prevent overemphasizing sparsity during the training process [30]. Another approach is the Dirichlet VAE Sparse (DVAE.Sp) model [3], which employs a sigmoid activation to select the topics relevant to each document, aiming to decouple sparsity and smoothness in the Dirichlet distribution. However, these modifications only impact the training process and do not incorporate topic selection within the generative process of LDA. Given the limitations of the Dirichlet prior in VAE-LDA models, it may be more appropriate to integrate sparsity considerations into the generative process of LDA.

Due to the limitations of existing works, we propose a new **Sparsity Reinforced and Non-Mean-Field Topic Model (SpareNTM)** in the framework of VAE-LDA, including two essential and novel methods. First, we need auxiliary prior beyond Dirichlet prior for sparsity modeling. In the autoencoding framework, a possible way is using Beta distribution as CRNTM [10], but it cannot produce real sparse representations. Another way is the 'spike and slab' [20] prior adopted by [9,32] and the binary latents by [8] in VAE. Although these studies use the sparse prior for image generation, we can incorporate the idea within VAE-LDA models. Therefore, we propose simply using the binary latents to model the sparsity in document-topic distributions, which introduces Bernoulli priors into the generative process of LDA. Our approach constructs a *topic selector* for each document using Bernoulli variables, which filter out irrelevant topics. In this way, the Dirichlet prior to each document will be constrained to the range of selected topics.

Second, to conduct the inference process of SpareNTM, we design a novel VAE network that employs a non-mean-field approximation for the true posterior. To the best of our knowledge, SpareNTM is among the first to use the non-mean-field inference for neural topic models. Previous neural topic models [5,10,27,28] adopt mean-field theory [1] for easy optimization when introducing auxiliary latent variables into VAE-LDA. However, the negative mean-field effects have been discussed in many works [7,33] since it fails to explain the correlation between latent variables. Instead, our model SpareNTM can preserve the connection between document-topic distributions and Bernoulli topic selectors. Then, we apply the 'reparameterization trick' [13] with Gumbel-Softmax Estimator [12] to generate posterior topic selectors. Extensive experiments demonstrate our method's superiority in topic quality and sparsity. The main contributions[1] of this paper can be concluded as follows:

- We propose a neural topic model modeling sparsity with Bernoulli prior to obtain a better balance between the topic quality and the sparsity of representations.
- We develop an effective network structure under the VAE framework to learn the inference process, which realizes a non-mean-field inference in posterior approximation to capture the correlation in latent variables.
- Experiments demonstrate that our model can achieve higher topic quality than state-of-the-art models and generate sparser document representations.

The rest of this paper is organized as follows. We discuss relevant research work in Sect. 2. In Sect. 3, we propose our model and give the inference details. Experimental settings and results are presented in Sect. 4. Finally, we draw the conclusion in Sect. 5.

## 2   Related Work

**VAE-LDA Models:** Recent advances in generative models have been largely attributed to the success of variational AutoEncoders (VAE) [13]. The Neural Variational Document Model (NVDM) [19] is a notable example that adopts a Gaussian distribution as prior and demonstrates the feasibility of using VAE for topic models. Other extensions have also been investigated, such as the Gaussian Softmax Construction (GSM) explored in [18]. Additionally, the Product of Expert LDA (ProdLDA) proposed by [29] uses Laplace approximation for Dirichlet distribution. On the other hand, [3] successfully uses the Dirichlet prior on latent variables by applying the rejection sampling variational inference [21], resulting in competitive coherent topics. However, despite these efforts, the majority of the aforementioned works focus on constructing effective VAEs for the LDA model without taking into account the issue of sparsity in the representation space.

**Sparse Topic Models:** Several sparse topic models have been proposed to extract sparse latent representations of texts. A 'Spike and Slab' prior is introduced in a hierarchical Dirichlet process by [34,38] to model the sparsity of topic-word distributions. Sparse topical coding (STC) [42] utilizes the Laplacian prior to directly control the sparsity of latent variables. However, the inference

---

[1] The code is available at https://github.com/Nazzcjy/SpareNTM.

process of these models involves high computation complexity due to their complicated structures. To address this issue, [25] proposes neural sparse topical coding (NSTC) by jointly utilizing word embeddings and neural networks with STC. Meanwhile, the Sparsemax function is suggested in [16] to replace the softmax in GSM. Moreover, [4] produces a neural framework based on sparse additive generative models, which flexibly incorporates the metadata of documents and achieves strong performance on several metrics. Nevertheless, recent studies [36,37] have shown that prior distributions used in the above models, such as Gaussian prior, fail to capture a document's multi-modality aspects and semantic patterns. Besides, the above models are not directly related solutions to model the sparsity in VAE-LDA models.

Our model relies on the binary latents to further discrete the latent representations in the VAE-LDA framework with Gumble-Softmax estimation [12]. Although recent works of VAE have focused on the non-mean-field approximation between the binary or "spike and slab" latents for image generation [8,9,32], we incorporate the binary latents with Dirichlet prior and concern with the mutual influence between the discrete and continuous latents in topic modeling.

## 3     Approach

In this section, the proposed method is described. We first introduce the generative process of SpareNTM. Then we put forward the adapted VAE topic model, explain how the none-mean-field inference is applied, and cover the neural network architecture in detail.

We first make some definitions. Given a corpus of $D$ texts with vocabulary $W$ of $V$ words, each document $x$ is processed into a bag-of-words (BOW) vectors as $x = [x_1, x_2, \ldots, x_V]$, where $x_i$ represents the number of times for $i^{th}$ word appearing in document $x$.

### 3.1   VAE-LDA

We first review the VAE-LDA framework. Following [31], each document $x$ of the corpus is represented as a document-topic distribution $\theta \sim Dir(\alpha)$ over $K$ topics with a Dirichlet prior, and a topic-word distribution $\beta_z$ models topic $z$ over $V$ words in vocabulary $W$. Using $\beta$ to denote the matrix $\beta = (\beta_1, \beta_2, \ldots, \beta_K)^T$, the words in a document is drawn i.i.d from the distribution of $p(x|\theta; \beta) =$ Multinomial$(1, \text{Softmax}(\theta^T \beta))$, referred to as "product of experts" in [29].

When applying VAE to an LDA model, the model is augmented with an *encoder* network $f_{enc}$. Specifically, the encoder takes the BOW $x$ as the input and outputs $\hat{\alpha}$, and then the Dirichlet distribution or other distributions $q(\theta|x; \hat{\alpha})$ with parameter $\hat{\alpha}$ is taken to approximate the true posterior distribution $p(\theta|x)$:

$$\hat{\alpha} := f_{enc}(x; \Pi) \tag{1}$$

$$\tilde{\theta} \sim q(\theta|x; \hat{\alpha}) \tag{2}$$

$$f_{dec}(\tilde{\theta}; \beta) := \text{Softmax}(\tilde{\theta}^T \beta) \tag{3}$$

Under the VAE framework, the parameters of the encoder and the decoder are optimized by maximizing the Evidence Lower Bound (ELBO):

$$\mathcal{L}(\Pi, \beta; x) = E_{q(\theta|x)}[\log p(x|\theta)] - KL(q(\theta|x; \hat{\alpha})\|p(\theta; \alpha)) \tag{4}$$

Under the one sample strategy [13], $E_{q(\theta|x)}[\log p(x|\theta)] \simeq x^T \log f_{dec}(\tilde{\theta})$.

## 3.2   SpareNTM

In SpareNTM, for each document, we construct a Bernoulli variable for each topic that determines whether the topic appears in the document and then model the topic probabilities on that subset of topics. Formally, each document $x$ has a document-topic distribution $\theta \sim Dir(b \cdot \alpha)$ over $K$ topics with a *topic selector* $b$. The *topic selector* $b = (b_1, \ldots, b_K)$ is a $K$-length binary vector composed of $K$ Bernoulli variables with parameter $\lambda = (\lambda_1, \ldots, \lambda_K)$. Thus, vector $b_d$ encourages each document to focus on some silent topics. When $b_d$ is set to a vector of only ones, SpareNTM will degenerate to the standard LDA model. Thus, the autoencoding framework of SpareNTM is:

$$\hat{\alpha}, \hat{\lambda} := f_{enc}(x; \Pi) \tag{5}$$

$$\tilde{\theta} \sim q(\theta, b|x; \hat{\alpha}, \hat{\lambda}) \tag{6}$$

$$f_{dec}(\tilde{\theta}; \beta) := \text{Softmax}(\tilde{\theta}^T \beta) \tag{7}$$

## 3.3   Objective Function

In this section, we develop a new neural inference method for the variational distribution $q(\theta, b|x; \hat{\alpha}, \hat{\lambda})$. Traditional variational inference uses a mean-field theory to make strong independence assumptions among latent variables for scalable and easy optimization [1]. Previous neural topic models, like [5,10,27,28], adopt mean-field theory when introducing auxiliary latent variables into VAE-LDA. However, the negative mean-field effects have been discussed in many works [7,33] since it fails to explain the correlation between latent variables. In contrast, we define a non-mean-field variational distribution Eq. (8) to capture the correlation between $\theta$ and $b$ in the true posterior $p(\theta, b|x)$

$$q(\theta, b|x) = q(b|x; \hat{\lambda})q(\theta|x, b; \hat{\alpha}) \tag{8}$$

Here we assume that $q(b|x; \hat{\lambda}) = \prod_{k=1}^K q(b_k|\hat{\lambda}_k)$, and $q(b_k|\hat{\lambda}_k)$ is a Bernoulli distribution with the selected rate $\hat{\lambda}_k$. We also define the $q(\theta|x, b; \hat{\alpha})$ similarly to $p(\theta|b, \alpha)$: $q(\theta|x, b; \hat{\alpha}) = \text{Dir}(b \cdot \hat{\alpha})$. We have overlooked the dependency relationship between $b_k$. This is because we are more concerned with the mutual influence between the global variables $\theta$ and $b$, which is crucial in obtaining sparse results. As mentioned before, the Dirichlet distribution also plays a role in promoting sparse representation. Unlike models that rely solely on binary latents as priors, the term $b \cdot \hat{\alpha}$ helps alleviate the negative impact of not explicitly modeling the dependencies among $b_k$.

The ELBO of SpareNTM is given by Eq. (9). This objective can be decomposed into separate loss functions and written as $\mathcal{L} = \mathcal{L}_{rec} + \mathcal{L}_\theta + \mathcal{L}_b$, where $\mathcal{L}_{rec} = E_{q(\theta,b|x)}[\log p(x|\theta)]$, $\mathcal{L}_\theta = -E_{q(\theta,b|x)}\left[\log \frac{q(\theta|x,b)}{p(\theta|b)}\right]$, and $\mathcal{L}_b = -E_{q(\theta,b|x)}\left[\log \frac{q(b|x)}{p(b)}\right]$. We aim to maximize $\mathcal{L}$ to find the best variational and model parameters. To shed light on what the ELBO is showing, we describe each term below.

$$\log(p(x,\theta,b|\alpha,\lambda,\beta)) \geq \mathcal{L}(\Pi,\beta;x) = E_{q(\theta,b|x)}[\log p(x,\theta,b|\alpha,\lambda,\beta) - \log q(\theta,b|x)]$$
$$= E_{q(\theta,b|x)}[\log p(x|\theta)] - E_{q(\theta,b|x)}\left[\log \frac{q(\theta|x,b)}{p(\theta|b)}\right] - E_{q(\theta,b|x)}\left[\log \frac{q(b|x)}{p(b)}\right] \quad (9)$$

$\mathcal{L}_b$ $\mathcal{L}_b = -\sum_{k=1}^{K} KL(q(b_k|x)\|p(b_k))$ (Show in the supplementary material[2]), can be calculated analytically by the KL divergence of $KL(q(b_k|x;\hat{\lambda}_k)\|p(b_k;\lambda_k)) = \hat{\lambda}_k \log \frac{\hat{\lambda}_k}{\lambda_k} + (1-\hat{\lambda}_k)\log\frac{1-\hat{\lambda}_k}{1-\lambda_k}$.

$\mathcal{L}_\theta$. The $\mathcal{L}_\theta$ can be written to $\mathcal{L}_\theta = -E_{q(b|x)}[KL(q(\theta|x,b)\|p(\theta|b))]$ (Show in the Appendix[2] for more details). Although there is an analytical calculation for this expectation, we decide to estimate it by reparameterization trick [13] due to the large discrete state space ($2^K$) of the vector $b$ composed of $K$ Bernoulli variables. We sample $\tilde{b}_k$ from Bernoulli($\hat{\lambda}_k$), $k = 1,\ldots,K$ using Gumbel-Softmax estimation [12], then the $\mathcal{L}_\theta$ term can be approximated as $\mathcal{L}_\theta \approx -KL(q(\theta|x,\tilde{b})\|p(\theta|\tilde{b}))$. And the KL divergence between $Dir(\tilde{b}\cdot\hat{\alpha})$ and $Dir(\tilde{b}\cdot\alpha)$ has an analytical form as follow:

$$KL(q(\theta|x,\tilde{b})\|p(\theta|\tilde{b})) = \log\Gamma(\sum_k \tilde{b}_k \cdot \hat{\alpha}_k) - \log\Gamma(\sum_k \tilde{b}_k \cdot \alpha_k) + \sum_k \log\Gamma(\tilde{b}_k \cdot \alpha_k)$$
$$- \sum_k \log\Gamma(\tilde{b}_k \cdot \hat{\alpha}_k) + \sum_k \tilde{b}_k \cdot (\hat{\alpha}_k - \alpha_k)(\psi(\tilde{b}_k \cdot \hat{\alpha}_k) - \psi(\sum_k \tilde{b}_k \cdot \hat{\alpha}_k)) \quad (10)$$

$\mathcal{L}_{rec}$. The reconstruction term is $\mathcal{L}_{rec} = E_{q(\theta,b|x)}[\log p(x|\theta)]$. Since the vector $b$ has been sampled in $\mathcal{L}_\theta$ and the variational distribution is $q(\theta,b|x) = q(b|x)q(\theta|x,b)$, we apply two steps to sample $\theta$ from $q(\theta,b|x)$. We first sample $\tilde{b}_k$ and then sample $\tilde{\theta} \sim Dir(\tilde{b}\cdot\hat{\alpha})$. So the $\mathcal{L}_{rec}$ term can be approximated as $\mathcal{L}_{rec} \approx \log p(x|\tilde{\theta}) = x^T \log f_{dec}(\tilde{\theta})$.

After applying SGVB for the variation lower bound (9), we can now reconstruct our objective function $\tilde{\mathcal{L}} \approx \mathcal{L}$ as:

$$\tilde{\mathcal{L}}(\Pi,\beta;x) = x^T \log f_{dec}(\tilde{\theta}) - KL(q(\theta|x,\tilde{b})\|p(\theta|\tilde{b})) - \sum_{k=1}^{K} KL(q(b_k)\|p(b_k)) \quad (11)$$

where $\tilde{b}_k \sim$ Bernoulli($\hat{\lambda}_k$), $k = 1,2,\ldots K$ and $\tilde{\theta} \sim Dir(\tilde{b}\cdot\hat{\alpha})$. A connection with auto-encoders becomes clear when looking at this objective function. The

---

[2] https://github.com/Nazzcjy/SpareNTM.

encoder network of our model will map a document bag-of-words $x$ to the variational parameters $\hat{\alpha}$ and $\hat{\lambda}$, and then sample $\tilde{b}$ and $\tilde{\theta}$ from the related distributions. Subsequently, the decoder network takes the sample $\tilde{\theta}$ as the input to function $\log p(x|\tilde{\theta})$, which equals the probability density of the observation $x$. The details are described in the next section.

### 3.4   Neural Network Architecture

The architecture of the neural network SpareNTM is illustrated in Fig. 1. The input $x$ is linearly transformed using a Relu-layer with dropout. The result then goes through branch ① to generate the variational parameter $\hat{\alpha}$ by a linear transformation and batch normalization. A softplus transformation is then applied because the Dirichlet parameter needs to be positive. Branch ② goes into the Topic Selector module, where linear transformations and batch normalization are utilized again to generate $u_1$ and $u_2$ that separately represent the proportions of whether the topics are selected. So the variational parameter $\hat{\lambda}$ is calculated by a softmax function in $u_1$ and $u_2$. We can now sample the topic selector $\tilde{b}$ from Bernoulli($\hat{\lambda}$) using Gumbel-Softmax estimation [12]. For topic $k$, denote $(\pi_{k1}, \pi_{k2}) = (\hat{\lambda}_k, 1 - \hat{\lambda}_k)$:

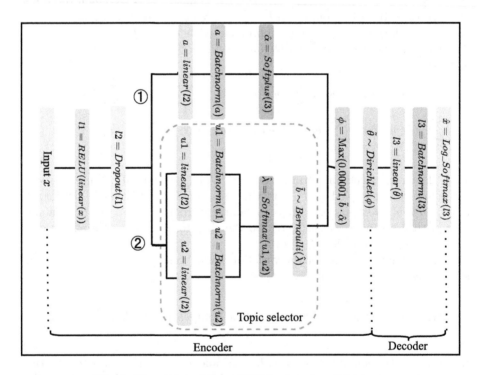

**Fig. 1.** The proposed SparseNTM network architecture

$$\tilde{b}_k = \frac{\exp\left((\log(\pi_{k1}) + g_1)/\tau\right)}{\sum_{i=1}^{2} \exp\left((\log(\pi_{ki}) + g_i)/\tau\right)} \tag{12}$$

where $g_1, g_2$ are i.i.d samples from Gumbel$(0, 1)$[3], and $\tau$ is set to 1 in the experiments. After generating the topic selector $\tilde{b} = (\tilde{b}_1, \ldots, \tilde{b}_K)$, we then sample the sparse $\tilde{\theta} \sim \text{Dir}(\tilde{b} \cdot \hat{\alpha})$ using rejection sampling and shape augmentation for Gamma distribution following [3,21].

## 4   Experiment

### 4.1   Datasets

The performances are reported over three text datasets, 20NewsGroups (20NG) [14], Wikitext-103 (Wiki) [17] and SearchSnippets [40]. The details are listed as

- **20NG**[4] consists of about 18,000 news articles that are grouped into 20 different categories.
- **Wiki**[4] is a version of WikiText dataset, which includes about 28,500 articles from the Good and Featured section on Wikipedia. We follow the preprocess and keep the top 20,000 words as in [17].
- **SearchSnippets**[5] is selected from the results of web search transaction using predefined phrases of 8 different domains by [26]. The eight domains are Business, Computers, Culture-Arts, Education-Science, Engineering, Health, Politics-Society, and Sports.

Following [23], we remove stopwords and words whose length is equal to 1 or whose frequency is less than 100. The key information of the datasets is summarized in Table 1, where $L$ shows the average length of each document, and $V$ indicates the vocabulary size.

**Table 1.** The basic information of the three datasets. $N$ is the number of documents in each dataset, $L$ shows the average length of each document, and $V$ indicates the vocabulary size.

| Dataset | $N$ | $L$ | $V$ |
|---|---|---|---|
| 20NG | 18,846 | 87.5 | 2,000 |
| Wiki | 28,532 | 133.4 | 20,000 |
| SearchSnippets | 12,295 | 14.4 | 5,547 |

---

[3] The Gumbel$(0, 1)$ distribution can be sampled using inverse transform sampling by drawing $u \sim \text{Uniform}(0, 1)$ and computing $g = -\log(-\log(u))$.

[4] https://github.com/nguyentthong/CLNTM.

[5] https://github.com/qiang2100/STTM.

## 4.2   Baseline Methods and Parameter Settings

We compare the SpareNTM with several different topic models, including LDA[5] and neural models. We do not consider NSTC [25] because our model aims to improve topic modeling without extra information (e.g., word embeddings). For regular topic models, we consider **ProdLDA**[6] [29], **DVAE**[7] [3]. Regarding models considering sparsity, we compare our model with **DVAE.Sp** [3], **GSM** [18], **NSMDM** [16], **SCHOLAR**[8] [4], and **SBVAE** [24]. For SearchSnippets, we also evaluate **NQTM**[9] [39]. DVAE and SCHOLAR are state-of-the-art neural topic models, while NQTM outperforms traditional topic modeling in short texts. We also evaluate SpareNTM-MF (SpareNTM using mean-field assumption) to demonstrate the effectiveness of non-mean-field inference.

Network structures and parameter settings of baseline models are constructed following their authors. The number of hidden units is set to 500, and s batch size of 200 is used for all datasets. We use a learning rate of 0.0001 and the Adam optimizer for optimization.

## 4.3   Evaluation Metric

To provide an evaluation, we focus on evaluating topic quality from two commonly-used measures, topic coherence, and diversity. Topic coherence is a quantitative measure of the interpretability of a topic. In computing topic coherence, an external dataset is needed to score word pairs using term co-occurrence. Here, we adopt normalized pointwise mutual information[10] (NPMI) [15] to evaluate the topic coherence over English Wikipedia articles[11]. NPMI implies that the most probable words of a topic tend to occur together within the same documents. The averaged value of NPMI on the top 5 and 10 words for all topics is computed as the final result. The topic diversity corresponds to the average probability of each word occurring in one of the other topics of the same model [3]. We use the topic unique (TU) metric [22] for topic diversity evaluation. TU close to 0 indicates redundant topics; TU close to 1 indicates more varied topics.

Intuitively, a higher NPMI often leads to a lower TU since coherent topics tend to be redundantly discovered, and a higher TU brings a lower NPMI since more marginal topics are encouraged to be discovered [39]. Hence, topics with a good trade-off between the above two aspects are preferred. To measure this, we adopt the Topic Quality (TQ) score which is defined as the product of NPMI and TU values in our evaluation by following [6,35]. For all metrics, t-tests show whether the performance difference between SpareNTM and each baseline is statistically significant regarding mean values over chunks. We consider the

---

[6] https://github.com/akashgit/autoencoding_vi_for_topic_models.

[7] https://github.com/sophieburkhardt/dirichlet-vae-topic-models.

[8] https://github.com/dallascard/SCHOLAR.

[9] https://github.com/bobxwu/NQTM.

[10] Instead of using a sliding window, we consider a whole document to identify co-occurrence.

[11] http://deepdive.stanford.edu/opendata/.

pairwise performance difference significant if the $P$-value obtained from $t$-test is lower than 0.05.

## 4.4    Experimental Results

**Comparison with Baselines.** In this section, we compare SpareNTM with the baseline models. The Dirichlet prior is set to 0.02. For SBVAE, the stick-breaking prior and the learning rate are set to 10 and 0.01. Besides, the Bernoulli prior for SpareNTM is set to 0.05 for 20NG and Wiki, while 0.2 in SeachSnippets. Table 2 presents the overall quality of topic coherence and uniqueness.

**20NG and Wiki.** We observe that SpareNTM and NSMDM achieve the top quality on 20NG followed by SCHOLAR and LDA. Although NSMDM performs slightly better than SpareNTM on 20NG at $K = 100$, SpareNTM has a great advantage at $K = 50$. On the longer Wiki dataset, SpareNTM outperforms other models by a large margin. Our model can discover more meaningful and diverse topics. Compared to models that do not consider sparsity, where DVAE has the best topic quality, SpareNTM exhibits significantly better topic quality. This indicates that the Dirichlet prior is superior to other prior assumptions. At the same time, SpareNTM, a sparsity-enhanced version of DVAE, proves that the Dirichlet prior is insufficient to meet the requirements of sparse modeling. Models that account for sparsity can achieve better topic quality. In a nutshell, SpareNTM incorporates Dirichlet prior and introduces additional prior to model sparsity, resulting in a great synergy.

**SearchSnippets.** GSM achieves the highest overall quality, followed by SpareNTM and NQTM. Models that incorporate sparsity achieve better topic quality than those that do not again. However, these models are a bit sensitive to the number of topics $K$ due to the sparse characteristic of short texts. All models, except for SpareNTM, show a decline in topic quality when $K = 50$, which implies that our model is stable in modeling short text. Besides, GSM performs well in SearchSnippets but underperforms in 20NG and Wiki. Although NQTM has a natural advantage in short text modeling using the discrete Autoencoder, its high memory requirements render it unsuitable for 20NG and Wiki. In summary, SpareNTM has broader applicability and is more stable than others, as the assumption that a text focuses only on a few topics is practical and reasonable.

**Ablation Study.** To evaluate the effectiveness of incorporating sparsity into the generative network and the non-mean-field inference approach used in our model, we compare our model with DVAE and SpareNTM-mean-field (SpareNTM-MF). Although DVAE has higher NPMI scores than SpareNTM-MF, it performs much worse regarding TU scores. Therefore, SpareNTM-MF achieves better topic quality in all datasets than DVAE, which implies that introducing sparsity enhances the performance. Furthermore, SpareNTM attains the highest topic quality, especially TU scores, among them, indicating the superiority of the proposed method, which is attributed to the topic selectors and non-mean-field inference technique applied in our model.

**Table 2.** Topic quality of the three corpora under different models, where the best values are marked by boldface. For each baseline, ↑ or ↓ after the result indicates that the baseline performs better or worse than our SpareNTM significantly according to t-tests with 5% significance level. The average rank in $K = 50$ and $K = 100$ is denoted as av.rank.

| Models | 20News | | | | | | |
| | K = 50 | | | K = 100 | | | |
| | NPMI | TU | TQ | NPMI | TU | TQ | av.rank |
|---|---|---|---|---|---|---|---|
| LDA [2] | 0.248 | 0.580↓ | 0.144↓ | 0.249↑ | 0.494↓ | 0.123 | 3.5 |
| ProdLDA [29] | 0.271↑ | 0.475↓ | 0.129↓ | 0.250↑ | 0.356↓ | 0.089↓ | 7.0 |
| DVAE [3] | **0.272↑** | 0.530↓ | 0.144↓ | **0.262↑** | 0.385↓ | 0.101↓ | 5.0 |
| DVAE.Sp [3] | 0.225↓ | 0.525↓ | 0.118↓ | 0.218↓ | 0.359↓ | 0.078↓ | 8.0 |
| SBVAE [24] | 0.171↓ | 0.524↓ | 0.090↓ | 0.148↓ | 0.363↓ | 0.054↓ | 9.0 |
| GSM [18] | 0.210↓ | 0.644↓ | 0.135↓ | 0.200↓ | 0.519↓ | 0.104↓ | 5.0 |
| NSMDM [16] | 0.222↓ | **0.784** | 0.174↓ | 0.200↓ | **0.651↑** | 0.130 | 1.5 |
| SCHOLAR [4] | 0.258↑ | 0.603↓ | 0.156↓ | 0.239↑ | 0.424↓ | 0.101↓ | 4.5 |
| SpareNTM | 0.244 | 0.763 | **0.186** | 0.229 | 0.549 | **0.126** | 1.5 |
| SpareNTM-MF | 0.236↓ | 0.684↓ | 0.161↓ | 0.232 | 0.490↓ | 0.114↓ | - |

| Models | Wiki | | | | | | |
| | K = 50 | | | K = 100 | | | |
| | NPMI | TU | TQ | NPMI | TU | TQ | av.rank |
|---|---|---|---|---|---|---|---|
| LDA | 0.280↓ | 0.617↓ | 0.173↓ | 0.286↓ | 0.596↓ | 0.170↓ | 6.0 |
| ProdLDA | 0.357↓ | 0.471↓ | 0.168↓ | 0.377↑ | 0.405↓ | 0.153↓ | 7.0 |
| DVAE | **0.403** | 0.669↓ | 0.270↓ | **0.396↑** | 0.491↓ | 0.194↓ | 5.0 |
| DVAE.Sp | 0.197↓ | 0.841↓ | 0.166↓ | 0.168↓ | 0.701↓ | 0.118↓ | 9.5 |
| SBVAE | 0.287↓ | 0.967 | 0.278↓ | 0.224↓ | 0.580↓ | 0.130↓ | 6.5 |
| GSM | 0.300↓ | 0.974 | 0.292↓ | 0.279↓ | **0.877↑** | 0.245↓ | 3.5 |
| NSMDM | 0.354↓ | **0.979** | 0.347↓ | 0.220↓ | 0.625↓ | 0.138↓ | 5.0 |
| SCHOLAR | 0.398 | 0.937↓ | 0.373↓ | 0.366 | 0.691↓ | 0.253↓ | 2.0 |
| SpareNTM | 0.401 | 0.973 | **0.390** | 0.364 | 0.831 | **0.302** | 1.0 |
| SpareNTM-MF | 0.379↓ | 0.940↓ | 0.356↓ | 0.390↑ | 0.737↓ | 0.287↓ | - |

| Models | SearchSnippets | | | | | | |
| | K = 25 | | | K = 50 | | | |
| | NPMI | TU | TQ | NPMI | TU | TQ | av.rank |
|---|---|---|---|---|---|---|---|
| LDA | 0.252↑ | 0.844↓ | 0.213↓ | 0.237 | 0.804↓ | 0.191↓ | 5.5 |
| ProdLDA | 0.140↓ | 0.840↓ | 0.118↓ | 0.138 | 0.728↓ | 0.100↓ | 9.0 |
| DVAE | 0.239↑ | 0.915↓ | 0.219↓ | **0.246** | 0.690↓ | 0.170↓ | 6.0 |
| DVAE.Sp | 0.190↓ | 0.868↓ | 0.165↓ | 0.172↓ | 0.708↓ | 0.122↓ | 7.5 |
| SBVAE | 0.230 | 0.969↓ | 0.223↓ | 0.173↓ | 0.702↓ | 0.121↓ | 6.5 |
| GSM | 0.256↑ | 0.968↓ | **0.248↑** | 0.236 | 0.960↓ | 0.227↓ | 1.5 |
| NSMDM | **0.261↑** | 0.947↓ | 0.247↑ | 0.214↓ | 0.887↓ | 0.190↓ | 3.5 |
| SCHOLAR | 0.253↑ | 0.975↓ | 0.247↑ | 0.239 | 0.863↓ | 0.206↓ | 2.5 |
| NQTM [39] | 0.245↑ | 0.992 | 0.243↑ | 0.238 | 0.944↓ | 0.225↓ | 2.5 |
| SpareNTM | 0.230 | **0.998** | 0.230 | 0.244 | **0.978** | **0.239** | 2.0 |
| SpareNTM-MF | 0.213↓ | 0.937↓ | 0.200↓ | 0.214↓ | 1.000↑ | 0.214↓ | - |

**Influence of** $\lambda$. In this part, we first investigate the influence of Bernoulli prior $\lambda$. We run SpareNTM on 20NG with Dirichlet prior $\alpha = 0.02$. Table 3 shows the average number of selected topics on test data with different values of $\lambda$. We can observe that the number of topics chosen found by SpareNTM grows when we enlarge $\lambda$, and nearly follows the expectation of Binomial distribution $E[\mathrm{B}(K, \lambda)] = \lambda \cdot K$, while DVAE.Sp can only choose half of K topics in fixed. By incorporating the Bernoulli prior, our model can flexibly enforce each document to focus on the part of K topics.

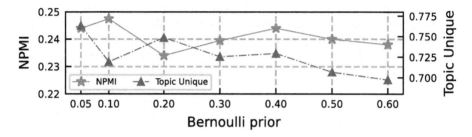

**Fig. 2.** NPMI and TU of SpareNTM with different values of Bernoulli prior $\lambda$ under K = 50 on 20News.

**Table 3.** The average number of selected topics of SpareNTM with different $\lambda$ and DVAE.Sp on 20NG.

|  | SpareNTM |  |  |  |  |  |  | DVAE.Sp |  |  |
|---|---|---|---|---|---|---|---|---|---|---|
| K | 50 |  |  |  |  | 100 | 200 | 50 | 100 | 200 |
| $\lambda$ | 0.2 | 0.4 | 0.5 | 0.6 | 0.8 | 0.1 | 0.1 | – | – | – |
| Avg.num | 10 | 21 | 27 | 31 | 41 | 11 | 20 | 25 | 46 | 102 |

Figure 2 shows NPMI and TU scores of SpareNTM with different values of $\lambda$ and $K = 50$. We can observe NPMI varies in a minor range from 0.230 to 0.250, demonstrating how we consider sparsity in the LDA model is stable in discovering semantic information. In contrast, the TU score declines when $\lambda$ grows up and gets the best value when $\lambda = 0.05$ with an average of 3 selected topics for each document, which is smaller than the topic number $K$ in parameter settings and even the actual number of categories in 20NG. This is because the assumption of each document focusing on a few topics is realistic.

**Document Representation Examples.** For example, we randomly chose a religion-related document from the 20NG and analyzed its document-topic representations produced by various models when K = 50. Figure 3 clearly illustrates that our proposed model generates sharper document representations, which is attributed to the fact that SpareNTM can capture more precise semantic information in each document. While some baseline models can also produce sparse topic distributions, our proposed model achieves better topic quality with sparser topic distributions.

**Topic Examples Evaluation.** To qualitatively illustrate the high-quality topics generated by our model, Table 4 presents the topic words associated with religion in 20NG, yielded by LDA, DVAE, NSMDM, SCHOLAR, and SpareNTM. Additionally, We bold the two topics with the highest probability corresponding to each topic distribution in Sect. 4.4. Baseline models tend to generate repetitive topics with repeated words. LDA and NSMDM will assign unrelated topics to the document. In contrast, SpareNTM generates coherent and diverse topics corresponding to the associated topic, and the quality of the topics generated by SpareNTM is higher.

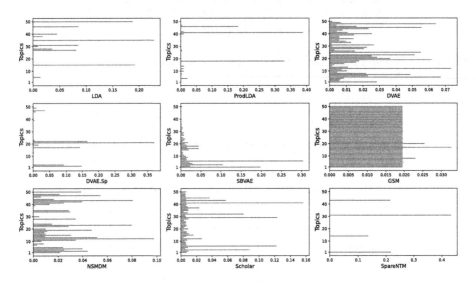

**Fig. 3.** The document-topic representations of a random text from the 20NG dataset produced by different models when K = 50. The y-axis of each subplot represents the topic $T = [1, 2, \ldots, 50]$, while the x-axis corresponds to the topic probability.

**Table 4.** Topics related to religion generated by different models. The top 2 topics of the selected document in Sect. 4.4 by different models are bolded.

| Model | Topics related to religion |
|---|---|
| LDA | **god believe truth one evidence** |
| | god jesus christian church christ |
| | **writes system morality keith organization** |
| DVAE | **god Christians gods faith bible** |
| | jesus god bible christ faith |
| | heaven christ jesus sin lord |
| | christians god israel christian |
| | **god Christians bible christ sin** |
| | morality objective evidence moral definition |
| | morality objective nsa crypto keith |
| NSMDM | **christians biblical holy jesus sin** |
| | god gods faith atheist heaven |
| | morality objective absolute values mac |
| | **constitution government catholic amendment moral** |
| SCHOLAR | god belief faith existence evidence |
| | god bible jesus christians christian |
| | christian christians god christ church |
| | **jesus christ church faith christians** |
| | **morality moral keith objective definition** |
| SpareNTM | **jesus sin christians christ bible** |
| | christ mary lord jesus heaven |
| | existence atheist belief islam exist |
| | **morality objective moral values keith** |

## 5 Conclusion

This paper proposes a SpareNTM topic model with auxiliary Bernoulli variables to better model sparsity in latent semantic structures of texts and develops an effective VAE network to learn the inference process. The proposed approaches can discover the document-topic sparsity by identifying which topics appear in it, performing better than existing methods in terms of both the quality of topics and the generalization. Experimental results on 20NewsGroups, Wikitext-103, and SearchSnippets corpora demonstrate that access to Bernoulli priors with a non-mean-field approximation in the neural inference process permits an intelligent neural topic model, which consistently achieves higher NPMI scores and more diverse topics than other methods. In future work, we plan to evaluate SpareNTM on more datasets, such as larger text collections, and determine the impact when the mutual influence in Bernoulli latent variables is considered in SpareNTM. We hope this study can shed some light on neural topic modeling and related applications.

**Acknowledgment.** This work was supported by the National Natural Science Foundation of China (61972261), Natural Science Foundation of Guangdong Province (2023A1515011667), Key Basic Research Foundation of Shenzhen (JCYJ20220818100205012), and Basic Research Foundations of Shenzhen (JCYJ20210324093609026).

**Ethical Statement.** This paper doesn't involve unethical tasks. All the experiment was done in public datasets.

# References

1. Blei, D.M., Kucukelbir, A., McAuliffe, J.D.: Variational inference: a review for statisticians. J. Am. Stat. Assoc. **112**(518), 859–877 (2017)
2. Blei, D.M., Ng, A.Y., Jordan, M.I.: Latent Dirichlet allocation. JMLR **3**(Jan), 993–1022 (2003)
3. Burkhardt, S., Kramer, S.: Decoupling sparsity and smoothness in the Dirichlet variational autoencoder topic model. JMLR **20**, 131:1–131:27 (2019)
4. Card, D., Tan, C., Smith, N.A.: Neural models for documents with metadata. In: Proceedings of the 56th Annual Meeting of the Association for Computational Linguistics, ACL 2018, Melbourne, Australia, 15–20 July 2018, pp. 2031–2040. Association for Computational Linguistics (2018)
5. Dieng, A.B., Wang, C., Gao, J., Paisley, J.W.: TopicRNN: a recurrent neural network with long-range semantic dependency. In: 5th International Conference on Learning Representations, ICLR 2017, Toulon, France, 24–26 April 2017, Conference Track Proceedings. OpenReview.net (2017)
6. Dieng, A.B., Ruiz, F.J.R., Blei, D.M.: Topic modeling in embedding spaces. Trans. Assoc. Comput. Linguist. **8**, 439–453 (2020)
7. Drefs, J., Guiraud, E., Lücke, J.: Evolutionary variational optimization of generative models. J. Mach. Learn. Res. **23**, 21:1–21:51 (2022)
8. Drefs, J., Guiraud, E., Panagiotou, F., Lücke, J.: Direct evolutionary optimization of variational autoencoders with binary latents. In: Amini, M.R., Canu, S., Fischer, A., Guns, T., Kralj Novak, P., Tsoumakas, G. (eds.) ECML PKDD 2022. LNCS, vol. 13715, pp. 357–372. Springer, Cham (2022). https://doi.org/10.1007/978-3-031-26409-2_22
9. Fallah, K., Rozell, C.J.: Variational sparse coding with learned thresholding. In: ICML. Proceedings of Machine Learning Research, vol. 162, pp. 6034–6058. PMLR (2022)
10. Feng, J., Zhang, Z., Ding, C., Rao, Y., Xie, H., Wang, F.L.: Context reinforced neural topic modeling over short texts. Inf. Sci. **607**, 79–91 (2022)
11. Griffiths, T.L., Steyvers, M.: Finding scientific topics. Proc. Natl. Acad. Sci. **101**(suppl_1), 5228–5235 (2004)
12. Jang, E., Gu, S., Poole, B.: Categorical reparameterization with gumbel-softmax. In: ICLR (2017)
13. Kingma, D.P., Welling, M.: Auto-encoding variational Bayes. In: ICLR (2014)
14. Lang, K.: Newsweeder: learning to filter netnews. In: Machine Learning, Proceedings of the Twelfth International Conference on Machine Learning, Tahoe City, California, USA, 9–12 July 1995, pp. 331–339 (1995). https://doi.org/10.1016/b978-1-55860-377-6.50048-7

15. Lau, J.H., Newman, D., Baldwin, T.: Machine reading tea leaves: automatically evaluating topic coherence and topic model quality. In: EACL, pp. 530–539 (2014)
16. Lin, T., Hu, Z., Guo, X.: Sparsemax and relaxed Wasserstein for topic sparsity. In: WSDM, pp. 141–149 (2019)
17. Merity, S., Xiong, C., Bradbury, J., Socher, R.: Pointer sentinel mixture models. In: 5th International Conference on Learning Representations, ICLR 2017, Toulon, France, 24–26 April 2017, Conference Track Proceedings (2017)
18. Miao, Y., Grefenstette, E., Blunsom, P.: Discovering discrete latent topics with neural variational inference. In: ICML, vol. 70, pp. 2410–2419 (2017)
19. Miao, Y., Yu, L., Blunsom, P.: Neural variational inference for text processing. In: ICML, vol. 48, pp. 1727–1736 (2016)
20. Mitchell, T.J., Beauchamp, J.J.: Bayesian variable selection in linear regression. J. Am. Stat. Assoc. **83**(404), 1023–1032 (1988)
21. Naesseth, C.A., Ruiz, F.J.R., Linderman, S.W., Blei, D.M.: Reparameterization gradients through acceptance-rejection sampling algorithms. In: AISTATS. Proceedings of Machine Learning Research, vol. 54, pp. 489–498 (2017)
22. Nan, F., Ding, R., Nallapati, R., Xiang, B.: Topic modeling with Wasserstein autoencoders. In: Proceedings of the 57th Conference of the Association for Computational Linguistics, ACL 2019, Florence, Italy, 28 July–2 August 2019, pp. 6345–6381 (2019)
23. Nguyen, T., Luu, A.T.: Contrastive learning for neural topic model. In: Advances in Neural Information Processing Systems 34: Annual Conference on Neural Information Processing Systems 2021, NeurIPS 2021, 6–14 December 2021, Virtual, pp. 11974–11986 (2021)
24. Ning, X., et al.: Nonparametric topic modeling with neural inference. Neurocomputing **399**, 296–306 (2020)
25. Peng, M., et al.: Neural sparse topical coding. In: ACL, pp. 2332–2340 (2018)
26. Phan, X.H., Nguyen, L., Horiguchi, S.: Learning to classify short and sparse text & web with hidden topics from large-scale data collections. In: Proceedings of the 17th International Conference on World Wide Web, WWW 2008, Beijing, China, 21–25 April 2008, pp. 91–100 (2008). https://doi.org/10.1145/1367497.1367510
27. Rezaee, M., Ferraro, F.: A discrete variational recurrent topic model without the reparametrization trick. In: Larochelle, H., Ranzato, M., Hadsell, R., Balcan, M., Lin, H. (eds.) Advances in Neural Information Processing Systems 33: Annual Conference on Neural Information Processing Systems 2020, NeurIPS 2020, 6–12 December 2020, Virtual (2020)
28. Song, Z., Hu, Y., Verma, A., Buckeridge, D.L., Li, Y.: Automatic phenotyping by a seed-guided topic model. In: KDD, pp. 4713–4723. ACM (2022)
29. Srivastava, A., Sutton, C.: Autoencoding variational inference for topic models. In: ICLR (2017)
30. Srivastava, A., Sutton, C.: Variational inference in pachinko allocation machines. CoRR (2018)
31. Tian, R., Mao, Y., Zhang, R.: Learning VAE-LDA models with rounded reparameterization trick. In: EMNLP, pp. 1315–1325 (2020)
32. Tonolini, F., Jensen, B.S., Murray-Smith, R.: Variational sparse coding. In: UAI. Proceedings of Machine Learning Research, vol. 115, pp. 690–700. AUAI Press (2019)
33. Turner, R.E., Sahani, M.: Two problems with variational expectation maximisation for time-series models. In: Barber, D., Cemgil, T., Chiappa, S. (eds.) Bayesian Time Series Models, chap. 5, pp. 109–130. Cambridge University Press (2011)

34. Wang, C., Blei, D.M.: Decoupling sparsity and smoothness in the discrete hierarchical Dirichlet process. In: NeurIPS, pp. 1982–1989 (2009)
35. Wang, D., et al.: Representing mixtures of word embeddings with mixtures of topic embeddings. In: ICLR. OpenReview.net (2022)
36. Wang, R., et al.: Neural topic modeling with bidirectional adversarial training. In: Proceedings of the 58th Annual Meeting of the Association for Computational Linguistics, ACL 2020, Online, 5–10 July 2020, pp. 340–350 (2020)
37. Wang, R., Zhou, D., He, Y.: ATM: adversarial-neural topic model. Inf. Process. Manag. **56**(6) (2019)
38. Williamson, S., Wang, C., Heller, K.A., Blei, D.M.: The IBP compound Dirichlet process and its application to focused topic modeling. In: ICML, pp. 1151–1158 (2010)
39. Wu, X., Li, C., Zhu, Y., Miao, Y.: Short text topic modeling with topic distribution quantization and negative sampling decoder. In: Proceedings of the 2020 Conference on Empirical Methods in Natural Language Processing, EMNLP, pp. 1772–1782 (2020)
40. Xu, J., Xu, B., Wang, P., Zheng, S., Tian, G., Zhao, J.: Self-taught convolutional neural networks for short text clustering. Neural Netw. **88**, 22–31 (2017)
41. Zhao, H., Phung, D.Q., Huynh, V., Jin, Y., Du, L., Buntine, W.L.: Topic modelling meets deep neural networks: a survey. In: IJCAI, pp. 4713–4720 (2021)
42. Zhu, J., Xing, E.P.: Sparse topical coding. In: UAI, pp. 831–838 (2011)

# Neuro/Symbolic Learning

# The Metric is the Message: Benchmarking Challenges for Neural Symbolic Regression

Amanda Bertschinger$^{(\boxtimes)}$, Q. Tyrell Davis, James Bagrow, and Joshua Bongard

University of Vermont, Burlington, VT 05405, USA
ambertsc@uvm.edu

**Abstract.** The neural symbolic regression (NSR) literature has thus far been hindered by an over-reliance on individual, *ad hoc* evaluation metrics, producing seemingly favorable performance for the method using it but making comparison between methods difficult. Here we compare the performance of several NSR methods using diverse metrics reported in the literature, and some of our own devising. We show that reliance on a single metric can hide an NSR method's shortcomings, causing performance rankings between methods to change as the evaluation metric changes. We further show that metrics which consider the structure of equations generated after training can help reveal these shortcomings, and suggest ways to correct for them. Given our results, we suggest best practices on what metrics to use to best advance this new field.

**Keywords:** Benchmarks · Interpretability and explainability · Symbolic regression · Deep learning

## 1 Introduction

Classical regression encompasses a range of methods that fit an equation to given data. In classical regression, the data and an equation skeleton is provided, to which coefficients are then fit. The limitation of this approach is the need to formulate an appropriate equation, which requires manual analysis of the data to determine an appropriate formal representation. One solution to this issue is symbolic regression (SR) [14]. SR searches over the space of possible equations to explain a given data set, removing the need for manual formulation of the equation and thus avoiding human bias. Traditionally, SR is conducted with genetic programming (GP) [2,12–14,26,27,35]. Advances in GPSR were hard to discern due to a lack of common metrics and benchmark equations. Throughout its history since the 19901990ss, a variety of metrics and best practices for GPSR have been studied [1,16,17]. However, it was not until 2012 that the lack of standardization began to be discussed and benchmarks proposed [15,19,36]. This delay in recognizing the problem a lack of standardized metrics and benchmarks creates hindered the progress of GPSR, and to date there still exist GPSR methods that rely on non-standard metrics and toy datasets that are not a part of established benchmarks.

D. Koutra et al. (Eds.): ECML PKDD 2023, LNAI 14172, pp. 161–177, 2023.
https://doi.org/10.1007/978-3-031-43421-1_10

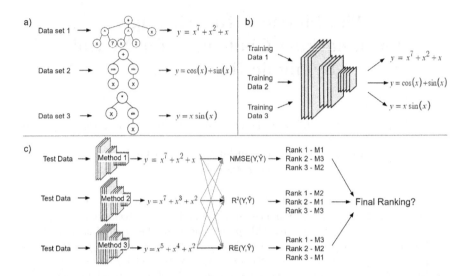

**Fig. 1.** a) Genetic Programming Symbolic Regression. Each instance is trained on a dataset of (x,y) values to describe a separate equation. b) Neural Symbolic Regression. A network is trained on multiple datasets of (x,y) values that describe a variety of equations. c) NSR methods' use of different metrics obscures how well networks perform in comparison to each other, so a final ranking of the best performing method is unclear.

Regardless of the speed of progress in evolutionary algorithm-based SR, it generally remains the standard for SR. However, such gradient-free search approaches require considerable computation, and they only fit one set of equations to one data set, rather than learning the more general problem of how to transform different data sets into different equations.

Deep learning methods offer a potential approach for achieving this generality. AI models such as large language models [7,25,34] show promise for this generalized form of SR by transforming data into equations [3,4,11,32,33]. This is possible because an equation can be considered a statement composed in the language of mathematical operators and variables. Indeed, recent literature shows progress in using transformers [4,11,32,33], a type of large language model, to generate an equation when fed a given data set.

Currently, however, NSR studies use *ad hoc* metrics on non-standardized benchmark sets, making comparison across methods difficult (Fig. 1c). This is similar to the issues faced by GPSR, which we seek to preemptively avoid. Similar studies have been done in other fields of machine learning in order to help ensure trustworthy benchmarks and comparisons between methods [5]. In order to better compare across methods, here we compare NSR methods (Table 1) using some metrics drawn from the literature and some created by us, and find that this reveals limitations in these current methods that are hidden when only one metric is used. Given our results, we suggest best practices on what benchmark equations and metrics to use to best advance this new field.

## 2    Methods

Five NSR methods have been reported in the literature to date [3,4,11,32,33]. Each method trains some kind of differentiable network to transform multiple data sets into multiple equations such that, post training, it can transform unseen data sets into equations accurately reflecting that data. This requires a set of training equations and a set of testing equations, and data generated from both. As GPSR is specialized per equation instead of being generalized for any equation, comparison between neural and GPSR methods is unfair given GPSR will always be more accurate than NSR. As such, evolutionary methods are not considered in this paper.

First, we define post generation coefficient fitting (PEGCF) and the role it plays in NSR. Second, benchmark equations in NSR are discussed. Third, the variety of metrics implimented are defined and analyzed. Fourth, details of the NSR methods and are outlined. Finally, we define the control equations that are used for comparison against NSR generated equations.

### 2.1    Post Equation Generation Coefficient Fitting

It has been found that training a transformer to generate coefficients and equation structure simultaneously is difficult, so some of these models [4,32] are only trained to generate equation structure, and rely on coefficient fitting methods [6,8,10,28] post inference. Even the NSR methods that do predict coefficients during training [11,33] still use PEGCF during and after training to further refine the coefficients in generated equations.

In theory, a trained model could learn to ignore data and instead always generate the same, sufficiently long equation that could be fit to various new data sets by PEGCF. Thus, as an initial demonstration of the utility of employing multiple NSR metrics, we reran some of the NSR methods reported in the literature [4,32,33] but denied them access to PEGCF. Target equations were generated with coefficients of 1, and coefficients in generated equations were replaced with 1; this allows NSR methods to not have to guess or fit coefficients at all. Numeric metrics reveal that several of these methods are overly reliant on PEGCF as the PEGCF-denied methods suffered deteriorations against these metrics; a symbolic metric—equation length—reveals how this over reliance might be manifesting (Sect. 3.1).

### 2.2    Benchmarks

In NSR there is a lack of commonly-agreed upon benchmark equations. Though some methods [4,33] test on benchmark equations such as the Nguyen equations [31], on their own, these equations tend to lack diversity and complexity. Thus, we propose a set of additional benchmark equations with increasing diversity and complexity (Appendix A).

## 2.3   Metrics

Choosing appropriate metrics for NSR is complicated by the fact that, unlike most forms of supervised learning, SR investigators face a dilemma between using numeric or symbolic metrics. The former rewards for prediction accuracy while the latter rewards for structural accuracy.

**Numeric Metrics.** Numeric evaluation metrics measure, in different ways, the distance between the dependent variable values of a given data set $(Y)$ and dependent variable values predicted by the equation generated by a model $(\hat{Y})$ when provided with independent variable values $X$. Use of such metrics implies the authors are interested in the predictive power of generated equations, rather than their form.

Biggio [4] uses numpy's `isclose` method. Here, we use `isclose` with the specifications reported in [4]: an absolute tolerance of 0.001, relative tolerance of 0.05, and a threshold of 0.95. This means that a generated equation that differs from the target equation at less than 5% of points is considered accurate. This metric is reported as the percentage of equations that are accurate. This metric has the advantage of being able to deal with values of $\pm\infty$ and `NaN`, however the multiple layers of error allowance do slightly obscure the model's true performance.

We also implement Valipour's [32] "protected" normalized mean square error (NMSE)—a different numeric metric—given by

$$\text{NMSE}(Y, \hat{Y}) = \frac{1}{n} \sum_{i=1}^{n} \frac{(y_i - \hat{y}_i)^2}{\|y_i + \epsilon\|_2}, \tag{1}$$

where $\epsilon = 10^{-5}$ [32] is a small factor used to avoid divide by zero errors. Mean squared error is a common metric in general, and using normalization keeps any extreme values from contributing overly much to the individual error. One disadvantage to this metric is that it ranges over $[0, +\infty]$. This can cause large outliers to have an outsized effect on the final mean NMSE, as it can take many perfect scores of 0 to balance one very large score.

Finally, we employ several versions of the coefficient of determination, $R^2$ [9]. Interpreting raw $R^2$ can be challenging, as outliers can have a significant effect on the final average. There are various ways to compensate for this. First is the mean raw $R^2$ score, as used in Vastl [33], given by

$$R^2(Y, \hat{Y}) = 1 - \frac{\sum_{i=1}^{n} (y_i - \hat{y}_i)^2}{\sum_{i=1}^{n} (y_i - \bar{y})^2}. \tag{2}$$

This shares a similar disadvantage to NMSE: perfect accuracy results in a value of 1.0, but poor accuracy can incur infinitely negative values. To alleviate the outsized effect outliers can have, median $R^2$ can be used. Alternately to median, $R^2$ over a threshold has been reported in the literature as an accuracy metric, but there is no consensus on what threshold to use: Biggio [4] used a threshold of 0.95, Kamienny [11] used 0.99, and La Cava [15] used 0.999.

**Symbolic Metrics.** Another version of accuracy is to consider the structural distance between a generated equation and a known target equation. Usage of symbolic metrics implies the authors wish to create a method that can 'explain' a data set, in mathematical form, to a human reader. To compare two equations symbolically, they must first be simplified, as NSR models can generate equations with duplicate terms during inference. Due to how symbolic comparison of two equations works, it is necessary to group matching terms and ensure that the equations are always written in the same order (e.g. a polynomial is always written highest to lowest order first). To do this we employ sympy's `simplify` method. This simplifies an equation and allows it to be accessed in string or tree form. This is important as some symbolic metrics require conversion of a string into a tokenized representation in order to calculate error, while other methods require the tree form of an equation.

Cross-entropy is commonly used for symbolic loss during training, and can be similarly used as an evaluation metric for equations generated by a trained model. To use cross-entropy, equations are transformed into a tokenized representation, and then processed using pytorch's `CrossEntropyLoss`.

La Cava [15] and Petersen [24] used another symbolic metric: exact symbolic equivalence. For this metric, first, target and predicted equations are compared in their tree representations $(f(x), \hat{f}(x))$ to determine whether they are the same tree: `simplify(f - f_hat) == 0`. This metric then reports the proportion of exact matches across the training equations or testing equations. La Cava [15] used a slightly more lenient definition of symbolic equivalence that includes equations that differ by a constant or are proportional. It is worth noting that [15,24] report evolutionary SR methods; exact equivalence has not yet been used as a metric in NSR. For the sake of parity with other symbolic metrics (the lower the metric the better the method is performing), we here report symbolic inequivalence- the proportion of equations that do not exactly match across training or testing equations.

The unforgiving nature of exact symbolic equivalence can foil comparisons between partially-working NSR methods because they all achieve a score of zero. So, the final symbolic metric we consider is tree edit distance (TED), a symbolic metric not yet used by any NSR methods. TED algorithms [20–23,37] calculate how many edits it would take to transform one equation's tree representation into another's. Ordered and unordered TED algorithms are possible. In an ordered algorithm, the order in which the nodes appear in the tree matters, so if a term appears in both equations, but different places in the tree, this is considered a necessary edit. Unordered TED does not make this distinction: so long as the term is present in both trees it is correct and does not require an edit. Here, we use APTED [23], an ordered TED. We report this TED normalized by the number of nodes in the target equation tree because generated equations will require, on average, more edits to transform them into longer target equations.

## 2.4    NSR Methods

We now summarize the methods considered in this study. Biggio 2021 [4], Valipour 2021 [32], and Vastl 2022 [33] are all implemented. Biggio 2020 [3] and Kamienny 2022 [11] were not implemented in this study due to a lack of models provided by the authors.

**Biggio 2020.** [3] implement a fully-convolutional model with gated recurrent units, residual connections and attention. The model uses cross-entropy loss for training and is evaluated on root mean squared error. It is trained on equations generated by their own equation generation program, and is tested on a combination of equations seen during training, and new equations, still produced by their equation generator. Despite significant effort we were unable to reimplement this method, so it is not included in the cross-method comparison below.

**Biggio 2021.** [4] use a set transformer encoder with a standard transformer decoder model, trained on cross-entropy loss using millions of equations from their equation generator. The trained model is evaluated by their own numerical metric using `np.isclose` (detailed below) on a combination of the AI Feynman equations [30], Nguyen equations [31], and their own generator-produced equations unseen during training. They provided a pretrained model to the community, which we use below.

**Valipour 2021.** [32] use a two transformer model, first passing data through a transformer to produce an order-invariant representation then used to train a second transformer that generates equations. The entire model is trained using cross-entropy loss and tested on NMSE. They use their own equation generator to generate training and testing equations. For our testing, we trained their model on equations generated by their generator.

**Kamienny 2022.** [11] use a fully connected feedforward network to reduce data dimensionality and then feed the lower dimensional data to the transformer model to generate equations from them. Their model predicts equations and coefficients, the latter of which are then refined using a coefficient fitter. The model is trained on cross-entropy loss and tested on both the coefficient of determination ($R^2$) and accuracy to tolerance.

They use their own equation generator for generating training and part of their testing equations (the rest come from the Feynman [30] and ODE-Strogatz [29] equations). They do not provide their model (code or pretrained), and as such we were unable to implement their method.

**Vastl 2022.** [33] use a transformer architecture with a cross-attention encoder and self-attention decoder. Their model uses cross-entropy and mean squared error losses for equation structure and coefficients respectively during training, and is tested on both $R^2$ and relative error. They generate their own training equations, and their testing equations are a combination of their training equations and benchmark equations drawn from the SR literature. They provide a pretrained model, which we use below.

In addition, we considered but did not ultimately test the NSR methods by Biggio [3] and Kamienny [11] as we were unable to implement either method and thus do not report results from them.

### 2.5   Control Equations

If PEGCF can fit randomly or systematically generated equations to a data set with similar success as it does for an NSR-generated equation, this would indicate that NSR method is not generating structurally correct equations. Thus, we compared NSR-generated equations against three types of control equations: polynomials, Fourier series, and randomly-generated equations. All equations were designed with 10°C of freedom in order to allow sufficient ability to fit to data. The polynomials are

$$f(x) = \sum_{i=0}^{10} c_i x^i, \tag{3}$$

where $c_i$ are the fit coefficients. The Fourier series used was

$$f(x) = c_0 + \sum_{i=1}^{5} c_{i,1} * \sin(ix + c_{i,2}). \tag{4}$$

Lastly, the random equations are generated using Valipour's [32] tree based equation generation with access to the mathematical operations $[+, *, \backslash, \sin, \cos, \sqrt{\cdot}, \exp, \log]$ and a maximum tree depth of 9.

## 3   Results

We use a variety of numeric and symbolic metrics to analyze the predictive and structural accuracies of equations generated by various methods. Methods that provide pre-trained networks use those saved weights for evaluation. Other methods that do not provide such are trained from scratch using the network architecture provided.[1] All methods' networks are trained on their own generated equations and are evaluated on our benchmark equations (Appendix A).

### 3.1   Numeric Metrics

**Cross-Method Comparison.** Results obtained against the numeric metrics are shown in columns 2–4 of Table 1. Biggio [4], with the `isclose` metric, outperforms Vastl [33] with this metric ($p \ll 0.001$). No significant performance advantage over Valipour [32] was detected ($p > 0.05$) with this metric. Similarly, although it appears that Valipour [32] performs best using their NMSE metric, there is no significant difference compared to other NSR methods using NMSE. Overall, Table 1 shows that the relative ranking of NSR methods is dependent on the evaluation metric used.

[1] https://github.com/mec-lab/metric_message.

**Table 1.** Comparison of testing metrics for NSR methods. Bold values indicate that it was the metric used in that method. Bracketed values denote the 95% confidence interval for the metric. Mann-Whitney U [18] tests for significance were performed within each column. Bonferroni correction was employed to compensate for the 12 pairwise comparisons. In the case of NMSE and $R^2$, the median is reported instead of the mean due to unbounded ranges.

| Reference | NMSE | $R^2 > 0.99$ | $R^2$ | np.isclose | Cross entropy | Symb Equiv | Tree Edit Dist.Prop |
|-----------|------|--------------|-------|------------|---------------|------------|---------------------|
| Biggio et al. (2021) | 0.20 (0.16, 0.25) | 0.34 (0.33, 0.36) | 0.95 (0.93, 0.96) | **0.24** *** (0.23, 0.26) | 0.60 (0.60, 0.60) | 0.18 (0.17, 0.19) | 1.01 (0.99, 1.02) |
| Valipour et al. (2021) | **0.03** (0.003, 0.07) | 0.37 (0.19, 0.59) | 0.91 (0.29, 0.99) | 0.07 (0.01, 0.31) | 1.96 (1.56, 2.30) | 0.07 (0.00, 0.30) | 1.05 (0.83, 1.18) |
| Vastl et al. (2022) | 0.72 (0.64, 0.84) | 0.15 (0.31, 0.47) | **0.38** (0.18, 0.20) | 0.13 (0.12, 0.15) | 0.48 (0.46, 0.49) | 0.05 (0.05, 0.07) | 1.69 (1.64, 1.75) |

**With and Without PEGCF.** Here we compare NSR methods with and without PEGCF, providing insight into how much data-to-equation effort is performed by skeleton generation (NSR) and coefficient fitting (PEGCF). We found that, when denied access to PEGCF, Biggio [4] and Valipour [32] suffered significant deterioration according to two numerical metrics during testing. This is similar to Kamienny [11], which reports a better $R^2$ value when PEGCF is used compared to when it is not. Vastl [33] however does not suffer any statistically significant deterioration according to either metric (Table 2).

**Equation Length Comparison.** One hypothesis for how NSR methods come to overly rely on PEGCF is that the models learn to generate equations that have too many terms and rely on PEGCF to lessen the contribution of these extra terms. We can check whether this occurs by examining the lengths of generated equations compared to our benchmark targets. Table 3 shows comparisons between generated and target equation length. In all methods, there is a significant difference between the two. Valipour's method [32] tends to generate overly-long equations while Biggio [4] and Vastl [33] tend to generate overly-short equations. Figure 2 shows the distribution of coefficient magnitudes across all methods, showing that while the correct coefficient of 1.0 is frequently predicted, there are many occurrences of the coefficients predicted being close to zero or very large.

**Table 2.** Median results over all benchmark equations for two different numeric evaluations metrics, with and without optimization techniques. Median is used for all metrics due to unbounded ranges. The bracketed pairs of values denote the 95% confidence interval for each median. *** denotes $p \ll 0.001$ after the Bonferroni correction is applied to compensate for the six pairwise comparisons.

|  | NMSE | | $R^2$ | |
|---|---|---|---|---|
|  | PEGCF | no PEGCF | PEGCF | no PEGCF |
| Biggio et al | 0.20*** | 0.43 | 0.95*** | 0.47 |
| (2021) | (0.16, 0.25) | (0.38, 0.47) | (0.93, 0.96) | (0.39, 0.54) |
| Valipour et al | 0.03*** | 0.52 | 0.91*** | -0.12 |
| (2021) | (0.003, 0.07) | (0.15, 1.45) | (0.29, 0.99) | ($-1.03$, 0.51) |
| Vastl et al | 0.72 | 0.77 | 0.38 | 0.33 |
| (2022) | (0.64, 0.84) | (0.69, 0.91) | (0.31, 0.47) | (0.26, 0.42) |

**Table 3.** Comparison of equation length for equations predicted by networks. *** denotes $p \ll 0.001$ after the Bonferroni correction is applied to compensate for the three pairwise comparisons.

| Reference | Target | | Predicted |
|---|---|---|---|
| Biggio | 10.625 (10.51, 10.75) | *** | 7.45 (7.36, 7.54) |
| Valipour | 12.74 (12.69, 12.78) | *** | 17.92 (17.87, 17.99) |
| Vastl | 11.11 (10.94, 11.26) | *** | 9.69 (9.41, 10.02) |

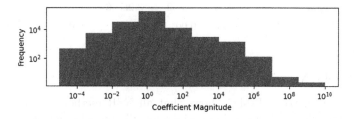

**Fig. 2.** Distribution of PEGCF coefficients across all equations generated by implimented NSR methods. The horizontal axis is the magnitude of the coefficients $|c_i|$. The vertical axis reports the number of appearances of that coefficient magnitude across all equations.

**Comparison to Control Equations.** The reliance of NSR methods on PEGCF can be so great that, in some cases, NSR-generated equations require no less coefficient fitting effort than is required to fit random equations, Fourier series, or polynonimals with near-equivalent degrees of freedom (Table 4). With enough terms, these control equations become competitive with NSR-generated networks, if numeric metrics are used to the compare them. Here we take competitive to mean that the reported median $R^2$ score is within or above the confidence interval of the NSR models for that benchmark equation.

**Table 4.** Performance of NSR methods and control equations on $R^2$ with PEGCF for benchmark equations [31]. Highlighted are cases where the control methods are competitive with the NSR methods, where competitive is defined as the control median above or equal to the best performing NSR method median. Median is used for all cases due to unbounded ranges in $R^2$.

| | | Random | Fourier | Polynomials | Valipour | Biggio | Vastl |
|---|---|---|---|---|---|---|---|
| Nguyen | | | | | | | |
| 1 | $x^3 + x^2 + x$ | −0.03 | −1.22 | **1.0** | 1.0 | 1.0 | 1.0 |
| 2 | $x^4 + x^3 + x^2 + x$ | 0.54 | −0.09 | **1.0** | 1.0 | 0.99 | 1.0 |
| 3 | $x^5 + x^4 + x^3 + x^2 + x$ | 0.36 | −0.21 | **1.0** | 1.0 | 1.0 | 0.89 |
| 4 | $x^6 + x^5 + x^4 + x^3 + x^2 + x$ | 0.16 | −0.14 | **1.0** | 1.0 | 0.90 | 0.80 |
| 5 | $\sin x^2 \cos x - 1$ | 0.08 | -22.62 | **0.71** | 0.51 | −3.08 | −0.5 |
| 6 | $\sin x + \sin x + x^2$ | 0.40 | −1.67 | **0.48** | 0.47 | 0.06 | 0.07 |
| 7 | $\log x + 1 + \log x^2 + 1$ | −0.41 | **1.0** | −2.7E+5 | 1.0 | 0.98 | 0.86 |
| 8 | $\sqrt{x}$ | 0.27 | – | 0.03 | 1.0 | 1.0 | -8.92 |
| Complexity spanning | | | | | | | |
| 1 | $\sin(x * e^x)$ | 0.11 | −0.57 | 0.27 | 0.14 | 1.0 | −0.30 |
| 2 | $x + \log(x^4)$ | -0.19 | 0.86 | −7.0E+4 | 0.98 | 1.0 | 1.0 |
| 3 | $1 + x\sin(\frac{1}{x})$ | 0.13 | 0.76 | −0.06 | 0.96 | 0.63 | 0.82 |
| 4 | $\sqrt{x^3}\log(x^2)$ | **−0.40** | **−0.09** | −1.3E+5 | −0.57 | – | – |
| 5 | $\frac{x}{\sqrt{x^2+\sin x}}$ | −0.01 | −9.63 | 0.02 | −0.01 | −0.33 | −0.08 |
| 6 | $\frac{x+x^3}{1+x\cos x^2}$ | 0.91 | 0.85 | **0.99** | 0.92 | −1.24 | −0.94 |
| 7 | $\frac{e^x(1+\sqrt{1+x}+\cos x^2)}{x^2}$ | −13.10 | −9.62 | −3.2E+6 | 0.58 | 0.07 | 0.26 |
| 8 | $\cos\left(\frac{x+\sin x}{x^3+x\log x^2}\right)$ | −0.03 | 0.00 | −0.03 | 0.0 | – | – |

### 3.2    Symbolic Metrics

Unlike numeric metrics, Table 5 shows that all NSR methods statistically significantly outperform all control equations for all symbolic metrics apart from Valipour [32], which does not outperform random equations when measured with cross-entropy loss.

## 4    Discussion

NSR models are not performing as well as the statistics reported in their literature would seem to imply. First, varied metrics make cross-method comparison difficult. Second, PEGCF artificially makes NSR models' performance seem better. Third, we show that use of symbolic metrics can help reveal the true performance of the models though the metric must be carefully chosen. Finally, we show why it is important to consider both numeric and symbolic metrics.

The relative ranking of methods is fluid. Because of the change in relative performances when switching metrics, it is near impossible to compare models

**Table 5.** A comparison of symbolic metrics on control methods and NSR methods for a) cross-entropy loss, b) symbolic inequivalence, and c) tree edit distance proportion, showing the lower values for across all metrics for NSR methods. The bracketed pairs of values denote the 95% confidence interval for each median. *** denotes $p \ll 0.001$ for the NSR model after the Bonferroni correction is applied to compensate for the 27 pairwise comparisons. In all but one case, the pairwise comparison shows the NSR method out-competing the control methods.

a)

| | Biggio [3] 0.6 (0.6,0.6) | Valipour [27] 1.96 (1.56, 2.30) | Vastl [28] 0.48 (0.46, 0.49) |
|---|---|---|---|
| Random 1.8 (1.75, 1.85) | *** | p¿0.05 | *** |
| Fourier 3.48 (3.48,3.48) | *** | *** | *** |
| Polynomial 3.67 (3.61,3.72) | *** | *** | *** |

b)

| | Biggio [3] 98.99 (98.98, 99.01) | Valipour [27] 98.95 (98.82, 99.17) | Vastl [28] 98.31 (98.25, 98.36) |
|---|---|---|---|
| Random 100 (100, 100) | *** | *** | *** |
| Fourier 100 (100, 100) | *** | *** | *** |
| Polynomial 100 (100, 100) | *** | *** | *** |

c)

| | Biggio [3] 0.18 (0.17, 0.19) | Valipour [27] 0.07 (0.0, 0.3) | Vastl [28] 0.05 (0.05, 0.07) |
|---|---|---|---|
| Random 2.83 (2.51, 3.16) | *** | *** | *** |
| Fourier 14.76 (14.52, 15.0) | *** | *** | *** |
| Polynomial 3.26 (2.69, 1.02) | *** | *** | *** |

cross-method. These metrics, when used on their own, are also problematic in that arbitrary hyperparameters must be chosen (as in the case of $R^2 > 0.99$ and $R^2 > 0.95$) or are hidden within software libraries (as in the case of `np.isclose`).

The decrease in predictive performance of most NSR methods when PEGCF is not allowed (as indicated by the numeric metrics) indicates that the methods are not generating equations with appropriate skeletons. We hypothesize that PEGCF may be performing the bulk of fitting here because NSR learns to either generate very long equations and then PEGCF removes extra terms by setting the coefficients on said terms sufficiently small that they contribute negligibly to numeric metrics, or generate only the part of an equation that contributes most to the data and the PEGCF emphasizes it with sufficiently large coefficients. To test this assertion, we measured the difference in mean number of nodes in the tree representation of the target and NSR generated equations. Shown in

Table 3, the significant disparity between these lengths for all methods shows that the trained models do not generate the structurally correct equations. Instead, good performance of the models is due to PEGCF being able to fit structurally incorrect equations well to the provided data. Overly long equations imply a relationship that is not present in data, while equations missing terms fail to report some relationships. Seen in Table 3, [32] suffers from errors of commission while [4,33] suffers from errors of omission. Across all methods, Fig. 2 shows that PEGCF is often "removing" terms from predicted equations by setting the coefficients for such terms close to zero, and emphasizing contribution from the correctly predicted terms by setting the coefficients for these to be much larger than 1. For those methods where there is no significant effect of PEGCF denial, the networks predict the starting coefficients when generating equations. These coefficients are then further refined by use of PEGCF after training. Presumably, the insignificant change observed in both methods are due to the effects of this during-training coefficient prediction reducing the effects of PEGCF withdrawal.

Symbolic metrics are important in showing how accurately an NSR method is performing on its primary task: automating the distillation of data into equations. Unlike numeric metrics, symbolic metrics are not influenced by PEGCF as they directly compare the symbolic structure of the equation. Of the symbolic metrics, TED is most meaningful as it has the advantages of absolute equivalence, as well as the ability to reveal a gradient in how "close" two equations are. A TED of 0 shows absolute equivalence just as symbolic equivalence does, but TED is not restricted to binary outcomes and could thus show that a particular change to an NSR method improves or harms it.

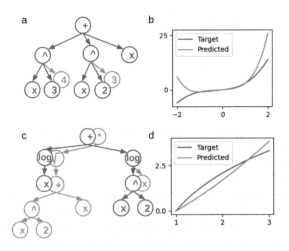

**Fig. 3.** a) Target versus predicted equation trees for the equations $x^3 + x^2 + x$ and $x^4 + x^3 + x$ respectively. b) Graph of aforementioned equations. c) Target versus predicted equation trees for the equations $\log(x) + \log(x^2)$ and $(\sqrt{x^2 + x})\log(x)$ respectively. d) Graph of these equations.

However, only using symbolic metrics is insufficient to determine how well a network is performing. While symbolic metrics do hold advantages over numeric metrics, the opposite is also true. Foremost is that numeric evaluation metrics do not require a ground truth equation while symbolic ones do. In practice, after training, most data sets will not have a ground truth equation. In such a situation only numeric metrics can be used.

Additionally, there are situations in which two equations can be close symbolically but distant numerically. Figure 3a,b shows two such equations. The TED between $x^3 + x^2 + x$ and $x^4 + x^3 + x$ is 2 (Fig. 3a). However, Fig. 3b shows that the two are quite far numerically, particularly in the negative $x$ range. In a case like this, it would be particularly important to also consider a numeric metric, as that would reveal where the network's failings are more than the symbolic metric. Figure 3c,d show the opposite case: the TED score is large (Fig. 3c), but within the tested range, the equations are numerically close (Fig. 3d). In either case, looking at only the symbolic or numeric metric would be deceptive.

## 5   Conclusion

NSR is a relatively new field, and like early ML research, it is suffering not just from a lack of commonly-agreed upon metrics, but an assumption that a single metric will suffice. Based on the results we obtained, it is important to report both numeric and symbolic metric scores. We recommend use of median $R^2$ as a numeric metric and TED (tree edit distance) proportion as a symbolic metric. $R^2$ is a commonly used, informative, and understandable metric by which to tell how close predictions made by generated equations are to target data. The weakness of $R^2$ to outliers is mitigated by use of the median instead of the mean. TED proportion is similarly informative and understandable in revealing a generated equation's structural proximity to a target equation. Together, the two metrics give a comprehensive view of a NSR model's accuracy.

Given this, multi-objective optimization for training and testing should be pursued. Common multi-objective optimization methods may help balance the importance of numeric and symbolic metrics depending on the goal of the specific model: some methods may wish to emphasize prediction while others may wish to reveal discovered relationships. Multi-objective optimization can go beyond just evaluation metrics; it may allow for training the models against all of the objectives by using a multi-objective loss function.

We also recommend the NSR field use common training sets. Cross-method comparison may be possible with standardized metrics, but will still be obstructed by training and testing on different equations. As such, we recommend the use of the Nguyen equations [31] as well as our benchmark equations (Table 4) which are designed to offer a diversity of mathematical operations and incrementally increasing complexity.

The history of machine learning demonstrates that no one metric will ever perfectly capture the goals of a community. Diminishing returns against technical metrics like accuracy, over time, revealed to the ML community that other metrics like time, compute, and carbon are also relevant. For the NSR field, acknowledging the importance of numeric and symbolic metrics, as well as standardization of evaluation equations, is the first step. An early acceptance of multi-objective metrics and methods could allow the field to accelerate and prepare for as-of-yet undiscovered metrics of import.

**Acknowledgment.** This research is based upon work supported by the Broad Agency Announcement Program and Cold Regions Research and Engineering Laboratory (ERDC CRREL) under Contract No. W913E521C0003. Computations were performed on the Vermont Advanced Computing Center supported in part by NSF award No. OAC-1827314. QTD was supported by the NSF under the EFRI program (EFMA-1830870).

## A   Appendix

See Table 6.

We use a description length definition of equation complexity: the length of a node traversal for the expression tree representation after applying SymPy's `simplify` function to the equation. Shannon's diversity operates on the same

**Table 6.** Complexities, Shannon's Diversities for Nguyen benchmark [31] and equations designed for this paper to have a steady ramp in complexity and diversity.

| Number | Equation | Complexity | Shannon's Diversity |
|---|---|---|---|
| Nguyen-1 | $x^3 + x^2 + x$ | 8 | 1.93 |
| Nguyen-2 | $x^4 + x^3 + x^2 + x$ | 11 | 2.17 |
| Nguyen-3 | $x^5 x^4 + x^3 + x^2 + x$ | 14 | 2.34 |
| Nguyen-4 | $x^6 + x^5 + x^4 + x^3 + x^2 + x$ | 17 | 2.48 |
| Nguyen-5 | $\sin x^2 \cos x - 1$ | 9 | 2.15 |
| Nguyen-6 | $\sin x + \sin x + x^2$ | 9 | 2.05 |
| Nguyen-7 | $\log x + 1 + \log x^2 + 1$ | 11 | 2.34 |
| Nguyen-8 | $\sqrt{x}$ | 3 | 1.10 |
| C.S.-1 | $sin(x * e^x)$ | 5 | 1.61 |
| C.S.-2 | $x + \log(x^4)$ | 6 | 1.73 |
| C.S.-3 | $1 + x \sin(\frac{1}{x})$ | 8 | 2.03 |
| C.S.-4 | $\sqrt{x^3} \log(x^2)$ | 10 | 2.25 |
| C.S.-5 | $\frac{x}{\sqrt{x^2 + \sin x}}$ | 10 | 2.15 |
| C.S.-6 | $\frac{x + x^3}{1 + x \cos x^2}$ | 14 | 2.40 |
| C.S.-7 | $\frac{e^x (1 + \sqrt{1 + x} + \cos x^2)}{x^2}$ | 17 | 2.71 |
| C.S.-8 | $\cos\left(\frac{x + \sin x}{x^3 + x \log x^2}\right)$ | 19 | 2.76 |

tree representation nodes, and is defined as

$$H = -\sum_{i=1}^{n} p_i \ln(p_i) \tag{5}$$

where $p_i$ is the relative incidence of the $ith$ node label.

# B  Ethics

Symbolic regression has far reaching applications, as any field that requires the collection of data that then needs to be understood in a compact format can benefit from the automatic distillation of said data into an equation. It is the belief of the authors that the ethics of said applications is an important subject to consider. As an application of AI that uses neural networks, it suffers from the general ethics concerns that AI does: bias in both data and perception of results, as well as potential for discriminatory practices.

A key ethical issue in all AI is bias and discrimination. Like other AI networks, symbolic regression networks could easily perpetuate biases and discriminatory practices if trained on biased or incomplete datasets. As an equation that describes a biased dataset would inherently be biased, SR networks could produce equations that accurately describe biased data without it being clear that there is a bias at all. Equations are almost never the true end goal of analyzing data. Instead, said equations are used to further understand the data it describes. The broad applications of neural SR are a key way that potential discriminatory data and practices could be introduced. Potential underlying biases in data could lead to networks that produce equations that are used to perpetuate discriminatory practices.

The ethical concerns that are more unique to SR are generally centered around the people who will be using the network and its resulting equations. There is a cognitive bias toward authority in people, and generally this bias is toward a trust in perceived authority. Through schooling, we have been trained to trust math as an authority, and as SR produces equations- which are math- users will be biased toward trusting the equation without verifying accuracy. Through this, SR can create an illusion of authority where there may not be one. Another user bias that must be considered is the accessibility of SR networks. By nature, an SR network is geared toward the mathematically literate, which presents an exclusionary bias toward people who are not.

Misunderstanding NSR methods and results, such as underestimating the effects of PEGCF discussed in this paper, can exacerbate these problems. Misunderstanding the potential flaws in the validity of the results contributes toward users finding authority in the equations produced regardless of the potential lack of any true accuracy. Our paper seeks to bring to light what contributes to NSR performance with explicit comparisons and test. In doing so, it has the potential to help prevent the false authority that NSR produced equations could cause by making users aware of the potential flaws. Overall, it will be critical to continue to address ethical issues and ensure any research in this field is done carefully and with full awareness of necessary precautions around the potential applications.

# References

1. Aldeia, G.S.I., de França, F.O.: Interpretability in symbolic regression: a benchmark of explanatory methods using the Feynman data set. Genet. Program Evolvable Mach. **23**(3), 309–349 (2022)
2. Arnaldo, I., Krawiec, K., O'Reilly, U.M.: Multiple regression genetic programming. In: Proceedings of the 2014 Annual Conference on Genetic and Evolutionary Computation, pp. 879–886 (2014)
3. Biggio, L., Bendinelli, T., Lucchi, A., Parascandolo, G.: A seq2seq approach to symbolic regression. In: Learning Meets Combinatorial Algorithms at NeurIPS2020 (2020)
4. Biggio, L., Bendinelli, T., Neitz, A., Lucchi, A., Parascandolo, G.: Neural symbolic regression that scales. In: International Conference on Machine Learning, pp. 936–945. PMLR (2021)
5. Bouthillier, X., et al.: Accounting for variance in machine learning benchmarks. CoRR abs/2103.03098 (2021). https://arxiv.org/abs/2103.03098
6. Broyden, C.G.: The convergence of a class of double-rank minimization algorithms 1. General considerations. IMA J. Appl. Math. **6**(1), 76–90 (1970). https://doi.org/10.1093/imamat/6.1.76
7. Collobert, R., Weston, J., Bottou, L., Karlen, M., Kavukcuoglu, K., Kuksa, P.: Natural language processing (almost) from scratch (2011)
8. Fletcher, R.: A new approach to variable metric algorithms. Comput. J. **13**(3), 317–322 (1970). https://doi.org/10.1093/comjnl/13.3.317
9. Glantz, S.A., Slinker, B.K.: Primer of Applied Regression & Analysis of Variance, 3rd edn (2016)
10. Goldfarb, D.: A family of variable-metric methods derived by variational means. Math. Comput. **24**(109), 23–26 (1970). http://www.jstor.org/stable/2004873
11. Kamienny, P.A., d'Ascoli, S., Lample, G., Charton, F.: End-to-end symbolic regression with transformers. arXiv preprint arXiv:2204.10532 (2022)
12. Kommenda, M., Burlacu, B., Kronberger, G., Affenzeller, M.: Parameter identification for symbolic regression using nonlinear least squares. Genet. Program Evolvable Mach. **21**(3), 471–501 (2020)
13. Koza, J.R.: Genetic Programming II: Automatic Discovery of Reusable Programs. MIT Press, Cambridge (1994)
14. Koza, J., Koza, J.: Genetic Programming: On the Programming of Computers by Means of Natural Selection. A Bradford Book, Bradford (1992). https://books.google.com/books?id=Bhtxo60BV0EC
15. La Cava, W., et al.: Contemporary symbolic regression methods and their relative performance. In: Thirty-Fifth Conference on Neural Information Processing Systems Datasets and Benchmarks Track (Round 1) (2021)
16. La Cava, W., Spector, L., Danai, K.: Epsilon-lexicase selection for regression. In: Proceedings of the Genetic and Evolutionary Computation Conference 2016. GECCO '16, pp. 741–748. Association for Computing Machinery, New York, NY, USA (2016). https://doi.org/10.1145/2908812.2908898, https://doi-org.ezproxy.uvm.edu/10.1145/2908812.2908898
17. Liskowski, P., Krawiec, K.: Discovery of search objectives in continuous domains. In: Proceedings of the Genetic and Evolutionary Computation Conference. GECCO '17, pp. 969–976. Association for Computing Machinery, New York, NY, USA (2017). https://doi.org/10.1145/3071178.3071344

18. Mann, H.B., Whitney, D.R.: On a test of whether one of two random variables is stochastically larger than the other. Ann. Math. Stat. **18**(1), 50–60 (1947)
19. McDermott, J., et al.: Genetic programming needs better benchmarks. In: Proceedings of the 14th Annual Conference on Genetic and Evolutionary Computation. GECCO '12, pp. 791–798. Association for Computing Machinery, New York, NY, USA (2012). https://doi.org/10.1145/2330163.2330273, https://doi-org.ezproxy.uvm.edu/10.1145/2330163.2330273
20. Ouangraoua, A., Ferraro, P.: A constrained edit distance algorithm between semi-ordered trees. Theoret. Comput. Sci. **410**(8), 837–846 (2009). https://doi.org/10.1016/j.tcs.2008.11.022, https://www.sciencedirect.com/science/article/pii/S0304397508008621
21. Pawlik, M., Augsten, N.: RTED: a robust algorithm for the tree edit distance. Proc. VLDB Endow. **5**(4), 334–345 (2011)
22. Pawlik, M., Augsten, N.: Efficient computation of the tree edit distance. ACM Trans. Database Syst. **40**(1), 1–40 (2015)
23. Pawlik, M., Augsten, N.: Tree edit distance: robust and memory-efficient. Inf. Syst. **56**, 157–173 (2016)
24. Petersen, B.K., Larma, M.L., Mundhenk, T.N., Santiago, C.P., Kim, S.K., Kim, J.T.: Deep symbolic regression: recovering mathematical expressions from data via risk-seeking policy gradients. In: International Conference on Learning Representations (2020)
25. Radford, A., Narasimhan, K.: Improving language understanding by generative pre-training (2018)
26. Schmidt, M., Lipson, H.: Distilling free-form natural laws from experimental data. Science (Am. Assoc. Adv. Sci.) **324**(5923), 81–85 (2009)
27. Schmidt, M.D., Lipson, H.: Coevolution of fitness predictors. IEEE Trans. Evol. Comput. **12**(6), 736–749 (2008). https://doi.org/10.1109/TEVC.2008.919006
28. Shanno, D.F.: Conditioning of quasi-Newton methods for function minimization. Math. Comput. **24**(111), 647–656 (1970). http://www.jstor.org/stable/2004840
29. Strogatz, S.H.: Nonlinear Dynamics and Chaos: With Applications to Physics, Biology, Chemistry, and Engineering. CRC Press, Boca Raton (2018)
30. Udrescu, S.M., Tegmark, M.: AI Feynman: a physics-inspired method for symbolic regression. Sci. Adva. **6**(16), eaay2631 (2020)
31. Uy, N.Q., Hoai, N.X., O'Neill, M., McKay, R.I., Galván-López, E.: Semantically-based crossover in genetic programming: application to real-valued symbolic regression. Genet. Program Evolvable Mach. **12**(2), 91–119 (2011)
32. Valipour, M., You, B., Panju, M., Ghodsi, A.: SymbolicGPT: a generative transformer model for symbolic regression. arXiv preprint arXiv:2106.14131 (2021)
33. Vastl, M., Kulhánek, J., Kubalík, J., Derner, E., Babuška, R.: SymFormer: end-to-end symbolic regression using transformer-based architecture. arXiv preprint arXiv:2205.15764 (2022)
34. Vaswani, A., et al.: Attention is all you need (2017)
35. Virgolin, M., Alderliesten, T., Witteveen, C., Bosman, P.A.: Improving model-based genetic programming for symbolic regression of small expressions. Evol. Comput. **29**(2), 211–237 (2021)
36. White, D.R., et al.: Better GP benchmarks: community survey results and proposals. Genet. Program Evolvable Mach. **14**(1), 3–29 (2013)
37. Zhang, K.: A constrained edit distance between unordered labeled trees. Algorithmica **15**, 205–222 (1996). https://doi.org/10.1007/BF01975866

# Symbolic Regression via Control Variable Genetic Programming

Nan Jiang[✉][iD] and Yexiang Xue[iD]

Department of Computer Science, Purdue University,
West Lafayette, IN, USA
{jiang631,yexiang}@purdue.edu

**Abstract.** Learning symbolic expressions directly from experiment data is a vital step in AI-driven scientific discovery. Nevertheless, state-of-the-art approaches are limited to learning simple expressions. Regressing expressions involving many independent variables still remain out of reach. Motivated by the control variable experiments widely utilized in science, we propose **C**ontrol **V**ariable **G**enetic **P**rogramming (CVGP) for symbolic regression over many independent variables. CVGP expedites symbolic expression discovery via customized experiment design, rather than learning from a fixed dataset collected a priori. CVGP starts by fitting simple expressions involving a small set of independent variables using genetic programming, under controlled experiments where other variables are held as constants. It then extends expressions learned in previous generations by adding new independent variables, using new control variable experiments in which these variables are allowed to vary. Theoretically, we show CVGP as an incremental building approach can yield an exponential reduction in the search space when learning a class of expressions. Experimentally, CVGP outperforms several baselines in learning symbolic expressions involving multiple independent variables.

**Keywords:** Control Variable Experiment · Symbolic Regression

## 1 Introduction

Discovering scientific laws automatically from experiment data has been a grand goal of Artificial Intelligence (AI). Its success will greatly accelerate the pace of scientific discovery. Symbolic regression, *i.e.*, learning symbolic expressions from data, consists of a vital step in realizing this grand goal. Recently, exciting progress [20, 22, 43, 45, 45, 48, 51, 52, 57] has been made in this domain, especially with the aid of deep neural networks. Despite great achievements, state-of-the-art approaches are limited to learning relatively simple expressions, often involving a few independent variables. Regressing symbolic expressions involving multiple independent variables still remains out of reach of current approaches. The difficulty mainly lies in the exponentially large search space of symbolic expressions.

Our work attacks this major gap of symbolic regression, leveraging control variable experimentation – a classic procedure widely implemented in the science

D. Koutra et al. (Eds.): ECML PKDD 2023, LNAI 14172, pp. 178–195, 2023.
https://doi.org/10.1007/978-3-031-43421-1_11

community [38,50]. In the analysis of complex scientific phenomena involving many contributing factors, control variable experiments are conducted where a set of factors are held constant (*i.e.*, controlled variables), and the dependence between the output variable and the remaining input variables is studied [27,34]. The result is a reduced-form expression that models the relationship only between the output and the non-controlled variables. Once the reduced-form equation is validated, scientists introduce more variables into play by freeing a few controlled variables in previous experiments. The new goal is to extend the previous equation to a general one including the newly introduced variables. This process continues until all independent variables are introduced.

Our proposed **C**ontrol **V**ariable **G**enetic **P**rogramming (CVGP) approach implements the aforementioned scientific discovery process using Genetic Programming (GP) for symbolic regression over many independent variables. The key insight of CVGP is to learn from *a customized set of control variable experiments*; in other words, the experiment data collection adapts to the learning process. This is in contrast to the current learning paradigm of most symbolic regression approaches, where they learn from a fixed dataset collected a priori. In CVGP, first, we hold all independent variables except for one as constants and learn an expression that maps the single variable to the dependent variable using GP. GP maintains a pool of candidate expressions and improves the fitness of these equations via mating, mutating, and selection over several generations. Mapping the dependence of one independent variable is easy. Hence GP can usually recover the ground-truth reduced-form equation. Then, CVGP frees one independent variable at a time. In each iteration, GP is used to modify the equations learned in previous generations to incorporate the new independent variable, via mating, mutating, and selection. Such a procedure repeats until all the independent variables have been incorporated into the symbolic expression.

After discovering CVGP independently, the authors learned in private communications a line of research work [9,28,29,31,32,36] that also implemented the human scientific discovery process using AI, pioneered by the BACON systems developed by Langley, P. in 1978–1981 [31,32,36]. While BACON's discovery was driven by rule-based engines and our CVGP uses modern machine-learning approaches such as genetic programming. Indeed, both approaches share a common vision - the *integration of experiment design and model learning* can further expedite scientific discovery.

Theoretically, we show CVGP as an incremental builder can reduce the exponential-sized search space for candidate expressions into a polynomial one when fitting a class of symbolic expressions. Experimentally, we show CVGP outperforms a number of state-of-the-art approaches on symbolic regression over multiple independent variables. Our contributions can be summarized as:

1. We propose CVGP, an incremental builder for symbolic regression over many independent variables. CVGP fits increasingly more complex equations via conducting control variable experiments with fewer and fewer controlled variables.
2. Theoretically, we show such an incremental builder as CVGP can reduce exponential-sized search spaces for symbolic regression to polynomial ones when searching for a class of symbolic expressions.

3. Empirically, we demonstrate CVGP outperforms state-of-the-art symbolic regression approaches in discovering multi-variable equations from data[1].

## 2  Preliminaries

**Symbolic Expression.** A symbolic expression $\phi$ is expressed as variables and constants connected by a set of operators. Variables are allowed to vary while constants remain the same. Each operand of an operator is either a variable, a constant, or a self-contained symbolic expression. A symbolic expression can also be drawn as a tree, where variables and constants reside in leaves, and operators reside in inner nodes. See Fig. 1(a) for an example. In this paper, we deal with expressions involving real numbers. The semantic meaning of a symbolic expression follows its standard definition in arithmetics.

**Symbolic Regression.** Given a dataset $\{(\mathbf{x}_i, y_i)\}_{i=1}^n$ and a loss function $\ell(\cdot, \cdot)$, where $\mathbf{x}_i \in \mathbb{R}^m$ and $y_i \in \mathbb{R}$, the objective of symbolic regression (SR) is to search for the optimal symbolic expression $\phi^*$ within the space of all candidate expressions $\Pi$ that minimizes the average loss:

$$\phi^* = \arg\min_{\phi \in \Pi} \frac{1}{n} \sum_{i=1}^n \ell(\phi(\mathbf{x}_i), y_i), \tag{1}$$

in addition to regularizers. Symbolic regression is challenging and is in NP-hard [58], due to the exponentially large space of candidate symbolic expressions.

**Genetic Programming for Symbolic Regression.** Genetic Programming (GP) has been a popular method to solve symbolic regression. Recently, a few other approaches based on neural networks surpassed the performance of GP in symbolic regression. We leave the discussions of these methods to the related work section. The high-level idea of GP is to maintain a pool of candidate symbolic expressions. In each generation, candidate expressions are *mutated* with probability $P_{mu}$ and *mated* with probability $P_{ma}$. Then in the *selection* step, those with the highest fitness scores, measured by how each expression predicts the output from the input, are selected as the candidates for the next generation, together with a few randomly chosen ones to maintain diversity. After several generations, expressions with high fitness scores, *i.e.*, those fit data well survive in the pool of candidate solutions. The best expressions found in all generations are recorded as *hall-of-fame* solutions.

## 3  Control Variable Genetic Programming

In this section, we present our control variable genetic programming algorithm. Before we dive into the algorithm description, we first need to study what are the outcomes of a control variable experiment and what conclusions we can draw on the symbolic regression expression by observing such outcomes.

---

[1] The code is at: https://github.com/jiangnanhugo/cvgp/. Please refer to the extended version (https://arxiv.org/abs/2306.08057) for the Appendix.

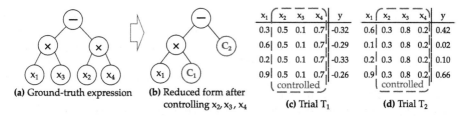

| $x_1$ | $x_2$ | $x_3$ | $x_4$ | y |
|---|---|---|---|---|
| 0.3 | 0.5 | 0.1 | 0.7 | -0.32 |
| 0.6 | 0.5 | 0.1 | 0.7 | -0.29 |
| 0.2 | 0.5 | 0.1 | 0.7 | -0.33 |
| 0.9 | 0.5 | 0.1 | 0.7 | -0.26 |

| $x_1$ | $x_2$ | $x_3$ | $x_4$ | y |
|---|---|---|---|---|
| 0.6 | 0.3 | 0.8 | 0.2 | 0.42 |
| 0.1 | 0.3 | 0.8 | 0.2 | 0.02 |
| 0.2 | 0.3 | 0.8 | 0.2 | 0.10 |
| 0.9 | 0.3 | 0.8 | 0.2 | 0.66 |

**(a)** Ground-truth expression     **(b)** Reduced form after controlling $x_2, x_3, x_4$     **(c)** Trial $T_1$     **(d)** Trial $T_2$

**Fig. 1.** An example of two trials of a control variable experiment. **(a)** The data of the experiment is generated by the ground-truth expression $\phi = x_1 x_3 - x_2 x_4$. **(b)** If we control $\mathbf{v}_c = \{x_2, x_3, x_4\}$ and only allow $\mathbf{v}_f = \{x_1\}$ to vary, it *looks like* the data are generated from the reduced-form equation $\phi' = C_1 x_1 - C_2$. **(c, d)** The generated data in two trials of the control variable experiments. The controlled variables are fixed within each trial but vary across trials.

### 3.1 Control Variable Experiment

A control variable experiment $\texttt{CVExp}(\phi, \mathbf{v}_c, \mathbf{v}_f, \{T_k\}_{k=1}^K)$ consists of the trial symbolic expression $\phi$, a set of controlled variables $\mathbf{v}_c$, a set of free variables $\mathbf{v}_f$, and $K$ trial experiments $T_1, \ldots, T_K$. The expression $\phi$ may have zero or multiple *open constants*. The values of open constants are determined by fitting the equation to the training data.

**One Trial in a Control Variable Experiment.** A single trial of a control variable experiment $T_k$ fits the symbolic expression $\phi$ with a batch of data. To avoid abusing notations, we also use $T_k$ to denote the batch of data. In the generated data $T_k$, every controlled variable is fixed to the same value while the free variables are set randomly. We assume the values of the dependent variables in a batch are (noisy observations) of the ground-truth expressions with the values of independent variables set in the batch. In science, this step is achieved by conducting real-world experiments, *i.e.*, controlling independent variables and performing measurements on the dependent variable.

For example, Fig. 1(c,d) demonstrates two trials ($K = 2$) of a control variable experiment in which variable $x_2, x_3, x_4$ are controlled, *i.e.*, $\mathbf{v}_c = \{x_2, x_3, x_4\}$. They are fixed to one value in trial $T_1$ (in Fig. 1(c)) and another value in trial $T_2$ (in Fig. 1(d)). $x_1$ is the only free variable, *i.e.*, $\mathbf{v}_f = \{x_1\}$.

**Reduced-Form Expression in a Control Variable Setting.** We assume there is a ground-truth symbolic expression that produces the experiment data. In other words, the observed output is the execution of the ground-truth expression from the input, possibly in addition to some noise. In control variable experiments, because the values of controlled variables are fixed in each trial, what we observe is the ground-truth expression in its *reduced form*, where sub-expressions involving only controlled variables are replaced with constants.

Figure 1(b) provides an example of the reduced form expression. Assume the data is generated from the ground-truth expression in Fig. (a): $\phi = x_1 x_3 - x_2 x_4$. When we control the values of variable in $\mathbf{v}_c = \{x_2, x_3, x_4\}$, the data *looks like* they are generated from the *reduced* expression: $\phi' = C_1 x_1 - C_2$. We can see both $C_1$ and $C_2$ hold constant values in each trial. However, their values vary across trials because the values of controlled variables change. In trial $T_1$, when $x_2$, $x_3$, and $x_4$ are fixed to 0.5, 0.1, 0.7, $C_1$ takes the value of $x_3$, *i.e.*, 0.1. $C_2$ takes the value of $x_2 x_4$, *i.e.*, 0.35. In trial $T_2$, $C_1 = 0.8$ and $C_2 = 0.06$.

We call constants which represent sub-expressions involving controlled variables in the ground-truth expression *summary constants*, and refer to constants in the ground-truth expression *stand-alone constants*. For example, $C_1$ and $C_2$ in Fig. 1(b) are both summary constants, because $C_1$ replaces the controlled variable $x_3$ and $C_2$ replaces a sub-expression $x_2 x_4$ in the ground-truth expression. Notice the types of constants are *unknown* in the process of fitting an expression to control variable experiment data. However, the best-fitted values of these constants across several trials reveal important information: a constant is probably a summary constant if its fitted values vary greatly across trials, while a constant that remains the almost same value across trials is probably stand-alone.

**Outcome of One Trial.** The outcomes of one trial are two-fold: (1) the values of the constants which best fit the given batch of data. We denote these values as vector $\mathbf{c}$. (2) the fitness score measuring the goodness-of-fit, denoted as $o$. One typical fitness score is the mean squared error (MSE). See Appendix B.2 for the exact definition of MSE. For the example in Fig. 1, if we fit the reduced expression in (b) to data in trial $T_1$, the best-fitted values are $\mathbf{c}_1 = (C_1 = 0.1, C_2 = 0.35)$. For trial $T_2$, the best-fitted values are $\mathbf{c}_2 = (C_1 = 0.8, C_2 = 0.06)$. In both trials, the fitness scores (i.e., the MSE value) are 0, indicating no errors.

**Outcome of Multiple Trials.** We let the values of control variables vary across different trials. This corresponds to changing experimental conditions in real science experiments. The outcomes of an experiment with $K$ trials are: (1) $\phi.\mathbf{o} = (o_1, \ldots, o_K)$, where each $o_k$ is the fitness score of trial $k$ and (2) $\phi.\mathbf{c} = (\mathbf{c}_1, \ldots, \mathbf{c}_K)$, the best-fitted values to open constants across trials.

Key information is obtained by examining the outcomes of multi-trials control variable experiments: (1) consistent close-to-zero fitness scores $\phi.\mathbf{o}$ suggest the fitted expression is close to the ground-truth equation in the reduced form. (2) given the equation is close to the ground truth, an open constant having similar best-fitted values across $K$ trials $\phi.\mathbf{c}$ suggests the open constants are stand-alone.

### 3.2 Control Variable Genetic Programming

The high-level idea of the CVGP algorithm is to build more complex symbolic expressions involving more and more variables based on control variable experiments with fewer and fewer controlled variables.

To fit an expression of $m$ variables, initially, we control the values of all $m - 1$ variables and allow only one variable to vary. Using Genetic Programming (GP), we find a pool of expressions $\{\phi_{1,1}, \ldots, \phi_{1,M}\}$ which best fit the data from this controlled experiment. Notice $\{\phi_{1,1}, \ldots, \phi_{1,M}\}$ are restricted to contain the only one free variable. This fact renders fitting them a lot easier

---

**Algorithm 1.** Control Variable Genetic Programming (CVGP)

---

**Input:** GP pool size $M$; #generations #Gen; #trials $K$; #expressions in hall-of-fame
set #Hof; mutate probability $P_{mu}$; mate probability $P_{ma}$; operator set $O_p$.

1: $\mathbf{v}_c \leftarrow \{x_1, \ldots, x_m\};$         $\mathbf{v}_f \leftarrow \emptyset.$
2: $\mathcal{P}_{gp} \leftarrow \texttt{CreateInitGPPool}(M).$
3: **for** $x_i \in \{x_1, \ldots, x_m\}$ **do**
4:     $\mathbf{v}_c \leftarrow \mathbf{v}_c \setminus \{x_i\};$   $\mathbf{v}_f \leftarrow \mathbf{v}_f \cup \{x_i\}.$          ▷ Set $x_i$ to be free variable
5:     $\mathcal{D}^o \leftarrow \texttt{DataOracle}(\mathbf{v}_c, \mathbf{v}_f).$
6:     **for** $\phi \in \mathcal{P}_{gp}$ **do**
7:         $\{T_k\}_{k=1}^{K} \leftarrow \texttt{GenData}(\mathcal{D}^o).$          ▷ Query Oracle for the trial data
8:         $\phi.\mathbf{o}, \phi.\mathbf{c} \leftarrow \texttt{CVExp}(\phi, \mathbf{v}_c, \mathbf{v}_f, \{T_k\}_{k=1}^{K}).$       ▷ Control variable experiments
9:     $\mathcal{P}_{gp}, \mathcal{H} \leftarrow \texttt{GP}(\mathcal{P}_{gp}, \mathcal{D}_i^o, K, M, \texttt{\#Gen}, \texttt{\#Hof}, P_{mu}, P_{ma}, O_p \cup \{\text{const}, x_i\}).$
10:    **for** $\phi \in \mathcal{P}_{gp}$ **do**
11:        $\texttt{FreezeEquation}(\phi, \phi.\mathbf{o}, \phi.\mathbf{c}).$
    **return** The set of hall-of-fame equations $\mathcal{H}$.

---

than fitting the expressions involving all $m$ variables. Next, for each $\phi_{1,l}$, we examine (1) if the errors of the fitting are consistently small across all trials. A small error implies $\phi_{1,l}$ is close to the ground-truth formula reduced to the one free variable. We hence freeze all operators of $\phi_{1,l}$ in this case. Freezing means GP in later steps cannot change these operators. (2) In the case of a small fitting error, we also inspect the best-fitted values of each open constant in $\phi_{1,l}$ across different trials. The constant is probably a summary constant if its values vary across trials. In other words, these constants represent sub-expressions involving the controlled variables. We thus mark these constants as *expandable* for later steps. The remaining constants are probably stand-alone. Therefore we also freeze them.

After the first step, CVGP adds a second free variable and starts fitting $\{\phi_{2,1}, \ldots, \phi_{2,M}\}$ using the data from control variable experiments involving the two free variables. Similar to the previous step, all $\phi_{2,l}$ are restricted to only contain the two free variables. Moreover, they can only be mated or mutated by GP from the first generation $\{\phi_{1,1}, \ldots, \phi_{1,M}\}$. The mutation can only happen on non-frozen nodes. After GP, a similar inspection is conducted for every equation in the GP pool, and corresponding variables and/or operators are frozen. This process continues to involve more and more variables. Eventually, the expressions in the GP pool consider all $m$ variables.

The whole procedure of CVGP is shown in Algorithm 1. Here, $x_1, \ldots, x_m$ are moved from the controlled to free variables in numerical order. We agree other orders may boost its performance even further. However, we leave the exploration of this direction as future work. When a new variable becomes free, the control variable experiment CVExp needs to be repeated for every equation $\phi$ in the GP pool $\mathcal{P}_{gp}$ (Line 5–9 in Algorithm 1). This is because the fitness scores and the fitted open constant values will both change when the set of controlled variables is updated. Then function GP is called. GP is a minimally modified genetic programming algorithm for symbolic regression whose pseudo-

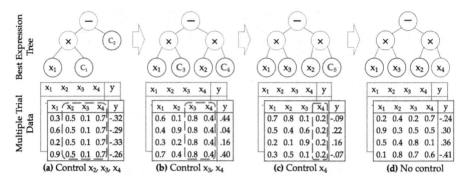

**Fig. 2.** Running example of Algorithm 1. **(a)** Initially, a reduced-form equation $\phi' = C_1 x_1 - C_2$ is found via fitting control variable data in which $x_2, x_3, x_4$ are held as constants and only $x_1$ is allowed to vary. Two leaves nodes $C_1, C_2$ are as summary constants (colored blue). **(b)** This equation is expanded to $C_3 x_1 - C_4 x_2$ in the second stage via fitting the data in which only $x_3, x_4$ are held as constants. **(c,d)** This process continues until the ground-truth equation $\phi = x_1 x_3 - x_2 x_4$ is found. The data generated for control variable experiment trials in each stage are shown at the bottom.

code is in Algorithm 2. The only differences are that it uses data from control variable experiments and the mutation operation at step $i$ only allows to use all the operators, the constant node, and variable $x_i$ at non-frozen nodes. Finally, in Lines 12–14 of Algorithm 1, `FreezeEquation` is called for every equation in the GP pool. The high-level idea of freezing is discussed above. $\mathcal{H}$ is returned as the set of "hall of fame" expressions.

Figure 2 shows the high-level idea of fitting an equation using CVGP. Here the process has four stages, each stage with a decreased number of controlled variables. The trial data in each stage is shown at the bottom and the best expression found is shown at the top. The expandable constants are bold and blue. The readers can see how the fitted equations grow into the final ground-truth equation, with one free variable added at a time.

**The Availability of a Data Oracle.** A crucial assumption behind the success of CVGP is the availability of a data oracle $\mathcal{D}^o$ that returns a (noisy) observation of the dependent output variable with input variables in $\mathbf{v}_c$ controlled and $\mathbf{v}_f$ free. This differs from the classical setting of symbolic regression, where a dataset is obtained before learning [41,49]. Such a data oracle represents conducting control variable experiments in the real world, which can be expensive.

However, we argue that the integration of experiment design in the discovery of scientific knowledge is indeed the main driver of the successes of CVGP. This idea has received tremendous success in early works [31,32,36] but unfortunately has been largely forgotten in today's symbolic regression community. Our work does not intend to show the superiority of one approach. Instead, we would like to point out that carefully designed experiments can improve any method, and GP is used as an example. We acknowledge that fully controlled experiments may be difficult in some scenarios. In cases where it is difficult to obtain such a data oracle, one possible solution is to use deep neural networks to learn a data generator for the given set of controlled variables. We leave it as future work.

---

**Algorithm 2.** GP($\mathcal{P}_{gp}, \mathcal{D}^o, K, M$, #Gen, #Hof, $P_{mu}, P_{ma}, O_p$)

---

**Input:** Initial GP Pool $\mathcal{P}_{gp}$; data Oracle $\mathcal{D}^o$; #trials $K$; GP pool size $M$; #genera-
tions #Gen; #expressions in hall-of-fame set #Hof; mutate probability $P_{mu}$; mate
probability $P_{ma}$; mutation node library $O_p$.

1: **for** $j \leftarrow 1$ *to* #Gen **do**
2:     $\mathcal{P}_{new} \leftarrow \emptyset$;
3:     **for** $\phi \in \mathcal{P}_{gp}$ **do**
4:         **if** with probability $P_{mu}$ **then**                          ▷ Mutation
5:             $\phi \leftarrow$ Mutate($\phi, O_p$);
6:             $\{T_k\}_{k=1}^{K} \leftarrow$ GenData($\mathcal{D}^o$);
7:             $\phi.\mathbf{o}, \phi.\mathbf{c} \leftarrow$ CVExp($\phi, \mathbf{v}_c, \mathbf{v}_f, \{T_k\}_{k=1}^{K}$);
8:         $\mathcal{P}_{new} \leftarrow \mathcal{P}_{new} \cup \{\phi\}$;
9:     $\mathcal{P}_{gp} \leftarrow \mathcal{P}_{new}$; $\mathcal{P}_{new} \leftarrow \emptyset$;
10:    **for** $\phi_l, \phi_{l+1} \in \mathcal{P}_{gp}$ **do**
11:        **if** with probability $P_{ma}$ **then**                          ▷ Mating
12:            $\phi_l, \phi_{l+1} \leftarrow$ Mate($\phi_l, \phi_{l+1}$);
13:            $\{T_k\}_{k=1}^{K} \leftarrow$ genData($\mathcal{D}^o$);
14:            $\phi_l.\mathbf{o}, \phi_l.\mathbf{c} \leftarrow$ CVExp($\phi_l, \mathbf{v}_c, \mathbf{v}_f, \{T_k\}_{k=1}^{K}$).
15:            $\phi_{l+1}.\mathbf{o}, \phi_{l+1}.\mathbf{c} \leftarrow$ CVExp($\phi_{l+1}, \mathbf{v}_c, \mathbf{v}_f, \{T_k\}_{k=1}^{K}$).
16:        $\mathcal{P}_{new} \leftarrow \mathcal{P}_{new} \cup \{\phi_l, \phi_{l+1}\}$;
17:    $\mathcal{H} \leftarrow$ TopK($\mathcal{P}_{new} \cup \mathcal{H}, K =$ #Hof);         ▷ Update the hall of fame set
18:    $\mathcal{P}_{gp} \leftarrow$ selection($\mathcal{P}_{new}, M$);
       **return** GP pool and hall-of-fame $\mathcal{P}_{gp}, \mathcal{H}$.

---

### 3.3 Theoretical Analysis

We show in this section that the idea of control variable experiments may bring
an exponential reduction in the search space for particular classes of symbolic
expressions. To see this, we assume the learning algorithm follows a search order
from simple to complex symbolic expressions and the data is noiseless.

**Definition 1.** *The search space of symbolic expression trees of $l$ nodes $S(l)$ is
the set of all symbolic expression trees involving at most $l$ nodes.*

**Lemma 1.** *For simplicity, assume all operators are binary, and let $o$ be the
number of operators and $m$ be the number of input variables. The size of the
search space of symbolic expression trees of $l$ nodes scales exponentially; more
precisely at $\mathcal{O}((4(m+1)o)^{\frac{l-1}{2}})$ and $\Omega((4(m+1)o)^{\frac{l-1}{4}})$.*

The proof of Lemma 1 mainly involves counting binary trees. We leave its detailed
proof in Appendix A. For our purposes, it is sufficient to know the size is exponential in the size of expression tree $l$.

**Definition 2 (Simple to complex search order).** *A symbolic regression
algorithm follows a simple to complex search order if it expands its search space
from short to long symbolic expressions; i.e., first search for the best symbolic
expressions in $S(1)$, then in $S(2) \setminus S(1)$, etc.*

In general, it is difficult to quantify the search order of any symbolic regression algorithms. However, we believe the simple to complex order reflects the search procedures of a large class of symbolic regression algorithms, including our CVGP. In fact, [12] explicitly use regularizers to promote the search of simple and short expressions. Our CVGP follows the simple to complex search order approximately. Indeed, it is possible that genetic programming encounters more complex equations before their simpler counterparts. However, in general, the expressions are built from simple to complex equations by mating and mutating operations in genetic programming algorithms.

**Proposition 1 (Exponential Reduction in the Search Space).** *There exists a symbolic expression $\phi$ of $(4m - 1)$ nodes, a normal symbolic regression algorithm following the simple to complex search order has to explore a search space whose size is exponential in $m$ to find the expression, while CVGP following the simple to complex order only expands $\mathcal{O}(m)$ constant-sized search spaces.*

*Proof.* Consider a dataset generated by the ground-truth symbolic expression made up of 2 operators $(+, \times)$, $2m$ input variables, and $(4m - 1)$ nodes:

$$(x_1 + x_2)(x_3 + x_4) \ldots (x_{2m-1} + x_{2m}). \tag{2}$$

To search for this symbolic regression, a normal algorithm following the simple to complex order needs to consider all expression trees up to $(4m - 1)$ nodes. According to Lemma 1, the normal algorithm has a search space of at least $\Omega((16m + 8)^{m-1/2})$, which is exponential in $m$.

On the other hand, in the first step of CVGP, $x_2, \ldots, x_{2m}$ are controlled and only $x_1$ is free. In this case, the ground-truth equation in the reduced form is

$$(x_1 + C_1)D_1, \tag{3}$$

in which both $C_1$ and $D_1$ are summary constants. Here $C_1$ represents $x_2$ and $D_1$ represents $(x_3 + x_4) \ldots (x_{2m-1} + x_{2m})$ in the control variable experiments. The reduced equation is quite simple under the controlled environment. CVGP should be able to find the ground-truth expression exploring search space $S(5)$.

Proving using induction. In step $2i$ $(1 \leq i \leq m)$, variables $x_{2i+1}, x_{2i+2}, \ldots, x_{2m}$ are held as constants, $x_1, \ldots, x_{2i}$ are allowed to vary. The ground-truth expression in the reduced form found in the previous $(2i - 1)$-th step is:

$$(x_1 + x_2) \ldots (x_{2i-1} + C_{2i-1})D_{2i-1}. \tag{4}$$

CVGP needs to extend this equation to be the ground-truth expression in the reduced form for the $2i$-th step, which is:

$$(x_1 + x_2) \ldots (x_{2i-1} + x_{2i})D_{2i}. \tag{5}$$

We can see the change is to replace the summary constant $C_{2i-1}$ to $x_{2i}$. Assume the data is noiseless and CVGP can confirm expression (4) is the ground-truth reduced-form expression for the previous step. This means all the operators and variables will be frozen by CVGP, and only $C_{2i-1}$ and $D_{2i-1}$ are allowed to be replaced by new expressions. Assume CVGP follows the simple to complex search order, it should find the ground-truth expression (5) by searching replacement expressions of lengths up to 1.

Similarly, in step $2i+1$, assume CVGP confirms the ground-truth expression in the reduced form in step $2i$, CVGP also only needs to search in constant-sized spaces to find the new ground-truth expression. Overall, we can see only $\mathcal{O}(m)$ searches in constant-sized spaces are required for CVGP to find the final ground-truth expression.

## 4 Related Work

**Symbolic Regression.** Symbolic Regression is proven to be NP-hard [58], due to the search space of all possible symbolic expressions being exponential in the number of input variables. Early works in this domain are based on heuristic search [33,39]. Genetic programming turns out to be effective in searching for good candidates of symbolic expressions [22,51,54,57]. RL-based methods propose a risk-seeking policy gradient to find the expressions [43,45,51]. Other works use RL to adjust the probabilities of genetic operations [11]. Also, there are works that reduced the search space by considering the composition of base functions, *e.g.* Fast function extraction [42] and elite bases regression [10]. In terms of the families of expressions, research efforts have been devoted to searching for polynomials with single or two variables [55], time series equations [3], and also equations in physics [54]. Existing works for multi-variable regression are mainly based on pre-trained encoder-decoder methods with a massive training dataset (e.g., millions of datasets [4]), and even larger generative models (e.g., about 100 million parameters [26]). Our CVGP is a tailored algorithm to solve multi-variable symbolic regression problems.

**AI-Driven Scientific Discovery.** Recently AI has been highlighted to enable scientific discoveries in diverse domains [37,59]. Early work in this domain focuses on learning logic (symbolic) representations [6,7]. Recently, learning Partial Differential Equations (PDEs) from data has also been studied extensively [8,13,14,16,23,40,46,47,61–63]. In this domain, a line of works develops robots that automatically refine the hypothesis space, some with human interactions [28,29,56]. These works are relevant to ours because they actively probe the hypothesis spaces, albeit they are in biology and chemistry.

**Active Learning and Reasoning.** Active learning considers querying data points actively to maximize the learning performance [19,21]. Our approach is related to active learning because control variable experiments can be viewed as a way to actively collect data. However, besides active data collection, our CVGP builds simple to complex models, which is not in active learning.

**Meta-reasoning – Thinking Fast and Slow.** The co-existence of fast and slow cognition systems marks an interesting side of human intelligence [2,5,25].

Our CVGP is motivated by this dual cognition process. In essence, we argue instead of entirely relying on the brute-force way of learning using big data and heavy computation (fast thinking), incrementally expanding from reduced-form equations to the full equation may result in better outcomes (slow thinking).

**Causality.** Control variable experiments are closely related to the idea of intervention, which is commonly used to discover causal relationships [18,24,35,44, 53]. However, we mainly use control variable experiments to accelerate symbolic regression, which still identifies correlations.

## 5   Experiments

In this section, we demonstrate CVGP finds the symbolic expressions with the smallest Normalized Mean-Square Errors (NMSE) among all 7 competing approaches on 21 noiseless benchmark datasets (in Table 1) and 20 noisy benchmark datasets (in Table 2). In the ablation studies, we show our CVGP is consistently better than the baselines when evaluated in different evaluation metrics, evaluating different quantiles of the NMSE metric, with different amounts of Gaussian noise added to the data (Fig. 3, more complete results in Fig. 4 and 5 in the appendix). In Table 3, we show our CVGP has a higher rate of recovering the ground-truth expressions than baselines.

### 5.1   Experimental Settings

**Datasets.** To highlight the performance of CVGP in regressing multi-variable expressions, we consider synthesized datasets, involving randomly generated expressions with multiple variables. A dataset is labeled by the ground-truth equation that generates it. The ground-truth equations we consider are multi-variable polynomials characterized by their operators and a tuple $(a, b, c)$. Here $a$ is the number of independent variables. $b$ is the number of singular terms. A singular term can be an independent variable (like $x_1$), or a unary operator with a variable (like $\sin(x_1)$). $c$ is the number of cross terms. They look like $C_1 x_3 x_4$ or $C_2 \sin(x_1)\texttt{inv}(x_5)$, etc. Here $C_1, C_2$ are randomly generated constants. The tuples and operators listed in different tables and charts indicate how the ground-truth expressions are generated. For each dataset configuration, we repeat our experiments 10 times, each time with a randomly generated symbolic expression of the given configuration. For noiseless datasets, the output is exactly the evaluation of the ground-truth expression. For noisy datasets, the output is further perturbed by Gaussian noise of zero means and a given standard deviation.

**Remarks on Public Available Datasets.** Most public datasets are black-box [30], containing randomly generated input and output pairs of an unknown symbolic equation. The point of our paper is to show customized collected control variable experiment data improves symbolic regression, and hence we cannot use these randomly generated data. In addition, most datasets are on equations of a small number of independent variables. We intentionally test on benchmark sets involving many variables to highlight our approach.

**Table 1.** Median (50%) and 75%-quantile NMSE values of the symbolic expressions found by all the algorithms on several *noiseless* benchmark datasets. Our CVGP finds symbolic expressions with the smallest NMSEs.

| Dataset | CVGP (ours) | | GP | | DSR | | PQT | | VPG | | GPMeld | | Eureqa | |
|---|---|---|---|---|---|---|---|---|---|---|---|---|---|---|
| configs | 50% | 75% | 50% | 75% | 50% | 75% | 50% | 75% | 50% | 75% | 50% | 75% | 50% | 75% |
| (3,2,2) | **0.001** | **0.004** | 0.015 | 0.135 | 1.53 | 43.09 | 0.58 | 1.13 | 0.83 | 1.32 | 1.06 | 2.18 | < 1e-6 | < 1e-6 |
| (4,4,6) | **0.008** | 0.059 | 0.012 | **0.054** | 1.006 | 1.249 | 1.006 | 2.459 | 1.221 | 2.322 | 1.127 | 2.286 | 1.191 | 6.001 |
| (5,5,5) | **0.011** | **0.019** | 0.025 | 0.177 | 1.038 | 8.805 | 1.048 | 4.736 | 1.401 | 38.26 | 1.008 | 1.969 | 0.996 | 6.340 |
| (5,5,8) | **0.007** | **0.013** | 0.010 | 0.017 | 1.403 | 5.161 | 1.530 | 41.27 | 4.133 | 27.42 | 1.386 | 8.092 | 1.002 | 1.495 |
| (6,6,8) | **0.044** | **0.074** | 0.058 | 0.200 | 1.963 | 90.53 | 4.212 | 8.194 | 4.425 | 22.91 | 15.58 | 269.6 | 1.005 | 1.150 |
| (6,6,10) | **0.012** | **0.027** | 0.381 | 0.820 | 1.021 | 1.036 | 1.006 | 1.048 | 1.003 | 1.020 | 1.022 | 1.689 | 1.764 | 49.041 |
| **(a)** Datasets containing operators $\{\texttt{inv}, +, -, \times\}$ | | | | | | | | | | | | | | |
| (3,2,2) | 0.005 | 0.123 | 0.023 | 0.374 | 0.087 | 0.392 | 0.161 | 0.469 | 0.277 | 0.493 | 0.112 | 0.183 | < 1e-6 | < 1e-6 |
| (4,4,6) | **0.028** | 0.132 | 0.044 | **0.106** | 2.815 | 9.958 | 2.381 | 13.844 | 2.990 | 11.316 | 1.670 | 2.697 | 0.024 | 0.122 |
| (5,5,5) | 0.086 | 0.402 | **0.063** | **0.232** | 2.558 | 3.313 | 2.168 | 2.679 | 1.903 | 2.780 | 1.501 | 2.295 | 0.158 | 0.377 |
| (5,5,8) | **0.014** | **0.066** | 0.102 | 0.683 | 2.535 | 2.933 | 2.482 | 2.773 | 2.440 | 3.062 | 2.422 | 3.853 | 0.284 | 0.514 |
| (6,6,8) | **0.066** | **0.166** | 0.127 | 0.591 | 0.936 | 1.079 | 0.983 | 1.053 | 0.900 | 1.018 | 0.964 | 1.428 | 0.433 | 1.564 |
| (6,6,10) | **0.104** | **0.177** | 0.159 | 0.230 | 6.121 | 16.32 | 5.750 | 16.29 | 3.857 | 19.82 | 7.393 | 21.709 | 0.910 | 1.927 |
| **(b)** Datasets containing operators $\{\sin, \cos, +, -, \times\}$. | | | | | | | | | | | | | | |
| (3,2,2) | 0.039 | 0.083 | 0.043 | 0.551 | 0.227 | 7.856 | 0.855 | 2.885 | 0.233 | 0.400 | 0.944 | 1.263 | < 1e-6 | < 1e-6 |
| (4,4,6) | **0.015** | **0.121** | 0.042 | 0.347 | 1.040 | 1.155 | 1.039 | 1.055 | 1.049 | 1.068 | 1.886 | 4.104 | 0.984 | 1.196 |
| (5,5,5) | **0.038** | **0.097** | 0.197 | 0.514 | 3.892 | 69.98 | 4.311 | 23.66 | 5.542 | 8.839 | 9.553 | 16.92 | 0.901 | 1.007 |
| (5,5,8) | **0.050** | **0.102** | 0.111 | 0.177 | 2.379 | 2.526 | 1.205 | 2.336 | 1.824 | 2.481 | 1.142 | 1.874 | 1.002 | 2.445 |
| (6,6,8) | **0.029** | **0.038** | 0.091 | 0.151 | 1.605 | 8.005 | 1.718 | 7.783 | 4.691 | 39.03 | 1.398 | 16.60 | 1.001 | 1.008 |
| (6,6,10) | **0.018** | **0.113** | 0.087 | 0.194 | 2.083 | 23.57 | 1.797 | 4.521 | 1.888 | 35.45 | 2.590 | 8.784 | 1.001 | 1.008 |
| **(c)** Datasets containing operators $\{\sin, \cos, \texttt{inv}, +, -, \times\}$. | | | | | | | | | | | | | | |

**Evaluation.** In terms of the evaluation metric, the median (50%) and 75%-percentile of the NMSE across these 10 experiments are reported. We choose to report median values instead of mean due to outliers (see box plots in Fig. 3(a–d)). This is a common practice for combinatorial optimization problems. The mathematical definition of NMSE and other metrics are in Appendix B.2.

**Baselines.** We consider the following baselines based on evolutionary algorithms: 1) Genetic Programming (GP) [17]. 2) Eureqa [15]. We also consider a series of baselines using reinforcement learning: 3) Priority queue training (PQT) [1]. 4) Vanilla Policy Gradient (VPG) that uses the REINFORCE algorithm [60] to train the model. 5) Deep Symbolic Regression (DSR) [45]. 6) Neural-Guided Genetic Programming Population Seeding (GPMeld) [43].

We leave detailed descriptions of the configurations of our CVGP and baseline algorithms in Appendix B and only mention a few implementation notes here. We implemented GP and CVGP. They use a data oracle, which returns (noisy) observations of the ground-truth equation when queried with inputs. We cannot implement the same Oracle for other baselines because of code complexity and/or no available code. To ensure fairness, the sizes of the training datasets we use for those baselines are larger than the total number of data points accessed in the full execution of those algorithms. In other words, their access to data would have no difference if the same oracle has been implemented for them because

**Table 2.** Median (50%) and 75%-quantile NMSE values of the symbolic expressions found by all the algorithms on several *noisy* benchmark datasets (Gaussian noise with zero mean and standard deviation 0.1 is added). Our CVGP finds symbolic expressions with the smallest NMSEs.

| Dataset | CVGP (ours) | | GP | | DSR | | PQT | | VPG | | GPMeld | |
|---|---|---|---|---|---|---|---|---|---|---|---|---|
| configs | 50% | 75% | 50% | 75% | 50% | 75% | 50% | 75% | 50% | 75% | 50% | 75% |
| (4,4,6) | **0.036** | **0.088** | 0.038 | 0.108 | 1.163 | 3.714 | 1.016 | 1.122 | 1.087 | 1.275 | 1.058 | 1.374 |
| (5,5,5) | 0.076 | 0.126 | **0.075** | **0.102** | 1.028 | 2.270 | 1.983 | 4.637 | 1.075 | 2.811 | 1.479 | 2.855 |
| (5,5,8) | **0.061** | **0.118** | 0.121 | 0.186 | 1.004 | 1.013 | 1.005 | 1.006 | 1.002 | 1.009 | 1.108 | 2.399 |
| (6,6,8) | **0.098** | **0.144** | 0.104 | 0.167 | 1.006 | 1.027 | 1.006 | 1.020 | 1.009 | 1.066 | 1.035 | 2.671 |
| (6,6,10) | **0.055** | **0.097** | 0.074 | 0.132 | 1.003 | 1.009 | 1.005 | 1.008 | 1.004 | 1.015 | 1.021 | 1.126 |

(a) Datasets containing operators $\{\sin, \cos, \mathtt{inv}, +, -, \times\}$.

| | | | | | | | | | | | | |
|---|---|---|---|---|---|---|---|---|---|---|---|---|
| (3,2,2) | **0.098** | **0.165** | 0.108 | 0.425 | 0.350 | 0.713 | 0.351 | 1.831 | 0.439 | 0.581 | 0.102 | 0.597 |
| (4,4,6) | **0.078** | **0.121** | 0.120 | 0.305 | 7.056 | 16.321 | 5.093 | 19.429 | 2.458 | 13.762 | 2.225 | 3.754 |
| (5,5,5) | **0.067** | **0.230** | 0.091 | 0.313 | 32.45 | 234.31 | 36.797 | 229.529 | 14.435 | 46.191 | 28.440 | 421.63 |
| (5,5,8) | **0.113** | **0.207** | 0.119 | 0.388 | 195.22 | 573.33 | 449.83 | 565.69 | 206.06 | 629.41 | 363.79 | 666.57 |
| (6,6,8) | **0.170** | **0.481** | 0.186 | 0.727 | 1.752 | 3.824 | 4.887 | 15.248 | 2.396 | 7.051 | 1.478 | 6.271 |
| (6,6,10) | **0.161** | **0.251** | 0.312 | 0.342 | 11.678 | 26.941 | 5.667 | 24.042 | 7.398 | 25.156 | 11.513 | 28.439 |

(b) Datasets containing operators $\{\sin, \cos, +, -, \times\}$.

| | | | | | | | | | | | | |
|---|---|---|---|---|---|---|---|---|---|---|---|---|
| (3,2,2) | 0.049 | **0.113** | **0.023** | 0.166 | 0.663 | 2.773 | 1.002 | 1.992 | 0.969 | 1.310 | 0.413 | 2.510 |
| (4,4,6) | **0.141** | **0.220** | 0.238 | 0.662 | 1.031 | 1.051 | 1.297 | 1.463 | 1.051 | 1.774 | 1.093 | 1.769 |
| (5,5,5) | 0.157 | 0.438 | 0.195 | **0.337** | 1.098 | 3.617 | 1.018 | 5.296 | 1.012 | 1.27 | 1.036 | 3.617 |
| (5,5,8) | **0.122** | **0.153** | 0.166 | 0.186 | 1.009 | 1.103 | 1.017 | 1.429 | 1.007 | 1.132 | 1.07 | 2.904 |
| (6,6,8) | 0.209 | **0.590** | **0.209** | 0.646 | 1.003 | 1.153 | 1.047 | 1.134 | 1.059 | 1.302 | 1.029 | 3.365 |
| (6,6,10) | 0.139 | 0.232 | **0.073** | **0.159** | 1.654 | 3.408 | 1.027 | 1.069 | 1.009 | 1.654 | 1.445 | 2.106 |

(c) Datasets containing operators $\{\sin, \cos, \mathtt{inv}, +, -, \times\}$.

it does not affect the executions whether the data is generated ahead of the execution or on the fly. The reported NMSE scores in all charts and tables are based on separately generated data that have never been used in training. The threshold to freeze operators in CVGP is if the MSE to fit a data batch is below 0.01. The threshold to freeze the value of a constant in CVGP is if the variance of best-fitted values of the constant across trials drops below 0.001.

## 5.2 Experimental Analysis

**Learning Result.** Our CVGP attains the smallest median (50%) and 75%-quantile NMSE values among all the baselines mentioned in Sect. 5.1, when evaluated on noiseless datasets (Table 1) and noisy datasets (Table 2). This shows our method can better handle multiple variables symbolic regression problems than the current best algorithms in this area.

**Ablation Studies.** We use box plots in Fig. 3(a–d) to show that the superiority of our CVGP generalizes to other quantiles beyond the 50% and 75%-quantile. We also show the performance is consistent under the variations of evaluation metrics in Fig. 3(a–d), and noise levels in Fig. 3(e–f).

**Recovering Ground-Truth Equations.** For relatively less challenging noise-less datasets (*i.e.*, $(2, 1, 1)$ with various operators sets), our CVGP sometimes recovers ground-truth expressions. We evaluate the percentage that each algorithm successfully detects the ground-truth expressions on 50 randomly generated benchmark datasets. Table 3 shows that our CVGP algorithm has a higher chance to recover ground-truth expressions than the GP method.

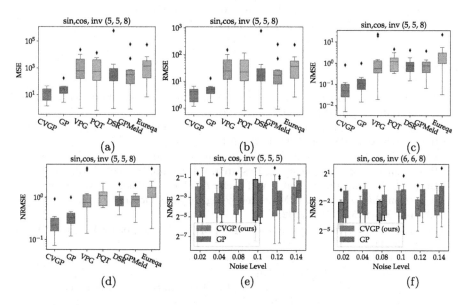

**Fig. 3.** (**a–d**) Box plots of evaluation metrics for the expressions found by different algorithms on the noiseless dataset. (**e–f**) Box plots in NMSE values for the expressions found by CVGP and GP over benchmark datasets with different noise levels. Our CVGP is consistently the best regardless of the evaluation metrics and noise levels.

**Table 3.** Ground-truth recovery rate comparison. Our CVGP has a higher rate to recover the ground-truth expressions compared to GP on 3 simple datasets.

| Operator set | Dataset configs | CVGP (ours) | GP |
|---|---|---|---|
| $\{\texttt{inv}, +, -, \times\}$ | $(2,1,1)$ | **64%** | 44% |
| $\{\sin, \cos, +, -, \times\}$ | | **46%** | 22% |
| $\{\sin, \cos, \texttt{inv}, +, -, \times\}$ | | **44%** | 32% |

## 6   Conclusion

In this research, we propose Control Variable Genetic Programming (CVGP) for symbolic regression with many independent variables. This is beyond current state-of-the-art approaches mostly tested on equations with one or two variables. CVGP builds equations involving more and more independent variables via control variable experimentation. Theoretically, we show CVGP as an incremental building approach can bring an exponential reduction in the search spaces when learning a class of expressions. In experiments, CVGP finds the best-fitted expressions among 7 competing approaches and on dozens of benchmarks.

**Acknowledgments.** We thank all the reviewers for their constructive comments. This research was supported by NSF grant CCF-1918327.

# References

1. Abolafia, D.A., Norouzi, M., Le, Q.V.: Neural program synthesis with priority queue training. CoRR abs/1801.03526 (2018)
2. Anthony, T., Tian, Z., Barber, D.: Thinking fast and slow with deep learning and tree search. In: NIPS, pp. 5360–5370 (2017)
3. Balcan, M., Dick, T., Sandholm, T., Vitercik, E.: Learning to branch. In: ICML. Proceedings of Machine Learning Research, vol. 80, pp. 353–362. PMLR (2018)
4. Biggio, L., Bendinelli, T., Neitz, A., Lucchi, A., Parascandolo, G.: Neural symbolic regression that scales. In: ICML. Proceedings of Machine Learning Research, vol. 139, pp. 936–945. PMLR (2021)
5. Booch, G., et al.: Thinking fast and slow in AI. In: AAAI, pp. 15042–15046. AAAI Press (2021)
6. Bradley, E., Easley, M., Stolle, R.: Reasoning about nonlinear system identification. Artif. Intell. **133**(1), 139–188 (2001)
7. Bridewell, W., Langley, P., Todorovski, L., Džeroski, S.: Inductive process modeling. Mach. Learn. **71**, 1–32 (2008)
8. Brunton, S.L., Proctor, J.L., Kutz, J.N.: Discovering governing equations from data by sparse identification of nonlinear dynamical systems. Proc. Natl. Acad. Sci. **113**(15), 3932–3937 (2016)
9. Cerrato, M., Brugger, J., Schmitt, N., Kramer, S.: Reinforcement learning for automated scientific discovery. In: AAAI Spring Symposium on Computational Approaches to Scientific Discovery (2023)
10. Chen, C., Luo, C., Jiang, Z.: Elite bases regression: a real-time algorithm for symbolic regression. In: ICNC-FSKD, pp. 529–535. IEEE (2017)
11. Chen, D., Wang, Y., Gao, W.: Combining a gradient-based method and an evolution strategy for multi-objective reinforcement learning. Appl. Intell. **50**(10), 3301–3317 (2020)
12. Chen, Q., Xue, B., Zhang, M.: Rademacher complexity for enhancing the generalization of genetic programming for symbolic regression. IEEE Trans. Cybern. **52**(4), 2382–2395 (2022)
13. Chen, R.T., Rubanova, Y., Bettencourt, J., Duvenaud, D.K.: Neural ordinary differential equations. In: Advances in Neural Information Processing Systems, vol. 31 (2018)
14. Cranmer, M.D., et al.: Discovering symbolic models from deep learning with inductive biases. In: NeurIPS (2020)
15. Dubčáková, R.: Eureqa: software review. Genet. Program Evolvable Mach. **12**(2), 173–178 (2011)

16. Dzeroski, S., Todorovski, L.: Discovering dynamics: from inductive logic programming to machine discovery. J. Intell. Inf. Syst. **4**(1), 89–108 (1995)
17. Fortin, F.A., De Rainville, F.M., Gardner, M.A., Parizeau, M., Gagné, C.: DEAP: evolutionary algorithms made easy. J. Mach. Learn. Res. **13**, 2171–2175 (2012)
18. Glymour, C., Scheines, R., Spirtes, P.: Discovering Causal Structure: Artificial Intelligence, Philosophy of Science, and Statistical Modeling. Academic Press, London (2014)
19. Golovin, D., Krause, A., Ray, D.: Near-optimal Bayesian active learning with noisy observations. In: Advances in Neural Information Processing Systems, vol. 23 (2010)
20. Guimerà, R., et al.: A Bayesian machine scientist to aid in the solution of challenging scientific problems. Sci. Adv. **6**(5), eaav6971 (2020)
21. Hanneke, S.: Theory of disagreement-based active learning. Found. Trends Mach. Learn. **7**(2–3), 131–309 (2014)
22. He, B., Lu, Q., Yang, Q., Luo, J., Wang, Z.: Taylor genetic programming for symbolic regression. In: GECCO, pp. 946–954. ACM (2022)
23. Iten, R., Metger, T., Wilming, H., Del Rio, L., Renner, R.: Discovering physical concepts with neural networks. Phys. Rev. Lett. **124**(1), 010508 (2020)
24. Jaber, A., Ribeiro, A., Zhang, J., Bareinboim, E.: Causal identification under Markov equivalence: calculus, algorithm, and completeness. Adv. Neural. Inf. Process. Syst. **35**, 3679–3690 (2022)
25. Kahneman, D.: Thinking, Fast and Slow. Macmillan, New York (2011)
26. Kamienny, P., d'Ascoli, S., Lample, G., Charton, F.: End-to-end symbolic regression with transformers. In: NeurIPS (2022)
27. Kibler, D.F., Langley, P.: The experimental study of machine learning (1991)
28. King, R.D., et al.: The automation of science. Science **324**(5923), 85–89 (2009)
29. King, R.D., et al.: Functional genomic hypothesis generation and experimentation by a robot scientist. Nature **427**(6971), 247–252 (2004)
30. La Cava, W., et al.: Contemporary symbolic regression methods and their relative performance. arXiv preprint arXiv:2107.14351 (2021)
31. Langley, P.: BACON: a production system that discovers empirical laws. In: IJCAI, p. 344. William Kaufmann (1977)
32. Langley, P.: Rediscovering physics with BACON.3. In: IJCAI, pp. 505–507. William Kaufmann (1979)
33. Langley, P.: Data-driven discovery of physical laws. Cogn. Sci. **5**(1), 31–54 (1981)
34. Langley, P.: Machine learning as an experimental science. Mach. Learn. **3**, 5–8 (1988)
35. Langley, P.: Scientific discovery, causal explanation, and process model induction. Mind Soc. **18**(1), 43–56 (2019)
36. Langley, P., Bradshaw, G.L., Simon, H.A.: BACON.5: the discovery of conservation laws. In: IJCAI, pp. 121–126. William Kaufmann (1981)
37. Langley, P.W., Simon, H.A., Bradshaw, G., Zytkow, J.M.: Scientific Discovery: Computational Explorations of the Creative Process. The MIT Press, Cambridge (1987)
38. Lehman, J.S., Santner, T.J., Notz, W.I.: Designing computer experiments to determine robust control variables. Statistica Sinica, 571–590 (2004)
39. Lenat, D.B.: The ubiquity of discovery. Artif. Intell. **9**(3), 257–285 (1977)
40. Liu, Z., Tegmark, M.: Machine learning conservation laws from trajectories. Phys. Rev. Lett. **126**, 180604 (2021)

41. Matsubara, Y., Chiba, N., Igarashi, R., Taniai, T., Ushiku, Y.: Rethinking symbolic regression datasets and benchmarks for scientific discovery. arXiv preprint arXiv:2206.10540 (2022)
42. McConaghy, T.: FFX: fast, scalable, deterministic symbolic regression technology. In: Riolo, R., Vladislavleva, E., Moore, J. (eds.) Genetic Programming Theory and Practice IX. Genetic and Evolutionary Computation, pp. 235–260. Springer, New York (2011). https://doi.org/10.1007/978-1-4614-1770-5_13
43. Mundhenk, T.N., Landajuela, M., Glatt, R., Santiago, C.P., Faissol, D.M., Petersen, B.K.: Symbolic regression via deep reinforcement learning enhanced genetic programming seeding. In: NeurIPS, pp. 24912–24923 (2021)
44. Pearl, J.: Causality. Cambridge University Press, Cambridge (2009)
45. Petersen, B.K., Landajuela, M., Mundhenk, T.N., Santiago, C.P., Kim, S., Kim, J.T.: Deep symbolic regression: recovering mathematical expressions from data via risk-seeking policy gradients. In: ICLR. OpenReview.net (2021)
46. Raissi, M., Perdikaris, P., Karniadakis, G.: Physics-informed neural networks: a deep learning framework for solving forward and inverse problems involving nonlinear partial differential equations. J. Comput. Phys. **378**, 686–707 (2019)
47. Raissi, M., Yazdani, A., Karniadakis, G.E.: Hidden fluid mechanics: learning velocity and pressure fields from flow visualizations. Science **367**(6481), 1026–1030 (2020)
48. Razavi, S., Gamazon, E.R.: Neural-network-directed genetic programmer for discovery of governing equations. CoRR abs/2203.08808 (2022)
49. Ryan, T.P., Morgan, J.P.: Modern experimental design. J. Stat. Theory Pract. **1**(3–4), 501–506 (2007)
50. Santner, T.J., Williams, B.J., Notz, W.I.: The Design and Analysis of Computer Experiments. Springer Series in Statistics, Springer, New York (2003). https://doi.org/10.1007/978-1-4757-3799-8
51. Scavuzzo, L., et al.: Learning to branch with tree MDPs. In: NeurIPS (2022)
52. Schmidt, M., Lipson, H.: Distilling free-form natural laws from experimental data. Science **324**(5923), 81–85 (2009)
53. Simon, H.A.: Spurious correlation: a causal interpretation. J. Am. Stat. Assoc. **49**(267), 467–479 (1954)
54. Udrescu, S.M., Tegmark, M.: AI Feynman: a physics-inspired method for symbolic regression. Sci. Adv. **6**(16) (2020)
55. Uy, N.Q., Hoai, N.X., O'Neill, M., McKay, R.I., López, E.G.: Semantically-based crossover in genetic programming: application to real-valued symbolic regression. Genet. Program Evolvable Mach. **12**(2), 91–119 (2011)
56. Valdés-Pérez, R.: Human/computer interactive elucidation of reaction mechanisms: application to catalyzed hydrogenolysis of ethane. Catal. Lett. **28**, 79–87 (1994)
57. Virgolin, M., Alderliesten, T., Bosman, P.A.N.: Linear scaling with and within semantic backpropagation-based genetic programming for symbolic regression. In: GECCO, pp. 1084–1092. ACM (2019)
58. Virgolin, M., Pissis, S.P.: Symbolic regression is NP-hard. Trans. Mach. Learn. Res. (2022)
59. Wang, H., et al.: Enabling scientific discovery with artificial intelligence. Nature (2022)
60. Williams, R.J.: Simple statistical gradient-following algorithms for connectionist reinforcement learning. Mach. Learn. **8**, 229–256 (1992)
61. Wu, T., Tegmark, M.: Toward an artificial intelligence physicist for unsupervised learning. Phys. Rev. E **100**, 033311 (Sep2019)

62. Xue, Y., Nasim, Md., Zhang, M., Fan, C., Zhang, X., El-Azab, A.: Physics knowledge discovery via neural differential equation embedding. In: Dong, Y., Kourtellis, N., Hammer, B., Lozano, J.A. (eds.) ECML PKDD 2021. LNCS (LNAI), vol. 12979, pp. 118–134. Springer, Cham (2021). https://doi.org/10.1007/978-3-030-86517-7_8
63. Zhang, S., Lin, G.: Robust data-driven discovery of governing physical laws with error bars. Proc. Roy. Soc. A Math. Phys. Eng. Sci. **474**(2217), 20180305 (2018)

# Neural Class Expression Synthesis in $\mathcal{ALCHIQ}(\mathcal{D})$

N'Dah Jean Kouagou$^{(\boxtimes)}$ ⓘ, Stefan Heindorf ⓘ, Caglar Demir ⓘ,
and Axel-Cyrille Ngonga Ngomo ⓘ

Department of Computer Science, Paderborn University,
Paderborn, Germany
{ndah.jean.kouagou,heindorf,caglar.demir,axel.ngonga}@upb.de

**Abstract.** Class expression learning in description logics has long been regarded as an iterative search problem in an infinite conceptual space. Each iteration of the search process invokes a reasoner and a heuristic function. The reasoner finds the instances of the current expression, and the heuristic function computes the information gain and decides on the next step to be taken. As the size of the background knowledge base grows, search-based approaches for class expression learning become prohibitively slow. Current neural class expression synthesis (NCES) approaches investigate the use of neural networks for class expression learning in the attributive language with complement ($\mathcal{ALC}$). While they show significant improvements over search-based approaches in runtime and quality of the computed solutions, they rely on the availability of pretrained embeddings for the input knowledge base. Moreover, they are not applicable to ontologies in more expressive description logics. In this paper, we propose a novel NCES approach which extends the state of the art to the description logic $\mathcal{ALCHIQ}(\mathcal{D})$. Our extension, dubbed NCES2, comes with an improved training data generator and does not require pretrained embeddings for the input knowledge base as both the embedding model and the class expression synthesizer are trained jointly. Empirical results on benchmark datasets suggest that our approach inherits the scalability capability of current NCES instances with the additional advantage that it supports more complex learning problems. NCES2 achieves the highest performance overall when compared to search-based approaches and to its predecessor NCES. We provide our source code, datasets, and pretrained models at https://github.com/dice-group/NCES2.

**Keywords:** Neural network · Description logic · Class expression learning

This work has received funding from the European Union's Horizon 2020 research and innovation programme under the Marie Skłodowska-Curie grant No 860801 and the European Union's Horizon Europe research and innovation programme under the grant No 101070305. This work has also been supported by the Ministry of Culture and Science of North Rhine-Westphalia (MKW NRW) within the project SAIL under the grant No NW21-059D and by the Deutsche Forschungsgemeinschaft (DFG, German Research Foundation): TRR 318/1 2021 – 438445824.

D. Koutra et al. (Eds.): ECML PKDD 2023, LNAI 14172, pp. 196–212, 2023.
https://doi.org/10.1007/978-3-031-43421-1_12

# 1   Introduction

Class expression learning approaches [13,14,22,24,30,35] are supervised machine learning approaches that learn class expressions in description logics: Given a knowledge base, and a subset of the individuals in the knowledge base, the goal is to learn a class expression that holds for the given individuals, i.e., describes them. For example, given the set of individuals {Marie Curie, Linus Pauling, John Bardeen, Frederick Sanger}, a learner should compute the class expression $\geq 2hasWon.\{NobelPrize\}$ (i.e., individuals who have won at least two Nobel prizes). As the learned class expressions provide a concise and human-readable explanation for why individuals are classified as positives or negatives, class expressions can be considered explainable, interpretable white-box models. Class expression learning has important applications in ontology engineering [23], biomedicine [25] and Industry 4.0 [4].

Although several approaches have been developed to solve class expression learning problems, most of them do not scale to large knowledge bases. In particular, approaches based on refinement operators [13,17,21,22,24,30] and evolutionary algorithms [14] suffer from the exploration of an infinite conceptual space where each step invokes a reasoner to compute the instances of numerous intermediary refinements. Moreover, the reasoning complexity grows with the expressivity of the underlying description logic [16,29], and existing search-based approaches cannot leverage previously solved learning problems [18].

To alleviate the aforementioned issues, Kouagou et al. [18] proposed a new family of approaches, dubbed neural class expression synthesis (NCES) approaches. These approaches work in a fashion akin to neural machine translation [9,39] and translate (embeddings of) sets of positive/negative examples to class expressions. Extensive experiments on different datasets showed that post-training, NCES approaches do not suffer the costly exploration encountered by search-based approaches as they directly synthesize class expressions in a single forward pass in approximately one second on average. Moreover, these approaches have the ability to solve multiple learning problems at the same time as they accept batches of inputs. NCES approaches are therefore well suited for deployment in large-scale applications of class expression learning, e.g., on the web.

Despite their effectiveness, current implementations of NCES have some important limitations. First, they cannot solve learning problems beyond $\mathcal{ALC}$, e.g., data properties are not supported. Second, they assume the availability of pretrained embeddings for each input knowledge base. In this work, we propose a novel implementation of NCES that goes beyond existing instantiations in three directions: (1) We extend the supported description logic to $\mathcal{ALCHIQ}(\mathcal{D})$ to increase reasoning capabilities, (2) we improve the training data generation method, and (3) we incorporate an embedding model into the approach so that embeddings for the input knowledge base can be jointly learned with class expressions. As a result, our approach works in an end-to-end manner and does not require pretrained embeddings. Our approach achieves the highest performance overall when compared to search-based approaches and current NCES implementations.

We organize the rest of the paper as follows: First, we present related works for class expression learning and the background needed throughout the paper. Next, we describe our proposed approach and evaluate it with respect to existing state-of-the-art approaches on four benchmark datasets. Finally, we conclude the paper and introduce new directions for future work.

## 2    Related Work

Many approaches for class expression learning have been developed in the last decade [7,13,22,23], and even recently [14,17,18,32]. The former are based on refinement operators while the most recent approaches use additional techniques such as evolutionary algorithms [14] or neural networks [17,18]. The state-of-the-art EvoLearner [14] initializes its population by random walks on the input knowledge graph where nodes are atomic classes or data values, and edges are abstract or concrete roles. The results of the random walks are then converted to description logic concepts and further refined by means of mutation and crossover operations. CELOE [23] is a state-of-the-art class expression learning algorithm tailored towards ontology engineering. It is implemented in DL-Learner [21] alongside other search-based algorithms such as OCEL [22]—which formed the basis for CELOE, and ELTL [7]—which learns concepts in the lightweight description logic $\mathcal{EL}$. ECII [32] is a search-based algorithm, too, but it does not use a refinement operator and only invokes a reasoner once for each run. CLIP [17] is an extension of CELOE that uses neural networks to predict an approximate length of the solution during concept learning. NCES (neural class expression synthesis) approaches were proposed by Kouagou et al. [18] to overcome the runtime limitations of search-based approaches. NCES instances use pretrained embeddings of input knowledge bases and translate them into class expressions in $\mathcal{ALC}$. They can solve hundreds of learning problems at a time because they accept batches of inputs.

Apart from the recent family of approaches NCES, the rest of the well-known approaches for class expression learning are search-based. Hence, these approaches need to perform numerous expensive entailment checks [29] and evaluations of candidate concepts during concept learning. Our approach inherits the scalability capability of current NCES instances and achieves superior performance on complex learning problems, i.e., learning problems involving data properties, cardinality restrictions, or inverse properties.

## 3    Background

In the rest of the paper, we denote a knowledge base by $\mathcal{K} = (TBox, ABox)$, i.e., a pair consisting of a terminological box, and an assertion box [18,27]. Its sets of individuals, roles, and atomic classes are denoted by $\mathcal{N}_I$, $\mathcal{N}_R$, and $\mathcal{N}_C$, respectively. $|.|$ denotes the cardinality of a set or the size of an array. Given a non-empty one-dimensional array $A$ and an integer $i$ such that $0 < i \leq |A|$, both $A[i]$ and $A_i$ denote the element of $A$ at position $i$. We adopt similar notations for

**Table 1.** Description logic constructs supported by NCES2.

| Syntax | Construct | Syntax | Construct |
|---|---|---|---|
| $\mathcal{ALC}$ | | $\mathcal{Q}$ | |
| $r$ | Abstract role | $\leq n\ r.C$ | Max. cardinality restriction |
| $\neg C$ | Negation | $\geq n\ r.C$ | Min. cardinality restriction |
| $C \sqcup C$ | Disjunction | | |
| $C \sqcap C$ | Conjunction | $(\mathcal{D})$ | |
| $\exists\ r.C$ | Existential restriction | | |
| $\forall\ r.C$ | Universal restriction | $b$ | Boolean concrete role |
| $\mathcal{H}$ | | $d$ | Numeric concrete role |
| $r_1 \sqsubseteq r_2$ | Role inclusion | $d \leq v$ | Max. numeric restriction |
| $\mathcal{I}$ | | $d \geq v$ | Min. numeric restriction |
| $r^-$ | Inverse role | $b = \mathit{True}; b = \mathit{False}$ | Boolean value restriction |

high-dimensional arrays. As in [18], we convert input knowledge bases into sets of triples with RDFLib [19]. These triples are used as inputs to the embedding model in NCES2 during training, see Sect. 4.4.

### 3.1 Description Logics

Description logics [27] are a family of knowledge representation systems that are widely used in artificial intelligence, the semantic web, and automated reasoning. They are designed to express the meaning of a statement in a formal language that is then used for automated reasoning. Indeed, the web ontology language, OWL, uses description logics to represent the *TBox* of RDF ontologies. Our approach runs in $\mathcal{ALCHIQ}(\mathcal{D})$, i.e., $\mathcal{ALC}$ [33] extended with property hierarchies (used during training data generation), inverse properties, cardinality restrictions, and data properties. We present the syntax of $\mathcal{ALCHIQ}(\mathcal{D})$ in Table 1. For its semantics, we refer to Lehmann [22].

### 3.2 Refinement Operators

**Definition 1 [18,24].** *Given a quasi-ordered space $(\mathcal{S}, \preceq)$, a downward (respectively upward) refinement operator on $\mathcal{S}$ is a mapping $\rho : \mathcal{S} \rightarrow 2^{\mathcal{S}}$ such that for all $C \in \mathcal{S}$, $C' \in \rho(C)$ implies $C' \preceq C$ (respectively $C \preceq C'$).*

In this work, we extend the refinement operator by Kouagou et al. [17] to the description logic $\mathcal{ALCHIQ}(\mathcal{D})$ and use the latter to generate training data for our approach, see Sect. 5.1 for more details.

### 3.3    Class Expression Learning

**Definition 2 (Theoretical Solution).**  *Given a knowledge base $\mathcal{K}$, a target concept $T$, a set of positive examples $E^+ = \{e_1^+, e_2^+, \ldots, e_{n_1}^+\}$, and a set of negative examples $E^- = \{e_1^-, e_2^-, \ldots, e_{n_2}^-\}$, the learning problem is to find a class expression $C$ such that for $\mathcal{K}' = \mathcal{K} \cup \{T \equiv C\}$, we have $\forall e^+ \in E^+ \, \forall e^- \in E^-$, $\mathcal{K}' \models C(e^+)$ and $\mathcal{K}' \not\models C(e^-)$.*

While search-based approaches such as CELOE and EvoLearner repeatedly invoke a reasoner and a heuristic function to incrementally construct the solution $C$, our approach directly synthesizes the solution by mapping the output (computed in approximately one second) of its neural network component to the vocabulary of tokens. In Sect. 4.2, we adapt Definition 2 to our approach.

### 3.4    Knowledge Graph Embedding

A knowledge graph is a collection of assertions. In this paper, we consider knowledge graphs $\mathcal{G} \subseteq \mathcal{E} \times \mathcal{R} \times \mathcal{E}$, where $\mathcal{E}$ is a finite set of entities and $\mathcal{R}$ is a finite set of relations. Knowledge graph embeddings are mappings of entities (and relations) into a vector space. Embeddings can be used for a variety of tasks such as link prediction [6], recommendation systems [43], and natural language processing [8]. A large number of embedding approaches have been developed in the recent past [10,36]. They can be classified in two main categories: (1) Approaches that use only facts observed in the knowledge graph [5,28], and (2) approaches that leverage additional available information about entities and relations, such as textual descriptions [37,40]. Our approach uses the state-of-the-art approach ConEx [11], which belongs to the first category, as its default embedding model. We also conduct additional experiments with DistMult [41]. The results obtained with DistMult are similar to those of ConEx. They are omitted due to space constraints and can be found in our supplementary material.

### 3.5    The Set Transformer Architecture

Class expression learning from examples deals with set-structured inputs (see Definition 2). Several neural network architectures have been proposed to solve set-structured input tasks, the most prominent of which include Deep Set [42] and Set Transformer [20]. Deep Set encodes the elements of the input set independently and applies a pooling function, usually a summation, to represent the entire set. Contrarily, Set Transformer computes an encoding of the input set via a self-attention mechanism on its elements. In its original paper, Set Transformer outperforms other set-compatible architectures on most tasks [20], including Deep Set. For this reason, the neural network component of our approach uses the Set Transformer architecture. Its building blocks are the Multi-head Attention Block (MAB), the Set Attention Block (SAB), the Induced Set Attention Block (ISAB), and the Pooling by Multi-head Attention (PMA). Due to space constraints, we refer to [20] for more details on the Set Transformer architecture.

# 4   Proposed Approach (NCES2)

## 4.1   Preliminaries

We create a vocabulary of tokens $\mathcal{V_K}$ (we simply write $\mathcal{V}$ when there is no ambiguity) for each input knowledge base $\mathcal{K}$. The vocabulary consists of all atomic concept and role names in $\mathcal{K}$ in addition to the following constructs: "⊤" (top concept), "⊥" (bottom concept), "False", "True" (Boolean values), "−" (for inverse properties), ":", "xsd", "double", "integer", "date" (for time data values), "≤", "≥", "" (white space), "." (dot), "⊔", "⊓", "∃", "∀", "¬", "[", "]", "{", "}", "(", and ")". We add the special token "PAD" to pad all class expressions in a batch of training examples to the same length. The token also serves as the end token at inference time when parsing the output of NCES2. Finally, we add numeric data values to the vocabulary. These values are obtained by creating evenly spaced bins ranging from the lowest to the highest value observed in the knowledge base.

We now choose a fixed ordering for the elements of $\mathcal{V_K}$ and use them to synthesize class expressions (more details in Sect. 4.6). In fact, class expressions in $\mathcal{ALCHIQ(D)}$ are written using tokens in $\mathcal{V_K}$ as can be seen in the learning problems below, which are extracted from test datasets: $LP_1 =$ Man ⊓ (∀ knows.(¬SonOfGod)) ⊓ (≤ 2 visitedPlace.⊤) (Semantic Bible), $LP_2 =$ Fluorine-92 ⊔ Sulfur-74 ⊔ (∃ drosophila_rt.{False}) (Carcinogenesis), $LP_3 =$ (Atom ⊓ (Tin ⊔ (¬Carbon-25))) ⊔ (∃ inBond.(¬Carbon-10)) (Mutagenesis), and $LP_4 =$ Measurable-Trend ⊔ (∃ related.(Idea ⊔ Uprising)) (Vicodi). We discuss the solutions computed by different class expression learning approaches for each of these learning problems in Sect. 5.

## 4.2   Learning Problem

**Definition 3 (Solution by NCES2).** *Given a knowledge base $\mathcal{K}$ and sets of positive/negative examples $E^+ = \{e_1^+, e_2^+, \ldots, e_{n_1}^+\}$ and $E^- = \{e_1^-, e_2^-, \ldots, e_{n_2}^-\}$, the learning problem is to compute a class expression $C$ in $\mathcal{ALCHIQ(D)}$ (using tokens in $\mathcal{V_K}$) that maximizes the F-measure and Accuracy defined by*

$$\mathbf{F}_1 = 2 \times \frac{\text{Precision} \times \text{Recall}}{\text{Precision} + \text{Recall}}, \tag{1}$$

$$\text{Precision} = \frac{|C_I \cap E^+|}{|C_I \cap E^+| + |C_I \cap E^-|}, \quad \text{Recall} = \frac{|C_I \cap E^+|}{|E^+|}, \tag{2}$$

$$\text{Accuracy} = \frac{|C_I \cap E^+| + |(\mathcal{N}_I \setminus C_I) \cap E^-|}{|E^+| + |E^-|}, \tag{3}$$

*where $C_I$ denotes the set of instances of $C$, and $\mathcal{N}_I$ the set of all individuals.*

The metrics **Accuracy** and **$\mathbf{F}_1$** are used to compare different approaches on class expression learning problems—see Table 4. One difference between Definition 2 and Definition 3 is for example that the latter targets a specific description logic (in this case $\mathcal{ALCHIQ}(\mathcal{D})$) while the former is general, i.e., applicable to any description logic. Moreover, Definition 3 allows for approximate solutions to be returned when the exact solution is not found, while Definition 2 does not. In theory, there can be multiple solutions to the learning problem; NCES2 generates only one.

## 4.3   Encoding Positive and Negative Examples

Set Transformer is an encoder-decoder architecture. The encoder $Enc$ consists of two ISAB layers. The decoder $Dec$ is composed of one PMA layer (with $k = 1$), and a linear layer for the desired output shape. During training, the embedding model component provides embeddings for positive examples $x_{pos}$ and negative examples $x_{neg}$. These two embeddings are fed to the encoder independently. The outputs are then concatenated row-wise and fed to the decoder which produces the final scores $s$ for all tokens in the vocabulary $\mathcal{V}$:

$$O_{pos} = Enc(x_{pos}), \; O_{neg} = Enc(x_{neg}), \tag{4}$$

$$s = Dec(\text{Concat}(O_{pos}, O_{neg})). \tag{5}$$

## 4.4   Loss Function

Our approach is trained by minimizing two joint loss functions: (1) The loss $\mathcal{L}_1$ from the embedding model, and (2) the loss $\mathcal{L}_2$ from the class expression synthesizer. Formally, let $\mathcal{G} \subseteq \mathcal{E} \times \mathcal{R} \times \mathcal{E}$ be the knowledge graph representation of the input knowledge base, and let $h \in \mathcal{E}, r \in \mathcal{R}$ be a head entity and a relation. We define $\mathcal{L}_1$ to be the binary cross-entropy loss:

$$\mathcal{L}_1(y^{hr}, \hat{y}^{hr}) = -\frac{1}{|\mathcal{E}|} \sum_{i=1}^{|\mathcal{E}|} y_i^{hr} \log(\hat{y}_i^{hr}) + (1 - y_i^{hr}) \log(1 - \hat{y}_i^{hr}). \tag{6}$$

Here, $y^{hr} \in \{0, 1\}^{|\mathcal{E}|}$ is the binary representation of $\{(h, r, t)|t \in \mathcal{E}\}$ in $\mathcal{G}$, i.e., $y^{hr}[\text{id}(t)] = 1$ if $(h, r, t) \in \mathcal{G}$, and $y^{hr}[\text{id}(t)] = 0$ otherwise. Accordingly, $\hat{y}^{hr} \in [0, 1]^{|\mathcal{E}|}$ is the vector of scores predicted by the embedding model for all candidate tail entities. On the other hand, $\mathcal{L}_2$ is defined by

$$\mathcal{L}_2(s, t) = -\frac{1}{L} \sum_{i=1}^{L} \log \left( \frac{\exp(s_{t_i, i})}{\sum_{c=1}^{|\mathcal{V}|} \exp(s_{c, i})} \right), \tag{7}$$

where $L$ is the maximum length of class expressions our approach can generate, $|\mathcal{V}|$ the total number of tokens in the vocabulary, $s \in \mathbb{R}^{|\mathcal{V}| \times L}$ the matrix of predicted scores for each position in the target sequence of tokens, and $t \in \{1, 2, \ldots, |\mathcal{V}|\}^L$ the vector of target token indices in the input class expression.

Our total loss $\mathcal{L}$ is defined as the average of $\mathcal{L}_1$ and $\mathcal{L}_2$, computed on the inputs $(y^{hr}, \hat{y}^{hr})$ and $(s, t)$:

$$\mathcal{L}(y^{hr}, \hat{y}^{hr}, s, t) = \frac{\mathcal{L}_1(y^{hr}, \hat{y}^{hr}) + \mathcal{L}_2(s, t)}{2}. \tag{8}$$

During training, we alternatively sample a minibatch of $N_1$ training datapoints for the embedding model, and a minibatch of $N_2$ training datapoints for the neural synthesizer to compute $\mathcal{L}_1$ and $\mathcal{L}_2$, respectively. We then compute the gradient of $\mathcal{L}$ w.r.t. both the parameters of the embedding model and those of the synthesizer. To prevent gradient explosion and to reduce overfitting, we use gradient clipping [44], and dropout [34]. Both parameter sets are updated using the Adam [15] optimization algorithm. Note that the embeddings of positive and negative examples used by the synthesizer—see Sect. 4.3—come from the embedding model and are hence dynamically updated during training. This way, we are able to learn embeddings that are not only finetuned for class expression learning, but also faithful to the input background knowledge.

### 4.5 Measuring Performance During Training

In our previous work [18], we introduced two metrics to quantify the performance of neural synthesizers during training[1]. We use the same metrics in this work. The first metric is called *"Soft Accuracy"* and is equivalent to the *Jaccard index* between the set of predicted tokens and the set of true tokens in the input expression. The second metric is called *"Hard Accuracy"*, and compares the tokens in the prediction and target expressions position-wise, i.e., taking into account their order of appearance. We refer to [18] for the mathematical expressions of these metrics.

### 4.6 Class Expression Synthesis

We synthesize class expressions by mapping the output scores $s$ (see Eq. 5) to the vocabulary. Specifically, we select the highest-scoring token in the vocabulary for each position $i$ along the sequence dimension:

$$\text{id}_i = \underset{c \in \{1,\ldots,|\mathcal{V}|\}}{\arg\max} \ s_{c,i}, \tag{9}$$

$$\texttt{synthesized\_token}_i = \mathcal{V}[\text{id}_i]. \tag{10}$$

The predicted tokens are concatenated to construct a class expression. Note that we ignore all tokens appearing after the special token "PAD".

### 4.7 Model Ensembling

Several works have highlighted that combining different neural models trained even on the same dataset usually performs better than each individual model [12, 31]. This technique is known as model ensembling. In this work, we trained three instances of our approach, NCES2, which all use the Set Transformer architecture

---

[1] These metrics are only used during training. When comparing NCES2 to state-of-the-art approaches on class expression learning on the test sets, we use metrics based on the number of covered/ruled-out positive/negative examples for all approaches.

but with different numbers of inducing points: $m = 32$, $m = 64$, and $m = 128$. We compute ensemble predictions by averaging the predicted scores for each token post training. Overall, we consider four ensemble models: $NCES2_{m=\{32,64\}}$, $NCES2_{m=\{32,128\}}$, $NCES2_{m=\{64,128\}}$, and $NCES2_{m=\{32,64,128\}}$. A class expression is then synthesized as described in Sect. 4.6 using the average scores.

## 5    Evaluation

### 5.1    Experimental Setup

**Datasets.** We used four benchmark datasets in our experiments: Vicodi [26], Carcinogenesis [38], Mutagenesis [38], and Semantic Bible[2]. The Carcinogenesis and Mutagenesis knowledge bases describe chemical compounds and how they relate to each other. The Semantic Bible knowledge base describes the New Testament, and the Vicodi knowledge base describes the European history. We summarize the statistics of each dataset in Table 2.

**Training Data Generation.** Training NCES2 requires numerous class expressions with their sets of positive and negative examples[3]. To this end, we extend the refinement operator by Kouagou et al. [17] to the description logic $\mathcal{ALCHIQ}(\mathcal{D})$ so that we can generate all forms of class expressions supported by NCES2 (see Table 1). Moreover, we improve upon the training data generation method used in [18]. Since most knowledge bases contain thousands to millions of individuals, current NCES approaches subsample the initial sets of positive/negative examples for each learning problem in the training set. This technique is inefficient because only a few examples are seen during training which results in poor performance on learning problems where, e.g., a different random seed is used to construct the sets of examples. To alleviate this issue, we construct multiple copies (2 copies in our experiments) of a given learning problem and assign different subsets of examples to each copy. The clear advantage of this new sampling technique is that it allows each learning problem to be seen from different perspectives and hence better understood. Note that this sampling technique is only applied to the training set. The statistics of the generated data are given in Table 2.

**Hyper-Parameter Search.** Following [18], we employ a random search [2] to find the best hyper-parameter values for NCES2. Specifically, we find highly performing values on one dataset (we used Carcinogenesis for this purpose) and use them on the rest of the datasets. Note that the total number of examples $n$ is an exception as it depends on the size of $\mathcal{N}_I$, i.e., the total number of individuals in the given knowledge base. Nonetheless, we used the same formula to compute the

---

[2]  https://www.semanticbible.com/ntn/ntn-overview.html.

[3]  Positive examples are instances of the class expression while negative examples are the rest of the individuals in $\mathcal{N}_I$.

**Table 2.** Statistics of the benchmark datasets. In the table, we use the following notations and abbreviations: Set of individuals ($\mathcal{N}_I$), set of atomic classes ($\mathcal{N}_C$), object properties (*Obj. Pr.*), data properties (*D. Pr.*), vocabulary ($\mathcal{V}$), and learning problems in the test set (*LPs*).

| Dataset | $|\mathcal{N}_I|$ | $|\mathcal{N}_C|$ | $|Obj.\ Pr.|$ | $|D.\ Pr.|$ | $|TBox|$ | $|ABox|$ | $|\mathcal{V}|$ | $|Train|$ | $|LPs|$ |
|---|---|---|---|---|---|---|---|---|---|
| Carcinogenesis | 22,372 | 142 | 4 | 15 | 144 | 74,223 | 198 | 19,635 | 100 |
| Mutagenesis | 14,145 | 86 | 5 | 6 | 82 | 47,722 | 133 | 9,705 | 100 |
| Semantic Bible | 724 | 48 | 29 | 9 | 56 | 3,106 | 125 | 11,069 | 100 |
| Vicodi | 33,238 | 194 | 10 | 2 | 204 | 116,181 | 242 | 46,094 | 100 |

**Table 3.** Hyper-parameter settings per dataset. $L$ is the maximum length of expressions synthesized by NCES2, $lr$ the learning rate, $N_1$ the minibatch size for the embedding model, $N_2$ the minibatch size for the synthesizer, $n$ the number of (positive and negative) examples, $d$ the embedding dimension, $gc$ the gradient clipping value.

| Dataset | epochs | optimizer | lr | d | $N_1$ | $N_2$ | L | n | gc |
|---|---|---|---|---|---|---|---|---|---|
| Carcinogenesis | 200 | Adam | 0.001 | 50 | 1,024 | 512 | 48 | 1,000 | 5 |
| Mutagenesis | 200 | Adam | 0.001 | 50 | 1,024 | 512 | 48 | 1,000 | 5 |
| Semantic Bible | 200 | Adam | 0.001 | 50 | 1,024 | 512 | 48 | 362 | 5 |
| Vicodi | 200 | Adam | 0.001 | 50 | 1,024 | 512 | 48 | 1,000 | 5 |

optimal value for $n$ : min $\left( \frac{|\mathcal{N}_I|}{2}, 1000 \right)$. The selected values for hyper-parameters are presented in Table 3.

**Hardware.** We trained NCES2 using 24 GB RAM, 16 AMD EPYC 7713 CPUs @3.10 GHz, and a single NVIDIA RTX A5000 GPU with 24 GB memory. Because search-based approaches do not support GPU computation, we conduct experiments on class expression learning on the test sets (see Table 4) using a server with 16 Intel Xeon E5-2695 CPUs @2.30 GHz and 128 GB RAM. Due to space constraints, we report the number of parameters and the training time in our supplementary material.[4]

### 5.2   Results and Discussion

**Training Curves.** NCES2 was trained for 200 epochs on each dataset. Training curves are shown in Fig. 1. From the figure, we can observe that NCES2 is able to accurately map instance data (positive/negative examples) to the corresponding class expressions on the training set. This is witnessed by a performance of over 95% *Hard Accuracy* (recall the definition in Sect. 4.5) on all datasets. In addition, the convergence rates are higher on the largest datasets (Carcinogenesis and Vicodi), which suggests that NCES2 learns faster on large datasets. Similar

---

[4] https://github.com/dice-group/NCES2/blob/main/supplement_material.pdf.

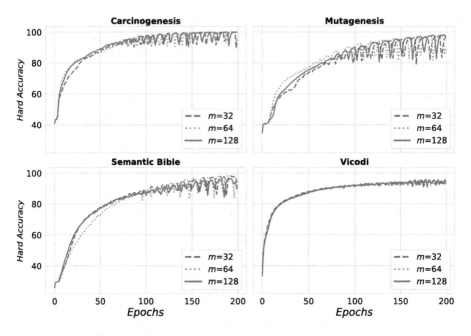

**Fig. 1.** Training accuracy curves using the ConEx embedding model. $m$ is the number of inducing points.

observations hold for the *Soft Accuracy* curves which we do not report due to space constraints; in particular, the *Soft Accuracy* is over 95% on all datasets. The training curves for this metric can be found in our supplementary material. The exact values during training can be found in our repository[5].

## Comparison to Baseline Approaches.

*NCES2 vs. Search-Based Approaches.* We ran extensive experiments comparing NCES2 to the search-based approaches EvoLearner, CELOE, ELTL, and ECII. The results are presented in Table 4. As done in [14,18], we employ a timeout of 5 min per approach on each learning problem. ECII and ELTL do not support a timeout configuration and were therefore executed with their default settings. On the one side, the results in Table 4 suggest that NCES2 significantly outperforms search-based approaches in runtime on all datasets as it synthesizes a solution in less than a second on average. The standard deviation of NCES2's prediction runtime is zero because it computes solutions for all learning problems at the same time as a single forward pass of a batch of inputs. This leads to the same prediction time for all learning problems and therefore a zero standard deviation. We employed the Wilcoxon Rank Sum Test to check for performance difference significance. The significance level is 5% and the null hypothesis that the compared

---
[5] https://github.com/dice-group/NCES2.

**Table 4.** Evaluation results per dataset. The star (*) indicates statistically significant differences between the best search-based and the best synthesis-based approaches. Underlined values are the second best. Here, NCES2 uses the embedding model ConEx.

| | $\mathbf{F_1}$ (%) | | | |
| --- | --- | --- | --- | --- |
| | Carcinogenesis | Mutagenesis | Semantic Bible | Vicodi |
| CELOE | $29.24 \pm 39.22$ | $74.46 \pm 37.59$ | $\mathbf{88.60^*} \pm 19.50$ | $22.63 \pm 35.21$ |
| EvoLearner | $89.34 \pm 15.80$ | $\mathbf{95.37} \pm 8.02$ | $\underline{88.38} \pm 12.50$ | $76.99 \pm 26.37$ |
| ELTL | $14.46 \pm 28.48$ | $36.33 \pm 34.98$ | $35.21 \pm 31.74$ | $8.58 \pm 22.94$ |
| ECII | $18.91 \pm 31.46$ | $34.33 \pm 31.53$ | $32.79 \pm 32.18$ | $29.20 \pm 30.81$ |
| $\text{NCES2}_{m=32}$ | $83.56 \pm 33.11$ | $76.79 \pm 38.61$ | $70.77 \pm 33.73$ | $82.36 \pm 32.05$ |
| $\text{NCES2}_{m=64}$ | $83.92 \pm 33.16$ | $78.25 \pm 37.18$ | $71.77 \pm 34.03$ | $82.64 \pm 31.28$ |
| $\text{NCES2}_{m=128}$ | $86.06 \pm 32.63$ | $73.21 \pm 38.31$ | $69.95 \pm 36.13$ | $83.50 \pm 30.85$ |
| $\text{NCES2}_{m=\{32,64\}}$ | $\underline{92.13} \pm 24.61$ | $83.09 \pm 34.04$ | $79.40 \pm 32.22$ | $\underline{90.67} \pm 24.07$ |
| $\text{NCES2}_{m=\{32,128\}}$ | $91.01 \pm 26.80$ | $\underline{86.33} \pm 31.54$ | $77.80 \pm 34.52$ | $87.68 \pm 26.48$ |
| $\text{NCES2}_{m=\{64,128\}}$ | $\mathbf{92.57^*} \pm 24.08$ | $84.18 \pm 32.30$ | $78.92 \pm 32.84$ | $86.49 \pm 29.33$ |
| $\text{NCES2}_{m=\{32,64,128\}}$ | $91.29 \pm 24.96$ | $85.12 \pm 32.28$ | $77.00 \pm 35.25$ | $\mathbf{91.06^*} \pm 23.97$ |
| | **Accuracy** (%) | | | |
| | Carcinogenesis | Mutagenesis | Semantic Bible | Vicodi |
| CELOE | $62.96 \pm 22.56$ | $87.33 \pm 17.80$ | $95.85 \pm 8.71$ | $78.59 \pm 15.83$ |
| EvoLearner | $\mathbf{99.68^*} \pm 0.81$ | $\mathbf{99.52^*} \pm 2.17$ | $\mathbf{97.43} \pm 4.74$ | $\mathbf{97.79^*} \pm 6.74$ |
| ELTL | $19.37 \pm 32.31$ | $40.58 \pm 35.33$ | $39.40 \pm 29.92$ | $41.67 \pm 44.29$ |
| ECII | $27.17 \pm 38.40$ | $32.52 \pm 33.31$ | $29.06 \pm 33.37$ | $71.05 \pm 39.43$ |
| $\text{NCES2}_{m=32}$ | $93.86 \pm 19.54$ | $88.77 \pm 25.13$ | $88.03 \pm 20.40$ | $93.87 \pm 21.39$ |
| $\text{NCES2}_{m=64}$ | $95.16 \pm 17.13$ | $88.95 \pm 26.21$ | $85.89 \pm 24.03$ | $95.21 \pm 18.43$ |
| $\text{NCES2}_{m=128}$ | $92.56 \pm 22.01$ | $89.09 \pm 24.20$ | $88.99 \pm 20.81$ | $96.29 \pm 16.11$ |
| $\text{NCES2}_{m=\{32,64\}}$ | $95.64 \pm 18.42$ | $90.75 \pm 24.83$ | $88.32 \pm 24.55$ | $96.04 \pm 17.30$ |
| $\text{NCES2}_{m=\{32,128\}}$ | $95.15 \pm 16.76$ | $\underline{92.22} \pm 22.65$ | $\underline{91.13} \pm 20.23$ | $95.93 \pm 17.39$ |
| $\text{NCES2}_{m=\{64,128\}}$ | $\underline{95.77} \pm 17.03$ | $90.81 \pm 23.69$ | $90.45 \pm 21.98$ | $95.78 \pm 18.67$ |
| $\text{NCES2}_{m=\{32,64,128\}}$ | $95.39 \pm 18.33$ | $90.55 \pm 24.19$ | $88.99 \pm 24.11$ | $\underline{96.43} \pm 17.01$ |
| | **Runtime** (sec.) | | | |
| | Carcinogenesis | Mutagenesis | Semantic Bible | Vicodi |
| CELOE | $268.90 \pm 116.04$ | $165.27 \pm 145.11$ | $172.04 \pm 140.27$ | $334.99 \pm 43.87$ |
| EvoLearner | $62.21 \pm 26.11$ | $70.77 \pm 47.53$ | $18.44 \pm 5.53$ | $236.92 \pm 80.90$ |
| ELTL | $26.15 \pm 2.11$ | $15.83 \pm 16.56$ | $4.73 \pm 0.98$ | $335.90 \pm 205.39$ |
| ECII | $25.62 \pm 6.11$ | $20.40 \pm 4.00$ | $6.73 \pm 1.67$ | $37.12 \pm 25.12$ |
| $\text{NCES2}_{m=32}$ | $\mathbf{0.02^*} \pm 0.00$ | $\mathbf{0.02^*} \pm 0.00$ | $\mathbf{0.01^*} \pm 0.00$ | $\mathbf{0.03^*} \pm 0.00$ |
| $\text{NCES2}_{m=64}$ | $\underline{0.03} \pm 0.00$ | $\underline{0.03} \pm 0.00$ | $\underline{0.01} \pm 0.00$ | $\underline{0.03} \pm 0.00$ |
| $\text{NCES2}_{m=128}$ | $0.03 \pm 0.00$ | $0.03 \pm 0.00$ | $0.02 \pm 0.00$ | $0.04 \pm 0.00$ |
| $\text{NCES2}_{m=\{32,64\}}$ | $0.05 \pm 0.00$ | $0.05 \pm 0.00$ | $0.03 \pm 0.00$ | $0.06 \pm 0.00$ |
| $\text{NCES2}_{m=\{32,128\}}$ | $0.06 \pm 0.00$ | $0.06 \pm 0.00$ | $0.03 \pm 0.00$ | $0.06 \pm 0.00$ |
| $\text{NCES2}_{m=\{64,128\}}$ | $0.06 \pm 0.00$ | $0.06 \pm 0.00$ | $0.03 \pm 0.00$ | $0.07 \pm 0.00$ |
| $\text{NCES2}_{m=\{32,64,128\}}$ | $0.09 \pm 0.00$ | $0.09 \pm 0.00$ | $0.05 \pm 0.00$ | $0.10 \pm 0.00$ |

**Table 5.** Solution per approach for learning problems $LP_1$, $LP_2$, $LP_3$, and $LP_4$ presented in Sect. 4.1. We consider the three best approaches NCES2, CELOE, and EvoLearner.

| | Prediction | $F_1$ (%) |
|---|---|---|
| | CELOE | |
| $LP_1$ | Man | 99.70 |
| $LP_2$ | ¬Bond | 0.72 |
| $LP_3$ | Bond ⊔ (Atom ⊓ (¬Carbon-25)) | 99.79 |
| $LP_4$ | Flavour ⊔ (¬War) | 1.14 |
| | EvoLearner | |
| $LP_1$ | Man | 99.70 |
| $LP_2$ | Sulfur-74 ⊔ (∃ drosophila_slrl.{True}) | 83.33 |
| $LP_3$ | Atom ⊔ (∃ inBond.Atom) | 99.78 |
| $LP_4$ | Intellectual-Construct | 92.59 |
| | NCES2 | |
| $LP_1$ | Man | 99.70 |
| $LP_2$ | Fluorine-92 ⊔ Sulfur-74 ⊔ (∃ drosophila_rt.{False}) | 100.00 |
| $LP_3$ | (Atom ⊓ (Oxygen-45 ⊔ (¬Oxygen))) ⊔ (∃ inBond.(¬Carbon-10)) | 97.10 |
| $LP_4$ | Measurable-Trend ⊔ (∃ related.(Idea ⊔ Uprising)) | 100.00 |

quantities share the same distribution. We also achieve better performance in terms of F-measure on large datasets (Carcinogenesis and Vicodi) while remaining the second best on the Mutagenesis dataset with $NCES2_{m=\{32,128\}}$ behind EvoLearner. Meanwhile, we observe a poor performance on the Semantic Bible dataset with an average F-measure of 79.40% ($NCES2_{m=\{32,64\}}$) compared to 88.60% for CELOE. We attribute this to the data hunger of deep learning models since Semantic Bible is the smallest dataset with only 724 individuals and 48 atomic classes (cf. Table 2).

On the other side, Table 5 presents the predictive performance of the three best approaches NCES2, EvoLearner, and CELOE on the learning problems introduced in Sect. 4.1. NCES2 outperforms its competitors in F-measure on $LP_2$ and $LP_4$ as it computes the exact solutions for these learning problems. CELOE fails to find suitable solutions and achieves 0.72% and 1.14% F-measure on $LP_2$ and $LP_4$, respectively. EvoLearner computes approximate solutions with 83.33% and 92.59% F-measure for $LP_2$ and $LP_4$, respectively. All three approaches achieve comparable performance on $LP_1$ and $LP_3$.

The effectiveness of NCES2 is demonstrated by its ability to compute (i.e. synthesize) expressions it has never seen during training, e.g., $LP_2$ and $LP_4$. We hence believe that NCES2 should serve as a robust alternative on large knowledge bases where search-based approaches are prohibitively slow.

**Table 6.** Comparison of NCES2 and NCES on test datasets. NCES2$^{*}$ and NCES2$^{\mathcal{ALC}}$ are ablations of NCES2. The first ablation corresponds to NCES2 without the improved data generator. The second ablation corresponds to NCES2 trained on the same data as NCES, i.e., data in $\mathcal{ALC}$ on which we apply the improved data generator. All approaches use 32 inducing points and the ConEx embedding model.

| | $\mathbf{F}_1$ (%) | | | |
| --- | --- | --- | --- | --- |
| | NCES2 | NCES2$^{*}$ | NCES2$^{\mathcal{ALC}}$ | NCES |
| Carcinogenesis | **83.56*** $\pm$ 33.11 | 78.52 $\pm$ 36.72 | 71.24 $\pm$ 38.43 | 67.86 $\pm$ 41.47 |
| Mutagenesis | **76.79*** $\pm$ 38.61 | 52.70 $\pm$ 44.07 | 53.08 $\pm$ 43.78 | 68.20 $\pm$ 41.70 |
| Semantic Bible | **70.77*** $\pm$ 33.73 | 66.33 $\pm$ 37.02 | 64.33 $\pm$ 37.15 | 63.61 $\pm$ 35.60 |
| Vicodi | **82.36*** $\pm$ 32.05 | 75.86 $\pm$ 34.50 | 52.57 $\pm$ 40.85 | 50.28 $\pm$ 43.68 |

*NCES2 vs. NCES.* To quantify the main differences between NCES2 and current NCES approaches, we compare them on the test sets (the 100 unseen learning problems on each knowledge base). Some of these learning problems have solutions in $\mathcal{ALC}$ while others can only be solved in $\mathcal{ALCHIQ}(\mathcal{D})$. Both approaches use the ConEx embedding model, and the Set Transformer architecture with 32 inducing points as the synthesizer. The results given by the two approaches are reported in Table 6. From the table, we can observe that NCES2 significantly outperforms NCES on all datasets with an absolute difference of up to 32.08% F-measure on the Vicodi dataset. These large differences in performance show the superiority of NCES2 over NCES; in particular, they reveal the impact of the improved training data generator and the expressiveness of $\mathcal{ALCHIQ}(\mathcal{D})$ as an ablation of any of these leads to a decrease in performance, see the results achieved by NCES2$^{*}$ and NCES2$^{\mathcal{ALC}}$ in Table 6. Nevertheless, the two approaches have comparable prediction time. NCES2 should therefore be preferred over NCES on most class expression learning tasks.

## 6    Conclusion and Future Work

We proposed an extension of NCES, a recent and scalable approach for class expression learning in $\mathcal{ALC}$. Our approach is called NCES2 and it supports the description logic $\mathcal{ALCHIQ}(\mathcal{D})$. NCES2 encodes positive and negative examples into real-valued vectors via its embedding model component, and uses a Set Transformer model to synthesize class expressions. This way, we reduce the expensive task of class expression learning, which is usually regarded as a search problem in an infinite conceptual space, to additions and multiplications in vector spaces. Our experiments demonstrated that NCES2 significantly outperforms all search-based approaches in runtime while synthesizing high-quality solutions for most learning problems. Moreover, NCES2 outperforms current NCES instances w.r.t. the F-measure of the computed solutions. NCES2 should therefore serve as a strong alternative to existing approaches especially when many learning problems are to be solved on a single knowledge base.

Currently, the training data generator in NCES2 uses an OWL reasoner to compute instances of the generated expressions. This is impractical for large knowledge bases such as DBpedia [1]. In the future, we will investigate ways to replace the reasoner by a SPARQL query-based method, such as the one by Bin et al. [3], to scale NCES2 to large datasets.

# References

1. Auer, S., Bizer, C., Kobilarov, G., Lehmann, J., Cyganiak, R., Ives, Z.: DBpedia: a nucleus for a web of open data. In: Aberer, K., et al. (eds.) ASWC/ISWC -2007. LNCS, vol. 4825, pp. 722–735. Springer, Heidelberg (2007). https://doi.org/10. 1007/978-3-540-76298-0_52
2. Bergstra, J., Bengio, Y.: Random search for hyper-parameter optimization. J. Mach. Learn. Res. **13**, 281–305 (2012)
3. Bin, S., Bühmann, L., Lehmann, J., Ngonga Ngomo, A.C.: Towards sparql-based induction for large-scale RDF data sets. In: ECAI 2016, pp. 1551–1552. IOS Press (2016)
4. Bin, S., Westphal, P., Lehmann, J., Ngonga, A.: Implementing scalable structured machine learning for big data in the sake project. In: 2017 IEEE International Conference on Big Data (Big Data), pp. 1400–1407. IEEE (2017)
5. Bordes, A., Glorot, X., Weston, J., Bengio, Y.: A semantic matching energy function for learning with multi-relational data - application to word-sense disambiguation. Mach. Learn. **94**(2), 233–259 (2014)
6. Bordes, A., Usunier, N., García-Durán, A., Weston, J., Yakhnenko, O.: Translating embeddings for modeling multi-relational data. In: NIPS, pp. 2787–2795 (2013)
7. Bühmann, L., Lehmann, J., Westphal, P.: Dl-learner-a framework for inductive learning on the semantic web. J. Web Semant. **39**, 15–24 (2016)
8. Chen, M., Zaniolo, C.: Learning multi-faceted knowledge graph embeddings for natural language processing. In: IJCAI, pp. 5169–5170 (2017)
9. Cho, K., van Merrienboer, B., Bahdanau, D., Bengio, Y.: On the properties of neural machine translation: encoder-decoder approaches. In: SSST@EMNLP, pp. 103–111. Association for Computational Linguistics (2014)
10. Dai, Y., Wang, S., Xiong, N.N., Guo, W.: A survey on knowledge graph embedding: approaches, applications and benchmarks. Electronics **9**(5), 750 (2020)
11. Demir, C., Ngomo, A.-C.N.: Convolutional complex knowledge graph embeddings. In: Verborgh, R., et al. (eds.) ESWC 2021. LNCS, vol. 12731, pp. 409–424. Springer, Cham (2021). https://doi.org/10.1007/978-3-030-77385-4_24
12. Dong, X., Yu, Z., Cao, W., Shi, Y., Ma, Q.: A survey on ensemble learning. Front. Comput. Sci. **14**(2), 241–258 (2020)
13. Fanizzi, N., d'Amato, C., Esposito, F.: DL-FOIL concept learning in description logics. In: Železný, F., Lavrač, N. (eds.) ILP 2008. LNCS (LNAI), vol. 5194, pp. 107–121. Springer, Heidelberg (2008). https://doi.org/10.1007/978-3-540-85928-4_12
14. Heindorf, S., et al.: Evolearner: learning description logics with evolutionary algorithms. In: WWW, pp. 818–828. ACM (2022)
15. Kingma, D.P., Ba, J.: Adam: a method for stochastic optimization. arXiv preprint arXiv:1412.6980 (2014)
16. Konev, B., Ozaki, A., Wolter, F.: A model for learning description logic ontologies based on exact learning. In: AAAI, pp. 1008–1015. AAAI Press (2016)

17. Kouagou, N.J., Heindorf, S., Demir, C., Ngomo, A.N.: Learning concept lengths accelerates concept learning in ALC. In: Groth, P., et al. (eds.) ESWC 2022. LNCS, vol. 13261, pp. 236–252. Springer, Cham (2022). https://doi.org/10.1007/978-3-031-06981-9_14
18. Kouagou, N.J., Heindorf, S., Demir, C., Ngonga Ngomo, A.C.: Neural class expression synthesis. In: Pesquita, C., et al. (eds.) ESWC 2023. LNCS, vol. 13870, pp. 209–226. Springer, Cham (2023). https://doi.org/10.1007/978-3-031-33455-9_13
19. Krech, D.: RDFlib: a Python library for working with RDF (2006). https://github.com/RDFLib/rdflib
20. Lee, J., Lee, Y., Kim, J., Kosiorek, A., Choi, S., Teh, Y.W.: Set transformer: a framework for attention-based permutation-invariant neural networks. In: International Conference on Machine Learning, pp. 3744–3753. PMLR (2019)
21. Lehmann, J.: Dl-learner: learning concepts in description logics. J. Mach. Learn. Res. (2009)
22. Lehmann, J.: Learning OWL Class Expressions, vol. 22. IOS Press, Amsterdam (2010)
23. Lehmann, J., Auer, S., Bühmann, L., Tramp, S.: Class expression learning for ontology engineering. J. Web Semant. (2011)
24. Lehmann, J., Hitzler, P.: Concept learning in description logics using refinement operators. Mach. Learn. **78** (2010)
25. Lehmann, J., Völker, J.: Perspectives on Ontology Learning, vol. 18. IOS Press, Amsterdam (2014)
26. Nagypál, G.: History ontology building: the technical view. Human. Comput. Cult. Herit. 207 (2005)
27. Nardi, D., Brachman, R.J., et al.: An introduction to description logics. In: Description Logic Handbook, vol. 1 (2003)
28. Nickel, M., Tresp, V., Kriegel, H.: Factorizing yago: scalable machine learning for linked data. In: Proceedings of WWW (2012)
29. Ozaki, A.: Learning description logic ontologies: five approaches. where do they stand? KI-Künstliche Intelligenz (2020)
30. Rizzo, G., Fanizzi, N., d'Amato, C.: Class expression induction as concept space exploration: from dl-foil to dl-focl. Future Gener. Comput. Syst. (2020)
31. Sagi, O., Rokach, L.: Ensemble learning: a survey. Wiley Interdisc. Rev. Data Min. Knowl. Discov. **8**(4), e1249 (2018)
32. Sarker, M.K., Hitzler, P.: Efficient concept induction for description logics. In: Proceedings of AAAI (2019)
33. Schmidt-Schauß, M., Smolka, G.: Attributive concept descriptions with complements. Artif. Intell. 1–26 (1991)
34. Srivastava, N., Hinton, G., Krizhevsky, A., Sutskever, I., Salakhutdinov, R.: Dropout: a simple way to prevent neural networks from overfitting. J. Mach. Learn. Res. **15**(1), 1929–1958 (2014)
35. Tran, T.L., Ha, Q.T., Hoang, T.L.G., Nguyen, L.A., Nguyen, H.S.: Bisimulation-based concept learning in description logics. Fund. Inform. **133**(2–3), 287–303 (2014)
36. Wang, Q., Mao, Z., Wang, B., Guo, L.: Knowledge graph embedding: a survey of approaches and applications. IEEE Trans. Knowl. Data Eng. (2017)
37. Wang, Z., Li, J., Liu, Z., Tang, J.: Text-enhanced representation learning for knowledge graph. In: Proceedings of IJCAI (2016)
38. Westphal, P., Bühmann, L., Bin, S., Jabeen, H., Lehmann, J.: SML-bench-a benchmarking framework for structured machine learning. Semant. Web **10**(2), 231–245 (2019)

39. Wu, Y., Schuster, M., Chen, Z., et al.: Google's neural machine translation system: bridging the gap between human and machine translation. arXiv preprint arXiv:1609.08144 (2016)
40. Xie, R., Liu, Z., Jia, J., Luan, H., Sun, M.: Representation learning of knowledge graphs with entity descriptions. In: Proceedings of AAAI (2016)
41. Yang, B., Yih, S.W.t., He, X., Gao, J., Deng, L.: Embedding entities and relations for learning and inference in knowledge bases. In: Proceedings of the International Conference on Learning Representations (ICLR) 2015 (2015)
42. Zaheer, M., Kottur, S., Ravanbakhsh, S., Poczos, B., Salakhutdinov, R.R., Smola, A.J.: Deep sets. In: Advances in Neural Information Processing Systems, vol. 30 (2017)
43. Zhang, F., Yuan, N.J., Lian, D., Xie, X., Ma, W.Y.: Collaborative knowledge base embedding for recommender systems. In: Proceedings of the 22nd ACM SIGKDD International Conference on Knowledge Discovery and Data Mining, pp. 353–362 (2016)
44. Zhang, J., He, T., Sra, S., Jadbabaie, A.: Why gradient clipping accelerates training: a theoretical justification for adaptivity. arXiv preprint arXiv:1905.11881 (2019)

# Deep Explainable Relational Reinforcement Learning: A Neuro-Symbolic Approach

Rishi Hazra[(✉)] and Luc De Raedt

Centre for Applied Autonomous Sensor Systems (AASS), Örebro University,
Örebro, Sweden
{rishi.hazra,luc.de-raedt}@oru.se

**Abstract.** Despite its successes, Deep Reinforcement Learning (DRL) yields non-interpretable policies. Moreover, since DRL does not exploit symbolic relational representations, it has difficulties in coping with structural changes in its environment (such as increasing the number of objects). Meanwhile, Relational Reinforcement Learning inherits the relational representations from symbolic planning to learn reusable policies. However, it has so far been unable to scale up and exploit the power of deep neural networks. We propose Deep Explainable Relational Reinforcement Learning (DERRL), a framework that exploits the best of both – *neural* and *symbolic* worlds. By resorting to a neuro-symbolic approach, DERRL combines relational representations and constraints from symbolic planning with deep learning to extract interpretable policies. These policies are in the form of logical rules that explain why each decision (or action) is arrived at. Through several experiments, in setups like the Countdown Game, Blocks World, Gridworld, Traffic, and Mingrid, we show that the policies learned by DERRL are adaptable to varying configurations and environmental changes.

**Keywords:** Neuro-Symbolic AI · Relational Reinforcement Learning · Deep Reinforcement Learning · Explainability

## 1 Introduction

Deep Reinforcement Learning (DRL) [1] has gained great success in many domains. However, so far, it has had limited success in relational domains, which are typically used in symbolic planning [34]. In the prototypical blocks world game (Fig. 1), one goal is to place block $a$ on block $b$. An obvious plan for achieving this is to *unstack* the blocks until both blocks $a$ and $b$ are at the top, upon which block $a$ can be moved atop block $b$. Standard DRL approaches struggle to adapt to out-of-domain data, such as placing block $c$ on $d$, or applying the learned strategies to changes in the stack size or the number of stacks, thus failing to learn generalized policies. Furthermore, the black-box nature of the learned policies makes it difficult to interpret action choices, especially in domains involving

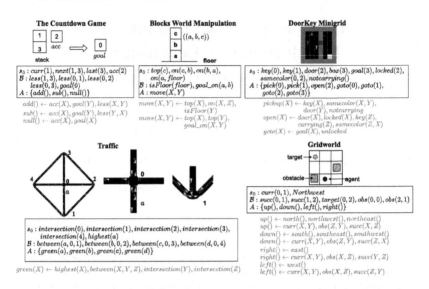

**Fig. 1.** Learned rules in all environments. [Row 1] left to right. Countdown Game: select operations (addition, subtraction, null) to make accumulated = target; Blocks World: place a specific block on another; DoorKey: unlock a door with a matching key to reach a goal. [Row 2] Traffic: minimize traffic at grid intersections. The figure shows a 5-agent grid with intersections 0 and 1 connected by lane $a$; Gridworld: navigate a grid to reach the goal. Descriptions in Sect. 5.1.

transparency and safety [16, 27, 38]. Understanding a machine's decision-making is crucial for human operators to eliminate irrational reasoning [14, 40].

Relational Reinforcement Learning (RRL) [5, 39] combines symbolic planning and reinforcement learning and has origins in Statistical Relational AI and Inductive Logic Programming (ILP) [3, 33]. RRL uses logic programs to represent interpretable policies that are similar to symbolic planning languages [8, 12, 13]. These policies use relations and objects, rather than specific states and actions, allowing agents to reason about their actions at a higher level of abstraction, and applying the learned knowledge to different situations. Earlier RRL approaches were purely symbolic [4, 5, 20, 32], searching policy spaces guided by performance estimates, but did not exploit deep learning advancements and were not robust to noisy data. Recent approaches [45] use neural networks for scalability and improved internal representations, but learned policies are not human-readable.

We introduce **D**eep **E**xplainable **R**elational **R**einforcement **L**earning (DERRL: neural DRL + symbolic RRL), a neuro-symbolic RRL approach that combines the strengths of neural (differentiability and representational power) and symbolic methods (generalizability and interpretability) while addressing their respective shortcomings. Concretely, DERRL uses a neural network to search the space of policies represented using First-Order Logic (FOL)-based rules[1]. Like other ILP methods, our framework provides interpretable solutions. However, instead of using search-based methods, we leverage the representational capacity of

---

[1] DERRL uses a relational representation akin to Quinlan's FOIL [36] with background knowledge comprising ground facts and non-recursive Datalog-formulated rules.

neural networks to generate interpretations of actions (called rules), while entirely bypassing the need to interpret the network itself. Specifically, we propose a parameterized rule generation framework where a neural network learns to generate a set of generalized *discriminative* rules that are representations of the policy. For e.g., in the blocks world game in Fig. 1, the two rules corresponding to *move* action are: $move(X,Y) \leftarrow top(X), on(X,Z), isFloor(Y)$, which triggers an *unstacking* process, and $move(X,Y) \leftarrow top(X), top(Y), goal\_on(X,Y)$, which puts block $a$ on $b$ when both are top blocks in the stacks. Note, that the same rules apply for a new goal ($goal\_on(c,d)$) or when blocks increase to 10.

Additionally, we formulate a semantic loss [42] to guide the rule learning and restrict the hypothesis space. This loss uses a differentiable relaxation of semantic refinement [2] to enforce semantic constraints on rule structure, allowing users to encode background knowledge as axioms to mitigate rule redundancy. For e.g., in the rule $r \leftarrow less(X,Y), less(Y,Z), less(X,Z)$, due to the transitive relation $less(X,Z) \leftarrow less(X,Y), less(Y,Z)$, the term $less(X,Z)$ is redundant. DERRL enables predefining such knowledge as axioms, penalizing models that violate them. We compare our framework with Neural Logic Reinforcement Learning (NLRL) [19] which uses FOL to represent RL policies and is based on Differentiable Inductive Logic Programming ($\partial$ILP) [7]. Like DERRL, NLRL uses policy gradients to train a differentiable ILP module by assigning *learnable weights to rules* enhancing policy interpretability and adaptability across varied problem configurations. Due to the potentially exponential number of rules, finding the optimal set is challenging. Instead, we assign *learnable weights to member terms* – learning the best membership of rules. We demonstrate DERRL's advantages in terms of computational efficiency, accuracy, and semantic constraint enforcement. **Contributions.** (i) A neuro-symbolic framework **DERRL** for learning interpretable RL policies in on-policy, model-free settings, demonstrating their adaptability to environmental changes; (ii) A differentiable relaxation of semantic refinement for guiding rule generation and constraining the hypothesis space.

## 2    Related Works

**Integrating Symbolic Planning and RL.** Recent research has sought to merge symbolic planning with DRL to improve data efficiency and performance, as seen in works like PEORL [44], RePReL [24], and SDRL [30]. These approaches aim to integrate a high-level planner that suggests sub-goals to be executed by a low-level DRL model, thus relying on predefined environment dynamics, such as high-level action schemas with pre and postconditions. DERRL differs from planning-based methods as it is purely a RL approach, i.e. it does not have access to precise handcrafted action schemas or the reward function, and instead learns suitable control policies through trial-and-error interactions with the environment. Therefore, we only compare DERRL with other RL baselines. **Explainable RL.** Previous studies on interpretable RL have utilized decision trees for their interpretability. Standard decision trees consist of nested if-then rules, are non-differentiable, and cannot be trained using gradient descent methods. The online nature of RL problems, combined with the non-stationarity introduced by an improving policy, presents additional challenges for decision trees in an interactive environment. While entirely re-learning decision trees is a possible but inefficient solution [6], recent studies have explored the use of differentiable functions in decision trees [9]. Differentiable Decision Trees have also been adapted for the RL framework [28,37], although their performance does not match that of deep neural networks. **Concurrent Works.** Our work on integrating differentiable logic programming into RL is concurrent with efforts such as NLRL [19] and dNL-ILP [35]. While dNL-ILP lacks goal generalization, we use the recent NLRL as our baseline. Recent research has also employed Graph Neural Networks [23] to capture relational representations [10,11] with applications to DRL [18] demonstrating zero-shot generalization to varying problem sizes. DERRL additionally learns interpretable policies. **Adjusting Language Bias** The possible hypothesis space expands exponentially with input space, necessitating user adjustments to language biases based on domain knowledge. Relational learning systems use declarative bias via semantic refinement [2]. Differentiable rule learning methods like $\partial$ILP [7] and NLRL [19] use rule templates to limit rule body atoms to 2. However, these methods overlook background knowledge and face redundancies. DERRL mitigates redundancies and shrinks the search space through a differentiable relaxation of semantic refinement.

## 3    Preliminaries

### 3.1    Logic Programming

Logic Programming [29] rules are written as **clauses** of the form $\alpha \leftarrow \alpha_1, \ldots, \alpha_m$ composed of a **head** atom $\alpha$ and a **body** $\alpha_1, \ldots, \alpha_m$. These clauses are defined using the standard *if-then* rules, wherein, if the body is satisfied, the head is true. Each **atom** is a tuple $p(v_1, \ldots, v_n)$ where $p$ is a n-ary **predicate** and $v_1, \ldots, v_n$ are either **variables** or **constants**. A **ground** atom is one that contains only constants. A predicate can either be **extensional** when it is defined by a set of ground atoms, or **target** (intensional) when it is defined by a set of clauses.

An **alphabet** $\mathcal{L}$ is defined by the tuple $\mathcal{L} := (\mathrm{P}_{\mathrm{tar}}, \mathrm{P}_{\mathrm{ext}}, arity, C, V)$ where, $\mathrm{P}_{\mathrm{tar}}$ is a set of target predicates, $\mathrm{P}_{\mathrm{ext}}$ is a set of extensional predicates, $arity :$ $\mathrm{P}_{\mathrm{ext}} \cup \mathrm{P}_{\mathrm{tar}} \mapsto \mathbb{N}$ is the number of arguments (variables or constants) that the predicate can take, $C$ is a set of constants and $V$ is a set of variables allowed in the clause. For the blocks world game in Fig. 1, $\mathrm{P}_{\mathrm{tar}} = \{move/2\}$, $\mathrm{P}_{\mathrm{ext}} = \{top/1, on/2, goal\_on/2, isFloor/1\}$, $V = \{X, Y, Z\}$, $C = \{a, b, c\}$.

### 3.2    Relational Markov Decision Process

We model our problem as a Relational MDP (RMDP) given by the tuple $\mathcal{E} := (S, \mathcal{B}, A, \delta, r, \gamma)$ which is just like a regular MDP, but with relational states and actions. Here, $S$ is a set of states, where each state is represented as a set of ground atoms consisting of predicates in $\mathrm{P}_{\mathrm{ext}}$ and constants in $C$; $\mathcal{B}$ is the background knowledge also represented in form of ground atoms consisting of predicates and constants, but unlike the state, it remains fixed over the episode; $A$ is a set of actions consisting of ground atoms from predicates in $\mathrm{P_{tar}}$ and constants in $C$; $\delta : S \times A \mapsto S$ is an **unknown** transition function; $r : S \times A \mapsto R$ is an **unknown** real-valued reward function; $\gamma$ is the discount factor.

In blocks world (Fig. 1), for the tuple $((a, b, c))^2$, the initial state $s_0$ and $\mathcal{B}$ are $\{top(c), on(c, b), on(b, a), on(a, floor)\}$ and $\{isFloor(floor), goal\_on(a, b)\}$, respectively. The actions are $move(X, Y)$ where variables $X$ and $Y$ can be substituted with constants in $C$. Although underlying models often use logical transition and reward rules [21], our approach is model-free, so we ignore them here.

### 3.3    Problem Statement

**Given**, a tuple $(\mathcal{L}, \mathcal{E})$ where $\mathcal{L}$ is an alphabet, and $\mathcal{E}$ is an RMDP;
**Find** an optimal policy $\pi_\theta : S \cup \mathcal{B} \mapsto A$ as a set of clauses (also called **rules**) that maximizes the expected reward $\mathbb{E}_{\tau \sim \pi_\theta}[R_\tau]$, where $R_\tau := \sum_{k=t+1}^{T-1} \gamma^{k-t-1} R_k$. Here, an episode trajectory is denoted by $\tau$.

More formally, the rules are selected from the hypotheses space, which is the set of all possible clauses. The head atom of each such rule is an action and the body is the definition of the action. As shown in Fig. 1, a rule for $move(X, Y)$ in the blocks world environment is given as $move(X, Y) \leftarrow top(X), on(X, Z),$ $isFloor(Y)$ which states that $move(X, Y)$ is triggered when the rule definition (i.e., the body) is satisfied. Thus, if the policy selects the action $move(c, floor)$, one can quickly inspect the body to find out **why** that action was taken. The rules are *discriminative* (i.e. that help select the correct action by distinguishing it from alternative actions) and together provide an interpretation of the policy. A set of rules is learned for each action. Once trained, the rules for actions do not change and the rule body decides which action should be triggered at each time-step. In what follows, we provide a detailed explanation of rule generation and inference for each time-step of an episode. For simplicity, we expunge the time-step notation (for e.g., state at $t^{th}$ time-step $s_t$ is now $s$).

## 4    Proposed Approach

Consider an alphabet $\mathcal{L}$ where $\mathrm{P_{tar}} = \{r/0, s/0\}, \mathrm{P_{ext}} = \{p/1, q/2\}, V = \{X, Y\}, C = \{a, b\}$. The set of all ground atoms $G$ formed from the predicates in $\mathrm{P_{ext}}$ and constants in $C$ is $\{p(a), p(b), q(a, a), q(a, b), q(b, a), q(b, b)\}$. We represent each ground atom $g_j \in G$ along with its index $j$ in Table 1.

Recall, that both state $s$ and background knowledge $\mathcal{B}$ are represented using ground atoms. Given a state $s = \{p(a), q(a, a), q(a, b)\}$ at each time-step, and an empty background knowledge $\mathcal{B}$, we encode it to a state vector $\boldsymbol{v}$, such that each element $v_j = 1$ if $g_j \in \{s, \mathcal{B}\}$ (i.e. if the current state $s$ or the background

---

[2] Here, the outer tuple denotes stacks and the inner tuples denote the blocks in the stack. For e.g., $((a, b), (c, d))$ has two stacks: $(a, b)$ is stack 1 and $(c, d)$ is stack 2.

**Table 1.** Table of all ground atoms $G$ and their indices $j$.

| $j$ | 0 | 1 | 2 | 3 | 4 | 5 | |
|---|---|---|---|---|---|---|---|
| $g_j$ | $p(a)$ | $p(b)$ | $q(a,a)$ | $q(a,b)$ | $q(b,a)$ | $q(b,b)$ | $s = \{p(a), q(a,a), q(a,b)\}$ |
| $v_j$ | 1 | 0 | 1 | 1 | 0 | 0 | $v = [1,0,1,1,0,0]$ |

**Table 2.** All atoms $K$, their indices $j$, the generated rule vectors $b^r, b^s$, and corresponding probability vectors $P^r, P^s$ for target actions $P_{tar} = r/0, s/0$.

| $j$ | 0 | 1 | 2 | 3 | 4 | 5 | |
|---|---|---|---|---|---|---|---|
| $k_j$ | $p(X)$ | $p(Y)$ | $q(X,X)$ | $q(X,Y)$ | $q(Y,X)$ | $q(Y,Y)$ | |
| $b^r_j$ | 0 | 1 | 0 | 0 | 1 | 0 | $r \leftarrow p(Y), q(Y,X)$ |
| $P^r_j$ | 0.1 | 0.8 | 0.3 | 0.4 | 0.7 | 0.2 | $w^r = [0.8, 0.7]^\top$ |
| $b^s_j$ | 1 | 0 | 0 | 0 | 0 | 1 | $s \leftarrow p(X), q(Y,Y)$ |
| $P^s_j$ | 0.6 | 0.3 | 0.4 | 0.2 | 0.1 | 0.9 | $w^s = [0.6, 0.9]^\top$ |

knowledge $\mathcal{B}$ contains the ground atom $g_j$), else 0. Let us now consider the set of all atoms $K$ formed from the predicates in $P_{ext}$ and variables in $V$ (instead of the constants in $C$). Table 2 lists the atoms $k_j \in K$ and the corresponding $v$.

We represent rules using rule vectors. As shown in Table 2, the rule vector for each action $i \in A$ is given as $b^i \in \{0,1\}^m$, where $m = |K|$ (i.e. the cardinality of the set of all atoms formed from the predicates in $P_{ext}$ and variables in $V$). Here, $b^i_j = 1$, if the $j^{th}$ atom is in the body of the $i^{th}$ rule. From Table 2, $b^r = [0,1,0,0,1,0]^\top$ corresponds to the rule $r \leftarrow p(Y), q(Y,X)$.

We impose the Object Identity (OI) assumption [22] which states that during grounding and unification, distinct variables must be mapped to distinct constants. For instance, ground rules for $r \leftarrow p(Y), q(Y,X)$ are $r \leftarrow p(b), q(b,a)$ and $r \leftarrow p(a), q(a,b)$ under substitutions $\phi_0 = \{a/X, b/Y\}$ and $\phi_1 = \{b/X, a/Y\}$, respectively, but a substitution $\phi_2 = \{a/X, a/Y\}$ is not allowed. Without loss of generality, one can model nullary predicates and negated atoms, by simply including additional dimensions (corresponding to atoms in $K$) in the vector $b^i$.

The DERRL framework learns a rule vector $b^i$ for each action $i \in A$ by associating it with a trainable weight vector $w^i$. Each element $w^i_j \in w^i$ indicates the membership of the corresponding atom in the rule definition (i.e., if the weight of the atom is high, it is more likely to belong to the rule definition). Given the state vector $v$, action probabilities $\pi_\theta(i \mid s, \mathcal{B})$ are calculated by performing a fuzzy conjunction on the rules (Sect. 4.2). The whole framework is trained end-to-end using the REINFORCE algorithm [41], with the loss function given as $J(\pi_\theta) = -\mathbb{E}_{\tau \sim \pi_\theta}[R_\tau]$. Here, $R_\tau$ is the discounted sum of rewards over trajectory $\tau$, and $\theta$ is the set of trainable parameters.

Algorithm 1 summarizes the DERRL framework. The two main components of DERRL are **(i)** Rule Generator (Sect. 4.1), which at every time-step $t$ and for each action $i \in A$, generates a rule vector $b^i$, and a weight vector $w^i$; **(ii)**

Forward chaining Inference (Sect. 4.2) that takes the generated rules vectors for all actions $\{b^i\}_{i=1}^{|A|}$, the corresponding weight vectors $\{w^i\}_{i=1}^{|A|}$, and the state valuation vector $v$ for the $t^{th}$ time-step, and returns the action probabilities $\pi_\theta(. \mid s, \mathcal{B})$. Note, that the rule generator parameters $\theta$ are trained by calculating the gradients of the loss function with respect to weight vectors $w^i$.

## 4.1 Rule Generation

The rule $\mathcal{R}_\theta : i \mapsto b^i, w^i$ uses a parameterized network $\mathcal{R}_\theta$ to map each action (index) $i$ to a rule vector $b^i$ and weight vector $w^i$. Here, $b_j^i = 1$ indicates the $j^{th}$ atom is in the rule body. The rule generator outputs a probability vector $P^i$ where $P_j^i$ represents the probability of the $j^{th}$ atom in $K$ belonging to the rule body. We use the Gumbel-max trick [17] on $P^i$ to sample the binary vector $b^i$.

$$b_j^i = arg\,max(\log(P_j^i) + u_0, \log(1 - P_j^i) + u_1) \text{ where } u \sim Gumbel(0,1)$$

Here, $Gumbel(0,1)$ is the standard Gumbel distribution given by the probability density function $f(x) = e^{-(x+e^{-x})}$. During evaluation, we use $arg\,max(.)$ operation without sampling. From $P^i$, we also obtain the weight vector $w^i \in \mathbb{R}^{\|b^i\|_1}$ comprising the probabilities of only those atoms which have $b_j^i = 1$. From Table 2, the generated rule vector $b^r = [0,1,0,0,1,0]^\top$, the probability vector $P^r = [0.1, 0.8, 0.3, 0.4, 0.7, 0.2]^\top$, and the corresponding weight vector $w^r = [0.8, 0.7]^\top$.

## 4.2 Inference

| $i$ | $\mathbf{X}^i$ | $\mathbf{Y}^i$ | $w^i$ | $z^i$ | $\mathcal{F}^i$ | $\pi_\theta(i \mid s, \mathcal{B})$ |
|---|---|---|---|---|---|---|
| $r \leftarrow p(Y), q(Y, X)$ | $\begin{bmatrix} 0,3 \\ 1,4 \end{bmatrix}$ | $\begin{bmatrix} 1,1 \\ 0,0 \end{bmatrix}$ | $\begin{bmatrix} 0.8 \\ 0.7 \end{bmatrix}$ | $\begin{bmatrix} 0.5 \\ 0 \end{bmatrix}$ | 0.5 | 0.62 |
| $s \leftarrow p(X), q(Y, Y)$ | $\begin{bmatrix} 0,5 \\ 1,2 \end{bmatrix}$ | $\begin{bmatrix} 1,0 \\ 0,1 \end{bmatrix}$ | $\begin{bmatrix} 0.6 \\ 0.9 \end{bmatrix}$ | $\begin{bmatrix} 0 \\ 0 \end{bmatrix}$ | 0 | 0.38 |

Consider the following rules generated by the rule generator. Each rule is passed through a substitution $\phi : V \mapsto C$ to produce ground rules. Let, $\mathbf{X}^i \in \mathbb{Z}_{\geq 0}^{N(\phi) \times \|b^i\|_1}$ be the matrix representation of the ground rules. Here, $\mathbb{Z}_{\geq 0}$ and $N(\phi)$ are the set of non-negative integers and the number of possible substitutions, respectively. Each row in $\mathbf{X}^i$ is a vector of ground atom indices that belong to the ground rules. Using a substitution $\phi = \{b/X, a/Y\}$, we obtain the ground rule $r \leftarrow p(a), q(a, b)$. From Table 1, this rule definition can be written as the vector $[0, 3]$ (i.e., indices of $p(a)$ and $q(a, b)$ are 0, 3, respectively). Similarly, the substitution $\phi = \{a/X, b/Y\}$ gives us $r \leftarrow p(b), q(b, a)$, and the vector $[1, 4]$.

Next, the $value(.)$ operation takes each element $\mathbf{X}_j^i$ and returns its state value $v_j$. From Table 1, $\mathbf{Y}^r = value(\mathbf{X}^r) = value(\begin{bmatrix} 0,3 \\ 1,4 \end{bmatrix}) = \begin{bmatrix} v_0, v_3 \\ v_1, v_4 \end{bmatrix} = \begin{bmatrix} 1,1 \\ 0,0 \end{bmatrix}$.

The row vectors of $\mathbf{Y}^i = [\mathbf{y}^i_1, \ldots, \mathbf{y}^i_{N(\phi)}] \in \mathbb{R}^{N(\phi) \times \|\mathbf{b}^i\|_1}$ can be regarded as truth values of the grounded rule (i.e., for each substitution $\phi$), based on $\{s, \mathcal{B}\}$. If the rule definition is not satisfied, the corresponding row vectors will have sparse entries. To ensure differentiability, we use fuzzy norms for our rules.

**Fuzzy Conjunction Operators.** Fuzzy norms integrate logic reasoning with deep learning by approximating the truth values of predicates [7,31]. Fuzzy conjunction operators $* : [0,1]^{\|\mathbf{b}^i\|_1} \mapsto [0,1]$ can be of various types like Godel t-norm and Product t-norm (refer to our full paper [15]). We use Lukasiewicz t-norm ($\top_{\text{Luk}}(a,b) := max\{0, a+b-1\}$) to compute the action values for each rule[3]. To encourage the rule generator to generate more precise rules with higher probability, we calculate a valuation vector by weighing each row $\mathbf{y}^i_k \in \mathbb{R}^{\|\mathbf{b}^i\|_1}$ with the weight vector $\mathbf{w}^i \in \mathbb{R}^{\|\mathbf{b}^i\|_1}$, and using the Lukasiewicz operator as $z^i_k = max(0, \langle \mathbf{y}^i_k, \mathbf{w}^i \rangle - |\mathbf{w}^i| + 1)$. Intuitively, the inner product $\langle \mathbf{y}^i_k, \mathbf{w}^i \rangle$ is a weighted sum over all atoms in the rule body that are true in $s \cup \mathcal{B}$. This is akin to performing $(a+b)$ in t-norm operator. For $\mathbf{y}^r_0 = [1,1]^\top, \mathbf{w}^r = [0.8, 0.7]$:

$$z^r_0 = max(0, \langle \begin{bmatrix} 1 \\ 1 \end{bmatrix}, \begin{bmatrix} 0.8 \\ 0.7 \end{bmatrix} \rangle - 1) = 0.5$$

With multiple substitutions (or groundings) for a generated rule, we find the maximum valuation as $\mathcal{F}^i = max(\mathbf{z}^i)$. The final action probability is calculated as $\pi_\theta(i \mid s, \mathcal{B}) = softmax(\mathcal{F}^i)$. Note, that if the generated rule is not satisfied for any substitution (i.e., has a sparse row vector in the matrix $\mathbf{Y}^i$), the valuation of the generated rule is lower (for e.g., from the above table $\mathcal{F}^s < \mathcal{F}^r$).

**Multiple Rules for a Single Action.** We generalize DERRL to learn policies with multiple rules for each action, allowing it to switch between rules based on input (for e.g. in the blocks world game, the "move" action uses two rules executed at different steps depending on the goal blocks' position). We allow multiple rule networks per action, adjusting the final computation step to determine action probabilities based on the best-satisfied rule. Given $\mathcal{F}^i_1$ and $\mathcal{F}^i_2$ for two different rules for the same action, we first compute $\tilde{\mathcal{F}}^i = max(\mathcal{F}^i_1, \mathcal{F}^i_2)$ to determine which rule is more appropriate at a given time-step. Consider two different rules generated for action $r$ with arbitrary $\mathbf{Y}^i$:

| $i$ | $\mathbf{Y}^i$ | $\mathbf{w}^i$ | $\mathbf{z}^i$ | $\mathcal{F}^i$ |
|---|---|---|---|---|
| $r_1 \leftarrow p(Y), q(Y, X)$ | $\begin{bmatrix} 1,1 \\ 0,0 \end{bmatrix}$ | $\begin{bmatrix} 0.8 \\ 0.7 \end{bmatrix}$ | $\begin{bmatrix} 0.5 \\ 0 \end{bmatrix}$ | $0.5$ |
| $r_2 \leftarrow p(X), p(Y), q(X, X)$ | $\begin{bmatrix} 1,0,1 \\ 0,1,1 \end{bmatrix}$ | $\begin{bmatrix} 0.6 \\ 0.8 \\ 0.8 \end{bmatrix}$ | $\begin{bmatrix} 0 \\ 0 \\ 0 \end{bmatrix}$ | $0$ |

---

[3] More generally, given a vector $\mathbf{y} \in [0,1]^n$, Lukasiewicz t-norm $\top_{\text{Luk}}\mathbf{y} := max(0, \langle \mathbf{y}, \mathbb{1} \rangle - n + 1)$. See Appendix in [15] for proof.

---

**Algorithm 1.** Deep Explainable Relational Reinforcement Learning (DERRL)

---

**Input:** Alphabet: $\mathcal{L}$, RMDP: $\mathcal{E}$
**Output:** (set of) rules that encode the policy $\pi_\theta$
Initialize rule generator parameters $\theta$

    **for** each episode **do**
        **for** $t = 0$ to $T - 1$ **do**
            $v = encode(s, \mathcal{B})$                                   ▷ state vector
            **for** each action $i$ **do**
                $b^i, w^i \sim \mathcal{R}_\theta(i)$                     ▷ Rule Generation (Section 4.1)
            **end for**
            $\pi_\theta(. \mid s, \mathcal{B}) = Inference(v, \{b^i\}_{i=1}^{|A|}, \{w^i\}_{i=1}^{|A|})$       ▷ (Section 4.2)
            $a \sim \pi_\theta(. \mid s, \mathcal{B});$   $s' \leftarrow \delta(s, a);$   $R_t \leftarrow r(s, a)$
        **end for**
        $R_\tau \leftarrow \sum_{t+1}^{T-1} \gamma^{k-t-1} R_k$
        $\theta \leftarrow \theta - \eta \nabla_\theta \mathbb{E}_{\tau \sim \pi_\theta}[R_\tau]$
    **end for**

---

Here, $\tilde{\mathcal{F}}^r = max(0.5, 0) = 0.5$ is the valuation for rule $r$. Intuitively, depending on the current state $s$ and background knowledge $\mathcal{B}$, one of the rules will be more appropriate (i.e., lower sparsity in rows of $\mathbf{Y}^i$) than the others, prompting the policy to switch to that rule for decision making[4].

## 4.3 Semantic Constraints

The set of possible rules to consider grows exponentially with the number of predicates and their arity. While traditional relational learning systems have used declarative bias in form of semantic refinement [2], prior works in differentiable rule learning [7,19] employ rule templates to restrict the hypothesis space (e.g. rules of size 2). However, these methods frequently encounter redundancies. For example, rules $r \leftarrow less(X, Y), less(Y, Z), less(X, Z)$ and $s \leftarrow equal(X, Y), equal(Y, X)$ exhibit transitive and symmetric relations, respectively, making some atoms redundant. A rule $r$ is redundant w.r.t. a constraint $h \leftarrow b_1, ..., b_n$ if the rule $false \leftarrow h, b_1, ..., b_n$ subsumes the rule $r$. To avoid redundancies, generated rule vectors with $b_j^i = 1$ for both atoms $equal(X, Y)$ and $equal(Y, X)$ should be penalized. To this end, we propose a differentiable relaxation of semantic refinement by applying a supervised loss on probability vectors $\{P^i\}_{i=1}^{|A|}$. We declare semantic constraints $\mathcal{S}_c$ as axioms which can either be a relation (symmetric or transitive), or some background fact (like $false \leftarrow on(X, Y), on(Y, X)$). Then we calculate the semantic loss as $\mathcal{L}_{sem} = \sum_{x \in \mathcal{S}_c} \sum_{i \in A} \prod_{j \in x} P_j^i$.

Here, the outer summation is over each semantic constraint $x \in \mathcal{S}_c$, and the inner summation is over each generated rule $i \in A$. The product is over the probability of each atom (with index $j$) in the body of axiom $x$. For instance, given

---

[4] This assumes a specified upper bound on the number of rules for each action, similar to selecting the number of clusters in a clustering algorithm [43].

a single axiom $false \leftarrow p(Y), q(Y, X)$, for the generated rule $r \leftarrow p(Y), q(Y, X)$, from Table 2, the loss is $\mathcal{L}_{sem} = P_1^i \times P_4^i = 0.56$. Here, the loss is high because according to the given constraint, $p(Y)$ and $q(Y, X)$ should not appear together in the body of the rule. Intuitively, the loss is highest if the membership probabilities of both atoms are high warranting a penalization. $\mathcal{L}_{sem}$ is summed over the entire episode and the final loss is given as $\bar{J}(\pi_\theta) = J(\pi_\theta) + \lambda_{sem}\mathcal{L}_{sem}$. Here, $\lambda_{sem}$ is a regularization term. See [15] for constraints in all environments.

# 5   Experiments

Through our experiments, we aim to answer the following questions: Q1. Can the proposed approach learn interpretable policies while performing on par with neural-based baselines? (§ 5.2); Q2. Are the learned rules agnostic to modifications in the environment? (§ 5.2); Q3. How efficient and scalable is the proposed approach compared to the current state-of-the-art NLRL? (§ 5.2)

## 5.1   Experimental Setup

**The Countdown Game.** The agent manipulates a stack of numbers and an initial accumulated value $acc(X)$ to match a target number $goal(X)$ by applying operations like addition ($add$), subtraction ($sub$), or no operation ($null$). The stack comprises of the top number ($curr(X)$), number below it ($next(X, Y)$), and bottom-most number ($last(X)$). From Fig. 1, the state $s_t$ includes the stack, accumulated number, and goal number. Operations are performed between the accumulated value and the top number of the stack[5]. The background knowledge $\mathcal{B}$ comprises the target number[6], and atoms of the form $less(X, Y)$ which denote that number $X$ is less than $Y$. A reward of $r = 1$ is given when the target and accumulated values match at the end of the episode, otherwise $r = -\frac{|goal - acc|}{N_1}$ where $N_1$ is a normalizing constant. An initial range of numbers $[-4, 6]$ and stack of length$= 2$ is used for training. The learned models are tested for generalization on the following tasks (i) dynamic stack lengths of $\{3, 4, 5\}$; (ii) held-out target unseen during training; (iii) held-out initial stack sequences. We also train a stochastic game version with 10% probability of altering an action to null.

**Blocks World Manipulation.** Here, the objective is to put a specified block atop another specified block (Fig. 1). Stacks are represented using predicates: $top(X)$ means that block $X$ is the top block, $on(X, Y)$ means that block $X$ is on top of block $Y$. The actions are $move(X, Y)$ with $X = \{a, b, c\}$ and $Y = \{a, b, c, floor\}$. A reward $r = 1$ is provided if the task is achieved. We impose a penalty of $r = -0.02$ for every action. Training includes a fixed number of blocks $= 3$ and a fixed goal – to stack block $a$ on block $b$ ($goal\_on(a, b)$). We train it with initial configurations: $((a, b, c)); ((c, a, b)); ((a, c), (b)); ((b, c), (a))$. Here, each tuple is a stack. For generalization, we use variations like (i) held-out configuration unseen during training like $((a, b), (c)); ((b, c, a)); ((b, a, c));$

---

[5] $add$: acc $+=$ top, $sub$: acc $-=$ top, $null$: acc.
[6] $goal(X)$ is provided as background since it does not change during the episode.

(ii) dynamic (number of) blocks $\{4, 5\}$; (iii) dynamic (number of) stacks $\{2, 3, 4\}$; (iv) unseen goals like $goal\_on(b, a)$ and $goal\_on(a, c)$.

**Gridworld.** The agent navigates a grid with obstacles to reach the goal and can move vertically ($up/down$) or sideways ($left/right$). The state consists of the current X, Y coordinates of the agent $curr(X, Y)$, and the compass direction of the target (*North, South, East, West, NE, NW, SE, SW*). The background information consists of target coordinates ($target(X, Y)$), obstacle coordinates ($obs(X, Y)$), and successor information $succ(X, Y)$ where $Y = X + 1$. The action space is $\{up, down, left, right\}$. The agent receives a reward of $r = 1$ for reaching the target, otherwise $r = -\frac{\|position_{goal} - position_{agent}\|_2}{N_2}$. Here $N_2$ is a normalizing constant. During training, a fixed size grid of $3 \times 3$ and $5 \times 5$ is used with 2 obstacles. For generalization, we use variations like: (i) dynamic (number of) obstacles $\{3, 4\}$; (ii) held-out (agent-goal) configurations. Unlike search algorithms like A* that use a dynamics model, DERRL learns actions through exploration.

**Traffic.** We used the Simulation of Urban MObility (SUMO) traffic simulator [25] to simulate traffic flow, where intersections (3-way and 4-way) function as agents denoted by $intersection(Y)$, and are connected by a network of 2-way lanes represented as $between(X, Y, Z)$, indicating a connection between intersections $Y$ and $Z$ by lane $X$. The goal is to minimize the traffic at the intersections, hence reward is the negative queue length at each intersection. Each agent is provided with the lane that has the highest traffic, labeled as $highest(X)$ for lane $X$, and is responsible for controlling the traffic lights (i.e. turn the lights green ($green(X)$)) for lane $X$. Therefore, 3 and 4-way intersections have an action space of size 3, 4 respectively. We train each intersection independently on a 5-agent grid, then apply the learned rules to an 8-agent grid. The mean rewards of all agents are shown in Table 3 – note, that the best possible reward $\approx 0$.

**DoorKey Minigrid.** The agent task is to unlock a locked door ($locked(Y), door(Y)$) and reach a goal ($goal(Z)$). Various colored keys ($key(X)$) are scattered throughout the room, and the agent must select the key that matches the color of the door ($samecolor(X, Y)$) to unlock it. We use high-level actions. The agent is only allowed to carry one key at a time and can navigate to and pick up a key $X$ using the $pick(X)$ action if it is not carrying any keys ($notcarrying$), otherwise, it drops the key before picking the new one. The $open(X)$ action enables it to unlock a door $X$ if it carries the key that matches the door's color. The $goto(X)$ action enables the agent to navigate to a specific object $X$. The reward $= 1$ for successfully reaching the goal, else 0. The learned model is tested for generalization with additional doors and keys of varying colors.

We evaluate our DERRL against **NLRL** baseline. We also compare with model-free DRL approaches with variations in the deep learning module like (i) Graph Convolution Network (**GCN**) [23] that perform well at relational learning [26]; (ii) Multilayer Perceptron (**MLP**). Finally, we compare with an untrained Random (**Random**) baseline to establish a performance minimum. Our rule generator employs a single-layer neural network ($2m$ parameters), while for the GCN and MLP baselines, we used 2-layer networks ($O(m^3)$ parameters).

**Table 3.** Generalization Scores (average rewards over 50 episodes across 3 runs) compare DERRL to other baselines. DERRL outperforms baselines, including the state-of-the-art NLRL. In Traffic, the mean reward for all agents is reported.

| Setup | | DERRL | NLRL | GCN | MLP | Random |
|---|---|---|---|---|---|---|
| Countdown Game | training | 0.98 | 0.95 | 0.98 | **1.00** | 0.30 |
| | dynamic stack | **0.98** | 0.95 | 0.95 | 0.54 | 0.38 |
| | held-out target | **0.98** | 0.85 | 0.95 | 0.35 | 0.33 |
| | held-out initial | 0.98 | 0.55 | **1.00** | 0.35 | 0.18 |
| Countdown Game(stochastic) | training | 0.98 | 0.95 | 0.98 | **1.00** | 0.15 |
| Blocks World Manipulation | training | **0.97** | **0.97** | **0.97** | **0.97** | -0.18 |
| | held-out config. | **0.97** | 0.70 | 0.55 | 0.45 | -0.18 |
| | dynamic blocks | **0.92** | 0.51 | -0.20 | -0.21 | -0.22 |
| | dynamic stacks | **0.96** | 0.90 | 0.90 | 0.85 | -0.18 |
| | unseen goal | **0.96** | 0.45 | -0.18 | -0.18 | -0.18 |
| DoorKey Minigrid | training | 0.80 | 0.45 | 0.75 | **0.90** | 0.10 |
| | dynamic keys/doors | **0.78** | 0.25 | 0.35 | 0.20 | 0.05 |
| Traffic | training (5-agents) | **-0.76** | -0.91 | -0.90 | -0.95 | -1.54 |
| | 8-agents | **-1.02** | -1.28 | -1.45 | -1.75 | -2.17 |
| Gridworld Game | training | 0.75 | 0.72 | 0.70 | **0.81** | 0.03 |
| | dynamic obstacles | **0.70** | 0.55 | 0.46 | 0.51 | -0.15 |
| | held-out config | **0.81** | 0.70 | 0.17 | -0.61 | -0.70 |

## 5.2   Results

**Interpretation of Policies (Q1).** Here, we provide interpretations of the learned rules in each training environment, as shown in Fig. 1. **The Countdown Game**: The policy selects *add* action when $acc(X) < goal(Y)$, *sub* action when $acc(X) > goal(Y)$, and null action when both are equal. **Blocks World Manipulation**: The model learns two rules for $move(X, Y)$. Given a goal to put block $a$ atop block $b$, the first rule is applicable when at least one of the blocks is not the top block. Hence, the model learns to unstack the blocks – the top block $X$ of the stack is moved to the floor $Y$. The second rule is applied when both $a$ and $b$ are at the top. **Traffic**: The general rule for each intersection is $green(X) \leftarrow highest(X), between(X, Y, Z), intersection(Y), intersection(Z)$. Intuitively, the lights corresponding to the lane with the highest traffic $X$, connecting intersections $Y$ and $Z$, are turned green. **DoorKey Minigrid**: The learned rule for action $pickup(X)$ tells the agent to pickup the key $X$ that matches the color of the door $Y$, provided that it is not carrying any other items (*notcarrying*). Similarly, for $open(X)$, the learned rule states that the agent can unlock a locked door $X$ using the key $Y$ only if the colors of the door and the key match. The $goto(X)$ action directs the agent to navigate to the goal object $X$ when the door is *unlocked*. **Gridworld Game**: In this setting, the model learns two rules for each action. The first is used for navigation to the target, such as moving *up* if the target is to the north (or northeast and northwest) of the grid.

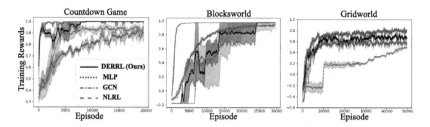

**Fig. 2.** [Best viewed in color] Comparison of training rewards at convergence for different baselines plotted by averaging the rewards over 3 independent runs. [Left to right] Countdown Game, Blocks World, and Gridworld.

The second helps navigate around obstacles, e.g. move *up* if the obstacle (given by $(Z, Y)$) is to the immediate right of the agent (given by $(X, Y)$). However, the policy may not follow the shortest path[7] or have consistent traversal strategies, resulting in varied rules for different instances without performance loss. We also observed that DERRL fails to learn accurate rules when trained on $8 \times 8$ grid, suggesting that it does not scale well to larger state spaces.

**Generalization Performance (Q2).** From Table 3, we observe that DERRL exceeds baselines in generalization tasks by learning general rules. Unlike symbolic planning, DERRL's performance remains unaffected by noisy training, such as stochastic Countdown. Secondly, although GCNs excel in relational learning, their generalization is marginally better than MLP, potentially failing to capture task-agnostic relational patterns, yet they outperform MLP and NLRL in the Countdown game. Lastly, DERRL's training performance and convergence speed match MLP (Fig. 2), but it outperforms MLP in generalization tasks, where MLP is akin to the Random baseline.

**Comparison with NLRL (Q3).** (i) Computational Complexity: NLRL assigns trainable weights to all possible rules with a body size of 2, while DERRL allocates weights to each atom in the rule body. Given, $m$ atoms from $P_{ext}$ and $V$, NLRL has C(m,2) learnable weights, while DERRL has $2m$. Therefore, the training reduces from learning the best set of rules (in NLRL) to learning the best membership of the rules (in DERRL), leading to a lower computation time in DERRL. The computation time per episode is reduced by a factor of $\approx 10$ (Fig. 3). (ii) Comparing Learned Rules: NLRL learned rules in blocksworld:

$$move(X,Y) \leftarrow top(X), pred(X,Y); \quad move(X,Y) \leftarrow top(X), goal\_on(X,Y)$$
$$pred(X,Y) \leftarrow isFloor(Y), pred2(X); \quad pred2(X) \leftarrow on(X,Y), on(Y,Z)$$

---

[7] When the target is to the southeast, and the agent encounters a target to its right, it will travel north (*up*) rather than south (*down*).

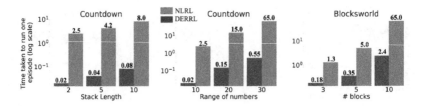

**Fig. 3.** Run-time comparison (in seconds) per episode between DERRL and NLRL as problems scale. Left to right: Countdown game (stack size), Countdown game (range of numbers), Blocks World (number of blocks). Y-axis in log scale. Plots show NLRL takes approximately 10 times longer per episode compared to DERRL. See additional plots in Appendix of [15].

With invented predicates *pred* and *pred2*, this plan differs from DERRL in that the second rule doesn't verify if both X and Y are movable, failing to solve configurations where block b is below block a. (iii) Size of hypothesis space: DERRL restricts the hypothesis space through the use of semantic constraints, whereas large hypothesis space in NLRL limits its convergence in DoorKey and Traffic domains. The convergence in DERRL is slower without semantic constraints (see Appendix in [15] for details). (iv) Expressiveness: NLRL can learn recursive rules by using templates as in meta-interpretive learning and predicate invention. While this is expressive, it can be hard to master. In contrast, DERRL learns non-recursive Datalog as Quinlan's FOIL [36] but combines it with constraints that can be recursive to rule out redundancies.

## 6    Conclusion

We proposed a neuro-symbolic approach to learn interpretable policies that are also generalizable. The representations that DERRL and RRL use are very similar to those used in the planning community. Upgrading the approach to enable automatic learning of the required number of rules can be a potential research direction. While being significantly more scalable than state-of-the-art NLRL, DERRL fails to learn accurate interpretable solutions for more complex environments with larger state spaces (more variables and constants) and a higher number of actions. As a part of future work, it will be interesting to explore ways in which the proposed approach can be scaled to such complex applications.

**Acknowledgements.** This work was partially supported by the Wallenberg AI, Autonomous Systems and Software Program (WASP) funded by the Knut and Alice Wallenberg Foundation.

# References

1. Arulkumaran, K., Deisenroth, M.P., Brundage, M., Bharath, A.A.: Deep reinforcement learning: a brief survey. IEEE Signal Process. Mag. **34**(6), 26–38 (2017)
2. Raedt, L.: Logical and relational learning. In: Zaverucha, G., da Costa, A.L. (eds.) SBIA 2008. LNCS (LNAI), vol. 5249, pp. 1–1. Springer, Heidelberg (2008). https://doi.org/10.1007/978-3-540-88190-2_1
3. De Raedt, L., Kersting, K., Natarajan, S., Poole, D.: Statistical Relational Artificial Intelligence: Logic, Probability, and Computation, Synthesis Lectures on Artificial Intelligence and Machine Learning, vol. 32. Morgan & Claypool, San Rafael (2016)
4. Driessens, K., Džeroski, S.: Integrating guidance into relational reinforcement learning. Mach. Learn. **57**(3), 271–304 (2004)
5. Dzeroski, S., Raedt, L.D., Blockeel, H.: Relational reinforcement learning. In: Proceedings of the Fifteenth International Conference on Machine Learning, ICML 1998, pp. 136–143. Morgan Kaufmann Publishers Inc., San Francisco (1998)
6. Ernst, D., Geurts, P., Wehenkel, L.: Tree-based batch mode reinforcement learning. J. Mach. Learn. Res. **6**(18), 503–556 (2005)
7. Evans, R., Grefenstette, E.: Learning explanatory rules from noisy data. J. Artif. Int. Res. **61**(1), 1–64 (2018)
8. Fikes, R.E., Nilsson, N.J.: Strips: a new approach to the application of theorem proving to problem solving. Artif. Intell. **2**(3), 189–208 (1971)
9. Frosst, N., Hinton, G.E.: Distilling a neural network into a soft decision tree. CoRR abs/1711.09784 (2017)
10. Garg, S., Bajpai, A., et al.: Size independent neural transfer for rddl planning. In: Proceedings of the International Conference on Automated Planning and Scheduling, vol. 29, pp. 631–636 (2019)
11. Garg, S., Bajpai, A., et al.: Symbolic network: generalized neural policies for relational mdps. In: International Conference on Machine Learning, pp. 3397–3407. PMLR (2020)
12. Gelfond, M., Lifschitz, V.: Action languages. Electron. Trans. Artif. Intell. **3**, 195–210 (1998)
13. Ghallab, M., et al.: PDDL–The Planning Domain Definition Language (1998)
14. Gilpin, L.H., Bau, D., Yuan, B.Z., Bajwa, A., Specter, M.A., Kagal, L.: Explaining explanations: an approach to evaluating interpretability of machine learning. CoRR abs/1806.00069 (2018)
15. Hazra, R., De Raedt, L.: Deep explainable relational reinforcement learning: a neuro-symbolic approach. arXiv preprint arXiv:2304.08349 (2023)
16. Iyer, R., Li, Y., Li, H., Lewis, M., Sundar, R., Sycara, K.: Transparency and explanation in deep reinforcement learning neural networks. In: Proceedings of the 2018 AAAI/ACM Conference on AI, Ethics, and Society, AIES 2018, pp. 144–150. Association for Computing Machinery, New York (2018)
17. Jang, E., Gu, S., Poole, B.: Categorical reparameterization with gumbel-softmax. In: 5th International Conference on Learning Representations, ICLR 2017, Toulon, France, April 24–26, 2017, Conference Track Proceedings. p. 0. OpenReview.net, Palais des Congrès Neptune, Toulon, France (2017)
18. Janisch, J., Pevný, T., Lisý, V.: Symbolic relational deep reinforcement learning based on graph neural networks. arXiv preprint arXiv:2009.12462 (2020)
19. Jiang, Z., Luo, S.: Neural logic reinforcement learning. In: Proceedings of the 36th International Conference on Machine Learning. Proceedings of Machine Learning Research, vol. 97, pp. 3110–3119. PMLR, Long Beach, USA (09–15 Jun 2019)

20. Kersting, K., Driessens, K.: Non-parametric policy gradients: A unified treatment of propositional and relational domains. In: Proceedings of the 25th International Conference on Machine Learning, pp. 456–463 (2008)
21. Kersting, K., Otterlo, M.V., De Raedt, L.: Bellman goes relational. In: Proceedings of the Twenty-First International Conference on Machine Learning, p. 59 (2004)
22. Khoshafian, S.N., Copeland, G.P.: Object identity. ACM SIGPLAN Notices **21**(11), 406–416 (1986)
23. Kipf, T.N., Welling, M.: Semi-supervised classification with graph convolutional networks. In: Proceedings of the 5th International Conference on Learning Representations, ICLR 2017 (2017)
24. Kokel, H., Manoharan, A., Natarajan, S., Ravindran, B., Tadepalli, P.: Reprel: Integrating relational planning and reinforcement learning for effective abstraction. In: Proceedings of the International Conference on Automated Planning and Scheduling, vol. 31, pp. 533–541 (2021)
25. Krajzewicz, D., Erdmann, J., Behrisch, M., Bieker, L.: Recent development and applications of sumo-simulation of urban mobility. Int. J. Adv. Syst. Measur. **5**(3&4) (2012)
26. Lamb, L.C., Garcez, A.d., Gori, M., Prates, M.O., Avelar, P.H., Vardi, M.Y.: Graph neural networks meet neural-symbolic computing: A survey and perspective. In: Bessiere, C. (ed.) Proceedings of the Twenty-Ninth International Joint Conference on Artificial Intelligence, IJCAI-20, pp. 4877–4884. International Joint Conferences on Artificial Intelligence Organization, Yokohama, Japan (7 2020), survey track
27. Lee, J.D., See, K.A.: Trust in automation: designing for appropriate reliance. Hum. Factors **46**(1), 50–80 (2004)
28. Liu, G., Schulte, O., Zhu, W., Li, Q.: Toward interpretable deep reinforcement learning with linear model u-trees. In: ECML/PKDD (2018)
29. Lloyd, J.W.: Foundations of Logic Programming. Springer, Heidelberg (1984)
30. Lyu, D., Yang, F., Liu, B., Gustafson, S.: Sdrl: Interpretable and data-efficient deep reinforcement learning leveraging symbolic planning. In: Proceedings of the Thirty-Third AAAI Conference on Artificial Intelligence and Thirty-First Innovative Applications of Artificial Intelligence Conference and Ninth AAAI Symposium on Educational Advances in Artificial Intelligence. AAAI'19/IAAI'19/EAAI'19, AAAI Press, Honolulu, Hawaii, USA (2019)
31. Marra, G., Giannini, F., Diligenti, M., Maggini, M., Gori, M.: T-norms driven loss functions for machine learning. arXiv: Artificial Intelligence (2019)
32. Martínez, D., Alenya, G., Torras, C.: Relational reinforcement learning with guided demonstrations. Artif. Intell. **247**, 295–312 (2017)
33. Muggleton, S., De Raedt, L.: Inductive logic programming: theory and methods. J. Log. Program. **19**(20), 629–679 (1994)
34. Nau, D., Ghallab, M., Traverso, P.: Automated Planning: Theory & Practice. Morgan Kaufmann Publishers Inc., San Francisco (2004)
35. Payani, A., Fekri, F.: Incorporating relational background knowledge into reinforcement learning via differentiable inductive logic programming. arXiv preprint arXiv:2003.10386 (2020)
36. Quinlan, J.R.: Learning logical definitions from relations. Mach. Learn. 5(3), 239–266 (sep 1990)
37. Silva, A., Gombolay, M., Killian, T., Jimenez, I., Son, S.H.: Optimization methods for interpretable differentiable decision trees applied to reinforcement learning. In: Chiappa, S., Calandra, R. (eds.) Proceedings of the Twenty Third International Conference on Artificial Intelligence and Statistics. Proceedings of Machine Learning Research, vol. 108, pp. 1855–1865. PMLR, Palermo, Italy, 26–28 Aug 2020

38. Stowers, K., Kasdaglis, N., Newton, O.B., Lakhmani, S.G., Wohleber, R.W., Chen, J.Y.: Intelligent agent transparency. Proceedings of the Human Factors and Ergonomics Society Annual Meeting **60**, 1706–1710 (2016)
39. Tadepalli, P., Givan, R., Driessens, K.: Relational reinforcement learning: an overview. In: Proceedings of the ICML'04 Workshop on Relational Reinforcement Learning (2004)
40. de Visser, E.J., Cohen, M., Freedy, A., Parasuraman, R.: A design methodology for trust cue calibration in cognitive agents. In: Shumaker, R., Lackey, S. (eds.) Virtual, Augmented and Mixed Reality. Designing and Developing Virtual and Augmented Environments, pp. 251–262. Springer International Publishing, Cham (2014)
41. Williams, R.J.: Simple statistical gradient following algorithms for connectionist reinforcement learning. Mach. Learn. **8**, 229–256 (1992)
42. Xu, J., Zhang, Z., Friedman, T., Liang, Y., Broeck, G.: A semantic loss function for deep learning with symbolic knowledge. In: International Conference on Machine Learning, pp. 5502–5511. PMLR (2018)
43. Xu, R., Wunsch, D.: Survey of clustering algorithms. IEEE Trans. Neural Networks **16**(3), 645–678 (2005). https://doi.org/10.1109/TNN.2005.845141
44. Yang, F., Lyu, D., Liu, B., Gustafson, S.: Peorl: integrating symbolic planning and hierarchical reinforcement learning for robust decision-making. In: Proceedings of the 27th International Joint Conference on Artificial Intelligence, IJCAI 2018, pp. 4860–4866. AAAI Press, Stockholm, Sweden (2018)
45. Zambaldi, V., et al.: Deep reinforcement learning with relational inductive biases. In: International Conference on Learning Representations (2019)

# ReOnto: A Neuro-Symbolic Approach for Biomedical Relation Extraction

Monika Jain[1(✉)], Kuldeep Singh[2], and Raghava Mutharaju[1]

[1] Knowledgeable Computing and Reasoning (KRaCR) Lab, IIIT -Delhi, Delhi, India
{monikaja,raghava.mutharaju}@iiitd.ac.in
[2] Cerence GmbH and Zerotha Research, Aachen, Germany
kuldeep.singh1@cerence.com

**Abstract.** Relation Extraction (RE) is the task of extracting semantic relationships between entities in a sentence and aligning them to relations defined in a vocabulary, which is generally in the form of a Knowledge Graph (KG) or an ontology. Various approaches have been proposed so far to address this task. However, applying these techniques to biomedical text often yields unsatisfactory results because it is hard to infer relations directly from sentences due to the nature of the biomedical relations. To address these issues, we present a novel technique called ReOnto, that makes use of neuro symbolic knowledge for the RE task. ReOnto employs a graph neural network to acquire the sentence representation and leverages publicly accessible ontologies as prior knowledge to identify the sentential relation between two entities. The approach involves extracting the relation path between the two entities from the ontology. We evaluate the effect of using symbolic knowledge from ontologies with graph neural networks. Experimental results on two public biomedical datasets, BioRel and ADE, show that our method outperforms all the baselines (approximately by 3%).

**Keywords:** ontology · neuro-symbolic integration · graph neural network · domain knowledge · relation extraction

## 1   Introduction

In recent times, due to the exponential increase in data, knowledge bases have gained popularity as a means to efficiently store and organize information [11]. Although considerable efforts are invested in updating and maintaining knowledge bases, their incompleteness persists due to the dynamic nature of facts, which constantly evolve over the Web and other sources. Hence, there is a need to automate the process of extracting knowledge from text. Relation Extraction (RE) is task of predicting the relation given a sentence and an entity pair [5]. In domains such as biomedicine, relation extraction task poses a few critical domain-specific challenges. Consider a sentence, *atrio ventricular (C0018827) conduction defects and arrhythmias by selective perfusion of a-v conduction system in the canine heart (C0018787)*, with entities C0018827 (ventricular) and

C0018787 (heart) linked to UMLS [6]. Here target relation is *hasPhysicalPartO-fAnatomicStructure*. The RE task aims to infer the semantic relationships. As demonstrated in the example, working with biomedical corpora poses several challenges. These include: complex input sentences that may require extensive parsing and interpretation to extract relevant information. Indirectly inferred relations between entities in the text, which may require sophisticated natural language processing techniques. Difficulty obtaining domain knowledge of the specific entities mentioned in the text, which may require specialized expertise and additional research. Moreover, in the biomedical domain, entities are intricately interlinked, resulting in numerous densely linked entities with high degrees and multiple paths connecting them [2]. Hence, inferring the correct relation from a given sentence may require reasoning about the potential path.

**Limitation of Existing Works and Hypothesis.** The existing approaches employ various techniques for relation extraction such as multi-task learning [9], transformers [10], Graph Neural Network (GNN) models [5,42] have been used to process complex relationships between entities. While deep learning models [22,31] can incorporate semantic information of entities. Albeit effective, these models employ standard message-passing or attention-based approaches (transformers, GNNs) which are inherently focused on homophilic signals [3,4] (i.e., only on neighborhood interactions) and ignore long-range interactions that may be required to infer the semantic relationship between two biomedical entities. Furthermore, sufficient domain-specific knowledge is available in various biomedical ontologies to be used as background knowledge for relation extraction. It is also evident in the literature that reasoning over ontologies [7,34] allow capturing long-range dependencies between two entities [24,41], which further helps in making predictions. For instance, in [16], ontology information was utilized as a tuple and transformed into a 3-D vector for predicting compound relations. Hence, it remains an open **research question**: for biomedical relation extraction, can we combine reasoning ability over publicly available biomedical ontologies to enrich an underlying deep learning model which is inherently homophilic?

**Contributions:** To tackle this research question, to our knowledge our approach represents the first neuro-symbolic method for extracting relations in the biomedical domain. Our method is two-fold. Firstly, we aim to aggregate the symbolic knowledge in the form of axioms (facts) consisting of logical constructs and quantifiers such as *there exist, for all, union* and *intersection* between entities present in various public ontologies and build background knowledge. In the second step, we incorporate background knowledge into a Graph Neural Network (GNN) to enhance its capabilities to capture long-range dependencies. The rationale behind using a GNN is to exploit the correlations between entities and predicates due to its message-passing ability between the nodes. Inducing external symbolic knowledge makes our approach transparent as we can backtrack the paths used for inducing long-range dependencies between entities. Hence, we empower the GNN by externally induced symbolic knowledge to capture long-range interactions needed to infer biomedical relations between two given entities and a sentence. We name our approach as "ReOnto" containing following key contributions.

- Our novel relation extraction method, ReOnto, utilizes an ontology model to learn subgraphs containing expressive axioms connecting the given entities. It consists of a symbolic module incorporating domain-specific knowledge into a GNN, enabling the prediction of required relations between two entities within a biomedical knowledge graph.
- We study the effect of symbolic knowledge on the performance of the underlying deep learning model by considering several key characteristics such as 1) entity coverage from ontology, 2) the number of hops, etc. We provide conclusive evidence that aggregating knowledge from various sources to build the symbolic component (instead of using just one ontology for background knowledge) has a positive impact on the overall performance.
- We provide an exhaustive evaluation on two standard datasets, and our proposed method outperforms all baselines for biomedical relation extraction.

## 2   Related Work

**Muti-instance RE:** Multi-instance relation extraction aims to utilize previous mentions of entities in a given document to infer the semantic relationship between them. Some approaches leverage attention-based convolution neural network [29], multi-level CNN attention [33] and by ranking with CNN to classify relation [27]. In contrast, alternative approaches employ recurrent neural networks for relation classification [40] and hierarchical RNN with attention. Besides this, some works also use entity context information such as type and descriptions to improve the performance [32]. To deal with the noise at the sentence-level and bag level, [37] proposed a distant supervision approach incorporating intra-bag and inter-bag attentions.

**Sentential and Biomedical RE:** GP-GNN [42] proposed a graph neural network with generated parameters which solves the relational message-passing task by encoding natural language as parameters and performing propagation from layer to layer. RECON [5] is an extended approach which uses the entity details like alias, labels, description and instance in an underlying GNN model for sentential RE. As discussed in [22], not all facts contribute to improved performance, and therefore, the context must be dynamically selected based on the given sentence. However, these works are limited to general domain and finds their limitation in the biomedical domain. In the biomedical domain, [9] introduced a multi-task learning approach that utilizes joint signals from entity extraction task to improve relation extraction. [31] enriched the performance of biomedical relation extraction by incorporating linguistic information and entity types into a BERT model. [8] employed an end-to-end seq2seq model for biomedical RE.

**Ontology Based RE:** The authors of reference [20] proposed using an ontology as a hyperlink structure for the web to facilitate relation extraction. Authors utilize the web structure using a breadth-first search for relation extraction. [1] uses RNN with a convolutional neural network to process three features: tokens, types, and graphs. Work claim that entity type and ontology graph structure provide better representations than simple token-based representations for RE. We point readers to [18] for details on ontology-powered information systems.

## 3    Problem Formulation and Approach

We define a KG as a tuple $KG = (\mathcal{E}, \mathcal{R}, \mathcal{T}^+)$ where $\mathcal{E}$ denotes the set of entities (vertices), $\mathcal{R}$ is the set of relations (edges), and $\mathcal{T}^+ \subseteq \mathcal{E} \times \mathcal{R} \times \mathcal{E}$ is a set of all triples. The *RE Task* aims to find the target relation $r^c \in \mathcal{R}$ for a given pair of entities $\langle e_i, e_j \rangle$ within the sentence $\mathcal{W}$. If no relation is inferred, it returns *NA* label. In this section, we first discuss the ReOnto framework, which integrates the power of the graph neural network (GNN) [5] with that of symbolic knowledge. A GNN primarily employs three modules, which are encoding, propagation, and classification. Symbolic knowledge is integrated with the GNN score in the aggregation module (Fig. 1).

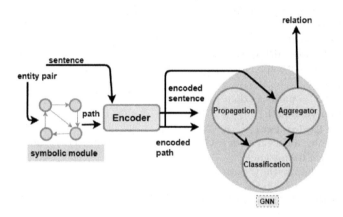

**Fig. 1.** ReOnto Approach. The role of the symbolic module is to aggregate symbolic knowledge. It takes the entity pair and gives path information. 1) Encoding module accepts input vectors of sentence and path information to provide transition matrix. 2) Propagation module shares the hidden states of generated transition matrix with its neighbors 3) Classification module provides scores of prediction 4) Aggregator module integrates the score of the biased relation (from ontology reasoning) with that of the one from GNN to calculate loss.

### 3.1    Symbolic Module

As a first step, we aggregate symbolic knowledge(SK), available in public ontologies for extracting long-range dependencies between entity pairs. We build a connected graph G of the symbolic knowledge derived from ontologies. We define $G = (V, E, T_+)$ where V has a set of entities such that each edge $(v_s, v_o) \in$

E and $v_s$, $v_o \in V$ corresponds to a sequence $s = s_0^{s,o} s_1^{s,o} s_2^{s,o} \ldots s_{l-1}^{s,o}$ extracted from the text where s, o represent the source and destination entities. We also consider related SK of entity pair $SK^{s,o}$ which consist of path information ($\sum path_0^i; \sum axiom\_path_0^i) \in SK^{s,o}$ where i is the number of hops traversed to get the path. Path consists of multi hop details, each containing detailed information, while the axiom path contains path information enriched with expressive axioms. We identify the, directly and indirectly, connecting paths between the entities $v_s$ and $v_o$ (Algorithm 1).

---

**Algorithm 1:** Path generation via ontology

---

**Input**  : entity pair ($v_s$,$v_o$), Number of hops (N)
**Output:** finalpath
**Initialization:**
    $i = 1$, source= $v_s$, $path_{i-1}$, $axiom\_path_{i-1}$, finalpath, adjacent node,
  hop_path$_i$, axiom_path$_i$ = {}
finalpath = PathGeneration($v_s$, $v_o$, N)
**Function PathGeneration($v_s$, $v_o$, N):**
   path, axiom_path, finalpath = {}
   **foreach** *entity pair* $v_s, v_o \in$ *ontology* **do**
      path.append(ExplorePath($v_s$, $v_o$, N))
      axiom_path.append(ExploreSymbolicPath($v_s$, $v_o$, N))
   **end**
   finalpath = path $\cup$ axiom_path
   **return** {finalpath}
**Function ExplorePath($v_s$, $v_o$, N):**
   hop_path$_i$, adjacent node= GetNHopFromSource($v_s$, 1)  // calculates 1 hop distance from source
   $path_i$ = hop_path$_i \cup path_{i-1}$
   **if** $v_o \neq$ *adjacent node and* $i \neq N$ **then**
      $path_i$= ExplorePath(adjacent node, $v_o$, N)
      $i = i + 1$
   **end**
   **return** {path$_i$}
**Function ExploreSymbolicPath($v_s$, $v_o$, N):**
   axiom_path$_i$, adjacent node = GetNHopFromSource($v_s$, 2)   // calculates 2 hop distance from source containing there exist and for all quantifier
   axiom_path$_i$ = hop_path$_i \cup$ axiom_path$_{i-1}$
   **if** $v_o \neq$ *adjacent node and* $i \neq N$ **then**
      axiom_path$_i$= ExploreSymbolicPath(adjacent node, $v_o$, N)
      $i = i + 1$
   **end**
   **return** {axiom_path$_i$}

---

**Single Hop.** For retrieving the direct path, we query on the ontology using SPARQL to check if a path exists between entity pair ($e_s$, $e_o$). The study examined the potential interactions in a sentence <u>Sandimmun,</u>

<u>a medication formulated as</u> cyclosporin *(cya) in cremophor and ethanol, and the muscle relaxants atracurium and vecuronium in anesthetized cats.* The correct relation label between sandimmun and cyclosporin is *hasTradename.* Upon querying this entity pair from the ontology, it was found that the direct path between given entity pairs is *synonymOf* relation which is similar to the correct relation label *hasTradename* present in the dataset. As depicted in Fig. 2, the direct path between two given entities (if they exist) is extricated using path$(y; e) \rightarrow$ cui$(x; y) \sqcap$ edge$(x; z) \sqcap$cui$(z; e)$, where cui is concept unique identifier which uniquely identifies entity (assuming x is entity1, y is cui of entity1, z is entity2 and e is cui of entity2). It retrieves the connecting edge between two given entities. Once assimilating the path *synonymOf* between entity pairs, the aggregator module in ReOnto computes the similarity between the extracted path and all relations, assigning the correct label *hasTradename* as the similarity score reaches its maximum.

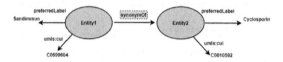

**Fig. 2.** Subgraph of ontology illustrating direct connection between two entities

**Multi Hop.** Multi-hop path reasoning over the knowledge base aims at finding a relation path for an entity pair by traversing along a path of triples from graph structure data [21]. For retrieving indirect path relation, we query on the ontology if a n-hop distance path exists between entity pair $(e_s, e_o)$ starting from 1-hop distance path. Consider the sentence *Intravenous azithromycin-induced ototoxicity* with its relation label as *hasAdverseEffect.* From ontologies, we get the path as a concatenation of *causative agent of, has adverse reaction* using path$(y;e) \rightarrow$ cui$(x;y) \sqcap$ edge$(x;z) \sqcap$ edge$(z;a) \sqcap$ cui$(a;e)$. The aggregator module receives this path as input and using a similarity score, assigns the target relation label *adverseEffect.* Refer to Fig. 3 for details.

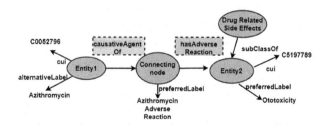

**Fig. 3.** Subgraph of ontology depicting two hop distance between two entities

**Using Axioms.** So far, we have considered only shallow and transitive relationships among the concepts. However, the biomedical domain consists of several complex relations. We argue that those relations can be captured using expressive axioms from ontology. Expressive axioms consist of logical quantifiers such as *there exist*($\exists$), *for all*($\forall$), *union*($\sqcup$), *intersection*($\sqcap$) which are part of popular biomedical ontologies. These expressive axioms enrich an ontology and play an essential role in the performance of downstream applications [24]. Our objective is to determine the relation label between two entities by tracing the corresponding multi-hop triplet path that contains these axioms, starting from the first entity in the graph and continuing up to a specified distance until we reach the second entity. Note that when multiple paths are available between two entities, we have taken into account all the paths that are available which consist of unique keywords Consider the sentence, *A 73-year-old woman presented with fever and* <u>*cough*</u> *2 weeks after completing the third cycle of* <u>*fludarabine*</u> *for chronic lymphocytic leukemia*. Here, correct relation label is *adverse effect*. From the ontology, we get following sub-graph enriched with axioms.

$$Fludaraline \xrightarrow{causativeAgentOf} Fludaraline\ Adverse\ Reaction$$
$$Fludaraline\ Adverse\ Reaction \sqsubseteq \exists hasFinding.Finding$$
$$Cough \sqsubseteq Finding$$

From the above relations, one can see that Fludaraline and Fludaraline Adverse Reaction (FADR) has a relation *causativeAgentOf*. Moreover, there exists a *hasFinding* relation between FADR and Finding. Therefore, with ontology reasoning, we can interpret that Fludaraline has an axiom path consisting of *causativeAgentOf, hasSomeFinding*, which is closest to the relation label adverseEffect. Similarly, consider another sentence, *concentrations were significantly related to the degree of apocrine differentiation of the* <u>*tumour*</u> *and, in a subset of the* <u>*cancers*</u>, *capacity to release gcdfp-15 was positively correlated with incidence of progestogen and androgen receptors*. The labeled relation for this sentence is has *nichdParentOf* .

$$Tumor \xrightarrow{qualifierBy} Diagnostic\ Imaging$$
$$Diagnostic\ Imaging \xrightarrow{allowedQualifier} Neoplasms$$
$$Neoplasms \sqsubseteq \exists parent.Post\text{-}Traumatic\ Cancer$$
$$Post\text{-}Traumatic\ Cancer \sqsubseteq Cancer$$

For the above case, the derived path is *qualifierBy, allowedQualifier, subClass* and there exist some *parent* and *subClass*.

## 3.2   Encoding Module

Entity pairs are encoded by concatenating the position embedding with the word embedding in the sentence (Eq. 1), represented as $En(s_t^{s,o})$ where $s_t$ is the word embedding and $p_t^{s,o}$ is the position embedding at word position $t$ relative to the entity pair position $(s, o)$. Similarly, symbolic path information from the Symbolic Module $(SK)$ is encoded by concatenating path $(path_0^i)$ and axiom path details $(axiom\_path_0^i)$ where $i$ represents the number of hops reaching destination.

$$En(s_t^{s,o}) = [s_t; p_t^{s,o}] \tag{1}$$

$$En(SK^{s,o}) = [\sum path_0^i; \sum axiom\_path_0^i]^{s,o} \tag{2}$$

The entity pairs representation and path information, after encoding with BioBERT are forwarded to a multi layer perceptron with non linear activation $\sigma$ (Eq. 3 and 4). We concatenate them as a shown in Eq. 5. Since our dataset are from biomedical domain, we have used BioBERT for encoding.

$$A_{s,o}^n = MLP_n(BioBERT(En(s_0^{s,o}), En(s_1^{s,o}), .., En(s_l - 1^{s,o})) \tag{3}$$

$$SP_{s,o}^n = MLP_n(BioBERT(En(SK^{s,o}))) \tag{4}$$

$$M_{s,o}^n = SP_{s,o}^{(n)} + A_{s,o}^{(n)} \tag{5}$$

### 3.3 Graph Neural Network

**Propagation Module.** In this module, we propagate information among graph nodes using Eq. 6, where given the representation of layer $n$ , representation of layer $n + 1$ is calculated. Here $n$ represents the index, $B$ represents neighbors of $v_o$, and $\sigma$ is the nonlinear activation function.

$$h_s^{n+1} = \sum_{v_o \in B(v_o)} \sigma(M_{s,o}^{(n)} h_o^{(n)}) \tag{6}$$

**Classification Module.** In the classification module, embeddings of entity pair are the input. Now, ReOnto performs element wise multiplication on input and then passed into multi layer perceptron using Eq. 7. Here $\cdot$ represent element wise multiplication.

$$MLP(v_s, v_o) = [h_{v_s}^{(1)} \cdot h_{v_o}^{(1)}]^T; [h_{v_s}^{(2)} \cdot h_{v_o}^{(2)}]^T; ...; [h_{v_s}^{(K)} \cdot h_{v_o}^{(K)}]^T \tag{7}$$

**Aggregator Module.** Path information $(path_0^i; axiom\_path_0^i) \in SK^{s,o}$ from Symbolic Module is separately encoded using BioBERT[1] model, which is pretrained on biomedical text corpora. At first, we perform encoding of path information and total relation label $R_1^i$ where $i$ is the total number of potential relations (refer Eq. 8 and 9). Then, we evaluate the semantic similarity between path information and complete labeled relation list. We get the relation label with the maximum similarity score and add it as a weighted bias as given in Eq. 10. An important observation to make is that the weights generated by the GNN undergo modification by incorporating the knowledge of the Symbolic Module. This step is crucial as it involves combining the symbolic and sub-symbolic components. We employ the softmax function to obtain probabilities and compute

---

[1] https://www.sbert.net/.

the cross entropy loss (refer Eqs. 11 and 12), where S denotes whole corpus and n are total entity pairs such that $s \neq o$. It is worth noting that if no path exists between two entities, the bias score is set to 0, and loss is computed accordingly.

$$Renc = enc(R_1^i) \tag{8}$$

$$Penc = enc(SK^{s,o}) \tag{9}$$

$$biasedscore_r = max(cosSim(Renc, Penc)) \tag{10}$$

$$P(v_s, v_o) = softmax((MLP(v_s, v_o) + biasedscore_r) \tag{11}$$

$$L = \sum_{t=0}^{S} \sum_{s,o=0}^{n} (log P(v_s, v_o))_t \tag{12}$$

## 4   Experimental Setup

We conduct our evaluation in response to following research questions.

**RQ1**: What is the effectiveness of ReOnto that combines symbolic knowledge with a neural model in solving biomedical relation extraction task?

**RQ2**: How does knowledge encoded in different ontologies impact performance of ReOnto?

**Datasets.** Our initial biomedical dataset is BioRel [35], which includes a total of 533,560 sentences, 69,513 entities, and 125 relations. The second dataset we use is the Adverse Drug Effect (ADE) dataset [12]. We treat the RE problem in this dataset as binary classification, where sentences are categorized as either positive adverse-related or negative adverse-related. Positive adverse relations are established when drug and reaction entities are associated in the given context, while negative relations involve drugs that are not accountable for a specific reaction. The ADE dataset comprises 6,821 labeled adverse sentences and 16,695 labeled negative adverse sentences, with a total of 5,063 entities. We consider two types of relations in this dataset: adverse-related and not adverse-related. The first entity is viewed as the drug, while the second entity is retrieved using named entity recognition. Table 1 provides details of the public ontologies utilized for constructing symbolic knowledge.

**Baseline Models for Comparison.** We used several competitive baselines: 1) Multi-instance models such as [23,38,39], 2) Sentential RE models such as

**Table 1.** Ontologies used for Symbolic Knowledge

| Ontology | Classes | Properties | Maximum depth |
|---|---|---|---|
| DINTO [7] | 28,178 | 12 | 2 |
| OAE [14] | 10,589 | 123 | 17 |
| NDF-RT [34] | 36,202 | 90 | 9 |
| MEDLINE [36] | 2,254 | 12 | 2 |
| NCIt [19] | 177,762 | 97 | 21 |

**Table 2.** Hyper parameters setting

| Hyper-parameters | Value |
|---|---|
| learning rate | 0.001 |
| batch size | 50 |
| dropout ratio | 0.5 |
| hidden state size | 256 |
| non linear activation | relu |

[4,30,42]. For Recon [4], we used its EAC variant for fair comparison. Please note, we adapted these models to biomedical domain by re-training and inducing biomedical context needed for these models such as entity descriptions and types. 3) Biomedical relation extraction works such as [13,17,26,28,35]. For biomedical RE works, values are obtained from original papers, and for other works (sentential and multi-instance), if code is available, we executed them on both datasets.

**Hyper-parameters and Metrics.** Table 2 outlines the best parameter setting. We employ GloVe embedding of dimension 50 for initialization. Since the datasets are from the biomedical domain for evaluating semantic similarity, we have used BioBERT model (see Footnote 1). The size of position embedding is also kept at 50. We have used the open-source ontology (.owl) from BioPortal to

**Table 3.** Biomedical Relation Extraction Results. ReOnto outperforms baselines on both datasets. We've left precision column blank for baselines that does not report it.

| Dataset | Model | Accuracy(in%) | F1 scores |
|---------|-------|---------------|-----------|
| ADE | CNN [23] | 68 | 0.71 |
| | PCNN [38] | 76.9 | 0.73 |
| | ContextAware [30] | 93 | 0.93 |
| | RGCN [28] | 86 | 0.83 |
| | GPGNN [42] | 92.1 | 0.90 |
| | CRNN [17] | – | 0.87 |
| | CNN-Embedding [26] | – | 0.89 |
| | SparkNLP [13] | – | 0.85 |
| | T5 [25] | 92 | 0.86 |
| | RECON [5] | 93.5 | 0.92 |
| | ReOnto (**Ours**) | **97** | **0.96** |
| Dataset | Model | Accuracy(in%) | F1 scores |
| BioRel | CNN [23] | 48 | 0.47 |
| | PCNN [38] | 64.6 | 0.57 |
| | RGCN [28] | 72 | 0.78 |
| | GPGNN [42] | 85 | 0.84 |
| | CNN+ATT [35] | – | 0.72 |
| | PCNN+AVG [35] | – | 0.76 |
| | RNN+AVG [35] | – | 0.74 |
| | ContextAware [30] | 89 | 0.87 |
| | T5 [25] | 88 | 0.86 |
| | RECON [5] | 89.6 | 0.86 |
| | ReOnto (**Ours**) | **92** | **0.90** |

extract the paths using the SPARQL query. We have followed [42] for experiment settings. We evaluated the accuracy (precision) and F1 score for both datasets.

## 5   Results

ReOnto outperforms all the baseline models on both datasets (From Table 3). These results indicate that our model could successfully conduct reasoning with a neuro-symbolic graph on the fully connected graph and combine it with the underlying deep learning model (GNN in our case). Observed results successfully answer **RQ1**. Methods such as [5, 30] use contexts such as entity types and descriptions. Similarly, RECON and T5 include additional explicit information of long entity descriptions, its type that allows offline learning of entity context. However, in a real-world setting of the biomedical domain, it is viable that such context may not be present for each entity. In contrast, our model discards the necessity of available entity context and learns purely using reasoning over connected entity graphs. Furthermore, multi-instance baselines try to learn relations using previous occurrences of entities in the document. In both cases, missing reasoning to capture long-range dependencies of entities hampers their performance. One possible reason for CNN and PCNN not performing well is that the biomedical sentence is complex and direct adherence to relation is impossible in this type of text. We can also notice that the context-aware model is performing better than multi-instance on these datasets because entity contexts are helping up to an extent. Presently, we have added context information(symbolic knowledge) via ontology into the model. If enough context details are given our model can work on generalised datasets as well. Figure 4 presents plots a, b, c, d, which depict the training and validation F1 scores on both datasets, while plots e, f show the loss graph. Our observations indicate that ReOnto delivers consistent performance on these graphs within the considered timeframe.

## 6   Ablation Study

### 6.1   Effectiveness of Number of Ontologies

To better understand the contribution of each ontology on ReOnto's performance, we conducted an ablation study. Table 4 presents a summary of our findings, which indicate a significant decrease in performance when considering individual ontologies. This validates our approach of merging knowledge from multiple ontologies to create symbolic knowledge.

For the ADE dataset, we have a lesser entity coverage of 22% using DRON ontology. However, we found that the performance significantly improves when we increase the entity coverage by incorporating the OAE and DINTO ontologies. This increase in entity coverage results in corresponding improvements in F1 scores. Similarly, for the BioRel dataset, we tested with MEDLINE ontology with entity coverage of 42% and then NCIt ontology with coverage of 34%, leading to corresponding improvements in F1 scores. Results also provide conclusive evidence that ReOnto's performance depends on the coverage of entities aligned with the dataset and combining encoded knowledge has positive impact on overall performance (answering **RQ2**).

**Table 4.** Effect of ontology on F1 scores

| Dataset | Ontology | Entity coverage(approx.) | F1 scores |
|---------|----------|--------------------------|-----------|
| ADE | DRON [7] | 22% | 0.92 |
| | OAE [14] | 34% | 0.93 |
| | DINTO [15] | 41% | 0.95 |
| BioRel | MEDLINE [36] | 42% | 0.88 |
| | NCIt [19] | 34% | 0.84 |

## 6.2   Effectiveness of Number of Hops

We separately study the effect of the number of hops on the performance of ReOnto. Figure 5 shows the impact of the number of hops on the model. Increasing hops initially improve F1 scores until reaching a plateau. This is because

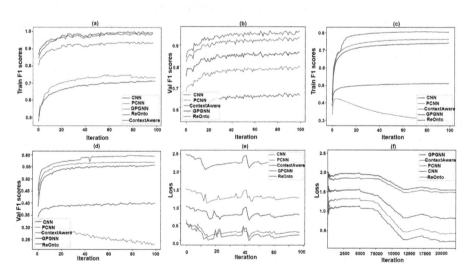

**Fig. 4.** For the ADE dataset, Figures a) and b) show the training and validation F1 scores with baseline, respectively. Figure e) illustrates the cross-entropy loss for the iteration. For the BioRel dataset, Figures c) and d) show the training and validation F1 scores with baseline, respectively. Figure f) illustrates the cross-entropy loss concerning the iteration. ReOnto exhibits consistent and stable performance on both datasets, as indicated by the plotted F1 scores and loss.

additional hops don't provide new relevant information. Table 6 summarizes the extracted hops from the MEDLINE ontology, supporting our observation. Interestingly, increasing hops leads to redundant information that doesn't contribute to performance. To maintain context and meaningful connections, we preserved multi-hop information up to five hops in our experiment. Furthermore, Table 5 illustrates the relationship between ontology size, parsing time, and the number of hops, indicating an increase in time as hops increase.

**Table 5.** Time taken to parse ontology and evaluate respective path. Parsing time increase w.r.t size of ontology

| Ontology | Size (in KB) | Time taken (in seconds) | | | | | |
|---|---|---|---|---|---|---|---|
| | | Parsing | Direct hop | One hop | Two hop | Axiom path1 | Axiom path2 |
| OAE | 9286 | 6.75 | 0.11 | 2.73 | 7.47 | 2.19 | 5.92 |
| NDFRT | 69387 | 123.11 | 1.21 | 0.003 | 7.629 | 44.79 | 103.36 |
| DINTO | 1,10,865 | 137.4 | 1.6 | 3.8 | 8.54 | 5.67 | 11.32 |
| MEDLINE | 6975 | 2.19 | 0.002 | 0.0023 | 0.003 | 3.118 | 6.09 |
| NCI | 5,71,434 | 758.9 | 1034.5 | 1294.5 | 3454.1 | 2485 | 5569 |

## 7   Case Study

Table 7 shows qualitative results that compare the ReOnto model with the baseline models. We report a few results showing ReOnto can surmise the relationship with reasoning. ReOnto retrieved the relevant derived path from the ontology in the first case. ReOnto implicitly learns from the facts and captures the derived path to provide the correct relation label, even if it is not explicitly mentioned as *isPrimaryAnatomicSiteOfDisease*.

$$CUI{:}C0262950 \xrightarrow{preferredLabel} Bone$$
$$Bone \sqsubseteq \exists anatomicSiteOfDisease.Rickets$$
$$Rickets \xrightarrow{CUI} CUI{:}C0035579$$
$$Bone \xrightarrow{semanticType} Anatomic\ Structure$$

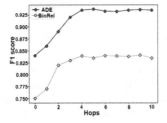

**Fig. 5.** Effectiveness of hops on performance

**Table 6.** Derived path obtained by connecting "protein" and "dietary protein" entity

| Hops | Path |
|---|---|
| path1 | classifies |
| path2 | mapped from dietary proteins, classifies |
| path3 | classifies proteins, classifies dietary proteins, classifies |
| path4 | classifies proteins, classifies dietary proteins, mapped from dietary proteins, classifies |
| path5 | classifies proteins, classifies dietary proteins, related to carbs, related to dietary proteins, classifies |
| path6 | classifies Proteins, classifies dietary proteins, mapped from dietary proteins, related to carbs, related to dietary proteins, classifies |
| path7 | classifies Proteins, classifies dietary proteins, mapped from dietary proteins, related to carbs, related to dietary proteins classifies dietary proteins |

**Table 7.** Sample sentences and predictions of various models. ReOnto using reasoning is able to predict the relations which are not explicitly observable from the sentence itself and requires long-range entity interactions.

| Sentence | Relation | GPGNN | Context Aware | ReOnto |
|---|---|---|---|---|
| Both compounds are equally potent in the stimulation of intestinal calcium transport, bone(C0262950) calcium mobilization , in the elevation of serum phosphorus, and in the healing of rickets(C0035579) in the rat | is primary anatomic site of disease | may be associated disease of disease | may be finding of disease | is primary anatomic site of disease |
| The ventricular effective refractory period, as well as the vt cycle length(C0042514), increased after propranolol(C0033497) and was further prolonged after the addition of a type i agent | may be treated by | may diagnose | may treat | may be treated by |
| dsip and clip [acth(18–39)] immunoreactive(ir) neurons and fibers were examined in the human(C0086418) hypophysis and pituitary stalk using immunmohistofluorescence and peroxidase(C4522012) antiperoxidase methods | is organism source of gene product | nichd parent of | organism has gene | is organism source of gene product |

In the second case, ReOnto produces the following path by utilizing the expressive axiom of the ontology. ReOnto captures the long-range dependencies between entities and provides the correct relation label.

$$CUI{:}C0042514 \xrightarrow{preferredLabel} Ventricular\ Tachycardia$$
$$Ventricular\ Tachycardia \equiv Techycardia$$
$$Techycardia \sqsubseteq \exists mayBeTreatedBy.Propranolol$$
$$Propranolol \xrightarrow{CUI} CUI{:}C0033497$$

In the last case study, several paths are derived from the ontology for the *Human* entity. It can be observed that ReOnto derives and asserts the dependency path between *Human* and *Peroxidase*, and concludes that the target relation label *isOrganismSourceOfGeneProduct* applies, as compared to other baseline models. Such complex ontology reasoning provides long-range interactions between entities, which is inherently not possible in baseline models.

$$CUI\text{:}C0086418 \xrightarrow{preferredLabel} Human$$
$$\exists Human \sqsubseteq geneProductHasOrganismSource.Myeloperoxidase$$
$$Myeloperoxidase \xrightarrow{hasDisposition} Peroxidase\,(disposition)$$
$$Peroxidase\,(disposition) \xrightarrow{preferredName} Peroxidase$$
$$Peroxidase \xrightarrow{CUI} CUI\text{:}C4522012$$

## 8    Conclusion and Future Work

We proposed a novel neuro-symbolic approach ReOnto that leverages path-based reasoning, including expressive axiom path with GNN. We apply our model to complex biomedical text and compare the approach with baselines. With empirical results, there are three key takeaways. Firstly, existing baseline models with any form of context only capture short-range dependencies of entities. In contrast, our model uses long-range entity dependencies derived from ontology reasoning to outperform all baselines on both biomedical datasets. Code is available at https://github.com/kracr/reonto-relation-extraction.

ReOnto provides effective reasoning on given text and entity pair, which can tackle the challenges of biomedical text. It also considers expressive axioms of ontology to reason on RE. The aggregation of these axioms outperformed the baselines. As a next step, we can consider using background knowlege on unsupervised data. An ontology reasoner can be used to infer more paths and perhaps these additional axioms can improve the performance further.

**Acknowledgements.** We express our sincere gratitude to the Infosys Centre for Artificial Intelligence (CAI) at IIIT-Delhi for their support throughout the duration of this project.

## References

1. Aghaebrahimian, A., Anisimova, M., Gil, M.: Ontology-aware biomedical relation extraction. bioRxiv (2022)
2. Angell, R., Monath, N., Mohan, S., Yadav, N., McCallum, A.: Clustering-based inference for biomedical entity linking. In: Proceedings of the 2021 Conference of the North American Chapter of the Association for Computational Linguistics: Human Language Technologies, pp. 2598–2608 (2021)
3. Balcilar, M., Renton, G., Héroux, P., Gaüzère, B., Adam, S., Honeine, P.: Analyzing the expressive power of graph neural networks in a spectral perspective. In: International Conference on Learning Representations (2020)
4. Bastos, A., Nadgeri, A., Singh, K., Kanezashi, H., Suzumura, T., Mulang', I.O.: How expressive are transformers in spectral domain for graphs? Trans. Mach. Learn. Res. (2022)
5. Bastos, A., et al.: Recon: relation extraction using knowledge graph context in a graph neural network. In: Proceedings of the Web Conference 2021, pp. 1673–1685 (2021)

6. Bodenreider, O.: The unified medical language system (UMLs): integrating biomedical terminology. Nucleic Acids Res. **32**(suppl_1), D267–D270 (2004)
7. Bona, J.P., Brochhausen, M., Hogan, W.R.: Enhancing the drug ontology with semantically-rich representations of national drug codes and RxNorm unique concept identifiers. BMC Bioinf. **20**(21) (2019). https://doi.org/10.1186/s12859-019-3192-8
8. Cabot, P.L.H., Navigli, R.: Rebel: relation extraction by end-to-end language generation. In: Findings of the Association for Computational Linguistics: EMNLP 2021, pp. 2370–2381 (2021)
9. Crone, P.: Deeper task-specificity improves joint entity and relation extraction. arXiv preprint arXiv:2002.06424 (2020)
10. Eberts, M., Ulges, A.: Span-based joint entity and relation extraction with transformer pre-training. In: ECAI 2020, pp. 2006–2013. IOS Press (2020)
11. Fensel, D., et al.: Why we need knowledge graphs: applications. In: Knowledge Graphs, pp. 95–112. Springer, Cham (2020). https://doi.org/10.1007/978-3-030-37439-6_4
12. Gurulingappa, H., Rajput, A.M., Roberts, A., Fluck, J., Hofmann-Apitius, M., Toldo, L.: Development of a benchmark corpus to support the automatic extraction of drug-related adverse effects from medical case reports. J. Biomed. Inf. **45**(5), 885–892 (2012). https://doi.org/10.1016/j.jbi.2012.04.008, www.sciencedirect.com/science/article/pii/S1532046412000615, text Mining and Natural Language Processing in Pharmacogenomics
13. Haq, H.U., Kocaman, V., Talby, D.: Mining adverse drug reactions from unstructured mediums at scale (2022). arxiv.org/abs/2201.01405, version: 2
14. He, Y., et al.: OAE: the ontology of adverse events. J. Biomed. Seman. **5** 29 (2014). https://doi.org/10.1186/2041-1480-5-29, www.ncbi.nlm.nih.gov/pmc/articles/PMC4120740/
15. Herrero-Zazo, M., Segura-Bedmar, I., Hastings, J., Martínez, P.: DINTO: using OWL ontologies and SWRL rules to infer drug-drug interactions and their mechanisms. J. Chem. Inf. Model. **55**(8), 1698–1707 (2015). https://doi.org/10.1021/acs.jcim.5b00119, publisher: American Chemical Society
16. Hong, J.F., Li, X.B., Huang, C.R.: Ontology-based prediction of compound relations : a study based on SUMO. In: Proceedings of the 18th Pacific Asia Conference on Language, Information and Computation, pp. 151–160. Logico-Linguistic Society of Japan, December 2004. http://hdl.handle.net/2065/568,https://aclanthology.org/Y04-1015
17. Huynh, T.T., He, Y., Willis, A., Rüger, S.M.: Adverse drug reaction classification with deep neural networks. In: International Conference on Computational Linguistics (2016)
18. Karkaletsis, V., Fragkou, P., Petasis, G., Iosif, E.: Ontology based information extraction from text. In: Paliouras, G., Spyropoulos, C.D., Tsatsaronis, G. (eds.) Knowledge-Driven Multimedia Information Extraction and Ontology Evolution. LNCS (LNAI), vol. 6050, pp. 89–109. Springer, Heidelberg (2011). https://doi.org/10.1007/978-3-642-20795-2_4
19. Kumar, A., Smith, B.: Oncology ontology in the NCI thesaurus. In: Miksch, S., Hunter, J., Keravnou, E.T. (eds.) AIME 2005. LNCS (LNAI), vol. 3581, pp. 213–220. Springer, Heidelberg (2005). https://doi.org/10.1007/11527770_30
20. Li, D., Huan, L.: The ontology relation extraction for semantic web annotation. In: IEEE International Symposium on Cluster Computing and the Grid, pp. 534–541. IEEE Computer Society, Los Alamitos, CA, USA, May 2008. https://doi.org/10.1109/CCGRID.2008.97

21. Lv, X., Cao, Y., Hou, L., Li, J., Liu, Z., Zhang, Y., Dai, Z.: Is multi-hop reasoning really explainable? towards benchmarking reasoning interpretability. In: Proceedings of the 2021 Conference on Empirical Methods in Natural Language Processing, pp. 8899–8911 (2021)

22. Nadgeri, A., et al.: KGPool: dynamic knowledge graph context selection for relation extraction. In: Findings of the Association for Computational Linguistics: ACL-IJCNLP 2021, pp. 535–548. Association for Computational Linguistics, August 2021. https://doi.org/10.18653/v1/2021.findings-acl.48, www.aclanthology.org/2021.findings-acl.48

23. Nguyen, T.H., Grishman, R.: Relation extraction: perspective from convolutional neural networks. In: VS@HLT-NAACL (2015)

24. Pan, J.Z., Zhang, M., Singh, K., Harmelen, F., Gu, J., Zhang, Z.: Entity enabled relation linking. In: Ghidini, C., et al. (eds.) ISWC 2019. LNCS, vol. 11778, pp. 523–538. Springer, Cham (2019). https://doi.org/10.1007/978-3-030-30793-6_30

25. Raffel, C., et al.: Exploring the limits of transfer learning with a unified text-to-text transformer (2020)

26. Rawat, A., Wani, M.A., ElAffendi, M., Imran, A.S., Kastrati, Z., Daudpota, S.M.: Drug adverse event detection using text-based convolutional neural networks (textcnn) technique. Electronics 11(20) (2022). https://doi.org/10.3390/electronics11203336, www.mdpi.com/2079-9292/11/20/3336

27. Santos, C.N.D., Xiang, B., Zhou, B.: Classifying relations by ranking with convolutional neural networks (2015). https://doi.org/10.48550/ARXIV.1504.06580, arxiv.org/abs/1504.06580

28. Schlichtkrull, M., Kipf, T.N., Bloem, P., Berg, R.V.D., Titov, I., Welling, M.: Modeling relational data with graph convolutional networks. arXiv preprint arXiv:1703.06103 (2017)

29. Shen, Y., Huang, X.: Attention-based convolutional neural network for semantic relation extraction. In: Proceedings of COLING 2016, the 26th International Conference on Computational Linguistics: Technical Papers, pp. 2526–2536. The COLING 2016 Organizing Committee, Osaka, Japan, December 2016. www.aclanthology.org/C16-1238

30. Sorokin, D., Gurevych, I.: Context-aware representations for knowledge base relation extraction. In: Proceedings of the 2017 Conference on Empirical Methods in Natural Language Processing, pp. 1784–1789. Association for Computational Linguistics, Copenhagen, Denmark, September 2017. https://doi.org/10.18653/v1/D17-1188, www.aclanthology.org/D17-1188

31. Santosh, T.Y.S.S., Chakraborty, P., Dutta, S., Sanyal, D.K., Das, P.P.: Joint entity and relation extraction from scientific documents: Role of linguistic information and entity types. In: EEKE@JCDL (2021)

32. Vashishth, S., Joshi, R., Prayaga, S.S., Bhattacharyya, C., Talukdar, P.: RESIDE: improving distantly-supervised neural relation extraction using side information. In: Proceedings of the 2018 Conference on Empirical Methods in Natural Language Processing, pp. 1257–1266. Association for Computational Linguistics, Brussels, Belgium, Oct–Nov 2018. https://doi.org/10.18653/v1/D18-1157, www.aclanthology.org/D18-1157

33. Wang, L., Cao, Z., de Melo, G., Liu, Z.: Relation classification via multi-level attention CNNs. In: Proceedings of the 54th Annual Meeting of the Association for Computational Linguistics (Volume 1: Long Papers), pp. 1298–1307. Association for Computational Linguistics, Berlin, Germany, August 2016. https://doi.org/10.18653/v1/P16-1123, www.aclanthology.org/P16-1123

34. Winnenburg, R., Mortensen, J.M., Bodenreider, O.: Using description logics to evaluate the consistency of drug-class membership relations in NDF-RT. J. Biomed. Seman. **6**https://doi.org/10.1186/s13326-015-0007-3, www.ncbi.nlm.nih. gov/pmc/articles/PMC4392727/(2015)

35. Xing, R., Luo, J., Song, T.: BioRel: towards large-scale biomedical relation extraction. BMC Bioinf. **21**(16), 543 (2020). https://doi.org/10.1186/s12859-020-03889-5

36. Yang, J.-J.: An ontology-based intelligent agent system for semantic search in medicine. In: Lee, J., Barley, M. (eds.) PRIMA 2003. LNCS (LNAI), vol. 2891, pp. 182–193. Springer, Heidelberg (2003). https://doi.org/10.1007/978-3-540-39896-7_16

37. Ye, Z.X., Ling, Z.H.: Distant supervision relation extraction with intra-bag and inter-bag attentions (2019). https://doi.org/10.48550/ARXIV.1904.00143, arxiv.org/abs/1904.00143

38. Zeng, D., Liu, K., Chen, Y., Zhao, J.: Distant supervision for relation extraction via piecewise convolutional neural networks. In: Proceedings of the 2015 Conference on Empirical Methods in Natural Language Processing, pp. 1753–1762. Association for Computational Linguistics, Lisbon, Portugal, September 2015. https://doi.org/10.18653/v1/D15-1203, www.aclanthology.org/D15-1203

39. Zeng, D., Liu, K., Lai, S., Zhou, G., Zhao, J.: Relation classification via convolutional deep neural network. In: Proceedings of COLING 2014, the 25th International Conference on Computational Linguistics: Technical Papers, pp. 2335–2344. Dublin City University and Association for Computational Linguistics, Dublin, Ireland, August 2014. www.aclanthology.org/C14-1220

40. Zhang, D., Wang, D.: Relation classification via recurrent neural network (2015). https://doi.org/10.48550/ARXIV.1508.01006, arxiv.org/abs/1508.01006

41. Zhang, W., Chen, J., Li, J., Xu, Z., Pan, J.Z., Chen, H.: Knowledge graph reasoning with logics and embeddings: survey and perspective. arXiv preprint arXiv:2202.07412 (2022)

42. Zhu, H., Lin, Y., Liu, Z., Fu, J., Chua, T.S., Sun, M.: Graph neural networks with generated parameters for relation extraction. In: Proceedings of the 57th Annual Meeting of the Association for Computational Linguistics, pp. 1331–1339. Association for Computational Linguistics, Florence, Italy, July 2019. https://doi.org/10.18653/v1/P19-1128, www.aclanthology.org/P19-1128

# Optimization

# NKFAC: A Fast and Stable KFAC Optimizer for Deep Neural Networks

Ying Sun[1], Hongwei Yong[1], and Lei Zhang[1,2(✉)]

[1] The Hong Kong Polytechnic University, Hong Hum, Kowloon, Hong Kong, China
{csysun,cslzhang}@comp.polyu.edu.hk, hongwei.yong@polyu.edu.hk
[2] OPPO Research Institute, Shenzhen, Guangdong, China

**Abstract.** In recent advances in second-order optimizers, computing the inverse of second-order statistics matrices has become critical. One such example is the Kronecker-factorized approximate curvature (KFAC) algorithm, where the inverse computation of the two second-order statistics to approximate the Fisher information matrix (FIM) is essential. However, the time-consuming nature of this inversion process often limits the extensive application of KFAC. What's more, improper choice of the inversion method or hyper-parameters can lead to instability and fail the entire optimization process. To address these issues, this paper proposes the Newton-Kronecker factorized approximate curvature (NKFAC) algorithm, which incorporates Newton's iteration method for inverting second-order statistics. As the FIM between adjacent iterations changes little, Newton's iteration can be initialized by the inverse obtained from the previous step, producing accurate results within a few iterations thanks to its fast local convergence. This approach reduces computation time and inherits the property of second-order optimizers, enabling practical applications. The proposed algorithm is further enhanced with several useful implementations, resulting in state-of-the-art generalization performance without the need for extensive parameter tuning. The efficacy of NKFAC is demonstrated through experiments on various computer vision tasks. The code is publicly available at https://github.com/myingysun/NKFAC.

**Keywords:** Second-order optimizer · Nature gradient method · Newton method

## 1 Introduction

Benefited from the convenient back-propagation (BP) process, the first-order gradient-based algorithms [17,25,32,43] have occupied the mainstream of deep neural networks (DNNs) optimization. Due to the appealing property of fast convergence, second-order optimizers have been continuously developed for training DNNs. At this stage, the research on second-order optimizers has achieved fruitful results by different approaches of design (e.g., [7,12,26–28,40,41]). They usually need fewer epochs than first-order optimizers to reach a specified loss or accuracy, confirming their broad application prospects in training DNNs.

© The Author(s), under exclusive license to Springer Nature Switzerland AG 2023
D. Koutra et al. (Eds.): ECML PKDD 2023, LNAI 14172, pp. 251–267, 2023.
https://doi.org/10.1007/978-3-031-43421-1_15

Optimizing deep neural networks (DNNs) in a second-order manner usually requires addressing the challenging problem of approximating the matrix inverse, which is usually time-consuming and sometimes unstable. Two popular ways to utilize the second-order information are Hessian-based methods, which rely on the inverse of second-order Hessian matrix, and nature gradient based methods, which require the inversion of the Fisher information matrix (FIM). However, dealing with the inversion of these matrices can be complex and resource-intensive. Therefore, second-order optimizers usually encounter greater challenges than first-order methods in applications.

In recent decades, natural gradient (NG) methods have received considerable attention due to their "Hessian-free" computation, specifically, only first-order information (i.e., gradients) is required in their computation. From a design perspective, the NG descent algorithm is based on minimizing the KL-divergence of two distributions, with the Fisher Information Matrix (FIM) serving as auxiliary information to aid in optimization. However, as a statistic that summarizes the information of stochastic parameters through observations, FIM is shown to be the expected value of the Hessian under certain regular assumptions [37]. As a result, NG methods are a specific kind of second-order optimizer, and they generally exhibit fast convergence.

The most popular way for applying the NG method is the Kronecker-factorized approximate curvature (KFAC) algorithm [27], which decouples the computation of FIM into a series of matrices of input and matrices of gradient under some assumptions. Thus, the computation cost of the inverse can be reduced from a greatly large FIM to a series of small matrices. Recent works [3,8–10,18,40] have improved KFAC with better approximations. However, computing the inverse of the decoupled matrices of FIM remains an area that requires further study. A recent work [40] proposed SKFAC, which randomly selects (or averages) samples in spatial dimension for convolutional layers and adopts the Sherman-Morrison formula to reduce the dimension of inversion and shorten the computation time. However, besides the loss of information from random sampling and averaging, the moving average of input and gradient instead of second-order statistics in this method may also lead to a considerable loss of information. Consequently, although the inversion time can be significantly reduced, SKFAC's convergence speed and performance may drop more severely if the number of samples is reduced. Additionally, since the Sherman-Morrison formula cannot reduce the time of matrix inversion when two matrix dimensions are close, SKFAC cannot speed up the optimization process under such circumstances.

Besides reducing the computational time to narrow the gap between first-order and second-order algorithms, the stability of second-order methods is also an issue that requires attention. From one aspect, several commonly used inversion approaches such as those relying on eigenvalue decomposition are not stable or not well optimized in build-in functions, which may greatly prevent the widespread application of the corresponding optimizers. From another aspect, the instability of second-order optimizers can also arise from an improper dampening parameter that is added to the matrix, which requires a careful parameter tuning process.

In this paper, based on the popular KFAC optimizer, we propose KFAC with Newton's iteration (in short, **NKFAC**), which is practical, stable and time-saving with state-of-the-art generalization results. By combining the property of slow change of FIM in training and the local fast convergence of Newton's iteration, NKFAC narrows the time gap between first-order and second-order methods caused by inversion, while inherits the convergence property of second-order optimizers, and is not inferior to first-order methods in generalization performance. We verify the effectiveness and efficiency of NKFAC by extensive experiments on different tasks in computer vision.

## 2    Backgrounds and Preliminaries

### 2.1    Matrix Inverse

The efficient computation of matrix inverses is a longstanding and critical research topic due to the universality and time-consuming nature of inversion. In DNNs optimization, there are two main techniques used to reduce the computational cost of matrix inversion. One is the equivalent matrix transformation [2,18,40], which reduces the inversion to a small dimension matrix by rigorous mathematics equations like the Sherman-Morrison formula. The other one is the application of iteration methods (e.g., [1,35]), which combines DNN training with some common iteration methods (e.g., conjugate gradient (CG) [15] and GMRES [31]).

Proper inversion methods are critical to the success of training DNNs with second-order optimizers. Using an improper method can lead to the failure of the entire training process. For example, when the input matrix has repeated eigenvalues, eigenvalue decomposition-based inversion often fails and disrupts the optimization process. Another concern about the stability of inversion arises from the poor condition number of the matrix. Some matrices encountered in DNNs training may have poor condition numbers that cause difficulties with inversion, regardless of the method used. Numerical operations can mitigate this problem to some extent, for example, by minimizing division in the inversion process to reduce the risk of numerical overflow. Meanwhile, a proper dampening parameter is usually necessary to improve the condition number. The classic KFAC [27] also stresses the importance of the dampening parameter for second-order optimizers in detail. In this paper, we are motivated to design a stable algorithm with a suitable inversion method and adaptive dampening parameter.

### 2.2    KFAC Algorithm

First, we introduce the classic KFAC [11,27]. For a fully connected network, denote $\mathbf{F}$ as the Fisher information matrix (FIM), which is computed only by the first-order derivatives (denote the derivative operation as $\mathcal{D}\cdot$) without additional back-propagation and saves plenty of time as a second-order optimizer. With the advantage of being "Hessian-free" to save computational cost, NG methods only need to solve the storage problem cost by the highly large dimension of $\mathbf{F}$. Each block of $\mathbf{F}$, denoted by $\mathbf{F}_{i,j}$ (defined in Eq. (1)), can be approximated with the assumption of the statistic independence between the inputs $\mathbf{X}$ and their gradients $\mathbf{\Delta}$, i.e.,

$$\mathbf{F}_{i,j} := \mathbb{E}[\text{vec}(\mathcal{D}\mathbf{W}_i)\text{vec}(\mathcal{D}\mathbf{W}_j)] = \mathbb{E}[\mathbf{X}_i\mathbf{X}_j^\top \otimes \mathbf{\Delta}_i\mathbf{\Delta}_j^\top] \approx \mathbb{E}[\mathbf{X}_i\mathbf{X}_j^\top] \otimes \mathbb{E}[\mathbf{\Delta}_i\mathbf{\Delta}_j^\top]. \quad (1)$$

For convenience, we use the notation $\mathbf{L}_{i,j} := \mathbb{E}[\mathbf{\Delta}_i\mathbf{\Delta}_j^\top]$ and $\mathbf{R}_{i,j} := \mathbb{E}[\mathbf{X}_i\mathbf{X}_j^\top]$. Therefore, by the block diagonal approximation of the FIM $\mathbf{F} \approx \text{Diag}(\mathbf{F}_{11}, \cdots, \mathbf{F}_{ll})$, together with the computation rules of Kronecker product, we get that for the $t$-th iteration, the update formula of KFAC, converted to the tensor operation related to the weight $\mathbf{W}$, takes the form

$$\mathbf{W}_{t+1} = \mathbf{W}_t - \tau_t \mathbf{L}_{t+1}^{-1}\mathbf{G}_t\mathbf{R}_{t+1}^{-1}, \quad (2)$$

where $\mathbf{L} = \text{Diag}(\mathbf{L}_{11}, \cdots, \mathbf{L}_{ll})$, $\mathbf{R} = \text{Diag}(\mathbf{R}_{11}, \cdots, \mathbf{R}_{ll})$, and $\mathbf{G}$ is the gradient of the weight $\mathbf{W}$ in tensor form.

The update Eq. (2) is derived only for fully-connected layers [27]. After this, with the help of $im2col$ function, a similar equation is derived for convolutional layers in [11] under some other assumptions, in which two matrix inverses related to the gradients $(\mathbf{L}^{-1})$ and the inputs $(\mathbf{R}^{-1})$ are also required. Although the periodic strategy can be adapted to update the inverse [30], the computation time of the inverse is still an important question that deserves consideration to maximize the performance of the optimizer.

## 2.3   About Other Second-Order Optimizers

There are many other recently proposed second-order optimizers, e.g., GGT [2], Shampoo [12], AdaHessian [41] and M-FAC [7]. Apart from AdaHessian, the other three optimizers all require matrix inversion, which suffer from the instability and time-consuming problems that will be specified in Sect. 3.1 without exception. Unfortunately, AdaHessian requires the second-time back-propagation, which is the most time-consuming (over 4 times compared with SGD). Besides, GGT and M-FAC both import a significant hyper-parameter related to matrix dimension, i.e., the window size $r$. This parameter $r$ has a great influence on the computational cost and storage, and when using the default number $r = 512$, M-FAC even cannot train ResNet50 on CIFAR100 within a 48G storage GPU. Therefore, the design of the second-order optimizer is still a research hot spot.

## 3   Methodology

### 3.1   Motivation

Apart from reducing the time cost of matrix inversion, the toolbox and built-in functions of different machine learning frameworks have also been updated to meet the need for stability as well as time. However, when we tried to reproduce some second-order optimizers, we found that there were still some unstable built-in functions related to the inversion that may kill the optimization process. For example, to deal with matrix inversion, many implementations of second-order optimizers first apply eigenvalue decomposition to the matrix and then use matrix multiplication to obtain the corresponding inverse. By this implementation, the maximum and minimum eigenvalues can also be obtained for some parameter tuning use. When using a previous version of PyTorch, eigenvalue decomposition sometimes failed, halting the optimization process. Although using the *torch.linalg.inv()* function in PyTorch 1.9 alleviated this issue, some complex matrix inversion algorithms still suffer from numerical overflow problems, particularly when the input matrix is ill-conditioned. Furthermore, parallel processing on GPUs for matrix inversion is not as feasible as for other optimized operations (e.g., matrix multiplication).

In addition, the time cost of computing inverse within a single optimization step for KFAC is very large. For example, when training ResNet50 on CIFAR100, computing the inverse takes up over 90% of the time cost of an optimization step. However, previous research [30] has shown that the Fisher Information Matrix (FIM) changes slowly. Our experiments have confirmed this property, especially once the training process stabilizes. Moreover, taking the momentum of second-order statistics into consideration, the inverse of FIM approximated by these statistics also change little between iterations. Therefore, if we adopt an iterative approach to solve the inverses each time, we can use the inverses computed in the previous iteration as good initialization points for the current computation. This property, to our best knowledge, has not been well-utilized in previous works.

Considering the above facts, we are motivated to design an iterative method that can quickly converge locally to maximize the utilization of the previous inverse, and keep only well-optimized matrix multiplications in our method to maximize stability. Here, we consider Newton's iteration, which is described in detail in Sect. 3.2.

## 3.2   Newton's Iteration of Matrix Inverse

For a given real matrix $\mathbf{A}$, an iterative method [4, 36] of computing matrix inverse $\mathbf{A}^{-1}$, which is a generalization of Newton's iterative method and also known as Schultz iteration, obtains a sequence $\{\mathbf{B}_k\}$ that performed simply by

$$\mathbf{B}_{k+1} = 2\mathbf{B}_k - \mathbf{B}_k\mathbf{A}\mathbf{B}_k. \tag{3}$$

Assume $\mathbf{A}$ is an invertible matrix, and $\mathbf{B}_0$ is an initialization close to $\mathbf{A}^{-1}$. Now we state the following **Proposition 1**.

**Proposition 1.** [29, Section 2.3] *If* $\|\mathbf{B}_0\| \neq 0$ *and* $\|\mathbf{I} - \mathbf{A}\mathbf{B}_0\| < 1$, *then the sequence* $\{\mathbf{B}_k\}$ *generated by* (3) *converges to* $\mathbf{A}^{-1}$ *with an order of at least 2.*

For the case that $\|\mathbf{I} - \mathbf{A}\mathbf{B}_0\| \geq 1$, we add a stepsize $\alpha_k$ in the $k$-th iteration. Thus, the Newton's iteration becomes

$$\mathbf{B}_{k+1} = (1 + \alpha_{k+1})\mathbf{B}_k - \alpha_{k+1}\mathbf{B}_k\mathbf{A}\mathbf{B}_k. \tag{4}$$

---

**Algorithm 1.** Newton's Iteration for solving matrix inverse

---

**Inputs:** $(\mathbf{A}, \mathbf{B}_0, K)$;
**Output:** $\mathbf{B}_K$.

1: **for** $k = 1, \ldots, K$ **do**
2:    **if** $\|\mathbf{I} - \mathbf{A}\mathbf{B}_0\| < 1$ **then**
3:        $\mathbf{B}_k = 2\mathbf{B}_{k-1} - \mathbf{B}_{k-1}\mathbf{A}\mathbf{B}_{k-1}$;
4:    **else**
5:        $\alpha_k = \frac{1}{\|\mathbf{A}\mathbf{B}_{k-1}\|}$,    $\mathbf{B}_k = (1 + \alpha_k)\mathbf{B}_{k-1} - \alpha_k \mathbf{B}_{k-1}\mathbf{A}\mathbf{B}_{k-1}$.
6:    **end if**
7: **end for**

---

Note that if $\alpha_{k+1} = 1$, the update iteration is exactly the classic Eq. (3). In our experiments, we empirically set an stepsize $\alpha_{k+1} = \frac{1}{\|\mathbf{A}\mathbf{B}_k\|}$ and it works well throughout our experiments. Ablation study about the stepsize $\alpha_{k+1}$ under the case $\|\mathbf{I} - \mathbf{A}\mathbf{B}_0\| \geq 1$ can be found in **Supplementary Materials** [1].

The fast convergence of Newton's method relies heavily on the request of a good initialized point (see supplementary materials for examples). Thus, when applying Newton's methods to solve traditional optimization problems, first-order methods are usually adopted for some iterations as a warm-up to acquire a good initialized point for Newton's method, and in principle, a series $\{\mathbf{B}_k\}$ should be generated to reach a good approximation of $\mathbf{A}^{-1}$. However, as we explained in Sect. 3.1, the change of the second-order statistic between iterations is quite small, which states that the inversion result of the last iteration is exactly a satisfactory initialized point of the current iteration. This ensures the efficiency of Newton's method with few iterations. Although in the recent research, a series of improved iterative methods with the order of convergence rate from cubic to seventh has been developed (e.g., [20,38]), we still adopt the above Newton's iteration with a substituted stepsize, since it has just several simple matrix multiplications and is easy to achieve a balance between computational cost and performance.

The detailed steps of the Newton's iteration for solving matrix inverse is stated in **Algorithm 1**.

## 3.3    NKFAC

As mentioned in Sect. 2.2, KFAC can be applied on both linear and convolutional layers with updating formula Eq. (2). Thus, with Newton's iteration to update the matrix inverse $\mathbf{L}^{-1}$ and $\mathbf{R}^{-1}$, we combine **Algorithm 1** with classic KFAC, and propose KFAC with Newton iteration (**NKFAC**). Again, since the FIM changes slow, we apply periodical strategy to update the second order statistics $\mathbf{L}, \mathbf{R}$ and their inverses, i.e., $T_{stat}$ and $T_{inv}$ steps, respectively. The periodical strategy is also adopted in some existing works, e.g., [40,42]. Moreover, at the very beginning stage or certain larger intervals $CT_{inv}$, we recalculate the exact

---

[1] Please visit https://github.com/myingysun/NKFAC for the supplementary file.

---

**Algorithm 2.** Periodical inversion updating strategy at the $t$-th iteration

---

**Inputs:** Tensors $\mathbf{L}_t, \mathbf{R}_t, \widehat{\mathbf{L}}_t, \widehat{\mathbf{R}}_t, \mathbf{X}_t, \boldsymbol{\Delta}_t$; floats $\eta, \alpha$; integers $T_{stat}, T_{inv}, C, K$.
**Outputs:** $(\widehat{\mathbf{L}}_{t+1}, \widehat{\mathbf{R}}_{t+1})$.

 1: **if** $t \% T_{stat} = 0$ **then**
 2:    $\mathbf{L}_{t+1} = \alpha \mathbf{L}_t + (1 - \alpha)\boldsymbol{\Delta}_t \boldsymbol{\Delta}_t^\top$, $\mathbf{R}_{t+1} = \alpha \mathbf{R}_t + (1 - \alpha)\mathbf{X}_t \mathbf{X}_t^\top$;
 3: **else**
 4:    $\mathbf{L}_{t+1} = \mathbf{L}_t$, $\mathbf{R}_{t+1} = \mathbf{R}_t$;
 5: **end if**                      *%periodical update the statistics*
 6: **if** $t \% (CT_{inv}) = 0$ or $t < 2T_{inv}$ **then**
 7:    $\widehat{\mathbf{L}}_{t+1} := (\mathbf{L}_{t+1} + \eta \lambda_{\mathrm{Lmax}}\mathbf{I})^{-1}$, $\widehat{\mathbf{R}}_{t+1} := (\mathbf{R}_{t+1} + \eta \lambda_{\mathrm{Rmax}}\mathbf{I})^{-1}$;
 8: **else if** $t \% T_{inv} = 0$ **then**
 9:    $\widehat{\mathbf{L}}_{t+1} := \mathbf{Alg.1}(\mathbf{L}_{t+1} + \eta \lambda_{\mathrm{Lmax}}\mathbf{I}, \widehat{\mathbf{L}}_t, K)$, $\widehat{\mathbf{R}}_{t+1} := \mathbf{Alg.1}(\mathbf{R}_{t+1} + \eta \lambda_{\mathrm{Rmax}}\mathbf{I}, \widehat{\mathbf{R}}_t, K)$;
10: **else**
11:    $\widehat{\mathbf{L}}_{t+1} = \widehat{\mathbf{L}}_t$, $\widehat{\mathbf{R}}_{t+1} = \widehat{\mathbf{R}}_t$;
12: **end if**                      *%periodical update the inverse*

---

inverse to prevent the approximation from getting too far from the exact inverse. For the slow change of $\mathbf{L}$ and $\mathbf{R}$, one can also refer to the supplementary materials for an example of experimental verification.

Different from the existing works, we do not reduce the inversion dimension by random sampling or averaging, so the comprehensiveness of the input information is preserved to the greatest extent. This also allows us to maximally inherit the fast convergence properties of the second-order optimizer while accelerating the inversion process. Meanwhile, **Algorithm 1** has only matrix product operations, which, from a numerical perspective, is stable in computation compared with other inversion methods that may need division. The possibility of numerical overflow is reduced, which also makes the training process more stable.

Before stating the whole structure of NKFAC, from a simple and practical point of view, we will introduce some useful implementations in Sect. 3.4.

### 3.4 Implementations and AdaNKFAC

Before introducing the implementations of our NKFAC, it is worth mentioning that these techniques can be implemented in other second-order optimizers to avoid the tedious tuning process and improve the stability of the algorithms. We also report some ablation studies of them on classic KFAC and the generalized SKFAC in supplementary materials.

**Gradient Norm Recovery:** Parameter tuning is a very important but tedious part of training DNNs. At this stage, first-order optimizers have been widely used in DNNs training. In the deep learning tasks, most of the commonly used parameters and tuning schedules, including learning rate and weight decay, have been finely tuned by many existing works, so their performances are generally satisfactory. However, for the second-order optimizers, the best parameters and tuning schedules may vary greatly from the first-order optimizers. Carefully tuning parameters will cost a lot of time and resources. However, without tuning parameters, second-order optimizers are easy to fail since they are usually more sensitive to changes in parameters. To solve the parameter tuning question of second-order algorithms, we adopt the gradient norm recovery technique, which can also be found in [42]. Specifically, the descent direction $\widehat{\mathbf{G}} = \mathbf{L}^{-1}\mathbf{G}\mathbf{R}^{-1}$ is recovered by

$$\widetilde{\mathbf{G}} = \widehat{\mathbf{G}}\frac{\|\mathbf{G}\|}{\|\widehat{\mathbf{G}}\|}. \tag{5}$$

After implementing this technique, the finely tuned parameters and tuning schedules can be adopted with just small changes, and even be applied directly. This allows us to maximize the use of the existing parameter tuning results without much tedious and repetitive work.

**Adaptive Dampening:** In computing matrix inverse, the property of the matrix itself has a great influence on the difficulty of solving the inverse and the stability of the inversion algorithm. For example, if the matrix is ill-conditioned, most algorithms may easy to fail numerically, and if the minimum eigenvalue of the matrix is close to zero, the magnitude of the inverse may become quite large, which may also fail the whole optimization process. For second-order optimizers, dampening parameters can greatly influence the training performance. Here, for each matrix $\mathbf{L}$ and $\mathbf{R}$, we adopt the adaptive dampening parameters related to the maximum eigenvalue $\lambda_{\mathrm{Lmax}}$ and $\lambda_{\mathrm{Rmax}}$ respectively, i.e.,

$$\mathbf{L} := \mathbf{L} + \eta\lambda_{\mathrm{Lmax}}\mathbf{I}, \quad \mathbf{R} := \mathbf{R} + \eta\lambda_{\mathrm{Rmax}}\mathbf{I}, \tag{6}$$

where $\eta \in (0,1)$ is a given hyper-parameter. This technique can also be found in [42] to improve the property of matrices with different magnitudes. With this technique, the matrix to be inverted becomes more stable.

**Statistics Momentum:** The second-order statistics used to help optimization are stored in two matrices $\mathbf{L}$ and $\mathbf{R}$, which are exactly the approximations of FIM and also the matrices that need inversion. To sum up all the information of different batches of input, we add momentum to the second-order statistics, i.e., for each iteration $t + 1$, we compute and store the matrix $\mathbf{L}_{t+1}$ and $\mathbf{R}_{t+1}$ by

$$\mathbf{L}_{t+1} = \alpha\mathbf{L}_t + (1 - \alpha)\boldsymbol{\Delta}_t\boldsymbol{\Delta}_t^\top, \quad \mathbf{R}_{t+1} = \alpha\mathbf{R}_t + (1 - \alpha)\mathbf{X}_t\mathbf{X}_t^\top. \tag{7}$$

In application, the hyper-parameter $\alpha$ is usually chosen close to 1, which leads to the slow change of FIM. Therefore, we design **Algorithm 2**, which shows our periodical inversion updating strategy. To prevent the probability of the statistics changing too fast at the beginning stage, we compute exact inversion in the first $2T_{inv}$ iterations, and one can decide whether to use this case by case.

**Adaptive Stepsize (AdaNKFAC):** Inspired by the success of adaptive stepsize methods especially in training transformers, we also add the adaptive stepsize and weight decouple technique into NKFAC and propose AdaNKFAC (stated in supplementary materials), which can also be regarded as a combination of NKFAC and AdamW [25]. Thus, without tedious parameter-tuning,

---

**Algorithm 3. NKFAC**

---

**Inputs:** Initialization $\mathbf{W}_0, \mathbf{L}_0 = \epsilon \mathbf{I}_{C_{out}}, \mathbf{R}_0 = \epsilon \mathbf{I}_{C_{in}}, \widehat{\mathbf{L}}_0 = \mathbf{0}_{C_{out}}, \widehat{\mathbf{R}}_0 = \mathbf{0}_{C_{in}}$; float numbers $\tau, \eta$; integer constants $T_{stat}, T_{inv}, C, K$;

**Outputs:** $\mathbf{W}_T$.

1: **for** $t = 0, 1, \ldots, T-1$ **do**
2:    compute the gradient $\mathbf{G}_t$;
3:    save $\mathbf{X}_t = [x_{ti}]_{i=1}^n$ and $\mathbf{\Delta}_t = [\delta_{ti}]_{i=1}^n$;    %by forward and backward propagation, respectively
4:    $(\widehat{\mathbf{L}}_{t+1}, \widehat{\mathbf{R}}_{t+1}) = \mathbf{Alg.2}(\mathbf{L}_t, \mathbf{R}_t, \widehat{\mathbf{L}}_t, \widehat{\mathbf{R}}_t, \mathbf{X}_t, \mathbf{\Delta}_t, \eta, \alpha, T_{stat}, T_{inv}, C, K)$;
5:    $\widehat{\mathbf{G}}_{t+1} = \widehat{\mathbf{L}}_{t+1} \mathbf{G}_t \widehat{\mathbf{R}}_{t+1}$;
6:    $\widetilde{\mathbf{G}}_{t+1} = \widehat{\mathbf{G}}_{t+1} \frac{\|\mathbf{G}_t\|}{\|\widehat{\mathbf{G}}_{t+1}\|}$;
7:    $\mathbf{W}_{t+1} = \mathbf{W}_t - \tau \widetilde{\mathbf{G}}_{t+1}$.
8: **end for**

---

we easily achieve higher performance compared with classical adaptive stepsize methods (e.g., AdamW) as we reported in Sect. 4.

Overall, the detailed NKFAC algorithm is stated in **Algorithm 3**.

# 4  Experiments

## 4.1  Experimental Setup

**Hyper-parameters Settings:** Due to the fast local convergence of Newton's method, together with the numerical performance, we take $K = 1$ in **Algorithm 1**. Although the step seems few, it works well through all our experiments. In classification tasks that NKFAC is compared with KFAC and SKFAC, we take $T_{stat} = 20$ and $T_{inv} = 200$, which keeps the same interval parameters as in [40] for a fair comparison. In other tasks, we adopt $T_{stat} = 100$ and $T_{inv} = 1000$, which not only shows the wide applicability and satisfactory performance but also states the robustness of our proposed NKFAC. The integer interval $C$ takes 500, the gradient momentum takes 0.9, the second-order statistics momentum is set to 0.95, and the dampening parameter $\eta = 0.01$. Please refer to supplementary materials for more ablation studies about these hyper-parameters.

**Choice of NKFAC and AdaNKFAC:** For experiments on transformers, the adaptive momentum methods often obtain more satisfactory results than SGDM, and the default optimizer of training transformers are often AdamW. To keep satisfactory results without tedious parameter tuning, we choose AdaNKFAC for these experiments, while for traditional CNNs with default optimizer SGD, we choose NKFAC as a comparison. Thus, we can gain the performance with the same or just slightly different hyper-parameters.

**Baseline Optimizers:** The baseline optimizers (Opt) in this section are KFAC, SKFAC, and the first-order optimizers SGDM [32], AdamW [25], RAdam [23] and Adabelief [43]. For SKFAC, a too-small number of random sampling will affect the performance, so we take the random sampling number to be 8, which

**Table 1.** Testing accuracies (%) of different optimizers on CIFAR100/10. * means at least one of the four repeated experiments fails to converge.

| | | | CIFAR100 | | | | |
|---|---|---|---|---|---|---|---|
| Opt | SGDM | AdamW | RAdam | Adabelief | KFAC | SKFAC | NKFAC |
| D121 | 80.26 ± .32 | 78.92 ± .17 | 79.29 ± .19 | 80.21 ± .24 | 79.32 ± .05 | 80.44 ± .35 | **81.13** ± .16 |
| R18 | 78.41 ± .25 | 77.63 ± .18 | 77.54 ± .11 | 78.41 ± .29 | 79.96 ± .21 | 78.91 ± .14 | **80.23** ± .24 |
| R50 | 78.87 ± .35 | 78.85 ± .50 | 79.15 ± .24 | 80.61 ± .44 | 80.77 ± .17 | 81.16 ± .16 | **81.78** ± .06 |
| GLN | 80.26 ± .15 | 79.83 ± .22 | 79.90 ± .07 | 80.98 ± .15 | 81.47 ± .24 | 79.68 ± .19 | **81.65** ± .10 |
| | | | CIFAR10 | | | | |
| D121 | 95.73 ± .12 | 95.11 ± .14 | 95.17 ± .24 | 95.68 ± .14 | 95.17 ± .11 | **95.77** ± .20 | 95.72 ± .07 |
| R18 | 95.50 ± .07 | 95.05 ± .14 | 95.04 ± .10 | 95.34 ± .10 | **95.84** ± .12 | 95.82 ± .05 | 95.80 ± .10 |
| R50 | 95.43 ± .21 | 95.20 ± .07 | 95.19 ± .15 | 95.77 ± .11 | 95.93 ± .09 | **96.11** ± .16 | 96.07 ± .10 |
| GLN | 95.56 ± .09 | 95.05 ± .14 | 95.17 ± .10 | 95.67 ± .11 | 95.52 ± .00* | 95.57 ± .16 | **96.23** ± .06 |

is still within the suggested range in [40]. Meanwhile, since our experiments are accomplished on Pytorch 1.9 framework, by noticing that the inverse function runs much faster than computing the inverse with the help of the eigenvalue decomposition function, we implement the computation of maximum eigenvalue by Newton-Schulz iterations to save running time in each step. It is worth mentioning that we have tested the second-order optimizers mentioned in Sect. 2.3, i.e., GGT [2], Shampoo [12], AdaHessian [41] and M-FAC [7]. However, as we mentioned that second-order optimizers usually need parameter-tuning from scratch, in our experiments, even after the tedious parameter-tuning, their performances are still not satisfactory and sometimes fail to converge. Therefore, we do not contain these optimizers in our comparison in this section.

## 4.2   Results on CIFAR100/10

In this section, our experiments are conducted on CIFAR100/10 [19] datasets with 4 Geforce RTX 2080Ti GPUs. In our experiments, we train DenseNet121 (D121) [16], ResNet18 (R18), ResNet50 (R50) [14], and GoogLeNet (GLN) [39] for 200 epochs with batch size 128 on one single GPU. We use cosine learning rate schedule, the detailed settings of which are reported in supplementary materials. Each experiment is repeated four times to eliminate randomness. The generalization performance is reported in the "mean ± std" format, and the time is reported by taking the average.

From the aspect of generalization performance, we see from Table 1 that NKFAC performs the best on CIFAR100 compared with all the other optimizers. After careful hyper-parameters tuning, KFAC performs better than the default first-order SGDM optimizer under most circumstances. With the proposed useful implementations, our NKFAC inherits this property with even better accuracy and faster convergence speed than KFAC as shown in Fig. 1. SKFAC, however, may suffer from information loss and does not perform as well as NKFAC and KFAC. For experiments on CIFAR10, we notice from the training process that after 200 epochs, all the optimizers reach nearly 100% training accuracy with the

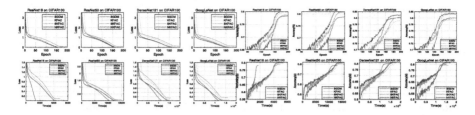

**Fig. 1.** Training loss and testing accuracy curves with respect to epoch and time on CIFAR100 for different optimizers, respectively.

training loss very close to zero, which means that all the networks are trained well under these circumstances. Therefore, there may not be a big difference in the generalization performance of different optimizers on CIFAR10 for the DNNs we tested, as we show in Table 1.

Table 2 demonstrates our superior ability to approximate the inverse from a time perspective. In most of the DNNs we tested, NKFAC outperforms other optimizers. Particularly, when the Sherman-Morrison formula cannot significantly reduce the dimension of inversion, SKFAC may not be powerful enough, whereas NKFAC consistently demonstrates its effectiveness. Across all experiments, NKFAC reduces inversion time from 31% to 86% compared to KFAC, while SKFAC achieves a reduction of 3% to 61%. These results demonstrate the time-saving benefit of using Newton's iteration in NKFAC.

From the aspect of convergence, we plot Fig. 1 about the training loss and testing accuracy curves with respect to epoch and total training time for different optimizers, respectively. When train the same number of epochs, NKFAC always gains the performance among all the optimizers in both training loss and testing accuracy. Meanwhile, considering total training time, NKFAC reduces the loss quicker and gains the generalization performance at most of the time compared with KFAC, NKFAC under most cases, while compared with the first-order optimizer SGDM, it is usually better than SGDM in the early stage but surpassed by SGDM in the later stage. Here, as shown in Fig. 1, first-order optimizer still shows its advantage in less training time.

### 4.3 Results on ImageNet

ImageNet [34] is an image classification dataset that contains 1k categories with 1.28 million images for training and 50k images for validation. Our experiments on ImageNet are accomplished on GeForce RTX 2080Ti GPUs. The initial learning rate and weight decay are reported in supplementary materials.

**Results on Transformers:** During our tests, we utilize Geforce RTX A6000 GPUs and the official MMClassification toolbox [6][2] to train the Swin-T and Swin-B transformers. Since the adaptive momentum optimizers are widely used

---

[2] https://github.com/open-mmlab/mmclassification.

**Table 2.** Time cost by inversion (s) of optimizers on CIFAR100.

| Optimizer | KFAC | SKFAC | NKFAC |
|-----------|------|-------|-------|
| DenseNet121 | 264.68 | 244.16 | **35.56** |
| ResNet18 | 136.41 | **53.32** | 54.24 |
| ResNet50 | 248.84 | 155.23 | **74.13** |
| GoogLeNet | 102.83 | 99.32 | **70.69** |

**Table 3.** Top 1 accuracy (%) with Swin-T and Swin-B.

| Optimizer | AdamW | AdaNKFAC |
|-----------|-------|----------|
| Swin-T | 81.18 | **81.63** |
| Swin-B | **83.36** | 83.30 |

**Table 4.** Top 1 accuracy (%) for different optimizers on ImageNet with ResNet18/50.

| Optimizer | SGDM | AdamW | RAdam | Adabelief | KFAC | SKFAC | NKFAC |
|-----------|------|-------|-------|-----------|------|-------|-------|
| ResNet18 | 70.49 | 70.01 | 69.92 | 70.08 | 70.51 | 10.28 | **71.12** |
| ResNet50 | 76.31 | 76.02 | 76.12 | 76.22 | 76.66 | 29.09 | **77.07** |

for training transformers, we apply the adaptive momentum optimizer AdaNK-FAC and compare it with the default optimizer AdamW, which we directly cite the official results of in Table 3[3]. For AdaNKFAC, we set the initial learning rate and weight decay to be 0.002 and 0.025, respectively, with other hyper-parameters keeping the same as default settings. Our AdaNKFAC inherits the quick convergence property as a second-order optimizer for both networks and converges faster than AdamW (as seen in Fig. 2 for the training loss and validating accuracy curves). By the final validation performance in Table 3, we see AdaNKFAC gains 0.45% and loses 0.06% on Swin-T and Swin-B, respectively, compared with the default AdamW. These results demonstrate the suitability of the second-order algorithm for training transformers. More experiment results on the training of transformers will be presented in Sect. 4.4.

**Results on CNNs:** In our testing, we train ResNet18 and ResNet50 networks [14] for a total of 100 epochs across 4 GPUs. The total batch size is set at 256, and the learning rate is decreased by a factor of 0.1 every 30 epochs. The top-1 accuracy results of ResNet18/50 are displayed in Table 4. While the same parameters prove effective for KFAC, SKFAC struggles to optimize the network despite the random sampling number being increased to 8, which could be due to information loss. In contrast, our NKFAC method successfully inherits most of the valuable information from KFAC, and with the help of our useful implementations and well-tuned parameters for first-order optimizers, it achieves the best performance among all optimizers with 0.61% and 0.41% higher than the second best one.

---

[3] The results can be found from https://github.com/open-mmlab/mmclassification/tree/master/configs/swin_transformer.

**Table 5.** Detection results on COCO. * means the default optimizer, and $\Delta$ means the improvement of NKFAC compared with the default one.

| Model, Backbone, Learning Schedule | Algorithm | AP | AP.5 | AP.75 | APs | APm | APl |
|---|---|---|---|---|---|---|---|
| | SGDM* | 37.4 | 58.1 | 40.4 | 21.2 | 41.0 | 48.1 |
| Faster-RCNN, ResNet50, 1× | NKFAC | 39.7 | 60.7 | 43.0 | 23.4 | 43.3 | 51.5 |
| | $\Delta$ | ↑2.3 | ↑ 2.6 | ↑2.6 | ↑2.2 | ↑2.3 | ↑3.4 |
| | SGDM* | 39.4 | 60.1 | 43.1 | 22.4 | 43.7 | 51.1 |
| Faster-RCNN, ResNet101, 1× | NKFAC | 41.3 | 62.0 | 45.0 | 24.4 | 44.7 | 54.9 |
| | $\Delta$ | ↑1.9 | ↑ 1.9 | ↑1.9 | ↑2.0 | ↑1.0 | ↑3.8 |
| | SGDM* | 37.3 | 57.4 | 39.6 | 22.2 | 40.7 | 50.6 |
| RetinaNet, Swin-T, 1× | NKFAC | 40.7 | 61.7 | 43.3 | 25.2 | 43.9 | 53.9 |
| | $\Delta$ | ↑3.4 | ↑ 4.3 | ↑3.7 | ↑3.0 | ↑ 3.2 | ↑ 3.3 |

## 4.4 Results on COCO

In this section, we will show the applicability and robustness of NKFAC on detection and segmentation tasks on COCO [22], which is a large-scale dataset of detection, segmentation and captioning tasks. In this section, we accomplish experiments with Faster-RCNN [33], RetinaNet [21] and Mask-RCNN [13] with backbones ResNet50, ResNet101 and Swin-T transformer [24] to show the stable and efficient performance of our NKFAC/AdaNKFAC on these tasks. Our experiments are accomplished under the sketch of the official MMDetection toolbox [5][4]. For the default optimizers, if the official results are given, we cite the official results directly for comparison[5]. Otherwise, we reproduce the results[6] under the official settings of MMDetection toolbox. Our experiments are accomplished on RTX A6000, Geforce RTX 3090Ti and Quadro RTX 8000 GPUs.

The hyperparameters of NKFAC/AdaNKFAC are the same as the default optimizers without any tuning. Specifically, for NKFAC in Faster-RCNN and Mask-RCNN, the initial learning rate takes 0.02 while the weight decay takes 0.0001, and for RetinaNet, the learning rate takes 0.01 while the weight decay takes 0.0001. For AdaNKFAC, the initial learning rate takes 0.0001 while the weight decay takes 0.2. Our results show that NKFAC performs much better than the default optimizers in all the experiments regardless of model and backbone. Table 5 reports the Average Precision (AP) of detection by Faster-RCNN and RetinaNet, from which we can see NKFAC improves the AP by 1.9% ∼ 3.4% compared to the default SGDM. Meanwhile, in Table 6, we report the detection and segmentation results of Mask-RCNN with different backbones, while

---

[4] https://github.com/open-mmlab/mmdetection.

[5] The results can be found from https://github.com/open-mmlab/mmdetection/tree/master/configs/faster_rcnn, https://github.com/open-mmlab/mmdetection/tree/master/configs/mask_rcnn, and https://github.com/open-mmlab/mmdetection/tree/master/configs/swin.

[6] For Swin-T 2× of Mask-RCNN, the decay epochs of learning rate are set to be 16 and 22, with total 24 epochs.

**Table 6.** Detection and segmentation results of Mask-RCNN on COCO. * and Δ mean the same as in Table 5.

| Backbone, Learning Schedule | Algorithm | $AP^b$ | $AP^b_{.5}$ | $AP^b_{.75}$ | $AP^m$ | $AP^m_{.5}$ | $AP^m_{.75}$ |
|---|---|---|---|---|---|---|---|
| | SGDM* | 38.2 | 58.8 | 41.4 | 34.7 | 55.7 | 37.2 |
| ResNet50, 1× | NKFAC | 40.1 | 60.9 | 43.9 | 36.6 | 57.9 | 39.2 |
| | Δ | ↑1.9 | ↑2.1 | ↑2.5 | ↑1.9 | ↑2.2 | ↑2.0 |
| | SGDM* | 40.0 | 60.5 | 44.0 | 36.1 | 57.5 | 38.6 |
| ResNet101, 1× | NKFAC | 41.8 | 62.1 | 45.9 | 37.8 | 59.2 | 40.3 |
| | Δ | ↑1.8 | ↑1.6 | ↑1.9 | ↑1.7 | ↑1.7 | ↑1.7 |
| | AdamW* | 42.7 | 65.2 | 46.8 | 39.3 | 62.2 | 42.2 |
| Swin-T, 1× | AdaNKFAC | 43.6 | 65.7 | 47.5 | 40.1 | 62.9 | 43.4 |
| | Δ | ↑0.9 | ↑0.5 | ↑0.7 | ↑0.8 | ↑0.7 | ↑1.2 |
| | AdamW* | 45.2 | 67.3 | 49.4 | 41.0 | 64.3 | 44.0 |
| Swin-T, 2× | AdaNKFAC | 46.2 | 68.2 | 50.5 | 41.7 | 65.1 | 45.0 |
| | Δ | ↑1.0 | ↑0.9 | ↑1.1 | ↑0.7 | ↑0.8 | ↑1.0 |
| | AdamW* | 46.0 | 68.2 | 50.3 | 41.6 | 65.3 | 44.7 |
| Swin-T, 3× | AdaNKFAC | 46.9 | 68.6 | 51.5 | 42.3 | 65.8 | 45.6 |
| | Δ | ↑0.9 | ↑0.4 | ↑1.2 | ↑0.7 | ↑0.5 | ↑0.9 |

NKFAC gains 0.9% ∼ 1.9% $AP^b$ and 0.7% ∼ 1.9% $AP^m$ over the default optimizers. These results can well demonstrate the effectiveness of our proposed NKFAC.

Further considering the convergence performance, we plot Fig. 3 to clearly show the training loss curves of different optimizers on Faster-RCNN with ResNet-101 backbone, RetinaNet with Swin-T backbone, Mask-RCNN with ResNet101 and Swin-T backbone. It can be shown from Fig. 3 that NKFAC/AdaNKFAC converges faster than the default optimizer in all the cases. Therefore, we are optimistic about the application of NKFAC on various tasks.

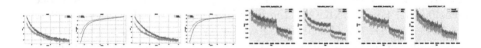

**Fig. 2.** Training loss and validating accuracy curves w.r.t epoch for different optimizers on ImageNet with Swin-T/Swin-B.

**Fig. 3.** Loss curves w.r.t iteration for different deep neural networks with different optimizers on COCO.

## 5   Conclusion

In this work, we propose NKFAC, a generalized KFAC optimizer that combines classic KFAC with Newton's iteration. With the help of a good initialization obtained from the last iteration and the fast local convergence of New-ton's iteration, we reduce the computational cost of the second-order statistics inversion while maintaining satisfactory performance. Meanwhile, since Newton's iteration contains only matrix product operations, the probability of numerical problems can be reduced and the stability of inversion can be improved. More-over, without random selection or taking an average to reduce the dimension of the second-order statistics, we preserve the information obtained from the samples to the greatest extent, ensuring a speedy convergence rate. Last but not least, through some useful implementations, the generalization performance of NKFAC achieves SOTA without tedious hyper-parameter tuning. NKFAC reduces the gap between first-order and second-order methods in terms of time cost by inversion and hyper-parameters tuning, while still keeping satisfactory convergence performance. Sufficient experiments on image classification, detec-tion and segmentation tasks have been conducted to confirm the effectiveness of our proposed NKFAC.

**Ethics Statements:.** Proposing a new optimizer NKFAC as the main contribution, this work does not involve collecting data or inferring personal information. So far, this work does not involve any ethical implications after the author's best consideration.

# References

1. Adya, S., Palakkode, V., Tuzel, O.: Nonlinear conjugate gradients for scaling syn-chronous distributed dnn training. arXiv preprint arXiv:1812.02886 (2018)
2. Agarwal, N., et al.: Efficient full-matrix adaptive regularization. arXiv preprint arXiv:1806.02958 (2018)
3. Bahamou, A., Goldfarb, D., Ren, Y.: A mini-block natural gradient method for deep neural networks. arXiv preprint arXiv:2202.04124 (2022)
4. Ben-Israel, A.: An iterative method for computing the generalized inverse of an arbitrary matrix. Mathematics of Computation, pp. 452–455 (1965)
5. Chen, K., et al.: MMDetection: open mmlab detection toolbox and benchmark. arXiv preprint arXiv:1906.07155 (2019)
6. Contributors, M.: Openmmlab's image classification toolbox and benchmark (2020). www.github.com/open-mmlab/mmclassification
7. Frantar, E., Kurtic, E., Alistarh, D.: M-fac: Efficient matrix-free approximations of second-order information. Adv. Neural. Inf. Process. Syst. **34**, 14873–14886 (2021)
8. Gao, K.X., et al.: Eigenvalue-corrected natural gradient based on a new approxi-mation. arXiv preprint arXiv:2011.13609 (2020)
9. Gao, K., Liu, X., Huang, Z., Wang, M., Wang, Z., Xu, D., Yu, F.: A trace-restricted kronecker-factored approximation to natural gradient. In: Proceedings of the AAAI Conference on Artificial Intelligence, vol. 35, pp. 7519–7527 (2021)
10. George, T., Laurent, C., Bouthillier, X., Ballas, N., Vincent, P.: Fast approximate natural gradient descent in a kronecker factored eigenbasis. Advances in Neural Information Processing Systems 31 (2018)
11. Grosse, R., Martens, J.: A kronecker-factored approximate fisher matrix for con-volution layers. In: International Conference on Machine Learning, pp. 573–582. PMLR (2016)

12. Gupta, V., Koren, T., Singer, Y.: Shampoo: preconditioned stochastic tensor opti-
    mization. In: International Conference on Machine Learning, pp. 1842–1850. PMLR
    (2018)
13. He, K., Gkioxari, G., Dollar, P., Girshick, R.: Mask r-cnn. In: 2017 IEEE Interna-
    tional Conference on Computer Vision (ICCV), October 2017
14. He, K., Zhang, X., Ren, S., Sun, J.: Deep residual learning for image recognition. In:
    Proceedings of the IEEE Conference on Computer Vision and Pattern Recognition,
    pp. 770–778 (2016)
15. Hestenes, M.R., Stiefel, E.: Methods of conjugate gradients for solving. J. Res.
    Natl. Bur. Stand. **49**(6), 409 (1952)
16. Huang, G., Liu, Z., Van Der Maaten, L., Weinberger, K.Q.: Densely connected
    convolutional networks. In: Proceedings of the IEEE Conference on Computer
    Vision and Pattern Recognition, pp. 4700–4708 (2017)
17. Kingma, D.P., Ba, J.: Adam: A method for stochastic optimization. arXiv preprint
    arXiv:1412.6980 (2014)
18. Koroko, A., Anciaux-Sedastrian, A., Gharbia, I., Garès, V., Haddou, M., Tran,
    Q.H.: Efficient approximations of the fisher matrix in neural networks using kro-
    necker product singular value decomposition. arXiv preprint arXiv:2201.10285
    (2022)
19. Krizhevsky, A., Hinton, G., et al.: Learning multiple layers of features from tiny
    images (2009)
20. Li, W., Li, Z.: A family of iterative methods for computing the approximate inverse
    of a square matrix and inner inverse of a non-square matrix. Appl. Math. Comput.
    **215**(9), 3433–3442 (2010)
21. Lin, T.Y., Goyal, P., Girshick, R., He, K., Dollár, P.: Focal loss for dense object
    detection. In: Proceedings of the IEEE International Conference on Computer
    Vision, pp. 2980–2988 (2017)
22. Lin, T.-Y., et al.: Microsoft COCO: common objects in context. In: Fleet, D.,
    Pajdla, T., Schiele, B., Tuytelaars, T. (eds.) ECCV 2014. LNCS, vol. 8693, pp.
    740–755. Springer, Cham (2014). https://doi.org/10.1007/978-3-319-10602-1_48
23. Liu, L., et al.: On the variance of the adaptive learning rate and beyond. In:
    Proceedings of the Eighth International Conference on Learning Representations
    (ICLR 2020), April 2020
24. Liu, Z., et al.: Swin transformer: Hierarchical vision transformer using shifted win-
    dows. arXiv preprint arXiv:2103.14030 (2021)
25. Loshchilov, I., Hutter, F.: Decoupled weight decay regularization. arXiv preprint
    arXiv:1711.05101 (2017)
26. Ma, X.: Apollo: An adaptive parameter-wise diagonal quasi-newton method for
    nonconvex stochastic optimization. arXiv preprint arXiv:2009.13586 (2020)
27. Martens, J., Grosse, R.: Optimizing neural networks with kronecker-factored
    approximate curvature. In: International Conference on Machine Learning, pp.
    2408–2417. PMLR (2015)
28. Martens, J., et al.: Deep learning via hessian-free optimization. In: ICML, vol. 27,
    pp. 735–742 (2010)
29. Najafi, H.S., Solary, M.S.: Computational algorithms for computing the inverse of
    a square matrix, quasi-inverse of a non-square matrix and block matrices. Appl.
    Math. Comput. **183**(1), 539–550 (2006)
30. Osawa, K., Tsuji, Y., Ueno, Y., Naruse, A., Yokota, R., Matsuoka, S.: Large-scale
    distributed second-order optimization using kronecker-factored approximate cur-
    vature for deep convolutional neural networks. In: Proceedings of the IEEE/CVF
    Conference on Computer Vision and Pattern Recognition, pp. 12359–12367 (2019)

31. Paige, C.C., Saunders, M.A.: Solution of sparse indefinite systems of linear equations. SIAM J. Numer. Anal. **12**(4), 617–629 (1975)
32. Qian, N.: On the momentum term in gradient descent learning algorithms. Neural Netw. **12**(1), 145–151 (1999)
33. Ren, S., He, K., Girshick, R., Sun, J.: Faster r-cnn: towards real-time object detection with region proposal networks. IEEE Trans. Pattern Anal. Mach. Intell., June 2017
34. Russakovsky, O., Deng, J., Su, H., Krause, J., Satheesh, S., Ma, S., Huang, Z., Karpathy, A., Khosla, A., Bernstein, M., et al.: Imagenet large scale visual recognition challenge. Int. J. Comput. Vision **115**(3), 211–252 (2015)
35. Sainath, T.N., Horesh, L., Kingsbury, B., Aravkin, A.Y., Ramabhadran, B.: Accelerating hessian-free optimization for deep neural networks by implicit preconditioning and sampling. In: 2013 IEEE Workshop on Automatic Speech Recognition and Understanding, pp. 303–308. IEEE (2013)
36. Schulz, G.: Iterative berechnung der reziproken matrix. Z. Angew. Math. Mech. **13**, 57–59 (1933)
37. Shewhart, W.A., Wilks, S.S.: Wiley series in probability and mathematical statistics. Wiley (1975)
38. Soleymani, F.: On a fast iterative method for approximate inverse of matrices. Commun. Korean Math. Soc. **28**(2), 407–418 (2013)
39. Szegedy, C., et al.: Going deeper with convolutions. In: Proceedings of the IEEE Conference on Computer Vision and Pattern Recognition, pp. 1–9 (2015)
40. Tang, Z., et al.: Skfac: training neural networks with faster kronecker-factored approximate curvature. In: Proceedings of the IEEE/CVF Conference on Computer Vision and Pattern Recognition, pp. 13479–13487 (2021)
41. Yao, Z., Gholami, A., Shen, S., Mustafa, M., Keutzer, K., Mahoney, M.: Adahessian: an adaptive second order optimizer for machine learning. In: Proceedings of the AAAI Conference on Artificial Intelligence, vol. 35, pp. 10665–10673 (2021)
42. Yong, H., Zhang, L.: An embedded feature whitening approach to deep neural network optimization. In: The European Conference on Conputer Vision (2022)
43. Zhuang, J., et al.: Adabelief optimizer: adapting stepsizes by the belief in observed gradients. Adv. Neural. Inf. Process. Syst. **33**, 18795–18806 (2020)

# Exact Combinatorial Optimization with Temporo-Attentional Graph Neural Networks

Mehdi Seyfi, Amin Banitalebi-Dehkordi[✉], Zirui Zhou, and Yong Zhang

Huawei Technologies Canada Co., Ltd., Shenzhen, China
amin.banitalebi@gmail.com, yong.zhang3@huawei.com

**Abstract.** Combinatorial optimization finds an optimal solution within a discrete set of variables and constraints. The field has seen tremendous progress both in research and industry. With the success of deep learning in the past decade, a recent trend in combinatorial optimization has been to improve state-of-the-art combinatorial optimization solvers by replacing key heuristic components with machine learning (ML) models. In this paper, we investigate two essential aspects of machine learning algorithms for combinatorial optimization: temporal characteristics and attention. We argue that for the task of variable selection in the branch-and-bound (B&B) algorithm, incorporating the temporal information as well as the bipartite graph attention improves the solver's performance. We support our claims with intuitions and numerical results over several standard datasets used in the literature and competitions. (Code is available at: https://developer.huaweicloud.com/develop/aigallery/notebook/detail?id=047c6cf2-8463-40d7-b92f-7b2ca998e935.)

**Keywords:** Combinatorial optimization · Graph Neural Networks · Temporal Attention · Mixed Integer Linear Program

## 1 Introduction

Combinatorial optimization is the process of searching for extrema of an objective function with a discrete domain when the optimized variables satisfy some pre-defined constraints. Typical examples of such problems include: the Traveling Salesman Problem (TSP) [18], finding the Minimum Spanning Tree (MST) [24], and the Knapsack problem [46].

Combinatorial optimization is adopted in many critical applications affecting day-to-day lives. Examples include: daily electric grid power distribution [35,39], airport flights scheduling [6], and etc. Due to the importance of such applications, there has been a tremendous amount of effort from both academia [1,17,49] and industry [8,20,38] to build advanced and reliable solutions.

In general, many combinatorial optimization problems can be reduced to Mixed-Integer Linear Programs (MILPs) in which at least some of the variables in the feasible domain are integral and the objective function and constraints are linear [28]. The existing MILP solutions, for the most part, are general-purpose

© The Author(s), under exclusive license to Springer Nature Switzerland AG 2023
D. Koutra et al. (Eds.): ECML PKDD 2023, LNAI 14172, pp. 268–283, 2023.
https://doi.org/10.1007/978-3-031-43421-1_16

one-size-fits-all products that target a variety of applications. However, in many applications, the data only changes slightly over time (e.g. daily electricity consumption in the same city should not change drastically day over day in a fixed network). These changes are hard to capture with hand-designed rules. This has motivated researchers to investigate the possibility of training machine learning models from the historical data, and use these models to help solve MILPs [22,25,32,40].

The standard well-established and exact approach to solving MILPs is the Branch and Bound (B&B) algorithm [36]. Variable selection within B&B is an essential step in which a fractional variable is selected in each LP relaxation iteration. The gold standard to perform variable selection is the Full Strong Branching (FSB) rule, which is unfortunately computationally expensive [38]. Consequently, many algorithms try to propose a fast approximation of the FSB [2].

In this paper, we focus on variable selection in the B&B algorithm by mimicking the full strong branching via imitation learning [30]. Our intention is to use the statistical properties of the MILP data samples to train a neural network model that can learn to imitate the variable branching from the FSB algorithm with much less computational complexity. Building on the former attempts in the literature to tackle this problem [4,25,33,40], by adopting a bipartite graph representation for MILP problems, we propose to engage with variable selection via two novel contributions. First, we embed the MILP graph into representation vectors utilizing the Graph Attention Networks (GAT), which are the state-of-the-art structures for representation learning [11,50]. We argue that as opposed to the traditional Graph Convolutional Neural Network (GCNN) structures, our model allows for *implicitly* assigning different gravity to nodes of the same neighborhood, enabling a surge in the model capacity. This would let our policy to capture information about the node embeddings that are more interesting to the expert solver (here FSB agent) to perform a branching action. Second, by dividing the process of solving a MILP instance into consecutive episodes of a Markov decision process [29], we propose to incorporate the temporal variations of representations associated to consecutive MILP episodes, into our smart branching scenario. To this end, we propose a Gated Recurrent Unit (GRU) to capture the temporal information concealed in the representation vectors associated with each episode of a MILP instance solution. We compare our results against the previous variable selection strategies in the literature and show that our method performs competitively compared to the existing branching mechanisms.

## 2   Related Work

Previous attempts to replace components of MILP solvers with machine learning models include:

*Learning Primal Heuristics:* Authors in [15,33,47] introduced methods to learn the primal heuristics; *i.e.,* methods with which a feasible but not necessarily optimal solution may be found. The task of learning primal heuristics is known as *primal task* in the research community [21].

*Node Selection:* Moreover, authors in [27,48] studied the node selection. He *et al.*[27] through imitation learning, learned a policy to select a candidate node with the optimal solution in its sub-tree. Song *et al.*[48] learned node selection and a good search policy via retrospective imitation learning, which is a self-correcting imitation learning algorithm by ruling out previous bad decisions.

*Learn to Branch:* Authors in [21,22,44] trained neural networks that imitate the internal gold standard full strong branching mechanism for variable selection. Alvarez *et al.* proposed to approximate a branching function on hand-crafted features using Extremely Randomized Trees (ExtraTrees) [23], a modified version of random forest [10], which is based on an ensemble of regression trees. The authors in [22] modeled the MILP-solving process by a Markov decision process [29]. At each state, the policy makes a decision on the optimal variable to branch on. They encode each MILP state by a GCNN and train their model with behavioral cloning [42] and a cross-entropy loss. This task is known as the *dual task* in the research community [21].

In the Machine Learning for Combinatorial Optimization (ML4CO) competition [16] held in 2021, the organizers challenged the participants in different tracks *i.e.,* the primal, the dual, and configuration tasks. In the *dual task* scenario which lies within the scope of this paper, the competition results revealed that the GCNN architecture used for branching can achieve a strong performance when combined with other techniques and tricks. For example, the winner solution proposed Knowledge Inheriting Dataset Aggregation (KIDA) along with a Model Weight Averaging (MWA) mechanism [21] to be applied on the GCNN architecture. This solution used the GCNN model proposed by [22] on an aggregated dataset using the techniques in [45]. It trained multiple parent models and performed a greedy search to select the final model from the trained parent models and their children weight averaging models [21]. The runner-up team (EI-OROAS) in the same task also used the baseline GCNN [22] and argued that the GCNN approach could be very effective if it was tuned and trained properly on the right kind of training samples [5]. In a later approach, the authors in [40] combined a learned primal heuristic and a branching policy in the solver environment together in order to tackle more practical real-world problems. In particular, they proposed neural diving that learns primal heuristics and neural branching that learns a branching policy to achieve a better performance in terms of latency and accuracy.

Although the GCNN-based methods set a good standard for selecting fractional variables in the B&B algorithm, there is still room for developing lightweight models that can imitate the full strong branching rule more accurately. To this end, we investigate two essential aspects of machine learning algorithms for branching in combinatorial optimization: temporal characteristics and attention. We argue that for the task of variable selection in the branch-and-bound (B&B) algorithm, incorporating the temporal information as well as the bipartite graph attention improves the solver's performance.

# 3   Background

*Preliminaries and Definitions:* A mixed-integer linear program is defined as:

$$\arg \min_{\mathbf{x}} \{ \mathbf{c}^T \mathbf{x} | \mathbf{A}\mathbf{x} \leq \mathbf{b}, \mathbf{l} \leq \mathbf{x} \leq \mathbf{u}, \mathbf{x} \in \mathbb{Z}^p \times \mathbb{R}^{n-p} \}, \tag{1}$$

where $\mathbf{c} \in \mathbb{R}^n$ denotes the coefficients of the linear objective, and $\mathbf{A} \in \mathbb{R}^{m \times n}$ and $\mathbf{b} \in \mathbb{R}^m$ respectively represent the coefficients and upper bounds of the linear constraints. There are $m$ linear constraints and $n$ variables where $p \leq n$ is the number of integer variables. $\mathbf{l}$ and $\mathbf{u}$ are both vectors in the $\mathbb{R}^n$ space and are the lower and upper bound vectors on variables $\mathbf{x} = [x_1, \ldots, x_n]$.

A *feasible solution* is a solution that satisfies all the constraints in (1). A linear programming relaxation is when we relax the last constraint in (1), *i.e.*, $\mathbf{x} \in \mathbb{R}^n$. This will turn the MILP to a *Linear Program* (LP) [9]. The value of the objective function $\mathbf{c}^T \mathbf{x}$ with the LP solution is a lower bound to the original MILP. Any lower bound for the MILP is referred to as a *dual bound*. The LP solution can be a feasible solution if it satisfies the integral constraints, *i.e.*, $\mathbf{x} \in \mathbb{Z}^p \times \mathbb{R}^{n-p}$. The *primal bound* is the objective value of a solution that is feasible for (1), but not necessarily optimal. This could be an upper bound to the objective value of the MILP. Finally, the dual-primal gap is the gap between the dual bound and the primal bound.

*The Branch and Bound Algorithm:* It is common in practice to solve the MILPs sequentially by building a search tree at each node with partial assignment of integer values to the variables, and use the information obtained at the node to converge to an optimal or a near-optimal solution [3,15,36]. At each step, we choose a leaf node to branch from (choose a variable to branch). We solve the LP relaxation problem at this node where we constrain the previously branched variables to be fixed at their integer value. Therefore at each node, we relax $p - r$ variables where $r \leq p$ and make a decision on which variable to branch on. The LP solution at this node provides us with a lower bound to the objective value of the original MILP solution as well as any further child nodes down the road. If this lower bound is larger than the objective value of any known feasible solution then we can safely cutout this branch of the search tree as it is guaranteed that the child nodes of this particular node will provide us with a larger (worse) objective value. If the LP relaxation at this node is not larger than the objective value of a known feasible solution then we may decide to expand this node. We do that by branching on a variable from the remaining fractional variables at that node. Once a variable is selected, the tree ramifies into two branches, and two child nodes are added to the search tree. We divide the domain of the selected variable into two non-overlapping intervals. We choose the solution of the LP relaxation problem at the parent node for that particular variable as a reference. If $x_i^{lp}$ is the LP relaxation solution of the variable with index $i$ at the parent node, the non-overlapping domains of child nodes will be $x_i \geq \lceil x_i^{lp} \rceil$ and $x_i \leq \lfloor x_i^{lp} \rfloor$, where $\lceil \cdot \rceil$ and $\lfloor \cdot \rfloor$ are the ceiling and floor operators, respectively. A new MILP the sample is generated from the MILP instance once branching on one variable is performed. The tree is updated and this procedure is resumed until convergence. LP is the backbone of the branch and bound algorithm. It is used for both finding the dual bounds at each node and deciding on the variable to branch on with the help of some primal heuristics. Practically the size of a search tree is in the exponential order with respect to the number of variables, therefore in some cases the search tree can be huge, and therefore time-consuming to traverse through.

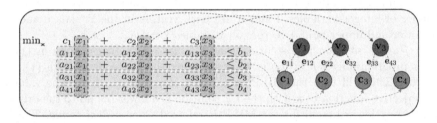

**Fig. 1.** An example representing a MILP instance of 3 variables and 4 constraints with a bipartite graph [40]. $\mathbf{v}_j \in \mathbb{R}^v$, $\mathbf{c}_i \in \mathbb{R}^c$, and $\mathbf{e}_{ij} \in \mathbb{R}^e$ denote the $j^{\text{th}}$ variable, $i^{\text{th}}$ constraint, and the edge connecting the two. In this example $a_{13} = a_{21} = a_{23} = a_{31} = a_{41} = a_{42} = 0$; therefore, there is no connecting edge between their representing graph nodes. For brevity of illustration, we have ignored the time-dependent nature of the node/edge features.

## 4   Methodology

In this section, we elaborate on the mechanics of our method for addressing variable selection in the B&B algorithm within a time-limit $T$. As introduced by [27] and later followed by [22, 25, 40] we can model the sequential selections made by the B&B algorithm with a Markov decision process [29]. Letting the solver be the environment and the brancher the agent, [22] denotes the solver state at the $t^{th}$ decision by $\mathbf{s}_t$, which contains information about the current dual bound, primal bound, the LP solution of each node, the current leaf node, etc. Let the action set $\mathcal{A}_t \subseteq \{1, \ldots, p\}$ be a set including the index of the fractional variables at the current LP relaxation node at the state $\mathbf{s}_t$. During a branching episode; the agent, based on the environment variables, and a selection policy $\pi_\theta(\cdot)$ with learning parameters $\theta$, takes an action $\tilde{a}_t \in \mathcal{A}_t$ which points to the index of a *desirably* optimal fractional variable to branch on; performs the branching-and-bounding as stated in Sect. 3 and moves to the next state $\mathbf{s}_{t+1}$. The authors in [22, 25, 40, 52] encode each state $\mathbf{s}_t$ of the B&B Markov process at time slot $t$ as a bipartite graph $\mathcal{G}$ with node and edge features $(\mathcal{G}, \mathbf{C}_t, \mathbf{V}_t, \mathbf{E}_t)$. At the current node's LP relaxation, each row in the feature matrices $\mathbf{C}_t \in \mathbb{R}^{m \times c}$ and $\mathbf{V}_t \in \mathbb{R}^{n \times v}$ represents a row and a column of the MILP instance at the state $\mathbf{s}_t$, respectively (ref to Fig. 1). In this setting, $\mathbf{v}_{j,t}$ and $\mathbf{c}_{i,t}$ refer to the $j^{\text{th}}$ and the $i^{\text{th}}$ rows from $\mathbf{C}_t$ and $\mathbf{V}_t$, respectively. Besides, node $\mathbf{c}_{i,t}$ is connected to the node $\mathbf{v}_{j,t}$ via the edge $\mathbf{e}_{ij,t} \in \mathbb{R}^e$ if and only if $a_{ij} \neq 0$ (ref. Fig. 1).

Subsequently, the sparse feature tensor $\mathbf{E}_t \in \mathbb{R}^{m \times n \times e}$ concatenates all $\mathbf{e}_{ij,t}$ features. $c$, $v$, and $e$ represent the dimensions of the feature vectors for constraints, variables, and edges, respectively. The aforementioned feature vectors are obtained by extracting some hand-crafted features from the solver environment. The authors in [22,31] studied and proposed engineering such features. We leverage the same set of features proposed in [22] in our work. In the following sub-sections we elaborate on our methodology and the components of our neural branching mechanism to imitate the FSB in the solver environment.

*Embedding Layers:* To increase the modeling capacity and also to be able to manipulate the node interactions with our proposed neural architecture, following [5,22,25] we use embedding layers to map each node and edge to space $\mathbb{R}^d$. For brevity and simplicity of notation, in the forthcoming sections, we assume that the embedding layers are already applied to $(\mathcal{G}, \mathbf{C}_t, \mathbf{V}_t, \mathbf{E}_t)$ and therefore, $(\mathbf{c}_{i,t}, \mathbf{v}_{j,t}, \mathbf{e}_{ij,t}) \in \mathbb{R}^{d \times d \times d}, \forall (i,j,t) : 1 \leq i \leq m, 1 \leq j \leq n, 0 \leq t \leq T$.

*Attention Mechanism:* Neighborhood normalization, in many cases, is known to be useful for improving the AGGREGATE operator in the Message Passing Networks (MPN) [34]. The intuition behind this normalization is that higher-degree neighbors might be bearing more generic and less precise information; therefore, the model should put less stress on such nodes. On the other hand, in some cases, normalization may lead to loss of information by removing key structural information from the graph nodes. Specifically, the embedding learned from nodes with different degrees might be indistinguishable [26]. Intuitively, some kind of node normalization for a graph representation of a MILP instance may be justifiable. The variables participating in many constraints might be less information-bearing than the ones engaging in only a few (ref. Fig. 2). At the same time, by normalizing the node degrees, we might be removing some structural information from the graph representation $(\mathcal{G}, \mathbf{C}_t, \mathbf{V}_t, \mathbf{E}_t)$. Therefore, we propose to use an attention mechanism to extract the information associated with the interplay between the nodes. By using attention, we give the model the freedom to prioritize each node according to its neighborhood structure and embedding features. Doing so will let the model decide how much participation a node should have in the final decision-making policy.

Considering the bipartite nature of $(\mathcal{G}, \mathbf{C}_t, \mathbf{V}_t, \mathbf{E}_t)$, we use a pair of back-to-back attention structures to encode the node interactions. Each constraint node $\mathbf{c}_{i,t}$ attends to its neighborhood $\mathcal{N}_i$ in the first round via an attention structure with number of $H$ attention heads:

$$\mathbf{c}_{i,t} = \frac{1}{H} \sum_{h=1}^{H} \left( \alpha_{ii}^{(h)} \mathbf{\Theta}_c^{(h)} \mathbf{c}_{i,t} + \sum_{j \in \mathcal{N}_i} \alpha_{ij}^{(h)} \mathbf{\Theta}_v^{(h)} \mathbf{v}_{j,t} \right), \qquad (2)$$

with learnable weights $\mathbf{\Theta}_c^{(h)}, \mathbf{\Theta}_v^{(h)} \in \mathbb{R}^{d' \times d}$ and LeakyRelu [51] being the activation function. The updated constraint embeddings are averaged across multiple

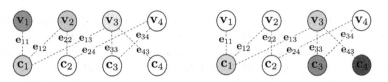

**Fig. 2.** (left) Intuitively, since $v_1$ only appears in the first constraint; therefore $c_1$ attends to $v_1$ more, rather than $v_3$ that participates in multiple constraints. It is mainly because the information about $v_3$ flows in the graph not only via its connection to $c_1$, but also via other connecting nodes to $v_3$ other than $c_1$. (right) With a similar intuition $v_3$ attends to $c_4$ the most and $c_2$ the least. In both figures darker color means more attention.

attention heads using attention weights [11]:

$$\alpha_{ij}^{(h)} = \frac{\exp\left(\mathbf{a}_c^{(h)^\top} \text{LeakyReLU}\left([\Theta_c^{(h)}\mathbf{c}_{i,t}, \Theta_v^{(h)}\mathbf{v}_{k,t}, \Theta_e^{(h)}\mathbf{e}_{ik,t}]\right)\right)}{\sum_{k\in\mathcal{N}_i\cup\{i\}} \exp\left(\mathbf{a}_c^{(h)^\top} \text{LeakyReLU}\left([\Theta_c^{(h)}\mathbf{c}_{i,t}, \Theta_v^{(h)}\mathbf{v}_{k,t}, \Theta_e^{(h)}\mathbf{e}_{ik,t}]\right)\right)}, \tag{3}$$

where $\Theta_e^{(h)} \in \mathbb{R}^{d'\times d}$ is a learnable weight. The attention coefficients vector $\mathbf{a}_c^{(h)} \in \mathbb{R}^{3d'}$, is automatically learned to encode both feature level and structure level information flow in the graph and "," denotes vector concatenation. Similarly, the variable nodes are encoded via:

$$\mathbf{v}_{j,t} = \frac{1}{H}\sum_{h=1}^{H}\left(\beta_{jj}^{(h)}\Psi_v^{(h)}\mathbf{v}_{j,t} + \sum_{i\in N_j}\beta_{ji}^{(h)}\Psi_c^{(h)}\mathbf{c}_{i,t}\right), \tag{4}$$

with learnable weights $\Psi_v^{(h)} \in \mathbb{R}^{d\times d}$, $\Psi_c^{(h)} \in \mathbb{R}^{d\times d'}$, and:

$$\beta_{ji}^{(h)} = \frac{\exp\left(\mathbf{a}_v^{(h)^\top} \text{LeakyReLU}\left([\Psi_v^{(h)}\mathbf{v}_{j,t}, \Psi_c^{(h)}\mathbf{c}_{i,t}, \Psi_e^{(h)}\mathbf{e}_{ji,t}]\right)\right)}{\sum_{k\in\mathcal{N}_j\cup\{j\}} \exp\left(\mathbf{a}_v^{(h)^\top} \text{LeakyReLU}\left([\Psi_v^{(h)}\mathbf{v}_{j,t}, \Psi_c^{(h)}\mathbf{c}_{k,t}, \Psi_e^{(h)}\mathbf{e}_{jk,t}]\right)\right)}, \tag{5}$$

where $\Psi_e^{(h)} \in \mathbb{R}^{d\times d}$ and $\mathbf{a}_v^{(h)} \in \mathbb{R}^{3d}$ are learnable weights and attention coefficients vector. The constraint feature nodes in (4) and (5) are replaced by their updated value in (2).

Feature nodes $\mathbf{v}_{i,t}$ encode the LP relaxation state of each variable in the current node $\forall i \in [0,n]$. These encoded representations hold information about the graph structure and node embeddings of the MILP instance at the state $\mathbf{s}_t$.

*Temporal Encoding:* After the $t^{\text{th}}$ branching episode the solver state $\mathbf{s}_t$ which was represented by the graph $(\mathcal{G}, \mathbf{V}_t, \mathbf{C}_t, \mathbf{E}_t)$ is further encoded to a set of variable features $\mathbf{v}_{i,t}, \forall i \in \{1,\ldots,n\}$ via passing the bipartite graph through a back-to-back attention module. This graph representation of the solver state; however, encodes only the current B&B tree state and lacks the temporal information about the past node/edge features that have led the graph representations to the current state. To better imitate the agent in the solver environment, monitoring the temporal variations of the encoded graph carries critical information about the temporal variations in the node/edge embeddings and their relative temporo-structural interplay. To this end, we can inject crucial information about the variation of the features associated to the B&B tree, and what sequential features have led the tree to the current status, into our model. To capture this temporal interaction between the graph nodes/edges we utilize a single-layer GRU recurrent neural network (RNN) to a sequence of $L$ consecutive variable embeddings $\mathbf{v}_{i,t}, \forall t \in \{t - L + 1, \ldots, t\}$. Specifically for each variable node $\mathbf{v}_{i,t}$ in the input sequence and $t \in \{t - L + 1, \ldots, t\}$, the model computes:

$$\mathbf{z}_{i,t} = \sigma_g(\mathbf{W}_z\mathbf{v}_{i,t} + \mathbf{U}_z\mathbf{h}_{t-1} + \mathbf{b}_z),$$
$$\mathbf{r}_{i,t} = \sigma_g(\mathbf{W}_r\mathbf{v}_{i,t} + \mathbf{U}_r\mathbf{h}_{i,t-1} + \mathbf{b}_r),$$
$$\hat{\mathbf{h}}_t = \phi_h(\mathbf{W}_h\mathbf{v}_{i,t} + \mathbf{U}_h(\mathbf{r}_{i,t} \odot \mathbf{h}_{i,t-1}) + \mathbf{b}_h),$$
$$\mathbf{h}_{i,t} = (1 - \mathbf{z}_{i,t}) \odot \mathbf{h}_{i,t-1} + \mathbf{z}_{i,t} \odot \hat{\mathbf{h}}_t, \qquad (6)$$

where $\odot$ is the Hadamard product operator, $\mathbf{h}_t \in \mathbb{R}^{d''}$ is the output vector, $\hat{\mathbf{h}}_t \in \mathbb{R}^{d''}$ is the candidate activation vector, $\mathbf{z}_t \in \mathbb{R}^{d''}$ is the update gate vector, and $\mathbf{r}_t \in \mathbb{R}^{d''}$ is the reset gate vector. $\mathbf{W}, \mathbf{U} \in \mathbb{R}^{d'' \times d}$, and $\mathbf{b} \in \mathbb{R}^{d''}$ are GRU parameter matrices/vector, and $\sigma_g$ and $\phi_h$ are sigmoid and hyperbolic tangent activation functions. Finally our branching policy models variable selection via:

$$\pi_\theta(\tilde{a}_t|\mathbf{s}_t, \ldots, \mathbf{s}_{t+1-L}) = \arg\max_i \frac{\exp(F_\mathcal{V}(\mathbf{h}_{i,t}))}{\sum_{j=1}^n \exp(F_\mathcal{V}(\mathbf{h}_{j,t}))}, \qquad (7)$$

where $F_\mathcal{V} : \mathbb{R}^{d''} \to \mathbb{R}$ is a multi-layer perceptron. In the training time the model weights are updated via a gradient decent algorithm by minimizing the loss function:

$$\mathcal{L}(\theta) = -\frac{1}{L} \sum_{l=t-L+1}^{t} \log(\pi_\theta(\tilde{a}_l|\mathbf{s}_l, \ldots, \mathbf{s}_{l+1-L})). \qquad (8)$$

## 5   Experiments

In this section, we present experiments and ablations to validate our theoretical propositions. We use SCIP 7.0 optimization suite [19] as the backend solver, along with the Ecole [43] library to run experiments on a V100 GPU card with 32 GB memory. For both generating the training set and solving the MILP instances we use a solver time-limit of 3600 s seconds unless otherwise stated. All results are reported by averaging 5 separate runs with different seeds in the inference time. More details and ablation studies are provided in the *appendix*.

*Datasets:* We evaluate our method on six different datasets that cover a good range of variations in terms of difficulty among the available MILP benchmarks. These datasets include: Set Covering (SC) [22], Combinatorial Auctions (CA) [22,37], Capacitated Facility Locations (CFL) [14], Maximum Independent Set (MIS) [7,22], work load appointments/Load Balancing (LB) [21], and Maritime Inventory Routing (MIR) [41]. Details on how each benchmark is created are provided in the *appendix*.

*Remark:* It is worth noting that, since solvers rely heavily on the underlying hardware of the testing machine (CPU, memory, GPU, etc.), a truly fair evaluation is only achieved when all baseline methods are run on the same machine with the same set of MILP instance; for this, we either trained the baselines from scratch on the same MILP samples or evaluated the checkpoint provided by the authors on the same MILP instances in our environment.

*Baselines:* We compare our results with SCIP's internal branching: FSB, reliability pseudocost branching (RPB) [2], and the pseudo cost branching rule (PB). Additionally, for the first 4 benchmarks, we compare our results with the GCNN approach of Gasse *et al.* [22], LambdaMART [12], SVMRank [33] and finally the ExtraTrees method proposed by [23]. For this, we used the code base provided by [25] in our environment. For the last two benchmarks we compare our results with the internal branching rules of SCIP and also the method proposed by [13] and EI-OROAS from the ML4CO competition [21].

*Training:* For training our temporo-attentional branching policy, we run a training data collection phase in which the instances are solved with a time-limit of 3600 s seconds using the FSB rule from SCIP as our expert agent. For each benchmark, we generate 160k samples from the training set instances for all the benchmarks except for maritime inventory routing dataset that we generated only 5.7k MILP samples due to lack of enough training MILP instances. In particular we record the states of the first $L$ *consecutive* episodes of each MILP instance in the form of bipartite graph representations along with the branching choices associated to each episode. The agents are then trained with the collected datasets. Further details of the training procedure is given in the *appendix*.

*Metrics of Performance:* For the first 4 benchmarks we use the same evaluation metrics as in [22,25]. Specifically, we report: Time: the 1-shifted geometric mean of solving time across the Easy, Medium, and Hard segments of each benchmark. Node: 1-shifted geometric mean of B&B node count of the instances solved by each strategy. Win: number of times each branching agent wins the other strategies based on the solving time across multiple validation runs.

   *Remark:* It is worth noting that the metrics mentioned above, each one alone, doesn't fully capture the solvers performance; since for each MILP instance the rate with which the policy approaches to the optimal solution is important. In other words, a good solution should be able to reduce the gap to the optimal value in a short amount of time. Therefore, it makes sense to include the rate

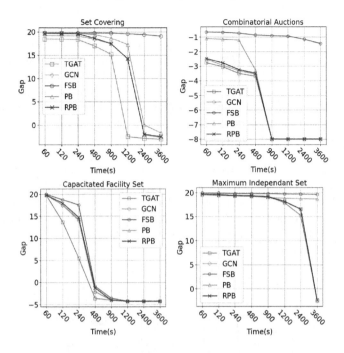

**Fig. 3.** Average dual-primal gap (logarithmic scale) vs solving time-limit (seconds).

with which the gap is reduced in the evaluation metric. To this end, the ML4CO competition [21] incorporated a 'reward' metric to address this for the last two benchmarks. This metric is defined as:

$$\mathcal{R} = \int_{t=0}^{T} \mathbf{z}_t^\star \, \mathrm{d}t - T \mathbf{c}^\top \mathbf{x}^\star, \tag{9}$$

where $\mathbf{z}_t^\star$ is the best dual bound at time $t$, $\mathbf{x}^\star$ is the optimal solution and $T$ is the time-limit. The reward, within a time-limit of $T$, is maximized if the gap between the optimal solution and the dual bound is decreased with a higher rate during consecutive episodes of the branching process.

*Results and Discussions:* Table 1 shows the results on the first 4 benchmark datasets compared to the baselines in three segments of the datasets *i.e.*, Easy, Medium, and Hard instances, where the GAT structure is parameterized with $(d, H)$ where $d = d' = d''$, and $H$ is the number of attention heads. Consequently, the temporo-attentional (TGAT) method is parameterized with $(d, H, L)$ with $L$ being the GRU sequence length. Ablation study on the hyper-parameters is provided in the *appendix*. The *Node* and *Time* metrics are reported when applying the policies on 20 test instances per dataset per difficulty segment, averaged over 5 runs(total 100 instances). As it can be seen our method outperforms the other baselines in terms of the evaluation metrics Wins, and Time for the set covering, capacitated facility locations, and maximum independent set benchmarks. In all the cases our model outperforms the baseline GCNN method [22]. Amongst other baselines LambdaMart performs better in Easy evaluation instances; however, its performance degrades in Hard problems. Figure 3, shows the dual-primal gap [40] across the branching policies. As observed, our methods perform better than the other internal branching rules, as well as the GCNN baseline in closing the gap between the dual bound and the primal bound during a given solving time-limit. Among the internal branching rules FSB is the slowest and RPB is the fastest in closing the dual-primal gap.

*Ablation on TGAT vs GAT:* To evaluate the effect of incorporating the temporal characteristics of the variable embeddings we evaluate the GAT-only agent by bypassing the GRU structure in our model. Figure 4, shows the top-1 validation accuracy of our proposed methods vs GCNN for different benchmarks. For all the datasets TGAT outperforms both GCNN and GAT in terms of imitating the FSB branching expert.

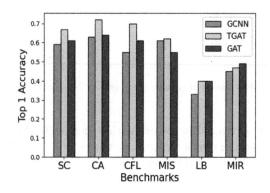

**Fig. 4.** Top-1 accuracy for different branching policies.

Additionally, Table 1 shows that TGAT outperforms the GAT agent except for the combinatorial auctions dataset. We argue that since this benchmark has relatively smaller MILP instances, adding a GRU structure to the model increases the policy complexity and thus the inference time. According to our metrics, the policy that can close the dual gap (reach the optimal solution) in a shorter solving time wins. For small and easy MILP instances a lightweight policy with less branching accuracy may win if it can solve B&B nodes at a higher rate. Our GAT version of the proposed algorithm, however, still outperforms other branching baselines. Although adding to the sequence length $L$, helps the TGAT policy to branch more accurately, it adds to the model complexity and increases the inference time, which as discussed above may degrade the branching performance; therefore, the sequence length should be tuned according to the MILP dataset complexity (More details in the *appendix*).

**Table 1.** Evaluation of branching strategies for sets of easy, medium, and hard MILP instances in terms of time, wins, and nodes metrics along with the standard deviation across runs. The $^†$ superscript indicates our methods.

| Model | Easy | | | Medium | | | Hard | | |
|---|---|---|---|---|---|---|---|---|---|
| | Time↓ | Wins↑ | Nodes↓ | Time↓ | Wins↑ | Nodes↓ | Time↓ | Wins↑ | Nodes↓ |
| Set Covering | | | | | | | | | |
| FSB | 21.2±6.5 | 0/100 | 19±0 | 488.6±145.4 | 0/100 | 183±4 | 3,601±58 | 0/100 | n/a |
| PB | 9.1±2.6 | 5/100 | 286±5 | 75.5±14.6 | 0/100 | 2,532±32 | 2,351±52 | 0/100 | 83,329±1453 |
| RPB | 11.9±5.7 | 0/100 | **56±1** | 74.8±15.7 | 0/100 | 1,892±47 | 1,858±20 | 0/100 | 49,321±1065 |
| SVMRANK [33] | 10.8±3.0 | 0/100 | 170±1 | 91.4±2.6 | 0/100 | 1,982±44 | 2,719±29 | 0/100 | 42,913±1085 |
| L-MART [12] | 9.5±4.6 | 4/100 | 168±28 | 77.8±13.1 | 0/100 | 2,005±55 | 2,432±40 | 0/100 | 45,823±991 |
| EX-TREES [23] | 12.3±1.3 | 0/100 | 174±4 | 122.1±3.3 | 0/100 | 2,281±58 | 3,033±64 | 0/100 | 60,123±1080 |
| GCNN [22] | 8.3±1.6 | 10/100 | 140±3 | 65.5±1.1 | 8/100 | 1,586±45 | 1,745±39 | 0/100 | 31,234±487 |
| FILM | 8.7±2.5 | 2/100 | 145±3 | 67.2±1.2 | 3/100 | 1,626±16 | 1,995±38 | 0/100 | 37,234±820 |
| GAT$^†$(32,2) | 9.8±2.7 | 9/100 | 141±8 | 57.4±14.8 | 11/100 | 1,467±19 | 1,574±47 | 8/100 | 30,812±811 |
| TGAT$^†$(32,2,4) | **6.8±0.20** | **70/100** | 126±9 | **45.6±1.2** | **78/100** | **1,332±25** | **1,376±24** | **92/100** | **29,452±313** |
| Combinatorial Auctions | | | | | | | | | |
| FSB | 5.8±2.2 | 0/100 | 7±0 | 101.0±22.0 | 0/100 | 79±1 | 2,034±25 | 0/100 | 437±5 |
| PB | 3.1±1.0 | 3/100 | 271±4 | 22.2±2.9 | 1/100 | 2,844±37 | 297±5 | 0/100 | 14,130±206 |
| RPB | 4.2±1.2 | 0/100 | **12±0** | 21.2±2.2 | 2/100 | 717±10 | 161±3 | 0/100 | 5,664±71 |
| SVMRANK [33] | 3.4±1.3 | 2/100 | 79±1 | 26.4±2.8 | 0/100 | 911±12 | 442±7 | 0/100 | 6,964±137 |
| L-MART [12] | 2.9±0.8 | 40/100 | 81±1 | 16.0±4.4 | 63/100 | 919±17 | 241±4 | 0/100 | 7,179±135 |
| EX-TREES [23] | 3.9±1.9 | 1/100 | 89±1 | 37.6±10.6 | 0/100 | 1,022±15 | 908±15 | 0/100 | 11,387±207 |
| GCNN [22] | 3.3±1.6 | 2/100 | 78±0 | 24.6±3.5 | 0/100 | 708±10 | 143±1 | 2/100 | 5,929±94 |
| FILM | 3.7±1.3 | 0/100 | 74±0 | 30.2±7.8 | 0/100 | 705±13 | 265±2 | 0/100 | 6,421±66 |
| GAT$^†$(32,2) | **2.7±1.3** | 42/100 | 67±0 | **17.3±4.4** | 34/100 | **675±7** | **89±1** | **95/100** | **5,635±74** |
| TGAT$^†$(32,2,2) | 3.1±1.1 | 10/100 | 76±0 | 22.1±2.8 | 2/100 | 690±7 | 142±1 | 3/100 | 5,900±83 |
| Capacitated Facility Location | | | | | | | | | |
| FSB | 33.2±8.4 | 0/100 | 16±0 | 229.4±67.8 | 0/100 | 82±0 | 784±11 | 0/100 | 61±1 |
| PB | 25.1±10.0 | 0/100 | 157±1 | 143.5±31.8 | 0/100 | 411±8 | 544±7 | 0/100 | 408±5 |
| RPB | 28.9±9.5 | 0/100 | **24±0** | 169.9±37.7 | 0/100 | **131±2** | 607±6 | 0/100 | **121±4** |
| SVMRANK [33] | 26.4±10.5 | 1/100 | 125±1 | 136.3±39.1 | 1/100 | 348±6 | 536±6 | 0/100 | 340±6 |
| L-MART [12] | 27.8±9.7 | 0/100 | 121±1 | 141.6±21.2 | 0/100 | 355±4 | 550±10 | 0/100 | 332±6 |
| EX-TREES [23] | 33.9±8.7 | 0/100 | 143±1 | 194.1±21.7 | 0/100 | 412±7 | 758±11 | 0/100 | 399±6 |
| GCNN [22] | 24.6±10.9 | 5/100 | 112±1 | 130.2±38.3 | 2/100 | 345±5 | 519±7 | 1/100 | 348±6 |
| FILM | 22.1±8.1 | 6/100 | 110±2 | 127.1±25.9 | 3/100 | 361±7 | 501±9 | 1/100 | 340±5 |
| GAT$^†$(32,2,2) | 20.4±9.0 | 18/100 | 107±2 | 123.3±14.2 | 15/100 | 329±5 | 432±8 | 8/100 | 328±5 |
| TGAT$^†$(32,2,2) | **17.9±8.7** | **70/100** | 99±1 | **110.4±22.6** | **79/100** | 304±3 | **349±5** | **90/100** | 301±3 |
| Maximum Independent Set | | | | | | | | | |
| FSB | 28.7±13.1 | 0/100 | 9±0 | 1,550.4±341.9 | 0/100 | 41±0 | 3,601±55 | 0/100 | n/a |
| PB | 11.1±3.7 | 0/100 | 6194±79 | 834.8±83.7 | 0/100 | 1,889±20 | 3,483±34 | 0/100 | 51,230±677 |
| RPB | 11.8±5.7 | 0/100 | **29±0** | 143.8±27.4 | 1/100 | 742±9 | 2,210±32 | 0/100 | 2,742±30 |
| SVMRANK [33] | 13.5±5.1 | 0/100 | 59±1 | 273.9±75.4 | 0/100 | **583±9** | 3,036±42 | 0/100 | 6,852±127 |
| L-MART [12] | 9.8±2.7 | 7/100 | 61±1 | 190.8±20.8 | 0/100 | 795±9 | 3,071±32 | 0/100 | 9,171±132 |
| EX-TREES [23] | 13.1±4.3 | 0/100 | 81±1 | 1,730.4±203.4 | 0/100 | 5,123±85 | 3,601±64 | 0/100 | 40,562±674 |
| GCNN [22] | 11.6±5.5 | 0/100 | 51±0 | 144.2±32.9 | 1/100 | 1,870±23 | 2,192±40 | 7/100 | 2,839±51 |
| FILM | 17.5±7.0 | 0/100 | 67±0 | 230.2±23.7 | 0/100 | 981±10 | 3,142±43 | 0/100 | 41,234±760 |
| GAT$^†$(32,2,4) | 8.8±3.6 | 23/100 | 47±0 | 137.0±39.0 | 3/100 | 1,611±16 | 2,171±25 | 9/100 | **2,736±49** |
| TGAT$^†$(32,2,4) | **8.5±3.4** | **70/100** | 44±0 | **96.1±14.7** | **95/100** | 1,464±14 | **2,126±23** | **84/100** | 2,753±53 |

*Dual Integral Reward:* Following the metric proposed in [21] we report the dual integral rewards for the load balancing and the maritime inventory routing benchmarks in Tables 2 and 3, respectively.

**Table 2.** Dual Integral Reward for the load balancing Dataset.

| Method \| Time | 60 s | 120 s | 240 s | 480 s | 900 s | 1200 s | 2400 s | 3600 s |
|---|---|---|---|---|---|---|---|---|
| FSB | **42236** | **84200** | 168,058 | 335,839 | 629,429 | 839,126 | 1,678,126 | 2,517,404 |
| PB | 41951 | 83933 | 168,003 | 336,290 | 630,968 | 841,510 | 1,683,792 | 2,526,330 |
| GCNN [22] | 41,960 | 83,944 | 167,997 | 336,272 | 630,889 | 841,383 | 1,683,626 | 2,526,162 |
| EI-OROAS [5] | 41,938 | 83,921 | 168,066 | 336,539 | 631,460 | 842,240 | 1,685,519 | 2,529,120 |
| Nuri [13] | 41,951 | 83,934 | 168,034 | 336,299 | 630,989 | 841,546 | 1,683,857 | 2,527,290 |
| GAT$^\dagger$(32, 3) | 41,952 | 83,949 | 168,068 | 336,408 | 631,120 | 841,685 | 1,684,149 | 2,527,838 |
| TGAT$^\dagger$(32, 3, 4) | 41,952 | 83,950 | **168,123** | **336,654** | **631,675** | **842,527** | **1,686,093** | **2,529,981** |

We evaluate the results on the same test set used by [21] in the ML4CO challenge. We compare our results with the SCIP's internal branching rules, the GCNN [22], team Nuri [13], and team EI-OROAS [5] of the competition (Nuri & El-OROAS results are reproduced in our environment using the checkpoints provided by the authors). We observe that FSB outperforms other policies in small time-limits. For such time-limits, none of the policies can completely solve the harder instances in the underlying benchmarks; however, FSB initially outperforms other policies in achieving a better dual gap for smaller problems; but with time, the slowness factor of FSB kicks in and it falls behind other policies in solving harder instances in terms of dual integral reward. A similar argument applies to the Nuri method in Table 3. The results suggest that in general our TGAT method generalizes better to the larger instances than other baselines.

**Table 3.** Dual Integral Reward for the maritime inventory routing Dataset.

| Method \| Time | 60 s | 240 s | 480 s | 900 s | 1200 ss | 2400 ss | 3600 ss |
|---|---|---|---|---|---|---|---|
| FSB | **1,828,117** | 7,084,200 | 13,506,208 | 24,812,337 | 33,215,861 | 66,904,807 | 100,815,459 |
| PB | 1,624,580 | 6,621,338 | 13,392,385 | 25,288,001 | 33,830,325 | 67,957,522 | 102,177,927 |
| GCNN [22] | 1,627,863 | 6,576,079 | 13,248,266 | 25,123,252 | 33,705,099 | 69,139,207 | 103,991,280 |
| EL-OROAS [5] | 1,682,022 | 6,926,643 | 14,108,146 | 26,743,861 | 36,060,519 | 73,039,994 | 109,997,616 |
| Nuri [13] | 1,744,715 | **7,168,752** | **14,516,105** | **27,464,789** | 36,760,604 | 74,077,350 | 111,507,638 |
| GAT$^\dagger$(32, 2) | 1,690,743 | 6,971,475 | 14,163,826 | 26,606,932 | 36,171,609 | 73,413,862 | 109,926,566 |
| TGAT$^\dagger$(32, 2, 4) | 1,732,502 | 7,118,571 | 14,414,492 | 27,272,535 | **37,164,971** | **74,892,201** | **112,934,222** |

# 6   Conclusion

In this paper, we proposed to encode the bipartite graph representation of a MILP instance with two successive passes of the graph attention message passing network. We argued that through the attention mechanism, we can better represent both the feature level and structure level importance of the neighboring nodes. Later, we proposed to encode the temporal correlations of the node embeddings with a GRU structure. We reason that the past states of the graph embeddings contain information that can be used in the current branching episode. By experiments on 6 different datasets that are challenging for state-of-the-art solvers, we corroborate the validity of our proposed method. The experiment results show that in general, our temporo-attentional method generalizes better on larger MILP instances with more complex structures. We hope our work can facilitate further research on incorporating the attention and temporal mechanisms of MILPs into modern combinatorial optimization solvers.

# 7 Statement of Ethics

This paper does not introduce a new dataset, nor it leverages any personal data.

# References

1. Achterberg, T.: Scip: solving constraint integer programs. Math. Program. Comput. **1**(1), 1–41 (2009)
2. Achterberg, T., Koch, T., Martin, A.: Branching rules revisited. Oper. Res. Lett. **33**(1), 42–54 (2005)
3. Achterberg, T., Wunderling, R.: Mixed integer programming: Analyzing 12 years of progress. In: Facets of Combinatorial Optimization, pp. 449–481. Springer (2013)
4. Alvarez, A.M., Louveaux, Q., Wehenkel, L.: A machine learning-based approximation of strong branching. INFORMS J. Comput. **29**(1), 185–195 (2017)
5. Banitalebi-Dehkordi, A., Zhang, Y.: Ml4co: Is gcnn all you need? graph convolutional neural networks produce strong baselines for combinatorial optimization problems, if tuned and trained properly, on appropriate data. arXiv preprint arXiv:2112.12251 (2021)
6. Bennell, J.A., Mesgarpour, M., Potts, C.N.: Dynamic scheduling of aircraft landings. Eur. J. Oper. Res. **258**(1), 315–327 (2017)
7. Bergman, D., Cire, A.A., Van Hoeve, W.J., Hooker, J.: Decision diagrams for optimization, vol. 1. Springer (2016)
8. Bixby, B.: The gurobi optimizer. Transp. Res. Part B **41**(2), 159–178 (2007)
9. Boyd, S., Boyd, S.P., Vandenberghe, L.: Convex optimization. Cambridge University Press (2004)
10. Breiman, L.: Random forests. Mach. Learn. **45**(1), 5–32 (2001)
11. Brody, S., Alon, U., Yahav, E.: How attentive are graph attention networks? arXiv preprint arXiv:2105.14491 (2021)
12. Burges, C.J.: From ranknet to lambdarank to lambdamart: An overview. Learning **11**(23–581), 81 (2010)
13. Cao, Z., Xu, Y., Huang, Z., Zhou, S.: Ml4co-kida: Knowledge inheritance in dataset aggregation. arXiv preprint arXiv:2201.10328 (2022)
14. Cornuéjols, G., Sridharan, R., Thizy, J.M.: A comparison of heuristics and relaxations for the capacitated plant location problem. Eur. J. Oper. Res. **50**(3), 280–297 (1991)
15. Ding, J.Y., Zhang, C., Shen, L., Li, S., Wang, B., Xu, Y., Song, L.: Accelerating primal solution findings for mixed integer programs based on solution prediction. In: Proceedings of the AAAI Conference on Artificial Intelligence, vol. 34, pp. 1452–1459 (2020)

16. ecole.ai: Ml4co: 2021 neurips competition on machine learning for combinatorial optimization (2021). www.ecole.ai/2021/ml4co-competition/
17. Fiala, J., Kočvara, M., Stingl, M.: Penlab: A matlab solver for nonlinear semidefinite optimization. arXiv preprint arXiv:1311.5240 (2013)
18. Flood, M.M.: The traveling-salesman problem. Oper. Res. **4**(1), 61–75 (1956)
19. Gamrath, G., et al.: The SCIP Optimization Suite 7.0. ZIB-Report 20–10, Zuse Institute Berlin, March 2020. www.nbn-resolving.de/urn:nbn:de:0297-zib-78023
20. Gamrath, G., et al.: The scip optimization suite 7.0 (2020)
21. Gasse, M., et al.: The machine learning for combinatorial optimization competition (ml4co): Results and insights. arXiv preprint: 2203.02433 (2022)
22. Gasse, M., Chételat, D., Ferroni, N., Charlin, L., Lodi, A.: Exact combinatorial optimization with graph convolutional neural networks. Advances in Neural Information Processing Systems 32 (2019)
23. Geurts, P., Ernst, D., Wehenkel, L.: Extremely randomized trees. Mach. Learn. **63**(1), 3–42 (2006)
24. Graham, R.L., Hell, P.: On the history of the minimum spanning tree problem. Ann. History Comput. **7**(1), 43–57 (1985)
25. Gupta, P., Gasse, M., Khalil, E., Mudigonda, P., Lodi, A., Bengio, Y.: Hybrid models for learning to branch. Adv. Neural. Inf. Process. Syst. **33**, 18087–18097 (2020)
26. Hamilton, W.L.: Graph representation learning. Synthesis Lectures Artif. Intell. Mach. Learn. **14**(3), 1–159 (2020)
27. He, H., Daume III, H., Eisner, J.M.: Learning to search in branch and bound algorithms. Advances in neural information processing systems 27 (2014)
28. Hoffman, K.L., Ralphs, T.K.: Integer and combinatorial optimization. In: Encyclopedia of Operations Research and Management Science, pp. 771–783 (2013)
29. Howard, R.A.: Dynamic programming and markov processes. John Wiley (1960)
30. Hussein, A., Gaber, M.M., Elyan, E., Jayne, C.: Imitation learning: a survey of learning methods. ACM Comput. Surv. (CSUR) **50**(2), 1–35 (2017)
31. Hutter, F., Hoos, H.H., Leyton-Brown, K.: Sequential model-based optimization for general algorithm configuration. In: Coello, C.A.C. (ed.) LION 2011. LNCS, vol. 6683, pp. 507–523. Springer, Heidelberg (2011). https://doi.org/10.1007/978-3-642-25566-3_40
32. Khalil, E., Dai, H., Zhang, Y., Dilkina, B., Song, L.: Learning combinatorial optimization algorithms over graphs. Advances in neural information processing systems 30 (2017)
33. Khalil, E., Le Bodic, P., Song, L., Nemhauser, G., Dilkina, B.: Learning to branch in mixed integer programming. In: Proceedings of the AAAI Conference on Artificial Intelligence, vol. 30 (2016)
34. Kipf, T.N., Welling, M.: Semi-supervised classification with graph convolutional networks. In: International Conference on Learning Representations (ICLR) (2017)
35. Knueven, B., Ostrowski, J., Watson, J.P.: On mixed-integer programming formulations for the unit commitment problem. INFORMS J. Comput. **32**(4), 857–876 (2020)
36. Land, A.H., Doig, A.G.: An automatic method for solving discrete programming problems. In: Jünger, M., Liebling, T.M., Naddef, D., Nemhauser, G.L., Pulleyblank, W.R., Reinelt, G., Rinaldi, G., Wolsey, L.A. (eds.) 50 Years of Integer Programming 1958-2008, pp. 105–132. Springer, Heidelberg (2010). https://doi.org/10.1007/978-3-540-68279-0_5

37. Leyton-Brown, K., Pearson, M., Shoham, Y.: Towards a universal test suite for combinatorial auction algorithms. In: Proceedings of the 2nd ACM Conference on Electronic Commerce, pp. 66–76 (2000)
38. Manual, C.U.: Ibm ilog cplex optimization studio. Version **12**, 1987–2018 (1987)
39. Morais, H., Kádár, P., Faria, P., Vale, Z.A., Khodr, H.: Optimal scheduling of a renewable micro-grid in an isolated load area using mixed-integer linear programming. Renew. Energy **35**(1), 151–156 (2010)
40. Nair, V., et al.: Solving mixed integer programs using neural networks. arXiv preprint arXiv:2012.13349 (2020)
41. Papageorgiou, D.J., Nemhauser, G.L., Sokol, J., Cheon, M.S., Keha, A.B.: Mirplib - a library of maritime inventory routing problem instances: survey, core model, and benchmark results. Eur. J. Oper. Res. **235**(2), 350–366 (2014)
42. Pomerleau, D.A.: Efficient training of artificial neural networks for autonomous navigation. Neural Comput. **3**(1), 88–97 (1991)
43. Prouvost, A., Dumouchelle, J., Scavuzzo, L., Gasse, M., Chételat, D., Lodi, A.: Ecole: a gym-like library for machine learning in combinatorial optimization solvers. In: Learning Meets Combinatorial Algorithms at NeurIPS2020 (2020). www.openreview.net/forum?id=IVc9hqgibyB
44. Qu, Q., Li, X., Zhou, Y.: Yordle: an efficient imitation learning for branch and bound. arXiv preprint arXiv:2112.12251 (2022)
45. Ross, S., Gordon, G., Bagnell, D.: A reduction of imitation learning and structured prediction to no-regret online learning. In: Proceedings of the Fourteenth International Conference on Artificial Intelligence and Statistics, pp. 627–635. JMLR Workshop and Conference Proceedings (2011)
46. Salkin, H.M., De Kluyver, C.A.: The knapsack problem: a survey. Naval Res. Logistics Quarterly **22**(1), 127–144 (1975)
47. Shen, Y., Sun, Y., Eberhard, A., Li, X.: Learning primal heuristics for mixed integer programs. In: 2021 International Joint Conference on Neural Networks (IJCNN), pp. 1–8. IEEE (2021)
48. Song, J., Lanka, R., Zhao, A., Bhatnagar, A., Yue, Y., Ono, M.: Learning to search via retrospective imitation. arXiv preprint arXiv:1804.00846 (2018)
49. Vaz, A.I.F., Vicente, L.N.: Pswarm: a hybrid solver for linearly constrained global derivative-free optimization. Optimization Methods Softw. **24**(4–5), 669–685 (2009)
50. Velickovic, P., Cucurull, G., Casanova, A., Romero, A., Lio, P., Bengio, Y.: Graph attention networks. Stat **1050**, 20 (2017)
51. Xu, B., Wang, N., Chen, T., Li, M.: Empirical evaluation of rectified activations in convolutional network. arXiv preprint arXiv:1505.00853 (2015)
52. Zhang, T., Banitalebi-Dehkordi, A., Zhang, Y.: Deep reinforcement learning for exact combinatorial optimization: learning to branch. In: 26th International Conference on Pattern Recognition, ICPR (2022)

# Improved Multi-label Propagation for Small Data with Multi-objective Optimization

Khadija Musayeva[✉] and Mickaël Binois

Université Côte d'Azur, Inria, CNRS, LJAD, Sophia Antipolis, France
{khadija.musayeva,mickael.binois}@inria.fr

**Abstract.** This paper focuses on multi-label learning from small amounts of labelled data. We demonstrate that the binary-relevance extension of the interpolated label propagation algorithm, the harmonic function, is a competitive learning method with respect to many widely-used evaluation measures. This is achieved by a new transition matrix that better captures the underlying structure useful for classification coupled with the use of data dependent thresholding strategies. Furthermore, we show that in the case of label dependence, one can use the outputs of a competitive learning model as part of the input to the harmonic function to improve the performance of this model. Finally, since we are using multiple measures to thoroughly evaluate the performance of the algorithm, we propose to use the game-theory based method of Kalai and Smorodinsky to output a single compromise solution for all measures. This method can be applied to any learning model irrespective of the number of evaluation metrics used.

**Keywords:** Multi-label classification · Small data · Label propagation · Label dependence · Thresholding strategy · Multi-objective optimization

## 1 Introduction

Multi-label classification deals with the problems where an instance can be assigned to multiple labels simultaneously. Examples of such a problem are text and music categorization, semantic annotation of image and video, gene function prediction (see references in [39]), soil microbiome prediction [1]. Sometimes, however, only small amounts of labelled data are available because the labelling can be a costly task, and large amounts of unlabelled data can be obtained rather easily. In this context, semi-supervised learning [13] and transductive learning [23,37] are particularly suitable learning settings as they both allow one to make use of the unlabelled part of the data to construct a predictive model. If in the former setting, the goal of the learning process is to construct a model that makes accurate predictions on out-of-sample examples, in the latter, it is to find an accurate model only for the unlabelled part of the data. The current paper focuses on the latter setting.

D. Koutra et al. (Eds.): ECML PKDD 2023, LNAI 14172, pp. 284–300, 2023.
https://doi.org/10.1007/978-3-031-43421-1_17

One of the transductive learning approaches is the family of label propagation algorithms. These are manifold learners [2,3] where the goal is, using a suitable approximation of the underlying manifold, to propagate the labels from the labelled instances to the unlabelled ones. Label propagation algorithms are decades old and started with the works [34,40–43] in the binary setting, and continued by [16,33] in the multi-label one. Clearly, any binary label propagation can be straightforwardly extended to the $C$-label ($C > 2$) case by binary relevance transformation [31], i.e., decomposing the data into $C$ binary classification tasks and applying the binary method of interest to each task independently. The main purpose of the current work is to show that the binary relevance extension of the harmonic function and its iterative version [42,43] are competitive multi-label learners for small data when they operate on a propagation matrix better aligning with the classification goal.

Roughly speaking, the harmonic function computes the labels based on an absorbing Markov chain [12], where the absorbing states represent the labelled instances with no path between them. One starts from an unlabelled instance and makes transitions unless one reaches an absorbing state. In the iterative approach, one can control the number of transitions made between the unlabelled instances. Each absorbing state contributes to the computation of the label of a given unlabelled instance $a$ proportionally to the probability of reaching that absorbing state from $a$. Clearly, the performances of these algorithms depend crucially on how well the transition matrix is aligned with the classification task. In this paper, we construct a new transition matrix where the transition probability between any two points is influenced by the neighbourhood structure of both points. Such a construction is useful to weaken the links between the points belonging to different clusters. Although we deal with interpolated approaches, this construction and the absence of paths between the labelled instances can be regarded as an implicit regularization. Furthermore, in the case of label dependence, modeling which is a central issue in the multi-label learning [9–11], we can leverage it by computing a transition matrix based on the data combining the original input variables and the labels, where for the unlabelled points the predictions of a competitive learning model can be used. In other words, the harmonic function and the iterative label propagation can be used as stacking methods to improve the performances of competitive external models by operating on a new structure incorporating inputs from all labels. The experiments show that these methods with the proposed transition matrices are superior to [16,33,38], and in particular, to the multi-label extensions of regularized label propagations [34,40]. As stacking methods, they improve performances of inductive classifiers such as ensembles of classifier chains [24] and random k-labelsets [32], and in this context, they are superior to the instance-based logistic regression which can also be used as a stacking method [6].

In the multi-label setting, the performances of learning methods are simultaneously evaluated with respect to multiple evaluation metrics, the majority of which require thresholding the real-valued outputs to $\{0,1\}$. Our remaining contributions concern this subject. In this paper, along with the widely used thresholding approach of [23], we propose to use the class-mass normalization method of [43] in the multi-label setting. We show that, if the former, being based on the label cardinality, improves the family of $F1$-measures, a heuristic competitive to the exact-$F1$-plug-in classifier [8], the latter computes a threshold separately for each label, and thus is suitable to improve the Hamming loss. Finally, the multiple evaluation metrics used in this paper are usually of conflicting nature, meaning that they might favor different label outputs for a given instance. To find a single compromise solution, we propose to use the multi-objective optimization approach based on the game-theoretic method of Kalai and Smorodinsky [4,15]. Unlike the existing approach in the multi-label setting [28], it can be applied to any model irrespective of the number of evaluation metrics considered.

## 2    Theoretical Background

We describe the problem of interest of this paper formally as follows.

Let $\mathcal{X}$ be an input space and let $\mathcal{L} = \{l_1, \ldots, l_C\}$, $C > 2$, be a finite set of labels. In this paper, we assume that $\mathcal{X} = \mathbb{R}^d$. In the multi-label classification setting, an instance $\mathbf{x} \in \mathcal{X}$ is associated with a set of labels in $P(\mathcal{L}) = 2^{\mathcal{L}}$. Let $\mathcal{Y} = \{0, 1\}^C$ be the *relevance* set. We map the set of labels $L(\mathbf{x}) \in P(\mathcal{L})$ associated to $\mathbf{x}$ to the corresponding element $\mathbf{y} = (y_1, \ldots, y_C) \in \mathcal{Y}$ where $y_i = 1$ if and only if $l_i \in L(\mathbf{x})$. Let $X$ and $\mathbf{Y} = (Y_1, \ldots, Y_C)$ be random variables taking values in $\mathcal{X}$ and $\mathcal{Y}$, respectively. We assume that a random pair $(X, \mathbf{Y})$ is distributed according to a fixed but unknown probability distribution $P$ on $X \times \mathcal{Y}$. We denote the marginal and conditional distributions as $P_X$ and $P_{\mathbf{Y}|X}$. The only available information we have about $P$ is via an $n$-sample $((\mathbf{x}_1, \mathbf{y}_1), \ldots, (\mathbf{x}_n, \mathbf{y}_n))$, where $\mathbf{y}_i = (y_{i1}, \ldots, y_{iC})$, a realization of $n$ independent copies of $(X, \mathbf{Y})$.

In this paper we focus on the problem of learning from the partially labelled data $D = ((\mathbf{x}_1, \mathbf{y}_1), \ldots, (\mathbf{x}_l, \mathbf{y}_l), \mathbf{x}_{l+1}, \ldots, \mathbf{x}_n)$ where the goal is to predict the labels of $(\mathbf{x}_{l+1}, \ldots, \mathbf{x}_n)$ based on the information on the joint distribution $P(X, \mathbf{Y})$ as well as that provided by $(\mathbf{x}_i)_{i=1}^n$ on $P_X$. One of such learning algorithms is the label propagation.

Label propagation exploits the manifold structure of the input data where the manifold is represented as the weighted graph $G = (V, E)$, with $V = \{1, \ldots, n\}$ and $E \subseteq \{(i, j) \in V^2\}$. The default assumption is that if $\mathbf{x}$ and $\mathbf{x}'$ are close in the intrinsic geometry of $P_X$, then $P_{\mathbf{Y}|X}(\mathbf{y}|\mathbf{x})$ and $P_{\mathbf{Y}|X}(\mathbf{y}|\mathbf{x}')$ should be similar [3], or in terms of the cluster assumption, instances should share similar labels if there is a path connecting them passing through the high density region of $P_X$ [5]. Under such an assumption, we would like the corresponding graph to be a good approximation of this structure and to find a smooth function $f : G \to \mathbb{R}^C$ whose outputs are similar for the instances connected with the edges of large weights. We can express most label propagation approaches as the following graph regularization problem:

$$\min_{\mathbf{f}} tr(\mathbf{f}^T \tilde{\mathbf{L}} \mathbf{f} + (\mathbf{f} - \tilde{\mathbf{y}}^{(n)})^T \boldsymbol{\Lambda} (\mathbf{f} - \tilde{\mathbf{y}}^{(n)})), \tag{1}$$

where tr is the trace operator, $\mathbf{f} = [f(1)^T \dots f(n)^T]^T \in \mathbb{R}^{n \times C}$ with $f(i) = (f_1(i), \dots, f_C(i))$, $\tilde{\mathbf{y}}^{(n)} = [\mathbf{y}_1^T \dots \mathbf{y}_l^T; \mathbf{0}]^T \in \mathbb{R}^{n \times C}$ with $\mathbf{0}$ being zero matrix of the dimension $C \times (n-l)$, $\mathbf{\Lambda}$ is a diagonal matrix of regularization parameters, $\tilde{\mathbf{L}}$ is usually the normalized Laplacian $\tilde{\mathbf{L}} = \mathbf{I} - \mathbf{P}$ with $\mathbf{P} = \mathbf{D}^{-1/2}\mathbf{W}\mathbf{D}^{-1/2}$ or $\mathbf{P} = \mathbf{D}^{-1}\mathbf{W}$ [7], $\mathbf{W}$ is the $n \times n$ weight matrix and $\mathbf{D}$ the diagonal matrix with $D_{ii} = \sum_{j=1}^{n} W_{ij}$. One particular case, on which the current paper focuses, is the interpolated label propagation, where for all labelled points $\Lambda_l = \infty$, and for the unlabelled ones $\Lambda_u = 0$. Consequently, the values of $f$ on the labelled points are constrained to be equal to their labels. This solution is called the harmonic function. Below we show that it corresponds to the random walk on an absorbing Markov chain [12], i.e., a Markov chain with at least one state which once entered cannot be left. The main advantage of such a representation is the unified view of the harmonic function and the iterative label propagation, and the clear view of the structure of the transition matrix for which we provide a new computation.

## 3   Label Propagation on Absorbing Markov Chain

Representing the labelled points by absorbing states, the label propagation on an absorbing Markov chain is a process that starts in non-absorbing states, i.e., the states corresponding to the unlabelled points and makes transitions based on the following probabilities:

$$\mathbf{P} = \begin{bmatrix} \mathbf{I} & \mathbf{0} \\ \mathbf{P}_{ul} & \mathbf{P}_{uu} \end{bmatrix}, \tag{2}$$

where $\mathbf{I}$ is $l \times l$ identity matrix, and $\mathbf{P}_{uu}$ and $\mathbf{P}_{ul}$ stand for the sub-matrices of $\mathbf{P}$ denoting the transition probabilities from the unlabelled to unlabelled, and from the unlabelled to labelled instances, respectively. The first row of this matrix represents the absorbing states, i.e., the labelled instances, with self-transitions of probability one and no transitions to other states. On such a chain, the labels of the unlabelled points can be computed by the harmonic function:

$$\mathbf{f} = \mathbf{P}\mathbf{f}. \tag{3}$$

Partitioning $\mathbf{f}$ into the labelled and unlabelled parts as $\mathbf{f} = [\mathbf{f}_l \ \mathbf{f}_u]^T$ and solving the system (3) for $\mathbf{f}_u$ gives

$$\mathbf{f}_u = (\mathbf{I} - \mathbf{P}_{uu})^{-1}\mathbf{P}_{ul}\mathbf{f}_l. \tag{4}$$

This is exactly the solution of the problem (1) with the constraints $\Lambda_l = \infty$ and $\Lambda_u = 0$ yielding $\min_{\mathbf{f}} \text{tr}(\mathbf{f}^T \tilde{\mathbf{L}} \mathbf{f}) = \min_{\mathbf{f}} \text{tr}(\mathbf{f}^T \mathbf{f} - \mathbf{f}^T \mathbf{P} \mathbf{f})$.

   Now for the $t$-step transition, $t \geq 2$, based on (3), we have $\mathbf{f} = \mathbf{P}^{(t)}\mathbf{f}$, where $\mathbf{A}^{(t)}$ denotes the $t$-th power of $\mathbf{A}$, and thus using (2) we get $\mathbf{f}_u = \mathbf{P}_{uu}^{(t)}\mathbf{f}_u + \left(\mathbf{I} + \sum_{i=1}^{t-1} \mathbf{P}_{uu}^{(i)}\right)\mathbf{P}_{ul}\mathbf{f}_l$ whose solution is again (4) (to see this, consider the equality $(\mathbf{I} - \mathbf{P}_{uu})^{-1} = \sum_{i=0}^{\infty} \mathbf{P}_{uu}^{(i)}$). If we consider the $t$-step transition as an iterative procedure $\mathbf{f}^t = \mathbf{P}\mathbf{f}^{t-1}$ where $\mathbf{f}^t$ denotes the values for the iteration $t$, based on (2), we get the expression similar to the one just above:

$$\mathbf{f}_u^t = \mathbf{P}_{uu}^{(t)}\mathbf{f}_u^0 + \left(\mathbf{I} + \sum_{i=1}^{t-1}\mathbf{P}_{uu}^{(i)}\right)\mathbf{P}_{ul}\mathbf{f}_l, \tag{5}$$

where we initiate $\mathbf{f}_u^0 = \mathbf{0}$. Note that the harmonic function subsumes the infinite number of transitions (as $t \to \infty$, the expression (5) converges to (4)). However, as we show in the experiments section, in some cases, only a finite number of transitions is needed to improve the classification performance.

Although the harmonic function is an interpolated approach, the manipulation of the transition matrix (2) on which it operates can be seen as an implicit regularization which makes the harmonic function a competitive learning method. Our goal now is to compute the second row of the transition matrix (2). We provide a new way of doing so in the following section.

## 3.1    Computing Transition Probabilities

As we mentioned before, the performance of the label propagation algorithms depends crucially on how well the weighted graph models the manifold structure. The standard way of building such a graph is based on the use of a weighting function or kernel, in a general form given as $K_\sigma(\mathbf{x}, \mathbf{x}') = D\left(d(\mathbf{x}, \mathbf{x}')/\sigma\right)$, where $d$ is a metric on $\mathcal{X}$, usually the Euclidean metric, and $\sigma$ is the width of the kernel, for which the most widely used choice is the Gaussian one,

$$D(u) = \exp\left(-u^2/2\right). \tag{6}$$

Applying it to the data $(\mathbf{x}_i)_{i=1}^n$ gives the weight matrix $\mathbf{W}$ with $W_{ij} = K_\sigma(\mathbf{x}_i, \mathbf{x}_j)$. The Gaussian kernel has infinite support where the parameter $\sigma$ dictates how slowly the similarities fade. Then applying the $k$-nearest neighbour approach, we can cancel the long-range relationships which can be helpful in capturing the underlying clustering structure. This might look similar to using compact kernels, such as Epanechnikov or tricube kernel [14], but the neighbourhood structure they produce are more in the spirit of that obtained by $\epsilon$-neighbourhoods. Now let $\mathcal{N}_k(\mathbf{x}_i)$ denote the set of points which are the $k$-nearest neighbours of an unlabelled point $\mathbf{x}_i$ chosen based on the row $W_{i.}$ of $\mathbf{W}$. For all $\mathbf{x}_j \notin \mathcal{N}_k(\mathbf{x}_i)$, we set $W_{ij} = 0$. Furthermore, since this paper focuses on an absorbing Markov chain, we consider the neighbourhood structure only of the unlabelled instances. Thus we set $W_{ij} = 0$ for all labelled points $\mathbf{x}_i, \mathbf{x}_j$, but allow self-loops for all points. Notice that the obtained weight matrix is not necessarily symmetric, i.e., $W_{ij} \neq W_{ji}$, yielding a directed graph.

The next step is to construct the transition probabilities which will turn our graph into an absorbing Markov chain. The standard way of doing so is to row normalize $\mathbf{W}$. Then the transition probability from $\mathbf{x}_i$ to $\mathbf{x}_j$ is $P_{ij} = W_{ij}/\sum_{j=1}^n W_{ij}$, which we call the standard transition matrix. Instead, we propose to column normalize $\mathbf{W}$ first and then row normalize the obtained matrix, i.e.,

$$\mathbf{P} = \mathbf{D}^{-1}\mathbf{W}' \qquad (7)$$

where $\mathbf{D}$ is the diagonal matrix consisting of row summation of $\mathbf{W}'$ with $D_{ii} = \sum_j^n W_{ij}'$, $\mathbf{W}' = \mathbf{W}\mathbf{D}'^{-1}$, and $\mathbf{D}'$ is another diagonal matrix consisting of column summation of $\mathbf{W}$ with $D_{jj}' = \sum_i^{n-l} W_{ij}$. The column normalization can be understood as adjusting the transition from $\mathbf{x}_i$ to $\mathbf{x}_j$ by taking into account all incoming links to $\mathbf{x}_j$. Thus if $\mathbf{x}_i$ and $\mathbf{x}_j$ are in different clusters but there is an edge between them, then the weight of this edge will be reduced. This weakens the label propagation between these clusters. Our experiments demonstrate that constructing the transition matrix in this way produces decisively better results (with respect to the majority of evaluation metrics) compared to those obtained by the standard transition matrix. In our experiments, we also compare this approach to the regularized ones of [34,40] whose propagation matrices are inspired from spectral clustering [19], and locally linear embedding [26], respectively.

Furthermore, in the case of label dependence, we can improve the performance of the harmonic function by incorporating the label information into our transition matrix (7). This is demonstrated in the next section.

## 4   Leveraging Label Dependence: Interpolated Label Propagation as a Stacking Method

If the labels are correlated, leveraging this information can improve the predictive power of the learning method [11]. One of the ways of doing so, that we follow in this paper, is to treat the labels as features [6,23].

In the binary setting of the harmonic function, the authors [43] propose to attach the predicted labels as new vertices to the corresponding unlabelled instance nodes in the graph representation, where the transition probabilities from the unlabelled instance nodes to their label nodes are fixed to some value (which is the same for all these nodes). In this paper, instead of attaching the labels directly to the graph, we propose to use the original labels, $\mathbf{y}^{(l)} = [\mathbf{y}_1^T \ldots \mathbf{y}_l^T] \in \mathcal{Y}^{C \times l}$, and the predictions $\mathbf{y}^{(u)} = [\bar{\mathbf{y}}_{l+1}^T \ldots \bar{\mathbf{y}}_n^T] \in \mathcal{Y}^{C \times u}$ of an external classifier, i.e., the combined label matrix $\tilde{\mathbf{Y}} = [\mathbf{y}^{(l)}; \mathbf{y}^{(u)}]^T \in \mathcal{Y}^{n \times C}$ as new features and join them to the original input data $\mathbf{X} = [\mathbf{x}_1^T \ldots \mathbf{x}_n^T]^T \in \mathbb{R}^{n \times d}$. The original problem now has a new representation of the dimensionality $d + C$. Since this new representation incorporates the information from all labels, it is suitable to perform the label propagation on the resulting graph, which we construct as discussed in Sect. 3.1, when there exists inter-dependencies between the majority of the labels.

The important point here is that we are dealing with the real-valued data $\mathbf{X}$, and thus we need to transform the relevance matrix $\tilde{\mathbf{Y}}$ to a real-valued one before joining it to $\mathbf{X}$. The straightforward approach would be to row-normalize it, but this transformation is indifferent to the frequency of labels. Instead, inspired from the ecological study [18], we propose to do a chi-square metric based trans-formation of $\tilde{\mathbf{Y}}$ as $\hat{\mathbf{Y}}' = (\sum_{ij} \tilde{\mathbf{Y}}_{ij})^{1/2} \mathbf{A}^{-1} \tilde{\mathbf{Y}} \mathbf{B}^{-1/2}$, where $\mathbf{A}$ is the diagonal matrix consisting of row summation of $\tilde{\mathbf{Y}}$, i.e., $A_{ii} = \sum_{j=1}^{n} \tilde{y}_{ij}$, and $\mathbf{B}$ is the diagonal matrix consisting of column summation of $\tilde{\mathbf{Y}}$, i.e., $B_{jj} = \sum_{i=1}^{n} \tilde{y}_{ij}$. The advantage of this transformation is that it is sensitive to the frequencies of the labels where the relatively rare ones get more weight since their column sums are smaller. Consequently, when building the weight matrix (6), they con-tribute more to the Euclidean distance than it is the case with a simple row normalization.

It should be noted that the matrix $\tilde{\mathbf{Y}}$ is noisy because it combines the pre-dictions of an external classifier (the original labels might also be assumed to be noisy). Taking this into account, we control the contribution from $\tilde{\mathbf{Y}}$ by multiplying it by a regularization parameter $\alpha \in (0, 1)$. This simply reduces to $d((\mathbf{x}, \mathbf{x}'))^2 + \alpha \cdot d((\tilde{\mathbf{y}}, \tilde{\mathbf{y}}'))^2$ in the computation of the squared Euclidean dis-tance in (6) for any points $(\mathbf{x}, \tilde{\mathbf{y}})$ and $(\mathbf{x}', \tilde{\mathbf{y}}')$. The transition matrix is computed using (7) to which we then apply the harmonic function or the iterative label propagation.

# 5   Evaluation Measures and Thresholding Strategies

Since multi-label classification constitutes a more complex setting than the single-label one, the performance of a multi-label classifier is usually evaluated simultaneously according to multiple evaluation metrics, each of which cap-tures different aspect of this performance. This paper considers the following most widely used metrics: subset accuracy, Hamming loss, average precision, $F1$-measure, and the *macro* and *micro* variants of the latter as well as that of the area under the ROC curve (AUC). For the completeness of the paper, their definitions are given in Appendix A[1].

The label propagation approach that we are dealing with produces outputs in $[0, 1]$. Then, to compute the Hamming loss, the subset accuracy and the family of $F1$-measures, a decision rule/thresholding strategy is needed to map them to $\{0, 1\}$. In fact, the choice of the decision rule can drastically impact the values of these measures [13,35]. The default approach would be to treat the outputs of the harmonic function as class posterior probabilities and use the standard thresholding at 0.5, however this would lead to poor results if the outputs are not well calibrated probability estimates. We can address it by probability calibra-tion techniques [17,21,36], but they require an additional training step. Instead, in this paper we consider two efficient data-dependent approaches that do not require a learning/cross-validation step and is superior to the standard thresh-olding. Due to space limits, their definitions are delegated to Appendix B.

One of these approaches is the class-mass normalization (CMN) proposed in [43] which can be extended straightforwardly to the multi-label setting (9) (in Appendix B). It computes a threshold for each label (and for each instance)

---

[1] The appendices are available at github.com/kmusayeva/M-LP.

independently based on its frequency and thus it is suitable to optimize the Hamming loss. To the best of our knowledge, this strategy has not yet been considered in the multi-label classification setting. On the other hand, [24] uses a single threshold for all labels and is based on the notion of label cardinality. We refer to this rule as the label cardinality optimizer (LCO). If the cardinality of the unlabelled data is similar to that of the labelled data, this heuristic is suitable to improve the family of $F1$-measures, because by optimizing the label cardinality it improves the recall[2]. In our experiments, we also compare the $F1$-values obtained by this strategy to that obtained by the exact-$F1$-plug-in classifier (EFC) [8] which is designed to optimize just mentioned measure.

## 6    Finding Compromise Solution for Multiple Evaluation Measures

The problem that arises from using multiple evaluation metrics is that their optimal values might favor different label outputs. For instance, the conflicting nature of the Hamming loss and the subset accuracy has been demonstrated rigorously in [9]. However, it might be desirable to find a single output for multiple metrics without much compromising on any of them. This problem falls into the field of multi-objective optimization and can be handled in the context of *Pareto dominance*. Without loss of generality, consider a minimization problem. The solution $\mathbf{a} = (a_1, \ldots, a_p) \in \mathbb{R}^p$ is said to dominate the solution $\mathbf{b} = (b_1, \ldots, b_p) \in \mathbb{R}^p$ if for all $i, a_i \leq b_i$ and there exists $i$ such that $a_i < b_i$, and the corresponding set of non-dominated solutions is called the Pareto front. The goal then is to select a single solution from this set. To the best of our knowledge, the only work that addresses this task in the context of multi-label classification is [28]. It is based on the evolutionary algorithm whose computation depends on the considered approach and might not be applicable to any model: the authors choose a neural network due to the efficiency of the computation.

In this paper, we propose to use the game theory based method of Kalai and Smorodinsky (KS) [15] which can be briefly described as follows. This method searches for the solution which, for a chosen set of evaluation metrics or objectives of equal importance, is the solution $\mathbf{s} = (s_1, \ldots, s_p) \in \mathbb{R}^p$ centrally located on the Pareto front, where $s_i$ is the value of the $i$-th evaluation metric and $p$ is the number of the metrics considered. Given the minimum of each objective $\mathbf{u} = (u_1, \ldots, u_p) \in \mathbb{R}^p$ and a *disagreement* point $\mathbf{d} = (d_1, \ldots, d_p) \in \mathbb{R}^p$, defaulted to the worse value of each objective on the Pareto front, the idea is to move from $\mathbf{d}$ towards $\mathbf{u}$ while equally improving all objectives. More precisely, the idea is to improve the corresponding benefit ratios defined as $r(\mathbf{s}, i) = \dfrac{d_i - s_i}{d_i - u_i}$, $1 \leqslant i \leqslant p$, for any solution $\mathbf{s} \in \mathcal{S} \subset \mathbb{R}^p$ and objective $i$. If it exists, this process leads to the KS solution, i.e., the Pareto optimal solution for which all benefit ratios

---

[2] To see this let $(1, 0, 1, 1)$ be the true label set. Then, although both $(1, 0, 0, 0)$ and $(1, 1, 0, 1)$ predict two labels incorrectly, the latter provides a higher $F1$ value because it provides higher recall without much degrading the precision.

are equal, and if it does not, the authors [4] propose the efficient maxmin solution: it is the Pareto optimal solution maximizing the smallest benefit ratio over objectives, i.e., $\mathbf{s}_{KS}^* \in \text{argmax}_{\mathbf{s} \in \mathcal{S}} \min_{1 \leqslant i \leqslant p} r(\mathbf{s}, i)$.

This method is applied to the outputs of a learning method over a hyperparameter grid, thus it is independent of the method used. If [28] can optimize up to four objectives, the KS method can be applied to any number of objectives scaling only linearly. In this paper, we find the compromise solution for eight objectives/evaluation metrics mentioned in the previous section.

# 7    Experiments

The main goal of the experiments is to compare the overall performance on multiple evaluation measures, i.e., the KS compromise solution of the harmonic function (HF) and the iterative label propagation (ILP) using the proposed transition matrices to those of other label propagation (LP)/local methods and to evaluate its stacking performance using several competitive inductive learning methods[3].

## 7.1    Experimental Setup

To the best of our knowledge, in this paper we considered all existing LP methods: the straightforward multi-label extension of regularized label propagation approaches, consistency method (CM) [40] and linear neighbourhood label propagation (LNP) [34], and multi-label propagation approaches, dynamic label propagation (DLP) [33] and TRAM [16]. In TRAM, we do not row-normalize the label matrix which leads to a better performance, and also, since we work with data of small to moderate dimensionality we do not apply any dimensionality reduction approach as it is done in the original work. As the considered LP approaches model the manifold based on the $k$-nearest neighbour graph, we also compare their performances to ML-KNN [38].

For the stacking performance of HF/ILP, we use the predictions of the following competitive multi-label classifiers: binary relevance method (BR) [30], ensembles of classifier chains (ECC) [24] and random k-labelsets (RAKEL) [32]. For these methods the support-vector machine is chosen as the base algorithm. Since BR is tailored to improve the label-wise performance, it improves the Hamming loss. On the other hand, ECC and RAKEL are capable of modeling the label dependencies, and thus they improve the subset accuracy [9,11]. Then, the general view of their performances gives an idea about possible label dependencies. More precisely, when there is no label dependence, we can expect the Hamming loss and the subset accuracy to be optimized simultaneously by BR. In this case, using HF/ILP as a stacking method is useless. If there is a label dependence, then ECC or RAKEL is expected to improve the subset accuracy, and we use the predictions of the best performing (on most measures) method in HF/ILP as discussed in Sect. 4.

---

[3] The code and the data are available at github.com/kmusayeva/M-LP.

We compare the stacking performance of HF/ILP to that of the instance-base logistic regression (IBLR) method: first, we test the performance of IBLR as a standalone method, then apply it to the predictions of the inductive methods mentioned above. The neighbourhood structure in IBLR is based on the similarity matrix derived from the Gaussian kernel (6).

As a decision rule, for LNP, since the labels are in $\{-1, 1\}$, we use the sign function. TRAM method implements a label propagation to find the number of relevant labels for each unlabelled point: as we show in Appendix G, TRAM is equivalent to using HF with the standard transition matrix, where the same procedure is also used to find the number of relevant labels. Since IBLR is based on logistic regression, we do the thresholding at 0.5. The remaining methods use both CMN (9) and LCO (10) thresholding approaches.

For the quadratic optimization problem of LNP we use OSQP package [29], and for the KS solution the GPGame package [20]. We use the utiml package [25] for BR, ECC, RAKEL and ML-KNN. For the logistic regression problem of IBLR and EFC we use glm package. All methods are implemented in R programming language [22].

We selected five publicly available data sets[4] with the moderate number $n$ of observations and the low average class imbalance defined as avgImb$(D) = \frac{1}{C} \sum_{j=1}^{C} \frac{\max(F(j), n - F(j))}{\min(F(j), n - F(j))}$ where $F(j) = \sum_{i=1}^{n} y_{ij}$ [37]. Table 1 shows the values of these properties along with the number $C$ of labels, the number ls of unique labelsets, and the label density ld $= \frac{1}{nC} \sum_{i=1}^{n} \sum_{j=1}^{C} y_{ij}$. For all LP methods and ML-KNN, we normalize the features of all data sets to the range $[0, 1]$, because they are based on the use of the Euclidean distance which is sensitive to the magnitude of the values.

**Table 1.** The properties of the datasets used in the experiments.

| Data set | $n$ | $d$ | $C$ | ls | ld | avgImb |
|----------|-----|-----|-----|-----|-----|--------|
| Emotions | 593 | 72 | 6 | 27 | 0.311 | 2.146 |
| Fungi | 240 | 9 | 12 | 147 | 0.344 | 5.451 |
| Scene | 2407 | 294 | 6 | 15 | 0.179 | 4.662 |
| Yeast | 2417 | 103 | 14 | 198 | 0.325 | 8.867 |

Since the current paper focuses on small data, we sample only half of the observations from Scene and Yeast datasets by stratified sampling based on the label powerset approach [27] to guarantee the similar label distribution, thus similar ls, ld and avgImb to those of the entire dataset. This same approach is also used in $5 \times 2$-fold cross validation to tune the hyperparameters.

Finally, in HF, ILP and TRAM, the number of neighbours is chosen from the set $\{15, 20, \ldots, 50\}$. In general, LNP favors small number of neighbours: this is

---

[4] All datasets except for Fungi are taken from https://www.uco.es/kdis/mllresources/. The Fungi dataset has been kindly provided to us by C. Averill [1].

due to the fact that each point and its neighbourhood is represented by a locally linear patch of the underlying manifold. Thus for LNP, and also for ML-KNN, we choose $k$ from $\{3, 5, \ldots, 50\}$. The $\alpha$ parameter in LNP and CM is tuned from $\{0.2, 0.4, \ldots, 0.99\}$ and that in HF as a stacking method in $\{0.01, 0.1, 0.3, 0.5\}$. In DLP method, $\alpha$ takes its values in $\{0.001, 0.0001\}$ and $\lambda$ in $\{0.01, 0.1\}$, and the number of iterations are set from $\{1, 2, \ldots, 10\}$. In LP methods the width $\sigma$ of the kernel is chosen from $\{0.1, 0.2, \ldots, 3\}$ and in SVM (used in the inductive approaches) from $\{10^{-3}, 10^{-2}, \ldots, 10\}$.

## 7.2  Results

We first report the superior performance of HF using our new transition matrix (7) to that using the standard one in Table 2. Tables 3, 4, 5 and 6 report the results of the experiments comparing the performances of learning methods discussed in the previous section (the standard deviations are delegated to Appendix E).

In all experiments, we observed CMN to be a better minimizer of the Hamming loss compared to LCO. The latter, on the other hand, improves the family

**Table 2.** Comparison of the new transition matrix with the standard one for HF. The reported values are the KS compromise solutions. The up/down arrow next to the name of an evaluation metric means the higher/lower the value the better the performance. The best results are underlined.

| | Emotions | | Fungi | |
|---|---|---|---|---|
| Measures | new | standard | new | standard |
| Hamming loss ↓ | 0.1891 ± 0.0085 | 0.1997 ± 0.0107 | 0.2047 ± 0.0095 | 0.2060 ± 0.0099 |
| Subset-accuracy ↑ | 0.3305 ± 0.0151 | 0.3156 ± 0.0235 | 0.1534 ± 0.0199 | 0.1517 ± 0.0190 |
| F1 ↑ | 0.6730 ± 0.0133 | 0.6576 ± 0.0145 | 0.6654 ± 0.0174 | 0.6631 ± 0.0178 |
| Macro-F1 ↑ | 0.6792 ± 0.0146 | 0.6622 ± 0.0171 | 0.5455 ± 0.0233 | 0.5511 ± 0.0189 |
| Micro-F1 ↑ | 0.6975 ± 0.0141 | 0.6801 ± 0.0167 | 0.6696 ± 0.0154 | 0.6711 ± 0.0139 |
| Macro-AUC ↑ | 0.8503 ± 0.0087 | 0.8408 ± 0.0105 | 0.8046 ± 0.0128 | 0.8024 ± 0.0093 |
| Micro-AUC ↑ | 0.8662 ± 0.0081 | 0.8578 ± 0.0105 | 0.8612 ± 0.0064 | 0.8599 ± 0.0061 |
| Average precision↑ | 0.8081 ± 0.0056 | 0.8027 ± 0.0093 | 0.8434 ± 0.0082 | 0.8423 ± 0.0068 |
| | Scene | | Yeast | |
| Measures | new | standard | new | standard |
| Hamming loss ↓ | 0.0935 ± 0.0030 | 0.1031 ± 0.0049 | 0.2018 ± 0.0046 | 0.2066 ± 0.0057 |
| Subset-accuracy ↑ | 0.6879 ± 0.0104 | 0.6623 ± 0.0156 | 0.2051 ± 0.0097 | 0.2066 ± 0.0107 |
| F1 ↑ | 0.7338 ± 0.0094 | 0.7064 ± 0.0144 | 0.6515 ± 0.0063 | 0.6429 ± 0.0097 |
| Macro-F1 ↑ | 0.7428 ± 0.0077 | 0.7156 ± 0.0129 | 0.4248 ± 0.0084 | 0.4389 ± 0.0116 |
| Micro-F1 ↑ | 0.7297 ± 0.0087 | 0.7021 ± 0.0140 | 0.6676 ± 0.0065 | 0.6604 ± 0.0092 |
| Macro-AUC ↑ | 0.9333 ± 0.0026 | 0.9292 ± 0.0033 | 0.7122 ± 0.0110 | 0.7058 ± 0.0130 |
| Micro-AUC ↑ | 0.9342 ± 0.0036 | 0.9283 ± 0.0050 | 0.8439 ± 0.0037 | 0.8389 ± 0.0045 |
| Average precision↑ | 0.8556 ± 0.0056 | 0.8372 ± 0.0085 | 0.7579 ± 0.0061 | 0.7529 ± 0.0068 |

of $F1$-measures at the cost of degrading the Hamming loss. For simplicity of the presentation, we report the performances corresponding to one of these decision rules (homogeneous for all methods, except for LNP, TRAM and IBLR which use their own decision functions): we choose CMN over LCO if it substantially improves the Hamming loss and the subset accuracy without much degrading the family of $F1$-measures. We report both CMN and LCO results only for HF in Table 7 in Appendix C; the observed tendency holds for all methods. The competitive performance of (stacking) HF using LCO to that of EFC method with respect to $F1$-measure is given in Table 8 in Appendix D.

As the results demonstrate, the interpolated LP approach, HF, is superior to the regularized approaches, CM and LNP, with respect to most evaluation metrics on all datasets, except for Scene, which is indicative of the fact that, on these datasets, the transition matrix (7) is capable of capturing the structure useful for classification. On Scene dataset, which has the lowest label density, i.e., a sparse label matrix, in view of (12) (in Appendix E), the regularized label propagation approach, CM, achieves a superior performance if we highly penalize the fitting to the labels. This, however, comes at the cost of degraded AUC measures. Also, on this dataset, ILP performs better than HF, which means that by keeping the number of transitions between the unlabelled points small, one can respect the sparsity of the label matrix.

In particular, HF has superiority over all LP methods as well as ML-KNN on Emotions and Yeast datasets. This is particularly remarkable for the former dataset: it contains a small number of unique labelsets, the lowest class imbalance

**Table 3.** The results for Emotions dataset. The up/down arrow next to the name of an evaluation metric means the higher/lower the value the better the performance. The best results are underlined. The decision function used is LCO.

A) HF and LP/ML-KNN

| Measures | HF | CM | LNP | TRAM | DLP | ML-KNN |
|---|---|---|---|---|---|---|
| Hamming loss ↓ | 0.1891 | 0.2270 | 0.2330 | 0.2251 | 0.2387 | 0.2029 |
| Subset-accuracy ↑ | 0.3305 | 0.2090 | 0.2630 | 0.2472 | 0.2091 | 0.2906 |
| F1 ↑ | 0.6730 | 0.6210 | 0.5780 | 0.6519 | 0.6072 | 0.6482 |
| Macro-F1 ↑ | 0.6792 | 0.6420 | 0.6000 | 0.6660 | 0.6123 | 0.6471 |
| Micro-F1 ↑ | 0.6975 | 0.6530 | 0.6080 | 0.6757 | 0.6365 | 0.6746 |
| Macro-AUC ↑ | 0.8503 | 0.7870 | 0.7840 | 0.8431 | 0.7631 | 0.8229 |
| Micro-AUC ↑ | 0.8662 | 0.8000 | 0.7950 | 0.8598 | 0.7825 | 0.8484 |
| Average precision↑ | 0.8081 | 0.8080 | 0.7700 | 0.8034 | 0.7930 | 0.7968 |

B) Stacking: HF vs IBLR

| Measures | BR | ECC | RAKEL | RAKEL+HF | IBLR | RAKEL+IBLR |
|---|---|---|---|---|---|---|
| Hamming loss↓ | 0.1873 | 0.1857 | 0.1841 | 0.1799 | 0.1937 | 0.1877 |
| Subset accuracy↑ | 0.3292 | 0.3410 | 0.3568 | 0.3703 | 0.3197 | 0.3382 |
| F1↑ | 0.6747 | 0.6710 | 0.6809 | 0.6858 | 0.6419 | 0.6615 |
| Macro-F1↑ | 0.6822 | 0.6869 | 0.6905 | 0.6986 | 0.6515 | 0.6799 |
| Micro-F1↑ | 0.7003 | 0.6995 | 0.7060 | 0.7114 | 0.6748 | 0.6989 |
| Macro-AUC↑ | 0.8508 | 0.8385 | 0.8044 | 0.8515 | 0.8417 | 0.8463 |
| Micro-AUC↑ | 0.8704 | 0.8510 | 0.8162 | 0.8646 | 0.8602 | 0.8651 |
| Average precision↑ | 0.8244 | 0.8117 | 0.8001 | 0.8241 | 0.8107 | 0.8117 |

**Table 4.** The results for Fungi dataset. The up/down arrow next to the name of an evaluation metric means the higher/lower the value the better the performance. The best results are underlined. The decision function used is CMN.

### A) HF and LP/ML-KNN

| Measures | HF | CM | LNP | TRAM | DLP | ML-KNN |
|---|---|---|---|---|---|---|
| Hamming loss ↓ | 0.2020 | 0.2060 | 0.2140 | 0.2034 | 0.2051 | 0.2255 |
| Subset-accuracy ↑ | 0.1517 | 0.1509 | 0.1360 | 0.1537 | 0.1410 | 0.1200 |
| F1 ↑ | 0.6690 | 0.6435 | 0.6440 | 0.6661 | 0.6672 | 0.6158 |
| Macro-F1 ↑ | 0.5192 | 0.4859 | 0.5710 | 0.5248 | 0.5689 | 0.4878 |
| Micro-F1 ↑ | 0.6708 | 0.6495 | 0.6600 | 0.6720 | 0.6809 | 0.6286 |
| Macro-AUC ↑ | 0.8051 | 0.8042 | 0.7600 | 0.8034 | 0.8047 | 0.7485 |
| Micro-AUC ↑ | 0.8605 | 0.8581 | 0.8190 | 0.8611 | 0.8623 | 0.8316 |
| Average precision↑ | 0.8440 | 0.8412 | 0.8280 | 0.8417 | 0.8480 | 0.7929 |

### B) Stacking: HF vs IBLR

| Measures | BR | RAKEL | ECC | ECC+HF | HF+HF | IBLR | ECC+IBLR |
|---|---|---|---|---|---|---|---|
| Hamming loss ↓ | 0.2070 | 0.2095 | 0.2078 | 0.2065 | 0.2018 | 0.2265 | 0.2056 |
| Subset-accuracy ↑ | 0.1483 | 0.1548 | 0.1552 | 0.1567 | 0.1600 | 0.1165 | 0.1533 |
| F1 ↑ | 0.6453 | 0.638 | 0.6559 | 0.6593 | 0.6745 | 0.6238 | 0.6579 |
| Macro-F1↑ | 0.4828 | 0.5112 | 0.5626 | 0.5840 | 0.5708 | 0.5357 | 0.5561 |
| Micro-F1 ↑ | 0.6460 | 0.6463 | 0.6639 | 0.6749 | 0.6796 | 0.6417 | 0.6672 |
| Macro-AUC ↑ | 0.7364 | 0.7150 | 0.7638 | 0.7631 | 0.7956 | 0.7717 | 0.8084 |
| Micro-AUC ↑ | 0.8285 | 0.7974 | 0.8409 | 0.8373 | 0.8611 | 0.8327 | 0.8570 |
| Average precision↑ | 0.8092 | 0.7916 | 0.8170 | 0.8226 | 0.8372 | 0.8011 | 0.8361 |

**Table 5.** The results for Scene dataset. The up/down arrow next to the name of an evaluation metric means the higher/lower the value the better the performance. The best results are underlined. The decision function used is CMN. On this dataset ILP performs better than HF.

### A) ILP and LP/ML-KNN

| Measures | ILP | CM | LNP | TRAM | DLP | ML-KNN |
|---|---|---|---|---|---|---|
| Hamming loss ↓ | 0.0930 | 0.0920 | 0.0958 | 0.1009 | 0.0937 | 0.1030 |
| Subset-accuracy ↑ | 0.6879 | 0.6928 | 0.6851 | 0.6691 | 0.6884 | 0.6573 |
| F1 ↑ | 0.7338 | 0.7414 | 0.7301 | 0.7121 | 0.7329 | 0.7087 |
| Macro-F1 ↑ | 0.7297 | 0.7351 | 0.7336 | 0.7079 | 0.7287 | 0.7047 |
| Micro-F1 ↑ | 0.7428 | 0.7465 | 0.7245 | 0.7205 | 0.7413 | 0.7150 |
| Macro-AUC ↑ | 0.9333 | 0.8521 | 0.9225 | 0.9301 | 0.9097 | 0.8995 |
| Micro-AUC ↑ | 0.9342 | 0.8553 | 0.9264 | 0.9303 | 0.9126 | 0.9140 |
| Average precision↑ | 0.8556 | 0.8620 | 0.8538 | 0.8411 | 0.8564 | 0.8320 |

### B) Stacking: ILP vs IBLR

| Measures | BR | ECC | RAKEL | RAKEL+ILP | IBLR | RAKEL+IBLR |
|---|---|---|---|---|---|---|
| Hamming loss ↓ | 0.0848 | 0.0862 | 0.0805 | 0.0796 | 0.0989 | 0.0923 |
| Subset-accuracy ↑ | 0.6998 | 0.6936 | 0.7237 | 0.7304 | 0.6599 | 0.6838 |
| F1 ↑ | 0.7683 | 0.7653 | 0.7750 | 0.7752 | 0.7255 | 0.7439 |
| Macro-F1 ↑ | 0.7620 | 0.7588 | 0.7699 | 0.7702 | 0.7203 | 0.7378 |
| Micro-F1 ↑ | 0.7720 | 0.7693 | 0.7797 | 0.7794 | 0.7302 | 0.7470 |
| Macro-AUC ↑ | 0.9346 | 0.9247 | 0.8954 | 0.9192 | 0.9272 | 0.9290 |
| Micro-AUC ↑ | 0.9443 | 0.9287 | 0.8938 | 0.9248 | 0.9337 | 0.9360 |
| Average precision↑ | 0.8753 | 0.8624 | 0.8499 | 0.8742 | 0.8487 | 0.8583 |

among the datasets considered, and exhibits label dependence which can also be concluded from the performance of the RAKEL method. Such a dependence

**Table 6.** The results for Yeast dataset. The up/down arrow next to the name of an evaluation metric means the higher/lower the value the better the performance. The best results are underlined. The decision function used is LCO.

### A) HF and LP/ML-KNN

| Measures | HF | CM | LNP | TRAM | DLP | ML-KNN |
|---|---|---|---|---|---|---|
| Hamming loss ↓ | 0.2018 | 0.2164 | 0.2030 | 0.2061 | 0.2090 | 0.2143 |
| Subset-accuracy ↑ | 0.2051 | 0.1584 | 0.1840 | 0.1799 | 0.1709 | 0.1599 |
| F1 ↑ | 0.6515 | 0.6150 | 0.6010 | 0.6278 | 0.6405 | 0.6333 |
| Macro-F1 ↑ | 0.4248 | 0.4317 | 0.3930 | 0.3968 | 0.3899 | 0.3838 |
| Micro-F1 ↑ | 0.6676 | 0.6426 | 0.6300 | 0.6438 | 0.6569 | 0.6480 |
| Macro-AUC ↑ | 0.7122 | 0.6906 | 0.6690 | 0.7063 | 0.7088 | 0.6521 |
| Micro-AUC ↑ | 0.8439 | 0.8298 | 0.8220 | 0.8400 | 0.8335 | 0.8261 |
| Average precision↑ | 0.7579 | 0.7611 | 0.7500 | 0.7544 | 0.7486 | 0.7460 |

### B) Stacking: HF vs IBLR

| Measures | BR | ECC | RAKEL | RAKEL+HF | IBLR | RAKEL+IBLR |
|---|---|---|---|---|---|---|
| Hamming loss ↓ | 0.2019 | 0.2062 | 0.1992 | 0.1980 | 0.2038 | 0.2005 |
| Subset-accuracy ↑ | 0.1838 | 0.1883 | 0.2243 | 0.2477 | 0.1604 | 0.2008 |
| F1 ↑ | 0.6502 | 0.6470 | 0.6565 | 0.6595 | 0.6009 | 0.6312 |
| Macro-F1 ↑ | 0.4180 | 0.4341 | 0.4200 | 0.4183 | 0.3517 | 0.3779 |
| Micro-F1 ↑ | 0.6672 | 0.6633 | 0.6712 | 0.6736 | 0.6271 | 0.6518 |
| Macro-AUC ↑ | 0.7029 | 0.6552 | 0.6194 | 0.6909 | 0.6687 | 0.6856 |
| Micro-AUC ↑ | 0.8406 | 0.8152 | 0.7910 | 0.8385 | 0.8296 | 0.8366 |
| Average precision↑ | 0.7663 | 0.7577 | 0.7602 | 0.7585 | 0.7527 | 0.7596 |

is also observed for Scene and Yeast datasets. On these datasets, HF effectively leverages this dependence as a stacking method using the predictions of RAKEL.

Fungi dataset contains the smallest number of observations, and HF, TRAM and DLP, being transductive methods, outperform all inductive methods with respect to all evaluation metrics except subset accuracy because they do not take the label dependence into account. It also has the highest ratio ls $/n$ of unique labelsets to the number of observations, thus the inferior performance demonstrated by RAKEL. Moreover, this dataset contains independent subsets of correlated labels, and as can be judged from the value of the subset accuracy, ECC and RAKEL are capable of leveraging it. The predictions of ECC are further improved by HF. Since HF outperforms the inductive methods, for comparison we also use its own predictions in the stacking approach. Compared to the standalone HF, incorporating the label information simultaneously improves the Hamming loss, the subset accuracy and the family of $F1$ measures.

Finally, HF/ILP outperforms IBLR on all datasets. Using the predictions of the inductive methods, IBLR does improve its performance with respect to all measures, however this does not provide an improvement over that of the inductive method.

# 8  Conclusions

This paper extends the harmonic function and its iterative version to the multi-label setting via the binary relevance transformation. In particular, we construct a new transition matrix which better aligns with the classification task than the standard transition matrix. Furthermore, although it is a binary relevance approach, we can leverage the label dependence by incorporating the labels into this transition matrix, where for the unlabelled points the predictions of a competitive learning method can be used. We evaluated the performances of all models considered in the paper via multiple evaluation metrics. A subset of these measures requires a thresholding strategy to be applied to the real-valued outputs. Since it computes a threshold for each label independently based on its frequency, we propose using the class-mass normalization method in the multi-label setting to improve the Hamming loss. Finally, for multiple evaluation metrics, we report a single compromise solution using the game-theory based multi-objective optimization approach. This approach can be applied to any number of metrics, scaling only linearly. The obtained results show that, despite its simplicity, the label propagation on an absorbing Markov chain with the proposed transition matrices is a competitive approach capable of improving the outputs of an external model when there exists label dependence.

## Ethical Implications

We have considered the potential ethical implications of our research. This paper can not be used for disinformation, generating fake profiles, surveillance, adversarial attacks etc., since it deals with a shallow method designed for small data, and does not use any data with personal information. On the other hand, we acknowledge that the use of imbalanced data might lead to biases against historically disadvantaged groups. Since the considered method does not address the class imbalance problem, we advocate against its use for the problems with highly imbalanced data containing information about marginalized groups.

## References

1. Averill, C., Werbin, Z., Atherton, K., Bhatnagar, J., Dietze, M.: Soil microbiome predictability increases with spatial and taxonomic scale. Nature Ecol. Evol. 5(6), 747–756 (2021)
2. Belkin, M., Niyogi, P.: Semi-supervised learning on Riemannian manifolds. Mach. Learn. 56(1), 209–239 (2004)
3. Belkin, M., Niyogi, P., Sindhwani, V.: Manifold regularization: a geometric framework for learning from labeled and unlabeled examples. J. Mach. Learn. Res. 7(11) (2006)
4. Binois, M., Picheny, V., Taillandier, P., Habbal, A.: The Kalai-Smorodinsky solution for many-objective Bayesian optimization. J. Mach. Learn. Res. 21(150), 1–42 (2020)

5. Chapelle, O., Weston, J., Schölkopf, B.: Cluster kernels for semi-supervised learning. In: Advances in Neural Information Processing Systems. Citeseer (2002)
6. Cheng, W., Hüllermeier, E.: Combining instance-based learning and logistic regression for multilabel classification. Mach. Learn. **76**, 211–225 (2009)
7. Chung, F.: Spectral graph theory, vol. 92. American Mathematical Soc. (1997)
8. Dembczyński, K., Jachnik, A., Kotlowski, W., Waegeman, W., Hüllermeier, E.: Optimizing the F-measure in multi-label classification: Plug-in rule approach versus structured loss minimization. In: International Conference on Machine Learning, pp. 1130–1138. PMLR (2013)
9. Dembczyński, K., Waegeman, W., Cheng, W., Hüllermeier, W.: Regret analysis for performance metrics in multi-label classification: the case of Hamming and subset zero-one loss. In: Joint European Conference on Machine Learning and Knowledge Discovery in Databases, pp. 280–295. Springer (2010)
10. Dembczyński, K.K., Cheng, W., Hüllermeier, E.: Bayes optimal multilabel classification via probabilistic classifier chains. In: ICML (2010)
11. Dembczyński, K.K., Waegeman, W., Cheng, W., Hüllermeier, E.: On label dependence in multilabel classification. In: LastCFP: ICML Workshop on learning from multi-label data. Ghent University, KERMIT, Department of Applied Mathematics, Biometrics (2010)
12. Doyle, P., Snell, J.: Random walks and electric networks, vol. 22. American Mathematical Soc. (1984)
13. Fan, R., Lin, C.: A study on threshold selection for multi-label classification, pp. 1–23. Department of Computer Science, National Taiwan University pp (2007)
14. Hastie, T., Tibshirani, R., Friedman, J.H., Friedman, J.H.: The elements of statistical learning: data mining, inference, and prediction, vol. 2. Springer (2009)
15. Kalai, E., Smorodinsky, M.: Other solutions to Nash's bargaining problem. Econometrica: J. Econometric Soc., 513–518 (1975)
16. Kong, X., Ng, M., Zhou, Z.: Transductive multilabel learning via label set propagation. IEEE Trans. Knowl. Data Eng. **25**(3), 704–719 (2011)
17. Leathart, T., Frank, E., Holmes, G., Pfahringer, B.: Probability calibration trees. In: Asian Conference on Machine Learning, pp. 145–160 (2017)
18. Legendre, P., Gallagher, E.: Ecologically meaningful transformations for ordination of species data. Oecologia **129**(2), 271–280 (2001)
19. Ng, A., Jordan, M., Weiss, Y.: On spectral clustering: analysis and an algorithm. Advances in neural information processing systems 14 (2001)
20. Picheny, V., Binois, M.: GPGame: Solving Complex Game Problems using Gaussian Processes (2022). www.github.com/vpicheny/GPGame, R package version 1.2.0
21. Platt, J.: Probabilistic outputs for support vector machines and comparisons to regularized likelihood methods. Adv. Large Margin Classifiers **10**(3), 61–74 (1999)
22. R Core Team: R: A Language and Environment for Statistical Computing. R Foundation for Statistical Computing, Vienna, Austria (2021). www.R-project.org/
23. Read, J., Pfahringer, B., Holmes, G.: Generating synthetic multi-label data streams. In: ECML/PKKD 2009 Workshop on Learning from Multi-label Data (MLD 2009), pp. 69–84. Citeseer (2009)
24. Read, J., Pfahringer, B., Holmes, G., Frank, E.: Classifier chains for multi-label classification. Mach. Learn. **85**(3), 333–359 (2011)
25. Rivolli, A., de Carvalho, A.: The utiml package: Multi-label classification in R. R J. **10**(2), 24 (2018)
26. Roweis, S., Saul, L.: Nonlinear dimensionality reduction by locally linear embedding. Science **290**(5500), 2323–2326 (2000)

27. Sechidis, K., Tsoumakas, G., Vlahavas, I.: On the stratification of multi-label data. In: Gunopulos, D., Hofmann, T., Malerba, D., Vazirgiannis, M. (eds.) ECML PKDD 2011. LNCS (LNAI), vol. 6913, pp. 145–158. Springer, Heidelberg (2011). https://doi.org/10.1007/978-3-642-23808-6_10

28. Shi, C., Kong, X., Yu, P., Wang, B.: Multi-objective multi-label classification. In: Proceedings of the 2012 SIAM International Conference on Data Mining, pp. 355–366. SIAM (2012)

29. Stellato, B., Banjac, G., Goulart, P., Bemporad, A., Boyd, S.: OSQP: an operator splitting solver for quadratic programs. Math. Program. Comput. **12**(4), 637–672 (2020)

30. Tsoumakas, G., Katakis, I.: Multi-label classification: an overview. Int. J. Data Warehousing Mining (IJDWM) **3**(3), 1–13 (2007)

31. Tsoumakas, G., Katakis, I., Vlahavas, I.: Mining multi-label data. In: Data Mining and Knowledge Discovery Handbook, pp. 667–685. Springer (2009). https://doi.org/10.1007/978-0-387-09823-4_34

32. Tsoumakas, G., Katakis, I., Vlahavas, I.: Random k-labelsets for multilabel classification. IEEE Trans. Knowl. Data Eng. **23**(7), 1079–1089 (2010)

33. Wang, B., Tu, Z., Tsotsos, J.: Dynamic label propagation for semi-supervised multi-class multi-label classification. In: Proceedings of the IEEE International Conference on Computer Vision, pp. 425–432 (2013)

34. Wang, F., Zhang, C.: Label propagation through linear neighborhoods. IEEE Trans. Knowl. Data Eng. **20**(1), 55–67 (2007)

35. Yang, Y.: A study of thresholding strategies for text categorization. In: Proceedings of the 24th Annual International ACM SIGIR Conference on Research and Development in Information Retrieval, pp. 137–145 (2001)

36. Zadrozny, B., Elkan, C.: Transforming classifier scores into accurate multiclass probability estimates. In: Proceedings of the Eighth ACM SIGKDD International Conference on Knowledge Discovery and Data Mining, pp. 694–699 (2002)

37. Zhang, M., Li, Y., Yang, H., Liu, X.: Towards class-imbalance aware multi-label learning. IEEE Trans. Cybern. (2020)

38. Zhang, M., Zhou: ML-KNN: a lazy learning approach to multi-label learning. Pattern Recogn. **40**(7), 2038–2048 (2007)

39. Zhang, M., Zhou, Z.: A review on multi-label learning algorithms. IEEE Trans. Knowl. Data Eng. **26**(8), 1819–1837 (2013)

40. Zhou, D., Bousquet, O., Lal, T., Weston, J., Schölkopf, B.: Learning with local and global consistency. In: Advances in Neural Information Processing Systems, pp. 321–328 (2004)

41. Zhou, D., Schölkopf, B.: Learning from labeled and unlabeled data using random walks. In: Rasmussen, C.E., Bülthoff, H.H., Schölkopf, B., Giese, M.A. (eds.) DAGM 2004. LNCS, vol. 3175, pp. 237–244. Springer, Heidelberg (2004). https://doi.org/10.1007/978-3-540-28649-3_29

42. Zhu, X., Ghahramani, Z.: Learning from labeled and unlabeled data with label propagation (2002)

43. Zhu, X., Ghahramani, Z., Lafferty, J.: Semi-supervised learning using Gaussian fields and harmonic functions. In: Proceedings of the 20th International Conference on Machine Learning (ICML-03), pp. 912–919 (2003)

# Fast Convergence of Random Reshuffling Under Over-Parameterization and the Polyak-Łojasiewicz Condition

Chen Fan[1]([✉]), Christos Thrampoulidis[2], and Mark Schmidt[1,3]

[1] Department of Computer Science, University of British Columbia, Vancouver, BC, Canada
{fanchen2,schmidtm}@cs.ubc.ca, cthrampo@ece.ubc.ca
[2] Department of Electrical and Computer Engineering, University of British Columbia, Vancouver, BC, Canada
[3] Canada CIFAR AI Chair (Amii), Montreal, Canada

**Abstract.** Modern machine learning models are often over-parameterized and as a result they can interpolate the training data. Under such a scenario, we study the convergence properties of a sampling-without-replacement variant of stochastic gradient descent (SGD) known as random reshuffling (RR). Unlike SGD that samples data with replacement at every iteration, RR chooses a random permutation of data at the beginning of each epoch and each iteration chooses the next sample from the permutation. For under-parameterized models, it has been shown RR can converge faster than SGD under certain assumptions. However, previous works do not show that RR outperforms SGD in over-parameterized settings except in some highly-restrictive scenarios. For the class of Polyak-Łojasiewicz (PL) functions, we show that RR can outperform SGD in over-parameterized settings when either one of the following holds: (i) the number of samples ($n$) is less than the product of the condition number ($\kappa$) and the parameter ($\alpha$) of a weak growth condition (WGC), or (ii) $n$ is less than the parameter ($\rho$) of a strong growth condition (SGC).

## 1 Introduction

We consider finite-sum minimization problems of the form

$$\min\left\{ f(x) = \frac{1}{n}\sum_{i=1}^{n} f(x;i) \right\}. \tag{1}$$

Stochastic gradient descent (SGD) is a popular algorithm for solving machine learning problems of this form. A significant amount of effort has been made to understand its theoretical and empirical properties [5]. SGD has a simple update rule in which a sample $i_k$ is chosen randomly with replacement and at each iteration we compute $x^{k+1} = x^k - \eta^k \nabla f(x^k; i_k)$. This is cheaper than using the full gradient at each iteration. However, it is well known that the

D. Koutra et al. (Eds.): ECML PKDD 2023, LNAI 14172, pp. 301–315, 2023.
https://doi.org/10.1007/978-3-031-43421-1_18

convergence rate of SGD can be much worse than the convergence rate of full-gradient descent. For example, for strongly-convex functions SGD has a sublinear convergence rate while full-gradient descent has a linear convergence rate.

Given the increasing complexity of modern learning models, a practically-relevant question to ask is how SGD performs in over-parameterized settings, under which the model interpolates (exactly fits) the data. Previously, it has been shown that SGD can achieve a linear convergence rate like full-gradient descent under various interpolation conditions for strongly-convex functions [25, 27, 36, 38] such as the strong growth condition (SGC) and the weak growth condition (WGC). An assumption that is weaker than strong convexity which allows full gradient descent to achieve a linear rate is the Polyak-Lojasiewicz (PL) condition [30]. Recently, the PL condition has gained popularity in machine learning [13] and it has been shown that several overparameterized models that interpolate the data satisfy the PL condition [2]. Similar to the strongly-convex case, under interpolation and the PL condition SGD can achieve a linear rate similar to full gradient descent [2, 38].

A popular variation on SGD is random reshuffling (RR). At each epoch $t \in \{1, 2, ..., T\}$, the algorithm RR randomly chooses a permutation $\pi^t$. That is, $\pi_{j+1}^t$ is sampled without replacement from the set $\{1, 2, ..., n\}$ for $j \in \{0, 1, ..., n-1\}$. Then it performs the following update, going through the dataset in the order specified by $\pi^t$

$$x_{j+1}^t = x_j^t - \eta_j^t \nabla f(x_j^t; \pi_{j+1}^t). \tag{2}$$

Note that $x_0 \triangleq x_0^1$ is the initialization and $x_0^{t+1} = x_n^t$ $\forall t \geq 1$. We summarize the method in Algorithm 1. A variation on RR is the incremental gradient (IG) method where $\pi^t$ is deterministic and fixed over all epochs.

---

**Algorithm 1.** Random Reshuffling (RR)

---

**Input:** $x_0$, $T$, step sizes $\{\eta_j^t\}$

1: **for** $t = 1, 2, \ldots, T$ **do**
2:     Choose a permutation $\pi^t$ from the set of all permutations; set $x_0^t = x_0$ if $t = 1$; set $x_0^t = x_n^{t-1}$ if $t > 1$.
3:     **for** $j = 1, 2, \ldots, n-1$ **do**
4:         $x_{j+1}^t = x_j^t - \eta_j^t \nabla f(x_j^t; \pi_{j+1}^t)$
5:     **end for**
6: **end for**

---

RR has long been known to converge faster than SGD empirically for certain problems [3, 4]. However, analyzing RR is more difficult than SGD because (conditioned on the past iterates) each individual gradient is no longer an unbiased estimate of the full gradient. Thus, the analysis of RR has only emerged in a series of recent efforts [11, 12, 26, 34]. Previous works have shown that RR outperforms SGD for strongly-convex objectives in various under-parameterized settings, when the number of epochs $(T)$ is sufficiently large. However, these sublinear rates for RR are slower than the linear rates obtained for SGD in the over-parameterized setting. Further, current convergence rate analyses for RR in the over-parameterized setting either make unrealistic assumptions (see the next section) or are also slower than SGD unless we make very-strong assumptions.

In this work, we analyze RR and IG for PL functions under both the SGC and WGC over-parameterized assumptions. We give explicit convergence rates for RR that can be faster than the best known rate for SGD, under realistic assumptions that hold for situations like over-parameterized least squares. Our results also show IG can converge faster than SGD (though not RR) in some settings. We consider relaxations of the SGC and WGC where interpolation is only approximately satisfied, showing faster convergence of RR to a neighbourhood of the solution.

## 2 Related Work

*Optimization Under the PL Condition:* the PL inequality was first explored by Polyak [30] and Lojasiewicz [20]. It applies to a wide range of important machine learning problems such as least square and logistic regression (over a compact set) [13]. More generally, any function of the form $f(x) = g(Ax)$ for a matrix $A$ with a $\mu$-strongly convex function $g$ satisfies the $\mu$-PL condition [13]. Several recent works have argued that considering a local PL condition around minimizers can be used as a model for analyzing the effectiveness of SGD in training neural networks [9,18,29,37].

Polyak [30] showed that full gradient descent on smooth objective functions can achieve a linear convergence rate under the PL condition. But it has recently been highlighted that the PL condition can be used to show linear convergence rates for a variety of methods [13]. Typically, the PL condition leads to similar convergence rates as those obtained under the stronger condition of strong convexity. In the case of SGD under interpolation, it has been shown that the rate of SGD under the PL condition is linear [2,38]. However, the convergence rates for SGD under interpolation for $\mu$-PL functions are slower than those for strongly convex functions (see Table 1).

*RR for Strongly-Convex Under-Parameterized Problems:* in this paragraph we focus our discussion on the case of strongly-convex functions, the subject of most literature on the topic. Bottou conjectured that the convergence rate of RR is $O(\frac{1}{n^2 T^2})$ [3], where $T$ is the number of epochs. But it was several years before progress was made at showing this. The difficulty in the analysis of RR arises because of the bias in the conditional expectation of the gradients,

$$\mathbb{E}\left[\nabla f(x_i^t; \pi_{i+1}^t) \mid x_i^t\right] \neq \nabla f(x_i^t). \tag{3}$$

An early attempt to analyze RR [33] was not successful because their noncommutative arithmetic-geometric mean inequality conjecture was proven to be false [15]. An $\tilde{\mathcal{O}}(\frac{1}{n^2 T^2})$ rate was first shown asymptotically by Gürbüzbalaban et al.

[11] Haochen and Sra [12] give the first non-asymptotic convergence result of $\tilde{\mathcal{O}}(\frac{1}{\mu^4}(\frac{1}{n^2T^2} + \frac{1}{T^3}))$ with a strong-convexity constant $\mu$, under strong assumptions. Under weaker assumptions a rate of $\tilde{\mathcal{O}}(\frac{1}{\mu^3 nT^2})$ was shown when $T \gtrsim \frac{1}{\mu^2}$ by assuming component-wise convexity of each $f(\cdot; i)$ [26], matching a lower bound of $\Omega(\frac{1}{nT^2})$ [32].[1] Note that this rate is faster than the $\tilde{\mathcal{O}}(\frac{1}{nT})$ rate of SGD when the large epoch requirement is satisfied. Mischenko et al. [23] obtain the same rate of $\tilde{\mathcal{O}}(\frac{1}{\mu^3 nT^2})$ but only require $T \gtrsim \frac{1}{\mu}$. Their analysis is dependent on the underlying component-wise convexity structure. Ahn et al. [1] remove this dependence and obtain the same rate with $T \gtrsim \frac{1}{\mu}$. However, their analysis relies on each $f(\cdot; i)$ being $G$-Lipschitz ($\|\nabla f(\cdot; i)\| \leq G$ for all $i$), which may require a constraint on problem (1) and a projection operation is needed to ensure the iterates are bounded [1,28]. Nguyen et al. [28] give a unified analysis for shuffling schemes other than RR, while Safran and Shamir [34] show a lower bound of $\Omega(\frac{1}{\mu n^2 T^2} + \frac{1}{\mu n T^3})$ when $f$ is a sum of $n$ quadratics. In a more recent work, they have also shown that RR does not significantly improve over SGD unless $T$ is larger than $\Theta(\frac{1}{\mu})$ in the worst case [35]. We can also consider other shuffling schemes; Lu et al. [21] design the GraB algorithm that achieves a faster rate of $\tilde{\mathcal{O}}(\frac{1}{\mu^3 n^2 T^2})$ by incorporating previous gradient information into determining the current permutation. Furthermore, the matching lower bound for this algorithm is given by Cha et al. [7]. We note that all of these sublinear convergence rates are slower than the linear rates that are possible for SGD on over-parameterized problems.[2]

*RR for Strongly-Convex Over-Parameterized Problems:* despite the widespread use of RR for training over-parameterized models, there is relatively little literature analyzing this setting. Haochen and Sra [12] show that the convergence rate of RR is at least as fast as SGD under interpolation without any epoch requirements. However, their result does not show that a gap in the rates can exist and only applies in the degenerate case where each function is strongly-convex.[3] Ma and Zhou [22] show a faster rate than SGD for RR under over-parameterization and a "weak strong convexity" assumption, but their result is also somewhat degenerate as their assumption excludes standard problems like over-parameterized least squares.[4] We can obtain interpolation results under more-realistic assumptions as special cases of the results of Mischenko et al. [23]

---

[1] Following previous conventions in the literature [7,26,35], we take $\kappa = \Theta(\frac{1}{\mu})$ for comparisons.

[2] Since the first version of this work was released, Koloskova et al. [14] show that SGD with arbitrary data orderings including RR converges at least as fast as SGD in a general nonconvex setting irrespective of the number of epochs. However, only sublinear rates are possible in this general setting.

[3] In this setting we could solve the problem by simply applying gradient descent to any individual function and ignoring all other training examples.

[4] The usual "weak strong convexity" assumption is that for each $f_i$ the strong convexity inequality holds for the projection onto the minima with respect to $f_i$ which holds for least squares. But Ma and Zhou instead use the projection onto the intersection

and Nguyen et al. [28]. However, in the interpolation setting the rates obtained by these works for convex and strongly-convex functions are slower than the rate obtained by Vaswani et al. [38] for SGD (we summarize the known linear rates under over-parameterization in Table 1).

*RR for Polyak-Lojasiewicz Problems:* several works have presented convergence rates for RR on PL problems [1,12,23,28]. Haochen and Sra give the first non-asymptotic rate of $\tilde{\mathcal{O}}(\frac{1}{\mu^4}(\frac{1}{n^2 T^2} + \frac{1}{T^3}))$ for the under-parameterized setting but requiring each individual function to have Lipschitz continuous Hessian [12]. Ahn et al. improve the rate to $\tilde{\mathcal{O}}(\frac{1}{\mu^3 n T^2})$ when $T \gtrsim \frac{1}{\mu}$ assuming bounded gradients [1] but these sublinear rates for the under-parameterized setting are slower than the linear rates of SGD for over-parameterized problems. The result of Mischenko et al. on $\mu$-PL functions [23] can be used to obtain a linear rate under over-parameterization,[5] but only in the degenerate setting where all functions have the same gradient. The result of Nguyen et al. on PL functions [28, Theorem 1] concerns the under-parameterized setting. But in Appendix E we show how the proof of Theorem 1 of Nguyen et al. [28] can be modified to give a linear convergence rate of RR for the over-parameterized setting. This RR rate can be faster than SGD, but under a more restricted scenario than the results presented in this work (we discuss the precise details in Sect. 4). Besides these non-asymptotic rates, Li et al. [17] demonstrate the asymptotic convergence of RR for Kurdyka-Lojasiewicz problems which generalize PL.

# 3   Assumptions

In this section, we present the assumptions made in our analyses. Our first assumption is that the individual and overall functions are smooth and bounded below.

**Assumption 1 (Smoothness and Boundedness).** *The objective $f$ is $L$-smooth and each individual loss $f(\cdot; i)$ is $L_i$-smooth such that $\forall x, x' \in \operatorname{dom}(f)$,*

$$\|\nabla f(x) - \nabla f(x')\| \le L\|x - x'\|, \tag{4}$$
$$\|\nabla f(x; i) - \nabla f(x'; i)\| \le L_i\|x - x'\|, \forall i. \tag{5}$$

*We denote $L_{\max} \triangleq \max_i L_i$. We assume $f$ is lower bounded by $f^*$, which is achieved at some $x^*$, so $f^* = f(x^*)$. We also assume that each $f(\cdot; i)$ is lower bounded by some $f_i^*$.*

Next, we give the definition of the Polyak-Lojasiewicz (PL) inequality which lower bounds the size of the gradient as the value of $f$ increases.

---

of this set with the set of minima with respect to $f$, which does not hold in general for least squares.

[5] By taking $B = 0$ in Mischenko et al.'s Theorem 4.

**Assumption 2 ($\mu$-PL).** *There exists some $\mu > 0$ such that*

$$f(x) - f^* \leq \frac{1}{2\mu} \|\nabla f(x)\|^2 \quad \forall x \in \mathrm{dom}(f), \tag{6}$$

*where $f^*$ is the optimal value of $f$.*

All strongly-convex functions satisfy the PL inequality. However, many important functions satisfy the PL inequality that are not necessarily strongly-convex including the classic example of the squared prediction error with a linear prediction function [13]. PL functions can be non-convex but the condition implies invexity, a generalization of convexity. For smooth functions invexity is equivalent to every stationary point of $f$ being a global minimum (though unlike strongly-convex functions we may have multiple stationary points) [8]. Recent literature shows that the PL condition and variants of it can be used to help analyze a variety of complicated models [2,9,18,29,37].

Next, we formally define interpolation which is the key property of the optimization problem implied by over-parameterization.

**Assumption 3 (Interpolation).** *We are in the interpolating regime, which we take to mean that*

$$\nabla f(x^*) = 0 \implies \nabla f(x^*; i) = 0. \tag{7}$$

Thus, by interpolation we mean that stationary points with respect to the function $f$ are also stationary points with respect to the individual functions $f(\cdot; i)$. However, we do not assume that $x^*$ is unique. Our results also consider either the strong or weak growth conditions [36,38] regarding how the individual gradients change as $x$ moves away from $x^*$.

**Assumption 4 (SGC).** *There exists a constant $\rho \geq 1$ such that the following holds*

$$\frac{1}{n} \sum_{i=1}^{n} \|\nabla f(x; i)\|^2 \leq \rho \|\nabla f(x)\|^2, \quad \forall x \in \mathrm{dom}(f). \tag{8}$$

**Assumption 5 (WGC).** *There exists a constant $\alpha \geq 0$ such that the following holds*

$$\frac{1}{n} \sum_{i=1}^{n} \|\nabla f(x; i)\|^2 \leq 2\alpha L(f(x) - f(x^*)), \quad \forall x \in \mathrm{dom}(f), \tag{9}$$

*where $f$ is lower bounded by $f^*$ and $f^* = f(x^*)$.*

There are a close relationships between interpolation, the SGC, and the WGC. The SGC implies interpolation, while for smooth functions the SGC implies the WGC [24, Lemma 5]. Further, for functions satisfying smoothness and $\mu$-PL (Assumptions 2 and 1) all three conditions are equivalent if the $f_i$ are invex (SGC implies interpolation which implies WGC which implies SGC). In this setting of smooth $\mu$-PL functions with invex $f_i$, the constant $\alpha$ in the WGC is upper bounded by $\frac{L_{\max}}{L}$ and by $\rho$ [24, Lemmas 5-6],[6] while the value of the constant $\rho$ in the SGC is upper bounded by $\frac{\alpha L}{\mu}$ [38, Proposition 1] and is thus also bounded by $\frac{L_{\max}}{\mu}$. The value of $\rho$ in the SGC is lower bounded by 1 while in Appendix A we show that $\alpha$ in the WGC is lower-bounded by $\frac{\mu}{L}$.

A classical setting where we would expect these interpolation properties to hold is binary classification with a linear classifier when the data is linearly separable. In this setting the gradient of each example can be made to converge to zero due to the linear separability (under standard loss functions). In Appendix A, we give a generalization of an existing result [38, Lemma 1] showing that the SGC holds for a class of functions including the squared hinge loss and logistic regression in the linearly-separable setting.

In the most-general form of our results, we consider relaxations of the SGC and the WGC that do not require the data to be fit exactly [6,31].

**Assumption 6.** *There exists constants $\rho \geq 0$ and $\sigma \geq 0$ such that the following holds:* $\forall x \in \mathrm{dom}(f)$,

$$\frac{1}{n}\sum_{i=1}^{n}\|\nabla f(x;i)\|^2 \leq \rho\|\nabla f(x)\|^2 + \sigma^2. \tag{10}$$

**Assumption 7.** *There exists constants $\alpha \geq 0$ and $\sigma \geq 0$ such that the following holds:* $\forall x \in \mathrm{dom}(f)$,

$$\frac{1}{n}\sum_{i=1}^{n}\|\nabla f(x;i)\|^2 \leq 2\alpha L(f(x) - f(x^*)) + \sigma^2. \tag{11}$$

These assumptions reduce to the SGC and WGC when $\sigma = 0$, and we note that the relaxed WGC is related to the expected smoothness condition of Gower et al. [10]. We also note that Assumption 6 reduces to the bounded variance assumption $\frac{1}{n}\sum_{i=1}^{n}\|\nabla f(x;i) - \nabla f(x)\|^2 \leq \sigma^2$ when $\rho = 1$, which is commonly used in the analysis of SGD [5].

## 4    Contributions

Table 1 summarizes known and new convergence results for the convergence of SGD on strongly-convex and PL functions under the interpolation assumptions (Assumptions 3, 4, and 5). In this table we see that existing RR rates for strongly-convex functions are slower than for SGD. In contrast, the RR rates shown in this work can be faster than the SGD rates for $\mu$-PL objectives. Our main contributions are summarized as follows:

---

[6] We include the $\alpha \leq \rho$ result in Appendix A since it is shown under stronger assumptions [38] or stated differently [23] in prior work.

**Table 1.** Number of gradient evaluations required by each algorithm to obtain an $\epsilon$-accurate solution, which is defined as $\|x - x^*\|^2 \le \epsilon$ and $f(x) - f(x^*) \le \epsilon$ for $\mu$-strongly convex and $\mu$-PL objectives respectively. The contributions of this work are the rates highlighted in blue.[1][2][3]

|  | Interp | WGC | SGC | Interp+Invex |
|---|---|---|---|---|
| SGD/SC | - | $\alpha\frac{L}{\mu}$ [38] | $\rho\frac{L}{\mu}$ [36] | $\frac{L_{\max}}{\mu}$ [27] |
| RR/SC | - | - | - | $\frac{L_{\max}}{\mu}n$ [23] |
| SGD/PL | $\frac{L_{\max}^2}{\mu^2}$ [2] | $\alpha\frac{L^2}{\mu^2}$ | $\rho\frac{L}{\mu}$ [38] | $\frac{L_{\max}^2}{\mu^2}$ [2] |
| IG/PL | $\frac{L_{\max}^2}{\mu^2}n$ [28] | $\frac{L_{\max}}{\mu}n\sqrt{\frac{\alpha L}{\mu}}$ | $\frac{L_{\max}}{\mu}n\sqrt{\rho}$ | $(\frac{L_{\max}}{\mu})^{3/2}n$ |
| RR/PL | $\frac{L_{\max}^2}{\mu^2}n$ [28] | $\frac{L_{\max}}{\mu}\sqrt{n}(\sqrt{n}\vee\sqrt{\frac{\alpha L}{\mu}})$ | $\frac{L_{\max}}{\mu}\sqrt{n}(\sqrt{n}\vee\sqrt{\rho})$ | $\frac{L_{\max}}{\mu}\sqrt{n}(\sqrt{n}\vee\sqrt{\frac{L_{\max}}{\mu}})$ |

[1] We ignore numerical constants and logarithmic factors. Note that $\mu$-SC stands for $\mu$-strongly convex. Interp, SGC, and WGC refer to Assumption 3, 4, and 5 (respectively). Note that $L \le L_{\max}$, for the WGC constant $\alpha$ we have $\frac{\mu}{L} \le \alpha \le \rho$ [24, Appendix A], while for the SGC constant $\rho$ we have $\max\{1, \alpha\} \le \rho \le \frac{\alpha L}{\mu}$ [38], and if all functions are invex we also have $\alpha \le \frac{L_{\max}}{L}$ and $\rho \le \frac{L_{\max}}{\mu}$ [24].

[2] The "Interp+Invex" results assume each function is invex, and the strongly-convex results [23, 27] additionally assume each function is convex.

[3] The symbol "$\vee$" refers to taking the maximum of two values.

*RR Under WGC:* for $\mu$-PL functions satisfying the WGC, we derive the sample complexity of RR to be $\tilde{O}(\max\{\frac{L_{\max}}{\mu}n, \frac{L_{\max}}{\mu}\sqrt{n}\sqrt{\frac{\alpha L}{\mu}}\})$. In comparison, the sample complexity of SGD in this case is $\tilde{O}(\alpha\frac{L^2}{\mu^2})$ (we show this in Appendix B). Hence, RR outperforms SGD when $\alpha\frac{L}{\mu} > n$ and $L_{\max} \sim L$ without requiring a large number of epochs. Thus, for $\mu$-PL objectives satisfying the WGC, RR converges faster than SGD for sufficiently ill-conditioned problems when the Lipschitz constants are similar.

*RR Under SGC:* under the SGC we give a sample complexity for RR of $\tilde{O}(\max\{\frac{L_{\max}}{\mu}n, \frac{L_{\max}}{\mu}\sqrt{n}\sqrt{\rho}\})$, which is better than the $\tilde{O}(\rho\frac{L}{\mu})$ of SGD provided $\rho > n$ and $L_{\max} \sim L$. The situation $\rho > n$ happens when there is a large amount of disagreements in the gradients. Note that the rates of SGC can be faster than the WGC when $\rho \le \alpha\frac{L}{\mu}$. This can be satisfied for example when $\alpha \sim 1$ and $L_{\max} \sim L$.

*IG UNder WGC/SGC:* IG can also outperform SGD for $\mu$-PL objectives when $\rho > n^2$ and $L_{\max} \sim L$ under the SGC, or when $\alpha\frac{L}{\mu} > n^2$ and $L_{\max} \sim L$ under the WGC. The rates of RR for $\mu$-PL objectives can be better than IG by a factor of $\sqrt{n}$, and cannot be worse because $\rho \ge 1$ and $\alpha \ge \frac{\mu}{L}$ (see Proposition 3 in Appendix A).

*Experiments:* we conduct experiments on objectives satisfying our assumptions. We experimentally see that a condition like $\rho > n$ is important for RR to achieve a faster rate than SGD. For over-parameterized problems we demonstrate that in practice RR can converge faster than SGD even in the early training phase, but that RR has less of an advantage as $n$ grows.

*Comparisons with Existing Rates for $\mu$-PL Functions:* Appendix E discusses how the proof of Nguyen et al. [28, Theorem 1] can used to obtain convergence rates of RR on over-parameterized $\mu$-PL objectives. Under interpolation (Assumption 3), the analysis of Nguyen et al. implies a rate for RR of $\tilde{\mathcal{O}}((\frac{L_{\max}}{\mu})^2 n)$, which is always worse than the SGD rate of $\tilde{\mathcal{O}}((\frac{L_{\max}}{\mu})^2)$ and our RR rate under this assumption of $\tilde{\mathcal{O}}(\max\{\frac{L_{\max}}{\mu}n, (\frac{L_{\max}}{\mu})^{3/2}\sqrt{n}\})$ (although this rate requires assuming each function is invex). On the other hand, under the SGC (Assumption 4) the analysis of Nguyen et al. implies a rate of $\tilde{\mathcal{O}}(\max\{\frac{L_{\max}}{\mu}n, \frac{L_{\max}}{\mu^2}\sqrt{n}\sqrt{n+\rho-1}\})$, but this is worse than our SGC result of $\tilde{\mathcal{O}}(\max\{\frac{L_{\max}}{\mu}n, \frac{L_{\max}}{\mu}\sqrt{n}\sqrt{\rho}\})$ and only faster than SGD under a more-narrow range of problem constant settings.

## 5    Convergence Results

We present the convergence results of RR and IG for $\mu$-PL objectives under the SGC and the WGC. Below, we use a constant step size $\eta$. The proofs of Theorems 1 and 2 are given in Appendix D.

**Theorem 1 (RR + $\mu$-PL).** *Suppose $f$ satisfies Assumption 1 and 2, then RR with a learning rate $\eta$ satisfying*

$$\eta \leq \min\{\frac{1}{2nL_{\max}}, \frac{1}{2\sqrt{2}L_{\max}\sqrt{n\rho}}\} \quad under\ Assumption\ 6,$$

*or*

$$\eta \leq \min\{\frac{1}{2nL_{\max}}, \frac{1}{2\sqrt{2}L_{\max}\sqrt{n}\sqrt{\frac{\alpha L}{\mu}}}\} \quad under\ Assumption\ 7, \quad (12)$$

*achieves the following rate for $\mu$-PL objectives:*

$$\mathbb{E}[f(x_n^T) - f(x^*)] \leq (1 - \frac{1}{4}n\mu\eta)^T (f(x^0) - f(x^*)) + \frac{4L_{\max}^2 \eta^2 n\sigma^2}{\mu}. \quad (13)$$

*Remark 1.* Set $\sigma = 0$ in (13) and using Lemma 5 in Appendix C to solve the recursion, the sample complexity under the SGC is $\tilde{\mathcal{O}}(\max\{\frac{L_{\max}}{\mu}n, \frac{L_{\max}}{\mu}\sqrt{n}\sqrt{\rho}\})$, and the sample complexity under the WGC is $\tilde{\mathcal{O}}(\max\{\frac{L_{\max}}{\mu}n, \frac{L_{\max}}{\mu}\sqrt{n}\sqrt{\frac{\alpha L}{\mu}}\})$. These rates are faster than SGD under the corresponding assumption for $\mu$-PL objectives when either $n < \rho$ or $n < \alpha\frac{L}{\mu}$ holds and $L_{\max} \sim L$. In cases where $L_{\max}$ is not similar to $L$, RR can still outperform SGD when $n < \frac{\rho L^2}{L_{\max}^2}$ is satisfied under the SGC or $n < \frac{\alpha L^3}{\mu L_{\max}^2}$ is satisfied under the WGC.

**Theorem 2 (IG + $\mu$-PL).** *Suppose $f$ satisfies Assumption 1 and 2, then IG with a learning rate $\eta$ satisfying*

$$\eta \leq \min\{\frac{1}{\sqrt{2}nL_{\max}}, \frac{1}{2L_{\max}n\sqrt{\rho}}\} \quad \text{under Assumption 6,}$$

*or*

$$\eta \leq \min\{\frac{1}{\sqrt{2}nL_{\max}}, \frac{1}{2L_{\max}n\sqrt{\frac{\alpha L}{\mu}}}\} \quad \text{under Assumption 7,} \qquad (14)$$

*achieves the following rate for $\mu$-PL objectives:*

$$f(x_n^T) - f(x^*) \leq (1 - \frac{1}{2}n\mu\eta)^T (f(x^0) - f(x^*)) + \frac{2L_{\max}^2\eta^2 n^2 \sigma^2}{\mu}. \qquad (15)$$

*Remark 2.* Similar to Remark 1, we can follow the same approach to obtain the sample complexity for IG to be $\tilde{O}(\max\{\frac{L_{\max}}{\mu}n, \frac{L_{\max}}{\mu}n\sqrt{\rho})\}) = \tilde{O}(\frac{L_{\max}}{\mu}n\sqrt{\rho})$ under the SGC and $\tilde{O}(\max\{\frac{L_{\max}}{\mu}n, \frac{L_{\max}}{\mu}n\sqrt{\frac{\alpha L}{\mu}}\}) = \tilde{O}(\frac{L_{\max}}{\mu}n\sqrt{\frac{\alpha L}{\mu}})$ under the WGC. For $\mu$-PL objectives, these rates are worse than RR as the parameter $\rho$ in the SGC satisfies $\rho \geq 1$, and the parameter $\alpha$ in the WGC satisfies $\alpha \geq \frac{\mu}{L}$.

### 5.1   Proof Sketch

In this section, we provide a proof sketch of Theorems 1 and 2 under the SGC. A similar approach is taken for the WGC. To start with, we first express the descent on the objective $f$ in terms of epochs. For a step size $\eta \leq \frac{1}{nL}$ [28], we have the following

$$f(x_0^{t+1}) \leq f(x_0^t) - \frac{n\eta}{2}\|\nabla f(x_0^t)\|^2 + \frac{L_{\max}^2\eta}{2} \sum_{i=0}^{n}\|x_i^t - x_0^t\|^2. \qquad (16)$$

The key is to upper bound the sum of deviations of each step from its starting point within an epoch, i.e. $\sum_{i=0}^{n}\|x_i^t - x_0^t\|^2$. We want this term to be small to get a fast rate. To do so, we obtain the following results (see Lemma 3 and Lemma 4 in Appendix C by setting $\sigma = 0$) for IG and RR under the SGC.

$$\text{IG:} \quad \sum_{i=0}^{n-1}\|x_i^t - x_0^t\|^2 \leq 2\eta^2 n^2 (n\rho)\|\nabla f(x_0^t)\|^2,$$

$$\text{RR:} \quad \mathbb{E}[\sum_{i=0}^{n-1}\|x_i^t - x_0^t\|^2] \leq 2\eta^2 n^2 (\rho + n)\mathbb{E}[\|\nabla f(x_0^t)\|^2].$$

Neglecting the effects of taking expectations, the difference in the deviation bound between RR and IG is reflected in the factors $\rho + n$ and $n\rho$. After substituting these results into (16), we obtain

$$\text{IG:} \quad f(x_0^{t+1}) \overset{(a)}{\leq} f(x_0^t) - \frac{n\eta}{2}(1 - 2L_{\max}^2\eta^2 n^2 \rho)\|\nabla f(x_0^t)\|^2, \qquad (17)$$

$$\text{RR:} \quad \mathbb{E}[f(x_0^{t+1})] \overset{(b)}{\leq} \mathbb{E}[f(x_0^t)] - \frac{n\eta}{4}(1 - 4L_{\max}^2\eta^2 n\rho)\mathbb{E}[\|\nabla f(x_0^t)\|^2], \qquad (18)$$

where both (a) and (b) require $\eta \sim \tilde{\mathcal{O}}(\frac{1}{nL_{\max}})$. Note that for IG to make progress in decreasing $f$, we further require $\eta \sim \tilde{\mathcal{O}}(\min\{\frac{1}{nL_{\max}}, \frac{1}{L_{\max}n\sqrt{\rho}}\}) = \frac{1}{L_{\max}n\sqrt{\rho}})$ as $\rho \geq 1$; whereas for RR, we require $\eta \sim \tilde{\mathcal{O}}(\min\{\frac{1}{nL_{\max}}, \frac{1}{L_{\max}\sqrt{n\rho}}\})$. Hence, the learning rate of RR can be larger than IG under the SGC.

## 6    Experimental Results

In this section, we aim to address the following questions with our experiments: ① How do the empirical convergence rates of RR, SGD, and IG depend on $n$ and $\rho$? ② Is a large number of epochs required for RR to outperform SGD under interpolation? Unless otherwise stated, we choose a constant learning rate in the range $[10^{-3}, 10^{-1}]$ that minimizes the train loss.

### 6.1    Synthetic Experiments

We first conduct experiments on a binary classification synthetic dataset. Specifically, we use the code provided by Loizou et al. [19] to generate linearly-separable data with margin $\tau > 0$. For training, we use a squared hinge loss with or without $L_2$ regularization to simulate the convex and $\mu$-PL cases respectively. Note that squared hinge loss satisfies the SGC with $\rho \leq \frac{n}{\tau^2}$ (see Proposition 1 in Appendix A). Thus by varying $\tau$ we can investigate the convergence of SGD, RR, and IG as a function of the SGC constant $\rho$. The results are shown in Fig. 1. In agreement with our bounds, we observe that: (i) RR outperforms SGD when $\rho \gg n$, (ii) RR outperforms IG for all values of $\rho$, and (iii) the convergence (naturally) slows down for increasing $\rho$ (which corresponds to decreasing margin $\tau$).

### 6.2    Binary Classification Using RBF Kernels

Besides understanding the influence of $\rho$, we further conduct experiments to study the convergence rates of RR in minimizing convex losses under interpolation. To this end, we use squared hinge loss, squared loss and logistic loss on the mushrooms dataset from LIBSVM using RBF kernels [19]. We follow the procedure in Vaswani et al. [39] for choosing the bandwidths of the RBF kernels. As shown by our bounds, a large epoch is not required for RR to outperform SGD. This is observed in Fig. 2, in which RR outperforms SGD in the first few epochs of training, and the performance gap is significantly larger in the early training stage than the later.

### 6.3    Multi-class Classification Using Deep Networks

We conducted experiments to study the convergence rates of RR in non-convex settings under interpolation. To this end, we use a softmax loss and one hidden-layer multilayer perceptrons (1-MLP) of different widths on the MNIST image classification dataset [16]. The results in Fig. 3 show that RR can converge faster

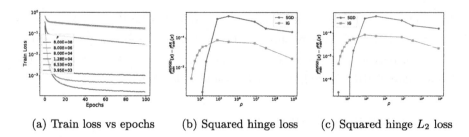

(a) Train loss vs epochs     (b) Squared hinge loss     (c) Squared hinge $L_2$ loss

**Fig. 1.** Binary classification on a linearly separable dataset with $n = 800$. (a) We plot train loss of RR as a function of epochs using squared hinge loss for different values of $\rho$. We observe that the training is very slow when $\rho > \mathcal{O}(10^4)$, and speeds up when $\rho$ approaches the order of magnitude of $n$ or less. (b) We plot minimum train loss difference between RR and SGD or IG as a function of $\rho$. For a convex objective such as squared hinge loss, we observe that the performance gain of RR over SGD predominantly occurs when $\rho \gtrsim \mathcal{O}(10^4)$. For $\rho < \mathcal{O}(10^4)$, SGD achieves a lower train loss than RR. We also observe that RR consistently performs better than IG for all $\rho$ values. (c) Similar observations are made as those of (b) for a $\mu$-PL objective: squared hinge loss with $L_2$ regularization.

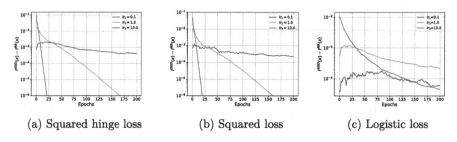

(a) Squared hinge loss     (b) Squared loss     (c) Logistic loss

**Fig. 2.** Binary classification on mushrooms dataset using RBF kernels. (a) We plot the difference in the squared loss between SGD and RR as a function of epochs for step sizes $(lr)$ 0.1, 1.0, and 10.0. (b)(c) Similar plot as (a) but for the squared loss and the logistic loss respectively. We observe that RR converges faster than SGD for all the step sizes, and the train loss difference is more significant in the initial training stage. Considering logistic loss and $lr = 10.0$, the train loss gap is $\tilde{\mathcal{O}}(10^{-2})$ after one epoch, and decreases to $\tilde{\mathcal{O}}(10^{-4})$ in the end. Similarly, we observe a faster decrease in the train loss difference within the first 25 epochs of training when squared hinge loss or squared loss is used. (Color figure online)

than SGD for a small $T$, and a small $n$ favors RR while for large $n$ there is less of an advantage to using RR.

The key take-aways from our experimental results is that for over-parameterized problems:

1. RR consistently outperforms IG.
2. The condition $n \ll \rho$ is crucial for RR to outperform SGD.

3. Under over-parametrization, RR can outperform SGD already at the early stage of training (a large epoch is not required as suggested by previous theory for under-parameterized models).

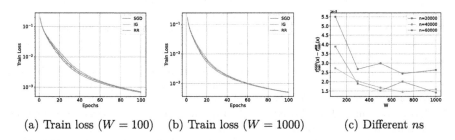

(a) Train loss ($W = 100$)    (b) Train loss ($W = 1000$)    (c) Different $n$s

**Fig. 3.** MNIST digits classification with a softmax loss. (a) (b) We plot train loss as a function of epochs for 1-MLP of width ($W$) 100 and 1000 respectively. In both cases, we observe that RR converges faster than SGD in the initial training stage. (c) We plot minimum train loss difference between RR and SGD for $n = 20000, 40000$ and $60000$ against different values of $W$. Despite RR outperforming SGD for all $W$s and $n$s, the performance gap is more significant when $n = 20000$.

## 7  Conclusion

In this paper, we have derived convergence rates of RR under interpolation as implied by the SGC or the WGC for $\mu$-PL objectives. In this setting, RR converge faster than SGD provided the key condition $\rho > n$ under the SGC or $\alpha \frac{L}{\mu} > n$ under the WGC holds (assuming the individual Lipschitz constants do not differ too much from the overall Lipschitz constant). Moreover, we show that RR outperforms IG for all values of $\rho$ and $\alpha$ under the SGC and WGC respectively. Besides this, we further demonstrate that IG can outperform SGD when $\rho > n^2$ holds under the SGC or $\alpha \frac{L}{\mu} > n^2$ holds under the WGC. We remark that none of these conclusions follows from previous analysis under the strong convexity assumption. Our experimental results support these theoretical findings.

**Acknowledgments.** This work was partially supported by the Canada CIFAR AI Chair Program, and the Natural Sciences and Engineering Research Council of Canada (NSERC) Discovery Grants RGPIN-2021-03677 and GPIN-2022-03669.

**Ethical Statement.** The contribution is the theoretical analysis of an existing algorithm, so it does not have direct societal or ethical implications.

# References

1. Ahn, K., Yun, C., Sra, S.: Sgd with shuffling: optimal rates without component convexity and large epoch requirements. Adv. Neural. Inf. Process. Syst. **33**, 17526–17535 (2020)
2. Bassily, R., Belkin, M., Ma, S.: On exponential convergence of SGD in non-convex over-parametrized learning. arXiv preprint arXiv:1811.02564 (2018)
3. Bottou, L.: Curiously fast convergence of some stochastic gradient descent algorithms. In: Proceedings of the Symposium on Learning and Data Science, Paris, vol. 8, pp. 2624–2633 (2009)
4. Bottou, L.: Stochastic gradient descent tricks. In: Montavon, G., Orr, G.B., Müller, K.-R. (eds.) Neural Networks: Tricks of the Trade. LNCS, vol. 7700, pp. 421–436. Springer, Heidelberg (2012). https://doi.org/10.1007/978-3-642-35289-8_25
5. Bottou, L., Curtis, F.E., Nocedal, J.: Optimization methods for large-scale machine learning. SIAM Rev. **60**(2), 223–311 (2018)
6. Cevher, V., Vũ, B.C.: On the linear convergence of the stochastic gradient method with constant step-size. Optim. Lett. **13**(5), 1177–1187 (2019)
7. Cha, J., Lee, J., Yun, C.: Tighter lower bounds for shuffling SGD: random permutations and beyond. arXiv preprint arXiv:2303.07160 (2023)
8. Craven, B.D., Glover, B.M.: Invex functions and duality. J. Aust. Math. Soc. **39**(1), 1–20 (1985)
9. Du, S.S., Zhai, X., Poczos, B., Singh, A.: Gradient descent provably optimizes over-parameterized neural networks. arXiv preprint arXiv:1810.02054 (2018)
10. Gower, R.M., Loizou, N., Qian, X., Sailanbayev, A., Shulgin, E., Richtárik, P.: SGD: general analysis and improved rates. In: International Conference on Machine Learning, pp. 5200–5209. PMLR (2019)
11. Gürbüzbalaban, M., Ozdaglar, A., Parrilo, P.A.: Why random reshuffling beats stochastic gradient descent. Math. Program. **186**(1), 49–84 (2021)
12. Haochen, J., Sra, S.: Random shuffling beats SGD after finite epochs. In: International Conference on Machine Learning, pp. 2624–2633. PMLR (2019)
13. Karimi, H., Nutini, J., Schmidt, M.: Linear convergence of gradient and proximal-gradient methods under the Polyak-Łojasiewicz Condition. In: Frasconi, P., Landwehr, N., Manco, G., Vreeken, J. (eds.) ECML PKDD 2016. LNCS (LNAI), vol. 9851, pp. 795–811. Springer, Cham (2016). https://doi.org/10.1007/978-3-319-46128-1_50
14. Koloskova, A., Doikov, N., Stich, S.U., Jaggi, M.: Shuffle SGD is always better than SGD: improved analysis of SGD with arbitrary data orders. arXiv preprint arXiv:2305.19259 (2023)
15. Lai, Z., Lim, L.H.: Recht-ré noncommutative arithmetic-geometric mean conjecture is false. In: International Conference on Machine Learning, pp. 5608–5617. PMLR (2020)
16. LeCun, Y., Bottou, L., Bengio, Y., Haffner, P.: Gradient-based learning applied to document recognition. Proc. IEEE **86**(11), 2278–2324 (1998)
17. Li, X., Milzarek, A., Qiu, J.: Convergence of random reshuffling under the kurdyka-{\L} ojasiewicz inequality. arXiv preprint arXiv:2110.04926 (2021)
18. Liu, C., Zhu, L., Belkin, M.: Loss landscapes and optimization in over-parameterized non-linear systems and neural networks. Appl. Comput. Harmon. Anal. **59**, 85–116 (2022)
19. Loizou, N., Vaswani, S., Laradji, I.H., Lacoste-Julien, S.: Stochastic polyak step-size for SGD: an adaptive learning rate for fast convergence. In: International Conference on Artificial Intelligence and Statistics, pp. 1306–1314. PMLR (2021)

20. Lojasiewicz, S.: A topological property of real analytic subsets. Coll. du CNRS, Les équations aux dérivées partielles **117**(87–89), 2 (1963)
21. Lu, Y., Guo, W., Sa, C.D.: Grab: Finding provably better data permutations than random reshuffling (2023)
22. Ma, S., Zhou, Y.: Understanding the impact of model incoherence on convergence of incremental SGD with random reshuffle. In: International Conference on Machine Learning, pp. 6565–6574. PMLR (2020)
23. Mishchenko, K., Khaled, A., Richtárik, P.: Random reshuffling: simple analysis with vast improvements. Adv. Neural. Inf. Process. Syst. **33**, 17309–17320 (2020)
24. Mishkin, A.: Interpolation, growth conditions, and stochastic gradient descent. Ph.D. thesis, University of British Columbia (2020)
25. Moulines, E., Bach, F.: Non-asymptotic analysis of stochastic approximation algorithms for machine learning. Advances in neural information processing systems 24 (2011)
26. Nagaraj, D., Jain, P., Netrapalli, P.: Sgd without replacement: sharper rates for general smooth convex functions. In: International Conference on Machine Learning, pp. 4703–4711. PMLR (2019)
27. Needell, D., Ward, R., Srebro, N.: Stochastic gradient descent, weighted sampling, and the randomized kaczmarz algorithm. Advances in neural information processing systems 27 (2014)
28. Nguyen, L.M., Tran-Dinh, Q., Phan, D.T., Nguyen, P.H., Van Dijk, M.: A unified convergence analysis for shuffling-type gradient methods. J. Mach. Learn. Res. **22**(1), 9397–9440 (2021)
29. Oymak, S., Soltanolkotabi, M.: Overparameterized nonlinear learning: gradient descent takes the shortest path? In: International Conference on Machine Learning, pp. 4951–4960. PMLR (2019)
30. Polyak, B.T.: Gradient methods for the minimisation of functionals. USSR Comput. Math. Math. Phys. **3**(4), 864–878 (1963)
31. Polyak, B., Tsypkin, Y.Z.: Pseudogradient adaptation and training algorithms. Autom. Remote. Control. **34**, 45–67 (1973)
32. Rajput, S., Gupta, A., Papailiopoulos, D.: Closing the convergence gap of SGD without replacement. In: International Conference on Machine Learning, pp. 7964–7973. PMLR (2020)
33. Recht, B., Ré, C.: Toward a noncommutative arithmetic-geometric mean inequality: Conjectures, case-studies, and consequences. In: Conference on Learning Theory, pp. 11–1. JMLR Workshop and Conference Proceedings (2012)
34. Safran, I., Shamir, O.: How good is sgd with random shuffling? In: Conference on Learning Theory, pp. 3250–3284. PMLR (2020)
35. Safran, I., Shamir, O.: Random shuffling beats SGD only after many epochs on ill-conditioned problems. Adv. Neural. Inf. Process. Syst. **34**, 15151–15161 (2021)
36. Schmidt, M., Roux, N.L.: Fast convergence of stochastic gradient descent under a strong growth condition. arXiv preprint arXiv:1308.6370 (2013)
37. Soltanolkotabi, M., Javanmard, A., Lee, J.D.: Theoretical insights into the optimization landscape of over-parameterized shallow neural networks. IEEE Trans. Inf. Theory **65**(2), 742–769 (2018)
38. Vaswani, S., Bach, F., Schmidt, M.: Fast and faster convergence of SGD for over-parameterized models and an accelerated perceptron. In: The 22nd International Conference on Artificial Intelligence and Statistics, pp. 1195–1204. PMLR (2019)
39. Vaswani, S., Mishkin, A., Laradji, I., Schmidt, M., Gidel, G., Lacoste-Julien, S.: Painless stochastic gradient: interpolation, line-search, and convergence rates. Advances in neural information processing systems 32 (2019)

# A Scalable Solution for the Extended Multi-channel Facility Location Problem

Etika Agarwal[(✉)], Karthik S. Gurumoorthy, Ankit Ajit Jain,
and Shantala Manchenahally

Walmart Global Tech, Bangalore, India
{etika.agarwal,karthik.gurumoorthy,ankit.ajit.jain,
shantala.manchenahally}@walmart.com

**Abstract.** We study the extended version of the non-uniform, capacitated facility location problem with multiple fulfilment channels between the facilities and clients, each with their own channel capacities and service cost. Though the problem has been extensively studied in the literature, all the prior works assume a single channel of fulfilment, and the existing methods based on linear programming, primal-dual relationships, local search heuristics etc. do not scale for a large supply chain system involving millions of decision variables. Using the concepts of submodularity and optimal transport theory, we present a scalable algorithm for determining the set of facilities to be opened under a cardinality constraint. By introducing various schemes such as: (i) iterative facility selection using incremental gain, (ii) approximation of the linear program using novel multi-stage Sinkhorn iterations, (iii) creation of facilities one for each fulfilment channel etc., we develop a fast but a tight approximate solution, requiring $O\left(\frac{3+k}{2}m\ln\left(\frac{1}{\epsilon}\right)\right)$ instances of optimal transport problems to select $k$ facilities from $m$ options, each solvable in linear time. Our algorithm is implicitly endowed with all the theoretical guarantees enjoyed by submodular maximisation problems and the Sinkhorn distances. When compared against the state-of-the-art commercial MILP solvers, we obtain a 100-fold speedup in computation, while the difference in objective values lies within a narrow range of **3%**.

**Keywords:** supply chain · facility location · submodular functions

## 1 Introduction

Most supply chains in the online retail system can be represented as a bi-partite graph between sets of facilities and clients. Typically, each client has a demand $d_j$ to be serviced by one or many facilities. Each facility has a capacity $fcap_i$ representing the maximum amount of demand it can satisfy. Each facility is also associated with a one time fixed opening cost $F_i$ and can serve the demands only when it is open. The primary problem of interest is in finding the subset of facilities to be opened, and the assignment of fraction of demand serviced by the facility $i$ for the client $j$, so that the overall cost of opening facilities (fixed cost)

© The Author(s), under exclusive license to Springer Nature Switzerland AG 2023
D. Koutra et al. (Eds.): ECML PKDD 2023, LNAI 14172, pp. 316–332, 2023.
https://doi.org/10.1007/978-3-031-43421-1_19

and assigning demand (variable cost) is minimized. This is popularly known as the *Facility Location Problem* (FLP) [9,14,24,32] and is studied under different variants as discussed in Sect. 4.

To the best of our knowledge, all the previous works on FLP assume a single channel of fulfilment—a single edge of one type in the bi-partite graph—between the facilities and clients which is used as a medium of service. The cost of servicing one unit of demand for the client $j$ by the facility $i$ using this one channel is denoted by the service cost $c_{ij}$. However, many real life scenarios exist where a facility can service a client via different channels, each with their own channel capacities and service cost. For instance, a source facility can send the required orders to the customers either through ground, 1-day air, or 2-day air shipments parcels etc. As opposed to a standard FLP, this introduces more complex constraints in the sense that the total outflow from a facility is not only limited by its capacity, but the capacities of individual shipment channels as well, leading to coupling constraints between the shipment channels.

In this paper, we study the extended version of non-uniform, capacitated facility location problem. We consider the scenario where: (i) the facility capacities are hard in that each facility can be opened at most once to serve a maximum demand of $fcap_i$, (ii) there are multiple fulfilment channels $e \in E$ between the facilities and clients, where the cost incurred to serve one unit of demand by facility $i$ to client $j$ via the fulfilment channel $e$ is $c_{i,j,e}$, (iii) each facility $i$ has a channel capacity $ccap_{i,e}$ denoting the maximum demand fulfilled by it using $e$, across all clients, (iv) the maximum number of facilities that can be opened is limited to a user input $k$ - this is referred to as the cardinality constraint. This extended FLP can be formulated as an MILP with one Boolean variable for each facility denoting its open status. However, it is known that even in the most basic forms, a capacitated FLP is $\mathcal{NP}$-hard [32], and the run time for the direct MILP solver grows exponentially in the number of facilities and hence is practically infeasible for a large-scale supply chain system.

## 1.1 Contributions

We present a scalable solution framework for the extended FLP by formulating it as a set selection problem. FLP problems in this form are known to be submodular [14]. We utilize the stochastic distorted greedy algorithm proposed in [18] for a special class of non-monotone submodular optimization problems, to arrive at a fast but good quality approximate solution for the FLP. The stochastic distorted greedy method incrementally selects the facility one at a time to maximize a distorted marginal gain. The calculation of best marginal gain requires repeatedly solving a demand allocation problem $\mathbb{P}_3$ in (8) which is an instance of Linear Program (LP). In the context of greedy algorithm for our FLP, any algorithm used to solve $\mathbb{P}_3$ is referred to as the *value oracle*. The complexity of applying greedy method is in the development of a *fast* value oracle. Though the LP can be solved in polynomial time [21,22], it does not scale for large-sized problems involving millions of decision variables, and more so when multiple instances of $\mathbb{P}_3$ need to be solved over many iterations. Our primary contribution is the development of a fast approximate algorithm for the value oracle to compute the solution of $\mathbb{P}_3$. We replace the direct LP solver by borrowing ideas from the domain of Optimal Transport (OT) theory [33]. Though OT studies the problem of optimal allocation of resources between supply (facilities) and demand (client) locations, the presence of multiple fulfilment channels between them precludes the direct application of efficient OT algorithms proposed in [1,2,10], referred to as the Sinkhorn iterations. Notwithstanding this difficulty, we show how the LP involved in the value oracle can still be approximated by a multi-stage OT problem. We first merge the multiple shipment channels into a single abstract channel between every facility-client pair. The stage-1 OT problem is solved for this approximate network to optimally allocate the client demand to facilities. Subsequently, the shipment channels are split again and stage-2 OT is solved, one for each facility, to determine the distribution of allocated demand from stage-1 OT on to multiple shipment channels. The second stage OT gives an approximate solution to the demand allocation problem $\mathbb{P}_3$ which is used in stochastic greedy algorithm. Although we incur an increase in the number of instances of OT problems compared to LP instances, each OT problem is computable in lightspeed using Sinkhorn iterations [1,2,10] and the overall computation time is much lower compared to executing a direct LP solver. Our work,

– is the first to combine the strengths of both the submodularity and the optimal transport theory, towards solving FLP.
– introduces an extended version of FLP involving multiple fulfilment channels and presents a scalable algorithm for a large-scale supply chain system.

## 1.2   Problem Formulation

Consider a supply chain network $\mathbf{T} = (\mathcal{M}, \mathcal{N}, E, \mathcal{E})$ with $n$ customers or clients, each with a demand $d_j$, $j \in \mathcal{N} = \{1, 2, \ldots, n\}$, and $m$ facilities serving these demand nodes. Each facility $i$ has a one-time fixed cost to open $F_i$, $i \in \mathcal{M} = \{1, 2, \ldots, m\}$, associated with its operation. Facilities can supply to the demand destinations via multiple shipment (fulfilment) channels $e \in E$. Let $c_{i,j,e}$ be the cost to ship unit item from facility $i$ to client $j$ using the channel $e$. Each facility has a channel capacity $ccap_{i,e}$ denoting the maximum demand that facility $i$ can fulfill using the channel $e$, across all clients. The total outflow from a facility $i$ cannot exceed the maximum fulfilment capacity of $fcap_i$, $i \in \mathcal{M} = \{1, 2, \ldots, m\}$. Without the loss of generality, we assume $ccap_{i,e} \leq fcap_i$. It is not required that all the demand from a client be serviced by a single facility, and not all facilities can serve a client location using all the shipment channels pertaining to the practical limitations on transport connectivity. Let $\mathcal{E}$ be the set of all edge connections $(i, j, e)$ where a shipment channel $e$ connects facility $i$ to client $j$, and $\mathcal{N}_i$ be the set of all clients that can be serviced by facility $i$. Denote by $E_i$, the shipment channels types available with the facility $i$. The sub-network formed by the facility $i$, clients $j \in \mathcal{N}_i$ and the shipment channels between them is represented by $\mathbf{T}_i = (\mathcal{N}_i, E_i, \mathcal{E}_i)$.

We aim to solve a facility location problem where the objective is to select an optimal set of facilities $\mathcal{S}^* \subseteq \mathcal{M}$, with a cardinality constraint $|\mathcal{S}^*| \leq k$, to meet maximum demand with minimum costs incurred in shipment and opening new facilities, while adhering to the dynamics of the supply chain network. We consider a soft constraint on the demand, in the sense that it is allowed to fulfil only partial demand, but a penalty is incurred for any unfulfilled demand. Given the supply chain network described above, the optimal set of facilities $S^*$ is obtained by solving the set selection problem $\mathbb{P}_1$ namely,

$$\mathbb{P}_1 : S^* = \underset{S \subseteq \mathcal{M}, \ |S| \leq k}{\arg\min} \left( \sum_{i \in S} F_i + \underset{x_{i,j,e}}{\min} \left( \sum_{i \in S} \sum_{(i,j,e) \in \mathcal{E}_i} c_{i,j,e} x_{i,j,e} d_j + \right. \right.$$
$$\left. \left. C \left( \sum_{j \in \mathcal{N}} d_j - \sum_{i \in S} \sum_{(i,j,e) \in \mathcal{E}_i} x_{i,j,e} d_j \right) \right) \right) \tag{1}$$

$$\sum_{i \in S} \sum_{e \in E_i} x_{i,j,e} \leq 1 \qquad\qquad \forall j \in \mathcal{N} \tag{2}$$

$$\sum_{j \in \mathcal{N}_i} \sum_{e \in E_i} x_{i,j,e} d_j \leq fcap_i \qquad\qquad \forall i \in S \tag{3}$$

$$\sum_{j \in \mathcal{N}_i} x_{i,j,e} d_j \leq ccap_{i,e} \qquad\qquad \forall i \in S, \quad \forall e \in E_i \tag{4}$$

$$x_{i,j,e} \geq 0 \qquad\qquad \forall (i,j,e) \in \mathcal{E} \tag{5}$$

$$x_{i,j,e} \leq 0 \qquad\qquad \forall (i,j,e) \in \{S \times \mathcal{N} \times E\} \backslash \mathcal{E}. \tag{6}$$

The value $x_{i,j,e}$ is the proportion of demand $d_j$ at the $j^{th}$ client fulfilled by the $i^{th}$ facility using the shipment channel $e$. The constraints in (3) and (4) enforce the facility capacity and channel capacity constraints on the outflow from the selected facilities $S$, and (5) and (6) ensure that the network connectivity constraints are followed. The cardinality constraint on the total number of selected facilities is imposed as $|S| \leq k$. The optimization objective of the FLP given in (1) has three components: (i) first term is the fixed cost to open the selected facilities $S$, (ii) the middle term denotes the total cost to ship, and (iii) lastly a penalty on any unfulfilled demand. The parameter $C > \underset{(i,j,e) \in \mathcal{E}}{\max} c_{i,j,e}$ controls the trade-off between the fulfilled and unfulfilled demand. Some times an FLP solution may not be able to meet all the demand either due to insufficient capacity, or insufficient supply due to transportation restrictions (network constraints). Allowing a slack on the fulfilled demand in (2) ensures the feasibility of the problem. For $(i,j,e) \in \mathcal{E}$, define $p_{i,j,e} = C - c_{i,j,e} \geq 0$ as the *profit* to ship unit item from facility $i$ to client $j$ using the channel $e$, and 0 otherwise. Using $p_{i,j,e}$ and dropping the constant $C \sum_{j \in \mathcal{N}} d_j$, the set selection problem $\mathbb{P}_1$ can be re-stated as a maximization problem over a set function,

$$\mathbb{P}_2 : \quad S^* = \underset{S \subseteq \mathcal{M}, \ |S| \leq k}{\arg\max} \quad g(S) - h(S) \tag{7}$$

where $h\left(\mathcal{S}\right) = \sum_{i \in \mathcal{S}} F_i$ is the total cost of opening the facilities in $\mathcal{S}$ and steadily increases as more facilities are included. The component $g\left(\mathcal{S}\right)$ is the optimal cost of demand allocation obtained by solving the sub-problem namely,

$$\mathbb{P}_3 : g\left(\mathcal{S}\right) = \max_{x_{i,j,e}} \sum_{i \in \mathcal{S}} \sum_{(i,j,e) \in \mathcal{E}_i} p_{i,j,e} x_{i,j,e} d_j \qquad (8)$$

subject to the constraints in (2)–(6). The objective here is to fulfill demand using the facilities $\mathcal{S}$ at the most profitable shipment value $p_{i,j,e}$. As any unfulfilled demand has profit 0, it must be minimized for profit maximization in (8). It is easy to see that $g\left(.\right) \geq 0$ and non-decreasing as for $\mathcal{S}_1 \subseteq \mathcal{S}_2, g\left(\mathcal{S}_1\right) \leq g\left(\mathcal{S}_2\right)$. This definition of FLP will allow us to utilize the concept of submodularity for a fast solution in the subsequent sections.

## 2   Background

### 2.1   Submodularity

We briefly review the concept of submodular functions, which we later use to develop our algorithm. For a set function $f(\cdot)$, a subset $\mathcal{A} \subseteq \mathcal{M}$ and an element $i \in \mathcal{M}$, define the incremental gain as $f_{\mathcal{A}}(i) = f\left(\mathcal{A} \cup \{i\}\right) - f(\mathcal{A})$.

**Definition 1.** *(Modularity, Submodularity and Monotonicity)   Consider any two sets $\mathcal{A} \subseteq \mathcal{B} \subseteq \mathcal{M}$. A set function $f(\cdot)$ is submodular iff for any $i \notin \mathcal{B}$, $f_{\mathcal{A}}(i) \geq f_{\mathcal{B}}(i)$. It is called monotone when $f(\mathcal{A}) \leq f(\mathcal{B})$ and modular when $f_{\mathcal{A}}(i)$ is independent of $\mathcal{A}$.*

Submodularity implies diminishing returns where the incremental gain in adding a new element $i$ to a set $\mathcal{A}$ is at least as high as adding to its superset $\mathcal{B}$ [15,27]. Submodular functions enjoy provable, tight performance bounds when the set elements are selected incrementally and greedily [13,17,31].

### 2.2   Optimal Transport (OT)

Let $\mathcal{M} = \{1, 2, \ldots, m\}$ and $\mathcal{N} = \{1, 2, \ldots, n\}$ be a set of supply and demand locations, associated with a capacity $\mathbf{p}_i$ and demand $\mathbf{q}_j$ at locations $i \in \mathcal{M}$ and $j \in \mathcal{N}$ respectively. The OT problem [20] aims at finding a most profitable transport plan $\gamma$ as a solution to[1] $\max_{\gamma \in \Gamma(\mathbf{p},\mathbf{q})} \langle \mathbf{P}, \gamma \rangle$, where $\Gamma(\mathbf{p}, \mathbf{q}) := \{\gamma \in \mathbb{R}_+^{m \times n} | \gamma \mathbf{1} \leq \mathbf{p}; \gamma^\top \mathbf{1} \leq \mathbf{q}\}$. Here, $\mathbf{P} \in \mathbb{R}_+^{m \times n}$ with entries $\mathbf{P}_{ij}$ representing the *profit* of transporting a unit mass from supply $i \in \mathcal{M}$ to demand $j \in \mathcal{N}$. Recently, [10] proposed an extremely fast solution for learning entropy regularized transport plan $\gamma$ using the Sinkhorn algorithm [23]. For a recent survey on OT, please refer to [33].

---

[1] When formulated as a minimisation problem, the objective is to find a transport plan that yields the minimal transporting effort.

# 3    A Scalable Approximate Solution

Facility location problems are known to be submodular [9,14]. In the context of FLP, the diminishing returns property of sub-modularity implies that it is more beneficial to open a new facility when there are fewer facilities already open. Maximisation of submodular set functions is a well studied problem. As they are $\mathcal{NP}$-hard in the general form, a variety of algorithms have been proposed to find approximate solutions to submodular optimization problems. One of the most popular category of algorithms are the variants of incremental selection of a set using greedy approaches [5,6,26,31,34]. These algorithms provide an approximation guarantee to the optimal solution if and only if the submodular objective is monotone and non-negative. However, in our case, while both $g\left(\mathcal{S}\right)$ and $h\left(\mathcal{S}\right)$ in (8) are monotone, the overall optimization objective in $\mathbb{P}_2$ is non-monotone and could also be negative. Therefore, a vanilla greedy algorithm does not give any guarantees on the quality of the solution. We note that the set function $g\left(\mathcal{S}\right)$, obtained as the output of the optimal demand allocation in $\mathbb{P}_3$ is non-negative monotone submodular function, and $h\left(\mathcal{S}\right)$ is monotone modular. This allows us to use a more recent *distorted greedy* algorithm proposed in [18].

A faster variation of the same algorithm called the *stochastic distorted greedy* progresses as follows. Let $\mathcal{S}$, $|\mathcal{S}| = \ell - 1$, represent the set of currently chosen facilities. The property of diminishing returns enables us to select facilities in an incremental fashion, where starting from the empty set $\mathcal{S} = \emptyset$, in every iteration we identify the next best facility $u_\ell$ from a random subset $\mathcal{M}^r$ of available facility options $\mathcal{M} - \mathcal{S}$. The selection is made to maximize a modified incremental gain $\left(1 - \frac{1}{k}\right)^{k-\ell} g_\mathcal{S}(u_\ell) - h_\mathcal{S}(u_\ell)$, where $\left(1 - \frac{1}{k}\right)^{k-\ell}$ is a continuously changing distortion factor applied to $g_\mathcal{S}(u_\ell) = g\left(\mathcal{S} \cup \{u_\ell\}\right) - g(\mathcal{S})$. The set $\mathcal{S}$ is grown incrementally by including the chosen facility $u_\ell$ and the entire process is repeated for $k$ iterations. This way of incrementally selecting the facility set eliminates the need of integrality constraints and is a major factor for reducing the solution complexity. The recommended size of the random set $\mathcal{M}^r$ is $r = \left\lceil \frac{m}{k} \log\left(\frac{1}{\epsilon}\right)\right\rceil$, where $\epsilon$ is a hyper-parameter which directly affects the approximation guarantees. The total number of invocations to set function $g(\cdot)$ over all the $k$ iterations is $O\left(m \ln\left(\frac{1}{\epsilon}\right)\right)$, and is independent of $k$. Let $\mathcal{S}$ be the approximate solution from stochastic distorted greedy algorithm, and $S^*$ the optimal solution. The stochastic distorted greedy algorithm gives guarantees on the optimality gap in an expected sense namely, $\mathbb{E}\left[g(\mathcal{S}) - h(\mathcal{S})\right] \geq \left(1 - \frac{1}{e} - \epsilon\right) g\left(S^*\right) - h\left(S^*\right)$. If all facilities have the same cost to open $\left(F_i\right)$, the approximation guarantee matches that in [30] for monotone sub-modular functions.

## 3.1    Fast Value Oracle

The greedy algorithm and its variants for the optimal set selection problem measure the computational complexity of the solution in terms of the number of calls to a *value oracle* [6,18,26,34]. Given a set of facilities $\mathcal{S}$, a *value oracle* is a system or an algorithm to compute the value of the submodular function. As the greedy algorithm and its variants require repeated evaluation of the incremental gain, *value oracle* is used multiple times in the set selection process. For the solution of FLP problem in $\mathbb{P}_2$ using the stochastic distorted greedy algorithm, the *value oracle* must solve the optimal demand allocation problem $\mathbb{P}_3$ for $O\left(m \ln\left(\frac{1}{\epsilon}\right)\right)$ different instance of LP, and hence can take significant amount of time for a large scale supply chain network involving millions of decision variables. In this section, we propose to solve the demand allocation problem using Sinkhorn iterations [10], popular in optimal transportation theory, for a fast, but good quality solution. As our problem is not an instance of a standard OT, we start by introducing methods to reduce the demand allocation problem $\mathbb{P}_3$ into a novel multi-stage OT problem using the steps below.

**Step 1: Channel Decoupling Under Favourable Conditions:** The presence of multiple fulfilment channels in the problem $\mathbb{P}_3$ introduces complexity by coupling the channels through the shared facility capacity $fcap_i$. If $fcap_i$ was large enough for all the facilities, it would no longer be a limiting constraint, and every facility and fulfilment channel pair could be treated independently. The limit over which the facility capacity in (3) plays no role to the demand allocation problem $\mathbb{P}_3$ is given in Lemma 1.

**Lemma 1.** *The facility capacity constraint is superfluous and trivially satisfied for all facilities $i$ satisfying $\sum_{e \in E_i} ccap_{i,e} \leq fcap_i$.*

It may further be possible to decouple the fulfilment channels of facilities with not enough facility capacity using the result below.

**Lemma 2.** *Consider a facility $i \in S$ such that $\sum_{e \in E_i} ccap_{i,e} > fcap_i$. If $\exists e' \in E_i$ satisfying $e' = \underset{e \in E_i}{\arg\min}\, p_{i,j,e}$,    $\forall j \in \mathcal{N}_i$, the channel capacity of $e'$ at the facility $i$ can be reduced to: $ccap_{i,e'} = \max\left(0, fcap_i - \left(\sum_{e \in E_i - \{e'\}} ccap_{i,e}\right)\right)$.*

Lemma 2 states that we can reduce the capacity requirement of the least profitable fulfilment channel $e'$ by modifying its $ccap$. However, this reduction is possible only when all the clients serviced by $e'$ are also serviced by all the other channels. Note that for clients not serviced by $e'$, the condition in Lemma 2 is trivially satisfied as $p_{i,j,e'} = 0$. If the facility capacity is still not enough, that is, $\sum_{e \in E_i} ccap_{i,e} > fcap_i$ even after the least profitable channel capacity reduction, the process can be repeated by applying Lemma 2 on the next least profitable channel-type with non-zero channel capacity satisfying (2). This way, a repeated application of Lemma 2, and lastly an application of Lemma 1 can be used to decouple the fulfilment channels. If the fulfilment channels at facility $i$ can be completely decoupled this way, then specific to the problem $\mathbb{P}_3$, each fulfilment channel associated with a facility $i$ can be treated as a separate facility indexed by (hyphenated letters) $i$-$e$, of capacity $fcap_{i-e} = ccap_{i,e}$, with profits on the *single* edge $e$ to client $j$ given by $p_{i-e,j} = p_{i,j,e}$. Henceforth in the paper we assume that the channel decoupling is already applied for problem $\mathbb{P}_3$ wherever possible, and for the sake of brevity continue to use the same original notations as before to represent this partially decoupled network model as well.

**Step 2: Reduced Channel Model:** Results from the last step can be used to decouple the shipment channels and make them independent of the outflow on other channels. However, such straightforward reductions are not always possible when the conditions in Lemmas 1 and 2 are not met. In this section we propose approximations for the remaining set of facilities with the non-trivial facility capacity constraint. Consider any facility $i \in \mathcal{M}$. We introduce a new abstract shipment channel $\alpha$ and replace multiple shipment channels $E_i$ at the facility $i$ with $\alpha$ to get an approximate network model $\overline{\mathbf{T}} = (\mathcal{M}, \mathcal{N}, \overline{\mathcal{E}})$ comprised of equivalent facilities with only single channel of shipment $E_i = \alpha$, $\forall i \in \mathcal{M}$, and edges $\overline{\mathcal{E}} = \{(i, j, \alpha) : i \in \mathcal{M} \text{ and } j \in \mathcal{N}_i\}$. Since there is only one channel $\alpha$, it is superfluous to impose its channel capacity as $ccap_{i,\alpha} = fcap_i$. The profit to ship one unit of item from the facility $i$ to a client $j$ through $\alpha$, is computed as a weighted sum of the profits on the original shipment channels $E_i$, namely $p_{i,j,\alpha} := \sum_{e \in E_i} w_{i,e} p_{i,j,e}$, $\forall j \in \mathcal{N}_i$, where $w_{i,e} = \frac{ccap_{i,e}}{\sum_{e \in E_i} ccap_{i,e}}$ $\forall i \in \mathcal{M}, e \in E_i$ represents the contribution of a channel to the total available channel capacity and is independent of the clients $j \in \mathcal{N}_i$. This definition ensures that the profit $p_{i,j,\alpha}$ on the abstract channel, is balanced between both the original channel profits $p_{i,j,e}$ and its capacity contribution proportion $w_{i,e}$. As the network $\overline{\mathbf{T}}$ only comprises of the facility capacities, the problem reduces into an instance of standard OT discussed in Sect. 2.2.

**Step 3: Multi-stage Sinkhorn Algorithm:** As discussed before, a quick solution to the FLP using the stochastic distorted greedy method would require *fast value oracle* to solve the demand allocation problem $\mathbb{P}_3$, especially when it is repeatedly invoked over several iterations. The optimal transportation literature [33] provides a linear time algorithm to compute approximate but good quality solution using Sinkhorn iterations [1,10] for LP instances arising in this field. We identify that the same algorithm can be applied to demand allocation problem for a supply chain network with single shipment channel. By adding an entropy maximization term $(-\mu \sum_{i,j} \gamma_{i,j} \log(\gamma_{i,j}))$ to the objective, the transport plan can be computed through an iterative method outlined in Algorithm 1 involving simple matrix operations. While the solution to the OT lies on one of the vertex of the polytope that forms the feasible region, the addition of entropy term shifts it to the interior of the polytope. In our context, this implies that a solution using Sinkhorn iterations is dense in terms of the used facility-client connections. The trade-off between sparsity and speed is controlled by the parameter $\mu > 0$. Building on this framework, we propose a novel multi-stage Sinkhorn algorithm as *the* fast value oracle for the multi-channel FLP.

Let $\overline{\mathbf{T}}_\mathcal{S}$ be the sub-network from $\overline{\mathbf{T}}$ formed of the facilities in $\mathcal{S}$, their clients, and the single shipment channel $\alpha$. The demand allocation problem in $\mathbb{P}_3$ is divided into two stages, namely demand allocation in (i) $\overline{\mathbf{T}}_\mathcal{S}$ and (ii) $\mathbf{T}_i$, $\forall i \in \mathcal{S}$, each modeled as an instance of OT. The demand allocation problem for $\overline{\mathbf{T}}$ with the selected set of facilities $\mathcal{S}$ can be posed as the OT below,

$$\mathbb{P}_4 : \quad \max_{\overline{\gamma} \in \Gamma(\overline{\mathbf{p}}, \overline{\mathbf{q}})} \langle \overline{\mathbf{P}}_\mathcal{S}, \overline{\gamma} \rangle, \tag{9}$$

---

**Algorithm 1.** Sinkhorn iterations $(\mathbf{p}, \mathbf{q}, \mathbf{P})$

1: If $\mathbf{1}^T\mathbf{p} < \mathbf{1}^T\mathbf{q}$, create a pseudo-supply node $\tilde{i}$ with capacity $\mathbf{p}_{\tilde{i}} = \mathbf{1}^T\mathbf{q} - \mathbf{1}^T\mathbf{p}$, and append it to $\mathbf{p}$. Set profit $P_{\tilde{i},j} = 0, \forall j$.

2: If $\mathbf{1}^T\mathbf{q} < \mathbf{1}^T\mathbf{p}$, create a pseudo-demand node $\tilde{j}$ with demand $\mathbf{q}_{\tilde{j}} = \mathbf{1}^T\mathbf{p} - \mathbf{1}^T\mathbf{q}$, and append it to $\mathbf{q}$. Set profit $P_{i,\tilde{j}} = 0, \forall i$.

3: Let $\kappa = \mathbf{1}^T\mathbf{p} = \mathbf{1}^T\mathbf{q}$. Define $\tilde{\mathbf{p}} = \mathbf{p}/\kappa$, $\tilde{\mathbf{q}} = \mathbf{q}/\kappa$.

4: Construct $\Omega$ with entries $\Omega_{ij} = \exp\left(\frac{P_{ij}}{\mu}\right)$.

5: **Initialize:** $\mathbf{a} = \tilde{\mathbf{p}}$, $\mathbf{b} = \tilde{\mathbf{q}}$.

6: **while** not convergence **do**

7:    $\mathbf{a} = \left(\mathbf{diag}(\Omega\mathbf{b})\right)^{-1}\tilde{\mathbf{p}}$

8:    $\mathbf{b} = \left(\mathbf{diag}(\Omega^T\mathbf{a})\right)^{-1}\tilde{\mathbf{q}}$

9: **end while**

10: **Return:** $\gamma = \kappa * (\mathbf{diag}(\mathbf{a}))\,\Omega\,(\mathbf{diag}(\mathbf{b}))$

---

**Algorithm 2.** Multi-stage Sinkhorn $(\mathcal{S})$

1: $\overline{\mathbf{q}}_j = d_j, \forall j \in \mathcal{N}$  ▷ Demand at the client locations

2: $\overline{\mathbf{p}}_i = fcap_i, \forall i \in \mathcal{S}$

3: $\overline{\mathbf{P}}_{\mathcal{S}_{i,j,\alpha}} = p_{i,j,\alpha}, \forall i \in \mathcal{S}, j \in \mathcal{N}$  ▷ Profits for abstract single channel $\alpha$

4: Solve $\mathbb{P}_4$ to get $\overline{\gamma}$: **run Algorithm 1** with $(\overline{\mathbf{p}}, \overline{\mathbf{q}}, \overline{\mathbf{P}}_{\mathcal{S}})$

5: **for** $i \in \mathcal{S}$ **do**

6:    $\mathbf{q}_j^i = \overline{\gamma}_{i,j}, \forall j \in \mathcal{N}_i$  ▷ Use output of Step 4 here

7:    $\mathbf{p}_e^i = ccap_{i,e}, \forall e \in E_i$

8:    $\mathbf{P}_{e,j}^i = p_{i,j,e}, \forall e \in E_i, j \in \mathcal{N}_i$

9:    Solve $\mathbb{P}_5^i$ to get $\gamma^i$: **run Algorithm 1** with $(\mathbf{p}^i, \mathbf{q}^i, \mathbf{P}^i)$

10:    $x_{i,j,e} = \dfrac{\gamma_{e,j}^i}{\overline{\gamma}_{i,j}}$

11: **end for**

---

where $\overline{\mathbf{p}}$ is the vector of facility capacities in $\mathcal{S}$, and $\overline{\mathbf{q}}$ is the vector of client demands $d_j$. $\overline{\mathbf{P}}_{\mathcal{S}}$ is the profit matrix with entries $\overline{\mathbf{P}}_{\mathcal{S}_{i,j,\alpha}} = p_{i,j,\alpha}$ on the edges in $\overline{\mathcal{E}}$ corresponding to the facilities in $\mathcal{S}$. We obtain the solution for $\mathbb{P}_4$ using the Sinkhorn iterations [10] outlined in Algorithm 1. It is adapted for a maximisation OT problem and differs slightly from the original algorithm proposed in [10]. The solution of this *stage-1 OT* problem is the desired proportion $\overline{x}_{i,j} = \frac{\overline{\gamma}_{i,j}}{d_j}$ of the demand $d_j$, to be fulfilled by the facilities $i \in \mathcal{S}$. The distribution of this demand among different fulfilment channels $x_{i,j,e}$ is not known yet.

A second round of Sinkhorn iterations are applied to each sub-network $\mathbf{T_i}$, $\forall i \in \mathcal{S}$ to optimally distribute the allocated demand portion $x_{i,j,\alpha}$ among multiple fulfilment channels which were abstracted using the channel $\alpha$. The *stage-2 optimal transportation* problem $\mathbb{P}_5^i$ is: $\max\limits_{\gamma^i \in \Gamma(\mathbf{p}^i, \mathbf{q}^i)} \langle \mathbf{P}^i, \gamma^i \rangle$, where $\mathbf{p}^i \in \mathbb{R}_+^{E_i}$ is the vector of channel capacities with $\mathbf{p}_e^i = ccap_{i,e}$, and $\mathbf{q}^i \in \mathbb{R}_+^{\mathcal{N}_i}$ is the stage-1 OT solution vector at the $i$-th facility with $\mathbf{q}_j^i = \overline{\gamma}_{i,j}$. The matrix $\mathbf{P}^i \in \mathbb{R}_+^{E_i \times \mathcal{N}_i}$ is the profit matrix with values $\mathbf{P}_{e,j}^i = p_{i,j,e}$. From the solution $\gamma^i$, the channel level distribution can be computed as: $x_{i,j,e} = \frac{\gamma_{e,j}^i}{\bar{\gamma}_{i,j}}$.

**Computational Complexity.** The multi-stage Sinkhorn method is outlined in Algorithm 2. When used as the value oracle in the stochastic distorted greedy technique described in Sect. 3, it requires utmost $\sum_{i=1}^{k}(i+1)r = \frac{3+k}{2}m\ln\left(\frac{1}{\epsilon}\right)$ calls to the Sinkhorn method in Algorithm 1, where $r = \left\lceil \frac{m}{k}\log\left(\frac{1}{\epsilon}\right)\right\rceil$ is the cardinality of the randomly selected set $\mathcal{M}^r \subseteq \mathcal{M} - \mathcal{S}$ in each iteration of stochastic distorted greedy algorithm. In particular, only $m\ln\left(\frac{1}{\epsilon}\right)$ invocations to Algorithm 1 are required in the stage-1 for the problem $\mathbb{P}_4$ in (9). A majority $\left(\frac{1+k}{2}m\ln\left(\frac{1}{\epsilon}\right)\right)$ calls are required only in the stage-2 OT for the problem $\mathbb{P}_5$ which are: (i) executed on the much smaller single facility sub-networks $\mathbf{T_i}$ and, (ii) can be computed in parallel across all the facilities. This results in an extremely fast value oracle to determine an approximate solution to the problem $\mathbb{P}_3$ in (8).

# 4 Related Work

Multiple variants of FLP are studied in the literature. In the uncapacitated FLP (UFLP), the facility capacity is assumed to be $\infty$ [11,16]. In the capacitated setting (CFLP), the capacities are finite and upper bound the quantum of demand that a facility can serve. Some papers investigate the specialised case of uniform facility capacities where $fcap_i = fcap$, $\forall i$ [9,24], while others consider the general scenario of non-uniform facility capacities [4,32]. FLPs are also classified based on whether the capacities are *hard* or *soft*. In case of hard capacities, each facility $i$ can be opened at most once and can serve a demand of at most $fcap_i$ [32], whereas the soft capacitated facilities can service demands marginally exceeding their $fcap_i$ but with an added penalty [3,7,8,19]. Another FLP variant allows facilities to be opened $k > 1$ times by replicating itself [8,9,11,29], and service demand up to $k * fcap_i$ at an opening cost of $kF_i$.

As solving the FLP directly as a MILP is $\mathcal{NP}$-hard [28], plethora of approximation algorithms based on techniques such as LP rounding, primal-dual algorithms, and local search heuristics have been developed to yield constant factor approximations. LP techniques are used in [11] to give the first 3.16 approximation algorithm for the UFLP, and subsequently are extended in [19] to handle soft capacitated FLPs. While the work in [8] develop an approximation algorithm for CFLP with uniform, soft capacities, [3] present a local search algorithm for the nonuniform, soft capacity variant. Local search heuristics have been the most popular approach for hard optimization problems. For the CFLP, [24] gave the first iterative approximation algorithm of value no more than $8 + \epsilon$ times optimum, for any $\epsilon > 0$ by using the simple local search heuristic originally proposed in [25]. By using the property of submodularity, [9] improved on the analysis of the same heuristic and proved a stronger $6(1 + \epsilon)$ approximation.

For the nonuniform CLP variant with hard capacities considered in this paper, [32] developed a approximation algorithm with a guarantee of $9 + \epsilon$

under the assumption of a single channel of fulfilment between facilities and client, unlike the extended multi-channel setup which is the focus of our work. Though the technique in [32] has a polynomial computational complexity, it is not designed for a large-scale network as it involves many computationally demanding subset selection operations in each iteration such as: (i) open one facility $i$ and close a subset of facilities $T \subseteq S - \{i\}$: open$(i, T)$, (ii) close one facility $i \in S$ and open a subset of facilities $T \subseteq M - \{i\}$: close$(i, T)$. The authors prove that their algorithm terminates after a polynomial number of these operations, and for each choice of $i$ identifies a set $T$ in polynomial time to execute open$(i, T)$ and close$(i, T)$ functions. Each of these operations require solving an instance of a LP, similar to the problem $\mathbb{P}_3$ in (8), referred here as the value oracle.

For a large-scale supply network running a large number of LP instances (invocations to the value oracle), though polynomial in number, will not scale. As explained in Sect. 1.1, our contribution is not only to study the extended nonuniform CFLP but to also design an efficient implementation of the value oracle, by solving these LPs via the proposed lightspeed *multi-stage* Sinkhorn iterations using concepts from OT [1,2,10,12,35]. Leveraging the recent advancements in submodular optimisation [5,6,18,26,34], we develop a scalable algorithm by incrementally selecting the facilities using the stochastic distorted greedy method [18]. Our approach does not require opening or closing subsets of facilities in each iteration as done in [32]. The approximation guarantee of $1 - \frac{1}{e} - \epsilon$ for the stochastic distorted greedy algorithm ensures that our solution will be closer to the global optimum.

## 5    Experiments

We first present results on a mid-size e-commerce network with $n = 2000$ client locations, $m = 150$ tentative facilities, and $|E| = 3$ different shipment channels. The network is fairly dense with a total of over 800,000 flow paths between the facility-client pairs, each with their own cost to ship per unit quantity. There is sufficient variation in the cost of opening the facilities with the ratio of std. dev. to its mean being 30%. The corresponding ratios for $fcap$ and $ccap$ are 28% and 24% respectively. The cost penalty for unfulfilled client demands is set to $C = 5 \times \max(c_{i,j,e})$. We solve the FLP problem for this network for different values of cardinality constraint $k$ using 4 different approaches:

(i) *Method 1*: A direct MILP solver,
(ii) The stochastic distorted greedy method, with $\epsilon = 0.01$ and following three different value oracles,
    (a) *Method 2*: a standard commercial LP solver,
    (b) *Method 3*: the proposed multi-stage Sinkhorn algorithm,
    (c) *Method 4*: single-stage Sinkhorn algorithm.

The *single-stage Sinkhorn* oracle in Method 4 outputs the objective value of stage-1 OT problem in (9), invoking the Algorithm 1 only for stage-1. This is equivalent to selecting all the facilities based on the reduced network $\overline{\mathbf{T}} = \left(\mathcal{M}, \mathcal{N}, \overline{\mathcal{E}}\right)$ constructed in Sect. 3.1. This oracle will incur the least computation time requiring only $m \ln\left(\frac{1}{\epsilon}\right)$ (independent of $k$) invocations to Algorithm 1. Though it cannot be used to obtain a solution for the problem $\mathbb{P}_3$ in (8) as the demand distribution among different fulfilment channels is not computed, we used it as a test bed to also assess the quality of our reduced network $\overline{\mathbf{T}}$.

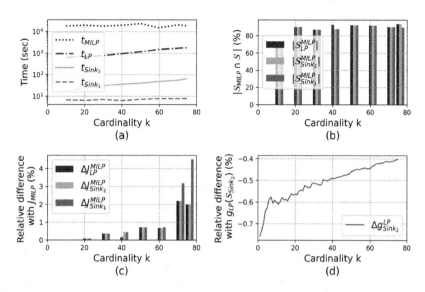

**Fig. 1.** Results for different $k$ values. (a) Time taken to select facilities, (b) percentage overlap between selected facilities, (c) relative difference between the objective values in (1), and (d) relative difference in objective (8) calculated with different value oracles.

After the facilities are selected, the demand allocation problem $\mathbb{P}_3$ is finally solved once using a standard LP solver with the final set of recommended facilities from these algorithms, and the objective value $J$ is calculated as per Eq. (1) for a fair comparison between approaches. Let $\mathcal{S}_{MILP}$, $\mathcal{S}_{LP}$, $\mathcal{S}_{Sink_2}$ and $\mathcal{S}_{Sink_1}$ be the sets of facilities selected using the above listed four approaches in order, $t_{MILP}$, $t_{LP}$, $t_{Sink_2}$ and $t_{Sink_1}$ be the solution times, and $J_{MILP}$, $J_{LP}$, $J_{Sink_2}$ and $J_{Sink_1}$ be the respective objective values. For different values of $k$, we assess the quality of our algorithm in terms of the following metrics: (i) the percentage overlaps on the final selected set of facilities, (ii) the time taken to select the all the facilities, (iii) the relative differences on the original objective function in (1), and (iv) the approximation of the demand allocation problem $\mathbb{P}_3$ by the multi-stage Sinkhorn oracle relative to standard LP solver.

In Fig. 1(b) we plot the percentage of facilities selected using the three oracles that are common with the solution from MILP, computed as: $\mathcal{S}_{algo}^{MILP} = \frac{|\mathcal{S}_{algo} \cap \mathcal{S}_{MILP}|}{|\mathcal{S}_{MILP}|} \times 100\%$, $\forall algo \in \{LP, Sink_2, Sink_1\}$. For most values of $k$ the over-

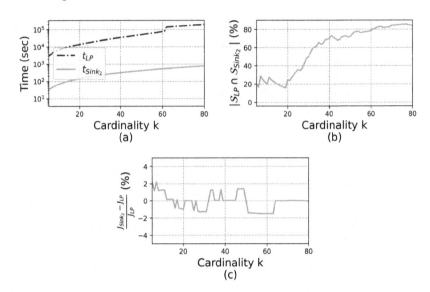

**Fig. 2.** Results for the large network with $n = 10000$, $m = 400$, $|\mathcal{E}| > 10^6$. (a) Time taken to select all the facilities, (b) Percentage overlap between the final set of selected facilities, and (c) Relative difference between the objective values.

lap is greater than 80%. In Fig. 1(c) we plot the relative difference in objective value against the MILP solution calculated as: $\Delta J_{algo}^{MILP} = \frac{J_{algo} - J_{MILP}}{J_{MILP}} \times 100\%$, $\forall algo \in \{LP, Sink_2, Sink_1\}$), and find that both the LP and the multi-stage Sinkhorn oracles are within **3%**. Any (acceptable) loss in optimality from the Sinkhorn oracles is compensated by the significant gain in computational time to select facilities as seen in Fig. 1(a). The execution time of the multi-stage Sinkhorn oracle can be further reduced by running the stage-2 OT instances in parallel, and also by making parallel calls to the value oracle for multiple facility options. Such a study is beyond the scope of this paper. As expected, the *single-stage* Sinkhorn oracle is faster than its multi-stage counterpart but also has a higher variation from the optimal objective value, as shown in Fig. 1(c).

We also make a stand-alone comparison of the proposed multi-stage Sinkhorn algorithm with a standard commercial LP solver, without any incremental facility selection algorithm. We execute the problem $\mathbb{P}_3$ with the selected set of facilities $\mathcal{S}_{Sink_2}$, for different values of cardinality constraint $k$, using: (i) an LP solver and, (ii) the multi-stage Sinkhorn Algorithm 2. Let the solution objectives be represented as $g_{LP}(\mathcal{S}_{Sink_2})$ and $g_{Sink_2}(\mathcal{S}_{Sink_2})$ respectively. The relative difference, $\Delta g_{Sink_2}^{LP} = \frac{g_{Sink_2}(\mathcal{S}_{Sink_2}) - g_{LP}(\mathcal{S}_{Sink_2})}{g_{LP}(\mathcal{S}_{Sink_2})} \times 100\%$, between the objective from multi-stage Sinkhorn and the optimal value from LP solver is less than 1%, as shown in Fig. 1(d). We thus obtain at least **20** fold speed up by replacing the LP solver with multi-stage Sinkhorn as the value oracle, without any significant compromise in the quality of the two results.

Lastly, we stress test the scalability of our approach by selecting facilities for a much larger network with 400 facilities, 10000 clients, and *more than 10 million flow paths* with three different shipment channels. It takes a tremendously large amount of time to solve an MILP for this scale of the FLP and is practically infeasible to be used even for comparison studies. For e.g., the best possible solution obtained using MILP in 48 hrs for $k = 80$ has an objective value which is worse by 40% than our approximate solution. We therefore use the stochastic distorted greedy algorithm with an LP value oracle to benchmark our solution in this case. The total time taken to select the facilities for different cardinality values $k$ is shown in Fig. 2(a). While the direct LP solver took more than 200000 secs to identify 80 facilities, the multi-stage Sinkhorn oracle was able to choose the same in $\approx 750$ s. The overlap between the solutions from using LP and multi-stage Sinkhorn as value oracles is shown in Fig. 2(b). While this overlap is less for lower values of $k$, the difference in objective values from the two solutions never exceeds 2.5% as seen in Fig. 2(c). In fact, since the subsets $\mathcal{M}^r \subseteq \mathcal{M} - \mathcal{S}$ in each iteration of the stochastic distorted greedy algorithm are chosen randomly, for some $k$ values the multi-stage Sinkhorn value oracle even does better than the LP solver. This re-establishes the significance of our method.

# 6  Conclusion

We introduced the novel multi-channel capacitated facility location problem, where the facilities can service the demand at the client locations using different fulfilment channels, each with their own service cost and channel capacities. As opposed to a standard FLP, this creates complex coupling constraints between the shipment channels. Though polynomial time iterative algorithms exists for the capacitated FLP, we argued that these methods do not scale as: (i) they perform complicated operations allowing to open or close a subset of facilities relative to the current solution which are computationally intensive, (ii) rely on using the LP solvers as the value oracle for determining the cost of demand allocation given the set of facilities $\mathcal{S}$, to which repeated invocations are made over multiple iterations. We proposed a scalable alternative by: (i) modelling the FLP as a submodular maximisation problem and using the well-known greedy technique which only performs the relatively simpler operation of incrementally adding a new facility to the current selection, (ii) replacing the direct LP solver in the value oracle by a multi-stage instances OT problem, each solvable in lightspeed using Sinkhorn iterations. The theoretical and convergence guarantees of these greedy and Sinkhorn approaches directly apply to our framework. As observed in our experiments, our OT based algorithm leads to a **20** fold decrease in computational time over state-of-the-art commercial LP solvers and over **100** fold decrease in the same as compared to the direct MILP solvers, with only a marginal variation of less than **3%** from the optimal objective value.

To the best of our knowledge, all the variants of FLP studied thus far are *static* in nature, where a one-time decision is made to open a facility given the various costs, capacity, and the demand values. However in the real world, client demands, facility capacities, service cost, etc. constantly vary over time. A straightforward approach for this *dynamic* setting would be to be to treat each time instance as a standalone static problem, and freshly determine the set of facilities to open for that time period. A number of operational constraints would preclude continuously opening and shutting down facilities. For instance, a supply chain system would not prefer to open a facility in the first year, close it down in the following year only to open it again. As our future work, we would like to investigate the multi-year, dynamic variant of FLP with changing input parameters over the years, where one could have the option to open a facility any time during the multi-year period, but constrained from closing it subsequently.

**Ethical Impact**

We do not foresee any scenario where our method would put a certain demographic, a specific organisation, or a particular location to a systematic disadvantage. We neither use any personal data in our experiments, nor think that our method will have policing or military applications. Our work is only focused on developing a fast, scalable algorithm to identify the set of facilities to be opened, to minimise the total cost associated with serving the demand from multiple client locations.

# References

1. Abid, B.K., Gower, R.: Stochastic algorithms for entropy-regularized optimal transport problems. In: Proceedings of the 21st International Conference on Artificial Intelligence and Statistics, vol. 84, pp. 1505–1512. PMLR (2018)
2. Altschuler, J., Niles-Weed, J., Rigollet, P.: Near-linear time approximation algorithms for optimal transport via sinkhorn iteration. In: Proceedings of the 31st Conference on Neural Information Processing Systems, vol. 30, pp. 1964–1974 (2017)
3. Arya, V., Garg, N., Khandekar, R., Meyerson, A., Mungala, K., Pandit, V.: Local search heuristic for K-median and facility location problems. In: 33rd ACM Symposium on Theory of Computing, pp. 21–29 (2001)
4. Barahona, F., Jensen, D.: Plant location with minimum inventory. Math. Program. **83**, 101–111 (1998)
5. Buchbinder, N., Feldman, M., Naor, J.S., Schwartz, R.: Submodular maximization with cardinality constraints. In: 25th ACM-SIAM Symposium on Discrete Algorithms, pp. 1433–1452 (2014)
6. Buchbinder, N., Feldman, M., Schwartz, R.: Comparing apples and oranges: query trade-off in submodular maximization. Math. Oper. Res. **42**(2), 308–329 (2017)
7. Charikar, M., Guha, S.: Improved combinatorial algorithms for facility location and K-median problems. In: 40th Annual Symposium on Foundations of Computer Science (1999)
8. Chudak, F., Shmoys, D.: Improved approximation algorithms for the capacitated facility location problem. In: 10th ACM-SIAM Symposium on Discrete Algorithms (1999)
9. Chudak, F., Williamson, D.: Improved approximation algorithms for capacitated facility location problems. Math. Program. **102**, 207–222 (2005)
10. Cuturi, M.: Sinkhorn distances: lightspeed computation of optimal transport. In: Advances in Neural Information Processing Systems, vol. 26 (2013)

11. Shmoys, D., Tardos, É., Aardal, K.: Approximation algorithms for the facility location problems. In: 29th ACM Symposium on Theory of Computing, pp. 265–274 (1997)
12. Dvurechensky, P., Gasnikov, A., Kroshnin, A.: Computational optimal transport: Complexity by accelerated gradient descent is better than by Sinkhorn's algorithm. In: Proceedings of the 35th International Conference on Machine Learning, vol. 80, pp. 1367–1376. PMLR (2018)
13. Elenberg, E., Khanna, R., Dimakis, A.G., Negahban, S.: Restricted strong convexity implies weak submodularity. Ann. Stat. **46**, 3539–3568 (2018)
14. Frieze, A.M.: A cost function property for plant location problems. Math. Program. **7**, 245–248 (1974)
15. Fujishige, S.: Submodular Functions and Optimization. Elsevier, Amsterdam (2005)
16. Cornuéjols, G., Nemhauser, G., Wolsey, L.: The Uncapacitated Facility Location Problem. Wiley, New York (1990)
17. Gurumoorthy, K.S., Dhurandhar, A., Cecchi, G., Aggarwal, C.: Efficient data representation by selecting prototypes with importance weights. In: IEEE ICDM (2019)
18. Harshaw, C., Feldman, M., Ward, J., Karbasi, A.: Submodular maximization beyond non-negativity: guarantees, fast algorithms, and applications. In: 36 International Conference on Machine Learning (2019)
19. Jain, K., Vazirani, V.: Primal-dual approximation algorithms for metric facility location and K-median problems. In: 40th Annual Symposium on Foundations of Computer Science (1999)
20. Kantorovich, L.: On the translocation of masses. Doklady Acad. Sci. USSR **37**, 199–201 (1942)
21. Karmarkar, N.: A new polynomial-time algorithm for linear programming. Combinatorica **4**(4), 373–395 (1984)
22. Khachiyan, L.: A polynomial algorithm for linear programming. Doklady Akademii Nauk SSSR **224**(5), 1093–1096 (1979)
23. Knight, P.A.: The Sinkhorn-Knopp algorithm: convergence and applications. SIAM J. Matrix Anal. Appl. **30**(1), 261–275 (2008)
24. Korupolu, M., Plaxton, C., Rajaraman, R.: Analysis of a local search heuristic for facility location problems. J. Algorithms **37**, 146–188 (2000)
25. Kuehn, A.A., Hamburger, M.J.: A heuristic program for locating warehouses. Manage. Sci. **9**, 643–666 (1963)
26. Kuhnle, A.: Interlaced greedy algorithm for maximization of submodular functions in nearly linear time. In: Advances in Neural Information Processing Systems, vol. 32 (2019)
27. Lovász, L.: Submodular functions and convexit. In: Bachem, A., Korte, B., Grötschel, M. (eds.) Mathematical Programming - The State of the Art, pp. 235–257. Springer, Heidelberg (1983). https://doi.org/10.1007/978-3-642-68874-4_10
28. Lund, C., Yannakakis, M.: On the hardness of approximating minimization problems. ACM **41**, 960–981 (1994)
29. Mahdian, M., Ye, Y., Zhang, J.: A 2-approximation algorithm for the soft-capacitated facility location problem. In: 6th International Workshop on Approximation Algorithms for Combinatorial Optimization, pp. 129–140 (2003)
30. Mirzasoleiman, B., Badanidiyuru, A., Karbasi, A., Vondrák, J., Krause, A.: Lazier than lazy greedy. In: Association for the Advancement of Artificial Intelligence (2015)
31. Nemhauser, G.L., Wolsey, L.A., Fisher, M.L.: An analysis of approximations for maximizing submodular set functions. Math. Program. **14**, 265–294 (1978)

32. Pál, M., Tardos, É., Wexler, T.: Facility location with nonuniform hard capacities. In: IEEE FOCS, pp. 329–338 (2001)
33. Peyré, G., Cuturi, M.: Computational optimal transport. Found. Trends Mach. Learn. **11**(5–6), 355–607 (2019)
34. Sakaue, S.: Guarantees of stochastic greedy algorithms for non-monotone submodular maximization with cardinality constraint. In: 23rd International Conference on Artificial Intelligence and Statistics (2020)
35. Xie, Y., Luo, Y., Huo, X.: An accelerated stochastic algorithm for solving the optimal transport problem. CoRR abs/2203.00813 (2022)

# Online State Exploration: Competitive Worst Case and Learning-Augmented Algorithms

Sungjin Im[1($\boxtimes$)], Benjamin Moseley[2($\boxtimes$)], Chenyang Xu[3($\boxtimes$)], and Ruilong Zhang[4($\boxtimes$)]

[1] Electrical Engineering and Computer Science, University of California at Merced, Merced, CA, USA
sim3@ucmerced.edu

[2] Tepper School of Business, Carnegie Mellon University, Pittsburgh, PA, USA
moseleyb@andrew.cmu.edu

[3] Shanghai Key Laboratory of Trustworthy Computing, East China Normal University, Shanghai, China
cyxu@sei.ecnu.edu.cn

[4] Department of Computer Science and Engineering, University at Buffalo, Buffalo, NY, USA
ruilongz@buffalo.edu

**Abstract.** This paper introduces the online state exploration problem. In the problem, there is a hidden $d$-dimensional target state. We are given a distance function between different states in the space and a penalty function depending on the current state for each incorrect guess. The goal is to move to a vector that dominates the target state starting from the origin in the $d$-dimensional space while minimizing the total distance and penalty cost. This problem generalizes several natural online discrete optimization problems such as multi-dimensional knapsack cover, cow path, online bidding, and online search. For online state exploration, the paper gives results in the worst-case competitive analysis model and in the online algorithms augmented with the prediction model. The results extend and generalize many known results in the online setting.

**Keywords:** Online Search · Online Algorithms · Competitive Ratio · Learning-augmented Algorithms · Worst-case Analysis

## 1 Introduction

A recent trend in algorithmic design under uncertainty is making use of machine learning to augment online algorithms [22]. In this emerging setting, we are given some predictions of the future. These predictions are learned from historical data, and thus, their actual accuracy is unknown. The goal is to develop

---

All authors (ordered alphabetically) have equal contributions.

D. Koutra et al. (Eds.): ECML PKDD 2023, LNAI 14172, pp. 333–348, 2023.
https://doi.org/10.1007/978-3-031-43421-1_20

an algorithm with these predictions so that the algorithm can outperform traditional algorithms (without predictions) if the predictions are accurate, while still retaining a theoretical worst-case guarantee even when the predictions are arbitrarily wrong. The performance measure of an algorithm is *competitive analysis*. Take a minimization problem as an example. An online algorithm is said to be *c*-competitive or have a competitive ratio *c* if the algorithm's objective value is at most a factor *c* larger than the optimal objective value *on any instance*. We also follow the standard terminology stated in [23]: an algorithm with predictions is said to be $\alpha$-*consistent* and $\beta$-*robust* if its competitive ratio is $\beta$ with any predictions and it improves to $\alpha$ with perfect predictions.

Many classical online problems have been considered in this novel model. For instance, see the work by [15,20,24] on caching; [5,12] on the classic secretary problem; [14,18] on scheduling; [3,23] on ski rental; and [8] on set cover. Among them, the recent two works [2,4] inspire our paper. In [2], the authors introduced the online search framework, and provided a 4-competitive algorithm and a learning-augmented algorithm that is $(1 + \epsilon)$-consistent and $5(1 + 1/\epsilon)$-robust for any $\epsilon > 0$. [4] considered the cow path problem with predictions and gave an algorithm with $(1+\epsilon)$-consistency and $(\epsilon(1+2/\epsilon)^2 +1)$-robustness. For both the two problems, we find that whether in their pure online algorithms or learning-augmented algorithms, the well-known *guess-and-double* technique is applied. This key observation motivates our paper.

*Guess-and-Double.* This technique is one of the most widely used techniques in the field of machine learning and algorithmic design under uncertainty. Many problems build on this technique to design algorithms, such as incremental clustering [9], online *k*-center [9] and online load balancing [6]. The basic algorithmic idea is first developing competitive algorithms parameterized by the optimal value (OPT) under the assumption that OPT is known, and then leveraging guess-and-double to remove the assumption. More specifically, we keep running the parameterized algorithm with a guessed value OPT, and once the guessed value is found to be wrong, we geometrically increase the guess. The analysis can guarantee that such an operation only loses a constant factor on the competitive ratio.

Due to the rich applications of the guess-and-double technique, a natural question then arises in the context of learning-augmented algorithms:

> *Is there any unified framework to integrate machine-learned predictions with the guess-and-double technique?*

The main contribution of this paper is proposing such a general framework. We first introduce the online state exploration problem, which unifies applications where guess-and-double is used, and then design learning-augmented algorithms for the problem.

## 1.1   The Online State Exploration Problem

The online state exploration problem (OSEP) is a generalization of many online discrete optimization problems. This problem is defined in $d$-dimensional (*state*) space $\mathbb{R}_{\geq 0}^d$, where each point $\mathbf{v} \in \mathbb{R}_{\geq 0}^d$ is referred to as a *state*. For any two states

$\mathbf{u} = (u_1, \ldots, u_d)$ and $\mathbf{v} = (v_1, \ldots, v_d)$, we define that $\mathbf{u}$ *dominates* $\mathbf{v}$ ($\mathbf{u} \succeq \mathbf{v}$) if $u_i \geq v_i \ \forall i \in [d]$. There is a hidden *target* state $\mathbf{t}$ known only to an oracle, and the algorithm is required to move from $\mathbf{0}$ to a state that dominates $\mathbf{t}$. When the algorithm moves from $\mathbf{u}$ to $\mathbf{v}$, it needs to pay the moving cost $c(\mathbf{u}, \mathbf{v})$ and then is told whether $\mathbf{v}$ dominates $\mathbf{t}$. The goal is to minimize the total moving cost.

To see how this captures the guess-and-double framework, intuitively think of $\mathbf{t}$ as the optimal value in the guess-and-double framework, which is generalized to multiple dimensions. Then, the moving cost captures how much an algorithm pays when using a particular guess of optimal.

Define that the moving cost $c(\mathbf{u}, \mathbf{v}) = \mathsf{D}(\mathbf{u}, \mathbf{v}) + \mathsf{P}(\mathbf{u})$ consists of two parts: the distance cost $\mathsf{D}(\mathbf{u}, \mathbf{v})$ and the penalty cost $\mathsf{P}(\mathbf{u})$. The distance function is assumed to satisfy the following three properties.

- (Identity) $\mathsf{D}(\mathbf{u}, \mathbf{u}) = 0$ for all $\mathbf{u}$. The distance of a point to itself is 0.
- (Domination Monotonicity) For any two states $\mathbf{u} \succeq \mathbf{v}$, $\mathsf{D}(\mathbf{0}, \mathbf{u}) \geq \mathsf{D}(\mathbf{0}, \mathbf{v})$. If $\mathbf{u}$ dominates $\mathbf{v}$ then $\mathbf{u}$ has no smaller distance from the origin than $\mathbf{v}$.
- (Domination Submodularity) For any two states $\mathbf{u} \succeq \mathbf{v}$ and any $\mathbf{w} \in \mathbb{R}_{\geq 0}^d$ with at most one non-zero entry, we have $\mathsf{D}(\mathbf{u}, \mathbf{u}+\mathbf{w}) \leq \mathsf{D}(\mathbf{v}, \mathbf{v}+\mathbf{w})$. In other words, making an affine move by $\mathbf{w}$ from $\mathbf{u}$ is no costlier than making the same move from $\mathbf{v}$. That is, distances are submodular.

For convenience, we call the last two assumptions *monotonicity* and *submodularity*, respectively. For a state $\mathbf{u}$ in the space, define its *distance vector* $\tilde{\mathbf{u}} = (\tilde{u}_1, \ldots, \tilde{u}_d)$, where $\tilde{u}_i = \mathsf{D}(\mathbf{0}, u_i\mathbf{e}_i)$ and $\mathbf{e}_i$ is the standard basis vectors where the 1 appears in the $i$-th position. We define penalty $\mathsf{P}(\mathbf{u}) \leq \gamma \cdot ||\tilde{\mathbf{u}}||_\infty$ where $\gamma \geq 0$ is an input *penalty factor*. Intuitively, the penalty is incurred when visiting an incorrect state $\mathbf{u}$. The penalty generalizes the cost function and is useful for capturing some applications that a submodular distance function is not general enough to capture. Given a target $\mathbf{t}$, we have a standard assumption that the optimal solution is moving from $\mathbf{0}$ to $\mathbf{t}$ directly, i.e., $\mathrm{OPT}(\mathbf{t}) = c(\mathbf{0}, \mathbf{t})$, and $\mathrm{OPT}(\mathbf{t})$ is scaled to always be at least 1.

In the learning-augmented algorithms model, the algorithm is given access to a prediction. We consider predicting the target state $\mathbf{t}'$. This prediction is constructed from data corresponding to prior instances of the problem considered. The prediction helps the algorithm cope with uncertainty in the online setting. As machine learning is often imperfect, the algorithm must cope with having an erroneous prediction.

## 1.2   Applications of Online State Exploration

Online state exploration captures many natural and known problems. We introduce three examples here. The detailed discussions of the reductions from these problems to online state exploration are omitted in this version.

*Online Bidding.* In this problem, an algorithm can make a bid $u$ for cost $u$. The algorithm must make bids until the algorithm bids larger than some unknown

**Table 1.** We only show the results of deterministic algorithms in the table. In the table, $d$ is the number of dimensions, $\gamma \geq 0$ is the penalty factor, and $e$ is the base of the natural logarithmic. The pair $(\alpha, \beta)$ represents an $\alpha$-consistent and $\beta$-robust algorithm. For the full spectrum of $(\alpha, \beta)$ pairs that can be obtained, see the theorems and corollaries below.

| Problems | Worst Case Algorithms | Learning-Augmented Algorithms |
|---|---|---|
| Online State Exploration | $(\gamma + 1)ed + e$ (Theorem 1) | $(2(1 + \gamma)d - \gamma, 2(1 + \gamma)e^2 d - \gamma e^2)$ (Theorem 3) |
| Online Bidding | 4 [10] | $(2, 4)$ (Theorem 5) |
| MD Cow Path | $2ed + 1$ [7] | $(2d + 1, 2ed + 1)$ (Corollary 3) |
| MD Knapsack Cover | $ed + e$ (Corollary 1) | $(2d, 2e^2 d)$ (Corollary 2) |

target $T$. In the online setting, the target is revealed only when the algorithm bids an amount larger than $T$. The goal is to minimize the summation of all bids. See [10,13]. The problem admits a 4-competitive deterministic algorithm and an $e$-competitive randomized algorithm, which are shown to be optimal.

*Multi-Directional Cow Path.* A cow is located at the meeting point of several rays. There is only one gate that is located on some ray. The cow must locate the gate by moving along the rays where each unit of distance traveled costs one unit. The gate is only discovered if the cow reaches that location. The goal is to discover the gate at a minimum cost. See [7,11,16,17]. The problem admits a deterministic algorithm that can achieve $2ed + 1$ and a randomized algorithm that can achieve $3.088d + o(d)$. Both ratios are optimal.

*Online Multi-dimensional Knapsack Cover.* In this problem, there is a collection of items that can be used to cover $d$ dimensional space. Each item $i$ costs $c_i$ units and covers dimension $j \in [d]$ by a non-negative amount $w_{i,j}$. Each dimension $j$ must be covered to an amount at least $h_j \geq 0$. We refer to vector $\mathbf{h} = (h_1, \ldots, h_d)$ as the *demand vector*. If a set of items $S$ are selected then dimension $j$ is covered by $\sum_{i \in S} w_{i,j}$ and the cost is $\sum_{i \in S} c_i$. The goal is to choose items of minimum cost to cover all dimensions. In the online setting, each dimension $i$ covering the amount $h_i$ is unknown, and it is only known when the algorithm purchases enough items to cover all dimensions. And we assume that every item can be used an infinite number of times, and the items cannot be revoked once they are included in the solution. This problem is a natural generalization of the Multi-Optional Ski-Rental problem. See [1,19,21,25] for the multi-optional ski-rental problem. To our best knowledge, we introduce this problem for the first time.

## 1.3   Our Contributions

Our main contributions are in the following two senses (Table 1):

- We introduce the online state exploration problem, which unifies many classical applications where guess-and-double is used, such as online bidding, multidimensional cow path, and multidimensional knapsack cover;
- We design learning-augmented algorithms for the problem which have good performance on each problem as long as the specific properties of each problem are utilized during the analysis.

We also consider the problem without a prediction in the traditional worst-case competitive analysis model. This paper develops a deterministic algorithm that has a competitive ratio linear in $d$ when the penalty factor $\gamma$ is given (Theorem 1). We show that this is essentially tight deterministically (Theorem 2). Then we show competitive ratio can be slightly improved via randomization.

We then consider the learning-augmented algorithm model. In this case, the algorithm is given a prediction $\mathbf{t}'$ of the target state that may be erroneous. We give a deterministic algorithm that has a trade-off on consistency and robustness with respect to the prediction error $||\tilde{\mathbf{t}} - \tilde{\mathbf{t}}'||_\infty$ (Theorem 3). We remark that the trade-off can also be improved by the randomized algorithm, which is omitted in this version. Finally, we show that any algorithm with a bounded robustness ratio has no smaller consistent ratio than ours (Theorem 2).

We show the consistency and robustness trade-offs can be further improved for some special cases by using the specific properties of specific problems.

For online bidding, we show that there is a deterministic algorithm that achieves the consistent ratio $(1 + \epsilon)$ and the robust ratio $\frac{2(1+\epsilon)^2}{\epsilon(1+\epsilon/2)}$ when $\epsilon < 1$ (Theorem 5), which slightly improves the previous result $(1 + \epsilon)$-consistency and $5(1+\frac{1}{\epsilon})$-robustness [2]. Moreover, if we do not pursue a consistency ratio smaller than 2, the robustness ratio can always be guaranteed no worse than the worst-case bound 4 [10]. We also remark that the trade-offs can be further improved if allowing for randomization.

For multi-directional cow path (MD cow path for short), we show that our algorithm achieves the consistency ratio $(1 + \epsilon)$ and the robustness ratio $(\epsilon(1 + \frac{2}{\epsilon})^d + 1)$ for any $\epsilon > 0$. Notice that if setting $\epsilon = 2d$, the robustness ratio is linearly dependent on $d$. When $d = 2$, our algorithm is $(1 + \epsilon)$-consistent and $(\epsilon(1 + \frac{2}{\epsilon})^2 + 1)$-robust, this matches the previous work [4] for 2-directional cow path which is shown to be Pareto optimal.

For online multi-dimensional knapsack cover (MD knapsack cover for short), we show that the problem is a special case of OSEP. Thus, we can directly get a worst-case algorithm and learning-augmented algorithm by setting the penalty factor $\gamma = 0$ (Corollary 1 and Corollary 2).

In Sect. 4, we verify the theory empirically. The experiments show that our algorithms can achieve desirable empirical trade-offs between consistency and robustness. We also discuss the learnability of our prediction. Say that $\mathbf{t}$ is drawn from an unknown distribution $\mathcal{D}$. Then we prove that only a small (polynomial in $d$) number of samples need to be drawn from $\mathcal{D}$ to efficiently learn $\mathbf{t}'$ that minimizes the expected prediction error. Due to space, this part and some proofs are omitted and can be found in the full version.

## 2    Algorithms and Analysis

In this section, we start by introducing an algorithmic framework that is used in our learning-augmented algorithms (Sect. 2.1). Then in Sect. 2.2, we discuss worst-case algorithms for OSEP as a warm-up. Finally, we show the main algorithmic results—the learning-augmented algorithms in Sect. 2.3.

**Algorithm 1.** Algorithmic Framework for Online State Exploration (Budget Solver)

---

**Input:** A target point $\mathbf{t}$; a budget sequence $\mathcal{B} = (B_1, B_2, \ldots)$; the cost function $c(\cdot, \cdot)$.
**Output:** A feasible solution $\mathcal{S}$.
1: $\mathcal{S} \leftarrow \{\mathbf{0}\}$; $k \leftarrow 0$; $\mathbf{u} \leftarrow \mathbf{0}$.
2: **while** the target point $\mathbf{t}$ has not been dominated **do**
3:    $\phi(k) \leftarrow 1 + k \pmod{d}$. // the current dimension
4:    Find the maximum $x$ such that $c(\mathbf{0}, x\mathbf{e}_{\phi(k)}) \leq B_k$.
5:    Move to $\mathbf{v}$, where $v_{\phi(k)} = x$ and $v_i = u_i$ for all $i \neq \phi(k)$.
6:    $\mathcal{S} \leftarrow \mathcal{S} \cup \{\mathbf{v}\}$; $\mathbf{u} \leftarrow \mathbf{v}$; $k \leftarrow k + 1$.
7: **end while**
8: **return** Solution $\mathcal{S}$.

---

## 2.1   Algorithmic Intuition and Framework

The main difficulty of online state exploration is that the algorithm has very little information available. Even if the algorithm arrives at a state with only one dimension's entry smaller than the target, the algorithm only knows that the current state is yet to dominate the target.

Thus, there is a trade-off between distance and penalty costs. If the algorithm increases all entries equally when deciding the next state, the total distance cost may be far from optimal because perhaps only one entry needs to increase. We call such a move a "big move" because all entries increase. Contrarily, if the algorithm explores one dimension at a time, this will control the distance cost, but the penalty is large. We refer to this strategy as a "small move" as only one entry increases.

*Algorithmic Intuition.* We will say that two states are *adjacent* if they differ in only one coordinate. Formally, $\mathbf{u}$ and $\mathbf{v}$ are adjacent if there exists a unique $r \in [d]$ such that $u_r \neq v_r$ and $u_i = v_i$ for all $i \neq r$. We first observe the following property for two adjacent states.

**Proposition 1.** *For any two adjacent states* $\mathbf{u}$ *and* $\mathbf{v}$, $c(\mathbf{u}, \mathbf{v}) \leq \gamma \cdot ||\tilde{\mathbf{u}}||_\infty + ||\tilde{\mathbf{v}}||_\infty$.

We can prove Proposition 1 easily by the monotonicity and submodularity. The proof is omitted in this version. We will use this property to carefully choose the next state each time so that the cost can be bounded. To see some intuition, say $||\tilde{\mathbf{u}}||_\infty$ doubles each time the algorithm moves. Then it is the case that the algorithm's total moving cost is bounded by $(2 + 2\gamma)$ times $||\tilde{\mathbf{u}}||_\infty$ where $\tilde{\mathbf{u}}$ is the final state the algorithm visits. If this cost is bounded by optimal, then we can bound the overall competitive ratio. Thus, we have the following framework.

*Algorithmic Framework.* Now, we present an algorithmic framework (Algorithm 1) that will be of use in several algorithms developed in this paper. The algorithm runs in rounds. Inspired by the intuition above, our algorithm will make a small move in each round. Based on the state selected by the previous round, the algorithm will increase the coordinate value of this state in a particular dimension. The key to the algorithm is selecting an upper bound of the moving cost (budget) each time the algorithm moves states. Once the budget is determined, Algorithm 1 will increase the coordinate value of the chosen dimension as much as possible under the budget constraint.

The framework specifies a family of algorithms depending on different budget sequences. All our algorithms will employ this algorithmic framework to obtain a feasible solution, and as such, the budget sequence is the main remaining technical challenge.

Our algorithms compute the budget sequence online, and together with Algorithm 1 this yields a fully online algorithm. We use BUDSOL($\mathcal{B}$) to denote the solution returned by Algorithm 1 when the budget sequence is $\mathcal{B}$.

## 2.2 Warm-Up: Worst Case Algorithms

For the completeness of the story, before stating the learning-augmented algorithm, we give a quick discussion of worst-case algorithms for the new defined problem. The deterministic worst-case algorithm is technically simple: we set the budget sequence $\mathcal{B}$ to be an infinite geometric progression, i.e., $\mathcal{B} = \{1, a, a^2, \ldots\}$, where $a$ is a parameter we can choose. The pseudo-code is omitted in this version. Use $\mathcal{A}$ to denote this algorithm.

**Theorem 1.** *Given an arbitrary target point* $\mathbf{t}$, *use* ALG($\mathbf{t}$) *to denote the objective value of* $\mathcal{A}$. *We have* ALG($\mathbf{t}$) $\leq ((\gamma + 1)ed + e) \cdot$ OPT($\mathbf{t}$), *where* $d$ *is the number of dimensions,* $\gamma \geq 0$ *is the penalty factor and* $e$ *is the base of natural logarithm.*

We only present the statements of two key lemmas in this version.

**Lemma 1.** *Given an arbitrary target point* $\mathbf{t}$, *algorithm* $\mathcal{A}$ *terminates in at most* $d + \lceil \log_a(\text{OPT}(\mathbf{t})) \rceil$ *iterations, where* OPT($\mathbf{t}$) *is the optimal cost.*

**Lemma 2.** *The competitive ratio of algorithm* $\mathcal{A}$ *is at most* $\left( \frac{a+\gamma}{a-1} \cdot a^d \right)$.

The first lemma shows that $\mathcal{A}$ terminates in a polynomial number of iterations. Then, by setting $a = 1 + 1/d$ in the second lemma, Theorem 1 can be proved. Notice that $1 + 1/d$ is not the best choice of $a$. By taking the derivation, one can find a better multiplier $a$.

## 2.3 Algorithms Leveraging Predictions

This section gives the learning-augmented algorithm where the algorithm is given an erroneous prediction of the target state. Given an arbitrary target point $\mathbf{t}$, let $\mathbf{t}' = (t'_1, \ldots, t'_d)$ be its predicted target point. We use a natural error measurement as the prediction error, namely the infinity norm. The formal definition can be found in Definition 1.

**Definition 1.** *(Prediction Error) Given a target point* $\mathbf{t}$ *and its prediction* $\mathbf{t}'$, *define the prediction error* $\eta(\mathbf{t}, \mathbf{t}') := ||\tilde{\mathbf{t}} - \tilde{\mathbf{t}}'||_\infty$.

When the parameter is clear in the context, write $\eta(\mathbf{t}, \mathbf{t}')$ as $\eta$ for short. We first prove a lower bound of the consistency ratio and then show that our algorithms can approach the bound arbitrarily close.

### Lower Bound of Consistency

We give an $\Omega(\gamma d)$ lower bound for (randomized) learning-augmented algorithms.

**Theorem 2.** *In online state exploration, given the predicted target, for any algorithm with a bounded robustness ratio, the consistency ratio is at least* $(1+\gamma)d-\gamma$.

The main idea of this proof is to construct a specific instance such that the moving cost between two non-adjacent states is infinitely large. Such an instance will force any algorithm to move to the adjacent state in each step. Otherwise, it cannot obtain a bounded robustness ratio. Thus, any algorithm has to go through the dimensions one by one and visit many incorrect states, which will incur an $\Omega(\gamma d)$ penalty cost.

*Remark.* Note that the lower bound $\Omega(\gamma d)$ also applies to traditional worst-case algorithms since a worst-case algorithm is essentially a special learning-augmented algorithm whose consistency and robustness are the same. From the proof sketch of Theorem 2, we see that a big move may make the competitive ratio unbounded. Thus, in our algorithms, only small moves are considered.

### Deterministic Learning-Augmented Algorithm

In this section, we give a deterministic learning-augmented algorithm for OSEP. For notational convenience, use $\psi(\gamma, d) := (1+\gamma)d-\gamma$ to denote the lower bound stated in Theorem 2.

**Theorem 3.** *Given any* $\epsilon > 0$, *there is a deterministic algorithm with a consistency ratio of* $\psi(\gamma, d) \cdot (1 + \epsilon)$ *and a robustness ratio of* $\psi(\gamma, d) \cdot (1 + \epsilon) \cdot$ $\left(1 + \frac{1+2/\epsilon}{d-\gamma/(\gamma+1)}\right)^{2d}$. *The ratio degrades at a rate of* $O(\gamma \epsilon^{-(2d+1)} d^{-(2d-1)})$ *as the error* $\eta$ *increases. Moreover, by setting appropriate parameters, the algorithm can be* $(2(1 + \gamma)d - \gamma)$-*consistent and* $(2(1 + \gamma)e^2d - \gamma e^2)$-*robust.*

Notice that for the online bidding problem, we have $\gamma = 1$ and $d = 1$. In this case, the algorithm is $(1 + \epsilon)$-consistent and $O(1/\epsilon^2)$-robust for any $\epsilon > 0$. Later in Sect. 3.1, we will show that by a more careful analysis specific to online bidding (online search), the algorithm obtains a robustness ratio of $O(1/\epsilon)$ when it is $(1+\epsilon)$-consistent, which has been proved to be the best possible trade-off [2].

To prove Theorem 3, we first state a parameterized algorithm, and then show that choosing appropriate parameters gives the claimed ratio. The algorithm is described in Algorithm 2.

The algorithm is parameterized by $a$ and $\theta$, where $a$ is the common ratio of the geometric progression. The parameter $\theta$ can be viewed as the degree of trusting the prediction with smaller values reflecting high confidence in the prediction. Define $\mathcal{B}^1 := \bigcup_{i \in [d-1]} \mathcal{B}_{(i)}$ and $\mathcal{B}^2 := \mathcal{B}_{(d)}$. The budgets in $\mathcal{B}^1$ are computed based on the prediction, while the budgets in $\mathcal{B}^2$ are computed following the manner of the deterministic worst-case algorithm.

Intuitively, $\mathcal{B}^1$ and $\mathcal{B}^2$ are two different types of budget sequences, and thus, they split Algorithm 2 into two different phases. In the first phase, Algorithm 2 is indicated by the predicted target state. Informally, the algorithm will utilize each coordinate of the predicted state to compute a initial budget (line 1 of Algorithm 2). Thus, there are $d$ initial budgets, one for each dimension. Starting from the smallest initial budget, Algorithm 2 grows the budget in a geometric manner until Algorithm 2 reaches a state that dominates the current coordinate of the predicted target point. At the end of each round, Algorithm 2 carefully choose the next initial budget. If the actual target state is still not dominated by Algorithm 2 at the end of $\mathcal{B}_{(d-1)}$, the algorithm will be switched to the traditional online deterministic algorithm and grow the budget in a pure geometric manner.

---

**Algorithm 2.** Deterministic Learning-Augmented Algorithm for Online State Exploration

---

**Input:** Parameter $a > 1$ and $\theta \in (0, 1]$; the predicted target point $\mathbf{t}'$; the cost function $c(\cdot, \cdot)$.

**Output:** A feasible solution $\mathcal{S}$.

1: $\forall j \in [d]$, compute the unique $r_j \in [-1, 0)$ such that $(r_j + z_j)d = T'_j + \theta d$ for some integer $z_j$, where $T'_j = \log_a(\tilde{t}'_j)$.
2: Reindex dimensions in the non-decreasing order of $r_j$.
3: $k \leftarrow 0; p \leftarrow 1; q \leftarrow 1;$
4: $B_0 \leftarrow a^{r_1 d}; \mathcal{B}_{(1)}, \ldots, \mathcal{B}_{(d)} \leftarrow \emptyset.$
5: **while** $q < d$ **do**
6:     $\phi(k) \leftarrow 1 + k \pmod{d}$. // the current dimension
7:     **if** $B_k \leq a^{T'_q + \theta d}$ **then**
8:         $\mathcal{B}_{(q)} \leftarrow \mathcal{B}_{(q)} \cup \{B_k\}; B_{k+1} \leftarrow B_k \cdot a.$
9:     **else**
10:         $q \leftarrow q + 1.$
11:         **if** $B_k/a < a^{T'_q + \theta d}$ **then**
12:             $B_k \leftarrow B_k \cdot a^{(r_q - r_p)d}; p \leftarrow q.$
13:         **end if**
14:         $\mathcal{B}_{(q)} \leftarrow \mathcal{B}_{(q)} \cup \{B_k/a\}; B_{k+1} \leftarrow B_k.$
15:     **end if**
16:     $k \leftarrow k + 1.$
17: **end while**
18: Let $\mathcal{B}_{(d)}$ be the infinite geometric progression $\{B_k, B_k \cdot a, B_k \cdot a^2, \ldots\}$.
19: $\mathcal{B} \leftarrow \mathcal{B}_{(1)} \cup \ldots \cup \mathcal{B}_{(d)}.$
20: $\mathcal{S} \leftarrow \text{BUDSOL}(\mathcal{B}).$
21: **return** Solution $\mathcal{S}$.

---

The algorithm is a bit subtle. So we first give two observations to help to understand why we design $\mathcal{B}$ in this way.

**Observation 1.** *For any $q \in [d]$, $\mathcal{B}_{(q)}$ contains at least one value and is a geometric sequence with a common ratio $a$.*

**Observation 2.** *For any $q \in [d-1]$, let $B_k$ and $B_{k+1}$ be the last term in $\mathcal{B}_{(q)}$ and the first term in $\mathcal{B}_{(q+1)}$ respectively. We have $B_k \leq B_{k+1}$.*

The first observation is because if $q$ increases by 1 in an iteration, we always add a budget into $\mathcal{B}_{(q)}$, while if $q$ does not increase, the budget added in that iteration must be $a$ times the budget added in the previous iteration. The second observation is due to $r_q \leq r_{q+1}$ for any $q \in [d-1]$. When $q$ increases, the added budget either remains the same or increases by a factor $a^{(r_q - r_p)d} \geq 1$. According to the two observations, if we remove the last term of each $\mathcal{B}_{(q)}$ ($q \in [d-1]$) from $\mathcal{B}$, we can round up each remaining term in $\{\mathcal{B}_{(q)}\}_{q \in [d-1]}$ such that the sequence becomes a geometric progression with common ratio $a$. Denote such a sequence by $\mathcal{B}'$. Note that the increase rate of these rounded terms is at most $a^d$ because $|r_j - r_i| \leq 1$ for any $i, j$.

Now we are ready to analyze the algorithm. We first prove that the algorithm always terminates in a polynomial number of iterations.

**Lemma 3.** *Algorithm 2 terminates in at most $3d - 1 + \lceil \log_a(\text{OPT}) \rceil$ iterations.*

*Proof.* Since the last term $\mathcal{B}_{(d)}$ is an infinite geometric progression, we can always find the term $B_h \in \mathcal{B}$ which is the first $B_h \geq \text{OPT}$. Following the proof of Lemma 1, the algorithm terminates within $h + d$ iterations. Now we show that $h \leq 2d - 1 + \lceil \log_a(\text{OPT}) \rceil$.

Due to Observation 1 and Observation 2, $\mathcal{B}$ is a non-decreasing sequence. If removing the last term of $\mathcal{B}_{(q)}$ for each $q \in [d-1]$, the ratio between any two neighboring budgets in the new sequence is at least $a$. Observing that the initial budget is at least $a^{-d}$, the index of $B_h$ in the new sequence is at most $d + \lceil \log_a(\text{OPT}) \rceil$. Since the number of removed budgets is at most $d-1$, we have $h \leq 2d - 1 + \lceil \log_a(\text{OPT}) \rceil$, completing the proof. $\square$

We bound the consistency and the robustness of the algorithm by the following two technical lemmas respectively.

**Lemma 4.** *Given any target point $\mathbf{t}$ and its predicted point $\mathbf{t}'$, let $\text{ALG}(\mathbf{t})$ be the solution returned by Algorithm 2. Then, we have*

$$\text{ALG}(\mathbf{t}) \leq f(a) \cdot a^{\theta d} \cdot \left( \text{OPT}(\mathbf{t}) + \frac{a^{2d} - a^{\theta d}}{a^{\theta d} - 1} \cdot \eta \right)$$

*where $a > 1, \theta \in (0,1]$ and $f(a) = \left( (1+\gamma)(\frac{1}{a-1} + d) - \gamma \right)$.*

**Lemma 5.** *Given an arbitrary target point $\mathbf{t}$ and its prediction $\mathbf{t}'$, let $\text{ALG}(\mathbf{t})$ be the solution returned by Algorithm 2. Then, we have: $\text{ALG}(\mathbf{t}) \leq f(a) \cdot a^{2d} \cdot \text{OPT}(\mathbf{t})$. where $a > 1$ is the parameter and $f(a) = \left( (1+\gamma)(\frac{1}{a-1} + d) - \gamma \right)$.*

Lemma 4 and Lemma 5 are sufficient to prove Theorem 3. By setting $a = 1 + \frac{2/\epsilon+1}{d-\gamma/(\gamma+1)}$ and $\theta = \frac{1}{d}\log_a(1 + \epsilon/2)$, the first claimed ratio in Theorem 3 can be proved. The second mentioned ratio is obtained by setting $a = 1 + 1/d$ and $\theta \to 0$.

*Remark for The Randomized Learning-Augmented Algorithm.* Note that we can also use the randomized technique to improve the competitive ratio in the learning-augmented setting. For Algorithm 2 with any $\epsilon > 0$, our randomized algorithm can improve both of the consistency ratio and robustness ratio by at least a factor of $(1 + 2/\epsilon)\ln(1 + \epsilon/2)$.

# 3   Applications of OSEP: Problem-Specific Analyses and Better Results

## 3.1   Online Bidding

We first give a formal reduction from online bidding to online state exploration.

**Theorem 4.** *A c-competitive algorithm for the OSEP implies a c-competitive ratio for online bidding.*

*Proof.* Given an arbitrary instance of online bidding, we construct an instance $I$ of OSEP as follows. There is only one dimension in the instance $I$. In the online bidding problem, every bid $u$ costs $u$. Thus, for every bid $u$ in the online bidding problem, we create a point $\mathbf{u} = u$. Given two points $\mathbf{u}$ and $\mathbf{v}$, we define the distance cost from the point $\mathbf{u}$ to $\mathbf{v}$ as follows: $\mathsf{D}(\mathbf{u}, \mathbf{v}) := |v - u|$. Note that, for an arbitrary point $\mathbf{u}$, the penalty cost $\mathsf{P}(\mathbf{u}) = u$ since there is only one dimension. Let the penalty factor $\gamma = 1$. Thus, the moving cost $c(\mathbf{u}, \mathbf{v}) = |v - u| + u$. Clearly, the distance function defined above satisfies the identity, monotonicity and submodularity property. Thus, the constructed instance is a special case of the online state exploration problem.

Given an arbitrary feasible solution $\mathcal{S}_b = \{v_1, v_2, \ldots, v_k\}$ of the online bidding problem, we can assume that $v_i \leq v_j$ if $i \leq j$ since any reasonable solution will not include a smaller bid in the next iteration. Now, we construct a solution $\mathcal{S}_e = \{\mathbf{v}^{(1)}, \mathbf{v}^{(2)}, \ldots, \mathbf{v}^{(k)}\}$ to the OSEP. Clearly, $\mathcal{S}_e$ is a feasible solution to the OSEP. Let $\mathsf{F}(\mathcal{S}_b)$ be the total cost of the solution $\mathcal{S}_b$. Then, we have $\mathsf{F}(\mathcal{S}_b) = \sum_{i\in[k]} v_i = \mathsf{F}(\mathcal{S}_e)$. Conversely, any reasonable solution $\mathcal{S}_e = \{\mathbf{v}^{(1)}, \mathbf{v}^{(2)}, \ldots, \mathbf{v}^{(k)}\}$ to the constructed online state exploration instance also satisfies $\mathbf{v}^{(i)} \preceq \mathbf{v}^{(j)}$ if $i \leq j$. Thus, $\mathcal{S}_e$ can also be easily converted into a feasible solution to the online bidding problem with the same cost.

Moreover, an arbitrary online bidding instance has the same optimal solution as the constructed online state exploration problem. Thus, a $c$-competitive algorithm for the general online state exploration problem will imply a $c$-competitive algorithm for the online bidding problem.

Due to the reduction, applying Algorithm 2 to online bidding directly gives a competitive ratio claimed in Theorem 3. We further show that a better analysis can be obtained by taking advantage of specific properties of online bidding.

**Theorem 5.** *Given an arbitrary instance of online bidding, if we want a near optimal consistency ratio $(1 + \epsilon)$ for a small $\epsilon > 0$, Algorithm 2 with appropriate parameters can obtain*

$$\text{ALG} \leq \min \left\{ \frac{2(1+\epsilon)^2}{\epsilon(1+\epsilon/2)} \text{OPT}, (1+\epsilon)\left(\text{OPT} + \left(\frac{4}{\epsilon^2} + \frac{2}{\epsilon} - 1\right)\eta\right) \right\}.$$

*On the other hand, if we want an optimal robustness ratio $4^1$, Algorithm 2 with appropriate parameters can obtain*

$$\text{ALG} \leq \min \left\{ 4\text{OPT}, 2(1+\epsilon)\text{OPT} + \left(\frac{1}{\epsilon} - \epsilon\right)\eta \right\}.$$

Since $\frac{2(1+\epsilon)^2}{\epsilon(1+\epsilon/2)} < 5(1 + \frac{1}{\epsilon})$, the trade-off is slightly better than [2]. Moreover, we can also use randomization to further improve the consistent and robust ratio by a factor of at least $(1 + \frac{2}{\epsilon})\ln(1 + \frac{\epsilon}{2})$. In Sect. 4, we show that both of these two algorithms beat the algorithm in [2] in practice. Note that the consistency and robustness trade-off is not unique.

*Extended to Online Search.* Our results for the online bidding problem can be directly extended to the online search problem considered by [2]. Online search is a generalization of online bidding, but we can show it is still captured by our framework. The reduction from online search to OSEP is similar to the reduction for online bidding.

## 3.2   Multi-dimensional Knapsack Cover

Multi-dimensional knapsack cover is a special case of the OSEP when $\gamma = 0$. Intuitively, if the demand vector $\mathbf{h}$ is known in advance, we can solve the multi-dimensional knapsack cover problem by standard dynamic programming (DP). The state in the dynamic programming is defined to be the optimal value of the sub-problem with a demand vector $\mathbf{x} \preceq \mathbf{h}$, which is denoted by $S(\mathbf{x})$. The key idea of the reduction is to map the DP's states to points in the OSEP. For a point $\mathbf{x}$ in online state exploration, we let the distance between $\mathbf{x}$ and the origin $\mathbf{0}$ be $S(\mathbf{x})$. For two different points $\mathbf{x}, \mathbf{y}$, we define their distance as $S(\mathbf{y} - \mathbf{x})$. Then, a $c$-competitive algorithm for the OSEP can imply a $c$-competitive algorithm for multi-dimensional knapsack cover.

**Corollary 1.** *Given an arbitrary instance of multi-dimensional knapsack cover and a target value vector $\mathbf{t}$, there exist a deterministic algorithm such that $\text{ALG}(\mathbf{t}) \leq (ed + e) \cdot \text{OPT}(\mathbf{t})$, where $d$ is the number of dimensions and $e$ is the base of natural logarithmic.*

---

[1] The lower bound 4 of worst case algorithms is the best possible robustness ratio.

**Corollary 2.** *Given any $\epsilon > 0$, there is a deterministic learning-augmented algorithm for multi-dimensional knapsack cover with a consistency ratio of $d(1 + \epsilon)$ and a robustness ratio of $d(1+\epsilon)(1 + \frac{1+2/\epsilon}{d})^{2d}$. The ratio degrades at a rate of $O(\epsilon^{-(2d+1)}d^{-(2d-1)})$ as the error $\eta$ increases. Moreover, by setting appropriate parameters, the algorithm can be $2d$-consistent and $2e^2d$-robust.*

### 3.3  Multi-directional Cow Path

This section shows that online state exploration captures the multi-directional cow path problem. Although both of them travel in a $d$-dimensional space, the reduction is not that obvious, because, in MD cow path, the algorithm can only visit a point with at most one non-zero entry while there is no such restriction for online state exploration.

To build the intuition of the reduction, we define states on MD cow path. Consider an algorithm $\mathcal{A}$ for MD cow path and an arbitrary time $t$ during $\mathcal{A}$'s travel. Define the state that $\mathcal{A}$ reaches at time $t$ to be a $d$-dimensional vector $\mathbf{v}$, where $v_i$ is the furthest point that $\mathcal{A}$ has visited in the $i$-th ray. Such a state definition implies that $\mathcal{A}$ will terminate if and only if it gets to a state $\mathbf{v}$ that dominates the target point $\mathbf{t}$. We can also obtain a better competitive ratio on MD cow path by more careful analysis.

**Corollary 3.** *Given an arbitrary instance of the multi-directions cow path problem and its prediction, for any $\epsilon > 0$, there exists a deterministic algorithm with $(1 + \epsilon)$-consistent and $(\epsilon(1 + \frac{2}{\epsilon})^d + 1)$-robust. When $\epsilon = 2d$, the algorithm is $(2d + 1)$-consistent and $(2ed + 1)$-robust.*

## 4   Experiments

This section shows the empirical performance of our algorithms. We investigate our algorithms' trade-offs between consistency and robustness on online bidding and multi-directional cow path. We only present experimental results for online bidding in this version. The experiments[2] are conducted on a machine running Ubuntu 18.04 with an i7-7800X CPU and 48 GB memory.

*Setup.* We compare the deterministic and randomized algorithm to the algorithm Predict-And-Double (PAD) [2] on the online bidding problem. To show the trade-off between consistency and robustness, we construct a set of $(T, T')$ pairs, where $T$ is the target bidding and $T'$ is the prediction, and test the worst empirical performance of each algorithm when they share the same consistency ratio $1 + \epsilon$. In the experiment, we let $T, T'$ be integers in $[1, 1000]$, thus, there are total $1000^2$ pairs. We investigate 10 different values of $\epsilon = 0.1, 0.2, \ldots, 1.0$.

---

[2] The code is available at https://github.com/Chenyang-1995/Online-State-Exploration.

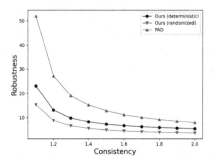

**Fig. 1.** The consistency and robustness trade-offs on online bidding.

*Results.* The results are given in Fig. 1. We see that the experiments corroborate the theory. For each learning-augmented algorithm, the curve in the figure matches our theoretical analysis, i.e., $(1 + \epsilon)$-consistency and $O(\frac{1}{\epsilon})$-robustness. Both of our algorithms obtain better consistency and robustness trade-offs than the baseline. Moreover, given the same consistency ratio, our randomized algorithm always obtains the best robustness ratio.

## 5    Conclusion

This paper introduces the online state exploration problem (OSEP), which generalizes many new and hitherto studied problems and gives online algorithms that can benefit from ML predictions. The problem formulation is distinguished from the previous work for its multidimensional aspect and thus can be used to capture a rich body of applications. Further, our results match or improve upon the best-known results for problems like cow path and online bidding. One interesting open problem is whether it is possible to further improve the trade-off between consistency and robustness for OSEP. Another direction would be to study the OSEP with different types of feedback. For example, if we get notified when the current state dominates the target state on each dimension, can we obtain stronger results? Also, it would be interesting to consider different types of predictions.

**Acknowledgements.** Chenyang Xu was supported in part by Science and Technology Innovation 2030 -"The Next Generation of Artificial Intelligence" Major Project No.2018AAA0100900, and the Dean's Fund of Shanghai Key Laboratory of Trustworthy Computing, East China Normal University. Sungjin Im was supported in part by NSF grants CCF-1844939 and CCF-2121745. Benjamin Moseley was supported in part by a Google Research Award, an Infor Research Award, a Carnegie Bosch Junior Faculty Chair, and NSF grants CCF-2121744 and CCF-1845146. Ruilong Zhang was supported by NSF grant CCF-1844890.

**Ethical Issues**

The current paper is a theoretical work that explores various ideas and concepts related to the topic which aims to strengthen the traditional worst-case algorithm via machine learning advice. As such, there are no ethical issues associated with the research presented here. The paper includes some experiments which aims to verify the efficiency of the proposed algorithms. But this paper does not involve any experiments or studies that involve human and no personal information or data is used in the analysis. Instead, the focus is on developing theoretical models and frameworks that can help to advance our understanding of the subject matter.

# References

1. Ai, L., Wu, X., Huang, L., Huang, L., Tang, P., Li, J.: The multi-shop ski rental problem. In: SIGMETRICS. pp. 463–475. ACM (2014)
2. Anand, K., Ge, R., Kumar, A., Panigrahi, D.: A regression approach to learning-augmented online algorithms. In: NeurIPS, vol. 34 (2021)
3. Anand, K., Ge, R., Panigrahi, D.: Customizing ML predictions for online algorithms. In: ICML. Proceedings of Machine Learning Research, vol. 119, pp. 303–313. PMLR (2020)
4. Angelopoulos, S.: Online search with a hint. In: ITCS. LIPIcs, vol. 185, pp. 51:1–51:16 (2021)
5. Antoniadis, A., Gouleakis, T., Kleer, P., Kolev, P.: Secretary and online matching problems with machine learned advice. In: NeurIPS (2020)
6. Azar, Y.: On-line load balancing. In: Fiat, A., Woeginger, G.J. (eds.) Online Algorithms. LNCS, vol. 1442, pp. 178–195. Springer, Heidelberg (1998). https://doi.org/10.1007/BFb0029569
7. Baeza-Yates, R.A., Culberson, J.C., Rawlins, G.J.E.: Searching in the plane. Inf. Comput. **106**(2), 234–252 (1993)
8. Bamas, É., Maggiori, A., Svensson, O.: The primal-dual method for learning augmented algorithms. In: NeurIPS (2020)
9. Charikar, M., Chekuri, C., Feder, T., Motwani, R.: Incremental clustering and dynamic information retrieval. SIAM J. Comput. **33**(6), 1417–1440 (2004)
10. Chrobak, M., Kenyon, C., Noga, J., Young, N.E.: Incremental medians via online bidding. Algorithmica **50**(4), 455–478 (2008)
11. Demaine, E.D., Fekete, S.P., Gal, S.: Online searching with turn cost. Theor. Comput. Sci. **361**(2–3), 342–355 (2006)
12. Dütting, P., Lattanzi, S., Leme, R.P., Vassilvitskii, S.: Secretaries with advice. In: EC, pp. 409–429. ACM (2021)
13. Epstein, L., Levin, A.: Randomized algorithms for online bounded bidding. Inf. Process. Lett. **110**(12–13), 503–506 (2010)
14. Im, S., Kumar, R., Qaem, M.M., Purohit, M.: Non-clairvoyant scheduling with predictions. In: SPAA, pp. 285–294. ACM (2021)
15. Jiang, Z., Panigrahi, D., Sun, K.: Online algorithms for weighted paging with predictions. In: ICALP, pp. 69:1–69:18 (2020)
16. Kao, M., Ma, Y., Sipser, M., Yin, Y.L.: Optimal constructions of hybrid algorithms. J. Algorithms **29**(1), 142–164 (1998)

17. Kao, M., Reif, J.H., Tate, S.R.: Searching in an unknown environment: an optimal randomized algorithm for the cow-path problem. Inf. Comput. **131**(1), 63–79 (1996)
18. Lattanzi, S., Lavastida, T., Moseley, B., Vassilvitskii, S.: Online scheduling via learned weights. In: SODA, pp. 1859–1877 (2020)
19. Lotker, Z., Patt-Shamir, B., Rawitz, D.: Rent, lease, or buy: randomized algorithms for multislope ski rental. SIAM J. Discret. Math. **26**(2), 718–736 (2012)
20. Lykouris, T., Vassilvitskii, S.: Competitive caching with machine learned advice. In: ICML, Proceedings of Machine Learning Research, vol. 80, pp. 3302–3311. PMLR (2018)
21. Meyerson, A.: The parking permit problem. In: FOCS, pp. 274–284. IEEE Computer Society (2005)
22. Mitzenmacher, M., Vassilvitskii, S.: Algorithms with predictions. In: Beyond the Worst-Case Analysis of Algorithms, pp. 646–662. Cambridge University Press (2020)
23. Purohit, M., Svitkina, Z., Kumar, R.: Improving online algorithms via ML predictions. In: NeurIPS, pp. 9684–9693 (2018)
24. Rohatgi, D.: Near-optimal bounds for online caching with machine learned advice. In: SODA, pp. 1834–1845 (2020)
25. Wang, S., Li, J., Wang, S.: Online algorithms for multi-shop ski rental with machine learned advice. In: NeurIPS (2020)

# Learning Graphical Factor Models
# with Riemannian Optimization

Alexandre Hippert-Ferrer[1](✉)(iD), Florent Bouchard[2](iD), Ammar Mian[3](iD),
Titouan Vayer[4](iD), and Arnaud Breloy[5](iD)

[1] Univ Gustave Eiffel, IGN, ENSG, LASTIG, 77454 Marne-la-Vallée, France
`alexandre.hippert-ferrer@univ-eiffel.fr`
[2] Univ Paris-Saclay, CNRS, CentraleSupélec, Laboratoire des signaux et systèmes,
Gif-sur-Yvette, France
[3] Univ Savoie Mont Blanc, LISTIC, Annecy, France
[4] Univ Lyon, Inria, CNRS, ENS de Lyon, UCB Lyon 1, LIP UMR 5668,
69342 Lyon, France
[5] Univ Paris-Nanterre, LEME, IUT Ville d'Avray, Ville d'Avray, France

**Abstract.** Graphical models and factor analysis are well-established tools in multivariate statistics. While these models can be both linked to structures exhibited by covariance and precision matrices, they are generally not jointly leveraged within graph learning processes. This paper therefore addresses this issue by proposing a flexible algorithmic framework for graph learning under low-rank structural constraints on the covariance matrix. The problem is expressed as penalized maximum likelihood estimation of an elliptical distribution (a generalization of Gaussian graphical models to possibly heavy-tailed distributions), where the covariance matrix is optionally constrained to be structured as low-rank plus diagonal (low-rank factor model). The resolution of this class of problems is then tackled with Riemannian optimization, where we leverage geometries of positive definite matrices and positive semi-definite matrices of fixed rank that are well suited to elliptical models. Numerical experiments on synthetic and real-world data sets illustrate the effectiveness of the proposed approach.

**Keywords:** Graph learning · Low-rank factor models · Riemannian optimization

## 1 Introduction

Graphical models allow us to represent specific correlation structures between any two variables (entries) of multivariate observations. Inferring the topology of this structure directly from the data is referred to as *graph learning*, which has been increasingly leveraged in numerous applications, such as biology [32,49,52], finance [34], or signal processing [23,47].

Within Gaussian graphical models (GGMs), graph learning boils down to the problem of estimating the precision (inverse covariance) matrix of a Gaussian Markov random field [18,27]. In practice, achieving an accurate covariance

© The Author(s), under exclusive license to Springer Nature Switzerland AG 2023
D. Koutra et al. (Eds.): ECML PKDD 2023, LNAI 14172, pp. 349–366, 2023.
https://doi.org/10.1007/978-3-031-43421-1_21

matrix estimation is often a difficult task due to low sample support. Thus, it is common to introduce prior assumptions on the structure of this matrix that guarantee a correct estimation with fewer samples. A popular approach is related to low-rank factorizations, which relies on the assumption that the data is driven by an underlying low-dimensional linear model, corrupted by an independent perturbation. The resulting covariance matrix decomposition then involves a core that is a low-rank positive semi-definite matrix. Such model is ubiquitous in statistics, and for example, at the heart of probabilistic principal component analysis [54], low-rank factor analysis [24, 44, 45], and their many generalizations.

Since GGMs and low-rank factorizations share a common root in structured covariance (or precision) matrix estimation, it appears desirable to leverage both approaches in a unified graph learning formulation. On one hand, linear dimension reduction approaches rely on particular spectral structures that can be beneficial for graph learning [26]. On the other hand, it also opens the way to graph-oriented view of sparse principal component analysis [37, 61]. Though theoretically appealing, such unification is challenging because it formulates optimization problems with objective functions and constraints that apply both on the covariance matrix and its inverse. Thus, deriving single-step learning algorithms for these models has only recently been addressed [8].

In this paper, we propose a new family of methods for graph learning with low-rank constraints on the covariance matrix, hereafter referred to as graphical factor models (GFM). First, we reformulate graph learning as a problem that encompasses both elliptical distributions and low-rank factor models. The main interest of generalizing Gaussian graphical models to elliptical ones is to ensure robustness to underlying heavy-tailed distributions [17, 39, 58, 62]. Moreover, additionally considering low-rank factor models allows for an effective dimensionality reduction. The main novelty of our approach is to tackle the resulting class of constrained and penalized maximum likelihood estimation in a unified way with Riemannian optimization [1, 7]. To do so, we leverage geometries of both the positive definite matrices [4], and positive semi-definite matrices of fixed rank [5, 6] that are well suited to the considered models. The corresponding tools allows us to develop optimization methods that ensure the desired structures for the covariance matrix, thus providing a flexible and numerically efficient framework for learning graphical factor models.

Finally, experiments[1] conducted on synthetic and real-world data sets demonstrate the interest of considering both elliptical distributions and factor model structures in a graph learning process. We observe that the proposed algorithms lead to more interpretable graphs compared to unstructured models. Notably, the factor model approaches compare well with the current state-of-the-art on Laplacian-constrained graph learning methods that require to set the number of components as additional prior information [26, 39]. The interest of our method is twofold: *i*) it requires less supervision to unveil meaningful clusters in the conditional correlation structure of the data; *ii*) the computational bottleneck is

---

[1] The code is available at: https://github.com/ahippert/graphfactormodel.

greatly reduced, as the proposed algorithm iterations only requires the thin-SVD of a low-rank factor, rather than the whole SVD of the Laplacian (or adjacency) matrix.

## 2   Background and Proposed Framework

### 2.1   Gaussian Graphical and Related Models

Gaussian graphical models assume that each observation is a centered multivariate Gaussian random vector $\boldsymbol{x} = [x_1, \ldots, x_p]^\top$ with covariance matrix $\mathbb{E}[\boldsymbol{x}\boldsymbol{x}^\top] = \boldsymbol{\Sigma}$, denoted $\boldsymbol{x} \sim \mathcal{N}(\boldsymbol{0}, \boldsymbol{\Sigma})$. For the corresponding Gaussian Markov random field, an undirected graph is matched to the variables as follows: each variable corresponds to a vertex, and an edge is present between two vertices if the corresponding random variables are conditionally dependent given the others [11,30]. The support of the precision matrix $\boldsymbol{\Theta} = \boldsymbol{\Sigma}^{-1}$ directly accounts for this conditional dependency, since

$$\mathrm{corr}\left[x_q x_\ell | \boldsymbol{x}_{[1,p]\setminus\{q,\ell\}}\right] = -\boldsymbol{\Theta}_{q\ell}/\sqrt{\boldsymbol{\Theta}_{qq}\boldsymbol{\Theta}_{\ell\ell}}. \tag{1}$$

Hence, a non-zero entry $\boldsymbol{\Theta}_{q\ell}$ implies a conditional dependency between the variables $x_q$ and $x_\ell$, underlined by an edge between vertices $q$ and $\ell$ of the graph. Within Gaussian graphical models, graph learning is therefore tied to the problem of estimating the precision matrix $\boldsymbol{\Theta}$ from a set of observations $\{\boldsymbol{x}_i\}_{i=1}^n \in (\mathbb{R}^p)^n$. In order to exhibit such correlation structure, a standard approach is to resort to regularized maximum likelihood estimation, *i.e.*, solving the problem:

$$\underset{\boldsymbol{\Theta} \in \mathcal{S}_p^{++}}{\mathrm{maximize}} \quad \log\det(\boldsymbol{\Theta}) - \mathrm{Tr}\{\boldsymbol{S}\boldsymbol{\Theta}\} - \lambda h(\boldsymbol{\Theta}), \tag{2}$$

where $\boldsymbol{S} = \frac{1}{n}\sum_{i=1}^n \boldsymbol{x}_i \boldsymbol{x}_i^\top$ is the sample covariance matrix, $h$ is a regularization penalty, and $\lambda \in \mathbb{R}^+$ is a regularization parameter. The $\ell_1$-norm if often used as penalty in order to promote a sparse structure in $\boldsymbol{\Theta}$, which is at the foundation of the well-known GLasso algorithm [16,18,27,36]. Many other convex on nonconvex penalties have been considered in this stetting [3,28,46]. Depending on the assumptions, it can also be beneficial to consider penalties that promote certain types of structured sparsity patterns [19,53]. Another main example of structure within the conditional correlations is total positivity, also known as attractive Gaussian graphical models, that assumes $\boldsymbol{\Theta}_{q\ell} \leq 0$, $\forall q \neq \ell$ [15,29]. In attractive Gaussian graphical models, the identifiability of the precision matrix to the graph Laplacian [9], has also attracted recent interest in graph learning [14,26,60].

### 2.2   Elliptical Distributions

A first shortcoming of graph learning as formulated in (2) is its lack of robustness to outliers, or heavy-tailed distributed samples. This is a consequence of the underlying Gaussian assumption, that cannot efficiently describe such data. A possible remedy is to consider a larger family of multivariate distributions. In this context, elliptical distributions [2,22] offer a good alternative, that are well-known to provide robust estimators of the covariance matrix [33,55,59]. In our present context, this framework has been successfully used to extend graphical models [17,39,58,62], as well as low-rank structured covariance matrices models [6,63,65] for corrupted or heavy-tailed data.

A vector is said to follow a centered elliptically symmetric distribution of scatter matrix $\boldsymbol{\Sigma}$ and density generator $g$, denoted $\boldsymbol{x} \sim \mathcal{ES}(\boldsymbol{0}, \boldsymbol{\Sigma}, g)$, if its density has the form

$$f(\boldsymbol{x}) \propto \det(\boldsymbol{\Sigma})^{-1/2} g(\boldsymbol{x}_i^\top \boldsymbol{\Sigma}^{-1} \boldsymbol{x}_i), \tag{3}$$

which yields the negative log-likelihood

$$\mathcal{L}(\boldsymbol{\Sigma}) \propto \frac{1}{n} \sum_{i=1}^n \rho(\boldsymbol{x}_i^\top \boldsymbol{\Sigma}^{-1} \boldsymbol{x}_i) + \frac{1}{2} \log |\boldsymbol{\Sigma}| + \text{const.} \tag{4}$$

for the sample set $\{\boldsymbol{x}_i\}_{i=1}^n$, where $\rho(t) = -\log g(t)$. Notice that using $g(t) = \exp(-t/2)$ allow us to recover the Gaussian case. However, the density generator $g$ enables more flexibility, and notably to encompass many heavy-tailed multivariate distributions. Among popular choices, elliptical distributions include the multivariate $t$-distribution with degree of freedom $\nu > 2$, which is obtained with $g(t) = (1 + t/\nu)^{-\frac{\nu+p}{2}}$. For this distribution, the parameter $\nu$ measures the rate of decay of the tails. The Gaussian case also corresponds to the limit case $\nu \to \infty$.

## 2.3   Low-Rank Factor Models

A second limitation of (2) is that it does not account for other potential structure exhibited by the covariance or precision matrices. This can problematic when the sample support is low ($n \simeq p$, or $n < p$) as the sample covariance matrix is not a reliable estimate in these setups [31,50,57]. In this context, a popular approach consists in imposing low-rank structures on the covariance matrix. These structures arise from the assumption that the data is driven by an underlying low-dimensional linear model, i.e., $\boldsymbol{x} = \boldsymbol{W}\boldsymbol{s} + \boldsymbol{\epsilon}$, where $\boldsymbol{W}$ is a rank-$k$ factor loading matrix, and $\boldsymbol{s} \in \mathbb{R}^k$ and $\boldsymbol{\epsilon} \in \mathbb{R}^p$ are independent random variables. Thus the resulting covariance matrix is of the form $\boldsymbol{\Sigma} \overset{\Delta}{=} \boldsymbol{H} + \boldsymbol{\Psi}$, where $\boldsymbol{H} = \boldsymbol{W}\mathbb{E}[\boldsymbol{s}\boldsymbol{s}^\top]\boldsymbol{W}^\top$ belongs to the set of positive semi-definite matrices of rank $k$, denoted $\mathcal{S}_{p,k}^+ = \{\boldsymbol{\Sigma} \in \mathcal{S}_p, \boldsymbol{\Sigma} \succcurlyeq \boldsymbol{0}, \text{rank}(\boldsymbol{\Sigma}) = k\}$. This model is well known in statistics, and for example, at the core of probabilistic principal component analysis, that assumes $\boldsymbol{\Psi} \propto \boldsymbol{I}_p$ [54]. Also notice that in Laplacian-constrained models, a rank-$k$ precision matrix implies a $(p-k)$-component graph [9]. Hence it is also interesting to leverage such spectral structures from the graph learning perspective [26].

In this paper, we will focus on the low-rank factor analysis models [24,44,45], that consider the general case $\boldsymbol{\Psi} \in \mathcal{D}_p^{++}$, where $\mathcal{D}_p^{++} = \{\boldsymbol{\Sigma} = \text{diag}(\boldsymbol{d}), \boldsymbol{d} \in \mathbb{R}_{+*}^p\}$ denotes the space of positive definite diagonal matrices. Given this model, the covariance matrix belongs to the space of rank-$k$ plus diagonal matrices, denoted as

$$\mathcal{M}_{p,k} = \left\{ \boldsymbol{\Sigma} = \boldsymbol{H} + \boldsymbol{\Psi}, \ \boldsymbol{H} \in \mathcal{S}_{p,k}^+, \boldsymbol{\Psi} \in \mathcal{D}_p^{++} \right\}. \tag{5}$$

Notice that this parameterization reduces the dimension of the estimation problem reduces from $p(p+1)/2$ to $p(k+1) - k(k-3)/2$, which is why it is often used in regimes with few samples, or high dimensional settings.

### 2.4   Learning Elliptical Graphical Factor Models

We cast the problem of graph learning for elliptical graphical factor models as

$$\begin{array}{c} \underset{\boldsymbol{\Sigma} \in \mathcal{S}_p^{++}}{\text{minimize}} \ \mathcal{L}(\boldsymbol{\Sigma}) + \lambda h(\boldsymbol{\Sigma}) \\ \text{subject to } \boldsymbol{\Sigma} \in \mathcal{M}_{p,k}, \end{array} \tag{6}$$

where $\mathcal{L}$ is the negative-log likelihood in (4), and $\mathcal{M}_{p,k}$ is the space of rank-$k$ plus diagonal positive definite matrices in (5). The penalty $h$ is a smooth function that promotes a sparse structure on the graph, and $\lambda \in \mathbb{R}_+$ is a regularization parameter. Although this formulation take into account many options, we focus on the usual element-wise penalty applied to the precision matrix $\boldsymbol{\Theta} = \boldsymbol{\Sigma}^{-1}$, defined as:

$$h(\boldsymbol{\Sigma}) = \sum_{q \neq \ell} \phi([\boldsymbol{\Sigma}^{-1}]_{q\ell}) \tag{7}$$

It is important to notice that the considered optimization framework will require $h$ to be smooth. This is why we presently use a surrogate of the $\ell_1$-norm defined as

$$\phi(t) = \varepsilon \log(\cosh(t/\varepsilon)), \tag{8}$$

with $\varepsilon > 0$ ($\lim_{\varepsilon \to 0} \phi(t)$ yields the $\ell_1$-norm). In practice, we use $\varepsilon = 1e^{-12}$. However, note that the output of the algorithm is not critically sensitive to this parameter: the obtained results were similar for $\varepsilon$ ranging from $1e^{-6}$ to the numerical tolerance.

In conclusion, the problem in (6) accounts for a low-rank structure in a graph learning formulation, which is also expected to be more robust to data following an underlying heavy-tailed distributions. We then introduce four main cases, and their corresponding acronyms:

GGM/GGFM: Gaussian graphical factor models (GGFM) are obtained with the Gaussian log-likelihood, i.e., setting $g(t) = \exp(-t/2)$ in (4). The standard Gaussian graphical models (GGM) as in (2) are recovered when dropping the constraint $\boldsymbol{\Sigma} \in \mathcal{M}_{p,k}$.

EGM/EGFM: elliptical graphical factor models (EGFM) are obtained for the more general case where $\mathcal{L}$ defines a negative log-likelihood of an elliptical distribution. Dropping the constraint $\boldsymbol{\Sigma} \in \mathcal{M}_{p,k}$ also yields a relaxed problem that we refer to as elliptical graphical models (EGM).

---

**Algorithm 1:** Graph learning with elliptical graphical (factor) models

---

**Input**: Data $\{x_i\}_{i=1}^n \in (\mathbb{R}^p)^n$
**Parameters** : GGM/GGFM/EGM/EGFM $\rightarrow$ density generator $g$, rank $k$
                    Regularization parameter $\lambda$ and penalty shape $\phi$
                    Tolerance threshold tol
**Output**: Learned graph adjacency $A$ (Boolean)

**if** $k{=}p$ **then**
> GGM/EGM initialization $\Sigma_0 = \frac{1}{n}\sum_{i=1}^n x_i x_i^\top$
> **for** $t = 0$ **to** *convergence* **do**
>> Compute the Riemannian gradient with (15) and (16)
>> Computes steps $\alpha_t$ and $\beta_t$ with ([20])
>> Update $\Sigma_{t+1}$ with (14) (transport in (12), retraction in (13))

**else**
> GGFM/EGFM initialization
> ($V_0 = k$ leading eigenvectors of $\frac{1}{n}\sum_{i=1}^n x_i x_i^\top$, $\Lambda_0 = I_k$, $\Psi_0 = I_p$)
> **for** $t = 0$ **to** *convergence* **do**
>> Compute the Riemannian gradient with (27)
>> Computes steps $\alpha_t$ and $\beta_t$ with ([20])
>> Update $(V_{t+1}, \Lambda_{t+1}, \Psi_{t+1})$ with (14) transposed to $\mathcal{M}_{p,k}$ (i.e., with transport in (27), retraction in (33))
>
> $\Sigma_{\text{end}} = V_{\text{end}} \Lambda_{\text{end}} V_{\text{end}}^\top + \Psi_{\text{end}}$

Compute $\Theta = \Sigma_{\text{end}}^{-1}$ and conditional correlations matrix $\tilde{\Theta}$ from (1)
Activate edges $(i,j)$ in adjacency $A$ for each $\tilde{\Theta}_{ij} \geq$ tol

---

# 3   Learning Graphs with Riemmanian Optimization

The optimization problem in (6) is non-convex and difficult to address. Indeed, it involves objective functions and constraints that apply on both the covariance matrix and its inverse. One approach to handle these multiple and complex constraints is to resort to variable splitting and alternating direction method of multipliers [25] which has, for example, been considered for Laplacian-constrained models in [39,64]. In this work, we propose a new and more direct approach by harnessing Riemannian optimization [1,7]. Besides being computationally efficient, this solution also has the advantage of not being an approximation of the original problem, nor requiring extra tuning parameters.

For GGM and EGM, the resolution of (6) requires to consider optimization on $\mathcal{S}_p^{++}$. This will be presented in Sect. 3.1, which will serve as both a short introduction to optimization on smooth Riemannian manifold, and as a building block for solving (6) for GGFM and EGFM. For these models, we will derive Riemannian optimization algorithms on $\Sigma \in \mathcal{M}_{p,k}$ in Sect. 3.2, which will be done by leveraging a suitable geometry for this space. The corresponding algorithms are summarized in Algorithm 1.

## 3.1   Learning GGM/EGM: Optimization on $\mathcal{S}_p^{++}$

When relaxing the constraint in (6), the problem still requires to be solved on $\mathcal{S}_p^{++}$. Since $\mathcal{S}_p^{++}$ is open in $\mathcal{S}_p$ the tangent space $T_{\Sigma}\mathcal{S}_p^{++}$ can simply be identified as $\mathcal{S}_p$, for any $\Sigma \in \mathcal{S}_p^{++}$. To be able to perform optimization, the first step is to define a Riemannian metric, $i.e.$, an inner product on this tangent space. In the case of $\mathcal{S}_p^{++}$, the most natural choice is the affine-invariant metric [4,48], that corresponds to the Fisher information metric of the Gaussian distribution and features very interesting properties from a geometrical point of view. It is defined for all $\Sigma \in \mathcal{S}_p^{++}$, $\xi, \eta \in \mathcal{S}_p$ as

$$\langle \xi, \eta \rangle_{\Sigma}^{\mathcal{S}_p^{++}} = \text{tr}(\Sigma^{-1}\xi\Sigma^{-1}\eta). \tag{9}$$

The Riemannian gradient [1] at $\Sigma \in \mathcal{S}_p^{++}$ of an objective function $f : \mathcal{S}_p^{++} \to \mathbb{R}$ is the only tangent vector such that for all $\xi \in \mathcal{S}_p$,

$$\langle \nabla^{\mathcal{S}_p^{++}} f(\Sigma), \xi \rangle_{\Sigma}^{\mathcal{S}_p^{++}} = \mathrm{D} f(\Sigma)[\xi], \tag{10}$$

where $\mathrm{D} f(\Sigma)[\xi]$ denotes the directional derivative of $f$ at $\Sigma$ in the direction $\xi$. The Riemannian gradient $\nabla^{\mathcal{S}_p^{++}} f(\Sigma)$ can also be obtained from the Euclidean gradient $\nabla^{\mathcal{E}} f(\Sigma)$ through the formula

$$\nabla^{\mathcal{S}_p^{++}} f(\Sigma) = \Sigma \,\text{sym}(\nabla^{\mathcal{E}} f(\Sigma))\Sigma, \tag{11}$$

where $\text{sym}(\cdot)$ returns the symmetrical part of its argument. The Riemannian gradient is sufficient in order to define a descent direction of $f$, $i.e.$, a tangent vector inducing a decrease of $f$, hence to define a proper Riemannian steepest descent algorithm. However, if one wants to resort to a more sophisticated optimization algorithm such as conjugate gradient or BFGS, vector transport [1] is required to transport a tangent vector from one tangent space to another. In the case of $\mathcal{S}_p^{++}$, we can employ the most natural one, $i.e.$, the one corresponding to the parallel transport associated with the affine-invariant metric [21]. The transport of the tangent vector $\xi$ of $\Sigma$ onto the tangent space of $\bar{\Sigma}$ is given by

$$T_{\Sigma \to \bar{\Sigma}}^{\mathcal{S}_p^{++}}(\xi) = (\bar{\Sigma}\Sigma^{-1})^{1/2}\xi(\Sigma^{-1}\bar{\Sigma})^{1/2}. \tag{12}$$

Now that we have all the tools needed to obtain a proper descent direction of some objective function $f$, it remains to be able to get from the tangent space back onto the manifold $\mathcal{S}_p^{++}$. This is achieved by means of a retraction map. The best solution on $\mathcal{S}_p^{++}$ in order to ensure numerical stability while taking into account the chosen geometry is

$$R_{\Sigma}^{\mathcal{S}_p^{++}}(\xi) = \Sigma + \xi + \frac{1}{2}\xi\Sigma^{-1}\xi. \tag{13}$$

This retraction corresponds to a second order approximation of the geodesics of $\mathcal{S}_p^{++}$ [21], which generalize the concept of straight lines for a manifold. We now have all the necessary elements to perform the optimization of $f$ on $\mathcal{S}_p^{++}$. For instance, the sequence of iterates $\{\boldsymbol{\Sigma}_t\}$ and descent directions $\{\boldsymbol{\xi}_t\}$ generated by a Riemannian conjugate gradient algorithm is

$$
\begin{aligned}
\boldsymbol{\Sigma}_{t+1} &= R_{\boldsymbol{\Sigma}_t}^{\mathcal{S}_p^{++}}(\boldsymbol{\xi}_t) \\
\boldsymbol{\xi}_t &= \alpha_t(-\nabla^{\mathcal{S}_p^{++}} f(\boldsymbol{\Sigma}_t) + \beta_t T_{\boldsymbol{\Sigma}_{t-1} \to \boldsymbol{\Sigma}_t}^{\mathcal{S}_p^{++}}(\boldsymbol{\xi}_{t-1})),
\end{aligned}
\tag{14}
$$

where $\alpha_t$ is a stepsize that can be computed through a linesearch [1] and $\beta_t$ can be computed using the rule in [20].

From there, to obtain a specific algorithm that solves (6) on $\mathcal{S}_p^{++}$, it only remains to provide the Riemannian gradients of the negative log-likelihood $\mathcal{L}$ and penalty $h$. The Riemannian gradient of $\mathcal{L}$ at $\boldsymbol{\Sigma} \in \mathcal{S}_p^{++}$ is

$$
\nabla^{\mathcal{S}_p^{++}} \mathcal{L}(\boldsymbol{\Sigma}) = \frac{1}{2}\boldsymbol{\Sigma} - \frac{1}{2n}\sum_i u(\boldsymbol{x}_i^\top \boldsymbol{\Sigma}^{-1} \boldsymbol{x}_i)\boldsymbol{x}_i \boldsymbol{x}_i^\top,
\tag{15}
$$

where $u(t) = -2g'(t)/g(t)$. For the Gaussian distribution, we have $u(t) = 1$. For the $t$-distribution with degree of freedom $\nu$, we have $u(t) = (\nu + p)/(\nu + t)$. Concerning $h$, the $q\ell$ element of its Riemannian gradient at $\boldsymbol{\Sigma} \in \mathcal{S}_p^{++}$ is

$$
[\nabla^{\mathcal{S}_p^{++}} h(\boldsymbol{\Sigma})]_{q\ell} = \begin{cases} 0 & \text{if } q = \ell \\ \phi'([\boldsymbol{\Sigma}^{-1}]_{q\ell}) & \text{if } q \neq \ell, \end{cases}
\tag{16}
$$

where $\phi'(t) = \tanh(t/\varepsilon)$. In the next section, the Euclidean gradients of $\mathcal{L}$ and $h$ in $\mathcal{S}_p^{++}$ are used. They are easily obtained from (11) and by noticing that the Euclidean gradient is already symmetric.

## 3.2  Learning GGFM/EGFM: Optimization on $\mathcal{M}_{p,k}$

When considering the factor model, we aim at finding a structured matrix $\boldsymbol{\Sigma}$ in $\mathcal{M}_{p,k}$, which is a smooth submanifold of $\mathcal{S}_p^{++}$. The Riemannian geometry of $\mathcal{M}_{p,k}$ is not straightforward. In fact, defining an adequate geometry for low-rank matrices is a rather difficult task and, while there were many attempts, see e.g., [5,6,35,38,40,56], no perfect solution has been found yet. Here, we choose the parametrization considered in [5,6,38]. From a geometrical perspective, the novelty here is to adopt the particular structure of $\mathcal{M}_{p,k}$, i.e., by combining a low-rank positive semi-definite matrix and a diagonal positive definite matrix. Each of the two manifolds of this product are well-known and the proofs of the following can easily be deduced from the proofs in [6]. All $\boldsymbol{\Sigma} \in \mathcal{M}_{p,k}$ can be written as

$$
\boldsymbol{\Sigma} = \boldsymbol{V}\boldsymbol{\Lambda}\boldsymbol{V}^\top + \boldsymbol{\Psi},
\tag{17}
$$

where $\boldsymbol{V} \in \mathrm{St}_{p,k} = \{\boldsymbol{V} \in \mathbb{R}^{p\times k} : \boldsymbol{V}^\top \boldsymbol{V} = \boldsymbol{I}_k\}$ (Stiefel manifold of $p \times k$ orthogonal matrices), $\boldsymbol{\Lambda} \in \mathcal{S}_k^{++}$ and $\boldsymbol{\Psi} \in \mathcal{D}_p^{++}$. Let $\mathcal{N}_{p,k} = \mathrm{St}_{p,k} \times \mathcal{S}_k^{++} \times \mathcal{D}_p^{++}$ and

$$
\begin{aligned}
\varphi: \quad & \mathcal{N}_{p,k} \to \mathcal{S}_p^{++} \\
& (\boldsymbol{V}, \boldsymbol{\Lambda}, \boldsymbol{\Psi}) \mapsto \boldsymbol{V}\boldsymbol{\Lambda}\boldsymbol{V}^\top + \boldsymbol{\Psi}.
\end{aligned}
\tag{18}
$$

It follows that $\mathcal{M}_{p,k} = \varphi(\mathcal{N}_{p,k})$. Therefore, to solve (6) on $\mathcal{M}_{p,k}$, one can exploit $\varphi$ and solve it on $\mathcal{N}_{p,k}$. However, $\mathcal{N}_{p,k}$ contains invariance classes with respect to $\varphi$, that is for any $\boldsymbol{O} \in \mathcal{O}_k$ (orthogonal group with $k \times k$ matrices),

$$\varphi(\boldsymbol{VO}, \boldsymbol{O}^\top \boldsymbol{\Lambda O}, \boldsymbol{\Psi}) = \varphi(\boldsymbol{V}, \boldsymbol{\Lambda}, \boldsymbol{\Psi}). \tag{19}$$

As a consequence, the space that best corresponds to $\mathcal{M}_{p,k}$ is the quotient manifold $\mathcal{N}_{p,k}/\mathcal{O}_k$ induced by equivalence classes on $\mathcal{N}_{p,k}$

$$\pi(\boldsymbol{V}, \boldsymbol{\Lambda}, \boldsymbol{\Psi}) = \{(\boldsymbol{V}, \boldsymbol{\Lambda}, \boldsymbol{\Psi}) * \boldsymbol{O} : \boldsymbol{O} \in \mathcal{O}_k\}, \tag{20}$$

where $(\boldsymbol{V}, \boldsymbol{\Lambda}, \boldsymbol{\Psi}) * \boldsymbol{O} = (\boldsymbol{VO}, \boldsymbol{O}^\top \boldsymbol{\Lambda O}, \boldsymbol{\Psi})$. To efficiently solve an optimization problem on $\mathcal{M}_{p,k}$ with the chosen parametrization, we thus need to consider the quotient $\mathcal{N}_{p,k}/\mathcal{O}_k$. In practice, rather than dealing with the quite abstract manifold $\mathcal{N}_{p,k}/\mathcal{O}_k$ directly, we will manipulate objects in $\mathcal{N}_{p,k}$, implying that the different points of an equivalence class (20) are, in fact, one and only point.

Our first task is to provide the tangent space of $\theta = (\boldsymbol{V}, \boldsymbol{\Lambda}, \boldsymbol{\Psi}) \in \mathcal{N}_{p,k}$. It is obtained by aggregating tangent spaces $T_V \mathrm{St}_{p,k}$, $T_\Lambda \mathcal{S}_k^{++}$ and $T_\Psi \mathcal{D}_p^{++}$, i.e.,

$$T_\theta \mathcal{N}_{p,k} = \{(\boldsymbol{\xi}_V, \boldsymbol{\xi}_\Lambda, \boldsymbol{\xi}_\Psi) \in \mathbb{R}^{p \times k} \times \mathcal{S}_k \times \mathcal{D}_p : \boldsymbol{V}^\top \boldsymbol{\xi}_V + \boldsymbol{\xi}_V^\top \boldsymbol{V} = \boldsymbol{0}\}. \tag{21}$$

Then, we define a Riemannian metric on $\mathcal{N}_{p,k}$. It needs to be invariant along equivalence classes, i.e., for all $\theta \in \mathcal{N}_{p,k}$, $\xi, \eta \in T_\theta \mathcal{N}_{p,k}$ and $\boldsymbol{O} \in \mathcal{O}_k$

$$\langle \xi, \eta \rangle_\theta^{\mathcal{N}_{p,k}} = \langle \xi * \boldsymbol{O}, \eta * \boldsymbol{O} \rangle_{\theta * \boldsymbol{O}}^{\mathcal{N}_{p,k}}. \tag{22}$$

In this work, the Riemannian metric $\mathcal{N}_{p,k}$ is chosen as the sum of metrics on $\mathrm{St}_{p,k}$, $\mathcal{S}_k^{++}$ and $\mathcal{D}_p^{++}$. The metric on $\mathrm{St}_{p,k}$ is the so-called canonical metric [13], which yields the simplest geometry of $\mathrm{St}_{p,k}$. The metrics on $\mathcal{S}_k^{++}$ and $\mathcal{D}_p^{++}$ are the affine-invariant ones. Hence, our chosen metric on $\mathcal{N}_{p,k}$ is

$$\langle \xi, \eta \rangle_\theta^{\mathcal{N}_{p,k}} = \mathrm{tr}(\boldsymbol{\xi}_V^\top (\boldsymbol{I}_p - \frac{1}{2}\boldsymbol{V}\boldsymbol{V}^\top)\boldsymbol{\eta}_V) + \mathrm{tr}(\boldsymbol{\Lambda}^{-1}\boldsymbol{\xi}_\Lambda \boldsymbol{\Lambda}^{-1}\boldsymbol{\eta}_\Lambda) + \mathrm{tr}(\boldsymbol{\Psi}^{-2}\boldsymbol{\xi}_\Psi \boldsymbol{\eta}_\Psi). \tag{23}$$

At $\theta \in \mathcal{N}_{p,k}$, $T_\theta \mathcal{N}_{p,k}$ contains tangent vectors inducing a move along the equivalence class $\pi(\theta)$. In our setting, these directions are to be eliminated. They are contained in the so-called vertical space $\mathcal{V}_\theta$, which is the tangent space $T_\theta \pi(\theta)$ to the equivalence class. In our case, it is

$$\mathcal{V}_\theta = \{(\boldsymbol{V\Omega}, \boldsymbol{\Lambda\Omega} - \boldsymbol{\Omega\Lambda}, \boldsymbol{0}) : \boldsymbol{\Omega} \in \mathcal{S}_k^\perp\}, \tag{24}$$

where $\mathcal{S}_k^\perp$ denotes the vector space of skew-symmetric matrices. Now that the unwanted vectors have been identified, we can deduce the ones of interest: they are contained in the orthogonal complement of $\mathcal{V}_\theta$ according to metric (23). This space is called the horizontal space $\mathcal{H}_\theta$ and is equal to

$$\mathcal{H}_\theta = \{\xi \in T_\theta \mathcal{N}_{p,k} : \boldsymbol{V}^\top \boldsymbol{\xi}_V = 2(\boldsymbol{\Lambda}^{-1}\boldsymbol{\xi}_\Lambda - \boldsymbol{\xi}_\Lambda \boldsymbol{\Lambda}^{-1})\}. \tag{25}$$

The Riemannian gradient of an objective function $\bar{f}$ on $\mathcal{N}_{p,k}$ is defined through the chosen metric as for $\mathcal{S}_p^{++}$ in (10). Again, it is possible to obtain the Riemannian gradient $\nabla^{\mathcal{N}_{p,k}} \bar{f}(\theta)$ on $\mathcal{N}_{p,k}$ from the Euclidean one $\nabla^{\mathcal{E}} \bar{f}(\theta)$. This is achieved by

$$\nabla^{\mathcal{N}_{p,k}} \bar{f}(\theta) = (\boldsymbol{G_V} - \boldsymbol{V G_V^\top V}, \boldsymbol{\Lambda G_\Lambda \Lambda}, \boldsymbol{\Psi}^2 \, \mathrm{ddiag}(\boldsymbol{G_\Psi})), \qquad (26)$$

where $\nabla^{\mathcal{E}} \bar{f}(\theta) = (\boldsymbol{G_V}, \boldsymbol{G_\Lambda}, \boldsymbol{G_\Psi})$ and $\mathrm{ddiag}(\cdot)$ cancels the off-diagonal elements of its argument. Furthermore, since the objective functions we are interested in are invariant along equivalence classes (20), their Riemannian gradient is naturally on the horizontal space $\mathcal{H}_\theta$ and we can use it directly. In this work, our focus is objective functions $\bar{f} : \mathcal{N}_{p,k} \to \mathbb{R}$ such that $\bar{f} = f \circ \varphi$, where $f : \mathcal{S}_p^{++} \to \mathbb{R}$; see (6). Hence, it is of great interest to be able to get the gradient of $\bar{f}$ directly from the one of $f$. The Euclidean gradient $\nabla^{\mathcal{E}} \bar{f}(\theta)$ as a function of the Euclidean gradient $\nabla^{\mathcal{E}} f(\varphi(\theta))$ is

$$\nabla^{\mathcal{E}} \bar{f}(\theta) = (2\nabla^{\mathcal{E}} f(\varphi(\theta)) \boldsymbol{V \Lambda}, \boldsymbol{V}^\top \nabla^{\mathcal{E}} f(\varphi(\theta)) \boldsymbol{V}, \mathrm{ddiag}(\nabla^{\mathcal{E}} f(\varphi(\theta)))). \qquad (27)$$

While it is not necessary for the gradient, the vector transport requires to be able to project elements from the ambient space $\mathbb{R}^{p \times k} \times \mathbb{R}^{k \times k} \times \mathbb{R}^{p \times p}$ onto the horizontal space. The first step is to provide the orthogonal projection from the ambient space onto $T_\theta \mathcal{N}_{p,k}$. For all $\theta \in \mathcal{N}_{p,k}$ and $\xi \in \mathbb{R}^{p \times k} \times \mathbb{R}^{k \times k} \times \mathbb{R}^{p \times p}$

$$P_\theta^{\mathcal{N}_{p,k}}(\xi) = (\boldsymbol{\xi_V} - \boldsymbol{V} \, \mathrm{sym}(\boldsymbol{V}^\top \boldsymbol{\xi_V}), \mathrm{sym}(\boldsymbol{\xi_\Lambda}), \mathrm{ddiag}(\boldsymbol{\xi_\Psi})). \qquad (28)$$

From there we can obtain the orthogonal projection from $T_\theta \mathcal{N}_{p,k}$ onto $\mathcal{H}_\theta$. Given $\xi \in T_\theta \mathcal{N}_{p,k}$, it is

$$\mathcal{P}_\theta^{\mathcal{N}_{p,k}}(\xi) = (\boldsymbol{\xi_V} - \boldsymbol{V \Omega}, \boldsymbol{\xi_\Lambda} + \boldsymbol{\Omega \Lambda} - \boldsymbol{\Lambda \Omega}, \boldsymbol{\xi_\Psi}), \qquad (29)$$

where $\boldsymbol{\Omega} \in \mathcal{S}_k^\perp$ is the unique solution to

$$2(\boldsymbol{\Lambda}^{-1} \boldsymbol{\Omega \Lambda} + \boldsymbol{\Lambda \Omega \Lambda}^{-1}) - 3\boldsymbol{\Omega} = \boldsymbol{V}^\top \boldsymbol{\xi_V} + 2(\boldsymbol{\xi_\Lambda \Lambda}^{-1} + \boldsymbol{\Lambda}^{-1} \boldsymbol{\xi_\Lambda}). \qquad (30)$$

We can now define an adequate vector transport operator. Given $\theta, \bar{\theta} \in \mathcal{N}_{p,k}$ and $\xi \in \mathcal{H}_\theta$, it is simply

$$\mathcal{T}_{\theta \to \bar{\theta}}^{\mathcal{N}_{p,k}}(\xi) = \mathcal{P}_{\bar{\theta}}^{\mathcal{N}_{p,k}}(P_{\bar{\theta}}^{\mathcal{N}_{p,k}}(\xi)). \qquad (31)$$

The last object that we need is a retraction on $\mathcal{N}_{p,k}$. To address the invariance requirement, the retraction needs to be invariant along equivalence classes, i.e., for all $\theta \in \mathcal{N}_{p,k}$, $\xi \in \mathcal{H}_\theta$ and $\boldsymbol{O} \in \mathcal{O}_k$

$$R_{\theta * \boldsymbol{O}}^{\mathcal{N}_{p,k}}(\xi * \boldsymbol{O}) = R_\theta^{\mathcal{N}_{p,k}}(\xi). \qquad (32)$$

In this paper, we choose a second order approximation of geodesics on $\mathcal{N}_{p,k}$ given by

$$R_\theta^{\mathcal{N}_{p,k}}(\xi) = (\mathrm{uf}(\boldsymbol{V} + \boldsymbol{\xi_V}), \boldsymbol{\Lambda} + \boldsymbol{\xi_\Lambda} + \frac{1}{2} \boldsymbol{\xi_\Lambda \Lambda}^{-1} \boldsymbol{\xi_\Lambda}, \boldsymbol{\Psi} + \boldsymbol{\xi_\Psi} + \frac{1}{2} \boldsymbol{\xi_\Psi}^2 \boldsymbol{\Psi}^{-1}), \qquad (33)$$

where uf$(\cdot)$ returns the orthogonal factor of the polar decomposition.

We finally have all the tools needed to solve problem (6) on $\mathcal{N}_{p,k}$ and thus to ensure the structure of $\mathcal{M}_{p,k}$. With all the objects given in this section, many Riemannian optimization algorithms can be employed to achieve the minimization (6), e.g., steepest descent, conjugate gradient or BFGS. In this work, we use in practice a conjugate gradient algorithm.

### 3.3   Algorithms Properties

In terms of convergence, the proposed algorithms inherit the standard properties from the Riemannian optimization framework [1,7]: each iterate satisfies the constraints and ensures a decrease of the objective function until a critical point is reached. Due to the inversion of $\Sigma$ at each step, the computational complexity of the Riemannian conjugate gradient for GGM/EGM is $\mathcal{O}(Tp^3)$, where $T$ is the number of iterations. This complexity has the same dependence in $p$ than GLasso [18] and more recent structured graph learning algorithms [26]. On the other hand, by relying on the structure of the factor models, the Riemannian conjugate gradient for GGFM/EGFM has a $\mathcal{O}(T(pk^2 + k^3))$ computational complexity[2]. As we usually set $k \ll p$, EGM/EGFM are therefore more suited to large dimensions.

While the question of statistical properties will not be explored in this paper, it is also worth mentioning that (6) appears as a regularized maximum likelihood estimation problem for elliptical models. Consequently, the algorithms presented in Algorithm 1 aim at solving a class of maximum a posteriori where a prior related to $\phi$ is set independently on the elements $\Theta_{ij}$. Thus, one can expect good statistical performance if the data falls within the class of elliptical distribution, and especially the algorithms to be robust to a mismatch related to the choice of $g$ [12,33].

## 4   Experiments

### 4.1   Validations on Synthetic Data

Due to space limitations, extensive experiments on synthetic data (ROC curves for edge detection, sensitivity to tuning parameters) are described in the supplementary material available at: https://tinyurl.com/5bv8wkc5. The short conclusions of these experiments are the following: (*i*) the proposed methods compare favorably to existing methods in terms of ROC curves for many underlying random graphs models (Erdős-Rényi, Barabási-Albert, Watts-Strogatz, and random geometric graph), especially when the sample support is limited; (*ii*) For the aforementioned graphs models, the covariance matrix does not always exhibit a low-rank structure, so factor models do not necessarily improve the ROC performance. However it is experienced to be extremely useful when applied to

---

[2] Note that GGFM/EGFM require the computation of the sample covariance matrix (SCM), which is in $\mathcal{O}(np^2)$. EGM/EGFM require to re-compute a weighted SCM at each step (i.e., $\mathcal{O}(Tnp^2)$). However, these operations consist only in matrix multiplications that can be parallelized, thus are not actual computational bottlenecks.

real-world data, as illustrated below (improved clustering capabilities); (iii) As all sparsity-promoting methods, the proposed algorithms require a proper set of the regularization parameter λ. However, the results are not critically sensitive to a change of this value when its order of magnitude is correctly set. The code for these experiments is available at: https://github.com/ahippert/graphfactormodel.

## 4.2   Real-World Data Sets

In this section, the performances of the proposed algorithms (GGM/GGFM and EGM/EGFM) are evaluated on three real-world data sets consisting of (i) animal species; (ii) GNSS time-series; (iii) concepts data. The purpose of the following experiments is to verify whether the factor model, which accounts for potential structures in the covariance matrix, provides an improved version of the learned graph topology. The latter is evaluated using both graph modularity $m$, for which high values measure high separability of a graph into sub-components [41], and visual inspection[3].

*Benchmarks and Parameter Setting:* The proposed algorithms are compared with state-of-the-art approaches for (i) *connected* graphs: GLasso [18], which uses $\ell_1$-norm as a sparse-promoting penalty, and NGL [60], which use a Gaussian Laplacian-constrained model with a concave penalty regularization; (ii) *multi-component* graphs: SGL [26], which constraints the number of graph components in an NGL-type formulation, and StGL [39], which generalizes the above to $t$-distributed data. For a fair comparison, the parameters of all tested algorithms (including competing methods) are tuned to display the best results. Notably, the proposed algorithms are set using Algorithm 1 with a tolerance threshold of tol $= 10^{-2}$. For EGM/EGFM, the chosen density generator relates to a $t$-distribution with degrees of freedom $\nu = 5$. The rank of factor models is chosen manually. Still, the results were similar for other ranks around the set value.

***Animals* Data:** In the *animals* data set [27,42] each node represents an animal, and is associated with binary features (categorical non-Gaussian data) consisting of answers to questions such as "has teeth?", "is poisonous?", *etc.* In total, there are $p = 33$ unique animals and $n = 102$ questions. Figure 1 displays the learned graphs of the *animals* data set. Following the recommendations of [14,26], the SGL algorithm is applied with $\beta = 0.5$ and $\alpha = 0$, GLasso with $\alpha = 0.05$ and the input for SGL and NGL is set to $\frac{1}{n} \sum_i \boldsymbol{x}_i^\top \boldsymbol{x}_i + \frac{1}{3} \boldsymbol{I}_p$. While EGM yields results similar to GLasso, GGM provides a clearer structure with (*trout, salmon*) and (*bee, butterfly*) clustered together. Interestingly, with no assumptions regarding the number of components, GGFM and EGFM reach similar structure and modularity compared to SGL and StGL, that require to set *a priori* the number of components in the graph.

---

[3] Note that there is no available ground truth for these data sets. Hence, to facilitate visualization, each graph node is then clustered into colors using a community detection algorithm based on label propagation [10].

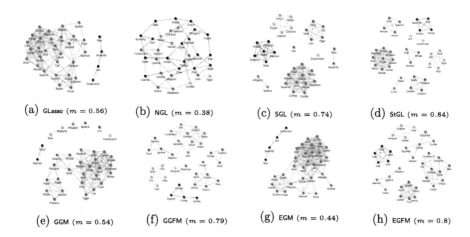

(a) GLasso ($m = 0.56$)    (b) NGL ($m = 0.38$)    (c) SGL ($m = 0.74$)    (d) StGL ($m = 0.84$)

(e) GGM ($m = 0.54$)    (f) GGFM ($m = 0.79$)    (g) EGM ($m = 0.44$)    (h) EGFM ($m = 0.8$)

**Fig. 1.** Learned graphs from the *animals* data set with various algorithms and their associated modularity $m$. For GGFM/EGFM, the rank is 10. For SGL and StGL, the number of components is fixed to 8.

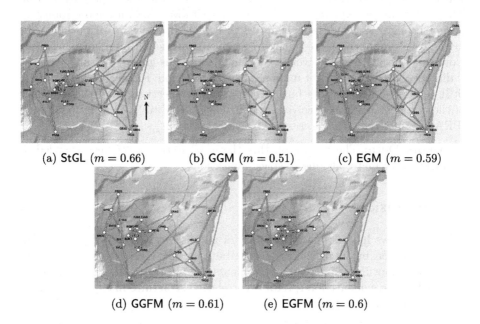

(a) StGL ($m = 0.66$)    (b) GGM ($m = 0.51$)    (c) EGM ($m = 0.59$)

(d) GGFM ($m = 0.61$)    (e) EGFM ($m = 0.6$)

**Fig. 2.** Learned graphs from the GNSS data with the StGL algorithm, our proposed approaches and their associated modularity $m$. For StGL, the number of components is fixed to 3. For GGFM and EGFM, the rank is fixed to 4. For the $t$-distribution, the degrees of freedom are set to $\nu = 5$. The red star in (a) points to the summit crater. ©WEBOBS/IPGP. (Color figure online)

**GNSS Data:** We present an application on Earth surface displacement data collected by a network of Global Navigation Satellite System (GNSS) receivers from the volcanological observatory of Piton de la Fournaise (OVPF-IPGP), located at La Réunion Island. The presented network is composed of $p = 22$ receivers recording daily vertical displacements from January 2014 to March 2017 [51], with a total of $n = 1106$ observations. During this time, vertical displacements induced by volcano eruptions have been recorded by the receivers network, sometimes leading to abrupt motion changes over time. Depending on their spatial position, some receivers might move in a particular direction (upwards or downwards), thus indicating (thin) spatial correlations. Results of the learned graphs are presented in Fig. 2. A general observation is that all graphs are mainly clustered into three groups: two located West (receivers 'GITG', 'FREG', etc.) and East ('BORG', 'FJAG', etc.) of the summit crater, and one extending from lower altitudes to the seashore ('CASG', 'TRCG', etc.). We call these groups *west*, *east* and *low* components, respectively. As described in [43], the four 2015 eruptions (February, May, July and August) are characterized by asymmetric displacement patterns with respect to the North-South eruptive fissures which extend slightly westward from the summit crater. Interestingly, this corresponds to the separation between *west* and *east* graph components, which is best evidenced by factor model-based algorithms, especially EGFM. This result can be explained by the fact that GGFM/EGFM are more robust to abrupt changes in the data as it occurs in heavy-tailed data distributions. The *low* graph component corresponds to receivers with small or no displacement. Note that the 'PRAG' receiver is also included in this group, probably because it did not record a significant motion during this period. Finally, GGM, EGM and StGL lead to similar results but with spurious connections from the west side of the crater to seashore receivers (*e.g.*, from 'BORG' to 'CASG' for StGL, and 'PRAG' connected to some *west* and/or *east* receivers).

**Concepts Data:** The results on this "large $p$" data set [27] are provided as supplementary materials due to space limitations.

## 5 Conclusion

In summary, we have proposed a family of graph learning algorithms in a unified formulation involving elliptical distributions, low-rank factor models, and Riemannian optimization. Our experiments demonstrated that the proposed approaches can evidence interpretable correlation structures in exploratory data analysis for various applications.

**Acknowledgements.** This work was supported by the MASSILIA project (ANR-21-CE23-0038-01) of the French National Research Agency (ANR). We thank V. Pinel for providing us the GNSS data set and D. Smittarello for insightful comments on the GNSS results. We also thank J. Ying for sharing the *concepts* data set.

# References

1. Absil, P.A., Mahony, R., Sepulchre, R.: Optimization Algorithms on Matrix Manifolds. Princeton University Press, Princeton (2008)
2. Anderson, T.W., Fang, K.T.: Theory and applications of elliptically contoured and related distributions (1990)
3. Benfenati, A., Chouzenoux, E., Pesquet, J.C.: Proximal approaches for matrix optimization problems: application to robust precision matrix estimation. Signal Process. **169**, 107417 (2020)
4. Bhatia, R.: Positive Definite Matrices. Princeton University Press, Princeton (2009)
5. Bonnabel, S., Sepulchre, R.: Riemannian metric and geometric mean for positive semidefinite matrices of fixed rank. SIAM J. Matrix Anal. Appl. **31**(3), 1055–1070 (2009)
6. Bouchard, F., Breloy, A., Ginolhac, G., Renaux, A., Pascal, F.: A Riemannian framework for low-rank structured elliptical models. IEEE Trans. Signal Process. **69**, 1185–1199 (2021)
7. Boumal, N.: An introduction to optimization on smooth manifolds. Available online, May 3 (2020)
8. Chandra, N.K., Mueller, P., Sarkar, A.: Bayesian scalable precision factor analysis for massive sparse Gaussian graphical models. arXiv preprint arXiv:2107.11316 (2021)
9. Chung, F.R.: Spectral Graph Theory, vol. 92. American Mathematical Soc. (1997)
10. Cordasco, G., Gargano, L.: Community detection via semi-synchronous label propagation algorithms. In: 2010 IEEE International Workshop on: Business Applications of Social Network Analysis (BASNA), pp. 1–8 (2010)
11. Dempster, A.P.: Covariance selection. Biometrics **28**, 157–175 (1972)
12. Drašković, G., Pascal, F.: New insights into the statistical properties of $M$-estimators. IEEE Trans. Signal Process. **66**(16), 4253–4263 (2018)
13. Edelman, A., Arias, T.A., Smith, S.T.: The geometry of algorithms with orthogonality constraints. SIAM J. Matrix Anal. Appl. **20**(2), 303–353 (1998)
14. Egilmez, H.E., Pavez, E., Ortega, A.: Graph learning from data under Laplacian and structural constraints. IEEE J. Sel. Topics Sig. Process. **11**(6), 825–841 (2017)
15. Fallat, S., Lauritzen, S., Sadeghi, K., Uhler, C., Wermuth, N., Zwiernik, P.: Total positivity in Markov structures. Ann. Stat. **45**, 1152–1184 (2017)
16. Fattahi, S., Sojoudi, S.: Graphical lasso and thresholding: equivalence and closed-form solutions. J. Mach. Learn. Res. **20**, 1–44 (2019)
17. Finegold, M.A., Drton, M.: Robust graphical modeling with $t$-distributions. arXiv preprint arXiv:1408.2033 (2014)
18. Friedman, J., Hastie, T., Tibshirani, R.: Sparse inverse covariance estimation with the graphical lasso. Biostatistics **9**(3), 432–441 (2008)
19. Heinävaara, O., Leppä-Aho, J., Corander, J., Honkela, A.: On the inconsistency of $\ell_1$-penalised sparse precision matrix estimation. BMC Bioinform. **17**(16), 99–107 (2016)
20. Hestenes, M.R., Stiefel, E.: Methods of conjugate gradients for solving linear equation. J. Res. Natl. Bur. Stand. **49**(6), 409 (1952)
21. Jeuris, B., Vandebril, R., Vandereycken, B.: A survey and comparison of contemporary algorithms for computing the matrix geometric mean. Electron. Trans. Numer. Anal. **39**, 379–402 (2012)

22. Kai-Tai, F., Yao-Ting, Z.: Generalized Multivariate Analysis, vol. 19. Science Press Beijing and Springer-Verlag, Berlin (1990)
23. Kalofolias, V.: How to learn a graph from smooth signals. In: Artificial Intelligence and Statistics, pp. 920–929. PMLR (2016)
24. Khamaru, K., Mazumder, R.: Computation of the maximum likelihood estimator in low-rank factor analysis. Math. Program. **176**(1), 279–310 (2019)
25. Kovnatsky, A., Glashoff, K., Bronstein, M.M.: MADMM: a generic algorithm for non-smooth optimization on manifolds. In: Leibe, B., Matas, J., Sebe, N., Welling, M. (eds.) ECCV 2016. LNCS, vol. 9909, pp. 680–696. Springer, Cham (2016). https://doi.org/10.1007/978-3-319-46454-1_41
26. Kumar, S., Ying, J., de Miranda Cardoso, J.V., Palomar, D.P.: A unified framework for structured graph learning via spectral constraints. J. Mach. Learn. Res. **21**(22), 1–60 (2020)
27. Lake, B., Tenenbaum, J.: Discovering structure by learning sparse graphs (2010)
28. Lam, C., Fan, J.: Sparsistency and rates of convergence in large covariance matrix estimation. Ann. Stat. **37**(6B), 4254–4278 (2009)
29. Lauritzen, S., Uhler, C., Zwiernik, P.: Maximum likelihood estimation in Gaussian models under total positivity. Ann. Stat. **47**(4), 1835–1863 (2019)
30. Lauritzen, S.L.: Graphical Models, vol. 17. Clarendon Press, Oxford (1996)
31. Ledoit, O., Wolf, M.: A well-conditioned estimator for large-dimensional covariance matrices. J. Multivar. Anal. **88**(2), 365–411 (2004)
32. Li, H., Gui, J.: Gradient directed regularization for sparse Gaussian concentration graphs, with applications to inference of genetic networks. Biostatistics **7**(2), 302–317 (2006)
33. Maronna, R.A.: Robust $M$-estimators of multivariate location and scatter. Ann. Stat. **4**, 51–67 (1976)
34. Marti, G., Nielsen, F., Bińkowski, M., Donnat, P.: A review of two decades of correlations, hierarchies, networks and clustering in financial markets. In: Nielsen, F. (ed.) Progress in Information Geometry. SCT, pp. 245–274. Springer, Cham (2021). https://doi.org/10.1007/978-3-030-65459-7_10
35. Massart, E., Absil, P.A.: Quotient geometry with simple geodesics for the manifold of fixed-rank positive-semidefinite matrices. Technical Report UCL-INMA-2018.06 (2018)
36. Mazumder, R., Hastie, T.: The graphical lasso: new insights and alternatives. Electron. J. Stat. **6**, 2125 (2012)
37. Meng, Z., Eriksson, B., Hero, A.: Learning latent variable Gaussian graphical models. In: International Conference on Machine Learning, pp. 1269–1277. PMLR (2014)
38. Meyer, G., Bonnabel, S., Sepulchre, R.: Regression on fixed-rank positive semidefinite matrices: a Riemannian approach. J. Mach. Learn. Res. **12**, 593–625 (2011)
39. de Miranda Cardoso, J.V., Ying, J., Palomar, D.: Graphical models in heavy-tailed markets. Adv. Neural. Inf. Process. Syst. **34**, 19989–20001 (2021)
40. Neuman, A.M., Xie, Y., Sun, Q.: Restricted Riemannian geometry for positive semidefinite matrices. arXiv preprint arXiv:2105.14691 (2021)
41. Newman, M.E.J.: Modularity and community structure in networks. Proc. Natl. Acad. Sci. **103**(23), 8577–8582 (2006)
42. Osherson, D.N., Stern, J., Wilkie, O., Stob, M., Smith, E.E.: Default probability. Cogn. Sci. **15**(2), 251–269 (1991)

43. Peltier, A., Froger, J.L., Villeneuve, N., Catry, T.: Assessing the reliability and consistency of InSAR and GNSS data for retrieving 3D-displacement rapid changes, the example of the 2015 Piton de la Fournaise eruptions. J. Volcanol. Geoth. Res. **344**, 106–120 (2017)
44. Robertson, D., Symons, J.: Maximum likelihood factor analysis with rank-deficient sample covariance matrices. J. Multivar. Anal. **98**(4), 813–828 (2007)
45. Rubin, D.B., Thayer, D.T.: EM algorithms for ML factor analysis. Psychometrika **47**(1), 69–76 (1982)
46. Shen, X., Pan, W., Zhu, Y.: Likelihood-based selection and sharp parameter estimation. J. Am. Stat. Assoc. **107**(497), 223–232 (2012)
47. Shuman, D.I., Narang, S.K., Frossard, P., Ortega, A., Vandergheynst, P.: The emerging field of signal processing on graphs: extending high-dimensional data analysis to networks and other irregular domains. IEEE Signal Process. Mag. **30**(3), 83–98 (2013)
48. Skovgaard, L.T.: A Riemannian geometry of the multivariate normal model. Scand. J. Stat. **11**, 211–223 (1984)
49. Smith, S.M., et al.: Network modelling methods for FMRI. Neuroimage **54**(2), 875–891 (2011)
50. Smith, S.T.: Covariance, subspace, and intrinsic Cramèr-Rao bounds. IEEE Trans. Signal Process. **53**(5), 1610–1630 (2005)
51. Smittarello, D., Cayol, V., Pinel, V., Peltier, A., Froger, J.L., Ferrazzini, V.: Magma propagation at Piton de la Fournaise from joint inversion of InSAR and GNSS. J. Geophys. Res. Solid Earth **124**(2), 1361–1387 (2019)
52. Stegle, O., Teichmann, S.A., Marioni, J.C.: Computational and analytical challenges in single-cell transcriptomics. Nat. Rev. Genet. **16**(3), 133–145 (2015)
53. Tarzanagh, D.A., Michailidis, G.: Estimation of graphical models through structured norm minimization. J. Mach. Learn. Res. **18**(1), 1–48 (2018)
54. Tipping, M.E., Bishop, C.M.: Probabilistic principal component analysis. J. Roy. Stat. Soc. Ser. B (Stat. Methodol.) **61**(3), 611–622 (1999)
55. Tyler, D.E.: A distribution-free $M$-estimator of multivariate scatter. Ann. Stat. **15**, 234–251 (1987)
56. Vandereycken, B., Absil, P.A., Vandewalle, S.: A Riemannian geometry with complete geodesics for the set of positive semidefinite matrices of fixed rank. IMA J. Numer. Anal. **33**(2), 481–514 (2012)
57. Vershynin, R.: How close is the sample covariance matrix to the actual covariance matrix? J. Theor. Probab. **25**(3), 655–686 (2012)
58. Vogel, D., Fried, R.: Elliptical graphical modelling. Biometrika **98**(4), 935–951 (2011)
59. Wald, Y., Noy, N., Elidan, G., Wiesel, A.: Globally optimal learning for structured elliptical losses. In: Advances in Neural Information Processing Systems, vol. 32 (2019)
60. Ying, J., de Miranda Cardoso, J.V., Palomar, D.: Nonconvex sparse graph learning under Laplacian constrained graphical model. Adv. Neural. Inf. Process. Syst. **33**, 7101–7113 (2020)
61. Yoshida, R., West, M.: Bayesian learning in sparse graphical factor models via variational mean-field annealing. J. Mach. Learn. Res. **11**, 1771–1798 (2010)
62. Zhang, T., Wiesel, A., Greco, M.S.: Multivariate generalized Gaussian distribution: convexity and graphical models. IEEE Trans. Signal Process. **61**(16), 4141–4148 (2013)
63. Zhao, J., Jiang, Q.: Probabilistic PCA for $t$-distributions. Neurocomputing **69**(16–18), 2217–2226 (2006)

64. Zhao, L., Wang, Y., Kumar, S., Palomar, D.P.: Optimization algorithms for graph Laplacian estimation via ADMM and MM. IEEE Trans. Signal Process. **67**(16), 4231–4244 (2019)
65. Zhou, R., Liu, J., Kumar, S., Palomar, D.P.: Robust factor analysis parameter estimation. In: Moreno-Díaz, R., Pichler, F., Quesada-Arencibia, A. (eds.) EURO-CAST 2019. LNCS, vol. 12014, pp. 3–11. Springer, Cham (2020). https://doi.org/10.1007/978-3-030-45096-0_1

# Recommender Systems

# ConGCN: Factorized Graph Convolutional Networks for Consensus Recommendation

Boyu Li[1], Ting Guo[1(✉)], Xingquan Zhu[2], Yang Wang[1], and Fang Chen[1]

[1] Data Science Institute, University of Technology Sydney, Sydney, Australia
boyu.li@student.uts.edu.au, {ting.guo,yang.wang,fang.chen}@uts.edu.au
[2] Department of Electrical Engineering and Computer Science,
Florida Atlantic University, Boca Raton, USA
xzhu@fau.edu

**Abstract.** An essential weakness of existing personalized recommender systems is that the learning is biased and dominated by popular items and users. Existing methods, particularly graph-based approaches, primarily focus on the "heterogeneous interaction" between user-item, leading to a disproportionately large influence of popular nodes during the graph learning process. Recently, popularity debiasing models have been proposed to address this issue, but they excessively concentrate on considering cause-effect or re-weighting the item/user popularity. These approaches artificially alter the nature of the data, inadvertently downplaying the representation learning of popular items/users. Consequently, balancing the trade-off between global recommendation accuracy and unpopular items/users exposure is challenging.

In this paper, we advocate the concept of "homogeneous effect" from both user and item perspectives to explore the intrinsic correlation and alleviate the bias effects. Our core theme is to simultaneously factorize user-item interactions, user-user similarity, and item-item correlation, thereby learning balanced representations for items and users. To pursue well-balanced representations, we propose a **Con**sensus factorized **G**raph **C**onvolution neural **N**etwork (ConGCN), which leverages graph-based nonlinear representation learning and manifold constraints to regulate the embedding learning. An inherent advantage of ConGCN is its consensus optimization nature, where item-item and user-user relationships ensure that unpopular items are well preserved in the embedding space. The experiments on four real-world datasets demonstrate that ConGCN outperforms existing single-task-oriented methods on two typical tasks with opposite goals (global recommendation and popularity debiasing recommendation), indicating that our model can perform a balanced recommendation with both higher global and debiasing recommendation accuracy with greater long-tail item/user exposure.

**Keywords:** Recommender System · Graph Neural Networks · Consensus Learning · Popularity Bias

# 1   Introduction

Recently, recommender systems serve as a crucial instrument in mitigating information overload problems. They help users make effective and efficient choices and also reduce service providers' costs in delivering interested and desirable items to potential users [20,27]. The core theme of a personalized recommender system is to learn high-quality representations (*a.k.a., embeddings*) of users and items, and integrate them to model the users' preferences on items for differentiated recommendations, known as Collaborative Filtering (CF) [15,24].

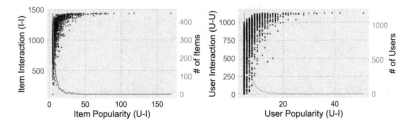

**Fig. 1.** The homogeneous effect (blue-colored points) *vs.* popularity bias (orange-colored curves) in the Automotive dataset. *X*-axis denotes item popularity/frequency (left plot) and user popularity/frequency (right plot) using the User-Item (U-I) graph, *i.e.*, the frequency of node interactions. Item interactions (I-I) refer to the number of items that appeared together with a certain item in the entire interaction records (*i.e.* shopping mix). User interactions (U-U) refer to the number of users interacted with the same items with a certain user. Red item/user popularity curves follow scale-free distributions, indicating very limited items/users possess high frequency.(Color figure online)

Real-world objects are often subject to explicit or implicit connections, forming a network. This characteristic is even more profound in recommender systems where objects such as users, items, attributes, context *etc.*, are connected and influence each other through different relations [34]. Noticing the power of such relations, graph-based recommendation methods start to get their places. A Neural Graph Collaborative Filtering framework (NGCF) [30] is proposed by integrating user-item interactions as a bipartite graph embedding process and using Graph Convolutional Networks (GCNs) to propagate information among neighbors. Later, He et al. [10] claim that GCNs with linear embedding propagation performs better than non-linearity on recommendation tasks and propose LightGCN to simplify GCN to make it more concise for collaborative filtering.

Despite the demonstrated effectiveness, existing methods largely suffer from the **popularity bias** problem: popular items receive much attention, yet the vast majority of less popular items get very limited exposure [3]. Items' under-recommendation bias are common because real-world data always have biased distributions due to the Pareto principle (*i.e.* 80–20 rule), as shown in Fig. 1 (the red-colored curves whose *y*-axis is shown on the right side of each plot). Considering that the long-tail distribution of user-item interactions essentially originates from the imbalance problem rooted in real-world data, it inspired a line of recent studies to give unpopular items/users a higher degree of exposure by adopting rebalancing techniques [28]. The ideas are to manually adjust the nature of the data, take the cause-effect into consideration by formulating a causal graph or reverse popularity scores (*i.e.,* reverse popularity scores or disregarding the popularity effect) [25,36]. In other words, they excessively emphasize discovering causal relationships between unpopular items and users. It causes another type of "bias": The learning process tends to decrease the impact of popular items and can lead to a downplaying of representation learning for popular items/users [1,18]. Therefore, how to achieve a balanced recommendation between global accuracy and unpopular item/user exposure is still challenging.

Meanwhile, the heterogeneous graph structure and the message-passing mode may lead to further deterioration of the popularity bias problem [2,37]. Specifically, most existing methods regard user-item interactions as a bipartite graph, in which the high-order connectivity is built up based on the relationship between heterogeneous nodes (User-Item) [26]. The one-hop neighbors of a target user are items and any two adjacent users sharing similar consumption habits are at least two-hop away (User-Item-User). It means popular items shared by more users have more influence in the message propagation process and the indirect connection between homogeneous nodes (User-User/Item-Item) hinders the learning model from exploring less popular preferences from homogeneous neighbors. Just imagine the message-passing mechanism between users and items, if the item is popular, it will show up in many passing paths like User-Item-User-Item yet uncommon items will not appear frequently.

The above observations motivate us to consider the underlying **Homogeneous Effect**: User-User similarity and Item-Item correlation, which can be obtained from side information or user-item historical interactions to enhance recommendation quality. Concerning the item homogeneous effect, when two unpopular items possess similar attributes (e.g., side information, such as identical movie genres) or are favored by certain users, they will connect in the item-item graph. This correlation helps capture unique patterns shared by a subgroup of users or the unexpected retail correlation of products (*e.g.* the classic case study of "beer and diapers" in marketing). Similarly, for user preference, distinctive preferences of unpopular items can be easily propagated through user-user connections if their overall preferences exhibit high similarity. As shown in Fig. 1, the majority of long-tail unpopular items also demonstrate high active item interactions which can augment their exposure and mitigate popularity bias. Although several latest studies tried to generate two homogeneous graphs (user-user/item-item graphs) for replacing the bipartite graph [12,29], all these methods straightforward aggregate the learned users and items embeddings to make final recommendations without any regulations. Given that user and item representations are obtained from two inconsistent feature spaces which leads to hard to converge, it hinders the final performance. Meanwhile, it is worth noting that these methods lack considering how homogeneous effects can mitigate the popularity bias problems.

Motivated by the homogeneous effect, we propose a **Con**sensus recommendation principle and a factorized **G**raph **C**onvolution **N**etwork (**ConGCN**) framework to simultaneously factorize two types of relationships, User-User similarity and Item-Item correlation, and enforce factorized embeddings to be consistent with user-item interactions. A dynamic weight average strategy is adopted for loss weighting over time by considering the rate of change for each component. Different from existing research that focuses on either global recommendations or popularity debiasing tasks separately, ConGCN demonstrates its strong generalized capability in improving both global recommendation accuracy and unpopular item/user exposure without requiring further model refinement. We summarize the main contributions as follows:

- *Consensus Recommendation*: While state-of-the-art (SOTA) approaches utilize the user-item feedback matrix for recommendations, the user-item feedback matrix alone cannot fully explore homogeneous effects. Alternatively, we construct homogeneous graphs and propose a consensus recommendation to investigate different kinds of relationships from users and items at the same time, to provide personalized recommendations.
- *Factorized GCN*: We propose a consensus recommendation model to factorize different types of relationships for optimal recommendation outcomes. Different from existing graph-based methods, like LightGCN and NGCF, our method learns embeddings from multi-relationships and then fuses them for better results with a novel latent matrix.
- *Balanced Recommendation*: Existing single-task-oriented methods either focus on global recommendation or improve the exposure of unpopular items, which are two typical recommendation tasks that seem conflict with each other. To the best of our knowledge, ConGCN is the first work that can perform beyond SOTA methods on both tasks without any further model modification or compromises, indicating that the proposed model can achieve a balanced recommendation with both global and debiasing recommendations.

## 2    Consensus Recommendation

### 2.1    Problem Statement

In the common paradigm of standard recommender systems, it involves two entities: a set of users $\mathcal{U}$ with $m$ users ($|\mathcal{U}| = m$) and item $\mathcal{V}$ with $n$ items ($|\mathcal{V}| = n$). User-item associations can be recorded in a feedback matrix $\mathcal{R} \in \mathbb{R}^{m \times n}$, where $r_{ai} = 1$ means that user $a$ interacted with (*e.g.* purchased or liked) item $i$, or 0 otherwise. With the feedback matrix, learning feature embeddings $\mathcal{G}$ and $\mathcal{F}$ to precisely represent users and items is critical, i.e., $\widehat{\mathcal{R}_a} = \mathcal{G}_a \times \mathcal{F}$ can be used to predict the user $a$'s potential preference on the item set for personalized recommendations. In this paper, we define two distinguished recommendation tasks: **Global recommendation** aims to provide personalized recommendations from the whole item sets to users, and **Popularity debiasing recommendation** focuses on recommending items based on users' genuine interests while eliminating the influence of popular items.

### 2.2    Consensus Recommendation

Given the growing success of graph learning methods, researchers formulated the user-item feedback matrix as a User-Item graph and applied GCNs to recommendation tasks [4]. As aforementioned, the User-Item bipartite graph is incapable of fully revealing the direct connections between homogeneous nodes, wherein adjacent users can exclusively interact via their mutually engaged items. This considerable limitation inhibits target users from learning potential preferences from analogous users who share particular tastes in items. Instead of only focusing on the "heterogeneous interaction", we formulate a novel *consensus recommendation* framework that takes both user-item heterogeneous interaction and homogeneous effect between user-user and item-item into consideration.

To exploit the homogeneous effect carefully, we introduce two relationships: User-User similarity ($\Theta_U =< \mathcal{U}, \mathcal{A}_U, \mathcal{X}_U >$) and Item-Item correlations ($\Theta_I =< \mathcal{V}, \mathcal{A}_I, \mathcal{X}_I >$), where $\mathcal{A}$ and $\mathcal{X}$ represent the adjacency matrix and node attribute matrix respectively. Consensus recommendation **aims** to simultaneously explore the valuable interactions under three relationships, $(\mathcal{R},\Theta_U,\Theta_I)$, and learns to minimize their reconstruction error with Eq. (1), where $|| \cdot ||_F^2$ is the Frobenius norm of the matrix $\mathcal{A}$ [7] and $\hat{\mathcal{R}}$ denotes reconstructed feedback matrix.

$$\ell(\mathcal{R}, \Theta_U, \Theta_I) = ||\mathcal{R} - \hat{\mathcal{R}}||_F^2 + ||\Theta_U - \hat{\Theta}_U||_F^2 + ||\Theta_I - \hat{\Theta}_I||_F^2 \qquad (1)$$

The rationale of Eq. (1) stems from its consensus on three relationships $(\mathcal{R},\Theta_U,\Theta_I)$ and their optimal reconstruction $(\hat{\mathcal{R}}, \hat{\Theta}_U, \hat{\Theta}_I)$. Under this objective, we are seeking solutions that not only minimize the reconstruction error of feedback matrix $(\mathcal{R},\hat{\mathcal{R}})$, but also the homogeneous relationships between users-users and items-items. If several unpopular users share a few items, such relationships are captured and preserved in Eq. (1), and therefore naturally alleviates the popularity bias.

Finding optimal solutions to Eq. (1) is, however, a nontrivial task, because it involves three types of graph relationships. In our research, we combine graph neural networks and factorization to solve Eq. (1). More specifically, assume $f_U(\cdot)$ and $f_I(\cdot)$ are the learnable functions which take augmented user-user relationships $\widetilde{\Theta}_U$ and item-item correlation $\widetilde{\Theta}_I$ as input, respectively. This will produce graph embedding for users $\mathcal{G} \in \mathbb{R}^{m \times u}$ with $\mathcal{G} = f_U(\widetilde{\Theta}_U)$ ($u$ denotes embedding vector size for each users). Similarity, $\mathcal{F} \in \mathbb{R}^{n \times \iota}$ with $\mathcal{F} = f_I(\widetilde{\Theta}_I)$ ($\iota$ denotes embedding vector size for each item). Then by introducing a matrix $\mathbf{S} \in \mathbb{R}^{m \times \iota}$, we can have:

$$\hat{\mathcal{R}} = \mathcal{G}\mathbf{S}\mathcal{F}^\top = f_U(\widetilde{\Theta}_U) \cdot \mathbf{S} \cdot f_I(\widetilde{\Theta}_I)^\top \qquad (2)$$

$\mathbf{S}$ essentially serves as turntable parameters for $f_U(\cdot)$ and $f_I(\cdot)$ such that, together with user embedding and item embedding results, they can optimally reconstruct $\mathcal{R}$. Because $f_U(\widetilde{\Theta}_U)$ and $f_I(\widetilde{\Theta}_I)$ inherently ensure user and item relationships are preserved, the learning is to find the balance between homogeneous and heterogeneous relations.

In practice, $\Theta_U$ can be generated based on users' features, such as their social status or demographic information. $\Theta_I$ can be constructed from items' properties, such as their usage, price range, and brands. Even If side information is not available, homogeneous relations can be extracted directly from the user-item feedback matrix ($\mathcal{R}$). The formulation details of homogeneous graphs are given in the experimental Sect. 4.2.

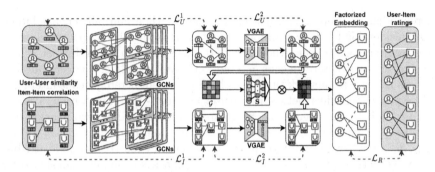

**Fig. 2.** An overview of the ConGCN framework. ConGCN carries out collaborative filtering by considering information from three perspectives: User-User similarity, Item-Item correlation, and User-Item interactions. ConGCN explores homogeneous relations and then reconstructs heterogeneous relations by consistently minimizing loss terms to achieve optimal recommendation results.

## 3    Factorized Graph Convolutional Network

In this paper, we propose **ConGCN** to incorporate both the homogeneous and heterogeneous interactions into the embedding process. The factorized embeddings ($\mathcal{G}_U$ and $\mathcal{F}_I$) of users and items are generated respectively by applying multi-layer GCN on User-User similarity graph $\Theta_U$ and Item-Item correlation graph $\Theta_I$. A nonlinear transformation of $\mathcal{G}_U$ and $\mathcal{F}_I$ is then applied to reconstruct the user-item interactions ($\mathcal{R}$) for consensus optimization. With delicate design, the loss functions of different components are consistently trained in our proposed model, and the overall framework architecture is shown in Fig. 2.

### 3.1    Homogeneous Effect Embedding

To consider the distinction between users and items and extract useful information from the relations between homogeneous objects (users/items), we generate the embeddings $\mathcal{G}_U$ and $\mathcal{F}_I$ by applying GCN layers on homogeneous graphs $\Theta_U$ and $\Theta_I$ respectively. For node embeddings of User-User similarity graph $\Theta_U$, we adopt an $L$-layer GCN with the following layer-wise propagation rule:

$$H_U^{(l+1)} = \sigma(\tilde{D}_U^{-\frac{1}{2}} \tilde{A}_U \tilde{D}_U^{-\frac{1}{2}} H_U^{(l)} \mathbf{W}_U^{(l)})  \tag{3}$$

Here, $\tilde{A}_U = A_U + I_m$ is the adjacency matrix of $\Theta_U$ with added self-connections. $I_m$ is the identity matrix, $\tilde{D}_{ii} = \sum_j \tilde{A}_{ij}$ and $\mathbf{W}^{(l)}$ is a layer-specific trainable weight matrix. To be consistent with non-negative matrix factorization (NFM), $\sigma(\cdot)$ is a non-negative activation function, such as the **ReLU**$(\cdot) = max(0, \cdot)$. $H^{(l)} \in \mathbb{R}^{m \times k}$ is the embedding matrix in the $l^{th}$ layer; $H_U^{(0)} = \mathcal{X}_U$. Therefore, the output of this component is $\mathcal{G}_U = H_U^{(L)}$ and the loss function is,

$$\mathcal{L}_U^1 = ||A_U - \sigma(\mathcal{G}_U \mathcal{G}_U^\top)||_F^2  \tag{4}$$

in which $\mathcal{G}_U$ is a non-linear factorized embedding by considering User-User similarity. Correspondingly, we can generate the embedding matrix for Item-Item correlation graph $\Theta_I$ with the corresponding loss function:

$$H_I^{(l+1)} = \sigma(\tilde{D}_I^{-\frac{1}{2}} \tilde{A}_I \tilde{D}_I^{-\frac{1}{2}} H_I^{(l)} \mathbf{W}_I^{(l)}), \text{ and } \mathcal{L}_I^1 = ||\mathcal{A}_I - \sigma(\mathcal{F}_I \mathcal{F}_I^\top)||_F^2 \quad (5)$$

where $H_I^{(0)} = \mathcal{X}_I$, $\mathcal{F}_I = H_I^{(L)}$. By constructing separate homogeneous graphs for users and items, the GCN layers can effectively capture collaborative signals between nodes of the same type (e.g., converting user-item-user chains into direct user-user-user relationships). This approach considerably enhances the representation learning for nodes that have fewer neighbors in the bipartite graph, as it allows them to acquire more comprehensive and informative from the same type of nodes. It effectively addresses the limitations of traditional bipartite graphs and fosters a more robust understanding of the underlying patterns and connections within the users and items.

## 3.2 Heterogeneous Interaction Reconstruction

To balance the homogeneous and heterogeneous relations, ConGCN aims to reconstruct $\mathcal{R}$ by using the embeddings learned from homogeneous graphs. But based on the experiments, we found that direct reconstruction of $\mathcal{R}$ from $\mathcal{G}_U$ and $\mathcal{F}_I$ leads to training difficulty and lower accuracy because of the intrinsic inconsistencies between homogeneous and heterogeneous nodes. More importantly, the collaborative signal within local communities, such as uncommon users sharing few items, is not encoded in the embedding process.

Accordingly, we adopt Variational Graph Auto-Encoders (VGAEs) [14] to learn $f_U(\cdot)$ and $f_I(\cdot)$ in Eq. (2). We use homogeneous embedding for users and items to generate augmented user-user and item-item graphs. Therefore, the augmented user-user relationship is $\widetilde{\Theta}_U =< \mathcal{U}, \mathcal{A}_U, \mathcal{G}_U >$ and the augmented item-item correlation is represented as $\widetilde{\Theta}_I =< \mathcal{V}, \mathcal{A}_I, \mathcal{F}_I >$.

Taking user embedding as an illustration, VGAEs extended the variational auto-encoder framework to graph structure. It utilizes a probabilistic model that involves latent variables $g_i$ for each node $i \in \mathcal{U}$. These latent variables are interpreted as node representations in an embedding space [13]. The inference model, which is the encoding part of VAE, is defined as:

$$q(\mathcal{G}|\mathcal{G}_U, \mathcal{A}_U) = \prod_{i=1}^{m} q(g_i|\mathcal{G}_U, \mathcal{A}_U) \quad (6)$$

where $q(g_i|\mathcal{G}_U, \mathcal{A}_U) = \mathcal{N}(g_i|\mu_i, diag(\sigma_i^2))$. Gaussian parameters are learned from two GCNs, i.e. $\mu = GCN_\mu(\mathcal{G}_U, \mathcal{A}_U)$, with $\mu$ the matrix stacking up mean vectors $\mu_i$; likewise, $log\sigma = GCN_\sigma(\mathcal{G}_U, \mathcal{A}_U)$. Latent vectors $g_i$ are samples drawn from this distribution. From these vectors, a generative model aims at reconstructing (decoding) $\mathcal{A}_U$, leveraging inner products: $p(\mathcal{A}_U|\mathcal{G}) = \prod_{i=1}^{M} \prod_{j=1}^{M} p([\mathcal{A}_U]_{ij}|g_i, g_j)$, where $p([\mathcal{A}_U]_{ij} = 1|g_i, g_j) = \sigma(g_i^\top g_j)$. The weights of VGAE are tuned by maximizing a tractable variational lower bound (ELBO) of the model's likelihood through gradient descent, with a Gaussian prior on the distribution of latent vectors and employing the reparameterization trick from [13]. Formally, for VGAE, the objective is to minimize the reconstruction error from $\mathcal{G}$ to $\mathcal{G}_U$ using:

$$\mathcal{L}_U^2 = \mathbb{E}_{q(\mathcal{G}|\mathcal{G}_U, \mathcal{A}_U)}[\log p(\mathcal{A}_U|\mathcal{G})] - D_{KL}[q(\mathcal{G}|\mathcal{G}_U, \mathcal{A}_U)\|p(\mathcal{G})] \qquad (7)$$

where $D_{KL}(\cdot\|\cdot)$ is the KL divergence of the approximate from the true posterior. Similarly, the loss function of the reconstruction from $\mathcal{F}$ to $\mathcal{F}_I$ is:

$$\mathcal{L}_I^2 = \mathbb{E}_{q(\mathcal{F}|\mathcal{F}_I, \mathcal{A}_I)}[\log p(\mathcal{A}_I|\mathcal{F})] - D_{KL}[q(\mathcal{F}|\mathcal{F}_I, \mathcal{A}_I)\|p(\mathcal{F})] \qquad (8)$$

With the aim to ensure the learned embedding of $\mathcal{F}$ and $\mathcal{G}$ are consistent with user-item interactions, our objective is to optimize the reconstruction loss introduced in Eq. (1). Here we introduce a neural network-based module that supplants the inner product with an advanced neural architecture in the ConGCN framework, which is able to learn an arbitrary function from data. Specifically,

$$\hat{\mathcal{R}} = \mathcal{G}\mathbf{S}\mathcal{F}^\top, \quad \text{and} \quad \mathcal{L}_R = \|\mathcal{R} - \hat{\mathcal{R}}\|_F^2 \qquad (9)$$

The latent $\mathbf{S}$ can be delicately considered as a learnable weight matrix under the neural network framework (as shown in Fig. 2), and its parameters can be automatically updated within typical backpropagation during the embedding process.

The factorized GCN components introduced above enable us to learn embeddings by taking into account different aspects. To ensure that the final embeddings are consistent with the final recommendation, we formulate all loss functions jointly as the unified loss of ConGCN. This loss function is a nonlinear variation of the objective function $\ell$ of consensus recommendation principle in Eq. (1):

$$\mathcal{L} = \lambda_1 \mathcal{L}_R + \lambda_2 \mathcal{L}_U^1 + \lambda_3 \mathcal{L}_I^1 + \lambda_4 (\mathcal{L}_U^2 + \mathcal{L}_I^2) \qquad (10)$$

The whole ConGCN framework parameters are jointly trained by optimizing the loss function $\mathcal{L}$. As a result, the final output embedding matrices for users and items are $\mathcal{G}$ and $\mathcal{F}$, respectively.

### 3.3 Dynamic Loss Fusion

Considering that our model consists of multiple components, it is critical to identify the appropriate equilibrium among them, *i.e.* $\lambda$ in Eq. 10. In this paper, we employ a straightforward yet efficacious adaptive weighting technique, referred to as Dynamic Weight Average (DWA), as proposed in [19]. This method facilitates averaging task weighting over time by accounting for the fluctuation in loss for each task. As it solely necessitates the numerical task loss, its implementation is considerably more simplistic.

$$w_k(t-1) = \frac{\mathcal{L}_k(t-1)}{\mathcal{L}_k(t-2)}, \lambda_k(t) = \frac{K \exp(w_k(t-1)/T)}{\sum_i \exp(w_i(t-1)/T)} \qquad (11)$$

**Table 1.** Statistics of the datasets & parameter setting.

| Dataset | #User | #Items | Interactions | $\delta_U$ | $\delta_I$ | $u$ | $\iota$ |
|---|---|---|---|---|---|---|---|
| ML-100k | 943 | 1,349 | 99,286 | 2 | 4 | 16 | 32 |
| Automotive | 2,928 | 1,835 | 20,473 | 2 | 3 | 16 | 32 |
| Movies & TV | 44,439 | 25,047 | 1,070,860 | 5 | 5 | 32 | 32 |
| Gowalla | 29,858 | 40,981 | 1,027,370 | 3 | 5 | 32 | 64 |

where $\mathcal{L}_k \in \{\mathcal{L}_R, \mathcal{L}_U^1, \mathcal{L}_I^1, (\mathcal{L}_U^2 + \mathcal{L}_I^2)\}$ and $\lambda_k \in \{\lambda_1, \lambda_2, \lambda_3, \lambda_4\}$. $t$ refers to the iteration index, and $T$ represents a temperature that controls the softness of task weighting.

# 4 Experiments

## 4.1 Benchmark Datasets

In the experiment, we adopt four public benchmark datasets widely used in recommender systems evaluations. Table 1 delineates the details of these datasets, where the $u$ and $\iota$ refer to the user and item output embedding dimensions, respectively.

- **MovieLens-100k**: This dataset was collected from MovieLens review websites [8]. We opt for the ML-100k and adopt the 5-core setting to guarantee the user and item have at least 5 interactions [9]. Regarding the side information, user attributes include gender, age, and occupation; item characteristics include film genres and eras.
- **Amazon-Automotive/Movies & TV**: The Amazon review datasets have been extensively employed in various product recommendation tasks. In this study, we select two datasets which are the Automotive and Movies & TV. We apply a 5-core setting for Automotive and a 10-core setting for Movies & TV. For the Amazon dataset, user reviews[1], as well as item categories and prices, can be regarded as side information.
- **Gowalla**: This dataset originates from Gowalla, a renowned location-based social network with over 600,000 users [17], where the locations can be considered as items based on user geographical records. A 10-core setting is employed to ensure data reliability. It is noteworthy that there is no side information contained in the Gowalla dataset.

## 4.2 Homogeneous Graph Generation

In ConGCN, the key concept is the homogeneous effect. The homogeneous graphs ($\Theta_U$ and $\Theta_I$) can be generated from various side information, as introduced

---

[1] Following prior research, we extract users' reviews, eliminate stop words, and select the top 5,000 frequent unigram features as item features [35].

in the dataset section. By given the feature embedding of users/items in side information space $\mathcal{E} = \{\mathcal{E}_U, \mathcal{E}_I\}$, the similarity/correlation can be formulated as:

$$[\mathcal{A}_U^S]_{ij} = \begin{cases} 1, & \mathcal{E}_{Ui}\mathcal{E}_{Uj}^\top \geq \delta_U \\ 0, & \text{otherwise} \end{cases} ; \quad [\mathcal{A}_I^S]_{ij} = \begin{cases} 1, & \mathcal{E}_{Ii}\mathcal{E}_{Ij}^\top \geq \delta_I \\ 0, & \text{otherwise} \end{cases} \quad (12)$$

where $\delta$ refers to the hyper-parameter that controls the degree of graph connectivity and is given in Table. 1. However, side information is not always available (*e.g.* Gowalla). Based on our experiments, the homogeneous graph can also be extracted from user-item interaction, as user preference and the audience for items show strong homogeneous effects between users/items.

$$[\mathcal{A}_U^R]_{ij} = \begin{cases} 1, & \mathcal{R}_{i\cdot}\mathcal{R}_{j\cdot}^\top \geq \delta_U \\ 0, & \text{otherwise} \end{cases} ; \quad [\mathcal{A}_I^R]_{ij} = \begin{cases} 1, & \mathcal{R}_{\cdot i}^\top \mathcal{R}_{\cdot j} \geq \delta_I \\ 0, & \text{otherwise} \end{cases} \quad (13)$$

In particular, as user preferences and shopping mix can also be treated as a kind of side information extractable from user-item interactions, we incorporate them into the homogeneous graph generation process when such information is accessible. Specifically, $\mathcal{A}_U = \mathcal{A}_U^S \cup \mathcal{A}_U^R$ and $\mathcal{A}_U = \mathcal{A}_I^S \cup \mathcal{A}_I^R$, where "$\cup$" represents the element-wise union operation. Concomitantly, the node attribute matrices are constructed as $\mathcal{X}_U = \mathcal{E}_U||\mathcal{R}$ and $\mathcal{X}_I = \mathcal{E}_I||\mathcal{R}^\top$, with "$||$" denoting the concatenation operation.

### 4.3   Experimental Settings

**Evaluation Metrics.** *Global recommendation*: We adopt two widely used evaluation protocols to evaluate our methods and other baseline methods: *recall@k* and *ndcg@k* (Normalized discounted cumulative gain) [33], $k = 20$. For global recommendation, we use the regular split rule by randomly selecting the exposed items for each user into training/validation/test sets, following 70/10/20 proportions. *Popularity debiasing recommendation*: While for the popularity debiasing task, we follow the widely adopted experimental setting outlined in [16], in which datasets are skewed split: Initially, we sample 20% items from total items with the uniform probability of items as test sets. Subsequently, we randomly divide the remaining data into training and validation sets, employing a ratio of 70%: 10% through a random split.

**Baseline Methods.** To reveal the value of our proposed method, we adopt the representative and SOTA methods as baselines for performance comparison. *General CF methods* - **BPR-MF** [23]; **NeuMF** [11]: These are the general matrix factorization method to factorize the user-item interaction matrix directly, where NeuMF replaces the inner product operation of MF with MLP (Multilayer perceptron). *Graph-based CF methods* - **GC-MC** [4]; **Gemini** [32]; **NGCF** [30]: These methods introduce deep graph learning approaches to learn the representations of users and items. Noted, Gemini introduces homogeneous graphs to learn node embedding. **LR-GCCF** [6]; **LightGCN** [10]: These

**Table 2.** Performance Comparison for Two Recommendation Tasks Between Baselines and ConGCN.

| Tasks | Methods | ML-100k | | Automotive | | Movies & TV | | Gowalla | |
|---|---|---|---|---|---|---|---|---|---|
| | | recall@20 | ndcg@20 | recall@20 | ndcg@20 | recall@20 | ndcg@20 | recall@20 | ndcg@20 |
| Global Recommendation | BPR-MF | 0.2897 | 0.3223 | 0.0742 | 0.0298 | 0.0625 | 0.0422 | 0.1291 | 0.1109 |
| | NeuMF | 0.3168 | 0.3647 | 0.0762 | 0.0311 | 0.0820 | 0.0511 | 0.1399 | 0.1212 |
| | GC-MC | 0.2544 | 0.3025 | 0.0990 | 0.0440 | 0.0638 | 0.0401 | 0.1395 | 0.1204 |
| | Gemini | 0.2724 | 0.3108 | 0.0874 | 0.0400 | 0.0718 | 0.0487 | 0.1351 | 0.1178 |
| | NGCF | 0.3382 | 0.4016 | 0.1127 | 0.0455 | 0.0866 | 0.0555 | 0.1569 | 0.1327 |
| | DICE-GCN | 0.3131 | 0.3568 | 0.1202 | 0.0513 | 0.0863 | 0.0549 | 0.1648 | 0.1433 |
| | LR-GCCF | 0.3174 | 0.3607 | 0.1189 | 0.0463 | 0.0873 | 0.0560 | 0.1605 | 0.1381 |
| | LightGCN | 0.3229 | 0.3805 | 0.1384 | 0.0598 | 0.0915 | 0.0599 | 0.1821 | 0.1537 |
| | SGL | 0.3238 | 0.3923 | 0.1401 | 0.0611 | 0.0932 | 0.0606 | 0.1824 | 0.1540 |
| | **ConGCN** | 0.3638 | 0.4203 | 0.1507 | 0.0648 | 0.0968 | 0.0631 | **0.1838** | **0.1561** |
| | **ConGCN-SI** | **0.3675** | **0.4234** | **0.1515** | **0.0657** | **0.0978** | **0.0642** | N/A | N/A |
| Popularity Debiasing | LightGCN | 0.1052 | 0.0844 | 0.0301 | 0.0187 | 0.0334 | 0.0256 | 0.0610 | 0.0401 |
| | SGL | 0.1063 | 0.0856 | 0.0304 | 0.0189 | 0.0340 | 0.0264 | 0.0617 | 0.0409 |
| | CausE-LightGCN | 0.1035 | 0.0822 | 0.0293 | 0.0176 | 0.0334 | 0.0257 | 0.0606 | 0.0397 |
| | IPW-LightGCN | 0.1067 | 0.0863 | 0.0302 | 0.0189 | 0.0338 | 0.0260 | 0.0609 | 0.0401 |
| | DICE-LightGCN | 0.1198 | 0.1087 | 0.0308 | 0.0190 | 0.0344 | 0.0283 | 0.0619 | 0.0425 |
| | **ConGCN** | 0.1210 | 0.1102 | 0.0345 | 0.0218 | 0.0352 | 0.0289 | **0.0624** | **0.0429** |
| | **ConGCN-SI** | **0.1228** | **0.1113** | **0.0355** | **0.0223** | **0.0359** | **0.0294** | N/A | N/A |

methods use linear GCN layers to learn the linear representations of node embedding. **SGL** [31]: This method adopts a contrastive learning method in the node embedding learning process to make the results more robust*Debiasing methods* - **IPW** [16]; **CausE** [5]; **DCIE** [36]: Existing debiasing methods address the popularity bias problem through introducing inverse propensity weight or causal embedding to disentangle the users' behaviors on items with a SOTA recommendation model as the backbone. *Proposed methods* - **ConGCN**: For a fair comparison, We generate the homogeneous graph from user-item interaction only. **ConGCN-SI**: Side information is integrated into homogeneous graph generation.

### 4.4   Experiment Results

The performance of ConGCN on global recommendation and popularity debiasing tasks is presented in Table 2. The results show ConGCN performs best in both two tasks. It indicates our model achieves balanced recommendations with the ability to make high recommendation quality and alleviate popularity bias. The detailed analysis is as follows.

**Global Recommendation Analysis.** Table 2 upper half presents the global recommendation performance of our model in comparison to other baseline methods. The results show that ConGCN consistently outperforms all other methods across all datasets. By incorporating side information (**ConGCN-SI**), the performance can be further improved with **8.66%** (ML-100k), **8.14%** (Automotive) and **4.94%** (Movies & TV) comparing with other methods. This demonstrates the effectiveness of incorporating both heterogeneous and homogeneous information under a consensus principle, with the consideration of side information. Additionally, our proposed method significantly outperforms Gemini, which provides evidence for the effectiveness of incorporating consensus constraints to balance the embedding learning process across two homogeneous graphs. These findings demonstrate the potential of our approach for improving the accuracy of recommendations and the importance of considering both heterogeneous and homogeneous information in recommendation systems.

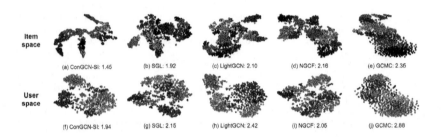

**Fig. 3.** Visualization comparison of learned t-SNE transformed representations for embeddings on ML-100k dataset. Every point represents a node. Nodes are color-coded based on their corresponding clusters, where 10 groups are formed. Sub-figure (a)-(e) refers to the clustering in item space, Sub-figure (f)-(j) refers to the clustering in user space, and the bottom indicators refer to the **intra-cluster distances**.

Moreover, we utilize the $t$-SNE algorithm [21] to project the learned embeddings $\mathcal{F}$ and $\mathcal{G}$ into a two-dimensional space, enabling the visualization of the embeddings for the ML-100K dataset as shown in Fig. 3. By employing the $k$-means clustering algorithm to partition the data into 10 unique clusters, we can observe that the user and item embeddings generated via ConGCN demonstrated the smallest intra-cluster distances compared with competitors. It substantiates the advantages of integrating homogeneous relationships between user-user and item-item within the ConGCN framework, facilitating the identification of user preferences and item associations.

**Popularity Debiasing Analysis.** We demonstrate the efficiency of ConGCN on popularity debiasing tasks. We can see from Table 2 that ConGCN continues to consistently yield the best performance on all benchmark datasets, which indicates that introducing homogeneous relations can significantly help debias the user preference interactions. Meanwhile, the experiments show that some debiasing methods even perform worse than general recommendation methods, as these methods are developed on some specific datasets which contain obvious causal-effect between users and items.

One remaining question is how popularity bias is alleviated by using Con-GCN from both user and item perspectives. We establish four distinct combinations of users and items based on their popularity, categorizing popular nodes

**Table 3.** Popularity debiasing analysis on Amazon Movies & TV dataset: PP/UP indicates popular/unpopular, and U/I indicates users and items, e.g., UP-I means unpopular items.

| Model | PP-U&PP-I | PP-U&UP-I | UP-U&PP-I | UP-U&UP-I |
|---|---|---|---|---|
| LightGCN | 0.3740 | 0.1203 | 0.6556 | 0.2513 |
| SGL | 0.3715 | 0.1163 | 0.6525 | 0.2422 |
| CausE-LightGCN | 0.4207 | 0.1359 | 0.6932 | 0.2744 |
| IPW-LightGCN | 0.3731 | 0.1151 | 0.6723 | 0.2486 |
| DCIE-LightGCN | 0.3812 | 0.1321 | 0.6601 | 0.2541 |
| **ConGCN** | 0.3711 | 0.0485 | 0.6504 | 0.1171 |
| **ConGCN-SI** | **0.3704** | **0.0471** | **0.6498** | **0.1162** |

(users/items) with their degrees in the top 20%, while unpopular nodes reside in the bottom 20%. The embedding quality reported in Table 3 is measured as $P = \frac{1}{m \times n} ||\mathcal{R}^* - \widehat{\mathcal{R}^*}||^2$, where $\mathcal{R}^* \in \mathbb{R}^{m \times n}$ refers to a submatrix of $\mathcal{R}$ that only contains the selected $m$ users and $n$ items. $\widehat{\mathcal{R}^*}$ is the reconstructed feedback matrix from $\mathcal{G}$, $\mathcal{F}$ and $\mathbf{S}$ in Eq. 9. Our ConGCN-SI excels in recommending unpopular items with a **59%** enhancement in Column 2 and **53%** in Column 4, demonstrating that incorporating homogeneous relations considerably helps in mitigating user preference interaction biases. For high-degree items, the performance of ConGCN-SI also outperforms SGL. It means ConGCN maintains a good balance between popular and unpopular items.

**Table 4.** Comparison of recommendation performance using side Information in the ML-100K dataset.

| Models | Global Recommendation | | Improv. | Popularity Debiasing | | Improv. |
|---|---|---|---|---|---|---|
| | recall@20 | ndcg@20 | | recall@20 | ndcg@20 | |
| BPR-MF-SI | 0.2914 | 0.3241 | 5.98% | 0.0834 | 0.0757 | 5.28% |
| LightGCN-SI | 0.3250 | 0.3833 | 6.74% | 0.1060 | 0.0851 | 8.42% |
| DICE-GCN-SI | 0.3139 | 0.3577 | 2.84% | 0.1201 | 0.1090 | 3.23% |
| SGL-SI | 0.3258 | 0.3987 | 6.17% | 0.1071 | 0.0863 | 7.52% |
| **ConGCN** | 0.3638 | 0.4203 | △ | 0.1210 | 0.1102 | △ |
| **ConGCN-SI** | **0.3675** | **0.4234** | 10.17% | **0.1228** | **0.1113** | 14.87% |

**Effectiveness of Side Information.** As mentioned, our method can effectively leverage side information to construct user-user/item-item graphs. In general recommendation systems, side information can be utilized to generate initial embeddings of users and items, *i.e.,* a weighted graph is constructed by using cosine similarity to calculate the similarity between different nodes based on their side information, and the nodes' embeddings are pre-trained using graph-learning models [22]. Therefore, to ensure fairness in comparison, we incorporate side information into other baseline methods. We select the MovieLens-100k dataset, which contains well-defined and rich side information such as user demographics (e.g., age, occupation) and movie genres, and the experimental results are shown in Table 4. We can observe that different models can benefit from using side information appropriately to improve their performance. However, the improvements are not significant, which is due to the fact that these models were not designed to learn the rich information contained in the features of users and items. In our model, it cleverly utilizes side information to construct connections between homogeneous nodes, thereby enhancing the transmission of information in the graph and improving the model's performance.

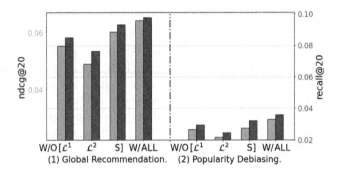

**Fig. 4.** Comparison of component effectiveness.

As ConGCN consists of multiple components, we conduct extensive experiences to demonstrate the analysis of component effectiveness on the Movie&TV dataset. The components are set as: (1) W/O $\mathcal{L}^1$ (Homogeneous Effect Embedding); (2) W/O $\mathcal{L}^2$ (Heterogeneous Interaction Reconstruction); (3) W/O S (Latent matrix); (4) **All** refers to ConGCN w/ all components activated. we report their performance on two recommendation tasks in Fig. 4. The experiments indicate that all components are effective in the proposed model: The homogeneous effect $\mathcal{L}^1$ enhances the learned representations of nodes under the homogeneous effect; The consideration of heterogeneous interaction $\mathcal{L}^2$ ensures the final recommendation results to be consistent with the user-item interactions; The latent matrix **S** can act as a transition gate to fuse the user/item embeddings with different scales.

**Running Time Comparison.** Figure 5 further illustrates the running time comparison, demonstrating that ConGCN remains an efficient recommendation model despite involving multiple components. This efficiency stems from the

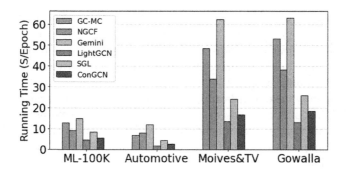

**Fig. 5.** Comparative analysis of running time.

parallel learning of $\mathcal{G}_U$ and $\mathcal{F}_I$. Additionally, the integration of VGAE enhances the reconstruction of $\mathcal{R}$ from $\Theta_U$ and $\Theta_I$, rendering the process more adaptable and expediting convergence. Although LightGCN exhibits swifter performance due to the omission of feature transformation and nonlinear activation components within the graph learning process, our experimental findings indicate that nonlinear transformations are essential for accurately representing the intricate relationships among user-item interactions, particularly in the context of.

## 5  Conclusion

In this work, we proposed a factorized graph convolution neural network for personalized recommendations. We introduce the homogeneous effect to construct the user-user and item-item graphs to model distinctive information of nodes and propose a consensus recommendation principle to simultaneously extract and incorporate both homogeneous and heterogeneous information for the final recommendation. Experiments demonstrated that ConGCN yields the best performance than SOTA methods on both global recommendation and popularity debiasing tasks and provides insightful discussion about the homogeneous effect.

## Ethics Statement

In this work, we focus on the research and practice of recommender systems. As researchers, we recognize our responsibility to adhere to ethical principles, comply with relevant laws and regulations, ensure data security and privacy, and protect the individuals involved in our research. We hereby declare that our paper presents no ethical risks or impacts, as detailed below:

- **Data source and processing:** The datasets adopted in this paper are all collected from public, legal, and authorized sources. All the information has been de-identified and anonymized to protect user privacy. We also adhere to relevant data protection regulations for secure data storage and use.

- **Positive social impact:** Our proposed method ConGCN is designed and implemented to prevent any form of discrimination. The introduction of the homogeneous effect can address potential negative consequences of recommender systems and take measures to avoid their occurrence, such as popularity bias amplification.
- **Transparency and explainability:** We emphasize the transparency and explainability of our proposed recommender model to help users understand the rationale behind recommendations and allow them to raise objections. Our paper explains the algorithm's principles and provides ample experimental validation.

In summary, we fully acknowledge our ethical responsibility in this research and will strictly adhere to relevant laws, regulations, and ethical principles to ensure the compliance and ethical standards of our paper. We commit to continuously monitoring ethical issues in recommender systems and following ethical guidelines in our future research.

**Acknowledgements.** This research is partially sponsored by the U.S. National Science Foundation under grant No. IIS-2302786.

# References

1. Abdollahpouri, H.: Popularity bias in ranking and recommendation. In: Proceedings of the 2019 AAAI/ACM Conference on AI, Ethics, and Society. pp. 529–530 (2019)
2. Abdollahpouri, H., Burke, R., Mobasher, B.: Managing popularity bias in recommender systems with personalized re-ranking. In: The thirty-second international flairs conference (2019)
3. Abdollahpouri, H., Mansoury, M., Burke, R., Mobasher, B.: The unfairness of popularity bias in recommendation. arXiv preprint arXiv:1907.13286 (2019)
4. Berg, R.v.d., Kipf, T.N., Welling, M.: Graph convolutional matrix completion. arXiv preprint arXiv:1706.02263 (2017)
5. Bonner, S., Vasile, F.: Causal embeddings for recommendation. In: Proceedings of the 12th ACM Conference on Recommender Systems. pp. 104–112 (2018)
6. Chen, L., Wu, L., Hong, R., Zhang, K., Wang, M.: Revisiting graph based collaborative filtering: a linear residual graph convolutional network approach. In: Proceedings of the AAAI conference on artificial intelligence. vol. 34, pp. 27–34 (2020)
7. Golub, G., Loan, C.V. (eds.): Matrix computations, vol. 3, 4th edn. Johns Hopkins University Press, Baltimore Maryland (2013)
8. Harper, F.M., Konstan, J.A.: The movielens datasets: history and context. ACM Trans. Interact. Intell. Syst. (TIIS) **5**(4), 1–19 (2015)
9. He, R., McAuley, J.: VBPR: visual Bayesian personalized ranking from implicit feedback. In: Proceedings of the AAAI Conference on Artificial Intelligence. vol. 30 (2016)
10. He, X., Deng, K., Wang, X., Li, Y., Zhang, Y., Wang, M.: LightGCN: simplifying and powering graph convolution network for recommendation. In: SIGIR. pp. 639–648 (2020)

11. He, X., Liao, L., Zhang, H., Nie, L., Hu, X., Chua, T.S.: Neural collaborative filtering. In: WWW. pp. 173–182 (2017)
12. Huang, C., et al.: Knowledge-aware coupled graph neural network for social recommendation. In: Proceedings of the AAAI Conference on Artificial Intelligence. vol. 35, pp. 4115–4122 (2021)
13. Kingma, D.P., Welling, M.: Auto-encoding variational bayes. arXiv preprint arXiv:1312.6114 (2013)
14. Kipf, T.N., Welling, M.: Variational graph auto-encoders. arXiv preprint arXiv:1611.07308 (2016)
15. Koren, Y., Bell, R., Volinsky, C.: Matrix factorization techniques for recommender systems. Computer 42(8), 30–37 (2009)
16. Liang, D., Charlin, L., Blei, D.M.: Causal inference for recommendation. In: Causation: Foundation to Application, Workshop at UAI. AUAI (2016)
17. Liang, D., Charlin, L., McInerney, J., Blei, D.M.: Modeling user exposure in recommendation. In: WWW. pp. 951–961 (2016)
18. Liu, D., Cheng, P., Dong, Z., He, X., Pan, W., Ming, Z.: A general knowledge distillation framework for counterfactual recommendation via uniform data. In: SIGIR. pp. 831–840 (2020)
19. Liu, S., Johns, E., Davison, A.J.: End-to-end multi-task learning with attention. In: Proceedings of the IEEE/CVF conference on computer vision and pattern recognition. pp. 1871–1880 (2019)
20. Lu, J., Wu, D., Mao, M., Wang, W., Zhang, G.: Recommender system application developments: a survey. Decis. Support Syst. 74, 12–32 (2015)
21. van der Maaten, L.: Accelerating t-SNE using tree-based algorithms. J. Mach. Learn. Res. 15(1), 3221–3245 (2014)
22. Meng, Z., Liu, S., Macdonald, C., Ounis, I.: Graph neural pre-training for enhancing recommendations using side information. arXiv preprint arXiv:2107.03936 (2021)
23. Rendle, S., Freudenthaler, C., Gantner, Z., Schmidt-Thieme, L.: BPR: Bayesian personalized ranking from implicit feedback. arXiv preprint arXiv:1205.2618 (2012)
24. Resnick, P., Varian, H.R.: Recommender systems. Commun. ACM 40(3), 56–58 (1997)
25. Sato, M., Singh, J., Takemori, S., Sonoda, T., Zhang, Q., Ohkuma, T.: Modeling user exposure with recommendation influence. In: Proceedings of the 35th Annual ACM Symposium on Applied Computing. pp. 1461–1464 (2020)
26. Shaikh, S., Rathi, S., Janrao, P.: Recommendation system in e-commerce websites: a graph based approached. In: 2017 IEEE 7th International Advance Computing Conference (IACC). pp. 931–934. IEEE (2017)
27. Sharma, L., Gera, A.: A survey of recommendation system: research challenges. Int. J. Eng. Trends Technol. (IJETT) 4(5), 1989–1992 (2013)
28. Steck, H.: Item popularity and recommendation accuracy. In: Proceedings of the Fifth ACM Conference on Recommender Systems. pp. 125–132 (2011)
29. Sun, J., Zhang, Y., Ma, C., Coates, M., Guo, H., Tang, R., He, X.: Multi-graph convolution collaborative filtering. In: ICDM. pp. 1306–1311. IEEE (2019)
30. Wang, X., He, X., Wang, M., Feng, F., Chua, T.S.: Neural graph collaborative filtering. In: SIGIR. pp. 165–174 (2019)
31. Wu, J., Wang, X., Feng, F., He, X., Chen, L., Lian, J., Xie, X.: Self-supervised graph learning for recommendation. In: SIGIR. pp. 726–735 (2021)
32. Xu, J., Zhu, Z., Zhao, J., Liu, X., Shan, M., Guo, J.: Gemini: a novel and universal heterogeneous graph information fusing framework for online recommendations. In: SIGKDD. pp. 3356–3365 (2020)

33. Yang, J.H., Chen, C.M., Wang, C.J., Tsai, M.F.: Hop-rec: high-order proximity for implicit recommendation. In: Proceedings of the 12th ACM Conference on Recommender Systems. pp. 140–144 (2018)
34. Zhang, M., Chen, Y.: Link prediction based on graph neural networks. Adv. Neural Inf. Process. Syst. **31**, 5165–5175 (2018)
35. Zhao, F., Guo, Y.: Learning discriminative recommendation systems with side information. In: IJCAI. vol. 2017, pp. 3469–3475 (2017)
36. Zheng, Y., Gao, C., Li, X., He, X., Li, Y., Jin, D.: Disentangling user interest and conformity for recommendation with causal embedding. In: WWW. pp. 2980–2991 (2021)
37. Zhu, Z., Wang, J., Caverlee, J.: Measuring and mitigating item under-recommendation bias in personalized ranking systems. In: SIGIR. pp. 449–458 (2020)

# Long-Tail Augmented Graph Contrastive Learning for Recommendation

Qian Zhao, Zhengwei Wu, Zhiqiang Zhang, and Jun Zhou$^{(\boxtimes)}$

Ant Group, Hangzhou, China
{zq317110,zejun.wzw,lingyao.zzq,jun.zhoujun}@antgroup.com

**Abstract.** Graph Convolutional Networks (GCNs) has demonstrated promising results for recommender systems, as they can effectively leverage high-order relationship. However, these methods usually encounter data sparsity issue in real-world scenarios. To address this issue, GCN-based recommendation methods employ contrastive learning to introduce self-supervised signals. Despite their effectiveness, these methods lack consideration of the significant degree disparity between head and tail nodes. This can lead to non-uniform representation distribution, which is a crucial factor for the performance of contrastive learning methods. To tackle the above issue, we propose a novel **L**ong-tail **A**ugmented **G**raph **C**ontrastive **L**earning (LAGCL) method for recommendation. Specifically, we introduce a learnable long-tail augmentation approach to enhance tail nodes by supplementing predicted neighbor information, and generate contrastive views based on the resulting augmented graph. To make the data augmentation schema learnable, we design an auto drop module to generate pseudo-tail nodes from head nodes and a knowledge transfer module to reconstruct the head nodes from pseudo-tail nodes. Additionally, we employ generative adversarial networks to ensure that the distribution of the generated tail/head nodes matches that of the original tail/head nodes. Extensive experiments conducted on three benchmark datasets demonstrate the significant improvement in performance of our model over the state-of-the-arts. Further analyses demonstrate the uniformity of learned representations and the superiority of LAGCL on long-tail performance.

**Keywords:** Recommender system · Graph neural networks · Contrastive learning · Self-supervised learning

## 1 Introduction

Recommender systems are a critical component of numerous online services, ranging from e-commerce to online advertising. As a classic approach, collaborative filtering (CF) [11,19] plays a vital role in personalized preference prediction by representing user and item embeddings from observed user-item interactions such as clicks and conversions. Recently, enhanced by the powerful Graph Convolutional Networks (GCNs) [13], GCN-based recommendation methods [10,22] have demonstrated significant potential in improving recommendation accuracy.

© The Author(s), under exclusive license to Springer Nature Switzerland AG 2023
D. Koutra et al. (Eds.): ECML PKDD 2023, LNAI 14172, pp. 387–403, 2023.
https://doi.org/10.1007/978-3-031-43421-1_23

GCN-based recommendation methods represent interaction data as graphs, such as the user-item interaction graph, and iteratively propagate neighborhood information to learn effective node representations. Compared to traditional CF methods, GCN-based recommendation methods are better equipped to capture higher-order collaborative signals, leading to improved user and item embedding learning.

Despite the effectiveness, GCN-based recommendation methods still face data sparsity issue in real-word scenarios. Most existing models follow the supervised learning paradigm [1,10,22,27], where the supervision signal is derived from the observed user-item interactions. However, the observed interactions are considerably sparse in contrast to the entire interaction space [24]. As a result, they may not be sufficient to acquire effective representations. Although several recent studies have attempted to alleviate the data sparsity of interaction data through contrastive learning [24,28], they generally rely on pre-defined data augmentation strategies, such as uniformly dropping edges or shuffling features. These methods lack consideration of the significant disparity in the graph structure between head and tail nodes and lack the ability to construct adaptive data augmentation tailored for various recommendation datasets. This can lead to non-uniform representation distribution, which is a crucial factor for the performance of contrastive learning methods [21,28].

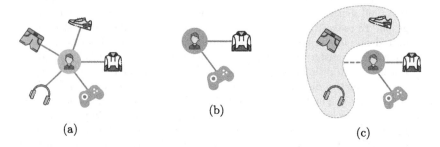

**Fig. 1.** An illustrated example depicting (a) a head node, (b) a tail node, and (c) a tail node augmented with predicted neighbor information.

In the light of the above limitations and challenges, we propose a novel **Long-tail Augmented Graph Contrastive Learning** (LAGCL) method for recommendation. To illustrate, consider the head user in Fig. 1(a) and the tail user in Fig. 1(b) who share similar preference. Our approach aims to extract informative transition patterns from head users and adapt to tail users effectively, as shown in Fig. 1(c). Specifically, we first design an auto drop module to convert head nodes into pseudo-tail nodes that mimic the patterns of real-tail nodes. Next, we leverage the dropped neighbor information of pseudo-tail nodes to learn the knowledge transfer module, which then augments the tail nodes as pseudo-head nodes by adding predicted neighbor information. These modules are updated using the adversarial training mechanism to ensure the distribution match between pseudo-head/tail nodes and real-head/tail nodes. Finally, we use an effective and efficient approach to generate contrastive views by injecting random noise into the graph embedding of both head nodes and augmented tail nodes, capitalizing on their uniformity to yield better contrastive performance.

The main contributions of this paper are summarized as follows:

- We propose a novel graph contrastive learning method, which encourages the model to learn the knowledge between head and tail nodes and generate uniform representation distribution for improving the GCN-based recommendation.
- We designed a learnable data augmentation scheme that can adaptively enhance tail nodes representation and easily generalize to different GCN-based recommendation scenarios.
- Extensive experiments are conducted on three public datasets, demonstrating our approach is consistently better than a number of competitive baselines, including GCN-based and graph contrastive learning-based recommendation methods.

## 2 Preliminaries

### 2.1 GCN-Based Recommendation

Given the user set $\mathcal{U} = \{u\}$ and the item set $\mathcal{I} = \{i\}$, the observed user-item interaction data is denoted as $\mathbf{R} \in \mathbb{R}^{|\mathcal{U}| \times |\mathcal{I}|}$, where each entry $r_{u,i} = 1$ if there exists an interaction between user $u$ and item $i$, otherwise $r_{u,i} = 0$. The number of nodes is $n = |\mathcal{U}| + |\mathcal{I}|$. GCN-based recommendation methods formulate the available data as a user-item bipartite graph $\mathcal{G} = (\mathcal{V}, \mathbf{A})$, where $\mathcal{V} = \mathcal{U} \cup \mathcal{I}$ and $\mathbf{A} \in \mathbb{R}^{n \times n}$ is the adjacent matrix defined as

$$\mathbf{A} = \begin{bmatrix} \mathbf{0}^{|\mathcal{U}| \times |\mathcal{U}|} & \mathbf{R} \\ \mathbf{R}^T & \mathbf{0}^{|\mathcal{I}| \times |\mathcal{I}|} \end{bmatrix}. \tag{1}$$

With a slight abuse of notation, we use $|\mathbf{A}_i|$ to refer to $\sum_{j \in \mathcal{N}_i} \mathbf{A}_{ij}$, where $\mathcal{N}_i$ denotes the neighbor set of node $i$. GCN-based recommendation methods utilize graph structure information to aggregate and produce the embedding of users and items on bipartite graph $\mathcal{G}$ through Eq. (2).

$$\mathbf{H}^{(l)} = \mathbf{D}^{-\frac{1}{2}} \mathbf{A} \mathbf{D}^{-\frac{1}{2}} \mathbf{H}^{(l-1)}, \tag{2}$$

where $\mathbf{D} \in \mathbb{R}^{n \times n}$ is the diagonal degree matrix of $\mathcal{G}$, in which each entry $\mathbf{D}_{ii}$ denotes the number of non-zeros in the $i$-th row of the matrix $\mathbf{A}$. $\mathbf{H}^{(l)} \in \mathbb{R}^{n \times d}$ denotes the $d$-dimensional node embedding matrix after $l$-th graph convolution layer, and $\mathbf{H}^{(0)}$ is the initial node embedding matrix that need to be learned. Finally, we combine all the $L$ layers output node embeddings, $i.e., \mathbf{H} = f_{\text{readout}}([\mathbf{H}^{(0)}; \mathbf{H}^{(1)}; \cdots ; \mathbf{H}^{(L)}])$, to generate preference scores between users and items for recommendation, while $f_{\text{readout}}(\cdot)$ is the mean pooling operation here.

## 2.2   Long-Tail Distribution in the Graph

Graph convolutional networks heavily rely on rich structural information to achieve high performance. However, for nodes with low degrees, their number of neighbors is typically very small, leading to unsatisfactory performance for these nodes. In this paper, in order to investigate the long-tail distribution in the graph, we partition nodes into head nodes $\mathcal{V}_{head}$ and tail nodes $\mathcal{V}_{tail}$ based on their degree with a predetermined threshold value $k$, i.e., $\mathcal{V}_{head} = \{i : \mathbf{D}_{ii} > k\}$ and $\mathcal{V}_{tail} = \{i : \mathbf{D}_{ii} \leq k\}$. Specifically, we have $\mathcal{V}_{head} \cap \mathcal{V}_{tail} = \emptyset$ and $\mathcal{V}_{head} \cup \mathcal{V}_{tail} = \mathcal{V}$.

# 3   Methodology

In this section, we introduce the proposed long-tail augmented graph contrastive learning (LAGCL) model for recommendation. First, we briefly exhibit the overall architecture of LAGCL. Then, we elaborate the detail implementation of LAGCL.

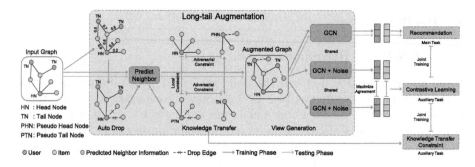

**Fig. 2.** Overall framework of our proposed long-tail augmented graph contrastive learning method for recommendation. To enhance readability, only user-side augmentation is shown. The core of the model is long-tail augmentation, which extracts informative transition from head nodes and augments tail nodes using the knowledge transfer module. The augmented graph is then used to generate the view pairs for contrastive learning. Finally, we train recommendation task, contrastive learning task and knowledge transfer constraints jointly using the multi-task training strategy.

## 3.1   Overview of LAGCL

Our framework follows the general contrastive learning paradigm, which aims to achieve maximum agreement between representations of different views. Figure 2 illustrates the overall framework. Firstly, we enhance tail node by a knowledge transfer module and then generate two graph views on the augmented graph. Next, we employ a contrastive loss function to conduct the contrastive learning task, which encourages representations of the same nodes in the two different views to be similar, while representations of different nodes in those views to be distinct. Finally, we adopt a multi-task training strategy to improve recommendation performance. Specifically, the main task is the recommendation task, while contrastive learning task and knowledge transfer constraints serve as auxiliary tasks.

## 3.2 Long-Tail Augmentation

Assuming that each node has a ground truth neighbor set, the difference between head and tail nodes lies in the former having a fully observed neighbor set while the latter has only partially observed neighbor information. This incomplete information adversely affects the performance of the model. Therefore, the technique of long-tail augmentation aims to supplement the tail nodes with missing neighbor information, with the aim of enforcing representation uniformity between head and tail nodes. However, conducting long-tail augmentation is a challenging task due to unavailability of ground truth labels for the missing neighbors of tail nodes. The intuition behind this approach is that head nodes have fully observed neighbor information. If we could generate pseudo-tail nodes by dropping the neighbor information of head nodes to mimic tail nodes, we could leverage the dropped neighbor information of pseudo-tail nodes to learn the long-tail augmentation strategy. Our long-tail augmentation boils down to three key modules: auto drop module, knowledge transfer module and generative adversarial learning module.

**Auto Drop Module.** An intuitive approach is to randomly sample neighbors from head nodes to generate pseudo-tail nodes. However, this method lacks an effective supervisory signal to guide the sampling process, leading to a distribution deviation between the enhanced data samples and the actual tail node samples. To improve the data augmentation process, we propose an auto drop module equipped with a trainable dropout strategy to minimize the distribution deviation between the enhanced data samples and the actual tail node samples. Specifically, the dropout strategy consists of two main steps: sorting by edge weight and selecting top-$K$ neighbors based on their importance weight, which is calculated between node pairs as:

$$\mathbf{S} = (\mathbf{H}^{(0)}\mathbf{W}_s\mathbf{H}^{(0)^T}) \odot \mathbf{A}, \tag{3}$$

where $\mathbf{S} \in \mathbb{R}^{n \times n}$, $\mathbf{W}_s \in \mathbb{R}^{d \times d}$ is trainable parameters and $\odot$ denotes the element-wise product. Then, to mimic real-tail nodes, we randomly choose the neighbor size $k_i$ of head nodes uniformly from the range of tail node neighbor sizes $[1, k]$:

$$k_i = \begin{cases} \text{Uniform}[1, k], & \mathbf{D}_{ii} > k, \\ \mathbf{D}_{ii}, & \mathbf{D}_{ii} \le k. \end{cases} \tag{4}$$

Finally, inspired by the top-rank selection method in [5,15], the new adjacency matrix $\hat{\mathbf{A}}$ is constructed by selecting the top-$K$ neighbors based on their importance weight, which will be used in the graph aggregation of tail nodes. The new adjacency matrix $\hat{\mathbf{A}}$ is defined as:

$$\hat{\mathbf{A}}_{ij} = \begin{cases} \frac{\exp(\delta \mathbf{S}_{ij})}{1+\exp(\delta \mathbf{S}_{ij})}, & \mathbf{S}_{ij} \in \text{top-}k_i(\mathbf{S}_i), \\ 0, & \mathbf{S}_{ij} \notin \text{top-}k_i(\mathbf{S}_i), \end{cases} \tag{5}$$

where $\delta$ is a hyperparameter that controls the smoothness of the adjacency matrix $\hat{\mathbf{A}}$, and the corresponding neighborhood of node $i$ is denoted as $\hat{\mathcal{N}}_i$.

**Knowledge Transfer Module.** After constructing the auto drop module, we can design a knowledge transfer module that leverages the dropped neighbor information of pseudo-tail nodes for predicting the missing neighbor information of real-tail nodes. Specifically, we use a multi-layer perceptron (MLP) function, denoted by $f_t(\mathbf{h}_i^{(l)}, \mathbf{h}_{\mathcal{N}_i}^{(l)}; \theta_t^{(l)}) = \mathbf{m}_i^{(l)}$, to predict the missing neighbor information based on the center node features and observed neighbor information. Here, $\mathbf{h}_i^{(l)}$ represents the $l$-layer graph embedding of node $i$, $\mathbf{h}_{\mathcal{N}_i}^{(l)}$ is the mean pooling representation of observable neighbors. Then, the predicted information is added to the neighbor aggregation process of real-tail node.

We can calculate the node embedding of head node $i$ in the sparse graph $\hat{\mathbf{A}}$ with predicted neighbor information by the knowledge transfer function:

$$\hat{\mathbf{h}}_i^{(l)} = \sum_{j \in \hat{\mathcal{N}}_i} \frac{1}{\sqrt{|\hat{\mathbf{A}}_i|}\sqrt{|\hat{\mathbf{A}}_j|}} \hat{\mathbf{h}}_j^{(l-1)} + f_t(\hat{\mathbf{h}}_i^{(l-1)}, \hat{\mathbf{h}}_{\hat{\mathcal{N}}_i}^{(l-1)}, \theta_t^{(l-1)}), \tag{6}$$

where $\hat{\mathbf{h}}^{(0)} = \mathbf{h}^{(0)}$. The embedding of head node $i$ in the original graph $\mathbf{A}$ is

$$\mathbf{h}_i^{(l)} = \sum_{j \in \mathcal{N}_i} \frac{1}{\sqrt{|\mathbf{A}_i|}\sqrt{|\mathbf{A}_j|}} \mathbf{h}_j^{(l-1)}. \tag{7}$$

In order to train the knowledge transfer function, we define the translation loss is defined as follows:

$$\mathcal{L}_{trans} = \sum_{i \in \mathcal{V}_{head}} \sum_{l=1}^{L} \|\mathbf{h}_i^{(l)} - \hat{\mathbf{h}}_i^{(l)}\|_2^2. \tag{8}$$

**Generative Adversarial Learning Module.** To learn effective long-tail augmentation, the representation distribution of real-tail nodes should match the representation distribution of pseudo-tail nodes generated by the auto drop module, which is calculated as follows:

$$\tilde{\mathbf{h}}_i^{(l)} = \sum_{j \in \hat{\mathcal{N}}_i} \frac{1}{\sqrt{|\hat{\mathbf{A}}_i|}\sqrt{|\hat{\mathbf{A}}_j|}} \tilde{\mathbf{h}}_j^{(l-1)}, \tag{9}$$

where $\tilde{\mathbf{h}}^{(0)} = \mathbf{h}^{(0)}$. Additionally, the distribution of pseudo-head nodes augmented by the knowledge transfer module should match that of real-head nodes. To achieve this, we use Generative Adversarial Networks [7]. The discriminator distinguishes pseudo-head/tail nodes from real-head/tail nodes based on the node representations, while the generator aims to provide information that is consistently classified as real nodes by the discriminator. Here we regard the output layer of LAGCL as the generator, which contests with the discriminator in the learning process. In particular, we use the following loss for the tail nodes adversarial constraint:

$$\mathcal{L}_{tail-disc} = \sum_{i \in \mathcal{V}} \mathbb{K}(i \notin \mathcal{V}_{tail})\text{CROSSENT}(\mathbf{0}, f_d(\tilde{\mathbf{h}}_i; \theta_d))$$
$$+ \mathbb{K}(i \in \mathcal{V}_{tail})\text{CROSSENT}(\mathbf{1}, f_d(\mathbf{h}_i; \theta_d)), \tag{10}$$

and use the following loss for the head nodes adversarial constraint:

$$\mathcal{L}_{head-disc} = \sum_{i \in \mathcal{V}} \text{CROSSENT}(\mathbf{0}, f_d(\hat{\mathbf{h}}_i; \theta_d))$$
$$+ \mathbb{K}(i \in \mathcal{V}_{head})\text{CROSSENT}(\mathbf{1}, f_d(\mathbf{h}_i; \theta_d)), \tag{11}$$

where $\text{CROSSENT}(\cdot)$ is the cross entropy function, $\mathbb{K}(\cdot)$ is the indicator function, $f_d(\cdot; \theta_d)$ is the discriminator function parameterized by $\theta_d$, which calculates the probability of a node being a head node, as

$$f_d(\mathbf{h}_i; \theta_d) = \sigma\Big(\mathbf{w}_d^\top \text{LEAKYRELU}(\mathbf{W}_d \mathbf{h}_i + \mathbf{b}_d)\Big), \tag{12}$$

where $\text{LEAKYRELU}(\cdot)$ is used as the activation function, $\sigma(\cdot)$ is the sigmoid function, $\theta_d = \{\mathbf{W}_d \in \mathbb{R}^{d \times d}, \mathbf{b}_d \in \mathbb{R}^{d \times 1}, \mathbf{w}_d \in \mathbb{R}^{d \times 1}\}$ contains the learnable parameters of the discriminator $f_d$.

### 3.3 Contrastive Learning

**View Generation.** With the knowledge transfer function mentioned above, we can obtain the augmented tail node embedding, as follows:

$$\mathbf{h}_i^{(l)} = \sum_{j \in \mathcal{N}_i} \frac{1}{\sqrt{|\mathbf{A}_i|}\sqrt{|\mathbf{A}_j|}} \mathbf{h}_j^{(l-1)} + f_t(\mathbf{h}_i^{(l-1)}, \mathbf{h}_{\mathcal{N}_i}^{(l-1)}; \theta_t^{(l-1)}). \tag{13}$$

Then, we follow the approach of SimGCL [28] and generate different views by slightly rotating refined node embeddings in space. This method retains original information while introducing the InfoNCE loss as an additional self-supervised task to improve robustness, as follows:

$$\mathbf{h}_i^{(l)'} = \mathbf{h}_i^{(l)} + \Delta_i^{(l)'}, \mathbf{h}_i^{(l)''} = \mathbf{h}_i^{(l)} + \Delta_i^{(l)''}, \tag{14}$$

where the noise vectors $\Delta_i'$ and $\Delta_i''$ are subject to $||\Delta||_2 = \epsilon$ and $\Delta = \bar{\Delta} \odot$ $\text{sign}(\mathbf{h}_i^{(l)})$, $\bar{\Delta} \in \mathbb{R}^d \sim U(0,1)$. We can use $\epsilon$ to control the rotation angle of

$\mathbf{h}_i^{(l)'}, \mathbf{h}_i^{(l)''}$ compared to $\mathbf{h}_i^{(l)}$. Since $\mathbf{h}_i^{(l)}, \mathbf{h}_i^{(l)'}, \mathbf{h}_i^{(l)''}$ always belong to the same hyperoctant, so adding noise will not cause significant deviation. The noise is injected into each convolution layer and we average each layer output as the final node embedding. To simply the notation, we denote $\mathbf{h}_i$ as the final node embedding after $L$ layers, $\mathbf{h}_i'$ and $\mathbf{h}_i''$ as two generated views.

**Contrastive Loss.** After obtaining the generated views of each node, we utilize the contrastive loss, InfoNCE [8], to maximize the agreement of positive pairs and minimize that of negative pairs:

$$\mathcal{L}_{cl}^U = \sum_{u \in \mathcal{U}} -\log \frac{\exp(s(\mathbf{h}_i', \mathbf{h}_i'')/\tau)}{\sum_{v \in \mathcal{U}} \exp(s(\mathbf{h}_i', \mathbf{h}_j'')/\tau)}, \tag{15}$$

where $s(\cdot)$ measures the similarity between two vectors, which is set as cosine similarity function; $\tau$ is the hyper-parameter, known as the temperature in softmax. Analogously, we obtain the contrastive loss of the item side $\mathcal{L}_{cl}^I$. Combining these two losses, we get the objective function of self-supervised task as $\mathcal{L}_{cl} = \mathcal{L}_{cl}^U + \mathcal{L}_{cl}^I$.

### 3.4   Multi-task Training

We leverage a multi-task training strategy to optimize the main recommendation task and the auxiliary tasks including translation task, discrimination task and contrastive learning task jointly:

$$\mathcal{L} = \mathcal{L}_{rec} + \lambda_1 \mathcal{L}_{trans} + \lambda_2 \mathcal{L}_{disc} + \lambda_3 \mathcal{L}_{cl} + \lambda_4 ||\Theta||^2, \tag{16}$$

where $\Theta$ is the set of model parameters, $\lambda_1, \lambda_2, \lambda_3, \lambda_4$ are hyperparameters to control the strengths of the diversity preserving loss. $\mathcal{L}_{rec}$ is the loss function of the main recommendation task. In this work, we adopt Bayesian Personalized Ranking (BPR) loss [18]:

$$\mathcal{L}_{rec} = \sum_{u,i,j \in \mathcal{O}} -\log \sigma(\hat{y}_{u,i} - \hat{y}_{u,j}), \tag{17}$$

where $\hat{y}_{u,i} = \mathbf{h}_u^\top \mathbf{h}_i$ is the preference score. $\sigma(\cdot)$ denotes the sigmoid function. $\mathcal{O} = \{(u,i,j)|(u,i) \in \mathcal{O}^+, (u,j) \in \mathcal{O}^-\}$ denotes the training data, and $\mathcal{O}^-$ is the unobserved interactions.

## 4   Experiments

To verify the effectiveness of the proposed LAGCL, we conduct extensive experiments and report detailed analysis results.

## 4.1   Experimental Setups

**Datasets.** We evaluate the LAGCL using three widely-used public benchmark datasets: Yelp2018[1], Amazon-Book[2] and Movielens-25M[3]. The statistics of these datasets are presented in Table 1.

**Evaluation Metrics.** Due to our focus on Top-N recommendation, following the convention in the previous research [29], we discard ratings less than 4 in Movielens-25M, and reset the rest to 1. We split the interactions into training, validation, and testing set with a ratio of 7:1:2. In the test set, we evaluate the performance of each model using the relevancy-based metric Recall@20 and the ranking-aware metric NDCG@20.

**Table 1.** The statistics of three datasets.

| Dataset | #Users | #Items | #Interactions | Density |
|---|---|---|---|---|
| Yelp2018 | 31,668 | 38,048 | 1,561,406 | 0.1296% |
| Amazon-Book | 52,643 | 91,599 | 2,984,108 | 0.0619% |
| Movielens-25M | 155,002 | 27,133 | 3,612,474 | 0.0859% |

**Baselines.** We compare LAGCL with other GCN-based recommendation methods, including:

- **LightGCN** [10] designs a light graph convolution to improve training efficiency and representation ability.
- **SGL** [24] designs an auxiliary tasks via perturbation to the graph structure (such as edge dropout), which achieves greater benifits in long-tail recommendation.
- **NCL** [16] improves the recommendation performance by clustering similar nodes to provide semantic neighbors and structural neighbors.
- **RGCF** [20] integrates a graph denoising module and a diversity preserving module to enhance the robustness of GCN-based recommendation.
- **SimGCL** [28] proves the positive correlation between the uniformity of representations and the ability to debias through feature-level perturbation and contrastive learning, and achieved greater long-tail performance than SGL.

**Settings and Hyperparameters.** We develop the model using the open-source SELFRec[4] [29]. For a fair comparison, we prioritize the hyperparameters reported in the original papers for each baseline when feasible. In cases where

---

[1]   https://www.yelp.com/dataset.
[2]   https://cseweb.ucsd.edu/~jmcauley/datasets.html#amazon_reviews.
[3]   https://grouplens.org/datasets/movielens/25m/.
[4]   https://github.com/Coder-Yu/SELFRec.

this information is not provided, we conduct a grid search to adjust the hyperparameters. As for the general settings of all the baselines, the Xavier initialization [6] is used on all embeddings. The embedding size is 64, the parameter for $L_2$ regularization is $10^{-4}$ and the batch size is 2048. We use Adam [12] with the learning rate 0.001 to optimize all the models. More settings can be found in https://github.com/im0qianqian/LAGCL.

**Table 2.** Overall performance comparsion. The percentage in brackets denote the relative performance improvement over LightGCN. The best results are bolded and the best results of baseline are underlined.

| Method | Yelp2018 | | Amazon Book | | MovieLens-25M | |
|---|---|---|---|---|---|---|
| | Recall@20 | NDCG@20 | Recall@20 | NDCG@20 | Recall@20 | NDCG@20 |
| LightGCN | 0.0583 | 0.0486 | 0.0323 | 0.0254 | 0.3267 | 0.2276 |
| SGL | 0.0659(+13.0%) | 0.0541(+11.4%) | 0.0443(+37.0%) | 0.0352(+38.5%) | 0.3471(+6.2%) | 0.2440(+7.2%) |
| NCL | 0.0663(+13.7%) | 0.0547(+12.5%) | 0.0426(+32.0%) | 0.0331(+30.2%) | 0.3292(+0.8%) | 0.2306(+1.3%) |
| RGCF | 0.0591(+1.5%) | 0.0487(+0.1%) | 0.0345(+6.9%) | 0.0274(+7.9%) | 0.3137(-4.0%) | 0.2060(-9.5%) |
| SimGCL | 0.0719(+23.4%) | 0.0600(+23.4%) | 0.0510(+57.9%) | 0.0406(+59.8%) | 0.3553(+8.8%) | 0.2468(+8.4%) |
| **LAGCL** | **0.0732(+25.6%)** | **0.0604(+24.3%)** | **0.0522(+61.8%)** | **0.0415(+63.4%)** | **0.3579(+9.6%)** | **0.2509(+10.2%)** |

## 4.2   Performance Comparison

Table 2 shows our comparison results with other baselines in three datasets. We have the following observations: (1) Our proposed LAGCL consistently outperforms all baselines in different datasets and metrics. Specifically, LAGCL achieves a relative improvement of 25.6%, 61.8%, and 9.6% on Recall@20 compared to LightGCN on the Yelp2018, Amazon Book, and Movielens-25M datasets, respectively. Compared to the strongest baseline (SimGCL), LAGCL also achieves better performance, e.g., about 1.81%, 2.35%, 0.73% performance improvement of Recall@20 on the same datasets. (2) All graph contrastive learning based methods e.g.,SGL, NCL, RGCF, SimGCL, show significant improvement compared to LightGCN on three datasets, which verifies the effectiveness of contrastive learning for collaborative filtering. SimGCL achieves better performance than other baselines, demonstrating that feature-level augmentation is more suitable for collaborative filtering tasks than structure-level augmentation. It is worth noting that our method predicts neighborhood information for tail nodes while preserving the original graph structure. LAGCL incorporates the advantages of feature-level augmentation and avoids the possibility of drastic changes in tail node information due to graph structural changes caused by structure-level augmentation. As a result, our method LAGCL achieves the state-of-the-art performance.

## 4.3   Ablation Study

We conduct an ablation study to compare several ablated variants, including the "w/o AD" variant that uses random dropout instead of the auto drop module. We also consider the "w/o KT" variant that do not use knowledge transfer module to augment the tail nodes, and the "w/o GAN" variants, which are generative adversarial networks proposed in Sect. 3.2. We have the following observations from Fig. 3. (1) Removing any of the components leads to a performance decrease, with the knowledge transfer module contributing the most. This demonstrates the importance of using knowledge transfer module to augment tail nodes is crucial in GCN-based recommendation scenarios. (2) Using random dropout instead of the auto drop module results in a decrease in performance. It indicates that auto drop module can help to extract informative transition patterns from head nodes that the random dropout strategy cannot learn. (3) Removing the generative adversarial networks significantly decreases the performance. This demonstrates that we cannot achieve meaningful data augmentation without the generative adversarial networks to ensure the distribution match between pseudo-head/tail nodes and real-head/tail nodes.

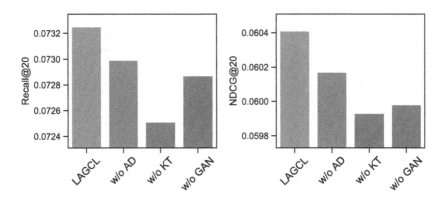

**Fig. 3.** Ablation study in the Yelp2018.

### 4.4   Further Analysis of LAGCL

**Distribution Uniformity Analysis.** A key contribution of the proposed LAGCL is the utilization of long-tail augmentation to supplement the neighbor information of tail nodes for GCN-based recommendation. To better understand the benefits brought by LAGCL, we visualize the learned embeddings in Fig 4 to illustrate how the proposed approach affects representation learning. We use Gaussian kernel density estimation (KDE) [2] to plot user and item embedding distributions in two-dimensional space. Additionally, we visualize each node's density estimations on angles on the unit hypersphere $\mathcal{S}^1$ (i.e., circle with radius 1). We can see that, the embeddings learned by LightGCN fall into serveral clusters located on narrow arcs. Graph contrastive learning-based methods exhibit a more uniform distribution than LightGCN, where SimGCL has a more uniform distribution than other structure-based graph contrastive learning-based methods (SGL, NCL and RGCF). When compared to the best baseline SimGCL, the

LAGCL distribution has fewer dark areas on the circle, indicating that LAGCL has a more uniform distribution that benefits the model performance. Previous studies [21,28] have shown a strong correlation between contrastive learning and the uniformity of learned representations. Thus, we speculate that a more uniform distribution of embeddings could endow the model with better capacity to capture diverse user preferences and item characteristics.

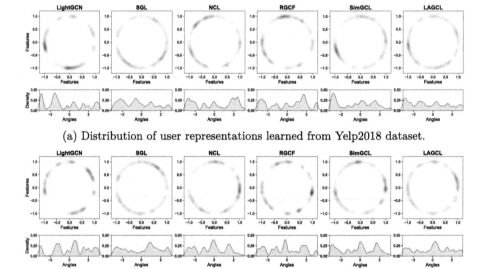

(a) Distribution of user representations learned from Yelp2018 dataset.

(b) Distribution of item representations learned from Yelp2018 dataset.

**Fig. 4.** The distribution of user and item representations learned from the Yelp2018 dataset. The top of each figure plots the Gaussian Kernel Density Estimation (KDE) in $\mathbb{R}^2$ (the darker the color is, the more points fall in that area). The bottom of each figure plots the KDE on angles (i.e., atan2$(y, x)$ for each point $(x, y) \in \mathcal{S}^1$)

**Long Tail Degree Analysis.** To verify whether LAGCL can provide additional performance gains for tail nodes, we divide each user into 10 groups of equally size based on their node degree in the user-item bipartite graph, as shown in Fig. 5. The smaller the Group Id, the lower node degree, and the lower user activity. We compare LAGCL with other baselines that alleviate long-tail distribution in graph, such as SGL employs structure-level augmentation and SimGCL utilizes feature-level augmentation. The results show that the performance of these methods are very similar for high-activity users, while for low-activity users, LAGCL exhibits better performance. This proves that our method has significant gains for modeling tail users.

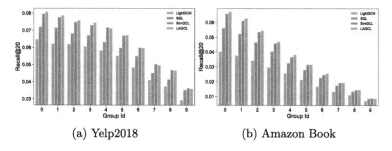

(a) Yelp2018          (b) Amazon Book

**Fig. 5.** Performance comparison of different user groups. In addition to the classic method LightGCN, we also select two different approaches to alleviate the long-tail distribution in the graph, namely SGL and SimGCL.

**Degree Threshold $k$.** As shown in Fig. 6, we conduct a parameter sensitivity experiment on the threshold for dividing the head and tail nodes using the Yelp2018 dataset. The results show that our model achieve the best performance at $k = 20$. We conclude that: (1) LAGCL can learn a transfer strategy through the head users to help bring benefits to tail users. (2) A larger $k$ will result in fewer number of the head users, which may cause the knowledge transfer module to be insufficiently learned. Conversely, a smaller $k$ will result in significant quality differences within the head users, causing inaccurate learning in the knowledge transfer module. Therefore, choosing a suitable threshold for division can maximize the overall benefit.

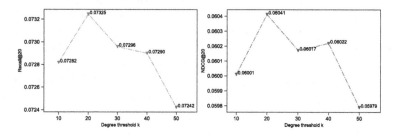

**Fig. 6.** Performance of LAGCL in the Yelp2018 when adjusting the degree threshold $k$.

## 5 Related Work

### 5.1 GCN-Based Recommendation

GCN-based recommendation methods have treated interaction data as a bipartite graph and applied graph neural networks to obtain embeddings while capturing high-order information. For example, GC-MC [1] applies the Graph Convolution Network (GCN) on the user-item graph and employs one convolutional layer to exploit the direct connections between users and items. PinSage [27] is an industrial solution that leverages efficient random walks and graph convolutions to generate item embeddings in Pinterest. NGCF [22] models high-order connectivities by effectively injecting the collaborative signal into the embedding process explicitly. LightGCN [10] simplifies the design of GCN by removing feature transformation and nonlinear activation, making it more effective for recommendation purpose.

However, all of these works perform training in the supervised learning paradigm, which heavily relies on labeled data. Since the observed interactions are considerably sparse compared to the entire interaction space, they may not be sufficient to acquire effective representations.

### 5.2    Self-supervised Learning in Recommender Systems

Self-supervised learning is an emerging technique that leverages unlabeled data to achieve impressive success in various fields, including computer vision [3,9], natural language processing [4,14] and graph learning [17,25,26]. Inspired by the success of these works, self-supervised learning has also been applied to recommender systems, where it has shown great improvement [29]. For instance, $S^3$-Rec utilizes four self-supervised objectives to learn the correlations among attribute, item, subsequence, and sequence by maximizing the mutual information [30]. Similarly, CLCRec further utilizes contrastive learning to mitigate the cold-start issue by maximizing the mutual dependencies between item content and collaborative signals [23]. Moreover, a promising line of research has incorporated contrastive learning into graph-based recommenders to tackle the label sparsity issue with self-supervision signals. For example, SGL [24] uses node dropout, edge dropout and random walk on the user-item interaction graph to generate different views and maximize the agreement between them. NCL [16] incorporates structural and semantic neighbors to enhance graph-based collaborative filtering. SimGCL [28] generates contrastive views by adding uniform noise in the embedding space instead of graph augmentations.

## 6    Conclusion

In this work, we propose a novel long-tail augmented graph contrastive learning (LAGCL) method for recommendation. Specifically, we introduce a learnable long-tail augmentation schema that enhances tail nodes by supplementing them with predicted neighbor information. To make the data augmentation schema learnable, we design an auto-drop strategy to generate pseudo-tail nodes from head nodes and a knowledge translation module to reconstruct the head nodes from pseudo-tail nodes. To ensure the effectiveness of the data augmentation, we leverage adversarial constraints to distinguish between pseudo-tail and real-tail nodes, as well as between augmented tail nodes and real-head nodes. Comprehensive experiments demonstrate the effectiveness of our proposed LAGCL.

## Ethics Statement

Our work aims to improve the accuracy of recommendations using only exposure and click data, without collecting or processing any personal information. We recognize the potential ethical implications of recommendation systems and their impact on user privacy, and we have taken steps to ensure that our work adheres to ethical standards.

We understand that recommendation systems have the potential to influence user behavior and may raise concerns related to user privacy. To address these concerns, we have designed our approach to rely solely on non-personal data, ensuring that our methods do not infringe on user privacy or rights.

In summary, our work focuses on improving recommendation accuracy while upholding ethical standards related to user privacy. We believe that our approach can contribute to the development of recommendation systems that are both effective and ethical.

## References

1. Berg, R.v.d., Kipf, T.N., Welling, M.: Graph convolutional matrix completion. arXiv preprint arXiv:1706.02263 (2017)
2. Botev, Z.I., Grotowski, J.F., Kroese, D.P.: Kernel density estimation via diffusion. Anna. Stat. **38**(5), 2916–2957 (2010). https://doi.org/10.1214/10-AOS799
3. Chen, T., Kornblith, S., Norouzi, M., Hinton, G.: A simple framework for contrastive learning of visual representations. In: International Conference on Machine Learning. pp. 1597–1607. PMLR (2020)
4. Devlin, J., Chang, M.W., Lee, K., Toutanova, K.: Bert: Pre-training of deep bidirectional transformers for language understanding. arXiv preprint arXiv:1810.04805 (2018)
5. Gao, H., Ji, S.: Graph u-nets. In: International Conference on Machine Learning. pp. 2083–2092. PMLR (2019)
6. Glorot, X., Bengio, Y.: Understanding the difficulty of training deep feedforward neural networks. In: Teh, Y.W., Titterington, M. (eds.) Proceedings of the Thirteenth International Conference on Artificial Intelligence and Statistics. Proceedings of Machine Learning Research, vol. 9, pp. 249–256. PMLR, Chia Laguna Resort, Sardinia, Italy (2010), www.proceedings.mlr.press/v9/glorot10a.html
7. Goodfellow, I., et al.: Generative adversarial nets. In: Ghahramani, Z., Welling, M., Cortes, C., Lawrence, N., Weinberger, K. (eds.) Adv. Neural Inf. Process. Syst. **27**. Curran Associates, Inc. (2014)
8. Gutmann, M., Hyvärinen, A.: Noise-contrastive estimation: A new estimation principle for unnormalized statistical models. In: Proceedings of the Thirteenth International Conference on Artificial Intelligence and Statistics. pp. 297–304. JMLR Workshop and Conference Proceedings (2010)
9. He, K., Fan, H., Wu, Y., Xie, S., Girshick, R.: Momentum contrast for unsupervised visual representation learning. In: Proceedings of the IEEE/CVF Conference on Computer Vision and Pattern Recognition. pp. 9729–9738 (2020)
10. He, X., Deng, K., Wang, X., Li, Y., Zhang, Y., Wang, M.: LightGCN: simplifying and powering graph convolution network for recommendation. In: Proceedings of the 43rd International ACM SIGIR conference on research and development in Information Retrieval. pp. 639–648 (2020)

11. He, X., Liao, L., Zhang, H., Nie, L., Hu, X., Chua, T.S.: Neural collaborative filtering. In: Proceedings of the 26th international conference on world wide web. pp. 173–182 (2017)
12. Kingma, D.P., Ba, J.: Adam: a method for stochastic optimization. In: International Conference on Learning Representations (ICLR) (2015)
13. Kipf, T.N., Welling, M.: Semi-supervised classification with graph convolutional networks. arXiv preprint arXiv:1609.02907 (2016)
14. Lan, Z., Chen, M., Goodman, S., Gimpel, K., Sharma, P., Soricut, R.: Albert: a lite BERT for self-supervised learning of language representations. arXiv preprint arXiv:1909.11942 (2019)
15. Lee, J., Lee, I., Kang, J.: Self-attention graph pooling. In: International conference on machine learning. pp. 3734–3743. PMLR (2019)
16. Lin, Z., Tian, C., Hou, Y., Zhao, W.X.: Improving graph collaborative filtering with neighborhood-enriched contrastive learning. In: Proceedings of the ACM Web Conference 2022. pp. 2320–2329 (2022)
17. Liu, Y., et al.: Graph self-supervised learning: a survey. IEEE Trans. Knowl. Data Eng. **35**, 5879–5900 (2022)
18. Rendle, S., Freudenthaler, C., Gantner, Z., Schmidt-Thieme, L.: BPR: Bayesian personalized ranking from implicit feedback. arXiv preprint arXiv:1205.2618 (2012)
19. Sarwar, B., Karypis, G., Konstan, J., Riedl, J.: Item-based collaborative filtering recommendation algorithms. In: Proceedings of the 10th international conference on World Wide Web. pp. 285–295 (2001)
20. Tian, C., Xie, Y., Li, Y., Yang, N., Zhao, W.X.: Learning to denoise unreliable interactions for graph collaborative filtering. In: Proceedings of the 45th International ACM SIGIR Conference on Research and Development in Information Retrieval. pp. 122–132 (2022)
21. Wang, T., Isola, P.: Understanding contrastive representation learning through alignment and uniformity on the hypersphere. In: International Conference on Machine Learning. pp. 9929–9939. PMLR (2020)
22. Wang, X., He, X., Wang, M., Feng, F., Chua, T.S.: Neural graph collaborative filtering. In: Proceedings of the 42nd international ACM SIGIR conference on Research and development in Information Retrieval. pp. 165–174 (2019)
23. Wei, Y., Wang, X., Li, Q., Nie, L., Li, Y., Li, X., Chua, T.S.: Contrastive learning for cold-start recommendation. In: Proceedings of the 29th ACM International Conference on Multimedia. pp. 5382–5390 (2021)
24. Wu, J., Wang, X., Feng, F., He, X., Chen, L., Lian, J., Xie, X.: Self-supervised graph learning for recommendation. In: Proceedings of the 44th international ACM SIGIR conference on research and development in information retrieval. pp. 726–735 (2021)
25. Wu, L., Lin, H., Tan, C., Gao, Z., Li, S.Z.: Self-supervised learning on graphs: contrastive, generative, or predictive. IEEE Transactions on Knowledge and Data Engineering (2021)
26. Xie, Y., Xu, Z., Zhang, J., Wang, Z., Ji, S.: Self-supervised learning of graph neural networks: a unified review. IEEE transactions on pattern analysis and machine intelligence (2022)
27. Ying, R., He, R., Chen, K., Eksombatchai, P., Hamilton, W.L., Leskovec, J.: Graph convolutional neural networks for web-scale recommender systems. In: SIGKDD. pp. 974–983 (2018)
28. Yu, J., Yin, H., Xia, X., Chen, T., Cui, L., Nguyen, Q.V.H.: Are graph augmentations necessary? Simple graph contrastive learning for recommendation. In: Pro-

ceedings of the 45th International ACM SIGIR Conference on Research and Development in Information Retrieval, pp. 1294–1303 (2022)

29. Yu, J., Yin, H., Xia, X., Chen, T., Li, J., Huang, Z.: Self-supervised learning for recommender systems: a survey. arXiv preprint arXiv:2203.15876 (2022)

30. Zhou, K., et al.: S3-rec: self-supervised learning for sequential recommendation with mutual information maximization. In: Proceedings of the 29th ACM International Conference on Information & Knowledge Management, pp. 1893–1902 (2020)

# News Recommendation via Jointly Modeling Event Matching and Style Matching

Pengyu Zhao[1], Shoujin Wang[2], Wenpeng Lu[1(✉)], Xueping Peng[3],
Weiyu Zhang[1], Chaoqun Zheng[1], and Yonggang Huang[4]

[1] School of Computer Science and Technology, Qilu University of Technology
(Shandong Academy of Sciences), Jinan, China
`pengyuzhao.h@gmail.com`, {`wenpeng.lu,zwy`}`@qlu.edu.cn`, `cqzhengWORK@163.com`
[2] Data Science Institute, University of Technology Sydney, Sydney, Australia
`shoujin.wang@uts.edu.au`
[3] Australian Artificial Intelligence Institute, University of Technology Sydney,
Sydney, Australia
`xueping.peng@uts.edu.au`
[4] School of Computer, Beijing Institute of Technology, Beijing, China
`yonggang.h@gmail.com`

**Abstract.** News recommendation is a valuable technology that helps users effectively and efficiently find news articles that interest them. However, most of existing approaches for news recommendation often model users' preferences by simply mixing all different information from news content together without in-depth analysis on news content. Such a practice often leads to significant information loss and thus impedes the recommendation performance. In practice, two factors which may significantly determine users' preferences towards news are news event and news style since users tend to read news articles that report events they are interested in, and they also prefer articles that are written in their preferred style. Such two factors are often overlooked by existing approaches. To address this issue, we propose a novel Event and Style Matching (ESM) model for improving the performance of news recommendation. The ESM model first uses an event-style disentangler to extract event and style information from news articles respectively. Then, a novel event matching module and a novel style matching module are designed to match the candidate news with users' preference from the event perspective and style perspective respectively. Finally, a unified score is calculated by aggregating the event matching score and style matching score for next news recommendation. Extensive experiments on real-world datasets demonstrate the superiority of ESM model and the rationality of our design (The source code and the splitted datasets are publicly available at https://github.com/ZQpengyu/ESM).

---

P. Zhao and S. Wang—Equal contribution.

This paper was partially supported by Nature Science Foundation of Shandong under Grant No. ZR2022MF243, National Nature Science Foundation of China under Grant No. 61502259, Key Program of Science and Technology of Shandong under Grant No. 2020CXGC010901, Program of Science and Technology of Qilu University of Technology under Grant No. 2021JC02010.

D. Koutra et al. (Eds.): ECML PKDD 2023, LNAI 14172, pp. 404–419, 2023.
https://doi.org/10.1007/978-3-031-43421-1_24

**Keywords:** News Recommendation · News Event · News Style

# 1   Introduction

Recent years have witnessed the increasing popularity of online news websites as the primary source of news of most individuals [6, 27]. A variety of news websites such as BBC News, CNN, Yahoo! News have been well established to provide massive news of various topics from politics to entertainment to millions of users around the world every day. While news websites bring convenience to people, they also bring challenges for individuals to navigate through the vast amount of available content and find articles that align with their interests [11,31,33]. As a dominated solution, news recommendation has playing an increasing important role [4,28].

There are some existing works on news recommendation in the literature. For example, some works first encode news content with deep neural network for generating news representation, and then encode news sequence into a unified user representation by using sequence models such as RNN [1] or attention networks [34–36]. However, since user's reading interests are usually diverse, the aforementioned unified user representation fails to accurately imitate the complicated interests of user. In order to alleviate this problem, some works attempt to model each user's multi-interest reading behaviors by capturing the news content interactions with complex matching modules [17,18,21], or generating multiple user representations with attention networks [8,23] or hierarchy modeling [16].

While great success has been achieved, most of existing approaches for news recommendations simply model each piece of news by learning a unified news representation [2,21,24,34,36]. They generally embed all relevant information (e.g., news article content, news topic, news title) together into the news representation without in-depth analysis [9,11,12]. However, such a practice may lose or weaken some implicit information which is significant for capturing users' preference towards news and thus news recommendation. In practice, users' preferences are usually driven by two underlying factors, i.e., news event and news style [3,32]. Specifically, on one hand, a user often read news with the purpose to obtain the information relevant to some events which interest her/him, e.g., US election. On the other hand, even for reporting the same event, there are usually a variety of news pieces with different writing styles from different sources (e.g., ABC news, Yahoo! news). In such a case, users often tend to read news with their preferred styles. Let us take the toy examples shown in Fig. 1 to illustrate such characteristics. In Fig. 1(a), a user Bob has read a series of news pieces which report the event of Russia-Ukraine War or NBA Regular Session, implying he may interest in such events. Then, he choose to read some news reporting the Nord Stream pipeline explosion which is a follow-up event closely related to the Russa-Ukraine War event. In Fig. 1(b), there are three news pieces reporting the Nord Stream pipeline explosion event. However, Bob prone to read the News 5 only which is written in a statement style, similar to the News 1 and News 4 which have been already browsed by Bob before as shown in Fig. 1(a).

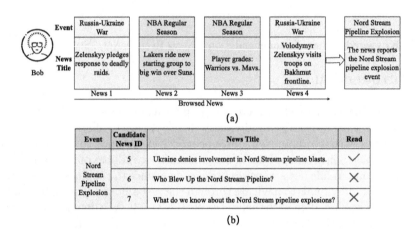

**Fig. 1.** (a) After reading a sequence of news, Bob preferred to read news about the Nord Stream pipeline explosion, which is related to the Russia-Ukraine War event. (b) Among the three news articles reporting the same event, Bob only read the News 5 that is written in his preferred style, similar to that of News 1 and 4.

Although news event and style are critical for learning users' preferences towards news as well as news recommendation, such two significant driving factors are mostly overlooked in the literature. To this end, in this paper, we aim to build a more powerful and accurate news recommender system to provide more accurate recommendations via well modeling news event and style respectively. To accommodate this idea, we propose a novel Event and Style Matching model for news recommendation, called ESM model for short. In ESM model, we first propose a novel event-style disentangler to effectively extract the event information and style information of news respectively from the input data (e.g., news article content, news title, category). Then, we design a novel event matching module to comprehensively model the matching degree between a set of a user's browsed historical news pieces and a given candidate news piece by taking the extracted event information as the input. To be specific, a novel fine-grained multi-channel matching module is proposed to model the possible multiple events covered by a set of historical news pieces browsed by each user, e.g., Russia-Ukraine war event and NBA Regular Session event shown in Fig. 1(a). At the same time, a novel style matching module is designed to measure the matching score between the user preferred news style revealed from her/his browsed news and the candidate news' style. Finally, both the event matching score and style matching score are well aggregated to a unified matching score between a user's preferred news and the candidate news for predicting the next news to the user. Extensive experiments on real-world datasets show that our proposed ESM model significantly improve the performance of news recommendation. The main contributions of this paper are summarized as follows:

- We propose modeling the event matching and style matching respectively for accurate news recommendation. A novel Event and Style Matching (ESM) model has been designed for implementing this idea. To the best of our knowledge, ESM is the first work to simultaneously model both event and style matching for news recommendation.

- We propose a novel event-style disentangler for effectively extracting event and style information respectively from the input news.
- We propose a novel and complicated event matching module and a style matching module for effectively identifying those candidate news of the user's interest w.r.t both news event and style.

## 2  Related Work

### 2.1  News Recommendation

**Methods modeling a single interest** usually first encode each of a user's browsed news pieces content into a news representation, and then generate a unified user representation based on these news representations for recommending the appropriate candidate news [1,34–36]. For example, Wu et al. [36] employed multi-head attention to encode news title and generate user representation for modeling the interaction among news. Although these methods achieve satisfactory performance, they encode user behavior into a unified user representation, which fails to capture the multiple interests of the user [10,22].

**Methods modeling multiple interests** aim to capture a user's diverse interests from browsed news sequences [16,18,19,21,23,26]. For example, Qi et al. [18] first encoded news piece into embedding representation, and then designed three kinds of candidate-aware components to generate the user representation for recommending diverse news. This type of methods well model the multiple interests of each user, and thus can achieve a significant improvement compared with the methods modeling the single interest only [30]. However, they embed the relevant information of news (e.g., title, content, topic) together into a simple unified news representation. Therefore, they lack the in-depth analysis of some important factors, such as news event and news style, which are important for driving users' preferences towards news.

### 2.2  News Event and Style Modeling

Since events are the essential content of news pieces, extracting event information from news content is beneficial to model news pieces. Some researchers have attempted to utilize news event information to enhance the performance of downstream tasks [3,32,40]. For example, Wang et al. [32] first utilized the event-veracity disentangler to obtain the event information and veracity information from news content, and then designed an event detection and transition module to predict which news event a user may prefer to know about. However, such study not only overlooked the multi-granularity nature of event information, but also ignored the significance of news style in modeling users' preference. Moreover, the method is specially built for fake news detection task, which relies on annotation of news veracity. Hence, it cannot be applied to general news recommendation tasks where news veracity label is not available.

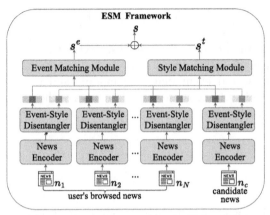 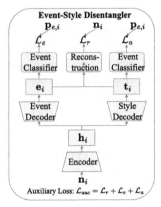

(a) The overall framework of ESM model.    (b) The structure of Event-Style Disentangler in ESM.

**Fig. 2.** (a) ESM consists of three main modules: Event-Style Disentangler, Event Matching Module, and Style Matching Module; (b) The Event-Style Distangler is built on the Encoder, Event and Style Decoder, and three auxiliary loss functions.

In addition to events, news style is also important for modeling news pieces. However, limited work has been done on exploring news style information for news representation [15,39]. For example, Zhou et al. [39] constructed a hierarchical linguistic tree and a recursive neural network for modeling the linguistic style of news and predicting their veracity. However, here the style information does not involve the content of the news. Therefore, merely relying on style information to model the user's representation makes it difficult to accurately capture the user's interests. Additionally, as far as we know, no research has been conducted to utilize news style for modeling news recommendation tasks. Different from the aforementioned methods, we attempt to jointly model new events and news style for news recommendation in this paper.

## 3    News Event and Style Matching Model

In this paper, the recommendation task is formalized as the next news prediction, which is similar to the next-item recommendation [20,25,29]. Specifically, given a sequence of $N$ news pieces which has been read by a given user, we aim to predict which news piece the user may like to read in the next by considering the matching degree between read news and candidate news in terms of both news event and news style.

Figure 2(a) presents the overall framework of our model, which consists of three main modules: an event-style disentangler, an event matching module, and a style matching module. First, given a news sequence which user browsed, the event-style disentangler disentangles the each news representation into event information and style information. Then, the event matching module generates the event-based user representation by modeling the event transition information, and matches it with events of candidate news to obtain the event matching score (i.e., fine- and coarse-granularity event matching score). Meanwhile, the style matching module aggregates the style information of the browsed news pieces into a style-based user representation, and matches it with styles of candidate news to obtain the style matching score. Finally, the recommendation score is achieved for predicting the next news by aggregating the event and style matching scores together.

## 3.1 News Encoder

In ESM, we encode each news piece into news representation using the news encoder proposed by [34]. Specifically, it first uses a CNN and attention network to encode the news title and content into corresponding text representations, and encodes the categories into feature representations using a dense network. Then, a view-level attention network is used to aggregate the representations of the title, content, and categories into a news representation $\mathbf{n}$.

## 3.2 Event-Style Disentangler

To extract the event and style information from news piece, and avoid interference between them [32], we propose an event-style disentangler to separate news representation into two kinds of information (i.e., event information and style information). As shown in Fig. 2(b), event-style disentangler consists of three modules: an encoder, an event and style decoder, and an auxiliary loss module.

**Encoder.** For the $i$-th browsed news, the encoder takes the news representation $\mathbf{n}_i$ as input, followed by a three-layer dense network with residual connections. Specifically,

$$\mathbf{n}_i^1 = ReLU(Dense(\mathbf{n}_i)), \mathbf{n}_i^2 = ReLU(Dense([\mathbf{n}_i; \mathbf{n}_i^1])), \mathbf{h}_i = ReLU(Dense([\mathbf{n}_i; \mathbf{n}_i^2])), \quad (1)$$

where $[;]$ stands for the concatenate operation, $\mathbf{n}_i$ is the representation of $i$-th browsed news, and $\mathbf{h}_i$ is the high-level representation extracted from $\mathbf{n}_i$.

**Event and Style Decoder.** The event and style decoder includes two decoders: an event decoder and a style decoder. The event decoder first takes the high-level representation of news $\mathbf{h}_i$ as input, and then utilizes a three-layer dense network with residual connections to capture the event information of news. Specifically,

$$\mathbf{h}_i^1 = ReLU(Dense(\mathbf{h}_i)), \mathbf{h}_i^2 = ReLU(Dense([\mathbf{h}_i; \mathbf{h}_i^1])), \mathbf{e}_i = ReLU(Dense([\mathbf{h}_i; \mathbf{h}_i^2])), \quad (2)$$

where $\mathbf{e}_i$ refers to the event information of news. Similar to event decoder, the style decoder also employs this structure to capture the style information of news, i.e., $\mathbf{t}_i$. Here, $\mathbf{e}_i$ and $\mathbf{t}_i$ could be viewed as event-based and style-based news representation, respectively.

In order to predict the event distribution of news, we further employ an event classifier to encode the event information $\mathbf{e}_i$. Specifically,

$$\widehat{\mathbf{p}}_{e,i} = softmax(Dense(\mathbf{e}_i)), \quad (3)$$

where $\widehat{\mathbf{p}}_{e,i}$ stands for the event distribution of the $i$-th browsed news.

**Auxiliary Loss Module.** To well train the event-style disentangler, we utilize three kinds of loss function to optimize it, i.e. reconstruction loss, event prediction loss and adversarial loss. The reconstruction loss is used to alleviate the information loss problem during the disentangling process. We first concatenate the event and style information, and then employ a dense layer to encode it for reconstructing the new representation. Formally,

$$\mathcal{L}_r = MSE(Dense([\mathbf{e}_i; \mathbf{t}_i]), \mathbf{n}_i). \tag{4}$$

Event prediction loss is to help the event classifier to correctly predict the event distribution of news. Formally,

$$\mathcal{L}_e = MSE(\widehat{\mathbf{p}}_{e,i}, \mathbf{p}_{e,i}), \tag{5}$$

where $\widehat{\mathbf{p}}_{e,i}$ is the output of event classifier, $\mathbf{p}_{e,i}$ is the real event distribution of $i$-th browsed news.

The aim of the adversarial loss is to ensure that the disentangled style information does not contain the event information. Specifically, we first take the style information as the input of event classifier to predict the event distribution, and then maximize the loss between it and the real event distribution of news,

$$\mathcal{L}_a = \frac{1}{K} \sum_{j=1}^{K} \frac{1}{1 + MSE(\widehat{\mathbf{p}}_{t,ij}, \mathbf{p}_{e,ij})}, \tag{6}$$

where $K$ represents the number of event channels, $\widehat{\mathbf{p}}_{t,ij}$ is the distribution probability of $j$-th event channel, which is predicted by style information and event classifier, and $\mathbf{p}_{e,ij}$ stands for the real distribution probability of $j$-th event channel for $i$-th browsed news.

Finally, the auxiliary loss function is the summation of the three loss function,

$$\mathcal{L}_{auc} = \mathcal{L}_r + \mathcal{L}_e + \mathcal{L}_a. \tag{7}$$

In this auxiliary loss module, we utilize the event prediction loss and adversarial loss to optimize the event-style disentangler. However, due to the dataset limitation, it is hard for us to obtain the real event distribution $\mathbf{p}_{e,i}$. Therefore, we propose a method to calculate the label of the news event distribution. Specifically, we first utilize TF-IDF to extract keywords of each piece of news, and then employ BERT to encode keywords into embeddings, followed by a $K$-means algorithm to cluster all keywords into $K$ event channels. For the $i$-th news, the distribution of $j$-th event channel $\mathbf{p}_{e,ij}$ is calculated as:

$$\mathbf{p}_{e,ij} = \frac{|N_{i,j}|}{|N_i|}, \tag{8}$$

where $|N_i|$ represents the number of keywords in the $i$-th news, and $|N_{i,j}|$ represents the number of keywords which belong to $i$-th news and $j$-th event channel.

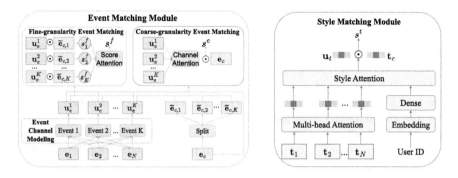

**Fig. 3.** The structure of Event Matching Module and Style Matching Module.

### 3.3 Event Matching Module

Users read a piece of news because the reported event may be one that they are interested in or has a potential relation to their interests. To measure the matching degree between user interest and candidate news event, we propose an event matching module. As shown in the left side of Fig. 3, the event matching module contains three modules: an event channel modeling module, a fine-granularity event matching module, and a coarse-granularity event matching module.

**Event Channel Modeling Module.** For generating the event-based user representation for each event channel, we employ attention networks to model the event information within the same event channel. Each event channel aggregates event information with potential connections. Specifically, according to the event distribution $\widehat{\mathbf{p}}_{e,i}$ calculated in Eq. (3), we first split the event information into different event channels. Formally,

$$\widetilde{\mathbf{e}}_i = \widehat{\mathbf{p}}_{e,i}\mathbf{e}_i, \tag{9}$$

where the event information $\mathbf{e}_i \in \mathbb{R}^{\dim}$ is split to $K$ event channels, the splitted event representation is $\widetilde{\mathbf{e}}_i \in \mathbb{R}^{K,\dim}$.

Since browsed news event may have different influences for generating event-based user representation, we separately utilize attention network to generate event-based user representation for each event channel. For the $j$-th event channel, the event-based user representation $\mathbf{u}_e^j$ is computed as below,

$$\alpha_{i,j}^e = \mathbf{q}_j^\top \tanh(\mathbf{V}_j \times \widetilde{\mathbf{e}}_{i,j} + \mathbf{v}_j), \quad \alpha_{i,j}^e = \frac{\exp(\alpha_{i,j}^e)}{\sum_{k=1}^N \exp(\alpha_{k,j}^e)}, \quad \mathbf{u}_e^j = \sum_{i=1}^N \alpha_{i,j}^e \widetilde{\mathbf{e}}_{i,j}, \tag{10}$$

where $\mathbf{V}_j$, $\mathbf{v}_j$ and $\mathbf{q}_j$ are trainable parameters, $N$ is the number of user browsed news, $\widetilde{\mathbf{e}}_{i,j}$ is the event information of $i$-th news on $j$-th event channels, and $\mathbf{u}_e^j$ is the event-based user representation on $j$-th event channel.

**Fine-Granularity Event Matching Module.** To model the possible multiple events covered by a set of historical news pieces browsed by each user, we first calculate the matching score on different event channels, and then aggregate them into a fine-granularity matching score by a score attention network.

The matching score of $j$-th event channel is computed by the event-based user representation and the event representation of candidate news on the $j$-th event channel,

$$s_j^f = \mathbf{u}_e^j \widetilde{\mathbf{e}}_{c,j}. \tag{11}$$

Afterward, we design a score attention network to aggregate all matching score on different event channels. Considering the event distribution of candidate news may influence the score aggregation, we incorporate it into score attention network. Specifically, we map the event distribution of candidate news $\widehat{\mathbf{p}}_{e,c}$ into a discrete value vector $\widetilde{\mathbf{p}}_{e,c}$ with the function $\widetilde{\mathbf{p}}_{e,c} = \text{round}(10 \times \widehat{\mathbf{p}}_{e,c})$. Then, we obtain the representation of $\widehat{\mathbf{p}}_{e,c}'$ via a dense layer:

$$\widehat{\mathbf{P}}_{e,c}'' = Dense(\widehat{\mathbf{P}}_{e,c}'), \tag{12}$$

where $\widehat{\mathbf{P}}_{e,c}'$ is the embedding of $\widetilde{\mathbf{p}}_{e,c}$.

Finally, we fuse $\widehat{\mathbf{P}}_{e,c}''$ with the event-based user representation to generate the attention weight of score attention network for aggregating all scores:

$$\alpha_j^s = \mathbf{q}_s^\top \tanh(\mathbf{V_s} \times [\mathbf{u}_e^j; \widehat{\mathbf{P}}_{e,cj}''] + \mathbf{v}_s), \quad \alpha_j^s = \frac{\exp(\alpha_j^s)}{\sum_{i=1}^K \exp(\alpha_i^s)}, \quad s^f = \sum_{j=1}^K \alpha_j^s s_j^f, \tag{13}$$

where $\mathbf{q}_s$, $\mathbf{V_s}$, and $\mathbf{v}_s$ are trainable parameters, $K$ is the number of event channels, and $s^f$ represents the fine-granularity event matching score.

**Coarse-Granularity Event Matching Module.** Since the user may focus on all the event information covered by candidate news, we match the overall event-based user representation with the candidate news event.

To generate the overall event-based user representation, we devise a channel attention network that aggregates all user representations across different event channels. More specifically, the number of news articles on an event channel likely reflects its importance in generating the overall user representation. We assume that a news belongs to the $j$-th event channel when its distribution $\widehat{\mathbf{p}}_{e,ij}$ is greater than $1/K$. We first convert the number of news on each event channel into embedding representation $R$. Then, we merge it with event-based user representation to construct the channel attention network for generating overall user representation,

$$\alpha_j^c = \mathbf{q}_c^\top \tanh(\mathbf{V}_c \times [\mathbf{u}_e^j; \mathbf{r}_j] + \mathbf{v}_c), \quad \alpha_j^c = \frac{\exp(\alpha_j^c)}{\sum_{i=1}^K \exp(\alpha_i^c)}, \quad \mathbf{u}_e^o = \sum_{j=1}^K \alpha_j^c \mathbf{u}_e^j, \tag{14}$$

where $\mathbf{q}_c$, $\mathbf{V}_c$ and $\mathbf{v}_c$ are trainable parameters, $\mathbf{u}_e^o$ is the overall event-based user representation. The coarse-granularity matching score is calculated by the overall event-based user representation $\mathbf{u}_e^o$ and event-based candidate news representation $\mathbf{e}_c$ from the event-style disentangler,

$$s^c = \mathbf{u}_e^{o\top} \mathbf{e}_c. \tag{15}$$

### 3.4   Style Matching Module

For each event, there exist abundant news to describe it. However, users only like to read the news pieces that are written in their preferred style. Therefore, we devise a style matching module to measure the matching score between the style of user preferred news and candidate news.

Specifically, we first utilize the multi-head attention to capture the interaction of style information among browsed news $\mathbf{T} = \{\mathbf{t}_i\}_{i=1}^N$,

$$[\mathbf{t}_1', \mathbf{t}_2', \cdots, \mathbf{t}_N'] = MultiHeadAttention(\mathbf{T}). \tag{16}$$

Next, we aggregate them into a style-based user representation by a style attention network. Since user IDs may contain user preferred style feature, we merge it with style information of browsed news to construct the style attention network:

$$\mathbf{u}_d' = ReLU(Dense(\mathbf{u}_d)), \quad \alpha_i^t = \mathbf{q}_t^\top \tanh(\mathbf{V}_t \mathbf{t}_i' + \mathbf{V}_d \mathbf{u}_d' + \mathbf{v}),$$

$$\alpha_i^t = \frac{\exp(\alpha_i^t)}{\sum_{j=1}^N \exp(\alpha_j^t)}, \quad \mathbf{u}_t = \sum_{i=1}^N \alpha_i^t \mathbf{t}_i', \tag{17}$$

where $\mathbf{q}_t$, $\mathbf{V}_t$, $\mathbf{V}_d$, $\mathbf{v}$ are trainable parameters, $\mathbf{u}_d$ stands for the embedding of user IDs, $\mathbf{u}_t$ refers to the style-based user representation.

Finally, the style matching score is calculated by the style-based user representation $\mathbf{u}_t$ and the style-based candidate news representation $\mathbf{t}_c$,

$$s^t = \mathbf{u}_t^\top \mathbf{t}_c. \tag{18}$$

### 3.5   News Recommendation

For each candidate news, its final recommendation score is obtained by merging the event and style matching scores, i.e., $s = s^e + \beta s^t$, where $s^e = s^f + s^c$. Besides, following [5], we employ the NCE loss $\mathcal{L}_{rec}$ to optimize our model.

Since the $\mathcal{L}_{auc}$ is utilized to optimize the event-style disentangler, we combine it with the $\mathcal{L}_{rec}$ as the total loss:

$$\mathcal{L} = \mathcal{L}_{rec} + \gamma \mathcal{L}_{auc}, \tag{19}$$

where $\gamma$ is a hyperparmeter.

## 4   Experiment

### 4.1   Dataset and Experimental Settings

We carried out extensive experiments on two datasets, namely MIND-large and MIND-500K. The MIND-large[1] is an official benchmark dataset [38], consisting of around 877k users and approximately 130k news articles. Each news article

---

[1] https://msnews.github.io/.

comprises the news title, abstract, entity, and categories. Considering the large scale of MIND-large, following common practice [13,37], we randomly sampled 500k users and their associated news browsing logs from MIND-large to constitute the MIND-500K dataset. The original test set of MIND-large cannot be used for testing since it did not have any released labels, we submitted our predictions to the official evaluation platform[2] to assess our model's performance. For MIND-500K, we divided the original validation set equally into an experimental validation set and a test set for validation and test.

In our model, the news titles and abstracts were truncated to a maximum length of 20 and 128 words, respectively. The user's browsing history was restricted to a maximum of 50 news articles. Glove embedding [14] with 300 dimensions was used as word embedding. In the auxiliary loss function module, the max number of keywords for each piece of news was set to 5. The number of event channels $K$ was set to 10 and 17 for MIND-large and MIND-500K respectively. In news recommendation module, the weight of style loss $\beta$ (resp. auxiliary loss $\gamma$) was set to 0.6 (resp. 1) and 1.9 (resp. 1.6) for MIND-large and MIND-500K respectively. The dropout and negative sampling rate was set to 0.2 and 4 respectively. Adam [7] was selected as the optimizer and the learning rate was set to 1e-4. All experiments were ran on one RTX 2080Ti GPU. Three commonly used evaluation metrics, i.e., AUC, MRR, nDCG were used.

### 4.2    Comparison with Competing Methods

**Baselines.** Six representative and/or state-of-the-art news recommendation approaches were used as baselines. They can be classified into two categories: single-interest approaches including NPA, NAML, LSTUR, and NRMS, and multiple-interest approaches including FIM and MINS. The details are as follows: (1) NPA [35] employs a personalized attention network to encode news content and user behavior; (2) NAML [34] aggregates multiple kinds of information together into the news representation; (3) LSTUR [1] combines the long- and short-term user interest for news recommendation; (4) NRMS [36] models user interactions on news content and sequence levels respectively by multi-head self-attention networks; (5) FIM [21] extracts fine-granularity interest with 3D-CNN network; (6) MINS [26] applies multi-head self-attention and GRU to model news sequence based on different interest channels.

**Baseline Settings.** To ensure a fair comparison between our ESM model and the baseline models, we fine-tuned all models' parameters consistently on the validation dataset. Specifically, we initialized the parameters of each baseline model with the values reported in the original paper and then fine-tuned them on the target dataset to achieve optimal performance. For NPA and NRMS, we fused category information to improve their performance. Additionally, we set the number of filters in CNN to 400 (resp. 150) and the filter size to 3 (resp. 3) for NAML and LSTUR (resp. FIM). Furthermore, we set the number of heads for multi-head self-attention to 20 and 15 for NRMS and MINS, respectively.

---

[2] https://codalab.lisn.upsaclay.fr/competitions/420.

**Table 1.** Comparison of our model with baseline methods (%).

| Models | MIND-large | | | | MIND-500K | | | |
|---|---|---|---|---|---|---|---|---|
| | AUC | MRR | nDCG@5 | nDCG@10 | AUC | MRR | nDCG@5 | nDCG@10 |
| NPA | 67.30 | 32.75 | 35.58 | 41.33 | 67.64 | 32.70 | 36.21 | 42.47 |
| NAML | 68.25 | 33.53 | 36.52 | 42.28 | 68.65 | 33.08 | 36.82 | 43.18 |
| LSTUR | 68.41 | 33.58 | 36.58 | 42.31 | 68.60 | 33.48 | 37.10 | 43.46 |
| NRMS | 68.62 | 33.69 | 36.72 | 42.46 | 68.58 | 33.32 | 36.85 | 43.35 |
| FIM | 68.98 | 34.18 | 37.33 | 43.02 | 69.03 | 33.45 | 37.19 | 43.50 |
| MINS | 69.03 | 33.90 | 36.96 | 42.74 | 68.98 | 33.22 | 36.99 | 43.41 |
| ESM | **69.38** | **34.23** | **37.38** | **43.11** | **69.87** | **33.63** | **37.52** | **43.90** |

The comparison results are shown in Table 1, and the following observations can be made. First, all metrics indicate that the approaches that model multiple interests (i.e. FIM, MINS, and ESM) performed better than those that model a single interest (i.e., NPA, NAML, LSTUR, and NRMS). This outcome may be due to the limited ability of single-interest models to comprehensively representing users via well capturing the wide range of reading interests (cf. Sect. 2) that a user may have. Second, our proposed ESM method demonstrated superior performance in all metrics compared to the other methods. This can possibly be attributed to the fact that these baseline methods solely embed relevant news information, such as the title, content, and categories, into a unified news representation, without conducting a thorough analysis of news events and styles, which are crucial factors influencing user preferences towards news. Conversely, ESM can effectively extract event and style information from news, and comprehensively calculate the matching score based on both the news event and news style perspectives, resulting in better performance.

### 4.3 Ablation Study

To show the effectiveness of ESM's core components, we customized ESM into five variants, referred to as $ESM^{-dise}$, $ESM^{-fine}$, $ESM^{-coarse}$, $ESM^{-event}$, and $ESM^{-style}$. These variants exclude event-style disentangler (cf. Sect. 3.2), fine-granularity event matching module (cf. Eq. (11)–Eq. (13)), coarse-granularity event matching module (cf. Eq. (14)–Eq. (16)), event matching module (cf. Sect. 3.3), and style matching module (cf. Sect. 3.4), respectively.

**Table 2.** Comparison of ESM with its variants on MIND-500K dataset (%).

| | AUC | MRR | nDCG@5 | nDCG@10 |
|---|---|---|---|---|
| $ESM^{-dise}$ | 69.11 | 33.48 | 37.13 | 43.58 |
| $ESM^{-fine}$ | 69.63 | 33.38 | 37.30 | 43.72 |
| $ESM^{-coarse}$ | 69.30 | 33.30 | 37.13 | 43.57 |
| $ESM^{-event}$ | 69.15 | 33.06 | 36.83 | 43.33 |
| $ESM^{-style}$ | 68.17 | 32.20 | 35.87 | 42.42 |
| ESM | **69.87** | **33.63** | **37.52** | **43.90** |

Table 2 shows the experimental results of ESM and its five variants. Based on these results, we make the following observations. First, the performance of ESM$^{-dise}$ was lower than that of the standard ESM, possibly due to the fact that ESM$^{-dise}$ does not separate the event and style information from the news representation. Second, both ESM$^{-fine}$ and ESM$^{-coarse}$ achieved worse results than ESM. This is because ESM$^{-fine}$ only considers the coarse-granularity event matching in the event matching module, neglecting the fine-granular multi-event matching. Similarly, ESM$^{-coarse}$ ignores the coarse-granularity event matching score, which also weakens the model's ability. Third, ESM$^{-event}$ was outperformed by ESM, possibly due to the fact that ESM$^{-event}$ only takes into account the style information of news, while ignoring the event information. Last, ESM$^{-style}$ exhibited inferior performance compared to ESM. This is primarily due to the fact that this variant only concentrates on matching news events, disregarding news style matching, resulting in unsatisfactory performance. In summary, the five components of ESM are advantageous in improving the performance of news recommendation tasks.

### 4.4   Comparison with Different News Encoders

To show the generalization of our model, we replaced the news encoder used in ESM with four news encoders that are respectively utilized in four representative baselines, namely NPA, LSTUR, NRMS, and MINS to obtain four more ESM variants. We then compared their performance with that of their corresponding baseline methods. As shown in Fig. 4, ESM variants (denoted as w/ ESM) significantly outperform the corresponding baseline methods in terms of AUC and nDCG@10. This could be attributed to the fact that ESM emphasizes the modeling of event and style information, which are critical to the news recommendation task. Furthermore, compared with all the four ESM variants here, the standard ESM delivered the best performance, likely because ESM's encoder (i.e., the NAML encoder) can effectively aggregate news content and category information into news representation, laying a robust foundation for extracting news event and style information.

### 4.5   Hyperparameter Analysis

Figure 5 provides a detailed analysis of the impact of key hyperparameters on the performance of ESM model. The hyperparameters examined include the number

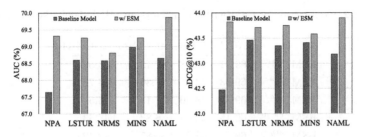

**Fig. 4.** Impact of news encoder in terms of AUC and nDCG@10 on MIND-500K.

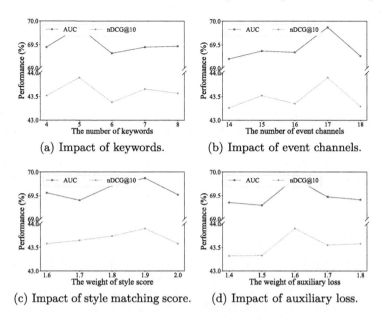

(a) Impact of keywords.          (b) Impact of event channels.

(c) Impact of style matching score.   (d) Impact of auxiliary loss.

**Fig. 5.** The performance of hyperparameter analysis on MIND-500K dataset.

of keywords, the number of event channels, the weight of style matching score, and the weight of the auxiliary loss function. ESM performs best on the MIND-500K dataset when the number of keywords and the number of event channels are set to 5 and 17 respectively. More keywords benefits accurately calculating the event distribution, but too many can introduce noise and reduce accuracy similarly, more channels can help to aggregate event information accurately, but too many can lead to overfitting and limited performance. The best results are achieved when the weight of style matching score is set to 1.9. Although style information can improve performance, a too-large weight will weaken the influence of event information. Lastly, the weight of the auxiliary loss function plays a crucial role in disentangling event and style information and ESM performs optimally when the weight is set to 1.6.

## 5   Conclusion

In this paper, we propose a novel news recommendation method via jointly modeling event matching and style matching (ESM). ESM considers news events and styles as two essential factors in recommending news to users. To achieve this, an event-style disentangler is devised to separate event and style information from news articles. Besides, an event matching module and a style matching module are designed to match news articles with users' preferences from the event and style perspectives, respectively. Extensive experiments have demonstrated the superiority of ESM over the representative and state-of-the-art methods.

Future work will focus on explicitly modeling news style features to enhance performance.

## 6 Ethics Consideration

In this paper, we conducted experiment on two datasets, i.e., MIND-large and MIND-500K. MIND-large is a publicly available news recommendation dataset, which is constructed by Wu et al. [38]. In MIND-large, the privacy of each user was protected by mapping user into an anonymized ID. Since MIND-500K was extracted from MIND-large, it also protects user privacy. Therefore, we ensure that this work will not lead to any privacy issues.

## References

1. An, M., Wu, F., Wu, C., et al.: Neural news recommendation with long- and short-term user representations. In: ACL, pp. 336–345 (2019)
2. Ge, S., Wu, C., Wu, F., Qi, T., Huang, Y.: Graph enhanced representation learning for news recommendation. In: WWW, pp. 2863–2869 (2020)
3. Han, S., Huang, H., Liu, J.: Neural news recommendation with event extraction. arXiv preprint arXiv:2111.05068 (2021)
4. Hu, L., Xu, S., Li, C., et al.: Graph neural news recommendation with unsupervised preference disentanglement. In: ACL, pp. 4255–4264 (2020)
5. Huang, P.S., He, X., Gao, J., et al.: Learning deep structured semantic models for web search using clickthrough data. In: CIKM, pp. 2333–2338 (2013)
6. Khattar, D., Kumar, V., et al.: Weave&Rec: a word embedding based 3-D convolutional network for news recommendation. In: CIKM, pp. 1855–1858 (2018)
7. Kingma, D.P., Ba, J.: Adam: a method for stochastic optimization. In: ICLR, pp. 1–15 (2015)
8. Li, J., Zhu, J., Bi, Q., et al.: Miner: multi-interest matching network for news recommendation. In: ACL Findings, pp. 343–352 (2022)
9. Liu, D., Lian, J., Liu, Z., et al.: Reinforced anchor knowledge graph generation for news recommendation reasoning. In: KDD, pp. 1055–1065 (2021)
10. Liu, D., Lian, J., Wang, S., et al.: KRED: knowledge-aware document representation for news recommendations. In: RecSys, pp. 200–209 (2020)
11. Lu, W., Wang, R., Wang, S., et al.: Aspect-driven user preference and news representation learning for news recommendation. TITS **23**(12), 25297–25307 (2022)
12. Mao, Z., Li, J., Wang, H., Zeng, X., Wong, K.: DIGAT: modeling news recommendation with dual graph interaction. In: EMNLP Findings, pp. 6595–6607 (2022)
13. Mao, Z., Zeng, X., Wong, K.F.: Neural news recommendation with collaborative news encoding and structural user encoding. In: EMNLP Findings, pp. 46–55 (2021)
14. Pennington, J., Socher, R., Manning, C.D.: GloVe: global vectors for word representation. In: EMNLP, pp. 1532–1543 (2014)
15. Przybyla, P.: Capturing the style of fake news. In: AAAI, pp. 490–497 (2020)
16. Qi, T., Wu, F., Wu, C., et al.: HieRec: hierarchical user interest modeling for personalized news recommendation. In: ACL, pp. 5446–5456 (2021)
17. Qi, T., Wu, F., Wu, C., Huang, Y.: Personalized news recommendation with knowledge-aware interactive matching. In: SIGIR, pp. 61–70 (2021)

18. Qi, T., Wu, F., Wu, C., Huang, Y.: News recommendation with candidate-aware user modeling. In: SIGIR, pp. 1917–1921 (2022)
19. Qiu, Z., Hu, Y., Wu, X.: Graph neural news recommendation with user existing and potential interest modeling. TKDD **16**(5), 1–17 (2022)
20. Song, W., Wang, S., Wang, Y., Wang, S.: Next-item recommendations in short sessions. In: RecSys, pp. 282–291 (2021)
21. Wang, H., Wu, F., Liu, Z., Xie, X.: Fine-grained interest matching for neural news recommendation. In: ACL, pp. 836–845 (2020)
22. Wang, H., Zhang, F., Xie, X., Guo, M.: DKN: deep knowledge-aware network for news recommendation. In: WWW, pp. 1835–1844 (2018)
23. Wang, J., Chen, Y., Wang, Z., Zhao, W.: Popularity-enhanced news recommendation with multi-view interest representation. In: CIKM, pp. 1949–1958 (2021)
24. Wang, J., Jiang, Y., Li, H., Zhao, W.: Improving news recommendation with channel-wise dynamic representations and contrastive user modeling. In: WSDM, pp. 562–570 (2023)
25. Wang, N., Wang, S., Wang, Y., et al.: Exploiting intra- and inter-session dependencies for session-based recommendations. World Wide Web **25**(1), 425–443 (2022)
26. Wang, R., Wang, S., Lu, W., Peng, X.: News recommendation via multi-interest news sequence modelling. In: ICASSP, pp. 7942–7946 (2022)
27. Wang, R., et al.: Intention-aware user modeling for personalized news recommendation. In: DASFAA, pp. 179–194 (2023)
28. Wang, S., Guo, S., Wang, L., et al.: Multi-interest extraction joint with contrastive learning for news recommendation. In: ECML-PKDD, pp. 606–621 (2022)
29. Wang, S., Cao, L., Wang, Y., Sheng, Q.Z., Orgun, M.A., Lian, D.: A survey on session-based recommender systems. CSUR **54**(7), 1–38 (2021)
30. Wang, S., Hu, L., Wang, Y., Sheng, Q.Z., Orgun, M., Cao, L.: Modeling multi-purpose sessions for next-item recommendations via mixture-channel purpose routing networks. In: IJCAI, pp. 3771–3777 (2019)
31. Wang, S., Pasi, G., Hu, L., Cao, L.: The era of intelligent recommendation: editorial on intelligent recommendation with advanced AI and learning. IEEE Intell. Syst. **35**(5), 3–6 (2020)
32. Wang, S., Xu, X., Zhang, X., et al.: Veracity-aware and event-driven personalized news recommendation for fake news mitigation. In: WWW, pp. 3673–3684 (2022)
33. Wang, S., Zhang, X., Wang, Y., Liu, H., Ricci, F.: Trustworthy recommender systems. arXiv preprint arXiv:2208.06265 (2022)
34. Wu, C., Wu, F., An, M., Huang, J., Huang, Y., Xie, X.: Neural news recommendation with attentive multi-view learning. In: IJCAI, pp. 3863–3869 (2019)
35. Wu, C., Wu, F., An, M., Huang, J., Huang, Y., Xie, X.: NPA: neural news recommendation with personalized attention. In: KDD, pp. 2576–2584 (2019)
36. Wu, C., Wu, F., Ge, S., Qi, T., Huang, Y., Xie, X.: Neural news recommendation with multi-head self-attention. In: EMNLP, pp. 6389–6394 (2019)
37. Wu, C., Wu, F., Qi, T., Huang, Y.: Empowering news recommendation with pre-trained language models. In: SIGIR, pp. 1652–1656 (2021)
38. Wu, F., et al.: Mind: a large-scale dataset for news recommendation. In: ACL, pp. 3597–3606 (2020)
39. Zhou, X., Li, J., Li, Q., Zafarani, R.: Linguistic-style-aware neural networks for fake news detection. arXiv preprint arXiv:2301.02792 (2023)
40. Zhou, Z., Ma, L., Liu, H.: Trade the event: corporate events detection for news-based event-driven trading. In: ACL Findings, pp. 2114–2124 (2021)

# BalancedQR: A Framework for Balanced Query Recommendation

Harshit Mishra[✉] and Sucheta Soundarajan

Syracuse University, Syracuse, NY 13244, USA
harsh.dsdh@gmail.com, susounda@syr.edu

**Abstract.** Online search engines are an extremely popular tool for seeking information. However, the results returned sometimes exhibit undesirable or even wrongful forms of imbalance, such as with respect to gender or race. In this paper, we consider the problem of *balanced query recommendation*, in which the goal is to suggest queries that are relevant to a user's search query but exhibit less (or opposing) bias than the original query. We present a multi-objective optimization framework that uses word embeddings to suggest alternate keywords for biased keywords present in a search query. We perform a qualitative analysis on pairs of subReddits from Reddit.com (r/Republican vs. r/democrats) as well as a quantitative analysis on data collected from Twitter. Our results demonstrate the efficacy of the proposed method and illustrate subtle linguistic differences between words used by sources with different political leanings.

**Keywords:** search engine · bias · recommender systems

## 1 Introduction

Online search engines are an extremely popular tool for individuals seeking information. However, as is well known, the results returned by search engines may over- or under-represent results in a way that exhibits undesirable or even wrongful forms of bias [26]. This occurs because search engines commonly use word embeddings to determine the relevance of a document to a search query, which can cause bias: e.g., as argued in [5], a hypothetical query for *CMU computer science phd student* may downrank results for female CS PhD students because male names are closer than female names to the search keywords in the embedding space. In addition to being ethically problematic, this phenomenon may also be unwanted by the user, who may not be aware of the latent bias embedded in their query. In the literature, this problem has been addressed in two main ways: by debiasing a word embedding [5,8] or by re-ranking search results to eliminate such bias [9, 34, 35].

In this paper, we consider an alternative solution, which we refer to as *balanced query recommendation*, in which an algorithm suggests less or oppositely-biased alternatives to a query. As we observe, if an individual is searching online for a particular query, nuanced, non-obvious differences in keyword choice may

© The Author(s), under exclusive license to Springer Nature Switzerland AG 2023
D. Koutra et al. (Eds.): ECML PKDD 2023, LNAI 14172, pp. 420–435, 2023.
https://doi.org/10.1007/978-3-031-43421-1_25

result in major differences in the bias exhibited by the results. For example, as we will see, searching Reddit for the term 'rioting' returns results that are disproportionately from the Republican party subReddit vs. the Democratic party subReddit by a factor of 4:1. However, the term 'protests' gives results that are still highly relevant to the original query, but are much less biased.

While the existing approaches of debiasing search terms or re-ranking search results are valid approaches to the general issue of biased search results, these methods accomplish different goals than what we seek here. First, although forcing debiasing on a user may be desirable in some cases, there are other cases when it is less clearly desirable. For example, in the 'rioting' example above, it is quite possible that a user *wants* results that disproportionately represent one political party. In such cases, providing a query recommendation is a 'gentler' alternative to a behind-the-scenes debiasing, because it allows the user to decide whether she wants to see different results. Second, existing methods of debiasing terms or results do not help the document creators debias their own documents. For example, in the job recruitment application described above, it is certainly useful to the recruiter to have a less biased set of results; but it is also important that the candidates themselves know how to modify their keywords so that they are less likely to be harmed by algorithmic bias.

We present BalancedQR, a novel algorithm for balanced query recommendation. BalancedQR works in conjunction with existing search algorithms. BalancedQR first computes the bias of the results returned in response to a query. It then uses a word embedding to identify related terms, and then measures the bias and relevance of those keywords. Finally, it presents a Pareto front of results of varying bias and relevance. Importantly, BalancedQR does *not* require a debiased word embedding: one can use it with respect to any attribute (e.g., gender, race, political alignment, preferred hobby, etc.), as long as there is some way of measuring the bias of a document set with respect to that attribute.

We demonstrate use of BalancedQR on pairs of subReddits from reddit.com. In particular, we consider results from r/AskMen and r/AskWomen and r/Republican and r/Democrats. We perform a qualitative evaluation across several queries on these subReddits. We also perform a quantitative evaluation using popular Google Trends search queries on Twitter data.

An early proof-of-concept of BalancedQR was published in [24]. Here, we present the full version of BalancedQR, including on multi-word queries, and perform a comprehensive evaluation across numerous search algorithms, word embeddings, and datasets.

## 2   Related Work

To our knowledge, this is the first work to approach the problem of balanced query recommendation. However, there is a large and recent body of work that has addressed group fairness concerns in rankings, including greedy algorithms for fair ranking [23] and a framework for mitigating bias in ranking [11], a re-ranking algorithm that balances personalization with fairness [20], and diversification-focused approaches for ranking [1]. [17] observed search bias in rankings, and proposed a framework to measure the bias of the results of a search engine. Ranking algorithms have only recently been used to increase fairness. For a set of items with given relevance scores, such algorithms generally extract partial ranking to mitigate bias [4, 7, 30, 33, 35].

In contrast to these existing works, our paper focuses on generating balanced query recommendation, as opposed to modifying or auditing the search results directly.

Also related to our work is the problem of debiasing word embeddings [5, 18, 27, 36]. These methods rely on maximizing and minimizing certain sub-vectors of words in a word embedding. [5] examines gender bias, and propose an algorithm that achieves fairness by modifying the underlying data. [36] proposed a learning scheme, Gender-Neutral Global Vectors (GN-GloVe), for training word embedding models based on GloVe [27]. This algorithm protects attributes in certain dimensions while neutralizing other attributes during the training process, thus ensuring that gender-related information is confined to a subvector. [21] proposed a new filtering technique which uses the Z-order prefix, based on the cosine similarity measure that decreases the number of comparisons between the query set and the search set to find highly similar documents. In this paper, we use cosine similarity to find the keywords similar to our search query.

## 3    Problem and Framework

In this paper, we explore the *balanced query recommendation* problem, in which a user enters a query into a search engine that may return results that are biased with respect to some attribute. These attributes may be those traditionally considered 'protected', such as gender or race; or may be other attributes of interest, such as political alignment.[1] For example, as we will see, the query 'privilege' gives results that are disproportionately from a Republican-associated subreddit.

Balanced query recommendation has similar high-level goals as debiasing search rankings, including reducing 'bubbles' and echo chambers, which can create a divide between people with different views [10, 15, 25]. However, it provides a 'gentler' approach than directly re-ranking results, in that the user may choose whether to accept a recommended query.

More formally, the goal of the balanced query recommendation problem is to provide a set of query recommendations to the user that are *relevant* to user's original search query, and exhibit greater *diversity*. As discussed below, 'diversity' can be quantified in different ways: here, we measure it with respect to the source of a document, but the framework allows for other approaches.

BalancedQR is a general framework for balanced query recommendation, and can be instantiated with the user's choice of relevance and bias measures. BalancedQR is intended to supplement an existing search engine, and does not itself perform searches.

---

[1] Like all work on fairness, we acknowledge that this algorithm must be used judiciously. There exist topics for which 'balance' is not always desirable.

The output of BalancedQR is a set of queries that, ideally, have high relevance to the original query but are more diverse/more balanced (for example, if the original query produced results with a strong male bias, the alternatives should be less so, or should exhibit a strong female bias). BalancedQR uses no prior information about the dataset and therefore can be used alone or as part of a larger architecture to reduce biases present in social media.

### 3.1  Problem Setup

In this paper, we will refer to the user's input query as the *original query*. A query is performed on a *dataset* consisting of a set of text documents. This query is performed by an existing search engine (not provided by BalancedQR).

For a given search query $Q$, performing query $Q$ using search engine $S$ on database $D$ results in a set of documents $S(Q)$ (depending on context, one might define this set as, e.g., the first page of documents shown in a browser window). Here, we assume that we are given a fixed search engine and document database, and so drop $S$ and $D$ from the notation when it would not lead to confusion.

There are two components to characterizing a set of documents– diversity and relevance, measured through appropriate user-provided functions $g$ and $Rel$, respectively. Both of these functions are discussed further below. Ideally, the relevance $Rel$ of $S(Q)$ would be measured by click-through rate, which is the fraction of returned documents clicked by the user. However, in practice, click-through rate is not known ahead of time, and so a different relevance function is required.

We then treat this problem as a multi-objective maximization problem over $g$ and $Rel$. There are many ways in which this problem can be formulated: for example, maximize $g$ subject to a constraint on $Rel$ (e.g., $Rel(Q') \geq \alpha Rel(Q)$, where $\alpha \in [0, 1]$ is specified by the user); maximize $Rel$ subject to a constraint on $g$ (e.g., $g(Q') \geq \beta$, where $\beta$ is specified by the user); and others.

The BalancedQR framework takes a Pareto front-based approach that returns the Pareto front of terms, as measured by the diversity function $g$ and the relevance function $Rel$, which are defined as desired by the user.

## 4  Proposed Method

Using a word embedding, BalancedQR creates a list of candidate words for the original search query, and scores words in this list based on relevance and diversity to create a set of suggested words which can be used in place of a biased word to achieve a more diverse set of recommendations.

**Measuring Diversity:** We measure diversity in terms of *bias*. Each document returned from the search engine for a query $Q$ has a *bias* between -1 and 1. These bias scores could be derived from, for instance, bias annotations on the sources of news articles, such as those provided by www.allsides.com. The bias for a query $Q$ is then simply the average of the *bias* scores of the returned documents. A low *bias* means most of the documents returned were from different sets, leading to high diversity; and vice versa.

**Measuring Relevance:** We define the *relevance* of a candidate query $Q'$ to an original query $Q$ in terms of the similarity between the document sets returned for each query. There are various similarity measures that can be used such as Euclidean distance, Manhattan distance, Cosine similarity, Jaccard similarity, and others. In this work, we use Cosine similarity (bag of words representation), in which for each document in the two sets, we find the most similar document in the other set, and so define a mean Cosine similarity for each set. The overall similarity is the harmonic mean of these values (akin to F1-score).

## 4.1    Recommendation Framework

Denote the original query as $Q$ and the dataset as $D$. As described before, BalancedQR works in conjunction with an existing search algorithm, which is used to perform the keyword searches. As before, denote this search algorithm as $S$. Without loss of generality, we assume that the search algorithm returns the top-$n$ results for some fixed $n$. In the following discussion, we assume that the dataset and search algorithm are fixed. As before, let $g(d)$ be the bias of a particular document $d$, and $Rel(d)$ be the relevance of document $d$ to keyword $Q$. Denote the word embedding used by BalancedQR as $W$.

At a high level, BalancedQR performs the following steps:

(1) Given query $Q$, BalancedQR applies the search algorithm $S$ to document set $D$ and fetches $S(Q)$, the top-$n$ most relevant documents to $Q$ from $D$.

(2) BalancedQR then performs an iterative process in which it identifies the $k$ alternative keywords $Q_1, ..., Q_k$ nearest to $Q$ in the embedding space defined by $W$ (the choice of $k$ depends on the termination criteria, see below). For a multi-word query, it uses a large language model to fetch alternative multi-word queries based on keywords fetched from $W$.[2] It then uses search engine $S$ to perform a search of each $Q_i$ on dataset $D$ to obtain set $S(Q_i)$. For each of these $i$ sets, BalancedQR computes the bias and relevance of those sets, where relevance is measured with respect to the *original* query $Q$. Using these values, BalancedQR produces a Pareto front along the bias-relevance axes. This Pareto front contains an alternative query $Q_i$ if $Q_i$ is not dominated by any of the other alternatives or by $Q$ itself. A query is non-dominated if there is no other query whose search results have both a lower bias and higher relevance score. (Note that it may sometimes be more appropriate to use a 'pseudo'-Pareto front that allows for queries that are highly biased, but in the opposite direction.)

(3) BalancedQR repeats the above step until a satisfactory Pareto front has been defined, and outputs the Pareto front (or a desired subset) to the user. In our experiments we continue until 10 recommended keywords are found, or no more are available. In our analysis, we highlight both the Pareto front as well as high-relevance words with opposing bias.

Through this process, the end user is made aware that by using an alternate query she can still get relevant results, but from a different point of view (Table 1).

---

[2] LLMs are known to exhibit their own bias, and, if desired, debiasing may be applied at that stage [14,19]. The bias of LLMs is outside the scope of this paper.

**Table 1.** Collective Inputs and Outputs of Algorithm

| Inputs | $Q$: Input Query |
|--------|------------------|
|        | $Q_i$: Alternative Query |
|        | $d, D$: Document, set of documents |
|        | $S$: Search algorithm |
|        | $S(Q)$: Top-$n$ most relevant documents to query $Q$ from document set $D$, as found by algorithm $S$ |
|        | $g(d), g(D)$: Diversity of a document $d$ or document set $D$ |
|        | $Rel(d), Rel(D)$: Relevance of a document $d$ or document set $D$ to query $Q$ |
|        | $W$: Word embedding |

## 4.2  Our Implementation

**Measuring Relevance.** We compute relevance using a cosine similarity-based approach that compares the documents returned for $Q_i$ to those returned for $Q$. In this approach, we compute a variant of F1 by measuring the precision and recall as follows: First, for each document $d' \in S(Q_i)$ (the top-$n$ documents returned in response to $Q_i$), we compute the greatest similarity between $d'$ and a document $d \in S(Q)$ (the top-$n$ documents returned in response to $Q$). This similarity is measured using cosine similarity between the bag-of-words corresponding to the documents. The *precision* is then the average of these maximum similarities. *Recall* is computed similarly, but in the other direction (i.e., finding the closest document from $S(Q_i)$ to each document in $S(Q)$). Then the F1-score, or relevance, is the harmonic mean of precision and recall.

**Measuring Bias.** In the bulk of our analysis (described in Sect. 5), we use a dataset scraped from Reddit.com. We consider posts (documents) from pairs of subReddits in which each subReddit corresponds to a particular group (e.g., Republican vs. Democrats). In this case, the bias function follows directly from the dataset. For a given document/post, that document has bias of either $+1$ (indicating that it was posted in one subReddit) or $-1$ (indicating that it was posted in the other). We also perform an analysis on Twitter data. Here, we use the AllSides media bias annotations [2] to label the bias of sources (the bias calculation for Twitter is described in Sect. 6.2).

The bias of a set of documents $D$ is simply the average of the biases of the individual documents.

**Termination.** We find the top-$k$ closest keywords based on the word embedding. In our experiments, we set $k = 10$: this appeared empirically to be sufficient to identify alternative queries. In our analysis, we highlight both the Pareto front (computed using the scalar version of bias), as well as high-relevance words with opposing bias. Also, It is possible that in certain situations no alternative queries are found and in those cases, no alternative queries are returned.

---

**Algorithm 1 .** Balanced query recommendation
_____

1: $Q$ = original query
2: $k$ = number of desired queries, $n$ = number of returned documents
3: $max\_iter$ = maximum number of iterations, $num\_iters = 0$
4: $Bias_Q = g_Q(D)$
5: $sim$ = list of $k$ most similar words from word embedding
6: **if** $Q$ is multi-word query **then**
7:     $sim$ = list of LLM($w'$) for each $w'$ in $sim$
8: **end if**
9: $recs = \{Q\}$
10: **while** $|num\_iters| < max\_iter$ and $|recs| < k$ **do**
11:     **for** each query $w'$ in $sim$ **do**
12:         $S_{w'}(D, n)$ = top-$n$ relevant documents from $D$ for $w'$
13:         $Bias_{w'} = g_{w'}(D)$
14:         $Rel(w')$ = F1-score between $S_{w'}(D, n)$ and $S_Q(D, n)$
15:         **if** $w'$ is not dominated by any query in $recs$ **then**
16:             Add $w'$ to $recs$
17:             Remove queries from $recs$ that are dominated by $w'$
18:         **end if**
19:     **end for**
20:     $sim = \{$next most similar word from word embedding$\}$
21:     $num\_iters + +$
22: **end while**
23: Return $recs$

_____

## 4.3   Limitations

The `BalancedQR` framework has a few important limitations. As explored in other works, word embeddings learned from collections of data often demonstrate a significant level of biases [12]. When these embeddings are used in low-level NLP tasks, it often amplifies the bias. Thus, it is quite likely that the GloVE embedding that we use is itself biased, reducing the efficacy of `BalancedQR`. Similarly, large language models may exhibit (sometimes substantial) bias as cited by Bender et al. in Sect. 4.3 of [3], which may also counter the efforts of `BalancedQR`. However, debiasing word embeddings and LLMs is a challenging problem that is the subject of much active research, and is outside the scope of this paper. `BalancedQR` is not inherently tied to any particular word embedding or LLM, and if less biased or unbiased word embeddings/LLMs are created, they can easily be used.

Second, `BalancedQR` only supports bias computations along one axis. In many cases, a query is biased along multiple dimensions. Dealing with this is challenging, but one solution is to define bias in a multidimensional space. For each candidate query, we can then calculate the final bias by finding the L2 norm of bias in this multidimensional space with respect to the original bias distribution of the dataset.

# 5  Experimental Setup

We conduct experiments on data from two sources– Reddit.com and Twitter.com, using multiple word embeddings and search engine/document retrieval strategies. The Reddit dataset consists of posts from pairs of subReddits (each of which can be thought of as a topic-specific discussion forum). Each pair represents a particular attribute of interest. The Twitter dataset consists of tweets from various news sources. Each of these tweets is assigned a specific bias based on political leaning of the news source according to AllSides media bias chart [2]. Later, we discuss these datasets as well as the simple search engine that we implemented to demonstrate `BalancedQR`. As described in Sect. 6.2, we use multiple word embeddings, including GloVe [28], GoogleNews [13], all-mpnet-base-v2 [31], as well as a word embedding created from the dataset, we used 'gensim' [29] to create the word embedding using it's implementation of word2vec algorithms. We also use multiple search engines for documents retrieval, including TF-IDF, BM25 [22] and FAISS [16].[3]

## 5.1  Data

**Reddit.** Given that there is no ground truth for which queries 'should' be returned, we perform a qualitative analysis in which we demonstrate the use of `BalancedQR` on real data. For our analysis, we compare pairs of contrasting subReddits from Reddit.com. Using the Python PRAW package, we crawled 'top' posts from the following pairs: (r/AskMen, r/AskWomen), and (r/Republican, r/Democrats). Additional pairs were considered, with similar results, but are not included here due to space constraints.

We collected a roughly equal number of posts from each subReddit in a pair. Dataset statistics– the number of posts collected and the total number of members of each subReddit– are shown in Table 2. Most of the data was collected in October, 2020 with additional political data collected in late January, 2021.

Next, we used data from Google Trends [32] to create a list of evaluation queries based on top trending queries. Most of these queries did not appear in the dataset or did not show substantial bias. For each pair of subReddits, we identified certain queries that showed interesting differences between the two subReddits.

**Table 2.** Dataset properties.

| subReddit | Posts Collected | Members |
|---|---|---|
| r/AskMen | 3618 | 2.2M |
| r/AskWomen | 2431 | 1.8M |
| r/democrats | 2445 | 143K |
| r/Republican | 2262 | 147K |

---

[3] https://github.com/harshdsdh/BalancedQR.

**Twitter.** We also perform an analysis on Twitter data. We collect tweets from major news sources between the period of Oct 2021 to Feb 2022. We used the AllSides media bias chart [2] to label the political leaning of each news source. We focused on tweets from news sources labeled as 'leaning left', 'left', 'center', 'leaning right' and 'right' by AllSides. We collected total 39k tweets from left and leaning-left sources, 17k tweets from leaning-right and right sources and 15k tweets from center sources.

Next, we again use data from Google Trends to create a list of evaluation queries based on top news/ political queries in years 2020, 2021 and 2022. We collect 50 relevant queries for the evaluation purpose.

## 5.2   Search Engines

To demonstrate `BalancedQR` on the datasets, we implement search engines based on tf-idf, Faiss and BM25.

In the case of tf-idf [22], we compute the tf-idf score of each document with respect to the original query $Q$, and return the 20 highest scoring documents (or fewer, if fewer than 20 documents use that query).

Faiss is a vector search library that provides a way to search for similar documents based on euclidean distance [16]. For `BalancedQR`, we convert query $Q$ and the dataset into vectors using a pre-trained sentence embedding. For this evaluation we use MPNet [31]. We then use Faiss to retrieve 20 similar documents for original query Q.

For BM25 [22], we compute the idf score of each document with respect to $Q$ and return the top 20 highest scoring documents.

Obviously, real-world search engines are much more sophisticated than these techniques, but our goal here is to demonstrate `BalancedQR` across a variety of search algorithms.

## 5.3   Word Embedding

For this analysis, we use multiple word embeddings, including GloVe [28], GoogleNews [13], and our own word2vec word embedding created from the Twitter dataset, we used 'gensim' [29] to create the word embedding using it's implementation of word2vec algorithms. We also use a pretrained MPNet based sentence transformer to get a sentence-embedding for the dataset [31]. `BalancedQR` uses embeddings to calculate document similarity as well as to create a set of potential recommended queries.

We use *gpt-3.5-turbo* in our analysis to retrieve multi-word queries, using cosine similarity in word embedding we create a set of similar keywords $w_i$ for a word $w$ in query $Q$ [6]. We then use *gpt-3.5-turbo* with the prompt *'I am a highly intelligent question answering bot. If you ask me a question that is nonsense, trickery, or has no clear answer, I will respond with Unknown. For original query Q, frame a new query using $w_i$. Be as brief as possible'* to fetch similar related queries. GPT and other large language models are prone to misinformation, so

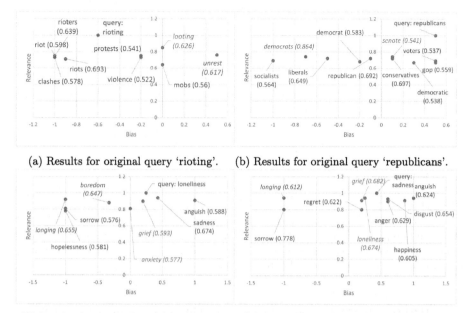

(a) Results for original query 'rioting'.     (b) Results for original query 'republicans'.

(c) Results for original query 'loneliness'.     (d) Results for original query 'sadness'.

**Fig. 1.** Potential keyword recommendations for queries on political (top) and gender (bottom) subReddits. Along the x-axis, positive values represent bias towards the r/Democrats (r/AskMen) subReddit, while negative values represent bias towards the r/Republican (r/AskWomen) subReddit. Words on the Pareto front (where bias is a scalar) are circled in green. High-relevance words with opposite bias are indicated in red. (Color figure online)

we provide a seed word $w_i$ for the new query, as a way to reduce wrongful or unrelated queries and to ground them in the context of the original query $Q$. We then use this generative query for `BalancedQR`. This is done purely for purposes of demonstrating `BalancedQR`: the user can use whatever technique is desired to find similar queries, and we make no specific recommendation on whether *gpt-3.5-turbo* should or should not be used in such a context.

## 6 Analysis and Discussion

### 6.1 Reddit

We first discuss the results of `BalancedQR` on the two pairs of subReddits described earlier. Results presented here use the document similarity-based relevance calculation, as discussed in Sect. 4.2. A bias of $\pm p$ indicates the sum of the document biases, divided by the total number of documents. A bias of 0 thus indicates that an equal number of documents from each subReddit were returned. A bias of $\pm 1$ indicates that all results were from one subReddit. In all

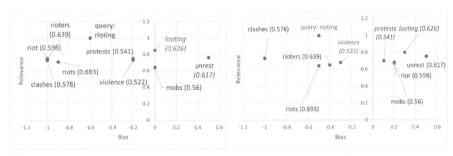

(a) Results for 'rioting' based on data col-    (b) Results for 'rioting' based on data collected in October, 2020.                        lected after Jan 6th, 2021.

**Fig. 2.** Potential keyword recommendations for 'rioting' on political subReddits. Along the x-axis, positive values represent bias towards the r/democrats subReddit, while negative values represent bias towards the r/Republican subReddit. Words on the Pareto front (where bias is a scalar) are circled in green. High-relevance words with opposite bias are indicated in red. (Color figure online)

plots, the original query is shown in boldface. This query always has a relevance of 1 to itself.

The Pareto front, computed by treating bias as a scalar (directionless) is circled in green, and includes the original keyword. We additionally note high-relevance words that are biased in the opposite direction.

Although our implementation of `BalancedQR` considers the 10 words closest to the original keyword (using the GloVe word embedding), in some cases, some of these words occurred 0 times in the dataset and do not appear in plots. For the results mentioned in following sections, we use tf-idf as our search algorithm and the GloVe word embedding is used to calculate word and document similarity. Results were similar for other search algorithms/embeddings.

**Politics.** For the political subReddits (r/Democrats, r/Republican), we considered the query keywords 'rioting' and 'republicans'. On these plots, a positive bias (right side of plots) indicates a bias towards r/Democrats, and a negative bias (left side of plots) indicates a bias towards r/Republican. Results for each of these keywords are shown in Fig. 1.

Results for the query 'rioting' are shown in Fig. 1a. The keyword itself returns results disproportionately from the Republicans subReddit (by a 4:1 ratio, giving a bias of $\frac{1-4}{5} = -0.6$). When considering words that are highly relevant, we observed that 'unrest' returns results disproportionately from the Democratic subReddit (by a 3:1 ratio, for a bias of 0.5), and 'riots' returns results biased towards Republicans subReddit (with no results from the Democratic subReddit). Interestingly, almost all related keywords are either neutral or Republican-biased: the only related word with a Democratic bias is 'unrest'. The keyword returned by `BalancedQR` on the Pareto front is 'looting', as this returns documents that are evenly balanced between the subReddits. If desired, `BalancedQR` can also return 'unrest' to provide a Democratic counterbalance to the original keyword.

For the 'rioting' keyword specifically, we were curious to see if there were any changes to the above results after the January 6th, 2021 insurrection. To answer this, we re-collected data and redid this analysis. Original results (collected in October 2020) are shown in Fig. 2a and new results (collected in early January 2021) are shown in Fig. 2a. As shown in Fig. 2b, the earlier data shows that posters in the Democratic party subReddit tended to use words such as 'unrest' instead of 'rioting', while individuals in the Republican subReddit were using words such as 'rioters' and 'riots'. Fig. 2b shows results from January 2021. People in the Democratic subReddit use words such as 'protests' and 'mobs' for this concept. Posters in the Republican subReddit still use words such as 'rioters' and 'riots', but there is a reduction in the bias of these words.

We also discuss results for the query 'republicans'. Interestingly, 'republicans' has a bias towards r/Democrats; but 'republican' has a slight bias towards r/Republican. Upon further inspection of posts, a possible explanation for this is that Democrats are more likely to discuss Republicans as a group, while individual Republicans may discuss their own identity as a (singular) Republican. In this case, BalancedQR suggests 'senate' on the Pareto front.

Next, we present sample results for the gender-based subReddits r/AskMen and r/AskWomen. We consider the original queries 'loneliness' and 'sadness'. Positive values of bias indicate bias towards r/AskMen, and negative values of bias indicate bias towards r/AskWomen. Results are shown in Fig. 1.

Figure 1c shows results for the query 'loneliness'. The original query returns results disproportionately from the r/AskMen (bias of 0.25). When considering words that are highly relevant, we observed that 'sadness' and 'anguish' were also biased towards r/AskMen, while 'boredom' was biased towards r/AskWomen (by a 2:1 ratio, for a bias of $-0.33$). The queries recommended by BalancedQR on the Pareto front are 'grief', which is slightly less r/AskMen-biased than 'loneliness'; and 'anxiety', which does not show bias towards either subReddit. Potential candidates with opposite bias include 'boredom' and 'longing', both of which are extremely relevant to 'loneliness'.

### 6.2  Twitter

Next, we perform a quantitative evaluation on Twitter data. We use a set of 50 queries, including 'Georgia Senate Race', 'Roe v Wade' and 'QAnon' applied on the dataset of 72k rows.

Figure 3 describes relevance and bias of results obtained for various implementations of BalancedQR. In this figure, bias under the 'Query', 'All Possible Recommend Queries', and 'BalancedQR Recommended Queries' columns refers to the average bias (cosine similarity) and relevance of the set of documents retrieved for the original query, queries produced via word embedding similarity alone (without care for bias), and by BalancedQR. Relevance is 1 when two queries retrieve the same documents and 0 when no documents are similar.

| Search Engines | Word/ Sentence Embedding | Document similarity Embedding | Query | | All Possible Recommended Queries | | BalanceQR Recommended Queries | |
|---|---|---|---|---|---|---|---|---|
| | | | Bias | Relevance | Bias | Relevance | Bias | Relevance |
| BM25 | GloVe | GloVe | 0.305 | 1 | 0.340 | 0.898 | 0.146 | 0.929 |
| | GoogleNews | GoogleNews | 0.276 | 1 | 0.332 | 0.728 | 0.178 | 0.822 |
| | Twitter_w2v | Twitter_w2v | 0.284 | 1 | 0.306 | 0.918 | **0.114** | 0.936 |
| | Twitter_w2v | all-mpnet-base-v2 | 0.276 | 1 | 0.306 | 0.465 | 0.117 | 0.604 |
| | Twitter_w2v + gpt-3.5-turbo | all-mpnet-base-v2 | 0.267 | 1 | 0.395 | 0.652 | 0.211 | 0.785 |
| | Twitter_w2v + gpt-3.5-turbo | Twitter_w2v | 0.267 | 1 | 0.395 | 0.944 | 0.216 | **0.965** |
| TF-IDF | GloVe | GloVe | 0.398 | 1 | 0.422 | 0.855 | **0.156** | 0.893 |
| | GoogleNews | GoogleNews | 0.398 | 1 | 0.500 | 0.575 | 0.182 | 0.724 |
| | Twitter_w2v | Twitter_w2v | 0.398 | 1 | 0.498 | 0.897 | 0.203 | 0.933 |
| | Twitter_w2v | all-mpnet-base-v2 | 0.398 | 1 | 0.498 | 0.360 | 0.190 | 0.547 |
| | Twitter_w2v + gpt-3.5-turbo | all-mpnet-base-v2 | 0.408 | 1 | 0.383 | 0.628 | 0.276 | 0.734 |
| | Twitter_w2v + gpt-3.5-turbo | Twitter_w2v | 0.408 | 1 | 0.395 | 0.937 | 0.270 | **0.953** |
| FAISS | GloVe | GloVe | 0.421 | 1 | 0.308 | 0.845 | 0.180 | 0.883 |
| | GoogleNews | GoogleNews | 0.421 | 1 | 0.27 | 0.577 | 0.215 | 0.668 |
| | Twitter_w2v | Twitter_w2v | 0.421 | 1 | 0.295 | 0.899 | 0.141 | 0.916 |
| | Twitter_w2v | all-mpnet-base-v2 | 0.421 | 1 | 0.295 | 0.342 | **0.133** | 0.477 |
| | Twitter_w2v + gpt-3.5-turbo | all-mpnet-base-v2 | 0.418 | 1 | 0.592 | 0.709 | 0.395 | 0.803 |
| | Twitter_w2v + gpt-3.5-turbo | Twitter_w2v | 0.421 | 1 | 0.295 | 0.889 | 0.391 | **0.963** |

**Fig. 3.** Analysis for bias and relevance for queries on Twitter data. `BalancedQR` recommends relevant queries with less bias compared to other queries.

As we compare values across the three query columns, we observe that `BalancedQR` produces less biased and highly relevant results. As we see, `BalancedQR` achieves highest relevance when used with a combination of word embedding created from the dataset and *gpt-3.5-turbo*. In this case, the average bias of the set of recommended queries is less than the bias of set of original queries as well as they are still relevant. We also observe that a higher relevance when we combine a word embedding with *gpt-3.5-turbo* for potential recommended queries.

Table 3 shows examples of several queries and recommended queries. Consider the query 'Stimulus Check'. During the COVID pandemic, stimulus checks were provided by the US government to its citizens. The list of related terms includes 'subscribe', 'list' and 'debunk'. The original query returns result that are disproportionately from left-leaning news sources (bias of 0.62). After observing highly relevant but less imbalanced queries, `BalancedQR` (using *gpt-3.5-turbo*) returns queries such as 'can I subscribe for updates on stimulus checks' (bias of

0.3, relevance of 0.91). These are still skewed towards left-leaning sources, but less so, and are still highly relevant.

**Table 3.** Sample results from LLM

| Original query | Suggested keyword from word embedding | Suggested query from LLM | Sample queries from `BalancedQR` |
|---|---|---|---|
| Roe v Wade | dobbs | What is the impact of dobbs v jackson womens health organization on roe v wade | which justices were on the supreme court for roe v wade |
| | alito | What is alitos stance on roe v wade | what would happen if roe v wade was overturned |
| QAnon | convincing | What is the convincing evidence for the claims made by qanon | What is the convincing evidence for the claims made by qanon |
| | conspiracy | What distinguishes qanon from other conspiracy theories | what are the chilling effects of qanon |
| Stimulus Check | drugmaker | What drugmakers have received stimulus funds | can i subscribe for updates on stimulus checks |
| | value | what is the value of the latest stimulus check | what is the value of the latest stimulus check |

# 7  Conclusion and Future Work

In this paper, we considered the problem of *balanced query recommendation*, and proposed `BalancedQR`, an algorithmic framework for identifying highly-relevant but less-biased query alternatives. A major application of this problem is on web search, where balanced query recommendation can be a step in addressing problems caused by echo chambers or filter bubbles. Search engines can leverage `BalancedQR` as a post-processing method using it to recommend less biased query alternatives to the end user. It can also be used as a plugin to any web browser. In future work, we will explore dealing with multiple dimensions of bias.

**Acknowledgements.** Soundarajan was supported in part by NSF #2047224.

# References

1. Abdollahpouri, H., Burke, R., Mobasher, B.: Managing popularity bias in recommender systems with personalized re-ranking. arXiv preprint arXiv:1901.07555 (2019)
2. allsides (2021)

3. Bender, E.M., Gebru, T., McMillan-Major, A., Shmitchell, S.: On the dangers of stochastic parrots: can language models be too big. In: Proceedings of the 2021 ACM Conference on Fairness, Accountability, and Transparency, FAccT 2021, pp. 610–623. Association for Computing Machinery, New York (2021). https://doi.org/10.1145/3442188.3445922

4. Beutel, A., et al.: Fairness in recommendation ranking through pairwise comparisons. In: Proceedings of the 25th ACM SIGKDD International Conference on Knowledge Discovery & Data Mining, pp. 2212–2220 (2019)

5. Bolukbasi, T., Chang, K.W., Zou, J.Y., Saligrama, V., Kalai, A.T.: Man is to computer programmer as woman is to homemaker? Debiasing word embeddings. In: Advances in Neural Information Processing Systems, pp. 4349–4357 (2016)

6. Brown, T.B., et al.: Language models are few-shot learners (2020)

7. Celis, L.E., Straszak, D., Vishnoi, N.K.: Ranking with fairness constraints. arXiv preprint arXiv:1704.06840 (2017)

8. Dev, S., Li, T., Phillips, J.M., Srikumar, V.: On measuring and mitigating biased inferences of word embeddings. In: AAAI, pp. 7659–7666 (2020)

9. Dutta, R.: System, method, and program for ranking search results using user category weighting (2002). US Patent App. 09/737,995

10. Flaxman, S., Goel, S., Rao, J.M.: Filter bubbles, echo chambers, and online news consumption. Public Opin. Q. **80**(S1), 298–320 (2016)

11. Geyik, S.C., Ambler, S., Kenthapadi, K.: Fairness-aware ranking in search & recommendation systems with application to linkedin talent search. In: Proceedings of the 25th ACM SIGKDD International Conference on Knowledge Discovery & Data Mining, pp. 2221–2231 (2019)

12. Gonen, H., Goldberg, Y.: Lipstick on a pig: debiasing methods cover up systematic gender biases in word embeddings but do not remove them. arXiv preprint arXiv:1903.03862 (2019)

13. Google

14. Guo, Y., Yang, Y., Abbasi, A.: Auto-debias: debiasing masked language models with automated biased prompts. In: Proceedings of the 60th Annual Meeting of the Association for Computational Linguistics (Volume 1: Long Papers), Dublin, Ireland, pp. 1012–1023. Association for Computational Linguistics (2022). https://doi.org/10.18653/v1/2022.acl-long.72. https://aclanthology.org/2022.acl-long.72/

15. Himelboim, I., McCreery, S., Smith, M.: Birds of a feather tweet together: integrating network and content analyses to examine cross-ideology exposure on twitter. J. Comput.-Mediat. Commun. **18**(2), 154–174 (2013)

16. Johnson, J., Douze, M., Jégou, H.: Billion-scale similarity search with GPUs. IEEE Trans. Big Data **7**(3), 535–547 (2019)

17. Kulshrestha, J., Eslami, M., Messias, J., Zafar, M.B., Ghosh, S., Gummadi, K.P., Karahalios, K.: Quantifying search bias: investigating sources of bias for political searches in social media (2017). https://arxiv.org/pdf/1704.01347.pdf

18. Kaneko, M., Bollegala, D.: Gender-preserving debiasing for pre-trained word embeddings. In: Proceedings of the 57th Annual Meeting of the Association for Computational Linguistics (ACL) (2019)

19. Khalifa, M., Elsahar, H., Dymetman, M.: A distributional approach to controlled text generation. In: International Conference on Learning Representations (2021). https://openreview.net/forum?id=jWkw45-9AbL

20. Liu, W., Burke, R.: Personalizing fairness-aware re-ranking. arXiv preprint arXiv:1809.02921 (2018)

21. Alewiwi, M., Orencik, C., Savas, E.: Efficient top-k similarity document search utilizing distributed file systems and cosine similarity (2017). https://arxiv.org/pdf/1704.01347.pdf
22. Manning, C.D., Raghavan, P., Schütze, H.: Introduction to Information Retrieval. Cambridge University Press, Cambridge (2008). https://doi.org/10.1017/CBO9780511809071
23. Zehlike, M., Bonchi, F., Castillo, C., Hajian, S., Megahed, M., Baeza-Yates, R.: Fa*ir: a fair top-k ranking algorithm (2018). https://arxiv.org/pdf/1706.06368.pdf
24. Mishra, H., Soundarajan, S.: Keyword recommendation for fair search. In: Boratto, L., Faralli, S., Marras, M., Stilo, G. (eds.) BIAS 2022, pp. 130–142. Springer, Cham (2022). https://doi.org/10.1007/978-3-031-09316-6_12
25. Nguyen, C.T.: Echo chambers and epistemic bubbles. Episteme **17**(2), 141–161 (2020)
26. Noble, S.U.: Algorithms of Oppression: How Search Engines Reinforce Racism. NYU Press, New York (2018)
27. Pennington, J., Socher, R., Manning, C.: Glove: global vectors for word representation. In: Proceedings of the 2014 Conference on Empirical Methods in Natural Language Processing (EMNLP), Doha, Qatar, pp. 1532–1543. Association for Computational Linguistics (2014). https://doi.org/10.3115/v1/D14-1162. https://www.aclweb.org/anthology/D14-1162
28. Pennington, J., Socher, R., Manning, C.D.: Glove: global vectors for word representation. In: Proceedings of the 2014 Conference on Empirical Methods in Natural Language Processing (EMNLP), pp. 1532–1543 (2014)
29. Řehůřek, R., Sojka, P.: Software framework for topic modelling with large corpora. In: Proceedings of the LREC 2010 Workshop on New Challenges for NLP Frameworks, Valletta, Malta, pp. 45–50. ELRA (2010)
30. Singh, A., Joachims, T.: Fairness of exposure in rankings. In: Proceedings of the 24th ACM SIGKDD International Conference on Knowledge Discovery & Data Mining, pp. 2219–2228 (2018)
31. Song, K., Tan, X., Qin, T., Lu, J., Liu, T.Y.: MPNet: masked and permuted pre-training for language understanding. In: NeurIPS 2020. ACM (2020). https://www.microsoft.com/en-us/research/publication/mpnet-masked-and-permuted-pre-training-for-language-understanding/
32. Google Trends (2021)
33. Vogel, R., Bellet, A., Clémençon, S.: Learning fair scoring functions: fairness definitions, algorithms and generalization bounds for bipartite ranking. arXiv preprint arXiv:2002.08159 (2020)
34. Zehlike, M., Castillo, C.: Reducing disparate exposure in ranking: a learning to rank approach. In: Proceedings of the Web Conference 2020, pp. 2849–2855 (2020)
35. Zehlike, M., Sühr, T., Castillo, C., Kitanovski, I.: Fairsearch: a tool for fairness in ranked search results. In: Companion Proceedings of the Web Conference 2020, pp. 172–175 (2020)
36. Zhao, J., Zhou, Y., Li, Z., Wang, W., Chang, K.: Learning gender-neutral word embeddings. CoRR abs/1809.01496 (2018). https://arxiv.org/abs/1809.01496

# Reinforcement Learning

# On the Distributional Convergence of Temporal Difference Learning

Jie Dai[1] and Xuguang Chen[2(✉)]

[1] Changsha, China
[2] College of Computer, National University of Defense Technology, Changsha, China
chenxuguang@nudt.edu.cn

**Abstract.** Temporal Difference (TD) learning is one of the most simple but efficient algorithms for policy evaluation in reinforcement learning. Although the finite-time convergence results of the TD algorithm are abundant now, the distributional convergence has still been blank. This paper shows that TD with constant step size simulates Markov chains converging to some stationary distribution under both i.i.d. and Markov chain observation models. We prove that TD enjoys the geometric distributional convergence rate and show how the step size affects the expectation and covariance of the stationary distribution. All assumptions used in our paper are mild and common in the TD community. Our proved results indicate a tradeoff between the convergence speed and accuracy for TD. Based on our theoretical findings, we explain why the Jacobi preconditioner can accelerate the TD algorithms.

**Keywords:** Temporal Difference Learning · Markov Chain Noise · Distributional Convergence

## 1 Introduction

Reinforcement learning is a mature but vibrant area in artificial intelligence that has been widely used in many fields, such as game theory, control theory, multi-agent systems, operations research [29]. In numerous cases, people need to evaluate whether a given policy is good enough, for which TD learning is one of the main workhorses [28]. Although the scheme of TD learning only uses an iterative procedure, the sampling cost and speed depend on the size of the state space. Thus in large-scale settings, the TD learning algorithm often becomes intractable, and researchers propose to combine function approximation techniques with TD [1,30]. The linear function approximation based TD stores the value function by a feature matrix and enjoys solid convergence [3,7,15]. In [7], the authors show a tight link between TD and the well-known Stochastic Gradient Descent (SGD) [21] when the state in each iteration is selected from

J. Dai–Independent Researcher.
This research is supported by the National Natural Science Foundation of China under the grant (12002382).

the stationary distribution. It has been proved that SGD with a constant step size simulates a Markov chain convergent to a stationary distribution [8,17]. A natural question is then

*Does TD with constant step size also simulate a Markov chain? If it does, how fast? How the step size affects the expectation and covariance of the stationary distribution?*

This paper presents affirmative answers to the above questions. Our theoretical findings show a tradeoff between the convergence speed of the Markov chain induced by TD and the covariance of the stationary distribution.

## 1.1  Related Works

We briefly review two kinds of works: TD and distributional convergence of stochastic algorithms.

**TD Learning.** The empirical successes inspire the theoretical development of TD algorithms. The early related works characterize the sequence asymptotically by the Ordinary Differential Equation (ODE) method [4] because the TD update is not the stochastic gradient direction of any fixed objective. Recently, the authors have presented the finite sample analysis of TD with linear function approximation under i.i.d. assumption on the received data [7]. In [15], a general linear stochastic system that includes TD is studied but with improved results. To get rid of the i.i.d. assumption, [3] present the finite-time analysis of a projected TD with Markov chain samplings; the projection operator is removed in [24] and [13]. The momentum-based TD is developed in [16]. Motivated by the adaptive schemes in the SGD community, the TD with adaptive step sizes updated by historical stochastic semi-gradients is developed with provable finite-time convergence results [26,32]. In [22], the authors proposed to use the Jacobi preconditioning method to improve the performance of TD.

**Distributional Convergence.** The SGD considered in the distributional convergence area is assumed to be associated with constant noise, i.e., the stochastic gradient can be decomposed into the gradient and random noise from a stationary distribution. It is worth mentioning that in the finite-sum optimization, the SGD might not follow such an assumption strictly. The distributional convergence about the SGD and its variants has been well studied based on the Markov chain theory. In [8], the authors present the distributional convergence analysis of SGD with constant step size when the objective is strongly convex. In [17], the authors pointed out that the SGD can be regarded as the approximate Bayesian inference and provided the property of the stationary distribution. In [5], the authors present detailed analyses of the Wasserstein distances analysis between stochastic gradient Langevin dynamics and its several variants. In [6], the distributional convergence of the accelerated SGD, including the Nesterov's and Polyak's versions, are studied. In [10], the authors proved the distribution convergence rate for the momentum SGD. Recently, a unified framework based on operator theory for the stationary convergence for a class of stochastic iterations has been developed in [11,12].

## 1.2   Contributions

In a nutshell, the contributions of this paper are summarized in fourfold:

- We show that the TD with linear function approximation under the steady-state distribution indeed simulates a Markov chain with an explicit geometric factor.
- We provide the properties about the expectation and covariance of the stationary distribution. Our results show that, in an interval, a larger step size accelerates the convergence speed of the Markov chain but yields a larger variance.
- We prove that in the Markov chain observation model, the distributions of TD with linear function approximation converge to the same distribution of i.i.d. case but with convergence speed being degraded.
- We explain that under some condition preconditioning method benefits the TD algorithm, i.e., accelerates the stationary convergence speed of TD.

## 2   Preliminaries

**Notation.** Given a vector $\mathbf{x}$, $\|\mathbf{x}\|$ denotes its $\ell_2$ norm; given a matrix $\mathbf{A}$, we denote $\|\mathbf{A}\|$ as its spectral norm. The Dirac delta function is denoted by $\delta_{\mathbf{x}}$. The vectorization from a matrix to a vector is denoted by $\mathbf{Vec}$ and its inverse is $\mathbf{Vec}^{-1}$. $\mathbf{A} \otimes \mathbf{B}$ represents the Kronecker product of matrices $\mathbf{A}$ and $\mathbf{B}$. $e^{\mathbf{A}}$ denotes the power series $e^{\mathbf{A}} = \sum_{k=0}^{+\infty} \frac{\mathbf{A}^k}{k!}$. We use $\mathcal{B}(\mathbb{R}^d)$ to represent the Borel set in the $\mathbb{R}^d$ space. All measures considered in the text are Borel measures on Polish spaces, which are complete and separable metric spaces, with the corresponding Borel $\sigma$-algebra. We use $\mathcal{P}_2(\mathbb{R}^d)$ to denote the space consisting of all the Borel probability measures $\kappa$ on $\mathbb{R}^d$ satisfying that $\int_{\mathbb{R}^d} \|\mathbf{x}\|^2 \kappa(d\mathbf{x}) < +\infty$. For all probability measures $\kappa$ and $\hat{\kappa}$ in $\mathcal{P}_2(\mathbb{R}^d)$, the Wasserstein distance of order 2 between $\kappa$ and $\hat{\kappa}$ is defined by $\mathcal{W}(\kappa, \hat{\kappa}) := \inf_{\mathfrak{m} \in \Pi(\kappa, \hat{\kappa})} \left( \int \|\mathbf{x} - \mathbf{y}\|^2 \mathfrak{m}(d\mathbf{x}, d\mathbf{y}) \right)^{1/2}$, where $\Pi(\kappa, \hat{\kappa})$ denotes the set of all joint probability distributions between $\kappa$ and $\hat{\kappa}$.

**Markov Decision Process.** This paper considers the Markov Decision Process (MDP) that involves a tuple $(\mathcal{S}, \mathcal{P}, \mathcal{R}, \gamma)$ associated with a fixed policy $\mu$, where $\mathcal{S}$ is the state space, $\mathcal{P}$ denotes the probability transition matrix, and $\mathcal{R}$ represents a reward function, and $0 < \gamma < 1$ is a discount factor. More specifically, given two states $s$ and $s'$, $\mathcal{P}(s' \mid s)$ and $\mathcal{R}(s, s')$ are the probability of the transition from $s$ to $s'$ and corresponding reward, respectively. The expected instantaneous reward about state $s$ is denoted as $\mathcal{R}(s) := \sum_{s' \in \mathcal{S}} \mathcal{P}(s' \mid s) \mathcal{R}(s, s')$. The value function associated with $\mu$ in this MDP is then $\mathbf{V}_\mu(s) := \mathbb{E}\left[\sum_{t=0}^{+\infty} \gamma^t \mathcal{R}(s_t) \mid s\right]$, which satisfies the well-known Bellman equation $\mathbf{V}_\mu = \mathcal{R} + \gamma \mathcal{P} \mathbf{V}_\mu$. The stationary distribution of the states is assumed to exist, denoted as $\vartheta$, and $\mathbf{D} := \mathrm{Diag}[(\vartheta(s))_{s \in \mathcal{S}}]$.

**Temporal Difference Learning.** Nevertheless, the curse of dimension destroys the routine of directly solving the Bellman equation. Alternatively, people employ a feature matrix $\Phi := [(\phi(s))_{s \in \mathcal{S}}]^\top$ and turn to the use of linear function approximation as $\mathbf{V}(s) \approx \langle \phi(s), \boldsymbol{\theta} \rangle$. The linear approximation directly results in the TD described as

$$\boldsymbol{\theta}^{t+1} = \boldsymbol{\theta}^t + \eta \mathbf{g}^t, \tag{1}$$

where $\eta > 0$ is the step size, and

$$\mathbf{g}^t := (\mathcal{R}(s_t, s_{t+1}) + \gamma \langle \phi(s_{t+1}), \boldsymbol{\theta}^t \rangle - \langle \phi(s_t), \boldsymbol{\theta}^t \rangle) \phi(s_t)$$

is the stochastic semi-gradient[1], and $(s_t, \mathcal{R}(s_t, s_{t+1}), s_{t+1})$ is a tuple observed in the $t$-th iteration under $\mu$. Under the i.i.d. observation model, $\{s_t\}_{t \geq 0}$ are drawn i.i.d. from the stationary distribution of the Markov process[2]. TD then can be reformulated as

$$\boldsymbol{\theta}^{t+1} = \boldsymbol{\theta}^t + \eta \mathbf{A}(s_t) \boldsymbol{\theta}^t + \eta \mathbf{b}(s_t), \tag{2}$$

where $\begin{cases} \mathbf{A}(s_t) := \gamma \phi(s_t)[\phi(s_{t+1})]^\top - \phi(s_t)[\phi(s_t)]^\top, \\ \mathbf{b}(s_t) := \mathcal{R}(s_t, s_{t+1}) \phi(s_t). \end{cases}$ Direct computations give us $\mathbb{E}\mathbf{A}(s_t) = \boldsymbol{\Phi}^\top \mathbf{D}(\gamma \mathcal{P} \boldsymbol{\Phi} - \boldsymbol{\Phi}) := \mathbf{A}$, and $\mathbb{E}\mathbf{b}(s_t) = \boldsymbol{\Phi}^\top \mathbf{D}\mathcal{R} := \mathbf{b}$. In [3], the authors proved that the sequence generated by TD with fixed step size will fall into an area around $\boldsymbol{\theta}^* := -\mathbf{A}^{-1}\mathbf{b}$ in expectation. Note that when $\boldsymbol{\Phi}$ is the identity matrix, $\boldsymbol{\theta}^*$ is exactly the solution of the Bellman equation.

**Tools.** We collect necessary notions in Markov chain theory for our analysis [18, 19]. Let $R_\eta(\boldsymbol{\theta}, \cdot)$ be the Markov kernel on $\mathcal{B}(\mathbb{R}^d)$ associated with TD iterates, almost surely

$$R_\eta(\boldsymbol{\theta}, C) = \mathbb{P}(\boldsymbol{\theta} + \eta \mathbf{A}(s)\boldsymbol{\theta} + \eta \mathbf{b}(s) \in C | \boldsymbol{\theta})$$

for any $C \in \mathcal{B}(\mathbb{R}^d)$ and $s \sim \vartheta$. The Markov kernel $R_\eta^t$ is defined as $R_\eta^1 = R_\eta$ and for $t \geq 1$, for all $\hat{\boldsymbol{\theta}} \in \mathbb{R}^d$ and $C \in \mathcal{B}(\mathbb{R}^d)$, $R_\eta^{t+1}(\hat{\boldsymbol{\theta}}, C) := \int_{\mathbb{R}^d} R_\eta^t(\hat{\boldsymbol{\theta}}, d\boldsymbol{\theta}) R_\eta(\boldsymbol{\theta}, C)$. Given a probability measure $\kappa$ on $\mathcal{B}(\mathbb{R}^d)$, the composite measure is defined by $\kappa R^t(C) := \int_{\mathbb{R}^d} \kappa(d\boldsymbol{\theta}) R_\eta^t(\boldsymbol{\theta}, C)$. We say probability measure $\pi_\eta$ on $\mathcal{B}(\mathbb{R}^d)$ is an invariant probability measure for $R_\eta$, if $\pi_\eta R_\eta = R_\eta$.

## 3    Distributional Convergence of TD

This section contains two parts: the first considers the i.i.d. sampling case, while the second considers the Markov chain sampling case.

### 3.1    The I.I.D. Observation Model

The part considers the i.i.d. observation model, i.e., the initial state follows the stationary distribution. We recall two necessary assumptions.

**Assumption 1.** *The stationary distribution of the state is $\vartheta$, and $\vartheta(s_i) > 0$ for any $i \in \{1, 2, \ldots, |\mathcal{S}|\}$.*

---

[1] We call it semi-gradient because the $\mathbf{g}^t$ does not follow the stochastic gradient direction of any fixed objective.

[2] The i.i.d. observation model happens if the initial state $s_0$ is drawn from the stationary distribution.

Assumption 1 is trivial: $\vartheta(s_i) = 0$ indicates that state $s_i$ contributes nothing and can be eliminated in the MDP.

**Assumption 2.** *The feature vectors are uniforms, i.e., $\|\phi(s_i)\| = 1$. And the matrix $\Phi \in \mathbb{R}^{|\mathcal{S}| \times d}$ is full row rank, i.e., there exists $\nu > 0$ such that $\|\Phi\theta\|^2 \geq \nu\|\theta\|^2$ for any $\theta \in \mathbb{R}^d$. The reward is uniformly bounded, i.e., $\max_{s,s' \in \mathcal{S}} |\mathcal{R}(s, s')| \leq \bar{r}$ for some $\bar{r} > 0$.*

If $\|\phi(s_i)\| \neq 1$ for some $s_i$, we can get a new feature as $\phi(s_i)/\|\phi(s_i)\|$. Thus, the uniform assumption can be easily satisfied. In the rest of the paper, we use the convention $\vartheta^* := \min_{1 \leq i \leq |\mathcal{S}|} \{\vartheta(s_i)\}$. In the analysis, we need an important property of the matrix $\mathbf{A}(s)$ in iterate (2).

**Lemma 1.** *Let Assumptions 1 and 2 hold. For any $\theta \in \mathbb{R}^d$, it holds $\|\mathbf{A}(s)\| \leq 1 + \gamma, -\theta^\top \mathbf{A}\theta \geq (1 - \gamma)\nu\vartheta^*\|\theta\|^2$.*

Let $\sigma$ be a singular of $-\mathbf{A}$, i.e., there exist two unit vectors $\mathbf{u}$ and $\mathbf{v}$ such that $-\mathbf{A}\mathbf{u} = \sigma\mathbf{v}$ and $-\mathbf{A}^\top\mathbf{v} = \sigma\mathbf{u}$. From Lemma 1, it holds $\sigma(\|\mathbf{u}\|^2 + \|\mathbf{v}\|^2) \geq 2\sigma\mathbf{u}\mathbf{v}^\top = -\mathbf{u}^\top\mathbf{A}\mathbf{u} - \mathbf{v}^\top\mathbf{A}^\top\mathbf{v} \geq (1 - \gamma)\nu\vartheta^*(\|\mathbf{u}\|^2 + \|\mathbf{v}\|^2)$, which means $\sigma \geq (1 - \gamma)\nu\vartheta^*$. Thus, all singular values of $-\mathbf{A}$ are not smaller than $(1 - \gamma)\nu\vartheta^*$. Similarly, all eigenvalues of $\mathbf{A}$ are negative. We now are prepared to prove that the sequence $(\theta^t)_{t \geq 0}$ generated by $R_\eta$ enjoys a unique asymptotic stationary distribution.

**Theorem 1.** *Assume the initial state follows the stationary distribution. Let Assumptions 1 and 2 hold. Given a step size $0 < \eta < \frac{2(1-\gamma)\nu\vartheta^*}{(1+\gamma)^2}$, the kernel $R_\eta$ admits a unique stationary distribution $\pi_\eta$ and $\pi_\eta R_\eta = \pi_\eta$. For any fixed $\theta^0 \in \mathbb{R}^d$,*

$$\mathcal{W}(R_\eta^t(\theta^0, \cdot), \pi_\eta) \leq \rho^t \cdot \left( \int_{\mathbb{R}^d} \|\theta - \theta^0\|^2 \pi_\eta(d\theta) \right)^{1/2},$$

$\rho = \sqrt{1 - 2(1 - \gamma)\eta\nu\vartheta^* + \eta^2(1 + \gamma)^2} < 1.$

The given point $\theta^0$ is indeed the initialization. Theorem 1 shows that distributions of $(\theta^t)_{t \geq 0}$ are convergent to some stationary distribution with a geometric speed. Theoretically, the step size $\eta$ that minimizes the geometric factor should be chosen as $\eta = \frac{(1-\gamma)\nu\vartheta^*}{(1+\gamma)^2}$. However, the current theory of the finite-time convergence requires $\eta$ to be as small as the desired error [3]. The contradiction comes from that the variance of $\pi_\eta$ increases as $\eta$ increases.

In the following, we provide several properties of $\pi_\eta$ including its expectation and covariance.

**Proposition 1.** *Assume conditions of Theorem 1 hold, it holds that $\int_{\mathbb{R}^d} \theta\pi_\eta(d\theta) = \theta^* = -\mathbf{A}^{-1}\mathbf{b}$. Denoting $\mathbf{C} := \mathbb{E}\Big( [\mathbf{b}(s) - \mathbf{A}(s)\theta^*][\mathbf{b}(s) - \mathbf{A}(s)\theta^*]^\top \Big)$, when $0 < \eta < \frac{2(1-\gamma)\nu\vartheta^*}{(1+\gamma)^2}$, the covariance satisfies $\int_{\mathbb{R}^d}[\theta - \theta^*][\theta - \theta^*]^\top\pi_\eta(d\theta) = -\eta\mathbf{Vec}^{-1}\Big\{ \big[ [\mathbf{A} \otimes \mathbf{I}] + [\mathbf{I} \otimes \mathbf{A}] + \mathbb{E}(\eta[\mathbf{A}(s) \otimes \mathbf{A}(s)]) \big]^{-1} \mathbf{Vec}(\mathbf{C}) \Big\}.*

From Proposition 1, the expectation of $\pi_\eta$ is independent of $\eta$ but the covariance is not. Proposition 1 also presents a very complicated form of the covariance. Fortunately, $\eta$ is often set very small in TD, the covariance enjoys a concise approximation. For sufficiently small $\eta > 0$, the covariance can be presented as

$$\underbrace{\mathbf{Vec}^{-1}\Big\{ -\big[[\mathbf{A} \otimes \mathbf{I}] + [\mathbf{I} \otimes \mathbf{A}]\big]^{-1} \mathbf{Vec}(\eta\mathbf{C})\Big\}}_{:=\mathbf{X}^\dagger} + \mathcal{O}(\eta^2).$$

It is easy to see that $\mathbf{X}^\dagger$ obeys the well-known continuous Lyapunov equation [23]

$$\mathbf{A}\mathbf{X}^\dagger + \mathbf{X}^\dagger\mathbf{A}^\top + \eta\mathbf{C} = \mathbf{0}, \tag{3}$$

whose solution is $\mathbf{X}^\dagger = \eta \int_0^{+\infty} e^{\mathbf{A}^\top t} \mathbf{C} e^{\mathbf{A}t} dt$. Note that the variance can be obtained by taking the trace of the covariance; the results then show that the variance decreases when the stepsize $\eta$ gets smaller. Such a result also answers the question before Proposition 1: although $\eta = \frac{(1-\gamma)\nu\vartheta^*}{(1+\gamma)^2}$ can yield the fastest convergence speed, the large variance of the stationary distribution cannot promise the use.

On the other hand, it holds $\mathbb{E}_{\theta \sim \pi_\eta}\|\theta - \theta^*\|^2 = |\mathrm{Tr}(\mathbf{X}^\dagger)| + \mathcal{O}(\eta^2)$. Let $(\theta^t)_{t \geq 0}$ be the sequence generated by the i.i.d. TD, we can have

$$\mathbb{E}\|\theta^t - \theta^*\|^2 \leq 2\mathbb{E}(\mathbb{E}_{\theta \sim \pi_\eta}\|\theta^t - \theta\|^2) + 2\mathbb{E}_{\theta \sim \pi_\eta}\|\theta - \theta^*\|^2$$
$$= 2|\mathrm{Tr}(\mathbf{X}^\dagger)| + \mathcal{O}(\rho^t) + \mathcal{O}(\eta^2) = \mathcal{O}(\rho^t) + \mathcal{O}(\eta).$$

To reach $\mathcal{O}(\epsilon)$ error, we need to set $\eta = \Theta(\epsilon)$ and

$$t = \frac{\ln\frac{1}{\epsilon}}{\ln\frac{1}{\rho}} = \mathcal{O}\Big(\frac{\ln\frac{1}{\epsilon}}{(1-\gamma)\nu\vartheta^*\epsilon}\Big).$$

## 3.2   The Markov Chain Observation Model

The TD algorithms studied in last subsection assume the state in each iteration follows i.i.d. samplings. However, in some literature the state is assumed to follow a Markov chain, i.e., non-i.i.d. case that the established theory in this paper cannot hold anymore. This subsection builds the distributional convergence under the non-i.i.d. case for TD. We recall a common assumption used in the analysis of the Markov chain observation model.

**Assumption 3.** *For any two states* $s, s' \in \mathcal{S}$, *it holds that* $\vartheta(s') = \lim_{t \to \infty} \mathbb{P}(s_t = s'|s_0 = s) > 0$ *and* $\sup_{s \in \mathcal{S}}\Big\{\sum_{s' \in \mathcal{S}} |\mathbb{P}(s_t = s' \mid s_0 = s) - \vartheta(s')|\Big\} \leq \zeta^t$ *with* $0 < \zeta < 1$.

**Theorem 2.** *Let Assumptions 1, 2 and 3 hold. Given a step size* $\eta > 0$ *sufficient small, and the initialization* $\theta^0$ *is selected from the bounded ball* $\mathbf{B}(\mathbf{0}, \eta)$. *Let*

$(\pi^t)_{\geq 1}$ be the distributions of sequence $(\boldsymbol{\theta}^t)_{\geq 1}$ generated by TD under Markov chain observation model, as $t \geq \lceil \frac{\ln \frac{1}{\eta}}{\ln \zeta} \rceil + 2$,

$$\mathcal{W}(\pi^t, \pi_\eta) \leq \rho^t \cdot \left( \int_{\mathbb{R}^d} \|\boldsymbol{\theta} - \boldsymbol{\theta}^0\|^2 \pi_\eta(d\boldsymbol{\theta}) \right)^{1/2}$$

$$+ \sqrt{2\rho^{t/2}C_\eta^2 + \frac{2\zeta^t}{1 - \rho} \frac{(\eta^2 \bar{r}^2 + \eta^2 (1+\gamma)^2 C_\eta^2)}{1 - \zeta^2}},$$

where $C_\eta$ is constant dependent on $\eta$ such that $C_\eta = \mathcal{O}(\sqrt{\frac{\ln \frac{1}{\eta}}{\eta \ln \frac{1}{\zeta}}})$, and $\pi_\eta$ is the distribution given in Theorem 1.

Theorem 2 indicates that the distributions of the sequence generated by TD under Markov chain observations also converge to the distribution $\pi_\eta$ but with convergence speed being degraded and a smaller fixed stepsize. Let $(\boldsymbol{\theta}^t)_{t \geq 0}$ be the sequence generated by the non-i.i.d. TD, similar to the i.i.d. case, we can have $\mathbb{E}\|\boldsymbol{\theta}^t - \boldsymbol{\theta}^*\|^2 \leq \underbrace{2|\mathbf{Tr}(\mathbf{X}^\dagger)|}_{\mathcal{O}(\eta)} + \mathcal{O}(\rho^t) + \mathcal{O}(\eta^2) + \mathcal{O}(\sqrt{\frac{\ln \frac{1}{\eta}}{\eta \ln \frac{1}{\zeta}}} \rho^{t/2} + \zeta^t)$. To reach $\mathcal{O}(\epsilon)$ error, we need to set $\eta = \Theta(\epsilon)$ and

$$t = \tilde{\mathcal{O}}\left( \frac{\ln \frac{1}{\epsilon}}{(1 - \gamma)\nu\vartheta^*\epsilon} + \frac{\ln \frac{1}{\epsilon}}{\ln \frac{1}{\zeta}} \right).$$

### 3.3   Jacobi Preconditioning Explanation

Our findings can be used to help the explanation of Jacobi preconditioning TD [22], in which

$$\boldsymbol{\theta}^{t+1} = \boldsymbol{\theta}^t + \eta \mathbf{J}^{-1}\mathbf{A}(s_t)\boldsymbol{\theta}^t + \eta \mathbf{J}^{-1}\mathbf{b}(s_t), \tag{4}$$

where $\mathbf{J}$ is a non-singular diagonal matrix[3]. We can denote a Markov kernel induced by this scheme and prove the geometric distributional convergence speed. If the geometric factor can be proved to be smaller than that of TD, we then get theoretical advantage of Jacobi preconditioning TD. We consider a condition for the preconditioner $\mathbf{J}^{-1}$.

**Condition 1.** For any $\boldsymbol{\theta} \in \mathbb{R}^d$, there exist $\hat{\vartheta} > 0$ such that $-\boldsymbol{\theta}^\top \mathbf{J}^{-1}\mathbf{A}\boldsymbol{\theta} \geq (1 - \gamma)\nu\hat{\vartheta}\|\boldsymbol{\theta}\|^2$.

We present the convergence speed and properties of the stationary distribution of Jacobi preconditioning TD with i.i.d. observations. Let $\hat{R}_\eta(\boldsymbol{\theta}, \cdot)$ be the Markov kernel on $\mathcal{B}(\mathbb{R}^d)$ associated with Jacobi preconditioning TD iterates, almost surely

$$\hat{R}_\eta(\boldsymbol{\theta}, C) = \mathbb{P}(\boldsymbol{\theta} + \eta \mathbf{J}^{-1}\mathbf{A}(s)\boldsymbol{\theta} + \eta \mathbf{J}^{-1}\mathbf{b}(s) \in C|\boldsymbol{\theta})$$

for any $C \in \mathcal{B}(\mathbb{R}^d)$ and $s \sim \vartheta$.

---

[3] In practice, $\mathbf{J}$ is approximated by a Monte Carlo method.

**Proposition 2.** *Assume the initial state follows the stationary distribution. Let Assumptions 1 and 2 hold, and condition (1) hold. Given a step size $0 < \eta < \frac{2(1-\gamma)\nu\hat{\vartheta}}{(1+\gamma)^2}$, the kernel $\hat{R}_\eta$ admits a unique stationary distribution $\hat{\pi}_\eta$ and $\hat{\pi}_\eta\hat{R}_\eta = \hat{\pi}_\eta$. For any fixed $\boldsymbol{\theta}^0 \in \mathbb{R}^d$,*

$$\mathcal{W}(\hat{R}_\eta^t(\boldsymbol{\theta}^0, \cdot), \pi_\eta) \leq \hat{\rho}^t \cdot \left( \int_{\mathbb{R}^d} \|\boldsymbol{\theta} - \boldsymbol{\theta}^0\|^2 \pi_\eta(d\boldsymbol{\theta}) \right)^{1/2},$$

*$\hat{\rho} = \sqrt{1 - 2(1-\gamma)\eta\nu\hat{\vartheta} + \eta^2\|\mathbf{J}^{-1}\|^2(1+\gamma)^2} < 1$. The expectation of $\hat{R}_\eta$ satisfies $\int_{\mathbb{R}^d} \boldsymbol{\theta}\hat{\pi}_\eta(d\boldsymbol{\theta}) = \boldsymbol{\theta}^*$, and its covariance is $\eta\mathbf{X}^{\ddagger} + \mathcal{O}(\eta^2)$ with $\mathbf{X}^{\ddagger}$ being the solution of $\mathbf{AX}^{\ddagger}\mathbf{J} + \mathbf{JX}^{\ddagger}\mathbf{A}^\top + \eta\mathbf{C} = \boldsymbol{0}$.*

In practice, the stepsize usually is set small, and the factor in Jacobi preconditioning TD is $\hat{\rho} = 1 - (1 - \gamma)\eta\nu\hat{\vartheta} + \mathcal{O}(\eta^2)$, while for TD the factor is $\rho = 1 - (1 - \gamma)\eta\nu\vartheta^* + \mathcal{O}(\eta^2)$. If $\hat{\vartheta} > \vartheta^*$, the Jacobi preconditioning TD enjoys a faster stationary convergence rate. Although the Jacobi one shares the same expectation as TD, the domain of covariance follows another equation; how $\mathbf{J}$ changes the covariance is unknown. Indeed, in the [22], $\mathbf{J}$ is unfixed and even a variable. Here, we present an attempt to understand how the preconditioner works. More challenging works including the variance and the changing preconditioner will be left a future work.

## 3.4   Discussions

Indeed, there are two kinds of notions of "Markov chain" in this paper: one is the style of samplings, and the other one is the tool used for the analysis.

The stationary convergence results of TD established in this paper are built on the Markov chain theory with a fixed kernel, in which step size is preset. Thus, we cannot extend our results to the TD with diminishing or adaptive step sizes [26, 32] currently. It is worth mentioning that even for the SGD, the changing step size issue in the stationary convergence has still been unsolved. The difficulty lies in the foundational theory of Markov chain.

The schemes considered in this paper are all projection free. Indeed, the projected version is also widely used [3], the projected TD reads as

$$\boldsymbol{\theta}^{t+1} = \mathbf{Proj}_\Omega\left[\boldsymbol{\theta}^t + \eta\mathbf{A}(s_t)\boldsymbol{\theta}^t + \eta\mathbf{b}(s_t)\right],$$

where $\Omega \subseteq \mathbb{R}^d$ is a convex closed set. In this case, we just need to define a Markov kernel on $\mathcal{B}(\mathbb{R}^d)$ almost surely $\bar{R}_\eta(\boldsymbol{\theta}, C) = \mathbb{P}\left(\mathbf{Proj}_\Omega[\boldsymbol{\theta} + \eta\mathbf{A}(s)\boldsymbol{\theta} + \eta\mathbf{b}(s) \in C|\boldsymbol{\theta}]\right)$ for any $C \in \mathcal{B}(\mathbb{R}^d)$ and $s \sim \vartheta$. Because $\mathbf{Proj}_\Omega(\cdot)$ is a contractive operator, we can prove that distributions of the projected schemes are also convergent with geometric factors. However, the analysis of the stationary distribution is nontrivial due to the nonlinearity of $\mathbf{Proj}_\Omega(\cdot)$. Some conditions on the set $\Omega$, e.g. large enough, benefit the detailed analysis of the stationary distribution.

Like TD, there has been a line of research that also using Markov chain to sample data, called Markov Chain Gradient Descent (MCGD[4]) [2,9,14,20,25, 27]. It is nontrivial to extend our results to MCGD because TD just involves quadratic objectives, which is much simpler to deal with. In some derivations, we can directly decompose the samples and variables, that cannot apply to the MCGD.

# 4 Proofs

## 4.1 Proof of Lemma 1

Let $s$ be a sample from the stationary distribution $\vartheta$ and $s'$ be a sample generated by Markov kernel $\mathcal{P}$ from $s$. And denote $z = (-\boldsymbol{\theta})^\top \phi(s)$, $z' = (-\boldsymbol{\theta})^\top \phi(s')$. It is easy to see that $\mathbb{E}(z^2) = \mathbb{E}((z')^2) = (-\boldsymbol{\theta})^\top \Phi^\top \mathbf{D}\Phi\boldsymbol{\theta}$. Noticing that $\mathbf{A}(s)(-\boldsymbol{\theta}) = \phi(s)(\gamma\phi(s') - \phi(s))^\top(-\boldsymbol{\theta})$, we then get

$$\|\mathbf{A}(s)\boldsymbol{\theta}\| = \|[\phi(s)(\gamma\phi(s') - \phi(s))^\top\boldsymbol{\theta}]\| \leq \|[\phi(s)(\gamma\phi(s') - \phi(s))^\top\boldsymbol{\theta}]\|$$
$$\leq (\|\phi(s)\| \cdot (\gamma\|\phi(s')\| + \|\phi(s)\|)\|\boldsymbol{\theta}\| \leq (1+\gamma)\|\boldsymbol{\theta}\|$$

and $(-\boldsymbol{\theta})^\top \mathbf{A}(\boldsymbol{\theta}) = \mathbb{E}[(-\boldsymbol{\theta})^\top\phi(s)(\gamma\phi(s') - \phi(s))^\top(\boldsymbol{\theta})] = \mathbb{E}[(\boldsymbol{\theta})^\top\phi(s)\phi(s)^\top(\boldsymbol{\theta})] - \gamma\mathbb{E}[(\boldsymbol{\theta})^\top\phi(s)\phi(s')^\top(\boldsymbol{\theta})] = \mathbb{E}(z^2) - \gamma\mathbb{E}(zz')$. With the Cauchy-Shwartz inequality $\mathbb{E}(zz') \leq \sqrt{\mathbb{E}(z^2)}\sqrt{\mathbb{E}[(z')^2]} = \mathbb{E}(z^2)$, we then get $(-\boldsymbol{\theta})^\top\mathbf{A}(\boldsymbol{\theta}) \geq (1-\gamma)\mathbb{E}(z^2) = (1-\gamma)(-\boldsymbol{\theta})^\top\Phi^\top\mathbf{D}\Phi(-\boldsymbol{\theta})^\top \geq (1-\gamma)\nu\vartheta^*\|\boldsymbol{\theta}\|^2$.

## 4.2 Proof of Theorem 1

For any $\kappa, \hat{\kappa} \in \mathcal{P}_2(\mathbb{R}^d)$, from [Theorem 4.1, [31]], there exists a couple of random variables $\boldsymbol{\theta}^0, \hat{\boldsymbol{\theta}}^0$ independent of $(s_t)_{t\geq 0}$ such that $\mathcal{W}^2(\kappa, \hat{\kappa}) = \mathbb{E}\|\boldsymbol{\theta}^0 - \hat{\boldsymbol{\theta}}^0\|^2$. Let $\boldsymbol{\theta}^0, \hat{\boldsymbol{\theta}}^0$ be the starting points and $(\boldsymbol{\theta}^t)_{\geq 1}, (\hat{\boldsymbol{\theta}}^t)_{\geq 1}$ be the sequence generated by TD(0) with step size $\eta$ with the same samples $(s_t)_{t\geq 1}$. When $t \geq 0$, we can see the joint distribution of $\boldsymbol{\theta}^t, \hat{\boldsymbol{\theta}}^t$ belongs to $\Pi(\kappa R_\eta^k, \hat{\kappa}R_\eta^k)$,

$$\mathcal{W}^2(\kappa R_\eta, \hat{\kappa}R_\eta) \leq \mathbb{E}\|\boldsymbol{\theta}^1 - \hat{\boldsymbol{\theta}}^1\|^2$$
$$= \mathbb{E}\left[\|\boldsymbol{\theta}^0 - \hat{\boldsymbol{\theta}}^0\|^2 + 2\eta\langle\boldsymbol{\theta}^0 - \hat{\boldsymbol{\theta}}^0, \mathbf{A}(s_t)(\boldsymbol{\theta}^0 - \hat{\boldsymbol{\theta}}^0)\rangle + \eta^2\|\mathbf{A}(s_t)(\boldsymbol{\theta}^0 - \hat{\boldsymbol{\theta}}^0)\|\right]$$
$$= \mathbb{E}\left[\|\boldsymbol{\theta}^0 - \hat{\boldsymbol{\theta}}^0\|^2 + 2\eta\langle\boldsymbol{\theta}^0 - \hat{\boldsymbol{\theta}}^0, \mathbf{A}(\boldsymbol{\theta}^0 - \hat{\boldsymbol{\theta}}^0)\rangle + \eta^2\|\mathbf{A}(s_t)(\boldsymbol{\theta}^0 - \hat{\boldsymbol{\theta}}^0)\|^2\right] \quad (5)$$
$$\overset{a)}{\leq} (1 - 2(1-\gamma)\eta\nu\vartheta^* + \eta^2(1+\gamma)^2) \cdot \mathbb{E}\|\boldsymbol{\theta}^0 - \hat{\boldsymbol{\theta}}^0\|^2 \leq \rho^2\mathcal{W}^2(\kappa, \hat{\kappa}),$$

where $a)$ comes from Lemma 1. With mathematical induction, we have

$$\mathcal{W}^2(\kappa R_\eta^t, \hat{\kappa}R_\eta^t) \leq \mathbb{E}\|\boldsymbol{\theta}^t - \hat{\boldsymbol{\theta}}^t\|^2 \leq \rho^{2t}\mathbb{E}\|\boldsymbol{\theta}^0 - \hat{\boldsymbol{\theta}}^0\|^2 = \rho^{2t}\mathcal{W}^2(\kappa, \hat{\kappa}). \quad (6)$$

---

[4] The random walk gradient descent can be regarded as a special MCGD because the random walk is a Markov chain process.

Hence, it follows $\sum_{t=1}^{+\infty} \mathcal{W}(\kappa R_\eta^t, \hat{\kappa} R_\eta^t) \leq (\sum_{t=1}^{+\infty} \rho^t) \mathcal{W}(\kappa, \hat{\kappa}) < +\infty$. By setting $\hat{\kappa} = \kappa R_\eta^t$, $\sum_{t=1}^{+\infty} \mathcal{W}(\kappa R_\eta^t, \kappa R_\eta^{t+1}) < +\infty$. With [Theorem 6.16, [31]], $\mathcal{P}_2(\mathbb{R}^d)$ endowed with $\mathcal{W}$ is a Polish space. Thus, $(\kappa R_\eta^t)_{t \geq 1}$ converges to some distribution $\pi_\eta^\kappa$, i.e.,

$$\lim_t \mathcal{W}(\pi_\eta^\kappa, \kappa R_\eta^t) = 0. \tag{7}$$

We now prove that $\pi_\eta^\kappa$ is independent of $\kappa$ and unique. For another $\hat{\kappa}$, we can get another $\pi_\eta^{\hat{\kappa}}$ and $\lim_t \mathcal{W}(\pi_\eta^{\hat{\kappa}}, \hat{\kappa} R_\eta^t) = 0$. With the triangle inequality,

$$\mathcal{W}(\pi_\eta^\kappa, \pi_\eta^{\hat{\kappa}}) \leq \mathcal{W}(\pi_\eta^\kappa, \kappa R_\eta^t) + \mathcal{W}(\pi_\eta^{\hat{\kappa}} R_\eta^t, \pi_\eta^{\hat{\kappa}} R_\eta^t) + \mathcal{W}(\pi_\eta^{\hat{\kappa}}, \hat{\kappa} R_\eta^t).$$

As $t \to +\infty$, $\mathcal{W}(\pi_\eta^\kappa, \pi_\eta^{\hat{\kappa}}) \to 0$. That means $\pi_\eta^\kappa = \pi_\eta^{\hat{\kappa}}$ and hence we can denote the limit distribution as $\pi_\eta$ due to they are the same for any initial. In (7), by setting $\kappa = \pi_\eta$, we have $\lim_t \mathcal{W}(\pi_\eta, \pi_\eta R_\eta^t) = 0$. On the other hand, from (5), for two distributions $\kappa, \hat{\kappa} \in \mathcal{P}_2(\mathbb{R}^d)$, $\mathcal{W}(\kappa R_\eta, \hat{\kappa} R_\eta) \leq \rho \mathcal{W}(\kappa, \hat{\kappa})$. By letting $\kappa = \pi_\eta$ and $\hat{\kappa} = \pi_\eta R_\eta^{t-1}$, we are then led to $\mathcal{W}(\pi_\eta R_\eta, \pi_\eta R_\eta^t) \leq \rho \mathcal{W}(\pi_\eta, \pi_\eta R_\eta^{t-1}) \to 0$. Hence, we get $\mathcal{W}(\pi_\eta, \pi_\eta R_\eta) \leq \mathcal{W}(\pi_\eta, \pi_\eta R_\eta^t) + \mathcal{W}(\pi_\eta R_\eta, \pi_\eta R_\eta^t) \to 0$, which indicates $\pi_\eta = \pi_\eta R_\eta$. In (6), letting $\hat{\kappa} = \pi_\eta$ and $\kappa = \delta_{\hat{\theta}}$, $\mathcal{W}(R_\eta^t(\hat{\theta}, \cdot), \pi_\eta) \leq \rho^t \mathcal{W}(\delta_{\hat{\theta}}, \pi_\eta) \leq \rho^t \left( \int_{\mathbb{R}^d} \|\theta - \hat{\theta}\|^2 \pi_\eta(d\theta) \right)^{1/2}$.

## 4.3    Proof of Proposition 1

Assume $\theta^0$ follows the distribution $\pi_\eta$, then $(\theta^t)_{t \geq 1}$ all follow $\pi_\eta$. Taking expectation of both sides of (2) and noticing that $s$ is selected i.i.d. from $\vartheta$, $0 = \eta \mathbf{b} + \eta \mathbf{A} \int_{\mathbb{R}^d} \theta \pi_\eta(d\theta)$. On the other hand, we have

$$\theta^{t+1} - \theta^* = \theta^t - \theta^* + \eta \mathbf{A}(s)(\theta^t - \theta^*) + \eta \hat{\mathbf{b}}(s),$$

where $\hat{\mathbf{b}}(s) := \mathbf{b}(s) - \mathbf{A}(s)\theta^*$ and $\mathbb{E}\hat{\mathbf{b}}(s) = \mathbf{0}$. Thus, we derive

$$[\theta^{t+1} - \theta^*][\theta^{t+1} - \theta^*]^\top = [\theta^t - \theta^* + \eta \mathbf{A}(s)(\theta^t - \theta^*) + \eta \hat{\mathbf{b}}(s)] \times [\theta^t - \theta^* + \eta \mathbf{A}(s)(\theta^t - \theta^*) + \eta \hat{\mathbf{b}}(s)]^\top.$$

Taking expectation of both sides on $\pi_\eta$ and $\vartheta$, and denoting $\Sigma := \int_{\mathbb{R}^d} [\theta - \theta^*][\theta - \theta^*]^\top \pi_\eta(d\theta)$,

$$0 = \mathbb{E}\left( \eta \mathbf{A}(s)\Sigma\mathbf{A}(s)^\top + \mathbf{A}(s)\Sigma + \Sigma\mathbf{A}(s)^\top \right) + \eta \mathbf{C}.$$

Taking vectorizations, we get $-\eta \mathbf{Vec}(\mathbf{C}) = \mathbb{E}\left( \eta[\mathbf{A}(s) \otimes \mathbf{A}(s)]\mathbf{Vec}(\Sigma) + [\mathbf{I} \otimes \mathbf{A}(s)]\mathbf{Vec}(\Sigma) + [\mathbf{A}(s) \otimes \mathbf{I}]\mathbf{Vec}(\Sigma) \right)$. We prove that $\mathbb{E}\left( \eta[\mathbf{A}(s) \otimes \mathbf{A}(s)] + [\mathbf{I} \otimes \mathbf{A}(s)] + [\mathbf{A}(s) \otimes \mathbf{I}] \right)$ is invertible when $\eta$ is small enough. First, it holds

$$-\mathbb{E}\left( [\mathbf{I} \otimes \mathbf{A}(s)] + [\mathbf{A}(s) \otimes \mathbf{I}] \right) = -(\mathbf{I} \otimes \mathbf{A} + \mathbf{A} \otimes \mathbf{I}),$$

whose singular values are $\sigma_i + \sigma_j$ $(i, j \in \{1, 2, \ldots, d\})$ and $\sigma_i$ is the $it$ singular value of $-\mathbf{A}$. From Lemma 1, $\sigma_i + \sigma_j \geq 2(1 - \gamma)\nu\vartheta^*$. On the other hand, from Lemma 1, we have $\|[\mathbf{A}(s) \otimes \mathbf{A}(s)]\| \leq \|\mathbf{A}(s)\|^2 \leq (1 + \gamma)^2$. Taking expectations, we get $\mathbb{E}\|[\mathbf{A}(s) \otimes \mathbf{A}(s)]\| \leq (1 + \gamma)^2$. For any nonzero $\mathbf{x} \in \mathbb{R}^{d^2}$,

$$
\begin{aligned}
&\|\mathbb{E}\big(\eta[\mathbf{A}(s) \otimes \mathbf{A}(s)] + [\mathbf{I} \otimes \mathbf{A}(s)] + [\mathbf{A}(s) \otimes \mathbf{I}]\big)\mathbf{x}\| \\
&\geq \|(\mathbf{I} \otimes \mathbf{A} + \mathbf{A} \otimes \mathbf{I})\mathbf{x}\| - \eta\|\mathbb{E}[\mathbf{A}(s) \otimes \mathbf{A}(s)]\mathbf{x}\| \\
&\geq \|(\mathbf{I} \otimes \mathbf{A} + \mathbf{A} \otimes \mathbf{I})\mathbf{x}\| - \eta\mathbb{E}\|[\mathbf{A}(s) \otimes \mathbf{A}(s)]\| \cdot \|\mathbf{x}\| \\
&= \| - (\mathbf{I} \otimes \mathbf{A} + \mathbf{A} \otimes \mathbf{I})\mathbf{x}\| - \eta\mathbb{E}\|[\mathbf{A}(s) \otimes \mathbf{A}(s)]\| \cdot \|\mathbf{x}\| \\
&\geq [2(1 - \gamma)\nu\vartheta^* - \eta(1 + \gamma)^2] \cdot \|\mathbf{x}\|.
\end{aligned}
$$

Thus, when $0 < \eta < \frac{2(1-\gamma)\nu\vartheta^*}{(1+\gamma)^2}$, we can derive $\mathbf{Vec}(\mathbf{\Sigma}) = -\eta\Big[\mathbb{E}\big(\eta[\mathbf{A}(s)\otimes\mathbf{A}(s)]\big) + [\mathbf{I} \otimes \mathbf{A}] + [\mathbf{A} \otimes \mathbf{I}]\Big]^{-1}\mathbf{Vec}(\mathbf{C})$.

### 4.4 Proof of Theorem 2

Let $(\hat{\boldsymbol{\theta}}^t)_{t\geq 1}$ be generated by $R_\eta$ with the starting point $\boldsymbol{\theta}^0$, i.e.,

$$
\hat{\boldsymbol{\theta}}^{t+1} = \hat{\boldsymbol{\theta}}^t + \eta\mathbf{A}(s)\hat{\boldsymbol{\theta}}^t + \eta\mathbf{b}(s)
$$

with $s \sim \vartheta$. Let $(\pi^t)_{t\geq 1}, (\hat{\pi}^t)_{t\geq 1}$ be the distributions of $(\boldsymbol{\theta}^t)_{t\geq 1}, (\hat{\boldsymbol{\theta}}^t)_{t\geq 1}$. We then have

$$
\begin{aligned}
\mathcal{W}^2(\pi^{t+1}, \hat{\pi}^{t+1}) &\leq \mathbb{E}\|\boldsymbol{\theta}^{t+1} - \hat{\boldsymbol{\theta}}^{t+1}\|^2 \\
&= \mathbb{E}\|\hat{\boldsymbol{\theta}}^t + \eta\mathbf{A}(s)\hat{\boldsymbol{\theta}}^t + \eta\mathbf{b}(s) - \hat{\boldsymbol{\theta}}^t - \eta\mathbf{A}(s_t)\hat{\boldsymbol{\theta}}^t - \eta\mathbf{b}(s_t)\|^2 \\
&\leq (1 + \alpha)\mathbb{E}\|\hat{\boldsymbol{\theta}}^t + \eta\mathbf{A}(s)\hat{\boldsymbol{\theta}}^t - \hat{\boldsymbol{\theta}}^t - \eta\mathbf{A}(s)\hat{\boldsymbol{\theta}}^t\|^2 \\
&\quad + (1 + \frac{1}{\alpha})\eta^2\mathbb{E}\|\mathbf{b}(s) - \mathbf{b}(s_t) + (\mathbf{A}(s) - \mathbf{A}(s_t))\hat{\boldsymbol{\theta}}^t\|^2 \\
&\leq (1 + \alpha)\mathbb{E}\|\hat{\boldsymbol{\theta}}^t + \eta\mathbf{A}(s)\hat{\boldsymbol{\theta}}^t - \hat{\boldsymbol{\theta}}^t - \eta\mathbf{A}(s)\hat{\boldsymbol{\theta}}^t\|^2 \\
&\quad + 2\eta^2(1 + \frac{1}{\alpha})\mathbb{E}\|\mathbf{b}(s) - \mathbf{b}(s_t)\|^2 + 2\eta^2(1 + \frac{1}{\alpha})\mathbb{E}\|(\mathbf{A}(s) - \mathbf{A}(s_t))\hat{\boldsymbol{\theta}}^t\|^2 \\
&\leq (1 + \alpha)\mathbb{E}\|\hat{\boldsymbol{\theta}}^t + \eta\mathbf{A}(s)\hat{\boldsymbol{\theta}}^t - \hat{\boldsymbol{\theta}}^t - \eta\mathbf{A}(s)\hat{\boldsymbol{\theta}}^t\|^2 + 2\eta^2(1 + \frac{1}{\alpha})\mathbb{E}\|\mathbf{b}(s) - \mathbf{b}(s_t)\|^2 \\
&\quad + 2\eta^2(1 + \frac{1}{\alpha})\sqrt{\mathbb{E}\|(\mathbf{A}(s) - \mathbf{A}(s_t))\|^4} \cdot \sqrt{\mathbb{E}\|\hat{\boldsymbol{\theta}}^t\|^4},
\end{aligned}
$$

(8)

where $\alpha > 0$ is a parameter to be determined. Noticing $\mathbb{E}[\mathbf{b}(s_t) \mid s_0] = \Phi^\top \mathrm{Diag}[(\mathbb{P}(s_t = s|s_0))_{s \in \mathcal{S}}]\mathcal{R}$, we can get

$$
\begin{aligned}
\mathbb{E}\Big( \|\mathbf{b}(s) - \mathbf{b}(s_t)\|^2 \mid s_0 \Big) &= \|\Phi^\top \mathrm{Diag}[(\mathbb{P}(s_t = s|s_0) - \vartheta(s))_{s \in \mathcal{S}}]\mathcal{R}\|^2 \\
&\leq (\sum_{s \in \mathcal{S}} \|\phi(s)\| \cdot |(\mathbb{P}(s_t = s|s_0) - \vartheta(s))| \cdot |\mathcal{R}(s)|)^2 \\
&= (\sum_{s \in \mathcal{S}} |(\mathbb{P}(s_t = s|s_0) - \vartheta(s))| \cdot |\mathcal{R}(s)|)^2 \\
&\leq \bar{r}^2 (\sum_{s \in \mathcal{S}} |(\mathbb{P}(s_t = s|s_0) - \vartheta(s))|)^2 \leq \bar{r}^2 \zeta^{2t},
\end{aligned}
$$

and thus $\mathbb{E}\|\mathbf{b}(s) - \mathbf{b}(s_t)\|^2 = \mathbb{E}\Big( \mathbb{E}(\|\mathbf{b}(s) - \mathbf{b}(s_t)\|^2 \mid s_0) \Big) \leq \bar{r}^2 \zeta^{2t}$. On the other hand, $\mathbb{E}(\mathbf{A}(s_t) \mid s_0) = \Phi^\top \mathrm{Diag}[(\mathbb{P}(s_t = s|s_0))_{s \in \mathcal{S}}](\gamma\mathcal{P} - \Phi)$, we then get

$$
\begin{aligned}
\mathbb{E}\Big( \|\mathbf{A}(s) - \mathbf{A}(s_t)\|^4 \mid s_0 \Big) &= \|\Phi^\top \mathrm{Diag}[(\mathbb{P}(s_t = s|s_0) - \vartheta(s))_{s \in \mathcal{S}}](\gamma\mathcal{P} - \Phi)\|^4 \\
&\leq (\sum_{s \in \mathcal{S}} \|\phi(s)\| \cdot |(\mathbb{P}(s_t = s|s_0) - \vartheta(s))| \cdot \|\gamma\mathcal{P}(s,:)^\top - \phi(s)\|)^4 \\
&\leq (\sum_{s \in \mathcal{S}} |(\mathbb{P}(s_t = s|s_0) - \vartheta(s))| \cdot (1 + \gamma))^4 \\
&\leq (1 + \gamma)^4 (\sum_{s \in \mathcal{S}} |(\mathbb{P}(s_t = s|s_0) - \vartheta(s))|)^4 \leq (1 + \gamma)^4 \zeta^{4t},
\end{aligned}
$$

In [Theorem 9, [24]], it show that for any sequence $(\boldsymbol{\theta}^t)_{t \geq 0}$ generated by TD(0) with a sufficient small $\eta$ and the initialization $\boldsymbol{\theta}^0$ being selected from the bounded ball $\mathbf{B}(\mathbf{0}, \eta)$, it holds

$$
\mathbb{E}\|\boldsymbol{\theta}^t\|^4 \leq C_\eta^4, \text{as } t \geq T, \tag{9}
$$

where $C_\eta$ is constant dependent on $\eta$ such that $C_\eta = \mathcal{O}(\sqrt{\frac{\ln\frac{1}{\eta}}{\eta\ln\frac{1}{\zeta}}})$, and if $T \geq \lceil \frac{\ln\frac{1}{\eta}}{\ln\zeta} \rceil$. Recall (8), we get

$$
\begin{aligned}
\mathbb{E}\|\boldsymbol{\theta}^{t+1} - \hat{\boldsymbol{\theta}}^{t+1}\|^2 \leq &(1 + \alpha)\mathbb{E}\|\hat{\boldsymbol{\theta}}^t + \eta\mathbf{A}(s)\hat{\boldsymbol{\theta}}^t - \hat{\boldsymbol{\theta}}^t - \eta\mathbf{A}(s)\hat{\boldsymbol{\theta}}^t\|^2 \\
&+ 2(1 + \frac{1}{\alpha})\eta^2\bar{r}^2\zeta^{2t} + 2(1 + \frac{1}{\alpha})\eta^2(1 + \gamma)^2 C_\eta^2\zeta^{2t}.
\end{aligned} \tag{10}
$$

Now, we turn to the analysis of $\xi_t := \mathbb{E}\|\hat{\boldsymbol{\theta}}^t + \eta\mathbf{A}(s)\hat{\boldsymbol{\theta}}^t - \hat{\boldsymbol{\theta}}^t - \eta\mathbf{A}(s)\hat{\boldsymbol{\theta}}^t\|^2$. With direct computations, we get

$$
\begin{aligned}
&\mathbb{E}\|\hat{\boldsymbol{\theta}}^t + \eta\mathbf{A}(s)\hat{\boldsymbol{\theta}}^t - \hat{\boldsymbol{\theta}}^t - \eta\mathbf{A}(s)\hat{\boldsymbol{\theta}}^t\|^2 \\
&= \mathbb{E}\Big[ \|\boldsymbol{\theta}^t - \hat{\boldsymbol{\theta}}^t\|^2 + 2\eta\langle\boldsymbol{\theta}^t - \hat{\boldsymbol{\theta}}^t, \mathbf{A}(s)(\boldsymbol{\theta}^t - \hat{\boldsymbol{\theta}}^t)\rangle + \eta^2\|\mathbf{A}(s)(\boldsymbol{\theta}^t - \hat{\boldsymbol{\theta}}^t)\|^2 \Big] \\
&= \mathbb{E}\Big[ \|\boldsymbol{\theta}^t - \hat{\boldsymbol{\theta}}^t\|^2 + 2\eta\langle\boldsymbol{\theta}^t - \hat{\boldsymbol{\theta}}^t, \mathbf{A}(\boldsymbol{\theta}^t - \hat{\boldsymbol{\theta}}^t)\rangle + \eta^2\|\mathbf{A}(s)(\boldsymbol{\theta}^t - \hat{\boldsymbol{\theta}}^t)\|^2 \Big] \\
&\overset{a)}{\leq} (1 - 2(1 - \gamma)\eta\nu\vartheta^* + \eta^2(1 + \gamma)^2) \times \mathbb{E}\|\boldsymbol{\theta}^t - \hat{\boldsymbol{\theta}}^t\|^2 \leq \rho^2\mathbb{E}\|\boldsymbol{\theta}^t - \hat{\boldsymbol{\theta}}^t\|^2,
\end{aligned}
$$

where $a$) comes from Lemma 1. Thus, we are led to $\mathbb{E}\|\boldsymbol{\theta}^{t+1} - \hat{\boldsymbol{\theta}}^{t+1}\|^2 \leq (1 + \alpha)\rho^2\mathbb{E}\|\boldsymbol{\theta}^t - \hat{\boldsymbol{\theta}}^t\|^2 + 2(1+\frac{1}{\alpha})\eta^2\bar{r}^2\zeta^{2t} + 2(1+\frac{1}{\alpha})\eta^2(1+\gamma)^2C_\eta^2\zeta^{2t}$. Letting $\alpha = \frac{1}{\rho} - 1$, it follows

$$\mathbb{E}\|\boldsymbol{\theta}^{t+1} - \hat{\boldsymbol{\theta}}^{t+1}\|^2 \leq \rho\mathbb{E}\|\boldsymbol{\theta}^t - \hat{\boldsymbol{\theta}}^t\|^2 + \frac{2}{1-\rho}\eta^2\bar{r}^2\zeta^{2t} + \frac{2}{1-\rho}\eta^2(1+\gamma)^2C_\eta^2\zeta^{2t}. \tag{11}$$

With Mathematical Induction method, we can get

$$\mathbb{E}\|\boldsymbol{\theta}^{t+1} - \hat{\boldsymbol{\theta}}^{t+1}\|^2 \leq \rho^{t+1-T}\mathbb{E}\|\boldsymbol{\theta}^T - \hat{\boldsymbol{\theta}}^T\|^2$$
$$+ \sum_{j=0}^{t-T}\left(\frac{2}{1-\rho}\eta^2\bar{r}^2\zeta^{2t-2j} + \frac{2}{1-\rho}\eta^2(1+\gamma)^2C_\eta^2\zeta^{2t-2j}\right)$$
$$\leq \rho^{t+1-T}\mathbb{E}\|\boldsymbol{\theta}^T - \hat{\boldsymbol{\theta}}^T\|^2 + \frac{2\zeta^{2T}}{1-\rho}\sum_{j=0}^{t-T}(\eta^2\bar{r}^2\zeta^{2j} + \eta^2(1+\gamma)^2C_\eta^2\zeta^{2j}) \tag{12}$$
$$\leq \rho^{t+1-T}\mathbb{E}\|\boldsymbol{\theta}^T - \hat{\boldsymbol{\theta}}^T\|^2 + \frac{2\zeta^{2T}}{1-\rho}\frac{(\eta^2\bar{r}^2 + \eta^2(1+\gamma)^2C_\eta^2)}{1-\zeta^2}$$
$$\leq \rho^{t+1-T}2(\mathbb{E}\|\boldsymbol{\theta}^T\|^2 + \mathbb{E}\|\hat{\boldsymbol{\theta}}^T\|^2) + \frac{2\zeta^{2T}}{1-\rho}\frac{(\eta^2\bar{r}^2 + \eta^2(1+\gamma)^2C_\eta^2)}{1-\zeta^2}.$$

With $\mathbb{E}\|\boldsymbol{\theta}^T\|^2 \leq \sqrt{\mathbb{E}\|\boldsymbol{\theta}^T\|^4} \leq C_\eta^2$ and $\mathbb{E}\|\hat{\boldsymbol{\theta}}^T\|^2 \leq \sqrt{\mathbb{E}\|\hat{\boldsymbol{\theta}}^T\|^4} \leq C_\eta^2$, we can get

$$\mathbb{E}\|\boldsymbol{\theta}^{t+1} - \hat{\boldsymbol{\theta}}^{t+1}\|^2 \leq 2\rho^{t+1-T}C_\eta^2 + \frac{2\lambda^{2T}}{1-\rho}\frac{(\eta^2\bar{r}^2 + \eta^2(1+\gamma)^2C_\eta^2)}{1-\zeta^2}. \tag{13}$$

Thus, it follows $\mathcal{W}(\pi^{t+1}, \hat{\pi}^{t+1}) \leq \sqrt{\mathbb{E}\|\boldsymbol{\theta}^{t+1} - \hat{\boldsymbol{\theta}}^{t+1}\|^2} \leq \sqrt{2\rho^{t+1-T}C_\eta^2 + \frac{2\lambda^{2T}}{1-\rho}\frac{(\eta^2\bar{r}^2 + \eta^2(1+\gamma)^2C_\eta^2)}{1-\zeta^2}}$. Replacing $t$ with $t-1$ above, we get

$$\mathcal{W}(\pi^t, \hat{\pi}^t) \leq \sqrt{2\rho^{t-T}C_\eta^2 + \frac{2\zeta^{2T}}{1-\rho}\frac{(\eta^2\bar{r}^2 + \eta^2(1+\gamma)^2C_\eta^2)}{1-\zeta^2}}.$$

Noticing $\mathcal{W}(\pi^t, \pi_\eta) \leq \mathcal{W}(\pi^t, \hat{\pi}^t) + \mathcal{W}(\hat{\pi}^t, \pi_\eta)$, with Theorem 1, we are then led to

$$\mathcal{W}(\pi^t, \pi_\eta) \leq \rho^t \cdot \left(\int_{\mathbb{R}^d}\|\boldsymbol{\theta} - \boldsymbol{\theta}^0\|^2\pi_\eta(d\boldsymbol{\theta})\right)^{1/2}$$
$$+ \sqrt{2\rho^{t-T}C_\eta^2 + \frac{2\zeta^{2T}}{1-\rho}\frac{(\eta^2\bar{r}^2 + \eta^2(1+\gamma)^2C_\eta^2)}{1-\zeta^2}},$$

as $t \geq T + 1$. Letting $T = t/2$, we then proved the result.

## 4.5    Proof of Proposition 2

Following the same procedure of Theorem 1, we just need to prove

$$\mathcal{W}^2(\kappa\hat{R}_\eta, \hat{\kappa}\hat{R}_\eta) \leq \mathbb{E}\|\boldsymbol{\theta}^1 - \hat{\boldsymbol{\theta}}^1\|^2$$

$$= \mathbb{E}\left[\|\boldsymbol{\theta}^0 - \hat{\boldsymbol{\theta}}^0\|^2 + 2\eta\langle\boldsymbol{\theta}^0 - \hat{\boldsymbol{\theta}}^0, \mathbf{J}^{-1}\mathbf{A}(s_t)(\boldsymbol{\theta}^0 - \hat{\boldsymbol{\theta}}^0)\rangle + \eta^2\|\mathbf{J}^{-1}\mathbf{A}(s_t)(\boldsymbol{\theta}^0 - \hat{\boldsymbol{\theta}}^0)\|\right]$$

$$= \mathbb{E}\left[\|\boldsymbol{\theta}^0 - \hat{\boldsymbol{\theta}}^0\|^2 + 2\eta\langle\boldsymbol{\theta}^0 - \hat{\boldsymbol{\theta}}^0, \mathbf{J}^{-1}\mathbf{A}(\boldsymbol{\theta}^0 - \hat{\boldsymbol{\theta}}^0)\rangle + \eta^2\|\mathbf{J}^{-1}\mathbf{A}(s_t)(\boldsymbol{\theta}^0 - \hat{\boldsymbol{\theta}}^0)\|^2\right]$$

$$\overset{a)}{\leq} (1 - 2(1-\gamma)\eta\nu\hat{\vartheta} + \eta^2(1+\gamma)^2\|\mathbf{J}^{-1}\|^2)\cdot\mathbb{E}\|\boldsymbol{\theta}^0 - \hat{\boldsymbol{\theta}}^0\|^2 \leq \hat{\rho}^2\mathcal{W}^2(\kappa, \hat{\kappa}),$$

where used $\|\mathbf{J}^{-1}\mathbf{A}(s_t)\| \leq \|\mathbf{J}^{-1}\|(1+\gamma)$. The rest of the proof about the convergence rate is almost identical to the proof of Theorem 1 and will not be repeated.

Now, we turn to the expectation and covariant of $\hat{\pi}_\eta$. Let $\boldsymbol{\theta}^0 \sim \hat{\pi}_\eta$, then $(\boldsymbol{\theta}^t)_{t\geq 0} \sim \hat{\pi}_\eta$. Taking expectations on both sides of (4), we then get $\int_{\mathbb{R}^d} \boldsymbol{\theta}\hat{\pi}_\eta(d\boldsymbol{\theta}) = \int_{\mathbb{R}^d} \boldsymbol{\theta}\hat{\pi}_\eta(d\boldsymbol{\theta}) + \eta\mathbf{J}^{-1}\mathbf{A}\int_{\mathbb{R}^d} \boldsymbol{\theta}\hat{\pi}_\eta(d\boldsymbol{\theta}) + \eta\mathbf{J}^{-1}\mathbf{b}$, which gives the result. On the other hand, similar to the proof of Proposition 1, we derive

$$[\boldsymbol{\theta}^{t+1} - \boldsymbol{\theta}^*][\boldsymbol{\theta}^{t+1} - \boldsymbol{\theta}^*]^\top = [\boldsymbol{\theta}^t - \boldsymbol{\theta}^* + \eta\mathbf{J}^{-1}\mathbf{A}(s)(\boldsymbol{\theta}^t - \boldsymbol{\theta}^*) + \eta\mathbf{J}^{-1}\hat{\mathbf{b}}(s)]$$

$$\times [\boldsymbol{\theta}^t - \boldsymbol{\theta}^* + \eta\mathbf{J}^{-1}\mathbf{A}(s)(\boldsymbol{\theta}^t - \boldsymbol{\theta}^*) + \eta\mathbf{J}^{-1}\hat{\mathbf{b}}(s)]^\top.$$

Taking expectation of both sides on $\hat{\pi}_\eta$, and denoting $\hat{\boldsymbol{\Sigma}} := \int_{\mathbb{R}^d}[\boldsymbol{\theta} - \boldsymbol{\theta}^*][\boldsymbol{\theta} - \boldsymbol{\theta}^*]^\top\hat{\pi}_\eta(d\boldsymbol{\theta})$ and noticing $\mathbb{E}\left([\mathbf{J}^{-1}\mathbf{b}(s) - \mathbf{J}^{-1}\mathbf{A}(s)\boldsymbol{\theta}^*][\mathbf{J}^{-1}\mathbf{b}(s) - \mathbf{J}^{-1}\mathbf{A}(s)\boldsymbol{\theta}^*]^\top\right) = \mathbf{J}^{-1}\mathbf{C}[\mathbf{J}^{-1}]^\top$, it holds $\mathbf{0} = \mathbb{E}\left(\eta\mathbf{J}^{-1}\mathbf{A}(s)\boldsymbol{\Sigma}\mathbf{A}(s)^\top[\mathbf{J}^{-1}]^\top + \mathbf{J}^{-1}\mathbf{A}(s)\boldsymbol{\Sigma} + \boldsymbol{\Sigma}\mathbf{A}(s)^\top[\mathbf{J}^{-1}]^\top\right) + \eta\mathbf{J}^{-1}\mathbf{C}[\mathbf{J}^{-1}]^\top$. That means the covariance can be presented $\mathbf{X}^\ddagger + \mathcal{O}(\eta^2)$ with $\mathbf{X}^\ddagger$ being the solution of $\mathbf{J}^{-1}\mathbf{A}\mathbf{X}^\ddagger + \mathbf{X}^\ddagger\mathbf{A}^\top[\mathbf{J}^{-1}]^\top + \eta\mathbf{J}^{-1}\mathbf{C}[\mathbf{J}^{-1}]^\top = \mathbf{0}$. Further, with the fact $\mathbf{J}$ is diagonal ($\mathbf{J}^\top = \mathbf{J}$), the equation can be simplified as

$$\mathbf{A}\mathbf{X}^\ddagger\mathbf{J} + \mathbf{J}\mathbf{X}^\ddagger\mathbf{A}^\top + \eta\mathbf{C} = \mathbf{0}.$$

It is worth mentioning that the above equation fails to be continuous Lyapunov equation provided that $\mathbf{X}^\ddagger\mathbf{J} = \mathbf{J}\mathbf{X}^\ddagger$.

## 5    Conclusion

We have presented the distributional convergence results of TD and studied the properties of the stationary distributions. The proved results show the tradeoff between the convergence speed and the accuracy of TD under both i.i.d. and Markov chain observation models. Using our findings, we make the first attempt to explain the superiority of the Jacobi preconditioning TD. The possible future work is to extend the proved results to the MCGD; the core difficulty may lay in dealing with non-quadratic objectives.

**Ethical Statement.** Our paper is devoted to the theoretical aspect of general stochastic algorithm, which does not present any foreseeable societal consequence.

# References

1. Baird, L.: Residual algorithms: reinforcement learning with function approximation. In: Machine Learning, pp. 30–37 (1995)
2. Bertsekas, D.P.: A new class of incremental gradient methods for least squares problems. SIAM J. Optim. **7**(4), 913–926 (1997)
3. Bhandari, J., Russo, D., Singal, R.: A finite time analysis of temporal difference learning with linear function approximation. In: Conference on learning theory (2018)
4. Borkar, V.S.: Stochastic approximation: a dynamical systems viewpoint, vol. 48. Springer (2009)
5. Brosse, N., Durmus, A., Moulines, E.: The promises and pitfalls of stochastic gradient langevin dynamics. In: Advances in Neural Information Processing Systems, vol. 31 (2018)
6. Can, B., Gurbuzbalaban, M., Zhu, L.: Accelerated linear convergence of stochastic momentum methods in Wasserstein distances. In: Proceedings of the 36th International Conference on Machine Learning, vol. 97, pp. 891–901. PMLR, 09–15 Jun 2019
7. Dalal, G., Szörényi, B., Thoppe, G., Mannor, S.: Finite sample analyses for td(0) with function approximation. In: Thirty-Second AAAI Conference on Artificial Intelligence (2018)
8. Dieuleveut, A., Durmus, A., Bach, F.: Bridging the gap between constant step size stochastic gradient descent and markov chains. Ann. Stat. **48**(3), 1348–1382 (2020)
9. Duchi, J.C., Agarwal, A., Johansson, M., Jordan, M.I.: Ergodic mirror descent. SIAM J. Optim. **22**(4), 1549–1578 (2012)
10. Gitman, I., Lang, H., Zhang, P., Xiao, L.: Understanding the role of momentum in stochastic gradient methods. In: Advances in Neural Information Processing Systems, vol. 32 (2019)
11. Gupta, A., Haskell, W.B.: Convergence of recursive stochastic algorithms using wasserstein divergence. SIAM J. Math. Data Sci. **3**(4), 1141–1167 (2021)
12. Gupta, A., Chen, H., Pi, J., Tendolkar, G.: Some limit properties of markov chains induced by recursive stochastic algorithms. SIAM J. Math. Data Sci. **2**(4), 967–1003 (2020)
13. Hu, B., Syed, U.: Characterizing the exact behaviors of temporal difference learning algorithms using markov jump linear system theory. In: Advances in Neural Information Processing Systems, pp. 8477–8488, Vancouver, Canada, December 2019
14. Johansson, B., Rabi, M., Johansson, M.: A randomized incremental subgradient method for distributed optimization in networked systems. SIAM J. Optim. **20**(3), 1157–1170 (2010)
15. Lakshminarayanan, C., Szepesvari, C.: Linear stochastic approximation: how far does constant step-size and iterate averaging go? In: International Conference on Artificial Intelligence and Statistics, pp. 1347–1355 (2018)
16. Lee, D., He, N.: Target-based temporal-difference learning. In: International Conference on Machine Learning, pp. 3713–3722. PMLR (2019)
17. Mandt, S., Hoffman, M.D., Blei, D.M.: Stochastic gradient descent as approximate bayesian inference. J. Mach. Learn. Res. **18**, 1–35 (2017)
18. Meyn, S.P.: Markov Chains and Stochastic Stability. Markov Chains and Stochastic Stability (1999)

19. Nlar, E.: Probability and stochastics. Probability and Stochastics (2011). https://doi.org/10.1007/978-0-387-87859-1
20. Ram, S.S., Nedić, A., Veeravalli, V.V.: Incremental stochastic subgradient algorithms for convex optimization. SIAM J. Optim. **20**(2), 691–717 (2009)
21. Robbins, H., Monro, S.: A stochastic approximation method. Ann. Math. Stat. 400–407 (1951)
22. Romoff, J., et al.: Tdprop: does adaptive optimization with jacobi preconditioning help temporal difference learning? In: Proceedings of the 20th International Conference on Autonomous Agents and MultiAgent Systems, pp. 1082–1090 (2021)
23. Simoncini, V.: Computational methods for linear matrix equations. SIAM Rev. **58**(3), 377–441 (2016)
24. Srikant, R., Ying, L.: Finite-time error bounds for linear stochastic approximation and TD learning. In: COLT (2019)
25. Sun, T., Li, D., Wang, B.: Adaptive random walk gradient descent for decentralized optimization. In: International Conference on Machine Learning, pp. 20790–20809. PMLR (2022)
26. Sun, T., Shen, H., Chen, T., Li, D.: Adaptive temporal difference learning with linear function approximation. IEEE Trans. Pattern Anal. Mach. Intell. **44**(12), 8812–8824 (2021)
27. Sun, T., Sun, Y., Yin, W.: On markov chain gradient descent. In: Advances in Neural Information Processing Systems, vol. 31 (2018)
28. Sutton, R.S.: Learning to predict by the methods of temporal differences. Mach. Learn. **3**(1), 9–44 (1988)
29. Sutton, R.S., Barto, A.G., et al.: Introduction to reinforcement learning, vol. 2. MIT Press, Cambridge (1998)
30. Tsitsiklis, J.N., Roy, B.V.: An analysis of temporal-difference learning with function approximation. IEEE Trans. Autom. Control (1997)
31. Villani, C.: Optimal Transport: Old and New, vol. 338. Springer, Berlin (2009). https://doi.org/10.1007/978-3-540-71050-9
32. Xiong, H., Tengyu, X., Liang, Y., Zhang, W.: Non-asymptotic convergence of adam-type reinforcement learning algorithms under markovian sampling. Proc. AAAI Conf. Artif. Intell. **35**, 10460–10468 (2021)

# Offline Reinforcement Learning with On-Policy Q-Function Regularization

Laixi Shi[1]([✉]) [ID], Robert Dadashi[2], Yuejie Chi[1] [ID], Pablo Samuel Castro[2], and Matthieu Geist[2]

[1] Carnegie Mellon University, Pittsburgh, PA, USA
{laixishi,yuejiechi}@cmu.edu
[2] Google Research, Brain Team, Pittsburgh, USA
{dadashi,mfgeist}@google.com

**Abstract.** The core challenge of offline reinforcement learning (RL) is dealing with the (potentially catastrophic) extrapolation error induced by the distribution shift between the history dataset and the desired policy. A large portion of prior work tackles this challenge by implicitly/explicitly regularizing the learning policy towards the behavior policy, which is hard to estimate reliably in practice. In this work, we propose to regularize towards the Q-function of the behavior policy instead of the behavior policy itself, under the premise that the Q-function can be estimated more reliably and easily by a SARSA-style estimate and handles the extrapolation error more straightforwardly. We propose two algorithms taking advantage of the estimated Q-function through regularizations, and demonstrate they exhibit strong performance on the D4RL benchmarks.

**Keywords:** offline reinforcement learning · actor-critic · SARSA

## 1 Introduction

Reinforcement learning (RL) has witnessed a surge of practical success recently, with widespread applications in games such as Go game and StarCraft II [30, 31], control, autonomous driving, etc. [1,25]. Online RL relies on sequentially collecting data through interactions with the environment. However, new sample collections or interactions might be infeasible due to privacy, safety, or cost, especially in real-world applications. To circumvent this,

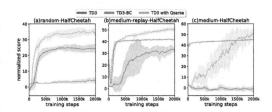

**Fig. 1.** A comparison between our $Q_{\text{sarsa}}$-regularized TD3 method (TD3 with Qsarsa), the vanilla TD3 method from online RL [11], and a strong baseline for offline RL TD3-BC [10] in the tasks of MuJoCo in D4RL.

offline/batch RL seeks to learn from an existing dataset, without further interaction with the environment [26].

D. Koutra et al. (Eds.): ECML PKDD 2023, LNAI 14172, pp. 455–471, 2023.
https://doi.org/10.1007/978-3-031-43421-1_27

The history dataset can be regarded as generated by some unknown behavior policy $\pi_b$, which is not necessarily of the desired quality or has insufficient coverage over the state-action space. This results in one of the major challenges of offline RL: *distribution shift.* Here, the state-action distribution under the behavior policy may heavily differ from that produced by a more desirable policy. As a result, the policy evaluation process presents considerable extrapolation error over the *out-of-distribution* (OOD) regions (state-action pairs) that are insufficiently visited or even unseen in the history dataset. To address the extrapolation error, prior works mainly follow three principles: 1) *behavior regularization:* regularizing the learning policy to be close to the behavior policy or to imitate the (weighted) offline dataset directly [10,12,22,33,34]; 2) *pessimism:* considering conservative value/Q-function by penalizing the values over OOD state-action pairs [4,20,23,27]; 3) *in-sample:* learning without querying any OOD actions [13,20].

To achieve behavior regularization, a large portion of prior works choose to regularize the policy towards the behavior policy. As the behavior policy is unknown, they usually rely on access to an approximation of the behavior policy, or on access to a distance metric between any policy and the behavior policy [8,22]. However, either estimating the behavior policy as a multimodal conditional distribution or estimating the distance between any policy and $\pi_b$ is a difficult task in practice, requiring tailored and complex designs such as conditional variational auto-encoders (CVAEs) [12,27] or restricted distance metrics [7]. To circumvent this, a natural question is: *Can we steer a learning policy towards the behavior policy without requiring access to the said policy?*

To answer this, we propose to rely on the Q-function of the behavior policy $\pi_b$, denoted as $Q^{\pi_b}$, instead of relying directly on $\pi_b$. The Q-function $Q^{\pi_b}$ can not only play a similar role as $\pi_b$ in pushing the learning policy towards the behavior policy, but can also provide additional information such as the quality of the dataset/actions (e.g., larger $Q^{\pi_b}$ represents better quality). In addition, harnessing $Q^{\pi_b}$ in offline RL is promising and has several essential advantages compared to prior works relying on (an estimate of) the behavior policy $\pi_b$:

**Estimating $Q^{\pi_b}$ is easier than $\pi_b$.** $Q^{\pi_b}$ can be estimated by $Q_{\mathsf{sarsa}}$ via minimizing a SARSA-style objective, while $\pi_b$ needs to be estimated as a multimodal conditional distribution, which is usually a more difficult problem.

**Regularizing towards $Q^{\pi_b}$ is more straightforward than $\pi_b$.** The goal of imitating the behavior policy is usually to restrict extrapolation errors when evaluating the Q-function of the learning policy. Thus, it is more direct and efficient to regularize the Q-function of the learning policy towards $Q^{\pi_b}$ than to do so indirectly in the bootstrapping step via a regularization towards $\pi_b$.

Despite these advantages, there are few works exploring the use of $Q^{\pi_b}$ for offline RL regularization. Indeed, OnestepRL [3] is, to the best of our knowledge, the only work that promotes the usage of $Q^{\pi_b}$ in continuous action tasks. However, Fig. 2 (more details are specified in Sect. 4.1) shows that although $Q_{\mathsf{sarsa}}$, the estimate of $Q^{\pi_b}$ using a SARSA-style objective, is one of the components in OnestepRL, it may not be the critical one that contributes to its success and hence, more investigations are warranted.

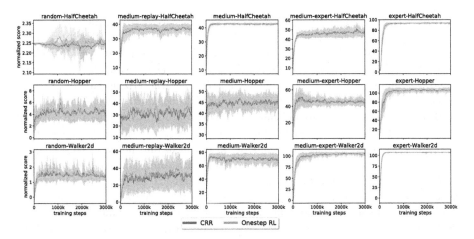

**Fig. 2.** The comparisions between OnestepRL [3] and CRR [33] over 15 tasks of MuJoCo in D4RL [9]. CRR and OnestepRL use the same actor with different critics (OnestepRL uses $Q_{sarsa}$ while CRR not). The similar performance implies that the actor plays a more important role compared to the critic $Q_{sarsa}$ in OnestepRL.

We suggest that a proper use of $Q^{\pi_b}$ has the potential to improve the performance in offline RL. As a warm-up study, by adding a slight regularization towards $Q_{sarsa}$ (the estimate of $Q^{\pi_b}$) in TD3 [11] without other modifications, we already observe a strong performance boost (see Fig. 1). Motivated by this potential, in this work, we propose to use $Q^{\pi_b}$ (estimated by $Q_{sarsa}$) as a promising regularization methodology for offline RL. We first demonstrate that $Q_{sarsa}$ is a reasonable estimate for $Q^{\pi_b}$ for *in-sample* state-action pairs and has controllable error over out-of-distribution regions. Equipped with these findings, we introduce two $Q_{sarsa}$-regularized algorithms based on TD3-BC, one of the state-of-the-art offline methods [10], and achieve strong performance on the D4RL benchmark [9], notably better than TD3-BC that we built on and OnestepRL.

## 2 Related Works

We shall discuss several lines of research on offline RL, with an emphasis on the most related works that make use of behavior regularization.

**Offline RL.** The major challenge of offline RL is the extrapolation error of policy evaluation induced by the distribution shift between the history dataset and the desired learning policy [12,22]. As a result, a large portion of works follow the approximate dynamic programming framework (e.g., actor-critic) to balance learning beyond the behavior policy and handling the distribution shift. They usually resort to behavior regularization/constraints [12,14,22,33,34], pessimistic value/Q-function estimation for out-of-distribution actions [20,23,27,29,36], or learning without querying any OOD actions [13,20]. In addition, prior works also leverage other techniques such as sequential modeling [5,19], representation learning [24], and diffusion models as policies [32].

**Offline RL with Behavior Regularization.** In order to handle distribution shift, besides restricting the learning of policy almost to be in-distribution/in-sample [28,33] or leveraging imitation learning and working directly with the dataset [6,10], many prior works regularize the policy to an explicit estimation of the behavior policy [12,14,22,27,35,37] or characterizing the discrepancy between policies based on special distance or tailored approaches [7,8,22].

However, the estimation of either the behavior policy or the distance between policies is difficult in practice or requires special design. In this work, we propose the Q-function of the behavior policy as an essential and helpful component in offline RL, which can be estimated easily but has almost not been studied in the literature. Only a few works [15,28,33] consider the usage of the Q-function of the behavior policy, but usually combined with some special optimization objective for the actor (e.g., advantage-weighted regression) which may take the most credit, or focusing on distinct tasks such as discrete action tasks [15]. To fill the gap, this work evaluates the reliability of estimating the Q-function of the behavior policy, and makes use of this estimate to design methods achieving competitive performance over the baselines.

## 3   Problem Formulation and Notations

**Discounted Infinite-Horizon MDP.** In this paper, we consider a discounted infinite-horizon Markov Decision Process (MDP) $\mathcal{M} = \{\mathcal{S}, \mathcal{A}, P, r, \gamma\}$. Here, $\mathcal{S}$ is the state space, $\mathcal{A}$ is the action space, $P : \mathcal{S} \times \mathcal{A} \to \Delta(\mathcal{S})$ represents the dynamics of this MDP (i.e., $P(\cdot \,|\, s, a)$ denote the transition probability from current state-action pair $(s, a)$ to the next state), $r : \mathcal{S} \times \mathcal{A} \to \mathbb{R}$ is the immediate reward function, $\gamma \in [0, 1)$ is the discount factor. We denote a stationary policy, also called an action selection rule, as $\pi : \mathcal{S} \to \Delta(\mathcal{A})$. The value function $V^\pi : \mathcal{S} \to \mathbb{R}$ and Q-value function $Q^\pi : \mathcal{S} \times \mathcal{A} \to \mathbb{R}$ associated with policy $\pi$ are defined as $V^\pi(s) = \mathbb{E}\left[\sum_{t=0}^{\infty} \gamma^t r(s_t, a_t) \,|\, s_0 = s; \pi\right]$ and $Q^\pi(s, a) = \mathbb{E}\left[\sum_{t=0}^{\infty} \gamma^t r(s_t, a_t) \,|\, s_0 = s, a_0 = a; \pi\right]$, where the expectation is taken over the sample trajectory $\{(s_t, a_t)\}_{t \geq 0}$ generated following that $a_t \sim \pi(\cdot \,|\, s_t)$ and $s_{t+1} \sim P(\cdot \,|\, s_t, a_t)$ for all $t \geq 0$.

**Offline/Batch Dataset.** We consider offline/batch RL, where we only have access to an offline dataset $\mathcal{D}$ consisting of $N$ sample tuples $\{s_i, a_i, r_i, s_i', a_i'\}_{i=1}^N$ generated following some behavior policy $\pi_b$ over the targeted environment. The goal of offline RL is to learn an optimal policy $\pi^\star$ given dataset $\mathcal{D}$ which maximizes the long-term cumulative rewards, $\pi^\star = \mathrm{argmax}_\pi \mathbb{E}_{s \sim \rho}[V^\pi(s)]$, where $\rho$ is the initial state distribution.

## 4   Introduction and Evaluation of $Q_{\mathsf{sarsa}}$

In this work, we propose to use an estimate of the Q-function of the behavior policy $(Q^{\pi_b})$ for algorithm design. Since the investigation of exploiting $Q^{\pi_b}$ or its estimate in offline RL methods is quite limited in the literature, we first

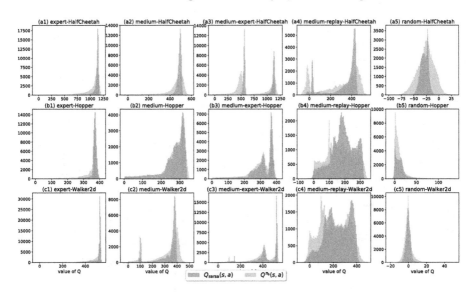

**Fig. 3.** The demonstration of $Q_{\text{sarsa}}$ and $Q^{\pi_b}$ over 15 tasks of MuJoCo in D4RL [9] with different tasks and diverse offline datasets. It shows that $Q_{\text{sarsa}}$ estimate the value of $Q^{\pi_b}$ reasonably regarding that their distribution largely overlap with each other (red and blue histogorams).

specify the form of the SARSA-style Q-estimate and then evaluate its reliability, characteristics, and possible benefits for prevalent offline algorithms.

**The SARSA-style Q-estimate** $Q_{\text{sarsa}}$. We estimate $Q^{\pi_b}$ by the following SARSA-style optimization problem [3] and denote the output as $Q_{\text{sarsa}}$:

$$Q_{\text{sarsa}} \leftarrow \min_{\theta_s} \mathbb{E}_{\mathcal{D}}[(r(s,a) + \gamma Q_{\bar{\theta}_s}(s',a') - Q_{\theta_s}(s,a))^2], \tag{1}$$

where $\theta_s$ (resp. $\bar{\theta}_s$) denotes the parameters of some neural network (resp. target network, a lagging version of $\theta_s$), the expectation is w.r.t. $(s,a,r,s',a') \sim \mathcal{D}$, and $Q_{\text{sarsa}} := Q_{\theta_s}$. Note that $Q_{\text{sarsa}}$ is estimated by *in-sample* learning, which only queries the samples inside the history dataset, without involving any OOD regions.

### 4.1   Evaluation of $Q_{\text{sarsa}}$

**An ablation for** OnestepRL. First, to verify the benefit of using $Q_{\text{sarsa}}$ directly as the critic in the actor-critic framework, proposed in OnestepRL [3], we conduct an ablation study by replacing the critic $Q_{\text{sarsa}}$ by the critic trained by vanilla temporal difference learning widely used in online RL (i.e., CRR [33]) and show the comparisons in Fig. 2. Figure 2 show the ablation study results over 15 MuJoCo tasks which include the main portion of the tasks considered in OnestepRL [3]. Note that to ensure a fair comparison, the actor component is the same for both methods — advantage-weighted regression/exponentially

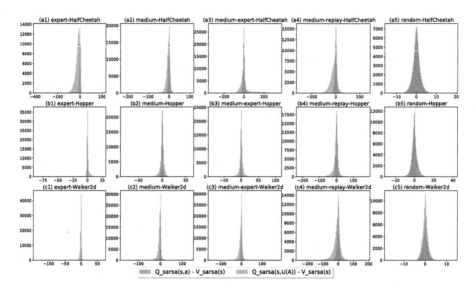

**Fig. 4.** The illustration of the histograms of the advantage $Q_{\text{sarsa}}(s,a) - V_{\text{sarsa}}(s)$ for *in-sample* state-action pairs $(s,a) \in \mathcal{D}$ and also the advantage $Q_{\text{sarsa}}(s, U(A)) - V_{\text{sarsa}}(s)$ for OOD state-action pairs $(s, U(A)) \notin \mathcal{D}$ over 15 tasks of MuJoCo in D4RL [9]. It indicates that $Q_{\text{sarsa}}$ usually xihas no/small OOD error, since $Q_{\text{sarsa}}$ over OOD state-action (purple histograms) won't exceed the value of in-distribution $Q_{\text{sarsa}}$ (green histograms) too often or too much.

weighted imitation [3,33]. Observing that the two methods perform almost the same in Fig. 2, it indicates that the key to the success of OnestepRL may be the objective function of the actor which restricts to *in-sample* learning but not $Q_{\text{sarsa}}$, since replacing $Q_{\text{sarsa}}$ does not impact the performance.

$Q_{\text{sarsa}}$ **estimates** $Q^{\pi_b}$ **reasonably well for** $(s,a) \in \mathcal{D}$. The goal of $Q_{\text{sarsa}}$ is to estimate the ground truth $Q^{\pi_b}$. With this in mind, taking the MuJoCo tasks for instance, we provide the histograms of $Q_{\text{sarsa}}(s,a)$ (in blue) and also $Q^{\pi_b}(s,a)$ estimated by reward-to-go[1] (in pink) in Fig. 3 for $(s,a) \in \mathcal{D}$ in different levels of history datasets. It shows that the distribution of the value of $Q_{\text{sarsa}}(s,a)$ almost coincide with $Q^{\pi_b}(s,a)$, indicating that $Q_{\text{sarsa}}$ estimates $Q^{\pi_b}$ accurately to some degree. The slight difference between $Q_{\text{sarsa}}$ (blue histograms) and $Q^{\pi_b}$ (red histograms) might result from that $Q_{\text{sarsa}}$ is estimating the Q-value of the behavior policy — may be a mixing of a set of policies (such as in the *medium-replay* case), while each point of the red histograms from $Q^{\pi_b}(s,a)$ is actually

---

[1] Note that $Q^{\pi_b}$ is unknown. So we utilize the reward-to-go function [19] starting from any state-action pair $(s,a) \in \mathcal{D}$ as $Q^{\pi_b}(s,a)$, i.e., $Q^{\pi_b}(s,a) := \sum_{t'=t}^{T} \gamma^{t'-t} r(s_{t'}, a_{t'})$ with $(s_t, a_t) = (s,a)$. The estimation can be filled by the trajectories in the entire dataset $\mathcal{D}$ with simple Monte Carlo return estimate, the same as the estimation of the value function used by [28].

the Q-value of one specific policy from the policy set but not the mixing policy (behavior policy).

In addition, the evaluation of $Q_{\mathsf{sarsa}}$ in Fig. 3 also provides useful intuition for the distribution of the dataset. For instance, the distribution of the *expert* datasets in Fig. 3(a1)-(c1) concentrate around the region with larger value/Q-function value since they are generated by some expert policy, while the *medium-replay* datasets in Fig. 3(a4)-(c4) have more diverse data over the entire space of the tasks (with more diverse Q-function values) due to they being sampled from some replay buffers generated by different policies.

$Q_{\mathsf{sarsa}}$ **has Controllable Out-of-Distribution (OOD) Error.** Before continuing, we first introduce a value function $V_{\mathsf{sarsa}} : \mathcal{S} \to \mathbb{R}$, where $V_{\mathsf{sarsa}}(s) := \mathbb{E}_{a \in \pi_b(s)} [Q_{\mathsf{sarsa}}(s, a)]$ for all $s \in \mathcal{S}$, learned by minimizing the following problem $\min_V \mathbb{E}_{(s,a) \in \mathcal{D}} \left[ |V(s) - Q_{\mathsf{sarsa}}(s, a)|^2 \right]$. As mentioned in the introduction (Sect. 1), extrapolation error of the Q-value estimation, especially the overestimation over the out-of-distribution (OOD) state-action pairs is the essential challenge for offline RL problems. To evaluate if $Q_{\mathsf{sarsa}}$ overestimate the Q-value in OOD regions, in Fig. 4, we demonstrate the deviations from $Q_{\mathsf{sarsa}}(s, a)$ to the expectation of $Q_{\mathsf{sarsa}}(s, a)$ ($V_{\mathsf{sarsa}}(s)$) for state action pairs $(s, a)$ over *in-distribution* region $\mathcal{D}$ (green histograms) and also OOD region $((s, U(A))$ in purple histograms). In particular, $U(A)$ denotes the uniform distribution over the action space $\mathcal{A}$.

Figure 4 indicates that $Q_{\mathsf{sarsa}}(s, a)$ **has controllable OOD error**. Specifically, the relative $Q_{\mathsf{sarsa}}(s, a) - V_{\mathsf{sarsa}}(s)$ value over OOD regions (purple histograms) generally has similar or smaller estimation value with comparisons to the maximum advantages over *in-sample* regions, i.e., $\max_{(s,a) \in \mathcal{D}} (Q_{\mathsf{sarsa}}(s, a) - V_{\mathsf{sarsa}}(s))$ (green histograms). It implies that $Q_{\mathsf{sarsa}}$ usually has no/only slight overestimation over OOD regions and probably has some implicit pessimistic regularization effects.

## 5    Offline RL with Q-sarsa (Qsarsa-AC)

Inspired by the potential of $Q_{\mathsf{sarsa}}$ shown in Sect. 4, we propose a new algorithm called **Qsarsa-AC** by taking advantage of $Q_{\mathsf{sarsa}}$ and designing regularizations based on it. To directly and clearly evaluate our changes around $Q_{\mathsf{sarsa}}$, **Qsarsa-AC** is prototyped against one of the state-of-the-art offline methods — TD3-BC [10] due to the simplicity of its algorithmic design. Specifically, among current offline state-of-the-art methods, we observe that TD3-BC has the minimal adjustments — by adding a BC term in the actor — compared to the existing off-policy method (used in online RL) [11]. As a result, it becomes much more straightforward and clear to evaluate the additional benefits, if any, indeed stem from our regularizations assisted by $Q_{\mathsf{sarsa}}$, rather than other components of the framework.

Before proceeding, we introduce several useful notations. We denote the parameter of two critic networks (resp. target critic networks) as $\{\theta_i\}_{i \in \{0,1\}}$

(resp. $\{\overline{\theta}_i\}_{i\in\{0,1\}}$). Similarly, $\phi$ (resp. $\overline{\phi}$) represents the parameter of the policy (actor) network (resp. policy target network).

## 5.1   Critic with $Q_{\mathsf{sarsa}}$

Before introducing our method, we recall the optimization problem of the two critics in prior arts TD3/TD3-BC [10,11], i.e., minimizing the temporal difference (TD) error: with $y(s_j, a_j) = r(s_j, a_j) + \gamma \min_{i \in \{1,2\}} Q_{\overline{\theta}_i}(s'_j, \tilde{a}'_j)$,

$$\theta_i \leftarrow \min \underbrace{B^{-1} \sum_{\mathcal{B}} |y(s_j, a_j) - Q_{\theta_i}(s_j, a_j)|^2}_{\text{TD-error}}, \quad i \in \{1, 2\}, \tag{2}$$

where $\mathcal{B} = \{s_j, a_j, r_j, s'_j, a'_j\}_{i=1}^{B}$ is a batch of data sampled from $\mathcal{D}$ with size $B$, $\tilde{a}'_j$ is the perturbed action [10,11] chosen by current target policy given state $s'_j$, i.e., $\tilde{a}'_j \approx \pi_{\overline{\phi}}(s'_j)$.

With the above in mind, we propose the following critic object of **Qsarsa-AC** by adding two natural regularization terms based on $Q_{\mathsf{sarsa}}$: for $i \in \{1, 2\}$,

$$\theta_i \leftarrow \min \text{TD-error} + \lambda B^{-1} \sum_{\mathcal{B}} \Big\{ \underbrace{\big[Q_{\theta_i}(s_j, a_j) - Q_{\mathsf{sarsa}}(s_j, a_j)\big]^2}_{\text{InD-sarsa}}$$

$$+ \underbrace{w(s'_j, \tilde{a}'_j) \cdot \big[Q_{\theta_i}(s'_j, \tilde{a}'_j) - Q_{\mathsf{sarsa}}(s'_j, \tilde{a}'_j)\big]^2}_{\text{OOD-sarsa}} \Big\}, \tag{3}$$

where $\lambda$ is a constant factor and $w(\cdot)$ is a mask function to be specified shortly.

Here, we choose the classic mean-squared error for both InD-sarsa and OOD-sarsa regularization terms. We introduce the role and intuition of the additional two regularizations separately. **(i) InD-sarsa: in-distribution regularization.** We highlight that this term regularizes the online learning Q-function (critic) $Q_{\theta_i}$ towards $Q_{\mathsf{sarsa}}$ only counting on *in-sample* state-action pairs $(s_j, a_j)$ from the offline dataset (i.e., $(s_j, a_j) \in \mathcal{D}$). Recalling that for all $(s_j, a_j) \in \mathcal{D}$, $Q_{\mathsf{sarsa}}(s_j, a_j) \approx Q^{\pi_b}(s_j, a_j)$ (see Fig. 3) is a reasonable target, this *in-sample* regularization plays the role of pushing $Q_{\theta_i}$ to $Q^{\pi_b}$ to avoid the overestimation of $Q_{\theta_i}$. Note that this regularization is unlikely to bring in OOD errors for $Q_{\theta_i}$ since it only acts on state-action pairs inside the dataset $((s_j, a_j) \in \mathcal{D})$. **(ii) OOD-sarsa: out-of-distribution regularization.** In contrast to InD-sarsa, this term pushes the Q-function $Q_{\theta_i}$ towards $Q_{\mathsf{sarsa}}$ by acting on OOD regions (i.e., $(s'_j, \tilde{a}'_j)$ perhaps not in $\mathcal{D}$). It is used to restrict/reduce the overestimation error of $Q_{\theta_i}$ over the OOD regions in order to circumvent the extrapolation error challenges.

Specifically, recall that the bootstrapping term $Q_{\overline{\theta}_i}(s'_j, \tilde{a}'_j)$ in (2) plays an essential role in estimating the Q-value, which has potentially catastrophic extrapolation error. The reason is that the state-action pair $(s'_j, \tilde{a}'_j)$ may appear scarcely or be unseen in the offline dataset, yielding large OOD errors since $Q_{\theta_i}(s'_j, \tilde{a}'_j)$ and/or $Q_{\overline{\theta}_i}(s'_j, \tilde{a}'_j)$ may not be sufficiently optimized during training. To address this, OOD-sarsa directly regularizes $Q_{\theta_i}(s'_j, \tilde{a}'_j)$ towards a more stable

Q-function $Q_{\mathsf{sarsa}}(s'_j, \widetilde{a}'_j)$, which generally does not incur large OOD errors (see Sect. 4), to restrict the overestimation error of the bootstrapping term. Last but not least, we specify the choice of $w(\cdot, \cdot)$, which is a hard mask to prevent the regularization term from being contaminated by extra OOD errors. Specifically, we remove *bad state-action pairs* in case $Q_{\mathsf{sarsa}}(s'_j, \widetilde{a}'_j)$ has relatively large OOD error: $w(\cdot, \cdot)$ is set as

$$w(s'_j, \widetilde{a}'_j) = \mathbb{K}\Big(Q_{\mathsf{sarsa}}(s'_j, \widetilde{a}'_j) > V_{\mathsf{sarsa}}(s'_j) - |Q_{\mathsf{sarsa}}(s'_j, a'_j) - V_{\mathsf{sarsa}}(s'_j)|\Big). \quad (4)$$

**Table 1.** The normalized score [9] of the final 10 evaluations over 5 random seeds. The highest performing scores are highlighted as pink and $\pm$ captures the standard deviation over seeds. For all the baselines, we re-run the implementations in the Acme framework [18] to keep an identical evaluation process for all methods. It shows that our two methods **Qsarsa-AC** and **Qsarsa-AC2** achieve better performance over the 15 tasks of MuJoCo benchmarks in D4RL [9].

| | | BC | CRR | OnestepRL | CQL | TD3-BC | Qsarsa-AC (Ours) | Qsarsa-AC2 (Ours) |
|---|---|---|---|---|---|---|---|---|
| Random | HalfCheetah | 2.3 ± 0.0 | 2.2 ± 0.1 | 2.3 ± 0.0 | 25.6 ± 1.8 | 6.0 ± 1.6 | 30.2 ±1.3 | 30.1 ±1.3 |
| | Hopper | 4.1 ± 1.9 | 3.9 ± 1.3 | 3.6 ± 1.0 | 8.7 ± 1.3 | 12.7 ±9.3 | 7.5 ± 0.9 | 8.1 ± 1.7 |
| | Walker2d | 1.3 ± 0.2 | 1.4 ± 0.2 | 1.6 ± 0.3 | 0.3 ± 0.5 | 5.4 ±6.3 | 5.9 ±8.1 | 4.5 ± 4.9 |
| Medium Replay | HalfCheetah | 34.4 ± 3.1 | 37.3 ± 2.1 | 38.1 ± 2.1 | −2.4 ± 1.9 | 42.5 ± 0.7 | 42.2 ± 0.7 | 54.4 ±1.8 |
| | Hopper | 30.0 ± 9.5 | 29.9 ± 7.8 | 43.2 ± 9.2 | 93.0 ±2.4 | 39.3 ± 8.4 | 92.6 ±10.2 | 68.1 ± 19.7 |
| | Walker2d | 21.3 ± 17.1 | 21.1 ± 12.2 | 28.6 ± 12.3 | 13.9 ± 13.0 | 67.6 ± 6.4 | 83.7 ±9.0 | 80.0 ± 11.4 |
| Medium Medium | HalfCheetah | 42.5 ± 2.0 | 42.7 ± 0.7 | 42.8 ± 0.7 | 48.7 ± 0.4 | 45.4 ± 0.4 | 44.1 ± 0.5 | 56.4 ±0.8 |
| | Hopper | 41.1 ± 10.2 | 43.3 ± 2.0 | 45.5 ± 3.2 | 55.6 ± 6.2 | 46.0 ± 3.3 | 78.6 ±15.7 | 66.6 ± 24.3 |
| | Walker2d | 67.4 ± 12.6 | 65.6 ± 11.5 | 70.7 ± 10.1 | 76.6 ± 6.6 | 82.5 ±0.9 | 79.0 ± 3.1 | 83.3 ±3.5 |
| Medium Expert | HalfCheetah | 50.2 ± 6.9 | 49.6 ± 8.2 | 47.9 ± 6.3 | 68.4 ± 16.0 | 91.8 ± 1.4 | 91.3 ±0.9 | 90.9 ± 1.0 |
| | Hopper | 48.7 ± 6.8 | 47.5 ± 3.2 | 45.6 ± 4.3 | 92.7 ±16.1 | 83.6 ± 17.6 | 56.9 ± 21.3 | 73.6 ± 25.5 |
| | Walker2d | 98.0 ± 14.3 | 105.6 ± 2.6 | 105.5 ± 3.4 | 106.2 ± 1.4 | 106.4 ± 5.2 | 105.2 ± 6.1 | 107.5 ±1.2 |
| Expert | HalfCheetah | 91.3 ± 2.4 | 93.9 ± 0.8 | 93.8 ± 1.2 | 72.6 ± 37.7 | 94.6 ±0.4 | 93.8 ± 1.0 | 93.7 ± 1.0 |
| | Hopper | 105.3 ± 6.6 | 107.3 ±4.9 | 105.9 ± 5.9 | 75.6 ± 26.9 | 104.2 ± 5.5 | 95.0 ± 21.1 | 97.8 ± 17.0 |
| | Walker2d | 107.5 ± 0.3 | 107.2 ± 0.6 | 107.3 ± 0.3 | 106.0 ± 5.0 | 108.1 ±0.3 | 107.0 ± 0.6 | 107.0 ± 0.8 |
| | Total | 745.3 ± 94.1 | 758.5 ± 58.1 | 782.4 ± 60.3 | 841.5 ± 137.2 | 936.2 ± 67.8 | 1013.2 ±100.3 | 1021.8 ±116.0 |

## 5.2  Actor with $Q_{\mathsf{sarsa}}$

Recall the ideal optimization problem for the learning policy (actor) in TD3-BC [10]: $\max_\pi \mathbb{E}_{\mathcal{D}}[\frac{\alpha}{\mathbb{E}_{\mathcal{D}}[Q(s,a)]} \cdot Q(s, \pi(s)) - (\pi(s) - a)^2]$, which directly adds a behavior cloning (BC) regularization towards the distribution of the dataset with a universal weight $\alpha$ for any offline dataset and any state-action pair. In this work, armed with $Q_{\mathsf{sarsa}}$, we propose the following optimization problem referring to $Q_{\mathsf{sarsa}}$-determined point-wise weights $f(Q_{\mathsf{sarsa}}, s, a)$ for BC instead of the fixed universal $\alpha$:

$$\max_\pi \mathbb{E}_{\mathcal{D}}\left[\frac{Q(s, \pi(s))}{\mathbb{E}_{\mathcal{D}}[Q(s,a)]} - f(Q_{\mathsf{sarsa}}, s, a)(\pi(s) - a)^2\right], \quad (5)$$

where $f(Q_{\mathsf{sarsa}}, s, a) := p_{s,a}(Q_{\mathsf{sarsa}})/g(Q_{\mathsf{sarsa}})$ is constructed by two terms given below. **(i) Global weight** $g(Q_{\mathsf{sarsa}})$ **for BC.** $g(Q_{\mathsf{sarsa}})$ serves as a global quantification of the dataset quality and determines the foundation of the weights on BC (keeping the same for all $(s, a) \in \mathcal{D}$). Intuitively, when the dataset is generated by some high-quality policies (e.g., the *expert* dataset), we are supposed to imitate the policy and put more weights on the BC regularization (bigger $1/g(Q_{\mathsf{sarsa}})$), otherwise smaller weights on BC. Towards this, we use $Q_{\mathsf{sarsa}}^{\mathsf{mean}} := \left| \mathbb{E}_{\mathcal{D}}[Q_{\mathsf{sarsa}}(s, a)] \right|$ as a global quantification for the behavior policy, which leads to

$$g(Q_{\mathsf{sarsa}}) = \mathrm{Clip}\left[\alpha \exp\left(\frac{\tau_1}{Q_{\mathsf{sarsa}}^{\mathsf{mean}}}\right), (1, 10^6)\right]. \tag{6}$$

Here, the clipping function $\mathrm{Clip}(\cdot)$ is just to normalize $g(Q_{\mathsf{sarsa}})$ between 1 and a huge number (e.g., $10^6$) to forbid it from being too big, which can cause numerical problems. **(ii) Point-wise weight** $p_{s,a}(Q_{\mathsf{sarsa}})$ **for BC.** $p_{s,a}(Q_{\mathsf{sarsa}}) \in [0, 1]$ is typically a point-wise normalized weight for different $(s, a)$ pairs, formed as

$$p_{s,a}(Q_{\mathsf{sarsa}}) = \max\left(\exp\left(\frac{\tau_2\,(Q_{\mathsf{sarsa}}(s, a) - V_{\mathsf{sarsa}}(s))}{|Q_{\mathsf{sarsa}}(s, a)|}\right), 1\right). \tag{7}$$

In particular, $p_{s,a}(Q_{\mathsf{sarsa}})$ puts larger weights on BC for *high-quality* state-action pair $(s, a)$ which deserves the learning policy to visit, otherwise reduces the weights for BC regularization. The quality of the state-action pairs is determined by the advantage $Q_{\mathsf{sarsa}}(s, a) - V_{\mathsf{sarsa}}(s)$ normalized by $Q_{\mathsf{sarsa}}(s, a)$.

## 5.3    A Variant Qsarsa-AC2

Given that the global weight $g(Q_{\mathsf{sarsa}})$ aims to evaluate the quality of the given dataset over some specific task, it is supposed to depend on the relative value of $Q^{\pi_b}$ w.r.t. the optimal Q-function $Q^\star$ over this task. However, $g(Q_{\mathsf{sarsa}})$ in (6) is calculated by the absolute value of $Q_{\mathsf{sarsa}} \approx Q^{\pi_b}$ without considering that $Q^\star$ may vary in different tasks (for example, $Q^\star$ of hopper or walker2d are different). So supposing that we have access to $\max_{s,a} Q^\star(s, a)$ for different tasks (can be approximated by the maximum of the reward function), we propose **Qsarsa-AC2** as a variant of **Qsarsa-AC** which only has a different form of $g(Q_{\mathsf{sarsa}})$ compared to **Qsarsa-AC** as follows:

$$g(Q_{\mathsf{sarsa}}) = \mathrm{Clip}\left[\alpha \exp\left(\frac{\tau_3 \max_{s,a} Q^\star(s, a)}{Q_{\mathsf{sarsa}}^{\mathsf{mean}}}\right), (1, 10^6)\right], \tag{8}$$

where $\max_{s,a} Q^\star(s, a)$ is estimated by $\frac{\max_{s,a} r_{\mathsf{expert}}(s,a)}{(1-\gamma)}$ with $r_{\mathsf{expert}}(s, a)$, the reward data from the *expert* dataset.

## 6    Experimental Evaluation

We first introduce the evaluation of our methods with comparisons to state-of-the-art baselines over the D4RL MuJoCo benchmarks [9], followed by ablation experiments to offer a more detailed analysis for the components based on $Q_{\mathsf{sarsa}}$.

## 6.1   Settings and Baselines

**Experimental Settings.** To evaluate the performance of the proposed methods, we conduct experiments on the D4RL benchmark of OpenAI gym MuJoCo tasks [9], constructed with various domains and dataset quality. Specifically, we conduct experiments on the recently released '-v2' version for MuJoCo in D4RL consisting of 5 different levels of offline datasets (*random, medium-replay, medium, medium-expert,* and *expert*) over 3 different environments, in total 15 tasks. All the baselines and our methods are trained for 3M steps.

**Baselines.** Besides behavior cloning (BC), we compare our performance to several state-of-the-art offline methods, namely CRR [33], OnestepRL [3], CQL [23], and TD3-BC [10]. We highlight that OnestepRL and TD3-BC are the most related baselines: 1) OnestepRL is the only prior work that exploit $Q_{\text{sarsa}}$ in offline methods by directly setting $Q_{\text{sarsa}}$ as the critic, whereas we adopt slight regularizations with the aid of $Q_{\text{sarsa}}$; 2) our methods are designed with TD3-BC as the prototype with additional $Q_{\text{sarsa}}$-assisted regularizations. For all the baselines, we use the implementations from the Acme framework [18] which maintains the designing details of the original papers with tuned hyper-parameters.

**Implementations and Hyperparameters.** Recall that the core of the proposed methods is $Q_{\text{sarsa}}$ — an estimate of $Q^{\pi_b}$ — can be learned from (1). Hence, the training of our methods is divided into two phases: 1) learning $Q_{\text{sarsa}}$ by solving (1) for 1M steps; 2) following the learning process of TD3-BC with a fixed $Q_{\text{sarsa}}$ for 3M training steps.

The hyperparameters of our methods defined in Sect. 5 are tuned in a small finite set using 5 random seeds that are different from those used in the final results reported in Table 1. In particular, we use $\lambda = 0.03$ for the critic and $\alpha = 10^{-4}$, $\tau_1 = 3000, \tau_2 = 4, \tau_3 = 4.5$ for the actor. We remark that $\tau_1$ is chosen according to the range of the value of $Q_{\text{sarsa}}$ as $\tau_1 \approx 2 \cdot \max_{s,a} Q_{\text{sarsa}}(s, a)$

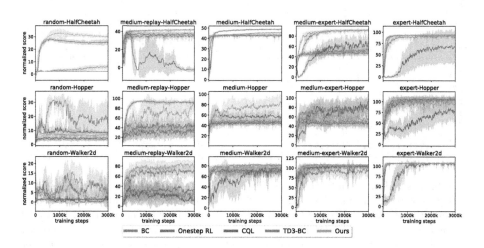

**Fig. 5.** Normalized scores [9] of the evaluations during the training process (5 seeds).

in MuJoCo. For the critic, we tune $\lambda$ in (3) within the set $\{0.01, 0.03, 0.05\}$. For the actor, $\tau_2$ is tuned inside $\{0.4, 2, 4\}$, and $\tau_1$ and $\tau_3$ are tuned across $\{2500, 3000, 3500\}$ and $\{4, 4.5, 5\}$ with a fixed $\alpha = 10^{-4}$ (Fig. 5).

## 6.2   Main Results

**Evaluation of** $Q_{\text{sarsa}}$. We evaluate our two methods **Qsarsa-AC** and **Qsarsa-AC2** with comparison to the baselines over the 15 tasks using 5 random seeds; the results are reported in Table 1. There are three key observations. **(i)** $Q_{\text{sarsa}}$ **brings benefits to existing offline methods.** Recall that our proposed methods are built on the framework of TD3-BC. The last 3 columns of Table 1 illustrate the comparisons between our two methods and TD3-BC. It indicates that the proposed **Qsarsa-AC** and **Qsarsa-AC2** methods, which take advantage of the information of $Q_{\text{sarsa}}$ (see Sect. 5), can bring additional benefits to the existing offline framework TD3-BC and outperform all the conducted baselines. It is also promising to integrate $Q_{\text{sarsa}}$ to other offline methods using approximate dynamic programming framework such as SAC [16] and IQL [21]. We also show that our methods has competitive results against some additional state-of-the-art methods (such as IQL and DT) in Table 2 since these baselines are not closely related. **(ii) Directly setting** $Q_{\text{sarsa}}$ **as the critic has no benefits.** To evaluate whether $Q_{\text{sarsa}}$ play an important role in the success of OnestepRL [3] more systematically, we also involve CRR as an ablation baseline to OnestepRL. As introduced in Sect. 4, we use variants of OnestepRL and CRR with the same actor

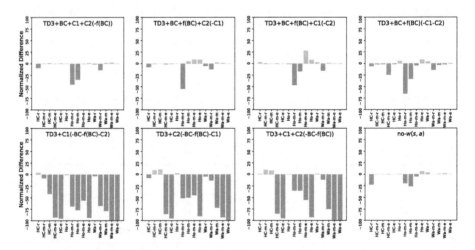

**Fig. 6.** The ablation study of **Qsarsa-AC** (denoted as TD3 + BC + f(BC) + C1 + C2), where f(BC) means the weight $f(Q_{\text{sarsa}}, s, a)$ for BC in (5), and C1 (resp. C2) denotes the $1^{\text{st}}$ (resp. $2^{\text{nd}}$) regularization term designed for the critic in (3). Here, the *Normalized Difference* is calculated as the difference of the normalized score [9] between one ablation and the full algorithm **Qsarsa-AC** (the mean score of 10 evaluations over 5 seeds).

loss (exponentially weighted imitation [3]), so that the only difference between OnestepRL and CRR is that OnestepRL uses $Q_{sarsa}$ as the critic, while CRR uses the critic learned by TD error (usually used in online RL). The similar scores in Table 1 and also the normalized training scores in Fig. 2 show that there is almost no difference between CRR and OnestepRL, indicating that the success of OnestepRL may be attributed to the actor loss. **(iii) Regularization strength for $Q_{sarsa}$.** Based on Table 1, it is noted that our methods achieve better performance with very small weights on the critic regularization terms ($\lambda = 0.03$ in (3)). $Q_{sarsa}$ typically doesn't influence the actor widely since it only determines the weights of the BC term. This observation implies that some small regularizations based on the Q-function of $\pi_b$ ($Q_{sarsa}$) may already achieve the goal of addressing the extrapolation and OOD error in offline RL.

**Ablation Study.** We also perform an ablation study for the components of our method **Qsarsa-AC**, illustrated in Fig. 6. Recall that the main components of **Qsarsa-AC** include $f(Q_{sarsa}, s, a)$ (denoted as f(BC)) for the actor and two regularizations for the critic — InD-sarsa (represented as C1) and OOD-sarsa (represented as C2). In Fig. 6, the first row shows that if we keep TD3-BC as the baseline, removing any of the three components based on $Q_{sarsa}$, especially removing the two critic regularizations together, leads to evident dropping of the

**Table 2.** This table displays the comparisons with two additional offline state-of-the-arts DT [5] and IQL [21] over the 15 tasks of MuJoCo benchmarks in D4RL [9].

| | | DT | IQL | Qsarsa-AC (Ours) | Qsarsa-AC2 (Ours) |
|---|---|---|---|---|---|
| Random | HalfCheetah | — | $13.1 \pm 1.1$ | $30.2 \pm 1.3$ | $30.1 \pm 1.3$ |
| | Hopper | — | $7.9 \pm 0.2$ | $7.5 \pm 0.9$ | $8.1 \pm 1.7$ |
| | Walker2d | — | $5.4 \pm 1.2$ | $5.9 \pm 8.1$ | $4.5 \pm 4.9$ |
| Medium Replay | HalfCheetah | $36.6 \pm 0.8$ | $44.2 \pm 1.2$ | $42.2 \pm 0.7$ | $54.4 \pm 1.8$ |
| | Hopper | $82.7 \pm 7.0$ | $94.7 \pm 8.6$ | $92.6 \pm 10.2$ | $68.1 \pm 19.7$ |
| | Walker2d | $66.6 \pm 3.0$ | $73.8 \pm 7.1$ | $83.7 \pm 9.0$ | $80.0 \pm 11.4$ |
| Medium | HalfCheetah | $42.6 \pm 0.1$ | $47.4 \pm 0.2$ | $44.1 \pm 0.5$ | $56.4 \pm 0.8$ |
| | Hopper | $67.6 \pm 1.0$ | $66.2 \pm 5.7$ | $78.6 \pm 15.7$ | $66.6 \pm 24.3$ |
| | Walker2d | $74.0 \pm 1.4$ | $78.3 \pm 8.7$ | $79.0 \pm 3.1$ | $83.3 \pm 3.5$ |
| Medium Expert | HalfCheetah | $86.8 \pm 1.3$ | $86.7 \pm 5.3$ | $91.3 \pm 0.9$ | $90.9 \pm 1.0$ |
| | Hopper | $107.6 \pm 1.8$ | $91.5 \pm 14.3$ | $56.9 \pm 21.3$ | $73.6 \pm 25.5$ |
| | Walker2d | $108.1 \pm 0.2$ | $110.1 \pm 0.5$ | $105.2 \pm 6.1$ | $107.5 \pm 1.2$ |
| Expert | HalfCheetah | — | $95.0 \pm 0.5$ | $93.8 \pm 1.0$ | $93.7 \pm 1.0$ |
| | Hopper | — | $109.4 \pm 0.5$ | $95.0 \pm 21.1$ | $97.8 \pm 17.0$ |
| | Walker2d | — | $109.0 \pm 1.2$ | $107.0 \pm 0.6$ | $107.0 \pm 0.8$ |
| Total (without random & expert) | | 672.6 | 692.8 | 673.6 | 680.8 |
| Total | | — | 1032.7 | 1013.2 | 1021.8 |

performance. It indicates that the information of $Q_{\text{sarsa}}$ inside the components brings significant benefits to the existing TD3-BC framework. We further evaluate the ablations of removing BC in the actor (as well as f(BC)), which lead to dramatic dropping of the performance, shown in the second row of Fig. 6. The performance drop is reasonable since the weights for the critic regularizations (C1 and C2) designed in (3) are tuned based on TD3-BC with BC in hand. Finally, the ablation of removing the mask $w(\cdot)$ inside the OOD-sarsa regularization in (3) implies that OOD error of $Q_{\text{sarsa}}$ may happen and harm the performance without $w(\cdot)$, but not often.

### 6.3    Additional Results

**The Comparisons to Additional Baselines.** Here, we provide the performance comparisons to two additional strong baselines DT [5] and IQL [21]. IQL is a well-known strong baseline using the same approximate dynamic programming framework as our methods, while DT resort to a different framework — sequential modeling. In Table 2, we directly report the scores in the original paper of DT [5] and the reported scores for IQL in a prior work [27]. Table 2 shows that our methods can not only bring significant benefits for some existing offline methods (such as TD3-BC) but also achieve competitive performance with comparisons to those strong offline methods.

**Auxiliary Implementation Details.** For our two methods **Qsarsa-AC** and **Qsarsa-AC2**, the models of the policies (actors) and the Q-functions (critics) are the same as the ones in TD3-BC [10]. The models for $Q_{\text{sarsa}}$ (including the networks parameterized by $\theta_s$ and $\bar{\theta}_s$) are MLPs with ReLU activations and with 2 hidden layers of width 1024. The training of the $Q_{\text{sarsa}}$ network parameterized by $\theta_s$ is completed in the first training phase using Adam with initial learning rate $10^{-4}$ and batch size as 512. The target of $Q_{\text{sarsa}}$ is updated smoothly with $\tau = 0.005$, i.e., $\bar{\theta}_s \leftarrow (1 - \tau)\bar{\theta}_s + \tau\theta_s$.

## 7    Conclusion

We propose to integrate a SARSA-style estimate of the Q-function of the behavior policy into offline RL for better performance. Given the limited use of the Q-function of the behavior policy in the current literature, we first evaluate the SARSA-style Q-estimate to establish its reliability in estimating the Q-function and potential to restrict OOD errors. We then propose two methods by taking advantage of the SARSA-style Q-estimate based on TD3-BC, one of the offline state-of-the-art methods. Our proposed methods achieve strong performance in D4RL MuJoCo benchmarks and outperform the baselines. It is our hope to inspire future works that exploit the benefit of Q/value-functions of the behavior policy in more offline methods, such as using different regularization loss functions beyond $\ell_2$, combining it with other regularization techniques, and in different schemes in the approximate dynamic programming framework, even sequential modeling.

**Acknowledgment.** Part of this work was completed when L. Shi was an intern at Google Research, Brain Team. The work of L. Shi and Y. Chi is supported in part by the grants NSF CCF-2106778 and CNS-2148212. L. Shi is also gratefully supported by the Leo Finzi Memorial Fellowship, Wei Shen and Xuehong Zhang Presidential Fellowship, and Liang Ji-Dian Graduate Fellowship at Carnegie Mellon University. The authors would like to thank Alexis Jacq for reviewing an early version of the paper. The authors would like to thank the anonymous reviewers for valuable feedback and suggestions. We would also like to thank the Python and RL community for useful tools that are widely used in this work, including Acme [18], Numpy [17], and JAX [2].

**Ethical Statement.** Offline RL methods may bring benefits for social application scenarios when collecting new data is infeasible due to cost, privacy or safety. For example, learning to diagnose from historical medical records or designing recommendations given existing clicking records of some advertisements. For negative social impact, offline methods may enable big data discriminatory pricing to yield unfair market or improve the recommendation techniques to make more people to be addicted to the social media. However, our proposed methods is more related to introducing scientific thoughts and investigations, which do not target such possible applications. Additionally, this work will only use public benchmarks and data, so no personal data will be acquired or inferred.

# References

1. Arulkumaran, K., Deisenroth, M.P., Brundage, M., Bharath, A.A.: A brief survey of deep reinforcement learning. arXiv preprint arXiv:1708.05866 (2017)
2. Bradbury, J., et al.: Jax: Autograd and xla. Astrophysics Source Code Library pp. ascl-2111 (2021)
3. Brandfonbrener, D., Whitney, W., Ranganath, R., Bruna, J.: Offline RL without off-policy evaluation. Adv. Neural Inf. Process. Syst. **34**, 4933–4946 (2021)
4. Buckman, J., Gelada, C., Bellemare, M.G.: The importance of pessimism in fixed-dataset policy optimization. In: International Conference on Learning Representations (2020)
5. Chen, L., et al.: Decision transformer: reinforcement learning via sequence modeling. Adv. Neural Inf. Process. Syst. **34**, 15084–15097 (2021)
6. Chen, X., Zhou, Z., Wang, Z., Wang, C., Wu, Y., Ross, K.: Bail: best-action imitation learning for batch deep reinforcement learning. Adv. Neural Inf. Process. Syst. **33**, 18353–18363 (2020)
7. Dadashi, R., Rezaeifar, S., Vieillard, N., Hussenot, L., Pietquin, O., Geist, M.: Offline reinforcement learning with pseudometric learning. In: International Conference on Machine Learning, pp. 2307–2318. PMLR (2021)
8. Fakoor, R., Mueller, J.W., Asadi, K., Chaudhari, P., Smola, A.J.: Continuous doubly constrained batch reinforcement learning. Adv. Neural Inf. Process. Syst. **34**, 11260–11273 (2021)
9. Fu, J., Kumar, A., Nachum, O., Tucker, G., Levine, S.: D4rl: datasets for deep data-driven reinforcement learning. arXiv preprint arXiv:2004.07219 (2020)
10. Fujimoto, S., Gu, S.S.: A minimalist approach to offline reinforcement learning. Adv. Neural Inf. Process. Syst. **34**, 20132–20145 (2021)

11. Fujimoto, S., Hoof, H., Meger, D.: Addressing function approximation error in actor-critic methods. In: International Conference on Machine Learning, pp. 1587–1596. PMLR (2018)
12. Fujimoto, S., Meger, D., Precup, D.: Off-policy deep reinforcement learning without exploration. In: International Conference on Machine Learning, pp. 2052–2062. PMLR (2019)
13. Garg, D., Hejna, J., Geist, M., Ermon, S.: Extreme q-learning: maxent RL without entropy. arXiv preprint arXiv:2301.02328 (2023)
14. Ghasemipour, S.K.S., Schuurmans, D., Gu, S.S.: EMaQ: expected-max Q-learning operator for simple yet effective offline and online RL. In: International Conference on Machine Learning, pp. 3682–3691. PMLR (2021)
15. Gulcehre, C., et al.: Regularized behavior value estimation. arXiv preprint arXiv:2103.09575 (2021)
16. Haarnoja, T., Zhou, A., Abbeel, P., Levine, S.: Soft actor-critic: off-policy maximum entropy deep reinforcement learning with a stochastic actor. In: International Conference on Machine Learning, pp. 1861–1870. PMLR (2018)
17. Harris, C.R., et al.: Array programming with numpy. Nature **585**(7825), 357–362 (2020)
18. Hoffman, M., et al.: Acme: a research framework for distributed reinforcement learning. arXiv preprint arXiv:2006.00979 (2020)
19. Janner, M., Li, Q., Levine, S.: Offline reinforcement learning as one big sequence modeling problem. Adv. Neural Inf. Process. Syst. **34**, 1273–1286 (2021)
20. Kostrikov, I., Fergus, R., Tompson, J., Nachum, O.: Offline reinforcement learning with fisher divergence critic regularization. In: International Conference on Machine Learning, pp. 5774–5783. PMLR (2021)
21. Kostrikov, I., Nair, A., Levine, S.: Offline reinforcement learning with implicit Q-learning. arXiv preprint arXiv:2110.06169 (2021)
22. Kumar, A., Fu, J., Soh, M., Tucker, G., Levine, S.: Stabilizing off-policy Q-learning via bootstrapping error reduction. In: Advances in Neural Information Processing Systems, vol. 32 (2019)
23. Kumar, A., Zhou, A., Tucker, G., Levine, S.: Conservative Q-learning for offline reinforcement learning. Adv. Neural Inf. Process. Syst. **33**, 1179–1191 (2020)
24. Lee, B.J., Lee, J., Kim, K.E.: Representation balancing offline model-based reinforcement learning. In: International Conference on Learning Representations (2020)
25. Levine, S.: Reinforcement learning and control as probabilistic inference: tutorial and review. arXiv preprint arXiv:1805.00909 (2018)
26. Levine, S., Kumar, A., Tucker, G., Fu, J.: Offline reinforcement learning: tutorial, review, and perspectives on open problems. arXiv preprint arXiv:2005.01643 (2020)
27. Lyu, J., Ma, X., Li, X., Lu, Z.: Mildly conservative Q-learning for offline reinforcement learning. Adv. Neural Inf. Process. Syst. **35**, 1711–1724 (2022)
28. Peng, X.B., Kumar, A., Zhang, G., Levine, S.: Advantage-weighted regression: simple and scalable off-policy reinforcement learning. arXiv preprint arXiv:1910.00177 (2019)
29. Rezaeifar, S., et al.: Offline reinforcement learning as anti-exploration. In: Proceedings of the AAAI Conference on Artificial Intelligence, vol. 36, pp. 8106–8114 (2022)
30. Silver, D., et al.: Mastering the game of go without human knowledge. Nature **550**(7676), 354–359 (2017)
31. Vinyals, O., et al.: Grandmaster level in starcraft ii using multi-agent reinforcement learning. Nature **575**(7782), 350–354 (2019)

32. Wang, Z., Hunt, J.J., Zhou, M.: Diffusion policies as an expressive policy class for offline reinforcement learning. arXiv preprint arXiv:2208.06193 (2022)
33. Wang, Z., et al.: Critic regularized regression. Adv. Neural Inf. Process. Syst. **33**, 7768–7778 (2020)
34. Wu, Y., Tucker, G., Nachum, O.: Behavior regularized offline reinforcement learning. arXiv preprint arXiv:1911.11361 (2019)
35. Yang, S., Wang, Z., Zheng, H., Feng, Y., Zhou, M.: A regularized implicit policy for offline reinforcement learning. arXiv preprint arXiv:2202.09673 (2022)
36. Yu, T., Kumar, A., Rafailov, R., Rajeswaran, A., Levine, S., Finn, C.: Combo: conservative offline model-based policy optimization. Adv. Neural Inf. Process. Syst. **34**, 28954–28967 (2021)
37. Zhang, G., Kashima, H.: Behavior estimation from multi-source data for offline reinforcement learning. In: Proceedings of the AAAI Conference on Artificial Intelligence, vol. 37, pp. 11201–11209 (2023)

# Alpha Elimination: Using Deep Reinforcement Learning to Reduce Fill-In During Sparse Matrix Decomposition

Arpan Dasgupta and Pawan Kumar$^{(\boxtimes)}$

IIIT Hyderabad, Hyderabad, India
arpan.dasgupta@research.iiit.ac.in, pawan.kumar@iiit.ac.in

**Abstract.** A large number of computational and scientific methods commonly require decomposing a sparse matrix into triangular factors as LU decomposition. A common problem faced during this decomposition is that even though the given matrix may be very sparse, the decomposition may lead to a denser triangular factors due to fill-in. A significant fill-in may lead to prohibitively larger computational costs and memory requirement during decomposition as well as during the solve phase. To this end, several heuristic sparse matrix reordering methods have been proposed to reduce fill-in before the decomposition. However, finding an optimal reordering algorithm that leads to minimal fill-in during such decomposition is known to be a NP-hard problem. A reinforcement learning based approach is proposed for this problem. The sparse matrix reordering problem is formulated as a single player game. More specifically, Monte-Carlo tree search in combination with neural network is used as a decision making algorithm to search for the best move in our game. The proposed method, Alpha Elimination is found to produce significantly lesser non-zeros in the LU decomposition as compared to existing state-of-the-art heuristic algorithms with little to no increase in overall running time of the algorithm. The code for the project is publicly available (https://github.com/misterpawan/alphaEliminationPaper).

**Keywords:** Reinforcement Learning · Sparse Matrices · Deep Learning · LU · MCTS

## 1 Introduction

Computations on large matrices are an essential component of several computational and scientific applications. In most cases, these matrices are sparse which, if exploited well, provide a significant reduction in computation time and memory consumption. Therefore, it is essential to ensure that any operation performed on these sparse matrices maintains their sparsity, so that subsequent operations remain efficient.

© The Author(s), under exclusive license to Springer Nature Switzerland AG 2023
D. Koutra et al. (Eds.): ECML PKDD 2023, LNAI 14172, pp. 472–488, 2023.
https://doi.org/10.1007/978-3-031-43421-1_28

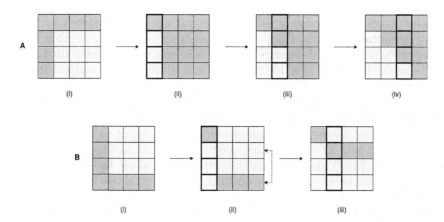

**Fig. 1.** Toy example demonstrating the effect of fill-in during LU decomposition on different permutations of the same matrix. The non-zero entries are denoted by red color and the column being eliminated is highlighted at each step. (A) The first column being eliminated causes all the other columns to become non-zeros, which are not eliminated in the subsequent steps. We end up with 10 non-zero entries in the $U$ matrix. (B) Using a different row permutation for the matrix, we obtain no fill-in, and end up with 4 non-zeros in the $U$ matrix.

*Challenges in LU decomposition for sparse matrices:* One of the most frequently performed operations on matrices is decomposition. Matrix decomposition in linear algebra refers to the factorization of a matrix into a product of multiple matrices; examples include LU, QR [15,18], SVD, etc. [9]. Matrix decomposition is also used in preconditioning [2,5,6,12,16,17,19–22,31]. Different types of decomposition may lead to factors with different properties or structures. In particular, in LU decomposition [9], the matrix $A$ is decomposed into a lower triangular and an upper triangular matrix, $L$ and $U$ respectively. The LU decomposition is useful in solving systems of linear equations stemming from numerous and wide variety of applications ranging from 3D reconstruction in vision, fluid dynamics, electromagnetic simulations, material science models, regression in machine learning and in a variety of optimization solvers that model numerous applications. Thus it is of essence that the $L$ and $U$ matrices after the decomposition of the sparse matrix are also sparse. However, it is possible that during the matrix decomposition, the $L$ and $U$ matrices become much denser than the initial matrix due to *fill-in* resulting from Gaussian elimination. The LU decomposition at each step requires choosing a pivot row, and then uses the diagonal entry on this row to eliminate all the elements in the same column in the following rows. The method is illustrated in Fig. 1. The figure shows that choosing the correct row is an important problem. The number of non-zeros created in the $U$ matrix (and similarly in the $L$ matrix) can be significantly reduced by choosing correct rows as pivot at each step.

The process of choosing a suitable row can also be formulated as finding a row permutation matrix $P_{\text{row}}$, which is pre-multiplied to the original matrix before performing the LU decomposition. The inverse of this permutation matrix can be multiplied back after the decomposition to obtain the original required decomposition without affecting the sparsity as follows $A = P_{\text{row}}^{-1}(P_{\text{row}}A) = P_{\text{row}}^{-1}(LU)$. Finding an optimal $P_{\text{row}}$ matrix which will minimize the fill-in is a very difficult task due to two reasons (1) Since the row chosen has to have a non-zero value at the column being eliminated, it is impossible to know in advance which row will have a non-zero value due to the non-zeros changing at each step of elimination (2) With larger matrices, the search space becomes impossible to traverse completely to find the optimal. In fact, [3] shows that solving this problem for a symmetric matrix is an NP-hard by converting it to a hypergraph partitioning problem. We aim to use Reinforcement Learning as a way to find a permutation matrix, which gives a lower fill-in than existing state-of-the-art algorithms.

***Deep Reinforcement Learning:*** Deep Reinforcement Learning (DRL) has become an effective method to find an efficient strategy to games wherever a large search space is involved. Algorithms have been developed which are capable of reacting and working around their environment successfully. The success of recent RL methods can be largely attributed to the development of function approximation and representation learning methods using Deep Learning. A landmark success in this field came when Deep Mind developed an algorithm AlphaGo [32], which was able to beat the reigning Go champion using DRL. The DRL methods have since been applied to several domains such as robotics, which find control policies directly from camera input [23,24]. RL has been used for several other applications such as playing video games [27–29], managing power consumption [35] and stowing objects [24]. One unique way to use DRL has been to aid discovery of optimal parameters in existing models such as machine translation models [36], and also for designing optimization functions [25]. To this end, work has been recently done on algorithm discovery for matrix multiplication [8] and discovery of protein structure [10]. Our work aims to use DRL to replace heuristic algorithms for sparse matrix permutation with an algorithm which can find a much better permutation, thus significantly saving time and memory in downstream tasks, in particular for LU.

***Contributions:*** Our main contributions can be summarized as follows.

- We formulate the problem of finding the row permutation matrix for reduced fill-in as a single player game complete with state, action and rewards. We then use MCTS to find a solution to the game.
- We perform extensive experiments on matrices from several real-world domains to show that our method performs better than the naive LU without reordering as well as existing heuristic reordering methods.

# 2    Related Work

Reduction of fill-in in LU and Cholesky decomposition of sparse matrices is a well studied problem. [13] provides an overview of the problem and describes the different algorithms in terms of a graph problem. Approximate Minimum Degree (AMD) [1] is an algorithm which permutes row and columns of the matrix by choosing the node at each step which has the minimum degree in the remaining graph. This was shown to perform well on an average. Column Approximate Minimum Degree (ColAMD) [7] performs approximate column permutations and uses a better heuristic than AMD. SymAMD is a derivative of ColAMD which is used on symmetric matrices. Sparse Reverse Cuthill-McKee (SymRCM) [26] is another method that is commonly used for ordering in symmetric matrices. It utilizes the reverse of the ordering produced by the Cuthill-McKee algorithm which is a graph based algorithm. However, all these algorithms utilize heuristics with some bound on the error, but no work involving machine learning has been done in this area.

Monte Carlo tree search (MCTS), a popular Reinforcement Learning algorithm has previously proven successful in a variety of domains such as playing games like Go [32], Chess and Shogi [33]. Applications have also been found in domains like qubit routing [34] and planning [30] where the problems can be formulated as a single player game. Recently, [8] used MCTS for discovering faster matrix multiplication algorithms. To our knowledge, there has been no attempt at application of RL in replacing heuristic algorithms for efficient LU decomposition on sparse matrices.

# 3    Alpha Elimination

This section will be organized as follows, in section one, we will talk about how we formulated the matrix decomposition problem as a single player game in the RL setting. In the next section, we will show how the Deep MCTS algorithm works in our problem, and in the third section we will talk about our choice of neural networks for the problem at hand.

## 3.1    Section 1: Formulating the Game

Figure 2 shows the state of the game at a certain point in the elimination. Let us assume that the matrix is denoted by $A$ and we are at step $i$ of the elimination, i.e., we are trying to eliminate entries below diagonal of the $i_{th}$ column. Elimination of column $i$ involves (i) Picking a row $j$ as a pivot where the value at column $i$ is non-zero (ii) Swapping row $j$ for the current row $i$ (iii) Using the value $A[i][i]$, we make all values $A[k][i] = 0$ for $k > i$ by performing elementary row operations. Figure 2 also shows the elimination procedure.

**Definition 1.** *(State) A state $S$ of the game provides entire configuration of the game and the environment at a certain timestep $t$. In our problem, this includes the matrix $A$ as well as the index $i$ which represents the current column to be eliminated.*

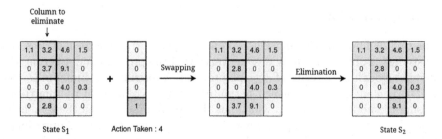

**Fig. 2.** Representation of a single step of the game, starting from a state. The action chosen determines the row pivot at each point. After the swapping of the row, the elimination is performed leading to the next step. The column in bold represents the next column to be eliminated.

Although the value of $i$ could be inferred from $A$, complete state information includes both the values.

**Definition 2.** *(Action) The action $a$ is the mechanism by which an agent transitions between the states. The agent has to choose one of several legal actions at the step. In our game, the action to be taken by the agent must be a row index $j$ where $j \geq i$ and $A[j][i] \neq 0$ or if no such value exists, $j = i$. The agent must thus choose which row to swap in for the current row as a pivot.*

As we have seen in the examples, choosing this pivot correctly at each step is essential to reduce the fill-in. The transition from one state to another is also done by using the procedure for elimination described previously.

**Definition 3.** *(Reward) Reward $R(S, a)$ is the numerical result of taking a certain action in a state. The final goal of the agent in our game is to reduce the number of non-zeros created in total during this elimination procedure.*

The reward can be provided to the agent in two different ways. We can provide the reward at the end of each step as negative of the number of non-zeros created at the current step based on the action. Alternatively, we can provide the total number of non-zeros created as a fraction of initial zeros in the matrix as a negative reward. While both these reward mechanisms are similar, the latter worked better in practice for us due to the ease of tuning the exploration factor $c$ for MCTS (Fig. 3).

## 3.2   Section 2: Applying Deep MCTS

Monte Carlo Tree Search progresses by executing four phases in repetition: select, expand, evaluate and backup. The entire algorithm for our problem is shown in form of pseudo-code in Algorithm 1.

**Algorithm 1.** Monte Carlo Tree Search Algorithm for Alpha Elimination

---

**Require:** Starting State $S$, Model $M$, Immediate reward function $R$

  **for** *loop* ← 1 to *num_mcts_loops* **do**

    root ← $S$

    cur_node ← $S$

    **while** True **do**                      ▷ Runs till expand phase reached

      Select best action $A$ which minimizes UCT  (See (4)).   ▷ **Select Phase**

      Compute UCT using prior values and noise

      **if** cur_node.children[$A$] ≠ null **then**    ▷ Move to next state if discovered

        cur_node ← cur_node.children[$A$]

      **else**

        new_state ← cur_state.**step**($A$)            ▷ **Expand Stage**

        **if** new_state = null **then**            ▷ Leaf Node

          break

        **end if**

        cur_state.children[$A$] ← new_state

        **store** reward[cur_state, $A$]

            ← $R$(new_state) - $R$(cur_state)

        break

      **end if**

    **end while**

    cur_reward ← model(cur_state)                ▷ **Evaluate Phase**

    **while** cur_node ≠ root **do**

      p_action ← action from cur_state to parent of cur_state

      cur_state ← cur_state.parent            ▷ **Backup Phase**

      cur_reward ← reward[cur_state, p_action] + $\gamma$ cur_reward  (see (2))

      **Update** cur_state.Q_value[$A$, p_action] with cur_reward  (See (2), (3))

      **Update** cur_state.N_value[$A$, p_action]  (See (1))

    **end while**

  **end for**

---

***Select:*** This step involves starting with a specific state and selecting a node to explore until a state node is reached which has not been explored yet. The selection starts at the root of the subtree to be explored at time $t$. The agent selects an action from a set of legal actions according to some criteria recursively. Assuming that $R(S, a)$ represents the immediate reward for taking action $a$ at state $S$, we keep track of two things during the MCTS procedure (over all passes during exploration):

1. $N$-values: $N(S, a)$ represents the number of times the state action pair has been taken in total.
2. $Q$-values: $Q(S, a)$ represents the expected long term reward for the state action pair $(S, a)$. To calculate this, we simply keep track of $W(S, a)$ which is the sum of all rewards received over the previous iterations. Here $N$, $W$ and $Q$ are updated as follows:

$$N(S, a) = N(S, a) + 1 \tag{1}$$

$$W(S, a) = R(S, a) + \gamma W(S, a) \tag{2}$$

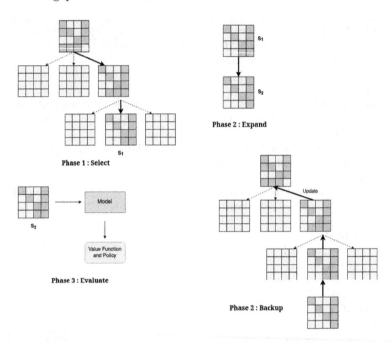

**Fig. 3.** Four Phases of the MCTS Algorithm

$$Q(S,a) = \frac{W(S,a)}{N(S,a)}. \tag{3}$$

These updates are actually performed in the backup stage.

We use an asymmetric formulation of Upper Confidence Bound on Trees (UCT) as a criteria for selection of the next action at each step

$$\text{UCT}(S,a) = Q(S,a) + c\frac{\sqrt{N(S,a)}}{N(S,a)} \times P(a|S), \tag{4}$$

where $c$ represents the exploration-exploitation constant (Higher $c$ encourages exploration) and $P(a|S)$ represents the prior probability of taking action $a$ given state $S$. $P(a|S)$ is calculated by adding Dirichlet noise to the function approximator $f$ (neural network in our case) prediction.

$$P(a|S) = (1-\epsilon)f(S') + \epsilon\eta_\alpha. \tag{5}$$

Here, $\eta_\alpha \sim Dir(\alpha)$ where $\alpha = 0.03$, $\epsilon = 0.25$, (values are the commonly used ones described in [34]) and $S'$ is the resulting state when action $a$ is taken at $S$. Here $Dir(\cdot)$ stands for Dirichlet distribution. This ensures that all moves are tried while search still overrules bad moves [32]. The prior estimate $P(a|S)$ improves as the MCTS continues to explore.

***Expand:*** The expand step is invoked when the select reaches a state and takes an action which has not been explored yet. The step involves creating a new node and adding it to the tree structure.

***Evaluate:*** On reaching a node newly created by the expand stage or reaching a leaf node, the evaluation phase is commenced. This involves estimating the long term reward for the current state using a neural network as an estimator. The neural network is provided the current state as the input, which estimates the expected reward and the prior probabilities for each action from the current state. The neural network architecture used for this purpose is described in the following section.

***Backup:*** Once the evaluation phase is completed, the reward value estimated at the last node in the tree is propagated backwards until the root is reached. At each of the ancestor nodes, the values of the expected reward for each action $Q$ and the number of times each action is taken $N$ are updated using the update equations described previously. As the MCTS probes the search space, it gets better estimates for the prior and the expected reward. The $N(S, a)$ represents the policies to take, and is thus used for training the policy (6), while the average $Q$ value is used to train the value estimator (7)

$$\pi(a|S) \propto N(S, a) \tag{6}$$

$$V(S) = \frac{\Sigma_a W(S, a)}{\Sigma_a N(S, a)}. \tag{7}$$

### 3.3    Section 3: Neural Network Architecture

The role of a neural network in the Deep MCTS algorithm is to be able to act as a function approximator which can estimate the expected reward ie. the $Q$-values for a certain state and the expected reward for each state-action pair for that state. Since actually calculating the $Q$-values is not feasible due to the intractable size of the search space, a neural network is used instead due to its ability to learn rules from the previous exploration data directly.

MCTS provides the neural network with a state $S$ and the network must output two values: (i) $\pi$, estimate of the $Q$ values for each action (ii) $V$, value function of that state. This is achieved by adding two output heads to the same neural network. The main challenge at this point was on how to provide the sparse matrix as an input to a neural network. For this, we considered several possible architectures.

Intuitively, a sparse matrix can be treated as an image with mostly zero pixels. CNNs have been successful in similar problems capturing row and column dependencies, for example, in board games such as Go [32], in Chess and Shogi [33]. While sparse layers for artificial neural networks are much more efficient than CNNs, a simple method of unrolling the matrix and providing it as single-dimensional input to the network does not work as most column information is lost. For example, any two vertically adjacent elements cannot preserve that information. Thus, positional embedding would need to be added with column information. However, this approach faces scaling issues, as the parameter count is proportional to matrix size $N$. Graph neural network could also be used, but

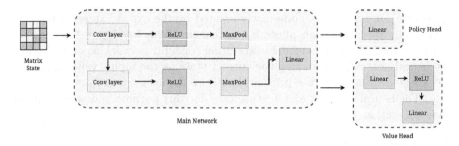

**Fig. 4.** Architecture of the neural network used for value and policy prediction. The first and second convolution layers have kernel sizes 3 and 5 respectively with a padding of 2 and stride 1 over 3 channels. The MaxPool layers have a kernel size of 2. Each of the linear layers have a single fully connected layer. The hidden layer dimensions are equal to the matrix size $N$, except for the last layers, where it corresponds to 1 for the value head and $N$ for the policy head.

it was unclear how to provide graph structure as GNN input. This idea remains a potential future direction.

We decide to use CNN as it emphasizes the row-column relationship, and is relatively simple to understand and implement. An issue with standard CNN is that it needs to densify the sparse matrix to be able to operate on it. Thus, we can use a sparse version of CNN [4] to run the CNN algorithm on larger matrices and take advantage of the sparsity. However, the benefit in running time while using sparse convolution only comes above a certain threshold of the matrix size $N$. However, as we will see at this threshold or above of matrix size, the time taken to train the network increases significantly due to large search space and alternative ways to scale the network have to be explored anyway. The final network architecture is denoted in Fig. 4. The problem of scaling to larger matrices will be discussed in detail in Sect. 4.4. We observed that masking of the input also led to a significant improvement in rate of learning by the model. We discuss this in detail in Sect. 4.3.

## 4   Alpha Elimination: Details

### 4.1   Training

We train our model on randomly generated matrices with a certain sparsity level. For each train matrix, the MCTS starts the self-play at time step 0 and generates a data point for every time step. Each data point consists of the state as input and the respective $Q$-values and updated value function as the output. These data points are added to a buffer which is used to train the neural network after a certain set of intervals. Prioritized experience replay (PER) [32] is used to efficiently train the neural network. The use of a buffer is necessary due to the fact that each data point must be independent from the previous.

**Size of Matrix to Train:** The size of the matrix on which we train the neural network must be fixed, since the input to the neural network cannot vary in size. However, the size of the matrix to be tested on is variable. Hence, we use the block property of LU decomposition to always change our problem into the same fixed size. For example, we train our Deep MCTS for a large matrix of size $N \times N$, but in practice we may get a matrix $A$ of size $n \times n$ where $n \leq N$. We can however, convert the smaller matrix to the size it was originally trained by adding an identity block as follows $\begin{bmatrix} I_{N-n} & 0 \\ 0 & A_{n \times n} \end{bmatrix}_{N \times N}$ . The LU decomposition of the above matrix is equivalent to that of $A$, and the row permutation matrix is also just a padded one. This procedure can also be interpreted as a intermediate time step of the LU decomposition of a larger matrix.

**Sparsity of Matrix:** The structure of the matrix received during testing must be similar to the ones in training, thus we need to make sure that the sparsity levels of the matrices match too. As a general rule, we see that the common matrices in practice have a sparsity level of $\geq 0.85$ (i.e. more than 85% of values are non-zeros). Thus, the network is trained on various levels of sparsity above this threshold.

### 4.2   Prediction

During prediction, instead of selecting the next action based on UCT, we directly utilize the output of the trained model as a prediction of the expected reward. We therefore choose optimal action $a^* = \max_a \pi(a|S)$ where $\pi$ is output of policy function of neural network. At each step, the algorithm outputs the row $j$ to be swapped with current row $i$. Using this information, we can reconstruct the row permutation matrix $P$ for final comparison with the other methods.

### 4.3   Remark on the Role of Masking

Neural networks are powerful learners; however, when presented with an abundance of information, they may struggle to discern the essential aspects of a problem and might establish spurious correlations. In our experiments, we observed that providing the original matrix with floating point entries to the neural network resulted in slow and erratic learning. Consequently, we employed masking of the non-zeros to minimize noise and ensure that the neural network focuses on the role of non-zero entries as pivots. More specifically, the non-zero entries are converted to a constant value of 1, whereas, the zeros (accounting for floating-point errors) are assigned a value of 0. This masking technique assumes that none of the non-zeros will become zero during elimination. Although this assumption may not be universally true, it is valid in most cases involving real-world matrices with floating-point values. Even in cases where the assumption does not hold, such instances are relatively rare and have minimal impact on the overall policy. Masking also has negligible effect on time complexity.

## 4.4   Scaling to Larger Matrices

The method effectively finds row permutation matrices, but the search space for even small matrices is vast. Matrix size $N$ and training data requirements increase with larger matrices. In real-life applications, matrix sizes can reach up to millions or higher. To address this, we employ a graph partitioning algorithm from the METIS library [11] to partition the matrix into parts of size 500, which allows for efficient learning within a reasonable time-frame. We remark here that most LU factorization for large matrices are anyway partitioned into small parts to achieve parallelism on modern day multi-core or multi-CPU architectures [9], and only "local" LU factorization of the smaller sub-matrices are required.

# 5   Experiments and Discussion

## 5.1   Experimental Setup

Experiments were conducted on a Linux machine equipped with 20 Intel(R) Xeon(R) CPU E5-2640 v4 cores @ 2.40GHz, 120GB RAM, and 2 RTX 2080Ti GPUs. The total number of non-zeros in the LU decomposition is used as the evaluation metric, as our method aims to minimize it. We compared our approach to the naive LU decomposition in sparse matrices and existing heuristic algorithms that minimize fill-in, such as ColAMD [7], SymRCM [26], and SymAMD. There are some specific re-ordering techniques, but due to lack of general applicability we do not compare with them. After exporting the matrix to MATLAB, where these methods are implemented, LU decomposition was performed. The final evaluation involved matrices from the SuiteSparse Matrix Collection [14]. Table 1 displays the selected matrices, which span various application areas, symmetry patterns, and sizes ranging from 400 to 11 million elements.

## 5.2   Experimental Results

**Comparison of Methods:** The comparison between Alpha Elimination and the baseline as well as the other methods is shown in Table 2. As it is evident from the results, Alpha Elimination obtains significant reduction in the number of non-zeros as compared to the other methods. This leads to significant reduction in storage space for the factors of the sparse matrices, and leads to reduction in solve time using LU factorization. The reduction in the number of non-zeros provides even more significant memory savings when the size of the matrices increases. Our method produced up to 61.5% less non-zeros on large matrices than the naive method and up to 39.9% less non-zeros than the best heuristic methods. While in some matrices our method gives a significant reduction, some matrices are much simpler in structure, providing much lesser time for improvement over simple algorithms. For example, the matrix *ohm500* has a very simple structure (almost already diagonal) and it is trivial for every row

**Table 1.** Matrices used for testing from Suite Sparse Matrix Market

| Matrix | Domain | Rows $N$ | Structurally Symmetric (Y/N) |
|---|---|---|---|
| west0479 | Chemical Process Simulation Problem | 479 | Yes |
| mbeause | Economic Problem | 496 | No |
| tomography | Computer Graphics/Vision Problem | 500 | No |
| Trefethen_500 | Combinatorial Problem | 500 | Yes |
| olm500 | Computational Fluid Dynamics Problem | 500 | Yes |
| Erdos991 | Undirected Graph | 492 | Yes |
| rbsb480 | Robotics Problem | 480 | No |
| ex27 | Computational Fluid Dynamics Problem | 974 | No |
| m_t1 | Structural Problem | 97,578 | Yes |
| Emilia_923 | Structural Problem | 923,136 | Yes |
| tx2010 | Undirected Weighted Graph | 914,231 | Yes |
| boneS10 | Model Reduction Problem | 914,898 | No |
| PFlow_742 | 2D/3D Problem | 742,793 | Yes |
| Hardesty1 | Computer Graphics/Vision Problem | 938,905 | Yes |
| vas_stokes_4M | Semiconductor Process Problem | 4,382,246 | No |
| stokes | Semiconductor Process Problem | 11,449,533 | No |

**Table 2.** Total Non-Zero Count in Lower and Upper Triangular Factors after reorderings for matrices from Suite Sparse Matrix Market Dataset.

| Matrix | LU Methods | | | | |
|---|---|---|---|---|---|
| | Naive LU | ColAMD | SymAMD | SymRCM | Proposed Method |
| west0479 | 16358 | 4475 | 4510 | 4352 | **3592** |
| mbeause | 166577 | 126077 | NA | NA | **94859** |
| tomography | 108444 | 41982 | NA | NA | **35690** |
| Trefethen_500 | 169618 | 150344 | 153170 | 119672 | **94632** |
| olm500 | 3984 | **3070** | **3070** | **3070** | 3070 |
| Erdos991 | 61857 | 4255 | 4287 | 4372 | **3584** |
| rbsb480 | 192928 | 63783 | NA | NA | **55185** |
| ex27 | 122464 | 104292 | NA | NA | **63948** |
| m_t1 | 9789931 | 9318461 | 8540363 | 8185236 | **7398266** |
| Emilia_923 | 5.67E08 | 4.49E08 | 4.29E08 | 4.56E08 | **3.9E08** |
| tx2010 | 1.48E10 | 3.83E09 | 2.34E09 | 2.44E09 | **1.3E09** |
| boneS10 | 3.98E08 | 1.89E08 | NA | NA | **1.1E08** |
| PFlow_742 | 1.98E08 | 9.20E07 | 8.43E07 | 8.92E07 | **8.3E07** |
| Hardesty1 | 6.03E08 | 5.91E08 | 5.90E08 | 5.92E08 | **4.9E08** |
| vas_stokes_4M | 1.35E09 | 8.71E+08 | NA | NA | **5.9E08** |
| stokes | 9.78E10 | 6.42E10 | NA | NA | **3.9E10** |

**Table 3.** Comparison of time (in seconds) taken for LU factorization after reordering by different methods.

| Matrix | Time taken for LU (s) | | | | |
|---|---|---|---|---|---|
| | Naive LU | ColAMD | SymAMD | SymRCM | Proposed Method |
| mbeause | 0.0326 | 0.0319 | NA | NA | **0.0302** |
| tomography | 0.04250 | 0.0394 | NA | NA | **0.0286** |
| Trefethen_500 | 0.0498 | 0.0419 | 0.0392 | 0.0347 | **0.0302** |
| m_t1 | 5.8790 | 4.7894 | 4.1321 | 3.7031 | **3.2820** |
| tx2010 | 24.3018 | 15.7040 | 14.5840 | 15.6194 | **12.9365** |

**Table 4.** Comparison of total time (in seconds) for LU (including reordering).

| Matrix | Time taken for LU (s) | | | | |
|---|---|---|---|---|---|
| | Naive LU | ColAMD | SymAMD | SymRCM | Proposed Method |
| mbeause | **0.0326** | 0.0345 | NA | NA | 0.0336 |
| tomography | 0.0425 | 0.0475 | NA | NA | **0.0391** |
| Trefethen_500 | 0.0498 | 0.0437 | 0.0404 | 0.0362 | **0.0334** |
| m_t1 | 5.8790 | 5.2174 | 4.5281 | 4.1161 | **3.9320** |
| tx2010 | 24.3018 | 16.2510 | 15.077 | 16.0324 | **13.7185** |

or column reordering algorithm to figure out the optimal ordering. Thus, all the methods end up having the same number of non-zeros. Some of these fill-reducing ordering methods are not applicable for non-symmetric matrices, hence applied on symmetric part $A + A^T$ of a matrix $A$; whereas, our proposed method is not restricted by structural assumptions on the matrix.

**Time Comparison:** Table 4 presents the total time taken for finding the permutation matrix and subsequently performing LU decomposition. The time required for LU decomposition decreases when the algorithm processes fewer non-zeros. As shown in Table 3, the time consumed for performing LU decomposition after reordering is proportional to the number of non-zeros generated during the decomposition process. For smaller matrices, the time saved during LU decomposition is overshadowed by the time required for ordering. However, with larger matrices, our method not only achieves a reduction in the number of non-zeros but also results in a noticeable decrease in LU decomposition time.

**Hyperparameter Tuning and Ablation Study:** The training is stopped when the average reward no longer improves or the average loss does not decrease. As a standard, either of these conditions were generally met for

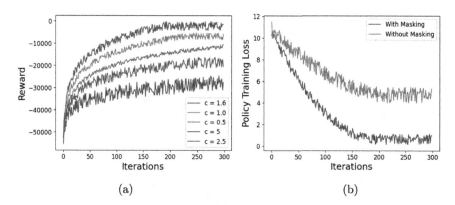

**Fig. 5.** (a) Reward plot versus iterations for different exploration factors $c$. (b) Training loss vs Iterations for masked and non-masked input.

$N = 500$ size matrices by iteration 300. The time taken for training matrices of size 10, 50, 100, 250, 500 and 1000 is 0.09, 1.2, 6.3, 13.1, 27.7 and 122.5 hours respectively for 100 iterations. The number of iterations also increases with increase in $N$. The most difficult hyperparameter to train is the exploration factor $c$. The correct value of $c$ determines how quickly the MCTS finds better solutions and how much it exploits those solutions to find better ones. This value is found experimentally. This is best demonstrated using Fig. 5a. The advantage of masking the matrix before providing it as input is demonstrated in Fig. 5b. The graph shows that masking helps the neural network learn better.

## 6   Conclusion and Future Work

In this paper, we demonstrated that the problem of identifying row permutations to minimize fill-in during LU decomposition of sparse matrices can be effectively formulated as a single-player game. Monte Carlo Tree Search combined with a deep neural network proves to be the optimal approach for addressing this problem. The neural network employed for the sparse matrix serves as a critical component of the algorithm. Further research focusing on the development of scalable architectures capable of handling large sparse matrix inputs may enhance the quality of the policy output. A combination of the heuristic methods along with MCTS for bootstrapping with additional training data can be explored in the future to get further improvements. For the stability of LU, the largest pivot is generally brought to the diagonal. Our method does not always follow this and how to improve numerical stability is left as a future research direction. Moreover, reinforcement learning methods can be potentially employed to either replace or improve upon existing heuristic algorithms, opening up new avenues for future investigation.

**Acknowledgment.** This work was done at IIIT-HYDERABAD, India. We thank the institute for HPC resources. We also thank Qualcomm faculty award.

**Ethical Considerations.** This work concerns algorithm development for sparse matrix factorization. To the best of our knowledge, we declare that there are no immediate or far reaching ethical considerations.

# References

1. Amestoy, P.R., Davis, T.A., Duff, I.S.: An approximate minimum degree ordering algorithm. SIAM J. Matrix Anal. Appl. **17**(4), 886–905 (1996)
2. Benzi, M.: Preconditioning techniques for large linear systems: a survey. J. Comput. Phys. **182**(2), 418–477 (2002)
3. Çatalyürek, Ü.V., Aykanat, C., Kayaaslan, E.: Hypergraph partitioning-based fill-reducing ordering for symmetric matrices. SIAM J. Sci. Comput. **33**(4), 1996–2023 (2011)
4. Contributors, S.: SpConv: spatially sparse convolution library. https://github.com/traveller59/spconv (2022)
5. Das, S., Katyan, S., Kumar, P.: Domain decomposition based preconditioned solver for bundle adjustment. In: Babu, R.V., Prasanna, M., Namboodiri, V.P. (eds.) Computer Vision, Pattern Recognition, Image Processing, and Graphics, pp. 64–75. Springer, Singapore (2020). https://doi.org/10.1007/978-981-15-8697-2_6
6. Das, S., Katyan, S., Kumar, P.: A deflation based fast and robust preconditioner for bundle adjustment. In: Proceedings of the IEEE/CVF Winter Conference on Applications of Computer Vision (WACV), pp. 1782–1789 (2021)
7. Davis, T.A., Gilbert, J.R., Larimore, S.I., Ng, E.G.: Algorithm 836: COLAMD, a column approximate minimum degree ordering algorithm. ACM Trans. Math. Softw. (TOMS) **30**(3), 377–380 (2004)
8. Fawzi, A., et al.: Discovering faster matrix multiplication algorithms with reinforcement learning. Nature **610**(7930), 47–53 (2022)
9. Golub, G.H., Van Loan, C.F.: Matrix Computations. JHU Press (2013)
10. Jumper, J., et al.: Highly accurate protein structure prediction with AlphaFold. Nature **596**(7873), 583–589 (2021)
11. Karypis, G., Kumar, V.: METIS: a software package for partitioning unstructured graphs, partitioning meshes, and computing fill-reducing orderings of sparse matrices. Technical report (1997)
12. Katyan, S., Das, S., Kumar, P.: Two-grid preconditioned solver for bundle adjustment. In: 2020 IEEE Winter Conference on Applications of Computer Vision (WACV), pp. 3588–3595 (2020)
13. Kaya, O., Kayaaslan, E., Uçar, B., Duff, I.S.: Fill-in reduction in sparse matrix factorizations using hypergraphs. Ph.D. thesis, INRIA (2014)
14. Kolodziej, S.P., et al.: The SuiteSparse matrix collection website interface. J. Open Source Softw. **4**(35), 1244 (2019)
15. Kumar, P.: Communication optimal least squares solver. In: 2014 IEEE International Conference on High Performance Computing and Communications, 2014 IEEE 6th International Symposium on Cyberspace Safety and Security, 2014 IEEE 11th International Conference on Embedded Software and Systems (HPCC, CSS, ICESS), pp. 316–319 (2014)

16. Kumar, P.: Aggregation based on graph matching and inexact coarse grid solve for algebraic two grid. Int. J. Comput. Math. **91**(5), 1061–1081 (2014)
17. Kumar, P.: Multithreaded direction preserving preconditioners. In: 2014 IEEE 13th International Symposium on Parallel and Distributed Computing, pp. 148–155 (2014)
18. Kumar, P.: Multilevel communication optimal least squares. In: Procedia Computer Science, International Conference On Computational Science, ICCS 2015, vol. 51, pp. 1838–1847 (2015)
19. Kumar, P.: Fast preconditioned solver for truncated saddle point problem in nonsmooth Cahn–Hilliard model. In: Fidanova, S. (ed.) Recent Advances in Computational Optimization. SCI, vol. 655, pp. 159–177. Springer, Cham (2016). https://doi.org/10.1007/978-3-319-40132-4_10
20. Kumar, P., Grigori, L., Nataf, F., Niu, Q.: On relaxed nested factorization and combination preconditioning. Int. J. Comput. Math. **93**(1), 179–199 (2016)
21. Kumar, P., Markidis, S., Lapenta, G., Meerbergen, K., Roose, D.: High performance solvers for implicit particle in cell simulation. In: Procedia Computer Science, 2013 International Conference on Computational Science, ICCS, vol. 18, pp. 2251–2258 (2013)
22. Kumar, P., Meerbergen, K., Roose, D.: Multi-threaded nested filtering factorization preconditioner. In: Manninen, P., Öster, P. (eds.) Applied Parallel and Scientific Computing, pp. 220–234. Springer, Berlin Heidelberg (2013). https://doi.org/10.1007/978-3-642-36803-5_16
23. Levine, S., Finn, C., Darrell, T., Abbeel, P.: End-to-end training of deep visuomotor policies. J. Mach. Learn. Res. **17**(1), 1334–1373 (2016)
24. Levine, S., Pastor, P., Krizhevsky, A., Ibarz, J., Quillen, D.: Learning hand-eye coordination for robotic grasping with deep learning and large-scale data collection. Int. J. Robot. Res. **37**(4–5), 421–436 (2018)
25. Li, K., Malik, J.: Learning to optimize. arXiv preprint arXiv:1606.01885 (2016)
26. Liu, W.H., Sherman, A.H.: Comparative analysis of the Cuthill-Mckee and the reverse Cuthill-Mckee ordering algorithms for sparse matrices. SIAM J. Numer. Anal. **13**(2), 198–213 (1976)
27. Mehta, K., Mahajan, A., Kumar, P.: Effects of spectral normalization in multi-agent reinforcement learning. In: IEEE International Joint Conference on Neural Networks, IJCNN, pp. 148–155 (2023)
28. Mehta, K., Mahajan, A., Kumar, P.: Marl-jax: Multi-agent reinforcement leaning framework for social generalization. In: ECML PKDD, pp. 148–155 (2023)
29. Mnih, V., et al.: Human-level control through deep reinforcement learning. Nature **518**(7540), 529–533 (2015)
30. Munos, R., et al.: From bandits to Monte-Carlo tree search: the optimistic principle applied to optimization and planning. Found. Trends® Mach. Learn. **7**(1), 1–129 (2014)
31. Niu, Q., Grigori, L., Kumar, P., Nataf, F.: Modified tangential frequency filtering decomposition and its fourier analysis. Numer. Math. **116**(1), 123–148 (2010)
32. Silver, D., et al.: Mastering the game of go with deep neural networks and tree search. Nature **529**(7587), 484–489 (2016)
33. Silver, D., et al.: Mastering chess and shogi by self-play with a general reinforcement learning algorithm. arXiv preprint arXiv:1712.01815 (2017)
34. Sinha, A., Azad, U., Singh, H.: Qubit routing using graph neural network aided Monte Carlo tree search. In: Proceedings of the AAAI Conference on Artificial Intelligence, vol. 36, pp. 9935–9943 (2022)

35. Tesauro, G., Das, R., Chan, H., Kephart, J., Levine, D., Rawson, F., Lefurgy, C.: Managing power consumption and performance of computing systems using reinforcement learning. In: Advances in Neural Information Processing Systems, vol. 20 (2007)
36. Zoph, B., Le, Q.V.: Neural architecture search with reinforcement learning. arXiv preprint arXiv:1611.01578 (2016)

# Learning Hierarchical Planning-Based Policies from Offline Data

Jan Wöhlke[1,2]($\boxtimes$)(ID), Felix Schmitt[3](ID), and Herke van Hoof[4](ID)

[1] Bosch Center for Artificial Intelligence, 71272 Renningen, Germany
JanGuenter.Woehlke@de.bosch.com
[2] UvA-Bosch DELTA Lab, University of Amsterdam, Amsterdam, The Netherlands
[3] Robert Bosch GmbH, 70469 Stuttgart, Germany
Felix.Schmitt@de.bosch.com
[4] AmLab, University of Amsterdam, Amsterdam, The Netherlands
h.c.vanhoof@uva.nl

**Abstract.** Hierarchical policy architectures incorporating some planning component into the top-level have shown superior performance and generalization in agent navigation tasks. Cost or safety reasons may, however, prevent training in an online (RL) fashion with continuous environment interaction. We therefore propose HORIBLe-VRN, an algorithm to learn a hierarchical policy with a top-level planning-based module from pre-collected data. A key challenge is to deal with the unknown, latent high-level (HL) actions. Our algorithm features an EM-style hierarchical imitation learning stage, incorporating HL action inference, and a subsequent offline RL refinement stage for the top-level policy. We empirically evaluate HORIBLe-VRN in a long horizon, sparse reward agent navigation task, investigating performance, generalization capabilities, and robustness with respect to sub-optimal demonstration data.

**Keywords:** Learning from Demonstrations · Imitation Learning · Reinforcement Learning · Hierarchical RL

## 1 Introduction

Reinforcement learning (RL) is a popular paradigm to learn control policies from interaction with the environment or a good simulation thereof. So far, much RL research went towards this online learning setting, which led to remarkable success in mastering video games from visual inputs [27] or solving sparse reward robotic manipulation tasks [1]. However, especially in industrial settings, continuous online training may not be possible for availability (of test benches) or safety reasons. Furthermore, sufficiently accurate simulations may not be readily available or too expensive to create for very specific use cases.

A solution to this dilemma might be to collect a limited dataset of demonstrations and use it for offline policy learning. For this objective, the literature presents a variety of solutions ranging from basic behavioral cloning (BC) [3] imitation learning (IL) to offline RL algorithms [13,14,23]. Despite their differences, these methods are commonly designed to learn a "flat" policy from data.

© The Author(s), under exclusive license to Springer Nature Switzerland AG 2023
D. Koutra et al. (Eds.): ECML PKDD 2023, LNAI 14172, pp. 489–505, 2023.
https://doi.org/10.1007/978-3-031-43421-1_29

For long horizon robot/vehicle navigation problems, Wöhlke et al. [38] showed that a hierarchical policy architecture with a top-level Value Refinement Network (VRN) policy that learns to refine a coarse prior plan shows superior performance. The planning component especially allows for better generalization towards new layouts, unseen during training. Fox et al. present in [10] a hierarchical imitation learning scheme, based on the options framework [32].

In this work, we combine the advantages of offline learning from data, not requiring environment interaction during training, with aforementioned effective hierarchical planning-based policy containing a VRN. Hence, we newly present the Hierarchical Offline Reinforcement and Imitation Batch Learning of VRN policies (HORIBLe-VRN) algorithm. It addresses the key challenge of latent high-level (HL) actions, which are the interface between policy levels but not part of the data (potentially collected with a flat policy), by performing hierarchical IL including HL action inference tailored to our architecture with a VRN. Furthermore, we add a novel offline RL refinement stage for the top-level VRN. In our empirical evaluation we investigate the following research hypotheses:

– *H.1*: Using a *planning-based* policy containing a VRN improves generalization (to unseen layouts) in the offline learning setting (as well).
– *H.2*: Learning a *hierarchical* policy architecture with temporal abstraction from offline data can further improve performance.
– *H.3*: Adding our offline RL *refinement stage* for the HL policy improves performance/robustness when the data is collected by sub-optimal policies.

## 2   Related Work

Our work combines aspects of imitation learning (IL), hierarchical (HRL), and offline RL. All of these are broad research fields in themselves. Hence, we refer the interested reader to recent surveys on IL [40], HRL [19], and offline RL [29].

We are particularly interested in hierarchical policy architectures that combine planning with RL. For robotic (navigation) tasks, these are commonly designed in a manager-worker "Feudal"-style [7,36], where a top-level planning policy sets sub-goals for some low-level, sub-goal-conditioned control policy: For the top-level planning, a sampling-based PRM planner [12], a differentiable ((M)VProp [28]) planning module [5], or value iteration (VI) with a learned transition model [37] have been used. In [38] VI is performed in a simpler state space abstraction, yielding a prior plan that is locally refined by a Value Refinement Network (VRN) using recent state information. The PAHRL approach [16] performs sub-goal planning on a graph of replay buffer states (like SoRB [9]). For the distance estimation, an (HAC-style [25]) Q-function hierarchy is trained via distributional RL, which is then also used for navigating the sub-goals.

Another related body of work focuses on learning hierarchical policy architectures from demonstrations. In [24] the algorithmic framework of "hierarchical guidance" is proposed, which allows utilizing different qualities of expert feedback to learn hierarchies of different combinations of IL and RL. Notably, hierarchical behavioral cloning (h-BC) is proposed. In contrast to our setting, where a static, pre-collected dataset is assumed, expert/environment interaction is possible during the policy learning. For h-BC, hierarchical demonstrations are assumed, which are generally not available. The HPIL approach [26] requires environment interaction as well. It performs an object-centric segmentation of demonstrations to then learn sub-policies for the segmented sub-tasks, in parallel, while simultaneously learning the meta-policy, leveraging the demonstrations for modified DDPG from Demonstrations [35]. For imitation learning parametrized hierarchical procedures (PHP), program-like structures that can invoke sub-procedures, variational inference methods are used in [11] to approximate a posterior distribution over the latent sequence of calls and terminations.

A line of research particularly relevant for our work investigates the hierarchical IL setting within the options framework [2,32], assuming the options to be latent variables. Modeling the data generation by an HMM, these approaches employ some EM-style [8] option inference. An early work [6], focusing on linear feature policies, employs a variant of the Baum-Welch (BW) algorithm [4] for the E-step to then perform a complete optimization in the M-step. Convergence guarantees for such an approach are investigated in [39]. An online BW algorithm, to process incoming data on the fly, is proposed in [15]. To allow for deep neural network policies, the DDO method in [10] uses an expectation gradient algorithm, similar to the ECG method in [30], to perform a gradient step on the policy parameters in the M-step. DDCO [22] extends DDO to continuous control settings and relaxes the pre-specification on the number of options. Option-GAIL [20] employs for the M-step option occupancy measurement matching, making use of adversarial learning to estimate the discrepancy between (inferred) expert and agent. A related online HRL approach is IOPG [31]: A policy gradient algorithm for the options framework assuming the options as latent variables and therefore containing a differentiable option inference procedure.

Offline learning of hierarchical planning-based policies has not been investigated, yet.

## 3    Technical Background and Problem Statement

### 3.1    Offline Learning Setting

Sequential decision-making problems can be modeled as Markov Decision Processes (MDPs). In this work, we look at goal-based MDPs, which we can denote as the tuple $\mathcal{M} = (\mathcal{S}, \mathcal{A}, \mathcal{P}, r, \mathcal{S}_0, \mathcal{S}_g, \gamma, T)$, where $\mathcal{S}$ is the state space, $\mathcal{A}$ is the action space, and $\mathcal{P}(s'|s,a)$ are the dynamics of transitioning from a state $s$ to a next state $s'$ as a result of taking action $a$. Start states $s_0$ and goal states $g$ are sampled from start and goal distributions $\mathcal{S}_0 \subseteq \mathcal{S}$ and $\mathcal{S}_g \subseteq \mathcal{S}$. The goal-dependent reward function $r(s,g)$ provides feedback and $\gamma$ is the discount factor. The time horizon $T$ determines the maximum number of steps to reach the goal.

In order to solve an MDP, we need to find a policy $\pi(a|s,g)$ that selects suitable actions $a$ given the current state $s$ and the goal state of the MDP $g$. Since we are in an offline learning setting, we cannot interact with the environment, hence have no access to $\mathcal{P}$ during training time. Instead, we need to learn $\pi$

from a dataset of collected demonstrations $\mathcal{D}$. We assume $\mathcal{D}$ to be a sequence of transition tuples from different demonstration episodes $e$. The tuples consist of state, action, next state, reward, termination flag, and goal state. With $|\mathcal{D}|$ being the size of the dataset (number of transition tuples), we can denote $\mathcal{D}$ as

$$\mathcal{D} = \left( (s_0, a_0, s_1, r_0, d_0, g_0) \ldots (s_{|\mathcal{D}|-1}, a_{|\mathcal{D}|-1}, s_{|\mathcal{D}|}, r_{|\mathcal{D}|-1}, d_{|\mathcal{D}|-1}, g_{|\mathcal{D}|-1}) \right)$$
$$= ((s_t, a_t, s_{t+1}, r_t, d_t, g_t))_{t=0}^{|\mathcal{D}|-1}. \quad (1)$$

### 3.2 Hierarchical Policy Architecture

We make use of a hierarchical policy architecture which is similar to the one presented in [37]. Figure 1 depicts the two-level hierarchy. It consists of a goal-conditioned high-level (HL) policy $\omega(o|z,g)$ that operates in a (discrete) state space abstraction with finite HL state space $\mathcal{Z}$ and finite HL action space $\mathcal{O}$. Transformations $f_{\mathcal{Z}}(s)$ and $f_{\mathcal{S}}(z)$, that are assumed known, transform low-level (LL) states $s$ into HL states $z$ and vice versa.

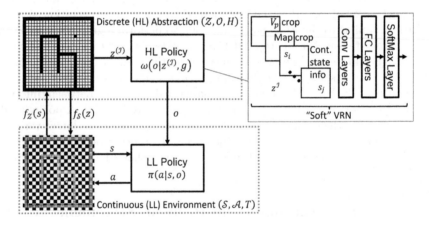

**Fig. 1.** Hierarchical policy architecture with "Soft" VRN.

The sub-goal conditioned low-level policy $\pi(a|s,o)$ directly interacts with the original MDP with state and action spaces $\mathcal{S}$ and $\mathcal{A}$. Please note that the LL policy receives a local sub-goal (tile) $z_{sg}$ derived from the current HL state $z$ and the chosen HL action $o$ (reflecting a relative direction in navigation so that $z_{sg}$ is the neighboring HL state $z$ in that direction). So, we have $\pi(a|s,z_{sg})$. Since $z_{sg}$ is a function of $s$ and $o$, we denote the LL policy, for simplicity, as $\pi(a|s,o)$.

Furthermore, the HL policy operates on a different timescale than the LL policy. A new HL action $o$ is selected when the HL state $z$ changes or the sub-goal horizon $H$ runs out. As a result, the LL policy experiences sub-episodes of maximum length $H$ until the horizon $T$ runs out or the MDP goal $g$ is achieved. We denote the parameters of the HL and LL policies as $\phi$ and $\theta$, respectively.

## 3.3   Value Refinement Network

For improved generalization across different environments, we employ a specific Value Refinement Network (VRN) [38] for the HL policy $\omega$. In short, the VRN is a specific convolutional neural network (CNN) architecture that locally refines a coarse prior plan $\widetilde{V}_p^{\mathcal{Z}}$. See top right of Fig. 1 for a depiction. The prior plan is obtained through value iteration (VI) in the HL abstraction, assuming HL transitions to be always successful, which results in a shortest path plan.

The VRN locally refines these prior values. Therefore, it receives a specific input representation $z^{\mathcal{I}} = f_{\mathcal{I}}(s, (z = f_{\mathcal{Z}}(s)), g, \Phi)$ based on the current LL (and HL) state, the goal, and the environment layout $\Phi$ so that we have $\omega^{\text{VRN}}(o|z^{\mathcal{I}})$. In the depicted robot navigation example, this input representation is composed as follows: The first input channel contains a local $(k \times k)$ crop of the value prior $\widehat{V}_p^z$, centered on the current HL state $z$. A local map crop $\widehat{\Phi}^z$ forms the second channel. Additional channels contain the continuous state information for refinement, broadcasting the numerical value of a state component (for example a velocity or orientation) across all entries of the corresponding channel. During data collection, the layouts $\Phi_e$ per episode are stored with the dataset $\mathcal{D}$.

In contrast to the original work, we employ a SoftMax output layer instead of an argmax to the refined values. This way, the "Soft-VRN" outputs probabilities for all HL actions $o$, which allows computing likelihoods of HL state-action pairs.

## 3.4   Problem Statement

In this work, we investigate the problem of learning a policy in an offline setting, using a dataset $\mathcal{D}$, such that it performs well on a distribution $\mathbb{M}$ of goal-based MDPs. Each MDP $m$ has the same $\mathcal{S}$ and $\mathcal{A}$ but may have different dynamics $\mathcal{P}_m$ (e.g. due to varying environment layout) as well as start and goal state distributions $\mathcal{S}_{0,m}$ and $\mathcal{S}_{g,m}$. The data $\mathcal{D}$ may only be collected on some of the MDPs and limited start-goal combinations. In summary, the objective is to learn a (hierarchical) policy that maximizes returns across all MDPs as well as starts and goals:

$$\max_{\omega, \pi} \mathbb{E}_{m \sim \mathbb{M}, s_0 \sim \mathcal{S}_{0,m}, g \sim \mathcal{S}_{g,m}, \mathcal{P}_m} \left[ \sum_{t=0}^{T-1} \gamma^t r(s_{t+1}, g) \right]. \tag{2}$$

The key challenge lies in inferring the latent HL actions $o$ of the HL policy $\omega$. Since they are the interface between the HL and LL policies, they need to be aligned between both for good performance.

# 4   HORIBLe-VRN Offline Learning Algorithm

This section presents our two-stage hierarchical offline learning scheme. We first take a look at the graphical model of our hierarchical policy in Sect. 4.1. Then Sect. 4.2 describes the pre-processing of the collected data. Sect. 4.3 presents the hierarchical IL stage of our algorithm, which is followed up by an offline RL refinement stage for the HL policy as described in Sect. 4.4. An overview over our algorithm HORIBLe-VRN is presented in Algorithm 2, at the end of the paper.

## 4.1   Graphical Model

We first need to understand how our hierarchical policy would have generated the data $\mathcal{D}$. Figure 2 depicts an exemplary state-action sequence, where LL states $s_t$ and LL actions $a_t$ are observed in the data. Please note the temporal abstraction, where the $h_i$ are the time stamps when new HL actions $o_{h_i}$ are selected based on the VRN inputs $z_{h_i}^{\mathcal{I}}$ at that time. As the VRN inputs deterministically depend on observed quantities like the state $s_{h_i}$, goal state $g_e$, and layout $\Phi_e$, they are also marked observed. In the example, $h_0 = 0$ and $h_1 = 2$. This means that the first (latent) HL action $o_{h_0}$, selected based on $z_{h_0}^{\mathcal{I}}$, results in two LL transitions.

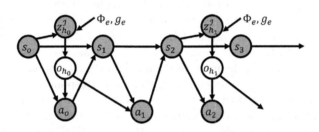

**Fig. 2.** Graphical model of the data generation process with our hierarchical policy architecture. Gray variables are observed from the data $\mathcal{D}$ or can be readily inferred from them, whereas white circles represent latent variables. (Color figure online)

Based on the graphical model, we can derive the probability of a latent HL action $o_{h_i}$ in the sequence taking a specific value $o$ given the data $\mathcal{D}$ as follows:

$$p\left(o_{h_i} = o|\mathcal{D}\right) = p\left(o_{h_i} = o|\mathcal{D}_{h_i}\right) =$$
$$\frac{p\left(o_{h_i} = o|z_{h_i}^{\mathcal{I}}\right) \prod_{t \in [h_i, h_{i+1}-1]} p\left(a_t|s_t, o\right)}{\sum_{o' \in \mathcal{O}} \left(p\left(o_{h_i} = o'|z_{h_i}^{\mathcal{I}}\right) \prod_{t \in [h_i, h_{i+1}-1]} p\left(a_t|s_t, o'\right)\right)}. \quad (3)$$

We notice from Fig. 2 that HL action $o_{h_i}$ only affects the LL transitions from $h_i$ to $h_{i+1}$, until the next HL action is selected in time step $h_{i+1}$. The probabilities can be replaced by the (hypothetically) data generating policies $\omega^{\mathcal{D}}$ and $\pi^{\mathcal{D}}$ with parameters $\phi^{\mathcal{D}}$ and $\theta^{\mathcal{D}}$, respectively. For improved numerical stability of our implementation, we furthermore apply an $\exp\left(\log\left(...\right)\right)$ transform, which results in

$$p\left(o_{h_i} = o|\mathcal{D}_{h_i}, \phi^{\mathcal{D}}, \theta^{\mathcal{D}}\right) =$$
$$\exp\left(\log \omega_{\phi^{\mathcal{D}}}^{\mathcal{D}} + \sum_{t \in [...]} \log \pi_{\theta^{\mathcal{D}}}^{\mathcal{D}} - \log\left(\sum_{o' \in \mathcal{O}} \exp\left(\log \omega_{\phi^{\mathcal{D}}}^{\mathcal{D}} + \sum_{t \in [...]} \log \pi_{\theta^{\mathcal{D}}}^{\mathcal{D}}\right)\right)\right),$$
$$(4)$$

dropping some notation for improved readability.

## 4.2 Dataset Pre-Processing

In a first pre-processing step, we need to determine the time stamps $h_i$, forming the set $\mathcal{H}$, at which new HL actions are selected. For that, we make use of our assumptions on the HL action selection process (Sect. 3.2): New $o$ are selected when the HL state $z$ changes, the sub-episode horizon $H$ runs out, or the episode terminates (episode termination flag $d = 1$). See Algorithm 1.

---

**Algorithm 1:** Computation of HL time stamps

---

1  $t \leftarrow 0, k \leftarrow 0, h_0 \leftarrow 0, \mathcal{H} \leftarrow \{h_0\}, i \leftarrow 1$
2  **while** $t < |\mathcal{D}|$ **do**
3    **if** $f_{\mathcal{Z}}\left(s_{h_{i-1}+k}\right) \neq f_{\mathcal{Z}}\left(s_{h_{i-1}}\right)$ **then** $h_i \leftarrow h_{i-1} + k$    // HL state change
4    **else if** $d_{h_{i-1}+k}$ **then** $h_i \leftarrow h_{i-1} + k + 1$      // episode end
5    **else if** $k = H - 1$ **then** $h_i \leftarrow h_{i-1} + H$      // sub-episode end
6    **if** $h_i$ *was assigned above* **then** $\mathcal{H} \leftarrow \mathcal{H} \cup \{h_i\}, i \leftarrow i+1, k \leftarrow 0,$ and $t \leftarrow t+1$
7    **else** $k \leftarrow k+1$ and $t \leftarrow t+1$
8  **end**
9  **return** $\mathcal{H}$

---

In the next step, the VRN inputs $z^{\mathcal{I}}_{h_i}$ at the time stamps $h_i$ are determined. For that, first, for every episode $e$ in the data the prior (shortest path) plan $\widetilde{V}^{\mathcal{Z}}_{p,e}$ is determined via value iteration (VI) using layout $\Phi_e$ and goal state $g_e$ from the data, as detailed in [38]. Finally, the accumulated HL rewards within a sub-episode and corresponding accumulated discount factors are calculated as

$$r^{\mathcal{Z}}_{h_i} = f_{r_{\mathcal{Z}}}\left(h_i, \mathcal{D}\right) = \sum_{t \in [h_i : h_{i+1}-1]} \gamma^{t-h_i} r_t \quad \text{and} \quad \gamma^{\mathcal{Z}}_{h_i} = \gamma^{h_{i+1} - h_i}. \tag{5}$$

As a result, the dataset $\mathcal{D}$ will have the following form after the pre-processing

$$\mathcal{D} = (\mathcal{D}_{h_i})_{h_i \in \mathcal{H}} = \left( \left( z^{\mathcal{I}}_{h_i}, r^{\mathcal{Z}}_{h_i}, \gamma^{\mathcal{Z}}_{h_i}, d_{h_i}, z^{\mathcal{I}}_{h_i+1}, ((s_t, a_t, s_{t+1}))^{h_{i+1}-1}_{t=h_i} \right) \right)_{h_i \in \mathcal{H}} \tag{6}$$

containing tuples $\mathcal{D}_{h_i}$ of HL VRN input transitions and corresponding subsequences of LL state-action transitions.

## 4.3 Stage 1: Hierarchical IL via EM Procedure

As a first step, we want to imitate the data $\mathcal{D}$ by finding parameters $\Theta^{\mathcal{D}} = \{\phi^{\mathcal{D}}, \theta^{\mathcal{D}}\}$ that maximize the likelihood. Since the HL action sequence $o = \{o_{h_0}, o_{h_1}, \dots\}$ is unknown, we employ an iterative Expectation-Maximization (EM) [8] scheme.

**Expectation (E-Step).** Following the EM scheme, we establish a lower bound

$$\mathcal{Q}\left(\Theta^{\mathcal{D}}|\Theta^{\text{old}}\right) = \mathbb{E}_{o|\mathcal{D},\Theta^{\text{old}}} \log p\left(\mathcal{D}, o|\Theta^{\mathcal{D}}\right)$$

$$= \mathbb{E}_{o|\mathcal{D},\Theta^{\text{old}}} \sum_{i\in[0,|\mathcal{H}|-1]} \left( \log \omega_{\phi^{\mathcal{D}}}^{\mathcal{D}}\left(o_{h_i}|z_{h_i}^{\mathcal{I}}\right) + \sum_{t\in[h_i,h_{i+1}-1]} \log \pi_{\theta^{\mathcal{D}}}^{\mathcal{D}}\left(a_t|s_t,o\right) \right)$$

$$= \sum_{i\in[0,|\mathcal{H}|-1]} \sum_{o\in\mathcal{O}} p\left(o_{h_i} = o|\mathcal{D}_{h_i},\Theta^{\text{old}}\right) \log \omega_{\phi^{\mathcal{D}}}^{\mathcal{D}}\left(o|z_{h_i}^{\mathcal{I}}\right) +$$

$$\sum_{i\in[0,|\mathcal{H}|-1]} \sum_{o\in\mathcal{O}} p\left(o_{h_i} = o|\mathcal{D}_{h_i},\Theta^{\text{old}}\right) \sum_{t\in[h_i,h_{i+1}-1]} \pi_{\theta^{\mathcal{D}}}^{\mathcal{D}}\left(a_t|s_t,o\right) \quad (7)$$

where the $p\left(o_{h_i} = o|\mathcal{D},\Theta^{\text{old}}\right)$ are obtained using Eq. (4) with the "old" parameters $\Theta^{\text{old}}$.

**Maximization (M-Step).** In the maximization step, we obtain new model parameters $\Theta^{\text{new}}$. Since the terms for the HL and LL parameters are separated from each other in Eq. (7), we can optimize these parameters separately with

$$\phi^{\mathcal{D},\text{new}} = \arg\max_{\phi^{\mathcal{D}}} \mathbb{E}_{o|\mathcal{D},\Theta^{\text{old}}} \log p\left(\mathcal{D}, o|\phi^{\mathcal{D}}\right) \quad (8)$$

and

$$\theta^{\mathcal{D},\text{new}} = \arg\max_{\theta^{\mathcal{D}}} \mathbb{E}_{o|\mathcal{D},\Theta^{\text{old}}} \log p\left(\mathcal{D}, o|\theta^{\mathcal{D}}\right). \quad (9)$$

We approximate the M-step, similar to [30], as a single gradient step, utilizing the Adam [21] optimizer. See Algorithm 2 for the parameter update formulas.

### 4.4    Stage 2: Offline RL HL Policy Refinement

In case the data $\mathcal{D}$ was collected by some non-optimal policy, the algorithm in the previous stage learns to imitate sub-optimal behavior. Therefore, we propose an offline RL refinement stage for the HL VRN policy, based on Batch-Constrained deep Q-learning (BCQ) [13]. BCQ is an offline DQN algorithm that at the core learns a state-action value function Q. Simultaneously, a state-conditioned generative model $G : \mathcal{S} \to \mathcal{A}$ of the data is learned, which is used to exclude actions from the action selection, which are unlikely under the data generating policy.

Our modified BCQ algorithm operates in the $(\mathcal{Z}, \mathcal{O}, H)$ HL problem abstraction. The generative model is readily available from *stage 1* as $G := \omega_{\phi^{\mathcal{D}}}\left(o|z^{\mathcal{I}}\right)$ and, therefore, does not need to be learned separately, which is our first modification. As a result, the constrained action selection can be written as

$$o = \arg\max_{\tilde{o}\in\tilde{\mathcal{O}}(z^{\mathcal{I}})} Q_{\phi_{\text{(target)}}}\left(z^{\mathcal{I}}, \tilde{o}\right) \quad (10)$$

with

$$\tilde{\mathcal{O}}\left(z^{\mathcal{I}}\right) = \left\{ o \in \mathcal{O} \middle| \frac{\omega_{\phi^{\mathcal{D}}}\left(o|z^{\mathcal{I}}\right)}{\max_{\hat{o}} \omega_{\phi^{\mathcal{D}}}\left(\hat{o}|z^{\mathcal{I}}\right)} > \tau_{\text{BCQ}} \right\}. \quad (11)$$

Our second modification affects the Q-function learning. While the VRN inputs $z^{\mathcal{I}}_{h_i}$ and $z^{\mathcal{I}}_{h_{i+1}}$ are part of the HL transition tuples $\mathcal{D}_{h_i}$ in our pre-processed dataset, the corresponding (latent) HL actions $o_{h_i}$ are, again, unknown. Therefore, we re-write the Q-learning update replacing the latent $o_{h_i}$ by their expectation with respect to the data generating policy parameters $\Theta^{\mathcal{D}}$, making use of our ability to compute $p\left(o_{h_i} = o | \mathcal{D}_{h_i}\right)$ according to Eq. (4), resulting in

$$\arg\min_{\phi} \mathbb{E}_{z^{\mathcal{I}}_{h_i}, o_{h_i}, r^{\mathcal{Z}}_{h_i}, \gamma^{\mathcal{Z}}_{h_i}, d_{h_i}, z^{\mathcal{I}}_{h_{i+1}} | \mathcal{D}} \left[ \mathcal{L}_{\mathrm{TD}}\left(h_i, o = o_{h_i} | \phi, \phi_{\mathrm{target}}\right)\right] =$$

$$\arg\min_{\phi} \mathbb{E}_{z^{\mathcal{I}}_{h_i}, r^{\mathcal{Z}}_{h_i}, \gamma^{\mathcal{Z}}_{h_i}, d_{h_i}, z^{\mathcal{I}}_{h_{i+1}} | \mathcal{D}} \left[ \sum_{o \in \mathcal{O}} p\left(o_{h_i} = o | \mathcal{D}_{h_i}, \Theta^{\mathcal{D}}\right) \mathcal{L}_{\mathrm{TD}}\left(h_i, o | \phi, \phi_{\mathrm{target}}\right) \right]$$
(12)

with the temporal-difference (TD) loss for the Q-function (network) denoting as

$$\mathcal{L}_{\mathrm{TD}}\left(h_i, o | \phi, \phi_{\mathrm{target}}\right) =$$
$$l_\kappa \left( r^{\mathcal{Z}}_{h_i} + (1 - d_{h_i}) \gamma^{\mathcal{Z}}_{h_i} Q_{\phi_{\mathrm{target}}} \left(z^{\mathcal{I}}_{h_{i+1}}, o'\right) - Q_\phi \left(z^{\mathcal{I}}_{h_i}, o\right)\right) \quad (13)$$

with

$$o' = \arg\max_{\tilde{o}' \in \tilde{\mathcal{O}}\left(z^{\mathcal{I}}_{h_{i+1}}\right)} Q_\phi \left(z^{\mathcal{I}}_{h_{i+1}}, \tilde{o}'\right) \quad (14)$$

and $l_\kappa$ being the Huber loss [18].

## 5   Empirical Evaluation

We will now empirically evaluate HORIBLe-VRN on a long-horizon agent navigation task, investigating the research hypotheses *H.1-3* from the introduction.

### 5.1   Environment

To investigate our research hypotheses, we need an environment with certain properties: Inherent task hierarchy, multiple layouts with different starts and goals requiring generalization, and agent dynamics that make simple HL shortest path planning insufficient. As a result, we implement, using MuJoCo [33], a point mass agent with an orientation influencing the motion that navigates different environment layouts. An example layout is shown in the bottom left of Fig. 1.

The continuous 6D state space $\mathcal{S}$ consists of the $x$ and $y$ position, orientation $\vartheta$, as well as the corresponding velocities $(\dot{x}, \dot{y}, \dot{\vartheta})$. The action space consists of a linear acceleration $a_v$ in orientation direction and the rotational acceleration $a_\vartheta = \ddot{\vartheta}$. The time horizon is $T = 500$ and the sparse reward signal results in $-1$ per step until the goal is reached (0). For the 2D (HL) abstraction $\mathcal{Z}$, the environment is tiled into $25 \times 25$ cells with $\bar{x}$ and $\bar{y}$ index. The HL VRN policy receives a $6 \times 7 \times 7$ input consisting of $7 \times 7$ (binary occupancy) layout and shortest path prior plan (value map) crops as well as $\vartheta, \dot{x}, \dot{y}, \dot{\vartheta}$ broadcasted across the remaining four channels, respectively (see Sect. 3.3 and [38]). The HL action space $\mathcal{O}$ contains four HL actions $o$ corresponding to the sub-task of moving to the neighboring HL state (tile) $z$ in direction 'North', 'East', 'South', or 'West', respectively. To address these sub-tasks, the low-level MLP policy receives as input the state $s$ alongside the tile representing the sub-goal, and an 8D binary occupancy vector for the neighboring tiles. The sub-goal horizon is $H = 10$.

Regarding the layouts as well as starts and goals, we distinguish 3 settings:

1. We have a first set of 12 layouts (also used for data collection) with 25 different pairs of start and goal tiles, each. The continuous start $s_0$ arises by uniformly sampling $x$ and $y$ from the start tile alongside an initial orientation $\in [-\pi, \pi]$.
2. To investigate generalization towards other starts and goals, we additionally allow start tiles being goal tiles and vice versa for the aforementioned setting.
3. To investigate generalization towards other layouts, we have a second set of 12 different layouts with 50 pairs of start and goal tiles, each.

## 5.2   Data Collection

For the purpose of data collection, we, first, train a hierarchical policy similar to the one described in Sect. 3.2 online, interacting with the environment (first layout setting): The HL VRN is trained (as in [38]) via double DQN [34] with HER [1] (featuring argmax action selection). The LL MLP policy is trained via SAC [17]. We use a hierarchical architecture for data collection because no flat policy was able to solve the multi layout navigation. Furthermore, this ensures that our HORIBLe-VRN conforms to the assumptions about the generative process. Using the obtained policy weights, we collect two different sets of data:

1. An "optimal" set of data, using the weights of the converged policy, which achieved 100 % success in reaching the goal tiles.
2. A "mediocre" dataset, using weights of an intermediate policy, which only achieved 70 % successful goal-reaching.

For each of these, we collect 20 rollouts for each start-goal tile combination (25) for each of the 12 layouts of the first layout setting (see previous section).

## 5.3   Baselines

**Flat Offline Learning Baselines.** We compare to two different flat behavioral cloning [3] baselines: The first (BC) uses the MLP architecture used as LL policy in our approach. The second (BC VRN) uses the VRN architecture used as HL policy in our approach, with two small modifications: 1) The number and size of the fully-connected layers is increased to match the LL MLP policy of our approach. 2) The SoftMax layer is replaced by a linear layer to output means and standard deviations for the 2D continuous actions. Besides that, we train the MLP architecture via TD3-BC [14] offline RL (ORL), as an additional baseline.

**Heuristic Hierarchical Imitation Learning (HHIM).** We compare the first stage of our approach (Sect. 4.3) to a hierarchical IL baseline, similar to h-BC [24]. We, however, first, need to infer the values of the latent HL actions $o_{h_i}$. For this, we use a simple heuristic that makes use of the (semantic) meaning the HL actions have in our navigation task: Requesting a HL state change in a certain direction (e.g. 'North') from the LL policy, which may or may not succeed at this sub-task. For this simple baseline, we assume that the HL state change from $z_{h_i}$ to $z_{h_{i+1}}$, seen in the data $\mathcal{D}$, is intentional, and choose $o_{h_i}$ accordingly. This may decently hold true for data collected with optimal policies. Using these approximate HL actions $\bar{o}_{h_i}$ allows to individually perform BC for both, the HL and the LL policy denoting as (with $f_{h_i}$ returning the HL time stamp corresponding to $t$)

$$\max_\phi \mathbb{E}_{z^{\mathcal{I}}_{h_i}, \bar{o}_{h_i} | \mathcal{D}} [\log \omega_\phi \left( \bar{o}_{h_i} | z^{\mathcal{I}}_{h_i} \right)] \tag{15}$$

and

$$\max_\theta \mathbb{E}_{s_t, a_t, \bar{o}_{f_{h_i}(t)} | \mathcal{D}} \left[ \log \pi_\theta \left( a_t | s_t, \bar{o}_{f_{h_i}(t)} \right) \right]. \tag{16}$$

**Heuristic HL BCQ Baseline (HBCQ).** We compare the second (HL refinement) stage of our approach (Sect. 4.4) to directly learning the HL policy via BCQ [13] offline RL, without using $\omega_{\phi^{\mathcal{D}}} \left( o | z^{\mathcal{I}} \right)$ as generative model. Again, we first need to infer the values of the latent HL actions $o_{h_i}$, using the same heuristic as for HHIM. With these approximate HL actions $\bar{o}_{h_i}$, Eq. 12 denotes as

$$\arg\min_\phi \mathbb{E}_{z^{\mathcal{I}}_{h_i}, \bar{o}_{h_i}, r^{\mathcal{Z}}_{h_i}, \gamma^{\mathcal{Z}}_{h_i}, d_{h_i}, z^{\mathcal{I}}_{h_{i+1}} | \mathcal{D}} [\mathcal{L}_{\text{TD}} (h_i, \bar{o}_{h_i} | \phi, \phi_{\text{target}})], \tag{17}$$

without the necessity of doing an expectation over all possible HL actions $o$. We use the same LL policy $\pi_{\theta^{\mathcal{D}}}$, from the previous step, as for our approach.

## 5.4    Results and Discussion

The results of evaluating the offline trained policies in the environment are presented in Table 1. We report results for both datasets ("optimal", "mediocre") and all three settings of layouts and starts/goals (as detailed in 5.1), each. The numerical values in the table reflect success rates of reaching the goal tile, reported as mean ± standard error across the best performing policies of 10 individual runs (seeds) of the respective algorithm. A success rate is determined by performing 10 rollouts each, with sampled start-goal pairs, for any of the 12 layouts. In the following, we will interpret these results in the light of our research hypotheses.

*H.1:* **Using a Planning-Based Policy Containing a VRN Improves Generalization in the Offline Learning Setting.** We, first, focus the discussion of the results on the (stage 1) imitation learning (IL) setting. Comparing the *flat* baselines BC, ORL, and BC VRN, it turns out that BC VRN incorporating

**Table 1.** Mean ± standard error across 10 seeds of success rates of best policies.

|  | Optimal Data | | | Mediocre Data | | |
|---|---|---|---|---|---|---|
|  | 1) collect | 2) add. $s_0/g$ | 3) other lay. | 1) collect | 2) add. $s_0/g$ | 3) other lay. |
| BC | 0.744 ± 0.006 | 0.614 ± 0.010 | 0.468 ± 0.006 | 0.457 ± 0.009 | 0.370 ± 0.005 | 0.270 ± 0.006 |
| BC VRN | 0.984 ± 0.003 | 0.880 ± 0.014 | 0.877 ± 0.012 | 0.633 ± 0.007 | 0.478 ± 0.012 | 0.422 ± 0.012 |
| ORL | 0.740 ± 0.009 | 0.602 ± 0.006 | 0.478 ± 0.011 | 0.443 ± 0.009 | 0.348 ± 0.011 | 0.203 ± 0.006 |
| HHIM | 0.744 ± 0.011 | 0.647 ± 0.014 | 0.638 ± 0.015 | 0.501 ± 0.007 | 0.419 ± 0.012 | 0.391 ± 0.009 |
| Stage 1 (Sect. 4.3) | 0.564 ± 0.019 | 0.428 ± 0.019 | 0.389 ± 0.017 | 0.520 ± 0.019 | 0.394 ± 0.015 | 0.344 ± 0.019 |
| Stage 1, w init | **1.000** ± **0.000** | 0.945 ± 0.004 | 0.959 ± 0.004 | 0.746 ± 0.003 | 0.665 ± 0.004 | 0.630 ± 0.008 |
| HORIBLe-VRN(Ours) | **1.000** ± **0.000** | **0.963** ± **0.002** | **0.983** ± **0.002** | **0.808** ± **0.003** | **0.744** ± **0.005** | **0.717** ± **0.010** |
| HBCQ | 0.439 ± 0.014 | 0.373 ± 0.007 | 0.370 ± 0.013 | 0.413 ± 0.008 | 0.323 ± 0.012 | 0.286 ± 0.009 |

planning clearly performs best while also generalizing better, dropping the least in success rate on the (unseen) other layouts 3). So, integrating planning in the form of a VRN into the policy improves performance and generalization.

*H.2:* **Learning a Hierarchical Policy with Temporal Abstraction from Offline Data Can Further Improve Performance.** With our stage 1 *hierarchical* IL scheme from Sect. 4.3 we add the aspects of hierarchy and temporal abstraction compared to the also planning-based BC VRN. Using the EM procedure from Sect. 4.3 for the necessary inference of unknown, latent HL actions, our stage 1 (with HHIM weight initialization) clearly outperforms the hierarchical HHIM baseline of similar architecture that only uses heuristic HL action inference[1]. Trained with optimal data, our stage 1 (w init) recovers the performance of the data collecting policy on the corresponding layouts 1). Incorporating the VRN planning, it furthermore generalizes well to different starts, goals, and layouts. Compared to the *flat* BC VRN, our stage 1 (w init) generalizes better to the settings 2) and 3), especially in case of the mediocre dataset, where it performs 0.266 to 0.295 better, despite the necessary HL action ($o$) inference.

---

[1] This is not due to additional optimization steps for initialization. The success rates of our approach and HHIM stop to significantly improve long before $N_{\text{iter}} = 10000$.

**Effect of Initialization.** For our stage 1 hierarchical IL from Sect. 4.3 to perform well, initializing the weights $\Theta$ is crucial. We do this by first running HHIM for $N_{\text{iter}} = 2500^2$. Afterwards, we initialize the first stage of our algorithm (Sect. 4.3) with these weights and run it for $N_{\text{iter}} = 10000$. Figure 3 shows the effect of the initialization on the (LL) policy behavior. We evaluate how it behaves for different HL actions $o$, in an empty environment, starting in the middle. With the initialization (Fig. 3a), the agent moves "North", "East", ... when the corresponding $o$ is selected. Without initialization (Fig. 3b), the stage 1 hierarchical IL from Sect. 4.3 can freely assign behaviors to the various $o$, which not only leads to different permutations ($o = 3$: "North" instead of "West"), but also to not any $o$ being clearly assigned to "West", in the example. The reasonable $o$ assignment in Fig. 3a might be explained by the weight initialization acting as a prior on the assignment. The HHIM algorithm used for initialization assigns an $o$ to its semantic meaning as a result of the heuristic rules used for the $o$-inference.

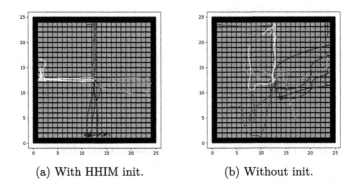

(a) With HHIM init.                    (b) Without init.

**Fig. 3.** LL policy behavior in empty maze for HL action $o \in \{0 : \text{"North"}, 1 : \text{"East"}, 2 : \text{"South"}, 3 : \text{"West"}\}$; colored blue, red, green, and orange, respectively. We did 4 rollouts with initial orientation $\vartheta \in \{0, \frac{\pi}{2}, \pi, -\frac{\pi}{2}\}$, for each $o$. (Color figure online)

### *H.3:* Adding our Offline RL Refinement Stage for the HL Policy Improves Performance/Robustness When the Data is Collected by Sub-Optimal Policies.

Our full HORIBLe-VRN algorithm adds our (stage 2) modified BCQ offline RL refinement (Sect. 4.4) for the HL VRN on top of the hierarchical IL (stage 1). The results in Table 1 show a further success rate improvement, especially for the mediocre dataset, where the imitation learned policy is not already close to optimal. The HBCQ baseline that learns the HL policy via offline RL from scratch, using heuristically inferred $o$-s, performs clearly worse.

---

[2] This is less than for a full training ($N_{\text{iter}} = 10000$ for BC (VRN), HHIM, stage 1).

---

**Algorithm 2:** Our HORIBLe-VRN Algorithm

---

   **Input**   : Dataset $\mathcal{D}$, initial parameters $\Theta^{\text{init}} = \{\phi^{\text{init}}, \theta^{\text{init}}\}$
   **Output**: Optimized policy parameters $\Theta^{\text{final}} = \{\phi^{\text{final}}, \theta^{\text{final}}\}$
   `/* Stage 0: Dataset pre-processing as outlined in Sect.4.2        */`
   `/* Stage 0.5: Optionally obtain initial parameters` $\Theta^{\text{init}}$ `using the`
     `HHIM algorithm described in Sect. 5.3        */`
   `/* Stage 1: Hierarchical Imitation Learning (Sect.4.3)        */`

1  $\Theta^{\text{old}} \leftarrow \Theta^{\text{init}}, \Theta^{\mathcal{D}} \leftarrow \Theta^{\text{init}}$

2  **for** $n = 1 : N_{iter}$ **do**

3    |  Sample batch $\mathcal{B}$ of time stamps $h_i$ ($\neq |\mathcal{H}|$), obtain tuples $\mathcal{D}_{h_i}$, and calculate, using Eq. (4), $p\left(o_{h_i} = o|\mathcal{D}_{h_i}, \Theta^{\text{old}}\right) \forall o \in \mathcal{O}$ and $\forall h_i \in \mathcal{B}$.

4    |  **if** $(n \mod k_{HL}) = 0$ **then**

        |  `/* HL param. gradient step to optim. Eq. (8) on` $\mathcal{B}$  `*/`

5       |  $\phi^{\mathcal{D}} \leftarrow \phi^{\mathcal{D}} + \alpha_{\text{HL}}\nabla_\phi \sum\limits_{o \in \mathcal{O}} \sum\limits_{h_i \in \mathcal{B}} p\left(o_{h_i} = o|\mathcal{D}_{h_i}, \Theta^{\text{old}}\right) \log \omega_\phi\left(o|z_{h_i}^{\mathcal{I}}\right)$

6    |  **end**

7    |  **if** $(n \mod k_{LL}) = 0$ **then**

        |  `/* LL param. gradient step to optim. Eq. (9) on` $\mathcal{B}$:  `*/`

8       |  $\pi^{\mathcal{D}} \leftarrow$
        $\pi^{\mathcal{D}} + \alpha_{\text{LL}}\nabla_\theta \sum\limits_{o \in \mathcal{O}} \sum\limits_{h_i \in \mathcal{B}} p\left(o_{h_i} = o|\mathcal{D}_{h_i}, \Theta^{\text{old}}\right) \sum\limits_{t \in \left[h_i, h_{i+1}-1\right]} \log \pi_\theta\left(a_t|s_t, o\right)$

9    |  **end**

10   |  $\Theta^{\text{old}} \leftarrow \Theta^{\mathcal{D}}$

11 **end**

12 $\phi = \phi_{\text{target}} \leftarrow \phi^{\mathcal{D}}, \theta^{\text{final}} \leftarrow \theta^{\mathcal{D}}$
    `/* Stage 2: Offline RL HL Policy Refinement (Sect.4.4)        */`

13 Calculate, using Eq. (4), $p\left(o_{h_i} = o|\mathcal{D}_{h_i}, \Theta^{\mathcal{D}}\right) \forall h_i \in \mathcal{H} \setminus |\mathcal{H}|$ and $\forall o \in \mathcal{O}$.

14 **for** $m = 1 : M_{iter}$ **do**

15  |  Sample batch $\mathcal{B}$ of HL time stamps $h_i$ ($\neq |\mathcal{H}|$)

      |  `/* Gradient step to optim. Eq. (12) on` $\mathcal{B}$; $\mathcal{L}_{\text{TD}}$: `Eq. (13)        */`

16  |  $\phi \leftarrow \phi - \alpha_{\text{BCQ}}\nabla_\phi\left[\sum\limits_{o \in \mathcal{O}} p\left(o_{h_i} = o|\mathcal{D}_{h_i}\right)\mathcal{L}_{\text{TD}}\left(o_{h_i} = o, h_i|\phi, \phi_{\text{target}}\right)\right]$

17  |  $\phi_{\text{target}} \leftarrow \tau \cdot \phi + (1 - \tau) \cdot \phi_{\text{target}}$    `// Polyak target network update`

18 **end**

19 $\phi^{\text{final}} \leftarrow \phi$

20 **return** $\Theta^{\text{final}} = \{\phi^{\text{final}}, \theta^{\text{final}}\}$

---

## 6   Conclusion

In this work, we propose HORIBLe-VRN, a two-stage algorithm to learn a hierarchical policy architecture containing a top-level Value Refinement Network purely from (offline) demonstration data: First, a hierarchical imitation learning stage incorporates inference of the unknown, latent HL actions and policy updates into an iterative EM-style algorithm tailored to our architecture. Subsequently, we use our proposed modified version of the offline RL BCQ algorithm to further refine the HL VRN policy. We empirically investigated several research hypotheses in long horizon, sparse reward agent navigation finding out that the planning-based VRN policy enables generalization (*H.1*), also in the offline setting, the hierarchical policy architecture with temporal abstraction further improves performance (*H.2*), and that our HL policy refinement improves robustness when demonstrations originate from sub-optimal policies (*H.3*).

An interesting direction for future work could be to scale up the approach to more complex problem settings by, for example, allowing for more flexible HL state space abstractions or even learning them as well.

**Ethical Statement.** We did not collect or process any personal data, for this work. All data was collected using a physics simulation of a point mass agent. There are several possible future applications for our research, like, for example, in autonomous vehicles or robotics, which hopefully have a positive impact on society. There are, however, also risks of negative societal impact, through the form of application itself, the impact on the job market, or real-world application without proper verification and validation. Such factors should be taken into consideration when designing applications.

# References

1. Andrychowicz, M., et al.: Hindsight experience replay. In: Advances in Neural Information Processing Systems (NeurIPS), pp. 5048–5058 (2017)
2. Bacon, P.L., Harb, J., Precup, D.: The option-critic architecture. In: AAAI Conference on Artificial Intelligence (2017)
3. Bain, M., Sammut, C.: A framework for behavioural cloning. In: Machine Intelligence, vol. 15, pp. 103–129 (1995)
4. Baum, L.E.: An inequality and associated maximization technique in statistical estimation for probabilistic functions of Markov processes. Inequalities **3**(1), 1–8 (1972)
5. Christen, S., Jendele, L., Aksan, E., Hilliges, O.: Learning functionally decomposed hierarchies for continuous control tasks with path planning. IEEE Robot. Autom. Lett. **6**(2), 3623–3630 (2021)
6. Daniel, C., Van Hoof, H., Peters, J., Neumann, G.: Probabilistic inference for determining options in reinforcement learning. Mach. Learn. **104**, 337–357 (2016)
7. Dayan, P., Hinton, G.E.: Feudal reinforcement learning. Adv. Neural Inf. Process. Syst. (NeurIPS) **5**, 271–278 (1992)
8. Dempster, A.P., Laird, N.M., Rubin, D.B.: Maximum likelihood from incomplete data via the EM algorithm. J. Royal Stat. Soc.: Ser. B (Methodological) **39**(1), 1–22 (1977)
9. Eysenbach, B., Salakhutdinov, R., Levine, S.: Search on the replay buffer: bridging planning and reinforcement learning. In: Advances in Neural Information Processing Systems (NeurIPS), vol. 32 (2019)
10. Fox, R., Krishnan, S., Stoica, I., Goldberg, K.: Multi-level discovery of deep options. arXiv preprint arXiv:1703.08294 (2017)
11. Fox, R., et al.: Hierarchical variational imitation learning of control programs. arXiv preprint arXiv:1912.12612 (2019)
12. Francis, A., et al.: Long-range indoor navigation with PRM-RL. IEEE Trans. Robot. (2020)
13. Fujimoto, S., Conti, E., Ghavamzadeh, M., Pineau, J.: Benchmarking batch deep reinforcement learning algorithms. arXiv preprint arXiv:1910.01708 (2019)

14. Fujimoto, S., Gu, S.: A minimalist approach to offline reinforcement learning. Adv. Neural Inf. Process. Syst. (NeurIPS) **34**, 20132–20145 (2021)
15. Giammarino, V., Paschalidis, I.: Online Baum-Welch algorithm for hierarchical imitation learning. In: Conference on Decision and Control (CDC), pp. 3717–3722. IEEE (2021)
16. Gieselmann, R., Pokorny, F.T.: Planning-augmented hierarchical reinforcement learning. IEEE Robot. Autom. Lett. **6**(3), 5097–5104 (2021)
17. Haarnoja, T., Zhou, A., Abbeel, P., Levine, S.: Soft actor-critic: off-policy maximum entropy deep reinforcement learning with a stochastic actor. In: International Conference on Machine Learning (ICML), pp. 1861–1870 (2018)
18. Huber, P.J.: Robust estimation of a location parameter. Ann. Math. Stat., 73–101 (1964)
19. Hutsebaut-Buysse, M., Mets, K., Latré, S.: Hierarchical reinforcement learning: a survey and open research challenges. Mach. Learn. Knowl. Extract. **4**(1), 172–221 (2022)
20. Jing, M., et al.: Adversarial option-aware hierarchical imitation learning. In: International Conference on Machine Learning (ICML), pp. 5097–5106 (2021)
21. Kingma, D.P., Ba, J.: ADAM: a method for stochastic optimization. arXiv preprint arXiv:1412.6980 (2014)
22. Krishnan, S., Fox, R., Stoica, I., Goldberg, K.: DDCO: discovery of deep continuous options for robot learning from demonstrations. In: Conference on Robot Learning (CoRL), pp. 418–437 (2017)
23. Kumar, A., Zhou, A., Tucker, G., Levine, S.: Conservative Q-learning for offline reinforcement learning. Adv. Neural Inf. Process. Syst. (NeurIPS) **33**, 1179–1191 (2020)
24. Le, H., Jiang, N., Agarwal, A., Dudík, M., Yue, Y., Daumé III, H.: Hierarchical imitation and reinforcement learning. In: International Conference on Machine Learning (ICML), pp. 2917–2926 (2018)
25. Levy, A., Konidaris, G., Platt, R., Saenko, K.: Learning multi-level hierarchies with hindsight. In: International Conference on Learning Representations (ICLR) (2019)
26. Li, B., Li, J., Lu, T., Cai, Y., Wang, S.: Hierarchical learning from demonstrations for long-horizon tasks. In: International Conference on Robotics and Automation (ICRA), pp. 4545–4551. IEEE (2021)
27. Mnih, V., et al.: Human-level control through deep reinforcement learning. Nature **518**(7540), 529 (2015)
28. Nardelli, N., Synnaeve, G., Lin, Z., Kohli, P., Torr, P.H., Usunier, N.: Value propagation networks. In: International Conference on Learning Representations (ICLR) (2019)
29. Prudencio, R.F., Maximo, M.R., Colombini, E.L.: A survey on offline reinforcement learning: taxonomy, review, and open problems. IEEE Trans. Neural Netw. Learn. Syst. (2023)
30. Salakhutdinov, R., Roweis, S.T., Ghahramani, Z.: Optimization with EM and expectation-conjugate-gradient. In: International Conference on Machine Learning (ICML), pp. 672–679 (2003)
31. Smith, M., Van Hoof, H., Pineau, J.: An inference-based policy gradient method for learning options. In: International Conference on Machine Learning (ICML), pp. 4703–4712. PMLR (2018)
32. Sutton, R.S., Precup, D., Singh, S.: Between MDPs and semi-MDPs: a framework for temporal abstraction in reinforcement learning. Artif. Intell. **112**(1–2), 181–211 (1999)

33. Todorov, E., Erez, T., Tassa, Y.: Mujoco: A physics engine for model-based control. In: International Conference on Intelligent Robots and Systems, pp. 5026–5033. IEEE (2012)
34. Van Hasselt, H., Guez, A., Silver, D.: Deep reinforcement learning with double Q-learning. In: AAAI Conference on Artificial Intelligence, vol. 30 (2016)
35. Vecerik, M., et al.: Leveraging demonstrations for deep reinforcement learning on robotics problems with sparse rewards. arXiv preprint arXiv:1707.08817 (2017)
36. Vezhnevets, A.S., et al.: FeUdal networks for hierarchical reinforcement learning. In: International Conference on Machine Learning (ICML), pp. 3540–3549 (2017)
37. Wöhlke, J., Schmitt, F., Van Hoof, H.: Hierarchies of planning and reinforcement learning for robot navigation. In: International Conference on Robotics and Automation (ICRA), pp. 10682–10688. IEEE (2021)
38. Wöhlke, J., Schmitt, F., Van Hoof, H.: Value refinement network (VRN). In: International Joint Conference on Artificial Intelligence (IJCAI), pp. 3558–3565 (2022)
39. Zhang, Z., Paschalidis, I.: Provable hierarchical imitation learning via EM. In: International Conference on Artificial Intelligence and Statistics (AISTATS), pp. 883–891 (2021)
40. Zheng, B., Verma, S., Zhou, J., Tsang, I.W., Chen, F.: Imitation learning: progress, taxonomies and challenges. IEEE Trans. Neural Netw. Learn. Syst., 1–16 (2022)

# Stepsize Learning for Policy Gradient Methods in Contextual Markov Decision Processes

Luca Sabbioni[✉], Francesco Corda, and Marcello Restelli

Politecnico di Milano, Milan, Italy
{luca.sabbioni,francesco.corda,marcello.restelli}@polimi.it

**Abstract.** Policy-based algorithms are among the most widely adopted techniques in model-free RL, thanks to their strong theoretical groundings and good properties in continuous action spaces. Unfortunately, these methods require precise and problem-specific hyperparameter tuning to achieve good performance, and tend to struggle when asked to accomplish a series of heterogeneous tasks. In particular, the selection of the step size has a crucial impact on their ability to learn a highly performing policy, affecting the speed and the stability of the training process, and often being the main culprit for poor results. In this paper, we tackle these issues with a Meta Reinforcement Learning approach, by introducing a new formulation, known as meta-MDP, that can be used to solve any hyperparameter selection problem in RL with contextual processes. After providing a theoretical Lipschitz bound to the difference of performance in different tasks, we adopt the proposed framework to train a batch RL algorithm to dynamically recommend the most adequate step size for different policies and tasks. In conclusion, we present an experimental campaign to show the advantages of selecting an adaptive learning rate in heterogeneous environments.

## 1 Introduction

Reinforcement Learning (RL, [51]) is a field of Machine Learning aimed at building agents capable of learning a behavior that maximizes the amount of reward collected while interacting with an environment. Typically, this interaction is modeled as a Markov Decision Process (MDP, [41]), where all trajectories share the same transition probability and reward function. Nevertheless, in many real-world scenarios, there may be exogenous variables that can affect the whole dynamics; one might think for example of a car race, where the road temperature or the tire choice may require different strategies. One of the most successful streams of model-free RL applications adopts policy-based algorithms, which provide solid theoretical groundings and good empirical properties in continuous-action spaces [2,7,56]. Unfortunately, these methods require precise and problem-specific hyperparameter tuning to achieve good performance, causing them to struggle when applied to a series of heterogeneous tasks. The fundamental parameter to tune is the step size, which has a crucial impact on the

D. Koutra et al. (Eds.): ECML PKDD 2023, LNAI 14172, pp. 506–523, 2023.
https://doi.org/10.1007/978-3-031-43421-1_30

ability to learn a performing policy, affecting the speed and the stability of the training process, and often being the main culprit for poor results. Similarly, widely used optimizers (e.g. Adam [27] and RMSProp [53]) and learning rate schedules have a narrow window of effective hyperparameters [20]. In this work, we consider the specific problem of learning how to dynamically select the best step size for each policy in case the MDP process might differ due to exogenous variables, here denoted as "tasks" or "contexts". This framework is accurately described by the definition of a Contextual Markov Decision Process (CMDP) introduced in [19] (Sect. 3).

Our first original contribution is the formalization of the Meta-RL problem, which we denoted as meta-MDP (Sect. 4). This general framework allows to solve a set of RL tasks, grouped as a CMDP. We discuss the main elements of the model, such as the objective function, which is performance learning, and the meta action, consisting of the hyperparameter selection for a policy update. In this framework, we then add an assumption of Lipschitz continuity of the meta-MDPs, in which trajectories sampled from similar contexts are similar. This is a reasonable assumption for real-world problems, where a small change in the settings slightly changes the effects on the dynamics of the environment. Under such conditions, it is possible to derive some guarantees on the Lipschitz continuity of the expected return and of its gradient (Sect. 5). This is relevant, as it gives insight into the generalization capabilities of meta-RL approaches, where the performance of policies selected by observing tasks in training can be bounded for test tasks. Subsequently, we propose in Sect. 6 to learn the step size of Policy Gradient methods in a meta-MDP. The idea of the approach is to apply a batch mode, value-based algorithm, known as Fitted Q-Iteration (FQI), to derive an estimate of the (meta) action-value function, based on the meta-features observed and of the hyperparameter selected. This approximation is used to dynamically recommend the most appropriate step size in the current scenario. The learning procedure is based on a regression through ExtraTrees [18], which shows low sensitivity to the choice of its own parameters. In conclusion, we evaluate our approach in various simulated environments shown in Sect. 7, highlighting its strengths and current limitations. The proofs and further results are reported in Appendix.[1]

## 2    Related Work

The importance of hyperparameter tuning is widely known in the general Machine Learning field, because it can significantly improve the performance of a model [20, 24, 57]. Therefore, Hyperparameter Optimization (HO) is a paramount component of Automated Machine Learning (AutoML, [22]) with a rich stream of research literature [37].

The tuning process is usually approached by practitioners as a black-box approach: the most common methods are grid search or random search [6]. More

---

[1] The full version of the paper, including the appendix, is available at http://arxiv.org/abs/2306.07741.

advanced methods are obtained by relying on sequential model-based Bayesian optimization [14,21,50], where a probabilistic model is trained to fit the underlying fitness function of the main learning algorithm. In some recent works [11,48], Genetic Algorithms are employed to automatically learn the most performing parameters on RL applications. The main limitation in this kind of approach consists of the need for complete learning instances to evaluate each hyperparameter, which is kept fixed throughout the whole process A completely different solution consists in training an outer network, typically an RNN [3,23,32,44] since it is often possible to compute the gradient of the objective function w.r.t. the hyperparameters through implicit differentiation, as shown in [30,31]. These methods are often referred to as *bilevel optimization* procedures, where the *outer* loop updates the hyperparameters on a validation set, and the *inner* one is used for training the models with a specific hyperparameter set.

Recent independent papers introduced the formal paradigm of Dynamic Algorithm Configuration and HO as a Sequential Decision Process [1,8,25], albeit many other works developed solutions in this direction, employing RL-based methods [28,58,60,61] or contextual bandits [29]. However, these works are rarely adopted in RL, as they become computationally intractable and sample inefficient. Furthermore, gradient-based methods [59] compute the gradient of the return function with respect to the hyperparameters: they rely on a strong assumption that the update function must be differentiable and the gradient must be computed on the whole chain of training updates. In addition, these approaches are typically online, with limited exploration (as discussed in [8]), or make use of gradient-based meta-algorithms, where the high level of sensitivity to new meta-hyperparameters makes the problem even more challenging, as the models may be harder to train and require more data. Within the specific task of learning rate tuning in a policy-gradient framework, [38] proposed a sample efficient algorithm to learn a hyperparameter schedule employing a Weighted Importance Sampling approach, while [35] deals with the offline hyperparameter selection for offline RL. In these proposed approaches, HO is meant to optimize the objective function in the next step, similar to a bandit problem, which favors convergence to local optima. In order to optimize over a longer horizon, [49] adopts an RL approach to select the learning rate through Guided Policy Search.

The concept of rapid adaptation to unseen tasks is usually denoted as meta-learning [45] and has recently emerged as a fertile and promising research field, especially with regard to gradient-based techniques. One of the cornerstones in this area is MAML [15], which learns a model initialization for fast adaptation and has been a starting point for several subsequent works [33,36]. PEARL [43] decouples the problem of making an inference on the probabilistic context and solving it by conditioning the policy in meta Reinforcement Learning problems. However, all these works heavily rely on choosing (multiple) learning rates.

# 3    Preliminaries

A discrete-time Markov Decision Process (MDP) is defined as a tuple $\langle \mathcal{S}, \mathcal{A}, \mathcal{P}, \mathcal{R}, \gamma, \mu \rangle$, where $\mathcal{S}$ is the (continuous) state space, $\mathcal{A}$ the (continuous) action space, $\mathcal{P}(\cdot|s, a)$ is the Markovian transition, which assigns to each state-action pair $(s, a)$ the probability of reaching the next state $s'$, $\mathcal{R}$ is the reward function, bounded by hypothesis, i.e. $\sup_{s \in \mathcal{S}, a \in \mathcal{A}} |\mathcal{R}(s, a)| \leq R_{max}$. Finally, $\gamma \in [0, 1]$ is the discount factor, and $\mu$ is the initial state distribution. The policy of an agent, denoted as $\pi(\cdot|s)$, assigns to each state $s$ the density distribution over the action space $\mathcal{A}$.

A trajectory $\tau := (s_0, a_0, s_1, a_1, s_2, a_2, ..., a_{H-1}, s_H)$ is a sequence of state-action pairs, where $H$ is the horizon, which may be infinite. The return of a trajectory $\tau$ is defined as the discounted sum of the rewards collected: $G_\tau = \sum_{t=0}^{H} \gamma^t \mathcal{R}(s_t, a_t)$. Consequently, it is possible to define the expected return $j_\pi$ as the expected performance under policy $\pi$. Similarly, we can define, for each state $s \in \mathcal{S}$ and action $a \in \mathcal{A}$, the (action)-value functions as:

$$Q_\pi(s, a) := \mathop{\mathbb{E}}_{\substack{s_{t+1} \sim \mathcal{P}(\cdot|s_t, a_t) \\ a_{t+1} \sim \pi(\cdot|s_{t+1})}} \left[ \sum_{t=0}^{\infty} \gamma^t \mathcal{R}(s_t, a_t) | s, a \right]$$

$$V_\pi(s) := \mathop{\mathbb{E}}_{a \sim \pi(\cdot|s)} [Q_\pi(s, a)].$$

For the rest of the paper, we consider parametric policies, where the policy $\pi_\theta$ is parameterized by a vector $\theta \in \Theta \subseteq \mathbb{R}^m$. In this case, the goal is to find the optimal parametric policy that maximizes the performance, i.e. $\theta^* = \arg\max_{\theta \in \Theta} j(\theta)^2$. Policy-based algorithms adopt a gradient-ascent approach: the Policy Gradient Theorem (PGT) [51] states that, for a given policy $\pi_\theta$, $\theta \in \Theta$:

$$\nabla_\theta j(\theta) = \mathop{\mathbb{E}}_{\substack{s \sim \delta_\mu^\theta \\ a \sim \pi_\theta(\cdot|s)}} \left[ \nabla_\theta \log \pi_\theta(a|s) Q_\pi(s, a) \right], \tag{1}$$

where $\delta_\mu^\theta$ is the state occupancy measure induced by the policy, in such a way that $\delta_\mu^\theta(s) := (1 - \gamma) \int_{\mathcal{S}} \mu(s_0) \sum_{t=0}^{T} \gamma^t p_\theta(s_0 \xrightarrow{t} s) ds_0$, with $p_\theta(s_0 \xrightarrow{t} s)$ being the probability of reaching state $s$ from $s_0$ in $t$ steps following $\pi_\theta$. In practice, the gradient in Eq. 1 can be computed only through an estimator $\widehat{\nabla}_N j_\theta$, such as PGT [52], that requires sampling a batch of trajectories $\{\tau_i\}_{i=1}^{N}$. A large family of algorithms is based on the Policy Optimization through Gradient Ascent, eventually with the inclusion of other methods, such as Trust Regions and constraints over the Kullback-Leibler divergence of the policies between consecutive iterations [46, 47]. An important variation on the approach consists in following the steepest ascent direction using the Natural Policy Gradient [26], which includes information regarding the curvature of the return manifold over the policy space in the form of the Fisher Information Matrix $F(\theta) = \mathbb{E}[\nabla_\theta \log \pi_\theta \nabla_\theta^\top \log \pi_\theta]$;

---

[2] For the sake of brevity, when a variable depends on the policy $\pi_\theta$, in the superscript only $\theta$ is shown.

its inverse is then multiplied by the gradient to obtain the natural gradient $g(\boldsymbol{\theta}) := F(\boldsymbol{\theta})^{-1}\nabla_\theta j(\boldsymbol{\theta})$, independent of the policy parameterization. A common approach to avoid long computational times for large policy spaces is to directly provide an estimate of the natural gradient $\widehat{g}_N(\boldsymbol{\theta})$ by using the same batch of trajectories adopted for the gradient estimation, and through the iteration of $k$ steps of conjugate gradient methods with the application of the Fisher-vector products [46].

*Lipschitz MDP.* This subsection introduces the concepts of Lipschitz Continuity (LC) and Lipschitz MDP. The notation is taken from [40]. Let $(\mathcal{X}, d_\mathcal{X})$ and $(\mathcal{Y}, d_\mathcal{Y})$ be two metric spaces; a function $f : \mathcal{X} \to \mathcal{Y}$ is called $L_f$-Lipschitz continuous ($L_f$-LC), with $L_f \geq 0$, if $d_\mathcal{Y}(f(x), f(x')) \leq L_f d_\mathcal{X}(x, x') \forall x, x' \in \mathcal{X}$. Furthermore, we define the Lipschitz semi-norm as $\|f\|_L = \sup_{x,x' \in \mathcal{X}: x \neq x'} \frac{d_\mathcal{Y}(f(x), f(x'))}{d_\mathcal{X}(x, x')}$. For real functions, the usual metric is the Euclidean distance while, for distributions, a common metric is the Kantorovich, or $L^1$-Wasserstein distance:

$$\mathcal{K}(p, q) := \sup_{f: \|f\|_L \leq 1} \left\{ \left\| \int_X f d(p - q) \right\| \right\}$$

[40,42] introduced some notion of smoothness in RL by defining the Lipschitz-MDP and the Lipschitz policies:

**Assumption 3.1.** *Let $\mathcal{M}$ be an MDP. $\mathcal{M}$ is called $(L_P, L_r)$-LC if for all $(s, a), (\overline{s}, \overline{a}) \in \mathcal{S} \times \mathcal{A}$:*

$$\mathcal{K}\left(P(\cdot|s, a), P(\cdot|\overline{s}, \overline{a})\right) \leq L_P \, d_{\mathcal{S} \times \mathcal{A}}\left((s, a), (\overline{s}, \overline{a})\right),$$
$$|r(s, a) - r(\overline{s}, \overline{a})| \leq L_r \, d_{\mathcal{S} \times \mathcal{A}}\left((s, a), (\overline{s}, \overline{a})\right).$$

**Assumption 3.2.** *Let $\pi \in \Pi$ be a Markovian stationary policy. $\pi$ is called $L_\pi$-LC if for all $s, \overline{s} \in \mathcal{S}$:*

$$\mathcal{K}\left(\pi(\cdot|s), \pi(\cdot|\overline{s})\right) \leq L_\pi \, d_\mathcal{S}\left(s, \overline{s}\right),$$

Since we are dealing with parametric policies, often other useful assumptions rely on the Lipschitz continuity w.r.t the policy parameters $\boldsymbol{\theta}$ and their gradient. In [40], it is shown that, under these Lipschitz continuity assumptions on the MDP and the policy model, also the expected return, the $Q$-function, and the gradient components are Lipschitz w.r.t. $\boldsymbol{\theta}$.[3]

**Meta Reinforcement Learning.** As the name suggests, meta-learning implies a higher level of abstraction than regular machine learning. In particular, meta reinforcement learning (meta-RL) consists in applying meta-learning techniques to RL tasks. Usually, these tasks are formalized in MDPs by a common set of parameters, known as the *context* $\boldsymbol{\omega}$. The natural candidate to represent the set of RL tasks is the Contextual Markov Decision Process (CMDP, [19]), defined as a tuple $(\Omega, \mathcal{S}, \mathcal{A}, \mathcal{M}(\boldsymbol{\omega}))$ where $\Omega$ is called the context space, $\mathcal{S}$ and $\mathcal{A}$ are the

---

[3] By assuming that the policy and its gradient is LC w.r.t. $\boldsymbol{\theta}$.

shared state and action spaces, and $\mathcal{M}$ is the function that maps any context $\omega \in \Omega$ to an MDP, such that $\mathcal{M}(\omega) = \langle \mathcal{S}, \mathcal{A}, P_\omega, R_\omega, \gamma_\omega, \mu_\omega \rangle$. In other words, a CMDP includes in a single entity a group of tasks. In the following, we will assume that $\gamma$ and $\mu$ are shared, too.

## 4    Meta-MDP

We now present the concept of meta-MDP, a framework for solving meta-RL tasks that extends the CMDP definition to include the learning model and the policy parameterization. Similar approaches can be found in [17] and in [28]. To start, let us consider the various tasks used in a meta-training procedure as a set of MDPs $\{\mathcal{M}_\omega\}_{\omega \in \Omega}$, such that each task $\mathcal{M}_\omega$ can be sampled from the distribution $\psi$ defined on the context space $\Omega$. This set can be seen equivalently as a CMDP $\mathscr{M} = \langle \Omega, \mathcal{S}, \mathcal{A}, \mathcal{M}(\omega) \rangle$, where $\mathcal{M}(\omega) = \mathcal{M}_\omega$. Similarly, we define a distribution $\rho$ over the policy space $\Theta$, so that at each iteration in an MDP $\mathcal{M}_\omega$, the policy parameters $\theta_0$ are initialized to a value sampled from $\rho$. In our case, we assume to be able to represent the task by the parameterized context itself $\omega$.

**Definition 4.1.** *A meta-MDP is a tuple $\langle \mathcal{X}, \mathcal{H}, \mathcal{L}, \widetilde{\gamma}, (\mathscr{M}, \psi), (\Theta, \rho), f \rangle$, where:*

- $\mathcal{X}$ *and* $\mathcal{H}$ *are respectively the meta observation space and learning action space;*
- $\mathcal{L} : \Theta \times \Omega \times \mathcal{H} \to \mathbb{R}$ *is the meta reward function;*
- $\widetilde{\gamma}$ *is the meta-discount factor;*
- $(\mathscr{M}, \psi)$ *and* $(\Theta, \rho)$ *contain respectively a CMDP $\mathscr{M}$ with distribution over tasks $\psi$, and the policy space $\Theta$, with initial distribution $\rho$;*
- $f$ *is the update rule of the learning model chosen.*

In particular, a meta-MDP attempts to enclose the general elements needed to learn an RL task into a model with properties similar to a classic MDP. The meta observation space $\mathcal{X}$ of a meta-MDP can be considered as the generalization of the observation space in classic Partially-Observable MDPs (POMDP) [4], and it is meant to include information regarding the current condition of the learning process, and it is (eventually implicitly) dependent on $\theta$ and on the context $\omega$.

Each action $h_k \in \mathcal{H}$ performed on the meta-MDP with policy parametrization $\theta_k$ at the $k$-th step, determines a specific hyperparameter that regulates the stochastic update rule $f$, i.e., $\theta_{k+1} = f(\theta_k, h_k, \tau_k)$, where $\tau_k$ is the current batch of trajectories. In general, we can consider any update function with a set of tunable hyperparameters; in particular, in this work we focus on (Normalized) Natural Gradient Ascent (NGA), in which the action $h$ determines the step size, and the update rule takes the form $f(\theta, h) = \theta + h \frac{\widehat{g}_n(\theta, \omega)}{\|\widehat{g}_n(\theta, \omega)\|_2}$, where $\widehat{g}_n(\theta, \omega)$ is the natural gradient of a policy $\theta$ estimated on $n$ episodes through the task $\mathcal{M}_\omega$.

As in a standard RL problem, the training of a meta-MDP is accomplished by optimizing a reward function. Meta-Learning has the main goal of learning to learn: as a consequence, we want to consider performance improvement as our reward. To accelerate the learning over the current MDP $\mathcal{M}_\omega$, this

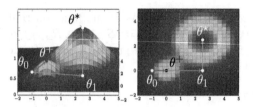

**Fig. 1.** Example of an optimization setting where a Bandit approach would be suboptimal: starting from $\theta_0$, the optimal bandit agent will choose to reach $\theta^+$, a local maximum. An RL agent, however, may plan to make a larger step, up to $\theta_1$, to reach the global optimum $\theta^*$ on the next update.

function should reflect variations between the returns obtained in different learning steps. To accomplish this, we define $\mathcal{L}(\boldsymbol{\theta}, \boldsymbol{\omega}, h)$ as a function of the current policy parameters $\boldsymbol{\theta}$ and of the meta-action $h$ once the context $\boldsymbol{\omega}$ is fixed:

$$\mathcal{L}(\boldsymbol{\theta}, \boldsymbol{\omega}, h) := j_{\boldsymbol{\omega}}(f(\boldsymbol{\theta}, h)) - j_{\boldsymbol{\omega}}(\boldsymbol{\theta});$$

where $j_{\boldsymbol{\omega}}(\boldsymbol{\theta})$ and $j_{\boldsymbol{\omega}}(f(\boldsymbol{\theta}, h))$ are respectively the expected returns in the task $\mathcal{M}_{\boldsymbol{\omega}}$ before and after one update step according to the function $f$, estimated through a batch of sampled trajectories. In the particular case of NGA, the function takes the following form:

$$\mathcal{L}(\boldsymbol{\theta}, \boldsymbol{\omega}, h) = j_{\boldsymbol{\omega}}\left(\boldsymbol{\theta} + h \frac{\widehat{g}_n(\boldsymbol{\theta}, \boldsymbol{\omega})}{\|\widehat{g}_n(\boldsymbol{\theta}, \boldsymbol{\omega})\|_2}\right) - j_{\boldsymbol{\omega}}(\boldsymbol{\theta}).$$

Unlike a standard MDP, a meta-MDP does not include a direct Markovian transition model that regulates its dynamics: given $x_k \in \mathcal{X}$, the stochastic transition to the next meta-state $x_{k+1}$ is induced by the distribution of the trajectories induced by the pair $(\theta_k, \mathcal{M}_{\boldsymbol{\omega}})$ and on the update rule $f$. The initial state hence implicitly depends on $\psi$ and $\rho$, and the transition to the next state is still Markovian, as it is independent of the previous states observed (once $x_k$ is known).

*Discount Factor, Contextual Bandit, and Meta-MDP.* The choice of the meta-discount factor $\widetilde{\gamma}$ is critical: meta-learning is very often considered as paired with *few-shot learning*, where a short horizon is taken into account for the learning process. $\widetilde{\gamma}$, if lower than 1, explicitly translates into an effective horizon of $\frac{1}{1-\widetilde{\gamma}}$. However, a myopic behavior induced by a low discount factor might lead the meta-agent to prefer actions leading to local optima, while sometimes it might be necessary to take more cautious steps to reach the global optima of the learning process. Setting $\widetilde{\gamma} = 0$, the problem degenerates into a contextual bandit, where the goal is to maximize the immediate reward, in a similar fashion as in [38]. However, it might be inefficient to directly maximize the immediate reward, as an agent might prefer to choose a different hyperparameter to reach the global optimum, which is possibly unreachable in just one step. Figure 1 provides an example in this direction, where a bi-dimensional parametrization is considered: starting from the initial parametrization $\boldsymbol{\theta}_0$, the maximization of the immediate return would lead to a local optimum $\boldsymbol{\theta}^+$. We want our agent to be able to plan the updates to maximize the final policy's performance: this is the main reason for the design of HO as a sequential decision-making problem.

*Meta-Space Features:* In this subsection, we deal with the choice of the features observed in the meta-observation $x_t$. Some properties are generally desirable for its formulation: first of all, it needs to include policy-specific information, as some form of knowledge about the current policy is necessary to adapt the meta-actions to the current setting of the model. Ideally, we can include all parameters of the current policy $\boldsymbol{\theta}_t$, even if this approach might be difficult for large policy spaces. Finding an informative set of meta-features remains an open problem for future research, as recalled in Sect. 8. Additionally, task-specific features may be informative. The information about the task $\boldsymbol{\omega}$ is used to achieve an *implicit task-identification*, a necessary step to optimize learning in new tasks, based on similarities to older ones. Finally, some relevant information could be included in the (natural) gradient $\widehat{g}_n(\theta_t, \boldsymbol{\omega})$: this vector is implicitly dependent on the stochasticity of the inner MDP $\mathcal{M}_\omega$ under policy $\boldsymbol{\theta}_t$ according to the batch of trajectories sampled for its estimation. In our experiments, we will consider the concatenation of all these features $x_t = \langle \boldsymbol{\theta}_t, \widehat{g}_n(\theta_t, \boldsymbol{\omega}), \boldsymbol{\omega} \rangle$. From a more technical point of view, a Meta-MDP can be considered as the conditional observation probability of a POMDP, where the true state consists of the pair $(\theta_t, \boldsymbol{\omega})$, and the meta-observation $x_t$ relies on a conditional observation probability $\mathcal{O}(\cdot|\theta_t, \boldsymbol{\omega})$.

## 5    Context Lipschitz Continuity

We consider a meta-MDP in which all inner tasks satisfy the Lipschitz continuity assumption. Under this condition, we can derive a set of bounds on the approximation errors obtained by the meta-agent when acting on unseen tasks. Among others, we obtain that the expected return $j_\omega(\boldsymbol{\theta})$ and its gradient are LC w.r.t. the context $\boldsymbol{\omega}$, providing useful theoretical foundations for the meta-RL general framework and inspiring motivation to look for solutions and models capable of generalizing on large task spaces. Let us suppose to be provided with a CMDP $(\Omega, \mathcal{S}, \mathcal{A}, \mathcal{M})$, such that Assumption 3.1 is verified $\forall \boldsymbol{\omega} \in \Omega$, meaning that $\forall \boldsymbol{\omega} \in \Omega$ the MDP $\mathcal{M}_\omega$ is $(L_P(\boldsymbol{\omega}) - L_r(\boldsymbol{\omega}))$-LC. Let us also assume that the set of MDPs is LC in the context $\boldsymbol{\omega}$:

**Assumption 5.1.** *Let $\mathcal{M}$ be a CMDP. $\mathcal{M}$ is called $(L_{\omega_P}, L_{\omega_r})$-Context Lipschitz Continuous $((L_{\omega_P}, L_{\omega_r})$-CLC) if for all $(s, a), (\overline{s}, \overline{a}) \in \mathcal{S} \times \mathcal{A}, \forall \boldsymbol{\omega}, \widehat{\boldsymbol{\omega}} \in \Omega$:*

$$\mathcal{K}\left(P_\omega(\cdot \mid s, a), P_{\widehat{\omega}}(\cdot \mid s, a))\right) \leq L_{\omega_P} d_\Omega(\boldsymbol{\omega}, \widehat{\boldsymbol{\omega}})$$

$$\left| R_\omega(s, a) - R_{\widehat{\omega}}(s, a) \right| \leq L_{\omega_r} d_\Omega(\boldsymbol{\omega}, \widehat{\boldsymbol{\omega}}).$$

This means we have some notion of task smoothness: when two MDPs with similar contexts are considered, their transition and reward processes are similar. These assumptions, along with Assumption 3.2, allow us to infer some considerations regarding the Q-value function:

**Theorem 5.1.** *Let $\mathcal{M}$ be a $(L_{\omega_P}, L_{\omega_r})$-CLC CMDP for which $\mathcal{M}(\omega)$ is $(L_P(\omega), L_r(\omega))$-LC $\forall \omega \in \Omega$. Given a $L_\pi$-LC policy $\pi$, the action value function $Q_\omega^\pi(s, a)$ is $L_{\omega_Q}$-CLC w.r.t. the context $\omega$, i.e., $\forall (s, a) \in \mathcal{S} \times \mathcal{A}:*

$$\left| Q_\omega^\pi(s, a) - Q_{\widehat{\omega}}^\pi(s, a) \right| \leq L_{\omega_Q}(\pi) d_\Omega(\omega, \widehat{\omega}),$$

*where*

$$L_{\omega_Q}(\pi) = \frac{L_{\omega_r} + \gamma L_{\omega_P} L_{V_\pi}(\omega)}{1 - \gamma},$$

$$L_{V_\pi}(\omega) = \frac{L_r(\omega)(1 + L_\pi)}{1 - \gamma L_P(\omega)(1 + L_\pi)} \tag{2}$$

As a consequence, the return function $j_\omega(\pi)$ is context-LC: $|j_\omega(\pi) - j_{\widehat{\omega}}(\pi)| \leq L_{\omega_Q}(\pi) d_\Omega(\omega, \widehat{\omega})$. In simpler terms, Theorem 5.1 exploits the LC property to derive an upper bound on the return distance in different tasks. This result represents an important guarantee on the generalization capabilities of the approach, as it provides a bound on the error obtained in testing unseen tasks. A proof for this theorem is provided in the supplementary material, where we also prove that the analytic gradient $\nabla j_\omega^\theta$ is CLC w.r.t. the context, too. In particular, a bound on the distance between the gradients of different tasks ensures regularity in the surface of the return function, which is important as the gradient is included in the meta state to capture information regarding the context space.

## 6  Fitted Q-Iteration on Meta-MDP

We now define our approach to learn a dynamic learning rate in the framework of a meta-MDP. As a meta-RL approach, the objectives of our algorithm are to improve the generalization capabilities of PG methods and to remove the need to manually tune the learning rate for each task. Finding an optimal dynamic step size serves two purposes: it maximizes the convergence speed by performing large updates when allowed and improves the overall training stability by selecting low values when the return is close to the optimum or the current region is uncertain. To accomplish these goals, we propose the adoption of the Fitted Q-Iteration (FQI, [12]) algorithm, which is an off-policy, and offline algorithm designed to learn a good approximation of the optimal action-value function by exploiting the Bellman optimality operator. The approach consists in applying Supervised Learning techniques as, in our case, Extra Trees [18], in order to generalize the $Q$ estimation over the entire state-action space. The algorithm considers a full dataset $\mathcal{F} = \{(x_t^k, h_t^k, l_t^k, x_{t+1}^k)\}_k$, where each tuple represents an interaction with the meta-MDP: in the $k$−th tuple, $x_t^k$ and $x_{t+1}^k$ are respectively the current

---

**Algorithm 1.** Meta-MDP Dataset Generation for NGA (trajectory method)

---

**Input:** CMDP $\mathcal{M}$, task distribution $\psi$, policy space $\boldsymbol{\Theta}$, initial policy distribution $\rho$, number of meta episodes $K$, learning steps $T$, inner trajectories $n$.
**Initialize:** $\mathcal{F} = \{\}$,
**for** $k = 1, \ldots, K$ **do**
    Sample context $\boldsymbol{\omega} \sim \psi(\Omega)$, initial policy $\boldsymbol{\theta}_0 \sim \rho(\boldsymbol{\Theta})$
    Sample $n$ trajectories in task $\mathcal{M}_{\boldsymbol{\omega}}$ under policy $\pi(\boldsymbol{\theta}_0)$
    Estimate $j_{\boldsymbol{\omega}}(\boldsymbol{\theta}_0)$, $\widehat{g}_n(\boldsymbol{\theta}_0, \boldsymbol{\omega})$
    **for** $t = 0, \ldots, T - 1$ **do**
        Sample meta-action $h \in \mathcal{H}$
        Update policy $\boldsymbol{\theta}_{t+1} = \boldsymbol{\theta}_t + h \frac{\widehat{g}_n(\boldsymbol{\theta}_t, \boldsymbol{\omega})}{\|\widehat{g}_n(\boldsymbol{\theta}_t, \boldsymbol{\omega})\|}$
        Sample $n$ trajectories in $(\mathcal{M}_{\boldsymbol{\omega}}, \pi(\boldsymbol{\theta}_t))$
        Estimate $j_{\boldsymbol{\omega}}(\boldsymbol{\theta}_{t+1})$, $\widehat{g}_n(\boldsymbol{\theta}_{t+1}, \boldsymbol{\omega})$
        Set $x = \langle \boldsymbol{\theta}_t, \widehat{g}_n(\boldsymbol{\theta}_t, \boldsymbol{\omega}), \boldsymbol{\omega} \rangle$;   $x' = \langle \boldsymbol{\theta}_{t+1}, \widehat{g}_n(\boldsymbol{\theta}_{t+1}, \boldsymbol{\omega}), \boldsymbol{\omega} \rangle$;   $l = j_{\boldsymbol{\omega}}(\boldsymbol{\theta}_{t+1}) - j_{\boldsymbol{\omega}}(\boldsymbol{\theta}_t)$.
        Append $\{(x, h, x', l)\}$ to $\mathcal{F}$
    **end for**
**end for**
**Output:** $\mathcal{F}$

---

and next meta-state, $h_t^k$ the meta-action and $l_t^k$ the meta reward function, as described in Sect. 4. To consider each meta-state $x$, there is the need to sample $n$ trajectories in the inner MDP to estimate return and gradient. At the iteration $N$ of the algorithm, given the (meta) action-value function $Q_{N-1}$, the training set $TS_N = \{(i^k, o^k)\}_k$ is built, where each input is equivalent to the state-action pair $i^k = (x_t^k, h_t^k)$, and the target is the result of the Bellman optimal operator: $o^k = l_t^k + \widetilde{\gamma} \max_{h \in \mathcal{H}} Q_{N-1}(x_{t+1}^k, h)$. In this way, the regression algorithm adopted is trained on $TS$ to learn $Q_N$ with the learning horizon increased by one step.

In general, the dataset is created by following $K$ learning trajectories over the CMDP: at the beginning of each meta-episode, a new context $\boldsymbol{\omega}$ and initial policy $\boldsymbol{\theta}_0$ are sampled from $\psi$ and $\rho$; then, for each of the $T$ learning steps, the meta action $h$ is randomly sampled to perform the policy update. In this way, the overall dataset is composed of $KT$ tuples. It is also possible to explore the overall task-policy space $\Omega \times \boldsymbol{\Theta}$ through a generative approach: instead of following the learning trajectories, both $\boldsymbol{\omega}, \boldsymbol{\theta}_0$ and $h$ are sampled every time. We refer to this method as "generative" approach, while the former will be referred to as "trajectory" approach. The pseudo-code for the dataset generation process with trajectories is provided in Algorithm 1.

*Double Clipped Q Function.* As mentioned, each FQI iteration approximates the $Q$-value function using the previous estimates. As the process goes on, the sequence of these compounding approximations can degrade the overall performance of the algorithm. In particular, FQI suffers from overestimation bias, similarly to other value-based approaches that rely on taking the maximum of a noisy $Q$ function. To countermeasure this tendency, we adopt a modified version of Clipped Double Q-learning, introduced by [16], to penalize uncertainties over future states. This approach consists in maintaining two parallel functions $Q_N^{\{1,2\}}$

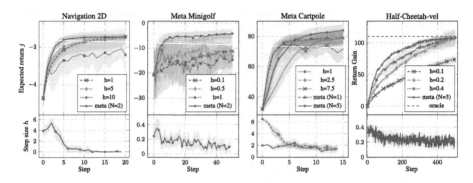

**Fig. 2.** FQI model performance against NGA with fixed step size $h$. The top plots show the expected returns or the return gain. The bottom plots show the meta actions chosen through learning iterations. $N$ represents the FQI iteration selected. (20 runs/random test contexts, avg $\pm$ 95 % c.i.)

for each iteration and choosing the action $h$ maximizing a convex combination of the minimum and the maximum between them:

$$l + \tilde{\gamma} \max_{h \in \mathcal{H}} \left[ \lambda \min_{j=1,2} Q^j \left( x', h \right) + (1 - \lambda) \max_{j=1,2} Q^j \left( x', h \right) \right],$$

with $\lambda > 0.5$. If we set $\lambda = 1$, the update corresponds to Clipped Double Q-learning. The minimum operator penalizes high variance estimates in regions of uncertainty and pushes the policy towards actions that lead to states already seen in the dataset.

The overall procedure introduces external hyperparameters,e.g. the number of decision trees, the minimum number of samples for a split (*min split*), and $\lambda$. However, the sensitivity on these parameters is minimal [18], as a different set of hyperparameters does not impact the ability of FQI to converge.

# 7 Experimental Evaluation

In this section, we show an empirical analysis of the performance of our approach in different environments. As we shall see, our agents are able to select the best step sizes and dynamically adapt them to fine-tune the learning procedure. As FQI iterations proceed, new estimation errors are gradually introduced, resulting in overfitting the model (with the *target loss* minimized on the training dataset), and consequently in degradation of out-of-sample performances over time. This is due to the error propagation w.r.t. the optimal $Q$−value function in the whole state-action space (and task space, in our case), as in [13]. As a consequence, the model iterations are evaluated in a validation process, as in the standard model selection procedure, on a set of out-of-sample tasks and policies. From this set, the number of iterations $N$ whose model obtains the best mean return is selected. The results of the selected models are shown in Fig. 2, along with NGA (with a fixed step size), tested on the same 20 trials (i.e., on the same random test tasks and initial policies), and performed with the same batch size for each trial. Our code is based upon OpenAI Gym [9] and Baselines [10] toolkits.

*Navigation2d:* For our first evaluation of the approach, we consider one of the environments presented in [15], called Navigation2D. This environment consists of a unit square space in which an agent aims to reach a random goal in the plane. The distribution of the tasks implemented is such that, at each episode, a different goal point is uniformly selected in the unit square. As we can note in the left plots of Fig. 2, the algorithm can select large step sizes with a good starting return gain without suffering from any drop. The algorithm can calibrate its action, starting with larger improvements and slowing down once the policy gets good results. In addition, all trajectories reach convergence in fewer steps than any other method.

*Minigolf:* In our second experiment, inspired by [39,54], we consider the scenario of a flat minigolf green, in which the agent has to hit the ball with a putter and place the ball inside the hole in the minimum number of strokes. The CMDP is built by varying the putter length and the friction coefficient. The environment is Lipschitz w.r.t. the context, but it is the only framework where the reward is non-Lipschitz, since for each step it can be either 0 if the shot is a success, -1 if the ball does not reach the goal (and the episode continues) or -100 for overshooting. The central plot in Fig. 2 illustrates the performance of our approach in the same set of random test tasks. We can see that the algorithm can consistently reach the optimal values by choosing an adaptive step size. In addition, the convergence to the global optimum is achieved in around 10 meta steps of training, a substantial improvement w.r.t. the choice of a fixed learning rate, which leads (when it converges) to a local minimum, meaning constantly undershooting until the end of the episode.

*CartPole:* For our third experiment, we examine the CartPole balancing task [5], which consists of a pole attached to a cart, where the agent has to move to balance the pole as long as possible. The CMDP is induced by varying the pole mass and length. To be more focused on the very first steps, and to better generalize on the overall policy and task space, the training dataset was built considering trajectories with only 15 total gradient updates. To have a fair comparison, the right plots of Fig. 2 illustrate an evaluation of the approach in the selected environment, where we have tested the resulting FQI model (and NGA with fixed step sizes) performing the same number of total updates as the training trajectories.[4] In the supplementary materials, we provide further results, where the models are tested for a longer horizon $T = 60$ and show the results closer to convergence. Differently from before, it is possible to see that the best model (blue solid line) is choosing to update the policy with small learning rates: this leads to a lower immediate return gain (high rates have a better learning curve in the first steps) but allows to improve the overall meta return. This is because the model is planning with a horizon of $N = 5$ policy updates. Indeed,

---

[4] Being an alteration of the classic Cartpole, standard results cannot be compared.

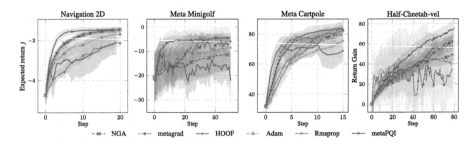

**Fig. 3.** FQI performance comparison against benchmarks (20 runs, 95% c.i.).

we included also the results of the first FQI iteration, which tries to optimize the immediate gain. As expected, the agent selects high step sizes for the first iterations, obtaining high immediate rewards only in the first learning steps.

*Half-Cheetah with Goal Velocity:* As a last environment, we considered the half-cheetah locomotion problem introduced in [15] with MuJoCo simulator [55], where a planar cheetah has to learn to run with a specific goal velocity. This is the most complex environment among the ones presented as the policy, albeit linear, is composed of 108 parameters. From the rightmost plot of Fig. 2 we can see the performance gain $j(\boldsymbol{\theta}_t) - j(\boldsymbol{\theta}_0)$.[5] The FQI model, trained with NGA trajectories with $T = 500$ total updates, is learning faster than benchmarks. The interesting fact is that the meta actions chosen by the model are within the range [0.2, 0.4], while the curves obtained with a fixed learning rate within those values are not able to obtain the same return gains. In the figure, we provide also the *oracle* value, as provided in [15].

*Benchmark Comparison.* In Fig. 2 we compared our approach with the choice of a fixed step size. There are, of course, many different schedules and optimization algorithms for the choice of the learning rate, and among the most widely adopted there are RMSprop and Adam [27]. The former considers an adaptive learning rate by introducing a momentum term and normalizing the step direction through a moving average of the square gradient. Adam, instead, takes also advantage of the exponentially decaying average of the second moments of the gradients. We compared our results (*metaFQI*) against tuned implementations of the mentioned update rules, and against the best fixed stepsize (*NGA*). Moreover, we include in the comparison also two other benchmarks for learning rate adaptation: *HOOF,* [38] and *metagrad,* [59], which have been implemented to optimize the stepsize for NGA (more details in the yy material). the results are shown in Fig. 3, in the same settings as the ones provided in Sect. 7. The only difference, for reasons of computational times, is the horizon of the Half-Cheetah environment, reduced to $T = 80$. We see that our approach outperforms the previous methods, showing improved learning with, in general, lower variance in

---

[5] The expected return changes deeply w.r.t. the task $\boldsymbol{\omega}$, hence the learning curves as in the other plots in Fig. 2 show very high variance, independently from the robustness of the models.

the returns obtained. Moreover, all the considered benchmarks heavily rely on the initial stepsize chosen and on the outer meta-hyperparameters, which deeply affect the learning capabilities.

# 8    Discussion, Limitations and Future Work

In this paper, we considered the problem of hyperparameter tuning for policy gradient-based algorithms in Contextual Markov Decision Processes, where heterogeneous contexts may require different solutions. In particular, we modeled the general problem through the meta-MDP definition, for which any policy-based update rule can be optimized using learning as reward. We analyzed the case of Lipschitz meta-MDPs, deriving some general guarantees that hold if the model is smooth with respect to the parameterization of the context and the transition processes. Finally, we implemented the Fitted Q-Iteration algorithm on the meta-MDP where the update rule is the Natural Gradient Ascent, and we used it to choose an adaptive step size through the learning process. The approach has been evaluated in different settings, where we observed good generalization capabilities of the model, which can reach fast convergence speed and robustness without the need for manual hyperparameter tuning.

Many challenges can be addressed in future work for this approach to be effective in real-life applications. More complex environments can be considered, and we can extend this method to different update rules and hyperparameters. One direct extension of our approach can be applied to the choice of the max Kullback-Leibler divergence constraints in Trust-Region-based approaches [46,47]: some results in this direction can already be observed in [34]. Moreover, the main limitation of our current approach is the same as for many hyperparameter tuning approaches: the computational time required to build the training dataset. One possible way to improve the sample efficiency might consist in evaluating the meta-reward by means of importance sampling, as in [38]. In realistic settings, where deep policies are required, the inclusion of all policy parameters in the meta-state might be inefficient; a solution might consist in compressing the representation of the policy through VAE or through the choice of specific informative meta-features: in this way, our approach would be independent on the policy architecture and scalable for large domains.

**Acknowledgments.** This paper is supported by FAIR (Future Artificial Intelligence Research) project, funded by the NextGenerationEU program within the PNRR-PE-AI scheme (M4C2, Investment 1.3, Line on Artificial Intelligence).

**Ethical Statement.** Hyperparameter selection for policy-based algorithms has a significant impact on the ability to learn a highly performing policy in RL, especially with heterogeneous tasks, where different contexts may require different solutions. Our approach shows that it is possible to learn an automatic selection of the best configurations that can be identified after a manual fine-tuning of the parameters. Consequently, our work can be seen as a further step in the AutoML direction, in which a practitioner could run the algorithm and, with some guidance, obtain optimal performance in just a few steps without the need for manual fine-tuning. Beyond this, we are not aware of any societal consequences of our work, such as welfare, fairness, or privacy.

# References

1. Adriaensen, S., et al.: Automated dynamic algorithm configuration. J. Artif. Intell. Res. **75**, 1633–1699 (2022)
2. Agarwal, A., Kakade, S.M., Lee, J.D., Mahajan, G.: On the theory of policy gradient methods: optimality, approximation, and distribution shift. J. Mach. Learn. Res. **22**(1), 4431–4506 (2021)
3. Andrychowicz, M., et al.: Learning to learn by gradient descent by gradient descent. In: Advances in Neural Information Processing Systems, pp. 3981–3989 (2016)
4. Åström, K.J.: Optimal control of Markov processes with incomplete state information. J. Math. Anal. Appl. **10**(1), 174–205 (1965)
5. Barto, A.G., Sutton, R.S., Anderson, C.W.: Neuronlike adaptive elements that can solve difficult learning control problems, pp. 81–93. IEEE Press (1990)
6. Bergstra, J., Bengio, Y.: Random search for hyper-parameter optimization. J. Mach. Learn. Res. **13**(2) (2012)
7. Bhandari, J., Russo, D.: Global optimality guarantees for policy gradient methods. arXiv preprint arXiv:1906.01786 (2019)
8. Biedenkapp, A., Bozkurt, H.F., Eimer, T., Hutter, F., Lindauer, M.: Dynamic algorithm configuration: foundation of a new meta-algorithmic framework. In: ECAI 2020, pp. 427–434. IOS Press (2020)
9. Brockman, G., et al.: Openai gym. arXiv preprint arXiv:1606.01540 (2016)
10. Dhariwal, P., et al.: Openai baselines. https://github.com/openai/baselines (2017)
11. Eiben, A.E., Horvath, M., Kowalczyk, W., Schut, M.C.: Reinforcement learning for online control of evolutionary algorithms. In: Brueckner, S.A., Hassas, S., Jelasity, M., Yamins, D. (eds.) ESOA 2006. LNCS (LNAI), vol. 4335, pp. 151–160. Springer, Heidelberg (2007). https://doi.org/10.1007/978-3-540-69868-5_10
12. Ernst, D., Geurts, P., Wehenkel, L.: Tree-based batch mode reinforcement learning. J. Mach. Learn. Res. **6**(Apr), 503–556 (2005)
13. Farahmand, A.M., Munos, R., Szepesvári, C.: Error propagation for approximate policy and value iteration. In: Advances in Neural Information Processing Systems (2010)
14. Feurer, M., Springenberg, J., Hutter, F.: Initializing Bayesian hyperparameter optimization via meta-learning. In: Proceedings of the AAAI Conference on Artificial Intelligence,vol. 29 (2015)
15. Finn, C., Abbeel, P., Levine, S.: Model-agnostic meta-learning for fast adaptation of deep networks. In: International Conference on Machine Learning, pp. 1126–1135. PMLR (2017)
16. Fujimoto, S., Meger, D., Precup, D.: Off-policy deep reinforcement learning without exploration. In: International Conference on Machine Learning, pp. 2052–2062. PMLR (2019)
17. Garcia, F.M., Thomas, P.S.: A Meta-MDP approach to exploration for lifelong reinforcement learning. In: Proceedings of the 18th International Conference on Autonomous Agents and MultiAgent Systems, pp. 1976–1978 (2019)
18. Geurts, P., Ernst, D., Wehenkel, L.: Extremely randomized trees. Mach. Learn. **63**(1), 3–42 (2006)

19. Hallak, A., Di Castro, D., Mannor, S.: Contextual Markov decision processes. arXiv preprint arXiv:1502.02259 (2015)
20. Henderson, P., Romoff, J., Pineau, J.: Where did my optimum go? An empirical analysis of gradient descent optimization in policy gradient methods. arXiv preprint arXiv:1810.02525 (2018)
21. Hutter, F., Hoos, H.H., Leyton-Brown, K.: Sequential model-based optimization for general algorithm configuration. In: International Conference on Learning and Intelligent Optimization, pp. 507–523. Springer (2011). https://doi.org/10.1007/978-3-642-25566-3_40
22. Hutter, F., Kotthoff, L., Vanschoren, J. (eds.): Automated Machine Learning. TSSCML, Springer, Cham (2019). https://doi.org/10.1007/978-3-030-05318-5
23. Im, D.J., Savin, C., Cho, K.: Online hyperparameter optimization by real-time recurrent learning. arXiv preprint arXiv:2102.07813 (2021)
24. Jastrzebski, S., et al.: The break-even point on optimization trajectories of deep neural networks. arXiv preprint arXiv:2002.09572 (2020)
25. Jomaa, H.S., Grabocka, J., Schmidt-Thieme, L.: Hyp-RL: hyperparameter optimization by reinforcement learning. arXiv preprint arXiv:1906.11527 (2019)
26. Kakade, S.M.: A natural policy gradient. In: Advances in Neural Information Processing Systems, vol. 14 (2001)
27. Kingma, D.P., Ba, J.: Adam: a method for stochastic optimization. arXiv preprint arXiv:1412.6980 (2014)
28. Li, K., Malik, J.: Learning to optimize. arXiv preprint arXiv:1606.01885 (2016)
29. Li, L., Jamieson, K., DeSalvo, G., Rostamizadeh, A., Talwalkar, A.: Hyperband: a novel bandit-based approach to hyperparameter optimization. J. Mach. Learn. Res. 18(1), 6765–6816 (2017)
30. Lorraine, J., Vicol, P., Duvenaud, D.: Optimizing millions of hyperparameters by implicit differentiation. In: International Conference on Artificial Intelligence and Statistics, pp. 1540–1552. PMLR (2020)
31. Maclaurin, D., Duvenaud, D., Adams, R.: Gradient-based hyperparameter optimization through reversible learning. In: International Conference on Machine Learning, pp. 2113–2122. PMLR (2015)
32. Meier, F., Kappler, D., Schaal, S.: Online learning of a memory for learning rates. In: 2018 IEEE International Conference on Robotics and Automation (ICRA), pp. 2425–2432. IEEE (2018)
33. Nichol, A., Schulman, J.: Reptile: a scalable metalearning algorithm, 2(2) 1 (2018). arXiv preprint arXiv:1803.02999
34. Occorso, M., Sabbioni, L., Metelli, A.M., Restelli, M.: Trust region meta learning for policy optimization. In: Brazdil, P., van Rijn, J.N., Gouk, H., Mohr, F. (eds.) ECMLPKDD Workshop on Meta-Knowledge Transfer. Proceedings of Machine Learning Research, vol. 191, pp. 62–74. PMLR (2022). https://proceedings.mlr.press/v191/occorso22a.html
35. Paine, T.L., et al.: Hyperparameter selection for offline reinforcement learning. arXiv preprint arXiv:2007.09055 (2020)
36. Park, E., Oliva, J.B.: Meta-curvature. In: Wallach, H., Larochelle, H., Beygelzimer, A., d'Alché-Buc, F., Fox, E., Garnett, R. (eds.) Advances in Neural Information Processing Systems, vol. 32. Curran Associates, Inc. (2019). https://proceedings.neurips.cc/paper/2019/file/57c0531e13f40b91b3b0f1a30b529a1d-Paper.pdf
37. Parker-Holder, J., et al.: Automated reinforcement learning (AutoRL): a survey and open problems. J. Artif. Intell. Res. 74, 517–568 (2022)

38. Paul, S., Kurin, V., Whiteson, S.: Fast efficient hyperparameter tuning for policy gradient methods. In: Wallach, H., Larochelle, H., Beygelzimer, A., d'Alché-Buc, F., Fox, E., Garnett, R. (eds.) Advances in Neural Information Processing Systems, vol. 32. Curran Associates, Inc. (2019). https://proceedings.neurips.cc/paper/2019/file/743c41a921516b04afde48bb48e28ce6-Paper.pdf
39. Penner, A.R.: The physics of golf. Rep. Progress Phys. **66**(2), 131 (2002)
40. Pirotta, M., Restelli, M., Bascetta, L.: Policy gradient in Lipschitz Markov decision processes. Mach. Learn. **100**(2), 255–283 (2015)
41. Puterman, M.L.: Markov Decision Processes: Discrete Stochastic Dynamic Programming. John Wiley & Sons (2014)
42. Rachelson, E., Lagoudakis, M.G.: On the locality of action domination in sequential decision making. In: International Symposium on Artificial Intelligence and Mathematics, ISAIM 2010, Fort Lauderdale, Florida, USA, January 6–8, 2010 (2010)
43. Rakelly, K., Zhou, A., Finn, C., Levine, S., Quillen, D.: Efficient off-policy meta-reinforcement learning via probabilistic context variables. In: International Conference on Machine Learning, pp. 5331–5340. PMLR (2019)
44. Ravi, S., Larochelle, H.: Optimization as a model for few-shot learning. In: 5th International Conference on Learning Representations, ICLR 2017, Toulon, France, April 24–26, 2017, Conference Track Proceedings. OpenReview.net (2017). https://openreview.net/forum?id=rJY0-Kcll
45. Schmidhuber, J.: Evolutionary principles in self-referential learning, or on learning how to learn: the meta-meta-... hook. Ph.D. thesis, Technische Universität München (1987)
46. Schulman, J., Levine, S., Abbeel, P., Jordan, M.I., Moritz, P.: Trust region policy optimization. In: ICML, JMLR Workshop and Conference Proceedings, vol. 37, pp. 1889–1897. JMLR.org (2015)
47. Schulman, J., Wolski, F., Dhariwal, P., Radford, A., Klimov, O.: Proximal policy optimization algorithms. CoRR abs/1707.06347 (2017)
48. Sehgal, A., La, H., Louis, S., Nguyen, H.: Deep reinforcement learning using genetic algorithm for parameter optimization. In: 2019 Third IEEE International Conference on Robotic Computing (IRC), pp. 596–601. IEEE (2019)
49. Shala, G., Biedenkapp, A., Awad, N., Adriaensen, S., Lindauer, M., Hutter, F.: Learning step-size adaptation in CMA-ES. In: Parallel Problem Solving from Nature-PPSN XVI: 16th International Conference, PPSN 2020, Leiden, The Netherlands, September 5–9, 2020, Proceedings, Part I 16, pp. 691–706. Springer (2020). https://doi.org/10.1007/978-3-030-58112-1_48
50. Snoek, J., Larochelle, H., Adams, R.P.: Practical Bayesian optimization of machine learning algorithms. arXiv preprint arXiv:1206.2944 (2012)
51. Sutton, R.S., Barto, A.G.: Introduction to Reinforcement Learning, 1st edn. MIT Press, Cambridge, MA, USA (1998)
52. Sutton, R.S., McAllester, D., Sidngh, S., Mansour, Y.: Policy gradient methods for reinforcement learning with function approximation. In: Solla, S., Leen, T., Müller, K. (eds.) Advances in Neural Information Processing Systems, vol. 12. MIT Press (2000). https://proceedings.neurips.cc/paper/1999/file/464d828b85b0bed98e80ade0a5c43b0f-Paper.pdf
53. Tieleman, T., Hinton, G.: Divide the gradient by a running average of its recent magnitude. COURSERA: Neural Networks for Machine Learning. Technical Report (2017)
54. Tirinzoni, A., Salvini, M., Restelli, M.: Transfer of samples in policy search via multiple importance sampling. In: Proceedings of the 36th International Conference

on Machine Learning. Proceedings of Machine Learning Research, vol. 97, pp. 6264–6274. PMLR (2019)

55. Todorov, E., Erez, T., Tassa, Y.: MuJoCo: a physics engine for model-based control. In: 2012 IEEE/RSJ International Conference on Intelligent Robots and Systems, pp. 5026–5033. IEEE (2012)

56. Wang, L., Cai, Q., Yang, Z., Wang, Z.: Neural policy gradient methods: global optimality and rates of convergence. arXiv preprint arXiv:1909.01150 (2019)

57. Weerts, H.J., Mueller, A.C., Vanschoren, J.: Importance of tuning hyperparameters of machine learning algorithms. arXiv preprint arXiv:2007.07588 (2020)

58. Xu, C., Qin, T., Wang, G., Liu, T.Y.: Reinforcement learning for learning rate control. arXiv preprint arXiv:1705.11159 (2017)

59. Xu, Z., van Hasselt, H., Silver, D.: Meta-gradient reinforcement learning. arXiv preprint arXiv:1805.09801 (2018)

60. Zhu, Y., Hayashi, T., Ohsawa, Y.: Gradient descent optimization by reinforcement learning. In: The 33rd Annual Conference of the Japanese Society for Artificial Intelligence (2019)

61. Zoph, B., Le, Q.V.: Neural architecture search with reinforcement learning. In: 5th International Conference on Learning Representations, ICLR 2017, Toulon, France, April 24–26, 2017, Conference Track Proceedings. OpenReview.net (2017). https://openreview.net/forum?id=r1Ue8Hcxg

# Invariant Lipschitz Bandits: A Side Observation Approach

Nam Phuong Tran$^{(\boxtimes)}$ and Long Tran-Thanh

University of Warwick, Coventry, UK
{nam.p.tran,long.tran-thanh}@warwick.ac.uk

**Abstract.** Symmetry arises in many optimization and decision-making problems, and has attracted considerable attention from the optimization community: by utilizing the existence of such symmetries, the process of searching for optimal solutions can be improved significantly. Despite its success in offline settings, the utilization of symmetries has not been well examined within online optimization problems, especially in the bandit literature. As such, in this paper, we study the invariant Lipschitz bandit setting, a subclass of the Lipschitz bandits in which a group acts on the set of arms and preserves the reward function. We introduce an algorithm named `UniformMesh-N`, which naturally integrates side observations using group orbits into the uniform discretization algorithm [15]. Using the side-observation approach, we prove an improved regret upper bound, which depends on the cardinality of the group, given that the group is finite. We also prove a matching regret's lower bound for the invariant Lipschitz bandit class (up to logarithmic factors). We hope that our work will ignite further investigation of symmetry in bandit theory and sequential decision-making theory in general.

**Keywords:** Bandit Theory · Symmetry · Group Theory

## 1 Introduction

Stochastic Multi-Armed Bandit (MAB) is a typical model of a sequential decision-making problem under uncertainty. The main challenge of these decision-making problems is uncertainty. That is, the outcome of a decision is only revealed after the decision is made with the possible presence of noise. Therefore, to achieve a high total reward, the agent (or the decision maker) must collect information along with trials and errors (i.e., *exploring*), while using this information to choose a decision with a high expected reward (i.e., *exploiting*). The exploration-exploitation trade-off is the main problem that one usually faces in such decision-making problems. The performance of a bandit strategy is typically evaluated in terms of regret which is the difference between the total expected reward of the used strategy and that of the optimal strategy. Stochastic MAB has been extensively studied since, and have achieved great success, both theoretically and practically [13,30]. For textbook treatment of the subject, see, e.g., [17,29].

© The Author(s), under exclusive license to Springer Nature Switzerland AG 2023
D. Koutra et al. (Eds.): ECML PKDD 2023, LNAI 14172, pp. 524–539, 2023.
https://doi.org/10.1007/978-3-031-43421-1_31

Classical stochastic MAB models assume a finite set of arms and unstructured environment, that is, information of an arm gives no information of others. This assumption is rather simple and might not capture the intrinsic relations between the arms. An immediate consequence is that MAB problems with a large or even infinite set of arms are difficult or intractable to address without any further assumption. This leads to a significant body of literature studying structured MAB, including linear bandits [1], convex optimizations with bandit feedback [28], and Lipschitz bandits [9,16]. With these additional assumptions, algorithms can be designed to exploit the underlying structures to achieve significantly smaller regret, compared to that of algorithms that are oblivious to these structures.

In addition to the abovementioned structures on the set of arms, many decision-making and optimization problems exhibit symmetry, that is, the expected reward function and the set of arms are invariant under certain group of transformations. For example, an important real-world application of continuous bandits, which naturally inherit symmetry, can be found in the context of online matrix factorization bandits [18]. The online matrix factorization bandit problem, in turn, has important machine learning applications, such as in interactive recommendation systems [14,33,34], or the online dictionary learning problem [20,21]. Briefly speaking, in recommender systems the matrix factorization method aims to decompose the user-item rating matrix $R$ into a product of small matrices, that is, $R = HW^\top$, where $H$ is the user-feature matrix and $W$ is the item-feature matrix. The goal is to find a pair $(H, W)$ such that the matrix $R$ can be recovered. Now, for any orthogonal matrix $\phi$ of the feature space, it can be easily seen that if any pair $(H, W)$ can recover matrix $R$, the pair $(H\phi, W\phi)$ can also recover matrix $R$. Therefore, this problem is invariant with respect to the action of the group of orthogonal matrices. In fact, as observed in [18], the appearance of symmetry in matrix factorization gives rise to infinitely many saddle points in the optimization landscape, causing a great challenge for an optimization algorithm that is oblivious to the existence of symmetry. We discuss matrix-factorization bandit and the implications of our result on this problem in the Appendix[1] as it might be of independent interest.

Another motivating example of symmetry in bandit settings is the online job-machine allocation problem with identical machines. In this problem, if the allocation is swapped among these identical machines, the total performance remains unchanged, and hence the problem is permutation-invariant. Intuitively, algorithms that are oblivious to this symmetry may waste time exploring many symmetric solutions, resulting in slower convergence.

While symmetry has not been investigated in the bandit literature, it has been studied extensively in the optimization domain, especially in Integer Linear Programming (ILP) [23]. In these problems, where the majority of algorithms are based on the branch-and-bound principle, the presence of symmetry causes an extremely waste of time in branching symmetric solutions, if it is not handled explicitly. The reason for this is that as symmetric solutions yield the same objective function, they cannot be pruned by the bounding principle. Therefore, the

---

[1] Appendix is available in the full version [31].

presence of symmetry causes great difficulty for existing combinatorial optimization algorithms that are oblivious to symmetry. As such, various approaches have been proposed to deal with existing symmetry in the model, including adding symmetry-breaking constraints or pruning symmetric nodes during the branch-and-bound process.

Despite its ubiquity in optimization problems, to date symmetry has not been extensively studied in bandit problems, which can be considered as the online counterpart of many optimization settings. Note that for unstructured $K$-armed bandit problems, if we assume a group $\mathcal{G}$ acts freely on the set of arms and the reward function is invariant under the action of $\mathcal{G}$, then we can compute the fundamental domain (i.e., a subset of arms whose orbit covers the original set) and restrict the bandit algorithm on the subset. As there are exactly $K/|\mathcal{G}|$ disjoint orbits, the regret of standard algorithms such as UCB1 [5] scales as $\tilde{\mathcal{O}}\left(\sqrt{\frac{Kn}{|\mathcal{G}|}}\right)$ where $n$ is the total number of rounds. Therefore, one could expect that the same improvement can be easily achieved in the case of other bandit settings. However, as we shall point out in detail in Subsect. 2.3, the same reasoning applied to the invariant $K$-armed bandits is not feasible in the case of Lipschitz bandits. This is due to two main reasons: (i) As the set of arms we consider is a dense subset of $\mathbb{R}^d$, simply counting disjoint orbits to show the reduction in cardinality of the fundamental domain is not feasible; (ii) The subgroup of Euclidean isometries we consider in this paper may admit uncountably infinite fixed points. Therefore, it is not trivial that the combination of symmetry with other structures such as Lipschitz continuity might help algorithms achieve better regret.

Now, in theory, if a Lipschitz bandit problem has the expected reward function to be invariant under the action of a finite group $\mathcal{G}$ of Euclidean isometries, one naive approach to exploit symmetry is to construct the fundamental domain and sample within the domain. However, sampling in the fundamental domain is computationally impractical, as we shall point out in detail in Sect. 2.3. Briefly, constructing a fundamental domain requires placing global inequalities on the original set of arms, and the problem of finding value for an arm that satisfies all global constraints is known as a NP-complete problem [8].

Against this background, we ask the question whether we can design an efficient bandit algorithm to tackle the Invariant Lipschitz Bandit (ILB) problem without the need of constructing the fundamental domain (to avoid facing the computationally expensive task of sampling from that domain). In particular, we ask that whether utilizing invariance can result in tighter regret bounds, if the only assumption of the model is that the set of arms is equipped with a distance, and the expected reward is Lipschitz continuous w.r.t. the set of arms.

## 1.1   Our Contributions

The contribution of this paper can be summarized as follows.

1. We introduce a new model for ILB problems, where the reward and the set of arms are invariant under a known finite group of transformations.

2. We introduce an algorithm, named UniformMesh-N, which naturally integrates side observations using group orbits into the uniform discretization algorithm.
3. We provide a regret analysis for the algorithm which shows an improvement in regret by a factor depending on the cardinality of the group. In particular, we show that if the number of rounds $n$ is large enough, the regret of UniformMesh-N algorithm is at most $\tilde{\mathcal{O}}\left(\left(\frac{1}{|\mathcal{G}|}\right)^{\frac{1}{d+2}} n^{\frac{d+1}{d+2}}\right)$, where $\mathcal{G}$ is the transformation group and $\tilde{\mathcal{O}}$ only hides logarithmic factor.
4. We provide a new lower bound for this bandit class, that is $\Omega\left(\left(\frac{1}{|\mathcal{G}|}\right)^{\frac{1}{d+2}} n^{\frac{d+1}{d+2}}\right)$, given $n$ is large enough. This lower bound essentially matches the upper bound of the algorithm up to a logarithimic factor.

Among these, our most important contribution is the regret analysis, which we proved a strict improvement of leveraging symmetry in designing algorithm. Note that, in supervised learning where symmetry is widely studied, while many empirical work showed that empirical work shows that integrating symmetry into learning can help reduce the generalization error, from a theoretical perspective, proving strict improvement when using symmetry is known as a challenging problem within the machine learning community [7,12,27]. To our knowledge, our analysis is novel and this paper is the first to show a strict improvement of using symmetry in the sequential decision-making context.

## 1.2   Related Works

Lipschitz MAB problem is referred to as continuum-armed bandit problems in early works [2,6,15], where the set of arms is the interval $[0,1]$. Within this context, [15] proposed a simple uniform discretization-based algorithm, which is later referred to as UniformMesh algorithm. Despite its simplicity, [15] showed that with the global Lipschitz continuous reward function, the UniformMesh algorithm achieves $\tilde{\mathcal{O}}(n^{2/3})$ regret, which essentially matches the minimax lower bound up to a logarithmic factor. However, uniform discretization is potentially wasteful as it keeps the approximation uniformly good over the whole space, while it is probably better to adapt the approximation so that the approximation is more precise around the maxima while being more loose in the rest of the space. With this in mind, [16] and [9] proposed adaptive discretization algorithms, which are referred to as Zooming algorithm and HOO algorithm, respectively. These adaptive discretization algorithms achieve better regret when dealing with benign instances, while not being deteriorated in the worst case. In particular, [9,16] showed that the regret of these algorithms is at most $\tilde{\mathcal{O}}(n^{\frac{d'+1}{d'+2}})$, where $d'$ is *near-optimal dimension* and is upper-bounded by *covering dimension*. Our algorithm is based on UniformMesh algorithm together with side observation. The rationale behind this choice is that UniformMesh fixes the set of played points and hence can easily combine with the group orbit to create a fixed undirected graph, which cannot be done if the set of played points (i.e., the set of vertices) varies every round. The combination of group orbit with adaptively discretizing algorithms such as HOO or Zooming algorithms may require a more complicated treatment and is left for future work.

Side-observation feedback was first introduced in the adversarial MAB context [22], and has been further studied by various authors [3,4,11]. Especially, the minimax lower bound as in [22] is $\Omega\left(\sqrt{\alpha n}\right)$, where $\alpha$ is the independent number of the graph. The first work that examines side observations in a stochastic MAB setting is [10], in which the observation graph is undirected and fixed over time. The authors introduced a naive algorithm named UCB-N, which chooses an arm $x$ that maximizes the index UCB, then observes all the rewards in the neighborhood of $x$. [10] proved the gap-dependent regret bound depends is at most $\mathcal{O}\left(\log(n)\sum_{C\in\mathcal{C}}\frac{\max_{x\in C}\Delta_x}{\min_{x\in C}\Delta_x^2}\right)$, where $\mathcal{C}$ is a clique covering of the graph and $\Delta_x$ is the subopitimality gap of arm $x$. More recently, [19] provided an alternative analysis to achieve a tighter regret for UCB-N, $\tilde{\mathcal{O}}\left(\log n\sum_{x\in\mathcal{I}}\frac{1}{\Delta_x}\right)$, where $\mathcal{I}$ is an independent set of $G$. From this, they also derived a minimax upper bound as $\tilde{\mathcal{O}}\left(\sqrt{\alpha n}\right)$. Similarly, [11] an algorithm based on arm elimination that achieves gap-dependent regret as $\mathcal{O}\left(\log n\sum_{x\in\mathcal{I}}\frac{1}{\Delta_x}\right)$, and minimax regret as $\tilde{\mathcal{O}}\left(\sqrt{\alpha n}\right)$. Our algorithm UniformMesh-N is based on UCB-N algorithm, and our analysis technique is similar to [10]. The reason for this choice is that the graph induced by group action is highly "regular", namely, the covering number of this graph is dependent on the covering number of the fundamental domain. Therefore, the result of [10] is sufficient to introduce the cardinality of the group into the regret.

Symmetry has been studied for decades in the literature of (Mixed) Integer Linear Programming in the case of subgroups of the group of permutation matrices [23]. There are two main approaches to dealing with symmetry; the main idea is to eliminate symmetric solutions to reduce search space. The first approach is to add symmetry-breaking constraints to the domain, making symmetric solutions infeasible [32]. The second approach is to incorporate symmetry information during the tree search procedure (e.g., branch and bound) to prune symmetric branches, for example, isomorphism pruning [24], orbital branching [25]. The concern of these works is to ensure that at least one of the optimal solutions remains feasible. However, these works did not compare the convergence rate of these algorithms, which uses symmetry information, with algorithms that are oblivious to symmetry information. In contrast, we analyze the convergence rate of the algorithm in terms of regret and are able to show an improvement of the algorithm which incorporates the group information. Although the simple mechanism of uniform discretization allows us to provide the regret bound, integrating group information with tree-based algorithms (e.g., isomorphism pruning [24] or orbital branching [25]) is an interesting research direction and is left for future work.

## 1.3   Outline

The rest of this paper is organized as follows. Notations and some important properties of subgroup Euclidean isometries are provided in Sect. 2, followed by the mathematical formulation of the ILB problem. In Sect. 3 we formalize the construction of the graph induced by the group action; then the `UniformMesh-N` algorithm is introduced, followed by its regret analysis. In Sect. 4, a regret lower bound for the ILB problem is provided. The limit of this paper and further work are discussed in Sect. 5. Due to the space limit, we defer the most of the proofs to the Appendix, as well as the more detailed description of our algorithm, and the application of our results to the matrix factorization bandit problem.

## 2  Preliminary and Problem Setup

### 2.1  Preliminary

Let $\mathcal{X}$ be a compact and convex subset of a $d$-dimensional Euclidean space $E^d$; denote $\mathcal{D}$ as Euclidean distance. For any $x \in \mathcal{X}$ and $\delta > 0$, define a $\delta$-open ball as $\mathcal{B}(x, \delta) = \{x' \in \mathcal{X} \mid \mathcal{D}(x, x') < \delta\}$.

*Packing and Covering Properties.* Consider $\delta > 0$, $S \subseteq \mathcal{X}$, and a finite subset $K \subset \mathcal{X}$. $K$ is called a $\delta$-*packing* of $S$ if and only if $K \subset S$ and $\mathcal{D}(i, j) > \delta$ for any two distinct points $i, j \in K$. $K$ is called a $\delta$-*covering* of $S$ if and only if for any $x \in S$, there is $i \in K$ such that $\mathcal{D}(i, x) < \delta$. $K$ is called $\delta$-*net* of $S$ if and only if $K$ is both a $\delta$-covering and $\delta$-packing of $S$. $K$ is called a *strictly $\delta$-packing* of $S$ if and only if $K$ is an $\delta$-packing of $S$ and $\mathcal{D}(i, \partial S) > \delta, \forall i \in K$, where $\partial S$ is the topological boundary of $S$ in $E^d$. The $\delta$-*packing number* $N^{\mathrm{pack}}(S, \mathcal{D}, \delta)$ of $S \subseteq \mathcal{X}$ with respect to the metric $\mathcal{D}$ is the largest integer $k$ such that there exists a $\delta$-packing of $S$ whose cardinality is $k$. The $\delta$-*covering number* $N^{\mathrm{cov}}(S, \mathcal{D}, \delta)$ of $S \subseteq \mathcal{X}$ with respect to the metric $\mathcal{D}$ is the smallest integer $k$ such that there exists a $\delta$-covering of $S$ whose cardinality is $k$. By the definitions of packing and covering number, if $K$ is a $\delta$-net of $S$, then $N^{\mathrm{cov}}(S, \mathcal{D}, \delta) \leq |K| \leq N^{\mathrm{pack}}(S, \mathcal{D}, \delta)$. Moreover, we can bound the packing and covering numbers of a compact set as follows.

**Proposition 1** ([35]). *Let $\mathcal{B}$ be the unit ball and $S$ be a compact subset of $E^d$. Then, for any $\delta > 0$, we have*

$$\left(\frac{1}{\delta}\right)^d \frac{\mathrm{Vol}(S)}{\mathrm{Vol}(\mathcal{B})} \leq N^{\mathrm{cov}}(S, \mathcal{D}, \delta) \leq N^{\mathrm{pack}}(S, \mathcal{D}, \delta) \leq \left(\frac{3}{\delta}\right)^d \frac{\mathrm{Vol}(S)}{\mathrm{Vol}(\mathcal{B})}.$$

*Euclidean Isometries.* A bijection mapping $\phi : E^d \to E^d$ is a *Euclidean isometry* if and only if it preserves the Euclidean distance, that is, $\mathcal{D}(\phi(x), \phi(x')) = \mathcal{D}(x, x')$. The symmetry group of $\mathcal{X}$, denoted as $\mathrm{Sym}(\mathcal{X})$, is the set of all Euclidean isometries that preserve $\mathcal{X}$, that is,

$$\mathrm{Sym}(\mathcal{X}) = \{\phi : E^d \to E^d \mid \phi \text{ is a Euclidean isometry and } \phi(\mathcal{X}) = \mathcal{X}\}.$$

For any group element $\phi \in \mathrm{Sym}(\mathcal{X})$, denote $\phi(x)$ as $\phi \cdot x$. Let $\mathcal{G}$ be a finite subgroup of $\mathrm{Sym}(\mathcal{X})$, we write $\mathcal{G} \leq \mathrm{Sym}(\mathcal{X})$, where $\leq$ denotes the subgroup relation. Denote the stabilizer of $x$ in $\mathcal{G}$ as $\mathcal{G}_x = \{g \in \mathcal{G} \mid g \cdot x = x\}$. Denote the $\mathcal{G}$-orbit of $x$ as $\mathcal{G} \cdot x = \{g \cdot x \mid g \in \mathcal{G}\}$ and the $\mathcal{G}$-orbit of a subset $S$ as $\mathcal{G} \cdot S = \{g \cdot x \mid g \in \mathcal{G}, x \in S\}$. As stated in [26], any finite group of isometries of Euclidean space must admit a point $x \in E^d$ whose stabilizer $\mathcal{G}_x$ is trivial.

For a subset $S \subset E^d$, denote the closure of $S$ in $E^d$ as $\overline{S}$. Note that since $\mathcal{X}$ is compact and then closed in $E^d$, the closure of $S$ in $\mathcal{X}$ is equivalent to the closure of $S$ in $E^d$. Next, we state the definition of the fundamental domain, an important notion that we use throughout the paper, especially in the regret analysis.

**Definition 1 (Fundamental domain).** *A subset* $\mathbf{F} \subset E^d$ *is a fundamental domain for a finite group* $\mathcal{G}$ *of isometries of a Euclidean space* $E^d$ *if and only if (1) the set* $\mathbf{F}$ *is open in* $E^d$; *(2) the members of the set* $\{g \cdot \mathbf{F} \mid g \in \mathcal{G}\}$ *are mutually disjoint; (3)* $E^d = \bigcup_{g \in \mathcal{G}} g \cdot \overline{\mathbf{F}}$; *(4)* $\mathbf{F}$ *is connected.*

Consider a finite subgroup $\mathcal{G}$ of isometries of $E^d$, we can explicitly construct a fundamental domain for $\mathcal{G}$. Recall that $\mathcal{G}$ admits a point $x^o \in E^d$ whose stabilizer $\mathcal{G}_{x^o}$ is trivial. As in [26], a fundamental domain can be constructed as follows.

**Definition 2 (Dirichlet domain).** *Let* $x^o$ *be a point in* $E^d$ *such that* $\mathcal{G}_{x^o}$ *is trivial. For each* $g \in \mathcal{G}$, *define an open half-space as*

$$H_g(x^o) = \{x \in E^d \mid \mathcal{D}(x, x^o) < \mathcal{D}(x, g \cdot x^o)\}. \tag{1}$$

*A Dirichlet domain is the intersection of those open half-spaces, particularly*

$$\mathbf{F} = \bigcap_{g \in \mathcal{G}} H_g(x^o). \tag{2}$$

As shown in [26], a Dirichlet domain is indeed a fundamental domain. Note that since the boundary of $\mathbf{F}$ is a subset of a finite union of some $(d-1)$-dimensional hyperplanes, it has volume zero.

Given Dirichlet domain $\mathbf{F}$ of $\mathcal{G}$ in $E^d$. Define $\mathbf{D} = \mathbf{F} \cap \mathcal{X}$. Now, we show that $\mathbf{D}$ is also a fundamental domain for $\mathcal{G}$ acting in $\mathcal{X}$.

**Proposition 2.** $\mathbf{D}$ *is a fundamental domain for* $\mathcal{G}$ *acting in* $\mathcal{X}$. *In particular, (i)* $\mathbf{D}$ *is open in* $\mathcal{X}$; *(ii) the members of* $\{g \cdot \mathbf{D}\}_{g \in \mathcal{G}}$ *are mutually disjoint; (iii)* $\mathbf{D}$ *is connected; (iv)* $\mathcal{X} = \bigcup_{g \in \mathcal{G}} g \cdot \overline{\mathbf{D}}$.

The Proof of Proposition 2 is deferred to the Appendix.

## 2.2   Problem Formulation

For any $k \in \mathbb{N}^+ \setminus \{1\}$, denote $[k]$ as $\{1, ..., k\}$. Denote the number of rounds as $n$, which is assumed to be known in advance. Each round $t \in [n]$, the agent chooses an arm $X_t \in \mathcal{X}$, then the nature returns a bounded stochastic reward that is sampled independently from an unknown distribution $Y_t \sim \mathbb{P}_{X_t}$. Define the expected reward function as $f(x) := \mathbb{E}[Y_t \mid X_t = x]$. Assume that $\mathbb{P}_x$ has support in $[0, 1]$ for all $x \in \mathcal{X}$. A bandit strategy is a decision rule for choosing an arm $X_t$ in round $t \in [n]$, given past observations up to round $t-1$. Formally, a bandit strategy is a mapping $\mathcal{A} : (\mathcal{X} \times [0, 1])^n \to \mathcal{P}(\mathcal{X})$, where $\mathcal{P}(\mathcal{X})$ is the set of probability measures over the set of arms $\mathcal{X}$. A bandit strategy is deterministic if $\mathcal{P}(\mathcal{X})$ is the set of Dirac probability measures.

Let $x^*$ be an optimal arm, associated with the optimal mean reward $f^* = f(x^*)$. In each round $t \in [n]$, the agent chooses an arm $X_t$ and incurs an immediate regret $f^* - f(X_t)$. The agent's goal is to minimize the regret over $n$, defined as

$$\mathbf{R}_n = \mathbb{E} \left[ \sum_{t=1}^n f^* - f(X_t) \right]. \tag{3}$$

Here, the expectation is taken over all random sources, including both the randomness in the rewards and the bandit strategy used by the agent. Next, we state the assumptions on the expected reward function that defines the ILB problems.

**Assumption 1 (Lipschitz continuity).** *For all $x, x' \in \mathcal{X}$, $\mathcal{D}(x, x') \geq |f(x) - f(x')|$.*

**Assumption 2 (Invariant expected reward function).** *Given a finite subgroup $\mathcal{G} \leq \mathrm{Sym}(\mathcal{X})$, the expected reward function $f$ is invariant under the group action of $\mathcal{G}$, that is, for all $g \in \mathcal{G}$, $f(x) = f(g \cdot x)$. Assume that $\mathcal{G}$ is revealed to the agent in advance.*

Note that while Lipschitz continuity Assumption 1 is the standard assumption that defines the class of Lipschitz bandits [16], the invariance Assumption 2 is new in the bandit's literature. As the agent knows $\mathcal{G}$ in advance, he can benefit from the information to learn the near-optimal arms more quickly.

### 2.3  A Warm-Up: Invariant Finite Unstructured MAB

*Invariant Unstructured K-Armed Bandit.* As a warm-up, consider the case of an invariant $K$-armed bandit with unstructured environment. The problem is almost the same as the problem described in Subsect. 2.2, however, there are only $K$ arms, and Lipschitz continuity (Assumption 1) is dropped. Now, assume that the group $\mathcal{G}$ acts freely on $[K]$, denote the quotient space as $[K]/\mathcal{G}$. As each orbit contains exactly $|\mathcal{G}|$ arms and these orbits are disjoint, it is obvious that the number of disjoint orbits $|[K]/\mathcal{G}|$ is $K/|\mathcal{G}|$.

For each element $q$ in the quotient space $[K]/\mathcal{G}$, denote the orbit $[K]_q \subset [K]$ as the orbit corresponding to $q$, and denote $k_q$ as the orbit representation of $[K]_q$. We have that the fundamental domain $\bigcup_{q \in [K]/\mathcal{G}} k_q$ must contain the optimal arm, and its cardinality is $K/\mathcal{G}$. Now, if we apply the standard MAB algorithm such as UCB1 [5] to the fundamental domain and ignore other arms, we can obtain the regret $\tilde{O} \left( \sqrt{\frac{Kn}{|\mathcal{G}|}} \right)$.

*Difficulties of Invariant Lipschitz Bandit.* The simplicity of the above result for invariant unstructured MAB is based on partitioning the set of arms into disjoint orbits, which in turn is based on two important assumptions that are not feasible in the case of the invariant and continuous Lipschitz bandit. First, as the set of arms $\mathcal{X}$ is a uncountable set, simply counting the cardinality of the quotient set $\mathcal{X}/\mathcal{G}$ to show the number of disjoint orbits as in the case of $K$-armed bandit is not possible. Second, as groups of Euclidean isometries might admit (uncountably infinite) fixed points (points which are fixed by all group elements) and non-effective point (points which are fixed by some group elements that are not identity). Therefore, applying group action on some points in $\mathcal{X}$ may result in the same points, or obtaining orbits whose points stay arbitrarily close to each other. In this case, the orbit of these nearly fixed points in the mesh might not produce useful information (e.g., see the Appendix).

A naive way to exploit symmetry in the ILB setting is to construct the Dirichlet domain and sampling within this subset. To show the reduction in terms of regret, proving that the covering number of the fundamental domain is $\mathcal{O}\left(\frac{\delta^{-d}}{|\mathcal{G}|}\right)$ as a direct consequence of our Lemma 1 is sufficient. However, as we mentioned in the introduction, sampling within the fundamental domain is computationally impractical. In particular, construction of the Dirichlet fundamental domain in the Lipschitz bandit case is equivalent to placing global inequality constraints on the set of arms as the construction in Definition 2. Given that verifying that a value of $x$ satisfies all $|\mathcal{G}|$ linear inequality constraints takes $|\mathcal{G}|d^2$ operation, [8] showed that the problem of finding a point $x \in \mathcal{X}$ that satisfies the global constraints is NP-complete, implying that sampling in the fundamental domain is computationally intractable. Against this background, we seek another approach that does not require sampling within the fundamental domain. Note that while in the rest of the paper we are not interested in the method of sampling within the fundamental domain, the geometric properties of the fundamental domain still play a crucial role in our analysis.

## 3    UniformMesh-N Algorithm and Regret Analysis

In this section, we first explain the construction of the graph induced by the group action of $\mathcal{G}$. According to this, UniformMesh-N algorithm is introduced, followed by its regret analysis.

### 3.1    Graph Structure Induced by the Group Action

We now explain how the group action can naturally induce a graph structure on the set of discretization points of $\mathcal{X}$. Intuitively, in round $t$, the agent chooses an arm $X_t$, and nature returns a reward $Y_t$, and the agent can then use the returned reward $Y_t$ to update the node along the orbit $(\mathcal{G} \cdot X_t)$. This is similar to the side-observation setting, where the nature returns not only a reward associating the chosen arm, but also the rewards of its neighbors in graph feedback. As a result, the orbit of $X_t$ can be treated as a neighborhood of $X_t$ in a graph formed by the group action. Moreover, it turns out that the graph's structure induced by the group action is highly regular, particularly its clique covering depends on the covering number of fundamental domain.

Given a number $\delta > 0$, let us denote $V$ as a $\delta$-net of $\mathcal{X}$. Given the Dirichlet domain $\mathbf{D}$ of $\mathcal{G}$ acting on $\mathcal{X}$, let $V_{\overline{\mathbf{D}}}$ denote a smallest subset of $V$ that covers $\overline{\mathbf{D}}$. By Proposition 1, it follows that $|V| = \Theta(\delta^{-d})$. We now compare the "size" of $\overline{\mathbf{D}}$ with $\mathcal{X}$ in terms of covering number as the follows.

**Lemma 1.** *For some numbers $c_1, c_2 > 0$, the cardinality of $V_{\overline{\mathbf{D}}}$ is bounded as*

$$|V_{\overline{\mathbf{D}}}| \leq \frac{c_1 \delta^{-d}}{|\mathcal{G}|} + c_2 \delta^{-(d-1)}. \tag{4}$$

*Moreover, there are constants $c_3, c_4 > 0$, such that for any $\delta : 0 < \delta < c_4/|\mathcal{G}|$, one has*

$$|V_{\overline{\mathbf{D}}}| \leq \frac{c_3 \delta^{-d}}{|\mathcal{G}|}. \tag{5}$$

Lemma 1 is in a similar vein as Lemma 1 in [27]. However, while [27] only proved for the permutation group, our Lemma 1 can be applied to any finite subgroup of $\mathrm{Sym}\,(\mathcal{X})$, and therefore the permutation group is treated as a special case. Thus, for our analysis is it essential to use Lemma 1 instead of the result from [27] (as our setting is more generic).

The generalization of Lemma 1 comes from a different technique that exploits the fact that the boundary of the Dirichlet domain has zero volume. The proof is deferred to the Appendix, but we provide the underlying idea of the proof here. First, we partition the set $V_{\overline{\mathbf{D}}}$ into two disjoint subsets. The first subset is points in $V_{\overline{\mathbf{D}}}$ lying "strictly" inside the fundamental domain (whose distance to the boundary greater than $\delta$), and the second subset is all points in $V_{\overline{\mathbf{D}}}$ lying near the boundary. Now, it is clear that the cardinality of the former is lesser than $|V|/|\mathcal{G}|$, since there are $|\mathcal{G}|$ disjoint images of $\mathbf{D}$ and we can always choose the image that contains the smallest number of points. The cardinality of the latter is derived from the fact that the volume of the area near the boundary shrinks as $\delta$ gets smaller; consequently, the packing number of this area is only bounded by $\mathcal{O}(\delta^{-(d-1)})$.

Lemma 1 implies that the covering number of the Dirichlet domain is proportional to $1/|\mathcal{G}|$ and can become significantly small when $|\mathcal{G}|$ is large. This is the key ingredient to the improvement in regret's bound. We give examples of some symmetry groups to highlight the importance and difficulty of Lemma 1 in the Appendix.

Before stating the definition of the graph, we first make an observation as follows.

**Proposition 3.** *Let $\mathcal{G}$ be a finite subgroup of $\mathrm{Sym}\,(\mathcal{X})$. For any $x, x' \in \mathcal{X}$ and a constant $\delta > 0$, if there is an action $g \in \mathcal{G}$ such that $\mathcal{D}(g \cdot x, x') < \delta$, then $\mathcal{D}(x, g^{-1} \cdot x') < \delta$.*

**Definition 3.** *Given a constant $\varepsilon > 0$, define the graph $G_\varepsilon = (V, E_\varepsilon)$, where $E_\varepsilon = \{(x, x') \mid x, x' \in V$ and $\exists g \in \mathcal{G}$ s.t. $\mathcal{D}(g \cdot x, x') < \varepsilon\}$.*

Note that as a result of Proposition 3, it follows that if $(x, x') \in E_\varepsilon$, then $(x', x) \in E_\varepsilon$. Therefore, $G_\varepsilon$ is an undirected graph.

**Definition 4.** *Given a constant $\varepsilon > 0$, a Neighborhood of Orbit $(\mathcal{G} \cdot x)$ in $V \subset \mathcal{X}$ with distance at most $\varepsilon$ is defined as*

$$\mathrm{N}(i, \varepsilon) = \{x \in V \mid \exists g \in \mathcal{G} \text{ s.t. } \mathcal{D}(g \cdot i, x) \leq \varepsilon\}.$$

It is obvious that $\mathrm{N}(i, \varepsilon)$ is the neighborhood of $i$ in $G_\varepsilon$. Besides, for a constant $\delta > 0$, suppose $x \in \mathrm{N}(i, 2\delta)$, let $g \in \mathcal{G}$ such that $\mathcal{D}(x, g \cdot i) < 2\delta$, we obtain

$$|f(x) - f(i)| = |f(x) - f(g \cdot i)| < \mathcal{D}(x, g \cdot i) < 2\delta. \tag{6}$$

Given a graph $G_\varepsilon$, a clique in $G_\varepsilon$ is a subset of vertices $C \subseteq V$ such that all arms in $C$ are neighbors. Moreover, a clique covering of $G_\varepsilon$ is a collection of cliques whose union is $V$. The clique covering number of the graph $G_\varepsilon$, denoted as $\chi(G_\varepsilon)$, is the smallest integer $k$ such that there exists a clique covering of $G_\varepsilon$ whose cardinality is $k$.

**Proposition 4.** *Given a constant $\delta > 0$ and $i \in V$, the set $\mathrm{N}(i, \delta)$ forms a clique of graph $G_{2\delta}$.*

*Remark 1.* In order to prove the regret bound using [10]'s analysis, we need to bound the clique covering of the graph induced by group action, which can be done by bounding the number of disjoint neighbors of orbits. However, due to the possibility of the existence of mutual neighbors of orbits, partitioning the graph into $|V|/|\mathcal{G}|$ disjoint neighbors of orbits is challenging. In particular, for an arbitrary $\delta$-net $V$ for $\mathcal{X}$, applying $g$ on $x \in V$ does not necessarily result in another point $x' \in V$. This leads to the situation where applying the action on two points in the mesh $V$ may end up in a same covering ball, implying that they might not have disjoint neighbors of orbits in $V$. To see this, let $x, x' \in V$ such that $\mathcal{D}(x, x') < 2\delta$, there could be a case where $g \cdot x, g' \cdot x'$ stay in the same covering ball $\mathcal{B}(z, \delta)$ whose diameter is $2\delta$, for some $z \in V$. The trivial reduction to $|V|/|\mathcal{G}|$ can only be achieved (as in the case of $K$-armed bandits) when we have a special mesh where each point in the mesh can map exactly to another point. If we only look at the combinatorial properties of the graph induced by group action, it is difficult to prove the number of disjoint dense neighbors of the graph (cliques). Instead, we need to look at the geometry of the problem. As a result of Proposition 4 and Lemma 1, the next lemma shows the upper bound of the clique covering number of the induced graph by utilising the connection between the clique covering of the graph and the covering of the fundamental domain.

**Lemma 2.** *There are constants $c_1, c_2 > 0$, such that for any $\delta : 0 < \delta < c_2/|\mathcal{G}|$, the clique covering number of graph $G_{2\delta}$ is bounded as*

$$\chi(G_{2\delta}) \leq \frac{c_1 \delta^{-d}}{|\mathcal{G}|}. \tag{7}$$

## 3.2    UniformMesh-N: Uniform Discretization with the Transformation Group

UniformMesh-N is a combination between UniformMesh [15] and UCB-N [10]. Roughly speaking, UniformMesh-N first uniformly discretizes the set of arms $\mathcal{X}$ into a $\delta$-net $V$. The algorithm then exploits the graph $G_{2\delta}$ induced by the group $\mathcal{G}$ as follows. In each round $t \in [n]$, it chooses an arm $x \in V$, observes a reward $Y_t$ and uses it to update the UCB index of all points within the neighborhood of $x$ in $G_{2\delta}$, that is, $\mathrm{N}(x, 2\delta)$. In this paper, we assume that there is an oracle such that in each round $t$, for a chosen arm $x \in V$, the oracle returns its neighbor of orbit $\mathrm{N}(x, 2\delta)$.

To formulate the algorithm, we need some additional notations. For each $x \in \mathcal{X}$, after round $t \in [n]$, let $T(x, t) := \sum_{s=1}^{t} \mathbb{I}_{\{X_s = x\}}$ be the number of times the arm $x$ is played, where $\mathbb{I}$ is the indicator random variable. After round $t$, given that the chosen arm is $X_t$, arm $x \in \mathcal{X}$ is *observed* if and only if $x \in \mathrm{N}(X_t, 2\delta)$. Denote the number of times arm $x$ is observed after the round $t$ as $O(x, t)$, that is,

$$O(x, t) := \sum_{s=1}^{t} \mathbb{I}_{\{x \in \mathrm{N}(X_s, 2\delta)\}}. \tag{8}$$

Denote $\hat{f}(x, t)$ as empirical mean reward of $x$, that is,

$$\hat{f}(x, t) := \sum_{s=1}^{t} Y_t \mathbb{I}_{\{x \in \mathrm{N}(X_s, 2\delta)\}}. \tag{9}$$

Let $\mathrm{U}(x, t)$ be the UCB index of arm $x$ after round $t$ as follows:

$$\mathrm{U}(x, t) := \hat{f}(x, t) + \sqrt{\frac{2 \log(n)}{O(x, t)}} + 3\delta. \tag{10}$$

The suboptimal gap of a point $i$ is defined as $\Delta_i = f^* - f(i)$. Let $\mathcal{C}$ be a clique covering of graph $G_{2\delta}$. For each clique $C \in \mathcal{C}$, define its played time as $T(C, t) = \sum_{i \in C} T(i, t)$. It is clear that $T(C, t) \leq O(i, t)$ for all $i \in C$. The pseudocode of UniformMesh-N is given in Algorithm 1.

While Algorithm 1 provides a general principle, we argue that the algorithm can be carried out efficiently with a carefully designed representation of $V$. In particular, since most of the computation burden is to search $\mathrm{N}(X_t, 2\delta)$, we can use a tree of coverings to represent $V$ as in [9], and implement tree search to find the neighbor of any point $x \in \mathrm{N}(X_t, 2\delta)$ within the tree with at most $\mathcal{O}(d)$ operations. We give a detailed description of how to represent $V$ and implement the search of $\mathrm{N}(X_t, 2\delta)$ in the Appendix. In each round, it takes only $\mathcal{O}(|\mathcal{G}|d)$ to find an approximation of $\mathrm{N}(X_t, 2\delta)$, and with a more refined design, we believe that one can find the exact $\mathrm{N}(X_t, 2\delta)$ with a similar strategy. Therefore, in contrast to sampling within the fundamental domain, which is computationally intractable, our algorithm is computationally efficient by carefully designing the data structure to facilitate searching for the neighbor of orbits.

---

**Algorithm 1.** `UniformMesh-N`

---
Require $n, V, \delta, \mathcal{G}$
**Init** $U(x,0) = \infty, O(x,0) = 0, \hat{f}(x,0) = 0$, for all $x \in V$.
**for** $t = 1 : n$ **do**
    Play $X_t = \arg\max_{x \in V} U(x, t-1)$ with ties broken arbitrarily.
    Receive a reward $Y_t$.
    Compute $N(X_t, 2\delta)$.
    **for** $i \in N(X_t, 2\delta)$ **do**
        Update $O(i,t)$ as (8).
        Update $\hat{f}(i,t)$ as (9).
        Update $U(i,t)$ as (10).
    **end for**
**end for**

---

**Theorem 3.** *Fix an invariant Lipschitz bandit instance with respect to a finite group $\mathcal{G}$. There are some numbers $a_1, a_2 > 0$ such that if $n = \Omega\left(|\mathcal{G}|^{2d+2}\right)$, the regret of* `UniformMesh-N` *algorithm satisfies*

$$\mathbf{R}_n \leq a_1 \left(\frac{\log(n)}{|\mathcal{G}|}\right)^{\frac{1}{d+2}} n^{\frac{d+1}{d+2}} + a_2 \left(\frac{|\mathcal{G}|}{\log(n)}\right)^{\frac{d}{d+2}} n^{\frac{d}{d+2}}. \tag{11}$$

Note that the second term on the right-hand side of (11) is insignificant, as it grows at a slower rate in $n$ compared to that of the first term. The proof of Theorem 3 is deferred to the Appendix, but we provide the intuition underlying the analysis here. First, using the analysis of [10], the regret bound increases at most $\mathcal{O}\left(\sum_{C \in \mathcal{C}} \log(n) \frac{\max_{i \in C} \Delta_i}{\min_{i \in C} \Delta_i^2}\right)$. In addition, we already proved that the clique covering number of the graph $G_{2\delta}$ is at most $|V|/|\mathcal{G}|$ when $n$ is sufficiently large. Moreover, for a "strongly suboptimal" clique, the factor $\frac{\max_{i \in C} \Delta_i}{\min_{i \in C} \Delta_i^2}$ can be reduced to $\mathcal{O}\left(\delta^{-1}\right)$ since the difference in the expected reward of nodes in any clique cannot be greater than $\delta$. Putting things together and choosing the suitable value for $\delta$, we obtain Theorem 3.

## 4    Regret Lower Bound

This section presents a minimax lower bound for the ILB class that matchs the upper bound in Theorem 3 up to a logarithmic factor, hence show that `UniformMesh-N` algorithm is near optimal in the minimax sense. The lower bound for ILB class can be stated formally as follows.

**Theorem 4.** *Consider the invariant Lipschitz bandit problems in $(\mathcal{X}, \mathcal{D})$ with respect to action of group $\mathcal{G}$. Suppose $n = \Omega(|\mathcal{G}|^{d+1})$, then any bandit strategy must suffer a regret at least $\Omega\left(\left(\frac{1}{|\mathcal{G}|}\right)^{\frac{1}{d+2}} n^{\frac{d+1}{d+2}}\right)$.*

While the full proof of Theorem 4 is deferred to the Appendix, we brief the main idea for the lower bound here. First, we prove that the (strictly) packing number of the fundamental domain $\mathbf{D}$ is at least $\Omega(\delta^{-d}/|\mathcal{G}|)$ when $\delta$ is small enough. Then, let $W$ be a strictly packing points in $\mathbf{D}$ that has maximum cardinality, we can construct a strictly packing points in $\mathcal{X}$ using the group action on those points in $\mathbf{D}$. Second, we construct a class of invariant problem instances that assigns the same expected reward for the image of each point in $W$ under the action of $\mathcal{G}$, and we show that this class has at least $\Omega(\delta^{-d}/|\mathcal{G}|)$ instances. Applying standard information-theoretic analysis we obtain the lower bound.

## 5   Conclusion

In this paper, we consider the class of invariant Lipschitz bandit problems. We first introduce a graph induced by the group action and prove that the clique covering number of this graph is only at most as $|\mathcal{G}|^{-1}$ large as the number of vertices. Using this graph, we propose the UniformMesh-N algorithm, utilizing group orbits as side observations. Furthermore, using side observation-based analysis, we provide an upper regret for UniformMesh-N, which shows that the improvement by a factor depends on the cardinality of the group $\mathcal{G}$; therefore, we are the first to show a strict statistical benefit of using group information to design algorithms. Finally, we derive a regret lower bound for the ILB class, closely matching the upper bound up to a logarithmic factor. This implies that UniformMesh-N algorithm is near-optimal in the worst case within the class of ILB problems. Note that as ILB has many important real-world applications (e.g., matrix factorization bandits, online dictionary learning) our results will open new research directions in those areas as well, providing new ideas to further improve the regret bounds of those respective domains.

As our current results use of uniform discretization instead of adaptive discretization, we conjecture that there is still room for improvement. In particular, as shown in [16] and [9], uniform discretization is less effective compared to adaptive discretization. We believe that by applying group orbit as side observation in adaptive discretization algorithms, one can achieve the regret bound whose "shape" is similar to that of Theorem 3, except that the covering dimension $d$ is replaced by the near-optimal dimension $d'$ [9]. However, the combination of side observations with adaptive discretization algorithms is significantly more challenging in terms of analysis. The reason is twofold: (i) While the analysis technique of side-observation setting requires the set of arms (i.e., feedback graph's vertices) to be fixed over time, the set of candidate arms in adaptive discretization algorithms vary each round; (ii) The proof of Lemma 1 heavily depends on the nice geometric properties of the Dirichlet domain, particularly, the set is full dimension with zero volume boundary. In contrast, a near-optimal set [9] can have an arbitrary shape. Therefore, without any further assumption, it is difficult to prove the upper bound for the covering number of the part of near-optimal set lying in the fundamental domain.

**Acknowledgments.** We would like to express our sincere gratitude to Dr. The Anh Ta for his numerous insightful suggestions.

# References

1. Abbasi-Yadkori, Y., Pál, D., Szepesvári, C.: Improved algorithms for linear stochastic bandits (2011)
2. Agrawal, R.: The continuum-armed bandit problem. SIAM J. Control. Optim. **33**, 1926–1951 (1995)
3. Alon, N., Cesa-Bianchi, N., Gentile, C., Mannor, S., Mansour, Y., Shamir, O.: Nonstochastic multi-armed bandits with graph-structured feedback. SIAM J. Comput. **46**, 1785–1826 (2017)
4. Alon, N., Cesa-Bianchi, N., Gentile, C., Mansour, Y.: From bandits to experts: a tale of domination and independence (2013)
5. Auer, P., Cesa-Bianchi, N., Fischer, P.: Finite-time analysis of the multiarmed bandit problem. Mach. Learn. **47**, 235–256 (2002)
6. Auer, P., Ortner, R., Szepesvári, C.: Improved rates for the stochastic continuum-armed bandit problem. In: Bshouty, N.H., Gentile, C. (eds.) COLT 2007. LNCS (LNAI), vol. 4539, pp. 454–468. Springer, Heidelberg (2007). https://doi.org/10.1007/978-3-540-72927-3_33
7. Behboodi, A., Cesa, G., Cohen, T.: A PAC-bayesian generalization bound for equivariant networks. In: Advances in Neural Information Processing Systems (2022)
8. Bessiere, C., Hebrard, E., Hnich, B., Walsh, T.: The complexity of reasoning with global constraints. Constraints **12** (2007). https://doi.org/10.1007/s10601-006-9007-3
9. Bubeck, S., Munos, R., Stoltz, G., Szepesvári, C.: X-armed bandits. J. Mach. Learn. Res. **12**, 1655–1695 (2011)
10. Caron, S., Kveton, B., Lelarge, M., Bhagat, S.: Leveraging side observations in stochastic bandits (2012)
11. Cohen, A., Hazan, T., Koren, T.: Online learning with feedback graphs without the graphs (2016)
12. Elesedy, B., Zaidi, S.: Provably strict generalisation benefit for equivariant models (2021)
13. Herbert, R.: Some aspects of the sequential design of experiments. Bull. Am. Math. Soc. **58** (1952). https://doi.org/10.1090/S0002-9904-1952-09620-8
14. Kawale, J., Bui, H., Kveton, B., Thanh, L.T., Chawla, S.: Efficient thompson sampling for online matrix-factorization recommendation, vol. 2015-January (2015)
15. Kleinberg, R.: Nearly tight bounds for the continuum-armed bandit problem (2005)
16. Kleinberg, R., Slivkins, A., Upfal, E.: Bandits and experts in metric spaces. J. ACM **66**, 1–77 (2019)
17. Lattimore, T., Szepesvári, C.: Bandit Algorithms. Cambridge University Press, Cambridge (2020)
18. Li, X., et al.: Symmetry, saddle points, and global optimization landscape of nonconvex matrix factorization. IEEE Trans. Inf. Theory **65** (2019). https://doi.org/10.1109/TIT.2019.2898663
19. Lykouris, T., Tardos, E., Wali, D.: Feedback graph regret bounds for Thompson sampling and UCB (2019)
20. Lyu, H., Needell, D., Balzano, L.: Online matrix factorization for Markovian data and applications to network dictionary learning. J. Mach. Learn. Res. **21**, 10148–10196 (2020)
21. Mairal, J., Bach, F., Ponce, J., Sapiro, G.: Online learning for matrix factorization and sparse coding. J. Mach. Learn. Res. **11**, 19–60 (2010)

22. Mannor, S., Shamir, O.: From bandits to experts: on the value of side-observations (2011)
23. Margot, F.: Symmetry in integer linear programming. In: Jünger, M., et al. (eds.) 50 Years of Integer Programming 1958-2008, pp. 647–686. Springer, Heidelberg (2010). https://doi.org/10.1007/978-3-540-68279-0_17
24. Margot, F.: Pruning by isomorphism in branch-and-cut. Math. Program. Seri. B **94** (2002). https://doi.org/10.1007/s10107-002-0358-2
25. Ostrowski, J., Linderoth, J., Rossi, F., Smriglio, S.: Orbital branching. Math. Program. **126** (2011). https://doi.org/10.1007/s10107-009-0273-x
26. Ratcliffe, J.G.: Foundations of Hyperbolic Manifolds (2007). https://doi.org/10.1007/978-0-387-47322-2
27. Sannai, A., Imaizumi, M., Kawano, M.: Improved generalization bounds of group invariant/equivariant deep networks via quotient feature spaces (2019)
28. Shamir, O.: On the complexity of bandit and derivative-free stochastic convex optimization, vol. 30 (2013)
29. Slivkins, A.: Introduction to multi-armed bandits. Found. Trends Mach. Learn. **12**, 1–286 (2019)
30. Thompson, W.R.: On the likelihood that one unknown probability exceeds another in view of the evidence of two samples. Biometrika **25**, 285–294 (1933)
31. Tran, N.P., Tran-Thanh, L.: Invariant lipschitz bandits: a side observation approach (2022). https://arxiv.org/abs/2212.07524v2
32. Walsh, T.: Symmetry breaking constraints: recent results, vol. 3 (2012). https://doi.org/10.1609/aaai.v26i1.8437
33. Wang, H., Wu, Q., Wang, H.: Factorization bandits for interactive recommendation (2017). https://doi.org/10.1609/aaai.v31i1.10936
34. Wang, Q., et al.: Online interactive collaborative filtering using multi-armed bandit with dependent arms. IEEE Trans. Knowl. Data Eng. **31** (2019). https://doi.org/10.1109/TKDE.2018.2866041
35. Wu, Y.: Lecture 14: Packing, covering, and consequences on minimax risk (2016). http://www.stat.yale.edu/yw562/teaching/598/lec14.pdf

# Filtered Observations for Model-Based Multi-agent Reinforcement Learning

Linghui Meng[1,2], Xuantang Xiong[1,2], Yifan Zang[1,2], Xi Zhang[1], Guoqi Li[1,2], Dengpeng Xing[1,2(✉)], and Bo Xu[1,2(✉)]

[1] Institute of Automation, Chinese Academy of Sciences, Beijing, China
{menglinghui2019,xiongxuantang2021,dengpeng.xing,xubo}@ia.ac.cn
[2] School of Artificial Intelligence, University of Chinese Academy of Sciences, Beijing, China

**Abstract.** Reinforcement learning (RL) pursues high sample efficiency in practical environments to avoid costly interactions. Learning to plan with a world model in a compact latent space for policy optimization significantly improves sample efficiency in single-agent RL. Although world model construction methods for single-agent can be naturally extended, existing multi-agent schemes fail to acquire world models effectively as redundant information increases rapidly with the number of agents. To address this issue, we in this paper leverage guided diffusion to filter this noisy information, which harms teamwork. Obtained purified global states are then used to build a unified world model. Based on the learned world model, we denoise each agent observation and plan for multi-agent policy optimization, facilitating efficient cooperation. We name our method UTOPIA, a model-based method for cooperative multi-agent reinforcement learning (MARL). Compared to strong model-free and model-based baselines, our method shows enhanced sample efficiency in various testbeds, including the challenging StarCraft Multi-Agent Challenge tasks.

**Keywords:** Model-based planning · Multi-agent reinforcement learning · Generative models

## 1 Introduction

Cooperative multi-agent reinforcement learning (MARL) has recently attracted much attention due to the success of its applications in many practical tasks, such as real-time strategy games [19], return-based card games [1,8], and unmanned aerial vehicles [32]. Despite the empirical success [18,20,30], the most extensively studied methods are built on the model-free reinforcement learning paradigm. They always face low sample efficiency since the policy optimization relies on a large number of costly interactions with the environment [28]. In addition, the policy exploration spaces which explode with the agent number in multi-agent systems further deteriorate this problem [29].

To rectify model-free RL's sample efficiency issue, a common practice of the alternative model-based RL in single-agent settings is to learn a world model [4,

© The Author(s), under exclusive license to Springer Nature Switzerland AG 2023
D. Koutra et al. (Eds.): ECML PKDD 2023, LNAI 14172, pp. 540–555, 2023.
https://doi.org/10.1007/978-3-031-43421-1_32

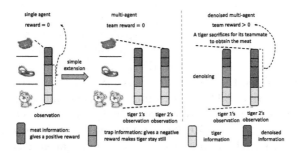

**Fig. 1. Illustrative example**: each tiger can see four kinds of information and aim to get the meat behind the trap. Each trapped tiger will die and receive negative feedback, which makes the tiger, in the left two cases, stay still to receive a zero reward. Once one tiger gets the meat, the team will receive maximum positive feedback.

6,13,26,27]. It builds transition and reward models to predict trajectories based on global states embedded in a compact latent space. By planning with the learned model rather than interacting with the environment as those model-free methods, these types of approaches efficiently optimize policies and achieve state-of-the-art performance in single-agent RL tasks.

When it comes to the multi-agent field, the embedded global state to construct the world model becomes the research concentration. Although the observation encoder in single-agent RL can be directly extended to embed multiple agents' observations by sharing and concatenating them, it ignores the cooperative relations in the team and leads to the fusion of noise, which hinders the system from getting higher rewards. An illustrative example in Fig. 1 describes an animal trap as noise. A single-agent tiger needs to avoid the trap and turn around for a living resulting in zero rewards. Once extending this problem by sharing and concatenating observations to the multi-agent case, two tigers unite as a multi-agent team to optimize the team reward, but the reward is still zero. A reasonable solution is to mask the noise (trap) in the observation of at least one agent to sacrifice it by covering the trap and finally cooperating for the meat to achieve a positive team reward. Accordingly, obtaining embedded global states and constructing a world model in a multi-agent scenario requires filtering out the above noise in the combination of each agent's local observations.

Following the above noise filtering intuition, we in this paper propose UTOPIA, a model-based method that denoises each agent observation to acquire the purified global states and learns a world model for the multi-agent system. Instead of building each agent a specific encoder that is impractical and unscalable, we designed a single conditioned noise filter for all agents. Concretely, we leverage a variational lower bound to train a diffusion model to represent the global states in the latent space. Moreover, we define the noise for a guided model to discriminate the noise given latent global states. It is learned from the perspectives of transition and reward for each agent. We conduct the noise filter using the gradient from the guided model to a diffusion model during sampling. The learned noise filter enables tailored denoising for each agent to purify global states. Our approach thus utilizes the purified global state to construct a multi-agent world model, which plans in latent space to improve sample efficiency.

In order to study the effectiveness of our method, we first examined its necessity on a toy multi-agent MDP (MMDP) example and then validated it on the challenging cooperative multi-agent task, Starcraft multi-agent challenges (SMAC). We show that UTOPIA can improve the sample efficiency compared to strong baselines in the toy example and challenging tasks. Our contributions are summarized as follows: 1) **Addressing model-based cooperative multi-agent reinforcement learning.** We propose a multi-agent algorithm based on a learnable world model and emphasize the model-based MARL to solve the low sample efficiency problem. 2) **Learning to denoise each agent observation for purified global states.** We explicitly propose the definition of task-relevant information. To utilize the explicit objective, we regard the definition as a condition and employ a guided model to enforce the diffusion model sampling. 3) **Empirical performance on cooperative MARL** Our experimental results show superior performance in sample efficiency compared to model-free baselines and a model-based approach extended from single-agent methods.

## 2   Related Work

The problem of learning to collaborate among multiple agents has been commonly addressed with the framework of the partially observed Markov decision process (POMDP) that partly masks the global state for each agent observation. Recent work has combined deep neural networks with multi-agent policy within this framework as centralized-training decentralized execution (CTDE) [15,18] or advantage decomposition approaches [10]. These approaches are based on value iteration or actor-critic even combined with sequential models, such as VDN [20], QMIX [18], MAPPO [30], MAT [25], which achieve remarkable performance in challenging tasks. However, these approaches are model-free methods limited by the low sample efficiency without accessing the environment [29]. An intuitive approach is to build model-based methods to augment the buffer generated for the policy learning [17,24]. In addition, it remains unclear whether these methods can incorporate the environment to construct a model-based method. In the single-agent field, a few works have attempted to abstract the input as global states via reconstruction loss to build a world model and plan it in the latent space, such as PlaNet, Dreamer, DreamerV2 [4–6]. [3] even leverages the goal as a condition to derive the imagined trajectories autoregressively. Although these methods have shown supreme performance on various single-agent tasks, the implicit relations and properties of partially observable limit their development to effectively represent the global states in the multi-agent domain [31]. [12] proposes that neighboring agents could have similar representations of observations in multi-agent. [21,22] claim the role-based method to represent the multi-agent observations via clustering them in latent space to discriminate each agent by sharing a role selector network automatically. These methods mainly focus on how to represent multi-agent observations well to be the policy input. We focus on abstracting the global states to construct the world model for planning. In contrast with directly abstracting the multi-agent observations for the global state extended from single-agent methods [6], we claim the noise fusion problem in the simple aggregation methods, which harms teamwork. The closest work emerges in the single-agent field, Denoised MDP, which splits latent states based on whether they are controllable or reward-relevant via reconstruction. Accordingly, we define noise based on teammate information from transition and reward perspectives and employ guided diffusion [2,7] to purify multi-agent observations conditionally. To combine with model-free MARL approaches, we also integrate prior works with multi-agent behavior learning. Our novelty lies in the definition of the noise in multi-agent observations and the method of conditionally purifying them to build a world model to improve the sample efficiency.

## 3    Background and Notations

### 3.1    Cooperative Multi-Agent Problem

We consider the formulation in cooperative multi-agent reinforcement learning, which is a partial observable extension of the standard Markov Decision Process (MDP) named partially-observed MDP (POMDP) [14]. $\hat{M} = (\mathcal{S}, \mathcal{O}, \mathcal{A}, \gamma, n, \mathcal{R}, \mathcal{T})$. $\mathcal{S}$ denotes the state space of multiple agents, $\mathcal{O} : \mathcal{S} \rightarrow \Omega$ denotes the observation function, where $\Omega$ represents the observation space, $\mathcal{A} = \{\mathcal{A}_1 \times \mathcal{A}_2 \times \cdots \times \mathcal{A}_n\}$ represents the joint action space of $n$ agents, respectively, $\mathcal{R}$ represents the reward function. To clarify the notation, we denote the time $t$ for variables of all agents by sub-scripts but the time for variables with agent index by super-scripts. We denote $s_t \in \mathcal{S}$ to refer to the global state of the environment. At time step $t$, let $\boldsymbol{o}_t = \{o_i^t\}_{i=1}^n$ with each $o_i^t \in \mathcal{O}(s_t, i)$ be the partial observation of agent $i$ accessing the global state $s_t$. Accordingly, let $\boldsymbol{a}_t = \{a_i^t\}_{i=1}^n$ with each $a_i^t \in \mathcal{A}_i$ indicating the action taken by the agent $i$. $\mathcal{T}(s_{t+1}|s_t, \boldsymbol{a}_t) : \mathcal{S} \times \mathcal{A} \times \mathcal{S} \rightarrow [0, 1]$ is the state transition function. $r(s_t, \boldsymbol{a}_t) \in \mathcal{R} : \mathcal{S} \times \mathcal{A} \rightarrow \mathbb{R}$ indicates the team reward function is shared across agents from the environment. $\gamma \in [0, 1)$ is the discount factor. Let $\pi_i(a_i^t|o_i^t)$ be a stochastic policy for agent $i$ and denote $\pi = \{\pi_i\}_{i=1}^n$. Let $J(\pi) = \mathbb{E}_t[R_t]$ with $R_t = \sum_{l=0}^{\infty} \gamma^l r_{t+l}(s_{t+l}, \{a_i^{t+l}\}_{i=1}^n)$ denoting the expected discounted reward, where $a_i^{t+l} \sim \pi_i(a_i^{t+l}|o_i^{t+l})$ for $i \in [1, n]$. The problem aims to find the optimal multi-agent policy $\pi^\star = \{\pi_i^\star\}_{i=1}^n$ that achieve the maximum expected team reward $J(\pi)$.

### 3.2    Latent Imagination for Learning Policy

Learning to plan via a predictive model named *world model* can facilitate learning complex behaviors [4,5]. The world model aims to estimate the real dynamics and reward conditioned on the input state with deep neural networks $p(s'|s)$ and $p(r|s)$, respectively, where $s$ denotes the global state usually encoded by the generative model VAEs in latent space. The behavior policy $\pi(a|s)$ is built on the latent states to control the agent. Once the world model is learned, it imagines batch trajectories starting from the true current state $s^t$, $\tau^t = \{s^j, a^j, r^j\}_{j=t}^{t+h}$, where $s^j \sim p(s^j|s^{j-1})$ and $a^j \sim \pi(a^j|s^j)$, $h$ denotes the imagination horizon. The objective is to maximize the expected reward on the imagined trajectories, $\mathbb{E}_\pi[\sum_{j=t}^\infty \gamma^{j-t} r(\tau^j)]$ with respect to the behavior policy, where $\gamma$ denotes the discount factor. To extend this mechanism to multi-agent fields, we follow the above procedure to build a world model and learn a policy for multi-agent from the trajectories planned by the world model. The challenges in the multi-agent case, mainly emerge in how to abstract the global states for the multi-agent world model and the policy learning.

## 3.3   Guided Diffusion Models

Score-based generative models, such as diffusion models [7], achieve great advancements in image synthesis tasks. The diffusion (forward) process gradually destroys inputs via a fixed Markov chain, such as adding weighted noise conditioned on the previous input, $x_d \sim \mathcal{N}(x_d; \sqrt{\bar{\alpha}_d} x_{d-1}, \sqrt{1 - \bar{\alpha}_d} \mathcal{I})$, where $\bar{\alpha}_d = \prod_{d=1}^D \alpha_d$, and $d$ denotes the index of the diffusion process, while $D$ denotes the diffusion horizon. To reconstruct the original input, we need to approximate the unknown posterior, $q(x_{d-1}|x_d)$ with a parameterized neural network, $p_\theta(x_{d-1}|x_d) = \mathcal{N}(x_{d-1}; \mu_\theta(x_d, d), \Sigma_d)$. The original inputs can be deblurred from the standard normal distribution. The induced data distribution is given by:

$$p_\theta(x_0) = \int p(x_D) \prod_{d=1}^D p_\theta(x_{d-1}|x_d) dx_{1:D} \tag{1}$$

Then the evidence lower bound can be derived based on the maximized likelihood estimation to optimize this generative model. The simplified loss is shown as:

$$L_{simple} = \mathbb{E}_{x_0, z_d}[||z_d - z_\theta(\sqrt{\bar{\alpha}_d} x_0 + \sqrt{1 - \bar{\alpha}_d} z_d, d)||] \tag{2}$$

where $z_d$ is the Gaussian noise. Recent works propose classifier-guided diffusion to generate a specified sample, such as generating an image with a label. The modified posterior $q(x_{d-1}|x_d, y)$ can be estimated with an integration between the diffusion model pre-trained and a classifier $p(y|x_d)$. Therefore, the reverse process can be approximated as the following prediction problem [2]:

$$p_\theta(x_{d-1}|x_d, y) \approx \mathcal{N}(x_{d-1}; \mu + \Sigma g, \Sigma) \tag{3}$$

where $\mu$ and $\Sigma$ are the output of the pre-trained diffusion model, $g = \nabla \log p(y|x)|_{x=x_d}$ denotes the gradient of the classifier. Therefore, we can guide the diffusion model with predefined objectives to generate samples of specific attributes without additionally retraining the diffusion model.

In this work, we define the task-relevant objective for the purified states in the multi-agent world model. UTOPIA guides the diffusion model to denoise each agent observation conditioned on the objective to filter out the noise that harms teamwork. The global purified states are composed of denoised observations to construct a multi-agent world model. By planning batch trajectories with the world model, the multi-agent policy is optimized based on the planned trajectories in a cooperative Markov Game.

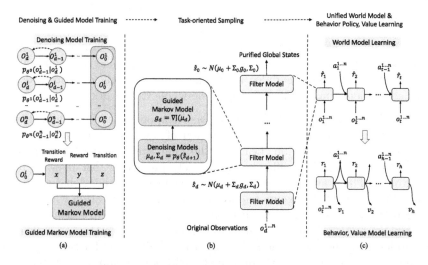

**Fig. 2.** Overview of UTOPIA learning process: (a) Denoising (up) and guided (down) model learning, where the original observations are fed into the diffusion model with the sub-scripts denoising index $d$ gradually decreasing, and the guided model learns to discriminate the noise; (b): Guide diffusion model purifies each agent original observation and concatenate them as purified global states; (c): Unified World (up) and behavior, value model (down) learning. The filter model in (b) is used to purify observations to predict the true reward and next state with a supervised style. Given observations in a time, the world model plans to roll out based on the purified global state, which fed for Behavior policy and Value model learning.

## 4    Methodology

In this section, we first highlight the critical motivation to learn a purified world model for model-based MARL. We then elaborate on each module of our method for learning to control multi-agent cooperation. In addition, we show the learning objective of the multi-agent world and behavior models. To illustrate the use of input-conditional guided sampling for each agent purified observation, we describe the training and sampling process of the task-oriented filter model.

### 4.1    Motivation

1) There exists much noise having no effect on the transition and reward functions, then noise increases the redundant exploration of the expanded policy space. To improve efficient cooperation, we need to filter it out to obtain the purified global states. 2) The noise in each agent observation should be eliminated conditioned on their local observations and global information rather than be denoised individually. Therefore, based on the above two points, we need to develop the conditioned denoising network for purifying the global states to construct the multi-agent world model.

## 4.2   Control with Denoised World Models

To resolve the problems that emerged in our motivation, we formulate the multi-agent behavior policy learning that takes input as the global states in a unified world model with several modules, mainly including the *unified world model* and *agent components* parts. Figure 2 shows the whole framework.

*Unified World Model.* We introduce six components for the unified world model learning and leave the demonstration of how to define and utilize the objective in the next section. Learning the joint world model for cooperation across multiple agents is difficult for precisely predicting task-relevant future trajectories. There are three main reasons: 1) Learning the global state from observations of multiple agents requires a purified representation without additional noise, as described in motivation. 2) The relationship among agents is implicit due to their identity, so how to define noisy information is difficult. 3) How to leverage the observation filtering process differently for each agent conditioned on the shared observation encoder and noise definition. Therefore, we introduce six components to construct the presented world model. The six components contain the sharing denoising model facilitated by the diffusion model, the guided model, the transition model, the reward prediction model, the available prediction model, and the mask prediction model. We formulate them as follows:

$$
\begin{aligned}
&\text{Denoising model:} && p(\hat{o}_i^t | o_i^t, a_i^{t-1}, \hat{s}_{t-1}) \\
&\text{Guided model:} && p(\mathcal{O}_t = 1 | o_i^t, a_i^{t-1}) \\
&\text{Transition model:} && q(\hat{s}_t | \hat{s}_{t-1}, \boldsymbol{a}_{t-1}) \\
&\text{Available model:} && q(ava_i^t | \hat{o}_i^t, a_i^{t-1}) \\
&\text{Reward model:} && q(r_t | \hat{s}_t, \boldsymbol{a}_t) \\
&\text{Masking model:} && q(m_t | \hat{s}_t)
\end{aligned}
\tag{4}
$$

1) The denoising model $p(\hat{o}_i^t | o_i^t, a_i^{t-1}, \hat{s}_{t-1})$ is shared across agents and aims to denoise each agent observation to the latent space. 2) The guided model $p(\mathcal{O}_t = 1 | o_i^t, a_i^{t-1})$ is input conditional on splitting the noisy information. In this model, we leverage the control-as-inference used in [9,11] to guide the denoising process by defining a binary variable $\mathcal{O}_t$ denoting the optimality of our defined objective which is described in the following sections. Conditioned on the learned guided model, the modified mean and variance for a permuted Gaussian distribution can be computed. The purified state is concatenated by all agents denoised observations $\hat{s} = \hat{o}_{i=1...n}$. 3) To predict the Markov transition, UTOPIA leverages the transition model $q(\hat{s}_t | \hat{s}_{t-1}, \boldsymbol{a}_{t-1})$ used in Dreamer [4] to predict the next global state based on the current ones. 4) The available models $q(ava_i^t | \hat{o}_i^t, a_i^{t-1})$ estimate the currently available actions given the global state, where $ava_i^t \in \mathbb{R}^{[\mathcal{A}_i]}$ represents the available action of agent $i$ at $t$ step, where each dimension denotes the corresponding action is actionable or not. 5) The reward model $q(r_t | \hat{s}_t, \boldsymbol{a}_t)$ is used to predict the current true reward given state and action. 6) The masking model $q(m_t | \hat{s}_t)$ predicts the end step for the whole episode, where $m^t$ is a binary

variable representing whether the game is over or not $0/1$ at $t$ step. They could emerge in a complicated environment like SMAC. We represent how to learn a specific model to tackle them for accurate planning, although they may be not necessary for many tasks. The denoised observation embeddings are concatenated together as the purified global state. The learned world model is leveraged to update the behavior and value models to maximize the expected reward in Markov games.

**Agent Components** We introduce two components used in UTOPIA, multi-agent behavior policy and value model.

$$\pi_i(a_i^t|\hat{o}_i^t) \quad \text{and} \quad V_\pi^t(\hat{s}_t) \tag{5}$$

where $\hat{o}_i^t$ denotes the denoised observation embedding for agent $i$ in timestep $t$, $\pi_i$ denotes the behavior policy of agent $i$ mapping the denoised observation $\hat{o}_i^t$ to the action space, $V_\pi^t$ denotes the value function base on the global state aims to estimate the expected reward at $t$. It should be noted that the conventional input of behavior policy for each agent in POMDP is local observation without global information integration in the inference period [18,30]. In the case of UTOPIA, the local observations are denoised as inputs with a guided denoising model optimized from the global information such as the team reward. Learning to estimate the team reward typically helps improve the policy update, where the value module takes as input the global information predefined. In contrast, the value model in UTOPIA evaluates the task-oriented global state $\hat{s} = \hat{o}_{i=1...n}$ concatenated by denoised observation embeddings. In the following section, we will introduce the corresponding objectives about how to optimize these presented modules.

### 4.3  Learning Objective

In this section, we first introduce how to define the noise information and how to learn to filter it from the local observations. Then the objective of the guided denoising model to learn to conditionally denoise each agent observation is introduced. Then we describe the objective of the multi-agent world model, including transition, reward, and other predictive models. Finally, based on the above world model, we introduce how to optimize the corresponding multi-agent action and value models are finally introduced.

**Guided Denoised Model Learning.** The denoised representations in latent space can be abstracted by the diffusion model beforementioned $p_\theta(\hat{o}_i^t|o_i^t, a_i^{t-1}, \hat{s}^{t-1})$. To simplify the training process, we send each agent observation as input and leverage the simple version of diffusion objective as follows:

$$\mathcal{L}_{denoising} = \sum_{i=1}^{n} \mathbb{E}_{\tau_i \sim \pi_i}[\sum_d ||z_d - z_\theta(\sqrt{\bar{\alpha}_d}\tau_i$$
$$+ \sqrt{1 - \bar{\alpha}_l}z_d, d)||], \quad \text{where } z_d \sim \mathcal{N}(0, \mathcal{I}) \tag{6}$$

where $n$ denotes the agent number, $\tau_i$ denotes the trajectory of agent $i$, and $z_\theta$ denotes the output of diffusion model $p_\theta$ described in Fig. 2.

Based on the denoising model above, to filter the noise information for each agent, we define the noise as long as it does not affect the transitions and reward predictions like in Denoised MDPs [23]. The guided model takes as input the diffusion representations and divides them into three parts, denoting $x$, $y$, and $z$ respectively, constructing the training set, where $y$ and $z$ denote the transition-irrelevant and reward-irrelevant noise. In terms of the two parts, which involve the global transition and reward, we set the following objective to train the guidance model:

$$
\begin{aligned}
\mathcal{L}_{guided} = {} & I(p(\hat{o}'_i|[x_i, y_i, z_i], a_i)||p(\hat{o}'_i|[x_i, z_i], a_i)) \\
& + I(p(r|[x_i, y_i, z_i]_{i=1\ldots n}, \boldsymbol{a})||p(r|[x_i, y_i, z_i]_{i=1\ldots n}], \boldsymbol{a}))
\end{aligned}
\tag{7}
$$

where the first term aims to minimize the distance of the posterior between the two conditions, and $y_i$ denotes the uncontrollable part in each agent. Similarly, the second term aims to learn to separate the reward-irrelevant part $z_i$, where $x$ denotes purified observation used to construct global states. When the objective is minimized, the noise $y$ and $z$ have no effect on the rollouts of the world model. Then we can generate $x$ of each agent to construct the purified global states for the unified multi-agent world model.

***World Model Learning.*** To further construct the world model based on the purified global states, we train the transition and prediction models for reward, available actions, and masks by reconstruction loss. We train a sequential model by taking as input the purified global state $\hat{s}$ concatenated from the diffusion outputs. The supervised learning process for the global world model can be optimized by minimizing the negative log-likelihood:

$$
\mathcal{L}_{world} \triangleq -\mathbb{E}_{i,t}\left[ \log p_\theta(\hat{s}_i^{t+1}, r^t, m_i^t, ava_i^t | \hat{s}_i^t, \boldsymbol{a}^t) \right]
\tag{8}
$$

where $\theta$ is the parameter of the global world transition model.

***Action and Value Model Learning.*** UTOPIA trains the behavior policy $\pi_i(a_i|\hat{o}_i)$ for each agent $i$ and value model $V(\hat{s})$ via backpropagating from additional roll-outs $\tau$ from the learned unified world model beforementioned. We adopt PPO-style algorithm for policy and value model optimization. To update the action and value models, we first compute the estimated state value $V_\psi^\pi(\hat{s}_\tau)$ for all states $s_\tau$ along the imagined trajectories. The objective for the action model $\pi(a_\tau|\hat{o}_\tau)$ is to predict actions that result in state trajectories with high-value estimates. The objective for the value model $V_\psi(\hat{s}_\tau)$, in turn, is to regress the cumulated reward. The objective of the action model is:

$$
\max_\phi \sum_{i=1}^n \mathbb{E}_{q_\phi, q_\psi}\left[ \sum_{j=t}^{t+h} \min\left( \frac{\pi_\phi(\tau_i^j)}{\pi_{\phi old}(\tau_i^j)}, \sigma \right) A(\tau_j) \right]
\tag{9}
$$

where $\sigma = \text{clip}(\frac{\pi_\phi(\tau_i^j)}{\pi_{\phi old}(\tau_i^j)}, 1 - \epsilon, 1 + \epsilon)$, $h$ represents the rollout horizon and $\tau_i^j = \{\hat{o}_i^m\}_{m=0}^j$, $\tau_j = \{\hat{s}_m\}_{m=0}^j$. The objective of the value model is:

$$\min_\psi \mathbb{E}_{q_\phi, q_\psi} \left[ \sum_{j=t}^{t+h} \frac{1}{2} \left\| \sum_{l=j}^{\infty} \gamma^l r_j - V_\psi^\pi(\tau_j)) \right\|^2 \right] \tag{10}$$

## 4.4 Training and Sampling

To describe the update procedure of each module described above, in this section, we demonstrate the training and sampling process in detail.

***Training Process.*** To filter the task-oriented global states in latent space and utilize the purified states as behavior and value model inputs, we train the diffusion model first and then optimize the guided model with the objective in Eq. 6, 7. The world model is learned from the rollout trajectories denoised by the guided diffusion model, then we train the critic model to estimate the true reward on each step. To predict optimal actions, we learn the behavior policy to maximize the total discounted values estimated by the critic model.

***Sampling Process.*** Then we derive the guided sampling in the presented denoising model with the explicit objective defined in Eq. 7. Let $\mathcal{O}_d$ be a binary random variable denoting the purity of timestep $t$ of a trajectory, with $p(\mathcal{O}_d = 1) = \exp(-\mathcal{L}_{guided})$. We can derive the conditional probability as follows:

$$p(\hat{o}_d | \hat{o}_{d+1}, \mathcal{O}_d = 1) = p_{\theta, \phi}(\hat{o}_d | \hat{o}_{d+1}, \mathcal{O}_d = 1) \tag{11}$$

By separating the diffusion model and the guided model, we split the reverse process as follows:

$$p_\theta(\hat{o}_d | \hat{o}_{d+1}, \mathcal{O}_d = 1) = p_\theta(\hat{o}_d | \hat{o}_{d+1}) p_\phi(\mathcal{O}_t = 1 | \hat{o}_t) \tag{12}$$

We ignore the superscript $i$ for succinct notation. By defining three variables $x$, $y$, and $z$, we propose to discriminate noise that is $y$ and $z$, which are irrelevant to the transition or reward. The guide sampling can be shown as follows:

$$\begin{aligned} \log p_\theta(\mathcal{O}_t = 1 | x_t) &\approx \log p_\phi(\mathcal{O}_d = 1 | \hat{o}_d)|_{\hat{o}_d = \mu} \\ &+ (\hat{o}_d - \mu)\nabla_{\hat{o}_d} \log p_\theta(\mathcal{O}_d = 1 | \hat{o}_d)|_{\hat{o}_d = \mu} \\ &= (\hat{o}_d - \mu)g + C_1 \end{aligned} \tag{13}$$

where $g = \nabla_{\hat{o}_d} \log p_\theta(\mathcal{O}_d = 1 | \hat{o}_d)|_{\hat{o}_d = \mu}$ is the gradients of the guided model at the specified value $\mu$. With the sampling proceeding, each agent observation can be purified by objective-oriented for constructing the world model subsequently.

## 5 Experiments

On top of the theoretic analysis, we tested UTOPIA on various environments. To illustrate the necessity of our method even in a simple case, we validated our method on a toy example, a multi-agent MDP (MMDP) (see Fig. 3(a)). To verify our method, we validate UTOPIA on both easy and (super-)hard maps of the StarCraft multi-agent challenge (SMAC) for efficient cooperation. All experimental results are obtained compared with popular multi-agent model-free and model-based MARL in terms of sample efficiency and performance. We mainly answer the following two research questions: **RQ1**: Can the world model help improve the sample efficiency of cooperative multi-agent tasks? **RQ2**: Can our method construct a purified world model to help multi-agent cooperation? Therefore, we set up different experiments to answer these two questions.

**Baselines.** We chose our baselines in MARL from two groups, namely model-free and model-based approaches. Since methods that worked well in POMDP belong to the model-free class, we compared several strong and representative model-free methods as our baselines. In the model-free group, the baselines include two policy and value-based methods, MAPPO and QMIX [18,30] that achieve state-of-the-art performance on the well-known challenging task, SMAC. In the model-based group, learning from multi-agent observations to construct the world model has been little addressed. We further extend the single-agent observation encoder used in Dreamer [4] by sharing it across agents for the global state abstraction as our model-based baseline. The latent global states are concatenated directly from the shared encoder outputs. The concatenated states conduct a world model for model-based MARL without denoising like that in Dreamer [4]. We named this approach Dreamer-MA as the model-based baseline.

**Evaluation Metrics.** On the toy example, we set up the end step as the evaluation metric, which denotes the maximum interactions of two players used to reach the goal state in the MMDP example, the end step can be intuitively evaluated the sample efficiency of all methods. It is also proportional to the reward defined in Fig. 3(a). On the metric of SMAC, in contrast to using the win rate, to compare these methods with a more fine-grained metric, we use average returns, which are normalized from 0 to 20 and proportion to the win rate. Therefore, we leverage *Average Returns* at each timestep in an episode as the evaluation metric to validate our method and baselines in SMAC.

**Implementation Details.** Our implementation uses PyTorch libarary [16]. All experiments run in 10 random seeds. We use a single Nvidia A100 GPU and 256 CPU cores for each training run. The baseline implementations are based on the official open source code. The world models are learned via reconstruction in Dreamer-MA. We reuse the architecture for estimating the world model in UTOPIA to the official implementation from Dreamer [4]. Concretely, we borrow the neural network architecture from QMIX, MAPPO, and Dreamer [4,18,30] as our baselines and train the behavior policy and value models as PPO methods. All of the other compared methods adopt exactly the same structure as the feature embedding from vectors of UTOPIA. For the hyperparameter selection, we have fine-tuned the key hyperparameters for our method and baselines in each experiment. In this section, we include details of our experiments.

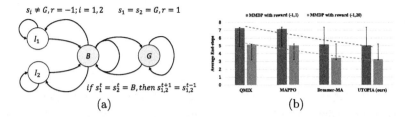

(a)    (b)

**Fig. 3.** (a) An illustration of Multi-agent MDP (MMDP): $I_i$ denotes the initial state of agent $i$, $B$ denotes the rebound state, $S$ denotes a normal state, and $G$ denotes the terminal goal state. Two players cooperate to reach the goal state together, rewarded with the above rule. (b) End-steps in MMDP after 50 interactions for our method and baselines. The blue and red data means the final reward is 1 or 20.

## 5.1 Toy Example

To illustrate the necessity of our method even in a simple multi-agent cooperation problem, we designed a two-player Multi-agent Markov decision process (MMDP) as a toy example, as shown in Fig. 3(a). We conduct a two-player multi-agent MDP to illustrate the necessity of our method, even in this simple case. This setup is arguably easier but more practical. Two players following the MMDP depicted in Fig. 3(a) cooperate to reach the same goal state together. This example can be regarded as a simplified version of many practical multi-agent cooperation problems, like vehicle collision avoidance. Each agent $i$ is initialized in the state $I_i$ and moves along the side in MMDP each timestep. Once two agents are headed to the rebound state $B$, they will return to their original states in the next step. The maximum episode length is set at 20 steps. The game ends when two agents reach the goal state $G$ together or the timestep exceeds the episode limit. Each agent receives a $-1$ reward if the two agents are still not in the goal state. To fully validate the effectiveness of our method compared with baselines, we set two different final rewards as 1 and 20 if they reach it together and denote the two MMDP as $(-1, 1)$ and $(-1, 20)$. The average end-steps of 10 experiments are shown in Fig. 3(b) on these two variants. In terms of the rule, the two agents need to plan together to avoid the collision in the rebound state to save the step to finish the game. Therefore, for this simple example, we see that the model-based method can achieve lower end-steps at the fixed rollout samples than the model-free methods. This indicates that planning in the latent space is crucial to improving the sample efficiency, even in a simple setting. When we dive into the model-based methods in Dreamer-MA, where the observation of each agent is shared across teammates to build a multi-agent shared world model, the noise can be included in the global states. By denoising task-irrelevant information, UTOPIA outperforms the naive model-based method, which also indicates the effectiveness of our method in Fig. 3(b). We analyze the reason for the limited improvement by comparing our method with Dreamer-MA mainly because of the finite noise that existed in this toy example.

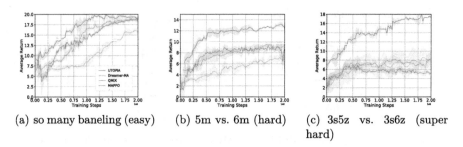

(a) so many baneling (easy)    (b) 5m vs. 6m (hard)    (c) 3s5z vs. 3s6z (super hard)

**Fig. 4.** The average returns of model-free and model-based MARL on three maps.

## 5.2   Cooperative Multi-agent Tasks on SMAC

Another more challenging benchmark we used as the testbed is StarCraft multi-agent challenge (SMAC) [19], where multiple agents are masked with the observation function and receive local observations, which can be modeled as a partially observed Markov decision process (POMDP). This partially observed property prevents multiple agents from collaborating to beat the opponents. Different maps include various entities with different observation and action spaces, which own a team reward normalized in $[0, 20]$. Multiple agents require discrete actions to cooperate to beat the enemy in the POMDP. The state-based input makes learning without denoising more difficult due to the high-level information in observations [18]. We compare UTOPIA with state-of-the-art model-free methods and an extension from single-agent model-based methods as described in baselines on three maps (easy, hard, and super hard) from SMAC. The results are shown in Fig. 4. Results suggest our method outperforms the other three baselines in terms of sample efficiency across all three difficulty maps. We also find that Dreamer-MA cannot compete with the performance of the other two model-free baselines. Dreamer-MA decreases the performance in the more complicated tasks, caused by the abundant noise with the increasing agent number and randomness of the environment. This also verifies the necessity of denoising the task-irrelevant information for each agent in UTOPIA.

## 5.3   Ablation Studies

To better analyze the importance of each component in UTOPIA, we have conducted an extensive ablation study as shown in Table 1. To clarify the ablation study, we claim several modifications in our method by dropping a module. We explain the modification in detail for the rows in Table 1. In the first row, we replace the behavior policy's objective from the clipped weighted advantage loss in PPO-style to the actor-critic method used in Dreamer [4], where the critic is to precisely estimate the expected rewards and the actor aims to maximize the critic value. In the second row, we use the generative model VAEs employed in Denoised MDP [23] to extract the global state via reconstruction loss and share this observation encoding network among agents. In the third row, we drop the guided denoising in UTOPIA to validate the effectiveness of the diffusion and guided models. In the last row, we use the fixed planning horizon for the latent roll-outs of the world model, where we claim the fixed horizon will limit behavior policy learning. The results in each row are obtained by replacing one component of UTOPIA and keeping other components unchanged. The first row shows the advantage of PPO in optimizing the behavior policy. The second row shows the degradation when our method shares the VAE encoder across agents, which is validated to be harmful to abstracting the global states and constructing the world model. The third row validates the effectiveness of the guided denoising models. Planning based on the fixed horizon step also struggles to compete with our method. We guess many hard tasks need more planning steps than the fixed horizon, which degrades behavior policy learning.

**Table 1.** Average returns of agents after training from 1M timesteps of UTOPIA variants by dropping different modules on two SMAC maps. All quantities are provided on a scale of 0.01, averaged under 10 random seeds. Standard deviations over these random seeds are provided in brackets.

| Method | 3m (easy) | MMM2 (super hard) |
|---|---|---|
| UTOPIA (our method) | **19.66** ($\pm$**0.25**) | **15.23** ($\pm$**2.37**) |
| with actor-critic | 17.26 ($\pm$0.15) | 14.47 ($\pm$1.72) |
| with VAE observation encoder | 15.74 ($\pm$0.62) | 11.37 ($\pm$2.68) |
| without guided denoising | 10.25 ($\pm$1.27) | 8.46 ($\pm$2.33) |
| without dynamic planning horizon | 8.26 ($\pm$2.15) | 7.14 ($\pm$3.43) |

# 6   Conclusion

In this paper, we presented UTOPIA, a new model-based MARL that improves sample efficiency by learning to filter multi-agent observations and building a purified world model. In a multi-agent setting, we highlight the necessity of denoising each agent observation differently and defining noise based on teammates' contributions to transitions and rewards. Considering the explicit definition, we encode each agent observation using a guided diffusion model to generate purified global states. Furthermore, our method shares an easily scalable condition-dependent guided diffusion model for each agent. By constructing a world model from purified states, we plan the trajectory in latent space, providing a buffer for learning policy and value models. Experimental results on a toy example and challenging tasks show that our method can outperform existing state-of-the-art mode-free methods and a multi-agent extension of the single-agent model-based approach. In summary, this method provides a feasible direction for model-based MARL and can be applied to many real-world tasks requiring planning with expensive interactions, such as robotic control tasks. In the future, we hope that the world model and behavior policy in multi-agent can be optimized together and avoid the extrapolation errors caused by insufficiently trained modules.

**Acknowledgements.** This work is supported by the National Key R&D Program of China (No. 2022ZD0116405), the Strategic Priority Research Program of the Chinese Academy of Sciences under Grant (No. XDA27030300), and the Program for National Nature Science Foundation of China (62073324).

# References

1. Bard, N.: The hanabi challenge: a new frontier for AI research. Artif. Intell. **280**, 103216 (2020)
2. Dhariwal, P., Nichol, A.: Diffusion models beat GANs on image synthesis. Adv. Neural. Inf. Process. Syst. **34**, 8780–8794 (2021)
3. Fang, K., Yin, P., Nair, A., Levine, S.: Planning to practice: efficient online fine-tuning by composing goals in latent space. arXiv preprint arXiv:2205.08129 (2022)
4. Hafner, D., Lillicrap, T., Ba, J., Norouzi, M.: Dream to control: learning behaviors by latent imagination. arXiv preprint arXiv:1912.01603 (2019)
5. Hafner, D., et al.: Learning latent dynamics for planning from pixels. arXiv preprint arXiv:1811.04551 (2018)
6. Hafner, D., Lillicrap, T., Norouzi, M., Ba, J.: Mastering Atari with discrete world models. arXiv preprint arXiv:2010.02193 (2020)
7. Ho, J., Jain, A., Abbeel, P.: Denoising diffusion probabilistic models. Adv. Neural. Inf. Process. Syst. **33**, 6840–6851 (2020)
8. Hu, H., Foerster, J.N.: Simplified action decoder for deep multi-agent reinforcement learning. arXiv preprint arXiv:1912.02288 (2019)
9. Janner, M., Du, Y., Tenenbaum, J.B., Levine, S.: Planning with diffusion for flexible behavior synthesis. arXiv preprint arXiv:2205.09991 (2022)
10. Kuba, J.G., et al.: Trust region policy optimisation in multi-agent reinforcement learning. arXiv preprint arXiv:2109.11251 (2021)
11. Levine, S.: Reinforcement learning and control as probabilistic inference: Tutorial and review. arXiv preprint arXiv:1805.00909 (2018)
12. Mao, H., et al.: Neighborhood cognition consistent multi-agent reinforcement learning. In: AAAI (2020)
13. Mendonca, R., Rybkin, O., Daniilidis, K., Hafner, D., Pathak, D.: Discovering and achieving goals via world models. Adv. Neural. Inf. Process. Syst. **34**, 24379–24391 (2021)
14. Oliehoek, F.A., Amato, C.: A Concise Introduction to Decentralized POMDPs. Springer, Cham (2016). https://doi.org/10.1007/978-3-319-28929-8
15. OroojlooyJadid, A., Hajinezhad, D.: A review of cooperative multi-agent deep reinforcement learning. arXiv preprint arXiv:1908.03963 (2019)
16. Paszke, A., et al.: Pytorch: an imperative style, high-performance deep learning library. In: Advances in Neural Information Processing Systems, vol. 32 (2019)
17. Pasztor, B., Bogunovic, I., Krause, A.: Efficient model-based multi-agent mean-field reinforcement learning. arXiv preprint arXiv:2107.04050 (2021)
18. Rashid, T., Samvelyan, M., Schroeder, C., Farquhar, G., Foerster, J., Whiteson, S.: Qmix: Monotonic value function factorisation for deep multi-agent reinforcement learning. In: International Conference on Machine Learning, pp. 4295–4304. PMLR (2018)

19. Samvelyan, M., et al.: The starcraft multi-agent challenge. arXiv preprint arXiv:1902.04043 (2019)
20. Sunehag, P., et al.: Value-decomposition networks for cooperative multi-agent learning. arXiv preprint arXiv:1706.05296 (2017)
21. Wang, T., Dong, H., Lesser, V.R., Zhang, C.: Roma: multi-agent reinforcement learning with emergent roles. arXiv:abs/2003.08039 (2020)
22. Wang, T., Gupta, T., Mahajan, A., Peng, B., Whiteson, S., Zhang, C.: Rode: learning roles to decompose multi-agent tasks. arXiv:abs/2010.01523 (2021)
23. Wang, T., Du, S.S., Torralba, A., Isola, P., Zhang, A., Tian, Y.: Denoised MDPs: learning world models better than the world itself. arXiv preprint arXiv:2206.15477 (2022)
24. Wang, X., Zhang, Z., Zhang, W.: Model-based multi-agent reinforcement learning: Recent progress and prospects. arXiv preprint arXiv:2203.10603 (2022)
25. Wen, M., et al.: Multi-agent reinforcement learning is a sequence modeling problem. arXiv preprint arXiv:2205.14953 (2022)
26. Wu, P., Escontrela, A., Hafner, D., Goldberg, K., Abbeel, P.: Daydreamer: world models for physical robot learning. arXiv preprint arXiv:2206.14176 (2022)
27. Xu, Y., et al.: Learning general world models in a handful of reward-free deployments. arXiv preprint arXiv:2210.12719 (2022)
28. Yarats, D., Zhang, A., Kostrikov, I., Amos, B., Pineau, J., Fergus, R.: Improving sample efficiency in model-free reinforcement learning from images. In: Proceedings of the AAAI Conference on Artificial Intelligence, vol. 35, pp. 10674–10681 (2021)
29. Ye, Z., Chen, Y., Jiang, X., Song, G., Yang, B., Fan, S.: Improving sample efficiency in multi-agent actor-critic methods. Appl. Intell. **52**(4), 3691–3704 (2022)
30. Yu, C., Velu, A., Vinitsky, E., Wang, Y., Bayen, A., Wu, Y.: The surprising effectiveness of PPO in cooperative, multi-agent games. arXiv preprint arXiv:2103.01955 (2021)
31. Zhang, K., Yang, Z., Başar, T.: Multi-agent reinforcement learning: a selective overview of theories and algorithms. In: Handbook of Reinforcement Learning and Control, pp. 321–384 (2021)
32. Zhou, M., et al.: Smarts: scalable multi-agent reinforcement learning training school for autonomous driving. arXiv preprint arXiv:2010.09776 (2020)

# Unsupervised Salient Patch Selection for Data-Efficient Reinforcement Learning

Zhaohui Jiang[ID] and Paul Weng[(✉)][ID]

UM-SJTU Joint Institute, Shanghai Jiao Tong University, Shanghai, China
{jiangzhaohui,paul.weng}@sjtu.edu.cn

**Abstract.** To improve the sample efficiency of vision-based deep reinforcement learning (RL), we propose a novel method, called SPIRL, to automatically extract important patches from input images. Following Masked Auto-Encoders, SPIRL is based on Vision Transformer models pre-trained in a self-supervised fashion to reconstruct images from randomly-sampled patches. These pre-trained models can then be exploited to detect and select salient patches, defined as hard to reconstruct from neighboring patches. In RL, the SPIRL agent processes selected salient patches via an attention module. We empirically validate SPIRL on Atari games to test its data-efficiency against relevant state-of-the-art methods, including some traditional model-based methods and keypoint-based models. In addition, we analyze our model's interpretability capabilities.

**Keywords:** image-based deep reinforcement learning · data efficiency · interpretability · keypoint

## 1 Introduction

Although deep reinforcement learning (RL) has shown a lot of promise [23,28], it is notoriously sample inefficient, especially with image inputs. Indeed, deep RL agents often need to be trained with millions of samples (or even more) before reaching an acceptable performance. Various techniques (see Related Work in Sect. 2) have been suggested to tackle this issue. In this paper, we consider two main causes, which we address in our novel method. First, most deep RL methods learn both end-to-end and from scratch, which is actually not realistic and practical. Second, the RL agent needs to learn to process a whole image, which may not be necessary since many parts are usually redundant.

Regarding the first point, inspired by recent successes in self-supervised learning in computer vision, we pre-train an adapted Masked Auto-Encoder (MAE) [12] to learn a feature extractor via self-supervision. Recall that in MAE (see Background in Sect. 3), an encoder and decoder, both based on Vision Transformer [5], are jointly trained to reconstruct images from a randomly-sampled

Partially supported by the program of National Natural Science Foundation of China (No. 62176154).

subset of its patches. Our adaptation of MAE help separate the background of an image from its other elements (e.g., moving objects in Atari games) by encouraging the encoder to focus only on those latter elements, while leaving irrelevant parts (e.g., background) to the decoder. Using such encoder can facilitate the training of the deep RL agent, since the agent does not need to learn to process the raw high-dimensional input anymore and a well-trained encoder should only embed relevant information.

Regarding the second point, we further exploit the same pre-trained MAE to determine the most salient image patches (i.e., those that are the hardest to reconstruct for the MAE decoder from their surrounding patches). Interestingly, our salient patch selection method can adaptively determine the number of salient patches depending on the image complexity. Our deep RL agent then only takes as inputs the selected salient patches, reducing further the dimensionality of its inputs. Intuitively, the RL agent may learn faster and better by focusing directly on important parts of an image.

For the deep RL agent itself, we adopt a simple network based on the Transformer architecture [36] to aggregate the embeddings of the selected salient patches. This architecture can accept a varying number of salient patches and intuitively learns to exploit their relationships to make decisions. We call our overall method *Salient Patch Input RL* (SPIRL) and demonstrate the whole approach on Atari games [4].

*Contributions.* Our contributions can be summarized as follows: We propose a novel deep RL method (Sect. 4) that learns to find salient image patches to improve data efficiency[1]. Compared to some alternative methods, our model can be pre-trained fast, with a relatively small dataset, and without specifying the number of patches to select. Moreover, our salient patch selection method is generic and could possibly be used for other downstream tasks. Since our goal is to improve sample complexity in RL, we propose in addition a simple Transformer-based architecture for the RL agent to process the selected salient patches, whose number can can vary from timestep to timestep. We experimentally demonstrate (Sect. 5) that our method can indeed improve sample efficiency in the low-data regime compared to state-of-the-art (SOTA) methods. Finally, we also discuss the interpretability of our method.

## 2   Related Work

Research has been very active in improving the data efficiency of deep RL. Various generic ideas have been explored, such as off-policy training [10,24,28], improved exploration [6,29], model-based RL [17,37], auxiliary tasks [15,41], or data augmentation [22,25,40] to cite a few. Most of these propositions are orthogonal to the idea explored in this paper and could be integrated to our method to further improve its performance. We leave such study to future work.

---

[1] Code and appendix are in https://github.com/AdaptiveAutonomousAgents/SPIRL.

Closer to our work are techniques proposed to learn more compact representations from images. We focus mainly on works related to vision-based RL. They range from keypoint extraction methods to object detection methods. Our proposed method can be understood as lying at the middle of this spectrum.

Regarding keypoint-based methods, most of them exploit *KeyNet* [16], which uses a convolutional neural network (CNN) and outputs different keypoints in different CNN channels as Gaussian heatmaps. For instance, Struct-VRNN [27] or WSDS [26] consider keypoints for learning a dynamic model. In addition, *Transporter* [21] and *PermaKey* [8], which both build on KeyNet, improve keypoint detection by considering changes between image pairs and local spatial predictability of CNN features, respectively. All these methods need the number $K$ of keypoints to be specified before pre-training, which can hinder their performance and applicability in situations where $K$ is unknown or dynamic, such as in video games.

Regarding object-based methods, various propositions have been made to learn object-centric representations for RL. For instance, [1] describe a technique notably combining image segmentation and object tracking. [7] pre-train a bottleneck-structured network, named *MOREL*, by unsupervised object segmentation with 100k consecutive game frames from a random policy. The bottleneck embedding is used as part of the input state for RL policy (PPO or A2C) to reduce the number of interactions with environments. [42] learn an object-centric latent representation via a compositional generative world model and proves that it can benefit downstream RL manipulation tasks with multiple objects. These methods are generally more complex, require more hyperparameters to tune, and are slower to train than our approach.

Following the success of Vision Transformer (ViT) [5] in computer vision, several recent works attempted to exploit it in deep RL. When applied on convolutional features, [18] report competitive performance in the model-free setting, while [32] present a successful model-based approach. However, current results [9,34] seem to suggest that convolutional layers outperform ViT for representation learning in standard RL algorithms, which may not be surprising since Transformer blocks [36] lack inductive biases like translation invariance encoded in convolutional layers. To the best of our knowledge, our method is the first demonstrating a promising application of ViT to deep RL without any convolutional layers.

In the context of vision-based deep RL, prior works used the Transformer model [36] for the RL agent's decision-making. For instance, [43] apply such model as a relational inductive bias to process elements of convolutional feature maps. [18] use such architecture on outputs of a ViT model. However, there are several differences with our architecture. Most notably, we use pre-layer normalization instead of post-layer normalization, which has been shown to be inferior [5,12,39]. More importantly, we only process embeddings of salient parts of the whole input image.

# 3    Background

We recall next some background on deep RL, the Transformer model, and the masked autoencoder architecture based on Vision Transformer.

*Notations.* Notation $d$ represents an embedding dimension. For any positive integer $n$, $[n]$ denotes the set $\{1, 2, \ldots, n\}$. For a sequence $\boldsymbol{x}_1, \boldsymbol{x}_2, \ldots \boldsymbol{x}_n \in \mathbb{R}^d$, $\boldsymbol{X} = (\boldsymbol{x}_i)_{i \in [n]} \in \mathbb{R}^{n \times d}$ denotes the matrix stacking them as row vectors.

## 3.1    Rainbow and Its Data-Efficient Version

RL is based on the Markov decision process (MDP) model [30] defined as a tuple $(\mathcal{S}, \mathcal{A}, T, R, d_0, \gamma)$ where $\mathcal{S}$ is a state space, $\mathcal{A}$ is an action space, $T : \mathcal{S} \times \mathcal{A} \times \mathcal{S} \rightarrow [0, 1]$ is a transition function, $R : \mathcal{S} \times \mathcal{A} \rightarrow \mathbb{R}$ is a reward function, $d_0$, is a distribution over initial states, and $\gamma \in (0, 1)$ is a discount factor. In this model, the goal is to find a policy $\pi : \mathcal{S} \rightarrow \mathcal{A}$ such that the expected discounted sum of rewards is maximized. Formally, this can be achieved by estimating the optimal Q-function defined by: $Q^*(s, a) = R(s, a) + \gamma \max_{a'} \mathbb{E}_{s'}[Q^*(s', a')]$.

Deep Q-Network (DQN) [28] approximates this Q-function by minimizing an L2 loss using transitions $(s, a, r, s')$ randomly sampled from a replay buffer storing samples obtained via interactions with the environment:

$$(r + \max_{a'} \gamma \hat{Q}_{\theta'}(s', a') - \hat{Q}_\theta(s, a))^2$$

where $\hat{Q}_\theta$ is the DQN network parametrized by $\boldsymbol{\theta}$ while parameter $\boldsymbol{\theta}'$ is a copy of $\boldsymbol{\theta}$, saved at a lower frequency.

Many techniques have been proposed to improve the efficiency of DQN: double Q-learning [11], prioritized replay [31], dueling network [38], multi-step bootstrap targets [33], distributional Q-learning [3], and noisy DQN [6]. Their combination called *Rainbow* [14] is a SOTA value-based method. By tuning its hyperparameters (i.e., earlier and more frequent updates, longer multi-step returns), the resulting algorithm called *Data-Efficient (DE) Rainbow* [35] can be very competitive in the low-data regime, which consists in training with 100K transitions. In particular, such optimized model-free approach can outperform some model-based methods [19,35].

## 3.2    Transformer Layers and Self-attention

A *Transformer* model [36] is defined as a stack of several identical layers, each comprised of a multi-head self-attention (MHSA) module followed by a multi-layer perceptron (MLP) module. Residual connections [13] are established around each of them and each module also includes a layer normalization [2].

Formally, one Transformer layer is defined as follows. For an input sequence of length $n$, $\boldsymbol{x}_1, \ldots, \boldsymbol{x}_n$, its output, $\boldsymbol{z}_1, \ldots, \boldsymbol{z}_n$, can be computed as follows:

$$\boldsymbol{x}'_i = \boldsymbol{x}_i + \text{MHSA}(\text{LN}(\boldsymbol{x}_i), \text{LN}(\boldsymbol{X}))$$
$$\boldsymbol{z}_i = \boldsymbol{x}'_i + \text{MLP}(\text{LN}(\boldsymbol{x}'_i))$$

where LN denotes a layer normalization and $\text{LN}(\boldsymbol{X}) = (\text{LN}(\boldsymbol{x}_j))_{j \in [n]}$. Note that we use pre-layer normalization (i.e., LN is applied on the inputs of the two modules, MHSA and MLP), instead of post-layer normalization like in the original Transformer. The former has been shown to be easier to train and to have better performance [5,12,39].

An MHSA is composed of several scaled dot-product attention (SDPA) heads. Each SDPA head specifies how an element $\boldsymbol{x}_i$ should attend to other elements of a sequence in $\boldsymbol{X}$. In practice, several heads are used to allow an element to simultaneously attend to different parts of a sequence.

An SDPA head uses an attention function, which can be understood as a soft associative map. Formally, given a query $\boldsymbol{q} \in \mathbb{R}^d$, keys $\boldsymbol{K} \in \mathbb{R}^{n \times d}$, and values $\boldsymbol{V} \in \mathbb{R}^{n \times d}$, this function computes the output associated to $\boldsymbol{q}$ as:

$$\text{Attention}(\boldsymbol{q}, \boldsymbol{K}, \boldsymbol{V}) = \text{softmax}(\frac{\boldsymbol{q}\boldsymbol{K}^\intercal}{\sqrt{d}})\boldsymbol{V}\,.$$

An SDPA head can then be defined as follows:

$$\text{SDPA}(\boldsymbol{x}_i, \boldsymbol{X}) = \text{Attention}(\boldsymbol{x}_i\boldsymbol{W}^Q, \boldsymbol{X}\boldsymbol{W}^K, \boldsymbol{X}\boldsymbol{W}^V)\,,$$

where $\boldsymbol{W}^Q, \boldsymbol{W}^K, \boldsymbol{W}^V \in \mathbb{R}^{d \times d}$ correspond to trainable projection matrices. An MHSA with $k$ heads is then defined by:

$$\text{MHSA}(\boldsymbol{x}_i, \boldsymbol{X}) = (\text{SDPA}_\ell(\boldsymbol{x}_i, \boldsymbol{X}))_{\ell \in [k]}\boldsymbol{W}^O\,,$$

where the $\text{SDPA}_\ell$'s denote different SDPAs with their own trainable weights, $(\text{SDPA}_\ell(\boldsymbol{x}_i, \boldsymbol{X}))_{\ell \in [k]}$ is seen as a row vector, and $\boldsymbol{W}^O \in \mathbb{R}^{kd \times d}$ is a trainable projection matrix.

### 3.3   Vision Transformer and Masked Autoencoder

*Vision Transformer* (ViT). [5] demonstrates that a Transformer-based architecture without any convolution layer can achieve SOTA performance on computer vision (CV) tasks. Given an image $\boldsymbol{X} \in \mathbb{R}^{h \times w \times c}$ of height $h$ and width $w$ with $c$ channels, the key idea is to split $\boldsymbol{X}$ into square patches $\{\boldsymbol{X}_{i,j} \in \mathbb{R}^{p^2 \times c} \mid (i,j) \in [\frac{w}{p}] \times [\frac{h}{p}]\}$ and linearly project each flattened patches to obtain $\{\boldsymbol{X}_{i,j}^{proj} \in \mathbb{R}^d \mid (i,j) \in [\frac{w}{p}] \times [\frac{h}{p}]\}$ as patch embeddings, where $(i,j)$ indicates the patch position in the image, $p$ is the side length of square patches, and $d$ is the embedding dimension for the Transformer layers. Since Transformer layers are invariant with respect to permutation of their inputs, positional embeddings are added to patch embeddings before feeding them to the Transformer layers.

While ViT originally relied on supervised training, Masked Auto-Encoder (MAE) [12] shows that it can also be trained via self-supervision using image reconstruction from image patches. MAE is composed of an encoder and decoder, whose architectures are both based on ViT. Given an image, the encoder receives 25% randomly selected patches, while the decoder receives the embedding of

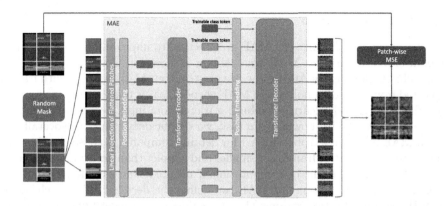

**Fig. 1.** Adaptation of MAE illustrated on *Seaquest*: a higher-capacity decoder can extract the background information, while a smaller encoder focuses on embedding only salient elements in images. Overall, its size is more than 50× smaller than in [12].

those patches with a shared trainable [mask] token replacing the 75% remaining masked patches. MAE uses 2-D sinusoidal positional embeddings $PE_{i,j}$ for position $(i, j)$. It therefore feeds $\{X_{i,j}^{proj} + PE_{i,j} \mid (i,j) \in [\frac{w}{p}] \times [\frac{h}{p}]\}$ to the Transformer layers.

The MAE model is trained to recover the whole image using a loss defined as a sum over patches of the mean-squared error (MSE) between a normalized patch from the original image and its corresponding patch reconstructed by the decoder. Formally, for a patch at position $(i, j)$,

$$\text{loss}(X_{i,j}, \hat{X}_{i,j}) = \frac{1}{p^2 c} \cdot \| X_{i,j}^{norm} - \hat{X}_{i,j} \|^2 \tag{1}$$

$$\text{where } X_{i,j}^{norm} = \frac{X_{i,j} - \overline{X}_{i,j}}{\hat{\sigma}_{X_{i,j}}} \text{ and}$$

$$\hat{X} = \text{MAE}(\text{RandomMask}(X)). \tag{2}$$

Here, $X_{i,j}^{norm}$ is a normalized patch ($\overline{X}_{i,j}$ and $\hat{\sigma}_{X_{i,j}}$ are the average and standard deviation resp. computed over a patch) and $\hat{X}_{i,j}$ is the corresponding patch extracted from the reconstructed image $\hat{X}$. After pre-training, the encoder can be fine-tuned for downstream tasks as a feature extractor.

## 4  Architecture

Our method, called SPIRL, is composed of three main components: MAE model, salient patch selection, and Transformer-based RL model. See Figs. 1 and 5 for an overview of MAE and SPIRL respectively. In Atari games, frames are usually square images. In the remaining, we use $P$ to denote the number of patches per row (i.e., $P = h/p = w/p$).

## 4.1   MAE Adaptation

We show how we specialize the MAE architecture to improve RL data-efficiency and interpretability The MAE pre-training is however mostly standard (see Appendix A): for a given Atari game, we pre-train our MAE network with frames collected from a random policy: the MAE encoder learns to encode frame patches and the MAE decoder learns to rebuilt a frame from input patch embeddings.

To facilitate the RL downstream task, we significantly reduce the overall size of our MAE model (see Appendix A.1 for details) compared to those used in computer vision since Atari frames are smaller and simpler than natural images. This leads to savings in terms of computational, memory, and sample costs. Moreover, in contrast to a standard MAE, we define the decoder to be much larger than the encoder for two reasons: (1) This enforces a stronger bottleneck where the encoder focuses on more essential information intrinsic to a patch, while (2) more global and repetitive information (e.g., background) can be learned by the decoder. The intuition is that the embeddings returned by the encoder would be easier for the RL agent to learn from.

We empirically justify those two points on some Atari games. We start with the second point, which is needed to discuss the first one. Our architecture can indeed separate the static background from other objects. The last 3 columns in Fig. 2 shows frames reconstructed by a decoder pre-trained in a specific game: *Frostbite*, *MsPacman*, *Seaquest*, and *BattleZone* (with frame size $w = h = 96$, patch size $p = 8$, and thus, $P = 12$) for three types of inputs: (a) positional embeddings alone, (b) trained $[mask]$ token added with positional embeddings, and (c) trained $[mask]$ token along. As expected, the decoder can reconstruct the whole background using only the trained $[mask]$ token with positional embeddings (i.e., all patches masked, see $4^{th}$ col. of Fig. 2). Interestingly, a finer analysis shows that the positional embeddings alone are necessary ($6^{th}$ col.) and sufficient ($5^{th}$ col.) for generating the background, suggesting that the background visual information is actually encoded in the parameters of the pre-trained decoder. Note that the colors in the reconstructed frames differ from the original ones ($1^{st}$ col.), because the MAE model processes normalized inputs (Eq. (2)).

Regarding the first point, to show that patch embeddings returned by an encoder contain useful local information, we use a pre-trained MAE to reconstruct each patch of a given frame from its surrounding patches as only input. Formally, for an image patch $X_{i,j}$ at position $(i, j) \in [P]^2$ of an image $X$, we denote its surrounding patches as: $\text{surr}(X_{i,j}) = \{X_{k,\ell} \,|\, (k, l) \in [P]^2, k = i \pm 1, \ell = j \pm 1\}$. Taking $\text{surr}(X_{i,j})$ as only input, the pre-trained MAE can reconstruct a whole frame $\text{MAE}(\text{surr}(X_{i,j}))$, from which we can extract the corresponding reconstructed patch $\hat{X}_{i,j}$:

$$\hat{Y}_{i,j} = \hat{X}_{i,j}, \quad \text{where } \hat{X} = \text{MAE}(\text{surr}(X_{i,j})). \tag{3}$$

The $2^{nd}$ column of Fig. 2 shows frames made of the reconstructed $\hat{Y}_{i,j}$ for all $(i, j) \in [P]^2$. Comparing with the original frames ($1^{st}$ column), more accurate details appear at their correct locations in the frames of the $2^{nd}$ column than

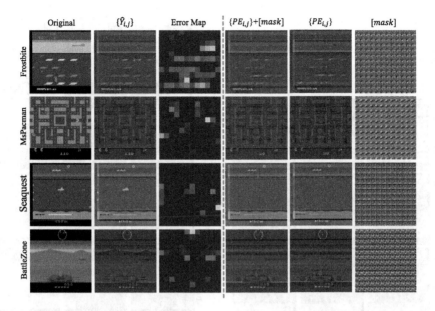

**Fig. 2.** Visualization from the pre-trained MAE model. The first 3 columns are visualizations related to a certain frame: ($1^{st}$ column) Original frames; ($2^{nd}$) Reconstruction from patch surroundings; ($3^{rd}$) Reconstruction error maps where brighter colors indicate larger values. The last 3 columns are obtained without frame patches, but with different inputs to the pre-trained MAE decoder: Reconstructions with ($4^{th}$) $\{PE_{i,j}\}$ added to $[mask]$ token; ($5^{th}$) only $\{PE_{i,j}\}$; ($6^{th}$) only $[mask]$ token.

in the background frames generated from the positional embeddings alone ($5^{th}$ column). This confirms that our MAE architecture achieves our first point.

## 4.2   Salient Patch Selection

As seen in the previous examples, in a given frame, most patches contain redundant or useless information (e.g., containing only static background). Since an RL agent could potentially learn faster by reducing the dimensionality of its inputs, a natural idea is to discard those irrelevant patches and only keep important ones (i.e., *salient patches*) to formulate the RL agent's input. We propose to exploit our pre-trained MAE to evaluate the saliency of a patch. Intuitively, a patch is salient if the decoder cannot reconstruct it from its surrounding patches. This idea can be formalized by (1) defining a reconstruction error map and (2) using it for selecting salient patches, which we explain next.

**Reconstruction Error Map.** Using a pre-trained MAE, we can calculate a reconstruction error map $\boldsymbol{E} \in \mathbb{R}^{P \times P}$ for any image $\boldsymbol{X}$. Intuitively, the reconstruction error of any patch $\boldsymbol{X}_{i,j}$ of $\boldsymbol{X}$ is obtained by comparing it with its

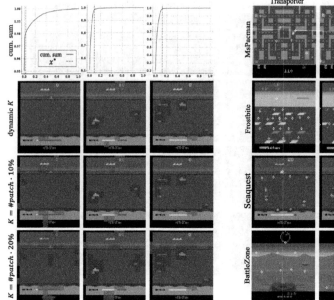

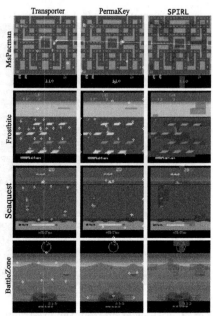

**Fig. 3.** Different salient patch selection strategies in three different frames (one per column) of *Seaquest*: ($1^{st}$ row) blue lines (resp. red dashed lines) are cumulative sum of errors in $E$ (resp. $p^*$); ($2^{nd}$) selected patches (red squares) with $K$ determined by $p^*$ from $1^{st}$ row; ($3^{rd}$ & $4^{th}$) selected patches with pre-defined $K$. (Color figure online)

**Fig. 4.** Comparison of key-point (represented as white crosses) / salient-patch (transparent red patches) selection using Transporter, PermaKey, or SPIRL. Each row corresponds to a same frame of a given game. Visualization for other frames can be found in Appendix A.4. (Color figure online)

reconstruction $\hat{Y}_{ij}$ (Eq. (3)) using only its surrounding patches surr($X_{ij}$). Formally, the reconstruction error map at position $(i, j)$ is simply the MSE between $X_{i,j}$ and $\hat{Y}_{i,j}$: $E_{i,j} = \frac{1}{p^2}\|X_{i,j} - \hat{Y}_{i,j}\|^2$. Using $E$, a patch is deemed more important than another if the $E$ score of the former is larger than latter.

As an illustration, the $2^{nd}$ column in Fig. 2 shows frames made of the reconstructed $\hat{Y}_{i,j}$ for all $(i, j) \in [P]^2$, and their corresponding reconstruction error maps ($3^{rd}$ column) where dark blue corresponds to smaller errors, while green (resp. yellow) corresponds to larger (resp. largest) errors. Interestingly, patches with larger errors roughly correspond to moving objects or objects with a complex hard-to-predict surface (i.e., Pacman, ghosts, floating ices, fishes, submarine, game score, or life count associated with higher error values), suggesting that the reconstruction error map can be exploited for salient patch selection.

**Salient Patch Selection.** Using the reconstruction error map $E$, salient patches can be selected, but one still needs to decide how many to keep. A

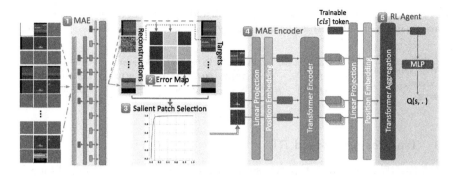

**Fig. 5.** Overview of SPIRL: (1) Pre-trained MAE rebuilds each patch from its surrounding, (2) a reconstruction error map is as MSE between pairs of reconstructed and target patches, (3) most salient patches are selected according to accumulated errors, (4) their embeddings are obtained from MAE encoder and concatenated to previous embeddings, and (5) A Transformer-based network aggregates them from which an MLP computes the estimated $Q$-values.

simple approach, as done in all previous works [8,16,21,27], would be to set a fixed pre-defined $K \in \mathbb{N}$ and select the top $K$ in terms of $\boldsymbol{E}$ scores. However, a suitable value for $K$ is not easy to choose: if too low, important information will be missing, but if too high, too many patches would need to be processed by the RL agent. Moreover, a pre-defined $K$ may be too simplistic, because the number of salient patches usually vary from games to games, but also from frames to frames for a given game. For instance, as Fig. 3 shows in *Seaquest*, objects may appear or disappear. Each column in Fig. 3 represents a frame at a different timestep and the $3^{rd}$ and $4^{th}$ rows depict the selected key frames for two different $K$'s expressed as a percentage of the total number of patches.

To be more adaptive, we propose instead a selection method, called *dynamic* $K$. A natural way to express it is via the absolute Lorenz curve [20] of $\boldsymbol{E}$. To define it formally, we first recall the cumulative distribution of the errors: $F(x) = \frac{1}{P^2} \sum_{i,j} \mathbb{I}_{\boldsymbol{E}_{i,j} \leq x}$, where $\mathbb{I}$ is the indicator function. Consider its left-continuous inverse (i.e., quantile function) for $p \in (0,1]$: $F^{-1}(p) = \inf\{x \in [0,1] \mid F(x) \geq p\}$. The absolute Lorenz curve $F^{-2}$ is defined as its integral: $F^{-2}(x) = \int_0^x F^{-1}(p)dp$. This curve, known to be concave, describes the allocation of errors over the population of patches. If this allocation were uniform, the curve would be a straight line from point $(0,0)$ to $(1,1)$. As expected, in practice, it is far from uniform ($1^{st}$ row of Fig. 3). There is a diminishing return for selecting more salient patches. We express the problem of selecting the best $K$ as finding $p$ such that the increase in the accumulated errors start to decrease. Formally, this point is approximately the point $(p^*, x^*)$ such that its slope is closest to $45°$.

**Table 1.** (Left) Pre-training time cost of SPIRL and baselines (averaged over the 4 Atari games); (Right) SPIRL with same configurations as in Table 2-*100K* v.s. MAE-All.

| Method | Time (h) |
| --- | --- |
| Transporter | 25.9 |
| PermaKey | 50.7 |
| SPIRL | 1.6 |

| Inputs for RL | Frostbite | MsPacman | Seaquest | BattleZone |
| --- | --- | --- | --- | --- |
| SPIRL | **669.5(731.7)** | **904.1(286.4)** | **557.9(148.1)** | **11980.0(3826.7)** |
| MAE-All | 405.7(382.3) | 760.3(210.0) | 538.4(79.8) | 10628.0(3176.9) |

### 4.3   Transformed-Based RL

After the dynamic salient patch selection, $K_t$ patches whose embeddings are given by the pre-trained embeddings are used as input for the downstream RL tasks. Note that we now index $K$ with time since this number can vary from frame to frame. We denote the set of selected salient patches at time $t$ as $O_t$.

The problem of how the embeddings in $O_t$ should be processed by the RL agent is not completely straightforward. Indeed, since our method does not guarantee temporal consistency across different frames (e.g., number or order of selected salient patches), the simple approach consisting in concatenating the embeddings is not feasible, in contrast to previous methods such as Transporter [21] or PermaKey [8]. In addition, concatenation is also not practical when $K$ becomes large. Moreover, a direct pooling (e.g., via a mean or max) over these embeddings would be a too lossy operation.

To solve this problem and obtain an architecture that is invariant with respect to permutations of its inputs, we propose the following simple Transformer-based architecture to aggregate the embeddings. A linear trainable projection is applied to each embeddings of $O_t$ to reduce their dimension. The resulting embeddings are then processed by several Transformer layers to obtain a global final embedding $o_t$, defined as MHSA($[cls], X_t$) where $[cls]$ is a trainable class token and $X_t$ contains the embeddings of patches in $O_t$. Embedding $o_t$ serves as input for the final decision-making part.

Although our method based on MAE and salient patch selection is generic, we instantiate it with DE Rainbow for simplicity. Therefore, following previous practice, the RL agent processes a concatenation of the four latest $o_t$ to account for partial observability using a simple MLP for the final decision-making part. Our overall proposition can be understood as replacing the convolutional layers of a standard Rainbow network by three components: a pre-trained MAE encoder, the dynamic $K$ salient patch selection, and MHSA layers.

## 5   Experimental Results

For the pre-training part, we mainly compare SPIRL against counterparts including Transporter [21], PermaKey [8], and MOREL [7], which also use pre-training to learn object-centric features to improve RL performance. For the RL training part, we focus on comparing with SOTA methods evaluated in the low-data regime, including SimPLe [17], Transporter, PermaKey. We further show examples about using attention to explain the learned policy with SPIRL.

**Table 2.** SPIRL v.s. baselines on Atari environments (Appendix B.4 for result sources).

| Games | 100K, average | | | | | 400K, median | |
|---|---|---|---|---|---|---|---|
| | SimPLe | Transporter | DE-Rainbow | DE-Rainbow-P | SPIRL | PermaKey | SPIRL |
| Frostbite | 254.7 | 388.3(142.1) | 341.4(277.8) | 483.7(710.7) | **669.5(731.7)** | 657.3(556.8) | **1194.0(1283.8)** |
| MsPacman | 762.8 | 999.4(145.4) | **1015.2(124.3)** | 985.4(129.6) | 904.1(286.4) | 1038.5(417.1) | **1186.0(193.9)** |
| Seaquest | 370.9 | 236.7(22.2) | 395.6(124.4) | 462.5(187.8) | **557.9(148.1)** | 520.0(169.9) | **534.0(88.2)** |
| BattleZone | 5184.4 | – | 10602.2(2299.6) | **13992.0(4713.5)** | 11980.0(3826.7) | 12566.7(3297.9) | **13500.0(1870.8)** |

**Pre-training.** SPIRL costs less than 50K interaction steps to collect pre-training data from a random policy, while other baselines either need to collect frames with trained agents or need at least 1.5 times more training data with higher or equal data quality requirement than us ( Appendix A.2 ). Although SPIRL is less demanding in terms of data quality and quantity for pre-training, its salient patch selection is qualitatively at least as good as other baselines (Fig. 4). While counterparts may not assign keypoints to important objects successfully (e.g., ghosts in *MsPacman*, small and semitransparent fishes in *Seaquest*, tiny bullet in the center in *BattleZone*), SPIRL manages to capture such patches correctly.

Table 1 (Left) shows that SPIRL can be pre-trained much faster than Transporter and PermaKey when using a same machine configuration (Appendix A.3).

Once our pre-training is finished, the reconstruction error map can be used to select varying numbers of salient patches in downstream tasks, which amortize the pre-training cost further. Recall that in contrast, previous keypoint methods would need to pre-train again if $K$ is changed.

**Atari Benchmark.** We test SPIRL on Atari games [4], a commonly-used RL benchmark, to demonstrate the performance of our framework. We choose the four games, *MsPacman, Frostbite, Seaquest,* and *BattleZone*, because they have various environment properties to demonstrate the ability of a data-efficient algorithm and they have also been adopted in PermaKey. We keep the hyper-parameters used in DE-Rainbow [35] (see Appendix B.2).

To illustrate SPIRL's data-efficiency, we focus on training in the low-data regime, which was already used to evaluate SimPLe. In this training regime, denoted *100K*, agents are trained with only 100K environment steps (i.e., 400K frames, since 4 frames are skipped every step). We also evaluate DE-Rainbow (denoted DE-Rainbow-P) trained with replay buffer initially filled with the same trajectory data as we pre-train our MAE before learning (see Appendix B.4 for more configuration details). Note that Permakey uses a variant of this low-data training regime, denoted *400K*: it allows the agent to interact with the environment 400K steps, but only updates the network 100K times. Although both regimes use the same number of updates, the latter one is more favorable and allows the agent to generate more data from more recent and better policies.

Since the number of selected salient patches may vary in an episode, we can not train the RL agent by sampling a batch of data, since the length of data inside a batch is not aligned. Moreover, diverging number of patches makes the training unstable and hurts the performance. As an implementation trick, in

**Table 3.** Ablation study to compare dynamic-$K$ (abbr. D-$K$) with $mr$ or simply using determined-$K$ on *100K* with average scores. (best results for each game in bold).

| Games | Frsotbite | | | MsPacman | | |
|---|---|---|---|---|---|---|
| ratio x | $mr^*$+5% | $mr^*$ = 60% | $mr^*$-5% | $mr^*$+5% | x* = 65% | $mr^*$-5% |
| D-$K$, $mr$ = x | 266.8(109.8) | 350.6(350.9) | **669.5(731.7)** | 847.9(314.3) | 735.9(196.8) | **904.1(286.4)** |
| $K = P^2 \times x$ | 410.6(373.6) | 565.4(538.7) | 563.0(720.7) | 859.3(311.2) | 909.2(512.2) | 710.5(146.4) |
| Games | Seaquest | | | BattleZone | | |
| ratio x | $mr^*$+5% | $mr^*$ = 80% | $mr^*$-5% | $mr^*$+5% | $mr^*$ = 70% | $mr^*$-5% |
| D-$K$, $mr$ = x | 371.6(89.5) | **557.9(148.1)** | 464.8(78.3) | 8624.0(2667.1) | **11980.0(3826.7)** | 9660.0(3462.8) |
| $K = P^2 \times x$ | 478.0(133.6) | 496.3(90.1) | 438.1(156.0) | 8035.3(2173.3) | 8700.0(2173.3) | 7600.0(3580.6) |

order to stabilize training and reduce the size of the replay buffer, we determine a maximal ratio $mr$ for the number of the selected patches based on counts of numbers of salient patches from the pre-training datasets. If more than $mr$ salient patches are selected, we simply drop the extra patches with the smallest error values. Otherwise we add dummy patches with zero padding. Detailed architecture and method to select $mr$ can be checked in Appendix B.5.

Table 2 compares SPIRL against other baselines. To make the results comparable, we run SPIRL according to the evaluation settings used in the baselines: average score for *100K* evaluated at the end of training, and the best median score for *400K* evaluated with the best policy during training. Further evaluation details are given in Appendix B.3. SPIRL can outperform Transporter and PermaKey without the need of tuning the number of selected patches in a wide range of candidates for different games. For *MsPacman* and *BattleZone*, SPIRL's performance is not as good as DE-Rainbow but is still reasonable. For *MsPacman*, the lower performance can be explained by the importance of the background, which we remove in SPIRL by design. Since we pre-train in MsPacman with a random policy, pebbles and corridors in the maze will be usually regarded as background. The performance of SPIRL, but also all key-point methods, will be limited if the background is important for decision-making. For *BattleZone*, DE-Rainbow-P can benefit a lot from richer transition data from replay buffer, while the performance decrease of SPIRL comes from the moving mountain backgrounds, which makes SPIRL select more irrelevant background patches than needed. For this kind of situation, the performance of SPIRL can be improved by using an optimized fixed pre-defined $K$ or tune the dynamic $K$ criterion (e.g., angle smaller than 45°).

**Ablation Study.** To understand the effect of our patch selection, we compare SPIRL with MAE-All where the RL agent processes all patch embeddings. Table 1 (Right) shows that selecting salient patches improves RL data-efficiency in low-data regime. Visualization of policy attention (Fig. 6) indicates that in contrast to SPIRL, MAE-All attends non-necessary patches, hurting its performance.

To understand Dynamic-$K$ (implemented with the $mr$ trick using zero-padding for unneeded patches), we compare SPIRL with fixed $K$ determined by

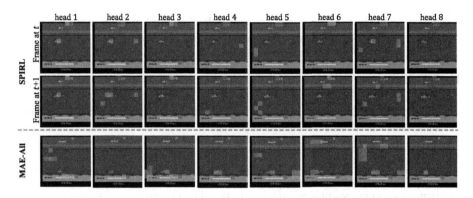

**Fig. 6.** Visualization for policy attention. Salient patches selected with dynamic-$K$ are highlighted with red squares, while policy-attended patches are marked with transparent yellow color. Patches selected and attended are highlighted with orange squares. (Color figure online)

$mr$, i.e., $K = \#patches \times mr$ patch embeddings provided to RL policy. Table 3 shows that our dynamic-$K$ method performs better.

We also tested some variations in the SPIRL architecture and implementation details. See Appendix C.1 and C.2 for those experimental results.

**Policy Interpretability via Policy Attention.** The learned policy can be interpreted to some extent from the policy attention scores w.r.t. $[cls]$ token, since we use $[cls]$ to pool the global information for downstream RL part. Figure 6 visualizes the policy-attended patches by maintaining 60% mass of softmax($\frac{q^{[cls]}K^{\top}}{\sqrt{d}}$). As illustrated in the top 2 rows in Fig. 6, the trained policy attends patches with useful objects (e.g., submarine, oxygen bar, enemies) than non-necessary patches (e.g., patches with the top rainbow bar), which explains why the shooting action is chosen (selected patches with enemy on the right). Moreover, by checking the policy-attention from a trained MAE-All policy as shown in the $3^{rd}$ row in Fig. 6, we find non-necessary policy-attention are assigned to non-salient patches, which could explain why MAE-All perform worse than SPIRL.

## 6    Conclusion

We presented a novel method to detect/select salient patches based on Vision Transformer without relying on convolutional features. In contrast to keypoint-based methods, our technique is fast, requires fewer pre-training data, and allows adaptive and varying number of salient patches. We showed how it can be exploited in RL to obtain a competitive method in the low-data training regime.

As future work, our salient patch selection technique could be applied on other downstream tasks. Moreover, it would be interesting to address the discussed shortcomings of SPIRL (but also other keypoint-based or object-based methods), e.g., how to exploit the static background if it is important for decision-making? how to drop irrelevant moving background elements?

# References

1. Agnew, W., Domingos, P.: Unsupervised object-level deep reinforcement learning. In: NeurIPS Workshop on Deep RL (2018)
2. Ba, J.L., Kiros, J.R., Hinton, G.E.: Layer normalization. arXiv preprint arXiv:1607.06450 (2016)
3. Bellemare, M.G., Dabney, W., Munos, R.: A distributional perspective on reinforcement learning. In: ICML (2017)
4. Bellemare, M.G., Naddaf, Y., Veness, J., Bowling, M.: The arcade learning environment: an evaluation platform for general agents. J. Artif. Intell. Res. **47**, 253–279 (2013)
5. Dosovitskiy, A., et al.: An image is worth 16x16 words: transformers for image recognition at scale. In: International Conference on Learning Representations (2020)
6. Fortunato, M., et al.: Noisy networks for exploration. In: ICLR (2018)
7. Goel, V., Weng, J., Poupart, P.: Unsupervised video object segmentation for deep reinforcement learning. In: Advances in Neural Information Processing Systems 31 (2018)
8. Gopalakrishnan, A., van Steenkiste, S., Schmidhuber, J.: Unsupervised object keypoint learning using local spatial predictability. In: International Conference on Learning Representations (2020)
9. Goulão, M., Oliveira, A.L.: Pretraining the vision transformer using self-supervised methods for vision based deep reinforcement learning (2022)
10. Haarnoja, T., Zhou, A., Abbeel, P., Levine, S.: Soft actor-critic: off-policy maximum entropy deep reinforcement learning with a stochastic actor. In: ICML (2018)
11. van Hasselt, H., Guez, A., Silver, D.: Deep reinforcement learning with double Q-learning. In: AAAI (2016)
12. He, K., Chen, X., Xie, S., Li, Y., Dollár, P., Girshick, R.: Masked autoencoders are scalable vision learners. In: Proceedings of the IEEE/CVF Conference on Computer Vision and Pattern Recognition, pp. 16000–16009 (2022)
13. He, K., Zhang, X., Ren, S., Sun, J.: Deep residual learning for image recognition. In: Proceedings of the IEEE Conference on Computer Vision and Pattern Recognition, pp. 770–778 (2016)
14. Hessel, M., et al.: Rainbow: combining improvements in deep reinforcement learning. In: Thirty-second AAAI Conference on Artificial Intelligence (2018)
15. Jaderberg, M., et al.: Reinforcement learning with unsupervised auxiliary tasks. In: International Conference on Learning Representations (2017)
16. Jakab, T., Gupta, A., Bilen, H., Vedaldi, A.: Unsupervised learning of object landmarks through conditional image generation. In: Advances in Neural Information Processing Systems 31 (2018)
17. Kaiser, Ł., et al.: Model based reinforcement learning for Atari. In: International Conference on Learning Representations (2019)
18. Kalantari, A.A., Amini, M., Chandar, S., Precup, D.: Improving sample efficiency of value based models using attention and vision transformers. arXiv preprint arXiv:2202.00710 (2022)

19. Kielak, K.P.: Do recent advancements in model-based deep reinforcement learning really improve data efficiency? In: ICLR, p. 6 (2020). https://openreview.net/forum?id=Bke9u1HFwB

20. Kostreva, M., Ogryczak, W., Wierzbicki, A.: Equitable aggregations and multiple criteria analysis. Eur. J. Operat. Res. **158**, 362–367 (2004)

21. Kulkarni, T.D., et al.: Unsupervised learning of object keypoints for perception and control. In: Advances in Neural Information Processing Systems 32 (2019)

22. Laskin, M., Lee, K., Stooke, A., Pinto, L., Abbeel, P., Srinivas, A.: Reinforcement learning with augmented data. In: NeurIPS (2020)

23. Levine, S., Finn, C., Darrell, T., Abbeel, P.: End-to-end training of deep visuomotor policies. In: JMLR (2016)

24. Lillicrap, T.P., et al.: Continuous control with deep reinforcement learning. In: ICLR (2016)

25. Lin, Y., Huang, J., Zimmer, M., Guan, Y., Rojas, J., Weng, P.: Invariant transform experience replay: Data augmentation for deep reinforcement learning. IEEE Robot. Autom. Lett. IROS **PP**, 1 (2020)

26. Manuelli, L., Li, Y., Florence, P., Tedrake, R.: Keypoints into the future: self-supervised correspondence in model-based reinforcement learning. In: CoRL (2020)

27. Minderer, M., Sun, C., Villegas, R., Cole, F., Murphy, K.P., Lee, H.: Unsupervised learning of object structure and dynamics from videos. In: Advances in Neural Information Processing Systems 32 (2019)

28. Mnih, V., et al.: Human-level control through deep reinforcement learning. Nature **518**(7540), 529–533 (2015)

29. Plappert, M., et al.: Parameter space noise for exploration. In: International Conference on Learning Representations (2018)

30. Puterman, M.: Markov decision processes: discrete stochastic dynamic programming. Wiley (1994)

31. Schaul, T., Quan, J., Antonoglou, I., Silver, D.: Prioritized experience replay. In: ICLR (2016)

32. Seo, Y., et al.: Masked world models for visual control. In: 6th Annual Conference on Robot Learning (2022)

33. Sutton, R., Barto, A.: Reinforcement learning: an introduction. MIT Press (2018)

34. Tao, T., Reda, D., van de Panne, M.: Evaluating vision transformer methods for deep reinforcement learning from pixels (2022)

35. Van Hasselt, H.P., Hessel, M., Aslanides, J.: When to use parametric models in reinforcement learning? In: Advances in Neural Information Processing Systems 32 (2019)

36. Vaswani, A., et al.: Attention is all you need. In: Advances in Neural Information Processing Systems 30 (2017)

37. Wang, T., et al.: Benchmarking model-based reinforcement learning (2019)

38. Wang, Z., Schaul, T., Hessel, M., Van Hasselt, H., Lanctot, M., De Freitas, N.: Dueling network architectures for deep reinforcement learning. In: ICML (2016)

39. Xiong, R., et al.: On layer normalization in the transformer architecture. In: International Conference on Machine Learning, pp. 10524–10533. PMLR (2020)

40. Yarats, D., Kostrikov, I., Fergus, R.: Image augmentation is all you need: regularizing deep reinforcement learning from pixels. In: International Conference on Learning Representations (2021). https://openreview.net/forum?id=GY6-6sTvGaf

41. Yarats, D., Zhang, A., Kostrikov, I., Amos, B., Pineau, J., Fergus, R.: Improving sample efficiency in model-free reinforcement learning from images. In: AAAI (2020)

42. Zadaianchuk, A., Seitzer, M., Martius, G.: Self-supervised visual reinforcement learning with object-centric representations. In: International Conference on Learning Representations (2021)
43. Zambaldi, V., et al.: Deep reinforcement learning with relational inductive biases. In: International conference on learning representations (2018)

# Eigensubspace of Temporal-Difference Dynamics and How It Improves Value Approximation in Reinforcement Learning

Qiang He[1(✉)], Tianyi Zhou[2], Meng Fang[3], and Setareh Maghsudi[1]

[1] University of Tübingen, Tübingen, Germany
{qiang.he,setareh.maghsudi}@uni-tuebingen.de
[2] University of Maryland, College Park, USA
tianyi@umd.edu
[3] University of Liverpool, Liverpool, UK
Meng.Fang@liverpool.ac.uk

**Abstract.** We propose a novel value approximation method, namely "Eigensubspace Regularized Critic (ERC)" for deep reinforcement learning (RL). ERC is motivated by an analysis of the dynamics of Q-value approximation error in the Temporal-Difference (TD) method, which follows a path defined by the 1-eigensubspace of the transition kernel associated with the Markov Decision Process (MDP). It reveals a fundamental property of TD learning that has remained unused in previous deep RL approaches. In ERC, we propose a regularizer that guides the approximation error tending towards the 1-eigensubspace, resulting in a more efficient and stable path of value approximation. Moreover, we theoretically prove the convergence of the ERC method. Besides, theoretical analysis and experiments demonstrate that ERC effectively reduces the variance of value functions. Among 26 tasks in the DMControl benchmark, ERC outperforms state-of-the-art methods for 20. Besides, it shows significant advantages in Q-value approximation and variance reduction. Our code is available at https://sites.google.com/view/erc-ecml23/.

## 1 Introduction

In recent years, deep reinforcement learning (RL), which is built upon the basis of the Markov decision process (MDP), has achieved remarkable success in a wide range of sequential decision-making tasks [29], including board games [27], video games [23,35], and robotics manipulation [11]. Leveraging the rich structural information in MDP, such as the Markov assumption [29], the stochasticity of transition kernel [1], and low-rank MDP [2,26,33,39], supports designing efficient RL algorithms.

Motivated by the potential benefits of utilizing structural information to design efficient RL algorithms [15,19–21,37], we investigate the dynamics of Q value approximation induced by the Temporal-Difference (TD) method. The Q value, commonly used to design DRL algorithms, is analyzed in the context of

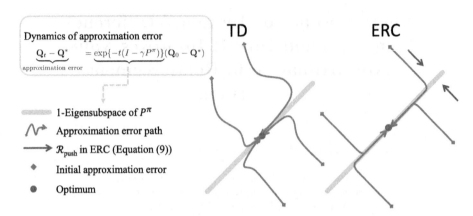

**Fig. 1.** Value approximation error $(Q - Q^*)$ path for TD and our proposed ERC algorithms. The approximation error of the TD method gradually approaches the 1-eigensubspace (as defined in Remark 3) before ultimately converging to the optimum. This path is referred to as the inherent path. ERC leverages this inherent path by directly pushing the approximation error towards the 1-eigensubspace through $\mathcal{R}_{\text{push}}$ (defined in Eq. (9)), resulting in a more efficient and stable learning process.

the matrix form of the Bellman equation. We study continuous learning dynamics. We also examine the crucial role of the transition kernel of MDP in the dynamics of the Bellman equation. We perform an eigenvalue decomposition of that dynamic process, which reveals that for any MDP, the TD method induces an inherent learning path of approximation error in the value approximation process.

Furthermore, as Fig. 1 shows, the approximation error of the TD method is optimized towards the 1-eigensubspace before ultimately converging to zero. It is in direct contrast with the optimum that the Monte Carlo (MC) method achieves [29]. Thus, such an inherent path is non-trivial. Such a path, which corresponds to prior knowledge of MDP, has been neglected in designing DRL algorithms [19–21,37], despite its great potential. Our main idea is utilizing the prior knowledge to improve the efficiency of value approximation by directly guiding the approximation error towards the 1-eigensubspace, leading to a more efficient and stable path. To that end, we propose a novel value approximation method, Eigensubspace Regularized Critic (ERC), as shown in Fig. 1. We also establish the convergence of our proposal. Theoretical analysis and experiments demonstrate that ERC effectively reduces the variance of value functions.

To evaluate the effectiveness of our proposed algorithm, ERC, we conduct extensive experiments on the continuous control suite DMControl [32]. Our empirical results demonstrate that ERC performs well in terms of approximation error. Moreover, by examining the ERC variance reduction, we verify its superior performance compared to the algorithms specifically designed for variance control (e.g., TQC [17], REDQ [5]), as consistent with our theoretical analysis. All in all, comparisons show that ERC outperforms the majority of the state-of-the-art methods (**20** out of **26** tasks) while achieving a similar performance otherwise. Specifically, on average, the ERC algorithm surpasses TQC, REDQ, SAC [11], and TD3 [9] by 13%, 25.6%, 16.6%, and 27.9%, respectively.

The main contributions of this work include i) identifying the existence of an inherent path of the approximation error for TD learning, ii) leveraging the inherent path to introduce a more efficient and stable method, ERC, with a convergence guarantee, and iii) demonstrating, through comparison with state-of-the-art deep RL methods, the superiority of ERC in terms of performance, variance, and approximation error.

## 2   Preliminaries

To formalize RL, one uses an MDP framework consisting of 6-tuple $(\mathcal{S}, \mathcal{A}, R, P, \gamma, \rho_0)$, where $\mathcal{S}$ denotes a state space, $\mathcal{A}$ an action space, $R : \mathcal{S} \times \mathcal{A} \rightarrow \mathbb{R}$ a reward function, $P : \mathcal{S} \times \mathcal{A} \rightarrow p(s)$ a transition kernel, $\gamma \in [0, 1)$ a discount factor, and $\rho_0$ an initial state distribution.

Deep RL focuses on optimizing the policy through return, defined as $R_t = \sum_{i=t}^{T} \gamma^{i-t} r(s_i, a_i)$. The action value (Q) function, $Q^\pi(s, a)$, represents the quality of a specific action, $a$, in a state, $s$, for a given policy $\pi$. Formally, the Q function is defined as

$$Q^\pi(s, a) = \mathbb{E}_{\tau \sim \pi, p}[R_\tau | s_0 = s, a_0 = a], \tag{1}$$

where $\tau$ is a state-action sequence $(s_0, a_0, s_1, a_1, s_2, a_2 \cdots)$ induced by a policy $\pi$ and $P$. The state value (V) function is $V^\pi(s) = \mathbb{E}_{\tau \sim \pi, p}[R_\tau | s_0 = s]$. A four-tuple $(s_t, a_t, r_t, s_{t+1})$ is referred to as a transition. The $Q$ value can be recursively computed by Bellman equation [29]

$$Q^\pi(s, a) = r(s, a) + \gamma \mathbb{E}_{s', a'}[Q^\pi(s', a')], \tag{2}$$

where $s' \sim p(\cdot|s, a)$ and $a \sim \pi(\cdot|s)$. The process of using a function approximator (e.g. neural networks) to estimate Q or V values is referred to as value approximation.

**Bellman Equation in Matrix Form.** Let $\mathbf{Q}^\pi$ denote the vector of all Q value with length $|\mathcal{S}| \cdot |\mathcal{A}|$, and $\mathbf{r}$ as vectors of the same length. We overload notation and let P refer to a matrix of dimension $(|\mathcal{S}| \cdot |\mathcal{A}|) \times |\mathcal{S}|$, with entry $P_{s,a,s'}$ equal to $P(s'|s, a)$. We define $P^\pi$ to be the transition matrix on state-action pairs induced by a stationary policy $\pi$

$$P^\pi_{s,a,s',a'} := P(s'|s, a)\pi(a'|s'). \tag{3}$$

Then, it is straightforward to verify

$$\mathbf{Q}^\pi = \mathbf{r} + \gamma P^\pi \mathbf{Q}^\pi, \tag{4}$$

where $P^\pi \in \mathbb{R}^{|\mathcal{S}| \cdot |\mathcal{A}| \times |\mathcal{S}| \cdot |\mathcal{A}|}$. The following famous eigenpair result holds.

*Remark 1. (Eigenpair for stochastic matrix $P^\pi$ [22]).* The spectral radius of $P^\pi$ is 1. The eigenvector corresponding to 1 is $\mathbf{e}$, where $\mathbf{e}$ is a column of all 1's.

## 3    Method

In this section, we start with the dynamics of Q value approximation induced by the TD method. This analysis reveals that in the value approximation, the approximation error has an inherent path. We leverage that path to design our proposed practical algorithm, ERC. We also investigate the convergence property of our method. All proofs are available in the appendix.

### 3.1    An Inherent Path of Value Approximation

Motivated by the potential benefits of using structural information to design novel RL algorithms [14, 19–21, 37], we examine the dynamics of Q value induced by the Bellman equation. Given Eq. (4) in matrix form, the true Q function of policy $\pi$ can be directly solved.

*Remark 2. (True Q value of a policy [1]).* Given a transition matrix induced by a policy $\pi$, as defined in Eq. (3), the true Q function of policy $\pi$ can be directly solved by

$$\mathbf{Q}^* = (I - \gamma P^\pi)^{-1}\mathbf{r}, \tag{5}$$

where $I$ is the identity matrix and $\mathbf{Q}^*$ is the true Q function of policy $\pi$.

To simplify the notation, let $X = (s, a)$. The one-step temporal difference (TD) continuous learning dynamics follows as

$$\partial_t Q_t(x) = \mathbb{E}_\pi[r_t + \gamma Q_t(x_{t+1})|x_t] - Q_t(x). \tag{6}$$

According to Eq. (4), we have the matrix form

$$\partial_t \mathbf{Q}_t = -(I - \gamma P^\pi)\mathbf{Q}_t + \mathbf{r}. \tag{7}$$

Equation (7) is a differential equation that is directly solvable using Remark 2.

**Lemma 1 (Dynamics of approximation error).** *Consider a continuous sequence* $\{Q_t|t \geq 0\}$, *satisfy Eq. (7) with initial condition* $\mathbf{Q}_0$ *at time step* $t = 0$, *then*

$$\mathbf{Q}_t - \mathbf{Q}^* = \exp\{-t(I - \gamma P^\pi)\}(\mathbf{Q}_0 - \mathbf{Q}^*). \tag{8}$$

From Lemma 1, $\mathbf{Q}_t$ converges to $\mathbf{Q}^*$, as $t \to \infty$. The approximation error, $\mathbf{Q}_t - \mathbf{Q}^*$, appears in Eq. (8), which reveals the dynamics of approximation error is related to the structure of transition kernel and policy $\pi$. Moreover, there is rich structural information in $P^\pi$, which inspires us to consider Eq. (8) in a more fine-grained way. To better understand the approximation error, following Ghosh and Bellemare [10], Lyle et al. [20, 21], we make the following assumption.

**Assumption 1.** $P^\pi$ *is a real-diagonalizable matrix with a strictly decreasing eigenvalue sequence* $|\lambda_1|, |\lambda_2|, \cdots, |\lambda_{|\mathcal{S}| \cdot |\mathcal{A}|}|$, *and the corresponding eigenvector* $H_1, H_2, \cdots, H_{|\mathcal{S}| \cdot |\mathcal{A}|}$.

Remark 1 shows that $\lambda_1 = 1$ because the $P^\pi$ is a stochastic matrix, and the eigenvector corresponding to 1 is $\mathbf{e}$. That inspires us to perform an eigenvalue decomposition for Eq. (8).

**Theorem 1.** *If Assumption 1 holds, we have* $\mathbf{Q}_t - \mathbf{Q}^* = \alpha_1 \exp\{t(\gamma\lambda_1 - 1)\}H_1 + \sum_{i=2}^{|\mathcal{S}| \cdot |\mathcal{A}|} \alpha_i \exp\{t(\gamma\lambda_i - 1)\}H_i = \alpha_1 \exp\{t(\gamma\lambda_1 - 1)\}H_1 + o\Big(\alpha_1 \exp\{t(\gamma\lambda_1 - 1)\}\Big),$ *where $\alpha_i$ is a constant.*

Theorem 1 states that the approximation error of the TD method can be decomposed into two components. One of the components is primarily influenced by the 1-eigensubspace. Thus, the approximation error of the value function in the TD method follows a path induced by the 1-eigensubspace, which is a result of the stochasticity inherent in MDP.

*Remark 3. (An inherent path of TD method).* Given an MDP consisting of 6-tuple $(\mathcal{S}, \mathcal{A}, R, P, \gamma, \rho_0)$, policy $\pi$, and a Banach space $(\mathcal{Q}, \|\cdot\|)$, there exists an inherent path that the Bellman approximation error, i.e., $\mathbf{Q}_t - \mathbf{Q}^*$, starts at the initial point and then approaches the 1-eigensubspace before ultimately converging to zero. The 1-eigensubspace, which is induced by $P^\pi$, is defined as $\{c\,\mathbf{e}\}$, where $c \in \mathbb{R}$ and $\mathbf{e}$ is a column of all ones.

**What Does a Theoretically Inherent Path Really Look Like in Practice?** The aforementioned content discusses the inherent path of approximation error. Does this occur in the practical scene? To empirically show the path of the approximation error, we visualize the path of approximation error given a fixed policy. The results are given in Fig. 2, where we perform experiments on FrozenLake-v1 environment since the true Q value $Q^*$ of this environment can be evaluated by the Monte Carlo Method.

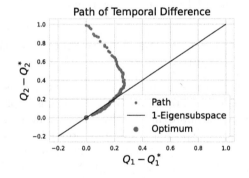

**Fig. 2.** Path of TD method. There exists an inherent path that approximation error approaches 1-eigensubspace before converging to zero. The empirical fact is consistent with our theoretical analysis in Theorem 1.

The approximation error of the TD method is optimized toward the 1-eigensubspace before ultimately converging to zero rather than directly toward the optimum. The inherent path in Fig. 2 is consistent with Remark 3. Thus, such a path is non-trivial and motivates us to improve the value approximation by guiding the approximation error to 1-eigensubspace, resulting in an efficient and robust path.

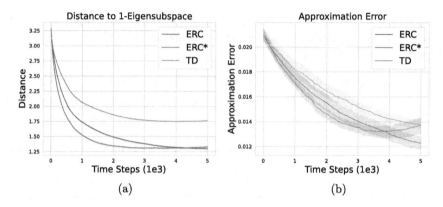

**Fig. 3.** Value function approximation process for various methods on FrozenLake-v1 environment. (a) illustrates the distance between the approximation error and the 1-eigensubspace for various methods, where ERC* denotes ERC utilizing an oracle true Q value, $Q^*$, to push the approximation error towards the 1-eigensubspace. The results demonstrate that the ERC method is closer to the 1-eigensubspace at the same time compared to the TD method. (b) represents the absolute approximation error for various algorithms. The result illustrates that the ERC method has a smaller approximation error at the same time than the TD method. For both metrics, ERC is observed to outperform or be at least as good as ERC* in later stages. The shaded area represents a standard deviation over ten trials.

## 3.2 Using Eigensubspace Regularization to Improve Value Approximation

The inherent path, which can be viewed as prior knowledge of MDP, has not been utilized to design DRL algorithms in previous work [19–21,37]. We improve the value approximation by directly guiding the approximation error towards the 1-eigensubspace, leading to a more efficient and stable path.

The true Q value, $Q^*$, is always unknown when designing DRL algorithms. However, we can use a target Q as an approximate substitute for $Q^*$ for two reasons. Firstly, from the perspective of value function optimization, the objective of the Bellman equation optimization is to make the learned Q-value as close as possible to $Q^*$. That is achievable by minimizing the distance between the learned Q and the target Q. Instead of using $Q^*$ directly in learning, the target Q is used to approximate $Q^*$ through a bootstrap approach. Similarly, we use target Q in our ERC algorithm design. Secondly, in our experiments, we find that using target Q to replace $Q^*$ produces an effect that approximates the effect produced by using $Q^*$, as illustrated in Fig. 3. We calculate the distance of the approximation error to the 1-eigensubspace and approximation error during the optimization of the value function, and we can see that: i) the ERC algorithm using target Q instead of $Q^*$ allows the approximation error to reach the 1-eigensubspace faster than the TD algorithm and the effect can be approximated to that of the ERC using $Q^*$ (ERC* algorithm). And ii) for the approximation error, the ERC algorithm obtains a relatively small approximation error compared to the TD method. The approximation error of ERC is smaller than that of ERC* in the later optimization stages. Therefore, it is reasonable to replace $Q^*$ with the target Q in the practical design of the algorithm. Using target Q-value is a feasible solution that allows us to achieve results similar or better to using $Q^*$, and it has the advantage of being more easily implemented in practice. Thus, the Bellman error is pushed to 1-eigensubspace in the ERC algorithm.

To push the Bellman error toward the 1-eigensubspace, it is essential to project the error onto that subspace. Therefore, one must determine the projected point in the 1-eigensubspace to the Bellman error.

**Lemma 2.** *Consider a Banach space* $(\mathfrak{B}, \| \cdot \|)$ *of dimension N, and let the N-dimensional Bellman error at timestep t, represented by* $\mathbf{B}^t$, *have coordinates* $(B_1, B_2, \cdots, B_N)$ *in* $(\mathfrak{B}, \| \cdot \|)$. *Within this Banach space, the projected point in the 1-eigensubspace, which is closest to* $B^t$, *is* $Z^t$ *whose coordinates are* $(z^t, z^t, \cdots, z^t)$, *where* $z^t = \frac{1}{N} \sum_{j=1}^{N} B_i^t$.

The Bellman error can be pushed towards 1-eigensubspace at each timestep with the help of Lemma 2. To accomplish this, we minimize the regularization term

$$\mathcal{R}_{\text{push}}(\theta) = \frac{1}{N} \sum_{i=1}^{N} \|B_i - Z\|_2^2, \tag{9}$$

where $B_i$ represents the Bellman error at the $i$-dimension and $Z = \frac{1}{N} \sum_{j=1}^{N} B_i(\theta)$. By combining Eq. (9) with policy evaluation loss $\mathcal{L}_{\mathbf{PE}}$, the Eigensubspace Regularized Critic (ERC) algorithm is defined as

$$\mathcal{L}_{\text{ERC}}(\theta) = \mathcal{L}_{\text{PE}}(\theta) + \beta \mathcal{R}_{\text{push}}(\theta), \tag{10}$$

where $\mathcal{L}_{\text{PE}}(\theta)$ is a policy evaluation phase loss such as

$$\mathcal{L}_{\text{PE}}(\theta) = \left[ Q(s, a; \theta) - \left( r(s, a) + \gamma \mathbb{E}_{s', a'} \left[ Q(s', a'; \theta') \right] \right) \right]^2,$$

and $\beta$ is a hyper-parameter that controls the degree to which the Bellman error is pushed toward the 1-eigensubspace. ERC enhances the value approximation by pushing the Bellman error to 1-eigensubspace, leading to a more stable and efficient value approximation path. To evaluate the effectiveness of ERC, a case study is conducted on the FrozenLake environment. The distance between the approximation error and the 1-eigensubspace, as well as the absolute approximation error, are used as metrics to compare the performance of ERC with that of the TD method and that of ERC* (ERC utilizing oracle $Q^*$). The results in Fig. 3 demonstrate that ERC is superior to the TD method, and is either superior to or at least as effective as ERC*.

The theoretical benefit of the ERC method can be understood by examining Eq. (9). Minimizing $\mathcal{R}_{\text{push}}$ explicitly reduces the variance of the Bellman error. This reduction in variance leads to two benefits: minimizing the variance of the Q-value and minimizing the variance of the target Q-value. That is observable by rewriting Eq. (9) as

$$
\begin{aligned}
\mathcal{R}_{\text{push}}(\theta) = {} & \mathbb{E}\left(\big(Q - \mathcal{B}Q\big) - \mathbb{E}[Q - \mathcal{B}Q]\right)^2 \\
= {} & \underbrace{\mathbb{E}[(Q - \mathbb{E}[Q])^2]}_{\text{variance of } Q} + \underbrace{\mathbb{E}[(\mathcal{B}Q - \mathbb{E}\mathcal{B}Q)^2]}_{\text{variance of } \mathcal{B}Q} - \\
& 2\underbrace{\mathbb{E}(Q - \mathbb{E}[Q])(\mathcal{B}Q - \mathbb{E}\mathcal{B}Q)}_{\text{covariance between } Q \text{ and } \mathcal{B}Q},
\end{aligned}
\tag{11}
$$

where $\mathcal{B}$ is a bellman backup operator and $\mathcal{B}Q$ is a target Q. These facts highlight the benefits of the ERC algorithm, as it leads to a more stable and efficient Q value approximation.

---

**Algorithm 1:** ERC (based on SAC [11]

---

**Initialize** actor network $\pi$, and critic network $Q$ with random parameters;
**Initialize** target networks and replay buffer $\mathcal{D}$;
**Initialize** $\beta$, total steps $T$, and $t = 0$;
Reset the environment and receive the initial state $s$;
**while** $t < T$ **do**
  Select action w.r.t. its policy $\pi$ and receive reward $r$, new state $s'$;
  Store transition tuple $(s, a, r, s')$ to $\mathcal{D}$;
  Sample $N$ transitions $(s, a, r, s')$ from $\mathcal{D}$;
  Compute $\hat{\mathcal{R}}_{\text{push}}$ by Eqs. (16) and (9);
  Update critic by minimizing Eq. (13);
  Update actor by minimizing Eq. (14);
  Update $\alpha$ by minimizing Eq. (15);
  Update target networks;
  $t \leftarrow t + 1, s \leftarrow s'$;
**end**

---

### 3.3   Theoretical Analysis

We are also interested in examining the convergence property of ERC. To do this, we first obtain the new Q value after one step of updating in tabular form.

**Lemma 3.** *Given the ERC update rules in Eq. (10), ERC updates the value function in tabular form in the following way*

$$
Q_{t+1} = (1 - \alpha_t(1 + \beta))Q_t + \alpha_t(1 + \beta)\mathcal{B}Q_t - \alpha_t\beta C_t,
\tag{12}
$$

*where* $\mathcal{B}Q_t(s_t, a_t) = r_t + \gamma\mathbb{E}_{s_{t+1}, a_{t+1}}Q_t(s_{t+1}, a_{t+1})$, $C_t = 2\mathbb{NG}(\mathbb{E}[\mathcal{B}Q_t - Q_t])$, *and* $\mathbb{NG}$ *means stopping gradient.*

To establish the convergence guarantee of ERC, we use an auxiliary lemma from stochastic approximation [28] and the results in Haarnoja et al. [11]. Theorem 2 states the convergence guarantee formally.

**Theorem 2. (Convergence of 1-Eigensubspace Regularized Value Approximation).** *Consider the Bellman backup operator $\mathcal{B}$ and a mapping $Q : \mathcal{S} \times \mathcal{A} \rightarrow \mathbb{R}$, and $Q^k$ is updated with Eq. (12). Then the sequence $\{Q^k\}_{k=0}^{\infty}$ will converge to 1-eigensubspace regularized optimal Q value of $\pi$ as $k \rightarrow \infty$.*

### 3.4 Practical Algorithm

The proposed ERC algorithm, which utilizes the structural information in MDP to improve value approximation, can be formulated as a practical algorithm. We combine the ERC with Soft Actor Critic (SAC) algorithm [11]. For the value approximation, ERC optimizes

$$J_{\text{ERC}}^Q(\theta) = \mathbb{E}_{(s,a)\sim\mathcal{D}}\left[\frac{1}{2}\Big(Q(s,a;\theta) - \big(r(s,a) + \gamma\mathbb{E}_{s'\sim P}[V(s';\theta')]\big)\Big)^2\right] + \beta\mathcal{R}_{\text{push}}, \tag{13}$$

where $V(s;\theta') = \mathbb{E}_{a\sim\pi(\cdot|s;\phi)}[Q(s,a;\theta') - \alpha\log\pi(a|s;\phi)]$. For policy improvement, ERC optimizes

$$J_{\text{ERC}}^\pi(\phi) = \mathbb{E}_{s\sim\mathcal{D}}[\mathbb{E}_{a\sim\pi(\cdot|s,\phi)}[\alpha\log(\pi(a \mid s;\phi)) - Q(s,a;\theta)]]. \tag{14}$$

Besides, we also use the automated entropy trick. The temperature $\alpha$ is learned by minimizing

$$J_{\text{ERC}}^\alpha(\alpha) = \mathbb{E}_{a\sim\pi^*}[-\alpha\log\pi^*(a|s;\alpha,\phi) - \alpha\mathcal{H}], \tag{15}$$

where $\mathcal{H}$ is a pre-selected target entropy. To help better stabilize the value approximation of ERC, we design a truncation mechanism for $\mathcal{R}_{\text{push}}$

$$\hat{\mathcal{R}}_{\text{push}} = \max\Big\{\min\Big\{\beta\mathcal{R}_{\text{push}}, \mathcal{R}_{\max}\Big\}, \mathcal{R}_{\min}\Big\}. \tag{16}$$

The practical algorithm is summarized in Algorithm 1.

## 4    Experiments

In this section, we thoroughly evaluate the performance of ERC by comparing it to a few baseline methods. Furthermore, we examine the value approximation error and the variance of the value function to gain a deeper understanding of ERC. Additionally, we analyze the individual contributions of each component of ERC to gain insight into its effectiveness.

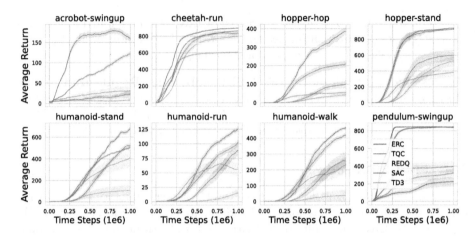

**Fig. 4.** Performance curves for OpenAI gym continuous control tasks on DeepMind Control suite. The proposed algorithm, ERC, is observed to significantly outperform the other tested algorithms. The shaded region represents half of the standard deviation of the average evaluation over 10 seeds. The curves are smoothed with a moving average window of size ten.

## 4.1   Evaluation Setting

**Baselines.** We conduct a comparative study of the proposed ERC algorithm with several well-established baselines in the literature. Specifically, we select TD3 [9] and SAC as our primary baselines as they are commonly used and perform well in various tasks. Additionally, we compare our method with REDQ [5] and TQC [17], which employ different techniques to improve value approximation and reduce the variance of the value function. To ensure a fair comparison, we use the authors' implementation of TD3 and REDQ available on Github, and the public implementation of SAC provided in PyTorch [38], which is also the basis of our ERC implementation. Besides, we use the implementation of TQC available in the stable baselines 3 library and use the default hyper-parameters as suggested by the authors.

**Environments.** The experimental suite is the state-based DMControl suite [32], which is for physics-based simulation, utilizing the MuJoCo physics engine [31]. We chose the DMControl suite as it offers a diverse range of environments to benchmark the capabilities of RL algorithms. We facilitate the interactions between the algorithm and environment using Gym [4]. We evaluate each algorithm over one million timesteps and obtain the average return of the algorithm every 10k timesteps over ten episodes.

**Setup.** The magnitude of the regularization effectiveness of ERC is controlled by a hyper-parameter, $\beta$, which is 5e–3. Additionally, $\mathcal{R}_{\max}$ and $\mathcal{R}_{\min}$ are 1e–2 and 0, respectively, for all experiments. The remaining hyper-parameters are consistent with the suggestions provided by Haarnoja et al. [11]. To ensure the validity and reproducibility of the experiments, unless otherwise specified, we evaluate each tested algorithm over ten fixed random seeds. For more implementation details, please refer to the appendix.

**Table 1.** Average Return after 1M timesteps of training on DMC. ERC demonstrates state-of-the-art performance on the majority (**20** out of **26**) tasks. If not, ERC is still observed to be comparable in performance. Additionally, ERC outperforms its backbone algorithm, SAC, on **all** tasks by a large margin. Specifically, the ERC algorithm outperforms TQC, REDQ, SAC, and TD3 by 13%, 25.6%, 16.6%, and 27.9%, respectively. The best score is marked with  colorbox.  $\pm$ corresponds to a standard deviation over ten trials.

| Domain | Task | ERC | TQC | REDQ | SAC | TD3 |
|---|---|---|---|---|---|---|
| Acrobot | Swingup | 151.0 ± 36.8 | 136.3 ± 51.9 | 31.1 ± 41.1 | 26.9 ± 47.7 | 5.3 ± 4.7 |
| BallInCup | Catch | 979.7 ± 1.3 | 981.6 ± 2.3 | 978.8 ± 3.7 | 980.3 ± 3.4 | 978.9 ± 3.6 |
| Cartpole | Balance | 998.8 ± 1.2 | 989.2 ± 25.8 | 984.0 ± 6.0 | 997.7 ± 1.5 | 997.9 ± 2.1 |
| Cartpole | BalanceSparse | 998.6 ± 4.5 | 899.9 ± 268.6 | 872.1 ± 262.7 | 997.6 ± 5.7 | 1000.0 ± 0.0 |
| Cartpole | Swingup | 867.8 ± 4.7 | 874.3 ± 5.8 | 828.1 ± 17.2 | 865.1 ± 1.6 | 867.2 ± 7.5 |
| Cartpole | SwingupSparse | 544.5 ± 356.9 | 797.6 ± 32.1 | 385.5 ± 374.7 | 234.4 ± 358.4 | 157.5 ± 314.9 |
| Cheetah | Run | 903.3 ± 5.9 | 853.8 ± 80.0 | 614.2 ± 58.2 | 873.4 ± 21.5 | 811.3 ± 102.2 |
| Finger | Spin | 988.1 ± 0.6 | 982.0 ± 9.1 | 940.1 ± 33.5 | 966.3 ± 27.1 | 947.6 ± 52.1 |
| Finger | TurnEasy | 981.1 ± 5.4 | 247.4 ± 133.6 | 962.6 ± 34.3 | 920.0 ± 91.8 | 856.5 ± 109.3 |
| Finger | TurnHard | 964.8 ± 27.5 | 299.2 ± 266.6 | 927.3 ± 99.8 | 874.1 ± 100.1 | 690.2 ± 167.6 |
| Fish | Upright | 936.0 ± 12.1 | 917.1 ± 25.6 | 799.6 ± 113.8 | 898.6 ± 50.4 | 873.6 ± 66.7 |
| Fish | Swim | 496.8 ± 61.6 | 526.6 ± 113.5 | 159.3 ± 100.1 | 342.4 ± 134.5 | 251.3 ± 107.7 |
| Hopper | Stand | 943.9 ± 8.9 | 941.6 ± 11.4 | 393.5 ± 225.8 | 597.8 ± 308.8 | 538.7 ± 256.2 |
| Hopper | Hop | 405.0 ± 91.1 | 221.8 ± 68.8 | 56.8 ± 36.2 | 117.4 ± 82.2 | 47.8 ± 46.2 |
| Humanoid | Stand | 804.5 ± 39.1 | 494.9 ± 145.5 | 407.2 ± 336.8 | 549.6 ± 201.0 | 110.6 ± 206.8 |
| Humanoid | Walk | 507.0 ± 37.0 | 376.4 ± 182.5 | 245.0 ± 222.6 | 248.4 ± 220.8 | 39.3 ± 101.9 |
| Humanoid | Run | 145.9 ± 10.1 | 115.6 ± 18.6 | 70.8 ± 57.0 | 83.4 ± 56.0 | 18.1 ± 33.9 |
| Pendulum | Swingup | 846.6 ± 14.1 | 834.0 ± 30.1 | 382.6 ± 297.0 | 226.2 ± 228.9 | 338.0 ± 232.0 |
| PointMass | Easy | 882.3 ± 18.2 | 793.7 ± 147.6 | 880.9 ± 16.7 | 889.9 ± 33.1 | 838.8 ± 158.5 |
| Reacher | Easy | 986.9 ± 2.3 | 964.5 ± 39.5 | 970.9 ± 24.4 | 983.5 ± 4.2 | 983.4 ± 3.7 |
| Reacher | Hard | 981.8 ± 1.7 | 971.8 ± 5.2 | 964.1 ± 24.0 | 958.6 ± 40.9 | 938.2 ± 63.0 |
| Swimmer | Swimmer6 | 422.0 ± 133.2 | 356.4 ± 107.5 | 215.8 ± 119.0 | 359.3 ± 130.9 | 289.2 ± 133.6 |
| Swimmer | Swimmer15 | 295.8 ± 113.7 | 222.8 ± 128.6 | 178.6 ± 116.6 | 264.6 ± 136.9 | 236.7 ± 150.1 |
| Walker | Stand | 989.6 ± 1.7 | 986.3 ± 4.5 | 974.0 ± 12.6 | 986.8 ± 2.7 | 983.4 ± 4.2 |
| Walker | Walk | 974.9 ± 1.6 | 971.9 ± 4.8 | 957.3 ± 10.6 | 973.5 ± 4.4 | 966.3 ± 10.4 |
| Walker | Run | 805.1 ± 19.4 | 770.5 ± 31.0 | 590.9 ± 51.6 | 773.0 ± 32.9 | 712.1 ± 65.6 |
| Average | Scores | 761.6 | 674.1 | 606.6 | 653.4 | 595.3 |

## 4.2   Performance Evaluation

Figure 4 shows the learning curves from scratch. Table 1 depicts the average performance after 1M timesteps training. The results demonstrate the following points: i) ERC outperforms the other tested algorithms in a majority (**20** out of **26**) of the environments. Specifically, it outperforms TQC, REDQ, SAC, and TD3 by 13%, 25.6%, 16.6%, and 27.9%, respectively; ii) ERC substantially improves upon its skeleton algorithm, SAC, by the addition of the $\mathcal{R}_{\text{push}}$ regularization term; iii) Additionally, although ERC does not employ complex techniques to eliminate estimation bias, it still substantially outperforms TQC and REDQ in most environments. Note that both REDQ and TQC leverage an ensemble mechanism to obtain a more accurate and unbiased Q estimation. ERC does not leverage any ensemble critic, distributional value functions, or high UTD ratio, yet it still outperforms them. The results above highlight the potential of utilizing structural information of MDP to improve DRL.

### 4.3   Variance and Approximation Error

We select four distinct environments 'acrobot-swing', 'humanoid-stand', 'finger-turn_easy', and 'fish-swim'. This selection is made because ERC has been demonstrated to perform well in the first two environments, while its performance is not as strong in the latter two. Thus, by evaluating ERC across these four environments, a comprehensive assessment of ERC can be obtained.

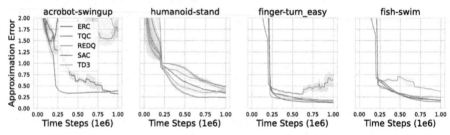

**Fig. 5.** Approximation error curves. The results demonstrate that the approximation error of ERC is empirically minimal when compared to other algorithms (such as TQC and REDQ) that are specifically designed to obtain accurate unbiased value estimation.

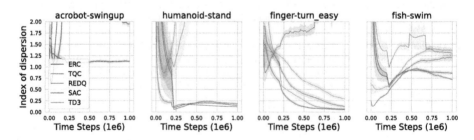

**Fig. 6.** Index of dispersion curves. The results demonstrate that ERC effectively controls the variance. Furthermore, the variance of ERC is observed to be minimal on the selected tasks, even in situations where the performance of ERC is not as good as TQC and REDQ.

**Approximation Error.** ERC aims to push the Bellman error to 1-eigensubspace to obtain an efficient and stable value approximation as discussed in Sect. 3.2. Thus we study the approximation error of ERC on the DMControl suite. We obtain the true value $Q^*$ using the Monte Carlo method and compare it to the estimated Q. We normalize the approximation error by the estimation value to eliminate the differences in scale, and the absolute value of the approximation error is used in each sample to eliminate inaccuracies caused by offsetting positive and negative errors. The results, presented in Fig. 5, indicate that ERC exhibits minimal approximation error compared to other methods that obtain accurate and unbiased value estimates.

**Table 2.** Average Return after 1M timesteps training on DMControl suite. $\beta = 5e - 3$-trunc means the truncation mechanism is used in the evaluation.

| 1M Steps Scores | $\beta$ =1e-4 | $\beta$ =5e-4 | $\beta$ =1e-3 | $\beta$ =5e-3 | $\beta$ =5e-3-trunc | $\beta$ =1e-2 | $\beta$ =5e-2 | SAC |
|---|---|---|---|---|---|---|---|---|
| Acrobot, Swingup | 151.2 ± 70.0 | 152.7 ± 43.4 | 91.4 ± 54.3 | 151.9 ± 69.3 | 151.0 ± 36.8 | 129.9 ± 58.7 | 114.7 ± 31.4 | 26.9 ± 47.7 |
| Humanoid, Stand | 418.2 ± 255.3 | 755.8 ± 88.3 | 692.1 ± 200.2 | 699.0 ± 129.3 | 804.5 ± 39.1 | 742.4 ± 130.8 | 550.0 ± 217.2 | 549.6 ± 201.0 |
| Finger, TurnEasy | 940.4 ± 49.5 | 919.8 ± 80.5 | 959.2 ± 37.3 | 979.4 ± 5.5 | 981.1 ± 5.4 | 979.9 ± 5.3 | 959.7 ± 43.7 | 920.0 ± 91.8 |
| Fish, Swim | 448.5 ± 102.8 | 436.9 ± 71.4 | 468.3 ± 130.5 | 390.0 ± 65.8 | 496.8 ± 61.6 | 414.4 ± 55.0 | 434.9 ± 61.4 | 342.4 ± 134.5 |

**Variance Reduction.** Above analysis shows that ERC reduces the value function variance. To investigate this claim in Sect. 3.2, we empirically analyze the variance of ERC. To eliminate the effect of the size of the value function on the variance, we use *index of dispersion* [16], which can be considered as a variance normalized by its mean, to evaluate the variance of algorithms. Our results, presented in Fig. 6, indicate that i) the variance of the value function of ERC is the lowest or equally low as other methods (TQC, and REDQ) specifically designed for variance reduction. And ii) ERC effectively controls variance even in environments where its performance is not as strong as other methods such as TQC and REDQ. These findings provide strong evidence for the theoretical claim that ERC reduces variance of the value function.

### 4.4 Ablation

The component introduced by ERC, as outlined in Eq. (10), is sole $\mathcal{R}_{push}$, in which $\beta$ regulates the efficiency of pushing the Bellman error towards the 1-eigensubspace. Therefore, investigating the selection of $\beta$ can aid in comprehending the impact of hyper-parameter on ERC. We vary $\beta$ and eliminate the truncation mechanism outlined in Eq. (16). Experiments are conducted on the same four environments as described in Sect. 4.3. The results, presented in Table 2, indicate the following: i) the value of $\beta$ influences the empirical performance of the ERC, yet ERC with various $\beta$ values consistently outperforms its skeleton algorithm, SAC, in most settings. That demonstrates the effectiveness of our proposed value approximation method; ii) Truncating parameters can improve the performance of ERC on specific tasks (Humanoid-Stand, Fish-Swim); iii) Carefully tuning both the hyper-parameter $\beta$ and the truncation mechanism ensures optimal performance.

# 5    Related Work

## 5.1    Value Function Approximation

Mnih et al. [23] utilizes neural networks (NN) to approximate value function by TD learning [30,36]. Combined with NN, several derivative value approximation methods [3,6,7,23] exist. Some [3,6,7,17] use a distributional view to obtain a better value function. Some reduce bias and variance of value function approximation [5,9,12,13,18,34]. Others [8,11,24] develop more robust value function approximation methods. ERC utilizes structural information from MDP to improve value approximation, which distinguishes it from previous work.

## 5.2    Using Structural Information of MDPs

Recent work [2,26,33,39] focus on the property of low-rank MDP. They study learning an optimal policy assuming a low-rank MDP given the optimal representation. Nevertheless, such a setting is not practical as the optimal representation is computationally intractable. Ren et al. [25] proposed a practical algorithm under low-rank MDP assumption, which, different from ERC, involves estimating the dynamics of MDP. Some other work [1,19,21] discuss the architecture of MDP from a matrix decomposition perspective. Lyle et al. [21] establishes a connection between the spectral decomposition of the transition operator and the representations of $V$ function induced by a variety of auxiliary tasks. ERC differs from Lyle et al. [21] in the following aspects: i) We analyze the dynamics of the Q approximation error, which is more commonly studied in DRL literature; ii) We consider the learning process of $Q$ function, whereas Lyle et al. [21] considers the dynamics of representations.

# 6    Conclusion

In this work, we examine the eigensubspace of the TD dynamics and its potential use in improving value approximation in DRL. We begin by analyzing the matrix form of the Bellman equation and subsequently derive the dynamics of the approximation error through the solution of a differential equation. This solution depends on the transition kernel of the MDP, which motivates us to perform eigenvalue decomposition, resulting in the inherent path of value approximation in TD. To the best of our knowledge, this inherent path has not been leveraged to design DRL algorithms in previous work. Our insight is to improve value approximation by directing the approximation error towards the 1-eigensubspace, resulting in a more efficient and stable path. Thus, we propose the ERC algorithm with a theoretical convergence guarantee. Theoretical analysis and experiments demonstrate ERC results in a variance reduction, which validates our insight. Extensive experiments on the DMControl suite demonstrate that ERC outperforms state-of-the-art algorithms in the majority of tasks. The limitation is that ERC is evaluated on the DMControl suite. Verifying the effectiveness of ERC on other suites is left for future work. Our contributions represent a significant step forward in leveraging the rich inherent structure of MDP to improve value approximation and ultimately enhance performance in RL.

**Acknowledgements.** Thanks to Xihuai Wang and Yucheng Yang for their helpful discussions. This research was supported by Grant 01IS20051 and Grant 16KISK035 from the German Federal Ministry of Education and Research (BMBF).

**Ethical Statement.** This work investigates the eigensubspace of the Temporal-Difference algorithm of reinforcement learning and how it improves DRL. The experimental part only uses a physical simulation engine DMControl. Therefore this work does not involve any personal information. This work may be used in areas such as autonomous vehicles, games, and robot control.

# References

1. Agarwal, A., Jiang, N., Kakade, S.M., Sun, W.: Reinforcement learning: theory and algorithms. CS Dept., UW Seattle, Seattle, WA, USA, Tech. Rep., pp. 10–4 (2019)
2. Agarwal, A., Kakade, S.M., Krishnamurthy, A., Sun, W.: FLAMBE: structural complexity and representation learning of low rank MDPs. In: Larochelle, H., Ranzato, M., Hadsell, R., Balcan, M., Lin, H. (eds.) Advances in Neural Information Processing Systems 33: Annual Conference on Neural Information Processing Systems 2020, NeurIPS 2020, 6–12 December 2020, virtual (2020)
3. Bellemare, M.G., Dabney, W., Munos, R.: A distributional perspective on reinforcement learning. In: Precup, D., Teh, Y.W. (eds.) Proceedings of the 34th International Conference on Machine Learning, ICML 2017, Sydney, NSW, Australia, 6–11 August 2017, Proceedings of Machine Learning Research, vol. 70, pp. 449–458, PMLR (2017)
4. Brockman, G., et al.: OpenAI gym (2016)
5. Chen, X., Wang, C., Zhou, Z., Ross, K.W.: Randomized ensembled double Q-learning: learning fast without a model. In: International Conference on Learning Representations (2020)
6. Dabney, W., Ostrovski, G., Silver, D., Munos, R.: Implicit quantile networks for distributional reinforcement learning. In: International Conference on Machine Learning, pp. 1096–1105. PMLR (2018)
7. Dabney, W., Rowland, M., Bellemare, M., Munos, R.: Distributional reinforcement learning with quantile regression. In: Proceedings of the AAAI Conference on Artificial Intelligence, vol. 32 (2018)
8. Espeholt, L., et al.: IMPALA: scalable distributed deep-RL with importance weighted actor-learner architectures. In: Dy, J.G., Krause, A. (eds.) Proceedings of the 35th International Conference on Machine Learning, ICML 2018, Stockholmsmässan, Stockholm, Sweden, 10–15 July 2018, Proceedings of Machine Learning Research, vol. 80, pp. 1406–1415. PMLR (2018)
9. Fujimoto, S., van Hoof, H., Meger, D.: Addressing function approximation error in actor-critic methods. In: Dy, J.G., Krause, A. (eds.) Proceedings of the 35th International Conference on Machine Learning, ICML 2018, Stockholmsmässan, Stockholm, Sweden, 10–15 July 2018, Proceedings of Machine Learning Research, vol. 80, pp. 1582–1591. PMLR (2018)

10. Ghosh, D., Bellemare, M.G.: Representations for stable off-policy reinforcement learning. In: International Conference on Machine Learning, pp. 3556–3565. PMLR (2020)
11. Haarnoja, T., Zhou, A., Abbeel, P., Levine, S.: Soft actor-critic: off-policy maximum entropy deep reinforcement learning with a stochastic actor. In: Dy, J.G., Krause, A. (eds.) Proceedings of the 35th International Conference on Machine Learning, ICML 2018, Stockholmsmässan, Stockholm, Sweden, 10–15 July 2018, Proceedings of Machine Learning Research, vol. 80, pp. 1856–1865. PMLR (2018)
12. Hasselt, H.: Double Q-learning. Adv. Neural. Inf. Process. Syst. **23**, 2613–2621 (2010)
13. He, Q., Hou, X.: WD3: taming the estimation bias in deep reinforcement learning. In: 2020 IEEE 32nd International Conference on Tools with Artificial Intelligence (ICTAI), pp. 391–398. IEEE (2020)
14. He, Q., Su, H., Zhang, J., Hou, X.: Representation gap in deep reinforcement learning. CoRR abs/2205.14557 (2022)
15. He, Q., Su, H., Zhang, J., Hou, X.: Frustratingly easy regularization on representation can boost deep reinforcement learning. In: Proceedings of the IEEE/CVF Conference on Computer Vision and Pattern Recognition, pp. 20215–20225 (2023)
16. Hoel, P.G.: On indices of dispersion. Ann. Math. Stat. **14**(2), 155–162 (1943)
17. Kuznetsov, A., Shvechikov, P., Grishin, A., Vetrov, D.: Controlling overestimation bias with truncated mixture of continuous distributional quantile critics. In: Proceedings of the 37th International Conference on Machine Learning, pp. 5556–5566 (2020)
18. Lan, Q., Pan, Y., Fyshe, A., White, M.: Maxmin Q-learning: Controlling the estimation bias of Q-learning. In: International Conference on Learning Representations (2019)
19. Lyle, C., Rowland, M., Dabney, W.: Understanding and preventing capacity loss in reinforcement learning. In: The Tenth International Conference on Learning Representations, ICLR 2022, Virtual Event, 25–29 April 2022. OpenReview.net (2022)
20. Lyle, C., Rowland, M., Dabney, W., Kwiatkowska, M., Gal, Y.: Learning dynamics and generalization in deep reinforcement learning. In: Chaudhuri, K., Jegelka, S., Song, L., Szepesvári, C., Niu, G., Sabato, S. (eds.) International Conference on Machine Learning, ICML 2022, 17–23 July 2022, Baltimore, Maryland, USA, Proceedings of Machine Learning Research, vol. 162, pp. 14560–14581. PMLR (2022)
21. Lyle, C., Rowland, M., Ostrovski, G., Dabney, W.: On the effect of auxiliary tasks on representation dynamics. In: International Conference on Artificial Intelligence and Statistics, pp. 1–9. PMLR (2021)
22. Meyer, C.D.: Matrix analysis and applied linear algebra, vol. 71. Siam (2000)
23. Mnih, V., et al.: Human-level control through deep reinforcement learning. Nature **518**(7540), 529–533 (2015)
24. Munos, R., Stepleton, T., Harutyunyan, A., Bellemare, M.G.: Safe and efficient off-policy reinforcement learning. In: Lee, D.D., Sugiyama, M., von Luxburg, U., Guyon, I., Garnett, R. (eds.) Advances in Neural Information Processing Systems 29: Annual Conference on Neural Information Processing Systems 2016, 5–10 December 2016, Barcelona, Spain, pp. 1046–1054 (2016)
25. Ren, T., Zhang, T., Lee, L., Gonzalez, J.E., Schuurmans, D., Dai, B.: Spectral decomposition representation for reinforcement learning. In: International Conference on Learning Representations (2023)

26. Sekhari, A., Dann, C., Mohri, M., Mansour, Y., Sridharan, K.: Agnostic rein-
    forcement learning with low-rank MDPs and rich observations. In: Ranzato, M.,
    Beygelzimer, A., Dauphin, Y.N., Liang, P., Vaughan, J.W. (eds.) Advances in Neu-
    ral Information Processing Systems 34: Annual Conference on Neural Information
    Processing Systems 2021, NeurIPS 2021, 6–14 December 2021, virtual, pp. 19033–
    19045 (2021)
27. Silver, D., et al.: A general reinforcement learning algorithm that masters chess,
    shogi, and go through self-play. Science 362(6419), 1140–1144 (2018)
28. Singh, S., Jaakkola, T., Littman, M.L., Szepesvári, C.: Convergence results for
    single-step on-policy reinforcement-learning algorithms. Mach. Learn. 38, 287–308
    (2000)
29. Sutton, R.S., Barto, A.G.: Reinforcement learning: an introduction. MIT Press
    (2018)
30. Tesauro, G.: Temporal difference learning and TD-Gammon. Commun. ACM
    38(3), 58–68 (1995)
31. Todorov, E., Erez, T., Tassa, Y.: MuJoCo: a physics engine for model-based con-
    trol. In: 2012 IEEE/RSJ International Conference on Intelligent Robots and Sys-
    tems, IROS 2012, Vilamoura, Algarve, Portugal, 7–12 October 2012, pp. 5026–
    5033. IEEE (2012)
32. Tunyasuvunakool, S., et al.: dm-control: software and tasks for continuous control.
    Softw. Impacts 6, 100022 (2020). ISSN 2665–9638
33. Uehara, M., Zhang, X., Sun, W.: Representation learning for online and offline RL
    in low-rank MDPs. In: The Tenth International Conference on Learning Represen-
    tations, ICLR 2022, Virtual Event, 25–29 April 2022. OpenReview.net (2022)
34. Van Hasselt, H., Guez, A., Silver, D.: Deep reinforcement learning with double
    Q-learning. In: Thirtieth AAAI Conference on Artificial Intelligence (2016)
35. Vinyals, O., et al.: Grandmaster level in StarCraft II using multi-agent reinforce-
    ment learning. Nature 575(7782), 350–354 (2019)
36. Watkins, C.J., Dayan, P.: Q-learning. Mach. Learn. 8(3), 279–292 (1992)
37. Yang, G., Ajay, A., Agrawal, P.: Overcoming the spectral bias of neural value
    approximation. In: The Tenth International Conference on Learning Representa-
    tions, ICLR 2022, Virtual Event, 25–29 April 2022. OpenReview.net (2022)
38. Yarats, D., Kostrikov, I.: Soft actor-critic (sac) implementation in PyTorch (2020)
39. Zhang, W., He, J., Zhou, D., Zhang, A., Gu, Q.: Provably efficient representation
    learning in low-rank Markov decision processes. arXiv preprint arXiv:2106.11935
    (2021)

# Representation Learning

# Learning Disentangled Discrete Representations

David Friede[1]([✉]), Christian Reimers[2], Heiner Stuckenschmidt[1],
and Mathias Niepert[3,4]

[1] University of Mannheim, Mannheim, Germany
{david,heiner}@informatik.uni-mannheim.de
[2] Max Planck Institute for Biogeochemistry, Jena, Germany
creimers@bgc-jena.mpg.de
[3] University of Stuttgart, Stuttgart, Germany
mathias.niepert@simtech.uni-stuttgart.de
[4] NEC Laboratories Europe, Heidelberg, Germany

**Abstract.** Recent successes in image generation, model-based reinforcement learning, and text-to-image generation have demonstrated the empirical advantages of discrete latent representations, although the reasons behind their benefits remain unclear. We explore the relationship between discrete latent spaces and disentangled representations by replacing the standard Gaussian variational autoencoder (VAE) with a tailored categorical variational autoencoder. We show that the underlying grid structure of categorical distributions mitigates the problem of rotational invariance associated with multivariate Gaussian distributions, acting as an efficient inductive prior for disentangled representations. We provide both analytical and empirical findings that demonstrate the advantages of discrete VAEs for learning disentangled representations. Furthermore, we introduce the first unsupervised model selection strategy that favors disentangled representations.

**Keywords:** Categorical VAE · Disentanglement

## 1 Introduction

Discrete variational autoencoders based on categorical distributions [17,28] or vector quantization [45] have enabled recent success in large-scale image generation [34,45], model-based reinforcement learning [13,14,31], and perhaps most notably, in text-to-image generation models like Dall-E [33] and Stable Diffusion [37]. Prior work has argued that discrete representations are a natural fit for complex reasoning or planning [17,31,33] and has shown empirically that a discrete latent space yields better generalization behavior [10,13,37]. Hafner et al. [13] hypothesize that the sparsity enforced by a vector of discrete latent variables could encourage generalization behavior. However, they admit that "we do not know the reason why the categorical variables are beneficial."

© The Author(s), under exclusive license to Springer Nature Switzerland AG 2023
D. Koutra et al. (Eds.): ECML PKDD 2023, LNAI 14172, pp. 593–609, 2023.
https://doi.org/10.1007/978-3-031-43421-1_35

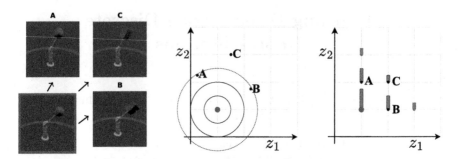

**Fig. 1.** Four observations and their latent representation with a Gaussian and discrete VAE. Both VAEs encourage similar inputs to be placed close to each other in latent space. **Left:** Four examples from the MPI3D dataset [11]. The horizontal axis depicts the object's shape, and the vertical axis depicts the angle of the arm. **Middle:** A 2-dimensional latent space of a Gaussian VAE representing the four examples. Distances in the Gaussian latent space are related to the Euclidean distance. **Right:** A categorical latent space augmented with an order of the categories representing the same examples. The grid structure of the discrete latent space makes it more robust against rotations constituting a stronger inductive prior for disentanglement.

We focus on an extensive study of the *structural impact* of discrete representations on the latent space. The disentanglement literature [3,15,25] provides a common approach to analyzing the structure of latent spaces. Disentangled representations [3] recover the low-dimensional and independent ground-truth factors of variation of high-dimensional observations. Such representations promise interpretability [1,15], fairness [7,24,42], and better sample complexity for learning [3,32,38,46]. State-of-the-art unsupervised disentanglement methods enrich *Gaussian* variational autoencoders [20] with regularizers encouraging disentangling properties [5,6,16,19,22]. Locatello et al. [25] showed that unsupervised disentanglement without inductive priors is theoretically impossible. Thus, a recent line of work has shifted to weakly-supervised disentanglement [21,26,27,40].

We focus on the impact on disentanglement of replacing the standard variational autoencoder with a slightly tailored *categorical* variational autoencoder [17,28]. Most disentanglement metrics assume an ordered latent space, which can be traversed and visualized by fixing all but one latent variable [6,9,16]. Conventional categorical variational autoencoders lack sortability since there is generally no order between the categories. For direct comparison via established disentanglement metrics, we modify the categorical variational autoencoder to represent each category with a *one-dimensional* representation. While regularization and supervision have been discussed extensively in the disentanglement literature, the variational autoencoder is a component that has mainly remained constant. At the same time, Watters et. al [50] have observed that Gaussian VAEs might suffer from rotations in the latent space, which can harm disentangling properties. We analyze the rotational invariance of multivariate Gaussian distributions in more detail and show that the underlying grid structure of categorical distributions mitigates this problem and acts as an efficient inductive prior for disentangled representations. We first show that the observation from

[5] still holds in the discrete case, in that neighboring points in the data space are encouraged to be also represented close together in the latent space. Second, the categorical latent space is less rotation-prone than its Gaussian counterpart and thus, constitutes a stronger inductive prior for disentanglement as illustrated in Fig. 1. Third, the categorical variational autoencoder admits an unsupervised disentangling score that is correlated with several disentanglement metrics. Hence, to the best of our knowledge, we present the first disentangling model selection based on unsupervised scores.

## 2    Disentangled Representations

The disentanglement literature is usually premised on the assumption that a high-dimensional observation $x$ from the data space $\mathcal{X}$ is generated from a low-dimensional latent variable $z$ whose entries correspond to the dataset's ground-truth factors of variation such as position, color, or shape [3,43]. First, the *independent* ground-truth factors are sampled from some distribution $z \sim p(z) = \prod p(z_i)$. The observation is then a sample from the conditional probability $x \sim p(x|z)$. The goal of disentanglement learning is to find a representation $r(x)$ such that each ground-truth factor $z_i$ is recovered in one and only one dimension of the representation. The formalism of variational autoencoders [20] enables an estimation of these distributions. Assuming a known prior $p(z)$, we can depict the conditional probability $p_\theta(x|z)$ as a parameterized probabilistic decoder. In general, the posterior $p_\theta(z|x)$ is intractable. Thus, we turn to variational inference and approximate the posterior by a parameterized probabilistic encoder $q_\phi(z|x)$ and minimize the Kullback-Leibler (KL) divergence $D_{\mathrm{KL}}\big(q_\phi(z|x) \parallel p_\theta(z|x)\big)$. This term, too, is intractable but can be minimized by maximizing the evidence lower bound (ELBO)

$$\mathcal{L}_{\theta,\phi}(x) = \mathbb{E}_{q_\phi(z|x)}\left[\log p_\theta(x|z)\right] - D_{\mathrm{KL}}\big(q_\phi(z|x) \parallel p(z)\big). \tag{1}$$

State-of-the-art unsupervised disentanglement methods assume a Normal prior $p(z) = \mathcal{N}(0, I)$ as well as an amortized diagonal Gaussian for the approximated posterior distribution $q_\phi(z|x) = \mathcal{N}(z \mid \mu_\phi(x), \sigma_\phi(x)I)$. They enrich the ELBO with regularizers encouraging disentangling [5,6,16,19,22] and choose the representation as the mean of the approximated posterior $r(x) = \mu_\phi(x)$ [25].

**Discrete VAE.** We propose a variant of the categorical VAE modeling a joint distribution of $n$ *Gumbel-Softmax* random variables [17,28]. Let $n$ be the dimension of $z$, $m$ be the number of categories, $\alpha_i^j \in (0,\infty)$ be the unnormalized probabilities of the categories and $g_i^j \sim \mathrm{Gumbel}(0,1)$ be i.i.d. samples drawn from the Gumbel distribution for $i \in [n], j \in [m]$. For each dimension $i \in [n]$, we sample a Gumbel-softmax random variable $z_i \sim \mathrm{GS}(\alpha_i)$ over the simplex $\Delta^{m-1} = \{y \in \mathbb{R}^n \mid y^j \in [0,1], \sum_{j=1}^m y^j = 1\}$ by setting

$$z_i^j = \frac{\exp(\log \alpha_i^j + g_i^j)}{\sum_{k=1}^m \exp(\log \alpha_i^k + g_i^k)} \tag{2}$$

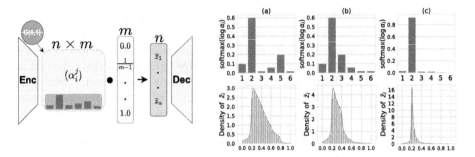

**Fig. 2.** We utilize $n$ Gumbel-softmax distributions (GS) to approximate the posterior distribution. **Left:** An encoder learns $nm$ parameters $a_i^j$ for the $n$ joint distributions. Each $m$-dimensional sample is mapped into the one-dimensional unit interval as described in Sect. 3.1. **Right:** Three examples of (normalized) parameters of a single Gumbel-softmax distribution and the corresponding one-dimensional distribution of $\bar{z}_i$.

for $j \in [m]$. We set the approximated posterior distribution to be a joint distribution of $n$ Gumbel-softmax distributions, i.e., $q_\phi(z|x) = \mathrm{GS}^n(z \mid \alpha_\phi(x))$ and assume a joint discrete uniform prior distribution $p(z) = \mathcal{U}^n\{1, m\}$. Note that $z$ is of dimension $n \times m$. To obtain the final $n$-dimensional latent variable $\bar{z}$, we define a function $f : \Delta^{m-1} \to [0,1]$ as the dot product of $z_i$ with the vector $v_m = (v_m^1, \ldots, v_m^m)$ of $m$ equidistant entries $v_m^j = \frac{j-1}{m-1}$ of the interval[1] $[0,1]$, i.e.,

$$\bar{z}_i = f(z_i) = z_i \cdot v_m = \frac{1}{m-1} \sum_{j=1}^m j z_i^j \tag{3}$$

as illustrated in Fig. 2. We will show in Sect. 3.2 that this choice of the latent variable $\bar{z}$ has favorable disentangling properties. The representation is obtained by the standard softmax function $r(x)_i = f\big(\mathrm{softmax}(\log \alpha_\phi(x)_i)\big)$.

## 3  Learning Disentangled Discrete Representations

Using a discrete distribution in the latent space is a strong inductive bias for disentanglement. In this section, we introduce some properties of the discrete latent space and compare it to the latent space of a Gaussian VAE. First, we show that mapping the discrete categories into a shared unit interval as in Eq. 3 causes an ordering of the discrete categories and, in turn, enable a definition of neighborhoods in the latent space. Second, we derive that, in the discrete case, neighboring points in the data space are encouraged to be represented close together in the latent space. Third, we show that the categorical latent space is less rotation-prone than its Gaussian counterpart and thus, constituting a stronger inductive prior for disentanglement. Finally, we describe how to select models with better disentanglement using the straight-through gap.

---

[1] The choice of the unit interval is arbitrary.

## 3.1  Neighborhoods in the Latent Space

In the Gaussian case, neighboring points in the observable space correspond to neighboring points in the latent space. The ELBO Loss Eq. 1, more precisely the reconstruction loss as part of the ELBO, implies a topology of the observable space. For more details on this topology, see Appendix 2. In the case, where the approximated posterior distribution, $q_\phi(z|x)$, is Gaussian and the covariance matrix, $\Sigma(x)$, is diagonal, the topology of the latent space can be defined in a similar way: The negative log-probability is the weighted Euclidean distance to the mean $\mu(x)$ of the distribution

$$C - \log q_\phi(z|x) = \frac{1}{2}\left[(z - \mu(x))^\intercal \Sigma(x)(z - \mu(x))\right]^2 = \sum_{i=1}^{n} \frac{(z_i - \mu_i(x))^2}{2\sigma_i(x)} \qquad (4)$$

where $C$ denotes the logarithm of the normalization factor in the Gaussian density function. Neighboring points in the observable space will be mapped to neighboring points in the latent space to reduce the log-likelihood cost of sampling in the latent space [5].

In the case of categorical latent distributions, the induced topology is not related to the euclidean distance and, hence, it does not encourage that points that are close in the observable space will be mapped to points that are close in the latent space. The problem becomes explicit if we consider a single categorical distribution. In the latent space, neighbourhoods entirely depend on the shared representation of the $m$ classes. The canonical representation maps a class $j$ into the one-hot vector $e^j = (e_1, e_2, \ldots, e_m)$ with $e_k = 1$ for $k = j$ and $e_k = 0$ otherwise. The representation space consists of the $m$-dimensional units vectors, and all classes have the same pairwise distance between each other.

To overcome this problem, we inherit the canonical order of $\mathbb{R}$ by depicting a 1-dimensional representation space. We consider the representation $\bar{z}_i = f(z_i)$ from Eq. 3 that maps a class $j$ on the value $\frac{j-1}{m-1}$ inside the unit interval. In this way, we create an ordering on the classes $1 < 2 < \cdots < m$ and define the distance between two classes by $d(j, k) = \frac{1}{m-1}|j - k|$. In the following, we discuss properties of a VAE using this representation space.

## 3.2  Disentangling Properties of the Discrete VAE

In this section, we show that neighboring points in the observable space are represented close together in the latent space and that each data point is represented discretely by a single category $j$ for each dimension $i \in \{1, \ldots, n\}$. First, we show that reconstructing under the latent variable $\bar{z}_i = f(z_i)$ encourages each data point to utilize neighboring categories rather than categories with a larger distance. Second, we discuss how the Gumbel-softmax distribution is encouraged to approximate the discrete categorical distribution. For the Gaussian case, this property was shown by [5]. Here, the ELBO (Eq. 1) depicts an inductive prior that encourages disentanglement by encouraging neighboring points in the data space to be represented close together in the latent space [5]. To show these properties for the D-VAE, we use the following proposition. The proof can be found in Appendix 1.

**Proposition 1.** Let $\alpha_i \in [0, \infty)^m$, $z_i \sim GS(\alpha_i)$ be as in Eq. 2 and $\bar{z}_i = f(z_i)$ be as in Eq. 3. Define $j_{min} = \operatorname{argmin}_j\{\alpha_i^j > 0\}$ and $j_{max} = \operatorname{argmax}_j\{\alpha_i^j > 0\}$. Then it holds that

(a) $\operatorname{supp}(f) = (\frac{j_{min}}{m-1}, \frac{j_{max}}{m-1})$

(b) $\frac{\alpha_i^j}{\sum_{k=1}^m \alpha_i^k} \to 1 \Rightarrow \mathbb{P}(z_i^j = 1) = 1 \wedge f(z_i) = \mathbb{1}_{\{\frac{j}{m-1}\}}$.

Proposition 1 has multiple consequences. First, a class $j$ might have a high density regarding $\bar{z}_i = f(z_i)$ although $\alpha_i^j \approx 0$. For example, if $j$ is positioned between two other classes with large $\alpha_i^k$ (e.g. $j = 3$ in Fig. 2(a)) Second, if there is a class $j$ such that $\alpha_i^k \approx 0$ for all $k \geq j$ or $k \leq j$, then the density of these classes is also almost zero (Figure 2(a-c)). Note that a small support benefits a small reconstruction loss since it reduces the probability of sampling a wrong class. The probabilities of Fig. 2 (a) and (b) are the same with the only exception that $\alpha_i^3 \leftrightarrow \alpha_i^5$ are swapped. Since the probability distribution in (b) yields a smaller support and consequently a smaller reconstruction loss while the KL divergence is the same for both probabilities,[2] the model is encouraged to utilize probability (b) over (a). This encourages the representation of similar inputs in neighboring classes rather than classes with a larger distance.

Consequently, we can apply the same argument as in [5] Sect. 4.2 about the connection of the posterior overlap with minimizing the ELBO. Since the posterior overlap is highest between neighboring classes, confusions caused by sampling are more likely in neighboring classes than those with a larger distance. To minimize the penalization of the reconstruction loss caused by these confusions, neighboring points in the data space are encouraged to be represented close together in the latent space. Similar to the Gaussian case [5], we observe an increase in the KL divergence loss during training while the reconstruction loss continually decreases. The probability of sampling confusion and, therefore, the posterior overlap must be reduced as much as possible to reduce the reconstruction loss. Thus, later in training, data points are encouraged to utilize exactly one category while accepting some penalization in the form of KL loss, meaning that $\alpha_i^j/(\sum_{k=1}^m \alpha_i^k) \to 1$. Consequently, the Gumbel-softmax distribution approximates the discrete categorical distribution, see Proposition 1 (b). An example is shown in Fig. 2(c). This training behavior results in the unique situation in which the latent space approximates a discrete representation while its classes maintain the discussed order and the property of having neighborhoods.

### 3.3   Structural Advantages of the Discrete VAE

In this section, we demonstrate that the properties discussed in Sect. 3.2 aid disentanglement. So far, we have only considered a single factor $z_i$ of the approximated posterior $q_\phi(z|x)$. To understand the disentangling properties regarding the full latent variable $z$, we first highlight the differences between the continuous and the discrete approach.

---

[2] The KL divergence is invariant under permutation.

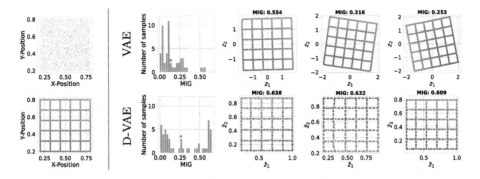

**Fig. 3.** Geometry analysis of the latent space of the circles experiment [50]. **Col 1, top:** The generative factor distribution of the circles dataset. **Bottom:** A selective grid of points in generative factor space spanning the data distribution. **Col 2:** The Mutual Information Gap (MIG) [6] for 50 Gaussian VAE (top) and a categorical VAE (bottom), respectively. The red star denotes the median value. **Col 3 - 5:** The latent space visualized by the representations of the selective grid of points. We show the best, 5th best, and 10th model determined by the MIG score of the Gaussian VAE (top) and the categorical VAE (bottom), respectively.

In the continuous case, neighboring points in the observable space are represented close together in the latent space. However, this does not imply disentanglement, since the first property is invariant under rotations over $\mathbb{R}^n$ while disentanglement is not. Even when utilizing a diagonal covariance matrix for the approximated posterior $q(z|x) = \mathcal{N}\big(z \mid \mu(x), \sigma(x)I\big)$, which, in general, is not invariant under rotation, there are cases where rotations are problematic, as the following proposition shows. We provide the proof in Appendix 1.

**Proposition 2 (Rotational Equivariance).** *Let $\alpha \in [0, 2\pi)$ and let $z \sim \mathcal{N}(\mu, \Sigma)$ with $\Sigma = \sigma I$, $\sigma = (\sigma_0, \dots, \sigma_n)$. If $\sigma_i = \sigma_j$ for some $i \neq j \in [n]$, then $z$ is equivariant under any $i, j$-rotation, i.e., $R_{ij}^\alpha z \overset{d}{=} y$ with $y \sim \mathcal{N}\big(R_{ij}^\alpha \mu, \Sigma\big)$.*

Since, in the Gaussian VAE, the KL-divergence term in Eq. 1 is invariant under rotations, Proposition 2 implies that its latent space can be arbitrarily rotated in dimensions $i, j$ that hold equal variances $\sigma_i = \sigma_j$. Equal variances can occur, for example, when different factors exert a similar influence on the data space, e.g., X-position and Y-position or for factors where high log-likelihood costs of potential confusion causes lead to variances close to zero. In contrast, the discrete latent space is invariant only under rotations that are axially aligned.

We illustrate this with an example in Fig. 3. Here we illustrate the 2-dimensional latent space of a Gaussian VAE model trained on a dataset generated from the two ground-truth factors, X-position and Y-position. We train 50 copies of the model and depicted the best, the 5th best, and the 10th best latent space regarding the Mutual Information Gap (MIG) [6]. All three latent spaces exhibit rotation, while the disentanglement score is strongly correlated with the angle of the rotation. In the discrete case, the latent space is, according to Proposition 1 (b), a subset of the regular grid $\mathbb{G}^n$ with $\mathbb{G} = \{\frac{j}{m-1}\}_{j=0}^{m-1}$ as illustrated in Fig. 1 (right). Distances and rotations exhibit different geometric properties on $\mathbb{G}^n$ than on $\mathbb{R}^n$. First, the closest neighbors are axially aligned. Non-aligned points have a distance at least $\sqrt{2}$ times larger. Consequently, representing neighboring points in the data space close together in the latent space encourages disentanglement. Secondly, $\mathbb{G}^n$ is invariant only under exactly those rotations that are axially aligned. Figure 3 (bottom right) illustrates the 2-dimensional latent space of a D-VAE model trained on the same dataset and with the same random seeds as the Gaussian VAE model. Contrary to the Gaussian latent spaces, the discrete latent spaces are sensible of the axes and generally yield better disentanglement scores. The set of all 100 latent spaces is available in Figs. 10 and 11 in Appendix 7.

### 3.4 The Straight-Through Gap

We have observed that sometimes the models approach local minima, for which $z$ is not entirely discrete. As per the previous discussion, those models have inferior disentangling properties. We leverage this property by selecting models that yield discrete latent spaces. Similar to the Straight-Through Estimator [4], we round $z$ off using argmax and measure the difference between the rounded and original ELBO, i.e., $\text{Gap}_{ST}(x) = |\mathcal{L}_{\theta,\phi}^{ST}(x) - \mathcal{L}_{\theta,\phi}(x)|$, which equals zero if $z$ is discrete. Figure 4 (left) illustrates the Spearman rank correlation between $\text{Gap}_{ST}$ and various disentangling metrics on different datasets. A smaller $\text{Gap}_{ST}$ value indicates high disentangling scores for most datasets and metrics.

## 4   Related Work

Previous studies have proposed various methods for utilizing discrete latent spaces. The REINFORCE algorithm [51] utilizes the log derivative trick. The Straight-Through estimator [4] back-propagates through hard samples by replacing the threshold function with the identity in the backward pass. Additional prior work employed the nearest neighbor look-up called vector quantization [45] to discretize the latent space. Other approaches use reparameterization tricks [20] that enable the gradient computation by removing the dependence of the density on the input parameters. Maddison et al. [28] and Jang et al. [17] propose the Gumbel-Softmax trick, a continuous reparameterization trick for categorical distributions. Extensions of the Gumbel-Softmax trick discussed control variates [12,44], the local reparameterization trick [39], or the behavior of multiple sequential discrete components [10]. In this work, we focus on the structural impact of discrete representations on the latent space from the viewpoint of disentanglement.

State-of-the-art unsupervised disentanglement methods enhance Gaussian VAEs with various regularizers that encourage disentangling properties. The $\beta$-VAE model [16] introduces a hyperparameter to control the trade-off between the

**Table 1.** The median MIG scores in % for state-of-the-art unsupervised methods compared to the discrete methods. Results taken from [25] are marked with an asterisk (*). We have re-implemented all other results with the same architecture as in [25] for the sake of fairness. The last row depicts the scores of the models selected by the smallest $Gap_{ST}$. The 25% and the 75% quantiles can be found in Table 5 in Appendix 7.

| Model | dSprites | C-dSprites | SmallNORB | Cars3D | Shapes3D | MPI3D |
|---|---|---|---|---|---|---|
| $\beta$-VAE [16] | 11.3* | 12.5* | 20.2* | 9.5* | n.a. | n.a. |
| $\beta$-TCVAE [6] | 17.6* | 14.6* | 21.5* | 12.0* | n.a. | n.a. |
| DIP-VAE-I [22] | 3.6* | 4.7* | 16.7* | 5.3* | n.a. | n.a. |
| DIP-VAE-II [22] | 6.2* | 4.9* | 24.1* | 4.2* | n.a. | n.a. |
| AnnealedVAE [5] | 7.8* | 10.7* | 4.6* | 6.7* | n.a. | n.a. |
| FactorVAE [19] | 17.4 | 14.3 | **25.3** | 9.0 | 34.7 | 11.1 |
| D-VAE | 17.4 | 9.4 | 19.0 | 8.5 | 28.8 | 12.8 |
| FactorDVAE | **21.7** | **15.5** | 23.2 | **14.9** | **42.4** | **30.5** |
| Selection | 39.5 | 20.0 | 22.7 | 19.1 | 40.1 | 32.3 |

reconstruction loss and the KL-divergence term, promoting disentangled latent representations. The annealedVAE [5] adapts to the $\beta$-VAE by annealing the $\beta$ hyperparameter during training. FactorVAE [19] and $\beta$-TCVAE [6] promote independence among latent variables by controlling the total correlation between them. DIP-VAE-I and DIP-VAE-II [22] are two variants that enforce disentangled latent factors by matching the covariance of the aggregated posterior to that of the prior. Previous research has focused on augmenting the standard variational autoencoder with discrete factors [8,18,29] to improve disentangling properties. In contrast, our goal is to replace the variational autoencoder with a categorical one, treating every ground-truth factor as a discrete representation.

## 5  Experimental Setup

**Methods.** The experiments aim to compare the Gaussian VAE with the discrete VAE. We consider the unregularized version and the total correlation penalizing method, VAE, D-VAE, FactorVAE [19] and FactorDVAE a version of FactorVAE for the D-VAE. We provide a detailed discussion of FactorDVAE in Appendix 3. For the semi-supervised experiments, we augment each loss function with the supervised regularizer $R_s$ as in Appendix 3. For the Gaussian VAE, we choose the BCE and the $L_2$ loss for $R_s$, respectively. For the discrete VAE, we select the cross-entropy loss, once without and once with masked attention where we incorporate the knowledge about the number of unique variations. We discuss the corresponding learning objectives in more detail in Appendix 3.

| BetaVAE | -13 | 17 | -13 | -2 | -30 | -36 |
|---|---|---|---|---|---|---|
| FactorVAE | -21 | 17 | -3 | -11 | -25 | -24 |
| MIG | -29 | -8 | 46 | -25 | -26 | -8 |
| DCI | -19 | 3 | -49 | -49 | -52 | -35 |
| Modularity | -35 | -8 | -20 | -22 | -22 | -14 |
| SAP | -4 | -23 | 7 | -15 | -14 | 4 |
| | (A) | (B) | (C) | (D) | (E) | (F) |

| BetaVAE | -20 | -17 | -38 | -36 | -53 | -67 |
|---|---|---|---|---|---|---|
| FactorVAE | -42 | -33 | -39 | -30 | -54 | -70 |
| MIG | 21 | 51 | 23 | 62 | 32 | 58 |
| DCI | 32 | 59 | 39 | 19 | -39 | -19 |
| Modularity | -62 | -76 | 28 | -27 | -37 | -68 |
| SAP | 2 | 59 | 7 | 27 | -37 | 33 |
| | (A) | (B) | (C) | (D) | (E) | (F) |

**Fig. 4.** The Spearman rank correlation between various disentanglment metrics and $Gap_{ST}$ (**left**) and the statistical sample efficiency, i.e., the downstream task accuracy based on 100 samples divided by the one on 10 000 samples (**right**) on different datasets: dSprites (A), C-dSprites (B), SmallNORB (C), Cars3D (D), Shapes3D (E), MPI3D (F). **Left:** Correlation to $Gap_{ST}$ indicates the disentanglement skill. **Right:** Only a high MIG score reliably leads to a higher sample efficiency over all six datasets.

**Datasets.** We consider six commonly used disentanglement datasets which offer explicit access to the ground-truth factors of variation: *dSprites* [16], *C-dSprites* [25], *SmallNORB* [23], *Cars3D* [35], *Shapes3D* [19] and *MPI3D* [11]. We provide a more detailed description of the datasets in Table 8 in Appendix 6.

**Metrics.** We consider the commonly used disentanglement metrics that have been discussed in detail in [25] to evaluate the representations: *BetaVAE* metric [16], *FactorVAE* metric [19], *Mutual Information Gap* (MIG) [6], *DCI Disentanglement* (DCI) [9], *Modularity* [36] and *SAP score* (SAP) [22]. As illustrated on the right side of Fig. 4, the MIG score seems to be the most reliable indicator of sample efficiency across different datasets. Therefore, we primarily focus on the MIG disentanglement score. We discuss this in more detail in Appendix 4.

**Experimental Protocol.** We adopt the experimental setup of prior work ([25,27]) for the unsupervised and for the semi-supervised experiments, respectively. Specifically, we utilize the same neural architecture for all methods so that all differences solely emerge from the distribution of the type of VAE. For the unsupervised case, we run each considered method on each dataset for 50 different random seeds. Since the two unregularized methods do not have any extra hyperparameters, we run them for 300 different random seeds instead. For the semi-supervised case, we consider two numbers (100/1000) of perfectly labeled examples and split the labeled examples (90%/10%) into a training and validation set. We choose 6 values for the correlation penalizing hyperparameter $\gamma$ and for the semi-supervising hyperparameter $\omega$ from Eq. 6 and 7 in Appendix 3, respectively. We present the full implementation details in Appendix 5.

## 6    Experimental Results

First, we investigate whether a discrete VAE offers advantages over Gaussian VAEs in terms of disentanglement properties, finding that the discrete model generally outperforms its Gaussian counterpart and showing that the FactorD-VAE achieves new state-of-the-art MIG scores on most datasets. Additionally, we

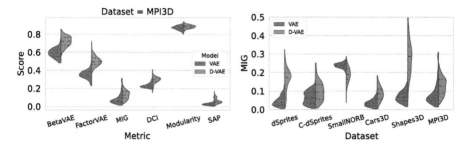

**Fig. 5.** Comparison between the unregularized Gaussian VAE and the discrete VAE by kernel density estimates of 300 runs, respectively. **Left:** Comparison on the MPI3D dataset w.r.t. the six disentanglement metrics. The discrete model yields a better score for each metric, with median improvements ranging from 2% for Modularity to 104% for MIG. **Right:** Comparison on all six datasets w.r.t. the MIG metric. With the exception of SmallNORB, the discrete VAE yields a better score for all datasets with improvements of the median score ranging from 50% on C-dSprites to 336% on dSprites.

propose a model selection criterion based on $\text{Gap}_{ST}$ to find good discrete models solely using unsupervised scores. Lastly, we examine how incorporating label information can further enhance discrete representations. The implementations are in JAX and Haiku and were run on a RTX A6000 GPU.[3]

## 6.1    Improvement in Unsupervised Disentanglement Properties

**Comparison of the Unregularized Models.** In the first experiment, we aim to answer our main research question of whether discrete latent spaces yield structural advantages over their Gaussian counterparts. Figure 5 depicts the comparison regarding the disentanglement scores (left) and the datasets (right). The discrete model achieves a better score on the MPI3D dataset for each metric with median improvements ranging from 2% for Modularity to 104% for MIG. Furthermore, the discrete model yields a better score for all datasets but Small-NORB with median improvements ranging from 50% on C-dSprites to 336% on dSprites. More detailed results can be found in Table 6, Fig. 12, and Fig. 13 in Appendix 7. Taking into account all datasets and metrics, the discrete VAE improves over its Gaussian counterpart in 31 out of 36 cases.

**Comparison of the Total Correlation Regularizing Models.** For each VAE, we choose the same 6 values of hyperparameter $\gamma$ for the total correlation penalizing method and train 50 copies, respectively. The right side of Fig. 6 depicts the comparison of FactorVAE and FactorDVAE w.r.t. the MIG metric. The discrete model achieves a better score for all datasets but SmallNORB with median improvements ranging from 8% on C-dSprites to 175% on MPI3D.

---

[3] The implementations and Appendix are at https://github.com/david-friede/lddr.

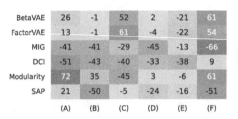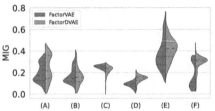

**Fig. 6.** Disentangling properties of FactorDVAE on different datasets: dSprites (A), C-dSprites (B), SmallNORB (C), Cars3D (D), Shapes3D (E), MPI3D (F). **Left:** The Spearman rank correlation between various disentangling metrics and $Gap_{ST}$ of D-VAE and FactorDVAE combined. A small $Gap_{ST}$ indicates high disentangling scores for most datasets regarding the MIG, DCI, and SAP metrics. **Right:** A comparison of the total correlation regularizing Gaussian and the discrete model w.r.t. the MIG metric. The discrete model yields a better score for all datasets but SmallNORB with median improvements ranging from 8% on C-dSprites to 175% on MPI3D.

## 6.2   Match State-of-the-Art Unsupervised Disentanglement Methods

Current state-of-the-art unsupervised disentanglement methods enrich Gaussian VAEs with various regularizers encouraging disentangling properties. Table 1 depicts the MIG scores of all methods as reported in [25] utilizing the same architecture as us. FactorDVAE achieves new state-of-the-art MIG scores on all datasets but SmallNORB, improving the previous best scores by over 17% on average. These findings suggest that incorporating results from the disentanglement literature might lead to even stronger models based on discrete representations.

## 6.3   Unsupervised Selection of Models with Strong Disentanglement

A remaining challenge in the disentanglement literature is selecting the hyperparameters and random seeds that lead to good disentanglement scores [27]. We propose a model selection based on an unsupervised score measuring the discreteness of the latent space utilizing $Gap_{ST}$ from Sect. 3.4. The left side of Fig. 6 depicts the Spearman rank correlation between various disentangling metrics and $Gap_{ST}$ of D-VAE and FactorDVAE combined. Note that the unregularized D-VAE model can be identified as a FactorDVAE model with $\gamma = 0$. A small Straight-Through Gap corresponds to high disentangling scores for most datasets regarding the MIG, DCI, and SAP metrics. This correlation is most vital for the MIG metric. We anticipate finding good hyperparameters by selecting those models yielding the smallest $Gap_{ST}$. The last row of Table 1 confirms this finding. This model selection yields MIG scores that are, on average, 22% better than the median score and not worse than 6%.

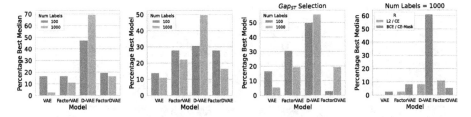

**Fig. 7.** The percentage of each semi-supervised method being the best over all datasets and disentanglement metrics for different selection methods: median, lowest $R_s$, lowest Gap$_{ST}$, median for 1000 labels. The unregularized discrete method outperforms the other methods in semi-supervised disentanglement task. Utilizing the masked regularizer improves over the unmasked one.

## 6.4  Utilize Label Information to Improve Discrete Representations

Locatello et al. [27] employ the semi-supervised regularizer $R_s$ by including 90% of the label information during training and utilizing the remaining 10% for a model selection. We also experiment with a model selection based on the Gap$_{ST}$ value. Figure 7 depicts the percentage of each semi-supervised method being the best over all datasets and disentanglement metrics. The unregularized discrete method surpasses the other methods on the semi-supervised disentanglement task. The advantage of the discrete models is more significant for the median values than for the model selection. Utilizing Gap$_{ST}$ for selecting the discrete models only partially mitigates this problem. Incorporating the number of unique variations by utilizing the masked regularizer improves the disentangling properties significantly, showcasing another advantage of the discrete latent space. The quantiles of the discrete models can be found in Table 7 in Appendix 7.

## 6.5  Visualization of the Latent Categories

Prior work uses latent space traversals for qualitative analysis of representations [5,16,19,50]. A latent vector $z \sim q_\phi(z|x)$ is sampled, and each dimension $z_i$ is traversed while keeping the other dimensions constant. The traversals are then reconstructed and visualized. Unlike the Gaussian case, the D-VAE's latent space is known beforehand, allowing straightforward traversal along the categories. Knowing the number of unique variations lets us use masked attention to determine the number of each factor's categories, improving latent space interpretability. Figure 8 illustrates the reconstructions of four random inputs and latent space traversals of the semi-supervised D-VAE utilizing masked attentions. While the reconstructions are easily recognizable, their details can be partially blurry, particularly concerning the object shape. The object color, object size, camera angle, and background color are visually disentangled, and their categories can be selected straightforwardly to create targeted observations.

Input   Recons                    Latent Category Traversals

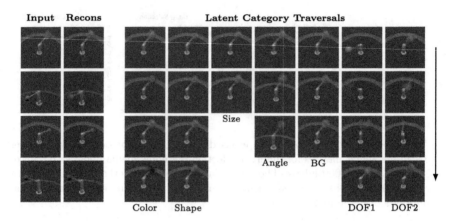

**Fig. 8.** Reconstructions and latent space traversals of the semi-supervised D-VAE, utilizing masked attentions with the lowest $R_s$ value. The masked attention allows for the incorporation of the number of unique variations, such as two for the object size. We visualize four degrees of freedom (DOF), selected equidistantly from the total of 40. **Left:** The reconstructions are easily recognizable, albeit with blurry details. **Right:** The object color, size, camera angle, and background color (BG) are visually disentangled. The object shape and the DOF factors remain partially entangled.

# 7   Conclusion

In this study, we investigated the benefits of discrete latent spaces in the context of learning disentangled representations by examining the effects of substituting the standard Gaussian VAE with a categorical VAE. Our findings revealed that the underlying grid structure of categorical distributions mitigates the rotational invariance issue associated with multivariate Gaussian distributions, thus serving as an efficient inductive prior for disentangled representations.

In multiple experiments, we demonstrated that categorical VAEs outperform their Gaussian counterparts in disentanglement. We also determined that the categorical VAE provides an unsupervised score, the Straight-Through Gap, which correlates with some disentanglement metrics, providing, to the best of our knowledge, the first unsupervised model selection score for disentanglement.

However, our study has limitations. We focused on discrete latent spaces, without investigating the impact of vector quantization on disentanglement. Furthermore, the Straight-Through Gap does not show strong correlation with disentanglement scores, affecting model selection accuracy. Additionally, our reconstructions can be somewhat blurry and may lack quality.

Our results offer a promising direction for future research in developing more powerful models with discrete latent spaces. Such future research could incorporate findings from the disentanglement literature and potentially develop novel regularizations tailored to discrete latent spaces.

# References

1. Adel, T., Ghahramani, Z., Weller, A.: Discovering interpretable representations for both deep generative and discriminative models. In: International Conference on Machine Learning, pp. 50–59. PMLR (2018)
2. Arcones, M.A., Gine, E.: On the bootstrap of $U$ and $V$ statistics. Annal. Statist. **20**, 655–674 (1992)
3. Bengio, Y., Courville, A., Vincent, P.: Representation learning: a review and new perspectives. IEEE Trans. Pattern Anal. Mach. Intell. **35**(8), 1798–1828 (2013)
4. Bengio, Y., Léonard, N., Courville, A.: Estimating or propagating gradients through stochastic neurons for conditional computation. arXiv:1308.3432 (2013)
5. Burgess, C.P., et al.: Understanding disentangling in $\beta$-vae. arXiv:1804.03599 (2018)
6. Chen, R.T., Li, X., Grosse, R.B., Duvenaud, D.K.: Isolating sources of disentanglement in variational autoencoders. In: Advances in Neural Information Processing Systems, vol. 31, pp. 2615–2625 (2018)
7. Creager, E., et al.: Flexibly fair representation learning by disentanglement. In: International Conference on Machine Learning, pp. 1436–1445. PMLR (2019)
8. Dupont, E.: Learning disentangled joint continuous and discrete representations. In: Advances in Neural Information Processing Systems, vol. 31 (2018)
9. Eastwood, C., Williams, C.K.: A framework for the quantitative evaluation of disentangled representations. In: International Conference on Learning Representations (2018)
10. Friede, D., Niepert, M.: Efficient learning of discrete-continuous computation graphs. In: Advances in Neural Information Processing Systems, vol. 34, pp. 6720–6732 (2021)
11. Gondal, M.W., et al.: On the transfer of inductive bias from simulation to the real world: a new disentanglement dataset. In: Advances in Neural Information Processing Systems, vol. 32 (2019)
12. Grathwohl, W., Choi, D., Wu, Y., Roeder, G., Duvenaud, D.: Backpropagation through the void: optimizing control variates for black-box gradient estimation. In: International Conference on Learning Representations (2018)
13. Hafner, D., Lillicrap, T., Norouzi, M., Ba, J.: Mastering Atari with discrete world models. arXiv:2010.02193 (2020)
14. Hafner, D., Pasukonis, J., Ba, J., Lillicrap, T.: Mastering diverse domains through world models. arXiv:2301.04104 (2023)
15. Higgins, I., et al.: Towards a definition of disentangled representations. arXiv:1812.02230 (2018)
16. Higgins, I., et al.: $\beta$-VAE: learning basic visual concepts with a constrained variational framework. In: International Conference on Learning Representations (2017)
17. Jang, E., Gu, S., Poole, B.: Categorical reparameterization with Gumbel-softmax. In: International Conference on Learning Representations (2017)
18. Jeong, Y., Song, H.O.: Learning discrete and continuous factors of data via alternating disentanglement. In: International Conference on Machine Learning, pp. 3091–3099. PMLR (2019)
19. Kim, H., Mnih, A.: Disentangling by factorising. In: International Conference on Machine Learning, pp. 2649–2658. PMLR (2018)
20. Kingma, D.P., Welling, M.: Auto-encoding variational Bayes. In: International Conference on Learning Representations (2013)

21. Klindt, D.A., et al.: Towards nonlinear disentanglement in natural data with temporal sparse coding. In: International Conference on Learning Representations (2021)
22. Kumar, A., Sattigeri, P., Balakrishnan, A.: Variational inference of disentangled latent concepts from unlabeled observations. In: International Conference on Learning Representations (2017)
23. LeCun, Y., Huang, F.J., Bottou, L.: Learning methods for generic object recognition with invariance to pose and lighting. In: Proceedings of the 2004 IEEE Computer Society Conference on Computer Vision and Pattern Recognition, 2004. CVPR 2004. vol. 2, pp. II-104. IEEE (2004)
24. Locatello, F., Abbati, G., Rainforth, T., Bauer, S., Schölkopf, B., Bachem, O.: On the fairness of disentangled representations. In: Advances in Neural Information Processing Systems, vol. 32 (2019)
25. Locatello, F., et al.: Challenging common assumptions in the unsupervised learning of disentangled representations. In: International Conference on Machine Learning, pp. 4114–4124. PMLR (2019)
26. Locatello, F., Poole, B., Rätsch, G., Schölkopf, B., Bachem, O., Tschannen, M.: Weakly-supervised disentanglement without compromises. In: International Conference on Machine Learning, pp. 6348–6359. PMLR (2020)
27. Locatello, F., Tschannen, M., Bauer, S., Rätsch, G., Schölkopf, B., Bachem, O.: Disentangling factors of variations using few labels. In: International Conference on Learning Representations (2020)
28. Maddison, C.J., Mnih, A., Teh, Y.W.: The concrete distribution: a continuous relaxation of discrete random variables. In: International Conference on Learning Representations (2017)
29. Makhzani, A., Shlens, J., Jaitly, N., Goodfellow, I., Frey, B.: Adversarial autoencoders. arXiv:1511.05644 (2015)
30. Nguyen, X., Wainwright, M.J., Jordan, M.I.: Estimating divergence functionals and the likelihood ratio by convex risk minimization. IEEE Trans. Inf. Theory 56(11), 5847–5861 (2010)
31. Ozair, S., Li, Y., Razavi, A., Antonoglou, I., Van Den Oord, A., Vinyals, O.: Vector quantized models for planning. In: International Conference on Machine Learning, pp. 8302–8313. PMLR (2021)
32. Peters, J., Janzing, D., Schölkopf, B.: Elements of causal inference: foundations and learning algorithms. The MIT Press (2017)
33. Ramesh, A., et al.: Zero-shot text-to-image generation. In: International Conference on Machine Learning, pp. 8821–8831. PMLR (2021)
34. Razavi, A., Van den Oord, A., Vinyals, O.: Generating diverse high-fidelity images with VQ-VAE-2. In: Advances in Neural Information Processing Systems, vol. 32 (2019)
35. Reed, S.E., Zhang, Y., Zhang, Y., Lee, H.: Deep visual analogy-making. In: Advances in Neural Information Processing Systems, vol. 28 (2015)
36. Ridgeway, K., Mozer, M.C.: Learning deep disentangled embeddings with the F-statistic loss. In: Advances in Neural Information Processing Systems, vol. 31 (2018)
37. Rombach, R., Blattmann, A., Lorenz, D., Esser, P., Ommer, B.: High-resolution image synthesis with latent diffusion models. IEEE 2022. In: CVF Conference on Computer Vision and Pattern Recognition (CVPR), pp. 10674–10685 (2022)
38. Schölkopf, B., Janzing, D., Peters, J., Sgouritsa, E., Zhang, K., Mooij, J.M.: On causal and anticausal learning. In: International Conference on Machine Learning (2012)

39. Shayer, O., Levi, D., Fetaya, E.: Learning discrete weights using the local reparameterization trick. In: International Conference on Learning Representations (2018)
40. Shu, R., Chen, Y., Kumar, A., Ermon, S., Poole, B.: Weakly supervised disentanglement with guarantees. In: International Conference on Learning Representations (2020)
41. Sugiyama, M., Suzuki, T., Kanamori, T.: Density-ratio matching under the Bregman divergence: a unified framework of density-ratio estimation. Ann. Inst. Stat. Math. **64**(5), 1009–1044 (2012)
42. Träuble, F., et al.: On disentangled representations learned from correlated data. In: International Conference on Machine Learning, pp. 10401–10412. PMLR (2021)
43. Tschannen, M., Bachem, O., Lucic, M.: Recent advances in autoencoder-based representation learning. arXiv:1812.05069 (2018)
44. Tucker, G., Mnih, A., Maddison, C.J., Lawson, J., Sohl-Dickstein, J.: REBAR: low-variance, unbiased gradient estimates for discrete latent variable models. In: Advances in Neural Information Processing Systems, vol. 30 (2017)
45. Van Den Oord, A., Vinyals, O., et al.: Neural discrete representation learning. In: Advances in Neural Information Processing Systems, vol. 30 (2017)
46. Van Steenkiste, S., Locatello, F., Schmidhuber, J., Bachem, O.: Are disentangled representations helpful for abstract visual reasoning? In: Advances in Neural Information Processing Systems, vol. 32 (2019)
47. Vaswani, A., et al.: Attention is all you need. In: Advances in Neural Information Processing Systems, vol. 30 (2017)
48. Watanabe, S.: Information theoretical analysis of multivariate correlation. IBM J. Res. Dev. **4**(1), 66–82 (1960)
49. Watters, N., Matthey, L., Borgeaud, S., Kabra, R., Lerchner, A.: Spriteworld: a flexible, configurable reinforcement learning environment (2019)
50. Watters, N., Matthey, L., Burgess, C.P., Lerchner, A.: Spatial broadcast decoder: a simple architecture for learning disentangled representations in VAEs. arXiv:1901.07017 (2019)
51. Williams, R.J.: Simple statistical gradient-following algorithms for connectionist reinforcement learning. Reinforcement Learning, pp. 5–32 (1992)

# Boosting Object Representation Learning via Motion and Object Continuity

Quentin Delfosse[1]([envelope]), Wolfgang Stammer[1,2], Thomas Rothenbächer[1], Dwarak Vittal[1], and Kristian Kersting[1,2,3,4]

[1] AI & ML Lab, TU Darmstadt, Darmstadt, Germany
`quentin.delfosse@cs.tu-darmstadt.de`
[2] Hessian Center for AI (hessian.AI), Darmstadt, Germany
[3] German Research Center for AI (DFKI), Kaiserslautern, Germany
[4] Centre for Cognitive Science, TU Darmstadt, Darmstadt, Germany

**Abstract.** Recent unsupervised multi-object detection models have shown impressive performance improvements, largely attributed to novel architectural inductive biases. Unfortunately, despite their good object localization and segmentation capabilities, their object encodings may still be suboptimal for downstream reasoning tasks, such as reinforcement learning. To overcome this, we propose to exploit object motion and continuity (objects do not pop in and out of existence). This is accomplished through two mechanisms: (i) providing temporal loss-based priors on object locations, and (ii) a contrastive object continuity loss across consecutive frames. Rather than developing an explicit deep architecture, the resulting unsupervised Motion and Object Continuity (MOC) training scheme can be instantiated using any object detection model baseline. Our results show large improvements in the performances of variational and slot-based models in terms of object discovery, convergence speed and overall latent object representations, particularly for playing Atari games. Overall, we show clear benefits of integrating motion and object continuity for downstream reasoning tasks, moving beyond object representation learning based only on reconstruction as well as evaluation based only on instance segmentation quality.

**Keywords:** Object Discovery · Motion Supervision · Object Continuity

## 1 Introduction

Our surroundings largely consist of objects and their relations. In fact, decomposing the world in terms of objects is considered an important property of human perception and reasoning. This insight has recently influenced a surge of research articles in the field of deep learning (DL), resulting in novel neural architectures and inductive biases for unsupervisedly decomposing a visual scene into objects (*e.g.* [6,15,16,20,33,39,41,49]). Integrating these modules into systems for downstream reasoning tasks, *e.g.* playing Atari games in reinforcement

D. Koutra et al. (Eds.): ECML PKDD 2023, LNAI 14172, pp. 610–628, 2023.
https://doi.org/10.1007/978-3-031-43421-1_36

**Fig. 1.** An object-centric reasoner playing Pong. The agent first extracts the object representation and then reasons on them to select an optimal action.

learning (RL) settings is a promising next step for human-centric AI (*cf.* Fig. 1). This integration could provide benefits both in overall performance and in terms of trustworthy human-machine interactions [32, 48].

However, although many of the previously mentioned works motivate their object discovery methods with the advantage of object-centric learning for complex downstream tasks, none of these explicitly optimize the object encodings for anything other than reconstruction. In fact, investigations of the object encodings of SPACE [39], SOTA on object detection for Atari games, reveal two shortcomings. First, although object detection does work for some games (*e.g.* Space Invaders), it shows significant issues on other, even as simple as Pong (*cf.* Fig. 2 for qualitative examples (top) and quantitative F-score evaluations (left)). Second, even for such a simple downstream task as object classification, its object encodings appear suboptimal even for games with high detection scores. This is exhibited by the accuracies of a ridge regression model [24, 25] trained on SPACE's encodings for object classification (Fig. 2 (left)). The encodings, mapped into a two-dimensional t-SNE [54] embedding and colored by their ground truth class labels (*cf.* Fig. 2 (right)), suggest a cluttered latent space.

These results indicate open issues from two types of errors: (**Type I**) failures in object detection per se and (**Type II**) sub-optimal object representations. Arguably, Type I is somewhat independent of Type II, as an optimal encoding is not a necessity for detecting objects in the first place. However, the Type II error is dependent on Type I, as an object representation can only exist for detected objects. Before integrating such recent modules into more general systems for reasoning tasks, we first need to tackle the remaining issues.

We therefore propose a novel model-agnostic, self-supervised training scheme for improving object representation learning, particularly for integration into downstream reasoning tasks. We refer to this scheme as Motion and Object Continuity supervision (MOC). MOC jointly tackles Type I and II errors by incorporating the inductive biases of object motion (*i.e.* objects tend to move in the real-world) and object continuity (*i.e.* objects tend to still exist over time and do not pop in and out of existence) into object discovery models.

It is based on the notion that visual input for humans is mainly perceived as image sequences. These contain rich object-based information signals, such as that objects tend to move over time, but also that an object identified in one frame will likely be present in the consecutive ones. We refer to the first property as *object motion* (M) and the second property as *object continuity*

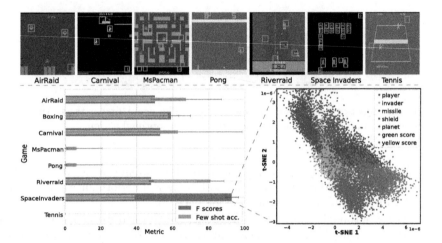

**Fig. 2.** Motivational example: unsupervised object detection models are insufficient for downstream tasks such as classification, exemplified here via SPACE [39] on Atari environments. Top: Example images of SPACE detecting objects on different Atari games. Left: F-score for object detection (blue) and few shot classification accuracy of object encodings via ridge regression (orange, 64 objects per class, 0% accuracy corresponds to no object detected). Right: Two-dimensional t-SNE embedding of object encodings produced by SPACE for Space Invaders. (Color figure online)

(OC). The concept of object continuity can be considered an extension of the Gestalt law of continuity [57] to the temporal dimension and has been identified to be an important property of infant and adult visual perception [51]. MOC specifically makes use of this underlying information via two mechanisms. The first mechanism produces accurate object location priors based on estimated optical flow. The second presents a contrastive loss term on the object encodings of consecutive images. Importantly, due to the model-agnostic approach, MOC can incorporate any object discovery model.

In our experimental evaluations, we show the benefits of the novel MOC training scheme for object-centric learning for downstream reasoning tasks. For this, we integrate the models SPACE [39] and Slot Attention [41] into MOC and quantify the benefits of MOC over the base models through a variety of metrics that highlight important properties of the training scheme. Importantly, and in contrast to previous works, we show the improved quality of MOC trained object encodings for downstream reasoning task performances such as playing Atari games and few-shot object classification. In summary, we show that **inductive biases extracted from motion and object continuity are enough to boost object encodings of a predisposed object discovery model for downstream reasoning tasks.**

Overall, our contributions are the following: (i) We identify two error sources of object discovery models, hindering their current integration into modules for downstream reasoning tasks. (ii) Introduce motion *and* object continuity to

DL as a novel self-supervised training scheme. (iii) Create a novel open-source dataset, Atari-OCTA, to train and evaluate object detection models on Atari games. (iv) Empirically show on the SPACE and Slot Attention architectures that motion and object continuity greatly boosts downstream task performance for object-centric DL and allow for object-centric RL.

We proceed as follows. We first give a brief introduction to object discovery methods, then explain our MOC scheme, detailing both Motion and Object Continuity supervision. We experimentally evaluate improvements on object detection and representations. Before concluding, we touch upon related work.

## 2   Motion and Object Continuity

The Motion and Object Continuity (MOC) training scheme utilizes two object properties for improving object detection and representation, both of which are required for good object representation learning for reasoning tasks and both of which can be discovered in visual observations over time. The first property corresponds to the fact that objects tend to move in an environment. Via optical flow estimations [50,53] this can be translated to a motion detection mechanism that guides object localization and transforms unsupervised object detection into a "motion supervised" one. The second property describes the observation that objects exist at consecutive time points in proximity to their initial location and do not simply disappear. This can be integrated into an object continuity constraint, enforcing encoding alignment of objects over time.

Our approach allows integrating any out-of-the-box object discovery method. For this work we have focused on providing MOC supervision to slot-based models [41] and to models that separately encode the background and the foreground via separate variational autoencoders (VAE) (*e.g.* [20,39]), where we specifically focus on SPACE [39] due to its SOTA object discovery performance on images from Atari games. We provide an overview of these methods in Fig. 7 (*cf.* App. B) and introduce the mathematical modelling of SPACE in the App. B.1 and of Slot Attention in the App. B.2. In the following, we present a high-level description of MOC supervision, illustrated in Fig. 3, independent of the base models implementation. MOC implementation details for each model can be found in App. C.2 and C.3. Let us first provide some details on notations.

In the following we denote **enc** as the object encoding obtained from a base model, *e.g.* the slot encodings for Slot Attention [41], or the $z_{what}$ encodings for SPACE [39]. We further denote **loc** as the positional representation of an object. Specifically, SPACE divides an image into a grid, and explicitly models the presence of an object in each cell using a $z_{pres}$ variable, and its position using a $z_{where}$ variable. For each object, **loc** can thus be obtained using the $z_{where}$ variable of each cell in which an object is present (*e.g.* $z_{pres} > 0.5$). For Slot Attention based models, on the other hand, the position information is implicitly contained within **enc**. However, the corresponding attention masks $\alpha$ also correspond to valid representations of object locations. We therefore denote these masks as the **loc** variables of Slot Attention in the MOC framework.

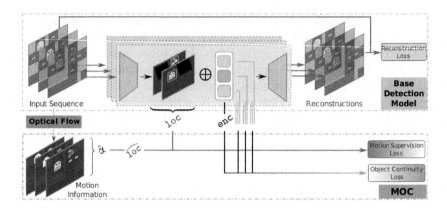

**Fig. 3.** An overview of the MOC training scheme applied to a base object detection model, which provides location and object representations. In our MOC training scheme, (i) motion information (dark blue), is extracted from each frame, allowing to detect objects and directly update the model's latent location variables (loc). (ii) Object continuity (black + cyan) aligns the encodings (enc) of spatially close objects of consecutive frames using a contrastive loss. (Color figure online)

Furthermore, we denote $\mathcal{L}^B$ to represent the original training loss function of the base model, *e.g.* reconstruction loss.

## 2.1   Motion Supervision

Let us now consider sequences of $T$ frames $\{\mathbf{x}_t\}_{t=1}^T$, whereby $\mathbf{x}_t$ corresponds to an RGB image ($\mathbf{x}_t \in \mathbb{R}^{3 \times h \times w}$), at time step $t$. Given such a sequence of images, MOC requires preprocessing via any suitable optical flow estimation method (*e.g.* [2,3,28,62]) which accurately detects the motion of objects for the given domain and provides us with sufficient binary masks $\hat{\alpha}$ of the moving objects from which location information, $\widehat{\text{loc}}$, can be obtained for each object.

MOC now integrates these masks to provide feedback on the locations of initial object representations. Specifically, for each frame $\mathbf{x}_t$ we compute:

$$\mathcal{L}^M(\mathbf{x}_t) := \sum_{i=1}^N \mathcal{L}^{M*}(\mathbf{x}_t, \hat{\alpha}_t), \qquad (1)$$

where $\mathcal{L}^{M*}$ refers to the exact implementation for the base model including a weighting hyperparameter (*cf.* App. C.2 and C.3 for SPACE and Slot Attention, respectively). In short, the masks obtained from optical flow ($\hat{\alpha}_t$) allow for direct supervision on the internal masks representation of Slot Attention based models, and allow us to construct $\widehat{\text{loc}}$ variables, to supervise $z_{pres}$ and $z_{where}$ in SPACE.

## 2.2   Object Continuity

Given that an object in consecutive image sequences tends to change its location only gradually and does not pop in and out of existence, we can integrate such bias by matching objects of similar position and latent encoding over consecutive frames. Particularly, we can make use of this information for explicitly improving the encoding space through a contrastive loss.

For detected entities in consecutive frames, we apply the object continuity loss, $\mathcal{L}^{OC}$, on the internal representations (*i.e.* enc) of the model. This loss makes the representations of the same object depicted over several frames similar, and of different objects heterogeneous. We estimate whether two objects in consecutive frames represent the same entity based on their loc and enc variables.

In detail, we denote $\Omega_t = \{o_t^j\}_{j=1}^{c_t}$ the set of object representations ($o_t^j = (\text{enc}_t^j, \text{loc}_t^j)$) that correspond to the $c_t$ detected objects in $\mathbf{x}_t$. Let $\text{enc}^*(o_t^j)$ denote a function providing the object in $\Omega_{t+1}$ with the most similar encoding to $o_t^j$ based on the cosine similarity ($S_C$). Correspondingly, $\text{loc}^*(o_t^j)$ is a function that provides the nearest object of $\Omega_{t+1}$ to $o_t^j$ based on the locations (*e.g.* via Euclidean distance). We thus introduce the contrastive object continuity loss as:

$$\mathcal{L}^{OC}(\mathbf{x}_t) = \sum_{o_t^i \in \Omega_t} \sum_{o_{t+1}^j \in \Omega_{t+1}} \lambda_{\text{differ}} \cdot S_C(o_t^i, o_{t+1}^j), \tag{2}$$

where $\lambda_{\text{differ}}$ is defined, using the hyperparameter $\beta \in \mathbb{R}^+$, as:

$$\lambda_{\text{differ}} = \begin{cases} -\beta & \text{if } o_{t+1}^j = \text{enc}^*(o_t^i) = \text{loc}^*(o_t^i) \\ 1 & \text{else} \end{cases} \tag{3}$$

This loss allows the models to have better internal representation of an object, for which the visual representation can vary across the frames.

## 2.3   General Training Scheme

The MOC scheme thus overall adds motion and object continuity supervision to a base object detection model, resulting in the final loss function:

$$\mathcal{L}^{MOC} := \mathcal{L}^B + (1 - \lambda_{align}) \cdot \mathcal{L}^M + \lambda_{align} \cdot \lambda_{OC} \cdot \mathcal{L}^{OC}. \tag{4}$$

$\mathcal{L}^M$ represents the batch-wise motion supervision loss and $\mathcal{L}^{OC}$ the batch-wise object continuity loss. We use $\lambda_{align} \in [0, 1]$, to balance the learning of object detection and object representation. We recommend using a scheduling approach for $\lambda_{align}$, described in the App. C.4. An additional $\lambda_{OC}$ hyperparameter can be used to balance image reconstruction capabilities and encoding improvements.

Concerning our previously suggested error types of object representation learning: the goal of $\mathcal{L}^{OC}$ is to improve on the Type II error. As previously identified, improvements on Type II also depend on improvements on the Type I error for which $\mathcal{L}^M$ was developed. The ultimate goal of MOC to improve deep object representation learning for downstream reasoning tasks is thus achieved by interdependently improving over both error types.

Lastly, MOC takes advantage of temporal information, while leaving the base architecture unchanged. In this way, it is possible to learn the concept of objects from image sequences, while still allowing for single image inference.

# 3   Experimental Evaluations

Let us now turn to the experimental evaluation of the MOC training scheme. With our experimental evaluations, we wish to investigate whether motion and object continuity biases can benefit object-centric DL for downstream reasoning tasks. Specifically, we investigate the effect of our MOC scheme on object discovery abilities and on object representation learning, such that these can be used for downstream tasks such as object-centric game playing and few-shot object classification. More precisely, we address the following research questions: (**Q1**) Does MOC benefit object discovery? (**Q2**) Does MOC improve latent object representations? (**Q3**) Does MOC improve representations for complex downstream reasoning tasks, such as game playing and few-shot object classification?

**Experimental Setup.** To this end, we consider the SPACE model [39] and a Slot Attention model [41] as base object discovery models, and compare performances of these trained with (+MOC) and without our MOC scheme (baseline, models only optimized for reconstruction). As we are ultimately interested in RL as downstream reasoning task, we train these models on images obtained from different reinforcement learning environments of the Atari 2600 domain [5]. As SPACE is the only object discovery model—to the best of our knowledge— trained on images obtained from different of the mostly used Atari environments, we focus the bulk of our evaluations on this, but provide results also on a Slot Attention model to show the generality and improvements across different base models. Both architectures are visualized in Fig. 7, with further details and training procedures (*cf.* App. B). We specifically focus on a subset of Atari games, namely AirRaid, Boxing, Carnival, MsPacman, Pong, Riverraid, SpaceInvaders and Tennis, many of which were investigated in the original work of SPACE. Note that this subset of Atari games contains a large variance in the complexity of objects, *i.e.* the number, shape, and size of objects, as well as games with both static and dynamic backgrounds, representing a valid test ground.

Overall, we evaluate 3 model settings: the original base models, SPACE and Slot Attention (SLAT), and both incorporated in our full MOC training scheme (SPACE+MOC and SLAT+MOC). We further provide specific ablation experiments in which the base model is only trained via $\mathcal{L}^B$ and $\mathcal{L}^M$, but without $\mathcal{L}^{OC}$. For each experiment, the results are averaged over converged (final) states of multiple seeded runs. We provide details on the hyperparameters in App. B for both models and on the evaluation metrics in each subsection, and further in App. E. Unless specified otherwise, the reported final evaluations are performed on a separated, unseen test set for each game.

As the aim of our work focuses on RL for Atari games, in our experimental evaluations we use a basic optical flow (OF) technique described in App. C.1 which provides us with sufficient masks $\hat{\alpha}$ of moving objects. As previously noted, the exact optical flow implementation, however, is not a core component of MOC and can be replaced with any other out-of-the-box OF approach such as [50,53]. All figures are best viewed in color.

**Atari-OCTA.** As the Atari dataset from [39] is not labelled and thus insufficient particularly for evaluating object encodings, we created a novel version of it.

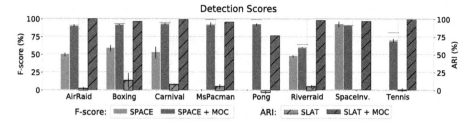

**Fig. 4.** MOC improves object detection. Final F-scores of SPACE models and Adjusted Random Index of Slot Attention (SLAT), both with and without MOC over frames of different Atari-OCTA games. Training via MOC leads to massive improvements over the set of investigated games. Optical flow F-scores are provided in red. They indicate the potential F-score upper-bound obtainable if using Motion supervision only. (Color figure online)

For this, we created one labelled dataset per game, where positions, sizes, and classes of all objects are provided. We used OC-Atari [10] to extract the objects properties. We separate classes of objects that are relevant for successful play from the objects of the HUD (*e.g.* scores, lives), and base our metrics on this first set, as we investigate MOC in the context of RL as reasoning task. Furthermore, we provide image sequences of $T = 4$ for the training data. For details on how Atari-OCTA (the resulting object-centric and time annotated version of Atari) was created, see App. A. Atari-OCTA and the generation code are provided along with this paper.[1] Our evaluations were performed on Atari-OCTA.

**MOC Benefits Object Discovery (Q1).** Let us now move to the actual research question evaluations. First, we evaluate the influence of our training scheme on a base model's performances in the originally intended task of object discovery, thus investigating the potential improvements over the Type I error alone. For this, we compute the foreground F-scores (further denoted as F-score) of SPACE as in the original work of [39] and compare to SPACE+MOC, *i.e.* SPACE incorporated in MOC. As Slot Attention is missing explicit variables for computing the F-scores, we revert to providing foreground Adjusted Rand Index (further denoted as ARI) scores for SLAT as well as SLAT+MOC, as also provided in the original work by Locatello et al. [41].

First, Fig. 4 presents the final foreground object detection scores (i.e. F-scores for versions of SPACE and ARI for versions of SLAT) of the different training setups for images from the eight Atari-OCTA games. Over the set of these, adding motion and object continuity supervision leads to great improvements in object discovery, with an average improvement from 38% to 85% and 4% to 95% over all games for SPACE+MOC and SLAT+MOC, respectively.

In particular, the base SPACE model on average performs quite unsatisfactorily. The base SLAT model performs even more poorly, importantly indicating SPACE's superiority over SLAT for Atari images, possibly due to the object size

---

[1] https://github.com/k4ntz/MOC.

**Table 1.** Faster convergence through MOC. The average number of steps needed to get an F-score > 0.5 (∞ if never reached) on the test set for SPACE, with and without MOC on Atari-OCTA. Lower values are better. For each model, we also provide the average. A complete evolution of the F-scores is given in App. D.

| Game | Airraid | Boxing | Canival | MsPac. | Pong | Riverraid | Sp.Inv. | Tennis | Avg |
|---|---|---|---|---|---|---|---|---|---|
| SPACE | 2600 | 2200 | 420 | ∞ | ∞ | 3400 | 430 | ∞ | 1800 |
| SP.+MOC | **300** | **240** | **350** | **350** | **270** | **270** | **290** | **260** | **280** |

prior of SPACE's and its grid-based approach. On games such as MsPacman and as arguably simple as Pong, SPACE and Slot Attention even appear to fail. Here, using our MOC scheme leads to more than 90% increase in object detection final performances. We also note the reduced performance variance of both +MOC models, suggesting more reliable training via MOC.

Furthermore, object biases via MOC not only improve final object detection performance, but also aid in obtaining such performances with fewer training iterations. Table 1 presents how many training steps are required for SPACE, on average, to obtain 50% of the validation F-scores of the different training schemes on the 8 Atari games. Over all games SPACE+MOC models approach convergence in much fewer number of steps. In fact, SPACE is able to reach an F-score above 50% on only 5 out of 8 games. For these games, it takes on average 1820 steps to reach this threshold, compared to 280 on average for SPACE+MOC on all games, hence leading to more than 7 times faster learning.

We provide detailed F-score progressions on all games, as well as final precision vs recall curves in App. (*cf.* Fig. 9 & 10). We also provide results with SPACE+MOC w/o OC indicating that updating object encodings via the OC loss in MOC on average shows equivalent object detection performances as without. This is an intuitive finding and shows that the motion loss, intentionally developed for tackling the Type I error, achieves its purpose. Our results in summary indicate a strong benefit of object location biases via MOC for object detection, thus affirming **Q1**.

**MOC Improves Latent Object Encodings (Q2).** In the previous section, we presented improvements of base object discovery models, SPACE and SLAT, via MOC, focusing on the task of object discovery for which these models were mainly developed for and evaluated on. However, our investigations in Fig. 2 exhibited that even when the object detection performance was promising (*e.g.* Space Invaders) the object representations themselves proved less useful for a downstream reasoning task as simple as object classification. Thus, apart from improvements in the detection itself, additional improvements need to be achieved in terms of optimal object representations for such models to actually be integrated into a more complex downstream setup. With **Q2**, we thus wish to investigate the effect of the MOC scheme on improving a base model's Type II errors, *i.e.* the usefulness of a model's latent object representations.

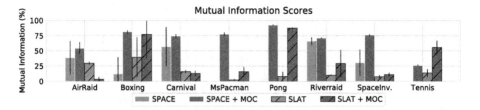

**Fig. 5.** MOC leads to more optimal object encodings as indicated via mutual information score. The adjusted mutual information of object encodings from SPACE and Slot Attention (SLAT), both with and without MOC, of Atari-OCTA are presented (mean ± std). Higher average values are better.

To answer **Q2**, we focus on the adjusted mutual information (AMI) of the encodings. Essentially, one computes a clustering on the latent object encodings and compares the clustering to a ground truth clustering (*cf.* App. F for details). Figure 5 presents the AMI for the two configurations: base model (i.e. SPACE and SLAT) and +MOC for training with MOC. One can observe immense improvements for MOC trained models in comparison to the base models. Averaged over all games we observe an increase in AMI from 26% to 69% and 16% to 37% for SPACE+MOC and SLAT+MOC, respectively.

In addition, one can observe the benefits of leveraging both $\mathcal{L}^{OC}$ *and* $\mathcal{L}^{M}$ in an ablation experiment for SPACE in which SPACE+MOC w/o OC is trained only via the motion supervision loss. Results can be found in App. D.5. As the object encodings in the original SPACE and in SPACE+MOC w/o OC are only optimized for reconstruction, there is little supervision to produce distinct object representations. Our results thus indicate that $\mathcal{L}^{OC}$ provides a strong supervisory signal on the latent encoding space. Lastly, as seen by the reduced cross validation variance, on average MOC produces less sensitive models (supporting the findings of Fig. 4). We provide detailed AMI scores in App. (*cf.* Fig. 13).

These results overall highlight the improvements of MOC, particularly the benefits of integrating both supervisory mechanisms into one training scheme, as well as $\mathcal{L}^{OC}$'s benefit for improving on Type II errors. Conclusively, we can affirm **Q2**: MOC does improve latent encodings.

**MOC Improves Object Encodings for Downstream Reasoning Tasks (Q3).** AMI is one way of measuring the quality of latent encodings. Ultimately, we are interested in integrating unsupervised object discovery models into more complex downstream tasks, *e.g.* integrating these into RL. In the following, we focus on evaluating object encodings for two specific downstream reasoning tasks, namely few-shot object classification and Atari game playing. The resulting performances in these downstream tasks thus act as important additional evaluations on the quality of learned object encodings and act as the main motivation behind our MOC scheme.

Let us begin with few-shot object classification. For each game, we optimize linear ridge regression models on 1, 4, 16 and 64 object encodings of each object

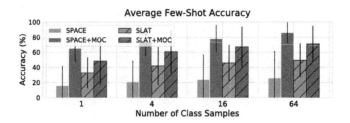

**Fig. 6.** MOC improves object representations for the few-shot classification task. Average few-shot accuracy performance (in %) based on latent object representations. We provide a ridge regression model with 1, 4, 16 and 64 encodings per class and test it on a held-out test set. The values are averaged over the 8 investigated Atari-OCTA games for SPACE and Slot Attention (SLAT), with and without MOC. Detailed, per game results are in App. G.2.

class and measure the classification accuracy on a separate held-out test set. We thus assume useful encodings to correspond to encodings that are similar for objects of the same class. As such, these representations should be easier to be differentiated by a simple (linear) classification method.

The results can be seen in Fig. 6. Specifically, we see a large boost in classification performance via the full MOC training scheme, visible both in SPACE+MOC and SLAT+MOC performances. Note the strong contrast, particularly for SPACE in test accuracy in the very small data regime, *e.g.* when the classifier has only seen 1 object encoding per class. Here, SPACE+MOC reaches 65% average accuracy, 3.5× higher than SPACE and 1.3× higher than SPACE+MOC w/o OC (*cf.* App. D.3). Detailed results on each game are provided in App. (*cf.* Fig. 12) and additional qualitative results can be found in App. D.6 and D.7.

We finally evaluate MOC in the context of RL for game playing as a representative complex downstream reasoning task and investigate in how far MOC can improve a base model's performance such that its learned representations can be used in playing Atari games, as done by [11] in logic oriented settings. We base our evaluations on concept-bottleneck [34] RL agents that are initially trained using perfect information (Info*) with the Dueling Q-learning algorithm [56] and focus here on playing a subset of the games from our previous evaluations (Boxing and Pong). These games are the only two from Atari-OCTA with a fixed number of objects, which allows for a very simple policy architecture, and for which perfect information obtained from the RAM using [1] is available. We note that although many RL agents might possibly provide higher overall game scores than the ones we focus on, the point to make here is that training object encodings via MOC can greatly improve *a* baseline (object-centric) RL agent.

For these experiments we focus only on SPACE as base model (rather than SLAT) due to its superior base performance on object detection in Atari images. We next replace the object extraction from RAM with object extraction performed by SPACE, and SPACE+MOC models but keep the initially learned

**Table 2.** MOC (via SPOC) allows object-centric playing via concept-bottleneck models. Average scores among all agents (avg) and of the best agent (best) of object-centric agents that detect objects based on SPACE and SPOC. Scores for each seed are in App. G.3. Additional base comparisons are agents with perfect information (Info*), random agents and human (from [55]).

|      | Method | SPACE | SP.+MOC | Info* | Random | Human |
|------|--------|-------|---------|-------|--------|-------|
| avg  | Boxing | $-3.5{\pm}4.3$ | $\mathbf{8.4}{\pm}9.9$ | $36{\pm}17$ | $-0.5{\pm}2.$ | 4.3 |
|      | Pong   | $-21{\pm}0.5$ | $\mathbf{-11}{\pm}12$ | $20{\pm}1.3$ | $-21{\pm}0.3$ | 9.3 |
| best | Boxing | $3.8{\pm}6.5$ | $\mathbf{22}{\pm}14$ | $52{\pm}3.5$ | $2.6{\pm}3.3$ | - |
|      | Pong   | $-20{\pm}0.8$ | $\mathbf{4.8}{\pm}11$ | $21{\pm}0.$ | $-20{\pm}0.7$ | - |

policies. For this, we transform the `loc` variables of these models into $(x, y)$ coordinates (ignore sizes). For object classes, we use the previously evaluated (same seeded) few-shot classification models on the object encodings (with 16 samples per class, *cf.* Fig. 12). The object coordinates are given to a 3 fully connected layers network, which predicts the Q-value for each action. We provide additional comparisons to human-level performance (H) and random agents (R).

As can be seen in Table 2, MOC greatly empowers the evaluated object-centric agents. On average, SPACE+MOC-based agents largely outperform SPACE-based agents, and even obtain higher average scores than humans on Boxing. For both games, the benefits of our approach is even more remarkable on mean scores obtained by best playing agents, due to the fact that a slightly more accurate object detector results in more reliable states, and thus better performing agent. Our experimental evaluations thus allow us to validate that MOC benefits object-centric reasoning tasks spanning from RL agents game playing capabilities to few-shot object classification (**Q3**).

# 4   Related Work

Our work touches upon several topics of ML research. In the following, we discuss related works from these areas.

**Unsupervised Object Detection.** Object-centric DL has recently brought forth several exciting avenues of unsupervised and self-supervised object discovery research by introducing inductive biases to neural networks to extract objects from visual scenes in an unsupervised manner [6,9,15,16,20,29,30,35, 39,41,47,49,60]. We refer to [21] for a detailed overview. However, until recently [45,46] these approaches have shown limited performances on more complex images. All of these mentioned works focus on object discovery from independent images. Importantly, although most of these approaches are motivated with the benefits of object representations for more complex downstream tasks, none of these apply additional constraints onto the latent object representations and only optimize object encodings for reconstruction. Lastly, among these works are more recent approaches that could provide improved baseline performances than SPACE and the vanilla Slot Attention model (*e.g.* [45,46]), however MOC can also be applied to these and these should be seen as orthogonal to our work.

**Unsupervised Object Detection from Videos.** Leveraging the supervisory signal within video data for object detection goes back several years *e.g.* to approaches based on conditional random fields [44]. More recently, DL approaches, *e.g.* [61] explicitly factorize images into background, foreground and segmentation masks. Also, [13] argue for the value of motion cues and showcasing this on physical reasoning tasks via a dynamics-based generative approach. [64] do multi-object segmentation via a carefully designed architecture of multiple submodules that handle certain aspects of the overall task. This idea is also taken up by [52] who introduce an approach for generative object-centric learning via the property of *common fate*. The recent works SAVi [33] and SAVI++ [14] improve the object discovery abilities of Slot Attention by using optical flow and depth signals, respectively, as a training target. Where many of these works present specifically designed architectures for video processing, MOC represents a model-agnostic scheme which, in principle, can incorporate any base object detection model and in this sense also be applicable to such tasks as semantic world modeling and object anchoring [43]. Additionally, although many mentioned works identify the importance and benefits of motion for object discovery, only [13] also focus on the advantages of learning good object representations for downstream tasks.

**Optical Flow.** Optical flow methods aim at finding translation vectors for each pixel in an input image to most accurately warp the current frame to the next frame. In other words, optical flow techniques try to find pixel groups with a common fate. Estimating optical flow is a fundamental problem of computer vision, starting with such approaches as the Gunnar-Farneback Algorithm [17] (for other traditional approaches, please refer to [18]). By now it is widely used in a variety of applications such as action recognition [7,37], object tracking [31,63], video segmentation [38,40]. Most recent works are based on DL approaches [12, 26–28,42,50,53]. Recently optical flow has also been applied to RL settings [19, 59] which hint the downstream RL agent at possibly important object locations, but do not perform object representation learning. As previously mentioned, optical flow is considered as a preprocessing step in MOC, thus any suitable OF method can in principle be used for a specific MOC implementation.

**Self-supervised Learning.** The idea of motion supervised learning is related to the large field of self-supervised learning. In fact the motion supervision aspect of MOC stands in line with other approaches [14,33,58] and notably [4] and confirms their findings on the general benefit of motion priors for object detection, however these works do not specifically improve or otherwise evaluate obtained object encodings for anything other than object detection. Aside from this, the $\mathcal{L}^{OC}$ loss of MOC can be considered as a form of contrastive loss, popularly used in self-supervised learning. Among other things, recent works apply patch-based contrasting [23], augmentations [8], cropping [22] or RL based contrasting

[36]. In comparison, MOC contrasts encodings between consecutive time steps. These approaches do not perform object representation learning, but rather try to improve the full encoding of an image.

## 5    Limitations and Future Work

As we focus evaluations on Atari environments for classification and game playing tasks, we make use of a very simple optical flow technique. A more advanced optical flow approach is necessary for more complex environments. The application of MOC to other types of object discovery models is a necessary next step in future work. Additionally, the $\mathcal{L}^{OC}$ of our SLAT+MOC implementation produces larger variances in AMI than that of SPACE+MOC (*cf.* Fig. 5). Future work should investigate ways of stabilizing this. MOC contains a bias towards moving objects, however it is desirable for a model to also detect stationary objects. Although the scheduling approach tackles this issue, additional investigations are necessary. The bottleneck-based [34] RL agents of **Q3** are somewhat limited, as additional techniques to increase detection robustness (*e.g.* Kalman filters) were not used. Certainly, more complicated models and RL algorithms would be worth investigating in future research. Lastly, certain environments also include static objects that are important to interact with, we would thus like to investigate object recognition based on agent-environment interactions. Following this idea, we think that performing representation learning based on the RL signal (*i.e.* cumulative reward) is another interesting line of research.

## 6    Conclusions

Already young children quickly develop a notion of object continuity: they know that objects do not pop in and out of existence. Here, we have demonstrated that deep networks also benefit from this knowledge. Specifically, we have shown that properties of objects that are observed from time can be leveraged to improve object representation learning for downstream tasks. This MOC training scheme, consisting of a motion supervision and object continuity contrastive loss, greatly improves a base model's object discovery and representation performances. In this way MOC collectively tackles two interdependent error sources of current object discovery models. Finally, along with this paper, we provide the novel dataset Atari-OCTA, an important step for evaluating object discovery in complex reasoning tasks such as game playing.

Apart from performance benefits that object-centric approaches can bring to deep learning, they particularly play an important role in human-centric AI, as such machines can perform inference and provide explanations on the same object-level as human-human communication [32]. Additional avenues for future work include investigating interactive object learning, such as agent-environment interactions, but also human-machine interactions for developing more reliable and trustworthy AI models.

**Acknowledgements.** The authors thank the anonymous reviewers for their valuable feedback. This research work has been funded by the German Federal Ministry of Education and Research and the Hessian Ministry of Higher Education, Research, Science and the Arts (HMWK) within their joint support of the National Research Center for Applied Cybersecurity ATHENE, via the "SenPai: XReLeaS" project. It also benefited from the HMWK cluster projects "The Third Wave of AI" and "The Adaptive Mind" as well as the Hessian research priority program LOEWE within the project "WhiteBox".

**Ethical Statement.** Our work aims to improve the object representations of object discovery models, specifically targeting the improvements of their use in additional modules in downstream reasoning tasks. With the improvements of our training scheme, it is feasible to integrate the findings of unsupervised object discovery methods into practical use-cases. A main motivation, as stated in our introduction, is that such an integration of high-quality object-centric representations is beneficial for more human-centric AI. Arguably, it seems beneficial for humans to perceive, communicate and explain the world on the level of objects. Integrating such level of abstraction and representation to AI agents is a necessary step for fruitful and reliable human-AI interactions.

Obviously, our work is not unaffected from the dual-use dilemma of foundational (AI) research. And a watchful eye should be kept, particularly on object detection research which can easily be misused, *e.g.* for involuntary human surveillance. However, our work or implications thereof do not, to the best of our knowledge, pose an obvious direct threat to any individuals or society in general.

# References

1. Anand, A., Racah, E., Ozair, S., Bengio, Y., Côté, M.-A., Hjelm, R.D.: Unsupervised state representation learning in atari. In: Wallach, H.M., Larochelle, H., Beygelzimer, A., d'Alché-Buc, F., Fox, E.B., Garnett, R. (eds.) Advances in Neural Information Processing Systems 32: Annual Conference on Neural Information Processing Systems 2019 (NeurIPS) (2019)
2. Anthwal, S., Ganotra, D.: An overview of optical flow-based approaches for motion segmentation. Imaging Sci. J. **67**(5), 284–294 (2019)
3. Bai, S., Geng, Z., Savani, Y., Kolter, J.Z.: Deep equilibrium optical flow estimation. In: 2022 IEEE/CVF Conference on Computer Vision and Pattern Recognition (CVPR) (2022)
4. Bao, Z., Tokmakov, P., Jabri, A., Wang, Y.-X., Gaidon, A., Hebert, M.: Discovering objects that can move. In: 2022 IEEE/CVF Conference on Computer Vision and Pattern Recognition (CVPR) (2022)
5. Brockman, G., et al.: OpenAI gym. CoRR (2016)
6. Burgess, C.P., et al.: MONet: unsupervised scene decomposition and representation. CoRR (2019)
7. Cai, Z., Neher, H., Vats, K., Clausi, D.A., Zelek, J.S.: Temporal hockey action recognition via pose and optical flows. In: 2019 IEEE/CVF Conference on Computer Vision and Pattern Recognition Workshops (CVPRW) (2019)

8. Chen, T., Kornblith, S., Norouzi, M., Hinton, G.E.: A simple framework for contrastive learning of visual representations. In: Proceedings of the 37th International Conference on Machine Learning (ICML) (2020)
9. Crawford, E., Pineau, J.: Exploiting spatial invariance for scalable unsupervised object tracking. In: The Thirty-Fourth AAAI Conference on Artificial Intelligence (AAAI) (2020)
10. Delfosse, Q., Blüml, J., Gregori, B., Sztwiertnia, S., Kersting, K.: OCAtari: object-centric atari 2600 reinforcement learning environments. CoRR (2021)
11. Delfosse, Q., Shindo, H., Dhami, D., Kersting, K.: Interpretable and explainable logical policies via neurally guided symbolic abstraction, CoRR (2023)
12. Dosovitskiy, A., et al.: Flownet: learning optical flow with convolutional networks. In: 2015 IEEE International Conference on Computer Vision (ICCV) (2015)
13. Du, Y., Smith, K., Ulman, T., Tenenbaum, J., Wu, J.: Unsupervised discovery of 3D physical objects from video. In: 9th International Conference on Learning Representations (ICLR) (2021)
14. Elsayed, G.F., Mahendran, A., van Steenkiste, S., Greff, K., Mozer, M.C., Kipf, T.: SAVi++: towards end-to-end object-centric learning from real-world videos. CoRR (2022)
15. Engelcke, M., Kosiorek, A.R., Jones, O.P., Posner, I.: GENESIS: generative scene inference and sampling with object-centric latent representations. In: 8th International Conference on Learning Representations (ICLR) (2020)
16. Eslami, S.M., Heess, N., Weber, T., Tassa, Y., Szepesvari, D., Hinton, G.E.: Attend, infer, repeat: fast scene understanding with generative models. In: Lee, D.D., Sugiyama, M., von Luxburg, U., Guyon, I., Garnett, R. (eds.) Advances in Neural Information Processing Systems 29: Annual Conference on Neural Information Processing Systems 2016 (NeurIPS) (2016)
17. Farnebäck, G.: Two-frame motion estimation based on polynomial expansion. In: Bigün, J., Gustavsson, T. (eds.) 13th Scandinavian Conference on Image Analysis 2003 (SCIA) (2003)
18. Fleet, D.J., Weiss, Y.: Optical flow estimation. In: Paragios, N., Chen, Y., Faugeras, O.D. (eds.) Handbook of Mathematical Models in Computer Vision (2006)
19. Goel, V., Weng, J., Poupart, P.: Unsupervised video object segmentation for deep reinforcement learning. In: Bengio, S., Wallach, H.M., Larochelle, H., Grauman, K., Cesa-Bianchi, N., Garnett, R. (eds.) Advances in Neural Information Processing Systems 31: Annual Conference on Neural Information Processing Systems 2018 (NeurIPS) (2018)
20. Greff, K., et al.: Multi-object representation learning with iterative variational inference. In: Chaudhuri, K., Salakhutdinov, R. (eds.) Proceedings of the 36th International Conference on Machine Learning (ICML) (2019)
21. Greff, K., van Steenkiste, S., Schmidhuber, J.: On the binding problem in artificial neural networks. CoRR (2020)
22. He, K., Fan, H., Wu, Y., Xie, S., Girshick, R.B.: Momentum contrast for unsupervised visual representation learning. In: 2020 IEEE/CVF Conference on Computer Vision and Pattern Recognition (CVPR) (2020)
23. Hénaff, O.J.: Data-efficient image recognition with contrastive predictive coding. In: Proceedings of the 37th International Conference on Machine Learning (ICML) (2020)
24. Hoerl, A.E., Kennard, R.W.: Ridge regression: applications to nonorthogonal problems. Technometrics $12(1)$, 69–82 (1970)
25. Hoerl, A.E., Kennard, R.W.: Ridge regression: biased estimation for nonorthogonal problems. Technometrics $12(1)$, 55–67 (2000)

26. Hur, J., Roth, S.: Optical flow estimation in the deep learning age. CoRR (2020)
27. Ilg, E., Mayer, N., Saikia, T., Keuper, M., Dosovitskiy, A., Brox, T.: Flownet 2.0: evolution of optical flow estimation with deep networks. In: 2017 IEEE Conference on Computer Vision and Pattern Recognition (CVPR) (2017)
28. Jeong, J., Lin, J.M., Porikli, F., Kwak, N.: Imposing consistency for optical flow estimation. In: 2022 IEEE/CVF Conference on Computer Vision and Pattern Recognition (CVPR) (2022)
29. Jiang, J., Ahn, S.: Generative neurosymbolic machines. In: Larochelle, H., Ranzato, M., Hadsell, R., Balcan, M.-F., Lin, H.-T. (eds.) Advances in Neural Information Processing Systems 33: Annual Conference on Neural Information Processing Systems 2020 (NeurIPS) (2020)
30. Jiang, J., Janghorbani, S., De Melo, G., Ahn, S.: SCALOR: generative world models with scalable object representations. In: 8th International Conference on Learning Representations (ICLR) (2020)
31. Kale, K., Pawar, S., Dhulekar, P.: Moving object tracking using optical flow and motion vector estimation. In: 4th International Conference on Reliability, Infocom Technologies and Optimization (ICRITO) (Trends and Future Directions) (2015)
32. Kambhampati, S., Sreedharan, S., Verma, M., Zha, Y., Guan, L.: Symbols as a lingua franca for bridging human-AI chasm for explainable and advisable AI systems. In: Thirty-Sixth AAAI Conference on Artificial Intelligence (AAAI) (2022)
33. Kipf, T., et al.: Conditional object-centric learning from video. In: The Tenth International Conference on Learning Representations (ICLR) (2022)
34. Koh, P.W., et al.: Concept bottleneck models. In: Proceedings of the 37th International Conference on Machine Learning (ICML) (2020)
35. Kosiorek, A., Kim, H., Teh, Y.W., Posner, I.: Sequential attend, infer, repeat: generative modelling of moving objects. In: Bengio, S., Wallach, H.M., Larochelle, H., Grauman, K., Cesa-Bianchi, N., Garnett, R. (eds.) Advances in Neural Information Processing Systems 31: Annual Conference on Neural Information Processing Systems 2018 (NeurIPS) (2018)
36. Laskin, M., Srinivas, A., Abbeel, P.: CURL: contrastive unsupervised representations for reinforcement learning. In: Proceedings of the 37th International Conference on Machine Learning (ICML) (2020)
37. Lee, M., Lee, S., Son, S., Park, G., Kwak, N.: Motion feature network: fixed motion filter for action recognition. In: Ferrari, V., Hebert, M., Sminchisescu, C., Weiss, Y. (eds.) 15th European Conference on Computer Vision 2018 (ECCV) (2018)
38. Li, J., Zhao, Y., He, X., Zhu, X., Liu, J.: Dynamic warping network for semantic video segmentation. Complexity (2021)
39. Lin, Z., et al.: SPACE: unsupervised object-oriented scene representation via spatial attention and decomposition. In: 8th International Conference on Learning Representations (ICLR) (2020)
40. Liu, Y., Shen, C., Yu, C., Wang, J.: Efficient semantic video segmentation with per-frame inference. In: Vedaldi, A., Bischof, H., Brox, T., Frahm, J.-M. (eds.) ECCV 2020. LNCS, vol. 12355, pp. 352–368. Springer, Cham (2020). https://doi.org/10.1007/978-3-030-58607-2_21
41. Locatello, F., et al.: Object-centric learning with slot attention. In: Larochelle, H., Ranzato, M., Hadsell, R., Balcan, M.-F., Lin, H.-T. (eds.) Advances in Neural Information Processing Systems 33: Annual Conference on Neural Information Processing Systems 2020, NeurIPS 2020, 6–12 December 2020, virtual (2020)
42. Luo, K., Wang, C., Liu, S., Fan, H., Wang, J., Sun, J.: Upflow: upsampling pyramid for unsupervised optical flow learning. In: 2021 IEEE/CVF Conference on Computer Vision and Pattern Recognition (CVPR) (2021)

43. Persson, A., Martires, P.Z.D., De Raedt, L., Loutfi, A.: Semantic relational object tracking. IEEE Trans. Cogn. Develop. Syst. **12**(1), 84–97 (2020)
44. Schulter, S., Leistner, C., Roth, P.M., Bischof, H.: Unsupervised object discovery and segmentation in videos. In: Burghardt, T., Damen, D., Mayol-Cuevas, W.W., Mirmehdi, M. (eds.) British Machine Vision Conference (BMVC) (2013)
45. Seitzer, M., et al.: Bridging the gap to real-world object-centric learning. CoRR (2022)
46. Singh, G., Deng, F., Ahn, S.: Illiterate DALL-E learns to compose. In: 10th International Conference on Learning Representations (ICLR) (2022)
47. Smirnov, D., Gharbi, M., Fisher, M., Guizilini, V., Efros, A., Solomon, J.M.: Marionette: self-supervised sprite learning. In: Ranzato, M., Beygelzimer, A., Dauphin, Y.N., Liang, P., Vaughan, J.W. (eds.) Advances in Neural Information Processing Systems 34: Annual Conference on Neural Information Processing Systems 2021 (NeurIPS) (2021)
48. Stammer, W., Schramowski, P., Kersting, K.: Right for the right concept: revising neuro-symbolic concepts by interacting with their explanations. In: 2021 IEEE/CVF Conference on Computer Vision and Pattern Recognition (CVPR) (2021)
49. Stelzner, K., Peharz, R., Kersting, K.: Faster attend-infer-repeat with tractable probabilistic models. In: Chaudhuri, K., Salakhutdinov, R. (eds.) Proceedings of the 36th International Conference on Machine Learning (ICML) (2019)
50. Stone, A., Maurer, D., Ayvaci, A., Angelova, A., Jonschkowski, R.: Smurf: self-teaching multi-frame unsupervised raft with full-image warping. In: 2021 IEEE/CVF Conference on Computer Vision and Pattern Recognition (CVPR) (2021)
51. Strickland, B., Wertz, A., Labouret, G., Keil, F., Izard, V.: The principles of object continuity and solidity in adult vision: some discrepancies in performance. J. Vis. **15**(12), 122 (2015)
52. Tangemann, M., et al.: Unsupervised object learning via common fate. CoRR (2021)
53. Teed, Z., Deng, J.: RAFT: recurrent all-pairs field transforms for optical flow. In: Vedaldi, A., Bischof, H., Brox, T., Frahm, J.-M. (eds.) ECCV 2020. LNCS, vol. 12347, pp. 402–419. Springer, Cham (2020). https://doi.org/10.1007/978-3-030-58536-5_24
54. Van der Maaten, L., Hinton, G.: Visualizing data using t-sne. J. Mach. Learn. Res. (2008)
55. Van Hasselt, H., Guez, A., Silver, D.: Deep reinforcement learning with double q-learning. In: Schuurmans, D., Wellman, M.P. (eds.) Proceedings of the Thirtieth AAAI Conference on Artificial Intelligence (2016)
56. Wang, Z., Schaul, T., Hessel, M., van Hasselt, H., Lanctot, M., de Freitas, N.: Dueling network architectures for deep reinforcement learning. In: Balcan, M.-F., Weinberger, K.Q. (eds.) Proceedings of the 33nd International Conference on Machine Learning (ICML) (2016)
57. Wertheimer, M.: Untersuchungen zur lehre von der gestalt. ii. Psychologische forschung (1923)
58. Yang, C., Lamdouar, H., Lu, E., Zisserman, A., Xie, W.: Self-supervised video object segmentation by motion grouping. In: 2021 IEEE/CVF International Conference on Computer Vision (ICCV) (2021)
59. Yuezhang, L., Zhang, R., Ballard, D.H.: An initial attempt of combining visual selective attention with deep reinforcement learning. CoRR (2018)

60. Zhang, Y., Hare, J., Prugel-Bennett, A.: Deep set prediction networks. In Wallach, H.M., Larochelle, H., Beygelzimer, A., d'Alché-Buc, F., Fox, E.B., Garnett, R. (eds.) Advances in Neural Information Processing Systems 32: Annual Conference on Neural Information Processing Systems 2019 (NeurIPS) (2019)
61. Zhao, D., Ding, B., Yulin, W., Chen, L., Zhou, H.: Unsupervised learning from videos for object discovery in single images. Symmetry **13**(1), 38 (2021)
62. Zheng, Z., et al.: DIP: deep inverse patchmatch for high-resolution optical flow. In: 2022 IEEE/CVF Conference on Computer Vision and Pattern Recognition (CVPR) (2022)
63. Zhou, H., Ummenhofer, B., Brox, T.: Deeptam: deep tracking and mapping. In: Ferrari, V., Hebert, M., Sminchisescu, C., Weiss, Y. (eds.) 15th European Conference on Computer Vision 2018 (ECCV) (2018)
64. Zhou, T., Li, J., Li, X., Shao, L.: Target-aware object discovery and association for unsupervised video multi-object segmentation. In: 2021 IEEE/CVF Conference on Computer Vision and Pattern Recognition (CVPR) (2021)

# Learning Geometric Representations of Objects via Interaction

Alfredo Reichlin[1]([✉]), Giovanni Luca Marchetti[1], Hang Yin[2],
Anastasiia Varava[1], and Danica Kragic[1]

[1] KTH Royal Institute of Technology, Stockholm, Sweden
{alfrei,glma}@kth.se
[2] University of Copenhagen, Copenhagen, Denmark

**Abstract.** We address the problem of learning representations from observations of a scene involving an agent and an external object the agent interacts with. To this end, we propose a representation learning framework extracting the location in physical space of both the agent and the object from unstructured observations of arbitrary nature. Our framework relies on the actions performed by the agent as the only source of supervision, while assuming that the object is displaced by the agent via unknown dynamics. We provide a theoretical foundation and formally prove that an ideal learner is guaranteed to infer an isometric representation, disentangling the agent from the object and correctly extracting their locations. We evaluate empirically our framework on a variety of scenarios, showing that it outperforms vision-based approaches such as a state-of-the-art keypoint extractor. We moreover demonstrate how the extracted representations enable the agent to solve downstream tasks via reinforcement learning in an efficient manner.

**Keywords:** Representation Learning · Equivariance · Interaction

## 1 Introduction

A fundamental aspect of intelligent behavior by part of an agent is building rich and structured *representations* of the surrounding world [10]. Through structure, in fact, a representation potentially leads to semantic understanding, efficient reasoning and generalization [17]. However, in a realistic scenario an agent perceives observations of the world that are high-dimensional and unstructured e.g., images. Therefore, the ultimate goal of inferring a representation consists of extracting structure from the observed data [3]. This is challenging and in some instances requires supervision or biases. For example, it is known that *disentangling* factors of variation in data is mathematically impossible in a completely unsupervised way [18]. In order to extract structure, it is therefore necessary to design methods and paradigms relying on additional information and specific assumptions.

A. Reichlin and G. L. Marchetti—Equal Contribution.

© The Author(s), under exclusive license to Springer Nature Switzerland AG 2023
D. Koutra et al. (Eds.): ECML PKDD 2023, LNAI 14172, pp. 629–644, 2023.
https://doi.org/10.1007/978-3-031-43421-1_37

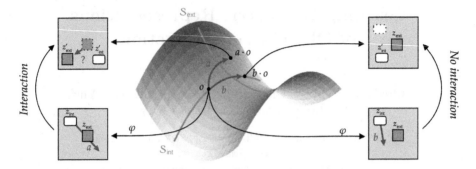

**Fig. 1.** Our framework enables to learn a representation $\varphi$ recovering the geometric and disentangled state of both an agent ($z_{\mathrm{int}}$, white) and an interactable object ($z_{\mathrm{ext}}$, brown) from unstructured observations $o$ (e.g., images). The only form of supervision comes from actions $a, b$ performed by the agent, while the transition of the object (question mark) in case of interaction is unknown. In case of no interaction, the object stays invariant.

In the context of an agent interacting with the world, a fruitful source of information is provided by the *actions* performed and collected together with the observations. Based on this, several recent works have explored the role of actions in representation learning and proposed methods to extract structure from interaction [15,22,25]. The common principle underlying this line of research is encouraging the representation to replicate the effect of actions in a structured space – a property referred to as *equivariance*[1]. In particular, it has been shown in [20] that equivariance enables to extract the location of the agent in physical space, resulting in a lossless and geometric representation. The question of how to represent features of the world which are extrinsic to the agent (e.g., objects) has been left open. Such features are dynamic since they change as a consequence of interaction. They are thus challenging to capture in the representation but are essential for understanding and reasoning by part of the agent.

In this work we consider the problem of learning representations of a scene involving an agent and an external rigid object the agent interacts with (see Fig. 1). We aim for a representation disentangling the agent from the object and extracting the locations of both of them in physical space. In order words, we aim for representations that are isometric w.r.t. to the geometry of the world. To this end, we focus on a scenario where the object displaces only when it comes in contact with the agent, which is realistic and practical. We make no additional assumption on the complexity of the interaction: the object is allowed to displace arbitrarily and its dynamics is unknown. Our assumption around the interaction enables to separate the problem of representing the agent – whose actions are known and available as a supervisory signal – from the problem of representing

---

[1] Alternative terminologies from the literature are *World Model* [15] and *Markov Decision Process Homomorphism* [26].

the object – whose displacement is unknown. Following this principle, we design an optimization objective relying on actions as the only form of supervision. This makes the framework general and in principle applicable to observations of arbitrary nature. We moreover provide a formalization of the problem and theoretical grounding for the method. Our core theoretical result guarantees that the representation inferred by an ideal learner recovers isometric representations as desired. We complement the theoretical analysis with an empirical investigation. Results show that our proposed representations outperform in quality of structure a state-of-the-art keypoint extractor and can be leveraged by the agent in order to solve control tasks efficiently by reinforcement learning. In summary, our contributions include:

- A representation learning framework extracting representations from observations of a scene involving an agent interacting with an object.
- A theoretical result guaranteeing that the above learning framework, when implemented by an ideal learner, infers an isometric representation for data of arbitrary nature.
- An empirical investigation of the framework on a variety of environments with comparisons to computer vision approaches (i.e., keypoint extraction) and applications to a control task.

We provide Python code implementing our framework together with all the experiments at the following public repository: https://github.com/reichlin/GeomRepObj. The repository additionally includes the Appendix of the present work.

## 2   Related Work

**Equivariant Representation Learning.** Several recent works have explored the idea of incorporating interactions into representation learning. The common principle is to infer a representation which is equivariant i.e., such that transitions in observations are replicated as transitions in the latent space. One option is to learn the latent transition end-to-end together with the representation [15,26,33]. This approach is however non-interpretable and the resulting representations are not guaranteed to extract any structure. Alternatively, the latent transition can be designed a priori. Linear and affine latent transitions have been considered in [9,22,25] while transitions defined by (the multiplication of) a Lie group have been discussed in [20,21]. As shown in [20], for static scenarios (i.e., with no interactive external objects) the resulting representations are structured and completely recover the geometry of the underlying state of the agent. Our framework adheres to this line of research by modelling the latent transitions via the additive Lie group $\mathbb{R}^n$. We however further extend the representation to include external objects. Our framework thus applies to more general scenarios and dynamics while still benefiting from the geometrical guarantees.

**Keypoint Extraction.** When observations are images, computer vision offers a spectrum of classical approaches to extract geometric structure. In particular, extracting keypoints enables to identify any object appearing in the observed images. Popular keypoint extractors include classical non-parametric methods [2,19] as well as modern self-supervised learning approaches [8,16]. However, keypoints from an image provide a representation based on the geometry of the field of view or, equivalently, of the pixel plane. This means that the intrinsic three-dimensional geometry of states of objects is not preserved since the representation differs from it by an unknown projective transformation. In specific situations such transformation can still be recovered by processing the extracted keypoints. This is the case when images are in first person view w.r.t. the observer: the keypoints can then be converted into three-dimensional landmarks via methods such as bundle adjustment [29,31]. Differently from computer vision approaches, our framework is data-agnostic and does not rely on specific priors tied to the nature of observations. It instead extracts representations based on the actions performed by the agent, which is possible due to the dynamical assumptions described in Sect. 3.

**Interactive Perception.** The role of interaction in perception has been extensively studied in cognitive sciences and neuroscience [7,12,23]. Inspired by those, the field of interactive perception from robotics aims to enhance the understanding of the world by part of an artificial system via interactions [5]. Applications include active control of cameras [1] and manipulators [32] in order to improve the perception of objects [4,13,28]. Our work fits into the program of interactive perception since we crucially rely on performed actions as a self-supervisory signal to learn the representation. We show that the location of objects can be extracted from actions alone, albeit in a particular dynamical setting. Without interaction, this would require strong assumptions and knowledge around the data and the environment as discussed in Sect. 2.

## 3    Formalism and Assumptions

In this section we introduce the relevant mathematical formalism together with the assumptions necessary for our framework. We consider the following scenario: an agent navigates in a Euclidean space and interacts in an unknown way with an external object. This means that the space of states $S$ is decomposed as

$$S = S_{\text{int}} \times S_{\text{ext}} \tag{1}$$

where $S_{\text{int}}$ is the space of states of the agent (*internal* states) and $S_{\text{ext}}$ is the space of states of the object (*external* states). We identify both the agent and the object with their location in the ambient space, meaning that $S_{\text{int}} \subseteq \mathbb{R}^n \supseteq S_{\text{ext}}$, where $n$ is the ambient dimension. The actions that the agent performs are displacements of its state i.e., the space of actions consists of translations $A = \mathbb{R}^n$. In our formalism we thus abstract objects as material points for simplicity of the theoretical analysis. The practical extension to volumetric objects together with their orientation is discussed in Sect. 4.3 while the extension of agent's actions to arbitrary Lie groups is briefly discussed in Sect. 6.

Our first assumption is that the agent can reach any position from any other via a sequence of actions. This translates in the following connectivity condition:

**Assumption 1** (Connectedness). *The space $\mathcal{S}_{\text{int}}$ is connected and open.*

When the agent performs an action $a \in \mathcal{A}$ the state $s = (s_{\text{int}}, s_{\text{ext}})$ transitions into a novel one denoted by $a \cdot s = (s'_{\text{int}}, s'_{\text{ext}})$. Since the actions displace the agent, the internal state gets translated as $s'_{\text{int}} = s_{\text{int}} + a$.[2] However, the law governing the transition of the object $s'_{\text{ext}} = T(s, a)$ is assumed to be unknown and can be arbitrarily complex and stochastic. We stick to deterministic transitions for simplicity of explanation. Crucially, the agent does not have access to the ground-truth state $s$. Instead it perceives unstructured and potentially high-dimensional observations $o \in \mathcal{O}$ (e.g., images) via an unknown emission map $\omega : \mathcal{S} \to \mathcal{O}$. We assume that $\omega$ is injective so that actions induce deterministic transitions of observations, which we denote as $o' = a \cdot o$. This assumption is equivalent to total observability of the scenario and again simplifies the forthcoming discussions by avoiding the need to model stochasticity in $\mathcal{O}$.

The fundamental assumption of this work is that the dynamics of the external object revolves around *contact* i.e., the object does not displace unless it is touched by the agent. This is natural and often satisfied in practice. In order to formalize it, note that when the agent in state $s_{\text{int}}$ performs an action $a \in \mathcal{A}$ we can imagine it moving along the open segment $\lfloor s_{\text{int}}, s_{\text{int}} + a \rfloor = \{s_{\text{int}} + ta\}_{0 < t < 1}$. Our assumption then translates into (see Fig. 1 for a graphical depiction):

**Assumption 2** (Interaction Occurs at Contact). *For all agent states $s_{\text{int}} \in S$ and actions $a \in \mathcal{A}$ it holds that $s'_{\text{ext}} = s_{\text{ext}}$ if and only if $s_{\text{ext}} \notin \lfloor s_{\text{int}}, s_{\text{int}} + a \rfloor$.*

As such, the dynamics of the external object can be summarized as follows:

$$s'_{\text{ext}} = \begin{cases} s_{\text{ext}} & \text{if } s_{\text{ext}} \notin \lfloor s_{\text{int}}, s_{\text{int}} + a \rfloor, \\ T(s, a) & \text{otherwise.} \end{cases} \tag{2}$$

Finally, we need to assume that interaction is possible for every state of the object i.e., the latter has to be always reachable by the agent. This is formalized via the following inclusion:

**Assumption 3** (Reachability). *It holds that $\mathcal{S}_{\text{ext}} \subseteq \mathcal{S}_{\text{int}}$.*

## 4   Method

### 4.1   Representations and Equivariance

We now outline the inference problem addressed in the present work. Given the setting introduced in Sect. 3, the overall goal is to infer a *representation* of observations $\varphi : \mathcal{O} \to \mathcal{Z} = \mathcal{Z}_{\text{int}} \times \mathcal{Z}_{\text{ext}}$, where $\mathcal{Z}_{\text{int}} = \mathcal{Z}_{\text{ext}} = \mathbb{R}^n$. Ideally $\varphi$ recovers the underlying inaccessible state in $\mathcal{S} \subseteq \mathcal{Z}$ and disentangles $\mathcal{S}_{\text{int}}$ from $\mathcal{S}_{\text{ext}}$. In order to achieve this, our central idea is to split the problem of representing

---

[2] Whenever we write $a \cdot s$ we implicitly assume that the action is valid i.e., that $s_{\text{int}} + a \in \mathcal{S}_{\text{int}}$.

the agent and the object. Since the actions of the agent are available, $z_{\text{int}} \in \mathcal{Z}_{\text{int}}$ can be inferred geometrically by existing representation learning methods. The representation of the object $z_{\text{ext}} \in \mathcal{Z}_{\text{ext}}$ can then be inferred based on the one of the agent by exploiting the relation between the dynamics of the two (Eq. 2). In order to represent the agent, we consider the fundamental concept of (translational) *equivariance*:

**Definition 1.** *The representation $\varphi$ is said to be* equivariant *(on internal states) if for all $a \in \mathcal{A}$ and $o \in \mathcal{O}$ it holds that $z'_{\text{int}} = z_{\text{int}} + a$ where $(z_{\text{int}}, z_{\text{ext}}) = \varphi(o)$ and $(z'_{\text{int}}, z'_{\text{ext}}) = \varphi(a \cdot o)$.*

We remark that Definition 1 refers to internal states only, making our terminology around equivariance unconventional. As observed in previous work [20], equivariance guarantees a faithful representation of internal states. Indeed if $\varphi$ is equivariant then $z_{\text{int}}$ differs from $s_{\text{int}}$ by a constant vector. This means that the representation of internal states is a translation of ground-truth ones and as such is lossless (i.e., bijective) and isometrically recovers the geometry of $\mathcal{S}_{\text{int}}$.

The above principle can be leveraged in order to learn a representation of external states with the same benefits as the representation of internal ones. Since the external object displaces only when it comes in contact with the agent (Assumption 2), the intuition is that $z_{\text{ext}}$ can be inferred by aligning it with $z_{\text{int}}$. The following theoretical result formalizes the possibility of learning such representations and traces the foundation of our learning framework.

**Theorem 4.** *Suppose that the representation $\varphi : \mathcal{O} \to \mathcal{Z}$ satisfies:*

1. *$\varphi$ is equivariant (Definition 1),*
2. *$\varphi$ is injective,*
3. *for all $o \in \mathcal{O}$ and $a \in \mathcal{A}$ it holds that either $z'_{\text{ext}} = z_{\text{ext}}$ or $z_{\text{ext}} \in \lfloor z_{\text{int}}, z_{\text{int}} + a \rfloor$ where $(z_{\text{int}}, z_{\text{ext}}) = \varphi(o)$ and $(z'_{\text{int}}, z'_{\text{ext}}) = \varphi(a \cdot o)$.*

*Then $\varphi \circ \omega$ is a translation i.e., there is a constant vector $h \in \mathbb{R}^n$ such that for all $s \in \mathcal{S}$ it holds that $\varphi(\omega(s)) = s + h$. In particular, $\varphi \circ \omega$ is an isometry w.r.t. the Euclidean metric on both $\mathcal{S}$ and $\mathcal{Z}$.*

We refer to the Appendix for a proof. Theorem 4 states that if the conditions 1. − 3. are satisfied (together with the assumptions stated in Sect. 3) then the representation recovers the inaccessible state up to a translation and thus isometrically preserves the geometry of the environment. All the conditions from Theorem 4 refer to properties of $\varphi$ depending on observations and the effect of actions on them, which are accessible in practice. The goal of the forthcoming section is to describe how these conditions can be enforced on $\varphi$ by optimizing a system of losses.

## 4.2   Learning the Representation

In this section we describe a viable implementation of a representation learning framework adhering to the conditions of Theorem 4. We model the representation learner $\varphi = (\varphi_{\text{int}}, \varphi_{\text{ext}})$ as two parameterized functions $\varphi_{\text{int}} : \mathcal{O} \to \mathcal{Z}_{\text{int}}$, $\varphi_{\text{ext}} :$ $\mathcal{O} \to \mathcal{Z}_{\text{ext}}$ e.g., two deep neural network models. In order to train the models, we assume that the dataset $\mathcal{D}$ consists of transitions observed by the agent in the form of $\mathcal{D} = \{(o, a, o' = a \cdot o)\} \subseteq \mathcal{O} \times \mathcal{A} \times \mathcal{O}$. Such data can be collected by the agent autonomously exploring its environment and randomly interacting with the external object. This implies that the only form of supervision required consists of the actions performed by the agent together with their effect on the observations.

First, we propose to enforce equivariance, condition 1 from Theorem 4, by minimizing the loss:

$$\mathcal{L}_{\text{int}}(o, a, o') = d(z'_{\text{int}}, z_{\text{int}} + a) \tag{3}$$

where $d$ is a measure of similarity on $\mathcal{Z}_{\text{int}} = \mathbb{R}^n$ and the notation is in accordance with Definition 1. Typically $d$ is chosen as the squared Euclidean distance as described in previous work [15,22].

Next, we focus on the representation of the external object. As stated before, the dataset consists of transitions either with or without interaction. When an interaction occurs, $z_{\text{ext}}$ should belong to the segment $\lfloor z_{\text{int}}, z_{\text{int}} + a \rfloor$. When it doesn't, the representation should be invariant i.e., $z_{\text{ext}} = z'_{\text{ext}}$. These two cases are outlined in condition 2 of Theorem 4 and can be enforced via the following losses:

$$\mathcal{L}_-(o, a, o') = d(z_{\text{ext}}, z'_{\text{ext}}) \qquad \mathcal{L}_+(o, a, o') = d(z_{\text{ext}}, \lfloor z_{\text{int}}, z_{\text{int}} + a \rfloor). \tag{4}$$

The distance involved in $\mathcal{L}_+$ represents a point-to-set metric and is typically set as $d(z, E) = \inf_{x \in E} d(z, x)$. The latter has a simple explicit expression in the case $E$ is a segment.

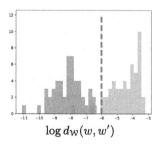

$$\log d_{\mathcal{W}}(w, w')$$

**Fig. 2.** Histograms of the log-distances in $\mathcal{W}$. Colors indicate whether interaction occurs (orange) or not (blue). The dotted line represents the threshold from Otsu's algorithm. (Color figure online)

However, the data contains no information on whether interaction occurs or not. It is, therefore, necessary to design a procedure determining when to optimize $\mathcal{L}_+$ and $\mathcal{L}_-$. To this end, we propose to train a parallel model $\varphi_{\text{cont}} :$ $\mathcal{O} \to \mathcal{W}$ with latent *contrastive representation* $\mathcal{W}$ (potentially different from $\mathcal{Z}$).

This is trained to attract $w = \varphi_{\text{cont}}(o)$ to $w' = \varphi_{\text{cont}}(o')$ while forcing injectivity of $\varphi$ (condition 2 from Theorem 4). To this end, we stick to the popular *InfoNCE* loss from contrastive learning literature [6]:

$$\mathcal{L}_{\text{cont}}(o, o') = d_{\mathcal{W}}(w, w') + \log \mathbb{E}_{o''} \left[ e^{-d_{\mathcal{W}}(w', w'') - d(z'_{\text{int}}, z''_{\text{int}})} \right] \tag{5}$$

where $o''$ is marginalized from $\mathcal{D}$. The second summand of Eq. 5 encourages the joint encodings $(z_{\text{int}}, w)$ to spread apart and thus encourages $\varphi$ to be injective. Since subsequent observations where interaction does not occur share the same external state, these will lie closer in $\mathcal{W}$ than the ones where interaction does not occur. This enables to exploit distances in $\mathcal{W}$ in order to choose whether to optimize $\mathcal{L}_-$ or $\mathcal{L}_+$. We propose to partition (the given batch of) the dataset in two disjoint classes $\mathcal{D} = C_- \sqcup C_+$ by applying a natural thresholding algorithm to the quantities $d_{\mathcal{W}}(w, w')$. This can be achieved via one-dimensional 2-means clustering, which is equivalent to Otsu's algorithm [24] (see Fig. 2 for an illustration). We then optimize:

$$\mathcal{L}_{\text{ext}}(o, a, o') = \begin{cases} \mathcal{L}_-(o, a, o') & \text{if } (o, a, o') \in C_-, \\ \mathcal{L}_+(o, a, o') & \text{if } (o, a, o') \in C_+. \end{cases} \tag{6}$$

In summary, the total loss minimized by the models $(\varphi_{\text{int}}, \varphi_{\text{ext}}, \varphi_{\text{cont}})$ w.r.t. the respective parameters is (see the pseudocode included in the Appendix):

$$\mathcal{L} = \mathbb{E}_{(o,a,o') \sim \mathcal{D}}[\mathcal{L}_{\text{int}}(o, a, o') + \mathcal{L}_{\text{ext}}(o, a, o') + \mathcal{L}_{\text{cont}}(o, o')]. \tag{7}$$

### 4.3   Incorporating Volumes of Objects

So far we have abstracted the external object as a point in Euclidean space. However, the object typically manifests with a body and thus occupies a volume. Interaction and consequent displacement (Assumption 3) occur when the agent comes in contact with the boundary of the object's body. The representation thus needs to take volumetric features into account in order to faithfully extract the geometry of states.

In order to incorporate volumetric objects into our framework we propose to rely on *stochastic* outputs i.e., to design $z_{\text{ext}}$ as a probability density over $\mathcal{Z}_{\text{ext}}$ representing (a fuzzy approximation of) the body of the object. More concretely, the output of $\varphi_{\text{ext}}$ consists of (parameters of) a Gaussian distribution whose covariance matrix represents the inertia ellipsoid of the object i.e., the ellipsoidal approximation of its shape. By diagonalizing the covariance matrix via an orthonormal frame, the orientation of the object can be extracted in the form of a rotation matrix in $SO(n)$. The losses of our model are naturally adapted to the stochastic setting as follows. The distance $d$ appearing in Eq. 4 is replaced with Kullback-Leibler divergence. The latter has an explicit simple expression for Gaussian densities which allows to compute $\mathcal{L}_-$ directly. In order to compute $\mathcal{L}_+$ we rely on a Monte Carlo approximation, meaning that we sample a point uniformly from the interval and set $\mathcal{L}^+$ as the negative log-likelihood of the point w.r.t. the density defining $z_{\text{ext}}$.

# 5    Experiments

We empirically investigate the performance of our framework in correctly identifying the position of an agent and of an interactive object. The overall goal of the experimental evaluation is to show that our representation is capable of extracting the geometry of states without relying on any prior knowledge of observations e.g., depth information. All the scenarios are normalized so that states lie in the unit cube. Observations are RGB images of resolution $100 \times 100$ in all the cases considered. We implement each of $\varphi_{\text{int}}$, $\varphi_{\text{ext}}$ and $\varphi_{\text{cont}}$ as a ResNet-18 [11] and train them for 100 epochs via the Adam optimizer with learning rate 0.001 and batch-size 128. We compare our framework with two baselines:

- *Transporter Network* [16]: a vision-based state-of-the-art unsupervised keypoint extractor. The approach heavily relies on image manipulation in order to infer regions of the pixel plane that are persistent between pairs of images. We train the model in order to extract two (normalized) keypoints representing $z_{\text{int}}$ and $z_{\text{ext}}$ respectively.
- *Variational AutoEncoder* (VAE) [14,27]: a popular representation learner with a standard Gaussian prior on its latent space. We impose the prior on $\mathcal{Z}_{\text{ext}}$ only, while $\varphi_{\text{int}}$ is still trained via the equivariance loss (Eq. 3). The decoder takes the joint latent space $\mathcal{Z}$ in input. We set $\dim(\mathcal{Z}_{\text{ext}}) = 32$. This makes the representations disentangled, so that $z_{\text{int}}$ and $z_{\text{ext}}$ are well-defined. The resulting representation of the object is generic and is not designed to extract any specific structure from observations.

In order to evaluate the preservation of geometry we rely on the following evaluation metric $\mathcal{L}_{\text{test}}$. Given a trained representation $\varphi : \mathcal{O} \to \mathcal{Z}$ and a test set $\mathcal{D}_{\text{test}}$ of observations with known ground-truth states, we define:

$$\mathcal{L}_{\text{test}} = \mathbb{E}_{o \sim \mathcal{D}_{\text{test}}} \left[ \, d(z_{\text{int}} - z_{\text{ext}}, s_{\text{int}} - s_{\text{ext}}) \, \right] \tag{8}$$

where $d$ is the squared Euclidean distance. Since both our framework and (the encoder of) VAE have stochastic outputs (see Sect. 4.3), we set $z_{\text{ext}}$ as the mean of the corresponding Gaussian distribution. Equation 8 measures the quality of preservation of the relative position between the agent and the object by part of the representation. When $\mathcal{L}_{\text{test}} = 0$, $\varphi$ is an isometry (w.r.t. the Euclidean metric) and thus recovers the geometry of states. The translational invariance of $\mathcal{L}_{\text{test}}$ makes the comparison agnostic to any reference frame eventually inferred by the given learner.

## 5.1    Sprites

For the first experiment we procedurally generate images of two sprites (the agent and the object) moving on a black background (see Fig. 3, top-left). Between images, the agent (red figure) moves according to a known action. If the agent comes in contact with the object (green diamond) during the execution of the action (see Assumption 2) the object is randomly displaced on the next image. In

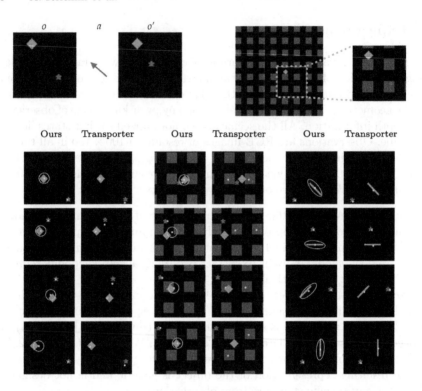

**Fig. 3. Top:** Visualization of the dataset from the Sprites experiment. On the left, an example of a datapoint $(o, a, o') \in \mathcal{D}$. On the right, an example of an observation from the second version of the dataset where a dynamic background is added as a visual distractor. **Bottom:** Comparison of $z_{\text{int}}$, $z_{\text{ext}}$ (gray dots, with the ellipse representing the learned std) extracted via our model and the Transporter network on the three versions of the Sprites dataset: vanilla version (left), with dynamic background (middle) and with anisotropic object (right).

other words, the object's transition function $T(s, a)$ is stochastic with a uniform distribution. Such a completely stochastic dynamics highlights the independence of the displacement of the agent w.r.t. the one of the object. We generate the following two additional versions of the dataset:

- A version with *dynamic background*. Images are now overlaid on top of a nine-times larger second image (blue squares in Fig. 3, top-right). The field of view and thus the background moves together with the agent. The background behaves as a visual distractor and makes it challenging to extract structure (e.g., keypoints) via computer vision.
- A version with *anisotropic object*. The latter is now a rectangle with one significantly longer side. Besides translating, the object rotates as well when interaction occurs. The goal here is showcasing the ability of our model in inferring the orientation of the object as described in Sect. 4.3.

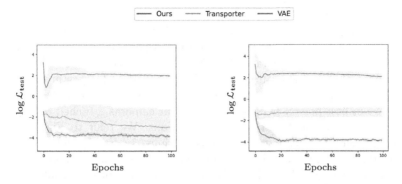

**Fig. 4.** Log-scale plots of the evaluation metric (Eq. 8) as the training progresses for the Sprite experiment. The curves display mean and std (for 10 experimental runs). **Left**: vanilla version of the dataset. **Right:** version with a dynamic background.

Figure 4 displays the analytic comparison of the performances between our model and the baselines in terms of the evaluation metric (Eq. 8). The plot is in log-scale for visualization purposes. Moreover, Fig. 3 (bottom) reports a qualitative comparison between our model and the Transporter network. As can be seen, for the simpler version of the experiment (plot on the left) both our model and the Transporter network successfully achieve low error and recover the geometry of both the agent and the object. Note that the Transporter network converges slowly and with high variance (Fig. 4, left). This is probably due to the presence of a decoder in its architecture. Our framework instead involves losses designed directly in the latent space, avoiding an additional model to decode observations. As expected, VAE achieves significantly worse performances because of the lack of structure in its representation. As can be seen from Fig. 3 (bottom-right), when the object is anisotropic our model correctly infers its orientation by encoding it into the covariance of the learned Gaussian distribution. The Transporter network instead places a keypoint on the barycenter of the object and is therefore unable to recover the orientation.

For the more challenging version of the experiment with dynamic background, the transporter is not able to extract the expected keypoints. As can be seen from Fig. 3 (bottom-middle), the distracting background causes the model to focus on regions of the image not corresponding to the agent and the object. This is reflected by a significantly higher error (and variance) w.r.t. our framework (Fig. 4, right). The latter still infers the correct representation and preserves geometry. This empirically confirms that our model is robust to visual distractors since it does not rely on any data-specific feature or structure.

## 5.2 Soccer

For the second experiment we test our framework on an environment consisting of an agent on a soccer field colliding with a ball (see Fig. 5, left). The scene is generated and rendered via the Unity engine. The physics of the ball is simulated realistically: in case of contact, rolling takes gravity and friction into account. Note that even though the scene is generated via three-dimensional rendering, the (inaccessible) state space is still two-dimensional since the agent navigates on the field. We generate two datasets of 10000 triples $(o, a, o' = a \cdot o)$ with observations of different nature. The first one consists of views in third-person perspective from a fixed external camera. In the second one, observations are four views in first-person perspective from four cameras attached on top of the agent and pointing in the 4 cardinal directions. We refer to Fig. 5 (left) for a visualization of the two types of observations. In Fig. 5 (right), we report visualizations of the learned representations. The extracted representation of our proposed method depends solely on the geometry of the problem at hand rather than the nature of the observation. The learned representation is thus identical when learned from the third-person dataset or the first-person one, as shown in 5 (right).

Figure 6 (left) displays the comparison of the performances between our model and the baselines in terms of the evaluation metric (Eq. 8). The Transporter network is trained on observations in third person and as can be seen, correctly extracts the keypoints on the *pixel plane*. As discussed in Sect. 2, such a plane differs from $S_{int}$ by an unknown projective (and thus non-isometric) transformation. This means that despite the successful keypoint extraction, the geometry of the state space is not preserved, which is reflected by the high error on the plot. This is a general limitation of vision-based approaches: they are unable to recover the intrinsic geometry due to perspective in the case of a three-dimensional scene. Differently from that, our framework extracts an isometric representation and achieves low error independently from the type of observations.

## 5.3   Control Task

In our last experiment we showcase the benefits of our representations in solving downstream control tasks. The motivation is that a geometric and low-dimensional representation improves efficiency and generalization compared to solving the task directly from observations. To this end we design a control task for the Soccer environment consisting in kicking the ball *into the goal*. The reward is given by the negative distance between the (barycenter of the) ball and the (barycenter of the) goal. Observations are views in third person perspective. In each episode the agent and the ball are initially placed in a random location while the ball is placed in the center. The maximum episode length is 20 steps.

We train a number of models via the popular reinforcement learning method *Proximal Policy Optimization* (PPO; [30]). One model (*End-to-End*) receives raw observations as inputs. The others operate on pre-trained representations $Z$ given by the Transporter network, the VAE and our method respectively. All the models implement a comparable architecture for a fair comparison.

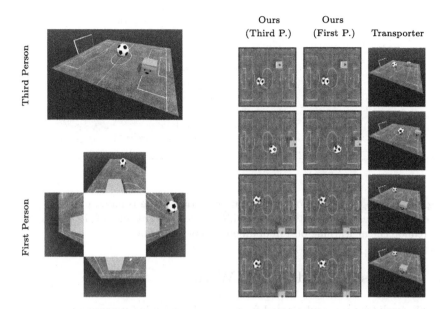

**Fig. 5. Left**: an example of the two types of observations (third and first person respectively) from the Soccer experiment. **Right**: visual comparison of $z_{\text{int}}$, $z_{\text{ext}}$ (red dots) extracted via our model (from third-person view and first-person view) and the Transporter network. For our model, we overlap the representation to a view of the scene from the top instead of the original observation.

Figure 6 (right) displays the reward gained on test episodic runs as the training by reinforcement learning progresses. As can be seen, our geometric representation enables to solve the task more efficiently than both the competing representations (Transporter and VAE) and the end-to-end model. Note that the Transporter not only does not preserve the geometry of the state space, but has the additional disadvantage that the keypoint corresponding to the agent and the object can get swapped in the output of $\varphi$. This causes indeterminacy in the representation and has a negative impact on solving the task. Due to this, the Transporter performs similarly to the end-to-end model and is outperformed by the generic and non-geometric representation given by the VAE. In conclusion, the results show that a downstream learner can significantly benefit from geometric representations of observations in order to solve downstream control tasks.

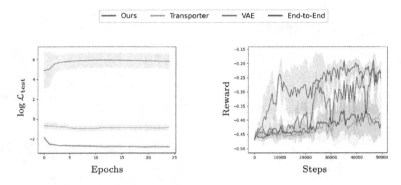

**Fig. 6. Left**: log-scale plot of the evaluation metric as the training progresses for the Soccer experiment. Observations are in third person. **Right**: plot of the reward gained via reinforcement learning on top of different representations.

# 6    Conclusions and Future Work

In this work we proposed a novel framework for learning representations of both an agent and an object the agent interacts with. We designed a system of losses based on a theoretical principle that guarantees isometric representations independently from the nature of observations and relying on supervision from performed actions alone. We empirically investigated our framework on multiple scenarios showcasing advantages over computer vision approaches.

Throughout the work we assumed that the agent interacts with a single object. An interesting line of future investigation is extending the framework to take multiple objects into account. In the stochastic context (see Sect. 4.3) an option is to model $z_{\text{ext}}$ via multi-modal densities, with each mode corresponding to an object. As an additional line for future investigation, our framework can be extended to actions beyond translations in Euclidean space. Lie groups other than $\mathbb{R}^n$ often arise in practice. For example, if the agent is able to rotate its body then (a factor of) the space of actions has to contain the group of rotations $SO(n)$, $n = 2, 3$. Thus, a framework where actions (and consequently states) are represented in general Lie groups defines a useful and interesting extension.

**Acknowledgements.** This work was supported by the Swedish Research Council, the Knut and Alice Wallenberg Foundation, the European Research Council (ERC-BIRD-884807) and the European Horizon 2020 CANOPIES project. Hang Yin would like to acknolwedge the support by the Pioneer Centre for AI, DNRF grant number P1.

**Ethical Statement.** We believe that the present work does not raise specific ethical concerns. Generally speaking, however, any system endowing artificial agents with intelligent behavior may be misused e.g., for military applications. Since we propose a representation learning method enabling an agent to locate objects in an environment, this can be potentially embedded into intelligent harmful systems and deployed for unethical applications.

# References

1. Bajcsy, R.: Active perception. Proc. IEEE **76**(8), 966–1005 (1988)
2. Bay, H., Tuytelaars, T., Van Gool, L.: SURF: speeded up robust features. In: Leonardis, A., Bischof, H., Pinz, A. (eds.) ECCV 2006. LNCS, vol. 3951, pp. 404–417. Springer, Heidelberg (2006). https://doi.org/10.1007/11744023_32
3. Bengio, Y., Courville, A., Vincent, P.: Representation learning: a review and new perspectives. IEEE Trans. Pattern Anal. Mach. Intell. **35**(8), 1798–1828 (2013)
4. Björkman, M., Bekiroglu, Y., Högman, V., Kragic, D.: Enhancing visual perception of shape through tactile glances. In: 2013 IEEE/RSJ International Conference on Intelligent Robots and Systems, pp. 3180–3186 (2013)
5. Bohg, J., et al.: Interactive perception: leveraging action in perception and perception in action. IEEE Trans. Rob. **33**(6), 1273–1291 (2017)
6. Chen, T., Kornblith, S., Norouzi, M., Hinton, G.: A simple framework for contrastive learning of visual representations. In: International Conference on Machine Learning, pp. 1597–1607. PMLR (2020)
7. Gibson, J.J., Carmichael, L.: The Senses Considered as Perceptual Systems, vol. 2. Houghton Mifflin, Boston (1966)
8. Gopalakrishnan, A., van Steenkiste, S., Schmidhuber, J.: Unsupervised object keypoint learning using local spatial predictability. In: ICLR 2021 (2020)
9. Guo, X., Zhu, E., Liu, X., Yin, J.: Affine equivariant autoencoder. In: IJCAI, pp. 2413–2419 (2019)
10. Ha, D., Schmidhuber, J.: World models. arXiv preprint arXiv:1803.10122 (2018)
11. He, K., Zhang, X., Ren, S., Sun, J.: Deep residual learning for image recognition. In: Proceedings of the IEEE Conference on Computer Vision and Pattern Recognition, pp. 770–778 (2016)
12. Held, R., Hein, A.: Movement-produced stimulation in the development of visually guided behavior. J. Comparat. Physiol. Psychol. **56**(5), 872 (1963)
13. Ilonen, J., Bohg, J., Kyrki, V.: Three-dimensional object reconstruction of symmetric objects by fusing visual and tactile sensing. Int. J. Rob. Res. **33**(2), 321–341 (2014)
14. Kingma, D.P., Welling, M.: Auto-encoding variational bayes. arXiv preprint arXiv:1312.6114 (2013)
15. Kipf, T., van der Pol, E., Welling, M.: Contrastive learning of structured world models. arXiv preprint arXiv:1911.12247 (2019)
16. Kulkarni, T.D., et al.: Unsupervised learning of object keypoints for perception and control. Adv. Neural Inf. Process. Syst. **32**, 1–11 (2019)
17. Lake, B.M., Ullman, T.D., Tenenbaum, J.B., Gershman, S.J.: Building machines that learn and think like people. Behav. Brain Sci. **40**, e253 (2017)
18. Locatello, F., et al.: Challenging common assumptions in the unsupervised learning of disentangled representations. In: International Conference on Machine Learning, pp. 4114–4124. PMLR (2019)
19. Lowe, D.G.: Object recognition from local scale-invariant features. In: Proceedings of the Seventh IEEE International Conference on Computer Vision, vol. 2, pp. 1150–1157. IEEE (1999)
20. Marchetti, G.L., Tegnér, G., Varava, A., Kragic, D.: Equivariant representation learning via class-pose decomposition. arXiv preprint arXiv:2207.03116 (2022)
21. Mondal, A.K., Jain, V., Siddiqi, K., Ravanbakhsh, S.: Eqr: equivariant representations for data-efficient reinforcement learning. In: International Conference on Machine Learning, pp. 15908–15926. PMLR (2022)

22. Mondal, A.K., Nair, P., Siddiqi, K.: Group equivariant deep reinforcement learning. arXiv preprint arXiv:2007.03437 (2020)
23. Noë, A., Noë, A., et al.: Action in Perception. MIT press, Cambridge (2004)
24. Otsu, N.: A threshold selection method from gray-level histograms. IEEE Trans. Syst. Man Cybern. **9**(1), 62–66 (1979)
25. Park, J.Y., Biza, O., Zhao, L., van de Meent, J.W., Walters, R.: Learning symmetric embeddings for equivariant world models. arXiv preprint arXiv:2204.11371 (2022)
26. van der Pol, E., Kipf, T., Oliehoek, F.A., Welling, M.: Plannable approximations to mdp homomorphisms: Equivariance under actions. arXiv preprint arXiv:2002.11963 (2020)
27. Rezende, D.J., Mohamed, S., Wierstra, D.: Stochastic backpropagation and approximate inference in deep generative models. In: International Conference on Machine Learning, pp. 1278–1286. PMLR (2014)
28. Schiebener, D., Morimoto, J., Asfour, T., Ude, A.: Integrating visual perception and manipulation for autonomous learning of object representations. Adapt. Behav. **21**(5), 328–345 (2013)
29. Schonberger, J.L., Frahm, J.M.: Structure-from-motion revisited. In: Proceedings of the IEEE Conference on Computer Vision and Pattern Recognition, pp. 4104–4113 (2016)
30. Schulman, J., Wolski, F., Dhariwal, P., Radford, A., Klimov, O.: Proximal policy optimization algorithms. arXiv preprint arXiv:1707.06347 (2017)
31. Triggs, B., McLauchlan, P.F., Hartley, R.I., Fitzgibbon, A.W.: Bundle adjustment—a modern synthesis. In: Triggs, B., Zisserman, A., Szeliski, R. (eds.) IWVA 1999. LNCS, vol. 1883, pp. 298–372. Springer, Heidelberg (2000). https://doi.org/10.1007/3-540-44480-7_21
32. Tsikos, C., Bajcsy, R.: Segmentation via manipulation. IEEE Trans. Rob. Autom. **7**(3), 306–319 (1991)
33. Watter, M., Springenberg, J., Boedecker, J., Riedmiller, M.: Embed to control: a locally linear latent dynamics model for control from raw images. Adv. Neural Inf. Process. Syst. **28**, 1–9 (2015)

# On the Good Behaviour of Extremely Randomized Trees in Random Forest-Distance Computation

Manuele Bicego[(⊠)] and Ferdinando Cicalese

Computer Science Department, University of Verona, Verona 37134, Italy
{manuele.bicego,ferdinando.cicalese}@univr.it

**Abstract.** Originally introduced in the context of supervised classification, ensembles of *Extremely Randomized Trees* (ERT) have shown to provide surprisingly effective models also in unsupervised settings, e.g., for anomaly detection (via Isolation Forests) and for distance computation. In this paper, we focus on this latter application of ERT, namely in the context of Random Forest (RF) distance computation. We aim at narrowing the gap between the established empirical evidence of the good behaviour of ERT and the still limited theoretical understanding of their (somehow) surprisingly good performance when compared to more involved methodologies. Our main contribution is the following: we assume the existence of a proper representation on a given domain, i.e., a vectorial representation of the objects which satisfies the *Compactness Hypothesis* formulated by Arkadev and Braverman in 1967. Under such a hypothesis, given the "true" distance between two objects, we show how to derive a bound on the approximation guaranteed by two main RF-distances obtained by employing ensembles of ERTs, with respect to such "true" distance. In other words, we show that there exists a constant $c$ such that if two objects are $\epsilon$-close in the true distance, then with high probability they are $(c \cdot \epsilon)$-close in the RF-distances computed with ERT forests.

**Keywords:** Random Forest-distances · Extremely Randomized Trees · Compactness hyphotesis

## 1 Introduction

Random Forests (RF) [7,10] are ensembles of decision trees [21], successfully applied in Pattern Recognition and Machine Learning as models for regression and classification, and more recently, for other tasks such as clustering or outlier detection [17,18,23]. Another exploitation of Random Forest, less investigated than previous ones, is for distance computation: starting from the seminal work of Breiman [7], it has been shown that powerful data-dependent distances can be extracted from RFs: the main idea is that it is possible to assess the similarity between two objects by looking at the way they answer to the tests of the different trees. In the basic version of [7,23], the similarity is proportional to the number

D. Koutra et al. (Eds.): ECML PKDD 2023, LNAI 14172, pp. 645–660, 2023.
https://doi.org/10.1007/978-3-031-43421-1_38

of times, over the total number of trees of the forest, the two objects reach the same leaf – thus answering in the same way to all questions in the path. Many different extensions have been proposed, exploiting different aspects like tests in the paths [32], probability masses [2, 29] or other concepts [6].

Typically, the RF-distance is extracted in two steps: i) a forest is learned from the available data and ii) the distance is defined given the trained forest. The solution of the first step typically depends on the task: the forest can be derived in a supervised way (i.e. using the labels, as in supervised RF-distances of [7, 23]), or in an unsupervised way. In this last case, different context specific solutions can be adopted (e.g. [23] or [5] for clustering), but a widely applied option is to use *Extremely Randomized Trees* (ERT) [16]. An ERT is a classic decision tree as CART [8], i.e. a binary tree in which questions in each node are defined with thresholds on a single feature. The difference with respect to CART is the way in which the tree is trained: instead of looking for "optimized" questions, the ERT is built in a completely random way: at each node, the question is defined by choosing a random feature and a random threshold inside the domain of that feature. These trees have shown to be surprisingly good for classification [16], but also for unsupervised domains, like anomaly detection [17, 18] or clustering [5, 20, 24].

In the context of RF-distance computation, ERT have been largely and successfully employed, for example in [2–5, 27, 29]. Training forests for RF-distance computation with ERT is attractive for many different reasons: i) it is an unsupervised, simple and efficient way to derive a forest: distances based on these forests have shown to outperform many other distances, also in semi-supervised settings [31]; ii) in the clustering case, authors of [5] have shown that this option is competitive with alternative more sophisticated strategies on datasets of moderate size, and better than all alternatives on datasets of larger size; iii) in the classification case, it has been shown in [28] that, when used with Support Vector Machines, distances computed from ERT are significantly better than RF-distances computed from supervisedly trained RF [9, 11], probably because of a reduced risk of overtraining.

From a theoretical point of view, only few studies characterize the good performances of RF-distances. For example, [9] shows how to derive a properly defined kernel from the RF-distance: such starting work has been further extended and integrated in [11, 22]. In these studies, the RF-distances were all based on supervisedly trained Random Forests. More in relation to ERT-based RF-distances, Ting and colleagues showed in recent papers such as [25, 26, 28] some theoretical properties of Isolation Kernels (kernels extracted from Isolation Forests, i.e. ERT-ensembles): for example it has been theoretically shown that the Isolation Kernel assigns a higher similarity to two points being in a sparse region than to two points of the same inter-point distance in a dense region, which is the main motivation behind the derivation of these data-dependent measures.

In this paper we make one step forward along this direction, proposing a novel theoretical characterization of RF-distances built from forests of ERT, aimed at providing evidences of the motivation behind the success of such RF distances in characterizing the distance between objects. In particular, in the paper we theoretically show that under some assumptions, if two objects $x$ and $y$ have a small "true distance", then also their RF-distance, built starting from a RF defined with ERT, is small. We provide such theoretical characterization for the original RF-distance introduced by Breiman [7,23] and for the recent RatioRF distance [6]. To show that, we assume that there is a representation which satisfies the "Compactness Hypothesis" of Arkadev and colleagues [1]; then, we derive a bound on the RF-distance, computed with ERT-forests based on such representation, with respect to the true distance. We also provide some simulations to understand the different aspects of the bounds, also suggesting a procedure to derive the minimum number of trees of the forest needed to get a given probabilistic guarantee.

The remainder of the paper is organized as follows: in Sect. 2 we provide the basic notation, whereas we present our main results in Sect. 3. We show some numerical simulations in Sect. 4, and we discuss our findings and conclude the paper in Sect. 5.

## 2    Background

In this section, we introduce the basic concepts needed to understand our main results. In the more general formulation [8], given a vectorial representation of $d$ features, a decision tree $t$ is a *complete* binary tree in which each internal node $j$ is associated to a test $\theta_j = (\nu_j, f_j)$, where $\nu_j$ is a threshold on a feature $f_j$; the two edges which link the node to the children represent the two possible results of the binary test $\theta_j = (\nu_j, f_j)$: an object $\mathbf{x} = [x_1, .., x_d]$ takes the left branch if $x_{f_j} < \nu_j$, the right one otherwise. Typically, decision trees are learned starting from a training set $X$, used to determine, at each node $j$, the optimal test $\theta_j = (\nu_j, f_j)$. Extremely Randomized Trees [16] are decision trees characterized by a high degree of randomness: in their extreme version, there is no optimization, and the tests $\theta_j = (\nu_j, f_j)$ are defined completely at random. More in detail, given a training set $X$, the training follows a recursive procedure: in a given node, i) a feature $f_j$ is randomly chosen among the $d$ features, ii) the threshold $\nu_j$ is uniformly sampled from the domain of the objects of $X$ arrived at that node, and iii) the objects are propagated to the left or the right node according to the test. This recursive procedure is repeated until a node contains a single object or a maximum depth is reached. The ERT-Random Forest is then obtained following the standard procedure [7]: $M$ different ERT are built starting from random subsamples of the problem training set. ERTs have been shown to be successful in different contexts, such as classification [16], distance computation [2–4,27,29], clustering [5,20,24] and anomaly detection - where ERTs are referred to as Isolation Trees, leading to Isolation Forests [17,18], one of the most powerful anomaly detection techniques ever introduced according to [12,15].

### 2.1    RF-Distances

Breiman was the first to point out that it is possible to derive highly descriptive data-dependent measures of similarity from Random Forests [7]. After his seminal work, many other powerful RF-distances have been presented (see, e.g., [2–6,23,27,29,32]) and proven to be very effective in a range of different applications such as classification, clustering, outlier detections and others. In all these measures, the main idea is that the relation between two objects $x$ and $y$ can be quantified by i) making the two objects traverse all trees of the trained Forest, and ii) comparing the answers they provide.

In this paper, we focus on two distances, briefly summarized in the following. Given a tree $t$, and an object $x$, let us denote as $\ell_t(x)$ the leaf where the object $x$ falls after traversing the tree $t$. Let us also denote as $P_t(x)$ the *path* of $x$ from the root to its leaf. The first distance, which we call *Shi* [7,23], represents the RF distance originally introduced by Breiman [7] and then exploited by Shi and colleagues for Random Forest Clustering [23]. The distance is firstly defined at the tree level by postulating the similarity between two objects $x$ and $y$ as 1 if the paths $P_t(x)$ and $P_t(y)$ are identical (i.e. if the two objects end in the same leaf of the tree), 0 otherwise. We have:

$$\text{Shi}_t(x,y) = \begin{cases} 1 & \text{if} \ell_t(x) = \ell_t(y) \\ 0 & \text{if} \ell_t(x) \neq \ell_t(y) \end{cases} \tag{1}$$

Given the similarity, the distance based on a forest of $M$ trees is then defined as[1]:

$$d_{Shi}(x,y) = 1 - \frac{1}{M} \sum_t \text{Shi}_t(x,y) \tag{2}$$

The second distance is the recently introduced RatioRF measure [6], a RF-distance defined on a set-based interpretation of the Tversky definition of similarity [30]. For simplicity, let us introduce here only the basic mechanism, referring to [6] the readers interested in the contextualization into the Tversky theory. Basically, within the RatioRF measure, two objects are compared on the basis of their answers to all the tests contained in the two paths $P_t(x)$ and $P_t(y)$ – these being the sole tests needed to characterize $x$ and $y$. More in detail, let us call $S_t^{xy}$ the set containing all tests in the two paths, i.e. $S_t^{xy} = S_t^x \cup S_t^y$, where $S_t^x$ is the set of tests $\{\theta_{\text{root}}, \cdots, \theta_{\ell_t(x)}\}$ in the path $P_t(x)$. Let us denote as $A_t^{xy}$ the set of tests in $S_t^{xy}$ for which $x$ and $y$ provide the same answer. At tree level, the RatioRF similarity between $x$ and $y$ is defined by:

$$\text{RRF}_t(x,y) = \frac{|A_t^{xy}|}{|S_t^{xy}|} \tag{3}$$

where $|\cdot|$ denote the cardinality of a set. Given this similarity, the distance based on a forest of $M$ trees is then defined as[2]:

$$d_{RRF}(x,y) = 1 - \frac{1}{M} \sum_t \text{RRF}_t(x,y) \tag{4}$$

---

[1] Please note that to ease the computation this formulation is the squared version of the original formulation of the distance, as given in [23].

[2] Also in this case, to simplify the computation, we remove the squared root from the original definition of the distance given in [6].

# 3   Main Result

We want to show that if two objects $x$ and $y$ have a small true distance, then their RF-distance, built starting from a RF defined with ERT, is also small. More precisely, if we denote by $d^*(x, y)$ the true distance between $x$ and $y$ and by $d^R(x, y)$ the distance obtained with a Random Forest $R$ built with *Extremely Randomized Trees*, e.g., as in (2) and in (4), then our goal is to show that

$$d^*(x, y) \leq \epsilon \quad \Rightarrow \quad Pr\left(d^R(x, y) \geq (1 + \delta_\epsilon)\epsilon\right) \leq P \tag{5}$$

where $\epsilon, \delta$, and $P$ are small numbers, i.e., with high probability the distance computed via the ERT random forest is a good approximation of the original distance.

## 3.1   Step 1: The Representation

We start our derivation by assuming that there exists a *proper representation* for our problem. To instantiate the concept of *proper representation*, we resort to the "Compactness Hypothesis", formulated by Arkadev and colleagues in 1967 [1], and then developed by Duin and Pekalska in [13]. Within such hypothesis, a representation is *proper* if two objects which are near in the real world are also near in the representation space. Arkadev and colleagues, together with Duin and Pekalska, showed that generalization is not possible if this hypothesis is not fulfilled. Please note that the definition only implies that similar objects have similar representations, and not that *dissimilar* objects have *dissimilar* representation. If this last is also true, then they refer to *true* representations, for which even a simple boundary-based classifier can permit zero-error classification. The principle is defined in a vague way (simply stating that near objects should have near representations), and can be formalized in different ways, depending on the goal: for example, Duin in [14] defined a measure to quantify the compactness of a given representation in case of nearest neighbour classification.

Here we provide the following formalization: let us assume that we have a representation based on a set of features $F$, i.e. every object $x$ of our problem is encoded with an $|F|$-dimensional vector $rep(x) = [x_1, \cdots, x_{|F|}] \in [0, 1]^{|F|}$. We assume, for the sake of the presentation, that the components of this vector are normalized to values in $[0, 1]$. Now, we formalize the property, for the representation, to be *proper*, i.e. to satisfy the "Compactness Hypothesis": if two objects $x$ and $y$ of our problem have a low distance, their representation $rep(x) = [x_1, \cdots, x_{|F|}]$ and $rep(y) = [y_1, \cdots, y_{|F|}]$ should be close. More precisely, we work with the following parameterized and more quantitative notion of a proper representation.

**Definition 1.** *Fix numbers* $\theta, \epsilon \in [0, 1]$. *The representation* $z \mapsto rep(z) = [z_1, \cdots, z_{|F|}]$ *is* $(\theta, \epsilon)$-**proper** *with respect to a (true) distance* $d^*$ *if the following condition holds:*

$$\forall x, y \ s.t. \ d^*(x, y) \leq \epsilon \quad \exists \tilde{F} \subset F \ s.t. \begin{cases} |\tilde{F}| \geq (1 - \theta)|F| \\ \forall f \in \tilde{F}, |x_f - y_f| \leq \epsilon. \end{cases} \tag{6}$$

*We say that the representation is $\theta$-proper, if it satisfies (6) for all $\epsilon > 0$. Finally, we say that the representation is simply proper if it is $\theta$-proper for some $\theta < 0.1$.*

## 3.2   Step 2: The Bounds

We can now show our probabilistic bounds on the approximation guarantee achievable by a ERT-based RF-distance computed over a proper representation. We assume that the forest is built based on a $(\theta, \epsilon)$-proper representation, over a set $F$ of features with values in $[0, 1]$. We let $M$ denote the number of trees in the forest, and we assume that each tree has height $h$. For the sake of the analysis it is easier to think that in each tree, each leaf is at depth $h$, although all the arguments remain valid under the hypothesis that $h$ is an upper bound on the maximum depth of a leaf.

**Theorem 1 (Shi distance).** *Given two objects $x$ and $y$, whose true distance is $d^*(x, y) \leq \epsilon$ and assuming an $(\theta, \epsilon)$-proper representation $rep(z)$, according to def. 1, let $d^R(x, y)$ be the RF-distance computed with Eq. (2) on the representation $rep(x), rep(y)$, starting from a forest of $M$ ERT trees. Then, for all $\delta \in (0, 1]$ and $\delta_\epsilon \geq 0$ such that*

$$(1 + \delta_\epsilon)\epsilon \geq (1 + \delta)\left[1 - ((1 - \theta)(1 - \epsilon))^h\right] \tag{7}$$

*it holds that*

$$Pr\left(d^R(x, y) \geq (1 + \delta_\epsilon)\epsilon\right) < \exp\left(\frac{-M\delta^2\left[1 - ((1 - \theta)(1 - \epsilon))^h\right]}{3}\right) \tag{8}$$

where $\exp(x)$ indicates $e^x$. The theorem says that under the condition stated in Eq. (7), the probability that the RF-distance is far away from the true distance – according to $\delta_\epsilon$ – can be made as small as possible by increasing the number of the trees $M$ of the forest.

**Theorem 2 (RatioRF distance).** *Given two objects $x$ and $y$, which true distance is $d^*(x, y) \leq \epsilon$ and assuming an $(\theta, \epsilon)$-proper representation $rep(z)$, according to def. 1, let $d^R(x, y)$ be the RF-distance computed with Eq. (4) on the representation $rep(x), rep(y)$, starting from a forest of $M$ ERT trees. Then, for all $\delta \in (0, 1]$ and $\delta_\epsilon \geq 0$ such that*

$$(1 + \delta_\epsilon)\epsilon \geq (1 + \delta)\left[1 - ((1 - \theta)(1 - \epsilon))\right] \tag{9}$$

*it holds that*

$$Pr(d^{RR}(x, y) \geq 2(1 + \delta_\epsilon)\epsilon) \leq 2\exp\left(\frac{-Mh\delta^2\left[1 - (1 - \theta)(1 - \epsilon)\right]}{3}\right) \tag{10}$$

## 3.3   The Proofs

Both proofs are based on the Chernoff bound (see, e.g., [19]). Among the several variants of the bound available, we use the following version: let $X_1, X_2, \ldots X_n$ be independent Poisson trials with $Pr[X_i = 1] = p_i$. Let $X$ be the sum of the $X_i$, and let $\mu$ be an upper bound on $E[X]$, i.e., $E[X] \leq \mu$. Then, for any $\delta \in (0, 1]$ we have that:

$$Pr(X > (1 + \delta)\mu) < \exp\left(\frac{-\mu\delta^2}{3}\right) \tag{11}$$

Let us derive the proof for Theorem 1.

*Proof (Theorem 1).* Given $x$ and $y$, let us define the random variable $X_t \in \{0, 1\}$ as:

$$X_t = \begin{cases} 1 & \text{if } x \text{ and } y \text{ fall in different leaves in the tree } t \\ 0 & \text{otherwise} \end{cases} \tag{12}$$

Given this definition, the RF-distance defined in Eq. (2) can be written as:

$$d^R(x, y) = \frac{1}{M} \sum_{t=1}^{M} X_t \tag{13}$$

Assume that a proper representation is given that uses the set of features $F$. The probability that $X_t = 0$ is the probability that the two objects fall in the same leaf, i.e. that they follow the same root-to-leaf path in the tree $t$, answering in the same way to all the questions along such a path. Let us consider the root. The probability that, in the root, two objects take the same branch is 1 minus the probability that they are separated, i.e. that the chosen threshold is exactly between their value on the feature tested in the root. Considering that the threshold is randomly chosen in the domain, if the feature $f$ used in the test belongs to $\tilde{F}$, then $|x_f - y_f| \leq \epsilon$, thus the probability that this happens is $\geq 1 - \epsilon$. Considering that there are at least $(1 - \theta)|F|$ such features, then the probability that $x$ and $y$ answer in the same way is $\geq (1 - \theta)(1 - \epsilon)$.

Now, let us consider the second node of the path. The reasoning is exactly the same, but for the fact that the domain of the feature tested at this node might be different from $[0, 1]$. Actually, if the feature used for the split is the same as the feature used in the root, then the domain is reduced: if $\tau$ is the threshold used in the root, the domain is $[0, \tau]$ or $[\tau, 1]$, depending on whether $x$ and $y$ took the left or the right path. However, if the feature in the second node of the path is different from the one used in the root, then the probability that $x$ and $y$ answer in the same way is again $\geq (1 - \theta)(1 - \epsilon)$. For the simplicity in the treatment let us for now assume that, on every root-to-leaf path, every split is done on a distinct feature, so that we can consider the threshold is always randomly chosen over the whole domain $[0, 1]$. We remark that this is not such a strong assumption since i) ERT trees used for RF-distances are very short — typically each tree is built with 128 or 256 objects, and the max depth is set to $\log(n)$, i.e., 7 or 8; ii) the contexts in which ERT-based RF-distances are more suitable are those characterized by high dimensional spaces, which implies that over a short path the probability of randomly choosing twice the same feature is very small. We will provide some arguments on the relaxation of this assumption in Sect. 5.

Since the path followed by $x$, has length at most $h$, we have that

$$Pr(X_t = 0) \geq [(1 - \theta)(1 - \epsilon)]^h \tag{14}$$

hence for the expected value $E[X_t]$ we have that:

$$E[X_t] = 0 \cdot Pr(X_t = 0) + 1 \cdot Pr(X_t = 1) \leq 1 - [(1 - \theta)(1 - \epsilon)]^h \tag{15}$$

First, let us rewrite the probability in the left part of Eq. (8) by using the definition of the Shi distance provided in Eq. (13):

$$Pr\left(d^R(x, y) \geq (1 + \delta_\epsilon)\epsilon\right) = Pr\left(\frac{1}{M}\sum_{t=1}^{M} X_t \geq (1 + \delta_\epsilon)\epsilon\right) = Pr\left(\sum_{t=1}^{M} X_t \geq M(1 + \delta_\epsilon)\epsilon\right)$$

Let $\mu = M\left[1 - ((1 - \theta)(1 - \epsilon))^h\right]$. Then, using (15), the Expected value of the variable $X = X_1 + X_2 + \ldots + X_M$ satisfies the inequality

$$E[X] = E\left[\sum_{t=1}^{M} X_t\right] = \sum_{t=1}^{M} E[X_t] \leq M\left[1 - ((1 - \theta)(1 - \epsilon))^h\right] = \mu \tag{16}$$

Now, from (9) it follows that $M(1 + \delta_\epsilon)\epsilon \geq (1 + \delta)\mu$ and by the Chernoff bound above (see Eq. (11)), we have

$$Pr\left(d^R(x, y) \geq (1 + \delta_\epsilon)\epsilon\right) = Pr\left(\sum_{t=1}^{M} X_t \geq M(1 + \delta_\epsilon)\epsilon\right) \leq Pr\left(\sum_{t=1}^{M} X_t \geq (1 + \delta)\mu\right)$$

$$< \exp\left(\frac{-\mu\delta^2}{3}\right) = \exp\left(\frac{-M\delta^2\left[1 - ((1 - \theta)(1 - \epsilon))^h\right]}{3}\right),$$

$$\square$$

Similarly we can provide the proof of the Theorem 2

*Proof (Theorem 2).* Recall that we assume a Forest $R$ with $M$ ERT trees, built on the feature set $F$ of a proper representation, where each feature has domain $[0, 1]$. Recall also that, given $x$ and $y$, the RatioRF distance is computed by considering the set $S_t^{xy}$ of the tests on the two root-to-leaf paths followed by $x$ and $y$ in the tree $t$. We start by defining the random variable $X_t^i \in \{0, 1\}$, for each tree $t = 1, \ldots, M$ and each test $i$ in the set $S_t^{xy}$, i.e., $1 \leq i \leq |S_t^{xy}|$:

$$X_t^i = \begin{cases} 1 & \text{if } x \text{ and } y \text{ give a different answer to the test } i \text{ in the set } S_t^{xy} \\ 0 & \text{otherwise} \end{cases} \tag{17}$$

Given this definition, the RF-distance can be reformulated as:

$$d^{RR}(x,y) = \frac{1}{M} \sum_{t=1}^{M} \frac{\sum_{i=1}^{|S_t^{xy}|} X_t^i}{|S_t^{xy}|} \tag{18}$$

Also in this case we can estimate the probability that $X_t^i = 0$. Under the assumption—see the discussion above in the part about the Shi distance—that all thresholds on the same root-to-leaf path are uniformly chosen in $[0,1]$, i.e., the features of the tests on the same root-to-leaf path are distinct, we have that for each $t$ and $i$,:

$$Pr(X_t^i = 0) \geq (1-\theta)(1-\epsilon) \tag{19}$$

hence,

$$E[X_t^i] \leq [1-(1-\theta)(1-\epsilon)] \tag{20}$$

We will now start with a reformulation of (18). Recall, from Sect. 2, that $S_t^x$ and $S_t^y$ represent the set of tests on the root-to-leaf paths associated to $x$ and $y$, respectively. Notice that on each node $\nu$ of the common part, $S_t^x \cap S_t^y$, of the these two paths–apart from the node where they separate– we have that $X_t^\nu = 0$. Then, from (18) it follows that

$$d^{RR}(x,y) \leq \frac{1}{M} \sum_{t=1}^{M} \frac{\sum_{i=1}^{|S_t^x|} X_t^i + \sum_{i=1}^{|S_t^y|} X_t^i}{|S_t^{xy}|} \tag{21}$$

Let us define

$$d_x^{RR}(y) = \frac{1}{M} \sum_{t=1}^{M} \frac{\sum_{i=1}^{|S_t^x|} X_t^i}{|S_t^x|}, \qquad d_y^{RR}(x) = \frac{1}{M} \sum_{t=1}^{M} \frac{\sum_{i=1}^{|S_t^y|} X_t^i}{|S_t^y|}. \tag{22}$$

Then, from (21) and (22) we have $d^{RR}(x,y) \leq d_x^{RR}(y) + d_y^{RR}(x)$. Hence,

$$Pr(d^{RR}(x,y) \geq 2(1+\delta_\epsilon)\epsilon) \leq Pr(d_x^{RR}(y) \geq (1+\delta_\epsilon)\epsilon) + Pr(d_y^{RR}(x) \geq (1+\delta_\epsilon)\epsilon) \tag{23}$$

where the inequality follows by noticing that, for every $a > 0$ the event $A = \{d^{RR}(x,y) > 2a\}$ implies at least one of the events: $B = \{d_x^{RR}(y) > a\}$, or $C = \{d_y^{RR}(x) > a\}$. I.e., we are using

$$A \subseteq B \cup C \Rightarrow Pr(A) \leq PR(B \cup C) \leq Pr(B) + Pr(C)$$

Under the assumption made above that both paths of $x$ and $y$ are of fixed length $h$, and that this length is the same for all trees, we can simplify the Eq. (22) as

$$d_x^{RR}(y) = \frac{\sum_{t=1}^{M} \sum_{i=1}^{h} X_t^i}{Mh}, \qquad d_y^{RR}(x) = \frac{\sum_{t=1}^{M} \sum_{i=1}^{h} X_t^i}{Mh} \tag{24}$$

Using (20), we can define an upper bound $\mu$ on the expected value of the sum in the enumerator of (24) as follows:

$$\mu = Mh(1 - (1 - \theta)(1 - \epsilon)) \geq \sum_{i=1}^{M} \sum_{i=1}^{h} E[X_t^i].$$

From (9) it follows that $Mh(1 + \delta_\epsilon)\epsilon \geq (1 + \delta)\mu$. Hence, by the Chernoff bound, we have

$$Pr\left(d_x^{RR}(y) \geq (1 + \delta_\epsilon)\epsilon\right) = Pr\left(\sum_{t=1}^{M} \sum_{i=1}^{h} X_t^i \geq Mh(1 + \delta_\epsilon)\epsilon\right)$$

$$\leq Pr\left(\sum_{t=1}^{M} \sum_{i=1}^{h} X_t^i \geq (1 + \delta)\mu\right) < \exp\left(\frac{-\mu\delta^2}{2 + \delta}\right) = \exp\left(\frac{-Mh\delta^2 [1 - (1 - \theta)(1 - \epsilon)]}{3}\right)$$

Analogously, we also obtain

$$Pr\left(d_y^{RR}(x) \geq (1 + \delta_\epsilon)\epsilon\right) \leq \exp\left(\frac{-Mh\delta^2 [1 - (1 - \theta)(1 - \epsilon)]}{3}\right) \qquad (25)$$

Therefore, recalling (23) we have the desired result

$$Pr(d^{RR}(x, y) \geq 2(1 + \delta_\epsilon)\epsilon) \leq 2\exp\left(\frac{-Mh\delta^2 [1 - (1 - \theta)(1 - \epsilon)]}{3}\right) \qquad (26)$$

$\square$

## 4    Understanding the Bounds

The two bounds say that the probability that the RF-based distance is significantly larger than the true distance can be made as small as possible by increasing the number of trees of the forest, as long as the conditions in Eq. (7) and in Eq. (9) are satisfied. In this section we discuss the relationship between $\delta_\epsilon$, $\delta$ and the size $M$ of the forest established by the bounds and the conditions. The parameters $\epsilon$ and $\theta$ are given by the proper representation available. We let $P^*$ be a desired upper bound on the probability in the right-hand side of Eqs. (8) and (10), i.e., $P^*$ is an upper bound on the probability that the RF-based distance $d^R$ is not a good approximation of the true distance $d^*$.

### 4.1    The Number of Trees $M$

From Eqs. (8) and (10) we can compute the minimum number of trees—henceforth denoted by $M_{\min}$—needed to guarantee the upper bound $P^*$.

**Shi Distance.** Let $\mu_t = \left[1 - ((1 - \theta)(1 - \epsilon))^h\right]$. Then, the upper bound $P^*$ is guaranteed by requiring $\exp\left(\frac{-M\delta^2\mu_t}{3}\right) \leq P^*$ which implies $M \geq \frac{-3 \ln P^*}{\mu_t\delta^2}$.

The last expression is minimized by $\delta = 1$, hence we have:

$$M_{\min}^{Sh} = \frac{-3 \ln P^*}{\mu_t} = \frac{-3 \ln P^*}{1 - ((1 - \theta)(1 - \epsilon))^h}. \tag{27}$$

**RatioRF Distance.** Analogously, we can compute the minimal number of trees $M_{\min}^{RR}$, necessary for guaranteeing the upper bound $P^*$ on the probability in the right side of Eq. (10), when the RatioRF distance is used. Let $\mu_t^i = [1 - (1 - \theta)(1 - \epsilon)]$ be the upper bound we obtained on the expected value of $X_t^i$ as defined in Eq. (20). Proceeding as for the Shi distance, we get the condition $M \geq \dfrac{-3 \ln(0.5P^*)}{h \mu_t^i \delta^2}$, from which (with $\delta = 1$) we have

$$M_{\min}^{RR} = \frac{-3 \ln(0.5P^*)}{h [1 - (1 - \theta)(1 - \epsilon)]} \tag{28}$$

For a better visualization of the relationship between $M_{\min}^{Sh}$ and $M_{\min}^{RR}$ and the parameter $\epsilon$, in Fig. 1(a), we provide such plots, for increasing $\epsilon \in [0.05, 0.5]$, assuming the other parameters in (27) and (28) fixed to $\theta = 0.01, P^* = 0.05$, and $h = 8$ which represents the expected height of the trees built on 256 samples (see e.g. [2,6]). As empirically accepted, these plots show that small forests are indeed sufficient. We can also observe that the curve for RatioRF is drastically better, especially for larger $\epsilon$.

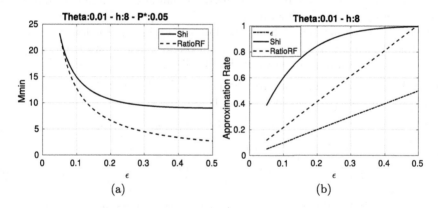

**Fig. 1.** (a) $M_{\min}^{Sh}$ and $M_{\min}^{RR}$ versus $\epsilon$; (b); Approximation versus $\epsilon$.

## 4.2   The Approximation $\delta_\epsilon$

From the conditions in Eqs. (7) and (9) we estimate the minimum $\delta_\epsilon$, which constraints the best approximation guarantee one can probabilistically achieve with the RF-distance.

**Shi Distance.** From the condition (7) we have that $\delta_\epsilon$ is lower bounded as

$$\delta_\epsilon \geq \frac{(1+\delta)\left[1 - ((1-\theta)(1-\epsilon))^h\right]}{\epsilon} - 1, \text{ and its minimum value—denoted by}$$

$\delta_{\epsilon(\min)}^{Sh}$— is achieved with $\delta \mapsto 0$, that is

$$\delta_\epsilon > \delta_{\epsilon(\min)}^{Sh} = \frac{\left[1 - ((1-\theta)(1-\epsilon))^h\right]}{\epsilon} - 1 \tag{29}$$

**RatioRF Distance.** Analogously, for the best approximation guarantee achievable in the case of the RatioRF distance, as given by the minimum value of $\delta_\epsilon$ in condition (9), here denoted $\delta_{\epsilon(\min)}^{RR}$, we have:

$$\delta_\epsilon > \delta_{\epsilon(\min)}^{RR} = \frac{[1 - (1-\theta)(1-\epsilon)]}{\epsilon} - 1 = \frac{\theta(1-\epsilon)}{\epsilon} \tag{30}$$

On the basis of (29) and (30), in Fig. 1(b), we plot the (best possible) approximation $(1+\delta_{\epsilon(\min)}^{Sh})\epsilon$ computed with the Shi distance and $2(1+\delta_{\epsilon(\min)}^{RR})\epsilon$ computed with the RatioRF distance as a function of the parameter $\epsilon$ taken as an estimate of the true distance. Also in this case the remaining parameters are fixed to $\theta = 0.01, P^* = 0.05$ and $h = 8$.

### 4.3  Using the Bounds for Estimating the Size of the Forest

Let us conclude our treatment with some practical considerations on how, in a given problem, the bounds can be used to compute the minimal number of trees required to get the guarantee with a given probability $P^*$ and a given approximation parameter $\delta_\epsilon$. The procedure is described in the following. Please note that we repeat and summarize some of the formulas shown before, in order to have a clear comparison between the two distances.

**Step 1.** Fix the required approximation on the distance $\delta_\epsilon$. Important, the conditions in Eqs. (29) and (30) should hold:

$$\text{Shi: } \delta_\epsilon > \delta_{\epsilon(\min)}^{Sh} = \frac{\left[1 - ((1-\theta)(1-\epsilon))^h\right]}{\epsilon} - 1 \tag{31}$$

$$\text{RatioRF: } \delta_\epsilon > \delta_{\epsilon(\min)}^{RR} = \frac{\theta(1-\epsilon)}{\epsilon} \tag{32}$$

It is possible that for some choices of $\theta, \epsilon, h$ the corresponding $\delta_\epsilon$ is too high.

**Step 2.** Compute the corresponding $\delta_{(\max)}$, i.e. the largest $\delta$ for which the validity conditions in Eqs. (7) and (9) for the bounds hold. Please note that we are looking for the maximum $\delta$ since this would permit to get the minimal amount of trees

$$\text{Shi: } \delta_{(\max)}^{Sh} = \frac{(1+\delta_\epsilon)\epsilon}{1 - ((1-\theta)(1-\epsilon))^h} - 1 \tag{33}$$

$$\text{RatioRF: } \delta_{(\max)}^{RR} = \frac{(1+\delta_\epsilon)\epsilon}{1 - (1-\theta)(1-\epsilon)} - 1 \tag{34}$$

**Step 3.** Compute the minimum number of trees for which the bound holds for a given probability $P^*$ and for the given approximation level $\delta_\epsilon$, which is:

$$\text{Shi:} \quad M_{\min}^{Sh} = \frac{-3 \ln P^*}{\left[ 1 - ((1-\theta)(1-\epsilon))^h \right] (\delta_{(\max)}^{Sh})^2} \tag{35}$$

$$\text{RatioRF:} \quad M_{\min}^{RR} = \frac{-3 \ln(0.5 P^*)}{h \left[ 1 - (1-\theta)(1-\epsilon) \right] (\delta_{(\max)}^{RR})^2} \tag{36}$$

In Fig. 2 we provide the number of required trees for different values of $\delta_\epsilon$. Also in this case let us keep fixed $\theta = 0.01$ and $P^* = 0.05$, and let us vary $\epsilon$ in the interval [0.05-0.5], with step 0.01, with $h = 8$. The behaviour is reported in Fig. 2. Please note that we report only the values for RatioRF, since $\delta_{\epsilon(\min)}$ for Shi is always larger than the required approximation $\delta_\epsilon$. This provides a further theoretical confirmation of the superiority of the RatioRF measure with respect to the Shi distance: for the latter measure, with the analysed configuration of $\theta, P^*$, it is not possible to have a reasonably low approximation rate.

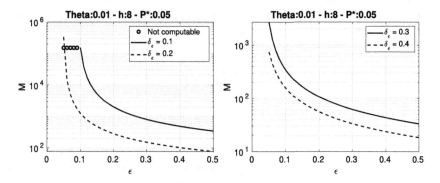

**Fig. 2.** Number of required trees, for a different approximation levels $\delta_\epsilon$. A circle denotes a value of $\epsilon$ for which the condition on $\delta_\epsilon$ was not satisfied (i.e. $\delta_\epsilon < \delta_{\epsilon(\min)}$)

## 5    Discussion and Final Remarks

In the paper we have shown that, given a proper representation, it is possible to approximate the true distance between two objects with a ERT-based RF-distance, an approximation which is guaranteed by choosing a sufficiently large number of trees. This provides a theoretical confirmation of the widely assessed empirical efficacy of such ERT-based RF distances. Moreover, we have also shown that the approximation rate is drastically better for the RatioRF distance, thus confirming the empirical results shown in [6].

In the presentation of our result, we assumed that the tests on the same root-to-leaf path are on distinct features, so that the thresholds are all uniformly randomly sampled in $[0, 1]$. Let us now concentrate on the general case, i.e. we can use many times the same feature. We will concentrate on the Shi distance, similar reasoning can also be applied in the RatioRF case. Suppose that two objects are at distance less than $\epsilon$; suppose first that all tests are on the same feature $f$, and that $f \in \tilde{F}$. In this case, the probability that the two objects are not split in the first $i$ tests is $\geq \max\{0, 1 - (2^i - 1)\epsilon\}$.

If we now assume that, along a root to leaf path (of length $h$), feature $f$ is tested $h_f$ times, we have:

$$P(X_t = 0) \geq \prod_{i=1}^{h_f} \max\left\{0, \left[1 - (2^i - 1)\epsilon\right]\right\}$$

Note that this probability is smaller than the probability defined in Eq. (14), possibly becoming 0: this is reasonable, since if we continue to split on the same feature $f$ we continue to reduce the domain, which will be at a certain level so small that $x$ and $y$ are split with probability 1.

If we have $|F|$ features, each one used $h_f$ times in the path, then the probability in (14) can be written as

$$Pr(X_t = 0) \geq (1 - \theta)^h \prod_{f=1}^{|F|} \left[\prod_{i=1}^{h_f} \max\left\{0, \left[1 - (2^i - 1)\epsilon\right]\right\}\right] \tag{37}$$

From this, we have that the expected value $E[X_t]$ satisfies:

$$E[X_t] \leq 1 - \left((1 - \theta)^h \prod_{f=1}^{|F|} \left[\prod_{i=1}^{h_f} \max\left\{0, \left[1 - (2^i - 1)\epsilon\right]\right\}\right]\right) \tag{38}$$

which can now be used in the place of the one defined in Eq. (15) to complete the proof also in this case.

Rather than re-deriving the resulting (much more involved) bound, we limit ourselves to observe that the bound worsens with the decrease of the expected value. On the other hand, this analysis provides additional interesting information. The fact that, when features are expected to be reused several times on the same root-to-leaf path induces a worst approximation guarantee of the RF-distance with respect to the true distance provides a theoretical justification for the empirical evidence that for most of the ERT-based RF-distances the good results are obtained i) by using small trees – e.g. [6, 25, 26, 28] and ii) on datasets with a large number of features – e.g. [5].

**Ethical Statement.** We do not see any evident ethical implication of our submission. Our paper is mainly theoretical, not involving the collection and processing of personal data, or the inference of personal information. We do not see any potential use of our work for military applications.

# References

1. Arkadev, A.G., Braverman, E.M.: Teaching Computers to Recognize Patterns. Academic, Transl. from the Russian by W. Turski and J.D. Cowan (1967)
2. Aryal, S., Ting, K., Washio, T., Haffari, G.: A comparative study of data-dependent approaches without learning in measuring similarities of data objects. Data Min. Knowl. Discov. **34**(1), 124–162 (2020)
3. Aryal, S., Ting, K.M., Haffari, G., Washio, T.: Mp-Dissimilarity: a data dependent dissimilarity measure. In: 2014 IEEE International Conference on Data Mining, pp. 707–712. IEEE (2014)
4. Aryal, S., Ting, K.M., Washio, T., Haffari, G.: Data-dependent dissimilarity measure: an effective alternative to geometric distance measures. Knowl. Inf. Syst. **53**(2), 479–506 (2017). https://doi.org/10.1007/s10115-017-1046-0
5. Bicego, M., Escolano, F.: On learning random forests for random forest-clustering. In: Proceedings of the International Conference on Pattern Recognition (ICPR), pp. 3451–3458. IEEE (2021)
6. Bicego, M., Cicalese, F., Mensi, A.: RatioRF: a novel measure for random forest clustering based on the Tversky's ratio model. IEEE Trans. Knowl. Data Eng. **35**(1), 830–841 (2023)
7. Breiman, L.: Random forests. Mach. Learn. **45**, 5–32 (2001)
8. Breiman, L., Friedman, J., Olshen, R., Stone, C.: Classification and regression trees. Wadsworth (1984)
9. Breiman, L.: Some infinity theory for predictor ensembles. Tech. Rep. CiteSeer (2000)
10. Criminisi, A., Shotton, J., Konukoglu, E.: Decision forests: a unified framework for classification, regression, density estimation, manifold learning and semi-supervised learning. Found. Trends Comput. Graph. Vis. **7**(2–3), 81–227 (2012)
11. Davies, A., Ghahramani, Z.: The random forest Kernel and other Kernels for big data from random partitions. arXiv preprint arXiv:1402.4293 (2014)
12. Domingues, R., Filippone, M., Michiardi, P., Zouaoui, J.: A comparative evaluation of outlier detection algorithms: experiments and analyses. Pattern Recognit. **74**, 406–421 (2018)
13. Duin, R.P., Pekalska, E.: Dissimilarity representation for pattern recognition. Foundations and applications, vol. 64. World scientific (2005)
14. Duin, R.: Compactness and complexity of pattern recognition problems. In: Proceedings of the International Symposium on Pattern Recognition "In Memoriam Pierre Devijver", pp. 124–128. Royal Military Academy (1999)
15. Emmott, A.F., Das, S., Dietterich, T., Fern, A., Wong, W.K.: Systematic construction of anomaly detection benchmarks from real data. In: Proceedings of the ACM SIGKDD Workshop on Outlier Detection and Description, pp. 16–21 (2013)
16. Geurts, P., Ernst, D., Wehenkel, L.: Extremely randomized trees. Mach. Learn. **63**(1), 3–42 (2006)

17. Liu, F.T., Ting, K.M., Zhou, Z.H.: Isolation forest. In: 2008 Eighth IEEE International Conference on Data Mining, pp. 413–422. IEEE (2008)
18. Liu, F.T., Ting, K.M., Zhou, Z.H.: Isolation-based anomaly detection. ACM Trans. Knowl. Discov. Data (TKDD) **6**(1), 1–39 (2012)
19. Mitzenmacher, M., Upfal, E.: Probability and computing: randomized algorithms and probabilistic analysis. Cambridge University Press (2005)
20. Moosmann, F., Triggs, B., Jurie, F.: Fast discriminative visual codebooks using randomized clustering forests. In: Advances in Neural Information Processing Systems 19, pp. 985–992 (2006)
21. Quinlan, J.: C4.5: programs for machine learning. Morgan Kaufmann Publishers Inc. (1993)
22. Scornet, E.: Random forests and Kernel methods. IEEE Trans. Inf. Theory **62**(3), 1485–1500 (2016)
23. Shi, T., Horvath, S.: Unsupervised learning with random forest predictors. J. Comput. Graph. Stat. **15**(1), 118–138 (2006)
24. Shotton, J., Johnson, M., Cipolla, R.: Semantic texton forests for image categorization and segmentation. In: IEEE Computer Society Conference on Computer Vision and Pattern Recognition (CVPR 2008) (2008)
25. Ting, K.M., Wells, J.R., Washio, T.: Isolation Kernel: the X factor in efficient and effective large scale online kernel learning. Data Min. Knowl. Disc. **35**(6), 2282–2312 (2021)
26. Ting, K.M., Xu, B.C., Washio, T., Zhou, Z.H.: Isolation distributional Kernel: a new tool for kernel based anomaly detection. In: Proceedings of the 26th ACM SIGKDD International Conference on Knowledge Discovery & Data Mining, pp. 198–206 (2020)
27. Ting, K.M., Zhu, Y., Carman, M., Zhu, Y., Washio, T., Zhou, Z.H.: Lowest probability mass neighbour algorithms: relaxing the metric constraint in distance-based neighbourhood algorithms. Mach. Learn. **108**, 331–376 (2019). https://doi.org/10.1007/s10994-018-5737-x
28. Ting, K.M., Zhu, Y., Zhou, Z.H.: Isolation Kernel and its effect on SVM. In: Proceedings of the 24th ACM SIGKDD International Conference on Knowledge Discovery & Data Mining, pp. 2329–2337 (2018)
29. Ting, K., Zhu, Y., Carman, M., Zhu, Y., Zhou, Z.H.: Overcoming key weaknesses of distance-based neighbourhood methods using a data dependent dissimilarity measure. In: Proceedings of the International Conference on Knowledge Discovery and Data Mining, pp. 1205–1214 (2016)
30. Tversky, A.: Features of similarity. Psychol. Rev. **84**(4), 327 (1977)
31. Wells, J.R., Aryal, S., Ting, K.M.: Simple supervised dissimilarity measure: bolstering iForest-induced similarity with class information without learning. Knowl. Inf. Syst. **62**, 3203–3216 (2020)
32. Zhu, X., Loy, C., Gong, S.: Constructing robust affinity graphs for spectral clustering. In: Proceedings of the International Conference on Computer Vision and Pattern Recognition, CVPR 2014, pp. 1450–1457 (2014)

# Hypernetworks Build Implicit Neural Representations of Sounds

Filip Szatkowski[1,3]($\boxtimes$) (iD), Karol J. Piczak[2] (iD), Przemysław Spurek[2] (iD),
Jacek Tabor[2,5] (iD), and Tomasz Trzciński[1,2,3,4] (iD)

[1] Warsaw University of Technology, Warsaw , Poland
{filip.szatkowski.dokt,tomasz.trzcinski}@pw.edu.pl
[2] Faculty of Mathematics and Computer Science, Jagiellonian University, Krakow,
Poland
{karol.piczak,przemyslaw.spurek,jacek.tabor}@uj.edu.pl
[3] IDEAS NCBR, Warsaw, Poland
[4] Tooploox, Wroclaw, Poland
[5] UES Ltd., Krakow, Poland

**Abstract.** Implicit Neural Representations (INRs) are nowadays used
to represent multimedia signals across various real-life applications,
including image super-resolution, image compression, or 3D rendering.
Existing methods that leverage INRs are predominantly focused on visual
data, as their application to other modalities, such as audio, is nontrivial
due to the inductive biases present in architectural attributes of image-
based INR models. To address this limitation, we introduce HyperSound,
the first meta-learning approach to produce INRs for audio samples that
leverages hypernetworks to generalize beyond samples observed in training. Our approach reconstructs audio samples with quality comparable to other state-of-the-art models and provides a viable alternative to
contemporary sound representations used in deep neural networks for
audio processing, such as spectrograms. Our code is publicly available at
https://github.com/WUT-AI/hypersound.

**Keywords:** Machine Learning · Hypernetworks · Audio Processing ·
Implicit Neural Representations

## 1 Introduction

The field of Implicit Neural Representations (INRs) is a rapidly growing area
of research, which aims to obtain functional, coordinate-based representations
of multimedia signals through the use of neural networks. These representations
are decoupled from the spatial resolution, so the signal can be resampled at any
arbitrary frequency without incurring additional memory storage requirements.
Applications of INRs include super-resolution [22,30], compression [22,30], 3D
rendering [23], and missing data imputation [10]. Furthermore, INRs can be used

---

F. Szatkowski and K. J. Piczak—Equal contribution.

D. Koutra et al. (Eds.): ECML PKDD 2023, LNAI 14172, pp. 661–676, 2023.
https://doi.org/10.1007/978-3-031-43421-1_39

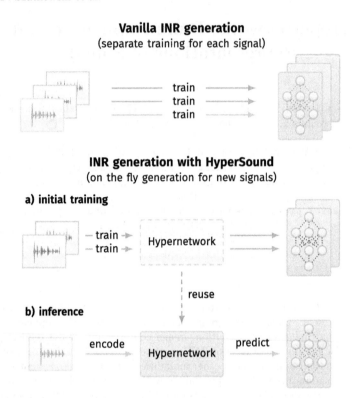

**Fig. 1.** We propose HyperSound, the first framework which produces Implicit Neural Representations for unseen audio signals, eliminating the need for retraining a model for each new example.

to synthesise data [44], and they show promise as an alternative to the traditional feature extraction techniques used in neural networks [8].

INRs are a promising research direction in audio processing, yet so far their applications in this domain remain limited. As the size of INR networks can be significantly smaller than the size of the represented signal, they can be used as a compression method [34]. They also provide an alternative to super-resolution algorithms such as ProGAN [15], which often require hand-crafting complex architectures for selected resolution. In contrast, in INRs the signal resolution is given by the granularity of input coordinates, so a single network represents the signal for any resolution we might require while remaining constant in size. Moreover, as [24] show that INRs can be used as features in other algorithms, this representation can be an alternative for current deep audio processing models that primarily operate on features obtained from mel spectrograms or raw audio waves [27].

In practice, architectures typically used for INRs struggle with modeling high frequencies inherent in audio signals [28] and require training a new model for every incoming data point, which is wasteful and greatly reduces their applicability. This issue is usually addressed by obtaining generalizable INRs through meta-learning methods, such as hypernetworks [12] – models that produce the weights for other models. The hypernetwork framework can be leveraged to obtain generalizable INRs for a variety of data types, including images [16,22,30], point clouds [22,33,36] 3D objects [14,43], videos [22] and time series [10]. However, obtaining generalizable INRs for audio signals remains an unsolved task due to the high dimensionality and variance of this type of data, which makes the standard methods for this task insufficient.

In our work, we propose a method that learns a general recipe for creating INRs for arbitrary audio samples not present in the training dataset. We adapt the hypernetwork framework for sound processing by introducing a domain-specific loss function and hypernetwork weight initialization. Additionally, we investigate various variants of the hypernetwork framework in order to achieve improved compression while maintaining audio quality. To our knowledge, our method, named HyperSound, is the first application of hypernetwork-based INR generation to the audio domain.

The main contributions of our work are:

- We introduce HyperSound, to our knowledge the first INR method for audio processing that builds functional representations of unseen audio signals, which eliminates the need of retraining the INR for each new data point.
- We show a successful adaptation of the hypernetwork paradigm to the audio processing through domain-specific modifications such as the spectral loss function.
- We empirically evaluate various approaches of using hypernetworks to build INRs for audio generation, e.g. by leveraging SIREN architecture or Fourier mapping.

## 2 Related Works

### 2.1 Implicit Neural Representations (INRs)

Implicit Neural Representations (INRs) are continuous, coordinate-based approximations of data obtained through neural networks. The decoupling of representation from spatial resolution makes INRs attractive for a wide range of applications in signal processing. However, functions represented by standard MLP networks with ReLU activation function show a strong bias towards low frequencies [28], which in practice make them infeasible as representations of multimedia signals. To mitigate this bias, most INRs use either Fourier features [37] or SIREN networks [30] with periodic activation functions. Later works improve SIREN networks, introducing various forms of modulation to sinusoidal layers [3,22]. INRs are currently used in many applications, such as super-resolution [22,30], compression [34], 3D rendering [23], missing data imputation [10] or data generation [44]. However, typical INRs are trained for each data point, and obtaining a representation for new signals requires retraining the network from scratch.

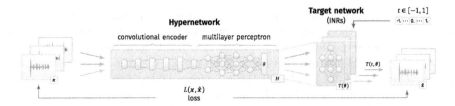

**Fig. 2.** Overview of the HyperSound framework. We use a single hypernetwork model to produce distinct INRs based on arbitrary audio signals provided as input.

## 2.2   Generalizable INRs

To obtain a way of generating INRs for new data without the need for model retraining, various meta-learning approaches were proposed. [31] leverage gradient-based meta-learning algorithms to solve the task of learning an INR space for shapes. [5] employ a transformer meta-learner to obtain INRs for unseen examples. Many methods of obtaining generalizable INRs also involve the use of hypernetworks [12], where one network (hypernetwork) generates the weights for another network (target network). More broadly, hypernetworks are employed in many applications, including model compression [42], continual learning [39] or generating INRs. In particular, hypernetworks were successfully used to generate INRs for images [16,22,30], shapes [30,33], videos [22] and time series [10]. To our knowledge, our work is the first application of hypernetworks for generating audio INRs.

## 2.3   Deep Neural Networks for Audio Processing

First successful attempts at raw waveform processing with deep neural networks were models such as WaveNet [26] and SampleRNN [21], but their autoregressive nature makes them slow and prone to accumulation of errors. Later architectures such as ParallelWaveNet [25], NSynth [9], MelGAN [17] or SING [7] proposed non-autoregressive architectures for audio generation. Recent autoencoder-based models such as RAVE [2] or SoundStream [41] are able to process high-resolution signals in an end-to-end fashion, producing audio of very good perceptual quality.

## 3   Method

Traditional digital representation of sound waves is a series of amplitude values sampled at regular time intervals, which approximates a continuous real function $x(t)$. Our goal is to obtain a meta-recipe for generating audio INRs approximating such functions. While the creation of INRs for particular audio samples can be successfully achieved with gradient descent, finding a general solution is much harder due to the inherent complexity of audio time series. Therefore, similar to

[16], we model such functions with neural networks $T$ (target networks), parameterized by weights generated by another neural network $H$ (hypernetwork). Our method, named HyperSound, can be described as

$$\boldsymbol{\theta}_x = H(\boldsymbol{x}),$$
$$\hat{x}(t) = T(t, \boldsymbol{\theta}_x). \tag{1}$$

We show the overview of our method in Fig. 2. In the following sections, we describe the architecture of the models used as Implicit Neural Representations and of the hypernetwork. Then, we present the details required for the successful application of the hypernetwork framework to the audio domain.

### 3.1 Implicit Neural Representations

We consider two variants of INR networks, inspired by NeRF [23] and SIREN [30] papers. Both models have a single input and a single output.

We refer to a NeRF-inspired network as a Fourier-mapped multilayer perceptron (FMLP). The network consists of a positional encoding layer followed by dense layers with biases and ReLU activation functions. Positional embedding vectors $\boldsymbol{\gamma}$ are obtained as

$$\boldsymbol{\gamma}(t) = \left[\sin(2^0\pi t), \cos(2^0\pi t), \ldots, \sin(2^{L-1}\pi t), \cos(2^{L-1}\pi t)\right] \tag{2}$$

where $t$ is the time coordinate and $L$ denotes the embedding size. We normalize input coordinates to a range of $[-1, 1]$ and use $L = 10$.

SIREN network consists of dense layers with a sinusoidal activation function. The output $\boldsymbol{y}_i$ of $i$-th SIREN layer is defined as:

$$\boldsymbol{y}_i = \sin\left(\omega_i \boldsymbol{x}_i \boldsymbol{W}_i^T + \boldsymbol{b}_i\right), \tag{3}$$

where $x_i$ is the input of the layer, $\boldsymbol{W}_i$ and $\boldsymbol{b}_i$ are layer weights and biases and $\omega_i$ is a scalar factor introduced in [30] to enable learning of higher signal frequencies. In practice, following the original paper, we set a distinct $\omega_0 \neq 1$ for the first layer and keep the same shared value of $\omega_i$ for all remaining layers.

[1] prove that FMLP networks are equal to single-layer SIREN networks. However, in our experiments, we see significant differences in the learning dynamics and representational capacity of both networks and thus explore both architectures in our experiments.

### 3.2 Hypernetwork

Typical audio recordings contain several thousands of samples, while hypernetworks generally use fully connected layers to produce target weights. Since we want to use raw audio recordings as input, using dense layers to process the signal directly leads to the explosion of the number of weights in the hypernetwork. To avoid this problem, we use a convolutional encoder to produce a latent, lower dimensional representation of the signal and then process this representation with fully connected layers. The hypernetwork outputs weights $\theta$ that parameterise the target network.

We use an encoder based on SoundStream [41]. The fully connected part of the hypernetwork is composed of six layers with biases and ELU [6] activation, where the last layer produces the flattened weights of the target network. Input of the hypernetwork is 32 768 samples of audio at a sampling rate of 22 050 Hz, the size of a latent representation is $103 \times 32$ and the layer sizes of the dense part are 400, 768, 768, 768, 768, 768, 400.

### 3.3    Hypernetwork Adaptation for Audio Data

Audio signals contain inherent high-frequency content, and neural networks in general tend to focus on low-frequency features [28]. Using a hypernetwork to produce INR weights introduces additional complexity to the optimization process. During training, small updates to the hypernetwork weights might disproportionally affect the function represented by the output weights, which makes the training process unstable. Moreover, the outputs of the neural network will always contain some inherent noise, which affects the high-frequency content more. Finally, in the case of training INRs, hypernetworks tend to overfit the training data, as they usually require over-parametrization to be able to solve a difficult problem of function generation. Combined, those issues make the straightforward application of the hypernetwork framework to our problem impossible.

To enable hypernetworks to model audio data, we introduce STFT loss function, which counters the hypernetworks tendency to ignore high-frequencies. The optimization process is described in detail in Sect. 3.4. The spectral loss component is crucial to obtain the INRs of sufficient quality, as using only standard reconstruction loss in the time domain leads to the network collapsing to trivial solutions such as uniform noise or silence. Additionally, we notice that our method tends to overfit the training dataset and find that in order to make hypernetwork generalize to the unseen data we have to introduce random data augmentations to the training process.

### 3.4    Optimization for Audio Reconstruction

We train the hypernetwork in a supervised fashion using backpropagation. To obtain audio results that are more perceptually pleasant, we use a loss function that penalizes the reconstruction error both in time and frequency domains. Given an original recording $x$ and its reconstruction $\hat{x}$ generated with a target network, we compute the loss function as:

$$L(x, \hat{x}) = \lambda_t L_t(x, \hat{x}) + \lambda_f L_f(x, \hat{x}), \tag{4}$$

**Table 1.** Comparison of different variants of computing target network pre-activation layer output.

| Network type | Instance-specific weights | Shared weights | Pre-activation layer output |
|---|---|---|---|
| standard | all layers | none | $y_i = x(W_i^h)^T + b_i^h$ |
| additive | all layers | all layers | $y_i = x(W_i^s + W_i^h)^T + b_i^s + b_i^h$ |
| multiplicative | all layers | all layers | $y_i = x(W_i^s \cdot W_i^h)^T + b_i^s \cdot b_i^h$ |
| shared | some layers | some layers | $y_i = \begin{cases} x(W_i^s)^T + b_i^s, & \text{if layer shared} \\ x(W_i^h)^T + b_i^h, & \text{otherwise} \end{cases}$ |

where $L_t$ is the L1 loss in time domain and $L_f$ is a multi-resolution mel-scale STFT loss in frequency domain as introduced in ParallelWaveGAN [40]. We use coefficients $\lambda_t$ and $\lambda_f$ to control the tradeoff between both losses.

For the STFT loss, we use 128 mel bins and FFT sizes of 2048, 1024, 512, 256, 128 with matching window sizes and an overlap of 75%. We set $\lambda_t = 1$ and $\lambda_f = 1$. Using both loss functions together allows us to optimize both quantitative metrics through L1 part of the loss and the perceptual quality of generated audio through the STFT part. We base this intuition on results from [10], which show that the FFT loss is crucial for learning INRs for time series.

Neural networks are naturally biased towards low-frequency features, and we notice that the target networks obtained with HyperSound suffer from the same problem. Therefore, in some experiments we modify the STFT loss by frequency-weighting the Fourier transforms of $x$ and $\hat{x}$. We compute the weightings $w_{f_i}$ for frequency bins $f_1, f_2, ..., f_N$ as:

$$w_{f_i} = \frac{N \cdot i^p}{\sum_{j=0}^{N} j^p}, \tag{5}$$

where $N$ is the number of frequency bins and $p \geq 0$ is a parameter that allows us to control the uniformity of this weighting. The weights are normalized so that they always sum to $N$, and the minimum value of $p$ yields a uniform weighting (no bias towards high frequencies). During training, we gradually move from uniform weighting to target weighting in 500 epochs.

## 3.5 Alternative Ways to Leverage Hypernetworks for INR Generation

In the standard variant of our framework, the hypernetwork generates weights and biases for target network layers and other parameters, such as frequencies of positional encoding in FMLP or $\omega_i$ in SIREN, remain fixed. However, we also consider learning a shared, generic set of weights and biases for target network layers and combining them with instance-specific weights and biases generated by the hypernetwork in other ways. We refer to the three variants of target networks explored in our work as shared, additive and multiplicative. We show a comparison of all the approaches in Table 1.

With a shared variant of the target network, we explicitly learn a shared set of weights $W_i^s$ and biases $b_i^s$ for some layers, and use the hypernetwork only for generating instance-specific weights $W_i^h$ and biases $b_i^h$ for the remaining layers. Target networks' outputs are then computed using either shared or instance-specific set of weights, depending on the layer.

In the additive and multiplicative variants of the target network, for each layer $i$ we explicitly learn shared weights $W_i^s$ and biases $b_i^s$. The hypernetwork learns to generate separate, instance-specific, weights $W_i^h$ and biases $b_i^h$. Both sets of weights and biases are then either added or multiplied and the results are used to compute layer output.

### 3.6   Hypernetwork Weight Initialization

Hypernetworks are very sensitive to the learning rate and require careful weight initialization to ensure stable learning. Xavier [11] or Kaiming [13] weight initializations typically used for deep neural networks are insufficient for hypernetworks, as we want to achieve the corresponding initial distribution of generated weights, but we can affect it only through the weights of the hypernetwork. To solve this issue, [4] propose hypernetwork weight initialization scheme which leads to the initial target network weights following the distribution given by either Xavier or Kaiming initialization. We adopt this process for our FMLP network, but find it insufficient for SIREN networks, as they require specific initialization described by [30]. Therefore, to simulate SIREN initialization in the initial stage of training, we set the starting weights for the last layer of the hypernetwork according to uniform distribution with boundaries close to zero. and set the distribution of biases to the one proposed in the SIREN paper. This makes the frequencies in the subsequent target network layers grow slowly in the initial stages of network training, which is crucial to stable learning with periodic activation functions.

## 4   Experiments

### 4.1   Setting

For most experiments, unless explicitly stated otherwise, we use the VCTK dataset downsampled to $f = 22\,050\,\text{Hz}$, with recording length set to 32 768 samples, which is around 1.5 seconds. We obtain inputs by cropping the original audio to the desired length. We use the recordings of the last 10 speakers in the VCTK dataset as a validation set. We set batch size to for all the models to 16, and train each model for 2500 epochs with 10 000 training samples per epoch. We use a OneCycleLR [32] optimizer, varying learning rate depending on the target network model type, as we observe that SIREN networks require smaller learning rates to maintain stability during training.

During the evaluation, we focus on the quality of reconstructions obtained with target networks. Example of these reconstructions can be seen in Fig. 3.

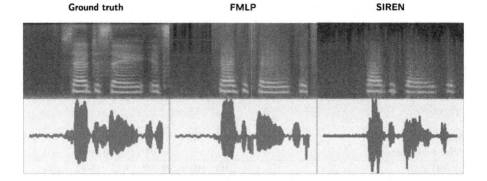

**Fig. 3.** Example of VCTK validation sample reconstructed with HyperSound.

Since there is no consensus on a single approach for the quantitative evaluation of audio quality, we assess the reconstruction results with multiple metrics. We use quantitative metrics such as MSE, Log-Spectral Distance (LSD) [18] and SI-SNR [19]. However, since these metrics do not fully capture the perceptual quality of the audio signal, we also include metrics such as PESQ [29], STOI [35] and CDPAM [20] to approximately measure how well the reconstructed signal sounds to the human ear.

Unless explicitly mentioned otherwise, all the network hyperparameters are set as described in Sect. 3. For training all of the hypernetworks, we use the same data augmentations as in RAVE[2], i.e. random crop, phase mangle, and dequantization.

## 4.2  Reconstruction Quality with FMLP Target Network

We measure the quality of reconstructions obtained on the VCTK dataset with HyperSound using different variants of the target network. We compare the quality of reconstructions with the state-of-the-art RAVE [2] autoencoder retrained with sampling rate of 22 050 Hz. We use the same set of data augmentations for training both RAVE and HyperSound, and train RAVE for $3 \times 10^6$ steps.

We consider multiple variants of target networks that match the desired compression ratio (measured as a ratio between the number of samples in the input recording and the number of target network parameters). We set the hypernetwork learning rate to $10^{-4}$ and use the AdamW optimizer. All target networks use five hidden dense layers with biases, and we set the width of each hidden layer to an equal value, so that we obtain the desired compression ratio. We explore more realistic scenarios with compression ratios above $1\times$, but also include the results for target networks with higher parameter counts as an insight into the representational capacities of over-parameterized networks.

We show the results for RAVE in Table 2a, and for our method with FMLP target network Table 2b. The results show that, while over-parameterization of the target network is beneficial for the reconstruction quality, the experiments

**Table 2.** HyperSound reconstruction error on the VCTK validation set compared with other methods. a) We compare our method with the state-of-the-art reconstruction model RAVE. b) We test different variants of the FMLP target network with different sizes as measured by the compression ratio (CR). c) We compare the reconstruction error obtained with SIREN target networks of size equal to FMLP with CR 1 and various values of $\omega_i$ and $\omega_0$. d) We also show the upper bound of INR reconstruction obtained by training a single model for each data point, using both FMLP and SIREN networks.

| Model | | | MSE | LSD | SI-SNR | PESQ | STOI | CDPAM |
|---|---|---|---|---|---|---|---|---|
| *Ideal metric behavior:* | | | $\to 0$ | $\to 0$ | $\to 100$ | $\to 4.5$ | $\to 1$ | $\to 0$ |
| a) *RAVE* [2] | | | 0.049 | 0.99 | -23.50 | 1.75 | 0.87 | 0.35 |
| b) *HyperSound FMLP* | **CR** | | | | | | | |
| | 10× | | 0.013 | 1.80 | -0.25 | 1.14 | 0.71 | 0.43 |
| | 4× | | 0.011 | 1.80 | 1.27 | 1.17 | 0.73 | 0.42 |
| | 2× | | 0.011 | 1.73 | 2.74 | 1.21 | 0.75 | 0.38 |
| | 1× | | 0.009 | 1.61 | 2.99 | 1.27 | 0.76 | 0.36 |
| | 0.5× | | 0.009 | 1.53 | 4.13 | 1.34 | 0.78 | **0.30** |
| | 0.125× | | **0.007** | **1.50** | **4.48** | **1.42** | **0.80** | **0.30** |
| c) *HyperSound SIREN* | $\omega_0$ | $\omega_i$ | | | | | | |
| | 30 | 30 | 0.020 | 4.14 | -4.82 | 1.18 | 0.66 | 0.39 |
| | 100 | 30 | **0.018** | 3.56 | **-3.66** | **1.19** | 0.65 | 0.38 |
| | 500 | 30 | 0.033 | 2.52 | -17.59 | 1.18 | 0.65 | **0.31** |
| | 1000 | 30 | 0.036 | 2.50 | -22.63 | **1.19** | 0.66 | 0.32 |
| | 2000 | 30 | 0.037 | 2.59 | -23.93 | **1.19** | **0.67** | 0.32 |
| | 2000 | 100 | 0.036 | **1.63** | -22.11 | 1.18 | **0.67** | 0.36 |
| d) *Individual INRs (upper bound)* | **Model** | | | | | | | |
| | FMLP | | 0.001 | 1.39 | 17.19 | 2.31 | 0.95 | 0.23 |
| | SIREN | | <0.001 | 1.40 | 27.53 | 3.05 | 0.97 | 0.28 |

with smaller target networks still obtain passable scores across all metrics. We also notice that our method outperforms RAVE in pure reconstruction metrics across all selected target network sizes, but obtains worse scores on metrics that measure spectral distance and perceptual quality.

## 4.3   Training SIREN Target Networks

Despite [1] showing a close relationship between SIREN and FMLP INRs, we observe that they behave very differently during training when compared to FMLP networks. First, we notice that without the hand-crafted hypernetwork weight initialization, as described in Sect. 3.3, SIREN networks fail to learn any meaningful signal. Additionally, we notice that SIRENs require significantly slower learning rates to converge, and we use a learning rate of $10^{-6}$ (1/100 the learning rate we use in FMLP networks). We would like to use high values of $\omega_0$ and $\omega_i$, which improve the network's capability to represent high frequencies,

**Table 3.** Comparison of different methods of generating INRs with hypernetworks described in Sect. 3.5. We notice that sharing initial layers of the target network is beneficial to reconstruction quality while making the effective size of both hypernetwork and target network smaller.

| model type | MSE | LSD | SI-SNR |
|---|---|---|---|
| *standard* | 0.009 | 1.61 | 2.99 |
| *multiplicative* | 0.009 | 1.61 | 2.77 |
| *additive* | **0.008** | **1.52** | 2.98 |
| *first layer shared* | **0.008** | 1.58 | **3.67** |
| *first two layers shared* | **0.008** | 1.60 | 3.44 |

but increasing those values makes training the network very unstable and often prevents convergence to any meaningful solution altogether.

Table 2c shows the results obtained for SIREN networks with different values of $\omega_0$ and $\omega_i$. We use network architecture corresponding to the FMLP model with a compression ratio of 1×. Increasing the frequencies $\omega_0$ and $\omega_i$ slightly improves the perceptual quality of the reconstructions, but makes the training process less stable. In further experiments, we focus on FMLP networks, as they produce better results and are easier to train.

### 4.4   Upper Bound of the INR Reconstruction Quality

We compute our metrics for SIREN and FMLP INRs trained in vanilla fashion to get an upper bound for reconstruction error. We select a subset of the validation data, train a model for each example minimizing the mean squared reconstruction error and report the mean metric values as an upper bound for HyperSound. We only use a subset of the validation dataset, as the mean of the metrics quickly stabilises after several recordings. We use basic variants of the FMLP and SIREN networks ($\omega_0 = 2000$, $\omega_i = 30$), with parameters other than layer weights and biases set at fixed values as described in Sect. 3.1 and the basic model size as described in previous Sections.

The comparison of our results is described in Table 2d. Unsurprisingly, vanilla INRs achieve significantly better quality compared to our method and RAVE. Contrary to results for HyperSound, SIREN INRs seem to work better than FMLP models when optimized directly for a single signal. We hypothesise that this can be explained by the increased complexity of hypernetwork optimization and ReLU nonlinearity being more robust to weight perturbations.

### 4.5   Exploring Different Ways to Use Weights Generated by the Hypernetwork

We explore possible extensions of the hypernetwork framework for INR generation, comparing three approaches described in Sect. 3.5 with the standard variant

**Table 4.** Impact of the frequency weighting. A higher value of $p$ indicates a stronger bias towards high frequencies in loss function, while $p = 0$ equals no weighting. Our results indicate that focusing on high-frequency content in signals leads to better reconstructions.

| p | MSE | LSD | SI-SNR |
|---|---|---|---|
| *0.0 [baseline]* | 0.009 | 1.61 | 2.99 |
| *0.2* | 0.008 | 1.50 | 3.38 |
| *0.5* | 0.008 | 1.57 | 3.09 |
| *1.0* | **0.007** | **1.48** | **3.60** |

**Table 5.** Comparison of HyperSound reconstruction quality on different datasets. Our method still performs reasonably well on datasets other than VCTK, without any additional hyperparameter tuning.

| Dataset | MSE | LSD | SI-SNR |
|---|---|---|---|
| *VCTK* | 0.009 | 1.61 | 2.99 |
| *LJ Speech* | 0.014 | 1.65 | −1.08 |
| *LibriSpeech* | 0.011 | 2.15 | 0.89 |

of the target network. We conduct experiments using the network architecture corresponding to the FMLP with compression ratio 1× from Sect. 4.2.

The results of our experiments are described in Table 3. We notice that learning a shared set of weights for the first layer in the target network leads to better results than in the case of the standard model, but sharing more than one layer is not beneficial. Sharing weights of the first layer can be thought of as learning a shared feature extractor for smaller hypernetwork and target network models, which means that effectively we reduce the computational cost of the method and provide more compressed representations. Other variants such as multiplicative and additive do not improve the results noticeably while inducing additional computational cost due to the added complexity.

### 4.6    Higher-Frequency Weighting in the Loss Function

We notice that our solution tends to produce representations that focus on lower frequencies, which lowers the perceptual quality of the reconstructions. We aim to improve this quality by assigning higher weights to the higher frequencies in the STFT loss, as described in Sect. 3.4. As shown in Table 4, this simple modification improves the reconstruction quality of the model, which indicates that audio processing can greatly benefit from domain-specific loss functions.

### 4.7    Results on Other Datasets

In our experiments, we focus on the VCTK dataset, as most publicly available audio datasets are either small, include data that does not match our sampling rate or input length requirements, or only include data from a single source or speaker. However, training hypernetworks requires large and diverse datasets and benefits from data augmentations, which are harder to apply in a reasonable way to music or environmental sound datasets. Therefore, we evaluate HyperSound reconstruction quality on additional speech datasets, i.e., LJ Speech and LibriSpeech *train-clean-360* datasets. We present the results of this evaluation

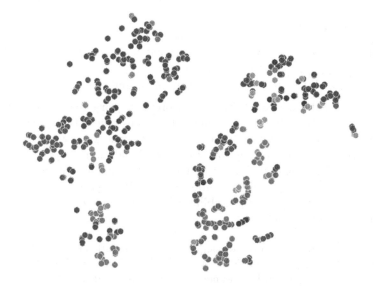

**Fig. 4.** t-SNE visualisation of the INR weights obtained on VCTK validation set. Different colors of the dots indicate different speakers. Speakers are generally clustered, and we notice a clear separation of the male and female recordings.

in Table 5, showing that HyperSound still achieves reasonable results despite no additional dataset-specific hyperparameter tuning apart from learning rate reduction for LibriSpeech.

### 4.8   Representational Capability of INRs

Finally, we conduct a simple experiment visualizing the weights of the INRs obtained on the validation set of VCTK with t-SNE [38] and show the results in Fig. 4. We group the INRs by speaker identity, as its the best-defined criterion to distinguish between recordings in the dataset. We notice that different speakers occupy distinct regions in the t-SNE subspace, with a clear separation between recordings of male and female speech. This proves that representations produced by HyperSound capture the underlying structure of the data.

## 5   Conclusions

We propose the first method of obtaining generalizable Implicit Neural Representations for audio signals, named HyperSound. We adapt the hypernetwork framework to audio processing through domain-specific modifications and demonstrate that our model performs reasonably well on the VCTK dataset, producing reconstructions quantitatively comparable to the state-of-the-art RAVE autoencoder. We investigate the use of SIREN and Fourier-mapped perceptron networks as INRs generated by the hypernetwork and try alternative ways of applying hypernetworks in the INR generation, which improve upon the standard method. INRs produced by our method can represent the signal in compressed way, using less weights than the number of samples in the original recording. Additionally, we demonstrate that our method performs reasonably across different datasets with minimal hyperparameter tuning and that the representations produced by the method align with the underlying structure of the data.

**Limitations and Future Work.** As theoretical guarantees of hypernetwork training are hard to define, we find our method sensitive to the hyperparameter choice and its training requires a lot of trial and error. Moreover, the misalignment between the human perception of the sound and metrics optimized in deep neural networks means that the perceptual quality of reconstructions generated with our method leaves room for improvement. We hope that further work in those directions can improve the stability of our method and better calibrate the results to human perception.

**Acknowledgements.** This work was supported by Foundation for Polish Science with Grant No POIR.04.04.00-00-14DE/18-00 carried out within the Team-Net program co-financed by the European Union under the European Regional Development Fund, and by the National Centre of Science (Poland) Grant No. 2020/39/B/ST6/01511. Filip Szatkowski and Tomasz Trzcinski are supported by National Centre of Science (Poland) Grant No. 2022/45/B/ST6/02817. Przemysław Spurek is supported by the National Centre of Science (Poland) Grant No. 2021/43/B/ST6/01456. Jacek Tabor research has been supported by a grant from the Priority Research Area DigiWorld under the Strategic Programme Excellence Initiative at Jagiellonian University.

**Ethical Statement.** This paper belongs to the line of fundamental research and all the experiments in this paper were performed using publicly available data. However, we acknowledge that there are potential ethical implications of our work that need to be considered.

As with all machine learning models, biases from the training data can be encoded into the model, leading to inaccurate or discriminatory behavior towards underrepresented groups.

Furthermore, the data reconstructed with Implicit Neural Representations always contains some degree of error, and models trained with different hyperparameters can produce varying representations. These properties make INRs a potential tool to evade copyright detection, and current detection algorithms are not equipped to work on data stored as INR weights, further compounding the issue.

# References

1. Benbarka, N., et al.: Seeing implicit neural representations as fourier series. In: Proceedings of the IEEE/CVF Winter Conference on Applications of Computer Vision (WACV), pp. 2041–2050 (Jan 2022)
2. Caillon, A., Esling, P.: RAVE: A variational autoencoder for fast and high-quality neural audio synthesis. arXiv: 2111.05011 (2021)
3. Chan, E.R., et al.: PI-GAN: periodic implicit generative adversarial networks for 3d-aware image synthesis. In: Proceedings of the IEEE/CVF conference on Computer Vision and Pattern Recognition, pp. 5799–5809 (2021)

4. Chang, O., Flokas, L., Lipson, H.: Principled weight initialization for hypernetworks. In: International Conference on Learning Representations (2019)

5. Chen, Y., Wang, X.: Transformers as meta-learners for implicit neural representations. In: Computer Vision-ECCV 2022: 17th European Conference, Tel Aviv, Israel, October 23–27, 2022, Proceedings, Part XVII, pp. 170–187. Springer (2022). https://doi.org/10.1007/978-3-031-19790-1_11

6. Clevert, D.-A., Unterthiner, T., Hochreiter, S.: Fast and Accurate Deep Network Learning by Exponential Linear Units (ELUs). arXiv preprint arXiv:1511.07289 (2015)

7. Défossez, A., et al.: SING: symbol-to-instrument neural generator. In: Advances in Neural Information Processing Systems 31 (2018)

8. Dupont, E., et al.: From data to functa: Your data point is a function and you should treat it like one. arXiv preprint arXiv:2201.12204 (2022)

9. Engel, J., et al.: Neural audio synthesis of musical notes with wavenet autoencoders. In: International Conference on Machine Learning, pp. 1068–1077. PMLR (2017)

10. Fons, E., et al.: HyperTime: Implicit Neural Representation for Time Series. arXiv preprint arXiv:2208.05836 (2022)

11. Glorot, X., Bengio, Y.: Understanding the difficulty of training deep feedforward neural networks. In: Proceedings of the Thirteenth International Conference on Artificial Intelligence and Statistics. JMLR Workshop and Conference Proceedings, pp. 249–256 (2010)

12. Ha, D., Dai, A., Le, Q.V.: HyperNetworks. arXiv preprint arXiv:1609.09106 (2016)

13. He, K., et al.: Delving deep into rectifiers: surpassing human-level performance on imagenet classification. In: Proceedings of the IEEE International Conference on Computer Vision, pp. 1026–1034 (2015)

14. Kania, A., et al.: Hypernerfgan: Hypernetwork approach to 3d nerf gan. arXiv preprint arXiv:2301.11631 (2023)

15. Karras, T., et al.: Progressive Growing of GANs for Improved Quality, Stability, And Variation. In: International Conference on Learning Representations (2018)

16. Klocek, S., Maziarka, Ł, Wołczyk, M., Tabor, J., Nowak, J., Śmieja, M.: Hypernetwork functional image representation. In: Tetko, I.V., Kůrková, V., Karpov, P., Theis, F. (eds.) ICANN 2019. LNCS, vol. 11731, pp. 496–510. Springer, Cham (2019). https://doi.org/10.1007/978-3-030-30493-5_48

17. Kumar, K., et al.: MelGAN: generative adversarial networks for conditional waveform synthesis. In: Advances in Neural Information Processing Systems 32 (2019)

18. Liu, H., et al.: Neural Vocoder is All You Need for Speech Superresolution. arXiv preprint arXiv:2203.14941 (2022)

19. Luo, Y., Mesgarani, N.: TasNet: time-domain audio separation network for realtime, single-channel speech separation. In: 2018 IEEE International Conference on Acoustics, Speech and Signal Processing (ICASSP), pp. 696–700. IEEE (2018)

20. Manocha, P., et al.: CDPAM: contrastive learning for perceptual audio similarity. In: ICASSP 2021–2021 IEEE International Conference on Acoustics, Speech and Signal Processing (ICASSP), pp. 196–200. IEEE (2021)

21. Mehri, S., et al.: SampleRNN: An Unconditional End-to-End Neural Audio Generation Model. arXiv preprint arXiv:1612.07837 (2016)

22. Mehta, I., et al.: Modulated periodic activations for generalizable local functional representations. In: Proceedings of the IEEE/CVF International Conference on Computer Vision, pp. 14214–14223 (2021)

23. Mildenhall, B., et al.: NeRF: representing scenes as neural radiance fields for view synthesis. Commun. ACM **65**(1), 99–106 (2021)

24. Müller, N., et al.: DiffRF: Rendering-Guided 3D Radiance Field Diffusion. arXiv preprint arXiv:2212.01206 (2022)
25. Oord, A., et al.: Parallel WaveNet: fast high-fidelity speech synthesis. In: International Conference on Machine Learning, pp. 3918–3926. PMLR (2018)
26. van den Oord, A., et al.: WaveNet: A Generative Model for Raw Audio. arXiv preprint arXiv:1609.03499 (2016)
27. Purwins, H., et al.: Deep learning for audio signal processing. IEEE J. Selected Topics Signal Process. **13**(2), 206–219 (2019)
28. Rahaman, N., et al.: On the spectral bias of neural networks. In: International Conference on Machine Learning, pp. 5301–5310. PMLR (2019)
29. Rix, A.W., et al.: Perceptual evaluation of speech quality (PESQ)-a new method for speech quality assessment of telephone networks and codecs. In: 2001 IEEE International Conference on Acoustics, Speech, and Signal Processing, Proceedings (Cat. No. 01CH37221), vol. 2, pp. 749–752. IEEE (2001)
30. Sitzmann, V., et al.: Implicit neural representations with periodic activation functions. Adv. Neural. Inf. Process. Syst. **33**, 7462–7473 (2020)
31. Sitzmann, V., et al.: Metasdf: Meta-learning signed distance functions. Adv. Neural. Inf. Process. Syst. **33**, 10136–10147 (2020)
32. Smith, L.N., Topin, N.: Super-convergence: very fast training of neural networks using large learning rates. In: Artificial Intelligence and Machine Learning for Multi-domain Operations Applications, vol. 11006, pp. 369–386. SPIE (2019)
33. Spurek, P., et al.: Hypernetwork approach to generating point clouds. In: Proceedings of Machine Learning Research, vol. 119 (2020)
34. Strümpler, Y., et al.: Implicit neural representations for image compression. In: Computer Vision-ECCV 2022: 17th European Conference, Tel Aviv, Israel, 23–27 October 2022, Proceedings, Part XXVI, pp. 74–91. Springer (2022). https://doi.org/10.1007/978-3-031-19809-0_5
35. Taal, C.H., et al.: A short-time objective intelligibility measure for time frequency weighted noisy speech. In: 2010 IEEE International Conference on Acoustics, Speech and Signal Processing, pp. 4214–4217. IEEE (2010)
36. Tabor, J., Trzciński, T., et al.: Hyperpocket: generative point cloud completion. In: 2022 IEEE/RSJ International Conference on Intelligent Robots and Systems (IROS), pp. 6848–6853. IEEE (2022)
37. Tancik, M., et al.: Fourier features let networks learn high frequency functions in low dimensional domains. Adv. Neural. Inf. Process. Syst. **33**, 7537–7547 (2020)
38. Van der Maaten, L., Hinton, G.: Visualizing data using t-SNE. J. Mach. Learn. Res. **9**(11) (2008)
39. Von Oswald, J., et al.: Continual learning with hypernetworks. arXiv preprint arXiv:1906.00695 (2019)
40. Yamamoto, R., Song, E., Kim, J.-M.: Parallel WaveGAN: a fast waveform generation model based on generative adversarial networks with multi-resolution spectrogram. In: ICASSP 2020–2020 IEEE International Conference on Acoustics, Speech and Signal Processing (ICASSP), pp. 6199–6203. IEEE (2020)
41. Zeghidour, N., et al.: SoundStream: an end-to-end neural audio codec. IEEE/ACM Trans. Audio, Speech Lang. Process. **30**, 495–507 (2021)
42. Zhao, D., et al.: Meta-Learning via Hypernetworks (2020)
43. Zimny, D., Trzciński, T., Spurek, P.: Points2NeRF: Generating Neural Radiance Fields from 3D point cloud. arXiv preprint arXiv:2206.01290 (2022)
44. Zuiderveld, J., Federici, M., Bekkers, E.J.: Towards Lightweight Controllable Audio Synthesis with Conditional Implicit Neural Representations. arXiv preprint arXiv:2111.08462 (2021)

# Contrastive Representation Through Angle and Distance Based Loss for Partial Label Learning

Priyanka Chudasama[⊠], Tushar Kadam, Rajat Patel, Aakarsh Malhotra, and Manoj Magam

AI Garage, Mastercard, India
{priyanka.chudasama,tushar.kadam,rajat.patel,aakarsh.malhotra, manoj.mangam}@mastercard.com

**Abstract.** Partial label learning (PLL) is a form of weakly supervised learning which aims to train a deep network from training instances and its corresponding label set. The label set, also known as the candidate set, is a group of labels associated with each training instance, out of which only one label is the ground truth for the training instance. Contrastive learning is one of the popular techniques used to learn from a partially labeled dataset, intending to reduce intra-class while maximizing inter-class distance. In this paper, we suggest improving the contrastive technique used in PiCO. The proposed **C**ontrastive **R**epresentation via **A**ngle and **D**istance based **L**oss (CRADL) segregates the contrastive loss into two parts, the angle based loss and the distance based loss. The former angle based loss covers the angular separation between two contrastive vectors. However, we showcase a scenario where such angular loss prefers one contrastive vector over the other despite having the same angle. Thus, the second loss term built on distance fixes the issue. We show experiments on CIFAR-10 and CIFAR-100, where the corresponding PLL databases are generated using uniform noise. The experiments show that the PLL algorithms learn better using the proposed CRADL-based learning and generate distinguishing representations, as observed by compact cluster formation with CRADL. This eventually results in CRADL outperforming the current state-of-the-art studies in PLL setup at different uniform noise rates.

**Keywords:** Partial label learning · Contrastive representation learning

## 1 Introduction

Modern deep networks have seen tremendous growth in the past decade. Most of these networks require a large amount of labeled data, becoming a significant obstacle to training them efficiently. Various weakly supervised learning [35] algorithms have been widely studied in recent years to tackle this challenge. For instance, such weakly supervised include semi-supervised learning [24], positive

D. Koutra et al. (Eds.): ECML PKDD 2023, LNAI 14172, pp. 677–692, 2023.
https://doi.org/10.1007/978-3-031-43421-1_40

unlabelled learning [22], learning with noisy labels [10], and partial label learning [12]. Partial Label Learning (PLL) focuses on scenarios where each instance of the dataset can have more than one label, of which only one is correct. Such scenarios naturally arise in various real-world applications, such as web mining [17], multimedia content analysis [32], and automatic image annotations [2]. PLL setup is also common and practical in scenarios of low-cost annotations, as required when labeling datasets in crowd-sourcing [1,19,20].

The ground-truth label of an instance is part of the candidate label set along with other noisy labels. Hence, during training, the ground truth label is not available. In literature, this challenge is tackled by identification-based label disambiguation. Here, the ground truth label is treated as a latent variable, and the actual label is identified based on confidence estimates on the candidate label set [6,30,31]. In many of these existing methods, error accumulation may arise due to inaccurate predictions in the early stages of training. Further, they are restricted to linear or kernel-based methods and can have considerable drawbacks while scaling to large datasets or high-dimensional features.

Recently, PLL has drawn the attention of deep learning researchers due to explosive growth in deep neural networks. PLL algorithms have particularly shown value when learning from labels from multiple sources, intending to learn to classify despite ambiguous labels. For instance, Feng et al. [8] proposed two risk and classifier consistency methods. Similarly, a classification risk estimator is proposed in Proden [18], which is minimized for progressive label disambiguation. Valen [29] assumes Dirichlet density for latent label distribution and uses a variational inference technique to arrive at the true posterior distribution for labels. These methods significantly improve over the baseline average-based label disambiguation strategy, where candidate labels are given equal weight. However, there is scope for improvement in utilizing feature representations more effectively, based on developments in representation learning [3,11,15,36].

More recently, PiCO [25] navigated the PLL setup using contrastive representation learning and class-prototype-based label disambiguation. It produces closely aligned representations for instances of the same class based on an adaptation of supervised contrastive learning [15] for PLL setup, producing better label disambiguation. The modified N-pair loss [21] term used in PiCO aims to reduce the inter-class similarity and increase the intra-class similarity in feature representation space. However, the chosen similarity metric is imbalanced for two instances equidistant and forming the same angle from another sample of the same class cluster. Indicating that this imbalanced loss can be improved for better aligned and compact clusters.

Hence, we propose Contrastive Representation via Angle and distance based Loss (CRADL) in this research. The proposed CRADL algorithm segregates the contrastive loss into angle based and distance based loss. The angle based loss focuses on the angular separation of instances by reducing intra-class angular separation and increasing inter-class angular separation. On the other hand, the distance based loss handles Euclidean distance separation. The loss terms are balanced in angular separation and distance, respectively. We show that the clusters formed are more compact and well-separated than the imbalanced loss. With more closely aligned representations for the same class and increased inter-class cluster separation, better class prototypes are produced along with less noisy predictions.

We also compare our proposed algorithm with the current state-of-the-art method for uniform partial label noise introduced by Wu et al. in [27]. Wu et al. introduce a regularisation term to match the output of multiple augmentations of an instance to a conformal label distribution. Framing it as a bi-level optimization problem, they achieve state-of-the-art results for uniform partial label noise. We show that CRADL performs better label disambiguation, reflecting improvement over state-of-the-art results and further narrowing the gap with the fully supervised counterpart.

The rest of this paper is organized as follows. We review related work in Sect. 2, and show the motivation of the CRADL in Sect. 3. The proposed method is introduced in Sect. 4; Sect. 5 presents the experimental setup, followed by the results and analysis in Sect. 6.

## 2 Background and Problem Formulation

### 2.1 Partial Label Learning (PLL): Notation and Preliminaries

Suppose we have a training dataset $\mathcal{D} := \{\mathcal{X}, Y_\mathcal{X}\}$. The dataset $\mathcal{D}$ consists of $n$ training pairs of d-dimensional instances $x \in \mathcal{X}$ and its corresponding partial label candidate set $y_x^p \in Y_\mathcal{X}$. The candidate (label) set, also known as the partial label, $y_x^p \subset L := \{1, 2, \ldots, c\}$ consists of ground truth label $y \in y_x^p$ along with remaining noisy labels $\overline{y} \in y_x^p \backslash \{y\}$. Here, $c$ is the total number of distinct classes present in the dataset. Hence, in a PLL setting, each instance has one ground truth label $y$ along with another set of incorrect labels $\overline{y}$. The aim is to learn the class properties using the pairs $(x, y_x^p) \in (\mathcal{X}, Y_\mathcal{X})$.

### 2.2 Literature Review

The difficulty in PLL comes from multiple labels for each instance. A similar challenging domain is learning from labeled and unlabeled data together. However, in PLL, only a subset of labels are candidates for target labels. This constraint makes it possible to develop a discriminative approach. The domain of PLL was pioneered by Jin et al. [13]. They formulated this problem as an unconstrained learning objective to minimize the KL divergence between the class prior and the model-based conditional distribution and solved it using the EM algorithm. It resulted in a procedure iterating between estimating the prior distribution and training the model.

The literature in PLL can be broadly categorized into either an average-based approach [4,12] or an identification-based approach for label disambiguation. The average-based method treats all candidate labels equally and averages the modeling outputs as the prediction. There are average-based approaches [4,12] where average model outputs of candidate labels are distinguished from the average model outputs of non-candidate labels.

In identification-based approaches [6,28,33], confidence estimates are derived for each label to narrow down on the correct label instead of giving all candidate labels equal weight. In this domain, Valen [29] method works in the space of instance-wise noise. It aims to recover the latent label distribution of the candidate label set by assuming Dirichlet density for latent label distribution and uses variational inference to arrive at the true posterior distribution for labels. PRODEN [18] proposed a novel classifier-consistent estimator and established an estimation error bound. They also presented a progressive identification algorithm for approximately minimizing the proposed risk estimator, where the model update and identification of true labels are conducted seamlessly. However, in many of these works, the inherent label uncertainty in PLL can undesirably manifest in the model features which in turn, prevents effective label disambiguation.

Unsupervised representation learning has been widely studied in recent years. For images, there has been effort [3,11,14] for generating better representations that can be fine-tuned for downstream tasks. Contrastive representation learning is one such way, where the effectiveness of the embedding is measured by how well it distinguishes between comparable (positive views) and dissimilar (negative views) samples. Contrastive learning techniques offer a straightforward yet effective strategy for learning representations in a discriminative way in both supervised and self-supervised settings. PiCO [25] uses unsupervised representation learning in the PLL setup for learning better embedding. They modify popular N-pair contrastive loss [21]) for a PLL setup. Their work produces closely aligned representations for examples from the same classes, facilitating better label disambiguation.

For a given instance, the modified N-pair loss contrasts its embedding against positive and negative embedding set as:

$$\mathcal{L}_{cont}(q_x, B, \Psi(x)) = \frac{-1}{|\Psi(x)|} \sum_{k_{x+} \in \Psi(x)} log \frac{exp\left(q_x^T k_{x+}\right)}{\sum\limits_{k_{x'} \in B \setminus \{q_x\}} exp\left(q_x^T k_{x'}\right)}, \tag{1}$$

where $q_x$ is embedding vector for instance $x$ and $B$ represents the entire batch's embedding. $\Psi(x)$ represents the embeddings of positive set for instance x.

Before feeding the embedding vectors in contrastive loss, we observed that all the representation vectors are $\mathcal{L}_2$ normalized instance-wise or $\mathcal{L}_2$ normalized dimension-wise. In the first instance-wise normalization scenario, not all embedding vectors are of the unit norm. That is, the length of the vector, and for each $q_x$, the angle it makes with the rest of the embedding vectors becomes significant through the contrastive loss. On the contrary, in the second scenario, each embedding vector has a unit norm. Hence, for two similar vectors, the contrastive loss will depend only on the angle between them. In contrast, the embedding vectors' actual positioning (length) around $x$ is not considered. We observe that contrastive loss could be improved in the first case, and using contrastive loss after normalizing all embeddings to the unit norm is not the best way around. We have explained in detail about problems mentioned above in the next section.

## 3   Motivation for Proposing CRADL Algorithm

We first analyze N-pair based contrastive loss [21], as used in PiCO. For each instance $x$, N-pair contrastive loss function uses the inner product to contrast between embedding of $x$ against positive and negative embeddings set of $x$ as:

$$\mathcal{L}_{cont}(g, \tau, A) = \frac{1}{|B_q|} \sum_{q_x \in B_q} \frac{-1}{|\Psi(x)|} \sum_{k_{x+} \in \Psi(x)} \log \frac{exp\left(q_x^T k_{x+}/\tau\right)}{\sum\limits_{k_{x'} \in A \backslash \{q_x\}} exp\left(q_x^T k_{x'}/\tau\right)}. \quad (2)$$

Here, $q_x$ is the feature embedding of $x$ and $\Psi(x)$ is the positive set of $x$ consisting of embeddings of instances in the same class as $x$. Set $A$ consists of all the representations of all the instances in the current mini-batch. It aims to increase intra-class similarity and reduce inter-class similarity.

### 3.1   Theoretical Analysis

In Eq. 2, there are a few challenges with the use of inner-product to contrast embedding vector $q_x$ of $x$ with other embedding vectors. To understand two such cases, let us call the part inside the logarithm of Eq. 2 as:

$$h(q_x, k_{x+}) = \frac{exp\left(q_x^T k_{x+}/\tau\right)}{exp\left(q_x^T k_{x+}/\tau\right) + \sum\limits_{k_{x'} \in A \backslash \{q_x, k_{x+}\}} exp\left(q_x^T k_{x'}/\tau\right)} \quad (3)$$

**Case 1** (refer to Fig. 1): Here, we contrast the embedding vector $q_x$ (referred to as anchor point from now on) with other contrasting vectors, say $k_1$ and $k_2$. As illustrated in Fig. 1, both $k_1$ and $k_2$ make the same angle with the anchor point. Furthermore, the distance of $k_1, k_2$ from $q_x$ is also same ($\|q_x - k_1\|_2 = \|q_x - k_1\|_2$). In such a scenario, they should contribute equally to the loss function and, consequently, to the model's parameter updation. However, without loss of generality, consider that $q_x, k_1$, and $k_2$ belongs to the same class ($\{k_1, k_2\} \subset \Psi(x)$). Using Eq. 3, we get that as $q_x^T k_2 < q_x^T k_1$, consequently implying $h(q_x, k_2) < h(q_x, k_1)$. Subsequently, the contribution of $(q_x, k_1)$ and $(q_x, k_2)$ in the Eq. 2 is different when ideally, it should be the same.

**Case 2** (refer to Fig. 2): Similar to Case 1, here we look at a much broader case. First, let us fix the angle of any contrasting vector with $q_x$, say $\theta$. The nearest contrasting vector to $q_x$ is the one whose line joining $q_x$ makes a right angle, which is $v_0$ in Fig. 2. The contrastive loss uses the most similar and dissimilar contrasting vectors to guide the loss. From the denominator of $h(.)$ in Eq. 3, the most similar vector will be the most confident vector to $q_x$ that can help in

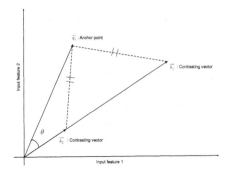

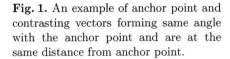

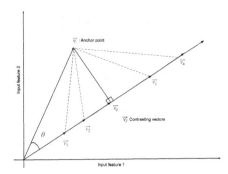

**Fig. 1.** An example of anchor point and contrasting vectors forming same angle with the anchor point and are at the same distance from anchor point.

**Fig. 2.** Example of anchor point and contrasting vectors forming same angle with anchor point. Here, $v_0$ is at the shortest distance from anchor point.

confidently contrasting, as chances of error are lower. Hence, in a PLL scenario with noisy labels alongside the ground truth label, giving higher weightage to $v_0$ can aid in learning better representation space.

Consider vectors $\{v_1, v_2, v_4\} \in \Psi(x)$ in Fig. 2. Since inner products $q_x^T v_1 < q_x^T v_2 < q_x^T v_4$, we will have $h(q_x, v_1) < h(q_x, v_2) < h(q_x, v_4)$. Eventually, in Eq. 2, the pair $(q_x, v_2)$ will have less contribution to inter-class separation in comparison with pair $(q_x, v_1)$ and $(q_x, v_4)$. However, the distance $\|q_x - v_2\|_2 < \|q_x - v_4\|_2$ and thus $v_2$ is a more confident positive pair, so ideally the pair $(q_x, v_2)$ should be weighed more. Thus, the inner product-based loss function 2 is not the ideal contrastive loss.

To solve the issues as pointed out in **case 1** and **case 2**, we introduce Contrastive **R**epresentation via **A**ngle and **D**istance based **L**oss (CRADL). The proposed CRADL consists of two loss functions, where the first term takes care of the angular separation between two contrasting vectors. On the other hand, the second loss term resolves the challenge illustrated in Fig. 1 and 2 using a distance based contrastive loss function.

### 3.2   Angle Based Contrastive Loss

Angle based contrastive loss is the same as the N-pair contrastive loss. Here, we feed in the normalized vectors to contrast with a normalised anchor point. Hence, instead of contrasting $q_x$ with the remainder of the pool $A$, we contrast $q_x/\|q_x\|_2$ with $unit - normalized\{A\}$, which contain unit vector embeddings.

$$\mathcal{L}_a(g, \tau, A) = \frac{1}{|B_q|} \sum_{q_x \in B_q} \frac{-1}{|\Psi(x)|} \sum_{k_x+ \in \Psi(x)} log \frac{exp\left(q_x^T k_x+/\tau \|q_x^T\|_2 \|k_x+\|_2\right)}{\sum\limits_{k_{x'} \in A\backslash\{x\}} exp\left(q_x^T k_{x'}/\tau \|q_x^T\|_2 \|k_{x'}\|_2\right)}.$$

The angle based loss defined above takes care of only the angle between $q_x$ and the remaining vector embeddings in set $A$.

### 3.3 Distance Based Contrastive Loss

To have the same similarity in the **case 1** and give the proper importance in **case 2** (pointed out in Sect. 3.1), we introduce a distance based contrastive loss. Here, we contrast the euclidean distance between $q_x$ and the rest of the embeddings in $A$ with reference to $q_x$. More specifically,

$$\mathcal{L}_d(g, \tau, A) = \frac{1}{|B_q|} \sum_{q_x \in B_q} \frac{-1}{|\Psi(x)|} \sum_{k_{x+} \in \Psi(x)} log \frac{exp\left(-\|q_x - k_{x+}\|_2 / \tau\right)}{\sum_{k_{x'} \in A \setminus \{x\}} exp\left(-\|q_x - k_{x'}\|_2 / \tau\right)}.$$

(4)

Thus, in situations illustrated in Fig. 1, the distance based loss term in the proposed CRADL algorithm will prioritize pairs $(q_x, k_1)$ and $(q_x, k_2)$ equally. Similarly, in Fig. 2, the distance loss term in the proposed CRADL algorithm gives maximum similarity to the pair $sim(q_x, v_0) > sim(q_x, v_2) = sim(q_x, v_3) > sim(q_x, v_1) = (q_x, v_4)$, which the N-pair contrastive loss failed to capture. The negative euclidean distance in the Eq. 4 will help the contrasting vector at shorter distances, which are most confident in a scenario of noisy labels, to contribute more to the inter-class separation.

## 4    Proposed Algorithm: CRADL

In this section, we first describe how to initialize the model's training in PLL setup in Sect. 4.1. In Sect. 4.2 we write the algorithmic details of our proposed method CRADL. Finally, the Sect. 4.3, is about how update related to labels in PLL setup can be done (Fig. 3).

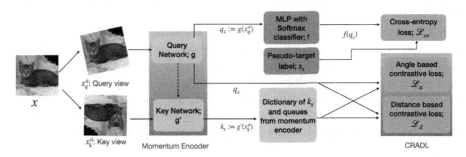

**Fig. 3.** Illustration of a forward pass in CRADL. Query and key views are obtained from two different augmentations of the input image. Cross entropy loss is calculated using pseudo labels and classifier output. CRADL loss is calculated from the query embedding and key dictionary.

### 4.1 Initialization

For each instance $x$ from dataset $\mathcal{D}$, we have a label set $y_x^p \subset L := \{1, 2, \ldots, c\}$, consisting of the ground truth label alongside other noisy labels. Thus, for each sample $x$, we create pseudo target $s_x \in [0,1]^c$, where $c = |L|$ number of distinct labels.

$$s_{x_i} = \begin{cases} 1/|y_x^p|, & \text{if } i \in y_x^p \\ 0 & \text{else} \end{cases} \quad (5)$$

Using $s_x$ we will train a classifier $f : \mathbf{R}^d \rightarrow [0,1]^c$. Lastly, we use cross-entropy loss [34] with the pseudo target defined above.

$$\mathcal{L}_{ce}(f,B) = \sum_{j=1}^{c} -(s_x)_j log(f(q_x)_j). \quad (6)$$

## 4.2   Algorithm

In an ideal scenario, the entire training data should be considered to contrast positive and negative views against a given sample. But given the computational complexity, this is unattainable. Hence, to overcome this challenge, we build upon Momentum Contrast for Unsupervised Visual Representation Learning (MoCo) [11]. MoCo creates a dynamic dictionary with a queue as a moving-average encoder. This results in building a large and consistent dictionary on-the-fly that facilitates better contrastive unsupervised learning.

We first create two augmentations for each sample $x$ to learn in the PLL setup. These augmentations are referred as query view, $x_q^a$, and key view $x_k^a$. These views are then fed to the momentum encoder to generate query representation $q_x = g(x_q^a)$ from the query network $g(.)$ and key representation $k_x = g'(x_k^a)$ from the key network $g'(.)$. Furthermore, we also have access to the queue, which stores the most current key embedding $k$ and is updated chronologically. Thus, we have a set $A$ consisting of queries, keys, and queue embedding to feed into the CRADL as:

$$A = B_q \cup B_k \cup queue, \quad (7)$$

where, $B_q$ and $B_k$ are m-dimensional vector embeddings corresponding to the query and key views of the current mini-batch, $B$. Given an instance $x$, we find per sample angle and distance based contrastive loss by contrasting query embedding $q_x$ with the remainder of the pool $A$. Given set $A$ has keys and queue as well, it gives a broader set to contrast. We define angle based loss (which is similar to N-pair loss [21] if we feed in unit vectors in the contrastive loss) as:

$$\mathcal{L}_a(g,\tau,A) = \frac{1}{|B_q|} \sum_{q_x \in B_q} \frac{-1}{|\Psi(x)|} \sum_{k_{x+} \in \Psi(x)} log \frac{exp\left(q_x^T k_{x+}/\tau \, \|q_x^T\|_2 \|k_{x+}\|_2\right)}{\sum_{k_{x'} \in A \setminus \{x\}} exp\left(q_x^T k_{x'}/\tau \, \|q_x^T\|_2 \|k_{x'}\|_2\right)}. \quad (8)$$

Furthermore, we define distance based loss as

$$\mathcal{L}_d(g,\tau,A) = \frac{1}{|B_q|} \sum_{q_x \in B_q} \frac{-1}{|\Psi(x)|} \sum_{k_{x+} \in \Psi(x)} log \frac{exp\left(-\|q_x - k_{x+}\|_2/\tau\right)}{\sum_{k_{x'} \in A \setminus \{x\}} exp\left(-\|q_x - k_{x'}\|_2/\tau\right)}, \quad (9)$$

---

**Algorithm 1:** Pseudo-code for CRADL algorithm

---

**Input:** Training Dataset $\mathcal{D} := \{\mathcal{X}, Y_{\mathcal{X}}\}$, classifier $f$, query network $g$, key network $g'$, momentum queue, uniform pseudo-labels $s_x$ for each $x \in \mathcal{X}$, class prototype $M_j$ for $j \in \{1, 2, 3 \ldots, c\}$

**for** $iter \in \{1, 2, \ldots\}$ **do**

    sample a mini-batch $B$ from $\mathcal{D}$ ;

    ▷generate query and key embeddings

    $B_q = \{q_x = g(x_q^a | x \in B\}$ ;

    $B_k = \{k_x = g'(x_k^a | x \in B\}$ ;

    $A = B_q \cup B_k \cup queue$ **for** $x \in B$ **do**

        ▷get prediction from classifier

        $\tilde{y} = \text{argmax}_{j \in y_x^p} f^j(x_q^a)$ ;

        ▷update class-prototype

        $M_j = \text{Normalize}\left(\gamma M_j + (1 - \gamma) q_x\right)$, if $\tilde{y} = j$ for $j \in \{1, 2, \ldots, c\}$;

        ▷positive set generation

        $\Psi(x) = \{a_{x'} \in A \backslash \{q_x\} | \tilde{y}' = \tilde{y}\}$

    **end**

    **for** $q_x \in B_q$ **do**

        ▷updating pseudo-target labels for each $x \in B$

        $s_{x_i} = \phi s_{x_i} + (1 - \phi)$, if $i = \text{argmax}_{j \in y_x^p} q^T M_j$ ;

        $s_{x_i} = \phi s_{x_i}$, otherwise;

    **end**

    ▷angle based contrastive loss calculation

    $\mathcal{L}_a(g, \tau, A) =$

    $\frac{1}{|B_q|} \sum\limits_{q_x \in B_q} -\frac{1}{|\Psi(x)|} \sum\limits_{k_{x+} \in \Psi(x)} log \frac{exp\left(q_x^T k_{x+} / \tau \|q_x^T\|_2 \|k_{x+}\|_2\right)}{\sum\limits_{k_{x'} \in A \backslash \{q_x\}} exp\left(q_x^T k_{x'} / \tau \|q_x^T\|_2 \|k_{x'}\|_2\right)}$ ;

    ▷distance based contrastive loss calculation

    $\mathcal{L}_d(g, \tau, A) = \frac{1}{|B_q|} \sum\limits_{q_x \in B_q} -\frac{1}{|\Psi(x)|} \sum\limits_{k_{x+} \in \Psi(x)} log \frac{exp\left(-\|q_x - k_{x+}\|_2 / \tau\right)}{\sum\limits_{k_{x'} \in A \backslash \{q_x\}} exp\left(-\|q_x - k_{x'}\|_2 / \tau\right)}$ ;

    ▷Cross-entropy loss calculation

    $\mathcal{L}_{ce}(f, B) = \frac{1}{|B|} \sum\limits_{x \in B} \sum\limits_{j=1}^{c} -s_{x_j} log(f(q_x)_j)$ ; ▷Network update

    minimize overall loss, $\mathcal{L} = \mathcal{L}_{ce} + \lambda (\mathcal{L}_a + \alpha \mathcal{L}_d)$;

    ▷update the key network and momentum queue

    update the key network; $g'$ using query network; $g$;

    remove previous key embeddings, $B_k$ & classifiers predictions from the queue and add updated $B_k$ & classifiers prediction to the queue.

**end**

---

where for each sample $x$, $\Psi(x)$ is the positive set of embedding vectors. The set

$$\Psi(x) := \{a_{x'} \in A \backslash \{q_x\} | \tilde{y}' = \tilde{y}\} \tag{10}$$

Here $\tilde{y}$ is the class probability vector produced by applying a classifier, $f$ on top of query network of momentum encoder. More specifically,

$$\tilde{y} := argmax_{j \in y_x^p}(f(q_x)_j). \tag{11}$$

Both $q_x$ and $k_x$ are two embedding vectors of same instance. Hence, we associate same $\tilde{y}$. Algorithm 1 provides the pseudo-code for the proposed CRADL algorithm.

### 4.3   Class-Prototype and Pseudo-target Update

We create a class prototype for each class, which can be considered class representative. To regularise the model, we create class-prototype and update them batch-wise as a moving average. Moreover, we use this class prototype to update the pseudo-target label associated with each image, consequently using it in the cross entropy loss instead of the actual label. For each class $i \in L := \{1, 2, 3, \ldots, c\}$ we define class-prototype as:

$$M_i = \text{unit-normalized}(\gamma(M_i) + (1 - \gamma)q_x), \text{ if } i = \tilde{y} \tag{12}$$

Further, we then update pseudo-target label for each sample $x$ as

$$s_{x_i} = \begin{cases} \phi s_{x_i} + (1 - \phi), & \text{if } i = \text{argmax}_{j \in y_x^p} q^T M_j \\ \phi s_{x_i}, & \text{else.} \end{cases} \tag{13}$$

Subsequently, for each sample $x$, we have an associated predicted label $\tilde{y}$ and a pseudo-target label $s_x$. To update the parameters in the classifier network, we use cross entropy loss, as suggested in Eq. 6,

$$\mathcal{L}_{ce}(f, B) = \frac{1}{|B|} \sum_{x \in B} \sum_{j=1}^{c} -s_{x_j} log(f(q_x)_j), \tag{14}$$

which ensures that for each sample $x$, the predicted and pseudo-target labels are synchronous.

## 5   Experimental Details

### 5.1   Model Architecture and Datasets

The proposed method uses two augmented views for each image. Query view and key view respectively. These views are passed through a neural network (ResNet) for getting representations. Representations for these two views should be close to each other in embedding space because these two views are generated from same image and these representations should be different from views of any other image. TO have a fair comparison with PiCO [25], in our experiments we use a similar base-architecture ResNet-18 trained from scratch.

The proposed architecture has two parts Momentum Contrast Encoder [11] and Encoder (ResNet-18) part for generating queries and keys for each image in batch. Given each sample $(X, y_x^p)$, we generate two views by randomized data augmentation: a query view $x_q^a$ and a key view $x_k^a$. The two views are fed into a query network $g(\cdot)$ and a key network $g'(\cdot)$, yielding a pair of feature-wise $L_2$-normalized embeddings $q_x = g\left(x_q^a\right)$ and $k_x = g'\left(x_k^a\right)$. For each query $q$ its contrastive loss is calculated with queries and keys of other images from batch as mentioned in Eq. 2. The difference between query $g(\cdot)$ and a key network $g'(\cdot)$ is that a key network uses momentum update with the query network. Proposed method also maintains a queue for storing the current key embeddings k, and then updates the queue chronologically, as shown in Sect. 4.

Query vectors that are generated are used for prototype vector generation $M_j$ which are representation vectors for each class and this vectors are used for label disambiguation. Embedding generated from query network are passed onto MLP with softmax-classifier and are used for cross entropy loss to update the parameters. We use a 18 layer ResNet as a backbone architecture. As most of the previous work uses 18 layer ResNet for benchmarking we have reported performance of proposed method with this back bone - ResNet-18 architecture. In implementations, the query network shares the same convolutional blocks as the classifier, followed by a prediction head. Following this, we evaluated our modification on two benchmark datasets: CIFAR 10 and CIFAR 100 [16].

## 5.2 Implementation Details

We developed our code-base over PiCO's implementation. Following the standard experimental setup in PLL, we split a clean validation set (10% of training data) to select the hyper-parameters. After that, we transform the validation set back to its original PLL form and incorporate it into the training set to accomplish the final model training. We use an untrained 18-layer ResNet as the backbone for feature extraction. We ran proposed architecture for hyper-parameters mentioned in PiCO [25]. The projection head of the contrastive network is a 2-layer MLP that outputs a 128-dimensional embedding.

**Generating Candidate Set:** We generate conventional partially labeled datasets by flipping negative labels $\bar{y} \neq y$ to false positive labels with a probability $z = P(\bar{y} \in L \mid \bar{y} \neq y)$. Here $y$ is the correct ground truth label. In other words, all $c-1$ negative labels have a uniform probability of being false positive, and we aggregate the flipped ones with the ground truth to form the candidate set $y_x^p$. We consider $z \in \{0.1, 0.3, 0.5\}$ for CIFAR-10 and $z \in \{0.01, 0.05, 0.1\}$ for CIFAR-100. For instance, a uniform noise rate of 0.5 means that on an average length of label set $y_x^p$ is $1 + (1 - |L|) * 0.5$ where L is the label set.

**Generating Query and Key Augmentations:** We use two data augmentation modules SimAugment [22] and RandAugment [5] for query and key data augmentation, respectively. The size of the queue that stores key embeddings is fixed to be 8,192. The momentum coefficients are set as 0.999 for contrastive network updating and $\gamma = 0.99$ for prototype calculation. For pseudo-label update parameter ($\phi$) and class prototype update parameter ($\gamma$) we used values reported in [25]. We have evaluated the proposed CRADL algorithm with different weights and have reported performance with the best hyper-parameters.

# 6    Results and Analysis

In this section, we present the experimental results to showcase the effectiveness of the proposed CRADL algorithm and compare it against the recent studies on PLL. Furthermore, we also present the ablation study.

## 6.1    Comparison with Recent PLL Methods

We compare our method CRADL with various algorithms used for partial label learning in Table 1 for CIFAR-10 and in Table 2 for the CIFAR-100 dataset at different noise rates. We also compare our model's performance with a fully supervised network for both datasets. A fully supervised method is when there is no noise in the label set. This will help us to compare the CRADL algorithm and set an upper bound on performance. For instance, when considering CIFAR-10 data in Table 1 with noise rate $z = 0.1$, we are only 0.03% in accuracy away from a fully supervised model. From Table 1 and 2, it is clear that the proposed CRADL algorithm gives the best accuracy.

**Table 1.** Performance comparisons of the proposed CRADL algorithm on the **CIFAR-10 dataset** [16], compared against recent popular PLL algorithms.

| Algorithm | Noise Rate ($z$) | | |
|---|---|---|---|
| | 0.1 | 0.3 | 0.5 |
| Fully Supervised | 94.91 | | |
| EXP | 79.23 | 75.79 | 70.34 |
| MSE [7] | 79.97 | 75.64 | 67.09 |
| CC [9] | 82.30 | 79.08 | 74.05 |
| Proden [18] | 90.24 | 89.38 | 87.78 |
| LWS [26] | 90.30 | 88.99 | 86.16 |
| PiCO [25] | 94.34 | 93.94 | 93.54 |
| **CRADL (Proposed)** | **94.88** | **94.65** | **94.11** |

**Table 2.** Performance comparisons of the proposed CRADL algorithm on the **CIFAR-100 dataset** [16], compared against recent popular PLL algorithms.

| Algorithm | Noise Rate ($z$) | | |
|---|---|---|---|
| | 0.01 | 0.05 | 0.1 |
| Fully Supervised | 73.56 | | |
| EXP | 44.45 | 41.05 | 29.27 |
| MSE [7] | 49.17 | 46.02 | 43.81 |
| CC [9] | 49.76 | 47.62 | 35.72 |
| Proden [18] | 62.60 | 60.73 | 56.80 |
| LWS [26] | 65.78 | 59.56 | 53.53 |
| PiCO [25] | 73.05 | 72.65 | 60.99 |
| **CRADL (Proposed)** | **73.23** | **73.07** | **72.49** |

Further, we compare our proposed CRADL method with the current state-of-the-art algorithm for PLL, namely Consistency-Regularisation (Consis-Reg) [27]. Since Consis-Reg uses different architectures and augmentations, it cannot be directly compared with CRADL and other algorithms presented in Table 1 and 2. Hence, we compare performance relative to their respective fully supervised accuracy in Table 3 for CIFAR-10 and in Table 4 for CIFAR-100. The values represent the performance dip in accuracy at different noise rates compared to

**Table 3.** Performance dip comparisons at various noise rate of the proposed CRADL algorithm with SOTA Consis-reg on CIFAR-10 [16] dataset when compared with fully supervised case. Fully supervised accuracy of CRADL 94.91% is and that of consis-reg is 96.43%

**Table 4.** Performance dip comparisons at various noise rate of the proposed CRADL algorithm with SOTA Consis-reg on CIFAR-100 [16] dataset when compared with fully supervised case. Fully supervised accuracy of CRADL is 73.56% and that of consis-reg is 79.88%

| Algorithm | Noise rate | | |
|---|---|---|---|
| | 0.1 | 0.3 | 0.5 |
| CRADL | **0.03%** | **0.26%** | **0.8%** |
| Consis-Reg | 0.20% | 0.61% | 1.01% |

| Algorithm | Noise rate | | |
|---|---|---|---|
| | 0.01 | 0.05 | 0.1 |
| CRADL | **0.33%** | **0.49%** | **1.07%** |
| Consis-Reg | 0.34% | 0.92% | 2.15% |

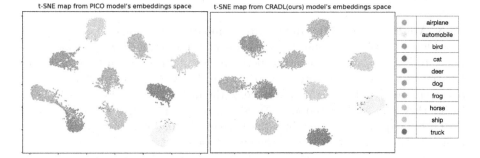

**Fig. 4.** T-SNE visualisation of the representation space on CIFAR-10 dataset at 0.05 noise rate from PiCO vs CRADL(our) algorithm.

their respective fully supervised case. We observe that our model has a lower dip than Consis-reg, showcasing the efficacy of the proposed CRADL algorithm.

In Fig. 4, we visualize the embedding vectors obtained by the embedding layer using t-SNE plots [23] for the CIFAR-10 dataset with uniform noise 0.5. Different colors represent ground-truth class labels, as mentioned on the right side of Fig. 4. We compare the t-SNE plots obtained using PiCO and the proposed CRADL algorithm. After comparing both the t-SNE maps, we observe that CRADL produces well-separated and more compact clusters than PiCO's t-SNE maps. This validates its effectiveness in learning high-quality image representation.

### 6.2 Ablation Study

**Impact of Weight Parameter:** While calculating overall loss, we multiply the distance based loss by a hyper-parameter $\alpha$, which we refer as weight parameter.

$$\text{Overall Loss: } \mathcal{L} = \mathcal{L}_{cls} + \lambda \left( \mathcal{L}_a + \alpha \mathcal{L}_d \right) \qquad (15)$$

The trend of weight factor with as we vary the noise rate for partial label in CIFAR-10 data can be seen in Table 5. We observe that for fixed noise rate,

**Table 5.** Trend of the weight parameter vs. noise rate for the CIFAR-10 dataset. The ablation results are compared with PiCO algorithm.

| Noise Rate | PiCO | Weight Parameter $\alpha$ | | | | | |
|---|---|---|---|---|---|---|---|
| | | 0.0 | 0.1 | 0.3 | 0.5 | 0.7 | 1.0 |
| 0.1 | 94.39 | 94.60 | 94.51 | 94.70 | 94.62 | **94.88** | 94.79 |
| 0.3 | 94.18 | 94.29 | **94.65** | 94.55 | 94.45 | 94.32 | 94.28 |
| 0.5 | 93.58 | 93.92 | 94.03 | 94.05 | **94.11** | 93.97 | 93.91 |

weight vs accuracy forms a concave function, that is it first increase and attains a maxima and then decreases.

**Only Angle vs only Distance:** After comparing only angle vs only distance based loss in CRADL we observed almost similar performance with various noise rates. In Table 5, we compare the performance of PiCO against the proposed CRADL. At weight parameter $\alpha = 0$, we see that CRADL outperforms PiCO. $\alpha = 0$ means that there is no influence of the distance based loss (Eq. 9), indicating that only angle based loss (Eq. 8) can result in a performance boost over PiCO. Subsequently, this justifies the problem we highlighted with the N-pair contrastive loss in Sect. 3. Hence, the angle based contrastive loss is better than N-pair contrastive loss (when un-normalized embedding vectors are fed into N-pair contrastive loss).

Furthermore, adding a distance based loss function in CRADL increases the performance even further at any weight parameter value, $\alpha \in (0, 1]$. Thus, justifying that our CRADL algorithm helps in better representation learning (refer to Sect. 6 and Fig. 4) and hence overall learning of the model.

# 7   Conclusion

This research proposes a contrastive loss setup titled **C**ontrastive **R**epresentation through **A**ngle and **D**istance based **L**oss for Partial Label Learning (CRADL) for partial label learning. In theoretical analysis Sect. 3.1, we explain the need for a new contrastive loss and why N-pair contrastive loss is not ideal. The proposed CRADL method helps in learning better representation vectors in embedding space associated with each instance. We compare our proposed CRADL algorithm with various PLL algorithms and current state-of-the-art algorithms, which shows the effectiveness of our proposed algorithm. CRADL generates compact and well-separated clusters, resulting in the best accuracy in PLL setup at different uniform noise rates.

**Ethics Statement.** Our proposed algorithm does not raise any ethical concerns. No database is collected in this research, and the experiments shown are on publicly available datasets. However, it is essential to note that partial label learning (PLL) algorithms, including the proposed one, aim to disambiguate and learn from labels that have some noise. Hence, while PLL aims to reduce its performance gap from fully supervised correct labels, the performance is typically lower. Therefore, while PLL research can benefit from our work, it is crucial to exercise caution and responsibility to ensure positive and socially beneficial outcomes of machine learning algorithms.

# References

1. Abhigna, B.S., Soni, N., Dixit, S.: Crowdsourcing - a step towards advanced machine learning. Procedia Comput. Sci. **132**, 632–642 (2018)
2. Chen, C.H., Patel, V.M., Chellappa, R.: Learning from ambiguously labeled face images. Trans. Pattern Anal. Mach. Intell. **40**(7), 1653–1667 (2017)
3. Chen, T., Kornblith, S., Norouzi, M., Hinton, G.: A simple framework for contrastive learning of visual representations. In: International conference on machine learning. PMLR (2020)
4. Cour, T., Sapp, B., Taskar, B.: Learning from partial labels. J. Mach. Learn. Res. **12**, 1501–1536 (2011)
5. Cubuk, E.D., Zoph, B., Shlens, J., Le, Q.V.: Randaugment: practical automated data augmentation with a reduced search space (2019)
6. Feng, L., An, B.: Leveraging latent label distributions for partial label learning. In: International Joint Conferences on Artificial Intelligence (2018)
7. Feng, L., Kaneko, T., Han, B., Niu, G., An, B., Sugiyama, M.: Learning with multiple complementary labels. In: International Conference on Machine Learning. PMLR (2020)
8. Feng, L., et al.: Provably consistent partial-label learning. In: Advances in Neural Information Processing Systems (2020)
9. Feng, L., et al.: Provably consistent partial-label learning (2020)
10. Feng, L., Shu, S., Lin, Z., Lv, F., Li, L., An, B.: Can cross entropy loss be robust to label noise? In: International Joint Conferences on Artificial Intelligence (2021)
11. He, K., Fan, H., Wu, Y., Xie, S., Girshick, R.: Momentum contrast for unsupervised visual representation learning. In: Computer Vision and Pattern Recognition (2020)
12. Hüllermeier, E., Beringer, J.: Learning from ambiguously labeled examples. Intell. Data Anal. **10**(5), 419–439 (2006)
13. Jin, R., Ghahramani, Z.: Learning with multiple labels. In: Advances in Neural Information Processing Systems (2002)
14. Jing, L., Vincent, P., LeCun, Y., Tian, Y.: Understanding dimensional collapse in contrastive self-supervised learning (2022)
15. Khosla, P., et al.: Supervised contrastive learning. In: Advances in Neural Information Processing Systems (2020)
16. Krizhevsky, A.: Learning multiple layers of features from tiny images. Master's thesis, University of Tront (2009)
17. Luo, J., Orabona, F.: Learning from candidate labeling sets. In: Advances in Neural Information Processing Systems (2010)
18. Lv, J., Xu, M., Feng, L., Niu, G., Geng, X., Sugiyama, M.: Progressive identification of true labels for partial-label learning. In: International Conference on Machine Learning. PMLR (2020)
19. Malhotra, A., Sankaran, A., Vatsa, M., Singh, R., Morris, K.B., Noore, A.: Understanding ACE-V latent fingerprint examination process via eye-gaze analysis. IEEE Trans. Biom. Behav. Identity Sci. **3**(1), 44–58 (2020)

20. Sheng, V., Zhang, J.: Machine learning with crowdsourcing: a brief summary of the past research and future directions. In: Proceedings of the AAAI Conference on Artificial Intelligence (2019)
21. Sohn, K.: Improved deep metric learning with multi-class n-pair loss objective. In: Advances in Neural Information Processing Systems (2016)
22. Su, G., Chen, W., Xu, M.: Positive-unlabeled learning from imbalanced data. In: International Joint Conferences on Artificial Intelligence (2021)
23. van der Maaten, L., Hinton, G.: Visualizing high-dimensional data using t-SNE. J. Mach. Learn. Res. (2008)
24. Van Engelen, J.E., Hoos, H.H.: A survey on semi-supervised learning. Mach. Learn. **109**(2), 373–440 (2020)
25. Wang, H., et al.: PiCO: contrastive label disambiguation for partial label learning. In: International Conference on Learning Representations (2022)
26. Wen, H., Cui, J., Hang, H., Liu, J., Wang, Y., Lin, Z.: Leveraged weighted loss for partial label learning. In: International Conference on Machine Learning. PMLR (2021)
27. Wu, D.D., Wang, D.B., Zhang, M.L.: Revisiting consistency regularization for deep partial label learning. In: International Conference on Machine Learning. PMLR (2022)
28. Xu, N., Lv, J., Geng, X.: Partial label learning via label enhancement. In: Conference on Artificial Intelligence. AAAI (2019)
29. Xu, N., Qiao, C., Geng, X., Zhang, M.L.: Instance-dependent partial label learning. In: Advances in Neural Information Processing Systems (2021)
30. Yao, Y., Gong, C., Deng, J., Yang, J.: Network cooperation with progressive disambiguation for partial label learning. In: Hutter, F., Kersting, K., Lijffijt, J., Valera, I. (eds.) ECML PKDD 2020. LNCS (LNAI), vol. 12458, pp. 471–488. Springer, Cham (2021). https://doi.org/10.1007/978-3-030-67661-2_28
31. Yu, F., Zhang, M.L.: Maximum margin partial label learning. In: Asian Conference on Machine Learning. PMLR (2016)
32. Zeng, Z., et al.: Learning by associating ambiguously labeled images. In: Computer Vision and Pattern Recognition. IEEE (2013)
33. Zhang, M.L., Zhou, B.B., Liu, X.Y.: Partial label learning via feature-aware disambiguation. In: Conference on Knowledge Discovery and Data Mining. ACM SIGKDD (2016)
34. Zhang, Z., Sabuncu, M.: Generalized cross entropy loss for training deep neural networks with noisy labels. In: Advances in Neural Information Processing Systems (2018)
35. Zhou, Z.H.: A brief introduction to weakly supervised learning. Natl. Sci. Rev. **5**(1), 44–53 (2018)
36. Zhuang, C., Zhai, A.L., Yamins, D.: Local aggregation for unsupervised learning of visual embeddings. In: International Conference on Computer Vision (2019)

# Equivariant Representation Learning in the Presence of Stabilizers

Luis Armando Pérez Rey[1,2,3]([⊠]), Giovanni Luca Marchetti[4], Danica Kragic[4], Dmitri Jarnikov[1,3], and Mike Holenderski[1]

[1] Eindhoven University of Technology, Eindhoven, The Netherlands
l.a.perez.rey@tue.nl
[2] Eindhoven Artificial Intelligence Systems Institute, Eindhoven, The Netherlands
[3] Prosus, Amsterdam, The Netherlands
[4] KTH Royal Institute of Technology, Stockholm, Sweden

**Abstract.** We introduce Equivariant Isomorphic Networks (EquIN) – a method for learning representations that are equivariant with respect to general group actions over data. Differently from existing equivariant representation learners, EquIN is suitable for group actions that are not free, i.e., that stabilize data via nontrivial symmetries. EquIN is theoretically grounded in the orbit-stabilizer theorem from group theory. This guarantees that an ideal learner infers isomorphic representations while trained on equivariance alone and thus fully extracts the geometric structure of data. We provide an empirical investigation on image datasets with rotational symmetries and show that taking stabilizers into account improves the quality of the representations.

**Keywords:** Representation Learning · Equivariance · Lie Groups

## 1 Introduction

Incorporating data symmetries into deep neural representations defines a fundamental challenge and has been addressed in several recent works [1,6,14,26,28]. The overall aim is to design representations that preserve symmetries and operate coherently with respect to them – a functional property known as *equivariance*. This is because the preservation of symmetries leads to the extraction of geometric and semantic structures in data, which can be exploited for data efficiency and generalization [2]. As an example, the problem of *disentangling* semantic factors of variation in data has been rephrased in terms of equivariant representations [3,12]. As disentanglement is known to be unfeasible with no inductive biases or supervision [18], symmetries of data arise as a geometric structure that can provide weak supervision and thus be leveraged in order to disentangle semantic factors.

The majority of models from the literature rely on the assumption that the group of symmetries acts *freely* on data [21] i.e., that no datapoint is stabilized

---

L. A. Pérez Rey and G. L. Marchetti—Equal Contribution.

D. Koutra et al. (Eds.): ECML PKDD 2023, LNAI 14172, pp. 693–708, 2023.
https://doi.org/10.1007/978-3-031-43421-1_41

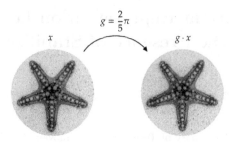

**Fig. 1.** An example of an action on data that is not free. The datapoint $x$ is stabilized by the symmetry $g \in G$.

by nontrivial symmetries. This avoids the need to model *stabilizers* of datapoints, which are unknown subgroups of the given symmetry group. However, non-free group actions arise in several practical scenarios. This happens, for example, when considering images of objects acted upon by the rotation group via a change of orientation. Such objects may be symmetrical, resulting in rotations leaving the image almost identical and consequently ambiguous in its orientation, see Fig. 1. Discerning the correct orientations of an object is important for applications such as pose estimation [20] and reinforcement learning [10]. This motivates the need to design equivariant representation learning frameworks that are capable of modeling stabilizers and therefore suit non-free group actions.

In this work, we propose a method for learning equivariant representation for general and potentially non-free group actions. Based on the Orbit-Stabilizer Theorem from group theory, we design a model that outputs subsets of the group, which represent the stabilizer subgroup up to a symmetry – a group theoretical construction known as *coset*. The representation learner optimizes an equivariance loss relying on supervision from symmetries alone. This means that we train our model on a dataset consisting of relative symmetries between pairs of datapoints, avoiding the need to know the whole group action over data a priori. From a theoretical perspective, the above-mentioned results from group theory guarantee that an ideal learner infers representations that are isomorphic to the original dataset. This implies that our representations completely preserve the symmetry structure while preventing any loss of information. We name our framework Equivariant Isomorphic Networks – EquIN for short. In summary, our contributions include:

- A novel equivariant representation learning framework suitable for non-free group actions.
- A discussion grounded on group theory with theoretical guarantees for iso-morphism representations.
- An empirical investigation with comparisons to competing equivariant repre-sentation learners on image datasets.

We provide Python code implementing our framework together with all the experiments at the following repository: luis-armando-perez-rey/non-free.

## 2    Related Work

In this section, we first briefly survey representation learning methods from the literature leveraging on equivariance. We then draw connections between equivariant representations and world models from reinforcement learning and discuss the role of equivariance in terms of disentangling semantic factors of data.

**Equivariant Representation Learning.** Several works in the literature have proposed and studied representation learning models that are equivariant with respect to a group of data symmetries. These models are typically trained via a loss encouraging equivariance on a dataset of relative symmetries between datapoints. What distinguishes the models is the choice of the latent space and of the group action over the latter. Euclidean latent spaces with linear or affine actions have been explored in [9,26,29]. However, the intrinsic data manifold is non-Euclidean in general, leading to representations that are non-isomorphic and that do not preserve the geometric structure of the data. To amend this, a number of works have proposed to design latent spaces that are isomorphic to disjoint copies of the symmetry group [8,15,21,28]. When the group action is free, this leads to isomorphic representations and thus completely recovers the geometric structure of the data [21]. However, the proposed latent spaces are unsuitable for non-free actions. Since they do not admit stabilizers, no equivariant map exists, and the model is thus unable to learn a suitable representation. In the present work, we extend this line of research by designing a latent space that enables learning equivariant representations in the presence of stabilizers. Our model implicitly represents stabilizer subgroups and leads to isomorphic representations for arbitrary group actions.

**Latent World Models.** Analogously to group actions, Markov Decision Processes (MDPs) from reinforcement learning and control theory involve a, possibly stochastic, interaction with an environment. This draws connections between MDPs and symmetries since the latter can be thought of as transformations and, thus, as a form of interaction. The core difference is that in an MDP, no algebraic structure, such as a group composition, is assumed on the set of interactions. In the context of MDPs, a representation that is equivariant with respect to the agent's actions is referred to as latent *World Model* [10,16,24] or *Markov Decision Process Homomorphism* (MDPH) [25]. In an MDPH the latent action is learned together with the representation by an additional model operating on the latent space. Although this makes MDPHs more general than group-equivariant models, the resulting representation is unstructured and uninterpretable. The additional assumptions of equivariant representations translate instead into the preservation of the geometric structure of data.

**Disentanglement.** As outlined in [2], a desirable property for representations is disentanglement, i.e., the ability to decompose in the representations the semantic factors of variations that explain the data. Although a number of methods have been proposed for this purpose [4,13], it has been shown that disentanglement is mathematically unachievable in an unbiased and unsupervised way

[18]. As an alternative, the notion has been rephrased in terms of symmetry and equivariance [12]. It follows that isomorphic equivariant representations are guaranteed to be disentangled in this sense [21,28]. Since we aim for general equivariant representations that are isomorphic, our proposed method achieves disentanglement as a by-product.

## 3    Group Theory Background

We review the fundamental group theory concepts necessary to formalize our representation learning framework. For a complete treatment, we refer to [27].

**Definition 1.** *A group is a set $G$ equipped with a composition map $G \times G \to G$ denoted by $(g, h) \mapsto gh$, an inversion map $G \to G$ denoted by $g \mapsto g^{-1}$, and a distinguished identity element $1 \in G$ such that for all $g, h, k \in G$:*

$$\begin{array}{ccc} \text{Associativity} & \text{Inversion} & \text{Identity} \\ g(hk) = (gh)k & g^{-1}g = gg^{-1} = 1 & g1 = 1g = g \end{array}$$

Elements of a group represent abstract symmetries. Spaces with a group of symmetries $G$ are said to be acted upon by $G$ in the following sense.

**Definition 2.** *An action by a group $G$ on a set $X$ is a map $G \times X \to X$ denoted by $(g, x) \mapsto g \cdot x$, satisfying for all $g, h \in G$, $x \in X$:*

$$\begin{array}{cc} \text{Associativity} & \text{Identity} \\ g \cdot (h \cdot x) = (gh) \cdot x & 1 \cdot x = x \end{array}$$

Suppose that $G$ acts on a set $X$. The action defines a set of *orbits* $X/G$ given by the equivalence classes of the relation $x \sim y$ iff $y = g \cdot x$ for some $g \in G$. For each $x \in X$, the *stabilizer* subgroup is defined as

$$G_x = \{g \in G \mid g \cdot x = x\}. \tag{1}$$

Stabilizers of elements in the same orbit are conjugate, meaning that for each $x, y$ belonging to the same orbit $O$ there exists $h \in G$ such that $G_y = hG_xh^{-1}$. By abuse of notation, we refer to the conjugacy class $G_O$ of stabilizers for $O \in X/G$. The action is said to be *free* if all the stabilizers are trivial, i.e., $G_O = \{1\}$ for every $O$.

We now recall the central notion for our representation learning framework.

**Definition 3.** *A map $\varphi : X \to Z$ between sets acted upon by $G$ is equivariant if $\varphi(g \cdot x) = g \cdot \varphi(x)$ for every $x \in X$ and $g \in G$. An equivariant bijection is referred to as isomorphism.*

Intuitively, an equivariant map between $X$ and $Z$ preserves their corresponding symmetries. The following is the fundamental result on group actions [27].

**Theorem 1 (Orbit-Stabilizer).** *The following holds:*

– *Each orbit $O$ is isomorphic to the set of (left) cosets $G/G_O = \{gG_O \mid g \in G\}$. In other words, there is an isomorphism:*

$$X \simeq \coprod_{O \in X/G} G/G_O \quad \subseteq 2^G \times X/G \tag{2}$$

*where $2^G$ denotes the power-set of $G$ on which $G$ acts by left multiplication i.e., $g \cdot A = \{ga \mid a \in A\}$.*
– *Any equivariant map*

$$\varphi : X \to \coprod_{O \in X/G} G/G_O \tag{3}$$

*that induces a bijection on orbits is an isomorphism.*

Theorem 1 describes arbitrary group actions completely and asserts that orbit-preserving equivariant maps are isomorphisms. Our central idea is to leverage on this in order to design a representation learner that is guaranteed to be isomorphic when trained on equivariance alone (Fig. 2).

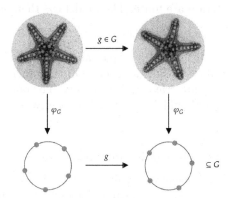

**Fig. 2.** An illustration of EquIN encoding data equivariantly as subsets of the symmetry group $G$. This results in representations that are suitable even when the action by $G$ on data is not free.

## 4    Equivariant Isomorphic Networks (EquIN)

Our goal is to design an equivariant representation learner based on Theorem 1. We aim to train a model

$$\varphi : X \to Z \tag{4}$$

with a latent space $Z$ on a loss encouraging equivariance. The ideal choice for $Z$ is given by $\coprod_{O \in X/G} G/G_O$ since the latter is isomorphic to $X$ (Theorem 1). In other words, $\varphi$ ideally outputs cosets of stabilizers of the input datapoints.

However, while we assume that $G$ is known a priori, its action on $\mathcal{X}$ is not and has to be inferred from data. Since the stabilizers depend on the group action, they are unknown a priori as well. In order to circumvent the modeling of stabilizers and their cosets, we rely on the following simple result:

**Proposition 1.** *Let $\varphi : \mathcal{X} \to 2^G$ be an equivariant map. Then for each $x \in \mathcal{X}$ belonging to an orbit $O$, $\varphi(x)$ contains a coset of (a conjugate of) $G_O$.*

*Proof.* Pick $x \in \mathcal{X}$. Then for every $g \in G_x$ it holds that $\varphi(x) = \varphi(g \cdot x) = g \cdot \varphi(x)$. In other words, $G_x h = hh^{-1}G_x h \subseteq \varphi(x)$ for each $h \in \varphi(x)$. Since $h^{-1}G_x h$ is conjugate to $G_x$ the thesis follows.

Proposition 1 enables $\varphi$ to output arbitrary subsets of $G$ instead of cosets of stabilizers. As long as those subsets are *minimal* w.r.t. to inclusion, they will coincide with the desired cosets.

Based on this, we define the latent space of EquIN as $\mathcal{Z} = \mathcal{Z}_G \times \mathcal{Z}_O$ and implement the map $\varphi$ as a pair of neural networks $\varphi_G : \mathcal{X} \to \mathcal{Z}_G$ and $\varphi_O : \mathcal{X} \to \mathcal{Z}_O$. The component $\mathcal{Z}_G$ represents cosets of stabilizers while $\mathcal{Z}_O$ represents orbits. Since the output space of a neural network is finite-dimensional, we assume that the stabilizers of the action are finite. The model $\varphi_G$ then outputs $N$ elements

$$\varphi_G(x) = \{\varphi_G^1(x), \cdots, \varphi_G^N(x)\} \subseteq G \tag{5}$$

where $\varphi_G^i(x) \in G$ for all $i$. The hyperparameter $N$ should be ideally chosen larger than the cardinality of the stabilizers. On the other hand, the output of $\varphi_O$ consists of a vector of arbitrary dimensionality. The only requirement is that the output space of $\varphi_O$ should have enough capacity to contain the space of orbits $\mathcal{X}/G$.

## 4.1   Parametrizing $G$ via the Exponential Map

The output space of usual machine learning models such as deep neural networks is Euclidean. However, $\varphi_G$ needs to output elements of the group $G$ (see Eq. 5), which may be non-Euclidean as in the case of $G = \mathrm{SO}(n)$. Therefore, in order to implement $\varphi_G$, it is necessary to parametrize $G$. To this end, we assume that $G$ is a differentiable manifold, with differentiable composition and inversion maps, i.e., that $G$ is a *Lie group*. One can then define the *Lie algebra* $\mathfrak{g}$ of $G$ as the tangent space to $G$ at $1$.

We propose to rely on the *exponential map* $\mathfrak{g} \to G$, denoted by $v \mapsto e^v$, to parametrize $G$. This means that $\varphi_G$ first outputs $N$ elements $\varphi_G(x) = \{v^1, \cdots, v^N\} \subseteq \mathfrak{g}$ that get subsequently mapped into $G$ as $\{e^{v^1}, \cdots, e^{v^N}\}$. Although the exponential map can be defined for general Lie groups by solving an appropriate ordinary differential equation, we focus on the case $G \subseteq \mathrm{GL}(n)$. The Lie algebra $\mathfrak{g}$ is then contained in the space of $n \times n$ matrices and the exponential map amounts to the matrix Taylor expansion

$$e^v = \sum_{k \geq 0} \frac{v^k}{k!} \tag{6}$$

where $v^k$ denotes the power of $v$ as a matrix. For specific groups, the latter can be simplified via simple closed formulas. For example, the exponential map of $\mathbb{R}^n$ is the identity while for SO(3) it can be efficiently computed via the Rodrigues' formula [17].

## 4.2  Training Objective

As mentioned, our dataset $\mathcal{D}$ consists of samples from the unknown group action. This means that datapoints are triplets $(x, g, y) \in X \times G \times X$ with $y = g \cdot x$. Given a datapoint $(x, g, y) \in \mathcal{D}$ the learner $\varphi_G$ optimizes the equivariance loss over its parameters:

$$\mathcal{L}_G(x, g, y) = d(g \cdot \varphi_G(x), \ \varphi_G(y)) \tag{7}$$

where $d$ is a semi-metric for sets. We opt for the asymmetric *Chamfer distance*

$$d(A, B) = \frac{1}{|A|} \sum_{a \in A} \min_{b \in B} d_G(a, b) \tag{8}$$

because of its differentiability properties. Any other differentiable distance between sets of points can be deployed as an alternative. Here $d_G$ is a metric on $G$ and is typically set as the squared Euclidean for $G = \mathbb{R}^n$ and as the squared Frobenius for $G = \mathrm{SO}(n)$. As previously discussed, we wish $\varphi_G(x)$, when seen as a set, to be minimal in cardinality. To this end, we add the following regularization term measuring the discrete entropy:

$$\widetilde{\mathcal{L}}_G(x) = \frac{\lambda}{N^2} \sum_{1 \leq i, j \leq N} d_G(\varphi_G^i(x), \ \varphi_G^j(x)) \tag{9}$$

where $\lambda$ is a weighting hyperparameter. On the other hand, since orbits are invariant to the group action $\varphi_O$ optimizes a *contrastive loss*. We opt for the popular InfoNCE loss from the literature [5]:

$$\mathcal{L}_O(x, y) = d_O(\varphi_O(x), \ \varphi_O(y)) + \log \mathbb{E}_{x'} \left[ e^{-d_O(\varphi_O(x'), \ \varphi_O(x))} \right] \tag{10}$$

where $x'$ is marginalized from $\mathcal{D}$. As customary for the InfoNCE loss, we normalize the output of $\varphi_O$ and set $d_O(a, b) = -\cos(\angle ab) = -a \cdot b$. The second summand of $\mathcal{L}_O$ encourages injectivity of $\varphi_O$ and as such prevents orbits from overlapping in the representation.

The Orbit-Stabilizer Theorem (Theorem 1) guarantees that if EquIN is implemented with ideal learners $\varphi_G, \varphi_O$ then it infers isomorphic representations in the following sense. If the $\mathcal{L}_G(x, g, y)$ and the first summand of $\mathcal{L}_O(x, y)$ vanish for every $(x, g, y)$ then $\varphi$ is equivariant. If moreover the regularizations, $\widetilde{\mathcal{L}}_G$ and the second summand of $\mathcal{L}_O$, are at a minimum then $\varphi_G(x)$ coincides with a coset of $G_O$ for every $x \in O$ (Proposition 1) and $\varphi_O$ is injective. The second claim of Theorem 1 implies then that the representation is isomorphic on its image, as desired.

## 5    Experiments

We empirically investigate EquIN on image data acted upon by a variety Lie groups. Our aim is to show both qualitatively and quantitatively that EquIN reliably infers isomorphic equivariant representations for non-free group actions.

We implement the neural networks $\varphi_G$ and $\varphi_O$ as a ResNet18 [11]. For a datapoint $x \in \mathcal{X}$, the network implements multiple heads to produce embeddings $\{\varphi_G^1(x), \cdots, \varphi_G^N(x)\} \subseteq G$. The output dimension of $\varphi_O$ is set to 3. We train the model for 50 epochs using the AdamW optimizer [19] with a learning rate of $10^{-4}$ and batches of 16 triplets $(x, g, y) \in \mathcal{D}$.

### 5.1    Datasets

We consider the following datasets consisting of $64 \times 64$ images subject to non-free group actions. Samples from these datasets are shown in Fig. 4.

- ROTATING ARROWS: images of radial configurations of $\nu \in \{1, 2, 3, 4, 5\}$ arrows rotated by $G = SO(2)$. The number of arrows $\nu$ determines the orbit and the corresponding stabilizer is (isomorphic to) the cyclic group $C_\nu$ of cardinality $\nu$. The dataset contains 2500 triplets $(x, g, y)$ per orbit.
- COLORED ARROWS: images similar to ROTATING ARROWS but with the arrows of five different colors. This extra factor produces additional orbits with the same stabilizer subgroups. The number of orbits is therefore 25. The dataset contains 2000 triplets per orbit.
- DOUBLE ARROWS: images of two radial configurations of $2, 3$ and $3, 5$ arrows respectively rotated by the torus $G = SO(2) \times SO(2)$. The action produces two orbits with stabilizers given by products of cyclic groups: $C_2 \times C_3$ and $C_3 \times C_5$ respectively. The dataset contains 2000 triplets per orbit.
- MODELNET: images of monochromatic objects from ModelNet40 [30] rotated by $G = SO(2)$ along an axis. We consider five objects: an airplane, a chair, a lamp, a bathtub and a stool. Each object corresponds to a single orbit. The lamp, the stool and the chair have the cyclic group $C_4$ as stabilizer while the action over the airplane and the bathub is free. The dataset contains 2500 triplets per orbit.
- SOLIDS: images of a monochromatic tetrahedron, cube and icosahedron [22] rotated by $G = SO(3)$. Each solid defines an orbit, and the stabilizers of the tetrahedron, the cube, and the icosahedron are subgroups of order 12, 24 and 60 respectively. The dataset contains 7500 triplets per orbit.

### 5.2    Comparisons

We compare EquIN with the following two equivariant representation learning models.

- *Baseline:* a model corresponding to EquIN with $N = 1$ where $\varphi_G$ outputs a single element of $G$. The latent space is $\mathcal{Z} = G \times \mathcal{Z}_O$, on which $G$ acts freely. We deploy this as the baseline since it has been proposed with minor variations in a number of previous works [3,21,23,28] assuming free group actions.

– *Equivariant Neural Renderer (ENR):* a model from [7] implementing a tensorial latent space $\mathcal{Z} = \mathbb{R}^{S^3}$, thought as a scalar signal space on a $S \times S \times S$ grid in $\mathbb{R}^3$. The group SO(3) act *approximately* on $\mathcal{Z}$ by rotating the grid and interpolating the obtained values. The model is trained jointly with a decoder $\psi : \mathcal{Z} \to \mathcal{X}$ and optimizes a variation of the equivariance loss that incorporates reconstruction: $\mathbb{E}_{x,g,y=g\cdot x}[d_{\mathcal{X}}(y, \; \psi(g \cdot \varphi(x)))]$ where $d_{\mathcal{X}}$ is the binary cross-entropy for normalized images. Although the action on $\mathcal{Z}$ is free, the latent discretization and consequent interpolation make the model only approximately equivariant. Similarly to EquIN, we implement ENR as ResNet18. As suggested in the original work [7] we deploy 3D convolutional layers around the latent and set to zero the latent dimensions outside a ball. We set $S = 8$ with 160 non-zero latent dimensions since this value is comparable to the latent dimensionality of EquIN, between 7 and 250 dimensions depending on $N$, making the comparison fair. Note that ENR is inapplicable to DOUBLE ARROWS since its symmetry group is not naturally embedded into SO(3).

## 5.3   Quantitative Results

In order to quantitatively compare the models, we rely on the following evaluation metrics computed on a test dataset $\mathcal{D}_{\text{test}}$ consisting of 10% of the corresponding training data:

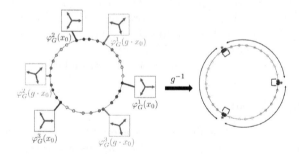

**Fig. 3.** Diagram explaining the estimation of the disentanglement metric for EquIN. This example assumes that $G = \mathrm{SO}(2)$ and that $A$ is the identity.

– *Hit-Rate:* a standard score comparing equivariant representations with different latent space geometries [16]. Given a test triple $(x, g, y = g \cdot x) \in \mathcal{D}_{\text{test}}$, we say that '$x$ hits $y$' if $\varphi(y)$ is the nearest neighbor in $\mathcal{Z}$ of $g \cdot \varphi(x)$ among a random batch of encodings $\{\varphi(x)\}_{x \in \mathcal{B}}$ with $|\mathcal{B}| = 20$. The hit-rate is then defined as the number of times $x$ hits $y$ divided by the test set size. For each model, the nearest neighbor is computed with respect to the same latent metric $d$ as the one used for training. Higher values of the metric are better.

– *Disentanglement:* an evaluation metric proposed in [28] to measure disentanglement according to the symmetry-based definition of [12]. This metric is designed for groups in the form $G = \mathrm{SO}(2)^T$ and therefore is inapplicable to the SOLIDS dataset. Per orbit, the test set is organized into datapoints of the form $y = g \cdot x_0$ where $x_0$ is an arbitrary point in the given orbit. In order to compute the metric, the test dataset is encoded into $\mathcal{Z}$ via the given representation and then projected to $\mathbb{R}^{2T}$ via principal component analysis. Then for each independent copy of $\mathrm{SO}(2) \subseteq G$, a group action on the corresponding copy of $\mathbb{R}^2$ is inferred by fitting parameters via a grid search. Finally, the metric computes the average dispersion of the transformed embeddings as the variance of $g^{-1} \cdot A\varphi_G(y)$. For EquIN, we propose a modified version accounting for the fact that $\varphi_G$ produces multiple points in $G$ using the Chamfer distance $d$ and averaging the dispersion with respect to each transformed embedding, see Fig. 3. The formula for computing the metric is given by:

$$\mathbb{E}_{y,y'}[d(h^{-1} \cdot A\varphi_G(y'),\ g^{-1} \cdot A\varphi_G(y))] \tag{11}$$

where $y = g \cdot x_0$ and $y' = h \cdot x_0$. Lower values of the metric are better.

The results are summarized in Table 1. EquIN achieves significantly better scores than the baseline. The latter is unable to model the stabilizers in its latent space, leading to representations of poor quality and loss of information. ENR is instead competitive with EquIN. Its latent space suits non-free group actions since stabilizers can be modelled as signals over the latent three-dimensional grid. ENR achieves similar values of hit-rate compared to EquIN. The latter generally outperforms ENR, especially on the MODELNET dataset, while is outpermformed on ROTATING ARROWS. According to the disentanglement metric, EquIN achieves significantly lower scores than ENR. This is probably due to the fact the latent group action in ENR is approximate, making the model unable to infer representations that are equivariant at a granular scale.

## 5.4   Qualitative Results

We provide a number of visualizations as a qualitative evaluation of EquIN. Figure 4 illustrates the output of $\varphi_G$ on the various datasets. As can be seen, EquIN correctly infers the stabilizers i.e., the cyclic subgroups of $\mathrm{SO}(2)$ and the subgroup of $\mathrm{SO}(3)$ of order 12. When $N$ is larger than the ground-truth cardinalities of stabilizers, the points $\varphi_G^i$ are overlapped and collapse to the number of stabilizers as expected. Figure 5 displays the output of $\varphi_O$ for data from COLORED ARROWS. The orbits are correctly separated in $\mathcal{Z}_O$. Therefore, the model is able to distinguish data due to variability in the number $\nu$ of arrows as well as in their color.

**Table 1.** Mean and standard deviation of the metrics across five repetitions. The number juxtaposed to the name of EquIN indicates the cardinality $N$ of the output of $\varphi_G$.

| Dataset | Model | Disentanglement ($\downarrow$) | Hit-Rate ($\uparrow$) |
|---|---|---|---|
| ROTATING ARROWS | Baseline | $1.582_{\pm 0.013}$ | $0.368_{\pm 0.004}$ |
| | EquIN5 | $\mathbf{0.009}_{\pm 0.005}$ | $0.880_{\pm 0.021}$ |
| | EquIN10 | $0.092_{\pm 0.063}$ | $0.857_{\pm 0.050}$ |
| | ENR | $0.077_{\pm 0.028}$ | $\mathbf{0.918}_{\pm 0.009}$ |
| COLORED ARROWS | Baseline | $1.574_{\pm 0.007}$ | $0.430_{\pm 0.004}$ |
| | EquIN5 | $0.021_{\pm 0.015}$ | $0.930_{\pm 0.055}$ |
| | EquIN10 | $\mathbf{0.001}_{\pm 0.001}$ | $\mathbf{0.976}_{\pm 0.005}$ |
| | ENR | $0.106_{\pm 0.032}$ | $0.949_{\pm 0.018}$ |
| DOUBLE ARROWS | Baseline | $1.926_{\pm 0.019}$ | $0.023_{\pm 0.004}$ |
| | EquIN6 | $0.028_{\pm 0.006}$ | $0.512_{\pm 0.011}$ |
| | EquIN15 | $0.004_{\pm 0.001}$ | $0.820_{\pm 0.104}$ |
| | EquIN20 | $\mathbf{0.002}_{\pm 0.001}$ | $\mathbf{0.934}_{\pm 0.020}$ |
| MODELNET | Baseline | $1.003_{\pm 0.228}$ | $0.538_{\pm 0.086}$ |
| | EquIN4 | $0.012_{\pm 0.022}$ | $0.917_{\pm 0.074}$ |
| | EquIN10 | $\mathbf{0.003}_{\pm 0.001}$ | $\mathbf{0.910}_{\pm 0.011}$ |
| | ENR | $0.037_{\pm 0.038}$ | $0.817_{\pm 0.085}$ |
| SOLIDS | Baseline | - | $0.123_{\pm 0.007}$ |
| | EquIN12 | - | $0.126_{\pm 0.004}$ |
| | EquIN24 | - | $0.139_{\pm 0.056}$ |
| | EquIN60 | - | $0.596_{\pm 0.106}$ |
| | EquIN80 | - | $\mathbf{0.795}_{\pm 0.230}$ |
| | ENR | - | $0.772_{\pm 0.095}$ |

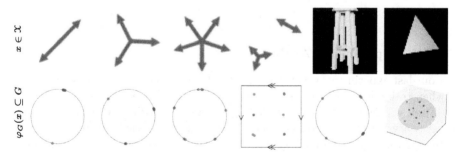

**Fig. 4.** Visualization of datapoints $x$ and the corresponding predicted (coset of the) stabilizer $\varphi_G(x)$. For DOUBLE ARROWS, the torus $G = SO(2) \times SO(2)$ is visualized as an identified square. For the tetrahedron from SOLIDS, $G$ is visualized as a projective space $\mathbb{RP}^3 \simeq SO(3)$.

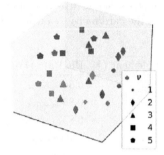

**Fig. 5.** Embeddings $\varphi_O(x) \in \mathcal{Z}_O \subseteq \mathbb{R}^3$ for $x$ in COLORED ARROWS. Each symbol represents the ground-truth cardinality $\nu = |G_x|$ of the stabilizer while the color of the symbol represents the corresponding color of the arrow (left). The same embeddings are projected onto $\mathbb{R}^2$ via principal component analysis (right).

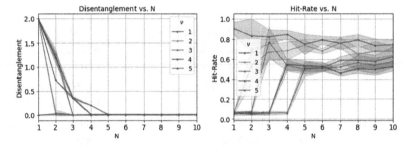

**Fig. 6.** Disentanglement and hit-rate for models trained with different values of $N$. Each line in the plot represents the results of a model trained on a dataset with a single orbit whose stabilizer has cardinality $\nu$. The plots show the mean and standard deviation across five repetitions.

## 5.5 Hyperparameter Analysis

For our last experiment, we investigate the effects of the hyperparameters $N$ and $\lambda$ when training EquIN on datasets with different numbers of stabilizers.

First, we show that a value of $N$ larger than the cardinality of the stabilizers is necessary to achieve good values of disentanglement, and hit-rate for datasets with non-free group action, see Fig. 6. However, large values of $N$ can result in non-collapsing embeddings $\varphi_G$ corresponding to non-minimal cosets of the stabilizers. In these cases, the regularization term of Eq. 9 and its corresponding weight $\lambda$ plays an important role.

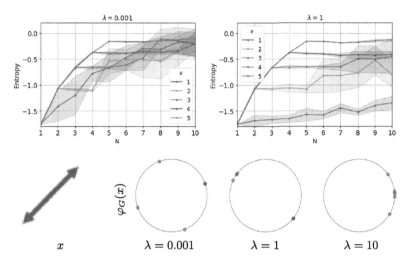

**Fig. 7.** Discrete entropy for models trained on the arrows dataset with different cardinalities of stabilizer $\nu$ and two distinct values of $\lambda$ (top row). Example embeddings $\varphi_G(x)$ obtained for a datapoint $x$ with two stabilizers obtained with models using $\lambda \in \{0.001, 1, 10\}$ (bottom row).

The bottom row of Fig. 7 shows the embeddings $\varphi_G(x)$ learnt for a datapoint $x \in X$ with stabilizer $G_x \simeq C_2$ of cardinality two. The plots show how for low values of $\lambda$, the network converges to a non-minimal set. When an optimal value is chosen, such as $\lambda = 1$, the embeddings obtained with $\varphi_G$ collapse to a set with the same cardinality as the stabilizers. If $\lambda$ is too large, the embeddings tend to degenerate and collapse to a single point.

If the value of $\lambda$ is too small, the discrete entropy of the learnt embeddings is not restricted. It continues to increase even if the number of embeddings matches the correct number of stabilizers. When an appropriate value of $\lambda$ is chosen, the entropy becomes more stable as the embeddings have converged to the correct cardinality.

The plots in Fig. 8 show the inverse relationship between $\lambda$ and the entropy of the encoder $\varphi_G$ that describes the collapse of the embeddings. The collapse of the embeddings also results in a lower performance of disentanglement and hit-rate by the models as seen for higher values of $\lambda > 1$. Throughout the experiments, we fix the value of $\lambda = 1$ except for SOLIDS where a value of $\lambda = 10$ was chosen since the number $N$ used is larger.

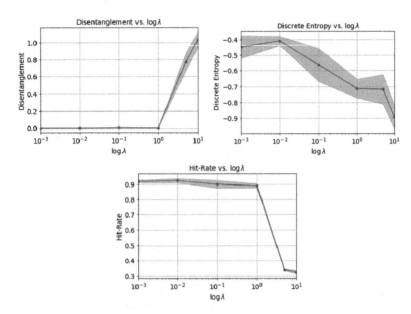

**Fig. 8.** Disentanglement, discrete entropy and hit-rate for models trained with different values of $\lambda$ and fixed $N = 5$. The training dataset corresponds to the rotating arrows with $\nu \in \{1, 2, 3, 4, 5\}$. Each line shows the mean and standard deviation across five repetitions.

## 6   Conclusions and Future Work

In this work, we introduced EquIN, a method for learning equivariant representations for possibly non-free group actions. We discussed the theoretical foundations and empirically investigated the method on images with rotational symmetries. We showed that our model can capture the cosets of the group stabilizers and separate the information characterizing multiple orbits.

EquIN relies on the assumption that the stabilizers of the group action are finite. However, non-discrete stabilizer subgroups sometimes occur in practice, e.g., in continuous symmetrical objects such as cones, cylinders or spheres. Therefore, an interesting future direction is designing an equivariant representation learner suitable for group actions with non-discrete stabilizers.

**Acknowledgements.** This work was supported by the Swedish Research Council, the Knut and Alice Wallenberg Foundation and the European Research Council (ERC-BIRD-884807). This work has also received funding from the NWO-TTW Programme "Efficient Deep Learning" (EDL) P16-25.

**Ethical Statement.** The work presented in this paper consists of a theoretical and practical analysis on learning representations that capture the information about symmetry transformations observed in data. Due to the nature of this work as fundamental research, it is challenging to determine any direct adverse ethical implications that might arise. However, we think that any possible ethical implications of these ideas would be a consequence of the possible applications to augmented reality, object recognition, or reinforcement learning among others. The datasets used in this work consist of procedurally generated images with no personal or sensitive information.

# References

1. Ahuja, K., Hartford, J., Bengio, Y.: Properties from mechanisms: an equivariance perspective on identifiable representation learning. In: International Conference on Learning Representations (2022)
2. Bengio, Y., Courville, A., Vincent, P.: Representation learning: a review and new perspectives. IEEE Trans. Pattern Anal. Mach. Intell. **35**(8), 1798–1828 (2013)
3. Caselles-Dupré, H., Garcia-Ortiz, M., Filliat, D.: Symmetry-based disentangled representation learning requires interaction with environments. In: Advances in Neural Information Processing Systems (2019)
4. Chen, R.T., Li, X., Grosse, R.B., Duvenaud, D.K.: Isolating sources of disentanglement in variational autoencoders. In: Advances in Neural Information Processing Systems (2018)
5. Chen, T., Kornblith, S., Norouzi, M., Hinton, G.: A simple framework for contrastive learning of visual representations. In: International Conference on Machine Learning (2020)
6. Cohen, T., Welling, M.: Learning the irreducible representations of commutative Lie groups. In: International Conference on Machine Learning (2014)
7. Dupont, E., Martin, M.B., Colburn, A., Sankar, A., Susskind, J., Shan, Q.: Equivariant neural rendering. In: International Conference on Machine Learning (2020)
8. Falorsi, L., et al.: Explorations in homeomorphic variational auto-encoding. In: ICML18 Workshop on Theoretical Foundations and Applications of Deep Generative Models (2018)
9. Guo, X., Zhu, E., Liu, X., Yin, J.: Affine equivariant autoencoder. In: International Joint Conference on Artificial Intelligence (2019)
10. Ha, D., Schmidhuber, J.: World models. arXiv preprint (2018)
11. He, K., Zhang, X., Ren, S., Sun, J.: Deep residual learning for image recognition. In: IEEE Conference on Computer Vision and Pattern Recognition (2016)
12. Higgins, I., et al.: Towards a definition of disentangled representations. arXiv preprint (2018)
13. Higgins, I., et al.: Beta-VAE: learning basic visual concepts with a constrained variational framework. In: International Conference on Learning Representations (2017)
14. Higgins, I., Racanière, S., Rezende, D.: Symmetry-based representations for artificial and biological general intelligence. Front. Comput. Neurosci. **16**, 836498 (2022)
15. Hinton, G.E., Krizhevsky, A., Wang, S.D.: Transforming auto-encoders. In: Honkela, T., Duch, W., Girolami, M., Kaski, S. (eds.) ICANN 2011. LNCS, vol. 6791, pp. 44–51. Springer, Heidelberg (2011). https://doi.org/10.1007/978-3-642-21735-7_6
16. Kipf, T., van der Pol, E., Welling, M.: Contrastive learning of structured world models. In: International Conference on Learning Representations (2020)
17. Liang, K.K.: Efficient conversion from rotating matrix to rotation axis and angle by extending rodrigues' formula. arXiv preprint (2018)

18. Locatello, F., et al.: Challenging common assumptions in the unsupervised learning of disentangled representations. In: International Conference on Machine Learning (2019)

19. Loshchilov, I., Hutter, F.: Decoupled weight decay regularization. In: International Conference on Learning Representations (2019)

20. Marchand, E., Uchiyama, H., Spindler, F.: Pose estimation for augmented reality: a hands-on survey. IEEE Trans. Vis. Comput. Graph. **22**(12), 2633–2651 (2016)

21. Marchetti, G.L., Tegnér, G., Varava, A., Kragic, D.: Equivariant Representation Learning via Class-Pose Decomposition. arXiv preprint (2022)

22. Murphy, K., Esteves, C., Jampani, V., Ramalingam, S., Makadia, A.: Implicit representation of probability distributions on the rotation manifold. In: International Conference on Machine Learning (2021)

23. Painter, M., Hare, J., Prügel-Bennett, A.: Linear disentangled representations and unsupervised action estimation. In: Advances in Neural Information Processing Systems (2020)

24. Park, J.Y., Biza, O., Zhao, L., van de Meent, J.W., Walters, R.: Learning symmetric embeddings for equivariant world models. In: International Conference on Machine Learning (2022)

25. van der Pol, E., Kipf, T., Oliehoek, F.A., Welling, M.: Plannable approximations to MDP homomorphisms: equivariance under actions. In: International Conference on Autonomous Agents and Multi-Agent Systems (2020)

26. Quessard, R., Barrett, T.D., Clements, W.R.: Learning disentangled representations and group structure of dynamical environments. In: Advances in Neural Information Processing Systems (2020)

27. Rotman, J.J.: An Introduction to the Theory of Groups, vol. 148. Springer, New York (2012). https://doi.org/10.1007/978-1-4612-4176-8

28. Tonnaer, L., Perez Rey, L.A., Menkovski, V., Holenderski, M., Portegies, J.: Quantifying and learning linear symmetry-based disentanglement. In: International Conference on Machine Learning (2022)

29. Worrall, D.E., Garbin, S.J., Turmukhambetov, D., Brostow, G.J.: Interpretable transformations with encoder-decoder networks. In: International Conference on Computer Vision (2017)

30. Wu, Z., et al.: 3D shapenets: a deep representation for volumetric shapes. In: IEEE Conference on Computer Vision and Pattern Recognition (2015)

# Towards Understanding the Mechanism of Contrastive Learning via Similarity Structure: A Theoretical Analysis

Hiroki Waida[1]([✉]), Yuichiro Wada[2,3], Léo Andéol[4,5,6,7], Takumi Nakagawa[1,3], Yuhui Zhang[1], and Takafumi Kanamori[1,3]

[1] Tokyo Institute of Technology, Tokyo, Japan
`waida.h.aa@m.titech.ac.jp`
[2] Fujitsu, Kanagawa, Japan
[3] RIKEN AIP, Tokyo, Japan
[4] Institut de Mathématiques de Toulouse, Toulouse, France
[5] SNCF, Saint-Denis, France
[6] Université de Toulouse, Toulouse, France
[7] CNRS, Toulouse, France

**Abstract.** Contrastive learning is an efficient approach to self-supervised representation learning. Although recent studies have made progress in the theoretical understanding of contrastive learning, the investigation of how to characterize the clusters of the learned representations is still limited. In this paper, we aim to elucidate the characterization from theoretical perspectives. To this end, we consider a kernel-based contrastive learning framework termed Kernel Contrastive Learning (KCL), where kernel functions play an important role when applying our theoretical results to other frameworks. We introduce a formulation of the similarity structure of learned representations by utilizing a statistical dependency viewpoint. We investigate the theoretical properties of the kernel-based contrastive loss via this formulation. We first prove that the formulation characterizes the structure of representations learned with the kernel-based contrastive learning framework. We show a new upper bound of the classification error of a downstream task, which explains that our theory is consistent with the empirical success of contrastive learning. We also establish a generalization error bound of KCL. Finally, we show a guarantee for the generalization ability of KCL to the downstream classification task via a surrogate bound.

**Keywords:** Contrastive Learning · Self-supervised Learning · Reproducing Kernels · Statistical Learning Theory · Representation Learning

## 1 Introduction

Recently, many studies on self-supervised representation learning have been paying much attention to contrastive learning [7,8,10,16,21,32]. Through contrastive learning, encoder functions acquire how to encode unlabeled data to

© The Author(s), under exclusive license to Springer Nature Switzerland AG 2023
D. Koutra et al. (Eds.): ECML PKDD 2023, LNAI 14172, pp. 709–727, 2023.
https://doi.org/10.1007/978-3-031-43421-1_42

good representations by utilizing some information of similarity behind the data, where recent works [8,10,16] use several data augmentation techniques to produce pairs of similar data. It is empirically shown by many works [7,8,10,16,21] that contrastive learning produces effective representations that are fully adaptable to downstream tasks, such as classification and transfer learning.

Besides the practical development of contrastive learning, the theoretical understanding is essential to construct more efficient self-supervised learning algorithms. In this paper, we tackle the following fundamental question of contrastive learning from the theoretical side: *How are the clusters of feature vectors output from an encoder model pretrained by contrastive learning characterized?*

Recently, several works have shed light on several theoretical perspectives on this problem to study the generalization guarantees of contrastive learning to downstream classification tasks [2,15,20,21,25,59,66]. One of the primary approaches of these works is to introduce some similarity measures in the data. Arora et al. [2] has introduced the conditional independence assumption, which assumes that data $x$ and its positive data $x^+$ are sampled independently according to the conditional probability distribution $\mathcal{D}_c$, given the *latent class* $c$ drawn from the latent class distribution. Although the concepts of latent classes and conditional independence assumption are often utilized to formulate semantic similarity of $x$ and $x^+$ [2–5,67], it is pointed out by several works [21,59] that this assumption can be violated in practice. Several works [21,59] have introduced different ideas about the similarity between data to alleviate this assumption. HaoChen et al. [21] have introduced the notion called *population augmentation graph* to provide a theoretical analysis for Spectral Contrastive Learning (SCL) without the conditional independence assumption on $x$ and $x^+$. Some works also focus on various graph structures [15,20,59]. Although these studies give interesting insights into contrastive learning, the applicable scope of their analyses is limited to specific objective functions. Recently, several works [25,66] consider the setup where raw data in the same latent class are aligned well in the sense that the *augmented distance* is small enough. Although their theoretical guarantees can apply to multiple contrastive learning frameworks, their assumptions on the function class of encoders are strong, and it needs to be elucidated whether their guarantees can hold in practice. Therefore, the investigation of the above question from unified viewpoints is ongoing, and more perspectives are required to understand the structure learned by contrastive learning.

## 1.1   Contributions

In this paper, we aim to theoretically investigate the above question from a unified perspective by introducing a formulation based on a statistical similarity between data. The main contributions of this paper are summarized below[1]:

1. Since we aim to elucidate the mechanism of contrastive learning, we need to consider a unified framework that can apply to others, not specific frameworks

---

[1] Supplementary material is available at https://github.com/hrkyd/KernelCL/tree/main/supplementary_material.

such as SimCLR [8] and SCL [21]. Li et al. [32] pointed out that kernel-based self-supervised learning objectives are related to other contrastive losses, such as the InfoNCE loss [8,38]. Therefore, via a kernel-based contrastive learning framework, other frameworks can be investigated through the lens of kernels. Motivated by this, we utilize the framework termed *Kernel Contrastive Learning* (KCL) as a tool for achieving the goal. The loss of KCL, which is called *kernel contrastive loss*, is a contrastive loss that has a simple and general form, where the similarity between two feature vectors is measured by a reproducing kernel [1,6,46] (Sect. 3). One of our contributions is employing KCL to study the mechanism of contrastive learning from a new unified theoretical perspective.

2. We introduce a new formulation of similarity between data (Sect. 4). Our formulation of similarity begins with the following intuition: if raw or augmented data $x$ and $x'$ belong to the same class, then the similarity measured by some function should be higher than a threshold. Following this, we introduce a formulation (Assumption 2) based on the similarity function (2).

3. We present the theoretical analyses towards elucidating the above question (Sect. 5). We first show that KCL can distinguish the clusters according to this formulation (Sect. 5.1). This result shows that our formulation is closely connected to the mechanism of contrastive learning. Next, we establish a new upper bound for the classification error of the downstream task (Sect. 5.2), which indicates that our formulation does not contradict the efficiency of contrastive learning shown by a line of work [8,10,16,21]. Notably, our upper bound is valid under more realistic assumptions on the encoders, compared to the previous works [25,66]. We also derive a generalization error bound for KCL (Sect. 5.3). Finally, applying our theoretical results, we show a guarantee for the generalization of KCL to the downstream classification task through a surrogate bound (Sect. 5.4).

## 1.2   Related Work

Contrastive learning methods have been investigated from the empirical side [7–10]. Chen et al. [8] propose a method called SimCLR, which utilizes a variant of InfoNCE [8,38]. Several works have recently improved contrastive methods from various viewpoints [7,16,41,42]. Contrastive learning is often utilized in several fundamental tasks, such as clustering [56] and domain adaptation [45], and applied to some domains such as vision [8], natural language processing [17], and speech [26]. Besides the contrastive methods, several works [11,19] also study non-contrastive methods. Investigation toward the theoretical understanding of contrastive learning is also a growing focus. For instance, the generalization ability of contrastive learning to the downstream classification task has been investigated from many kinds of settings [2,5,20,21,25,43,50,59,66]. Several works investigate contrastive learning from various theoretical and empirical viewpoints to elucidate its mechanism, such as the geometric properties of contrastive losses [25,58], formulation of similarity between data [2,15,21,25,30,59,66], inductive bias [20,43], transferablity [22,44,66], feature suppression [9,41], negative sampling methods [12,42], and optimization viewpoints [48,61].

Several works [15,28,29,32,51,63] study the connection between contrastive learning and the theory of kernels. Li et al. [32] investigate some contrastive losses, such as InfoNCE, from a kernel perspective. Zhang et al. [63] show a relation between the kernel method and $f$-mutual information and apply their theory to contrastive learning. Tsai et al. [51] tackle the conditional sampling problem using kernels as similarity measurements. Dufumier et al. [15] consider incorporating prior information in contrastive learning by using the theory of kernel functions. Kiani et al. [29] connect several self-supervised learning algorithms to kernel methods through optimization problem viewpoints. Note that different from these works, our work employs kernel functions to investigate a new unified perspective of contrastive learning via the statistical similarity.

Many previous works investigate various interpretations of self-supervised representation learning objectives. For instance, the InfoMax principle [40,54], spectral clustering [21] (see Ng et al. [35] for spectral clustering), and Hilbert-Schmidt Independence Criterion (HSIC) [32] (see Gretton et al. [18] for HSIC). However, the investigation of contrastive learning from unified perspectives is worth addressing to elucidate its mechanism, as recent works on self-supervised representation learning tackle it from the various standpoints [14,25,28,29,48].

## 2    Preliminaries

In this section, we present the problem setup and several notations.

### 2.1    Problem Setup

We give the standard setup of contrastive learning. Our setup closely follows that of HaoChen et al. [21], though we also introduce additional technically necessary settings to maintain the mathematical rigorousness. Let $\overline{\mathbb{X}} \subset \mathbb{R}^p$ be a topological space consisting of raw data, and let $P_{\overline{\mathbb{X}}}$ be a Borel probability measure on $\overline{\mathbb{X}}$. A line of work on contrastive learning [8,10,16,21] uses data augmentation techniques to obtain similar augmented data points. Hence, we define a set $\mathcal{T}$ of maps transforming a point $\overline{x} \in \overline{\mathbb{X}}$ into $\mathbb{R}^p$, where we assume that $\mathcal{T}$ includes the identity map on $\mathbb{R}^p$. Then, let us define $\mathbb{X} = \bigcup_{t \in \mathcal{T}} \{t(\overline{x}) : \overline{x} \in \overline{\mathbb{X}}\}$. Every element $t$ in $\mathcal{T}$ can be regarded as a map returning an augmented data $x = t(\overline{x})$ for a raw data point $\overline{x} \in \overline{\mathbb{X}}$. Note that since the identity map belongs to $\mathcal{T}$, $\overline{\mathbb{X}}$ is a subset of $\mathbb{X}$. We endow $\mathbb{X}$ with some topology. Let $\nu_{\mathbb{X}}$ be a $\sigma$-finite and nonnegative Borel measure in $\mathbb{X}$. Following the idea of HaoChen et al. [21], we denote $a(x|\overline{x})$ as the conditional probability density function of $x$ given $\overline{x} \sim P_{\overline{\mathbb{X}}}$ and define the weight function $w : \mathbb{X} \times \mathbb{X} \to \mathbb{R}$ as $w(x,x') = \mathbb{E}_{\overline{x} \sim P_{\overline{\mathbb{X}}}}[a(x|\overline{x})a(x'|\overline{x})]$. From the definition, $w$ is a joint probability density function on $\mathbb{X} \times \mathbb{X}$. Let us define the marginal $w(\cdot)$ of the weight function to be $w(x) = \int w(x,x')d\nu_{\mathbb{X}}(x')$. The marginal $w(\cdot)$ is also a probability density function on $\mathbb{X}$, and the corresponding probability measure is denoted by $dP_{\mathbb{X}}(x) = w(x)d\nu_{\mathbb{X}}(x)$. Denote by $\mathbb{E}_{x,x+}[\cdot], \mathbb{E}_{x,x-}[\cdot]$ respectively, the expectation w.r.t. the probability measure $w(x,x')d\nu_{\mathbb{X}}^{\otimes 2}(x,x'), w(x)w(x')d\nu_{\mathbb{X}}^{\otimes 2}(x,x')$ on $\mathbb{X} \times \mathbb{X}$, where $\nu_{\mathbb{X}}^{\otimes 2} := \nu_{\mathbb{X}} \otimes \nu_{\mathbb{X}}$ is the product measure on $\mathbb{X} \times \mathbb{X}$. To rigorously formulate our framework of contrastive learning, we assume that the marginal $w$ is positive on $\mathbb{X}$. Indeed, a point $x \in \mathbb{X}$ satisfying $w(x) = 0$ is not included in the support of $a(\cdot|\overline{x})$ for $P_{\overline{\mathbb{X}}}$-almost surely $\overline{x} \in \overline{\mathbb{X}}$, which means that such a point $x$ merely appears as augmented data.

Let $f_0 : \mathbb{X} \to \mathbb{R}^d$ be an encoder mapping augmented data to the feature space, and let $\mathcal{F}_0$ be a class of functions consisting of such encoders. In practice, $f_0$ is defined by a backbone architecture (e.g., ResNet [23]; see Chen et al. [8]), followed by the additional multi-layer perceptrons called *projection head* [8]. We assume that $\mathcal{F}_0$ is uniformly bounded, i.e., there exists a universal constant $c \in \mathbb{R}$ such that $\sup_{f_0 \in \mathcal{F}_0} \sup_{x \in \mathbb{X}} \|f_0(x)\|_2 \leq c$. For instance, a function space of bias-free fully connected neural networks on a bounded domain, where every neural network has the continuous activation function at each layer, satisfies this condition. Since a feature vector output from the encoder is normalized using the Euclidean norm in many empirical studies [8,16] and several theoretical studies [58,59], we consider the space of normalized functions $\mathcal{F} = \{f \mid \exists f_0 \in \mathcal{F}_0,\ f(x) = f_0(x)/\|f_0(x)\|_2 \text{ for } \forall x \in \mathbb{X}\}$. Here, to guarantee that every $f \in \mathcal{F}$ is well-defined, suppose that $\mathfrak{m}(\mathcal{F}_0) := \inf_{f \in \mathcal{F}} \inf_{x \in \mathbb{X}} \|f_0(x)\|_2 > 0$ holds.

Finally, we introduce several notations used throughout this paper. Let $\mathbb{M} \subset \mathbb{X}$ be a measurable set, then we write $\mathbb{E}[f(x)|\mathbb{M}] := \int_{\mathbb{X}} f(x) P_{\mathbb{X}}(dx|\mathbb{M})$, where we note that $\int_{\mathbb{X}} f(x) P_{\mathbb{X}}(dx|\mathbb{M}) = P_{\mathbb{X}}(\mathbb{M})^{-1} \int_{\mathbb{M}} f(x) w(x) d\nu_{\mathbb{X}}(x)$. We also use the notation $\mathbb{E}[f(x); \mathbb{M}] := \int_{\mathbb{M}} f(x) w(x) d\nu_{\mathbb{X}}(x)$. Denote by $\mathbb{1}_{\mathbb{M}}(\cdot)$, the indicator function of a set $\mathbb{M}$. We also use $[n] := \{1, \cdots, n\}$ for $n \in \mathbb{N}$.

## 2.2 Reproducing Kernels

We provide several notations of reproducing kernels [1,6,46]. Let $k : \mathbb{S}^{d-1} \times \mathbb{S}^{d-1} \to \mathbb{R}$ be a real-valued, continuous, symmetric, and positive-definite kernel, where $\mathbb{S}^{d-1}$ denotes the unit hypersphere centered at the origin $\mathbf{0} \in \mathbb{R}^d$, and the positive-definiteness means that for every $\{z_i\}_{i=1}^n \subset \mathbb{S}^{d-1}$ and $\{c_i\}_{i=1}^n \subset \mathbb{R}$, $\sum_{i,j=1}^n c_i c_j k(z_i, z_j) \geq 0$ holds [6]. Let $\mathcal{H}_k$ be the Reproducing Kernel Hilbert Space (RKHS) with kernel $k$ [1], which satisfies $\phi(z) = \langle \phi, k(\cdot, z) \rangle_{\mathcal{H}_k}$ for all $\phi \in \mathcal{H}_k$ and $z \in \mathbb{S}^{d-1}$. Denote $h(z) = k(\cdot, z)$ for $z \in \mathbb{S}^{d-1}$, where such a map is often called feature map [46]. Here, we impose the following condition.

**Assumption 1.** For the kernel function $k$, there exists some $\rho$-Lipschitz function $\psi : [-1, 1] \to \mathbb{R}$ such that for every $z, z' \in \mathbb{S}^{d-1}$, $k(z, z') = \psi(z^\top z')$ holds.

Several popular kernels in machine learning such as the linear kernel, quadratic kernel, and Gaussian kernel, satisfy Assumption 1. Note that the Lipschitz condition in Assumption 1 is useful to derive the generalization error bound for the kernel contrastive loss (see Sect. 5.3), and sometimes it can be removed when analyzing for a specific kernel. We use this assumption to present general results. Here, we also use the following notion in this paper:

**Proposition 1.** Let $\mathbb{M} \subset \mathbb{X}$ be a measurable set and $f \in \mathcal{F}$. Define $\mu_{\mathbb{M}}(f) := \mathbb{E}_{P_{\mathbb{X}}}[h(f(x))|\mathbb{M}]$. Then, $\mu_{\mathbb{M}}(f) \in \mathcal{H}_k$.

The quantity $\mu_{\mathbb{M}}(f)$ with a measurable subset $\mathbb{M}$ can be regarded as a variant of the kernel mean embedding [34]. The proof of Proposition 1 is a slight modification of Muandet et al. [34]; see Appendix A of the supplementary material.

## 3    Kernel Contrastive Learning

In this section, we introduce a contrastive learning framework to analyze the mechanism of contrastive learning. In representation learning, the InfoNCE loss [8,38] are widely used in application domains such as vision [8,9,16]. Following previous works [5,8,38], we define the InfoNCE loss as,

$$L_{\text{NCE}}(f;\tau) = -\mathbb{E}_{x,x^+,\{x_i^-\}} \left[ \log \frac{e^{f(x)^\top f(x^+)/\tau}}{e^{f(x)^\top f(x^+)/\tau} + \sum_{i=1}^{M} e^{f(x)^\top f(x_i^-)/\tau}} \right],$$

where $\{x_i^-\} \sim P_{\mathbb{X}}$ are i.i.d., $\tau > 0$, and $M$ is the number of negative samples. Wang and Isola [58] introduce the asymptotic of the InfoNCE loss:

$$L_{\infty\text{-NCE}}(f;\tau) = -\mathbb{E}_{x,x^+} \left[ \frac{f(x)^\top f(x^+)}{\tau} \right] + \mathbb{E}_x \left[ \log \mathbb{E}_{x'} \left[ e^{\frac{f(x)^\top f(x')}{\tau}} \right] \right].$$

According to the theoretical analysis of Wang and Isola [58], they show that the first term represents the *alignment*, i.e., the averaged closeness of feature vectors of the pair $(x, x^+)$, while the second one indicates the *uniformity*, i.e., how far apart the feature vectors of negative samples $x, x'$ are. Besides, Chen et al. [9] report the efficiency of the generalized contrastive losses, which have the additional weight hyperparameter. Meanwhile, since we aim to study the mechanism of contrastive learning, a simple and general form of contrastive losses related to other frameworks is required. Here, Li et al. [32] find the connection between self-supervised learning and kernels by showing that some HSIC criterion is proportional to the objective function $\mathbb{E}_{x,x^+}[k(f(x), f(x^+))] - \mathbb{E}_{x,x^-}[k(f(x), f(x^-))]$ (for more detail, see Appendix F.2 of the supplementary material). Motivated by this connection, we consider a contrastive learning objective where a kernel function measures the similarity of the feature vectors of augmented data points. More precisely, for the kernel function $k$ introduced in Sect. 2.2, we define the kernel contrastive loss as,

$$L_{\text{KCL}}(f;\lambda) = -\mathbb{E}_{x,x^+} \left[ k(f(x), f(x^+)) \right] + \lambda \mathbb{E}_{x,x^-} \left[ k(f(x), f(x^-)) \right],$$

where the weight hyperparameter $\lambda$ is inspired by Chen et al. [9]. Here, the kernel contrastive loss $L_{\text{KCL}}$ is minimized during the pretraining stage of contrastive learning. Throughout this paper, the contrastive learning framework with the kernel contrastive loss is called *Kernel Contrastive Learning* (KCL).

Next, we show the connections to other contrastive learning objectives. First, for the InfoNCE loss, we consider the linear kernel contrastive loss $L_{\text{LinKCL}}(f;\lambda)$ defined by selecting $k(z, z') = z^\top z'$. Note that $L_{\text{LinKCL}}$ and its empirical loss are also discussed in several works [25,57]. For $L_{\text{LinKCL}}(f;1)$, we have,

$$\tau^{-1} L_{\text{LinKCL}}(f;1) \le L_{\text{NCE}}(f;\tau) + \log M^{-1}. \tag{1}$$

In Appendix F.3 of the supplementary material, we show a generalized inequality of (1) for the generalized loss [9]. Note that similar relations hold when $L_{\text{NCE}}$ is replaced with the asymptotic loss [58] or decoupled contrastive learning loss [62]; see Appendix F.3 of the supplementary material. Therefore, it is possible to analyze the InfoNCE loss and its variants via $L_{\text{LinKCL}}(f; \lambda)$.

The kernel contrastive loss is also related to other objectives. For instance, the quadratic kernel contrastive loss with the quadratic kernel $k(z, z') = (z^\top z')^2$ becomes a lower bound of the spectral contrastive loss [21] up to an additive constant (see Appendix F.3 of the supplementary material). Thus, theoretical analyses of the kernel contrastive loss can apply to other objectives.

Note that we empirically demonstrate that the KCL frameworks with the Gaussian kernel and quadratic kernel work, although simple; see Appendix H.1 for the experimental setup and Appendix H.2 and H.3 for the results in the supplementary material[2]. The experimental results also motivate us to use KCL as a theoretical tool for studying contrastive learning.

## 4   A Formulation Based on Statistical Similarity

In this section, we introduce a formulation based on similarity of data.

### 4.1   Key Ingredient: Similarity Function

To study the mechanism of contrastive learning, we introduce a notion of similarity between two augmented data points, which is a key component in our analysis. Let us define,

$$\operatorname{sim}(x, x'; \lambda) := \frac{w(x, x')}{w(x)w(x')} - \lambda, \tag{2}$$

where $\lambda \geq 0$ is the weight parameter of $L_{\text{KCL}}$, and $w(x, x')$ and $w(x)$ have been introduced in Sect. 2.1. Note that (2) is well-defined since $w(x) > 0$ holds for every $x \in \mathbb{X}$. The quantity $\operatorname{sim}(x, x'; \lambda)$ represents how much statistical dependency $x$ and $x'$ have. The density ratio $w(x, x')/(w(x)w(x'))$ can be regarded as an instance of *point-wise dependency* introduced by Tsai et al. [53]. The hyperparameter $\lambda$ controls the degree of relevance between two augmented data $x, x'$ via their (in-)dependency. For instance, with the fixed $\lambda = 1$, $\operatorname{sim}(x, x'; 1)$ is positive if $w(x, x') > w(x)w(x')$, i.e., $x$ and $x'$ are correlated.

Note that several theoretical works [28,50,60] use the density ratio to study the optimal representations of several contrastive learning objectives. Tosh et al. [50] focus on the fact that the minimizer of a logistic loss can be written in terms of the density ratio and utilize it to study *landmark embedding* [49]. Johnson et al. [28] connect the density ratio to the minimizers of several contrastive learning objectives and investigate the quality of representations related to the minimizers. In addition, Wang et al. [60] study the minimizer of the spectral

---

[2] Code is available at https://github.com/hrkyd/KernelCL/tree/main/code.

contrastive loss [21]. Meanwhile, we emphasize that the purpose of using the density ratio in (2) is not to study the optimal representation of KCL but to give a formulation based on the statistical similarity between augmented data.

*Remark 1.* We can show that the kernel contrastive loss can be regarded as a relaxation of the population-level Normalized Cut problem [47], where the integral kernel is defined with (2). Thus, (2) defines the similarity structure utilized by KCL. Detailed arguments and comparison to related works [21,48] can be found in Appendix G of the supplementary material.

## 4.2    Formulation and Example

We introduce the following formulation based on our problem setting.

**Assumption 2.** There exist some $\delta \in \mathbb{R}$, number of clusters $K \in \mathbb{N}$, measurable subsets $\mathbb{M}_1, \cdots, \mathbb{M}_K \subset \mathbb{X}$, and a deterministic labeling function $y : \mathbb{X} \to [K]$ such that the following conditions hold:

**(A)** $\bigcup_{i=1}^{K} \mathbb{M}_i = \mathbb{X}$ holds.
**(B)** For every $i \in [K]$, any points $x, x' \in \mathbb{M}_i$ satisfy $\mathrm{sim}(x, x'; \lambda) \geq \delta$.
**(C)** For every $x \in \mathbb{X}$ and the set of indices $J_x = \{j \in [K] \mid x \in \mathbb{M}_j\}$, $y(x) \in J_x$ holds. Moreover, each set $\{x \in \mathbb{X} \mid y(x) = i\}$ is measurable.

Assumption 2 does not require that $\mathbb{M}_1, \cdots, \mathbb{M}_K$ are disjoint, which is a realistic setting, as Wang et al. [59] show that clusters of augmented data can have inter-cluster connections depending on the strength of data augmentation. The conditions **(A)** and **(B)** in Assumption 2 guarantee that each subset $\mathbb{M}_i$ consists of augmented data that have high similarity. The condition **(C)** enables to incorporate label information in our analysis. Note that several works on contrastive learning [20,21,43] also employ deterministic labeling functions.

These conditions are useful to analyze the theory of contrastive learning. To gain more intuition, we provide a simple example that satisfies Assumption 2.

*Example 1 (The proof and another example can be found in Appendix F.1 of the supplementary material).*    Suppose that $\mathbb{X}$ consists of disjoint open balls $\mathbb{B}_1, \cdots, \mathbb{B}_K$ of the same radius in $\mathbb{R}^p$, and $\overline{\mathbb{X}} = \mathbb{X}$. Let $p_{\overline{\mathbb{X}}}(\overline{x}) = (K\mathrm{vol}(\mathbb{B}_1))^{-1}$ be the probability density function of $P_{\overline{\mathbb{X}}}$, and $a(x|\overline{x}) = \mathrm{vol}(\mathbb{B}_1)^{-1} \sum_{i=1}^{K} \mathbb{1}_{\mathbb{B}_i \times \mathbb{B}_i}(x, \overline{x})$. Then, $w(x) > 0$ and $\mathrm{sim}(x, x'; \lambda) = K\mathbb{1}_{\bigcup_{i \in [K]} \mathbb{B}_i \times \mathbb{B}_i}(x, x') - \lambda$ hold. Hence, for instance, let $\lambda = 1$, $\delta = K - 1$, take $\mathbb{M}_i := \mathbb{B}_i$, and define $y : \mathbb{X} \to [K]$ as $y(x) = i$ if $x \in \mathbb{B}_i$ for some $i \in [K]$. Then, Assumption 2 is satisfied in this setting.

Theoretical formulations of similarity have been investigated by several works on contrastive learning [2,15,20,21,25,30,39,59,66]. The basic notions introduced by these works are: *latent classes* of unlabeled data and conditional independence assumption [2], graph structures of raw or augmented data [15,20,21,59], the decomposition of the latent variable of unlabled data into the *content* (i.e., invariant against data augmentation) and *style* (i.e., changeable

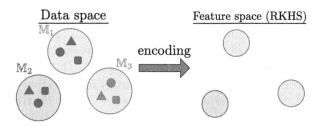

**Fig. 1.** An illustration of Theorem 1. The clusters $\mathbb{M}_1, \cdots, \mathbb{M}_K$ defined with $\mathrm{sim}(x, x'; \lambda)$ are mapped into the RKHS, where each cluster in the RKHS shrinks or expands (via $\mathfrak{a}(f)$) while maintaining the distance to other clusters (via $\mathfrak{c}(f)$).

by data augmentation) variables [30,39], and the geometric structure based on *augmented distance* and the concentration within class subsets [25,66]. Meanwhile, our formulation in Assumption 2 uses the similarity function (2), which differs from the previous works. Note that Assumption 2 has some relation to Assumption 3 in HaoChen and Ma [20]; see Appendix F.4 of the supplementary material. Our formulation gives deeper insights into contrastive learning, as shown in Sect. 5.

# 5  Theoretical Results

We present the theoretical analyses of KCL by utilizing the similarity structure.

## 5.1  KCL as Representation Learning with Statistical Similarity

The aim of this subsection is to see how the formulation based on the similarity $\mathrm{sim}(x, x'; \lambda)$ is related to representation learning by the KCL framework. To this end, we connect the kernel contrastive loss to the formulation. The following theorem indicates that KCL has two effects on the way of representation learning, where $\mathbb{M}_1, \cdots, \mathbb{M}_K$ defined with $\mathrm{sim}(x, x'; \lambda)$ involve to explain the relation.

**Theorem 1.** *Suppose that Assumption 1 and 2 hold. Take $\delta \in \mathbb{R}$, $K \in \mathbb{N}$, and $\mathbb{M}_1, \cdots, \mathbb{M}_K$ such that the conditions* **(A)** *and* **(B)** *in Assumption 2 are satisfied. Then, the following inequality holds for every $f \in \mathcal{F}$:*

$$\frac{\delta}{2} \cdot \mathfrak{a}(f) + \lambda \cdot \mathfrak{c}(f) \leq L_{\mathrm{KCL}}(f; \lambda) + R(\lambda). \tag{3}$$

*where $\mathfrak{a}(f) := \sum_{i=1}^{K} \mathbb{E}_{x, x^-} \left[ \| h(f(x)) - h(f(x^-)) \|_{\mathcal{H}_k}^2; \mathbb{M}_i \times \mathbb{M}_i \right]$, $\mu_i(f) = \mu_{\mathbb{M}_i}(f)$, $\mathfrak{c}(f) := \sum_{i \neq j} P_{\mathbb{X}}(\mathbb{M}_i) P_{\mathbb{X}}(\mathbb{M}_j) \langle \mu_i(f), \mu_j(f) \rangle_{\mathcal{H}_k}$, and $R(\lambda)$ is a function of $\lambda$.*

For the proof of Theorem 1, see Appendix B.2 of the supplementary material. Note that the key point of the proof is the following usage of Assumption 2: for any $x, x' \in \mathbb{M}_i$, the inequality $\mathrm{sim}(x, x'; \lambda) \geq \delta$ implies the relation $w(x, x') \geq (\lambda + \delta) w(x) w(x')$. Here we briefly explain each symbol in

**Theorem 1.** The value $\mathfrak{a}(f)$ quantifies the concentration within each cluster consisting of the representations of augmented data in $\mathbb{M}_i$. The quantity $\mathfrak{c}(f)$ measures how far the subsets $h(f(\mathbb{M}_1)), \cdots, h(f(\mathbb{M}_K))$ are, since $\langle \mu_i(f), \mu_j(f) \rangle_{\mathcal{H}_k} = \int_{\mathbb{M}_i} \int_{\mathbb{M}_j} k(f(x), f(x')) P_{\mathbb{X}}(dx|\mathbb{M}_i) P_{\mathbb{X}}(dx'|\mathbb{M}_j)$ holds (see Lemma 2 in Appendix B.1 of the supplementary material). These quantities indicate that representation learning by KCL can distinguish the subsets $\mathbb{M}_1, \cdots, \mathbb{M}_K$ in the RKHS (see Fig. 1 for illustration). The function $R(\lambda)$ includes the term that represents the hardness of the pretraining task in the space of augmented data $\mathbb{X}$: if the overlaps between two different subsets $\mathbb{M}_i$ and $\mathbb{M}_j$ expand, then $R(\lambda)$ increases (for the definition, see Definition 3 in Appendix B.2 of the supplementary material).

A key point of Theorem 1 is that $\delta$ and $\lambda$ can determine how learned representations distribute in the RKHS. If $\delta > 0$, then representations of augmented data in each $\mathbb{M}_i$ tend to align as controlling the trade-off between $\mathfrak{a}(f)$ and $\mathfrak{c}(f)$. For $\delta \leq 0$, not just the means $\mu_1(f), \cdots, \mu_K(f)$ but also the representations tend to scatter. We remark that $\delta$ depends on the fixed weight $\lambda$ due to the condition **(B)** in Assumption 2. Intuitively, larger $\lambda$ makes $\delta$ smaller and vice versa.

Here we remark that under several assumptions, the equality holds in (3).

**Corollary 1.** *In the setting of Theorem 1, suppose that $\mathbb{M}_1, \cdots, \mathbb{M}_K$ are disjoint, and for every pair $(i,j) \in [K] \times [K]$ such that $i \neq j$, every $(x, x') \in \mathbb{M}_i \times \mathbb{M}_j$ satisfies $w(x, x') = 0$. Suppose that for every $i \in [K]$, it holds that $\mathrm{sim}(x, x'; \lambda) = \delta$ for any $x, x' \in \mathbb{M}_i$. Then, for every $f \in \mathcal{F}$, the equality in (3) holds, i.e., $L_{\mathrm{KCL}}(f; \lambda) = \frac{\delta}{2} \cdot \mathfrak{a}(f) + \lambda \cdot \mathfrak{c}(f) - R(\lambda)$.*

The proof of Corollary 1 can be found in Appendix B.3 of the supplementary material. The above corollary means that, under these assumptions, the minimization of the kernel contrastive loss is equivalent to that of the objective function $(\delta/2) \cdot \mathfrak{a}(f) + \lambda \cdot \mathfrak{c}(f)$. Note that Example 1 satisfies all the assumptions enumerated in the statement. In summary, Theorem 1 and Corollary 1 imply that contrastive learning by the KCL framework is characterized as representation learning with the similarity structure of augmented data space $\mathbb{X}$.

Here, we make a comparison to related work. The quantity $\mathfrak{a}(f)$ is closely related to the property called *alignment* [58] since the representations of similar data are learned to be close in the RKHS. Also, the quantity $\mathfrak{c}(f)$ has some connection to *divergence property* [25] since it measures how far apart the means $\mu_i(f)$ and $\mu_j(f)$ are. Although the relations between these properties and contrastive learning have been pointed out by Wang and Isola [58]; Huang et al. [25], we emphasize that our result gives a new characterization of the clusters. Furthermore, this theorem also implies that the trade-off between $\mathfrak{a}(f)$ and $\mathfrak{c}(f)$ is determined with $\delta$ and $\lambda$. Therefore, Theorem 1 provides deeper insights into understanding the mechanism of contrastive learning.

## 5.2    A New Upper Bound of the Classification Error

Next, we show how minimization of the kernel contrastive loss guarantees good performance in the downstream classification task, according to our formulation of similarity. To this end, we prove that the properties of contrastive learning shown in Theorem 1 yield the linearly well-separable representations in the RKHS. First, we quantify the linear separability as follows: following HaoChen et al. [21]; Saunshi et al. [43], under Assumption 2, for a model $f \in \mathcal{F}$, a linear weight $W : \mathcal{H}_k \to \mathbb{R}^K$, and a bias $\beta \in \mathbb{R}^K$, we define the downstream classification error as $L_{\mathrm{Err}}(f, W, \beta; y) := P_{\mathbb{X}}(g_{f,W,\beta}(x) \neq y(x))$, where $g_{f,W,\beta}(x) := \arg\max_{i \in [K]} \{\langle W_i, h(f(x)) \rangle_{\mathcal{H}_k} + \beta_i\}$ for $W_i \in \mathcal{H}_k$ and $\beta_i \in \mathbb{R}$. Note that we let arg max and arg min break tie arbitrary as well as HaoChen et al. [21]. Note that in our definition, after augmented data $x \in \mathbb{X}$ is encoded to $f(x) \in \mathbb{S}^{d-1}$, $f(x)$ is further mapped to $h(f(x))$ in the RKHS, and then linear classification is performed using $W$ and $\beta$.

To derive a generalization guarantee for KCL, we focus on the 1-Nearest Neighbor (NN) classifier in the RKHS $\mathcal{H}_k$ as a technical tool, which is a generalization of the 1-NN classifiers utilized in Robinson et al. [42]; Huang et al. [25].

**Definition 1 (1-NN classifier in $\mathcal{H}_k$).** *Suppose $\mathbb{C}_1, \cdots, \mathbb{C}_K$ are subsets of $\mathbb{X}$. For a model $f : \mathbb{X} \to \mathbb{S}^{d-1}$, the 1-NN classifier $g_{1\text{-NN}} : \mathbb{X} \to [K]$ associated with the RKHS $\mathcal{H}_k$ is defined as $g_{1\text{-NN}}(x) := \arg\min_{i \in [K]} \|h(f(x)) - \mu_{\mathbb{C}_i}(f)\|_{\mathcal{H}_k}$.*

Huang et al. [25] show that the 1-NN classifier they consider can be regarded as a mean classifier [2,59] (see Appendix E in Huang et al. [25]). This fact can also apply to our setup: indeed, under Assumption 1, $g_{1\text{-NN}}$ is equal to $g_{f,W_\mu,\beta_\mu}(x) = \arg\max_{i \in [K]} \{\langle W_{\mu,i}, h(f(x)) \rangle_{\mathcal{H}_k} - \beta_{\mu,i}\}$, where $W_\mu : \mathcal{H}_k \to \mathbb{R}^K$ is defined as $W_\mu(\phi)_i := \langle W_{\mu,i}, \phi \rangle_{\mathcal{H}_k} = \langle \mu_{\mathbb{C}_i}(f), \phi \rangle_{\mathcal{H}_k}$ for each coordinate $i \in [K]$, and $\beta_{\mu,i} := (\|\mu_{\mathbb{C}_i}(f)\|_{\mathcal{H}_k}^2 + \psi(1))/2$ for $i \in [K]$. We also introduce the following:

**Definition 2 (Meaningful encoder).** *An encoder $f \in \mathcal{F}$ is said to be meaningful if $\min_{i \neq j} \|\mu_i(f) - \mu_j(f)\|_{\mathcal{H}_k}^2 > 0$ holds.*

Note that a meaningful encoder $f \in \mathcal{F}$ avoids the *complete collapse* of feature vectors [24,27], where many works on self-supervised representation learning [8, 11,19,21,32] introduce various architectures and algorithms to prevent it. Now, the theoretical guarantee is presented:

**Theorem 2.** *Suppose that Assumption 1 and 2 hold. Take $\delta \in \mathbb{R}$, $K \in \mathbb{N}$, $\mathbb{M}_1, \cdots, \mathbb{M}_K$, and $y$ such that the conditions (A), (B), and (C) in Assumption 2 are satisfied. Then, for each meaningful encoder $f \in \mathcal{F}$, we have*

$$L_{\mathrm{Err}}(f, W_\mu, \beta_\mu; y) \leq \frac{8(K-1)}{\Delta_{\min}(f) \cdot \min_{i \in [K]} P_{\mathbb{X}}(\mathbb{M}_i)} \mathfrak{a}(f)$$

*where $\Delta_{\min}(f) = \min_{i \neq j} \|\mu_i(f) - \mu_j(f)\|_{\mathcal{H}_k}^2$.*

The proof of Theorem 2 can be found in Appendix C of the supplementary material. The upper bound in Theorem 2 becomes smaller if the representations of any two points $x, x'$ belonging to $\mathbb{M}_i$ are closer for each $i \in [K]$ and the closest centers $\mu_i(f)$ and $\mu_j(f)$ of different subsets $\mathbb{M}_i$ and $\mathbb{M}_j$ become distant from each other. Since $\|\mu_i(f) - \mu_j(f)\|_{\mathcal{H}_k}^2 = -2\langle \mu_i(f), \mu_j(f) \rangle_{\mathcal{H}_k} + \|\mu_i(f)\|_{\mathcal{H}_k}^2 + \|\mu_j(f)\|_{\mathcal{H}_k}^2$,

Theorem 1 and 2 indicate that during the optimization for the kernel contrastive loss, the quantities $\mathfrak{a}(f)$ and $\mathfrak{c}(f)$ can contribute to making the learned representations linearly well-separable. Thus, our theory is consistent with the empirical success of contrastive learning shown by a line of research [8,10,16,21].

Next, we discuss Theorem 2 by comparing to related work. 1) Several works [25,42] also show that the classification loss or error is upper bounded by the quantity related to the alignment of feature vectors within each cluster. However, their results do not address the following conjecture: *Does the distance between the centers of each cluster consisting of feature vectors affect the linear separability?* Theorem 2 indicates that the answer is yes via the quantity $\Delta_{\min}(f)$. Note that Theorem 3.2 of Zhao et al. [66] implies a similar answer, but their result is for the squared loss and requires several strong assumptions on the encoder functions. Meanwhile, our Theorem 2 for the classification error requires the meaningfulness of encoder functions (Definition 2), which is more practical than those of Zhao et al. [66]. 2) Furthermore, our result is different from previous works [25,42,66] in the problem setup. Indeed, Robinson et al. [42] follow the setup of Arora et al. [2], and Huang et al. [25]; Zhao et al. [66] formulate their setup by imposing the $(\sigma, \delta)$-*augmentation* property to given latent class subsets. Meanwhile, our formulation is mainly based on the statistical similarity (2). Furthermore, we note that our Theorem 2 can be extended to the case that $K \in \mathbb{N}$, $\mathbb{M}_1, \cdots, \mathbb{M}_K \subset \mathbb{X}$, and $y$ are taken to satisfy the conditions **(A)** and **(C)** in Assumption 2 (see Theorem 5 in Appendix C of the supplementary material), implying that our result can apply to other problem setups of contrastive learning. Due to space limitations, we present more detailed explanations in Appendix F.6 and F.7 of the supplementary material.

### 5.3    A Generalization Error Bound for KCL

Since in practice we minimize the empirical kernel contrastive loss, we derive a generalization error bound for KCL. The empirical loss is defined as follows: denote $dP_+(x, x') = w(x, x')d\nu_{\mathbb{X}}^{\otimes 2}(x, x')$. Let $(X_1, X_1'), \cdots, (X_n, X_n')$ be pairs of random variables drawn independently from $P_+$, where $X_i$ and $X_j'$ are assumed to be independent for each pair of distinct indices $i, j \in [n]$. Following the standard setup that a pair of two augmented samples is obtained by randomly transforming the same raw sample, which is considered in many empirical works [8,10,16], for each $i \in [n]$, we consider the case that $X_i, X_i'$ are not necessarily independent. The empirical kernel contrastive loss is defined as,

$$\widehat{L}_{\mathrm{KCL}}(f; \lambda) = -\frac{1}{n} \sum_{i=1}^{n} k(f(X_i), f(X_i')) + \frac{\lambda}{n(n-1)} \sum_{i \neq j} k(f(X_i), f(X_j')). \quad (4)$$

In the statement below, denote $\mathcal{Q} = \{f(\cdot)^\top f(\cdot) : \mathbb{X} \times \mathbb{X} \to \mathbb{R} \mid f \in \mathcal{F}\}$. Define the Rademacher complexity [33] as, $\mathfrak{R}_n^+(\mathcal{Q}) := \mathbb{E}_{P_+, \sigma_{1:n}}[\sup_{q \in \mathcal{Q}} n^{-1} \sum_{i=1}^{n} \sigma_i q(X_i, X_i')]$, where $\sigma_1, \cdots, \sigma_n$ are independent random variables taking $\pm 1$ with probability 0.5 for each. We also define the Rademacher compexltiy $\mathfrak{R}_{n/2}^-(\mathcal{Q}; s^*)$ with the optimal choice $s^*$ from the symmetric group $S_n$ of degree $n$:

$\mathfrak{R}^-_{n/2}(\mathcal{Q}; s^*) := \max_{s \in S_n} \mathbb{E}_{X, X', \sigma_{1:(n/2)}}[\sup_{q \in \mathcal{Q}} 2n^{-1} \sum_{i=1}^{n/2} \sigma_i q(X_{s(2i-1)}, X'_{s(2i)})].$

Here $\mathfrak{R}^-_{n/2}(\mathcal{Q}; s^*)$ is related to the *average of "sums-of-i.i.d." blocks* technique for $U$-statistics explained in Clémençon et al. [13]; for more detail, see also Remark 3 in Appendix D.4 of the supplementary material. The generalization error bound for KCL is presented below:

**Theorem 3.** *Suppose that Assumption 1 holds, and $n$ is even. Furthermore, suppose that the minimizer $\widehat{f} \in \mathcal{F}$ of $\widehat{L}_{\mathrm{KCL}}(f; \lambda)$ exists. Then, with probability at least $1 - 2\varepsilon$ where $\varepsilon > 0$, we have*

$$L_{\mathrm{KCL}}(\widehat{f}; \lambda) \le L_{\mathrm{KCL}}(f; \lambda) + 2 \cdot \mathrm{Gen}(n, \lambda, \varepsilon),$$

*where* $\mathrm{Gen}(n, \lambda, \varepsilon) = O(\mathfrak{R}^+_n(\mathcal{Q}) + \lambda \mathfrak{R}^-_{n/2}(\mathcal{Q}; s^*) + (1 + \lambda)(\log(2/\varepsilon)/n)^{1/2}).$

*Remark 2.* Following Tu et al. [55], in Appendix D.2 of the supplementary material we show that under mild conditions, $\mathrm{Gen}(n, \lambda, \varepsilon) \downarrow 0$ holds as $n \to \infty$.

The proof of Theorem 3 can be found in Appendix D.1 of the supplementary material. Since $X_i, X'_i$ are not necessarily independent for each $i \in [n]$, the standard techniques (e.g., Theorem 3.3 in Mohri et al. [33]) are not applicable. We instead utilize the results by Zhang et al. [64] to overcome this difficulty, which is different from the previous bounds for contrastive learning [2,3,21,31, 36,60,63,67] (see Appendix F.5 for more detail). Here, if $\mathfrak{R}^+_n(\mathcal{Q})$ and $\mathfrak{R}^-_{n/2}(\mathcal{Q}; s^*)$ converge to 0 as $n \to \infty$, then by using our result, we can prove the consistency of the empirical contrastive loss to the population one for each $f \in \mathcal{F}$.

### 5.4 Application of the Theoretical Results: A New Surrogate Bound

Recent works [2–5,15,21,36,37,43,50,59,67] show that some contrastive learning objectives can be regarded as surrogate losses of the supervised loss or error in downstream tasks. Here, Arora et al. [2] show that, a contrastive loss $L_{\mathrm{CL}}$ *surrogates* a supervised loss or error $L_{\mathrm{sup}}$: for every $f \in \mathcal{F}$, $L_{\mathrm{sup}}(W \circ f) \lesssim L_{\mathrm{CL}}(f) + \alpha$ holds for some $\alpha \in \mathbb{R}$ and matrix $W$. This type of inequality is also called *surrogate bound* [5]. Arora et al. [2] show that the inequality guarantees that $L_{\mathrm{sup}}(W^* \circ \widehat{f}) \lesssim L_{\mathrm{CL}}(f) + \alpha$ holds with high probability, where $\widehat{f}$ is a minimizer of the empirical loss for $L_{\mathrm{CL}}$, $W^*$ is the optimal weight, and $\alpha$ is some term. Motivated by these works, we show a surrogate bound for KCL.

**Theorem 4.** *Suppose that Assumption 1 and 2 hold, $n$ is even, and there exists a minimizer $\widehat{f}$ of $\widehat{L}_{\mathrm{KCL}}(f; \lambda)$ such that $\widehat{f}$ is meaningful. Take $\delta \in \mathbb{R}$, $K \in \mathbb{N}$, $\mathbb{M}_1, \cdots, \mathbb{M}_K$, and $y$ such that the conditions (A), (B), and (C) in Assumption 2 are satisfied. Then, for any $f \in \mathcal{F}$ and $\varepsilon > 0$, with probability at least $1 - 2\varepsilon$,*

$$L_{\mathrm{Err}}(\widehat{f}, W^*, \beta^*; y) \lesssim L_{\mathrm{KCL}}(f; \lambda) + (1 - \frac{\delta}{2})\mathfrak{a}(\widehat{f}) - \lambda\mathfrak{c}(\widehat{f}) + R(\lambda) + 2\mathrm{Gen}(n, \lambda, \varepsilon),$$

*where $L_{\mathrm{Err}}(\widehat{f}, W^*, \beta^*; y) = \inf_{W, \beta} L_{\mathrm{Err}}(\widehat{f}, W, \beta; y)$, and $\lesssim$ omits the coefficient $8(K - 1)/(\Delta_{\min}(\widehat{f}) \cdot \min_{i \in [K]} P_{\mathbb{X}}(\mathbb{M}_i))$.*

The proof of Theorem 4 can be found in Appendix E of the supplementary material. This theorem indicates that minimization of the kernel contrastive loss in $\mathcal{F}$ can reduce the infimum of the classification error with high probability. Note that since larger $\lambda$ can make $\delta$ smaller due to the relation in condition **(B)** of Assumption 2, larger $\lambda$ may result in enlarging $(1 - \delta/2)\mathfrak{a}(\widehat{f}) - \lambda\mathfrak{c}(\widehat{f})$ and loosening the upper bound if $\mathfrak{a}(\widehat{f}) > 0$ and $\mathfrak{c}(\widehat{f}) < 0$. We empirically find that the KCL framework with larger $\lambda$ degrades its performance in the downstream classification task; see Appendix H.4 of the supplementary material.

Several works also establish the surrogate bounds for some contrastive learning objectives [2–5,15,21,36,37,43,50,59,67]. The main differences between the previous works and Theorem 4 are summarized in three points: 1) Theorem 4 indicates that the kernel contrastive loss is a surrogate loss of the classification error, while the previous works deal with other contrastive learning objectives. 2) Recent works [5,59] prove that the InfoNCE loss is a surrogate loss of the cross-entropy loss. However, since the theory of classification calibration losses (see e.g., Zhang [65]) indicates that the relation between the classification loss and others such as the cross-entropy loss is complicated under the multi-class setting, the relation between the InfoNCE loss and the classification error is non-trivial from the previous results. On the other hand, combining Theorem 4 and (1), we can show that the InfoNCE loss is also a surrogate loss of the classification error. Note that Theorem 4 can apply to other contrastive learning objectives. 3) The bound in Theorem 4 is established by introducing the formulation presented in Sect. 4. Especially, our bound includes the threshold $\delta$ and hyperparameter $\lambda$.

## 6 Conclusion and Discussion

In this paper, we studied the characterization of the structure of the representations learned by contrastive learning. By employing Kernel Contrastive Learning (KCL) as a unified framework, we showed that the formulation based on statistical similarity characterizes the clusters of learned representations and guarantees that the kernel contrastive loss minimization can yield good performance in the downstream classification task. As a limitation of this paper, it is hard to see the tightness of the bounds since computation of the true $\text{sim}(x, x'; \lambda)$ and $\delta$ for practical datasets is challenging. However, we believe that our theory promotes future research to investigate contrastive learning via the sets of augmented data defined by $\text{sim}(x, x'; \lambda)$ and $\delta$. Note that as recent works [52,53] tackle the estimation of the point-wise dependency by using neural networks, the estimation problem is an important future work. It is also worth studying how the selection of kernels affects the quality of representations via our theory. The investigation of transfer learning perspectives of KCL is an interesting future work, as recent works [22,44,66] address the problem for some contrastive learning frameworks.

**Acknowledgements.** The authors would like to thank Tomohiro Hayase and Takayuki Kawashima for useful comments. TK was partially supported by JSPS KAK-ENHI Grant Number 19H04071, 20H00576, and 23H03460.

**Ethical Statement.** Since this paper mainly studies theoretical analysis of contrastive learning, it will not be thought that there is a direct negative social impact. However, revealing detailed properties of contrastive learning could promote an opportunity to misuse the knowledge. We point out that such wrong usage is not straightforward with the proposed method, as the application is not discussed much in the paper.

# References

1. Aronszajn, N.: Theory of reproducing kernels. Trans. Am. Math. Soc. **68**(3), 337–404 (1950). https://doi.org/10.1090/s0002-9947-1950-0051437-7
2. Arora, S., Khandeparkar, H., Khodak, M., Plevrakis, O., Saunshi, N.: A theoretical analysis of contrastive unsupervised representation learning. In: Proceedings of the 36th International Conference on Machine Learning. Proceedings of Machine Learning Research, vol. 97, pp. 5628–5637. PMLR (2019)
3. Ash, J., Goel, S., Krishnamurthy, A., Misra, D.: Investigating the role of negatives in contrastive representation learning. In: Proceedings of The 25th International Conference on Artificial Intelligence and Statistics. Proceedings of Machine Learning Research, vol. 151, pp. 7187–7209. PMLR (2022)
4. Awasthi, P., Dikkala, N., Kamath, P.: Do more negative samples necessarily hurt in contrastive learning? In: Proceedings of the 39th International Conference on Machine Learning. Proceedings of Machine Learning Research, vol. 162, pp. 1101–1116. PMLR (2022)
5. Bao, H., Nagano, Y., Nozawa, K.: On the surrogate gap between contrastive and supervised losses. In: Proceedings of the 39th International Conference on Machine Learning. Proceedings of Machine Learning Research, vol. 162, pp. 1585–1606. PMLR (2022)
6. Berlinet, A., Thomas-Agnan, C.: Reproducing kernel Hilbert spaces in probability and statistics. Springer Science & Business Media (2004). https://doi.org/10.1007/978-1-4419-9096-9
7. Caron, M., Misra, I., Mairal, J., Goyal, P., Bojanowski, P., Joulin, A.: Unsupervised learning of visual features by contrasting cluster assignments. In: Advances in Neural Information Processing Systems. vol. 33, pp. 9912–9924. Curran Associates, Inc. (2020)
8. Chen, T., Kornblith, S., Norouzi, M., Hinton, G.: A simple framework for contrastive learning of visual representations. In: Proceedings of the 37th International Conference on Machine Learning. Proceedings of Machine Learning Research, vol. 119, pp. 1597–1607. PMLR (2020)
9. Chen, T., Luo, C., Li, L.: Intriguing properties of contrastive losses. In: Advances in Neural Information Processing Systems, vol. 34, pp. 11834–11845. Curran Associates, Inc. (2021)
10. Chen, X., Fan, H., Girshick, R., He, K.: Improved baselines with momentum contrastive learning. arXiv preprint arXiv:2003.04297v1 (2020)
11. Chen, X., He, K.: Exploring simple siamese representation learning. In: 2021 IEEE/CVF Conference on Computer Vision and Pattern Recognition (CVPR), pp. 15745–15753 (2021). https://doi.org/10.1109/CVPR46437.2021.01549
12. Chuang, C.Y., Robinson, J., Lin, Y.C., Torralba, A., Jegelka, S.: Debiased contrastive learning. In: Advances in Neural Information Processing Systems, vol. 33, pp. 8765–8775. Curran Associates, Inc. (2020)

13. Clémençon, S., Lugosi, G., Vayatis, N.: Ranking and empirical minimization of U-statistics. Ann. Stat. **36**(2), 844–874 (2008). https://doi.org/10.1214/009052607000000910
14. Dubois, Y., Ermon, S., Hashimoto, T.B., Liang, P.S.: Improving self-supervised learning by characterizing idealized representations. In: Advances in Neural Information Processing Systems, vol. 35, pp. 11279–11296. Curran Associates, Inc. (2022)
15. Dufumier, B., Barbano, C.A., Louiset, R., Duchesnay, E., Gori, P.: Rethinking positive sampling for contrastive learning with kernel. arXiv preprint arXiv:2206.01646v1 (2022)
16. Dwibedi, D., Aytar, Y., Tompson, J., Sermanet, P., Zisserman, A.: With a little help from my friends: Nearest-neighbor contrastive learning of visual representations. In: 2021 IEEE/CVF International Conference on Computer Vision (ICCV), pp. 9568–9577 (2021). https://doi.org/10.1109/ICCV48922.2021.00945
17. Gao, T., Yao, X., Chen, D.: SimCSE: simple contrastive learning of sentence embeddings. In: Proceedings of the 2021 Conference on Empirical Methods in Natural Language Processing, pp. 6894–6910. Association for Computational Linguistics (2021). https://doi.org/10.18653/v1/2021.emnlp-main.552
18. Gretton, A., Bousquet, O., Smola, A., Schölkopf, B.: Measuring statistical dependence with hilbert-schmidt norms. In: Algorithmic Learning Theory, pp. 63–77. Springer, Berlin Heidelberg (2005). https://doi.org/10.1007/11564089_7
19. Grill, J.B., et al.: Bootstrap your own latent - a new approach to self-supervised learning. In: Advances in Neural Information Processing Systems, vol. 33, pp. 21271–21284. Curran Associates, Inc. (2020)
20. HaoChen, J.Z., Ma, T.: A theoretical study of inductive biases in contrastive learning. In: The Eleventh International Conference on Learning Representations (2023). https://openreview.net/forum?id=AuEgNlEAmed
21. HaoChen, J.Z., Wei, C., Gaidon, A., Ma, T.: Provable guarantees for self-supervised deep learning with spectral contrastive loss. In: Advances in Neural Information Processing Systems, vol. 34, pp. 5000–5011. Curran Associates, Inc. (2021)
22. HaoChen, J.Z., Wei, C., Kumar, A., Ma, T.: Beyond separability: Analyzing the linear transferability of contrastive representations to related subpopulations. In: Advances in Neural Information Processing Systems, vol. 35, pp. 26889–26902. Curran Associates, Inc. (2022)
23. He, K., Zhang, X., Ren, S., Sun, J.: Deep residual learning for image recognition. In: 2016 IEEE Conference on Computer Vision and Pattern Recognition (CVPR), pp. 770–778 (2016). https://doi.org/10.1109/CVPR.2016.90
24. Hua, T., Wang, W., Xue, Z., Ren, S., Wang, Y., Zhao, H.: On feature decorrelation in self-supervised learning. In: 2021 IEEE/CVF International Conference on Computer Vision (ICCV), pp. 9578–9588 (2021). https://doi.org/10.1109/ICCV48922.2021.00946
25. Huang, W., Yi, M., Zhao, X., Jiang, Z.: Towards the generalization of contrastive self-supervised learning. In: The Eleventh International Conference on Learning Representations (2023). https://openreview.net/forum?id=XDJwuEYHhme
26. Jiang, D., Li, W., Cao, M., Zou, W., Li, X.: Speech SimCLR: combining contrastive and reconstruction objective for self-supervised speech representation learning. In: Proceedings of Interspeech 2021, pp. 1544–1548 (2021). https://doi.org/10.21437/Interspeech.2021-391
27. Jing, L., Vincent, P., LeCun, Y., Tian, Y.: Understanding dimensional collapse in contrastive self-supervised learning. In: International Conference on Learning Representations (2022). https://openreview.net/forum?id=YevsQ05DEN7

28. Johnson, D.D., Hanchi, A.E., Maddison, C.J.: Contrastive learning can find an optimal basis for approximately view-invariant functions. In: The Eleventh International Conference on Learning Representations (2023). https://openreview.net/forum?id=AjC0KBjiMu
29. Kiani, B.T., Balestriero, R., Chen, Y., Lloyd, S., LeCun, Y.: Joint embedding self-supervised learning in the kernel regime. arXiv preprint arXiv:2209.14884v1 (2022)
30. von Kügelgen, J., et al.: Self-supervised learning with data augmentations provably isolates content from style. In: Advances in Neural Information Processing Systems, vol. 34, pp. 16451–16467. Curran Associates, Inc. (2021)
31. Lei, Y., Yang, T., Ying, Y., Zhou, D.X.: Generalization analysis for contrastive representation learning. arXiv preprint arXiv:2302.12383v2 (2023)
32. Li, Y., Pogodin, R., Sutherland, D.J., Gretton, A.: Self-supervised learning with kernel dependence maximization. In: Advances in Neural Information Processing Systems, vol. 34, pp. 15543–15556. Curran Associates, Inc. (2021)
33. Mohri, M., Rostamizadeh, A., Talwalkar, A.: Foundations of machine learning. MIT press (2018)
34. Muandet, K., Fukumizu, K., Sriperumbudur, B., Schölkopf, B.: Kernel mean embedding of distributions: a review and beyond. Foundation Trends® Mach. Learn. **10**(1–2), 1–141 (2017)
35. Ng, A., Jordan, M., Weiss, Y.: On spectral clustering: Analysis and an algorithm. In: Advances in Neural Information Processing Systems, vol. 14. MIT Press (2001)
36. Nozawa, K., Germain, P., Guedj, B.: Pac-bayesian contrastive unsupervised representation learning. In: Proceedings of the 36th Conference on Uncertainty in Artificial Intelligence (UAI). Proceedings of Machine Learning Research, vol. 124, pp. 21–30. PMLR (2020)
37. Nozawa, K., Sato, I.: Understanding negative samples in instance discriminative self-supervised representation learning. In: Advances in Neural Information Processing Systems, vol. 34, pp. 5784–5797. Curran Associates, Inc. (2021)
38. van den Oord, A., Li, Y., Vinyals, O.: Representation learning with contrastive predictive coding. arXiv preprint arXiv:1807.03748v2 (2018)
39. Parulekar, A., Collins, L., Shanmugam, K., Mokhtari, A., Shakkottai, S.: Infonce loss provably learns cluster-preserving representations. arXiv preprint arXiv:2302.07920v1 (2023)
40. Poole, B., Ozair, S., Van Den Oord, A., Alemi, A., Tucker, G.: On variational bounds of mutual information. In: Proceedings of the 36th International Conference on Machine Learning. Proceedings of Machine Learning Research, vol. 97, pp. 5171–5180. PMLR (2019)
41. Robinson, J., Sun, L., Yu, K., Batmanghelich, K., Jegelka, S., Sra, S.: Can contrastive learning avoid shortcut solutions? In: Advances in Neural Information Processing Systems, vol. 34, pp. 4974–4986. Curran Associates, Inc. (2021)
42. Robinson, J.D., Chuang, C.Y., Sra, S., Jegelka, S.: Contrastive learning with hard negative samples. In: International Conference on Learning Representations (2021). https://openreview.net/forum?id=CR1XOQ0UTh-
43. Saunshi, N., et al.: Understanding contrastive learning requires incorporating inductive biases. In: Proceedings of the 39th International Conference on Machine Learning. Proceedings of Machine Learning Research, vol. 162, pp. 19250–19286. PMLR (2022)

44. Shen, K., et al.: Connect, not collapse: Explaining contrastive learning for unsupervised domain adaptation. In: Proceedings of the 39th International Conference on Machine Learning. Proceedings of Machine Learning Research, vol. 162, pp. 19847–19878. PMLR (2022)

45. Singh, A.: Clda: contrastive learning for semi-supervised domain adaptation. In: Advances in Neural Information Processing Systems, vol. 34, pp. 5089–5101. Curran Associates, Inc. (2021)

46. Steinwart, I., Christmann, A.: Support vector machines. Springer Science & Business Media (2008). https://doi.org/10.1007/978-0-387-77242-4

47. Terada, Y., Yamamoto, M.: Kernel normalized cut: a theoretical revisit. In: Proceedings of the 36th International Conference on Machine Learning. Proceedings of Machine Learning Research, vol. 97, pp. 6206–6214. PMLR (2019)

48. Tian, Y.: Understanding deep contrastive learning via coordinate-wise optimization. In: Advances in Neural Information Processing Systems. vol. 35, pp. 19511–19522. Curran Associates, Inc. (2022)

49. Tosh, C., Krishnamurthy, A., Hsu, D.: Contrastive estimation reveals topic posterior information to linear models. J. Mach. Learn. Res. **22**(281), 1–31 (2021)

50. Tosh, C., Krishnamurthy, A., Hsu, D.: Contrastive learning, multi-view redundancy, and linear models. In: Proceedings of the 32nd International Conference on Algorithmic Learning Theory. Proceedings of Machine Learning Research, vol. 132, pp. 1179–1206. PMLR (2021)

51. Tsai, Y.H.H., et al.: Conditional contrastive learning with kernel. In: International Conference on Learning Representations (2022). https://openreview.net/forum?id=AAJLBoGt0XM

52. Tsai, Y.H.H., Ma, M.Q., Yang, M., Zhao, H., Morency, L.P., Salakhutdinov, R.: Self-supervised representation learning with relative predictive coding. In: International Conference on Learning Representations (2021). https://openreview.net/forum?id=068E_JSq9O

53. Tsai, Y.H.H., Zhao, H., Yamada, M., Morency, L.P., Salakhutdinov, R.R.: Neural methods for point-wise dependency estimation. In: Advances in Neural Information Processing Systems, vol. 33, pp. 62–72. Curran Associates, Inc. (2020)

54. Tschannen, M., Djolonga, J., Rubenstein, P.K., Gelly, S., Lucic, M.: On mutual information maximization for representation learning. In: International Conference on Learning Representations (2020). https://openreview.net/forum?id=rkxoh24FPH

55. Tu, Z., Zhang, J., Tao, D.: Theoretical analysis of adversarial learning: A minimax approach. In: Advances in Neural Information Processing Systems, vol. 32. Curran Associates, Inc. (2019)

56. Van Gansbeke, W., Vandenhende, S., Georgoulis, S., Proesmans, M., Van Gool, L.: SCAN: learning to classify images without labels. In: Vedaldi, A., Bischof, H., Brox, T., Frahm, J.-M. (eds.) ECCV 2020. LNCS, vol. 12355, pp. 268–285. Springer, Cham (2020). https://doi.org/10.1007/978-3-030-58607-2_16

57. Wang, F., Liu, H.: Understanding the behaviour of contrastive loss. In: 2021 IEEE/CVF Conference on Computer Vision and Pattern Recognition (CVPR), pp. 2495–2504 (2021). https://doi.org/10.1109/CVPR46437.2021.00252

58. Wang, T., Isola, P.: Understanding contrastive representation learning through alignment and uniformity on the hypersphere. In: Proceedings of the 37th International Conference on Machine Learning. Proceedings of Machine Learning Research, vol. 119, pp. 9929–9939. PMLR (2020)

59. Wang, Y., Zhang, Q., Wang, Y., Yang, J., Lin, Z.: Chaos is a ladder: a new theoretical understanding of contrastive learning via augmentation overlap. In: International Conference on Learning Representations (2022). https://openreview.net/forum?id=ECvgmYVyeUz

60. Wang, Z., Luo, Y., Li, Y., Zhu, J., Schölkopf, B.: Spectral representation learning for conditional moment models. arXiv preprint arXiv:2210.16525v2 (2022)

61. Wen, Z., Li, Y.: Toward understanding the feature learning process of self-supervised contrastive learning. In: Proceedings of the 38th International Conference on Machine Learning. Proceedings of Machine Learning Research, vol. 139, pp. 11112–11122. PMLR (2021)

62. Yeh, C.H., Hong, C.Y., Hsu, Y.C., Liu, T.L., Chen, Y., LeCun, Y.: Decoupled contrastive learning. In: Computer Vision - ECCV 2022. pp. 668–684. Springer Nature Switzerland (2022). https://doi.org/10.1007/978-3-031-19809-0_38

63. Zhang, G., Lu, Y., Sun, S., Guo, H., Yu, Y.: $f$-mutual information contrastive learning (2022). https://openreview.net/forum?id=3kTt_W1_tgw

64. Zhang, R.R., Liu, X., Wang, Y., Wang, L.: Mcdiarmid-type inequalities for graph-dependent variables and stability bounds. In: Advances in Neural Information Processing Systems, vol. 32. Curran Associates, Inc. (2019)

65. Zhang, T.: Statistical analysis of some multi-category large margin classification methods. J. Mach. Learn. Res. **5**, 1225–1251 (2004)

66. Zhao, X., Du, T., Wang, Y., Yao, J., Huang, W.: ArCL: enhancing contrastive learning with augmentation-robust representations. In: The Eleventh International Conference on Learning Representations (2023). https://openreview.net/forum?id=n0Pb9T5kmb

67. Zou, X., Liu, W.: Generalization bounds for adversarial contrastive learning. J. Mach. Learn. Res. **24**(114), 1–54 (2023)

# BipNRL: Mutual Information Maximization on Bipartite Graphs for Node Representation Learning

Pranav Poduval$^{(\boxtimes)}$, Gaurav Oberoi, Sangam Verma, Ayush Agarwal, Karamjit Singh, and Siddhartha Asthana

Mastercard AI Garage, Mumbai, India
{pranav.poduval,gaurav.oberoi,sangam.verma,ayush.agarwal,karamjit.singh, siddhartha.asthana}@mastercard.com

**Abstract.** Unsupervised representation learning on bipartite graphs is of particular interest due to the lack of explicit labels and its application in a variety of domains. Several unsupervised representation learning methods make use of mutual information maximization between node-level and graph/sub-graph-level information. We argue that such methods are better suited to graph level tasks than node level tasks because local information in node representation is dominated by graph level information. Additionally, current approaches rely on building a global summary vector in which information diminishes as the graph scales. In this work, we concentrate on optimizing representations for node-level downstream tasks such as node classification/regression. The **Bi**partite **N**ode **R**epresentation **L**earning (BipNRL) method, which aims to learn the node embeddings by maximizing MI between the node's representation and self features without using summary vector is introduced. Furthermore, we propose the decoupled graph context loss on projected graphs to preserve the bipartite graph structure, enhancing representation for node-level tasks. Finally, we utilize attention-based neighborhood aggregation and modify the neighbourhood sampling algorithm to account for the high variance of node degree that is common in bipartite graphs. Extensive experiments show that BipNRL achieves cutting-edge results on multiple downstream tasks across diverse datasets.

**Keywords:** Node Representation Learning · Bipartite Graph

## 1 Introduction

Bipartite graphs have been shown to be useful for representing data relationships in domains with two types of entities, for example, an e-commerce domain can be represented by a user-product graph, where the edge corresponds to a user's purchase of a product; academic graphs of author-paper have an edge

Supported by organization Mastercard.

connecting the author(s) with a paper title. Because these domains frequently lack labelled data, researchers have to rely on unsupervised learning of bipartite graph embeddings [3,7]. We are particularly interested in unsupervised methods that employ Graph Neural Networks (GNNs) [9,12,20] over random walk based methods [5,7,8], because they can learn the representation while taking into account both graph structure and node attributes.

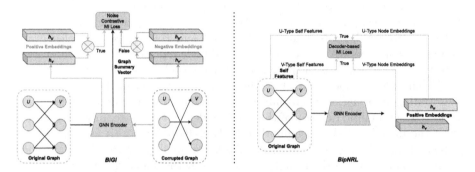

**Fig. 1.** As seen in the left figure, BiGI uses a corruption function to create negative samples and a readout function to create summary vectors. On the other hand, BipNRL (right) avoids computing the summary vector directly maximizing the MI between the learned representation and the self-features.

While previous GNN-based methods enforced neighbouring nodes to have similar representations, new approaches such as Deep Graph Infomax (DGI) [22] and Graph Mutual Information (GMI) [15] focus on maximising Mutual Information (MI) between the graph representation (global summary vector) and local node representation. BiGI [3], a recent work in bipartite graphs, extends DGI to the bipartite domain by generating a summary vector for each node type. These summary vectors are used in BiGI to compose a global graph representation. The MI between the global graph and local edge representations is then maximised to make the nodes globally relevant. BiGI is regarded as the state-of-the-art solution for bipartite graph recommendation and link prediction tasks. We contend that such objective function formulation lead to the dominance of global information in node representations, making them less useful for node level tasks. The use of non-injective (e.g. averaging) readout functions to create summary vectors in DGI and BiGI has a known limitation in that the graph information contained in the summary vector decreases as the size of the graph increases [15,21]. In this paper, we present BipNRL, a novel **Bip**artite **N**ode **R**epresentation **L**earning method that avoids the use of summary vector. Instead, BipNRL maximises the MI between the learned node's representation and its own feature vector. There are two benefits to doing so: First, the representation's quality does not deteriorate as the graph's size grows; Second, embeddings are more relevant for downstream tasks at the node level. Figure 1 highlights the difference between BiGI and BipNRL.

In a bipartite graph, only $u$-type node is directly connected to a $v$-type node and vice-versa. Therefore, an issue with using GNNs in bipartite graphs is that two $u$-type nodes with structurally similar $v$-type connections are never directly forced to have similar representation. As a result, two $u$-type nodes with similar $v$-type connections may have distinct embeddings. This could also apply to two $v$-type nodes. To preserve this topological similarity of the same type nodes in bipartite graph, we include [9] graph context loss in our optimisation function. In contrast to previous approaches, BipNRL decouples the bipartite graph into two projected graphs, one for each node type. The two projected graphs are then subjected to graph context loss. Unlike DGI and BiGI, this decoupled graph context loss necessitate smoothing of learned node representations within $u$-type or $v$-type nodes, which is projected to aid node-level downstream tasks [4].

Given that any node's direct neighbours will always be of the opposite type, aggregating information from only direct neighbours will not be sufficient to capture the semantic richness of the 'root' node. To aggregate information from both the direct and skip neighborhoods, BipNRL employs an attention-based neighbourhood aggregation function. Also, the quality of the neighbourhood aggregation function is significantly influenced by the underlying neighbourhood sampling strategy. Because many real-world bipartite graphs are skewed towards one of the partitions and have a high variance in node degree [7], naive uniform neighbourhood sampling is sub-optimal. As a result, we develop a biased neighbourhood sampling algorithm to address the issue of influential nodes (high degree).

We demonstrate BipNRL's efficacy by running experiments on three types of downstream tasks: node classification, node regression, and link prediction, using four publicly available datasets from different domains. We show that BipNRL significantly outperforms state-of-the-art algorithms. Our contributions are summarised below:

- Unsupervised learning of rich node embeddings for bipartite graphs by maximising MI between node representation and self features (without using the summary vector and readout function). We avoid a major weakness in BiGI, in which the information contained in the summary vectors decreases as the graph grows larger.
- Preserve the topological structure of the bipartite graph by applying decoupled graph context loss to the projected graph of each node type. This necessitates that nodes in the same neighbourhood have a similar representation.
- Attention-based mechanism in order to optimally aggregate neighbourhood information from direct and skip connections.
- Biased neighbourhood sampling that accounts for the high variance in node degree, which is common in bipartite graphs.

## 2   Related Works

Graph-based methods are broadly classified according to graph type (homogeneous & heterogeneous) [3]. The graph literature is replete with homogeneous methods, such as DeepWalk [16], LINE [18], Node2vec [8], GNN-based

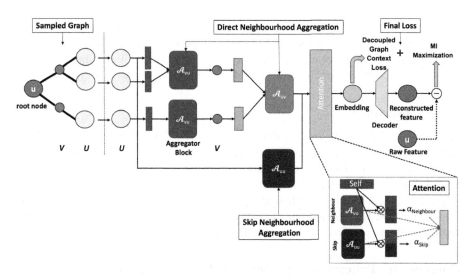

**Fig. 2.** BipNRL: For computing the embeddings of the root node $u$, we sample the direct and indirect/skip neighbors of $u$. We then use separate aggregator blocks and an attention mechanism to combine the information both the neighbor types. The aggregated node embeddings are then optimized via a combination of MI Maximization and Decoupled Graph Context Loss.

approaches [9,12,20], and heterogeneous methods such as metapath2vec [5], DMGI [14]. Despite the fact that bipartite graphs are a type of heterogeneous graph, the above mentioned heterogeneous methods are not directly applicable. Recognizing the limitations of heterogeneous methods, researchers proposed several bipartite graph methods. CascadeBGNN [10], a method for bipartite graphs, learns from opposite domains in a semi-supervised fashion using inter-domain message passing. BiNE [7] generates vertex sequences while maintaining the long tail distribution of vertices in the bipartite network. For bipartite graphs, algorithms such as IGE [25], PinSAGE [23], and FOBE [17] are designed.

Nonetheless, all of these algorithms are focused on learning a graph's local structure. BiGI [3], a recent work, extended the concept of MI maximisation to the bipartite domain from a homogeneous graph-based technique known as DGI [22]. DGI, however, is limited to coarse-grained maximisation of MI between the learned node representation and the entire graph summary vector, preventing the node representation from capturing the details of individual node features. This flaw is addressed by GMI [15], which aligns the learnt node representation with only the sampled sub-graph. None of these approaches, however, attempt to learn embeddings that are fine-tuned for node-level downstream tasks and are limited to graph or sub-graph level.

## 3   Methodology

In this section, we provide the details of our proposed approach BipNRL. The four major components of BipNRL are 1) mutual information maximization without readout and corruption function, 2) decoupled topology preserving graph context loss, 3) attention-based neighbourhood aggregation, and 4) biased neighbourhood sampling algorithm. For illustration, we will assume our model is learning embedding of the node $u$ (referred to as *root node*) in Fig. 2.

### 3.1   Background

**Notations.** *A bipartite graph* is defined as $G = (U, V, E)$, illustrated in Fig. 3(a), with $U$ and $V$ representing the sets containing two different types of nodes. Here, $u_i \in U$ and $v_j \in V$ denote the $i$-th and $j$-th node in $U$ and $V$, respectively, and $e_{ij} \in E$ denotes the edge between $u_i$ and $v_j$, where $i \in \{1, 2, ..., M\}$ and $j \in \{1, 2, ..., N\}$. Further, each edge $e_{ij}$ is represented by a weight $w_{ij}$ defining the strength of the connection. The features of the two types of nodes can be represented as $x_{u_i}$ and $x_{v_j}$, respectively, where $x_{u_i} \in \mathbb{R}^P$ and $x_{v_j} \in \mathbb{R}^Q$.

**Corruption Function.** Unsupervised learning typically uses a noise-contrastive formulation of the loss function, which calls for the use of negative samples that can be compared to positive samples. These negative samples can be created from the other training graphs in multi-graph settings, but in single-graph settings, a corruption function is necessary to create the negative graph samples from the same original graph.

A corruption function $C(X, A)$ for a $u$-type node in a bipartite graph can be defined as $C : \mathbb{R}^{U \times P} \times \mathbb{R}^{U \times V} \longrightarrow \mathbb{R}^{\tilde{U} \times P} \times \mathbb{R}^{\tilde{U} \times V}$. The function $C(X, A) = (\tilde{X}, \tilde{A})$ corrupts the graph such that a node $v_j$ now connected to $\tilde{u}_i$ instead of $u_i$. The type of corruption function governs the quality of representation generated and typically requires an expensive compute over adjacency matrix [22].

**Readout Function.** A readout function is used to summarize the local individual node representations into a global graph representation. In a bipartite graph, generally two prototype representations may be generated, one for each node type. $s_u = \mathcal{R}_u(\{u_i : u_i \in U\})$, $s_v = \mathcal{R}_v(\{v_j : v_j \in V\})$.

Previous works in graph have used simple average-based readouts

$$\mathcal{R}_u = \sigma(\frac{1}{U} \sum_{u \in U} h_u) \tag{1}$$

where $h_u$ is the latent representation of node $u$ and $\sigma$ is the sigmoid non-linearity. A strict condition imposed on readout function for the optimization algorithm to have upper bound on the error is that the readout function should be injective. Due to the non-injective reading function used by BiGI, the amount of information in the summary vector decreases as the size of the graph grows [15,22].

### 3.2   Mutual Information Maximization Without Readout Functions

In this section, we shall explain the intuition and details of our MI maximization approach. Let us assume we have a function that maps each node $u, v$ in the

Graph $(U, V, E)$ to embedding $h_u, h_v$, where $h_u, h_v \in \mathbb{R}^d$ (we shall explain the details of such mapping functions in upcoming Sub-sect. 3.4).

One of the primary goals is to make these embeddings capture the node-specific feature information that is critical for node-level downstream tasks. We achieve it by maximizing the mutual information between the node embeddings $(h_u, h_v)$ and self features $(x_u, x_v)$, i.e. maximizing $\mathcal{I}(x_u, h_u)$ and $\mathcal{I}(x_v, h_v)$. Maximizing the MI between two high-dimensional continuous variables is challenging, and the typical approach involves relying on Mutual Information Neural Estimation (MINE) [2]. MINE trains a classifier to distinguish samples from the joint distribution of two random variables and the product of their marginals. Training MINE requires a corruption function for generating "negative embeddings" that is expensive in large graphs. To avoid this corruption function, we rely on an alternative formulation of MI maximization [6], not so familiar in graph literature. To the best of our knowledge this is the first work to utilize alternative MI formulation [6] for graph mutual information maximization. Under this formulation, instead of a classifier we need to utilize two decoders $f_\theta(h_u)$, $f_\phi(h_v)$, that attempt to reconstruct the node features $x_u, x_v$, respectively. Let us restrict our discussion to maximizing $\mathcal{I}(x_u, h_u)$, without loss of generality. We have $x_u = f_\theta(h_u) + \delta$, where $\delta$ is the error of our decoder. Note that the estimated mean squared error (MSE) of the decoder can be formulated as $\mathbb{E}[|x_u - f_\theta(h_u)|^2] = \mathbb{E}[\delta^2] = |\Sigma|$, assuming that the error has a Gaussian distribution with covariance matrix $\Sigma$. Now the MI between $h_u$ and $x_u$, $I(x_u, h_u)$ can be rewritten in terms of entropy as $\mathcal{I}(x_u, h_u) = H(x_u) - H(x_u|h_u)$, hence our objective simplifies to minimizing $H(x_u|h_u)$.

$$
\begin{aligned}
H(x_u|h_u) &= \int_{\mathcal{H}} p(\tilde{h_u}) H(x_u|h_u = \tilde{h_u}) \, d\tilde{h_u} \\
&= \int_{\mathcal{H}} p(\tilde{h_u}) H((f_\theta(\tilde{h_u}) + \delta)|h_u = \tilde{h_u}) \, d\tilde{h_u} \\
&= \int_{\mathcal{H}} p(\tilde{h_u}) H(\delta|h_u = \tilde{h_u}) \, d\tilde{h_u} = \frac{\log[(2\pi e)^P |\Sigma|]}{2}
\end{aligned}
\tag{2}
$$

Thus maximizing $I(x_u, h_u)$ is the equivalent of minimizing expected MSE loss as

$$
|\Sigma| = \mathbb{E}[|x_u - f_\theta(h_u)|^2] = \frac{1}{(2\pi e)^P} \exp\left[2H(x_u|h_u)\right]
\tag{3}
$$

The above implies, minimizing expected MSE loss is equivalent to minimizing the conditional entropy $H(x_u|h_u)$, which maximizes our desired objective $I(x_u, h_u)$. This can be generalized to distributions beyond Gaussian [6]. Thus, the first component of our loss function $\mathcal{L}_1$, that maximizes the MI between the learnt representation of the node and its feature can be written as:

$$
\mathcal{L}_1 = \frac{1}{|U|} \sum_{u \in U} ||f_\theta(h_u) - x_u||^2 + \frac{1}{|V|} \sum_{v \in V} ||f_\phi(h_v) - x_v||^2
\tag{4}
$$

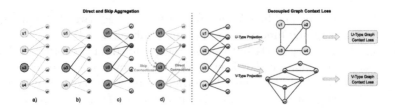

**Fig. 3.** Illustration of: A) Sampling the direct (one-hop) and skip neighbours over a bipartite graph (Left), B) Projecting the bipartite graph into $U$-type and $V$-type graphs and utilizing decoupled graph context loss (Right).

### 3.3   Decoupled Graph Context Loss

The use of graph context loss to preserve the topological structure of a graph in embedding space is frequently suggested in the literature. It cannot, however, be applied to the bipartite graph because the connecting nodes are of different types. Their features and/or embeddings may be in a completely different space and have a completely different contextual meaning. As a result, for each node type, we generate a decoupled projected homogeneous graph and apply the graph context loss used in [9] independently on both projected graphs, as shown in Fig. 3. This loss forces nodes of the same type with common neighbours to have embeddings closer together in euclidean space, while nodes with no common neighbours have embeddings farther apart. Our modified graph context loss can be summed up as follows:

$$\mathcal{L}_2 = - \log \sigma(h_{u_1}^T h_{u_2}) - Q * \log \left(1 - \sigma(h_{u_1}^T h_{u_3})\right) \tag{5}$$

where $u_1, u_2$ represent nodes with common neighbours and $u_1, u_3$ represent nodes with no common neighbours. The sigmoid activation function is denoted by $\sigma$. A loss based on the same logic as for the $v$-type nodes is added to $\mathcal{L}_2$. Our final loss becomes $\mathcal{L}_{final} = \mathcal{L}_1 + \lambda \mathcal{L}_2$ where $\lambda$ is a hyper-parameter. Our final loss is responsible for two tasks: a) preserving the bipartite graph structure, thereby enforcing smoothness [4] among nodes of the same type, and b) learning representations optimised for node-level downstream tasks. The Adam optimizer is used to learn all of the model parameters using stochastic gradient descent. The training iterations are repeated until convergence is reached. The learned embeddings when concatenated with the node's features can cater to a variety of domain-independent downstream tasks.

### 3.4   Attention-Based Neighbourhood Aggregation

In bipartite graphs, the direct neighbours of any node will always be of the other type. Therefore aggregating information only from direct neighbours will not be sufficient to capture the semantic richness of the 'root' node. As illustrated in Fig. 2, we sample two sets of neighbours $N(u)$ and $N(N(u))$, which represent direct and skip neighbours of the root node $u$, respectively. In order to capture the information from the direct neighbours (different type) and indirect neighbours (same type), we introduce two aggregator blocks, a direct neighbourhood aggregation and a skip neighbourhood aggregation, as illustrated in Fig. 2.

**Direct Aggregation:** We follow a two-step process to capture the information from direct neighbours of the root node $u$. Firstly, we find the aggregation vector for each neighbouring node of $u$. Let us say $v_i \in N(u)$ is the direct neighbour of $u$ and $\tilde{u}_{ij} \in N(v_i)$ is the direct neighbour of $v_i$. For each $v_i \in N(u)$, we apply the aggregation block:

$$
h_{N(v_i)} = \mathcal{A}_{vu}(X_{\tilde{u}_{ij}}, \forall \tilde{u}_{ij} \in N(v_i)) \\
= \frac{\sum_{\tilde{u} \in N(v_i)} FFN_{vu}(X_{\tilde{u}})}{|N(v_i)|}
\tag{6}
$$

where $\mathcal{A}$ represents the Aggregator block, an aggregator block consists of a Feed-Forward Network (FFN), followed by any aggregation function like Max, GCN, Mean, LSTM, etc. In this work, we use the mean aggregator, where we take the element-wise mean of output vectors of FFN. $h_{N(v_i)} \in \mathbb{R}^d$ is the aggregated vector of a node $v_i$ and $x_{\tilde{u}_{ij}} \in \mathbb{R}^P$ is the feature vector of $\tilde{u}_{ij} \in N(v_i)$. For each $v_i$ corresponding vector $h_{N(v_i)}, x_{v_i}$ is passed through the next aggregation block to get final *direct neighbourhood embedding* $h_{N(u)}$ of the root node $u$.

$$
h_{N(u)} = \mathcal{A}_{uv}([h_{N(v_i)}, x_{v_i}], \forall v_i \in N(u))
\tag{7}
$$

**Skip Aggregation:** In order to get *skip neighbourhood embedding* for node $u$, we aggregate the features of the nodes $\tilde{u} \in N(N(u))$ as follows:

$$
h_{\mathcal{N}(\mathcal{N}(u))} = \mathcal{A}_{uu}(X_{\tilde{u}_{ij}}, \forall \tilde{u}_{ij} \in N(N(u))
\tag{8}
$$

We use different aggregations for different combinations of nodes, e.g. $\mathcal{A}_{vu}$ is used for aggregating nodes of type $U$ when the root node is of type $V$.

**Combining Direct and Skip Embeddings:** We need to fuse the direct and skip neighbourhood embedding intelligently to learn a more comprehensive node embedding for the root node $u$. We address this challenge using a self-attention mechanism [20] to automatically learn the importance of embeddings emerging from two different types of neighbours. We design an attention mechanism [19] as below:

$$
h_u = \sum_{i \in [N(u), N(N(u))]} \alpha_i * h_i
\tag{9}
$$

$$
\alpha_i = \frac{\exp(LReLU(z^T[x_u, h_i]))}{\sum_{i \in [N(u), N(N(u))]} \exp(LReLU(z^T[x_u, h_i]))}
\tag{10}
$$

where $\alpha_i$ is the attention weight, and $z$ is a learnable GNN parameter. Apart from computing $\alpha_i$ using $x_u$, the above formulation of $h_u$ does not utilize $x_u$, keeping it safe from collapsing into an auto-encoder [1,11] when we try to maximize $\mathcal{I}(x_u, h_u)$ (as discussed in 3.2).

### 3.5   Biased Neighbourhood Sampling

Most GNNs function by aggregating information from the node's immediate surroundings. The neighbourhood is frequently sampled uniformly for each node [9]. This approach has several drawbacks, including a) the influences of high variance in node degree observed in real-life bipartite graphs and the high-degree nodes not being considered, and b) the same weightage for both strong and weak connections. To address these shortcomings, we devise a sampling strategy in which the probability of sampling a neighbour node 'n' for the root node 'm' is defined as follows:

$$p(n|m) \propto w_{nm}/\log(O(n)) \tag{11}$$

where $w_{nm}$ gives the strength of the connection between $n$ and $m$, $O(n)$ is the degree of node $n$. This strategy solves the aforementioned issues by penalising the nodes with a high degree ("super-popular" nodes) and supporting strongly connected nodes.

---

**Algorithm 1.** BipNRL embedding generation extended to K layers

---
1: **for** $u \in U$ **do**
2:     **for** $iteration = 1, 2, \ldots K$ **do**
3:         $h_{N(u)}^k = \mathcal{A}_{uv}([h_{N(v_i)}^k, h_{v_i}^{k-1}], \forall v_i \in N(u))$
4:         $h_{N(N(u))}^k = \mathcal{A}_{uu}(\boldsymbol{h}_{\tilde{u}}^{\boldsymbol{k-1}}, \forall \tilde{u} \in N(N(u)))$
5:     **end for**
6:     $h_u = \alpha_1 h_{N(u)}^K + \alpha_2 h_{N(N(u))}^K$
7: **end for**

---

## 4   Experiments

### 4.1   Datasets and Tasks

We experimented on three diverse tasks: 1) node classification, 2) node regression, and 3) link prediction using four datasets: Movielens $(ML)$[1], Amazon Movie $(AM)$[2], Amazon CDs $(AC)$ (see Footnote 2), Aminer Paper-Author $(PA)$[3]. Table 1 shows the detail of each dataset such as node types, number of nodes, and number of edges in the bipartite graph.

– **V-type Nodes**: Paper nodes in $PA$ dataset are associated with the text of paper abstract, while the item (movie/CD) nodes in $AM$ and $AC$ are associated with the text of title and description. We use Para2Vec [13] to generate these node' s features i.e. features of paper nodes in $PA$, and item nodes in $AM$ and $AC$. In $ML$ movie nodes are represented by their genre.

---

[1] https://grouplens.org/datasets/movielens/100k/.
[2] http://jmcauley.ucsd.edu/data/amazon/index.html.
[3] http://doc.aminer.org/.

– **U-type Nodes**: Features of author nodes in $PA$ and user nodes in $AM$ and $AC$ are created by taking the average of the features of connected nodes (paper/item nodes) respectively. In $ML$ dataset, user nodes are represented through demographics like occupation, gender etc.

**Table 1.** Datasets used in the work

| Datasets | Node Types $(U, V)$ | $|U|$ | $|V|$ | $|E|$ |
| --- | --- | --- | --- | --- |
| MovieLens 100 k(ML) | User, Movie | 1 k | 1.6 k | 110 k |
| MovieLens 500 k(ML2) | User, Movie | 6.04 k | 3.7 k | 500 k |
| MovieLens 1M(ML3) | User, Movie | 6.04 k | 3.7 k | 1M |
| Amazon CD (AC) | User, CD | 54 k | 55 k | 453 k |
| Amazon Movie (AM) | User, Movie | 44 k | 49 k | 946 k |
| Aminer (PA) | Author, Paper | 79 k | 47 k | 261 k |

## 4.2   Baselines

We compare our model rigorously against strong baselines -

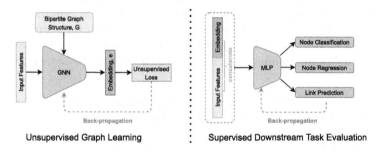

**Fig. 4.** Experiment Setting: We first learn node embeddings by training BipNRL in an unsupervised fashion. The embeddings are then evaluated by training three separate task-specific MLP models, with input being the concatenation of node features and embeddings.

– **Homogeneous graph embeddings**: Node2Vec [8], Attri2Vec [24], Graph-SAGE [9] and GAT [20]. Node2Vec uses Skip-Gram to learn node embeddings that preserve the graph structure without ever utilizing node' s features. Attri2Vec follows a similar principle as Node2Vec, but also uses the nodes features for learning the final embeddings. GraphSAGE and GAT attempts to aggregate neighbouring features with a similar aim of preserving the local graph structure.

– **Bipartite graph embeddings**: Metapath2Vec [5], C-BGNN [10], BiNE [7] and BiGI [3]. Metapath2Vec follows similar principle as Node2Vec, but follows metapath-based random walks to construct heterogeneous node neighbourhoods. C-BGNN utilizes a combination of inter-domain message passing and intra-domain alignment for learning embeddings from a bipartite graph. BiNE extends the ideas of Node2Vec to a Bipartite graph, by proposing a biased random walk and a new optimization framework for handling the specific challenges of Bipartite Graphs. BiGI maximizes the MI between the local representation and the global summary for each of the node types, using a dual infomax objective function, with a primary focus of capturing global properties of a graph rather than preserving node-level features.

For BiNE, BiGI and C-BGNN we use their official github codes and for all other algorithms we use the implementation available in Stellargraph.[4]

### 4.3 Experiment Setting

We use the experimental configuration of [4] to assess the quality of the node representations. The learned node embeddings are fed into a subsequent model that is trained in a supervised manner. We use multi layer preceptron (MLP) as done in [4], since MLP has the capability to capture higher non-linearity. This configuration is maintained across all baselines and our algorithm to guarantee fairness.

We have fixed the neighbourhood sample size per layer to 40. The default hidden dimension size is 128 for all the algorithms. Also, for random walk based baselines we have fixed the random walk length to 8 with the number of walks per node to 8. We use Adam optimizer with a learning rate of 0.0001, and a batch size of 512 for training the models. For supervised downstream tasks, we

**Table 2.** Performance of BipNRL & other baseline algorithms on multiple downstream tasks. BipNRL beats BiGI, the state-of-the-art for bipartite graphs in the all tasks.

| Method | Regression | | | | | | Link Prediction | | | | | | Classification | |
|---|---|---|---|---|---|---|---|---|---|---|---|---|---|---|
| | AC | | AM | | ML | | AC | | AM | | ML | | PA | |
| | MSE | MAE | MSE | MAE | MSE | MAE | AUC | F1 | AUC | F1 | AUC | F1 | ACC | F1 |
| BiNE | 0.33 | 0.28 | 0.52 | 0.42 | 0.69 | 0.68 | 0.87 | 0.77 | 0.89 | 0.80 | 0.76 | 0.7 | 0.54 | 0.56 |
| C-BGNN | 0.32 | 0.26 | 0.38 | 0.30 | 0.69 | 0.67 | 0.88 | 0.79 | 0.89 | 0.81 | 0.77 | 0.72 | 0.57 | 0.56 |
| Node2Vec | 0.47 | 0.38 | 0.54 | 0.45 | 0.68 | 0.67 | 0.89 | 0.76 | 0.85 | 0.75 | 0.54 | 0.55 | 0.50 | 0.52 |
| Attri2Vec | 0.31 | 0.25 | 0.37 | 0.30 | 0.69 | 0.67 | **0.90** | 0.78 | 0.93 | 0.87 | 0.63 | 0.61 | 0.56 | 0.57 |
| GSAGE | 0.32 | 0.25 | 0.41 | 0.32 | 0.67 | 0.67 | 0.87 | 0.73 | 0.92 | 0.84 | 0.64 | 0.63 | 0.54 | 0.55 |
| Metapath | 0.36 | 0.29 | 0.44 | 0.35 | 0.71 | 0.69 | 0.87 | 0.65 | 0.86 | 0.77 | 0.53 | 0.53 | 0.54 | 0.53 |
| GAT | 0.32 | 0.36 | 0.39 | 0.38 | 0.87 | 0.78 | 0.59 | 0.67 | 0.68 | 0.67 | 0.82 | 0.59 | 0.56 | 0.58 |
| BiGI | 0.33 | 0.28 | 0.40 | 0.39 | 0.64 | 0.67 | 0.88 | **0.80** | 0.92 | **0.88** | 0.80 | 0.74 | 0.55 | 0.51 |
| **BipNRL** | **0.30** | **0.23** | **0.36** | **0.28** | **0.61** | **0.62** | **0.90** | **0.80** | **0.94** | **0.88** | **0.86** | **0.78** | **0.59** | **0.59** |

---

[4] https://github.com/stellargraph/stellargraph.

use a 3 layer MLP model with 64 hidden units in each layer and ReLU activation function. All models were trained on Python 3.7 and tensorflow 2.3.0. We have used a single quadro rtx 6000, 16 GB with CUDA 10.1 and cuDNN 7.6.5.

## 4.4   Performance Evaluation

**Node Regression:** We use three datasets to perform node regression task. Our goal is to predict *average ratings* of CDs and movies in *AC* and *AM* respectively, whereas for *ML* dataset, we predict the *age* of a user. As shown in Table 2, BipNRL outperforms all the baseline models on all three datasets. We use mean square error (MSE) and Mean absolute error (MAE) as our primary metrics for comparing the model performances. We observe a relative improvement of 1.5% and 10% in MSE and MAE respectively in *AC*, and a relative gain of 10 % in both MSE and MAE in *AM*. Similar improvement is also seen for *ML* dataset.

**Link Prediction:** For link prediction task, the goal is to predict whether the link exists between two nodes. For *AC* dataset, a link between a user and a CD denotes that the user has rated the CD. Similarly for *AM* and *ML* datasets, link exists when a user rated a movie. For each dataset we follow a random split strategy of 90:10 for training and testing purposes. A link embedding is formed by concatenating embeddings and features of connected nodes and is then fed into the FFN. The test edges with an equal number of negative samples (non connected nodes) are used to evaluate the model performance. Table 2 demonstrates that in the case of link Prediction, BipNRL is able to show an approximate 5% improvement in AUC and F1-score for *ML*. For *AM* and *AC* we observe BiGI and BipNRL both achieve state of the art results, beating other baseline significantly with 5-10% relative gains in terms of F1-score.

**Node Classification:** We use *PA* dataset for node classification task where we choose a subset of the Aminer papers that have been published in top 10 venues. The goal is to predict the venue of a paper. Table 2 clearly demonstrate that BipNRL outperforms state-of-the-art baseline with a performance boost of 5.29% in terms of accuracy and 4.21% boost in terms of F1 score.

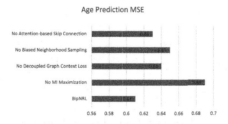

**Fig. 5.** Ablation Study: Comparing the performance of BipNRL after removing individual components. Mutual Information Maximization with Self features contributes the most to BipNRL performance, followed by Biased Sampling, Decoupled Graph Context Loss, and Attention-based Skip Connection.

## 4.5   Analysis and Discussion

**Ablation Study:** In BipNRL, we have four major components: 1) mutual information (MI) maximization with self features, 2) decoupled graph context loss, 3) attention-based neighbourhood aggregation and 4) biased sampling technique Following the removal of each of these particular components, we analyse Bip-NRL's performance. We perform this study on Movielens ($ML$) dataset for the task of node regression, where the goal is to predict age of a user. Fig. 5, shows the comparison of MSE after removing individual components and we can observe that, in each of the four scenarios, performance is always lower as compared to BipNRL. Removing the MI maximization component has the most significant impact of 13% increment in MSE, while removing the decoupled graph context loss, attention-based neighbourhood aggregation and the biased neighbourhood sampling lead a more relatively modest drop in performance (5%, 3.3% and 6.5% respectively). Highlighting that, although MI maximisation is the main factor improving node regression/classification performance, it is essential for the best node representation learning that all components work together in harmony.

**Graph Size vs Performance Gain:** A major limitation of our baseline BiGI is that the information contained in the summary vector diminishes as the graph scales. We demonstrate the effect of this limitation on Movielens datasets across 3 different graph scales - Movielens 100k, Movielens 500k and Movielens 1M. Movielens 500k is not an official dataset, but created from Movielens 1M by dropping 50% of it's edges at random. To prove this hypothesis, we conduct two experiments, a) user age prediction as done previously and b) average movie rating prediction. Fig. 6 clearly depicts in the case of user age prediction the performance gap between BiGI and BipNRL widens from 4.91% at Movielens 100k to 10.16% at Movielens 500k, and finally significantly widens to 13.8% at Movielens 1M. This indicates BipNRL offers significant performance gains over BiGI as graph scales especially for node level downstream tasks. Similar pattern can be observed for Movie's average rating prediction where at Movielens 100k BipNRL offers only a modest 9.3% boost in performance over BiGI, this gap

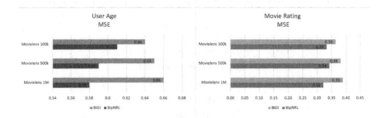

**Fig. 6.** Graph Size vs. Performance Gain: For both user age prediction and movie rating prediction tasks, MSE for BipNRL decreases as the graph scales. On the other hand, the MSE of BiGI rises. This is consistent with the theoretical limitation of BiGI's readout function.

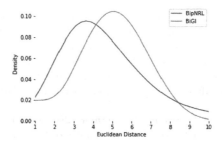

**Fig. 7.** Topology Preserving Embedding: In contrast to BiGI, BipNRL embeddings are smoother because their mean euclidean distance is significantly lower, indicating that indirectly connected user nodes are closer in the embedding space.

increases significantly to 11.5% and 21% as the graph scales to Movielens 500k and 1M respectively.

**Topology Preserving Embedding:** It is well known in the literature that smooth embeddings are a desired property for optimal node representation learning [4,9]. To understand the smoothing effect of our Decoupled Graph Context Loss, we compare the eucledian distance of embeddings of users connected by a common movie in Movielens-1M dataset. The distribution of the eucledian distance for both BiGI and BipNRL is shown in Fig. 7. BipNRL embeddings have a lower mean distance and are significantly smoother for connected user nodes.

## 5    Conclusion

BipNRL is a simple and effective node representation learning algorithm for bipartite graphs presented in our work. Rather than using the global graph summary used by previous approaches, we maximise the mutual information between the learned node representation and the input features. By applying graph context loss to a projected graph of each node type, BipNRL captures the unique structure of a bipartite graph. We take on with skip-information through attention-based aggregation and high variance through biased sampling. The BipNRL algorithm can learn representations that are optimised for node-level downstream tasks for bipartite graphs by combining all of these techniques, as empirically demonstrated by outperforming state-of-the-art baselines on multiple datasets.

## References

1. Ballard, D.H.: Modular learning in neural networks. In AAAI, vol. 647 (1987)
2. Belghazi, M.I.: Mine: mutual information neural estimation. arXiv preprint arXiv:1801.04062 (2018)

3. Cao, J., Lin, X., Guo, S., Liu, L., Liu, T., Wang, B.: Bipartite graph embedding via mutual information maximization. In: Proceedings of the 14th ACM International Conference on Web Search and Data Mining, pp. 635–643 (2021)
4. Dong, W., Wu, J., Luo, Y., Ge, Z., Wang, P.: Node representation learning in graph via node-to-neighbourhood mutual information maximization. In: Proceedings of the IEEE/CVF Conference on Computer Vision and Pattern Recognition, pp. 16620–16629 (2022)
5. Dong, Y., Chawla, N.V., Swami, A.: Metapath2vec: scalable representation learning for heterogeneous networks. In: Proceedings of the 23rd ACM SIGKDD International Conference on Knowledge Discovery and Data Mining, pp. 135–144 (2017)
6. Frénay, B., Doquire, G., Verleysen, M.: Is mutual information adequate for feature selection in regression? Neural Netw. **48**, 1–7 (2013)
7. Gao, M., Chen, L., He, X., Zhou, A.: Bine: bipartite network embedding. In: The 41st International ACM SIGIR Conference on Research & Development in Information Retrieval, pp. 715–724 (2018)
8. Grover, A., Leskovec, J.: Node2vec: scalable feature learning for networks. In Proceedings of the 22nd ACM SIGKDD International Conference on Knowledge Discovery and Data Mining, pp. 855–864 (2016)
9. Hamilton, W.L., Ying, R., Leskovec, J.: Inductive representation learning on large graphs. arXiv preprint arXiv:1706.02216 (2017)
10. He, C.: Bipartite graph neural networks for efficient node representation learning. arXiv preprint arXiv:1906.11994 (2019)
11. Kingma, P., Welling, M., et al.: An introduction to variational autoencoders. Foundations Trends® Mach. Learn. **12**(4), 307–392 (2019)
12. Kipf, T.N., Welling, M.: Semi-supervised classification with graph convolutional networks. arXiv preprint arXiv:1609.02907 (2016)
13. Le, Q., Mikolov, T.: Distributed representations of sentences and documents. In: International Conference on Machine Learning. PMLR (2014)
14. Park, C., Kim, D., Han, J., Hwanjo, Y.: Unsupervised attributed multiplex network embedding. In: Proceedings of the AAAI Conference on Artificial Intelligence, vol. 34,pp. 5371–5378 (2020)
15. Peng, Z.: Graph representation learning via graphical mutual information maximization. In: Proceedings of The Web Conference (2020)
16. Perozzi, B., Al-Rfou, R., Skiena, S.: Deepwalk: online learning of social representations. In: Proceedings of the 20th ACM SIGKDD International Conference on Knowledge Discovery and Data Mining, pp. 701–710 (2014)
17. Sybrandt, J., Safro, I.: Fobe and hobe: first-and high-order bipartite embeddings. arXiv preprint arXiv:1905.10953 (2019)
18. Tang, J., Qu, M., Wang, M., Zhang, M., Yan, J., Mei, Q.: Line: Large-scale information network embedding. In: Proceedings of the 24th International Conference on World Wide Web, pp. 1067–1077 (2015)
19. Vaswani, A.: Attention is all you need. In: Advances in Neural Information Processing Systems 30 (2017)
20. Veličković, P., Cucurull, G., Casanova, A., Romero, A., Lio, P., Bengio, Y.: Graph attention networks. arXiv preprint arXiv:1710.10903 (2017)
21. Veličković, P., Fedus, W., Hamilton, W.L., Liò, P., Bengio, Y., Hjelm, R.D.: Deep graph infomax. arXiv preprint arXiv:1809.10341 (2018)
22. Velickovic, P., Fedus, W., Hamilton, W.L., Liò, P., Bengio, Y., Hjelm, R.D.: Deep graph infomax. ICLR (Poster) **2**(3), 4 (2019)

23. Ying, R., He, R., Chen, K., Eksombatchai, P., Hamilton, W.L., Leskovec, J.: Graph convolutional neural networks for web-scale recommender systems. In: Proceedings of the 24th ACM SIGKDD International Conference on Knowledge Discovery & Data Mining, pp. 974–983 (2018)
24. Zhang, D., Yin, J., Zhu, X., Zhang, C.: Attributed network embedding via subspace discovery. Data Min. Knowl. Disc. **33**(6), 1953–1980 (2019). https://doi.org/10.1007/s10618-019-00650-2
25. Zhang, Y., Xiong, Y., Kong, X., Zhu, Y.: Learning node embeddings in interaction graphs. In: Proceedings of the 2017 ACM on Conference on Information and Knowledge Management, pp. 397–406 (2017)

# Author Index

D. Koutra et al. (Eds.): ECML PKDD 2023, LNAI 14172, pp. 745–747, 2023.
https://doi.org/10.1007/978-3-031-43421-1

Printed in the United States
by Baker & Taylor Publisher Services